Programming Python

Other resources from O'Reilly

Related titles

Learning Python	Python Pocket Reference
Python and XML	Python Standard Library
Python Cookbook™	Twisted Network
Python in a Nutshell	Programming Essentials

oreilly.com

oreilly.com is more than a complete catalog of O'Reilly books. You'll also find links to news, events, articles, weblogs, sample chapters, and code examples.

oreillynet.com is the essential portal for developers interested in open and emerging technologies, including new platforms, programming languages, and operating systems.

Conferences

O'Reilly brings diverse innovators together to nurture the ideas that spark revolutionary industries. We specialize in documenting the latest tools and systems, translating the innovator's knowledge into useful skills for those in the trenches. Visit *conferences.oreilly.com* for our upcoming events.

Safari Bookshelf (*safari.oreilly.com*) is the premier online reference library for programmers and IT professionals. Conduct searches across more than 1,000 books. Subscribers can zero in on answers to time-critical questions in a matter of seconds. Read the books on your Bookshelf from cover to cover or simply flip to the page you need. Try it today for free.

THIRD EDITION

Programming Python

Mark Lutz

O'REILLY®

Beijing · Cambridge · Farnham · Köln · Paris · Sebastopol · Taipei · Tokyo

Programming Python, Third Edition
by Mark Lutz

Copyright © 2006, 2001, 1996 O'Reilly Media, Inc. All rights reserved.
Printed in the United States of America.

Published by O'Reilly Media, Inc., 1005 Gravenstein Highway North, Sebastopol, CA 95472.

O'Reilly books may be purchased for educational, business, or sales promotional use. Online editions
are also available for most titles (*safari.oreilly.com*). For more information, contact our
corporate/institutional sales department: (800) 998-9938 or *corporate@oreilly.com*.

Editor: Mary O'Brien
Production Editor: Mary Brady
Copyeditor: Audrey Doyle
Proofreaders: Lydia Onofrei, Colleen Gorman,
and Mary Brady

Indexer: Johnna VanHoose Dinse
Cover Designer: Edie Freedman
Interior Designer: David Futato
Illustrators: Robert Romano and Jessamyn Read

Printing History:

October 1996:	First Edition.
March 2001:	Second Edition.
August 2006:	Third Edition.

ISBN-10: 0-596-00925-9
ISBN-13: 978-0-596-00925-0

[M]

Table of Contents

Part II. System Programming

Part V. Tools and Techniques

Part VI. Integration

Part VII. The End

Foreword

How Time Flies!

Ten years ago I completed the foreword for the first edition of this book. Python 1.3 was current then, and 1.4 was in beta. I wrote about Python's origins and philosophy, and about how its first six years changed my life. Python was still mostly a one-man show at the time, and I only mentioned other contributors and the Python community in one paragraph near the end.

Five years later the second edition came out, much improved and quite a bit heftier, and I wrote a new foreword. Python 2.0 was hot then, and the main topic of the foreword was evolution of the language. Python 2.0 added a lot of new features, and many were concerned that the pace of change would be unsustainable for the users of the language. I addressed this by promising feature-by-feature backward compatibility for several releases and by regulating change through a community process using Python Enhancement Proposals (PEPs).

By then, Python's development had become truly community-driven, with many developers (besides myself) having commit privileges into the source tree. This move toward community responsibility has continued ever since. My own role has become more limited over time, though have not yet been reduced to playing a purely ceremonial function like that of the Dutch Queen.

Perhaps the biggest change in recent years is the establishment of the Python Software Foundation (PSF), a non-profit organization that formally owns and manages the rights to the Python source code and owns the Python trademark. Its board and members (helped by many nonmember volunteers) also offer many services to the Python community, from the Python.org web site and mailing lists to the yearly Python Conference. Membership in the PSF is by invitation only, but donations are always welcome (and tax-deductible, at least in the U.S.).

The PSF does not directly control Python's development; however, the developers don't have to obey any rules set by the PSF. Rather, it's the other way around: active

Python developers make up the majority of the PSF's membership. This arrangement, together with the open source nature of Python's source code license, ensures that Python will continue to serve the goals of its users and developers.

Coming Attractions

What developments can Python users expect to see in the coming years? Python 3000, which is referred to in the foreword to the second edition as "intentionally vaporware," will see the light of day after all as Python 3.0. After half a decade of talk, it's finally time to start doing something about it. I've created a branch of the 2. 5 source tree, and, along with a handful of developers, I'm working on transforming the code base into my vision for Python 3000. At the same time, I'm working with the community on a detailed definition of Python 3000; there's a new mailing dedicated to Python 3000 and a series of PEPs, starting with PEP 3000.

This work is still in the early stages. Some changes, such as removing classic classes and string exceptions, adopting Unicode as the only character type, and changing integer division so that 1/2 returns 0.5 instead of truncating toward zero, have been planned for years. But many other changes are still being hotly debated, and new features are being proposed almost daily.

I see my own role in this debate as a force of moderation: there are many more good ideas than could possibly be implemented in the given time, and, taken together, they would change the language so much that it would be unrecognizable. My goal for Python 3000 is to fix some of my oldest design mistakes, especially the ones that can't be fixed without breaking backward compatibility. That alone will be a huge task. For example, a consequence of the choice to use Unicode everywhere is the need for a total rewrite of the standard I/O library and a new data type to represent binary ("noncharacter") data, dubbed "bytes."

The biggest potential danger for Python 3000 is that of an "accidental paradigm shift": a change, or perhaps a small set of changes that weren't considered together, that would unintentionally cause a huge change to the way people program in Python. For example, adding optional static type checking to the language could easily have the effect of turning Python into "Java without braces"—which is definitely not what most users would like to see happen! For this reason, I am making it my personal responsibility to guide the Python 3000 development process. The new language should continue to represent my own esthetics for language design, not a design-by-committee compromise or a radical departure from today's Python. And if we don't get everything right, well, there's always Python 4000....

The timeline for 3.0 is roughly as follows: I expect the first alpha release in about a year and the first production release a year later. I expect that it will then take another year to shake out various usability issues and get major third-party packages ported, and, finally, another year to gain widespread user acceptance. So, Mark should have about three to four years before he'll have to start the next revision of this book.

To learn more about Python 3000 and how we plan to help users convert their code, start by reading PEP 3000. (To find PEP 3000 online, search for it in Google.)

In the meantime, Python 2.x is not dead yet. Python 2.5 will be released around the same time as this book (it's in late alpha as I am writing this). Python's normal release cycle produces a new release every 12–18 months. I fully expect version 2.6 to see the light of day while Python 3000 is still in alpha, and it's likely that 2.7 will be released around the same time as 3.0 (and that more users will download 2.7 than 3.0). A 2.8 release is quite likely; such a release might back-port certain Python 3.0 features (while maintaining backward compatibility with 2.7) in order to help users migrate code. A 2.9 release might happen, depending on demand. But in any case, 2.10 will be right out!

(If you're not familiar with Python's release culture, releases like 2.4 and 2.5 are referred to as "major releases." There are also "bug-fix releases," such as 2.4.3. Bug-fix releases are just that: they fix bugs and, otherwise, maintain strict backward and forward compatibility within the same major release. Major releases introduce new features and maintain backward compatibility with at least one or two previous major releases, and, in most cases, many more than that. There's no specific name for "earth-shattering" releases like 3.0, since they happen so rarely.)

Concluding Remarks

Programming Python was the first or second book on Python ever published, and it's the only one of the early batch to endure to this day. I thank its author, Mark Lutz, for his unceasing efforts in keeping the book up-to-date, and its publisher, O'Reilly, for keeping the page count constant for this edition.

Some of my fondest memories are of the book's first editor, the late Frank Willison. Without Frank's inspiration and support, the first two editions would never have been. He would be proud of this third edition.

I must end in a fine tradition, with one of my favorite Monty Python quotes: "Take it away, Eric the orchestra leader!"

—Guido van Rossum
Belmont, California, May 2006

Foreword to the Second Edition (2001)

Less than five years ago, I wrote the Foreword for the first edition of Programming Python. Since then, the book has changed about as much as the language and the Python community! I no longer feel the need to defend Python: the statistics and developments listed in Mark's Preface speak for themselves.

In the past year, Python has made great strides. We released Python 2.0, a big step forward, with new standard library features such as Unicode and XML support, and several new syntactic constructs, including augmented assignment: you can now write x += 1 instead of x = x+1. A few people wondered what the big deal was (answer: instead of x, imagine dict[key] or list[index]), but overall this was a big hit with those users who were already used to augmented assignment in other languages.

Less warm was the welcome for the extended print statement, print>>file, a shortcut for printing to a different file object than standard output. Personally, it's the Python 2.0 feature I use most frequently, but most people who opened their mouths about it found it an abomination. The discussion thread on the newsgroup berating this simple language extension was one of the longest ever—apart from the never-ending Python versus Perl thread.

Which brings me to the next topic. (No, not Python versus Perl. There are better places to pick a fight than a Foreword.) I mean the speed of Python's evolution, a topic dear to the heart of the author of this book. Every time I add a feature to Python, another patch of Mark's hair turns gray—there goes another chapter out of date! Especially the slew of new features added to Python 2.0, which appeared just as he was working on this second edition, made him worry: what if Python 2.1 added as many new things? The book would be out of date as soon as it was published!

Relax, Mark. Python will continue to evolve, but I promise that I won't remove things that are in active use! For example, there was a lot of worry about the string module. Now that string objects have methods, the string module is mostly redundant. I wish I could declare it obsolete (or deprecated) to encourage Python programmers to start using string methods instead. But given that a large majority of existing Python code—even many standard library modules—imports the string module, this change is obviously not going to happen overnight. The first likely opportunity to remove the string module will be when we introduce Python 3000; and even at that point, there will probably be a string module in the backwards compatibility library for use with old code.

Python 3000?! Yes, that's the nickname for the next generation of the Python interpreter. The name may be considered a pun on Windows 2000, or a reference to Mystery Science Theater 3000, a suitably Pythonesque TV show with a cult following. When will Python 3000 be released? Not for a loooooong time—although you won't quite have to wait until the year 3000.

Originally, Python 3000 was intended to be a complete rewrite and redesign of the language. It would allow me to make incompatible changes in order to fix problems with the language design that weren't solvable in a backwards compatible way. The current plan, however, is that the necessary changes will be introduced gradually into the current Python 2.x line of development, with a clear transition path that includes a period of backwards compatibility support.

Take, for example, integer division. In line with C, Python currently defines x/y with two integer arguments to have an integer result. In other words, 1/2 yields 0! While most dyed-in-the-wool programmers expect this, it's a continuing source of confusion for newbies, who make up an ever-larger fraction of the (exponentially growing) Python user population. From a numerical perspective, it really makes more sense for the / operator to yield the same value regardless of the type of the operands: after all, that's what all other numeric operators do. But we can't simply change Python so that 1/2 yields 0.5, because (like removing the string module) it would break too much existing code. What to do?

The solution, too complex to describe here in detail, will have to span several Python releases, and involves gradually increasing pressure on Python programmers (first through documentation, then through deprecation warnings, and eventually through errors) to change their code. By the way, a framework for issuing warnings will be introduced as part of Python 2.1. Sorry, Mark!

So don't expect the announcement of the release of Python 3000 any time soon. Instead, one day you may find that you are *already* using Python 3000—only it won't be called that, but rather something like Python 2.8.7. And most of what you've learned in this book will still apply! Still, in the meantime, references to Python 3000 will abound; just know that this is intentionally vaporware in the purest sense of the word. Rather than worry about Python 3000, continue to use and learn more about the Python version that you do have.

I'd like to say a few words about Python's current development model. Until early 2000, there were hundreds of contributors to Python, but essentially all contributions had to go through my inbox. To propose a change to Python, you would mail me a context diff, which I would apply to my work version of Python, and if I liked it, I would check it into my CVS source tree. (CVS is a source code version management system, and the subject of several books.) Bug reports followed the same path, except I also ended up having to come up with the patch. Clearly, with the increasing number of contributions, my inbox became a bottleneck. What to do?

Fortunately, Python wasn't the only open source project with this problem, and a few smart people at VA Linux came up with a solution: SourceForge! This is a dynamic web site with a complete set of distributed project management tools available: a public CVS repository, mailing lists (using Mailman, a very popular Python application!), discussion forums, bug and patch managers, and a download area, all made available to any open source project for the asking.

We currently have a development group of 30 volunteers with SourceForge checkin privileges, and a development mailing list comprising twice as many folks. The privileged volunteers have all sworn their allegiance to the BDFL (Benevolent Dictator For Life—that's me :-). Introduction of major new features is regulated via a lightweight system of proposals and feedback called Python Enhancement Proposals (PEPs). Our PEP system proved so successful that it was copied almost verbatim by the Tcl community when they made a similar transition from Cathedral to Bazaar.

So, it is with confidence in Python's future that I give the floor to Mark Lutz. Excellent job, Mark. And to finish with my favorite Monty Python quote: Take it away, Eric, the orchestra leader!

—Guido van Rossum
Reston, Virginia, January 2001

Foreword from the First Edition (1996)

As Python's creator, I'd like to say a few words about its origins, adding a bit of personal philosophy.

Over six years ago, in December 1989, I was looking for a "hobby" programming project that would keep me occupied during the week around Christmas. My office (a government-run research lab in Amsterdam) would be closed, but I had a home computer, and not much else on my hands. I decided to write an interpreter for the new scripting language I had been thinking about lately: a descendant of ABC that would appeal to UNIX/C hackers. I chose Python as a working title for the project, being in a slightly irreverent mood (and a big fan of *Monty Python's Flying Circus*).

Today, I can safely say that Python has changed my life. I have moved to a different continent. I spend my working days developing large systems in Python, when I'm not hacking on Python or answering Python-related email. There are Python T-shirts, workshops, mailing lists, a newsgroup, and now a book. Frankly, my only unfulfilled wish right now is to have my picture on the front page of the *New York Times*. But before I get carried away daydreaming, here are a few tidbits from Python's past.

It all started with ABC, a wonderful teaching language that I had helped create in the early eighties. It was an incredibly elegant and powerful language aimed at nonprofessional programmers. Despite all its elegance and power and the availability of a free implementation, ABC never became popular in the UNIX/C world. I can only speculate about the reasons, but here's a likely one: the difficulty of adding new "primitive" operations to ABC. It was a monolithic closed system, with only the most basic I/O operations: read a string from the console, write a string to the console. I decided not to repeat this mistake in Python.

Besides this intention, I had a number of other ideas for a language that improved upon ABC, and was eager to try them out. For instance, ABC's powerful data types turned out to be less efficient than we hoped. There was too much emphasis on theoretically optimal algorithms, and not enough tuning for common cases. I also felt that some of ABC's features, aimed at novice programmers, were less desirable for the (then!) intended audience of experienced UNIX/C programmers. For instance: ABC's idiosyncratic syntax (all uppercase keywords!), some terminology (for example, "how-to" instead of "procedure"); and the integrated structured editor, which its users almost universally hated. Python would rely more on the UNIX infrastructure and conventions, without being UNIX-bound. And in fact, the first implementation was done on a Macintosh.

As it turned out, Python is remarkably free from many of the hang-ups of conventional programming languages. This is perhaps due to my choice of examples: besides ABC, my main influence was Modula-3. This is another language with remarkable elegance and power, designed by a small, strong-willed team (most of whom I had met during a summer internship at DEC's Systems Research Center in Palo Alto). Imagine what Python would have looked like if I had modeled it after the UNIX shell and C instead! (Yes, I borrowed from C too, but only its least controversial features, in my desire to please the UNIX/C audience.)

Any individual creation has its idiosyncracies, and occasionally its creator has to justify them. Perhaps Python's most controversial feature is its use of indentation for statement grouping, which derives directly from ABC. It is one of the language's features that is dearest to my heart. It makes Python code more readable in two ways. First, the use of indentation reduces visual clutter and makes programs shorter, thus reducing the attention span needed to take in a basic unit of code. Second, it allows the programmer less freedom in formatting, thereby enabling a more uniform style, which makes it easier to read someone else's code. (Compare, for instance, the three or four different conventions for the placement of braces in C, each with strong proponents.)

This emphasis on readability is no accident. As an object-oriented language, Python aims to encourage the creation of reusable code. Even if we all wrote perfect documentation all of the time, code can hardly be considered reusable if it's not readable. Many of Python's features, in addition to its use of indentation, conspire to make Python code highly readable. This reflects the philosophy of ABC, which was intended to teach programming in its purest form, and therefore placed a high value on clarity.

Readability is often enhanced by reducing unnecessary variability. When possible, there's a single, obvious way to code a particular construct. This reduces the number of choices facing the programmer who is writing the code, and increases the chance that it will appear familiar to a second programmer reading it. Yet another contribution to Python's readability is the choice to use punctuation mostly in a conservative, conventional manner. Most operator symbols are familiar to anyone with even a vague recollection of high school math, and no new meanings have to be learned for comic strip curse characters like @&$!.

I will gladly admit that Python is not the fastest running scripting language. It is a good runner-up, though. With ever-increasing hardware speed, the accumulated running time of a program during its lifetime is often negligible compared to the programmer time needed to write and debug it. This, of course, is where the real time savings can be made. While this is hard to assess objectively, Python is considered a winner in coding time by most programmers who have tried it. In addition, many consider using Python a pleasure—a better recommendation is hard to imagine.

I am solely responsible for Python's strengths and shortcomings, even when some of the code has been written by others. However, its success is the product of a community, starting with Python's early adopters who picked it up when I first published it on the Net, and who spread the word about it in their own environment. They sent me their praise, criticism, feature requests, code contributions, and personal revelations via email. They were willing to discuss every aspect of Python in the mailing list that I soon set up, and to educate me or nudge me in the right direction where my initial intuition failed me. There have been too many contributors to thank individually. I'll make one exception, however: this book's author was one of Python's early adopters and evangelists. With this book's publication, his longstanding wish (and mine!) of having a more accessible description of Python than the standard set of manuals, has been fulfilled.

But enough rambling. I highly recommend this book to anyone interested in learning Python, whether for personal improvement or as a career enhancement. Take it away, Eric, the orchestra leader! (If you don't understand this last sentence, you haven't watched enough Monty Python reruns.)

—Guido van Rossum
Reston, Virginia, May 1996

Preface

"And Now for Something Completely Different . . . Again"

This book teaches *application-level programming* with Python. That is, it is about what you can *do* with the language once you've mastered its fundamentals.

By reading this book, you will learn to use Python in some of its most common roles: to build GUIs, web sites, networked tools, scripting interfaces, system administration programs, database and text processing utilities, and more.

Along the way, you will also learn how to use the Python language in realistically scaled programs—concepts such as object-oriented programming (OOP) and code reuse are recurring side themes throughout this text. And you will gain enough information to further explore the application domains introduced in the book, as well as to explore others.

About This Book

Now that I've told you what this book is, I should tell you what it is not. First of all, this book is not a reference manual. Although the index can be used to hunt for information, this text is not a dry collection of facts; it is designed to be read. And while many larger examples are presented along the way, this book is also not just a collection of minimally documented code samples.

Rather, this book is a *tutorial* that teaches the most common Python application domains from the ground up. It covers each of Python's target domains gradually, beginning with in-depth discussions of core concepts in each domain, before progressing toward complete programs. Large examples do appear, but only after you've learned enough to understand their techniques and code.

For example, network scripting begins with coverage of network basics and protocols and progresses through sockets, client-side tools, HTML and CGI fundamentals, and web frameworks. GUI programming gets a similarly gentle presentation, with one introductory and two tutorial chapters, before reaching larger, complete programs. And system interfaces are explored carefully before being applied in real and useful scripts.

In a sense, this book is to application-level programming what the book *Learning Python* is to the core Python language—a learning resource that makes no assumptions about your prior experience in the domains it covers. Because of this focus, this book is designed to be a natural follow-up to the core language material in *Learning Python* and a next step on the way to mastering the many facets of Python programming.

In deference to all the topic suggestions I have received over the years, I should also point out that this book is not intended to be an in-depth look at specific systems or tools. With perhaps one million Python users in the world today, it would be impossible to cover in a useful way every Python-related system that is of interest to users.

Instead, this book is designed as a tutorial for readers new to the application domains covered. The web chapters, for instance, focus on core web scripting ideas, such as server-side scripts and state retention options, not on specific systems, such as SOAP, Twisted, and Plone. By reading this book, you will gain the groundwork necessary to move on to more specific tools such as these in the domains that interest you.

About This Edition

To some extent, this edition's structure is a result of this book's history. The first edition of this book, written in 1995 and 1996, was the first book project to present the Python language. Its focus was broad. It covered the core Python language, and it briefly introduced selected application domains. Over time, the core language and reference material in the first edition evolved into more focused books *Learning Python* and *Python Pocket Reference*.

Given that evolution, the second edition of this book, written from 1999 to 2000, was an almost completely new book on advanced Python topics. Its content was an expanded and more complete version of the first edition's application domain material, designed to be an application-level follow-up to the core language material in *Learning Python*, and supplemented by the reference material in *Python Pocket Reference*. The second edition focused on application libraries and tools rather than on the Python language itself, and it was oriented toward the practical needs of real developers and real tasks—GUIs, web sites, databases, text processing, and so on.

This third edition, which I wrote in 2005 and 2006, is exactly like the second in its scope and focus, but it has been updated to reflect Python version 2.4, and to be compatible with the upcoming Python 2.5. It is a minor update, and it retains the second edition's design and scope as well as much of its original material. However, its code and descriptions have been updated to incorporate both recent changes in the Python language, as well as current best practices in Python programming.

Python Changes

You'll find that new language features such as string methods, enclosing-function scope references, list comprehensions, and new standard library tools, such as the email package, have been integrated throughout this edition. Smaller code changes— for instance, replacing apply calls and exc_type usage with the newer func(*args) and exc_info( )—have been applied globally as well (and show up surprisingly often, because this book is concerned with building general tools).

All string-based, user-defined exceptions are now class-based, too; string exceptions appeared half a dozen times in the book's examples, but are documented as deprecated today. This is usually just a matter of changing to class MyExc(Exception): pass, though, in one case, exception constructor arguments must be extracted manually with the instance's args attribute. `X` also became repr(X) across all examples, and I've replaced some appearances of while 1: with the newer and more mnemonic while True:, though either form works as advertised and C programmers often find the former a natural pattern. Hopefully, these changes will future-proof the examples for as long as possible; be sure to watch the updates page described later for future Python changes.

One futurisms note: some purists might notice that I have not made all classes in this book derive from object to turn on new-style class features (e.g., class MyClass(object)). This is partly because the programs here don't employ the new-style model's slightly modified search pattern or advanced extensions. This is also because Python's creator, Guido van Rossum, told me that he believes this derivation will not be required in Python 3.0—standalone classes will simply be new-style too, automatically (in fact, the new-style class distinction is really just a temporary regression due to its incompatible search order in particular rare, multiple-inheritance trees). This is impossible to predict with certainty, of course, and Python 3.0 might abandon compatibility in other ways that break some examples in this book. Be sure to both watch for 3.0 release notes and keep an eye on this book's updates page over time.

Example Changes

You'll also notice that many of the second edition's larger examples have been upgraded substantially, especially the two larger GUI and CGI email-based examples (which are arguably the implicit goals of much of the book). For instance:

- The PyMailGUI email client is a complete rewrite and now supports sending and receiving attachments, offline viewing from mail save files, true transfer thread overlap, header-only fetches and mail caches, auto-open of attachments, detection of server inbox message number synchronization errors, and more.

- The PyMailCGI email web site was also augmented to support sending and receiving mail attachments, locate an email's main text intelligently, minimize mail fetches to run more efficiently, and use the PyCrypto extension for password encryption.

- The PyEdit text editor has grown a font dialog; unlimited undo and redo; a configuration module for fonts, colors, and sizes; intelligent modified tests on quit, open, new, and run; and case-insensitive searches.

- PyPhoto, a new, major example in Chapter 12, implements an image viewer GUI with Tkinter and the optional PIL extension. It supports cached image thumbnails, image resizing, saving images to files, and a variety of image formats thanks to PIL.

- PyClock has incorporated a countdown timer and a custom window icon; PyCalc has various cosmetic and functionality upgrades; and PyDemos now automatically pops up examples' source files.

In addition to the enhanced and new, major examples, you'll also find many other examples that demonstrate new and advanced topics such as thread queues.

Topic Changes

In addition to example changes, new topics have been added throughout. Among these are the following:

- Part II, *System Programming*, looks at the struct, mimetools, and StringIO modules and has been updated for newer tools such as file iterators.

- Part III, *GUI Programming*, has fresh coverage of threading and queues, the PIL imaging library, and techniques for linking a separately spawned GUI with pipes and sockets.

- Part IV, *Internet Programming*, now uses the new email package; covers running a web server on your local machine for CGI scripts; has substantially more on cookies, Zope, and XML parsing; and uses the PyCrypto encryption toolkit.

- Chapter 19, *Databases and Persistence*, has new ZODB examples and much-expanded coverage of the SQL API, including dozens of new pages on using MySQL and ZODB.
- Chapter 21, *Text and Language*, has a new, gentler introduction to pattern matching and mentions Python 2.4 templates.
- Chapter 22, *Extending Python*, now introduces Distutils and includes overviews of Pyrex, SIP, ctypes, Boost.Python, and CXX, in addition to offering updated SWIG coverage.

Beyond these specific kinds of changes, some material has been reorganized to simplify the overall structure. For example, a few chapters have been split up to make them less challenging; appendixes have been removed to save space (references are available separately); and the PyErrata web site example chapter has been removed (it didn't present many new concepts, so we've made it and its code available in the book's examples distribution as optional reading).

You'll also find a new "Sneak Preview" chapter for readers in a hurry—a throwback to the first edition. This chapter takes a single example from command line to GUI to web site, and introduces Python and its libraries along the way.

Focus Unchanged

Fundamentally, though, this edition, like the second, is still focused on ways to *use* Python rather than on the language itself. Python development concepts are explored along the way—in fact, they really become meaningful only in the context of larger examples like those in this edition. Code structure and reuse, for instance, are put into practice by refactoring and reusing examples throughout the book.

But in general, this text assumes that you already have at least a passing acquaintance with Python language fundamentals, and it moves on to present the rest of the Python story—its application to real tasks. If you find code in this book confusing, I encourage you to read *Learning Python* as a prelude to this text.

In the remainder of this preface, I'll explain some of the rationales for this design, describe the structure of this edition in more detail, and give a brief overview of how to use the Python programs shipped in the book examples package.

This Book's Motivation

Over the 10 years since the first edition of this book was written, Python has transitioned from an emerging language that was of interest primarily to pioneers to a widely accepted tool used by programmers for day-to-day development tasks. Along the way, the Python audience has changed as well, and this book has been refocused with this new readership in mind. You will find that it is a nuts-and-bolts text, geared

So, What's Python?

If you are looking for a concise definition of this book's topic, try this:

Python is a general-purpose, open source computer programming language optimized for quality, productivity, portability, and integration. It is used by hundreds of thousands of developers around the world in areas such as Internet scripting, systems programming, user interfaces, product customization, and more.

As a popular programming language that shrinks the development time, Python is used in a wide variety of products and roles. Counted among its current user base are Google, Industrial Light & Magic, ESRI, the BitTorrent file sharing system, NASA's Jet Propulsion Lab, and the U.S. National Weather Service. Python's application domains range from system administration, web site development, cell phone scripting, and education to hardware testing, investment analysis, computer games, and spacecraft control.

Among other things, Python sports OOP; a remarkably simple, readable, and maintainable syntax; integration with C components; and a vast collection of precoded interfaces and utilities. Its tool set makes it a flexible and agile language, ideal for both quick tactical tasks as well as longer-range strategic application development efforts.

Although it is a general-purpose language, Python is often called a *scripting language* because it makes it easy to utilize and direct other software components. Perhaps Python's best asset is simply that it makes software development more rapid and enjoyable. To truly understand how, read on; we'll expand on these concepts in the next chapter.

---

less toward introducing and popularizing the language and more toward showing you how to apply Python for realistically scaled programming tasks.

Since writing the first edition, I have also had the opportunity to teach Python classes in the U.S. and abroad some 170 times as of mid-2006, and this book reflects feedback garnered from these training sessions. The application domain examples, for instance, reflect interests and queries common among the thousands of students I have introduced to Python. Teaching Python to workers in the trenches, many of whom are now compelled to use Python on the job, also inspired a new level of practicality that you will notice in this book's examples and topics.

Other book examples are simply the result of me having fun programming Python. Yes, fun. One of the most common remarks I hear from Python newcomers is that Python is actually enjoyable to use—it is able to both kindle the excitement of programming among beginners and rekindle that excitement among those who have toiled for years with more demanding tools. When you can code as fast as you can think, programming becomes a very different proposition and feels more like pleasure than work.

As you will see in this book, Python makes it easy to play with advanced but practical tools such as threads, sockets, GUIs, web sites, and OOP—areas that can be both tedious and daunting in traditional languages such as C and C++. It enables things you may not have considered or attempted with other tools.

Frankly, even after 14 years as a bona fide *Pythonista*, I still find programming most enjoyable when I do it in Python. Python is a remarkably productive and flexible language, and witnessing its application firsthand is an aesthetic pleasure. I hope this edition, as much as the two before it, will both demonstrate how to reap Python's productivity benefits and communicate some of the excitement to be found in this rewarding tool.

This Book's Structure

Although code examples are reused throughout the book and later chapters build upon material in earlier chapters (e.g., GUIs), topics in this book are covered fairly independently and are grouped together in different parts. If a particular domain's part doesn't interest you, you can generally skip ahead to a part that does.

As a result, it's not too much of a stretch to consider this edition as akin to four or five books in one. Its top-level structure underscores its application-topics focus (see the Table of Contents for a more fine-grained look at the book's structure):

Part I, *The Beginning*
> I start off with an overview of some of the main ideas behind Python and a quick sneak-preview chapter to whet your appetite. The sneak preview doesn't teach much, but it serves as an introduction and demo for some of the topics to come, and as a refresher for core Python concepts such as OOP.

Part II, *System Programming*
> This section explores the system-level interfaces in Python as well as their realistic applications. We'll look at topics such as threading, directory walkers, processes, environment variables, and streams, and we will apply such tools to common system administration tasks such as directory searchers and file splitters.

Part III, *GUI Programming*
> In this section, you'll learn how to build portable GUIs with Python. The Tkinter toolkit is covered from the ground up as you move from basics to techniques to constructing complete programs. You'll build text editors, clocks, and more in this part. GUIs also show up throughout the rest of the book, and they often reuse some of the tools you'll build here.

Part IV, *Internet Programming*
> In this section, you'll learn all about using Python on the Internet. I begin with network basics and sockets, move through client-side tools like FTP and email, and end up using server-side tools to implement interactive web sites. Along the way, I'll contrast different ways to move bits around the Web with Python.

You'll code GUI and web-based email programs, for example, to help underscore trade-offs between client- and server-side techniques. A final chapter in this part surveys more advanced toolkits and techniques for Internet-related application development—Zope, Jython, XML, and the like.

Part V, *Tools and Techniques*

This part is a collection of tool topics that span application domains—database interfaces and object persistence, text and language processing, and data structure implementation. You'll build GUIs here for browsing databases, viewing data structures, and performing calculations.

Part VI, *Integration*

This part of the book looks at the interfaces available for mixing Python with programs written in C and C++. These interfaces allow Python to script existing libraries and to serve as an embedded customization tool. As you'll see, by combining Python with compiled languages, programs can be both flexible and efficient.

Part VII, *The End*

Finally, I'll wrap up with a conclusion that looks at some of the implications of Python's scripting role.

Two notes about the structure: first of all, don't let these titles fool you—although most have to do with application topics, Python language features and general design concepts are still explored along the way, in the context of real-world goals. Secondly, readers who use Python as a standalone tool can safely skip the integration part, though I still recommend a quick glance. C programming isn't nearly as fun or as easy as Python programming is. Yet, because integration is central to Python's role as a scripting tool, a cursory understanding can be useful, regardless of whether you do integrating, scripting, or both.

This Edition's Design

The best way to get a feel for any book is to read it, of course. But especially for people who are familiar with the prior edition, this section will clarify regarding what is new this time around.

It's Been Updated for Python 2.4 (and 2.5)

All of the example code has been upgraded to use the latest features of the Python language and its standard library. Python is still largely compatible with the code in the first two editions, but recent language additions such as nested scopes and list comprehensions simplify many coding tasks. For instance, default arguments are no longer required to pass objects into most lambda expressions, and the new email package greatly simplifies the tasks of parsing and adding email attachments. See the Python changes list earlier in this chapter for more on this subject.

Although the GUI examples in this book required almost no code changes, they have been updated to run on Tk 8.4, the library used by Python 2.4 as its standard portable GUI toolkit. Among other things, the latest Tk allows window icons to be set by the program. Although begun under 2.4, this edition is also compatible with the upcoming Python 2.5 release.

It's Been Reorganized

A few chapters have been moved to make the flow more logical; for example, the sections on files and directories and the PyMailGUI example are now in chapters of their own. In addition, all appendixes were cut (this book is neither a reference nor a Python changes log), and a new initial preview chapter was added to introduce topics explored throughout the book.

As mentioned earlier, in deference to space, one second-edition chapter—that on the PyErrata web site—has been cut in this edition. Its main, unique topics on state retention have been incorporated into other chapters. The original source code for the PyErrata site still appears on the book's examples package, as supplemental reading.*

It Covers New Topics

You'll find much-expanded coverage of Zope, the ZODB database, threading tools and techniques including the queue module, SQL interfaces, XML parsing, and more. See the example and topic changes lists provided earlier for additional details. Most of the new or expanded topics are a result of the evolution of common practice in the Python world. While this book doesn't address core language evolution directly (the basics of new language tools such as list comprehensions are the domain of the text *Learning Python*), it does employ it throughout its examples.

It's Still Mostly Platform-Neutral

Except for some C integration examples, the majority of the programs in this edition were developed on Windows XP computers, with an eye toward portability to Linux and other platforms. In fact, some of the examples were born of my desire to provide portable Python equivalents of tools missing on Windows (e.g., file splitters). When programs are shown in action, it's usually on Windows; they are demonstrated on the Linux platform only if they exercise Unix-specific interfaces.

This is not meant as a political statement; it is mostly a function of the fact that I wrote this book with Microsoft Word. When time is tight, it's more convenient to run scripts on the same platform as your publishing tools than to frequently switch

---

* I regret cutting this chapter, but new material was added, and as you can tell, this is already a substantial book. As my first editor, Frank Willison, famously said when the second edition came out, if this book were run over by a truck, it would do damage....

platforms. Luckily, because Python has become so portable, the underlying operating system is largely irrelevant to developers. Python, its libraries, and its Tkinter GUI framework work extremely well on all major platforms today.

Where platform issues do come into play, though, I've made the examples as platform-neutral as possible, and I point out platform-specific issues along the way. Generally speaking, most of the scripts should work unchanged on common Python platforms. For instance, all the GUI examples were tested on both Windows (ME, XP) and Linux (KDE, Gnome), and most of the command-line and thread examples were developed on Windows but work on Linux too. Because Python's system interfaces are built to be portable, this is easier than it may sound; it's largely automatic.

On the other hand, this book does delve into platform-specific topics where appropriate. For instance, there is coverage of many Windows-specific topics—Active Scripting, COM, program launch options, and so on. Linux and Unix readers will also find material geared toward their platforms—forks, pipes, and the like.

C integration code platform issues

The one place where readers may still catch a glimpse of platform biases is in the Python/C integration examples. For simplicity, the C compilation details covered in this text are still somewhat Unix/Linux-oriented. One can make a reasonable case for such a focus—not only does Linux come with C compilers, but the Unix development environment it provides grew up around that language. On standard Windows, the C code shown in this book will work, but you may need to use different build procedures (they vary per Windows compiler, some of which are very similar to Linux compilers).

In fact, for this third edition of the book, many of the C integration examples were run on the Cygwin system, not on Linux. Cygwin provides a complete, Unix-like environment and library for Windows. It includes C development tools, command-line utilities, and a version of Python that supports Unix tools not present in the standard Windows Python, including process forks and fifos. Unlike Linux, because it runs on Windows, Cygwin does not require a complete operating system installation (see *http://www.cygwin.com*).

Cygwin has a GPL-style, open source license that requires giving away code (more on this later in the book). If you do not wish to download and install Cygwin, you may have to translate some of the C integration build files for your platform; the standard C development concepts apply. On standard Windows, you'll have to translate for your C compiler. O'Reilly has published an outstanding text, *Python Programming on Win32*, that covers Windows-specific Python topics like this, and it should help address any disparity you may find here.

It's Still Focused for a More Advanced Audience

Becoming proficient in Python involves two distinct tasks: learning the core language itself, and then learning how to apply it in applications. This book addresses the latter (and larger) of these tasks by presenting Python libraries, tools, and programming techniques.

Learning Python syntax and datatypes is an important first step, and a prerequisite to this book. Very soon after you've learned how to slice a list, though, you'll find yourself wanting to do real things, like writing scripts to compare file directories, responding to user requests on the Internet, displaying images in a window, reading email, and so on. Most of the day-to-day action is in applying the language, not the language itself.

That's what this book is for. It covers libraries and tools beyond the core language, which become paramount when you begin writing real applications. It also addresses larger software design issues such as reusability and OOP, which can be illustrated only in the context of realistically scaled programs. Because it assumes you already know Python, this is a somewhat advanced text; again, if you find yourself lost, you might do well to learn the core language from other resources before returning here.

It's Still Example-Oriented

Although this book teaches concepts before applying them, it still contains many larger working programs that tie together concepts presented earlier in the book and demonstrate how to use Python for realistically scaled tasks. Among them:

PyEdit
: A Python/Tk text-file editor object and program

PyView
: A photo image and note-file slideshow

PyDraw
: A paint program for drawing and moving image objects

PyTree
: A tree data structure drawing program

PyClock
: A Python/Tk analog and digital clock widget

PyToe
: An AI-powered graphical tic-tac-toe program

PyForm
: A persistent object table browser

PyCalc
: A calculator widget in Python/Tk

PyMailGUI
> A Python/Tkinter POP and SMTP email client

PyFtp
> A simple Python/Tk file-transfer GUI

PyMailCGI
> A web-based email client interface

PyPhoto
> A new thumbnail picture viewer with resizing and saves

See the earlier example changes list for more about how some of these have mutated in this edition. Besides the major examples listed here, there are also mixed-mode C integration examples (e.g., callback registration and class object processing); SWIG examples (with and without "shadow" classes for C++); more Internet examples (FTP upload and download scripts, NNTP and HTTP examples, email tools, and socket and select module examples); many examples of Python threads and thread queues; and coverage of Jython, HTMLgen, Zope, COM, XML parsing, and Python ZODB and MySQL database interfaces. In addition, as mentioned earlier, the second edition's PyErrata web site example appears in the examples distribution.

But It's Still Not a Reference Manual

This edition, like the first, is still more of a *tutorial* than a reference manual (despite sharing a title pattern with a popular Perl reference text). This book aims to teach, not to document. You can use its table of contents and index to track down specifics, and the new structure helps make this easy to do. But this edition is still designed to be used in conjunction with, rather than to replace, Python reference manuals. Because Python's manuals are free, well written, available online, and change frequently, it would be folly to devote space to parroting their content. For an exhaustive list of all tools available in the Python system, consult other books (e.g., O'Reilly's *Python Pocket Reference* and *Python in a Nutshell*) or the standard manuals at Python's web site (see *http://www.python.org/doc*).

Using the Book's Examples

Because examples are central to the structure of this book, I want to briefly describe how to use them here. In general, though, see the following text files in the *examples* directory for more details:

README-root.txt
> Package structure notes

PP3E\README-PP3E.txt
> General usage notes

Of these, the *README-PP3E.txt* file is the most informative. In addition, the *PP3E\ Config* directory contains low-level configuration file examples for Windows and Linux, which may or may not be applicable to your usage. I give an overview of some setup details here, but the preceding files give the complete description.

The Book Examples Tree

In a sense, the directory containing the book's examples is *itself* a fairly sophisticated Python software system and the examples within it have been upgraded structurally in a number of important ways:

Examples directory tree: a package
> The entire examples distribution has been organized as one Python *module package* to facilitate cross-directory imports and avoid name clashes with other Python code installed on your computer. All cross-directory imports in book examples are package imports, relative to the examples root directory.

> Using directory paths in import statements (instead of a complex PYTHONPATH) also tends to make it easier to tell where modules come from. Moreover, you now need to add only one directory to your PYTHONPATH search-path setting for the entire book examples tree: the directory containing the *PP3E* examples root directory. To reuse code in this book within your own applications, simply import through the *PP3E* package root (e.g., from PP3E.Launcher import which, or import PP3E.Gui.Tools.threadtools).

Example filenames
> Module names are now descriptive and of arbitrary length (I punted on 8.3 DOS compatibility long ago), and any remaining all-uppercase filenames are long gone.

Example listing titles
> Labels of example listings give the full directory pathname of the example's source file to help you locate it in the examples distribution. For instance, an example source-code file whose name is given as *Example N-M: PP3E\Internet\ Ftp\sousa.py* refers to the file *sousa.py* in the *PP3E\Internet\Ftp* subdirectory of the *examples* directory. The *examples* directory is the directory containing the top-level *PP3E* directory of the book examples tree. The examples tree is simply the *Examples* directory of the book examples distribution, described further in the next section.

Example command lines
> Similarly, command lines give their directory context. For example, when a command line is shown typed after a system prompt, as in ...\PP3E\System\Streams>, it is really to be typed at a system command-line prompt, while working in the *PP3E\System\Streams* subdirectory in your *examples* directory. Unix and Linux users: think / when you see \ in filename paths.

Example launchers

Because it's just plain fun to click on things right away, there are also self-configuring demo launcher programs (described later), to give you a quick look at Python scripts in action with minimal configuration requirements. You can generally run them straight from the examples package without any configuration.

The Book Examples Distribution Package

You can find the book examples distribution package on the book's web page at O'Reilly's web site, *http://www.oreilly.com/catalog/python3/*. The book *examples* directory is located in the *PP3E* subdirectory of the topmost *Examples* directory in the package—that is, *Examples\PP3E* on Windows and *Examples/PP3E* on Linux.

If you've copied the examples to your machine, the examples directory is wherever you copied the *PP3E* root directory. Example titles reflect this tree's structure. For instance, an example title of *PP3E\Preview\mod.py* refers to the *Examples\PP3E\Preview\mod.py* file at the top level of the book examples distribution package.

You can run most of the examples from within the package directly, but if you obtained them on a CD, you'll want to copy them to a writable medium such as your hard drive to make changes, and to allow Python to save *.pyc* compiled bytecode files for quicker startups. See the example package's top-level README file for more details, or browse the examples directory in your favorite file explorer for a quick tour.

Depending on how often the book's distribution package is maintained, it may also contain extra open source packages such as the latest releases of Python, the SWIG code generator, and Windows extensions, but you can always find up-to-date releases of Python and other packages on the Web (see Python's web site, *http://www.python.org*, or search the Web). In fact, you should—most likely, the Web will very quickly become more current than any extra software included in the book's package.

Running Examples: The Short Story

Now the fun stuff—if you want to see some Python examples right away, do this:

1. Install Python from the book's distribution package or from Python's web site (*http://www.python.org*), unless it is already present on your computer. If you use a Linux or recent Macintosh, Python is probably already installed. On Windows, click on the name of the Python self-installer program and do a default install (click Yes or Next in response to every prompt). On other systems, see the README file.

2. Start one of the following self-configuring scripts located in the top-level *Examples\PP3E* directory of the book examples package. Either click on their icons in your file explorer, or run them from your system prompt (e.g., a Windows console box, or Linux xterm) using command lines of the form python *scriptname* (you may need to use the full path to python if it's not implicit on your system):

Launch_PyDemos.pyw
> The main Python/Tk demo launcher toolbar

Launch_PyGadgets_bar.pyw
> A Python/Tk utilities launcher bar

Launch_PyGadgets.py
> Starts the standard Python/Tk utilities

LaunchBrowser.py
> Opens the web examples index page in your web browser

The Launch_* scripts start Python programs portably* and require only that Python be installed—you don't need to set any environment variables first to run them. LaunchBrowser will work if it can find a web browser on your machine even if you don't have an Internet link (though some Internet examples won't work completely without a live link).

The demo launchers also include a number of web-based programs that use a web browser for their interface. When run, these programs launch a locally running web server coded in Python (we'll meet this server script later in this book). Although these programs can run on a remote server too, they still require a local Python installation to be used with a server running on your machine.

Running Examples: The Details

This section goes into a few additional details about running the book's example programs. If you're in a hurry, feel free to skip this and run the programs yourself now.

Demos and gadgets

To help organize the book's examples, I've provided a demo launcher program GUI, *PyDemos2.pyw*, in the top-level *PP3E* directory of the examples distribution. Figure P-1 shows PyDemos in action on Windows after pressing a few buttons. We'll

---

* All the demo and launcher scripts are written portably but are known to work only on Windows and Linux at the time of this writing; they may require minor changes on other platforms. Apologies if you're using a platform that I could not test: Tk runs on Windows, X Windows, and Macs; Python itself runs on everything from PDAs, iPods, and cell phones to real-time systems, mainframes, and supercomputers; and my advance for writing this book wasn't as big as you may think.

meet in this text all the programs shown in the figure. The launcher bar itself appears on the top right of the screen; with it, you can run most of the major graphical examples in the book with a mouse click, and view their source code in pop-up windows. The demo launcher bar can also be used to start major Internet book examples if a browser can be located on your machine and a Python-coded server can be started.

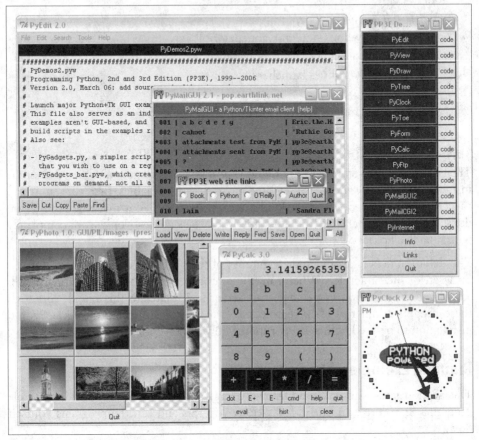

Figure P-1. The PyDemos launcher with gadgets and demos

Besides launching demos, the PyDemos source code provides pointers to major examples in the examples tree; see its code for details. You'll also find automated build scripts for the Python/C integration examples in the *Integration* examples directory, which serve as indexes to major C examples.

I've also included a top-level program called *PyGadgets.py*, and its relative, *PyGadgets_bar.pyw*, to launch some of the more useful GUI book examples for real use instead of demonstration (mostly, the programs I use; configure as desired). Run PyGadgets_bar to see how it looks—it's a simple row of buttons that pop up many of the same programs shown in Figure P-1, but for everyday use, not for demonstrations. All of its programs are presented in this book as well and are included in the examples distribution package. See the end of Chapter 10 for more on PyDemos and PyGadgets.

Setup requirements

Most demos and gadgets require a Python with Tkinter GUI support, but that is the default configuration for Python out-of-the-box on Windows. As a result, most of the demos and gadgets should "just work" on Windows. On some other platforms, you may need to install or enable Tkinter for your Python; try it and see—if you get an error about Tkinter not being found, you'll need to configure it. If it's not already present, Tkinter support can be had freely on the Web for all major platforms (more on this in the GUI part of this book, but search the Web with Google for quick pointers).

Two external dependency notes: PyPhoto will not run without PIL, and PyMailCGI runs without PyCrypto but uses it if installed. Both PIL and PyCrypto are open source third-party extension packages, but must be installed in addition to Python. Some book examples use additional third-party tools (for instance, ZODB and MySQL in the database chapter), but these are not launched from the demos and gadgets interfaces.

To run the files listed in the preceding section directly, you'll also need to set up your Python module search path, typically with your PYTHONPATH environment variable or a *.pth* file. The book examples tree ships as a simple directory and does not use Python's Distutils scripts to install itself in your Python's site packages directory (this system works well for packed software, but can add extra steps for viewing book examples).

If you want to run a collection of Python demos from the book right away, though, and you don't want to bother with setting up your environment first, simply run these self-launching utility scripts in the *PP3E* directory instead:

- *Launch_PyDemos.pyw*
- *Launch_PyGadgets_bar.pyw*
- *Launch_PyGadgets.py*

These Python-coded launcher scripts assume Python has already been installed, but will automatically find your Python executable and the book examples distribution and set up your Python module and system search paths as needed to run their programs. You can probably run these launcher scripts by simply clicking on their names in a file explorer, and you should be able to run them directly from the book's examples package tree (you can read more about these scripts in Part II of the book).

Web-based examples

Beginning with this edition of the book, its browser-based Internet examples are not installed on a remote server. Instead, we'll be using a Python-coded web server running locally to test these examples. If you launch this server, though, you can also test-drive browser-based examples too. You can find more on this in the Internet section of this book.

For a quick look, though, PyDemos attempts to launch both a web server and a web browser on your machine automatically for the major example web pages. You start the browser by running the *LaunchBrowser.py* script in the examples root directory. That script tries to find a usable browser on your machine, with generally good results; see the script for more details if it fails. The server is implemented by a Python script, assuming you have permission to run an HTTP server on your machine (you generally do on Windows).

Provided the server starts and LaunchBrowser can find a browser on your machine, some demo buttons will pop up web pages automatically. Figure P-2, for example, shows the web examples index page running under a local server and the Firefox browser.

Clicking this page's links runs various server-side Python CGI scripts presented in the book. Of special interest, the *getfile.html* link on this page allows you to view the source code of any other file in the book's web server directory—HTML code, Python CGI scripts, and so on; see Chapter 16 for details.

Top-level programs

To summarize, here is what you'll find in the top-level *Examples\PP3E* directory of the book's examples package:

PyDemos.pyw
> Button bar for starting major GUI and Internet examples in demo mode

PyGadgets_bar.pyw
> Button bar for starting GUIs in PyGadgets on demand

PyGadgets.py
> Starts programs in nondemo mode for regular use

*Launch_*.py**
> Starts the PyDemos and PyGadgets programs using *Launcher.py* to autoconfigure search paths (run these for a quick look)

LaunchBrowser.py
> Opens example web pages with an automatically located web browser

Launcher.py
> Utility used to start programs without environment settings—finds Python, sets PYTHONPATH, and spawns Python programs

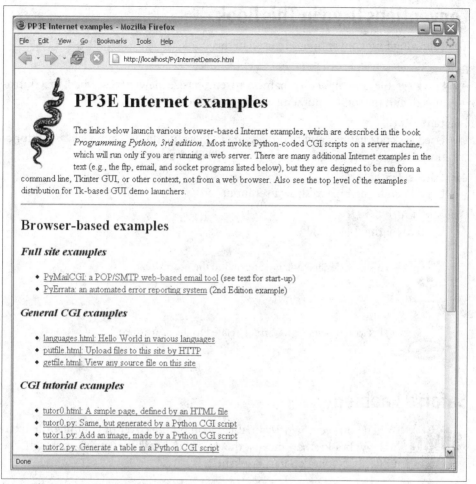

Figure P-2. The PyInternetDemos web page

You'll also find subdirectories for examples from each major topic area of the book. In addition, the top-level *PP3E\PyTools* directory contains Python-coded command-line utilities for converting line feeds in all example text files to DOS or Unix format (useful if they look odd in your text editor); making all example files writable (useful if you drag-and-drop off a CD on some platforms); deleting old *.pyc* bytecode files in the tree; and more. Again, see the example directory's *README-PP3E.txt* file for more details on all example issues.

Conventions Used in This Book

The following font conventions are used in this book:

Italic

Used for file and directory names, to emphasize new terms when first introduced, and for some comments within code sections

`Constant width`

Used for code listings and to designate modules, methods, options, classes, functions, statements, programs, objects, and HTML tags

`Constant width bold`

Used in code sections to show user input

`Constant width italic`

Used to mark replaceables

This icon designates a note related to the nearby text.

This icon designates a warning related to the nearby text.

Safari® Enabled

When you see a Safari® Enabled icon on the cover of your favorite technology book, that means the book is available online through the O'Reilly Network Safari Bookshelf.

Safari offers a solution that's better than e-books. It's a virtual library that lets you easily search thousands of top tech books, cut and paste code samples, download chapters, and find quick answers when you need the most accurate, current information. Try it for free at *http://safari.oreilly.com*.

Where to Look for Updates

As before, updates, corrections, and supplements for this book will be maintained at the author's web site, *http://www.rmi.net/~lutz*. Look for the third edition's link on that page for all supplemental information related to this version of the book. As for the first two editions, I will also be maintaining a log on this web site of Python changes over time, which you should consider a supplemental appendix to this text. O'Reilly's web site, *http://www.oreilly.com*, also has an errata report system, and you should consider the union of these two lists to be the official word on book bugs and updates.

Contacting O'Reilly

You can also address comments and questions about this book to the publisher:

O'Reilly Media, Inc.
1005 Gravenstein Highway North
Sebastopol, CA 95472
800-998-9938 (in the United States and Canada)
707-827-7000 (international/local)
707-829-0104 (fax)

O'Reilly has a web page for this book, which lists errata, examples, and any additional information. You can access this page at:

http://www.oreilly.com/catalog/python3

To comment or ask technical questions about this book, send email to:

bookquestions@oreilly.com

For more information about books, conferences, software, Resource Centers, and the O'Reilly Network, see the O'Reilly web site at:

http://www.oreilly.com

Using Code Examples

This book is here to help you get your job done. In general, you may use the code in this book in your programs and documentation. You do not need to contact us for permission unless you're reproducing a significant portion of the code. For example, writing a program that uses several chunks of code from this book does not require permission. Selling or distributing a CD-ROM of examples from O'Reilly books does require permission. Answering a question by citing this book and quoting example code does not require permission. Incorporating a significant amount of example code from this book into your product's documentation does require permission.

We appreciate, but do not require, attribution. An attribution usually includes the title, author, publisher, and ISBN. For example: "Python Programming, Third Edition, by Mark Lutz. Copyright 2006 O'Reilly Media, Inc., 978-0-596-00925-0."

Acknowledgments

In closing, I would like to extend appreciation to a few of the people who helped in some way during all the incarnations of this book project:

- To this book's first editor, the late Frank Willison, for the early years.
- To this book's later editors, for tolerating my nondeterministic schedule: Laura Lewin on the second edition, Jonathan Gennick on the third edition, and Mary O'Brien at the end.

- To the people who took part in a technical review of an early draft of this edition: Fredrik Lundh, Valentino Volonghi, Anna Ravenscroft, and Kyle VanderBeek.

- To Python creator Guido van Rossum, for making this stuff fun again.

- To Tim O'Reilly and the staff of O'Reilly, both for producing this book and for supporting open source software in general.

- To the Python community at large, for quality, simplicity, diligence, and humor.

- To C++, for frustrating me enough to compel me toward Python; I think I'd rather flip burgers than go back :-).

- To the thousands of students of the 170 Python classes I have taught so far, for your feedback on Python in general, and its applications. You taught me how to teach.

- To the scores of readers who took the time to send me comments about the first two editions of this book. Your opinions helped shape this book's evolution.

And finally, a few personal notes of thanks. To all the friends I've met on the training trail, for hospitality. To my mom, for wisdom and courage. To OQO, for toys. To my brothers and sister, for old days. To Guinness, for the beer in Dublin. To Birgit, for inspiration and spleenwurst. And to my children, Michael, Samantha, and Roxanne, for hope.

—Mark Lutz
April 2006
Somewhere in Colorado, or an airport near you

## PART I

The Beginning

This part of the book gets things started by introducing the Python language and taking us on a quick tour of some of the most common ways it is applied.

Chapter 1

Here, we'll take a "behind the scenes" look at Python and its world by presenting some of its history, its major uses, and the common reasons people choose it for their projects. This is essentially a management-level, nontechnical introduction to Python.

Chapter 2

This chapter uses a simple example—recording information about people—to briefly introduce some of the major Python application domains we'll be studying in this book. We'll migrate the same example through multiple steps. Along the way, we'll meet databases, GUIs, web sites, and more. This is something of a demo chapter, designed to pique your interest. We won't learn much here, but we'll have a chance to see Python in action before digging into the details. This chapter also serves as a review of some core language ideas you should be familiar with before starting this book, such as data representation and object-oriented programming (OOP).

The point of this part of the book is not to give you an in-depth look at Python, but just to let you sample its application. It will also provide you with a grounding in Python's broader goals and purpose.

CHAPTER 1

Introducing Python

"And Now for Something Completely Different"

This book is about using Python, an easy-to-use, flexible, object-oriented, mature, popular, and open source[*] programming language designed to optimize development speed. Although it is completely general purpose, Python is often called a *scripting language*, partly because of its sheer ease of use and partly because it is commonly used to orchestrate or "glue" other software components in an application. Python is also commonly known as a *high-level language*, because it automates most low-level tasks that programmers must handle manually in traditional languages such as C.

If you are new to Python, chances are you've heard about the language somewhere but are not quite sure what it is about. To help you get started, this chapter provides a general introduction to Python's features and roles. Most of it will make more sense once you have seen real Python programs, but let's first take a quick pass over the forest before wandering among the trees. In this chapter, we'll explore Python's philosophy, its history, and some of its most prominent benefits and uses, before digging into the details.

Python Philosophy 101

In the Preface, I mentioned that Python emphasizes concepts such as quality, productivity, portability, and integration. Since these four terms summarize most of the reasons for using Python, I'd like to define them in a bit more detail.

---

[*] Open source systems are sometimes called *freeware*, in that their source code is freely distributed and community controlled. Don't let that concept fool you, though; with roughly 1 million users in that community today, Python is very well supported. For more information on open source, see *http://opensource.org*.

Software quality

Python makes it easy to write software that can be understood, reused, and modified. It was deliberately designed to raise development quality expectations in the scripting world. Python's clear syntax and coherent design, for example, almost force programmers to write *readable code*—a critical feature for software that may be changed or reused by others in the future.

Of equal importance, because the Python language tries to do better, so too do Python developers and the Python community at large. In the Python world, one finds a refreshing focus on quality concepts such as simplicity, explicitness, and readability—ideas often given little more than a passing glance in some camps. (For more on this Python-inspired mindset, see the sidebar "The Python 'Secret Handshake'," near the end of this chapter.)

The Python language really does look like it was *designed* and not accumulated. It has an orthogonal, explicit, and minimalist design that makes code easy to understand and easy to predict. Python approaches complexity by providing a simple core language and splitting application-specific tools into a large set of modular library components.

As a popular slogan attests, the result is that Python "*fits your brain*"—it's possible to use the language without constantly flipping through reference manuals. This design makes Python ideal as a customization language for nonexperts. Perhaps most important is that by limiting the number of possible interactions in your code, Python reduces both program complexity and the potential for bugs.

Besides being well designed, Python is also well tooled for modern software methodologies such as structured, modular, and object-oriented design, which allow code to be written once and reused many times. In fact, due to the inherent power and flexibility of the language, writing high-quality Python components that may be applied in multiple contexts is almost automatic.

Developer productivity

Python is optimized for *speed of development*. It's easy to write programs fast in Python, because the interpreter handles details you must code explicitly in more complex, lower-level languages. Things such as type declarations, storage layout, memory management, common task implementations, and build procedures are nowhere to be found in Python scripts.

In fact, programs written in Python are typically one-third to one-fifth as large as they would be in a language like C++ or Java, and these ratios directly correlate to improved programmer speed. Because of Python's high-level design, Python developers have less to code, less to debug, and less to maintain.

The result is a remarkably *flexible* and *agile* language, useful for both quick *tactical* tasks such as testing and system administration, as well as larger and long-term *strategic* projects employing design and analysis tools.

Today, developers use Python for everything from five-line scripts to systems composed of more than 1 million lines of Python code (including IronPort's email security products suite). Its tool set allows it to scale up as needed. In both modes, Python programmers gain a crucial development speed advantage because of the language itself, as well as its library of precoded tools.

For instance, the lack of type declarations alone accounts for much of the conciseness and flexibility of Python code: because code is not restricted to a specific type, it is generally applicable to many types. Any object with a compatible interface will do. And although Python is *dynamically* typed—types are tracked automatically instead of being declared (it is still *strongly* typed)—every operation is sanity checked as your program runs. Odd type combinations are errors in Python, not invocations of arbitrary magic.

But fast initial development is only one component of productivity. In the real world, programmers must write code both for a computer to execute and for other programmers to read and maintain. Because Python's syntax resembles *executable pseudocode*, it yields programs that are easy to understand, change, and use long after they have been written. In addition, Python supports (but does not impose) advanced code reuse paradigms such as object-oriented programming, which further boost developer productivity and shrink development time.

Program portability

Most Python programs run without modification on nearly every computer system in use today—on Windows, Linux, Macintosh, and everything from IBM mainframes and Cray supercomputers to real-time systems and handheld PDAs. Python programs even run on more exotic devices such as game consoles, cell phones, and the Apple iPod. Although some platforms offer nonportable extensions, the core Python language and libraries are largely platform neutral and provide tools for dealing with platform differences when they arise.

For example, most Python scripts developed on Windows, Linux, or Macintosh will generally run on the other two platforms immediately—simply copy the script's source code over to the other platforms. Moreover, a GUI program written with Python's standard Tkinter library will run on the X Windows system, Microsoft Windows, and the Macintosh, with native look-and-feel on each and without modifying the program's source code. Alternative toolkits such as wxPython and PyQt offer similar GUI portability.

Component integration

Python is not a closed box: it is also designed to be integrated with other tools. Programs written in Python can be easily mixed with and can *script* (i.e., direct) other components of a system. This makes Python ideal as a control language and as a customization tool. When programs are augmented with a Python layer, their end users can configure and tailor them, without shipping the system's entire source code.

More specifically, today Python scripts can call out to existing C and C++ libraries; use Java classes; integrate with COM, .NET, and CORBA components; communicate with other components over network protocols such as sockets, HTTP, XML-RPC, and SOAP; and more. In addition, programs written in other languages can just as easily run Python scripts by calling C and Java API functions, accessing Python-coded COM and network servers, and so on. Python allows developers to open up their products to customization in a variety of ways.

In an era of increasingly short development schedules, faster machines, and heterogeneous applications, these strengths have proven to be powerful allies to hundreds of thousands of developers, in both small and large development projects.

Naturally, there are other aspects of Python that attract developers, such as its simple learning curve for developers and users alike, vast libraries of precoded tools to minimize upfront development, and a completely free nature that cuts product development and deployment costs.

Python's open source nature, for instance, means that it is controlled by its users, not by a financially vested company. To put that more forcefully, because Python's implementation is freely available, Python programmers can never be held hostage by a software vendor. Unlike commercial tools, Python can never be arbitrarily discontinued. Access to source code liberates programmers and provides a final form of documentation.

At the end of the day, though, Python's *productivity* focus is perhaps its most attractive and defining quality. As I started writing the second edition of this book in the Internet bubble era of 1999, the main problem facing the software development world was not just writing programs quickly, but finding developers with the time to write programs at all. As I write this third edition in the post-boom era of 2005, it is perhaps more common for programmers to be called on to accomplish the same tasks as before, but with fewer resources. In both scenarios, developers' time is paramount—in fact, it's usually much more critical than raw execution speed, especially given the speed of today's computers.

As a language optimized for developer productivity, Python seems to be the right answer to the questions asked by the development world. It allows programmers to accomplish more in less time. Not only can Python developers implement systems quickly, but the resulting systems will be reusable, maintainable by others, portable across platforms, and easily integrated with other application components.

Why Not Just Use C or C++?

I'm asked this question quite often, and if you're new to the scripting languages domain, you might be puzzling over this question yourself. After all, C runs very fast and is widely available. So how did Python become so popular?

The short story—one we'll see in action firsthand in this book—is that people use scripting languages rather than compiled languages like C and C++ because scripting languages are orders of magnitude easier and quicker to use. Python can be used in long-term strategic roles too, but unlike compiled languages, it also works well in quick, tactical mode. As an added benefit, the resulting systems you build are easier to change and reuse over time.

This is especially true in the web domain, for example, where text processing is so central, change is a constant, and development speed can make or break a project. In domains like these:

- Python's string objects and pattern matching make text processing a breeze—there is no need to limit the size of strings, and tasks like searching, splitting, concatenation, and slicing are trivial. In C, such tasks can be tedious, because everything is constrained by a type and a size.

- Python's general support for data structures helps here too—you just type a complex nested dictionary literal, for example, and Python builds it. There is no need to lay out memory, allocate and free space, and so on.

- The Python language itself is much simpler to code. Because you don't declare types, for instance, your code not only becomes shorter, but also can be applied and reused in a much wider range of contexts. When there is less to code, programming is quicker. And the runtime error checking provided by scripting languages like Python makes it easier to find and fix bugs.

- Just as important is that a vast collection of free, web-related software is available for Python programmers to use—everything from the client and server-side protocol modules in the standard library, to third-party web application frameworks such as Zope, Plone, CherryPy, Django, and Webware. These greatly simplify the task of building enterprise-level web sites.

In other domains, the same factors apply but with different available tool sets. In fact, after you use Python for awhile, you'll probably find that it enables things that you would have never considered doing in a compiled language because they would have been too difficult. Network scripting, GUIs, multitasking, and so on, can be cumbersome in C but are easy in Python.

—continued—

The bottom line is that C is just too complex, rigid, and slow, especially for web work. In such a dynamic domain, you need the flexibility and rapid development of a scripting language like Python. Compiled languages can run faster (depending on the sort of code you run), but speed of development tends to overshadow speed of execution on the Web. You should be warned, though—once you start using Python, you may never want to go back.

The Life of Python

Python was invented around 1990 by Guido van Rossum, when he was at CWI in Amsterdam. It is named after the BBC comedy series *Monty Python's Flying Circus*, of which Guido is a fan (see this chapter's sidebar "What's in a Name?"). Guido was also involved with the Amoeba distributed operating system and the ABC language. In fact, his original motivation for creating Python was to create an advanced scripting language for the Amoeba system. Moreover, Python borrowed many of the usability-study-inspired ideas in ABC, but added practicality in the form of libraries, datatypes, external interfaces, and more.

The net effect was that Python's design turned out to be general enough to address a wide variety of domains. It is now used in increasingly diverse roles by hundreds of thousands of engineers around the world. Companies use Python today in commercial products for tasks as diverse as web site construction, hardware testing, numeric analysis, customizing C++ and Java class libraries, movie animation, and much more (more on roles in the next section). In fact, because Python is a completely general-purpose language, its target domains are limited only by the scope of computers in general.

Since it first appeared on the public domain scene in 1991, Python has continued to attract a loyal following and has spawned a dedicated Internet newsgroup, comp.lang.python, in 1994. As the first edition of this book was being written in 1995, Python's home page debuted on the Web at *http://www.python.org*—still the official place to find all things Python. A supplemental site, the Vaults of Parnassus, serves as a library of third-party extensions for Python application development (see *http://www.vex.net/parnassus*). More recently, the Python Package Index site (PyPI at *http://www.python.org/pypi*—also known as the "Python Cheese Shop"—began providing a comprehensive and automated catalog of third-party Python packages.

To help manage Python's growth, organizations that are aimed at supporting Python developers have taken shape over the years: among them, the now defunct Python Software Activity (PSA) was formed to help facilitate Python conferences and web sites, and the Python Consortium was formed by organizations interested in helping to foster Python's growth. More recently, the Python Software Foundation (PSF) was formed to own the intellectual property of Python and coordinate community activities, and the Python Business Forum (PBF) nonprofit group addresses the needs of companies whose businesses are based on Python. Additional resources are available for Python training, consulting, and other services.

Today, Guido is employed by Google, the web search-engine maker and a major Python user, and he devotes a portion of his time to Python. A handful of key Python developers are also employed by Zope Corporation, home to the Python-based Zope web application toolkit (see *http://www.zope.org* and Chapter 18; Zope is also the basis of the Plone web content management system). However, the Python language is owned and managed by an independent body, and it remains a true open source, community-driven, and self-organizing system. Hundreds, if not thousands, of individuals contribute to Python's development, following a now formal Python Enhancement Proposal (PEP) procedure and coordinating their efforts online.

Other companies have Python efforts underway as well. For instance, ActiveState and PythonWare develop Python tools, O'Reilly (the publisher of this book) and the Python community organize annual Python conferences (OSCON, PyCon, and Euro-Python), and O'Reilly manages a supplemental Python web site (see the O'Reilly Network's Python DevCenter at *http://www.oreillynet.com/python*). Although the world of professional organizations and companies changes more frequently than do published books, the Python language will undoubtedly continue to meet the needs of its user community.

Signs of the Python Times

It's been an exciting decade in the Python world. Since I wrote the first edition of this book in 1995 and 1996, Python has grown from a new kid on the scripting-languages block to an established and widely used tool in companies around the world. In fact, today the real question is not who is using Python, but who is not. Python is now used in some fashion in almost every software organization—whether as a tactical tool for quick tasks or an implementation language for longer-range strategic projects.

Although measuring the popularity of an open source, freely distributed tool such as Python is not always easy (there are no licenses to be tallied), most available statistics reveal exponential growth in Python's popularity over the last decade. Among the most recent signs of Python's explosive growth are:

Users
> In 1999, one leading industry observer suggested that, based on various statistics, there were as many as 300,000 Python users worldwide. Other estimates are still more optimistic. In early 2000, for instance, the Python web site was already on track to service 500,000 new Python interpreter downloads by year end in

addition to other Python distribution media. Python is also a standard prein-stalled item on Linux, Macintosh, and some Windows computers today and is embedded in various applications and hardware.

Today, the best estimates, based on developer surveys and network activity, suggest that there are likely between 750,000 and 1 million Python users worldwide. A better estimate is impossible because of Python's open source nature, but Python clearly enjoys a large and active user community.

Applications

Real organizations have adopted Python and Python-focused systems for real projects. It has been used to:

- Animate movies (Industrial Light & Magic, Sony Pictures Imageworks, Disney, Pixar)
- Perform searches on the Internet (Google, Infoseek)
- Script GIS mapping products (ESRI)
- Distribute content downloads on the Internet (BitTorrent)
- Predict the weather (U.S. National Weather Service, NOAA)
- Test computer hardware (Seagate, Intel, Hewlett-Packard, Micron, KLA)
- Do numeric analysis (NASA, Los Alamos National Laboratory, Lawrence Livermore National Laboratory, Fermi)
- Perform cryptography and stock market analysis (NSA, Getco)
- Script games and graphics (Origin, Corel, Blender, PyGame)
- Navigate spacecraft and control experiments (Jet Propulsion Laboratory)
- Serve up maps and directories on the Web (Yahoo!)
- Guide users through Linux installation and maintenance (Red Hat)
- Implement web sites and content (Disney, JPL, Zope, Plone, Twisted)
- Design missile defense systems (Lockheed Martin)
- Manage mail lists (Mailman)
- Deliver eGreeting cards (American Greetings)
- Implement Personal Information Managers (Chandler)

...and much more.* Some of the Python-based systems in the preceding list are very popular in their own right. For example, the widely used Google search engine—arguably responsible for much of the Web's success—makes heavy use

---

* See *http://www.python.org/moin/OrganizationsUsingPython* or search Python.org (*http://www.python.org/about/success*) for more examples of Python-based applications. Some companies don't disclose their Python use for competitive reasons, though many eventually become known when one of their web pages crashes and displays a Python error message in a browser. O'Reilly has also published a list of Python success stories derived from a list of testimonials maintained by people interested in Python advocacy; see the advocacy group's list at *http://www.pythonology.com/success*.

of the Python language and is likely the most successful server-side application of Python so far. And in the latest release of its popular ArcGIS geographical information system (GIS), ESRI has begun recommending Python as the scripting tool for customization and automation to its reported 1 million licensees.

Of special note, BitTorrent, a distributed file-sharing system written in Python, is likely the most successful client-side Python program to date. It already records 42 million lifetime downloads on SourceForge.net as this chapter is being written, and it is listed as the number three package for all-time top downloads at that site (this does not include the roughly 2 million new downloads per month, or alternative clients that embed the BitTorrent Python backend). In addition, a late 2004 Reuters report noted that more than one-third of the Internet's traffic was based on BitTorrent. Per other reports, BitTorrent accounted for 53 percent of all peer-to-peer (P2P) Internet traffic in mid-2004, and P2P traffic may be two-thirds of all Internet traffic today.

Books

When I started the first edition of this book in 1995, no Python books were available. As I wrote the second edition of this book in 2000, more than a dozen were available, with almost that many more on the way. And as I write this third edition in 2005, far more than 50 Python books are on the market, not counting non-English translations (a simple search for "Python programming" books currently yields 91 hits on Amazon.com). Some of these books are focused on a particular domain such as Windows or the Web, and some are available in German, French, Japanese, and other language editions.

Domains

Python has grown to embrace Microsoft Windows developers, with support for .NET, COM, and Active Scripting; Java developers, with the Jython Java-based implementation of the language; Mac OS X developers, with integration of tools such as Cocoa and standard inclusion in the Mac OS; and web developers, with a variety of toolkits such as Zope and Plone.

As we'll see in this book, the COM support allows Python scripts to be both a server and a client of components and to interface with Microsoft Office products; Active Scripting allows Python code to be embedded in HTML web page code and run on either clients or servers. The Jython system compiles Python scripts to Java Virtual Machine (JVM) code so that they can be run in Java-aware systems and seamlessly integrate Java class libraries for use by Python code.

As an open source tool for simplifying web site construction, the Python-based Zope web application framework discussed in this edition has also captured the attention of webmasters and CGI coders. Dynamic behavior in Zope web sites is scripted with Python and rendered with a server-side templating system. By using a workflow model, the Plone web content management system, based on Zope and Python, also allows webmasters to delegate the management of web site content to people who produce the content. Other toolkits, such as Django, Twisted, CherryPy, and Webware, similarly support network-based applications.

Compilers

As I write this third edition, two Python compilers are under development for the Microsoft .NET framework and C# language environment—independent implementations of the Python language that provide seamless .NET integration for Python scripts.

For instance, the new IronPython implementation of Python for .NET and Mono compiles Python code for use in the .NET runtime environment (and is currently being developed in part by Microsoft employees). It promises to be a new, alternative implementation of Python, along with the standard C-based Python and the Jython Java-based implementation mentioned in the prior section.

Other systems, such as the Psyco just-in-time bytecode compiler and the PyPy project, which may subsume it the IronPython implementation, promise substantial speedups for Python programs. See this chapter's sidebar "How Python Runs Your Code" for more details on program execution and compilers.

Newsgroup

User traffic on the main Python Internet newsgroup, comp.lang.python, has risen dramatically too. For instance, according to Yahoo! Groups (see *http:// groups.yahoo.com/group/python-list*), 76 articles were posted on that list in January 1994 and 2,678 in January 2000—a 35-fold increase. Later months were busier still (e.g., 4,226 articles during June 2000, and 7,675 in February 2003— roughly 275 per day), and growth has been generally constant since the list's inception.

Python Internet newsgroup user traffic—along with all other user-base figures cited in this chapter—is likely to have increased by the time you read this text. But even at current traffic rates, Python forums are easily busy enough to consume the full-time attention of anyone with full-time attention to give. Other online forums, such as weblogs (blogs), host additional Python-oriented discussions.

Conferences

There are now two or more annual Python conferences in the U.S., including the annual PyCon event, organized by the Python community, and the Python conference held as part of the Open Source Convention, organized by O'Reilly. Attendance at Python conferences roughly doubled in size every year in their initial years. At least two annual conferences are also now held in Europe each year, including EuroPython and PythonUK. Furthermore, there is now a PyCon conference in Brazil, and conferences have also been held in other places around the world.

Press

Python is regularly featured in industry publications. In fact, since 1995, Python creator Guido van Rossum has appeared on the cover of prominent tech magazines such as *Linux Journal* and *Dr. Dobb's Journal*; the latter publication gave him a programming excellence award for Python. *Linux Journal* also published a special Python supplement with its May 2000 issue, and a Python-specific magazine, *PyZine*, was started up in recently.

Group therapy

Regional Python user groups have begun springing up in numerous sites in the U.S. and abroad, including Oregon, San Francisco, Washington D.C., Colorado, Italy, Korea, and England. Such groups work on Python-related enhancements, organize Python events, and more.

Services

On the pragmatics front, commercial support, consulting, prepackaged distributions, and professional training for Python are now readily available from a variety of sources. For instance, the Python interpreter can be obtained on CDs and packages sold by various companies (including ActiveState), and Python usually comes prebuilt and free with most Linux and recent Macintosh operating systems. In addition, there are now two primary sites for finding third-party add-ons for Python programming: the Vaults of Parnassus and PyPI (see *http://www.python.org* for links).

Jobs

It's now possible to make money as a Python programmer (without having to resort to writing large, seminal books). As I write this book, the Python job board at *http://www.python.org/Jobs.html* lists some 60 companies seeking Python programmers in the U.S. and abroad, in a wide variety of domains. Searches for Python at popular employment sites such as Monster.com and Dice.com yield hundreds of hits for Python-related jobs. And according to one report, the number of Python jobs available in the Silicon Valley area increased 400 percent to 600 percent in the year ending in mid-2005. Not that anyone should switch jobs, of course, but it's nice to know that you can now make a living by using a language that also happens to be fun.

Tools

Python has also played host to numerous tool development efforts. Among the most prominent are the Software Carpentry project, which developed new core software tools in Python; ActiveState, which provides a set of Windows- and Linux-focused Python development products; the Eclipse development environment; and PythonWare, which offers a handful of Python tools.

Education

Python has also begun attracting the attention of educators, many of whom see Python as the "Pascal of the 2000s"—an ideal language for teaching programming due to its simplicity and structure. Part of this appeal was spawned by

Guido van Rossum's proposed Computer Programming for Everybody (CP4E) project, aimed at making Python the language of choice for first-time programmers worldwide.

CP4E itself is now defunct, but an active Python Special Interest Group (SIG) has been formed to address education-related topics. Regardless of any particular initiative's outcome, Python promises to make programming more accessible to the masses. As people grow tired of clicking preprogrammed links, they may evolve from computer users to computer scripters.

Recent Growth (As of 2005, at Least)

As I was writing this third edition, I found that all signs pointed toward continued growth in the Python world:

- Python.org traffic had increased 30 percent for the year that ended in March 2005.

- PyCon conference attendance essentially doubled, increasing to 400–500 attendees in 2005 compared to 200–300 in 2004.

- Python 2.4 was given a Jolt productivity award in early 2005 by *Software Development Magazine*.

- Per a survey conducted by *InfoWorld*, Python popularity nearly doubled in 2004 (usage by developers grew to 14 percent in late 2004, versus 8 percent in the prior year; another survey in the same period measured Python use to be roughly 16 percent).

- Based on the *InfoWorld* survey and the number of all developers, the Python user base is now estimated to be from 750,000 to 1 million worldwide.

- Google, maker of the leading web search engine, launched an open source code site whose initially featured components were mostly Python code.

- The IronPython port being developed in part by Microsoft reported an 80 percent performance boost over the standard C-based Python 2.4 release on some benchmarks.

- As mentioned, the number of Python jobs available in Silicon Valley have reportedly increased by a factor of 4 to 6.

- A web site that automatically tracks the frequency of references to programming languages in online forums found that Python chatter more than doubled between 2004 and 2005. This site also found that among scripting languages, only Python traffic showed the early stages of a rapid growth curve.

- According to an article by O'Reilly, industry-wide book sales data shows that the Python book market grew to two-thirds the size of the Perl book market as of

April 2005. Two years earlier, the Python book market was approximately one-sixth the size of the Perl book market. (Perl is an older scripting language optimized for text processing tasks, which some see as being in competition with Python for mindshare.)

In other words, it's not 1995 anymore. Much of the preceding list was unimaginable when the first edition of this book was conceived. Naturally, this list is doomed to be out-of-date even before this book hits the shelves, but it is nonetheless representative of the sorts of milestones that have occurred over the last five years and will continue to occur for years to come. As a language optimized to address the productivity demands of today's software world, Python's best is undoubtedly yet to come.

What's in a Name?

Python gets its name from the 1970s British TV comedy series *Monty Python's Flying Circus*. According to Python folklore, Guido van Rossum, Python's creator, was watching reruns of the show at about the same time he needed a name for a new language he was developing. And as they say in show business, "the rest is history."

Because of this heritage, references to the comedy group's work often show up in examples and discussion. For instance, the words *spam*, *lumberjack*, and *shrubbery* have a special connotation to Python users, and confrontations are sometimes referred to as "The Spanish Inquisition." As a rule, if a Python user starts using phrases that have no relation to reality, they're probably borrowed from the Monty Python series or movies. Some of these phrases might even pop up in this book. You don't have to run out and rent *The Meaning of Life* or *The Holy Grail* to do useful work in Python, of course, but it can't hurt.

While "Python" turned out to be a distinctive name, it has also had some interesting side effects. For instance, when the Python newsgroup, comp.lang.python, came online in 1994, its first few weeks of activity were almost entirely taken up by people wanting to discuss topics from the TV show. More recently, a special Python supplement in the *Linux Journal* magazine featured photos of Guido garbed in an obligatory "nice red uniform."

Python's news list still receives an occasional post from fans of the show. For instance, one poster innocently offered to swap Monty Python scripts with other fans. Had he known the nature of the forum, he might have at least mentioned whether they ran on Windows or Unix.

The Compulsory Features List

One way to describe a language is by listing its features. Of course, this will be more meaningful after you've seen Python in action; the best I can do now is speak in the abstract. And it's really how Python's features work together that make it what it is. But looking at some of Python's attributes may help define it; Table 1-1 lists some of the common reasons cited for Python's appeal.

Table 1-1. Python language features

Features	Benefits
No manual compile or link steps	Rapid development cycle turnaround
No type declarations	Simpler, shorter, and more flexible programs
Automatic memory management	Garbage collection avoids bookkeeping code and errors
High-level datatypes and operations	Fast development using built-in object types
Object-oriented programming	Code reuse; C++, Java, COM, and .NET integration
Embedding and extending in C	Optimization, customization, legacy code, system "glue"
Classes, modules, exceptions	Modular "programming-in-the-large" support for large-scale projects
A simple, clear syntax and design	Readability, maintainability, ease of learning, less potential for bugs
Dynamic loading of C modules	Simplified extensions, smaller binary files
Dynamic reloading of Python modules	Programs can be modified without stopping
Universal "first-class" object model	Fewer restrictions, code flexibility
Runtime program construction	Handles unforeseen needs, end-user coding
Interactive, dynamic nature	Incremental development and testing
Access to interpreter information	Metaprogramming, introspective objects
Wide interpreter portability	Cross-platform programming without per-program ports
Compilation to portable bytecode	Execution speed, portability
Standard portable GUI framework	Tkinter scripts run on X, Windows, Macs; alternatives: wxPython, PyQt, etc.
Standard Internet protocol support	Easy access to email, FTP, HTTP, CGI, Telnet, etc.
Standard portable system calls	Platform-neutral system scripting and system administration
Built-in and third-party libraries	Vast collection of precoded software components
True open source software	May be freely embedded and shipped

To be fair, Python is really a conglomeration of features borrowed from other languages and combined into a coherent whole. It includes elements taken from C, C++, Modula-3, ABC, Icon, and others. For instance, Python's modules came from Modula and its slicing operation from Icon (as far as anyone can seem to remember, at least). And because of Guido's background, Python borrows many of ABC's ideas but adds practical features of its own, such as support for C-coded extensions. To many, Python's feature combination seems to be "just right"—it combines remarkable power with a readable syntax and coherent design.

What's Python Good For?

Because Python is used in a wide variety of ways, it's almost impossible to give an authoritative answer to this question. As a *general-purpose* language, Python can be used for almost anything computers are capable of. Its feature set applies to both rapid and longer-term development modes. And from an abstract perspective, any project that can benefit from the inclusion of a language optimized for speed of development is a good target Python application domain. Given the ever-shrinking schedules in software development, this is a very broad category.

A more specific answer is less easy to formulate. For instance, some use Python as an embedded extension language, and others use it exclusively as a standalone programming tool. To some extent, this entire book will answer this very question—it explores some of Python's most common roles. For now, here's a summary of some of the more common ways Python is being applied today:

System utilities
> Portable command-line tools, testing, system administration scripts

Internet scripting
> CGI web sites, Java applets, XML, email, Zope/Plone, CherryPy, Webware, Twisted

GUIs
> With tools such as Tk, wxPython, Qt, Gtk, PythonCard, Dabo, Swing, Anygui

Component integration
> C/C++ library frontends, product customization

Database access
> Persistent object stores, SQL database interfaces

Distributed programming
> With client/server APIs like CORBA, CGI, COM, .NET, SOAP, XML-RPC

Rapid-prototyping/development
> Tactical run-once programs or deliverable prototypes

Language-based modules
> Replacing special-purpose parsers with Python

And more
> Image processing, numeric programming, gaming, AI, etc.

On the other hand, Python is not really tied to any particular application area. For example, Python's integration support makes it useful for almost any system that can benefit from a frontend, programmable interface. In abstract terms, Python provides services that span domains. It is all of the things described in the following list.

"Buses Considered Harmful"

The PSA organization described earlier was originally formed in response to an early thread on the Python newsgroup that posed the semiserious question: "What would happen if Guido was hit by a bus?" The more recent PSF group has been tasked to address similar questions.

These days, Python creator Guido van Rossum is still the ultimate arbiter of proposed Python changes. He was officially anointed the BDFL—Benevolent Dictator For Life—of Python, at the first Python conference and still makes final yes and no decisions on language changes (and usually says no: a good thing in the programming languages domain, because Python tends to change slowly and in backward-compatible ways).

But Python's user base helps support the language, work on extensions, fix bugs, and so on. It is a true community project. In fact, Python development is now a completely open process—anyone can inspect the latest source-code files or submit patches by visiting a web site (see *http://www.python.org* for details).

As an open source package, Python development is really in the hands of a very large cast of developers working in concert around the world. Given Python's popularity, bus attacks seem less threatening now than they once did; of course, I can't speak for Guido.

- A dynamic programming language, ideal for situations in which a compile/link step is either impossible (on-site customization) or inconvenient (prototyping, rapid development, system utilities)
- A powerful but simple programming language designed for development speed, ideal for situations in which the complexity of larger languages can be a liability (prototyping, end-user coding, time to market)
- A generalized language tool, ideal for situations in which we might otherwise need to invent and implement yet another "little language" (programmable system interfaces, configuration tools)

Given these general properties, you can apply Python to any area you're interested in by extending it with domain libraries, embedding it in an application, or using it all by itself. For instance, Python's role as a system tools language is due as much to its built-in interfaces to operating system services as to the language itself.

In fact, because Python was built with integration in mind, it has naturally given rise to a growing library of extensions and tools, available as off-the-shelf components to Python developers. Table 1-2 names just a few as a random sample (with apologies to the very many systems omitted here). You can find more about most of these components in this book, on Python's web site, at the Vaults of Parnassus and PyPI web sites mentioned earlier in this chapter, and by a simple Google web search.

How Python Runs Your Code

Today, Python is "interpreted" in the same way Java is: Python source code is automatically compiled (translated) to an intermediate and platform-neutral form called bytecode, which is then executed by the Python virtual machine (that is, the Python runtime system). Translation to bytecode happens when a module is first imported, and it is avoided when possible to speed program startup: bytecode is automatically saved in *.pyc* files and, unless you change the corresponding source file, loaded directly the next time your program runs.

This bytecode compilation model makes Python scripts portable and faster than a pure interpreter that runs raw source code lines. But it also makes Python slower than true compilers that translate source code to binary machine code. Bytecode is not machine code and is ultimately run by the Python (or other) virtual machine program, not directly by your computer's hardware.

Keep in mind, though, that some of these details are specific to the standard Python implementation. For instance, the Jython system compiles Python scripts to Java bytecode, and the IronPython implementation compiles Python source code to the bytecode used by the C#/.NET environment. In addition, Python compiler-related projects have been spawned in the past and will likely continue into the future. For more details on this front, see the following:

- The Psyco just-in-time compiler for Python, which replaces portions of a running program's bytecode with optimized binary machine code tailored to specific datatypes. Psyco can speed Python programs by any factor from 2 to 100. The high end is more likely for heavily algorithmic code, whereas I/O-bound programs don't improve as much. (In my own experience, a 3x–5x speedup is common for typical programs—amazing for a simple install.)

- A related project, PyPy, which aims to reimplement the Python virtual machine to better support optimizations. The PyPy project may incorporate and subsume Psyco's techniques.

- The Parrot project, which seeks to develop a bytecode and virtual machine that will be shared by many languages, including Python.

- The Installer, Py2Exe, and Freeze systems, which package Python programs as standalone executables known as "frozen binaries"—a combination of your bytecode and the Python virtual machine. Frozen binaries do not require that Python be installed on the receiving end.

- Other program distribution formats, including zip archives (with modules automatically extracted on imports); Python eggs (an emerging package format); Distutils (an installation script system); and encrypted bytecode (for instance, using PyCrypto and the import hooks).

—continued—

- The emerging Shed Skin system, which translates Python source code to C++. This system assumes that your code will not use the full range of Python's dynamic typing, but this constraint allows highly efficient code to be generated, which is by some accounts faster than Psyco and much faster than standard Python. Shed Skin's own website reports speedups of 12 and 45 times faster on average than Psyco and standard CPython, respectively, though results can vary greatly.

Psyco may provide a simpler optimization path for some programs than linked-in C libraries, especially for algorithm-intensive code. Although Python's extreme dynamic nature makes compilation complex (the behavior of "x + 1" cannot be easily predicted until runtime), a future optimizing Python compiler might also make many of the performance notes in this chapter moot points.

Table 1-2. Popular Python domains, tools, and extensions

Domain	Tools and extensions
Systems programming: support for all common system-level tools	Sockets, processes, threads, signals, pipes, RPC, directories, POSIX bindings...
GUIs: a variety of portable GUI toolkits and builders	Tkinter, wxPython, PyQt, PyGTK, Anygui, Swing, PythonCard, Dabo...
Database interfaces: interfaces for both relational and object-oriented databases	MySQL, Oracle, Sybase, PostgreSQL, SQLite, persistence, ZODB, DBM...
Microsoft Windows tools: access to a variety of Windows-specific tools	MFC wrappers, COM interfaces, ActiveX scripting, ASP, ODBC drivers, .NET...
Internet tools: sockets, CGI, client tools, server tools, web frameworks, parsers, Apache support, Java integration	Jython, XML, email, ElementTree, htmllib, telnetlib, urllib, Zope, CherryPy, Twisted, Webware, Django, mod_python, SSL...
Distributed objects: SOAP web services, XML-RPC, CORBA, DCOM	PySOAP, SOAPy, xmlrpclib, ILU, Fnorb, omniORB, PyWin32...
Other popular tools: graphics, language, visualization, numerics, cryptography, integration, gaming, wikis...	PIL, VPython, Blender, PyOpenGL, NLTK, YAPPS, VTK, NumPy, PyCrypto, SWIG, ctypes, PyGame, MoinMoin...

What's Python Not Good For?

To be fair again, some tasks are outside of Python's scope. Like all dynamic interpreted languages, Python, as currently implemented, isn't generally as fast or efficient as static, compiled languages such as C (see the earlier sidebar, "How Python Runs Your Code," for the technical story). At least when nontypical benchmarks are compared line for line, Python code runs more slowly than C code.

Whether you will ever care about this difference in execution speed depends upon the sorts of applications you will write. In many domains, the difference doesn't matter at all; for programs that spend most of their time interacting with users or transferring data over networks, Python is usually more than adequate to meet the performance needs of the entire application by itself.

Moreover, most realistic Python programs tend to run very near the speed of the C language anyhow. Because system interactions such as accessing files or creating GUIs are implemented by linked-in C language code in the standard implementation, typical Python programs are often nearly as fast as equivalent C language programs. In fact, because Python programs use highly optimized data structures and libraries, they are sometimes quicker than C programs that must implement such tools manually.

In some domains, however, efficiency is still a main priority. Programs that spend most of their time in intense number crunching, for example, will usually be slower in Python than in fully compiled languages. Because it is interpreted today, Python alone usually isn't the best tool for the delivery of such performance-critical components. Instead, computationally intensive operations can be implemented as compiled *extensions* to Python and coded in a low-level language such as C. Python can't be used as the sole implementation language for such components, but it works well as a frontend scripting interface to them.

For example, numerical programming and image processing support has been added to Python by combining optimized extensions with a Python language interface. In such a system, once the optimized extensions have been developed, most of the programming occurs at the simpler level of Python scripting. The net result is a numerical programming tool that's both efficient and easy to use. The NumPy extension (and its NumArray and ScientificPython relatives), for instance, adds vector processing to Python, turning it into what has been called an open source equivalent to Matlab.

Python can also still serve as a prototyping tool in such domains. Systems may be implemented in Python first and later moved whole or piecemeal into a language such as C for delivery. C and Python have distinct strengths and roles; a hybrid approach using C for compute-intensive modules and Python for prototyping and frontend interfaces can leverage the benefits of both.

In some sense, Python solves the efficiency/flexibility trade-off by not solving it at all. It provides a language optimized for ease of use, along with tools needed to integrate with other languages. By combining components written in Python with compiled languages such as C and C++, developers may select an appropriate mix of usability and performance for each particular application.

On a more fundamental level, while it's unlikely that it will ever be as fast as C, Python's speed of development is at least as important as C's speed of execution in most modern software projects.

Truth in Advertising

In this book's conclusion—after we've had a chance to study Python in action—we will return to some of the bigger ideas introduced in this chapter. I want to point out up front, though, that my background is in computer science, not marketing. I plan to be brutally honest in this book, both about Python's features and about its downsides. Despite the fact that Python is one of the most easy-to-use and flexible programming languages ever created, there are indeed some pitfalls, which we will not gloss over in this book.

Let's start now. One of the first pitfalls you should know about, and a common remark made by Python newcomers, is this: *Python makes it incredibly easy to quickly throw together a bad design.* For some, it seems a genuine problem. Because developing programs in Python is so simple and fast compared with using traditional languages, it's easy to get wrapped up in the act of programming itself and pay less attention to the problem you are really trying to solve. If you haven't done any Python development yet, you'll find that it is an incremental, interactive, and rapid experience that encourages experimentation.

In fact, Python can be downright seductive—so much so that you may need to consciously resist the temptation to quickly implement a program in Python that works, is loaded with features, and is arguably "cool," but that leaves you as far from a maintainable implementation of your original conception as you were when you started. The natural delays built into compiled language development—fixing compiler error messages, linking libraries, and the like—aren't there in Python to apply the brakes. In fact, it's not uncommon for a Python program to run the first time you try it; there is much less syntax and there are far fewer procedures to get in your way.

This isn't necessarily all bad, of course. In most cases, the early designs that you throw together fast are steppingstones to better designs that you later keep. That is the nature of prototyping, after all, and often the reality of programming under tight schedules. But you should be warned: even with a rapid development language such as Python, there is no substitute for brains—it's always best to think before you start typing code. To date, at least, no computer programming language has managed to make "wetware" obsolete.

The Python "Secret Handshake"

I've been involved with Python for some 14 years now as of this writing, and I have seen it grow from an obscure language into one that is used in some fashion in almost every development organization. It has been a fun ride.

But looking back over the years, it seems to me that if Python truly has a single legacy, it is simply that Python has made quality a more central focus in the development world. It was almost inevitable. A language that requires its users to line up code for readability can't help but make people raise questions about good software practice in general.

Probably nothing summarizes this aspect of Python life better than the standard library this module—a sort of Easter egg in Python written by Python core developer, Tim Peters, which captures much of the design philosophy behind the language. To see this for yourself, go to any Python interactive prompt and import the module (naturally, it's available on all platforms):

```
>>> import this
The Zen of Python, by Tim Peters

Beautiful is better than ugly.
Explicit is better than implicit.
Simple is better than complex.
Complex is better than complicated.
Flat is better than nested.
Sparse is better than dense.
Readability counts.
Special cases aren't special enough to break the rules.
Although practicality beats purity.
Errors should never pass silently.
Unless explicitly silenced.
In the face of ambiguity, refuse the temptation to guess.
There should be one-- and preferably only one --obvious way to do it.
Although that way may not be obvious at first unless you're Dutch.
Now is better than never.
Although never is often better than *right* now.
If the implementation is hard to explain, it's a bad idea.
If the implementation is easy to explain, it may be a good idea.
Namespaces are one honking great idea -- let's do more of those!
>>>
```

Worth special mention, the "Explicit is better than implicit" rule has become known as "EIBTI" in the Python world—one of Python's defining ideas, and one of its sharpest contrasts with other languages. As anyone who has worked in this field for more than a few years can attest, magic and engineering do not mix. Python has not always followed all of these guidelines, of course, but it comes very close. And if Python's main contribution to the software world is getting people to think about such things, it seems like a win. Besides, it looked great on the T-shirt.

CHAPTER 2

A Sneak Preview

"Programming Python: The Short Story"

If you are like most people, when you pick up a book as large as this one, you'd like to know a little about what you're going to be learning before you roll up your sleeves. That's what this chapter is for—it provides a demonstration of some of the kinds of things you can do with Python, before getting into the details. You won't learn much here, and if you're looking for explanations of the tools and techniques applied in this chapter, you'll have to read on to later parts of the book. The point here is just to whet your appetite, review a few Python basics, and preview some of the topics to come.

To do this, I'll pick a fairly simple application task—constructing a database of records—and migrate it through multiple steps: interactive coding, command-line tools, console interfaces, GUIs, and simple web-based interfaces. Along the way, we'll also peek at concepts such as data representation, object persistence, and object-oriented programming (OOP); I'll mention some alternatives that we'll revisit later in the book; and I'll review some core Python ideas that you should be aware of before reading this book. Ultimately, we'll wind up with a database of Python class instances, which can be browsed and changed from a variety of interfaces.

I'll cover additional topics in this book, of course, but the techniques you will see here are representative of some of the domains we'll explore later. And again, if you don't completely understand the programs in this chapter, don't worry because you shouldn't—not yet anyway. This is just a Python demo. We'll fill in the details soon enough. For now, let's start off with a bit of fun.

The Task

Imagine, if you will, that you need to keep track of information about people for some reason; maybe you want to store an address book on your computer, or perhaps you need to keep track of employees in a small business. For whatever reason, you want to write a program that keeps track of details about these people. In other words, you want to keep records in a database—to permanently store lists of people's attributes on your computer.

Naturally, there are off-the-shelf programs for managing databases like these. By writing a program for this task yourself, however, you'll have complete control over its operation; you can add code for special cases and behaviors that precoded software may not have anticipated. You won't have to install and learn to use yet another database product. And you won't be at the mercy of a software vendor to fix bugs or add new features. You decide to write a Python program to manage your people.

Step 1: Representing Records

If we're going to store records in a database, the first step is probably deciding what those records will look like. There are a variety of ways to represent information about people in the Python language. Built-in object types such as lists and dictionaries are often sufficient, especially if we don't care about processing the data we store.

Using Lists

Lists, for example, can collect attributes about people in a positionally ordered way. Start up your Python interactive interpreter and type the following two statements (this works in the IDLE GUI, after typing **python** at a shell prompt, and so on, and the >>> characters are Python's prompt—if you've never run Python code this way before, see an introductory resource such as O'Reilly's *Learning Python* for help with getting started):

```
>>> bob = ['Bob Smith', 42, 30000, 'software']
>>> sue = ['Sue Jones', 45, 40000, 'music']
```

We've just made two records, albeit simple ones, to represent two people, Bob and Sue (my apologies if you really are Bob or Sue, generically or otherwise[*]). Each record is a list of four properties: name, age, pay, and job field. To access these fields, we simply index by position (the result is in parentheses here because it is a tuple of two results):

```
>>> bob[0], sue[2]              # fetch name, pay
('Bob Smith', 40000)
```

---

[*] No, I'm serious. For an example I present in Python classes I teach, I had for many years regularly used the named "Bob Smith," age 40.5, and jobs "developer" and "manager" as a supposedly fictitious database record—until a recent class in Chicago, where I met a student name Bob Smith who was 40.5 and was a developer and manager. The world is stranger than it seems.

Processing records is easy with this representation; we just use list operations. For example, we can extract a last name by splitting the name field on blanks and grabbing the last part, and we may give someone a raise by changing their list in-place:

```
>>> bob[0].split()[-1]          # what's bob's last name?
'Smith'
>>> sue[2] *= 1.25              # give sue a 25% raise
>>> sue
['Sue Jones', 45, 50000.0, 'music']
```

The last-name expression here proceeds from left to right: we fetch Bob's name, split it into a list of substrings around spaces, and index his last name (run it one step at a time to see how).

A database list

Of course, what we really have at this point is just two variables, not a database; to collect Bob and Sue into a unit, we might simply stuff them into another list:

```
>>> people = [bob, sue]
>>> for person in people:
        print person

['Bob Smith', 42, 30000, 'software']
['Sue Jones', 45, 50000.0, 'music']
```

Now, the people list represents our database. We can fetch specific records by their relative positions and process them one at a time, in loops:

```
>>> people[1][0]
'Sue Jones'

>>> for person in people:
        print person[0].split()[-1]          # print last names
        person[2] *= 1.20                     # give each a 20% raise

Smith
Jones

>>> for person in people: print person[2]     # check new pay

36000.0
60000.0
```

Now that we have a list, we can also collect values from records using some of Python's more powerful iteration tools, such as list comprehensions, maps, and generator expressions:

```
>>> pays = [person[2] for person in people]   # collect all pay
>>> pays
[36000.0, 60000.0]

>>> pays = map((lambda x: x[2]), people)      # ditto
>>> pays
```

```
[36000.0, 60000.0]

>>> sum(person[2] for person in people)          # generator expression sum (2.4)
96000.0
```

To add a record to the database, the usual list operations, such as append and extend, will suffice:

```
>>> people.append(['Tom', 50, 0, None])
>>> len(people)
3
>>> people[-1][0]
'Tom'
```

Lists work for our people database, and they might be sufficient for some programs, but they suffer from a few major flaws. For one thing, Bob and Sue, at this point, are just fleeting objects in memory that will disappear once we exit Python. For another, every time we want to extract a last name or give a raise, we'll have to repeat the kinds of code we just typed; that could become a problem if we ever change the way those operations work—we may have to update many places in our code. We'll address these issues in a few moments.

Field labels

Perhaps more fundamentally, accessing fields by position in a list requires us to memorize what each position means: if you see a bit of code indexing a record on magic position 2, how can you tell it is extracting a pay? In terms of understanding the code, it might be better to associate a field name with a field value.

We might try to associate names with relative positions by using the Python range built-in function, which builds a list of successive integers:

```
>>> NAME, AGE, PAY = range(3)                     # [0, 1, 2]
>>> bob = ['Bob Smith', 42, 10000]
>>> bob[NAME]
'Bob Smith'
>>> PAY, bob[PAY]
(2, 10000)
```

This addresses readability: the three variables essentially become field names. This makes our code dependent on the field position assignments, though—we have to remember to update the range assignments whenever we change record structure. Because they are not directly associated, the names and records may become out of sync over time and require a maintenance step.

Moreover, because the field names are independent variables, there is no direct mapping from a record list back to its field's names. A raw record, for instance, provides no way to label its values with field names in a formatted display. In the preceding record, without additional code, there is no path from value 42 to label AGE.

We might also try this by using lists of tuples, where the tuples record both a field name and a value; better yet, a list of lists would allow for updates (tuples are immutable). Here's what that idea translates to, with slightly simpler records:

```
>>> bob = [['name', 'Bob Smith'], ['age', 42], ['pay', 10000]]
>>> sue = [['name', 'Sue Jones'], ['age', 45], ['pay', 20000]]
>>> people = [bob, sue]
```

This really doesn't fix the problem, though, because we still have to index by position in order to fetch fields:

```
>>> for person in people:
        print person[0][1], person[2][1]      # name, pay

Bob Smith 10000
Sue Jones 20000

>>> [person[0][1] for person in people]       # collect names
['Bob Smith', 'Sue Jones']

>>> for person in people:
        print person[0][1].split()[-1]         # get last names
        person[2][1] *= 1.10                    # give a 10% raise

Smith
Jones
>>> for person in people: print person[2]

['pay', 11000.0]
['pay', 22000.0]
```

All we've really done here is add an extra level of positional indexing. To do better, we might inspect field names in loops to find the one we want (the loop uses tuple assignment here to unpack the name/value pairs):

```
>>> for person in people:
        for (name, value) in person:
            if name == 'name': print value      # find a specific field

Bob Smith
Sue Jones
```

Better yet, we can code a fetcher function to do the job for us:

```
>>> def field(record, label):
        for (fname, fvalue) in record:
            if fname == label:                   # find any field by name
                return fvalue

>>> field(bob, 'name')
'Bob Smith'
>>> field(sue, 'pay')
22000.0

>>> for rec in people:
```

```
    print field(rec, 'age')              # print all ages
```

42
45

If we proceed down this path, we'll eventually wind up with a set of record interface functions that generically map field names to field data. If you've done any Python coding in the past, you probably already know that there is an easier way to code this sort of association, and you can probably guess where we're headed in the next section.

Using Dictionaries

The list-based record representations in the prior section work, though not without some cost in terms of performance required to search for field names (assuming you need to care about milliseconds and such). But if you already know some Python, you also know that there are more convenient ways to associate property names and values. The built-in dictionary object is a natural:

```
>>> bob = {'name': 'Bob Smith', 'age': 42, 'pay': 30000, 'job': 'dev'}
>>> sue = {'name': 'Sue Jones', 'age': 45, 'pay': 40000, 'job': 'mus'}
```

Now, Bob and Sue are objects that map field names to values automatically, and they make our code more understandable and meaningful. We don't have to remember what a numeric offset means, and we let Python search for the value associated with a field's name with its efficient dictionary indexing:

```
>>> bob['name'], sue['pay']              # not bob[0], sue[2]
('Bob Smith', 40000)

>>> bob['name'].split()[-1]
'Smith'

>>> sue['pay'] *= 1.10
>>> sue['pay']
44000.0
```

Because fields are accessed mnemonically now, they are more meaningful to those who read your code (including you).

Other ways to make dictionaries

Dictionaries turn out to be so useful in Python programming that there are even more convenient ways to code them than the traditional literal syntax shown earlier—e.g., with keyword arguments and the type constructor:

```
>>> bob = dict(name='Bob Smith', age=42, pay=30000, job='dev')
>>> bob
{'pay': 30000, 'job': 'dev', 'age': 42, 'name': 'Bob Smith'}
```

Other Uses for Lists

Lists are convenient any time we need an ordered container of other objects that may need to change over time. A simple way to represent matrixes in Python, for instance, is as a list of nested lists—the top list is the matrix, and the nested lists are the rows:

```
>>> M = [[1, 2, 3],          # 3x3, 2-dimensional
         [4, 5, 6],
         [7, 8, 9]]

>>> N = [[2, 2, 2],
         [3, 3, 3],
         [4, 4, 4]]
```

Now, to combine one matrix's components with another's, step over their indexes with nested loops; here's a simple pairwise multiplication:

```
>>> for i in range(3):
        for j in range(3):
            print M[i][j] * N[i][j],
        print
2 4 6
12 15 18
28 32 36
```

To build up a new matrix with the results, we just need to create the nested list structure along the way:

```
>>> tbl = []
>>> for i in range(3):
        row = []
        for j in range(3):
            row.append(M[i][j] * N[i][j])
        tbl.append(row)

>>> tbl
[[2, 4, 6], [12, 15, 18], [28, 32, 36]]
```

Nested list comprehensions such as either of the following will do the same job, albeit at some cost in complexity (if you have to think hard about expressions like these, so will the next person who has to read your code!):

```
[[M[i][j] * N[i][j] for j in range(3)] for i in range(3)]

[[x * y for x, y in zip(row1, row2)]
        for row1, row2 in zip(M, N)]
```

—continued—

List comprehensions are powerful tools, provided you restrict them to simple tasks—for example, listing selected module functions, or stripping end-of-lines:

```
>>> import sys
>>> [x for x in dir(sys) if x.startswith('getr')]
['getrecursionlimit', 'getrefcount']

>>> lines = [line.rstrip() for line in open('README.txt')]
>>> lines[0]
'This is Python version 2.4 alpha 3'
```

If you are interested in matrix processing, also see the mathematical and scientific extensions available for Python in the public domain, such as those available through NumPy and SciPy. The code here works, but extensions provide optimized tools. NumPy, for instance, is seen by some as an open source Matlab equivalent.

by filling out a dictionary one field at a time:

```
>>> sue = {}
>>> sue['name'] = 'Sue Jones'
>>> sue['age']  = 45
>>> sue['pay']  = 40000
>>> sue['job']  = 'mus'
>>> sue
{'job': 'mus', 'pay': 40000, 'age': 45, 'name': 'Sue Jones'}
```

and by zipping together name/value lists:

```
>>> names  = ['name', 'age', 'pay', 'job']
>>> values = ['Sue Jones', 45, 40000, 'mus']
>>> zip(names, values)
[('name', 'Sue Jones'), ('age', 45), ('pay', 40000), ('job', 'mus')]
>>> sue = dict(zip(names, values))
>>> sue
{'job': 'mus', 'pay': 40000, 'age': 45, 'name': 'Sue Jones'}
```

We can even make dictionaries today from a sequence of key values and an optional starting value for all the keys (handy to initialize an empty dictionary):

```
>>> fields = ('name', 'age', 'job', 'pay')
>>> record = dict.fromkeys(fields, '?')
>>> record
{'job': '?', 'pay': '?', 'age': '?', 'name': '?'}
```

Lists of dictionaries

Regardless of how we code them, we still need to collect our records into a database; a list does the trick again, as long as we don't require access by key:

```
>>> people = [bob, sue]
>>> for person in people:
        print person['name'], person['pay']       # all name, pay
```

```
Bob Smith 30000
Sue Jones 44000.0

>>> for person in people:
        if person['name'] == 'Sue Jones':          # fetch sue's pay
            print person['pay']


44000.0
```

Iteration tools work just as well here, but we use keys rather than obscure positions (in database terms, the list comprehension and map in the following code project the database on the "name" field column):

```
>>> names = [person['name'] for person in people]     # collect names
>>> names
['Bob Smith', 'Sue Jones']

>>> map((lambda x: x['name']), people)                # ditto
['Bob Smith', 'Sue Jones']

>>> sum(person['pay'] for person in people)           # sum all pay
74000.0
```

And because dictionaries are normal Python objects, these records can also be accessed and updated with normal Python syntax:

```
>>> for person in people:
        print person['name'].split()[-1]      # last name
        person['pay'] *= 1.10                  # a 10% raise


Smith
Jones

>>> for person in people: print person['pay']


33000.0
48400.0
```

Nested structures

Incidentally, we could avoid the last-name extraction code in the prior examples by further structuring our records. Because all of Python's compound datatypes can be nested inside each other and as deeply as we like, we can build up fairly complex information structures easily—simply type the object's syntax, and Python does all the work of building the components, linking memory structures, and later reclaiming their space. This is one of the great advantages of a scripting language such as Python.

The following, for instance, represents a more structured record by nesting a dictionary, list, and tuple inside another dictionary:

```
>>> bob2 = {'name': {'first': 'Bob', 'last': 'Smith'},
            'age':  42,
```

```
                'job':  ['software', 'writing'],
                'pay':  (40000, 50000)}
```

Because this record contains nested structures, we simply index twice to go two levels deep:

```
>>> bob2['name']                    # bob's full name
{'last': 'Smith', 'first': 'Bob'}
>>> bob2['name']['last']            # bob's last name
'Smith'
>>> bob2['pay'][1]                  # bob's upper pay
50000
```

The name field is another dictionary here, so instead of splitting up a string, we simply index to fetch the last name. Moreover, people can have many jobs, as well as minimum and maximum pay limits. In fact, Python becomes a sort of query language in such cases—we can fetch or change nested data with the usual object operations:

```
>>> for job in bob2['job']: print job    # all of bob's jobs
software
writing

>> bob2['job'][-1]                       # bob's last job
'writing'
>>> bob2['job'].append('janitor')        # bob gets a new job
>>> bob2
{'job': ['software', 'writing', 'janitor'], 'pay': (40000, 50000), 'age': 42, 'name':
{'last': 'Smith', 'first': 'Bob'}}
```

It's OK to grow the nested list with append, because it is really an independent object. Such nesting can come in handy for more sophisticated applications; to keep ours simple, we'll stick to the original flat record structure.

Dictionaries of dictionaries

One last twist on our people database: we can get a little more mileage out of dictionaries here by using one to represent the database itself. That is, we can use a dictionary of dictionaries—the outer dictionary is the database, and the nested dictionaries are the records within it. Rather than a simple list of records, a dictionary-based database allows us to store and retrieve records by symbolic key:

```
>>> db = {}
>>> db['bob'] = bob
>>> db['sue'] = sue
>>>
>>> db['bob']['name']               # fetch bob's name
'Bob Smith'
>>> db['sue']['pay'] = 50000        # change sue's pay
>>> db['sue']['pay']                # fetch sue's pay
50000
```

Notice how this structure allows us to access a record directly instead of searching for it in a loop (we get to Bob's name immediately by indexing on key bob). This really is a dictionary of dictionaries, though you won't see all the gory details unless you display the database all at once:

```
>>> db
{'bob': {'pay': 33000.0, 'job': 'dev', 'age': 42, 'name': 'Bob Smith'},
 'sue': {'job': 'mus', 'pay': 50000, 'age': 45, 'name': 'Sue Jones'}}
```

If we still need to step through the database one record at a time, we can now rely on dictionary iterators. In recent Python releases, a dictionary iterator produces one key in a for loop each time through (in earlier releases, call the keys method explicitly in the for loop: say db.keys( ) rather than just db):

```
>>> for key in db:
        print key, '=>', db[key]['name']

bob => Bob Smith
sue => Sue Jones

>>> for key in db:
        print key, '=>', db[key]['pay']

bob => 33000.0
sue => 50000
```

To visit all records, either index by key as you go:

```
>>> for key in db:
        print db[key]['name'].split( )[-1]
        db[key]['pay'] *= 1.10

Smith
Jones
```

or step through the dictionary's values to access records directly:

```
>>> for record in db.values( ): print record['pay']

36300.0
55000.0

>>> x = [db[key]['name'] for key in db]
>>> x
['Bob Smith', 'Sue Jones']

>>> x = [rec['name'] for rec in db.values( )]
>>> x
['Bob Smith', 'Sue Jones']
```

And to add a new record, simply assign it to a new key; this is just a dictionary, after all:

```
>>> db['tom'] = dict(name='Tom', age=50, job=None, pay=0)
>>>
>>> db['tom']
{'pay': 0, 'job': None, 'age': 50, 'name': 'Tom'}
>>> db['tom']['name']
'Tom'
>>> db.keys()
['bob', 'sue', 'tom']
>>> len(db)
3
```

Although our database is still a transient object in memory, it turns out that this dictionary-of-dictionaries format corresponds exactly to a system that saves objects permanently—the shelve (yes, this should be *shelf* grammatically speaking, but the Python module name and term is *shelve*). To learn how, let's move on to the next section.

Step 2: Storing Records Persistently

So far, we've settled on a dictionary-based representation for our database of records, and we've reviewed some Python data structure concepts along the way. As mentioned, though, the objects we've seen so far are temporary—they live in memory and they go away as soon as we exit Python or the Python program that created them. To make our people persistent, they need to be stored in a file of some sort.

Using Formatted Files

One way to keep our data around between program runs is to write all the data out to a simple text file, in a formatted way. Provided the saving and loading tools agree on the format selected, we're free to use any custom scheme we like.

Test data script

So that we don't have to keep working interactively, let's first write a script that initializes the data we are going to store (if you've done any Python work in the past, you know that the interactive prompt tends to become tedious once you leave the realm of simple one-liners). Example 2-1 creates the sort of records and database dictionary we've been working with so far, but because it is a module, we can import it repeatedly without having to retype the code each time. In a sense, this module is a database itself, but its program code format doesn't support automatic or end-user updates as is.

Other Uses for Dictionaries

Besides allowing us to associate meaningful labels with data rather than numeric positions, dictionaries are often more flexible than lists, especially when there isn't a fixed size to our problem. For instance, suppose you need to sum up columns of data stored in a text file where the number of columns is not known or fixed:

```
>>> print open('data.txt').read( )
001.1 002.2 003.3
010.1 020.2 030.3 040.4
100.1 200.2 300.3
```

Here, we cannot preallocate a fixed-length list of sums because the number of columns may vary. Splitting on whitespace extracts the columns, and float converts to numbers, but a fixed-size list won't easily accommodate a set of sums (at least, not without extra code to manage its size). Dictionaries are more convenient here because we can use column positions as keys instead of using absolute offsets Most of this code uses tools added to Python in the last five years; see Chapter 4 for more on file iterators, Chapter 21 for text processing and alternative summers, and the library manual for the 2.3 enumerate and 2.4 sorted functions this code uses:

```
>>> sums = {}
>>> for line in open('data.txt'):
        cols = [float(col) for col in line.split( )]
        for pos, val in enumerate(cols):
            sums[pos] = sums.get(pos, 0.0) + val

>>> for key in sorted(sums):
        print key, '=', sums[key]

0 = 111.3
1 = 222.6
2 = 333.9
3 = 40.4

>>> sums
{0: 111.3, 1: 222.59999999999999, 2: 333.90000000000003,
3: 40.399999999999999}
```

Dictionaries are often also a handy way to represent matrixes, especially when they are mostly empty. The following two-entry dictionary, for example, suffices to represent a potentially very large three-dimensional matrix containing two nonempty values—the keys are coordinates and their values are data at the coordinates. You can use a similar structure to index people by their birthdays (use month, day, and year for the key), servers by their Internet Protocol (IP) numbers, and so on.

—continued—

```
>>> D = {}
>>> D[(2, 4, 6)] = 43                     # 43 at position (2, 4, 6)
>>> D[(5, 6, 7)] = 46
>>> X, Y, Z = (5, 6, 7)
>>> D.get((X, Y, Z), 'Missing')
46
>>> D.get((0, Y, Z), 'Missing')
'Missing'
>>> D
{(2, 4, 6): 43, (5, 6, 7): 46}
```

Example 2-1. PP3E\Preview\initdata.py

```
# initialize data to be stored in files, pickles, shelves

# records
bob = {'name': 'Bob Smith', 'age': 42, 'pay': 30000, 'job': 'dev'}
sue = {'name': 'Sue Jones', 'age': 45, 'pay': 40000, 'job': 'mus'}
tom = {'name': 'Tom',       'age': 50, 'pay': 0,      'job': None}

# database
db = {}
db['bob'] = bob
db['sue'] = sue
db['tom'] = tom

if __name__ == '__main__':          # when run as a script
    for key in db:
        print key, '=>\n ', db[key]
```

As usual, the __name__ test at the bottom of Example 2-1 is true only when this file is run, not when it is imported. When run as a top-level script (e.g., from a command line, via an icon click, or within the IDLE GUI), the file's self-test code under this test dumps the database's contents to the standard output stream (remember, that's what print statements do by default).

Here is the script in action being run from a system command line on Windows. Type the following command in a Command Prompt window after a cd to the directory where the file is stored, and use a similar console window on other types of computers:

```
...\PP3E\Preview> python initdata.py
bob =>
   {'job': 'dev', 'pay': 30000, 'age': 42, 'name': 'Bob Smith'}
sue =>
   {'job': 'mus', 'pay': 40000, 'age': 45, 'name': 'Sue Jones'}
tom =>
   {'job': None, 'pay': 0, 'age': 50, 'name': 'Tom'}
```

Now that we've started running script files, here are a few quick startup hints:

- On some platforms, you may need to type the full directory path to the Python program on your machine, and on recent Windows systems you don't need python on the command line at all (just type the file's name to run it).

- You can also run this file inside Python's standard IDLE GUI (open the file and use the Run menu in the text edit window), and in similar ways from any of the available third-party Python IDEs (e.g., Komodo, Eclipse, and the Wing IDE).

- If you click the program's file icon to launch it on Windows, be sure to add a raw_input( ) call to the bottom of the script to keep the output window up. On other systems, icon clicks may require a #! line at the top and executable permission via a chmod command.

I'll assume here that you're able to run Python code one way or another. Again, if you're stuck, see other books such as *Learning Python* for the full story on launching Python programs.

Data format script

Now, all we have to do is store all of this in-memory data on a file. There are a variety of ways to accomplish this; one of the most basic is to write one piece of data at a time, with separators between each that we can use to break the data apart when we reload. Example 2-2 shows one way to code this idea.

Example 2-2. PP3E\Preview\make_db_files.py

```
#####################################################################
# save in-memory database object to a file with custom formatting;
# assume 'endrec.', 'enddb.', and '=>' are not used in the data;
# assume db is dict of dict;  warning: eval can be dangerous - it
# runs strings as code;  could also eval() record dict all at once
#####################################################################

dbfilename = 'people-file'
ENDDB   = 'enddb.'
ENDREC  = 'endrec.'
RECSEP  = '=>'

def storeDbase(db, dbfilename=dbfilename):
    "formatted dump of database to flat file"
    dbfile = open(dbfilename, 'w')
    for key in db:
        print >> dbfile, key
        for (name, value) in db[key].items( ):
            print >> dbfile, name + RECSEP + repr(value)
        print >> dbfile, ENDREC
    print >> dbfile, ENDDB
    dbfile.close( )

def loadDbase(dbfilename=dbfilename):
```

Example 2-2. PP3E\Preview\make_db_files.py (continued)

```
    "parse data to reconstruct database"
    dbfile = open(dbfilename)
    import sys
    sys.stdin = dbfile
    db = {}
    key = raw_input( )
    while key != ENDDB:
        rec = {}
        field = raw_input( )
        while field != ENDREC:
            name, value = field.split(RECSEP)
            rec[name] = eval(value)
            field = raw_input( )
        db[key] = rec
        key = raw_input( )
    return db

if __name__ == '__main__':
    from initdata import db
    storeDbase(db)
```

This is a somewhat complex program, partly because it has both saving and loading logic and partly because it does its job the hard way; as we'll see in a moment, there are better ways to get objects into files than by manually formatting and parsing them. For simple tasks, though, this does work; running Example 2-2 as a script writes the database out to a flat file. It has no printed output, but we can inspect the database file interactively after this script is run, either within IDLE or from a console window where you're running these examples (as is, the database file shows up in the current working directory):

```
...\PP3E\Preview> python make_db_file.py
...\PP3E\Preview> python
>>> for line in open('people-file'):
...     print line,
...
bob
job=>'dev'
pay=>30000
age=>42
name=>'Bob Smith'
endrec.
sue
job=>'mus'
pay=>40000
age=>45
name=>'Sue Jones'
endrec.
tom
job=>None
pay=>0
age=>50
```

```
name=>'Tom'
endrec.
enddb.
```

This file is simply our database's content with added formatting. Its data originates from the test data initialization module we wrote in Example 2-1 because that is the module from which Example 2-2's self-test code imports its data. In practice, Example 2-2 itself could be imported and used to store a variety of databases and files.

Notice how data to be written is formatted with the as-code repr( ) call and is re-created with the eval( ) call which treats strings as Python code. That allows us to store and re-create things like the None object, but it is potentially unsafe; you shouldn't use eval( ) if you can't be sure that the database won't contain malicious code. For our purposes, however, there's probably no cause for alarm.

Utility scripts

To test further, Example 2-3 reloads the database from a file each time it is run.

Example 2-3. PP3E\Preview\dump_db_file.py

```
from make_db_file import loadDbase
db = loadDbase( )
for key in db:
    print key, '=>\n  ', db[key]
print db['sue']['name']
```

And Example 2-4 makes changes by loading, updating, and storing again.

Example 2-4. PP3E\Preview\update_db_file.py

```
from make_db_file import loadDbase, storeDbase
db = loadDbase( )
db['sue']['pay'] *= 1.10
db['tom']['name'] = 'Tom Tom'
storeDbase(db)
```

Here are the dump script and the update script in action at a system command line; both Sue's pay and Tom's name change between script runs. The main point to notice is that the data stays around after each script exits—our objects have become persistent simply because they are mapped to and from text files:

```
...\PP3E\Preview> python dump_db_file.py
bob =>
   {'pay': 30000, 'job': 'dev', 'age': 42, 'name': 'Bob Smith'}
sue =>
   {'pay': 40000, 'job': 'mus', 'age': 45, 'name': 'Sue Jones'}
tom =>
   {'pay': 0, 'job': None, 'age': 50, 'name': 'Tom'}
Sue Jones
```

```
...\PP3E\Preview> python update_db_file.py
...\PP3E\Preview> python dump_db_file.py
bob =>
    {'pay': 30000, 'job': 'dev', 'age': 42, 'name': 'Bob Smith'}
sue =>
    {'pay': 44000.0, 'job': 'mus', 'age': 45, 'name': 'Sue Jones'}
tom =>
    {'pay': 0, 'job': None, 'age': 50, 'name': 'Tom Tom'}
Sue Jones
```

As is, we'll have to write Python code in scripts or at the interactive command line
for each specific database update we need to perform (later in this chapter, we'll do
better by providing generalized console, GUI, and web-based interfaces instead). But
at a basic level, our text file is a database of records. As we'll learn in the next section, though, it turns out that we've just done a lot of pointless work.

Using Pickle Files

The formatted file scheme of the prior section works, but it has some major limitations. For one thing, it has to read the entire database from the file just to fetch one
record, and it must write the entire database back to the file after each set of updates.
For another, it assumes that the data separators it writes out to the file will not
appear in the data to be stored: if the characters => happen to appear in the data, for
example, the scheme will fail. Perhaps worse, the formatter is already complex without being general: it is tied to the dictionary-of-dictionaries structure, and it can't
handle anything else without being greatly expanded. It would be nice if a general
tool existed that could translate any sort of Python data to a format that could be
saved on a file in a single step.

That is exactly what the Python pickle module is designed to do. The pickle module translates an in-memory Python object into a *serialized* byte stream—a string of
bytes that can be written to any file-like object. The pickle module also knows how
to reconstruct the original object in memory, given the serialized byte stream: we get
back the exact same object. In a sense, the pickle module replaces proprietary data
formats—its serialized format is general and efficient enough for any program. With
pickle, there is no need to manually translate objects to data when storing them persistently.

The net effect is that pickling allows us to store and fetch native Python objects as
they are and in a single step—we use normal Python syntax to process pickled
records. Despite what it does, the pickle module is remarkably easy to use.
Example 2-5 shows how to store our records in a flat file, using pickle.

Example 2-5. PP3E\Preview\make_db_pickle.py

```
from initdata import db
import pickle
dbfile = open('people-pickle', 'w')
```

Example 2-5. PP3E\Preview\make_db_pickle.py (continued)

```
pickle.dump(db, dbfile)
dbfile.close()
```

When run, this script stores the entire database (the dictionary of dictionaries defined in Example 2-1) to a flat file named *people-pickle* in the current working directory. The pickle module handles the work of converting the object to a string. Example 2-6 shows how to access the pickled database after it has been created; we simply open the file and pass its content back to pickle to remake the object from its serialized string.

Example 2-6. PP3E\Preview\dump_db_pickle.py

```
import pickle
dbfile = open('people-pickle')
db = pickle.load(dbfile)
for key in db:
    print key, '=>\n  ', db[key]
print db['sue']['name']
```

Here are these two scripts at work, at the system command line again; naturally, they can also be run in IDLE, and you can open and inspect the pickle file by running the same sort of code interactively as well:

```
...\PP3E\Preview> python make_db_pickle.py
...\PP3E\Preview> python dump_db_pickle.py
bob =>
   {'pay': 30000, 'job': 'dev', 'age': 42, 'name': 'Bob Smith'}
sue =>
   {'pay': 40000, 'job': 'mus', 'age': 45, 'name': 'Sue Jones'}
tom =>
   {'pay': 0, 'job': None, 'age': 50, 'name': 'Tom'}
Sue Jones
```

Updating with a pickle file is similar to a manually formatted file, except that Python is doing all of the formatting work for us. Example 2-7 shows how.

Example 2-7. PP3E\Preview\update-db-pickle.py

```
import pickle
dbfile = open('people-pickle')
db = pickle.load(dbfile)
dbfile.close()

db['sue']['pay'] *= 1.10
db['tom']['name'] = 'Tom Tom'

dbfile = open('people-pickle', 'w')
pickle.dump(db, dbfile)
dbfile.close()
```

Notice how the entire database is written back to the file after the records are changed in memory, just as for the manually formatted approach; this might become slow for very large databases, but we'll ignore this for the moment. Here are our update and dump scripts in action—as in the prior section, Sue's pay and Tom's name change between scripts because they are written back to a file (this time, a pickle file):

```
...\PP3E\Preview> python update_db_pickle.py
...\PP3E\Preview> python dump_db_pickle.py
bob =>
    {'pay': 30000, 'job': 'dev', 'age': 42, 'name': 'Bob Smith'}
sue =>
    {'pay': 44000.0, 'job': 'mus', 'age': 45, 'name': 'Sue Jones'}
tom =>
    {'pay': 0, 'job': None, 'age': 50, 'name': 'Tom Tom'}
Sue Jones
```

As we'll learn in Chapter 19, the Python pickling system supports nearly arbitrary object types—lists, dictionaries, class instances, nested structures, and more. There, we'll also explore the faster cPickle module, as well as the pickler's binary storage protocols, which require files to be opened in binary mode; the default text protocol used in the preceding examples is slightly slower, but it generates readable ASCII data. As we'll see later in this chapter, the pickler also underlies shelves and ZODB databases, and pickled class instances provide both data and behavior for objects stored.

In fact, pickling is more general than these examples may imply. Because they accept any object that provides an interface compatible with files, pickling and unpickling may be used to transfer native Python objects to a variety of media. Using a wrapped network socket, for instance, allows us to ship pickled Python objects across a network and provides an alternative to larger protocols such as SOAP and XML-RPC.

Using Per-Record Pickle Files

As mentioned earlier, one potential disadvantage of this section's examples so far is that they may become slow for very large databases: because the entire database must be loaded and rewritten to update a single record, this approach can waste time. We could improve on this by storing each record in the database in a separate flat file. The next three examples show one way to do so; Example 2-8 stores each record in its own flat file, using each record's original key as its filename with a *.pkl* prepended (it creates the files *bob.pkl*, *sue.pkl*, and *tom.pkl* in the current working directory).

Example 2-8. PP3E\Preview\make_db_pickle_recs.py

```
from initdata import bob, sue, tom
import pickle
for (key, record) in [('bob', bob), ('tom', tom), ('sue', sue)]:
```

Example 2-8. PP3E\Preview\make_db_pickle_recs.py (continued)

```
    recfile = open(key+'.pkl', 'w')
    pickle.dump(record, recfile)
    recfile.close( )
```

Next, Example 2-9 dumps the entire database by using the standard library's glob module to do filename expansion and thus collect all the files in this directory with a *.pkl* extension. To load a single record, we open its file and deserialize with pickle; we must load only one record file, though, not the entire database, to fetch one record.

Example 2-9. PP3E\Preview\dump_db_pickle_recs.py

```
import pickle, glob
for filename in glob.glob('*.pkl'):          # for 'bob','sue','tom'
    recfile = open(filename)
    record  = pickle.load(recfile)
    print filename, '=>\n ', record

suefile = open('sue.pkl')
print pickle.load(suefile)['name']           # fetch sue's name
```

Finally, Example 2-10 updates the database by fetching a record from its file, changing it in memory, and then writing it back to its pickle file. This time, we have to fetch and rewrite only a single record file, not the full database, to update.

Example 2-10. PP3E\Preview\update_db_pickle_recs.py

```
import pickle
suefile = open('sue.pkl')
sue = pickle.load(suefile)
suefile.close( )

sue['pay'] *= 1.10
suefile = open('sue.pkl', 'w')
pickle.dump(sue, suefile)
suefile.close( )
```

Here are our file-per-record scripts in action; the results are about the same as in the prior section, but database keys become real filenames now. In a sense, the filesystem becomes our top-level dictionary—filenames provide direct access to each record.

```
...\PP3E\Preview> python make_db_pickle_recs.py
...\PP3E\Preview> python dump_db_pickle_recs.py
bob.pkl =>
    {'pay': 30000, 'job': 'dev', 'age': 42, 'name': 'Bob Smith'}
tom.pkl =>
    {'pay': 0, 'job': None, 'age': 50, 'name': 'Tom'}
sue.pkl =>
    {'pay': 40000, 'job': 'mus', 'age': 45, 'name': 'Sue Jones'}
Sue Jones
```

```
...\PP3E\Preview> python update_db_pickle_recs.py
...\PP3E\Preview> python dump_db_pickle_recs.py
bob.pkl =>
    {'pay': 30000, 'job': 'dev', 'age': 42, 'name': 'Bob Smith'}
tom.pkl =>
    {'pay': 0, 'job': None, 'age': 50, 'name': 'Tom'}
sue.pkl =>
    {'pay': 44000.0, 'job': 'mus', 'age': 45, 'name': 'Sue Jones'}
Sue Jones
```

Using Shelves

Pickling objects to files, as shown in the preceding section, is an optimal scheme in many applications. In fact, some applications use pickling of Python objects across network sockets as a simpler alternative to network protocols such as the SOAP and XML-RPC web services architectures (also supported by Python, but much heavier than pickle).

Moreover, assuming your filesystem can handle as many files as you'll need, pickling one record per file also obviates the need to load and store the entire database for each update. If we really want keyed access to records, though, the Python standard library offers an even higher-level tool: shelves.

Shelves automatically pickle objects to and from a keyed-access filesystem. They behave much like dictionaries that must be opened, and they persist after each program exits. Because they give us key-based access to stored records, there is no need to manually manage one flat file per record—the shelve system automatically splits up stored records and fetches and updates only those records that are accessed and changed. In this way, shelves provide utility similar to per-record pickle files, but are usually easier to code.

The shelve interface is just as simple as pickle: it is identical to dictionaries, with extra open and close calls. In fact, to your code, a shelve really does appear to be a persistent dictionary of persistent objects; Python does all the work of mapping its content to and from a file. For instance, Example 2-11 shows how to store our in-memory dictionary objects in a shelve for permanent keeping.

Example 2-11. make_db_shelve.py

```
from initdata import bob, sue
import shelve
db = shelve.open('people-shelve')
db['bob'] = bob
db['sue'] = sue
db.close( )
```

This script creates one or more files in the current directory with the name *people-shelve* as a prefix; you shouldn't delete these files (they are your database!), and you should be sure to use the same name in other scripts that access the shelve.

Example 2-12, for instance, reopens the shelve and indexes it by key to fetch its stored records.

Example 2-12. dump_db_shelve.py

```
import shelve
db = shelve.open('people-shelve')
for key in db:
    print key, '=>\n  ', db[key]
print db['sue']['name']
db.close()
```

We still have a dictionary of dictionaries here, but the top-level dictionary is really a shelve mapped onto a file. Much happens when you access a shelve's keys—it uses pickle to serialize and deserialize, and it interfaces with a keyed-access filesystem. From your perspective, though, it's just a persistent dictionary. Example 2-13 shows how to code shelve updates.

Example 2-13. update_db_shelve.py

```
from initdb import tom
import shelve
db = shelve.open('people-shelve')
sue = db['sue']                      # fetch sue
sue['pay'] *= 1.50
db['sue'] = sue                      # update sue
db['tom'] = tom                      # add a new record
db.close()
```

Notice how this code fetches sue by key, updates in memory, and then reassigns to the key to update the shelve; this is a requirement of shelves, but not always of more advanced shelve-like systems such as ZODB (covered in Chapter 19). Also note how shelve files are explicitly closed; some underlying keyed-access filesystems may require this in order to flush output buffers after changes.

Finally, here are the shelve-based scripts on the job, creating, changing, and fetching records. The records are still dictionaries, but the database is now a dictionary-like shelve which automatically retains its state in a file between program runs:

```
...\PP3E\Preview> python make_db_shelve.py
...\PP3E\Preview> python dump_db_shelve.py
bob =>
   {'pay': 30000, 'job': 'dev', 'age': 42, 'name': 'Bob Smith'}
sue =>
   {'pay': 40000, 'job': 'mus', 'age': 45, 'name': 'Sue Jones'}
Sue Jones

...\PP3E\Preview> python update_db_shelve.py
...\PP3E\Preview> python dump_db_shelve.py
tom =>
   {'pay': 0, 'job': None, 'age': 50, 'name': 'Tom'}
bob =>
```

```
        {'pay': 30000, 'job': 'dev', 'age': 42, 'name': 'Bob Smith'}
    sue =>
        {'pay': 60000.0, 'job': 'mus', 'age': 45, 'name': 'Sue Jones'}
    Sue Jones
```

When we ran the update and dump scripts here, we added a new record for key tom and increased Sue's pay field by 50 percent. These changes are permanent because the record dictionaries are mapped to an external file by shelve. (In fact, this is a particularly good script for Sue—something she might consider scheduling to run often, using a cron job on Unix, or a Startup folder or msconfig entry on Windows.)

Step 3: Stepping Up to OOP

Let's step back for a moment and consider how far we've come. At this point, we've created a database of records: the shelve, as well as per-record pickle file approaches of the prior section suffice for basic data storage tasks. As is, our records are represented as simple dictionaries, which provide easier-to-understand access to fields than do lists (by key, rather than by position). Dictionaries, however, still have some limitations that may become more critical as our program grows over time.

For one thing, there is no central place for us to collect record processing logic. Extracting last names and giving raises, for instance, can be accomplished with code like the following:

```
>>> import shelve
>>> db = shelve.open('people-shelve')
>>> bob = db['bob']
>>> bob['name'].split()[-1]          # get bob's last name
'Smith'
>>> sue = db['sue']
>>> sue['pay'] *= 1.25               # give sue a raise
>>> sue['pay']
75000.0
>>> db['sue'] = sue
>>> db.close()
```

This works, and it might suffice for some short programs. But if we ever need to change the way last names and raises are implemented, we might have to update this kind of code in many places in our program. In fact, even finding all such magical code snippets could be a challenge; hardcoding or cutting and pasting bits of logic redundantly like this in more than one place will almost always come back to haunt you eventually.

It would be better to somehow hide—that is, *encapsulate*—such bits of code. Functions in a module would allow us to implement such operations in a single place and thus avoid code redundancy, but still wouldn't naturally associate them with the records themselves. What we'd like is a way to bind processing logic with the data stored in the database in order to make it easier to understand, debug, and reuse.

Another downside to using dictionaries for records is that they are difficult to expand over time. For example, suppose that the set of data fields or the procedure for giving raises is different for different kinds of people (perhaps some people get a bonus each year and some do not). If we ever need to extend our program, there is no natural way to customize simple dictionaries. For future growth, we'd also like our software to support extension and customization in a natural way.

This is where Python's OOP support begins to become attractive:

Structure
> With OOP, we can naturally associate processing logic with record data—classes provide both a program unit that combines logic and data in a single package and a hierarchy that allows code to be easily factored to avoid redundancy.

Encapsulation
> With OOP, we can also wrap up details such as name processing and pay increases behind method functions—i.e., we are free to change method implementations without breaking their users.

Customization
> And with OOP, we have a natural growth path. Classes can be extended and customized by coding new subclasses, without changing or breaking already working code.

That is, under OOP, we program by customizing and reusing, not by rewriting. OOP is an option in Python and, frankly, is sometimes better suited for strategic than for tactical tasks. It tends to work best when you have time for upfront planning—something that might be a luxury if your users have already begun storming the gates.

But especially for larger systems that change over time, its code reuse and structuring advantages far outweigh its learning curve, and it can substantially cut development time. Even in our simple case, the customizability and reduced redundancy we gain from classes can be a decided advantage.

Using Classes

OOP is easy to use in Python, thanks largely to Python's dynamic typing model. In fact, it's so easy that we'll jump right into an example: Example 2-14 implements our database records as class instances rather than as dictionaries.

Example 2-14. PP3E\Preview\person_start.py

```
class Person:
    def __init__(self, name, age, pay=0, job=None):
        self.name = name
        self.age  = age
        self.pay  = pay
        self.job  = job
```

Example 2-14. PP3E\Preview\person_start.py (continued)

```
if __name__ == '__main__':
    bob = Person('Bob Smith', 42, 30000, 'sweng')
    sue = Person('Sue Jones', 45, 40000, 'music')
    print bob.name, sue.pay

    print bob.name.split()[-1]
    sue.pay *= 1.10
    print sue.pay
```

There is not much to this class—just a constructor method that fills out the instance with data passed in as arguments to the class name. It's sufficient to represent a database record, though, and it can already provide tools such as defaults for pay and job fields that dictionaries cannot. The self-test code at the bottom of this file creates two instances (records) and accesses their attributes (fields); here is this file being run under IDLE:

```
>>>
Bob Smith 40000
Smith
44000.0
```

This isn't a database yet, but we could stuff these objects into a list or dictionary as before in order to collect them as a unit:

```
>>> from person_start import Person
>>> bob = Person('Bob Smith', 42)
>>> sue = Person('Sue Jones', 45, 40000)

>>> people = [bob, sue]                    # a "database" list
>>> for person in people:
        print person.name, person.pay

Bob Smith 0
Sue Jones 40000

>>> x = [(person.name, person.pay) for person in people]
>>> x
[('Bob Smith', 0), ('Sue Jones', 40000)]
```

Notice that Bob's pay defaulted to zero this time because we didn't pass in a value for that argument (maybe Sue is supporting him now?). We might also implement a class that represents the database, perhaps as a subclass of the built-in list or dictionary types, with insert and delete methods that encapsulate the way the database is implemented. We'll abandon this path for now, though, because it will be more useful to store these records persistently in a shelve, which already encapsulates stores and fetches behind an interface for us. Before we do, though, let's add some logic.

Adding Behavior

So far, our class is just data: it replaces dictionary keys with object attributes, but it doesn't add much to what we had before. To really leverage the power of classes, we need to add some behavior. By wrapping up bits of behavior in class method functions, we can insulate clients from changes. And by packaging methods in classes along with data, we provide a natural place for readers to look for code. In a sense, classes combine records and the programs that process those records; methods provide logic that interprets and updates the data.

For instance, Example 2-15 adds the last-name and raise logic as class methods; methods use the self argument to access or update the instance (record) being processed.

Example 2-15. PP3E\Preview\person.py

```
class Person:
    def __init__(self, name, age, pay=0, job=None):
        self.name = name
        self.age  = age
        self.pay  = pay
        self.job  = job
    def lastName(self):
        return self.name.split()[-1]
    def giveRaise(self, percent):
        self.pay *= (1.0 + percent)

if __name__ == '__main__':
    bob = Person('Bob Smith', 42, 30000, 'sweng')
    sue = Person('Sue Jones', 45, 40000, 'music')
    print bob.name, sue.pay

    print bob.lastName()
    sue.giveRaise(.10)
    print sue.pay
```

The output of this script is the same as the last, but the results are being computed by methods now, not by hardcoded logic that appears redundantly wherever it is required:

```
>>>
Bob Smith 40000
Smith
44000.0
```

Adding Inheritance

One last enhancement to our records before they become permanent: because they are implemented as classes now, they naturally support customization through the inheritance search mechanism in Python. Example 2-16, for instance, customizes the last section's Person class in order to give a 10 percent bonus by default to managers whenever they receive a raise (any relation to practice in the real world is purely coincidental).

Example 2-16. PP3E\Preview\manager.py

```
from person import Person

class Manager(Person):
    def giveRaise(self, percent, bonus=0.1):
        self.pay *= (1.0 + percent + bonus)

if __name__ == '__main__':
    tom = Manager(name='Tom Doe', age=50, pay=50000)
    print tom.lastName()
    tom.giveRaise(.20)
    print tom.pay
```

```
>>>
Doe
65000.0
```

Here, the Manager class appears in a module of its own, but it could have been added to the person module instead (Python doesn't require just one class per file). It inherits the constructor and last-name methods from its superclass, but it customizes just the raise method. Because this change is being added as a new subclass, the original Person class, and any objects generated from it, will continue working unchanged. Bob and Sue, for example, inherit the original raise logic, but Tom gets the custom version because of the class from which he is created. In OOP, we program by *customizing*, not by changing.

In fact, code that uses our objects doesn't need to be at all ware of what the raise method does—it's up to the object to do the right thing based on the class from which it is created. As long as the object supports the expected interface (here, a method called giveRaise), it will be compatible with the calling code, regardless of its specific type, and even if its method works differently than others.

If you've already studied Python, you may know this behavior as polymorphism; it's a core property of the language, and it accounts for much of your code's flexibility. When the following code calls the giveRaise method, for example, what happens depends on the obj object being processed; Tom gets a 20 percent raise instead of 10 percent because of the Manager class's customization:

```
>>> from person import Person
>>> from manager import Manager

>>> bob = Person(name='Bob Smith', age=42, pay=10000)
>>> sue = Person(name='Sue Jones', age=45, pay=20000)
>>> tom = Manager(name='Tom Doe',  age=55, pay=30000)
>>> db = [bob, sue, tom]
```

```
>>> for obj in db:
        obj.giveRaise(.10)          # default or custom

>>> for obj in db:
        print obj.lastName( ), '=>', obj.pay

Smith => 11000.0
Jones => 22000.0
Doe => 36000.0
```

Refactoring Code

Before we move on, there are a few coding alternatives worth noting here. Most of these underscore the Python OOP model, and they serve as a quick review.

Augmenting methods

As a first alternative, notice that we have introduced some redundancy in Example 2-16: the raise calculation is now repeated in two places (in the two classes). We could also have implemented the customized Manager class by *augmenting* the inherited raise method instead of replacing it completely:

```
class Manager(Person):
    def giveRaise(self, percent, bonus=0.1):
        Person.giveRaise(self, percent + bonus)
```

The trick here is to call back the superclass's version of the method directly, passing in the self argument explicitly. We still redefine the method, but we simply run the general version after adding 10 percent (by default) to the passed-in percentage. This coding pattern can help reduce code redundancy (the original raise method's logic appears in only one place and so is easier to change) and is especially handy for kicking off superclass constructor methods in practice.

If you've already studied Python OOP, you know that this coding scheme works because we can always call methods through either an instance or the class name. In general, the following are equivalent, and both forms may be used explicitly:

```
instance.method(arg1, arg2)
class.method(instance, arg1, arg2)
```

In fact, the first form is mapped to the second—when calling through the instance, Python determines the class by searching the inheritance tree for the method name and passes in the instance automatically. Either way, within giveRaise, self refers to the instance that is the subject of the call.

Display format

For more object-oriented fun, we could also add a few operator overloading methods to our people classes. For example, a __str__ method, shown here, could return a string to give the display format for our objects when they are printed as a whole—much better than the default display we get for an instance:

```
class Person:
    def __str__(self):
        return '<%s => %s>' % (self.__class__.__name__, self.name)

tom = Manager('Tom Jones', 50)
print tom                              # prints: <Manager => Tom Jones>
```

Here __class__ gives the lowest class from which self was made, even though __str__ may be inherited. The net effect is that __str__ allows us to print instances directly instead of having to print specific attributes. We could extend this __str__ to loop through the instance's __dict__ attribute dictionary to display all attributes generically.

We might even code an __add__ method to make + expressions automatically call the giveRaise method. Whether we should is another question; the fact that a + expression gives a person a raise might seem more magical to the next person reading our code than it should.

Constructor customization

Finally, notice that we didn't pass the job argument when making a manager in Example 2-16; if we had, it would look like this with keyword arguments:

```
tom = Manager(name='Tom Doe', age=50, pay=50000, job='manager')
```

The reason we didn't include a job in the example is that it's redundant with the class of the object: if someone is a manager, their class should imply their job title. Instead of leaving this field blank, though, it may make more sense to provide an explicit constructor for managers, which fills in this field automatically:

```
class Manager(Person):
    def __init__(self, name, age, pay):
        Person.__init__(self, name, age, pay, 'manager')
```

Now when a manager is created, its job is filled in automatically. The trick here is to call to the superclass's version of the method explicitly, just as we did for the giveRaise method earlier in this section; the only difference here is the unusual name for the constructor method.

Alternative classes

We won't use any of this section's three extensions in later examples, but to demonstrate how they work, Example 2-17 collects these ideas in an alternative implementation of our Person classes.

Example 2-17. PP3E\Preview\people-alternative.py

```
"""
alternative implementation of person classes
data, behavior, and operator overloading
"""

class Person:
    """
    a general person: data+logic
    """
    def __init__(self, name, age, pay=0, job=None):
        self.name = name
        self.age  = age
        self.pay  = pay
        self.job  = job
    def lastName(self):
        return self.name.split( )[-1]
    def giveRaise(self, percent):
        self.pay *= (1.0 + percent)
    def __str__(self):
        return ('<%s => %s: %s, %s>' %
                (self.__class__.__name__, self.name, self.job, self.pay))

class Manager(Person):
    """
    a person with custom raise
    inherits general lastname, str
    """
    def __init__(self, name, age, pay):
        Person.__init__(self, name, age, pay, 'manager')
    def giveRaise(self, percent, bonus=0.1):
        Person.giveRaise(self, percent + bonus)

if __name__ == '__main__':
    bob = Person('Bob Smith', 44)
    sue = Person('Sue Jones', 47, 40000, 'music')
    tom = Manager(name='Tom Doe', age=50, pay=50000)
    print sue, sue.pay, sue.lastName( )
    for obj in (bob, sue, tom):
        obj.giveRaise(.10)                # run this obj's giveRaise
        print obj                         # run common __str__ method
```

Notice the polymorphism in this module's self-test loop: all three objects share the constructor, last-name, and printing methods, but the raise method called is dependent upon the class from which an instance is created. When run, Example 2-17 prints the following to standard output—the manager's job is filled in at construction, we get the new custom display format for our objects, and the new version of the manager's raise method works as before:

```
<Person => Sue Jones: music, 40000> 40000 Jones
<Person => Bob Smith: None, 0.0>
<Person => Sue Jones: music, 44000.0>
<Manager => Tom Doe: manager, 60000.0>
```

Such *refactoring* (restructuring) of code is common as class hierarchies grow and evolve. In fact, as is, we still can't give someone a raise if his pay is zero (Bob is out of luck); we probably need a way to set pay, too, but we'll leave such extensions for the next release. The good news is that Python's flexibility and readability make refactoring easy—it's simple and quick to restructure your code. If you haven't used the language yet, you'll find that Python development is largely an exercise in rapid, incremental, and interactive programming, which is well suited to the shifting needs of real-world projects.

Adding Persistence

It's time for a status update. We now have encapsulated in the form of classes customizable implementations of our records and their processing logic. Making our class-based records persistent is a minor last step. We could store them in per-record pickle files again; a shelve-based storage medium will do just as well for our goals and is often easier to code. Example 2-18 shows how.

Example 2-18. PP3E\Preview\make_db_classes.py

```python
import shelve
from person import Person
from manager import Manager

bob = Person('Bob Smith', 42, 30000, 'sweng')
sue = Person('Sue Jones', 45, 40000, 'music')
tom = Manager('Tom Doe',  50, 50000)

db = shelve.open('class-shelve')
db['bob'] = bob
db['sue'] = sue
db['tom'] = tom
db.close( )
```

This file creates three class instances (two from the original class and one from its customization) and assigns them to keys in a newly created shelve file to store them permanently. In other words, it creates a shelve of class instances; to our code, the database looks just like a dictionary of class instances, but the top-level dictionary is mapped to a shelve file again. To check our work, Example 2-19 reads the shelve and prints fields of its records.

Example 2-19. PP3E\Preview\dump_db_class.py

```python
import shelve
db = shelve.open('class-shelve')
for key in db:
    print key, '=>\n  ', db[key].name, db[key].pay

bob = db['bob']
print bob.lastName( )
print db['tom'].lastName( )
```

Note that we don't need to reimport the Person class here in order to fetch its instances from the shelve or run their methods. When instances are shelved or pickled, the underlying pickling system records both instance attributes and enough information to locate their classes automatically when they are later fetched (the class's module simply has to be on the module search path when an instance is loaded). This is on purpose; because the class and its instances in the shelve are stored separately, you can change the class to modify the way stored instances are interpreted when loaded (more on this later in the book). Here is the shelve dump script running under IDLE just after creating the shelve:

```
>>>
tom =>
    Tom Doe 50000
bob =>
    Bob Smith 30000
sue =>
    Sue Jones 40000
Smith
Doe
```

As shown in Example 2-20, database updates are as simple as before, but dictionary keys become object attributes and updates are implemented by method calls, not by hardcoded logic. Notice how we still fetch, update, and reassign to keys to update the shelve.

Example 2-20. PP3E\Preview\update_db_class.py

```
import shelve
db = shelve.open('class-shelve')

sue = db['sue']
sue.giveRaise(.25)
db['sue'] = sue

tom = db['tom']
tom.giveRaise(.20)
db['tom'] = tom
db.close( )
```

And last but not least, here is the dump script again after running the update script; Tom and Sue have new pay values, because these objects are now persistent in the shelve. We could also open and inspect the shelve by typing code at Python's interactive command line; despite its longevity, the shelve is just a Python object containing Python objects.

```
>>>
tom =>
    Tom Doe 65000.0
bob =>
    Bob Smith 30000
sue =>
```

```
      Sue Jones 50000.0
   Smith
   Doe
```

Tom and Sue both get a raise this time around, because they are persistent objects in the shelve database. Although shelves can store simpler object types such as lists and dictionaries, class instances allow us to combine both data and behavior for our stored items. In a sense, instance attributes and class methods take the place of records and processing programs in more traditional schemes.

Other Database Options

At this point, we have a full-fledged database system: our classes simultaneously implement record data and record processing, and they encapsulate the implementation of the behavior. And the Python `pickle` and `shelve` modules provide simple ways to store our database persistently between program executions. This is not a relational database (we store objects, not tables, and queries take the form of Python object processing code), but it is sufficient for many kinds of programs.

If we need more functionality, we could migrate this application to even more powerful tools. For example, should we ever need full-blown SQL query support, there are interfaces that allow Python scripts to communicate with relational databases such as MySQL, PostgreSQL, and Oracle in portable ways.

Moreover, the open source ZODB system provides a more comprehensive object database for Python, with support for features missing in shelves, including concurrent updates, transaction commits and rollbacks, automatic updates on in-memory component changes, and more. We'll explore these more advanced third-party tools in Chapter 19. For now, let's move on to putting a good face on our system.

Step 4: Adding Console Interaction

So far, our database program consists of class instances stored in a shelve file, as coded in the preceding section. It's sufficient as a storage medium, but it requires us to run scripts from the command line or type code interactively in order to view or process its content. Improving on this is straightforward: simply code more general programs that interact with users, either from a console window or from a full-blown graphical interface.

A Console Shelve Interface

Let's start with something simple. The most basic kind of interface we can code would allow users to type keys and values in a console window in order to process the database (instead of writing Python program code). Example 2-21, for instance, implements a simple interactive loop that allows a user to query multiple record objects in the shelve by key.

Example 2-21. PP3E\Preview\peopleinteract_query.py

```
# interactive queries
import shelve
fieldnames = ('name', 'age', 'job', 'pay')
maxfield   = max(len(f) for f in fieldnames)
db = shelve.open('class-shelve')

while True:
    key = raw_input('\nKey? => ')        # key or empty line, exc at eof
    if not key: break
    try:
        record = db[key]                 # fetch by key, show in console
    except:
        print 'No such key "%s"!' % key
    else:
        for field in fieldnames:
            print field.ljust(maxfield), '=>', getattr(record, field)
```

This script uses `getattr` to fetch an object's attribute when given its name string, and the `ljust` left-justify method of strings to align outputs (`maxfield`, derived from a comprehension expression, is the length of the longest field name). When run, this script goes into a loop, inputting keys from the interactive user (technically, from the standard input stream, which is usually a console window) and displaying the fetched records field by field. An empty line ends the session:

```
Key? => sue
name => Sue Jones
age  => 45
job  => music
pay  => 40000

Key? => nobody
No such key "nobody"!

Key? =>
```

Example 2-22 goes further and allows interactive updates. For an input key, it inputs values for each field and either updates an existing record or creates a new object and stores it under the key.

Example 2-22. PP3E\Preview\peopleinteract_update.py

```
# interactive updates
import shelve
from person import Person
fieldnames = ('name', 'age', 'job', 'pay')

db = shelve.open('class-shelve')
while True:
    key = raw_input('\nKey? => ')
    if not key: break
    if key in db.keys():
```

Example 2-22. PP3E\Preview\peopleinteract_update.py (continued)

```
        record = db[key]                    # update existing record
    else:                                   # or make/store new rec
        record = Person(name='?', age='?')  # eval: quote strings
    for field in fieldnames:
        currval = getattr(record, field)
        newtext = raw_input('\t[%s]=%s\n\t\tnew?=>' % (field, currval))
        if newtext:
            setattr(record, field, eval(newtext))
    db[key] = record
db.close( )
```

Notice the use of eval in this script to convert inputs (as usual, that allows any Python object type, but it means you must quote string inputs explicitly) and the use of setattr call to assign an attribute given its name string. When run, this script allows any number of records to be added and changed; to keep the current value of a record's field, press the Enter key when prompted for a new value:

```
Key? => tom
        [name]=Tom Doe
                new?=>
        [age]=55
                new?=>56
        [job]=mgr
                new?=>
        [pay]=65000.0
                new?=>90000

Key? => nobody
        [name]=?
                new?=>'John Doh'
        [age]=?
                new?=>55
        [job]=None
                new?=>
        [pay]=0
                new?=>None

Key? =>
```

This script is still fairly simplistic (e.g., errors aren't handled), but using it is much easier than manually opening and modifying the shelve at the Python interactive prompt, especially for nonprogrammers. Run the query script to check your work after an update (we could combine query and update into a single script if this becomes too cumbersome, albeit at some cost in code and user-experience complexity):

```
Key? => tom
name => Tom Doe
age  => 56
job  => mgr
pay  => 90000
```

```
Key? => nobody
name => John Doh
age  => 55
job  => None
pay  => None

Key? =>
```

Step 5: Adding a GUI

The console-based interface approach of the preceding section works, and it may be sufficient for some users assuming that they are comfortable with typing commands in a console window. With just a little extra work, though, we can add a GUI that is more modern, easier to use and less error prone, and arguably sexier.

GUI Basics

As we'll see later in this book, a variety of GUI toolkits and builders are available for Python programmers: Tkinter, wxPython, PyQt, PythonCard, Dabo, and more. Of these, Tkinter ships with Python, and it is something of a de facto standard.

Tkinter is a lightweight toolkit and so meshes well with a scripting language such as Python; it's easy to do basic things with Tkinter, and it's straightforward to do more advanced things with extensions and OOP-based code. As an added bonus, Tkinter GUIs are portable across Windows, Linux/Unix, and Macintosh; simply copy the source code to the machine on which you wish to use your GUI.

Because Tkinter is designed for scripting, coding GUIs with it is straightforward. We'll study all of its concepts and tools later in this book. But as a first example, the first program in Tkinter is just a few lines of code, as shown in Example 2-23.

Example 2-23. PP3E\Preview\tkinter001.py

```
from Tkinter import *
Label(text='Spam').pack()
mainloop()
```

This isn't the most useful GUI ever coded, but it demonstrates Tkinter basics and it builds the fully functional window shown in Figure 2-1 in just three simple lines of code. From the Tkinter module, we get widget (screen device) construction calls such as Label, geometry manager methods such as pack, widget configuration constants such as TOP and RIGHT side hints for pack, and the mainloop call, which starts event processing.

You can launch this example in IDLE from a console command line by clicking its icon the same way you can run other Python scripts. Tkinter itself is a standard part of Python and works out-of-the-box on Windows, though you may need to install extras on some computers (more details later in this book).

Figure 2-1. tkinter001.py window

It's not much more work to code a GUI that actually responds to a user: Example 2-24 implements a GUI with a button that runs the reply function each time it is pressed.

Example 2-24. PP3E\Preview\ tkinter101.py

```
from Tkinter import *
from tkMessageBox import showinfo

def reply():
    showinfo(title='popup', message='Button pressed!')

window = Tk()
button = Button(window, text='press', command=reply)
button.pack()
window.mainloop()
```

This example still isn't very sophisticated—it creates an explicit Tk main window for the application to serve as the parent container of the button, and it builds the simple window shown in Figure 2-2 (in Tkinter, containers are passed in as the first argument when making a new widget; they default to the main window). But this time, each time you click the "press" button, the program responds by running Python code that pops up the dialog window in Figure 2-3.

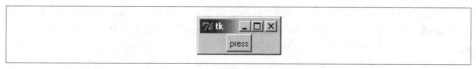

Figure 2-2. tkinter101.py main window

Figure 2-3. tkinter101.py common dialog pop up

Notice how the pop-up dialog looks like it should for Windows, the platform on which this screenshot was taken; Tkinter gives us a native look and feel that is appropriate for the machine on which it is running. We can customize this GUI in many ways (e.g., by changing colors and fonts, setting window titles and icons, using photos on buttons instead of text), but part of the power of Tkinter is that we need to set only the options we are interested in tailoring.

Using OOP for GUIs

All of our GUI examples so far have been top-level script code with a function for handling events. In larger programs, it is often more useful to code a GUI as a subclass of the Tkinter Frame widget—a container for other widgets. Example 2-25 shows our single-button GUI recoded in this way as a class.

Example 2-25. PP3E\Preview\tkinter102.py

```
from Tkinter import *
from tkMessageBox import showinfo

class MyGui(Frame):
    def __init__(self, parent=None):
        Frame.__init__(self, parent)
        button = Button(self, text='press', command=self.reply)
        button.pack()
    def reply(self):
        showinfo(title='popup', message='Button pressed!')

if __name__ == '__main__':
    window = MyGui()
    window.pack()
    window.mainloop()
```

The button's event handler is a *bound method*—self.reply, an object that remembers both self and reply when later called. This example generates the same window and pop up as Example 2-24 (Figures 2-2 and 2-3); but because it is now a subclass of Frame, it automatically becomes an attachable *component*—i.e., we can add all of the widgets this class creates, as a package, to any other GUI, just by attaching this Frame to the GUI. Example 2-26 shows how.

Example 2-26. PP3E\Preview\attachgui.py

```
from Tkinter import *
from tkinter102 import MyGui

# main app window
mainwin = Tk()
Label(mainwin, text=__name__).pack()

# popup window
popup = Toplevel()
Label(popup, text='Attach').pack(side=LEFT)
MyGui(popup).pack(side=RIGHT)                        # attach my frame
mainwin.mainloop()
```

This example attaches our one-button GUI to a larger window, here a Toplevel pop-up window created by the importing application and passed into the construction call as the explicit parent (you will also get a Tk main window; as we'll learn later, you always do, whether it is made explicit in your code or not). Our one-button widget package is attached to the right side of its container this time. If you run this live, you'll get the scene captured in Figure 2-4; the "press" button is our attached custom Frame.

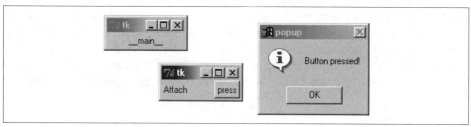

Figure 2-4. Attaching GUIs

Moreover, because MyGui is coded as a class, the GUI can be customized by the usual inheritance mechanism; simply define a subclass that replaces the parts that differ. The reply method, for example, can be customized this way to do something unique, as demonstrated in Example 2-27.

Example 2-27. PP3E\Preview\customizegui.py

```
from tkMessageBox import showinfo
from tkinter102 import MyGui

class CustomGui(MyGui):                          # inherit init
    def reply(self):                             # replace reply
        showinfo(title='popup', message='Ouch!')

if __name__ == '__main__':
    CustomGui().pack( )
    mainloop( )
```

When run, this script creates the same main window and button as the original MyGui class. But pressing its button generates a different reply, as shown in Figure 2-5, because the custom version of the reply method runs.

Figure 2-5. Customizing GUIs

Although these are still small GUIs, they illustrate some fairly large ideas. As we'll see later in the book, using OOP like this for inheritance and attachment allows us to reuse packages of widgets in other programs—calculators, text editors, and the like can be customized and added as components to other GUIs easily if they are classes.

Getting Input from a User

As a final introductory script, Example 2-28 shows how to input data from the user in an Entry widget and display it in a pop-up dialog. The lambda it uses defers the call to the reply function so that inputs can be passed in—a common Tkinter coding pattern (we could also use ent as a global variable within reply, but that makes it less general). This example also demonstrates how to change the icon and title of a top-level window; here, the window icon file is located in the same directory as the script.

Example 2-28. PP3E\Preview\tkinter103.py

```
from Tkinter import *
from tkMessageBox import showinfo

def reply(name):
    showinfo(title='Reply', message='Hello %s!' % name)

top = Tk()
top.title('Echo')
top.iconbitmap('py-blue-trans-out.ico')

Label(top, text="Enter your name:").pack(side=TOP)
ent = Entry(top)
ent.pack(side=TOP)
btn = Button(top, text="Submit", command=(lambda: reply(ent.get())))
btn.pack(side=LEFT)

top.mainloop()
```

As is, this example is just three widgets attached to the Tk main top-level window; later we'll learn how to use nested Frame container widgets in a window like this to achieve a variety of layouts for its three widgets. Figure 2-6 gives the resulting main and pop-up windows after the Submit button is pressed (shown here running on a different Windows machine). We'll see something very similar later in this chapter, but rendered in a web browser with HTML.

The code we've seen so far demonstrates many of the core concepts in GUI programming, but Tkinter is much more powerful than these examples imply. There are more than 20 widgets in Tkinter and many more ways to input data from a user, including multiple-line text, drawing canvases, pull-down menus, radio and check-buttons, scroll bars, as well as other layout and event handling mechanisms. Beyond

Figure 2-6. Fetching input from a user

Tkinter itself, extensions such as the open source PMW and Tix libraries add additional widgets we can use in our Python Tkinter GUIs and provide an even more professional look and feel. To hint at what is to come, let's put Tkinter to work on our database of people.

A GUI Shelve Interface

For our database application, the first thing we probably want is a GUI for viewing the stored data—a form with field names and values—and a way to fetch records by key. It would also be useful to be able to update a record with new field values given its key and to add new records from scratch by filling out the form. To keep this simple, we'll use a single GUI for all of these tasks. Figure 2-7 shows the window we are going to code as it looks in Windows; the record for the key sue has been fetched and displayed. This record is really an instance of our class in our shelve file, but the user doesn't need to care.

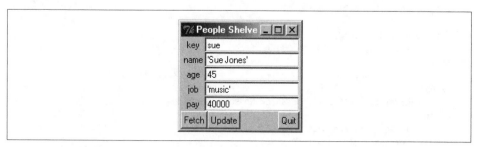

Figure 2-7. peoplegui.py main display/input window

Coding the GUI

Also, to keep this simple, we'll assume that all records in the database have the same sets of fields. It would be a minor extension to generalize this for any set of fields (and come up with a general form GUI constructor tool in the process, such as this book's PyForm example), but we'll defer such evolutions to later in this book. Example 2-29 implements the GUI shown in Figure 2-7.

Example 2-29. PP3E\Preview\peoplegui.py

```
##########################################################################
# implement a GUI for viewing/updating class instances stored in a shelve;
# the shelve lives on machine this script runs on, as 1 or more local files
##########################################################################

from Tkinter import *
from tkMessageBox import showerror
import shelve
shelvename = 'class-shelve'
fieldnames = ('name', 'age', 'job', 'pay')

def makeWidgets():
    global entries
    window = Tk()
    window.title('People Shelve')
    form   = Frame(window)
    labels = Frame(form)
    values = Frame(form)
    labels.pack(side=LEFT)
    values.pack(side=RIGHT)
    form.pack()
    entries = {}
    for label in ('key',) + fieldnames:
        Label(labels, text=label).pack()
        ent = Entry(values)
        ent.pack()
        entries[label] = ent
    Button(window, text="Fetch",  command=fetchRecord).pack(side=LEFT)
    Button(window, text="Update", command=updateRecord).pack(side=LEFT)
    Button(window, text="Quit",   command=window.quit).pack(side=RIGHT)
    return window

def fetchRecord():
    key = entries['key'].get()
    try:
        record = db[key]                       # fetch by key, show in GUI
    except:
        showerror(title='Error', message='No such key!')
    else:
        for field in fieldnames:
            entries[field].delete(0, END)
            entries[field].insert(0, repr(getattr(record, field)))

def updateRecord():
    key = entries['key'].get()
    if key in db.keys():
        record = db[key]                       # update existing record
    else:
        from person import Person              # make/store new one for key
        record = Person(name='?', age='?')     # eval: strings must be quoted
    for field in fieldnames:
```

Example 2-29. PP3E\Preview\peoplegui.py (continued)

```
        setattr(record, field, eval(entries[field].get( )))
    db[key] = record

db = shelve.open(shelvename)
window = makeWidgets( )
window.mainloop( )
db.close( ) # back here after quit or window close
```

Notice how the end of this script opens the shelve as a global variable and starts the GUI; the shelve remains open for the lifespan of the GUI (`mainloop` returns only after the main window is closed). As we'll see in the next section, this state retention is very different from the web model, where each interaction is normally a standalone program. Also notice that the use of global variables makes this code simple but unusable outside the context of our database; more on this later.

Using the GUI

The GUI we're building is fairly basic, but it provides a view on the shelve file and allows us to browse and update the file without typing any code. To fetch a record from the shelve and display it on the GUI, type its key into the GUI's "key" field and click Fetch. To change a record, type into its input fields after fetching it and click Update; the values in the GUI will be written to the record in the database. And to add a new record, fill out all of the GUI's fields with new values and click Update— the new record will be added to the shelve file using the key and field inputs you provide.

In other words, the GUI's fields are used for both display and input. Figure 2-8 shows the scene after adding a new record (via Update), and Figure 2-9 shows an error dialog pop up issued when users try to fetch a key that isn't present in the shelve.

Figure 2-8. peoplegui.py after adding a new persistent object

Notice how we're using `repr( )` again to display field values fetched from the shelve and `eval( )` to convert field values to Python objects before they are stored in the shelve. As mentioned previously, this is potentially dangerous if someone sneaks some malicious code into our shelve, but we'll finesse such concerns for now.

Figure 2-9. peoplegui.py common error dialog pop up

Keep in mind, though, that this scheme means that strings must be quoted in input fields other than the key—they are assumed to be Python code. In fact, you could type an arbitrary Python expression in an input field to specify a value for an update. (Typing "Tom"*3 in the name field, for instance, would set the name to TomTomTom after an update, though this was not by design! Fetch to see the result.)

Even though we now have a GUI for browsing and changing records, we can still check our work by interactively opening and inspecting the shelve file or by running scripts such as the dump utility in Example 2-19. Remember, despite the fact that we're now viewing records in a GUI's windows, the database is a Python shelve file containing native Python class instance objects, so any Python code can access it. Here is the dump script at work after adding and changing a few persistent objects in the GUI:

```
...\PP3E\Preview> python dump_db_class.py
tom =>
    Tom Doe 90000
peg =>
    1 4
tomtom =>
    Tom Tom 40000
bob =>
    Bob Smith 30000
sue =>
    Sue Jones 40000
bill =>
    bill 9999
nobody =>
    John Doh None
Smith
Doe
```

Future directions

Although this GUI does the job, there is plenty of room for improvement:

- As coded, this GUI is a simple set of functions that share the global list of input fields (entries) and a global shelve (db). We might instead pass these two objects in as function arguments using the lambda trick of the prior section; though not crucial in a script this small, as a rule of thumb, making your external dependencies explicit makes your code both easier to understand and reusable in other contexts.

- We could also structure this GUI as a class to support attachment and customization, though it's unlikely that we'll need to reuse such a specific GUI (but see *peoplegui_class.py* in the book examples directory for a start).

- More usefully, we could pass in the `fieldnames` tuple as an input parameter to the functions here to allow them to be used for other record types in the future. Code at the bottom of the file would similarly become a function with a passed-in shelve filename, and we would also need to pass in a new record construction call to the update function because `Person` could not be hardcoded. (Such generalization is beyond the scope of this preview, but see *people_general.py* in the book examples directory for a first implementation and the PyForm program later in this book for a more general approach.)

- To make this GUI more user friendly, it might also be nice to add an index window that displays all the keys in the database in order to make browsing easier. Some sort of verification before updates might be useful as well, and Delete and Clear buttons would be simple to code. Furthermore, assuming that inputs are Python code may be more bother than it is worth; a simpler input scheme might be easier and safer.

- We could also support window resizing (as we'll learn, widgets can grow and shrink with the window) and provide an interface for calling class methods (as is, the pay field can be updated, but there is no way to invoke the `giveRaise` method).

- If we plan to distribute this GUI widely, we might package it up as a standalone executable program—a *frozen binary* in Python terminology—using third-party tools such as Py2Exe, Installer, and Freeze (search the Web for pointers). Such a program can be run directly without installing Python on the receiving end.

We'll leave all such extensions as suggested exercises and revisit some of them later in this book.

Before we move on, two notes. First, I should mention that even more graphical packages are available to Python programmers. For instance, if you need to do graphics beyond basic windows, the Tkinter Canvas widget supports freeform graphics. Third-party extensions such as Blender, OpenGL, VPython, PIL, VTK, and PyGame provide even more advanced graphics, visualization, and animation tools for use in Python scripts. Moreover, the PMW and Tix widget kits mentioned earlier extend Tkinter itself. Try the Vaults of Parnassus, PyPI, and Google for third-party graphics extensions.

And in deference to fans of other GUI toolkits such as wxPython and PyQt, I should also note that there are other GUI options to choose from and that choice is sometimes very subjective. Tkinter is shown here because it is mature, robust, fully open source, well documented, well supported, lightweight, and a standard part of Python. By most accounts, it remains the standard for building portable GUIs in Python.

Other GUI toolkits for Python have pros and cons of their own, discussed later in this book. For example, some exchange simplicity for richer widget sets. By and large, though, they are variations on a theme—once you've learned one GUI toolkit, others are easy to pick up. Because of that, we'll focus fully on learning one toolkit in its entirety in this book instead of sampling many partially. Some consider web pages to be a kind of GUI as well, but you'll have to read the next and final section of this chapter to judge that for yourself.

Step 6: Adding a Web Interface

GUI interfaces are easier to use than command lines and are often all we need to simplify access to data. By making our database available on the Web, we can open it up to even wider use. Anyone with Internet access and a web browser can access the data, regardless of where they are located and which machine they are using. Anything from workstations to cell phones will suffice. Moreover, web-based interfaces require only a web browser; there is no need to install Python to access the data except on the single-server machine. Although web-based approaches may sacrifice some of the utility and speed of in-process GUI toolkits, their portability gain can be compelling.

As we'll also see later in this book, there are a variety of ways to go about scripting interactive web pages of the sort we'll need in order to access our data. Basic CGI scripting is more than adequate for simple tasks like ours. For more advanced applications, toolkits and frameworks such as Zope, Plone, Twisted, CherryPy, Webware, Django, TurboGears, mod_python, and Quixote can provide tools that we would otherwise need to code from scratch. Zope, for instance, simplifies many CGI scripting tasks and provides for security, load balancing on the server, and more. For now, let's keep things simple and code a CGI script.

CGI Basics

CGI scripting in Python is easy as long as you already have a handle on things like HTML forms, URLs, and the client/server model of the Web (all topics we'll address in detail later in this book). Whether you're aware of all the underlying details or not, the basic interaction model is probably familiar.

In a nutshell, a user visits a web site and receives a form, coded in HTML, to be filled out in her browser. After submitting the form, a script, identified within either the form or the address used to contact the server, is run on the server and produces another HTML page as a reply. Along the way, data typically passes through three programs: from the client browser, to the web server, to the CGI script, and back again to the browser. This is a natural model for the database access interaction we're after—users can submit a database key to the server and receive the corresponding record as a reply page.

We'll go into CGI basics in depth later in this book, but as a first example, let's start out with a simple interactive web page that requests, and then echoes back a user's name in a web browser. The first page in this interaction is just an input form produced by the HTML file shown in Example 2-30. This HTML file is stored on the web server machine and is transferred to the web browser when accessed.

Example 2-30. PP3E\Preview\cgi101.html

```
<html>
<title>Interactive Page</title>
<body>
<form method=POST action="cgi-bin/cgi101.py">
    <P><B>Enter your name:</B>
    <P><input type=text name=user>
    <P><input type=submit>
</form>
</body></html>
```

Notice how this HTML form names the script that will process its input on the server in its action attribute. The input form that this code produces is shown in Figure 2-10 (shown in the open source Firefox web browser running on Windows).

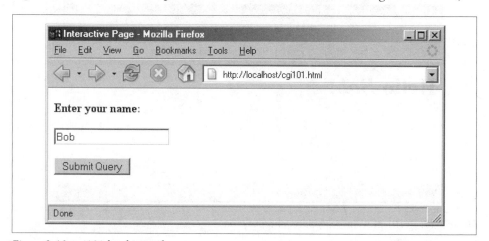

Figure 2-10. cgi101.html input form page

After the input form is submitted, the script in Example 2-31 is run on the web server machine to handle the inputs and generate a reply to the browser on the client machine. Like the HTML file, this Python script resides on the same machine as the web server; it uses the cgi module to parse the form's input and insert it into the HTML reply stream, properly escaped. The cgi module gives us a dictionary-like interface to form inputs sent by the browser, and the HTML code that this script prints winds up rendering the next page on the client's browser. In the CGI world, the standard output stream is connected to the client through a socket.

Example 2-31. PP3E\Preview\cgi-bin\cgi101.py

```
#!/usr/bin/python
import cgi
form = cgi.FieldStorage()                    # parse form data
print "Content-type: text/html\n"            # hdr plus blank line
print "<title>Reply Page</title>"            # html reply page
if not form.has_key('user'):
    print "<h1>Who are you?</h1>"
else:
    print "<h1>Hello <i>%s</i>!</h1>" % cgi.escape(form['user'].value)
```

And if all goes well, we receive the reply page shown in Figure 2-11—essentially, just an echo of the data we entered in the input page. The page in this figure is produced by the HTML printed by the Python CGI script running on the server. Along the way, the user's name was transferred from a client to a server and back again—potentially across networks and miles. This isn't much of a web site, of course, but the basic principles here apply, whether you're echoing inputs or doing full-blown e-whatever.

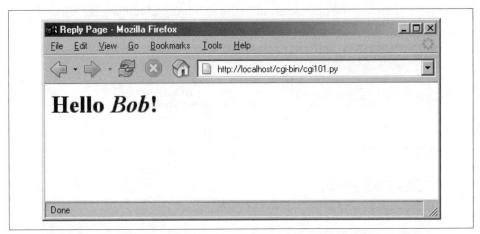

Figure 2-11. cgi101.py script reply page for input form

If you have trouble getting this interaction to run on Unix-like systems, you may need to modify the path to your Python in the #! line at the top of the script file and make it executable with a chmod command, but this is dependent on your web server (more on servers in the next section).

Also note that the CGI script in Example 2-31 isn't printing complete HTML: the <html> and <body> tags of the static HTML file in Example 2-30 are missing. Strictly speaking, such tags should be printed, but web browsers don't mind the omissions, and this book's goal is not to teach legalistic HTML; see other resources for more on HTML.

Before moving on, it's worth taking a moment to compare this basic CGI example with the simple GUI of Example 2-28 and Figure 2-6. Here, we're running scripts on a server to generate HTML that is rendered in a web browser. In the GUI, we make calls to build the display and respond to events within a single process and on a single machine. The GUI runs multiple layers of software, but not multiple programs. By contrast, the CGI approach is much more distributed—the server, the browser, and possibly the CGI script itself run as separate programs that usually communicate over a network.

Because of such differences, the GUI model may be simpler and more direct: there is no intermediate server, replies do not require invoking a new program, no HTML needs to be generated, and the full power of a GUI toolkit is at our disposal. On the other hand, a web-based interface can be viewed in any browser on any computer and only requires Python on the server machine. And just to muddle the waters further, a GUI can also employ Python's standard library networking tools to fetch and display data from a remote server (that's how web browsers do their work). We'll revisit the trade-offs of the GUI and CGI schemes later in this book. First, let's preview a handful of pragmatic issues related to CGI work before we apply it to our people database.

Running a Web Server

To run CGI scripts at all, we need a web server that will serve up our HTML and launch our Python scripts on request. The server is a required mediator between the browser and the CGI script. If you don't have an account on a machine that has such a server available, you'll want to run one of your own. We could configure and run a full-blown web server such as the open source Apache system (which, by the way, can be tailored with Python-specific support by the mod_python extension). For this chapter, however, I instead wrote a simple web server in Python using the code in Example 2-32.

We'll revisit the tools used in this example later in this book. In short, because Python provides precoded support for various types of network servers, we can build a CGI-capable and portable HTTP web server in roughly 20 lines of code (including comments, whitespace, and a workaround added to force the CGI script to run in-process because of a Windows problem I ran into on two of my test machines—more on this later).

As we'll see later in this book, it's also easy to build proprietary network servers with low-level socket calls in Python, but the standard library provides canned implementations for many common server types, web based or otherwise. The SocketServer module, for instance, provides threaded and forking versions of TCP and UDP servers. Third-party systems such as Twisted provide even more implementations. For serving up web content, the standard library modules used in Example 2-32 provide what we need.

Example 2-32. PP3E\Preview\webserver.py

```
#####################################################################
# implement HTTP web server in Python that knows how to run server-
# side CGI scripts;  serves files/scripts from current working dir;
# Python scripts must be stored in webdir\cgi-bin or webdir\htbin;
#####################################################################

webdir = '.'   # where your html files and cgi-bin script directory live
port   = 80    # default http://localhost/, else use http://localhost:xxxx/

import os, sys
from BaseHTTPServer import HTTPServer
from CGIHTTPServer  import CGIHTTPRequestHandler

# hack for Windows: os.environ not propagated
# to subprocess by os.popen2, force in-process
if sys.platform[:3] == 'win':
    CGIHTTPRequestHandler.have_popen2 = False
    CGIHTTPRequestHandler.have_popen3 = False

os.chdir(webdir)                                    # run in HTML root dir
srvraddr = ("", port)                               # my hostname, portnumber
srvrobj  = HTTPServer(srvraddr, CGIHTTPRequestHandler)
srvrobj.serve_forever()                             # run as perpetual demon
```

The classes this script uses assume that the HTML files to be served up reside in the current working directory and that the CGI scripts to be run live in a */cgi-bin* or */htbin* subdirectory there. We're using a */cgi-bin* subdirectory for scripts, as suggested by the filename of Example 2-31. Some web servers look at filename extensions to detect CGI scripts; our script uses this subdirectory-based scheme instead.

To launch the server, simply run this script (in a console window, by an icon click, or otherwise); it runs perpetually, waiting for requests to be submitted from browsers and other clients. The server listens for requests on the machine on which it runs and on the standard HTTP port number 80. To use this script to serve up other web sites, either launch it from the directory that contains your HTML files and a *cgi-bin* subdirectory that contains your CGI scripts, or change its webdir variable to reflect the site's root directory (it will automatically change to that directory and serve files located there).

But where in cyberspace do you actually run the server script? If you look closely enough, you'll notice that the server name in the addresses of the prior section's examples (near the top right of the browser after the "http://") is always *localhost*. To keep this simple, I am running the web server on the same machine as the web browser; that's what the server name "localhost" (and the equivalent IP address "127.0.0.1") means. That is, the client and server machines are the same: the client (web browser) and server (web server) are just different processes running at the same time on the same computer.

This turns out to be a great way to test CGI scripts—you can develop them on the same machine without having to transfer code back to a remote server machine after each change. Simply run this script from the directory that contains both your HTML files and a *cgi-bin* subdirectory for scripts and then use "http://localhost/..." in your browser to access your HTML and script files. Here is the trace output the web server script produces in a Windows console window that is running on the same machine as the web browser and launched from the directory where the HTML files reside:

```
...\PP3E\Preview> python webserver.py
localhost - - [17/Jan/2005 14:30:44] "GET /cgi101.html HTTP/1.1" 200 -
localhost - - [17/Jan/2005 14:30:45] code 404, message File not found
localhost - - [17/Jan/2005 14:30:45] "GET /favicon.ico HTTP/1.1" 404 -
localhost - - [17/Jan/2005 14:31:30] "POST /cgi-bin/cgi101.py HTTP/1.1" 200 -
localhost - - [17/Jan/2005 14:31:30] CGI script exited OK
localhost - - [17/Jan/2005 14:31:31] code 404, message File not found
localhost - - [17/Jan/2005 14:31:31] "GET /favicon.ico HTTP/1.1" 404 -
localhost - - [17/Jan/2005 14:32:31] "GET /cgi-bin/cgi101.py?name=Sue+Smith HTTP
/1.1" 200 -
localhost - - [17/Jan/2005 14:32:31] CGI script exited OK
```

To run this server on a different port, change the port number in the script and name it explicitly in the URL (e.g., "http://localhost:8888/"). To run this server on a remote computer, upload the HTML files and CGI scripts' subdirectory to the remote computer, launch the server script on that machine, and replace "localhost" in the URLs with the domain name or IP address of your server machine (e.g., "http://www.myserver.com/"). When running the server remotely, all the interaction will be as shown here, but inputs and replies will be automatically shipped across network connections, not routed between programs running in the same computer.

On systems that don't require custom code like the Windows workaround in our code, you can also start a CGI-capable web server by simply running the file *CGIHTTPServer.py* in the Python standard library (this script is located in the *C:\ Python24\Lib* directory on Windows, for instance, under Python 2.4). This file's test code is similar to our script, but it defaults to port number 8000 unless a port number is given on the command line as an argument. In Chapter 16, we'll expand Example 2-32 to allow the directory name and port numbers to be passed in on the command line, and we'll augment the module search path for platforms where the server runs the script in-process.*

Using Query Strings and urllib

In the basic CGI example shown earlier, we ran the Python script by filling out and submitting a form that contained the name of the script. Really, CGI scripts can be invoked in a variety of ways—either by submitting an input form as shown so far, or by sending the server an explicit URL (Internet address) string that contains inputs at the end. Such an explicit URL can be sent to a server either in or outside of a browser; in a sense, it bypasses the traditional input form page.

For instance, Figure 2-12 shows the reply generated by the server after typing a URL of the following form in the address field at the top of the web browser (+ means a space here):

> http://localhost/cgi-bin/cgi101.py?user=Sue+Smith

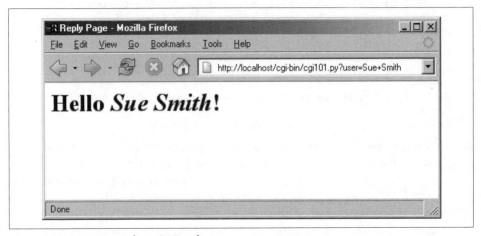

Figure 2-12. cgi101.py reply to GET-style query parameters

The inputs here, known as *query parameters*, show up at the end of the URL after the ?; they are not entered into a form's input fields. Adding inputs to URLs is sometimes called a GET request. Our original input form uses the POST method, which instead ships inputs in a separate step. Luckily, Python CGI scripts don't have to

---

* Technically speaking, the Windows workaround in Example 2-31 was related to a bug in the os.environ. update call, which was used by the server classes; it did not correctly update on Windows XP, but it may by the time you read this sentence. At the time of this writing, of the environment changes made by os.environ. update({'X': 'spam'}) and os.environ['Y'] = 'ni', only the second was propagated to the subprocess after a (i, o) = os.popen2('sub.py') call. This may seem obscure, but it underscores one of the nice things about having access to the source code of an open source system such as Python: I was not at the mercy of a software vendor to uncover this and provide me with a workaround.

distinguish between the two; the cgi module's input parser handles any data submission method differences for us.

It's even possible, and often useful, to submit URLs with inputs appended as query parameters completely outside any web browser. The Python urllib module, for instance, allows us to read the reply generated by a server for any valid URL. In effect, it allows us to visit a web page or invoke a CGI script from within another script; your Python code acts as the web client. Here is this module in action, run from the interactive command line:

```
>>> from urllib import urlopen
>>> conn = urlopen('http://localhost/cgi-bin/cgi101.py?user=Sue+Smith')
>>> reply = conn.read()
>>> reply
'<title>Reply Page</title>\n<h1>Hello <i>Sue Smith</i>!</h1>\n'

>>> urlopen('http://localhost/cgi-bin/cgi101.py').read()
'<title>Reply Page</title>\n<h1>Who are you?</h1>\n'

>>> urlopen('http://localhost/cgi-bin/cgi101.py?user=Bob').read()
'<title>Reply Page</title>\n<h1>Hello <i>Bob</i>!</h1>\n'
```

The urllib module gives us a file-like interface to the server's reply for a URL. Notice that the output we read from the server is raw HTML code (normally rendered by a browser). We can process this text with any of Python's text-processing tools, including string methods to search and split, the re regular expression pattern-matching module, or the full-blown HTML parsing support in the standard library. When combined with such tools, the urllib module is a natural for interactive testing and custom client-side GUIs, as well as implementing automated tools such as regression testing systems for remote server-side CGI scripts.

Formatting Reply Text

One last fine point: because CGI scripts use text to communicate with clients, they need to format their replies according to a set of rules. For instance, notice how Example 2-31 adds a blank line between the reply's header and its HTML by printing an explicit newline (\n) in addition to the one print adds automatically; this is a required separator.

Also note how the text inserted into the HTML reply is run through the cgi.escape call, just in case the input includes a character that is special in HTML. For example, Figure 2-13 shows the reply we receive on another machine for form input Bob </i> Smith—the </i> in the middle becomes </i> in the reply, and so doesn't interfere with real HTML code (if not escaped, the rest of the name would not be italicized).

Escaping text like this isn't always required, but it is a good rule of thumb when its content isn't known; scripts that generate HTML have to respect its rules. As we'll see later in this book, a related call, urllib.quote, applies URL escaping rules to text.

Figure 2-13. Escaping HTML characters

As we'll also see, larger frameworks such as Zope often handle text formatting tasks for us.

A Web-Based Shelve Interface

Now, to use the CGI techniques of the prior sections for our database application, we basically just need a bigger input and reply form. Figure 2-14 shows the form we'll implement for accessing our database in a web browser.

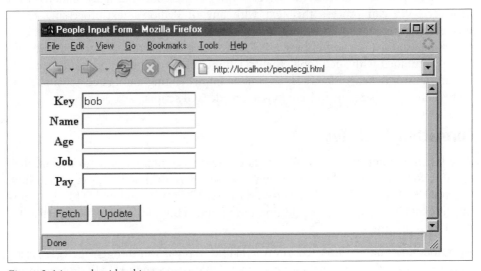

Figure 2-14. peoplecgi.html input page

Coding the web site

To implement the interaction, we'll code an initial HTML input form, as well as a Python CGI script for displaying fetch results and processing update requests. Example 2-33 shows the input form's HTML code that builds the page in Figure 2-14.

Example 2-33. PP3E\Preview\peoplecgi.html

```html
<html>
<title>People Input Form</title>
<body>
<form method=POST action="cgi-bin/peoplecgi.py">
    <table>
    <tr><th>Key <td><input type=text name=key>
    <tr><th>Name<td><input type=text name=name>
    <tr><th>Age <td><input type=text name=age>
    <tr><th>Job <td><input type=text name=job>
    <tr><th>Pay <td><input type=text name=pay>
    </table>
    <p>
    <input type=submit value="Fetch",  name=action>
    <input type=submit value="Update", name=action>
</form>
</body></html>
```

To handle form (and other) requests, Example 2-34 implements a Python CGI script that fetches and updates our shelve's records. It echoes back a page similar to that produced by Example 2-33, but with the form fields filled in from the attributes of actual class objects in the shelve database.

As in the GUI, the same web page is used for both displaying results and inputting updates. Unlike the GUI, this script is run anew for each step of user interaction, and it reopens the database each time (the reply page's action field is a link back to the script). The basic CGI model provides no automatic memory from page to page.

Example 2-34. PP3E\Preview\cgi-bin\peoplecgi.py

```python
#########################################################################
# implement a web-based interface for viewing/updating class instances
# stored in a shelve; shelve lives on server (same machine if localhost)
#########################################################################

import cgi, shelve                          # cgi.test() dumps inputs
form = cgi.FieldStorage()                   # parse form data
print "Content-type: text/html"            # hdr, blank line in string
shelvename = 'class-shelve'
fieldnames = ('name', 'age', 'job', 'pay')

# main html template
replyhtml = """
<html>
<title>People Input Form</title>
<body>
<form method=POST action="peoplecgi.py">
    <table>
    <tr><th>key<td><input type=text name=key value="%(key)s">
    $ROWS$
    </table>
    <p>
```

Example 2-34. PP3E\Preview\cgi-bin\peoplecgi.py (continued)

```
        <input type=submit value="Fetch",  name=action>
        <input type=submit value="Update", name=action>
</form>
</body></html>
"""


# insert html for data rows at $ROWS$
rowhtml  = '<tr><th>%s<td><input type=text name=%s value="%%(%s)s">\n'
rowshtml = ''
for fieldname in fieldnames:
    rowshtml += (rowhtml % ((fieldname,) * 3))
replyhtml = replyhtml.replace('$ROWS$', rowshtml)


def htmlize(adict):
    new = adict.copy()
    for field in fieldnames:                     # values may have &, >, etc.
        value = new[field]                       # display as code: quoted
        new[field] = cgi.escape(repr(value))     # html-escape special chars
    return new


def fetchRecord(db, form):
    try:
        key = form['key'].value
        record = db[key]
        fields = record.__dict__                 # use attribute dict
        fields['key'] = key                      # to fill reply string
    except:
        fields = dict.fromkeys(fieldnames, '?')
        fields['key'] = 'Missing or invalid key!'
    return fields


def updateRecord(db, form):
    if not form.has_key('key'):
        fields = dict.fromkeys(fieldnames, '?')
        fields['key'] = 'Missing key input!'
    else:
        key = form['key'].value
        if key in db.keys():
            record = db[key]                     # update existing record
        else:
            from person import Person            # make/store new one for key
            record = Person(name='?', age='?')   # eval: strings must be quoted
        for field in fieldnames:
            setattr(record, field, eval(form[field].value))
        db[key] = record
        fields = record.__dict__
        fields['key'] = key
    return fields


db = shelve.open(shelvename)
action = form.has_key('action') and form['action'].value
if action == 'Fetch':
```

Example 2-34. PP3E\Preview\cgi-bin\peoplecgi.py (continued)

```
    fields = fetchRecord(db, form)
elif action == 'Update':
    fields = updateRecord(db, form)
else:
    fields = dict.fromkeys(fieldnames, '?')        # bad submit button value
    fields['key'] = 'Missing or invalid action!'
db.close()
print replyhtml % htmlize(fields)                  # fill reply from dict
```

This is a fairly large script, because it has to handle user inputs, interface with the database, and generate HTML for the reply page. Its behavior is fairly straightforward, though, and similar to the GUI of the prior section.

The only feat of semimagic it relies on is using a record's attribute dictionary (__ dict__) as the source of values when applying string formatting to the HTML reply template string in the last line of the script. Recall that a %(key)code replacement target fetches a value by key from a dictionary:

```
>>> D = {'say': 5, 'get': 'shrubbery'}
>>> D['say']
5
>>> S = '%(say)s => %(get)s' % D
>>> S
'5 => shrubbery'
```

By using an object's attribute dictionary, we can refer to attributes by name in the format string. In fact, part of the reply template is generated by code. If its structure is confusing, simply insert statements to print replyhtml and to call sys.exit, and run from a simple command line. This is how the table's HTML in the middle of the reply is generated (slightly formatted here for readability):

```
<table>
<tr><th>key<td><input type=text name=key value="%(key)s">
<tr><th>name<td><input type=text name=name value="%(name)s">
<tr><th>age<td><input type=text name=age value="%(age)s">
<tr><th>job<td><input type=text name=job value="%(job)s">
<tr><th>pay<td><input type=text name=pay value="%(pay)s">
</table>
```

This text is then filled in with key values from the record's attribute dictionary by string formatting at the end of the script. This is done after running the dictionary through a utility to convert its values to code text with repr and escape that text per HTML conventions with cgi.escape (again, the last step isn't always required, but it's generally a good practice).

These HTML reply lines could have been hardcoded in the script, but generating them from a tuple of field names is a more general approach—we can add new fields in the future without having to update the HTML template each time. Python's string processing tools make this a snap.

Using the web site

Using the web interface is as simple as using the GUI. To fetch a record, fill in the Key field and click Fetch; the script populates the page with field data grabbed from the corresponding class instance in the shelve, as illustrated in Figure 2-15 for the key bob.

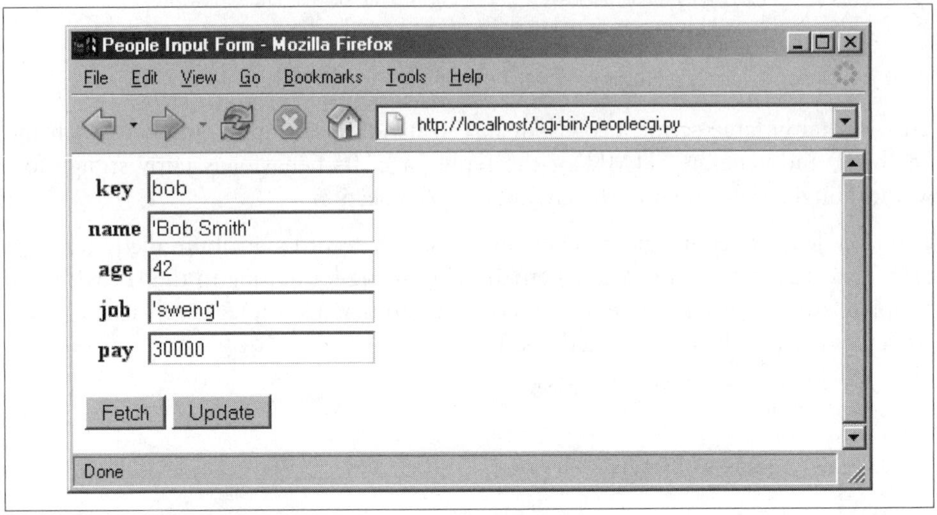

Figure 2-15. peoplecgi.py reply page

Figure 2-15 shows what happens when the key comes from the posted form. As usual, you can also invoke the CGI script by instead passing inputs on a query string at the end of the URL; Figure 2-16 shows the reply we get when accessing a URL of the following form:

```
http://localhost/cgi-bin/peoplecgi.py?action=Fetch&key=sue
```

As we've seen, such a URL can be submitted either within your browser, or by scripts that use tools such as the urllib module. Again, replace "localhost" with your server's domain name if you are running the script on a remote machine.

To update a record, fetch it by key, enter new values in the field inputs, and click Update; the script will take the input fields and store them in the attributes of the class instance in the shelve. Figure 2-17 shows the reply we get after updating sue.

Finally, adding a record works the same as in the GUI: fill in a new key and field values and click Update; the CGI script creates a new class instance, fills out its attributes, and stores it in the shelve under the new key. There really is a class object behind the web page here, but we don't have to deal with the logic used to generate it. Figure 2-18 shows a record added to the database in this way.

In principle, we could also update and add records by submitting a URL—either from a browser or from a script—such as:

```
http://localhost/cgi-bin/
    peoplecgi.py?action=Update&key=sue&pay=50000&name=Sue+Smith& ...more...
```

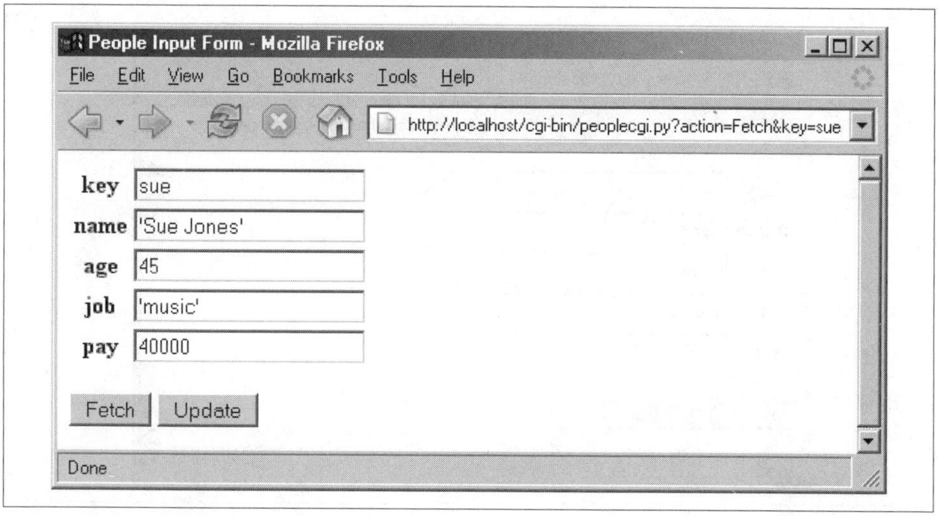

Figure 2-16. peoplecgi.py reply for query parameters

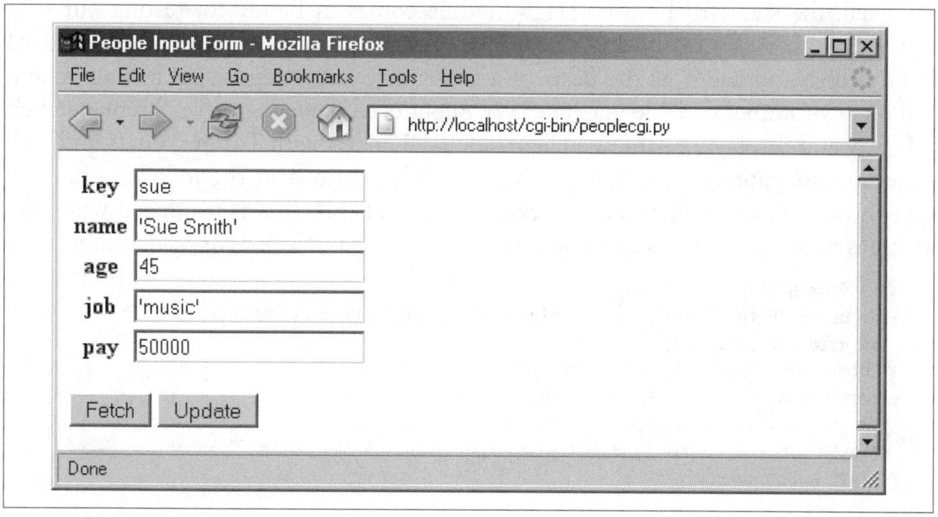

Figure 2-17. peoplecgi.py update reply

Except for automated tools, though, typing such a long URL will be noticeably more difficult than filling out the input page. Here is part of the reply page generated for the "guido" record's display of Figure 2-18 (use your browser's "view page source" option to see this for yourself). Note how the < and > characters are translated to HTML escapes with cgi.escape before being inserted into the reply:

```
<tr><th>key<td><input type=text name=key value="guido">
<tr><th>name<td><input type=text name=name value="'GvR'">
<tr><th>age<td><input type=text name=age value="None">
<tr><th>job<td><input type=text name=job value="'BDFL'">
<tr><th>pay<td><input type=text name=pay value="'&lt;?&gt;'">
```

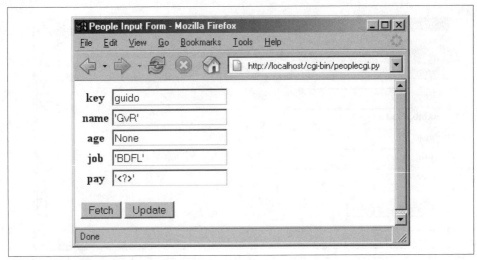

Figure 2-18. peoplecgi.py after adding a new record

As usual, the standard library urllib module comes in handy for testing our CGI script; the output we get back is raw HTML, but we can parse it with other standard library tools and use it as the basis of a server-side script regression testing system run on any Internet-capable machine. We might even parse the server's reply fetched this way and display its data in a client-side GUI coded with Tkinter; GUIs and web pages are not mutually exclusive techniques. The last test in the following interaction shows a portion of the error message page's HTML that is produced when the action is missing or invalid in the inputs, with line breaks added for readability:

```
>>> from urllib import urlopen
>>> url = 'http://localhost/cgi-bin/peoplecgi.py?action=Fetch&key=sue'
>>> urlopen(url).read()
'<html>\n<title>People Input Form</title>\n<body>\n
<form method=POST action="peoplecgi.py">\n    <table>\n
<tr><th>key<td><input type=text name=key value="sue">\n
<tr><th>name<td><input type=text name=name value="\'Sue Smith\'">\n
<tr><t ...more deleted...

>>> urlopen('http://localhost/cgi-bin/peoplecgi.py').read()
'<html>\n<title>People Input Form</title>\n<body>\n
<form method=POST action="peoplecgi.py">\n    <table>\n
<tr><th>key<td><input type=text name=key value="Missing or invalid action!">\n
<tr><th>name<td><input type=text name=name value="\'?\'">\n
<tr><th>age<td><input type=text name=age value="\'?\'">\n<tr><th>job ...more deleted...
```

In fact, if you're running this CGI script on "localhost," you can use both the last section's GUI and this section's web interface to view the same physical shelve file—these are just alternative interfaces to the same persistent Python objects. For comparison, Figure 2-19 shows what the record we saw in Figure 2-18 looks like in the GUI; it's the same object, but we are not contacting an intermediate server, starting other scripts, or generating HTML to view it.

Figure 2-19. Same object displayed in the GUI

And as before, we can always check our work on the server machine either interactively or by running scripts. We may be viewing a database through web browsers and GUIs, but, ultimately, it is just Python objects in a Python shelve file:

```
>>> import shelve
>>> db = shelve.open('class-shelve')
>>> db['sue'].name
'Sue Smith'
>>> db['guido'].job
'BDFL'
>>> list(db['guido'].name)
['G', 'v', 'R']
```

Future directions

Naturally, there are plenty of improvements we could make here too:

- The HTML code of the initial input page in Example 2-33, for instance, is somewhat redundant with the script in Example 2-34, and it could be automatically generated by another script that shares common information. In fact, we could avoid hardcoding HTML completely if we use an HTML generator tool such as HTMLgen, discussed later in this book.

- For ease of maintenance, it might also be better to split the CGI script's HTML code off to a separate file in order to better divide display from logic (different parties with possibly different skill sets could work on the different files).

- Moreover, if this web site might be accessed by many people simultaneously, we would have to add file locking or move to a database such as ZODB or MySQL to support concurrent updates. ZODB and other full-blown database systems would also provide transaction rollbacks in the event of failures. For basic file locking, the fcntl module and the os.open call and its flags provide the tools we need.

- In the end, if our site grows much beyond a few interactive pages, we might also migrate from basic CGI scripting to a more complete web framework such as Zope, CherryPy, Webware, Django, TurboGears, or Python Server Pages and mod_python, all Python-based systems. If we must retain information across pages, tools such as cookies, hidden inputs, mod_python session data, and FastCGI may help too.

- If our site eventually includes content produced by its own users, we might transition to Plone, a popular open source Python- and Zope-based site builder that, using a workflow model, delegates control of site content to its producers.

- And if wireless interfaces are on our agenda, we might eventually migrate our system to cell phones using a port such as that currently available for Nokia platforms. Python tends to go wherever technology trends lead.

For now, though, both the GUI and web-based interfaces we've coded get the job done.

The End of the Demo

And that concludes our sneak preview demo of Python in action. We've explored data representation, OOP, object persistence, GUIs, and web site basics. We haven't studied any of these topics in any sort of depth. Hopefully, though, this chapter has piqued your curiosity about Python applications programming.

In the rest of this book, we'll delve into these and other application programming tools and topics, in order to help you put Python to work in your own programs. In the next chapter, we begin our tour with the systems programming tools available to Python programmers.

System Programming

This first in-depth part of the book presents Python's system programming tools—interfaces to services in the underlying operating system as well as the context of an executing program. It consists of the following chapters:

Chapter 3, *System Tools*

> This chapter is a comprehensive look at commonly used system interface tools. This chapter teaches you how to process streams, command-line arguments, shell variables, and more. This chapter starts slowly and is meant in part as a reference for tools and techniques we'll be using later in the book.

Chapter 4, *File and Directory Tools*

> This chapter continues our survey of system interfaces by focusing on tools and techniques used to process files and directories in Python. We'll learn about binary files, tree walkers, and so on.

Chapter 5, *Parallel System Tools*

> This chapter is an introduction to Python's library support for running programs in parallel. Here, you'll find coverage of threads, process forks, pipes, signals, queues, and the like.

Chapter 6, *System Examples: Utilities and* Chapter 7, *System Examples: Directories*

> This is a two-chapter collection of typical system programming examples that draw upon the material of the prior three chapters. Among other things, Python scripts here demonstrate how to do things like split and join files, compare and copy directories, generate web pages from templates, and launch programs, files, and web browsers portably. The second of these chapters focuses on advanced file and directory examples; the first presents assorted system tools case studies.

Although this part of the book emphasizes systems programming tasks, the tools introduced are general-purpose and are used often in later chapters.

System Tools

"The os.path to Knowledge"

This chapter begins our in-depth look at ways to apply Python to real programming tasks. In this and the following chapters, you'll see how to use Python to write system tools, GUIs, database applications, Internet scripts, web sites, and more. Along the way, we'll also study larger Python programming concepts in action: code reuse, maintainability, object-oriented programming (OOP), and so on.

In this first part of the book, we begin our Python programming tour by exploring the *systems application domain*—scripts that deal with files, programs, and the general environment surrounding a program. Although the examples in this domain focus on particular kinds of tasks, the techniques they employ will prove to be useful in later parts of the book as well. In other words, you should begin your journey here, unless you are already a Python systems programming wizard.

Why Python Here?

Python's system interfaces span application domains, but for the next five chapters, most of our examples fall into the category of *system tools*—programs sometimes called command-line utilities, shell scripts, and other permutations of such words. Regardless of their title, you are probably already familiar with this sort of script; these scripts accomplish such tasks as processing files in a directory, launching test scripts, and so on. Such programs historically have been written in nonportable and syntactically obscure shell languages such as DOS batch files, csh, and awk.

Even in this relatively simple domain, though, some of Python's better attributes shine brightly. For instance, Python's ease of use and extensive built-in library make it simple (and even fun) to use advanced system tools such as threads, signals, forks, sockets, and their kin; such tools are much less accessible under the obscure syntax of shell languages and the slow development cycles of compiled languages. Python's support for concepts like code clarity and OOP also help us write shell tools that can be read, maintained, and reused. When using Python, there is no need to start every new script from scratch.

Moreover, we'll find that Python not only includes all the interfaces we need in order to write system tools, but also fosters script *portability*. By employing Python's standard library, most system scripts written in Python are automatically portable to all major platforms. For instance, you can usually run in Linux a Python directory-processing script written in Windows without changing its source code at all—simply copy over the source code. If used well, Python is the only system scripting tool you need to know.

The Next Five Chapters

To make this part of the book easier to study, I have broken it down into five chapters:

- In this chapter, I'll introduce the main system-related modules in overview fashion, and then use them to illustrate core system programming concepts: streams, command-line arguments, environment variables, and so on.
- In Chapter 4, we'll focus on the tools Python provides for processing files and directories, as well as focusing on directory trees.
- Chapter 5 moves on to cover Python's standard tools for parallel processing— processes, threads, queues, pipes, signals, and more.
- Chapters 6 and 7 wrap up by presenting larger and more realistic examples that use the tools introduced in the prior three chapters. Chapter 6 is a collection of general system scripts, and Chapter 7 focuses on scripts for processing directories of files.

Especially in the two example chapters at the end of this part of the book, we will be concerned as much with system interfaces as with general Python development concepts. We'll see non-object-oriented and object-oriented versions of some examples along the way, for instance, to help illustrate the benefits of thinking in more strategic ways.

System Scripting Overview

We will take a quick tour through the standard library sys and os modules in the first few sections of this chapter before moving on to larger system programming concepts. As you can tell from the length of their attribute lists, both of these are large modules (their content may vary slightly per Python version and platform):

```
>>> import sys, os
>>> len(dir(sys))          # 56 attributes
56
```

"Batteries Included"

This chapter, and those that follow, deal with both the Python language and its *standard library*—a collection of precoded modules written in Python and C that are installed with the Python interpreter. Although Python itself provides an easy-to-use scripting language, much of the real action in Python development involves this vast library of programming tools (a few hundred modules at last count) that ship with the Python package.

In fact, the standard library is so powerful that it is not uncommon to hear Python described with the phrase "batteries included"—a phrase generally credited to Frank Stajano meaning that most of what you need for real day-to-day work is already there for importing.

As we'll see, the standard library forms much of the challenge in Python programming. Once you've mastered the core language, you'll find that you'll spend most of your time applying the built-in functions and modules that come with the system. On the other hand, libraries are where most of the fun happens. In practice, programs become most interesting when they start using services external to the language interpreter: networks, files, GUIs, databases, and so on. All of these are supported in the Python standard library. Beyond the standard library, there is an additional collection of third-party packages for Python that must be fetched and installed separately. As of this writing, you can find most of these third-party extensions via searches and links at *http:// www.python.org* and at the PyPI and Vaults of Parnassus Python sites (also reachable from links at *http://www.python.org*). Some third-party extensions are large systems in their own right—NumPy and VPython, for instance, add vector processing and visualization, respectively.

If you have to do something special with Python, chances are good that you can find a free and open source module that will help. Most of the tools we'll employ in this text are a standard part of Python, but I'll be careful to point out things that must be installed separately.

```
>>> len(dir(os))            # 118 on Windows, more on Unix
118
>>> len(dir(os.path))       # a nested module within os
43
```

As I'm not going to demonstrate every item in every built-in module, the first thing I want to do is show you how to get more details on your own. Officially, this task also serves as an excuse for introducing a few core system scripting concepts; along the way, we'll code a first script to format documentation.

Python System Modules

Most system-level interfaces in Python are shipped in just two modules: sys and os. That's somewhat oversimplified; other standard modules belong to this domain too. Among them are the following:

glob
> For filename expansion

socket
> For network connections and Inter-Process Communication (IPC)

thread *and* queue
> For concurrent threads

time
> For accessing system time details

fcntl
> For low-level file control

In addition, some built-in functions are actually system interfaces as well (e.g., open). But sys and os together form the core of Python's system tools arsenal.

In principle at least, sys exports components related to the Python *interpreter* itself (e.g., the module search path), and os contains variables and functions that map to the operating system on which Python is run. In practice, this distinction may not always seem clear-cut (e.g., the standard input and output streams show up in sys, but they are arguably tied to operating system paradigms). The good news is that you'll soon use the tools in these modules so often that their locations will be permanently stamped on your memory.*

The os module also attempts to provide a *portable* programming interface to the underlying operating system; its functions may be implemented differently on different platforms, but to Python scripts, they look the same everywhere. In addition, the os module exports a nested submodule, os.path, which provides a portable interface to file and directory processing tools.

Module Documentation Sources

As you can probably deduce from the preceding paragraphs, learning to write system scripts in Python is mostly a matter of learning about Python's system modules. Luckily, there are a variety of information sources to make this task easier—from module attributes to published references and books.

---

* They may also work their way into your subconscious. Python newcomers sometimes appear on Internet discussion forums to discuss their experiences "dreaming in Python" for the first time.

For instance, if you want to know everything that a built-in module exports, you can read its library manual entry, study its source code (Python is open source software, after all), or fetch its attribute list and documentation string interactively. Let's import sys and see what it has:

```
C:\...\PP3E\System> python
>>> import sys
>>> dir(sys)
['__displayhook__', '__doc__', '__excepthook__', '__name__', '__stderr__',
'__stdin__', '__stdout__', '_getframe', 'api_version', 'argv',
'builtin_module_names', 'byteorder', 'call_tracing', 'callstats', 'copyright',
'displayhook', 'dllhandle', 'exc_clear', 'exc_info', 'exc_traceback', 'exc_type',
'exc_value', 'excepthook', 'exec_prefix', 'executable', 'exit', 'exitfunc',
'getcheckinterval', 'getdefaultencoding', 'getfilesystemencoding',
'getrecursionlimit', 'getrefcount', 'getwindowsversion', 'hexversion', 'maxint',
'maxunicode', 'meta_path', 'modules', 'path', 'path_hooks', 'path_importer_cache',
'platform', 'prefix', 'ps1', 'ps2', 'setcheckinterval', 'setprofile',
'setrecursionlimit', 'settrace', 'stderr', 'stdin', 'stdout', 'version', 'version_
info', 'warnoptions', 'winver']
```

The dir function simply returns a list containing the string names of all the attributes in any object with attributes; it's a handy memory jogger for modules at the interactive prompt. For example, we know there is something called sys.version, because the name version came back in the dir result. If that's not enough, we can always consult the __doc__ string of built-in modules:

```
>>> sys.__doc__
"This module provides access to some objects used or maintained by the\ninterpreter
and to functions that interact strongly with the interpreter.\n\nDynamic objects:\n\
nargv -- command line arguments; argv[0] is the script pathname if known\npath --
module search path; path[0] is the script directory, else ''\nmodules
...
...lots of text deleted here...
...
"
```

Paging Documentation Strings

The __doc__ built-in attribute usually contains a string of documentation, but it may look a bit weird when displayed this way—it's one long string with embedded endline characters that print as \n, not as a nice list of lines. To format these strings for a more humane display, you can simply use a print statement:

```
>>> print sys.__doc__
This module provides access to some objects used or maintained by the
interpreter and to functions that interact strongly with the interpreter.

Dynamic objects:

argv -- command line arguments; argv[0] is the script pathname if known
...
...lots of lines deleted here...
...
```

The print statement, unlike interactive displays, interprets end-line characters correctly. Unfortunately, print doesn't, by itself, do anything about scrolling or paging and so can still be unwieldy on some platforms. Tools such as the built-in help function can do better:

```
>>> help(sys)
Help on built-in module sys:

NAME
    sys

FILE
    (built-in)

MODULE DOCS
    http://www.python.org/doc/current/lib/module-sys.html

DESCRIPTION
    This module provides access to some objects used or maintained by the
    interpreter and to functions that interact strongly with the interpreter.

    Dynamic objects:

    argv -- command line arguments; argv[0] is the script pathname if known
...
...lots of lines deleted here...
...
```

The help function is one interface provided by the PyDoc system—code that ships with Python and renders documentation (documentation strings, as well as structural details) related to an object in a formatted way. The format is either like a Unix manpage, which we get for help, or an HTML page, which is more grandiose. It's a handy way to get basic information when working interactively, and it's a last resort before falling back on manuals and books. It is also fairly fixed in the way it displays information; although it attempts to page the display in some contexts, its page size isn't quite right on some of the machines I use. When I want more control over the way help text is printed, I usually use a utility script of my own, like the one in Example 3-1.

Example 3-1. PP3E\System\more.py

```
#########################################################
# split and interactively page a string or file of text;
#########################################################

def more(text, numlines=15):
    lines = text.split('\n')
    while lines:
        chunk = lines[:numlines]
        lines = lines[numlines:]
        for line in chunk: print line
```

Example 3-1. PP3E\System\more.py (continued)

```
        if lines and raw_input('More?') not in ['y', 'Y']: break

if __name__ == '__main__':
    import sys                          # when run, not imported
    more(open(sys.argv[1]).read( ), 10) # page contents of file on cmdline
```

The meat of this file is its more function, and if you know any Python at all, it should be fairly straightforward. It simply splits up a string around end-line characters, and then slices off and displays a few lines at a time (15 by default) to avoid scrolling off the screen. A slice expression, lines[:15], gets the first 15 items in a list, and lines[15:] gets the rest; to show a different number of lines each time, pass a number to the numlines argument (e.g., the last line in Example 3-1 passes 10 to the numlines argument of the more function).

The split string object method call that this script employs returns a list of substrings (e.g., ["line", "line",...]). In recent Python releases, a new splitlines method does similar work:

```
>>> line = 'aaa\nbbb\nccc\n'
>>> line.split('\n')
['aaa', 'bbb', 'ccc', '']
>>> line.splitlines( )
['aaa', 'bbb', 'ccc']
```

As we'll see in the next chapter, the end-of-line character is always \n (which stands for a byte having a binary value of 10) within a Python script, no matter what platform it is run upon. (If you don't already know why this matters, DOS \r characters are dropped when read.)

Introducing String Methods

Now, this is a simple Python program, but it already brings up three important topics that merit quick detours here: it uses string methods, reads from a file, and is set up to be run or imported. Python string methods are not a system-related tool per se, but they see action in most Python programs. In fact, they are going to show up throughout this chapter as well as those that follow, so here is a quick review of some of the more useful tools in this set. String methods include calls for searching and replacing:

```
>>> str = 'xxxSPAMxxx'
>>> str.find('SPAM')                    # return first offset
3
>>> str = 'xxaaxxaa'
>>> str.replace('aa', 'SPAM')           # global replacement
'xxSPAMxxSPAM'

>>> str = '\t  Ni\n'
>>> str.strip( )                        # remove whitespace
'Ni'
```

The find call returns the offset of the first occurrence of a substring, and replace does global search and replacement. Like all string operations, replace returns a new string instead of changing its subject in-place (recall that strings are immutable). With these methods, substrings are just strings; in Chapter 21, we'll also meet a module called re that allows regular expression *patterns* to show up in searches and replacements.

String methods also provide functions that are useful for things such as case conversions, and a standard library module named string defines some useful preset variables, among other things:

```
>>> str = 'SHRUBBERY'
>>> str.lower()                          # case converters
'shrubbery'

>>> str.isalpha()                        # content tests
True
>>> str.isdigit()
False

>>> import string                        # case constants
>>> string.lowercase
'abcdefghijklmnopqrstuvwxyz'
```

There are also methods for splitting up strings around a substring delimiter and putting them back together with a substring in between. We'll explore these tools later in this book, but as an introduction, here they are at work:

```
>>> str = 'aaa,bbb,ccc'
>>> str.split(',')                       # split into substrings list
['aaa', 'bbb', 'ccc']

>>> str = 'a  b\nc\nd'
>>> str.split()                          # default delimiter: whitespace
['a', 'b', 'c', 'd']

>>> delim = 'NI'
>>> delim.join(['aaa', 'bbb', 'ccc'])    # join substrings list
'aaaNIbbbNIccc'

>>> ' '.join(['A', 'dead', 'parrot'])    # add a space between
'A dead parrot'

>>> chars = list('Lorreta')              # covert to characters list
>>> chars
['L', 'o', 'r', 'r', 'e', 't', 'a']
>>> chars.append('!')
>>> ''.join(chars)                       # to string: empty delimiter
'Lorreta!'
```

These calls turn out to be surprisingly powerful. For example, a line of data columns separated by tabs can be parsed into its columns with a single split call; the *more.py* script uses it to split a string into a list of line strings. In fact, we can emulate the replace call we saw earlier in this section with a split/join combination:

```
>>> str = 'xxaaxxaa'
>>> 'SPAM'.join(str.split('aa'))          # replace, the hard way
'xxSPAMxxSPAM'
```

For future reference, also keep in mind that Python doesn't automatically convert strings to numbers, or vice versa; if you want to use one as you would use the other, you must say so with manual conversions:

```
>>> int("42"), eval("42")                 # string to int conversions
(42, 42)

>>> str(42), repr(42), ("%d" % 42)        # int to string conversions
('42', '42', '42')

>>> "42" + str(1), int("42") + 1          # concatenation, addition
('421', 43)
```

In the last command here, the first expression triggers string concatenation (since both sides are strings), and the second invokes integer addition (because both objects are numbers). Python doesn't assume you meant one or the other and convert automatically; as a rule of thumb, Python tries to avoid magic whenever possible. String tools will be covered in more detail later in this book (in fact, they get a full chapter in Part V), but be sure to also see the library manual for additional string method tools.

> A section on the original string module was removed in this edition. In the past, string method calls were also available by importing the string module and passing the string object as an argument to functions corresponding to the current methods. For instance, given a name str assigned to a string object, the older call form:
>
> ```
> import string
> string.replace(str, old, new)      # requires an import
> ```
>
> is the same as the more modern version:
>
> ```
> str.replace(old, new)
> ```
>
> But the latter form does not require a module import, and it will run quicker (the older module call form incurs an extra call along the way). You should use string object methods today, not string module functions, but you may still see the older function-based call pattern in some Python code. Although most of its functions are now deprecated, the original string module today still contains predefined constants (such as string.lowercase) and a new template interface in 2.4.

File Operation Basics

The *more.py* script also opens the external file whose name is listed on the command line using the built-in open function, and reads that file's text into memory all at once with the file object read method. Since file objects returned by open are part of the core Python language itself, I assume that you have at least a passing familiarity with them at this point in the text. But just in case you've flipped to this chapter early on in your Pythonhood, the calls:

```
open('file').read()          # read entire file into string
open('file').read(N)         # read next N bytes into string
open('file').readlines()     # read entire file into line strings list
open('file').readline()      # read next line, through '\n'
```

load a file's contents into a string, load a fixed-size set of bytes into a string, load a file's contents into a list of line strings, and load the next line in the file into a string, respectively. As we'll see in a moment, these calls can also be applied to shell commands in Python to read their output. File objects also have write methods for sending strings to the associated file. File-related topics are covered in depth in the next chapter, but making an output file and reading it back is easy in Python:

```
>>> file = open('spam.txt', 'w')          # create file spam.txt
>>> file.write(('spam' * 5) + '\n')
>>> file.close()

>>> file = open('spam.txt')               # or open('spam.txt').read()
>>> text = file.read()
>>> text
'spamspamspamspamspam\n'
```

Using Programs in Two Ways

The last few lines in the *more.py* file also introduce one of the first big concepts in shell tool programming. They instrument the file to be used in either of two ways: as a *script* or as a *library*. Every Python module has a built-in __name__ variable that Python sets to the __main__ string only when the file is run as a program, not when it's imported as a library. Because of that, the more function in this file is executed automatically by the last line in the file when this script is run as a top-level program, not when it is imported elsewhere. This simple trick turns out to be one key to writing reusable script code: by coding program logic as *functions* rather than as top-level code, you can also import and reuse it in other scripts.

The upshot is that we can run *more.py* by itself or import and call its more function elsewhere. When running the file as a top-level program, we list on the command line the name of a file to be read and paged: as I'll describe in depth later in this chapter, words typed in the command that is used to start a program show up in the built-in sys.argv list in Python. For example, here is the script file in action, paging itself (be sure to type this command line in your *PP3E\System* directory, or it won't find the input file; more on command lines later):

```
C:\...\PP3E\System>python more.py more.py
#########################################################
# split and interactively page a string or file of text;
#########################################################

def more(text, numlines=15):
    lines = text.split('\n')
    while lines:
        chunk = lines[:numlines]
        lines = lines[numlines:]
        for line in chunk: print line
More?y
        if lines and raw_input('More?') not in ['y', 'Y']: break

if __name__ == '__main__':
    import sys                          # when run, not imported
    more(open(sys.argv[1]).read(), 10)  # page contents of file on cmdline
```

When the *more.py* file is imported, we pass an explicit string to its more function, and this is exactly the sort of utility we need for documentation text. Running this utility on the sys module's documentation string gives us a bit more information in human-readable form about what's available to scripts:

```
C:\...\PP3E\System> python
>>> from more import more
>>> import sys
>>> more(sys.__doc__)
This module provides access to some objects used or maintained by the
interpreter and to functions that interact strongly with the interpreter.

Dynamic objects:

argv -- command line arguments; argv[0] is the script pathname if known
path -- module search path; path[0] is the script directory, else ''
modules -- dictionary of loaded modules

displayhook -- called to show results in an interactive session
excepthook -- called to handle any uncaught exception other than SystemExit
  To customize printing in an interactive session or to install a custom
  top-level exception handler, assign other functions to replace these.

exitfunc -- if sys.exitfunc exists, this routine is called when Python exits
More?
```

Pressing "y" or "Y" here makes the function display the next few lines of documentation, and then prompt again, unless you've run past the end of the lines list. Try this on your own machine to see what the rest of the module's documentation string looks like.

Python Library Manuals

If that still isn't enough detail, your next step is to read the Python library manual's entry for sys to get the full story. All of Python's standard manuals ship as HTML pages, so you should be able to read them in any web browser you have on your computer. They are installed with Python on Windows, but here are a few simple pointers:

- On Windows, click the Start button, pick Programs, select the Python entry there, and then choose the manuals item. The manuals should magically appear on your display within a browser like Internet Explorer. As of Python 2.4, the manuals are provided as a Windows help file and so support searching and navigation.

- On Linux, you may be able to click on the manuals' entries in a file explorer, or start your browser from a shell command line and navigate to the library manual's HTML files on your machine.

- If you can't find the manuals on your computer, you can always read them online. Go to Python's web site at *http://www.python.org* and follow the documentation links.

However you get started, be sure to pick the Library manual for things such as sys; Python's standard manual set also includes a short tutorial, language reference, extending references, and more.

Commercially Published References

At the risk of sounding like a marketing droid, I should mention that you can also purchase the Python manual set, printed and bound; see the book information page at *http://www.python.org* for details and links. Commercially published Python reference books are also available today, including *Python Essential Reference* (Sams) and *Python Pocket Reference* (O'Reilly). The former is more complete and comes with examples, but the latter serves as a convenient memory jogger once you've taken a library tour or two.* Also useful are O'Reilly's *Python in a Nutshell* and *Python Standard Library*.

Introducing the sys Module

On to module details; as mentioned earlier, the sys and os modules form the core of much of Python's system-related tool set. Let's now take a quick, interactive tour through some of the tools in these two modules before applying them in bigger examples. We'll start with sys, the smaller of the two; remember that to see a full list of all the attributes in sys, you need to pass it to the dir function (or see where we did so earlier in this chapter).

---

* I also wrote the latter as a replacement for the reference appendix that appeared in the first edition of this book; it's meant to be a supplement to the text you're reading. Insert self-serving plug here.

Platforms and Versions

Like most modules, sys includes both informational names and functions that take action. For instance, its attributes give us the name of the underlying operating system on which the platform code is running, the largest possible integer on this machine, and the version number of the Python interpreter running our code:

```
C:\...\PP3E\System>python
>>> import sys
>>> sys.platform, sys.maxint, sys.version
('win32', 2147483647, '2.4 (#60, Nov 30 2004, 11:49:19) [MSC v.1310 32 bit (Intel)]')
>>>
>>> if sys.platform[:3] == 'win': print 'hello windows'
...
hello windows
```

If you have code that must act differently on different machines, simply test the sys.platform string as done here; although most of Python is cross-platform, non-portable tools are usually wrapped in if tests like the one here. For instance, we'll see later that today's program launch and low-level console interaction tools vary per platform—simply test sys.platform to pick the right tool for the machine on which your script is running.

The Module Search Path

The sys module also lets us inspect the module search path both interactively and within a Python program. sys.path is a list of strings representing the true search path in a running Python interpreter. When a module is imported, Python scans this list from left to right, searching for the module's file on each directory named in the list. Because of that, this is the place to look to verify that your search path is really set as intended.*

The sys.path list is simply initialized from your PYTHONPATH setting—the content of any *.pth* path files located in Python's directories on your machine plus system defaults—when the interpreter is first started up. In fact, if you inspect sys.path interactively, you'll notice quite a few directories that are not on your PYTHONPATH—sys.path also includes an indicator for the script's home directory (an empty string—something I'll explain in more detail after we meet os.getcwd) and a set of standard library directories that may vary per installation:

```
>>> sys.path
['', 'C:\\PP3rdEd\\Examples', ...plus standard paths deleted... ]
```

---

* It's not impossible that Python sees PYTHONPATH differently than you do. A syntax error in your system shell configuration files may botch the setting of PYTHONPATH, even if it looks fine to you. On Windows, for example, if a space appears around the = of a DOS set command in your *autoexec.bat* file (e.g., set NAME = VALUE), you will actually set NAME to an empty string, not to VALUE!

Surprisingly, sys.path can actually be *changed* by a program, too. A script can use list operations such as append, del, and the like to configure the search path at runtime to include all the source directories to which it needs access. Python always uses the current sys.path setting to import, no matter what you've changed it to:

```
>>> sys.path.append(r'C:\mydir')
>>> sys.path
['', 'C:\\PP3rdEd\\Examples', ...more deleted..., 'C:\\mydir']
```

Changing sys.path directly like this is an alternative to setting your PYTHONPATH shell variable, but not a very good one. Changes to sys.path are retained only until the Python process ends, and they must be remade every time you start a new Python program or session. However, some types of programs (e.g., scripts that run on a web server) may not be able to depend on PYTHONPATH settings; such scripts can instead configure sys.path on startup to include all the directories from which they will need to import modules.

Windows Directory Paths

Because backslashes normally introduce escape code sequences in Python strings, Windows users should be sure to either double up on backslashes when using them in DOS directory path strings (e.g., in "C:\\dir", \\ is an escape sequence that really means \), or use raw string constants to retain backslashes literally (e.g., r"C:\dir").

If you inspect directory paths on Windows (as in the sys.path interaction listing), Python prints double \\ to mean a single \. Technically, you can get away with a single \ in a string if it is followed by a character Python does not recognize as the rest of an escape sequence, but doubles and raw strings are usually easier than memorizing escape code tables.

Also note that most Python library calls accept either forward (/) or backward (\) slashes as directory path separators, regardless of the underlying platform. That is, / usually works on Windows too and aids in making scripts portable to Unix. Tools in the os and os.path modules, described later in this chapter, further aid in script path portability.

The Loaded Modules Table

The sys module also contains hooks into the interpreter; sys.modules, for example, is a dictionary containing one *name:module* entry for every module imported in your Python session or program (really, in the calling Python process):

```
>>> sys.modules
{'os.path': <module 'ntpath' from 'C:\Program Files\Python\Lib\ntpath.pyc'>,...

>>> sys.modules.keys()
['os.path', 'os', 'exceptions', '__main__', 'ntpath', 'strop', 'nt', 'sys',
```

```
'__builtin__', 'site', 'signal', 'UserDict', 'string', 'stat']
>>> sys
<module 'sys' (built-in)>
>>> sys.modules['sys']
<module 'sys' (built-in)>
```

We might use such a hook to write programs that display or otherwise process all the modules loaded by a program (just iterate over the keys list of sys.modules). sys also exports tools for getting an object's reference count used by Python's garbage collector (getrefcount), checking which modules are built into this Python (builtin_module_names), and more.

Exception Details

Some of the sys module's attributes allow us to fetch all the information related to the most recently raised Python exception. This is handy if we want to process exceptions in a more generic fashion. For instance, the sys.exc_info function returns the latest exception's type, value, and traceback object:

```
>>> try:
...     raise IndexError
... except:
...     print sys.exc_info()
...
(<class exceptions.IndexError at 7698d0>, <exceptions.IndexError instance at 797140>, <traceback object at 7971a0>)
```

We might use such information to format our own error message to display in a GUI pop-up window or HTML web page (recall that by default, uncaught exceptions terminate programs with a Python error display). The first two items returned by this call have reasonable string displays when printed directly, and the third is a traceback object that can be processed with the standard traceback module:

```
>>> import traceback, sys
>>> def grail(x):
...     raise TypeError, 'already got one'
...
>>> try:
...     grail('arthur')
... except:
...     exc_info = sys.exc_info()
...     print exc_info[0]
...     print exc_info[1]
...     traceback.print_tb(exc_info[2])
...
exceptions.TypeError
already got one
  File "<stdin>", line 2, in ?
  File "<stdin>", line 2, in grail
```

The traceback module can also format messages as strings and route them to specific file objects; see the Python library manual for more details.

 I should make two portability notes. First, the most recent exception type, value, and traceback objects are also available via other names:

```
>>> try:
...     raise TypeError, "Bad Thing"
... except:
...     print sys.exc_type, sys.exc_value
...
exceptions.TypeError Bad Thing
```

But these names represent a single, global exception, and they are not specific to a particular thread (threads are covered in Chapter 5). If you mean to raise and catch exceptions in multiple threads, exc_info provides thread-specific exception details. In fact, you are better off using exc_info in all cases today, as the older tools are now documented as deprecated and may be removed in a future version of Python.

It has also been suggested (in the 2.4 library reference manual and the Python 3.0 PEP document) that string-based exceptions may be removed in a future Python release. This seems more radical and less certain. But if you want to avoid potential future work, use class-based exceptions instead. Because they allow you to define categories of exceptions, they are better than strings in terms of code maintenance anyhow; by listing categories, your exception handlers are immune to future changes. Built-in exceptions have been classes since Python 1.5.

Other sys Module Exports

The sys module exports additional tools that we will meet in the context of larger topics and examples introduced later in this chapter and book. For instance:

- Command-line arguments show up as a list of strings called sys.argv.
- Standard streams are available as sys.stdin, sys.stdout, and sys.stderr.
- Program exit can be forced with sys.exit calls.

Since all of these lead us to bigger topics, though, we will cover them in sections of their own.

Introducing the os Module

As mentioned, os is the larger of the two core system modules. It contains all of the usual operating-system calls you may have used in your C programs and shell scripts. Its calls deal with directories, processes, shell variables, and the like. Technically, this module provides POSIX tools—a portable standard for operating-system calls—along with platform-independent directory processing tools as the nested module os.path.

Operationally, os serves as a largely portable interface to your computer's system calls: scripts written with os and os.path can usually be run unchanged on any platform.

In fact, if you read the os module's source code, you'll notice that it really just imports whatever platform-specific system module you have on your computer (e.g., nt, mac, posix). See the *os.py* file in the Python source library directory—it simply runs a from* statement to copy all names out of a platform-specific module. By always importing os rather than platform-specific modules, though, your scripts are mostly immune to platform implementation differences. On some platforms, os includes extra tools available just for that platform (e.g., low-level process calls on Unix); by and large, though, it is as cross-platform as it is technically feasible.

The Big os Lists

Let's take a quick look at the basic interfaces in os. As a preview, Table 3-1 summarizes some of the most commonly used tools in the os module organized by functional area.

Table 3-1. Commonly used os module tools

Tasks	Tools
Shell variables	os.environ
Running programs	os.system, os.popen, os.popen2/3/4, os.startfile
Spawning processes	os.fork, os.pipe, os.exec, os.waitpid, os.kill
Descriptor files, locks	os.open, os.read, os.write
File processing	os.remove, os.rename, os.mkfifo, os.mkdir, os.rmdir
Administrative tools	os.getcwd, os.chdir, os.chmod, os.getpid, os.listdir
Portability tools	os.sep, os.pathsep, os.curdir, os.path.split, os.path.join
Pathname tools	os.path.exists('path'), os.path.isdir('path'), os.path.getsize('path')

If you inspect this module's attributes interactively, you get a huge list of names that will vary per Python release, will likely vary per platform, and isn't incredibly useful until you've learned what each name means (I've removed most of this list to save space—run the command on your own):

```
>>> import os
>>> dir(os)
['F_OK', 'O_APPEND', 'O_BINARY', 'O_CREAT', 'O_EXCL', 'O_NOINHERIT',
'O_RANDOM', 'O_RDONLY', 'O_RDWR', 'O_SEQUENTIAL', 'O_SHORT_LIVED',
'O_TEMPORARY', 'O_TEXT', 'O_TRUNC', 'O_WRONLY', 'P_DETACH', 'P_NOWAIT',
...
...10 lines removed here...
...
'popen4', 'putenv', 'read', 'remove', 'removedirs', 'rename', 'renames', 'rmdir',
'sep', 'spawnl', 'spawnle', 'spawnv', 'spawnve', 'startfile', 'stat',
```

```
'stat_float_times', 'stat_result', 'statvfs_result', 'strerror', 'sys', 'system',
'tempnam', 'times', 'tmpfile', 'tmpnam', 'umask', 'unlink', 'unsetenv', 'urandom',
'utime', 'waitpid', 'walk', 'write']
```

Besides all of these, the nested os.path module exports even more tools, most of which are related to processing file and directory names portably:

```
>>> dir(os.path)
['__all__', '__builtins__', '__doc__', '__file__', '__name__', 'abspath',
'altsep', 'basename', 'commonprefix', 'curdir', 'defpath', 'devnull', 'dirname',
'exists', 'expanduser', 'expandvars', 'extsep', 'getatime', 'getctime', 'getmtime',
'getsize', 'isabs', 'isdir', 'isfile', 'islink', 'ismount', 'join', 'lexists',
'normcase', 'normpath', 'os', 'pardir', 'pathsep', 'realpath', 'sep', 'split',
'splitdrive', 'splitext', 'splitunc', 'stat', 'supports_unicode_filenames', 'sys',
'walk']
```

Administrative Tools

Just in case those massive listings aren't quite enough to go on, let's experiment interactively with some of the simpler os tools. Like sys, the os module comes with a collection of informational and administrative tools:

```
>>> os.getpid()
-510737
>>> os.getcwd()
'C:\\PP3rdEd\\Examples\\PP3E\\System'

>>> os.chdir(r'c:\temp')
>>> os.getcwd()
'c:\\temp'
```

As shown here, the os.getpid function gives the calling process's process ID (a unique system-defined identifier for a running program), and os.getcwd returns the current working directory. The current working directory is where files opened by your script are assumed to live, unless their names include explicit directory paths. That's why earlier I told you to run the following command in the directory where *more.py* lives:

```
C:\...\PP3E\System>python more.py more.py
```

The input filename argument here is given without an explicit directory path (though you could add one to page files in another directory). If you need to run in a different working directory, call the os.chdir function to change to a new directory; your code will run relative to the new directory for the rest of the program (or until the next os.chdir call). This chapter will have more to say about the notion of a current working directory, and its relation to module imports when it explores script execution context.

Portability Constants

The os module also exports a set of names designed to make cross-platform programming simpler. The set includes platform-specific settings for path and directory separator characters, parent and current directory indicators, and the characters used to terminate lines on the underlying computer:[*]

```
>>> os.pathsep, os.sep, os.pardir, os.curdir, os.linesep
(';', '\\', '..', '.', '\r\n')
```

os.sep is whatever character is used to separate directory components on the platform on which Python is running; it is automatically preset to \ on Windows, / for POSIX machines, and : on the Mac. Similarly, os.pathsep provides the character that separates directories on directory lists—: for POSIX and ; for DOS and Windows.

By using such attributes when composing and decomposing system-related strings in our scripts, the scripts become fully portable. For instance, a call of the form os.sep.split(dirpath) will correctly split platform-specific directory names into components, even though dirpath may look like dir\dir on Windows, dir/dir on Linux, and dir:dir on Macintosh. As previously mentioned, on Windows you can usually use forward slashes rather than backward slashes when giving filenames to be opened; but these portability constants allow scripts to be platform neutral in directory processing code.

Basic os.path Tools

The nested module os.path provides a large set of directory-related tools of its own. For example, it includes portable functions for tasks such as checking a file's type (isdir, isfile, and others), testing file existence (exists), and fetching the size of a file by name (getsize):

```
>>> os.path.isdir(r'C:\temp'),        os.path.isfile(r'C:\temp')
(True, False)
>>> os.path.isdir(r'C:\config.sys'),  os.path.isfile(r'C:\config.sys')
(False, Tuue)
>>> os.path.isdir('nonesuch'),        os.path.isfile('nonesuch')
(False, False)

>>> os.path.exists(r'c:\temp\data.txt')
0
>>> os.path.getsize(r'C:\autoexec.bat')
260
```

---

[*] os.linesep comes back as \r\n here—the symbolic escape code equivalent of \015\012, which reflect the carriage-return + line-feed line terminator convention on Windows. In older versions of Python, you may still see these displayed in their octal or hexadecimal escape forms. See the discussion of end-of-line translations in the next chapter.

The os.path.isdir and os.path.isfile calls tell us whether a filename is a directory or a simple file; both return False if the named file does not exist. We also get calls for splitting and joining directory path strings, which automatically use the directory name conventions on the platform on which Python is running:

```
>>> os.path.split(r'C:\temp\data.txt')
('C:\\temp', 'data.txt')
>>> os.path.join(r'C:\temp', 'output.txt')
'C:\\temp\\output.txt'

>>> name = r'C:\temp\data.txt'                          # Windows paths
>>> os.path.basename(name), os.path.dirname(name)
('data.txt', 'C:\\temp')

>>> name = '/home/lutz/temp/data.txt'                   # Unix-style paths
>>> os.path.basename(name), os.path.dirname(name)
('data.txt', '/home/lutz/temp')

>>> os.path.splitext(r'C:\PP3rdEd\Examples\PP3E\PyDemos.pyw')
('C:\\PP3rdEd\\Examples\\PP3E\\PyDemos', '.pyw')
```

os.path.split separates a filename from its directory path, and os.path.join puts them back together—all in entirely portable fashion using the path conventions of the machine on which they are called. The basename and dirname calls here return the second and first items returned by a split simply as a convenience, and splitext strips the file extension (after the last .). The normpath call comes in handy if your paths become a jumble of Unix and Windows separators:

```
>>> mixed
'C:\\temp\\public/files/index.html'
>>> os.path.normpath(mixed)
'C:\\temp\\public\\files\\index.html'
>>> print os.path.normpath(r'C:\temp\\sub\.\file.ext')
C:\temp\sub\file.ext
```

This module also has an abspath call that portably returns the full directory pathname of a file; it accounts for adding the current directory, .. parents, and more:

```
>>> os.getcwd()
'C:\\PP3rdEd\\cdrom\\WindowsExt'
>>> os.path.abspath('temp')                       # expand to full pathname
'C:\\PP3rdEd\\cdrom\\WindowsExt\\temp'
>>> os.path.abspath(r'..\examples')               # relative paths expanded
'C:\\PP3rdEd\\examples'
>>> os.path.abspath(r'C:\PP3rdEd\chapters')       # absolute paths unchanged
'C:\\PP3rdEd\\chapters'
>>> os.path.abspath(r'C:\temp\spam.txt')          # ditto for filenames
'C:\\temp\\spam.txt'
>>> os.path.abspath('')                           # empty string means the cwd
'C:\\PP3rdEd\\cdrom\\WindowsExt'
```

Because filenames are relative to the current working directory when they aren't fully specified paths, the os.path.abspath function helps if you want to show users what directory is truly being used to store a file. On Windows, for example, when GUI-based programs are launched by clicking on file explorer icons and desktop short-cuts, the execution directory of the program is the clicked file's home directory, but that is not always obvious to the person doing the clicking; printing a file's abspath can help.

Running Shell Commands from Scripts

The os module is also the place where we run shell commands from within Python scripts. This concept is intertwined with others we won't cover until later in this chapter, but since this is a key concept employed throughout this part of the book, let's take a quick first look at the basics here. Two os functions allow scripts to run any command line that you can type in a console window:

os.system
> Runs a shell command from a Python script

os.popen
> Runs a shell command and connect to its input or output streams

What's a shell command?

To understand the scope of these calls, we first need to define a few terms. In this text, the term *shell* means the system that reads and runs command-line strings on your computer, and *shell command* means a command-line string that you would normally enter at your computer's shell prompt.

For example, on Windows, you can start an MS-DOS console window and type DOS commands there—commands such as dir to get a directory listing, and type to view a file, names of programs you wish to start, and so on. DOS is the system shell, and commands such as dir and type are shell commands. On Linux, you can start a new shell session by opening an xterm window and typing shell commands there too—ls to list directories, cat to view files, and so on. A variety of shells are available on Unix (e.g., csh, ksh), but they all read and run command lines. Here are two shell commands typed and run in an MS-DOS console box on Windows:

```
C:\temp>dir /B                    ...type a shell command line
about-pp.html                     ...its output shows up here
python1.5.tar.gz                  ...DOS is the shell on Windows
about-pp2e.html
about-ppr2e.html
newdir

C:\temp>type helloshell.py
# a Python program
print 'The Meaning of Life'
```

Running shell commands

None of this is directly related to Python, of course (despite the fact that Python command-line scripts are sometimes confusingly called "shell tools"). But because the os module's system and popen calls let Python scripts run any sort of command that the underlying system shell understands, our scripts can make use of every command-line tool available on the computer, whether it's coded in Python or not. For example, here is some Python code that runs the two DOS shell commands typed at the shell prompt shown previously:

```
C:\temp>python
>>> import os
>>> os.system('dir /B')
about-pp.html
python1.5.tar.gz
about-pp2e.html
about-ppr2e.html
newdir
0

>>> os.system('type helloshell.py')
# a Python program
print 'The Meaning of Life'
0
```

The 0s at the end here are just the return values of the system call itself. The system call can be used to run any command line that we could type at the shell's prompt (here, C:\temp>). The command's output normally shows up in the Python session's or program's standard output stream.

Communicating with shell commands

But what if we want to grab a command's output within a script? The os.system call simply runs a shell command line, but os.popen also connects to the standard input or output streams of the command; we get back a file-like object connected to the command's output by default (if we pass a w mode flag to popen, we connect to the command's input stream instead). By using this object to read the output of a command spawned with popen, we can intercept the text that would normally appear in the console window where a command line is typed:

```
>>> open('helloshell.py').read()
"# a Python program\nprint 'The Meaning of Life'\n"

>>> text = os.popen('type helloshell.py').read()
>>> text
"# a Python program\nprint 'The Meaning of Life'\n"

>>> listing = os.popen('dir /B').readlines()
>>> listing
['about-pp.html\n', 'python1.5.tar.gz\n', 'helloshell.py\n',
 'about-pp2e.html\n', 'about-ppr2e.html\n', 'newdir\n']
```

Here, we first fetch a file's content the usual way (using Python files), then as the output of a shell type command. Reading the output of a `dir` command lets us get a listing of files in a directory that we can then process in a loop (we'll learn other ways to obtain such a list in the next chapter[*]). So far, we've run basic DOS commands; because these calls can run any command line that we can type at a shell prompt, they can also be used to launch other Python scripts:

```
>>> os.system('python helloshell.py')        # run a Python program
The Meaning of Life
0
>>> output = os.popen('python helloshell.py').read()
>>> output
'The Meaning of Life\n'
```

In all of these examples, the command-line strings sent to `system` and `popen` are hard-coded, but there's no reason Python programs could not construct such strings at runtime using normal string operations (+, %, etc.). Given that commands can be dynamically built and run this way, `system` and `popen` turn Python scripts into flexible and portable tools for launching and orchestrating other programs. For example, a Python test "driver" script can be used to run programs coded in any language (e.g., C++, Java, Python) and analyze their output. We'll explore such a script in Chapter 6.

Shell command limitations

You should keep in mind two limitations of `system` and `popen`. First, although these two functions themselves are fairly portable, their use is really only as portable as the commands that they run. The preceding examples that run DOS `dir` and `type` shell commands, for instance, work only on Windows, and would have to be changed in order to run `ls` and `cat` commands on Unix-like platforms.

Second, it is important to remember that running Python files as programs this way is very different and generally much slower than importing program files and calling functions they define. When `os.system` and `os.popen` are called, they must start a brand-new, independent program running on your operating system (they generally run the command in a newly forked process). When importing a program file as a module, the Python interpreter simply loads and runs the file's code in the same process in order to generate a module object. No other program is spawned along the way.[†]

---

[*] In the next chapter, after we've learned about file iterators, we'll also learn that the popen objects have an *iterator* that reads one line at a time, often making the readlines method call superfluous.

[†] The Python execfile built-in function also runs a program file's code, but within the same process that called it. It's similar to an import in that regard, but it works more as if the file's text had been *pasted* into the calling program at the place where the execfile call appears (unless explicit global or local namespace dictionaries are passed). Unlike imports, execfile unconditionally reads and executes a file's code (it may be run more than once per process), no module object is generated by the file's execution, and unless optional namespace dictionaries are passed in, assignments in the file's code may overwrite variables in the scope where the execfile appears; see the Python library manual for more details.

There are good reasons to build systems as separate programs too, and we'll later explore things such as command-line arguments and streams that allow programs to pass information back and forth. But for most purposes, imported modules are a faster and more direct way to compose systems.

If you plan to use these calls in earnest, you should also know that the os.system call normally blocks—that is, pauses—its caller until the spawned command line exits. On Linux and Unix-like platforms, the spawned command can generally be made to run independently and in parallel with the caller by adding an & shell background operator at the end of the command line:

```
os.system("python program.py arg arg &")
```

On Windows, spawning with a DOS start command will usually launch the command in parallel too:

```
os.system("start program.py arg arg")
```

In fact, this is so useful that an os.startfile call was added in recent Python releases. This call opens a file with whatever program is listed in the Windows registry for the file's type—as though its icon has been clicked with the mouse cursor:

```
os.startfile("webpage.html")     # open file in your web browser
os.startfile("document.doc")     # open file in Microsoft Word
os.startfile("myscript.py")      # run file with Python
```

The os.popen call does not generally block its caller (by definition, the caller must be able to read or write the file object returned) but callers may still occasionally become blocked under both Windows and Linux if the pipe object is closed—e.g., when garbage is collected—before the spawned program exits or the pipe is read exhaustively (e.g., with its read( ) method). As we will see in the next chapter, the Unix os.fork/exec and Windows os.spawnv calls can also be used to run parallel programs without blocking.

Because the os module's system and popen calls also fall under the category of program launchers, stream redirectors, and cross-process communication devices, they will show up again in later parts of this chapter and in the following chapters, so we'll defer further details for the time being. If you're looking for more details right away, see the stream redirection section in this chapter and the directory listings section in the next.

Other os Module Exports

Since most other os module tools are even more difficult to appreciate outside the context of larger application topics, we'll postpone a deeper look at them until later sections. But to let you sample the flavor of this module, here is a quick preview for reference. Among the os module's other weapons are these:

`os.environ`
> Fetches and sets shell environment variables

`os.fork`
> Spawns a new child process on Unix

`os.pipe`
> Communicates between programs

`os.execlp`
> Starts new programs

`os.spawnv`
> Starts new programs with lower-level control

`os.open`
> Opens a low-level descriptor-based file

`os.mkdir`
> Creates a new directory

`os.mkfifo`
> Creates a new named pipe

`os.stat`
> Fetches low-level file information

`os.remove`
> Deletes a file by its pathname

`os.path.walk, os.walk`
> Applies a function or loop body to all parts of an entire directory tree

And so on. One caution up front: the os module provides a set of file `open`, `read`, and `write` calls, but all of these deal with low-level file access and are entirely distinct from Python's built-in `stdio` file objects that we create with the built-in `open` function. You should normally use the built-in `open` function (not the os module) for all but very special file-processing needs (e.g., opening with exclusive access file locking).

Throughout this chapter, we will apply sys and os tools such as these to implement common system-level tasks, but this book doesn't have space to provide an exhaustive list of the contents of modules we will meet along the way. If you have not already done so, you should become acquainted with the contents of modules such as os and sys by consulting the Python library manual. For now, let's move on to explore additional system tools in the context of broader system programming concepts.

Script Execution Context

Python scripts don't run in a vacuum. Depending on platforms and startup procedures, Python programs may have all sorts of enclosing context; information automatically passed in to the program by the operating system when the program starts up. For instance, scripts have access to the following sorts of system-level inputs and interfaces:

Current working directory
> os.getcwd gives access to the directory from which a script is started, and many file tools use its value implicitly.

Command-line arguments
> sys.argv gives access to words typed on the command line that are used to start the program and that serve as script inputs.

Shell variables
> os.environ provides an interface to names assigned in the enclosing shell (or a parent program) and passed in to the script.

Standard streams
> sys.stdin, stdout, and stderr export the three input/output streams that are at the heart of command-line shell tools.

Such tools can serve as inputs to scripts, configuration parameters, and so on. In the next few sections, we will explore these context tools—both their Python interfaces and their typical roles.

Current Working Directory

The notion of the current working directory (CWD) turns out to be a key concept in some scripts' execution: it's always the implicit place where files processed by the script are assumed to reside unless their names have absolute directory paths. As we saw earlier, os.getcwd lets a script fetch the CWD name explicitly, and os.chdir allows a script to move to a new CWD.

Keep in mind, though, that filenames without full pathnames map to the CWD and have nothing to do with your PYTHONPATH setting. Technically, a script is always launched from the CWD, not the directory containing the script file. Conversely, imports always first search the directory containing the script, not the CWD (unless the script happens to also be located in the CWD). Since this distinction is subtle and tends to trip up beginners, let's explore it in more detail.

CWD, Files, and Import Paths

When you run a Python script by typing a shell command line such as python dir1\ dir2\file.py, the CWD is the directory you were in when you typed this command, not *dir1\dir2*. On the other hand, Python automatically adds the identity of the script's home directory to the front of the module search path such that *file.py* can always import other files in *dir1\dir2* no matter where it is run from. To illustrate, let's write a simple script to echo both its CWD and its module search path:

```
C:\PP3rdEd\Examples\PP3E\System>type whereami.py
import os, sys
print 'my os.getcwd =>', os.getcwd()          # show my cwd execution dir
print 'my sys.path =>', sys.path[:6]           # show first 6 import paths
raw_input()                                     # wait for keypress if clicked
```

Now, running this script in the directory in which it resides sets the CWD as expected and adds an empty string ('') to the front of the module search path in order to designate the CWD (we met the sys.path module search path earlier):

```
C:\PP3rdEd\Examples\PP3E\System>set PYTHONPATH=C:\PP3rdEd\Examples
C:\PP3rdEd\Examples\PP3E\System>python whereami.py
my os.getcwd => C:\PP3rdEd\Examples\PP3E\System
my sys.path => ['', 'C:\\PP3rdEd\\Examples', 'C:\\Program Files\\Python
\\Lib\\plat-win', 'C:\\Program Files\\Python\\Lib', 'C:\\Program Files\\
Python\\DLLs', 'C:\\Program Files\\Python\\Lib\\lib-tk']
```

But if we run this script from other places, the CWD moves with us (it's the directory where we type commands), and Python adds a directory to the front of the module search path that allows the script to still see files in its own home directory. For instance, when running from one level up (..), the System name added to the front of sys.path will be the first directory that Python searches for imports within *whereami. py*; it points imports back to the directory containing the script that was run. Filenames without complete paths, though, will be mapped to the CWD (*C:\PP3rdEd\ Examples\PP3E*), not the *System* subdirectory nested there:

```
C:\PP3rdEd\Examples\PP3E\System>cd ..
C:\PP3rdEd\Examples\PP3E>python System\whereami.py
my os.getcwd => C:\PP3rdEd\Examples\PP3E
my sys.path => ['System', 'C:\\PP3rdEd\\Examples', ...rest same... ]

C:\PP3rdEd\Examples\PP3E>cd ..
C:\PP3rdEd\Examples>python PP3E\System\whereami.py
my os.getcwd => C:\PP3rdEd\Examples
my sys.path => ['PP3E\\System', 'C:\\PP3rdEd\\Examples', ...rest same... ]

C:\PP3rdEd\Examples\PP3E\System>cd PP3E\System\App
C:\PP3rdEd\Examples\PP3E\System\App>python ..\whereami.py
my os.getcwd => C:\PP3rdEd\Examples\PP3E\System\App
my sys.path => ['..', 'C:\\PP3rdEd\\Examples', ...rest same... ]
```

The net effect is that filenames without directory paths in a script will be mapped to the place where the command was typed (os.getcwd), but imports still have access to the directory of the script being run (via the front of sys.path). Finally, when a file is launched by clicking its icon, the CWD is just the directory that contains the clicked file. The following output, for example, appears in a new DOS console box when *whereami.py* is double-clicked in Windows Explorer:

```
my os.getcwd => C:\PP3rdEd\Examples\PP3E\System
my sys.path => ['C:\\PP3RDED\\EXAMPLES\\PP3E\\SYSTEM', 'C:\\PP3rdEd\\Examples',
'C:\\Program Files\\Python\\Lib\\plat-win', 'C:\\Program Files\\Python\\Lib',
'C:\\Program Files\\Python\\DLLs']
```

In this case, both the CWD used for filenames and the first import search directory are the directory containing the script file. This all usually works out just as you expect, but there are two pitfalls to avoid:

- Filenames might need to include complete directory paths if scripts cannot be sure from where they will be run.
- Command-line scripts cannot use the CWD to gain import visibility to files that are not in their own directories; instead, use PYTHONPATH settings and package import paths to access modules in other directories.

For example, files in this book, regardless of how they are run (import filehere), can always import other files in their own home directories without package path imports but must go through the PP3E package root to find files anywhere else in the examples tree (from PP3E.dir1.dir2 import filethere), even if they are run from the directory containing the desired external module. As usual for modules, the *PP3E\ dir1\dir2* directory name could also be added to PYTHONPATH to make files there visible everywhere without package path imports (though adding more directories to PYTHONPATH increases the likelihood of name clashes). In either case, though, imports are always resolved to the script's home directory or other Python search path settings, not to the CWD.

CWD and Command Lines

This distinction between the CWD and import search paths explains why many scripts in this book designed to operate in the current working directory (instead of one whose name is passed in) are run with command lines such as this one:

```
C:\temp>python %X%\PyTools\cleanpyc-py.py          process cwd
```

In this example, the Python script file itself lives in the directory *C:\PP3rdEd\ Examples\PP3E\PyTools*, but because it is run from *C:\temp*, it processes the files located in *C:\temp* (i.e., in the CWD, not in the script's home directory). To process files elsewhere with such a script, simply cd to the directory to be processed to change the CWD:

```
C:\temp>cd C:\PP2nEd\examples
C:\PP3rdEd\examples>python %X%\PyTools\cleanpyc-py.py       process cwd
```

Because the CWD is always implied, a cd command tells the script which directory to process in no less certain terms than passing a directory name to the script explicitly, like this:

```
C:\...\PP3E\PyTools>python find.py *.py C:\temp          process named dir
```

In this command line, the CWD is the directory containing the script to be run (notice that the script filename has no directory path prefix); but since this script processes a directory named explicitly on the command line (*C:\temp*), the CWD is irrelevant. Finally, if we want to run such a script located in some other directory in order to process files located in yet another directory, we can simply give directory paths to both:

```
C:\temp>python %X%\PyTools\find.py *.cxx C:\PP3rdEd\Examples\PP3E
```

Here, the script has import visibility to files in its *PP3E\PyTools* home directory and processes files in the PP3E root, but the CWD is something else entirely (*C:\temp*). This last form is more to type, of course, but watch for a variety of CWD and explicit script-path command lines like these in this book.

> Whenever you see a %X% in command lines such as those in the preceding examples, it refers to the value of the shell environment variable named X. It's just shorthand for the full directory pathname of the *PP3E* book examples package root directory, which I use to point to scripts' files. On my machines, it is preset in my *PP3E\Config setup-pp** files like this:
>
> ```
> set X=C:\PP3rdEd\Examples\PP3E              --DOS
> setenv X /home/mark/PP3rdEd/Examples/PP3E  --Unix/csh
> ```
>
> That is, it is assigned and expanded to the directory where *PP3E* lives on the system. See the next section in this chapter for more on shell variables. You can instead type full example root paths everywhere you see %X% in this book, but both your fingers and your keyboard are probably better off if you don't.

Command-Line Arguments

The sys module is also where Python makes available the words typed on the command that is used to start a Python script. These words are usually referred to as command-line arguments and show up in sys.argv, a built-in list of strings. C programmers may notice its similarity to the C argv array (an array of C strings). It's not much to look at interactively, because no command-line arguments are passed to start up Python in this mode:

```
>>> sys.argv
['']
```

To really see what arguments are about, we need to run a script from the shell command line. Example 3-2 shows an unreasonably simple one that just prints the argv list for inspection.

Example 3-2. PP3E\System\testargv.py

```
import sys
print sys.argv
```

Running this script prints the command-line arguments list; note that the first item is always the name of the executed Python script file itself, no matter how the script was started (see the sidebar titled "Executable Scripts on Unix," later in this chapter).

```
C:\...\PP3E\System>python testargv.py
['testargv.py']

C:\...\PP3E\System>python testargv.py spam eggs cheese
['testargv.py', 'spam', 'eggs', 'cheese']

C:\...\PP3E\System>python testargv.py -i data.txt -o results.txt
['testargv.py', '-i', 'data.txt', '-o', 'results.txt']
```

The last command here illustrates a common convention. Much like function arguments, command-line options are sometimes passed by position and sometimes by name using a "-name value" word pair. For instance, the pair -i data.txt means the -i option's value is data.txt (e.g., an input filename). Any words can be listed, but programs usually impose some sort of structure on them.

Command-line arguments play the same role in programs that function arguments do in functions: they are simply a way to pass information to a program that can vary per program run. Because they don't have to be hardcoded, they allow scripts to be more generally useful. For example, a file-processing script can use a command-line argument as the name of the file it should process; see the *more.py* script we met in Example 3-1 for a prime example. Other scripts might accept processing mode flags, Internet addresses, and so on.

Once you start using command-line arguments regularly, though, you'll probably find it inconvenient to keep writing code that fishes through the list looking for words. More typically, programs translate the arguments list on startup into structures that are more conveniently processed. Here's one way to do it: the script in Example 3-3 scans the argv list looking for -optionname optionvalue word pairs and stuffs them into a dictionary by option name for easy retrieval.

Example 3-3. PP3E\System\testargv2.py

```
# collect command-line options in a dictionary

def getopts(argv):
    opts = {}
    while argv:
        if argv[0][0] == '-':                  # find "-name value" pairs
            opts[argv[0]] = argv[1]            # dict key is "-name" arg
            argv = argv[2:]
        else:
            argv = argv[1:]
    return opts

if __name__ == '__main__':
    from sys import argv                        # example client code
    myargs = getopts(argv)
    if myargs.has_key('-i'):
        print myargs['-i']
    print myargs
```

You might import and use such a function in all your command-line tools. When run by itself, this file just prints the formatted argument dictionary:

```
C:\...\PP3E\System>python testargv2.py
{}

C:\...\PP3E\System>python testargv2.py -i data.txt -o results.txt
data.txt
{'-o': 'results.txt', '-i': 'data.txt'}
```

Naturally, we could get much more sophisticated here in terms of argument patterns, error checking, and the like. We could also use standard and more advanced command-line processing tools in the Python library to parse arguments; see the standard getopt library module and the newer optparse in the library manual for other options. In general, the more configurable your scripts, the more you must invest in command-line processing logic complexity.

Shell Environment Variables

Shell variables, sometimes known as environment variables, are made available to Python scripts as os.environ, a Python dictionary-like object with one entry per variable setting in the shell. Shell variables live outside the Python system; they are often set at your system prompt or within startup files and typically serve as system-wide configuration inputs to programs.

In fact, by now you should be familiar with a prime example: the PYTHONPATH module search path setting is a shell variable used by Python to import modules. By setting it once in your system startup files, its value is available every time a Python program is run. Shell variables can also be set by programs to serve as inputs to other programs in an application; because their values are normally inherited by spawned programs, they can be used as a simple form of interprocess communication.

Fetching Shell Variables

In Python, the surrounding shell environment becomes a simple preset object, not special syntax. Indexing os.environ by the desired shell variable's name string (e.g., os.environ['USER']) is the moral equivalent of adding a dollar sign before a variable name in most Unix shells (e.g., $USER), using surrounding percent signs on DOS (%USER%), and calling getenv("USER") in a C program. Let's start up an interactive session to experiment:

```
>>> import os
>>> os.environ.keys()
['WINBOOTDIR', 'PATH', 'USER', 'PP2HOME', 'CMDLINE', 'PYTHONPATH', 'BL*ER',
'X', 'TEMP', 'COMSPEC', 'PROMPT', 'WINDIR', 'TMP']
>>> os.environ['TEMP']
'C:\\windows\\TEMP'
```

Executable Scripts on Unix

Unix and Linux users: you can also make text files of Python source code directly executable by adding a special line at the top with the path to the Python interpreter and giving the file executable permission. For instance, type this code into a text file called *myscript*:

```
#!/usr/bin/python
print 'And nice red uniforms'
```

The first line is normally taken as a comment by Python (it starts with a #); but when this file is run, the operating system sends lines in this file to the interpreter listed after #! on line 1. If this file is made directly executable with a shell command of the form chmod +x myscript, it can be run directly without typing python in the command, as though it were a binary executable program:

```
% myscript a b c
And nice red uniforms
```

When run this way, sys.argv will still have the script's name as the first word in the list: ["myscript", "a", "b", "c"], exactly as if the script had been run with the more explicit and portable command form python myscript a b c. Making scripts directly executable is actually a Unix trick, not a Python feature, but it's worth pointing out that it can be made a bit less machine dependent by listing the Unix env command at the top instead of a hardcoded path to the Python executable:

```
#!/usr/bin/env python
print 'Wait for it...'
```

When coded this way, the operating system will employ your environment variable settings to locate your Python interpreter (your PATH variable, on most platforms). If you run the same script on many machines, you need only change your environment settings on each machine (you don't need to edit Python script code). Of course, you can always run Python files with a more explicit command line:

```
% python myscript a b c
```

This assumes that the python interpreter program is on your system's search path setting (otherwise, you need to type its full path), but it works on any Python platform with a command line. Since this is more portable, I generally use this convention in the book's examples, but consult your Unix manpages for more details on any of the topics mentioned here. Even so, these special #! lines will show up in many examples in this book just in case readers want to run them as executables on Unix or Linux; on other platforms, they are simply ignored as Python comments.

Note that on recent flavors of Windows, you can usually also type a script's filename directly (without the word *python*) to make it go, and you don't have to add a #! line at the top. Python uses the Windows registry on this platform to declare itself as the program that opens files with Python extensions (.*py* and others). This is also why you can launch files on Windows by clicking on them.

Here, the keys method returns a list of set variables, and indexing fetches the value of the shell variable TEMP on Windows. This works the same way on Linux, but other variables are generally preset when Python starts up. Since we know about PYTHONPATH, let's peek at its setting within Python to verify its content (as I wrote this, mine was set to the roots of the book examples trees for the third and second editions):

```
>>> os.environ['PYTHONPATH']
'C:\\Mark\\PP3E-cd\\Examples;C:\\Mark\\PP2E-cd\\Examples'
>>>
>>> for dir in os.environ['PYTHONPATH'].split(os.pathsep):
...     print dir
...
C:\Mark\PP3E-cd\Examples
C:\Mark\PP2E-cd\Examples
```

PYTHONPATH is a string of directory paths separated by whatever character is used to separate items in such paths on your platform (e.g., ; on DOS/Window, : on Unix and Linux). To split it into its components, we pass to the split string method an os.pathsep delimiter—a portable setting that gives the proper separator for the underlying machine.

Changing Shell Variables

Like normal dictionaries, the os.environ object supports both key indexing and *assignment*. As usual, assignments change the value of the key:

```
>>> os.environ['TEMP'] = r'c:\temp'
>>> os.environ['TEMP']
'c:\\temp'
```

But something extra happens here. In recent Python releases, values assigned to os.environ keys in this fashion are automatically *exported* to other parts of the application. That is, key assignments change both the os.environ object in the Python program as well as the associated variable in the enclosing *shell* environment of the running program's process. Its new value becomes visible to the Python program, all linked-in C modules, and any programs spawned by the Python process.

Internally, key assignments to os.environ call os.putenv—a function that changes the shell variable outside the boundaries of the Python interpreter. To demonstrate how this works, we need a couple of scripts that set and fetch shell variables; the first is shown in Example 3-4.

Example 3-4. PP3E\System\Environment\setenv.py

```
import os
print 'setenv...',
print os.environ['USER']                # show current shell variable value

os.environ['USER'] = 'Brian'            # runs os.putenv behind the scenes
os.system('python echoenv.py')

os.environ['USER'] = 'Arthur'           # changes passed to spawned programs
```

Example 3-4. PP3E\System\Environment\setenv.py (continued)

```
os.system('python echoenv.py')          # and linked-in C library modules

os.environ['USER'] = raw_input('?')
print os.popen('python echoenv.py').read( )
```

This *setenv.py* script simply changes a shell variable, USER, and spawns another script that echoes this variable's value, as shown in Example 3-5.

Example 3-5. PP3E\System\Environment\echoenv.py

```
import os
print 'echoenv...',
print 'Hello,', os.environ['USER']
```

No matter how we run *echoenv.py*, it displays the value of USER in the enclosing shell; when run from the command line, this value comes from whatever we've set the variable to in the shell itself:

```
C:\...\PP3E\System\Environment>set USER=Bob

C:\...\PP3E\System\Environment>python echoenv.py
echoenv... Hello, Bob
```

When spawned by another script such as *setenv.py*, though, *echoenv.py* gets whatever USER settings its parent program has made:

```
C:\...\PP3E\System\Environment>python setenv.py
setenv... Bob
echoenv... Hello, Brian
echoenv... Hello, Arthur
?Gumby
echoenv... Hello, Gumby

C:\...\PP3E\System\Environment>echo %USER%
Bob
```

This works the same way on Linux. In general terms, a spawned program always *inherits* environment settings from its parents. *Spawned* programs are programs started with Python tools such as os.spawnv on Windows, the os.fork/exec combination on Unix and Linux, and os.popen and os.system on a variety of platforms. All programs thus launched get the environment variable settings that exist in the parent at launch time.[*]

---

[*] This is by default. Some program-launching tools also let scripts pass environment settings that are different from their own to child programs. For instance, the os.spawnve call is like os.spawnv, but it accepts a dictionary argument representing the shell environment to be passed to the started program. Some os.exec* variants (ones with an "e" at the end of their names) similarly accept explicit environments; see the os.exec call formats in Chapter 5 for more details.

From a larger perspective, setting shell variables like this before starting a new program is one way to pass information into the new program. For instance, a Python configuration script might tailor the PYTHONPATH variable to include custom directories just before launching another Python script; the launched script will have the custom search path because shell variables are passed down to children (in fact, watch for such a launcher script to appear at the end of Chapter 6).

Shell Variable Details

Notice the last command in the preceding example—the USER variable is back to its original value after the top-level Python program exits. Assignments to os.environ keys are passed outside the interpreter and *down* the spawned programs chain, but never back *up* to parent program processes (including the system shell). This is also true in C programs that use the putenv library call, and it isn't a Python limitation per se.

It's also likely to be a nonissue if a Python script is at the top of your application. But keep in mind that shell settings made within a program usually endure only for that program's run and for the run of its spawned children. If you need to export a shell variable setting so that it lives on after Python exits, you may be able to find platform-specific extensions that do this; search *http://www.python.org* or the Web at large.

Another subtlety: currently, changes to os.environ automatically call os.putenv, which runs the putenv call in the C library if the later is available on your platform; this exports the setting outside Python to any linked-in C code too. However, direct calls to os.putenv do not update os.environ to reflect the change, so os.environ changes are preferred.

Also note that environment settings are loaded into os.environ on startup and not on each fetch; hence, changes made by linked-in C code after startup may not be reflected in os.environ. Python does have an os.getenv call today, but it is translated into an os.environ fetch on most platforms, not into a call to getenv in the C library. Most applications won't need to care, especially if they are pure Python code. On platforms without a putenv call, os.environ can be passed as a parameter to program startup tools to set the spawned program's environment.

Standard Streams

The sys module is also the place where the standard input, output, and error streams of your Python programs live:

```
>>> for f in (sys.stdin, sys.stdout, sys.stderr): print f
...
<open file '<stdin>', mode 'r' at 762210>
<open file '<stdout>', mode 'w' at 762270>
<open file '<stderr>', mode 'w' at 7622d0>
```

The standard streams are simply preopened Python file objects that are automatically connected to your program's standard streams when Python starts up. By default, all of them are tied to the console window where Python (or a Python program) was started. Because the `print` statement and `raw_input` functions are really nothing more than user-friendly interfaces to the standard output and input streams, they are similar to using `stdout` and `stdin` in sys directly:

```
>>> print 'hello stdout world'
hello stdout world

>>> sys.stdout.write('hello stdout world' + '\n')
hello stdout world

>>> raw_input('hello stdin world>')
hello stdin world>spam
'spam'

>>> print 'hello stdin world>',; sys.stdin.readline( )[:-1]
hello stdin world>eggs

'eggs'
```

Standard Streams on Windows

Windows users: if you click a *.py* Python program's filename in a Windows file explorer to start it (or launch it with `os.system`), a DOS console box automatically pops up to serve as the program's standard stream. If your program makes windows of its own, you can avoid this console pop-up window by naming your program's source-code file with a *.pyw* extension, not with a *.py* extension. The *.pyw* extension simply means a *.py* source file without a DOS pop up on Windows (it uses Windows registry settings to run a custom version of Python).

One historical note: in the Python 1.5.2 release and earlier, *.pyw* files could only be run, not imported—the *.pyw* was not recognized as a module name. If you wanted a program to be run without a DOS console pop up *and* be importable elsewhere, you needed both *.py* and *.pyw* files; the *.pyw* simply served as top-level script logic that imported and called the core logic in the *.py* file. This is no longer required today: *.pyw* files may be imported as usual.

Also note that because printed output goes to this DOS pop up when a program is clicked, scripts that simply print text and exit will generate an odd "flash"—the DOS console box pops up, output is printed into it, and the pop up goes away immediately (not the most user-friendly of features!). To keep the DOS pop-up box around so that you can read printed output, simply add a `raw_input( )` call at the bottom of your script to pause for an Enter key press before exiting.

Redirecting Streams to Files and Programs

Technically, standard output (and print) text appears in the console window where a program was started, standard input (and raw_input) text comes from the keyboard, and standard error text is used to print Python error messages to the console window. At least that's the default. It's also possible to *redirect* these streams both to files and to other programs at the system shell, as well as to arbitrary objects within a Python script. On most systems, such redirections make it easy to reuse and combine general-purpose command-line utilities.

Redirecting streams to files

Redirection is useful for things like canned (precoded) test inputs: we can apply a single test script to any set of inputs by simply redirecting the standard input stream to a different file each time the script is run. Similarly, redirecting the standard output stream lets us save and later analyze a program's output; for example, testing systems might compare the saved standard output of a script with a file of expected output to detect failures.

Although it's a powerful paradigm, redirection turns out to be straightforward to use. For instance, consider the simple read-evaluate-print loop program in Example 3-6.

Example 3-6. PP3E\System\Streams\teststreams.py

```
# read numbers till eof and show squares

def interact():
    print 'Hello stream world'                    # print sends to sys.stdout
    while 1:
        try:
            reply = raw_input('Enter a number>')  # raw_input reads sys.stdin
        except EOFError:
            break                                 # raises an except on eof
        else:                                     # input given as a string
            num = int(reply)
            print "%d squared is %d" % (num, num ** 2)
    print 'Bye'

if __name__ == '__main__':
    interact()                                    # when run, not imported
```

As usual, the interact function here is automatically executed when this file is run, not when it is imported. By default, running this file from a system command line makes that standard stream appear where you typed the Python command. The script simply reads numbers until it reaches end-of-file in the standard input stream (on Windows, end-of-file is usually the two-key combination Ctrl-Z; on Unix, type Ctrl-D instead[*]):

```
C:\...\PP3E\System\Streams>python teststreams.py
Hello stream world
Enter a number>12
12 squared is 144
Enter a number>10
10 squared is 100
Enter a number>
Bye
```

But on both Windows and Unix-like platforms, we can redirect the standard input stream to come from a file with the < *filename* shell syntax. Here is a command session in a DOS console box on Windows that forces the script to read its input from a text file, *input.txt*. It's the same on Linux, but replace the DOS type command with a Unix cat command:

```
C:\...\PP3E\System\Streams>type input.txt
8
6

C:\...\PP3E\System\Streams>python teststreams.py < input.txt
Hello stream world
Enter a number>8 squared is 64
Enter a number>6 squared is 36
Enter a number>Bye
```

Here, the *input.txt* file automates the input we would normally type interactively—the script reads from this file rather than from the keyboard. Standard output can be similarly redirected to go to a file with the > *filename* shell syntax. In fact, we can combine input and output redirection in a single command:

```
C:\...\PP3E\System\Streams>python teststreams.py < input.txt > output.txt

C:\...\PP3E\System\Streams>type output.txt
Hello stream world
Enter a number>8 squared is 64
Enter a number>6 squared is 36
Enter a number>Bye
```

This time, the Python script's input and output are both mapped to text files, not to the interactive console session.

---

[*] Notice that raw_input raises an exception to signal end-of-file, but file read methods simply return an empty string for this condition. Because raw_input also strips the end-of-line character at the end of lines, an empty string result means an empty line, so an exception is necessary to specify the end-of-file condition. File read methods retain the end-of-line character and denote an empty line as \n instead of "". This is one way in which reading sys.stdin directly differs from raw_input. The latter also accepts a prompt string that is automatically printed before input is accepted.

Chaining programs with pipes

On Windows and Unix-like platforms, it's also possible to send the standard output of one program to the standard input of another using the | shell character between two commands. This is usually called a "pipe" operation because the shell creates a pipeline that connects the output and input of two commands. Let's send the output of the Python script to the standard more command-line program's input to see how this works:

```
C:\...\PP3E\System\Streams>python teststreams.py < input.txt | more

Hello stream world
Enter a number>8 squared is 64
Enter a number>6 squared is 36
Enter a number>Bye
```

Here, teststreams's standard input comes from a file again, but its output (written by print statements) is sent to another program, not to a file or window. The receiving program is more, a standard command-line paging program available on Windows and Unix-like platforms. Because Python ties scripts into the standard stream model, though, Python scripts can be used on both ends. One Python script's output can always be piped into another Python script's input:

```
C:\...\PP3E\System\Streams>type writer.py
print "Help! Help! I'm being repressed!"
print 42

C:\...\PP3E\System\Streams>type reader.py
print 'Got this" "%s"' % raw_input()
import sys
data = sys.stdin.readline()[:-1]
print 'The meaning of life is', data, int(data) * 2

C:\...\PP3E\System\Streams>python writer.py | python reader.py
Got this" "Help! Help! I'm being repressed!"
The meaning of life is 42 84
```

This time, two Python programs are connected. Script reader gets input from script writer; both scripts simply read and write, oblivious to stream mechanics. In practice, such chaining of programs is a simple form of cross-program communications. It makes it easy to *reuse* utilities written to communicate via stdin and stdout in ways we never anticipated. For instance, a Python program that sorts stdin text could be applied to any data source we like, including the output of other scripts. Consider the Python command-line utility scripts in Examples 3-7 and 3-8 that sort and sum lines in the standard input stream.

Example 3-7. PP3E\System\Streams\sorter.py

```
import sys                        # or sorted(sys.stdin)
lines = sys.stdin.readlines()     # sort stdin input lines,
lines.sort()                      # send result to stdout
for line in lines: print line,    # for further processing
```

Example 3-8. PP3E\System\Streams\adder.py

```
import sys
sum = 0
while True:
    try:
        line = raw_input()          # or call sys.stdin.readlines()
    except EOFError:                 # or for line in sys.stdin:
        break                        # raw_input strips \n at end
    else:
        sum += int(line)             # was sting.atoi() in 2nd ed
print sum
```

We can apply such general-purpose tools in a variety of ways at the shell command
line to sort and sum arbitrary files and program outputs (Windows note: on my XP
machine, I have to type "python file.py" here, not just "file.py"; otherwise, the input
redirection fails):

```
C:\...\PP3E\System\Streams>type data.txt
123
000
999
042

C:\...\PP3E\System\Streams>python sorter.py < data.txt          sort a file
000
042
123
999

C:\...\PP3E\System\Streams>python sorter.py < data.txt          sum file
1164

C:\...\PP3E\System\Streams>type data.txt | python adder.py      sum type output
1164

C:\...\PP3E\System\Streams>type writer2.py
for data in (123, 0, 999, 42):
    print '%03d' % data

C:\...\PP3E\System\Streams>python writer2.py | python sorter.py     sort py output
000
042
123
999

C:\...\PP3E\System\Streams>python writer2.py | python sorter.py | python adder.py
1164
```

The last command here connects three Python scripts by standard streams—the output of each prior script is fed to the input of the next via pipeline shell syntax.

Coding alternatives

A few coding pointers here: if you look closely, you'll notice that sorter reads all of stdin at once with the readlines method, but adder reads one line at a time. If the input source is another program, some platforms run programs connected by pipes in *parallel*. On such systems, reading line by line works better if the data streams being passed about are large because readers don't have to wait until writers are completely finished to get busy processing data. Because raw_input just reads stdin, the line-by-line scheme used by adder can always be coded with sys.stdin too:

```
C:\...\PP3E\System\Streams>type adder2.py
import sys
sum = 0
while True:
    line = sys.stdin.readline( )
    if not line: break
    sum += int(line)
print sum
```

This version utilizes the fact that the int allows the digits to be surrounded by whitespace (readline returns a line including its \n, but we don't have to use [:-1] or rstrip( ) to remove it for int). In fact, we can use Python's more recent file iterators to achieve the same effect—the for loop, for example, automatically grabs one line each time through when we iterate over a file object directly (more on file iterators in the next chapter):

```
C:\...\PP3E\System\Streams>type adder3.py
import sys
sum = 0
for line in sys.stdin: sum += int(line)
print sum
```

Changing sorter to read line by line this way may not be a big performance boost, though, because the list sort method requires that the list already be complete. As we'll see in Chapter 20, manually coded sort algorithms are likely to be much slower than the Python list sorting method.

Interestingly, these two scripts can also be coded in a much more compact fashion in Python 2.4 by using the new sorted function, list comprehensions, and file iterators. The following work the same way as the originals:

```
C:\...\PP3E\System\Streams>type sorter24.py
import sys
for line in sorted(sys.stdin): print line,
```

```
C:\...\PP3E\System\Streams>type adder24.py
import sys
print sum(int(line) for line in sys.stdin)
```

The latter of these employs a generator expression, which is much like a list comprehension, but results are returned one at a time, not in a physical list. The net effect is space optimization.

Redirected streams and user interaction

At the start of the last section, we piped *teststreams.py* output into the standard more command-line program with a command similar to this one:

```
C:\...\PP3E\System\Streams>python teststreams.py < input.txt | more
```

But since we already wrote our own "more" paging utility in Python near the start of this chapter, why not set it up to accept input from stdin too? For example, if we change the last three lines of the *more.py* file listed earlier in this chapter to this...

```
if __name__ == '__main__':          # when run, not when imported
    if len(sys.argv) == 1:          # page stdin if no cmd args
        more(sys.stdin.read())
    else:
        more(open(sys.argv[1]).read())
```

...it almost seems as if we should be able to redirect the standard output of *teststreams.py* into the standard input of *more.py*:

```
C:\...\PP3E\System\Streams>python teststreams.py < input.txt | python ..\more.py
Hello stream world
Enter a number>8 squared is 64
Enter a number>6 squared is 36
Enter a number>Bye
```

This technique generally works for Python scripts. Here, *teststreams.py* takes input from a file again. And, as in the last section, one Python program's output is piped to another's input—the *more.py* script in the parent (..) directory.

Reading keyboard input

But there's a subtle problem lurking in the preceding more.py command. Really, chaining worked there only by sheer luck: if the first script's output is long enough that more has to ask the user if it should continue, the script will utterly fail. The problem is that the augmented *more.py* uses stdin for two disjointed purposes. It reads a reply from an interactive user on stdin by calling raw_input, but now it *also* accepts the main input text on stdin. When the stdin stream is really redirected to an input file or pipe, we can't use it to input a reply from an interactive user; it contains only the text of the input source. Moreover, because stdin is redirected before the program even starts up, there is no way to know what it meant prior to being redirected in the command line.

If we intend to accept input on stdin *and* use the console for user interaction, we have to do a bit more. Example 3-9 shows a modified version of the *more* script that pages the standard input stream if called with no arguments but also makes use of lower-level and platform-specific tools to converse with a user at a keyboard if needed.

Example 3-9. PP3E\System\moreplus.py

```
#############################################################
# split and interactively page a string, file, or stream of
# text to stdout; when run as a script, page stdin or file
# whose name is passed on cmdline; if input is stdin, can't
# use it for user reply--use platform-specific tools or GUI;
#############################################################

import sys

def getreply():
    """
    read a reply key from an interactive user
    even if stdin redirected to a file or pipe
    """
    if sys.stdin.isatty():                       # if stdin is console
        return raw_input('?')                    # read reply line from stdin
    else:
        if sys.platform[:3] == 'win':            # if stdin was redirected
            import msvcrt                         # can't use to ask a user
            msvcrt.putch('?')
            key = msvcrt.getche()                 # use windows console tools
            msvcrt.putch('\n')                    # getch() does not echo key
            return key
        elif sys.platform[:5] == 'linux':         # use linux console device
            print '?',                            # strip eoln at line end
            console = open('/dev/tty')
            line = console.readline()[:-1]
            return line
        else:
            print '[pause]'                       # else just pause--improve me
            import time                           # see also modules curses, tty
            time.sleep(5)                         # or copy to temp file, rerun
            return 'y'                            # or GUI pop up, tk key bind

def more(text, numlines=10):
    """
    split multiline string to stdout
    """
    lines = text.split('\n')
    while lines:
        chunk = lines[:numlines]
        lines = lines[numlines:]
        for line in chunk: print line
        if lines and getreply() not in ['y', 'Y']: break

if __name__ == '__main__':                        # when run, not when imported
    if len(sys.argv) == 1:                         # if no command-line arguments
        more(sys.stdin.read())                     # page stdin, no raw_inputs
    else:
        more(open(sys.argv[1]).read())             # else page filename argument
```

Most of the new code in this version shows up in its getreply function. The file's isatty method tells us whether stdin is connected to the console; if it is, we simply read replies on stdin as before. Unfortunately, there is no portable way to input a string from a console user independent of stdin, so we must wrap the non-stdin input logic of this script in a sys.platform test:

- On Windows, the built-in msvcrt module supplies low-level console input and output calls (e.g., msvcrt.getch( ) reads a single key press).

- On Linux, the system device file named */dev/tty* gives access to keyboard input (we can read it as though it were a simple file).

- On other platforms, we simply run a built-in time.sleep call to pause for five seconds between displays (this is not at all ideal, but it is better than not stopping at all and it serves until a better nonportable solution can be found).

Of course, we have to add such extra logic only to scripts that intend to interact with console users *and* take input on stdin. In a GUI application, for example, we could instead pop up dialogs, bind keyboard-press events to run callbacks, and so on (we'll meet GUIs in Chapter 8).

Armed with the reusable getreply function, though, we can safely run our moreplus utility in a variety of ways. As before, we can import and call this module's function directly, passing in whatever string we wish to page:

```
>>> from moreplus import more
>>> more(open('System.txt').read( ))
This directory contains operating system interface examples.

Many of the examples in this unit appear elsewhere in the examples
distribution tree, because they are actually used to manage other
programs. See the README.txt files in the subdirectories here
for pointers.
```

Also as before, when run with a command-line *argument*, this script interactively pages through the named file's text:

```
C:\...\PP3E\System>python moreplus.py System.txt
This directory contains operating system interface examples.

Many of the examples in this unit appear elsewhere in the examples
distribution tree, because they are actually used to manage other
programs. See the README.txt files in the subdirectories here
for pointers.

C:\...\PP3E\System>python moreplus.py moreplus.py
#############################################################
# split and interactively page a string, file, or stream of
# text to stdout; when run as a script, page stdin or file
# whose name is passed on cmdline; if input is stdin, can't
# use it for user reply--use platform-specific tools or GUI;
#############################################################
```

```
import sys, string

def getreply( ):
?n
```

But now the script also correctly pages text redirected into stdin from either a *file* or a command *pipe*, even if that text is too long to fit in a single display chunk. On most shells, we send such input via redirection or pipe operators like these:

```
C:\...\PP3E\System>python moreplus.py < moreplus.py
##############################################################
# split and interactively page a string, file, or stream of
# text to stdout; when run as a script, page stdin or file
# whose name is passed on cmdline; if input is stdin, can't
# use it for user reply--use platform-specific tools or GUI;
##############################################################

import sys, string

def getreply( ):
?n

C:\...\PP3E\System>type moreplus.py | python moreplus.py
##############################################################
# split and interactively page a string, file, or stream of
# text to stdout; when run as a script, page stdin or file
# whose name is passed on cmdline; if input is stdin, can't
# use it for user reply--use platform-specific tools or GUI;
##############################################################

import sys, string

def getreply( ):
?n
```

This works the same way on Linux, but, again, use the cat command rather than type. Finally, piping one Python script's output into this script's input now works as expected, without botching user interaction (and not just because we got lucky):

```
......\System\Streams>python teststreams.py < input.txt | python ..\moreplus.py
Hello stream world
Enter a number>8 squared is 64
Enter a number>6 squared is 36
Enter a number>Bye
```

Here, the standard *output* of one Python script is fed to the standard *input* of another Python script located in the parent directory: *moreplus.py* reads the output of *teststreams.py*.

All of the redirections in such command lines work only because scripts don't care what standard input and output really are—interactive users, files, or pipes between programs. For example, when run as a script, *moreplus.py* simply reads stream sys. stdin; the command-line shell (e.g., DOS on Windows, csh on Linux) attaches such streams to the source implied by the command line before the script is started. Scripts use the preopened stdin and stdout file objects to access those sources, regardless of their true nature.

And for readers keeping count, we have run this single more pager script in four different ways: by importing and calling its function, by passing a filename command-line argument, by redirecting stdin to a file, and by piping a command's output to stdin. By supporting importable functions, command-line arguments, and standard streams, Python system tools code can be reused in a wide variety of modes.

Redirecting Streams to Python Objects

All of the previous standard stream redirections work for programs written in any language that hooks into the standard streams and rely more on the shell's command-line processor than on Python itself. Command-line redirection syntax like < filename and | program is evaluated by the shell, not by Python. A more Pythonesque form of redirection can be done within scripts themselves by resetting sys.stdin and sys.stdout to file-like objects.

The main trick behind this mode is that anything that looks like a file in terms of methods will work as a standard stream in Python. The object's interface (sometimes called its protocol), and not the object's specific datatype, is all that matters. That is:

- Any object that provides file-like *read* methods can be assigned to sys.stdin to make input come from that object's read methods.
- Any object that defines file-like *write* methods can be assigned to sys.stdout; all standard output will be sent to that object's methods.

Because print and raw_input simply call the write and readline methods of whatever objects sys.stdout and sys.stdin happen to reference, we can use this technique to both provide and intercept standard stream text with objects implemented as classes.

Such plug-and-play compatibility is usually called *polymorphism*—i.e., it doesn't matter what an object is, and it doesn't matter what its interface does, as long as it provides the expected interface. This liberal approach to datatypes accounts for much of the conciseness and flexibility of Python code. Here, it provides a way for scripts to reset their own streams. Example 3-10 shows a utility module that demonstrates this concept.

Example 3-10. PP3E\System\Streams\redirect.py

```
###############################################################################
# file-like objects that save standard output text in a string and provide
# standard input text from a string; redirect runs a passed-in function
# with its output and input streams reset to these file-like class objects;
###############################################################################
```

Example 3-10. PP3E\System\Streams\redirect.py (continued)

```python
import sys                                    # get built-in modules

class Output:                                 # simulated output file
    def __init__(self):
        self.text = ''                        # empty string when created
    def write(self, string):                  # add a string of bytes
        self.text = self.text + string
    def writelines(self, lines):              # add each line in a list
        for line in lines: self.write(line)

class Input:                                  # simulated input file
    def __init__(self, input=''):             # default argument
        self.text = input                     # save string when created
    def read(self, *size):                    # optional argument
        if not size:                          # read N bytes, or all
            res, self.text = self.text, ''
        else:
            res, self.text = self.text[:size[0]], self.text[size[0]:]
        return res
    def readline(self):
        eoln = self.text.find('\n')           # find offset of next eoln
        if eoln == -1:                        # slice off through eoln
            res, self.text = self.text, ''
        else:
            res, self.text = self.text[:eoln+1], self.text[eoln+1:]
        return res

def redirect(function, args, input):          # redirect stdin/out
    savestreams = sys.stdin, sys.stdout       # run a function object
    sys.stdin  = Input(input)                 # return stdout text
    sys.stdout = Output()
    try:
        function(*args)                       # was apply(function, args)
    except:
        sys.stderr.write('error in function! ')
        sys.stderr.write("%s, %s\n" % tuple(sys.exc_info()[:2]))
    result = sys.stdout.text
    sys.stdin, sys.stdout = savestreams
    return result
```

This module defines two classes that masquerade as real files:

Output

Provides the write method interface (a.k.a. protocol) expected of output files but saves all output in an in-memory string as it is written.

Input

Provides the interface expected of input files, but provides input on demand from an in-memory string passed in at object construction time.

The redirect function at the bottom of this file combines these two objects to run a single function with input and output redirected entirely to Python class objects. The passed-in function to run need not know or care that its print statements, raw_input calls and stdin and stdout method calls, are talking to a class rather than to a real file, pipe, or user.

To demonstrate, import and run the interact function at the heart of the teststreams script of Example 3-6 that we've been running from the shell (to use the redirection utility function, we need to deal in terms of functions, not files). When run directly, the function reads from the keyboard and writes to the screen, just as if it were run as a program without redirection:

```
C:\...\PP3E\System\Streams>python
>>> from teststreams import interact
>>> interact( )
Hello stream world
Enter a number>2
2 squared is 4
Enter a number>3
3 squared is 9
Enter a number
>>>
```

Now, let's run this function under the control of the redirection function in *redirect. py* and pass in some canned input text. In this mode, the interact function takes its input from the string we pass in ('4\n5\n6\n'—three lines with explicit end-of-line characters), and the result of running the function is a string containing all the text written to the standard output stream:

```
>>> from redirect import redirect
>>> output = redirect(interact, (), '4\n5\n6\n')
>>> output
'Hello stream world\nEnter a number>4 squared is 16\nEnter a number>
5 squared is 25\nEnter a number>6 squared is 36\nEnter a number>Bye\n'
```

The result is a single, long string containing the concatenation of all text written to standard output. To make this look better, we can split it up with the string object's split method:

```
>>> for line in output.split('\n'): print line
...
Hello stream world
Enter a number>4 squared is 16
Enter a number>5 squared is 25
Enter a number>6 squared is 36
Enter a number>Bye
```

Better still, we can reuse the more.py module we saw earlier in this chapter; it's less to type and remember, and it's already known to work well:

```
>>> from PP3E.System.more import more
>>> more(output)
Hello stream world
Enter a number>4 squared is 16
Enter a number>5 squared is 25
```

```
Enter a number>6 squared is 36
Enter a number>Bye
```

This is an artificial example, of course, but the techniques illustrated are widely applicable. For example, it's straightforward to add a GUI interface to a program written to interact with a command-line user. Simply intercept standard output with an object such as the Output class shown earlier and throw the text string up in a window. Similarly, standard input can be reset to an object that fetches text from a graphical interface (e.g., a popped-up dialog box). Because classes are plug-and-play compatible with real files, we can use them in any tool that expects a file. Watch for a GUI stream-redirection module named guiStreams in Chapter 11.

 Notice the function(*args) syntax in the redirect function of Example 3-10. In the prior edition of this book, this was a built-in function call, apply(function, args), but the apply built-in has been marked as deprecated since that edition (in fact, it's not even listed in the functions section of the library manual). It's unclear whether apply will ever be removed completely, but the new call syntax is more general and concise, and it should be preferred today. The following equivalent calls, for instance, are more complex with apply; the new syntax allows normal arguments to be mixed with argument collection objects, but apply must merge manually:

```
>>> def m(self, a, b, c): print self, a, b, c

>>> m(1, *(2, 3, 4))
1 2 3 4

>>> apply(m, (1,) + (2, 3, 4))
1 2 3 4
```

This becomes more useful as call signatures grow more complex:

```
>>> a=1; b=2; c=3; d=4; e=5
>>> def func(a, *ps, **ks): print a, ps, ks

>>> func(a, b, c=1, *(d, e), **{'f':2})
1 (2, 4, 5) {'c': 1, 'f': 2}

>>> kargs = {'f':2}
>>> kargs.update({'c':1})
>>> apply(func, (a, b) + (d, e), kargs)
1 (2, 4, 5) {'c': 1, 'f': 2}
```

The StringIO Module

The prior section's technique of redirecting streams to objects proved so handy that now a standard library automates the task. It provides an object that maps a file object interface to and from in-memory strings. For example:

```
>>> from StringIO import StringIO
>>> buff = StringIO()                    # save written text to a string
```

```
>>> buff.write('spam\n')
>>> buff.write('eggs\n')
>>> buff.getvalue()
'spam\neggs\n'

>>> buff = StringIO('ham\nspam\n')          # provide input from a string
>>> buff.readline()
'ham\n'
>>> buff.readline()
'spam\n'
>>> buff.readline()
''
```

As in the prior section, instances of StringIO objects can be assigned to sys.stdin
and sys.stdout to redirect streams for raw_input and print and can be passed to any
code that was written to expect a real file object. Again, in Python, the object *interface*, not the concrete datatype, is the name of the game:

```
>>> from StringIO import StringIO
>>> import sys
>>> buff = StringIO()

>>> temp = sys.stdout
>>> sys.stdout = buff
>>> print 42, 'spam', 3.141          # or print >> buff, ...

>>> sys.stdout = temp                # restore original stream
>>> buff.getvalue()
'42 spam 3.141\n'
```

Capturing the stderr Stream

We've been focusing on stdin and stdout redirection, but stderr can be similarly
reset to files, pipes, and objects. This is straightforward within a Python script. For
instance, assigning sys.stderr to another instance of a class such as Output or a
StringIO object in the preceding section's example allows your script to intercept
text written to standard error too.

Python itself uses standard error for error message text (and the IDLE GUI interface
intercepts it and colors it red by default). However, no higher-level tools for standard error do what print and raw_input() do for the output and input streams. If
you wish to print to the error stream, you'll want to call sys.stderr.write() explicitly or read the next section for a print statement trick that makes this a bit simpler.

Redirecting standard errors from a shell command line is a bit more complex and less
portable. On most Unix-like systems, we can usually capture stderr output by using
shell-redirection syntax of the form command > output 2>&1. This may not work on
some flavors of Windows platforms, though, and can even vary per Unix shell; see
your shell's manpages for more details.

Redirection Syntax in Print Statements

Because resetting the stream attributes to new objects was so popular, as of Python 2.0 the print statement is also extended to include an explicit file to which output is to be sent. A statement of the form:

```
print >> file, stuff        # file is an object, not a string name
```

prints stuff to file instead of to stdout. The net effect is similar to simply assigning sys.stdout to an object, but there is no need to save and restore in order to return to the original output stream (as shown in the section on redirecting streams to objects). For example:

```
import sys
print >> sys.stderr, 'spam' * 2
```

will send text the standard error stream object rather than sys.stdout for the duration of this single print statement only. The next normal print statement (without >>) prints to standard output as usual.

Other Redirection Options

Earlier in this chapter, we studied the built-in os.popen function, which provides a way to redirect another command's streams from within a Python program. As we saw, this function runs a shell command line (e.g., a string we would normally type at a DOS or csh prompt) but returns a Python file-like object connected to the command's input or output stream.

Because of that, the os.popen tool is another way to redirect streams of spawned programs, and it is a cousin to the techniques we just met: its effect is much like the shell | command-line pipe syntax for redirecting streams to programs (in fact, its name means "pipe open"), but it is run within a script and provides a file-like interface to piped streams. It's similar in spirit to the redirect function, but it's based on running programs (not calling functions), and the command's streams are processed in the spawning script as files (not tied to class objects). That is, os.popen redirects the streams of a program that a script starts instead of redirecting the streams of the script itself.

By passing in the desired mode flag, we redirect a spawned program's input or output streams to a file in the calling scripts:

```
C:\...\PP3E\System\Streams>type hello-out.py
print 'Hello shell world'

C:\...\PP3E\System\Streams>type hello-in.py
input = raw_input( )
open('hello-in.txt', 'w').write('Hello ' + input + '\n')

C:\...\PP3E\System\Streams>python
>>> import os
```

```
>>> pipe = os.popen('python hello-out.py')          # 'r' is default--read stdout
>>> pipe.read()
'Hello shell world\n'

>>> pipe = os.popen('python hello-in.py', 'w')
>>> pipe.write('Gumby\n')                            # 'w'--write to program stdin
>>> pipe.close()                                     # \n at end is optional
>>> open('hello-in.txt').read()
'Hello Gumby\n'
```

The popen call is also smart enough to run the command string as an independent process on platforms that support such a notion. It accepts an optional third argument that can be used to control buffering of written text.

Additional popen-like tools in the Python library allow scripts to connect to more than one of the commands' streams. For instance, the os.open2 call includes functions for hooking into *both* a command's input and output streams:

```
childStdIn, childStdout = os.popen2('python hello-in-out.py')
childStdin.write(input)
output = childStdout.read()
```

os.popen3 is similar, but it returns a third pipe for connecting to standard error as well. A related call, os.popen4, returns two pipe file objects; it's like os.popen3, but the output and error streams are tied together into a single pipe:

```
childStdin, childStdout, childStderr = os.popen3('python hello-in-out.py')
childStdin, childStdout_and_err =      os.popen4('python hello-in-out.py')
```

The os.popen2/3/4 variants work much like os.popen, but they connect additional streams and accept an optional second argument that specifies text or binary-mode data (t or b—more on the distinction in the next chapter).

The os.popen calls are also Python's portable equivalent of Unix-like shell syntax for redirecting the streams of spawned programs. The Python versions also work on Windows, though, and are the most platform-neutral way to launch another program from a Python script. The command-line strings you pass to them may vary per platform (e.g., a directory listing requires an ls on Unix but a dir on Windows), but the call itself works on all major Python platforms.

On Unix-like platforms, the combination of the calls os.fork, os.pipe, os.dup, and some os.exec variants can be used to start a new independent program with streams connected to the parent program's streams. As such, it's another way to redirect streams and a low-level equivalent to tools such as os.popen.

As of this writing, the os.fork call does not work on the standard version of Python for Windows, however, because it is too much at odds with that system's process model. See Chapter 5 for more on all of these calls, especially its section on pipes, as well its sidebar on Cygwin, a third-party package that includes a library for use on Windows that adds Unix calls such as fork and a version of Python that contains such tools.*

In the next chapter, we'll continue our survey of Python system interfaces by exploring the tools available for processing files and directories. Although we'll be shifting focus somewhat, we'll find that some of what we've learned here will already begin to come in handy as general system-related tools. Spawning shell commands, for instance, provides ways to inspect directories, and the file interface we will expand on in the next chapter is at the heart of the stream processing techniques we have studied here.

---

* More historical anecdotes for users of older releases: as of Python 2.0, the popen2 and popen3 calls are made available in the os module, and this subsumes the older popen2 module. For example, os.popen2 is the same as the older popen2.popen2 except that the order of stdin and stdout in the call's result tuple is swapped.

CHAPTER 4

File and Directory Tools

"Erase Your Hard Drive in Five Easy Steps!"

This chapter continues our look at system interfaces in Python by focusing on file and directory-related tools. As you'll see, it's easy to process files and directory trees with Python's built-in and standard library support.

File Tools

External files are at the heart of much of what we do with shell utilities. For instance, a testing system may read its inputs from one file, store program results in another file, and check expected results by loading yet another file. Even user interface and Internet-oriented programs may load binary images and audio clips from files on the underlying computer. It's a core programming concept.

In Python, the built-in open function is the primary tool scripts use to access the files on the underlying computer system. Since this function is an inherent part of the Python language, you may already be familiar with its basic workings. Technically, open gives direct access to the stdio filesystem calls in the system's C library—it returns a new file object that is connected to the external file and has methods that map more or less directly to file calls on your machine. The open function also provides a portable interface to the underlying filesystem—it works the same way on every platform on which Python runs.

Other file-related interfaces in Python allow us to do things such as manipulate lower-level descriptor-based files (os module), store objects away in files by key (anydbm and shelve modules), and access SQL databases. Most of these are larger topics addressed in Chapter 19.

In this chapter, we'll take a brief tutorial look at the built-in file object and explore a handful of more advanced file-related topics. As usual, you should consult the library manual's file object entry for further details and methods we don't have space to cover here. Remember, for quick interactive help, you can also run dir(file) for an attributes list with methods, help(file) for general help, and help(file.read) for help on a specific method such as read. The built-in name file identifies the file datatype in recent Python releases.[*]

Built-In File Objects

For most purposes, the open function is all you need to remember to process files in your scripts. The file object returned by open has methods for reading data (read, readline, readlines), writing data (write, writelines), freeing system resources (close), moving about in the file (seek), forcing data to be transferred out of buffers (flush), fetching the underlying file handle (fileno), and more. Since the built-in file object is so easy to use, though, let's jump right into a few interactive examples.

Output files

To make a new file, call open with two arguments: the external *name* of the file to be created and a *mode* string w (short for *write*). To store data on the file, call the file object's write method with a string containing the data to store, and then call the close method to close the file if you wish to open it again within the same program or session:

```
C:\temp>python
>>> file = open('data.txt', 'w')         # open output file object: creates
>>> file.write('Hello file world!\n')    # writes strings verbatim
>>> file.write('Bye    file world.\n')
>>> file.close( )                        # closed on gc and exit too
```

And that's it—you've just generated a brand-new text file on your computer, regardless of the computer on which you type this code:

```
C:\temp>dir data.txt /B
data.txt

C:\temp>type data.txt
Hello file world!
Bye    file world.
```

There is nothing unusual about the new file; here, I use the DOS dir and type commands to list and display the new file, but it shows up in a file explorer GUI too.

---

[*] Technically, you can use the name file anywhere you use open, though open is still the generally preferred call unless you are subclassing to customize files. We'll use open in most of our examples. As for all built-in names, it's OK to use the name file for your own variables as long as you don't need direct access to the built-in file datatype (your file name will hide the built-in scope's file). In fact, this is such a common practice that we'll frequently follow it here. This is not a sin, but you should generally be careful about reusing built-in names in this way.

Opening. In the open function call shown in the preceding example, the first argument can optionally specify a complete directory path as part of the filename string. If we pass just a simple filename without a path, the file will appear in Python's current working directory. That is, it shows up in the place where the code is run. Here, the directory *C:\temp* on my machine is implied by the bare filename *data.txt*, so this actually creates a file at *C:\temp\data.txt*. More accurately, the filename is relative to the current working directory if it does not include a complete absolute directory path. See the section "Current Working Directory," in Chapter 3, for a refresher on this topic.

Also note that when opening in w mode, Python either creates the external file if it does not yet exist or erases the file's current contents if it is already present on your machine (so be careful out there—you'll delete whatever was in the file before).

Writing. Notice that we added an explicit \n end-of-line character to lines written to the file; unlike the print statement, file write methods write exactly what they are passed without adding any extra formatting. The string passed to write shows up byte for byte on the external file.

Output files also sport a writelines method, which simply writes all of the strings in a list one at a time without adding any extra formatting. For example, here is a writelines equivalent to the two write calls shown earlier:

```
file.writelines(['Hello file world!\n', 'Bye   file world.\n'])
```

This call isn't as commonly used (and can be emulated with a simple for loop), but it is convenient in scripts that save output in a list to be written later.

Closing. The file close method used earlier finalizes file contents and frees up system resources. For instance, closing forces buffered output data to be flushed out to disk. Normally, files are automatically closed when the file object is garbage collected by the interpreter (i.e., when it is no longer referenced) and when the Python session or program exits. Because of that, close calls are often optional. In fact, it's common to see file-processing code in Python like this:

```
open('somefile.txt', 'w').write("G'day Bruce\n")
```

Since this expression makes a temporary file object, writes to it immediately, and does not save a reference to it, the file object is reclaimed and closed right away without ever having called the close method explicitly.

But note that this *auto-close on reclaim* file feature may change in future Python releases. Moreover, the Jython Java-based Python implementation discussed later does not reclaim files as immediately as the standard Python system (it uses Java's garbage collector). If your script makes many files and your platform limits the number of open files per program, explicit close calls are a robust habit to form.

Also note that some IDEs, such as Python's standard IDLE GUI, may hold on to your file objects longer than you expect, and thus prevent them from being garbage collected. If you write to an output file in IDLE, be sure to explicitly close (or flush) your file if you need to read it back in the same IDLE session. Otherwise, output buffers won't be flushed to disk and your file may be incomplete when read.

Input files

Reading data from external files is just as easy as writing, but there are more methods that let us load data in a variety of modes. Input text files are opened with either a mode flag of r (for "read") or no mode flag at all—it defaults to r if omitted, and it commonly is. Once opened, we can read the lines of a text file with the readlines method:

```
>>> file = open('data.txt', 'r')        # open input file object
>>> for line in file.readlines():       # read into line string list
...     print line,                     # lines have '\n' at end
...
Hello file world!
Bye    file world.
```

The readlines method loads the entire contents of the file into memory and gives it to our scripts as a list of line strings that we can step through in a loop. In fact, there are many ways to read an input file:

file.read( )
Returns a string containing all the bytes stored in the file

file.read(N)
Returns a string containing the next N bytes from the file

file.readline( )
Reads through the next \n and returns a line string

file.readlines( )
Reads the entire file and returns a list of line strings

Let's run these method calls to read files, lines, and bytes (more on the seek call, used here to rewind the file, in a moment):

```
>>> file.seek(0)                        # go back to the front of file
>>> file.read( )                        # read entire file into string
'Hello file world!\nBye    file world.\n'

>>> file.seek(0)
```

```
>>> file.readlines( )
['Hello file world!\n', 'Bye    file world.\n']

>>> file.seek(0)
>>> file.readline( )                       # read one line at a time
'Hello file world!\n'
>>> file.readline( )
'Bye    file world.\n'
>>> file.readline( )                       # empty string at end-of-file
''

>>> file.seek(0)
>>> file.read(1), file.read(8)
('H', 'ello fil')
```

All of these input methods let us be specific about how much to fetch. Here are a few rules of thumb about which to choose:

- read( ) and readlines( ) load the *entire file* into memory all at once. That makes them handy for grabbing a file's contents with as little code as possible. It also makes them very fast, but costly for huge files—loading a multigigabyte file into memory is not generally a good thing to do.

- On the other hand, because the readline( ) and read(N) calls fetch just *part of the file* (the next line, or N-byte block), they are safer for potentially big files but a bit less convenient and usually much slower. Both return an empty string when they reach end-of-file. If speed matters and your files aren't huge, read or readlines may be a better choice.

- See also the discussion of the newer file iterators in the next section. Iterators provide the convenience of readlines( ) with the space efficiency of readline( ).

By the way, the seek(0) call used repeatedly here means "go back to the start of the file." In our example, it is an alternative to reopening the file each time. In files, all read and write operations take place at the current position; files normally start at offset 0 when opened and advance as data is transferred. The seek call simply lets us move to a new position for the next transfer operation.

Python's seek method also accepts an optional second argument that has one of three values—0 for absolute file positioning (the default), 1 to seek relative to the current position, and 2 to seek relative to the file's end. When seek is passed only an offset argument of 0, as shown earlier, it's roughly a file *rewind* operation.

Reading lines with file iterators

The traditional way to read a file line by line that you saw in the prior section:

```
>>> file = open('data.txt')                # open input file object
>>> for line in file.readlines( ):         # read into line string list
...     print line,
```

is actually more work than is needed today. In recent Pythons, the file object includes an iterator which is smart enough to grab just one more line per request in iteration contexts such as for loops and list comprehensions. Iterators are simply objects with next methods. The practical benefit of this extension is that you no longer need to call .readlines in a for loop to scan line by line; the iterator reads lines on request:

```
>>> file = open('data.txt')
>>> for line in file:              # no need to call readlines
...     print line,                # iterator reads next line each time
...
Hello file world!
Bye   file world.

>>> for line in open('data.txt'):    # even shorter: temporary file object
...     print line,
...
Hello file world!
Bye   file world.
```

Moreover, the iterator form does not load the entire file into a line's list all at once, so it will be more space efficient for large text files. Because of that, this is the prescribed way to read line by line today; when in doubt, let Python do your work automatically. If you want to see what really happens inside the for loop, you can use the iterator manually; it's similar to calling the readline method each time through, but read methods return an empty string at end-of-file (EOF), whereas the iterator raises an exception to end the iteration:

```
>>> file = open('data.txt')      # read methods: empty at EOF
>>> file.readline()
'Hello file world!\n'
>>> file.readline()
'Bye   file world.\n'
>>> file.readline()
''

>>> file = open('data.txt')      # iterators: exception at EOF
>>> file.next()
'Hello file world!\n'
>>> file.next()
'Bye   file world.\n'
>>> file.next()
Traceback (most recent call last):
  File "<stdin>", line 1, in ?
StopIteration
```

Interestingly, iterators are automatically used in all iteration contexts, including the list constructor call, list comprehension expressions, map calls, and in membership checks:

```
>>> open('data.txt').readlines()
['Hello file world!\n', 'Bye   file world.\n']
```

```
>>> list(open('data.txt'))
['Hello file world!\n', 'Bye    file world.\n']

>>> lines = [line.rstrip() for line in open('data.txt')]        # or [:-1]
>>> lines
['Hello file world!', 'Bye    file world.']

>>> lines = [line.upper() for line in open('data.txt')]
>>> lines
['HELLO FILE WORLD!\n', 'BYE    FILE WORLD.\n']

>>> map(str.split, open('data.txt'))
[['Hello', 'file', 'world!'], ['Bye', 'file', 'world.']]

>>> line = 'Hello file world!\n'
>>> line in open('data.txt')
True
```

Iterators may seem somewhat implicit at first glance, but they represent the ways that Python makes developers' lives easier over time.[*]

Other file object modes

Besides w and r, most platforms support an a open mode string, meaning "append." In this output mode, write methods add data to the end of the file, and the open call will not erase the current contents of the file:

```
>>> file = open('data.txt', 'a')        # open in append mode: doesn't erase
>>> file.write('The Life of Brian')     # added at end of existing data
>>> file.close()
>>>
>>> open('data.txt').read()             # open and read entire file
'Hello file world!\nBye    file world.\nThe Life of Brian'
```

Most files are opened using the sorts of calls we just ran, but open actually allows up to three arguments for more specific processing needs—the filename, the open mode, and a buffer size. All but the first of these are optional: if omitted, the open mode argument defaults to r (input), and the buffer size policy is to enable buffering on most platforms. Here are a few things you should know about all three open arguments:

Filename

As mentioned earlier, filenames can include an explicit directory path to refer to files in arbitrary places on your computer; if they do not, they are taken to be names relative to the current working directory (described in the prior chapter).

---

[*] This is so useful that I was able to remove an entire section from this chapter in this edition, which wrapped a file object in a class to allow iteration over lines in a for loop. In fact, that example became completely superfluous and no longer worked as described after the second edition of this book. Technically, its __getitem__ indexing overload method was never called anymore because for loops now look for a file object's __iter__ iteration method first. You don't have to know what that means, because iteration is a core feature of file objects today.

In general, any filename form you can type in your system shell will work in an open call. For instance, a filename argument r'..\temp\spam.txt' on Windows means *spam.txt* in the *temp* subdirectory of the current working directory's parent—up one, and down to directory *temp*.

Open mode

The open function accepts other modes too, some of which are not demonstrated in this book (e.g., r+, w+, and a+ to open for updating, and any mode string with a b to designate binary mode). For instance, mode r+ means both reads and writes are allowed on an existing file; w+ allows reads and writes but creates the file anew, erasing any prior content; and wb writes data in binary mode (more on this in the next section). Generally, whatever you could use as a mode string in the C language's fopen call on your platform will work in the Python open function, since it really just calls fopen internally. (If you don't know C, don't sweat this point.) Notice that the contents of files are always strings in Python programs, regardless of mode: read methods return a string, and we pass a string to write methods.

Buffer size

The open call also takes an optional third buffer size argument, which lets you control stdio buffering for the file—the way that data is queued up before being transferred to boost performance. If passed, 0 means file operations are unbuffered (data is transferred immediately), 1 means they are line buffered, any other positive value means to use a buffer of approximately that size, and a negative value means to use the system default (which you get if no third argument is passed and which generally means buffering is enabled). The buffer size argument works on most platforms, but it is currently ignored on platforms that don't provide the sevbuf system call.

Binary datafiles

All of the preceding examples process simple text files. Python scripts can also open and process files containing *binary* data—JPEG images, audio clips, packed binary data produced by FORTRAN and C programs, and anything else that can be stored in files. The primary difference in terms of your code is the *mode* argument passed to the built-in open function:

```
>>> file = open('data.txt', 'wb')      # open binary output file
>>> file = open('data.txt', 'rb')      # open binary input file
```

Once you've opened binary files in this way, you may read and write their contents using the same methods just illustrated: read, write, and so on. (readline and readlines don't make sense here, though: binary data isn't line oriented.)

In all cases, data transferred between files and your programs is represented as Python *strings* within scripts, even if it is binary data. This works because Python string objects can always contain character bytes of any value (though some may look odd if printed). Interestingly, even a byte of value zero can be embedded in a Python string; it's called \0 in escape-code notation and does not terminate strings in Python as it typically does in C. For instance:

```
>>> data = 'a\0b\0c'
>>> data
'a\x00b\x00c'
>>> len(data)
5
```

Instead of relying on a terminator character, Python keeps track of a string's length explicitly. Here, data references a string of length 5 that happens to contain two zero-value bytes; they print in hexadecimal escape sequence form as \x00 (Python uses escapes to display all nonprintable characters). Because no character codes are reserved, it's OK to read binary data with zero bytes (and other values) into a string in Python.

End-of-line translations on Windows

Strictly speaking, on some platforms you may not need the b at the end of the open mode argument to process binary files; the b is simply ignored, so modes r and w work just as well. In fact, the b in mode flag strings is usually required only for binary files on Windows. To understand why, though, you need to know how lines are terminated in text files.

For historical reasons, the end of a line of text in a file is represented by different characters on different platforms: it's a single \n character on Unix and Linux, but the two-character sequence \r\n on Windows.* That's why files moved between Linux and Windows may look odd in your text editor after transfer—they may still be stored using the original platform's end-of-line convention. For example, most Windows editors handle text in Unix format, but Notepad is a notable exception— text files copied from Unix or Linux usually look like one long line when viewed in Notepad, with strange characters inside (\n). Similarly, transferring a file from Windows to Unix in binary mode retains the \r characters (which usually appear as ^M in text editors).

Python scripts don't normally have to care, because the Windows port (actually, the underlying C compiler on Windows) automatically maps the DOS \r\n sequence to a single \n. It works like this—when scripts are run on Windows:

- For files opened in text mode, \r\n is translated to \n when input.
- For files opened in text mode, \n is translated to \r\n when output.

---

* Actually, it gets worse: on the classic Mac, lines in text files are terminated with a single \r (not \n or \r\n). The more modern Mac is a Unix-based machine and normally follows that platform's conventions instead. Whoever said proprietary software was good for the consumer probably wasn't speaking about users of multiple platforms, and certainly wasn't talking about programmers.

- For files opened in binary mode, no translation occurs on input or output.
- On Unix-like platforms, no translations occur, regardless of open modes.

You should keep in mind two important consequences of all of these rules. First, the end-of-line character is almost always represented as a single \n in all Python scripts, regardless of how it is stored in external files on the underlying platform. By mapping to and from \n on input and output, the Windows port hides the platform-specific difference.

The second consequence of the mapping is subtler: if you mean to process *binary data files* on Windows, you generally must be careful to open those files in binary mode (rb, wb), not in text mode (r, w). Otherwise, the translations listed previously could very well corrupt data as it is input or output. It's not impossible that binary data would by chance contain bytes with values the same as the DOS end-of-line characters, \r and \n. If you process such binary files in *text* mode on Windows, \r bytes may be incorrectly discarded when read and \n bytes may be erroneously expanded to \r\n when written. The net effect is that your binary data will be trashed when read and written—probably not quite what you want! For example, on Windows:

```
>>> len('a\0b\rc\r\nd')                     # 4 escape code bytes
8
>>> open('temp.bin', 'wb').write('a\0b\rc\r\nd')   # write binary data to file

>>> open('temp.bin', 'rb').read()           # intact if read as binary
'a\x00b\rc\r\nd'

>>> open('temp.bin', 'r').read()            # loses a \r in text mode!
'a\x00b\rc\nd'

>>> open('temp.bin', 'w').write('a\0b\rc\r\nd')    # adds a \r in text mode!
>>> open('temp.bin', 'rb').read()
'a\x00b\rc\r\r\nd'
```

This is an issue only when running on Windows, but using binary open modes rb and wb for binary files everywhere won't hurt on other platforms and will help make your scripts more portable (you never know when a Unix utility may wind up seeing action on your Windows machine).

You may want to use binary file open modes at other times as well. For instance, in Chapter 7, we'll meet a script called fixeoln_one that translates between DOS and Unix end-of-line character conventions in text files. Such a script also has to open *text* files in *binary* mode to see what end-of-line characters are truly present on the file; in text mode, they would already be translated to \n by the time they reached the script.

Parsing packed binary data with the struct module

By using the letter *b* in the open call, you can open binary datafiles in a platform-neutral way and read and write their content with normal file object methods. But how do you process binary data once it has been read? It will be returned to your script as a simple string of bytes, most of which are not printable characters (that's why Python displays them with \xNN hexadecimal escape sequences).

If you just need to pass binary data along to another file or program, your work is done. And if you just need to extract a number of bytes from a specific position, string slicing will do the job. To get at the deeper contents of binary data, though, as well as to construct its contents, the standard library struct module is more powerful.

The struct module provides calls to pack and unpack binary data, as though the data was laid out in a C-language struct declaration. It is also capable of composing and decomposing using any endian-ness you desire (endian-ness determines whether the most significant bits are on the left or on the right). Building a binary datafile, for instance, is straightforward: pack Python values into a string and write them to a file. The format string here in the pack call means big-endian (>), with an integer, four-character string, half integer, and float:

```
>>> import struct
>>> data = struct.pack('>i4shf', 2, 'spam', 3, 1.234)
>>> data
'\x00\x00\x00\x02spam\x00\x03?\x9d\xf3\xb6'
>>> file = open('data.bin', 'wb')
>>> file.write(data)
>>> file.close()
```

As usual, Python displays here most of the packed binary data's bytes with \xNN hexadecimal escape sequences, because the bytes are not printable characters. To parse data like that which we just produced, read it off the file and pass it to the struct module with the same format string; you get back a tuple containing the values parsed out of the string and converted to Python objects:

```
>>> import struct
>>> file   = open('data.bin', 'rb')
>>> bytes  = file.read()
>>> values = struct.unpack('>i4shf', data)
>>> values
(2, 'spam', 3, 1.2339999675750732)
```

For more details, see the struct module's entry in the Python library manual. Also note that slicing comes in handy in this domain; to grab just the four-character string in the middle of the packed binary data we just read, we can simply slice it out. Numeric values could similarly be sliced out and then passed to struct.unpack for conversion:

```
>>> bytes
'\x00\x00\x00\x02spam\x00\x03?\x9d\xf3\xb6'
>>> string = bytes[4:8]
```

```
>>> string
'spam'

>>> number = bytes[8:10]
>>> number
'\x00\x03'
>>> struct.unpack('>h', number)
(3,)
```

File Tools in the os Module

The os module contains an additional set of file-processing functions that are distinct from the built-in file *object* tools demonstrated in previous examples. For instance, here is a very partial list of os file-related calls:

os.open(*path, flags, mode*)
: Opens a file and returns its descriptor

os.read(*descriptor, N*)
: Reads at most *N* bytes and returns a string

os.write(*descriptor, string*)
: Writes bytes in *string* to the file

os.lseek(*descriptor, position*)
: Moves to *position* in the file

Technically, os calls process files by their *descriptors*, which are integer codes or "handles" that identify files in the operating system. Because the descriptor-based file tools in os are lower level and more complex than the built-in file objects created with the built-in open function, you should generally use the latter for all but very special file-processing needs.[*]

To give you the general flavor of this tool set, though, let's run a few interactive experiments. Although built-in file objects and os module descriptor files are processed with distinct tool sets, they are in fact related—the stdio filesystem used by file objects simply adds a layer of logic on top of descriptor-based files.

In fact, the fileno file object method returns the integer descriptor associated with a built-in file object. For instance, the standard stream file objects have descriptors 0, 1, and 2; calling the os.write function to send data to stdout by descriptor has the same effect as calling the sys.stdout.write method:

```
>>> import sys
>>> for stream in (sys.stdin, sys.stdout, sys.stderr):
...     print stream.fileno( ),
...
```

---

[*] For instance, to process *pipes*, described in Chapter 5. The Python pipe call returns two file descriptors, which can be processed with os module tools or wrapped in a file object with os.fdopen.

```
0 1 2

>>> sys.stdout.write('Hello stdio world\n')          # write via file method
Hello stdio world

>>> import os
>>> os.write(1, 'Hello descriptor world\n')          # write via os module
Hello descriptor world
23
```

Because file objects we open explicitly behave the same way, it's also possible to process a given real external file on the underlying computer through the built-in open function, tools in the os module, or both:

```
>>> file = open(r'C:\temp\spam.txt', 'w')            # create external file
>>> file.write('Hello stdio file\n')                 # write via file method
>>>
>>> fd = file.fileno( )
>>> print fd
3
>>> os.write(fd, 'Hello descriptor file\n')          # write via os module
22
>>> file.close( )
>>>
C:\WINDOWS>type c:\temp\spam.txt                     # both writes show up
Hello descriptor file
Hello stdio file
```

Open mode flags

So why the extra file tools in os? In short, they give more low-level control over file processing. The built-in open function is easy to use but is limited by the underlying stdio filesystem that it wraps; buffering, open modes, and so on, are all per-stdio defaults.[*] The os module lets scripts be more specific—for example, the following opens a descriptor-based file in read-write and binary modes by performing a binary "or" on two mode flags exported by os:

```
>>> fdfile = os.open(r'C:\temp\spam.txt', (os.O_RDWR | os.O_BINARY))
>>> os.read(fdfile, 20)
'Hello descriptor fil'
>>> os.lseek(fdfile, 0, 0)                           # go back to start of file
0
>>> os.read(fdfile, 100)                             # binary mode retains "\r\n"
'Hello descriptor file\r\nHello stdio file\r\n'

>>> os.lseek(fdfile, 0, 0)
0
>>> os.write(fdfile, 'HELLO')                        # overwrite first 5 bytes
5
```

---

[*] To be fair to the built-in file object, the open function accepts an rb+ mode, which is equivalent to the combined mode flags used here and can also be made nonbuffered with a buffer size argument. Whenever possible, use open, not os.open.

On some systems, such open flags let us specify more advanced things like *exclusive access* (O_EXCL) and *nonblocking* modes (O_NONBLOCK) when a file is opened. Some of these flags are not portable across platforms (another reason to use built-in file objects most of the time); see the library manual or run a dir(os) call on your machine for an exhaustive list of other open flags available.

We saw earlier how to go from file object to field descriptor with the fileno file method; we can also go the other way—the os.fdopen call wraps a file descriptor in a file object. Because conversions work both ways, we can generally use either tool set—file object or os module:

```
>>> objfile = os.fdopen(fdfile)
>>> objfile.seek(0)
>>> objfile.read( )
'HELLO descriptor file\r\nHello stdio file\r\n'
```

 Using os.open with the O_EXCL flag is the most portable way to lock files for concurrent updates or other process synchronization in Python today. Another module, fcntl, also provides file-locking tools but is not as widely available across platforms. As of this writing, locking with os.open is supported in Windows, Unix, and Macintosh; fcntl works only on Unix.

Other os file tools

The os module also includes an assortment of file tools that accept a file pathname string and accomplish file-related tasks such as renaming (os.rename), deleting (os.remove), and changing the file's owner and permission settings (os.chown, os.chmod). Let's step through a few examples of these tools in action:

```
>>> os.chmod('spam.txt', 0777)          # enabled all accesses
```

This os.chmod file permissions call passes a 9-bit string composed of three sets of three bits each. From left to right, the three sets represent the file's owning user, the file's group, and all others. Within each set, the three bits reflect read, write, and execute access permissions. When a bit is "1" in this string, it means that the corresponding operation is allowed for the assessor. For instance, octal 0777 is a string of nine "1" bits in binary, so it enables all three kinds of accesses for all three user groups; octal 0600 means that the file can be read and written only by the user that owns it (when written in binary, 0600 octal is really bits 110 000 000).

This scheme stems from Unix file permission settings, but it works on Windows as well. If it's puzzling, either check a Unix manpage for *chmod* or see the fixreadonly example in Chapter 7 for a practical application (it makes read-only files that are copied off a CD-ROM writable).

```
>>> os.rename(r'C:\temp\spam.txt', r'C:\temp\eggs.txt')      # (from, to)
>>>
>>> os.remove(r'C:\temp\spam.txt')                            # delete file
```

```
Traceback (innermost last):
  File "<stdin>", line 1, in ?
OSError: [Errno 2] No such file or directory: 'C:\\temp\\spam.txt'
>>>
>>> os.remove(r'C:\temp\eggs.txt')
```

The os.rename call used here changes a file's name; the os.remove file deletion call deletes a file from your system and is synonymous with os.unlink (the latter reflects the call's name on Unix but was obscure to users of other platforms). The os module also exports the stat system call:

```
>>> import os
>>> info = os.stat(r'C:\temp\spam.txt')
>>> info
(33206, 0, 2, 1, 0, 0, 41, 968133600, 968176258, 968176193)

>>> import stat
>>> info[stat.ST_MODE], info[stat.ST_SIZE]
(33206, 41)

>>> mode = info[stat.ST_MODE]
>>> stat.S_ISDIR(mode), stat.S_ISREG(mode)
(0, 1)
```

The os.stat call returns a tuple of values giving low-level information about the named file, and the stat module exports constants and functions for querying this information in a portable way. For instance, indexing an os.stat result on offset stat.ST_SIZE returns the file's size, and calling stat.S_ISDIR with the mode item from an os.stat result checks whether the file is a directory. As shown earlier, though, both of these operations are available in the os.path module too, so it's rarely necessary to use os.stat except for low-level file queries:

```
>>> path = r'C:\temp\spam.txt'
>>> os.path.isdir(path), os.path.isfile(path), os.path.getsize(path)
(0, 1, 41)
```

File Scanners

Unlike some shell-tool languages, Python doesn't have an implicit file-scanning loop procedure, but it's simple to write a general one that we can reuse for all time. The module in Example 4-1 defines a general file-scanning routine, which simply applies a passed-in Python function to each line in an external file.

Example 4-1. PP3E\System\Filetools\scanfile.py

```
def scanner(name, function):
    file = open(name, 'r')              # create a file object
    while 1:
        line = file.readline()          # call file methods
        if not line: break              # until end-of-file
        function(line)                  # call a function object
    file.close()
```

The scanner function doesn't care what line-processing function is passed in, and that accounts for most of its generality—it is happy to apply *any* single-argument function that exists now or in the future to all of the lines in a text file. If we code this module and put it in a directory on PYTHONPATH, we can use it any time we need to step through a file line by line. Example 4-2 is a client script that does simple line translations.

Example 4-2. PP3E\System\Filetools\commands.py

```
#!/usr/local/bin/python
from sys import argv
from scanfile import scanner
class UnknownCommand(Exception): pass

def processLine(line):                       # define a function
    if line[0] == '*':                       # applied to each line
        print "Ms.", line[1:-1]
    elif line[0] == '+':
        print "Mr.", line[1:-1]              # strip first and last char: \n
    else:
        raise UnknownCommand, line           # raise an exception

filename = 'data.txt'
if len(argv) == 2: filename = argv[1]        # allow filename cmd arg
scanner(filename, processLine)               # start the scanner
```

The text file *hillbillies.txt* contains the following lines:

```
*Granny
+Jethro
*Elly May
+"Uncle Jed"
```

and our commands script could be run as follows:

```
C:\...\PP3E\System\Filetools>python commands.py hillbillies.txt
Ms. Granny
Mr. Jethro
Ms. Elly May
Mr. "Uncle Jed"
```

Notice that we could also code the command processor in the following way; especially if the number of command options starts to become large, such a data-driven approach may be more concise and easier to maintain than a large if statement with essentially redundant actions (if you ever have to change the way output lines print, you'll have to change it in only one place with this form):

```
commands = {'*': 'Ms.', '+': 'Mr.'}     # data is easier to expand than code?

def processLine(line):
    try:
        print commands[line[0]], line[1:-1]
    except KeyError:
        raise UnknownCommand, line
```

As a rule of thumb, we can also usually speed things up by shifting processing from Python code to built-in tools. For instance, if we're concerned with speed (and memory space isn't tight), we can make our file scanner faster by using the readlines method to load the file into a list all at once instead of using the manual readline loop in Example 4-1:

```
def scanner(name, function):
    file = open(name, 'r')                # create a file object
    for line in file.readlines():        # get all lines at once
        function(line)                   # call a function object
    file.close()
```

A file iterator will do the same work but will not load the entire file into memory all at once:

```
def scanner(name, function):
    for line in open(name, 'r'):         # scan line by line
        function(line)                   # call a function object
    file.close()
```

And if we have a list of lines, we can work more magic with the map built-in function or list comprehension expression. Here are two minimalist's versions; the for loop is replaced by map or a comprehension, and we let Python close the file for us when it is garbage collected or the script exits (both of these build a temporary list of results along the way, which is likely trivial for all but the largest of files):

```
def scanner(name, function):
    map(function, open(name, 'r'))
```

```
def scanner(name, function):
    [function(line) for line in open(name, 'r')]
```

But what if we also want to *change* a file while scanning it? Example 4-3 shows two approaches: one uses explicit files, and the other uses the standard input/output streams to allow for redirection on the command line.

Example 4-3. PP3E\System\Filetools\filters.py

```
def filter_files(name, function):        # filter file through function
    input  = open(name, 'r')             # create file objects
    output = open(name + '.out', 'w')    # explicit output file too
    for line in input:
        output.write(function(line))     # write the modified line
    input.close()
    output.close()                       # output has a '.out' suffix

def filter_stream(function):
    import sys                           # no explicit files
    while 1:                            # use standard streams
        line = sys.stdin.readline()      # or: raw_input()
        if not line: break
        print function(line),            # or: sys.stdout.write()
```

Example 4-3. PP3E\System\Filetools\filters.py (continued)

```
if __name__ == '__main__':
    filter_stream(lambda line: line)      # copy stdin to stdout if run
```

Since the standard streams are preopened for us, they're often easier to use. This module is more useful when imported as a library (clients provide the line-processing function); when run standalone it simply parrots stdin to stdout:

```
C:\...\PP3E\System\Filetools>python filters.py < ..\System.txt
This directory contains operating system interface examples.

Many of the examples in this unit appear elsewhere in the examples
distribution tree, because they are actually used to manage other
programs. See the README.txt files in the subdirectories here
for pointers.
```

 Brutally observant readers may notice that this last file is named *filters.py* (with an *s*), not *filter.py*. I originally named it the latter but changed its name when I realized that a simple import of the filename (e.g., "import filter") assigns the module to a local name "filter," thereby hiding the built-in `filter` function. This is a built-in functional programming tool that is not used very often in typical scripts. And as mentioned earlier, redefining built-in names this way is not an issue unless you really need to use the built-in version of the name. But as a general rule of thumb, be careful to avoid picking built-in names for module files. I will if you will.

Directory Tools

One of the more common tasks in the shell utilities domain is applying an operation to a set of files in a *directory*—a "folder" in Windows-speak. By running a script on a batch of files, we can automate (that is, *script*) tasks we might have to otherwise run repeatedly by hand.

For instance, suppose you need to search all of your Python files in a development directory for a global variable name (perhaps you've forgotten where it is used). There are many platform-specific ways to do this (e.g., the grep command in Unix), but Python scripts that accomplish such tasks will work on every platform where Python works—Windows, Unix, Linux, Macintosh, and just about any other platform commonly used today. If you simply copy your script to any machine you wish to use it on, it will work regardless of which other tools are available there.

Walking One Directory

The most common way to go about writing such tools is to first grab a list of the names of the files you wish to process, and then step through that list with a Python for loop, processing each file in turn. The trick we need to learn here, then, is how to get such a directory list within our scripts. There are at least three options: running shell listing commands with os.popen, matching filename patterns with glob.glob, and getting directory listings with os.listdir. They vary in interface, result format, and portability.

Running shell listing commands with os.popen

Quick: how did you go about getting directory file listings before you heard of Python? If you're new to shell tools programming, the answer may be "Well, I started a Windows file explorer and clicked on stuff," but I'm thinking here in terms of less GUI-oriented command-line mechanisms (and answers submitted in Perl and Tcl get only partial credit).

On Unix, directory listings are usually obtained by typing ls in a shell; on Windows, they can be generated with a dir command typed in an MS-DOS console box. Because Python scripts may use os.popen to run any command line that we can type in a shell, they are the most general way to grab a directory listing inside a Python program. We met os.popen in the prior chapter; it runs a shell command string and gives us a file object from which we can read the command's output. To illustrate, let's first assume the following directory structures (yes, I have both dir and ls commands on my Windows laptop; old habits die hard):

```
C:\temp>dir /B
about-pp.html
python1.5.tar.gz
about-pp2e.html
about-ppr2e.html
newdir

C:\temp>ls
about-pp.html      about-ppr2e.html  python1.5.tar.gz
about-pp2e.html    newdir

C:\temp>ls newdir
more    temp1  temp2  temp3
```

The *newdir* name is a nested subdirectory in *C:\temp* here. Now, scripts can grab a listing of file and directory names at this level by simply spawning the appropriate platform-specific command line and reading its output (the text normally thrown up on the console window):

```
C:\temp>python
>>> import os
>>> os.popen('dir /B').readlines( )
['about-pp.html\n', 'python1.5.tar.gz\n', 'about-pp2e.html\n',
'about-ppr2e.html\n', 'newdir\n']
```

Lines read from a shell command come back with a trailing end-of-line character, but it's easy enough to slice off with a for loop or list comprehension expression as in the following code:

```
>>> for line in os.popen('dir /B').readlines():
...     print line[:-1]
...
about-pp.html
python1.5.tar.gz
about-pp2e.html
about-ppr2e.html
newdir

>>> lines = [line[:-1] for line in os.popen('dir /B')]
>>> lines
['about-pp.html', 'python1.5.tar.gz', 'about-pp2e.html',
'about-ppr2e.html', 'newdir']
```

One subtle thing: notice that the object returned by os.popen has an iterator that reads one line per request (i.e., per next( ) method call), just like normal files, so calling the readlines method is optional here unless you really need to extract the result list all at once (see the discussion of file iterators earlier in this chapter). For pipe objects, the effect of iterators is even more useful than simply avoiding loading the entire result into memory all at once: readlines will block the caller until the spawned program is completely finished, whereas the iterator might not.

The dir and ls commands let us be specific about filename patterns to be matched and directory names to be listed; again, we're just running shell commands here, so anything you can type at a shell prompt goes:

```
>>> os.popen('dir *.html /B').readlines()
['about-pp.html\n', 'about-pp2e.html\n', 'about-ppr2e.html\n']

>>> os.popen('ls *.html').readlines()
['about-pp.html\n', 'about-pp2e.html\n', 'about-ppr2e.html\n']

>>> os.popen('dir newdir /B').readlines()
['temp1\n', 'temp2\n', 'temp3\n', 'more\n']

>>> os.popen('ls newdir').readlines()
['more\n', 'temp1\n', 'temp2\n', 'temp3\n']
```

These calls use general tools and work as advertised. As I noted earlier, though, the downsides of os.popen are that it requires using a platform-specific shell command and it incurs a performance hit to start up an independent program. The following two alternative techniques do better on both counts.

The glob module

The term *globbing* comes from the * wildcard character in filename patterns; per computing folklore, a * matches a "glob" of characters. In less poetic terms, globbing simply means collecting the names of all entries in a directory—files and subdirectories—whose names match a given filename pattern. In Unix shells, globbing expands filename patterns within a command line into all matching filenames before the command is ever run. In Python, we can do something similar by calling the glob.glob built-in with a pattern to expand:

```
>>> import glob
>>> glob.glob('*')
['about-pp.html', 'python1.5.tar.gz', 'about-pp2e.html', 'about-ppr2e.html',
'newdir']

>>> glob.glob('*.html')
['about-pp.html', 'about-pp2e.html', 'about-ppr2e.html']

>>> glob.glob('newdir/*')
['newdir\\temp1', 'newdir\\temp2', 'newdir\\temp3', 'newdir\\more']
```

The glob call accepts the usual filename pattern syntax used in shells (e.g., ? means any one character, * means any number of characters, and [] is a character selection set).* The pattern should include a directory path if you wish to glob in something other than the current working directory, and the module accepts either Unix or DOS-style directory separators (/ or \). Also, this call is implemented without spawning a shell command and so is likely to be faster and more portable across all Python platforms than the os.popen schemes shown earlier.

Technically speaking, glob is a bit more powerful than described so far. In fact, using it to list files in one directory is just one use of its pattern-matching skills. For instance, it can also be used to collect matching names across multiple directories, simply because each level in a passed-in directory path can be a pattern too:

```
C:\temp>python
>>> import glob
>>> for name in glob.glob('*examples/L*.py'): print name
...
cpexamples\Launcher.py
cpexamples\Launch_PyGadgets.py
cpexamples\LaunchBrowser.py
cpexamples\launchmodes.py
examples\Launcher.py
examples\Launch_PyGadgets.py
examples\LaunchBrowser.py
examples\launchmodes.py

>>> for name in glob.glob(r'*\*\visitor_find*.py'): print name
...
cpexamples\PyTools\visitor_find.py
cpexamples\PyTools\visitor_find_quiet2.py
cpexamples\PyTools\visitor_find_quiet1.py
examples\PyTools\visitor_find.py
examples\PyTools\visitor_find_quiet2.py
examples\PyTools\visitor_find_quiet1.py
```

---

* In fact, glob just uses the standard fnmatch module to match name patterns; see the fnmatch description later in this chapter for more details.

In the first call here, we get back filenames from two different directories that match the *examples pattern; in the second, both of the first directory levels are wildcards, so Python collects all possible ways to reach the base filenames. Using os.popen to spawn shell commands achieves the same effect only if the underlying shell or listing command does too.

The os.listdir call

The os module's listdir call provides yet another way to collect filenames in a Python list. It takes a simple directory name string, not a filename pattern, and returns a list containing the names of all entries in that directory—both simple files and nested directories—for use in the calling script:

```
>>> os.listdir('.')
['about-pp.html', 'python1.5.tar.gz', 'about-pp2e.html', 'about-ppr2e.html',
'newdir']

>>> os.listdir(os.curdir)
['about-pp.html', 'python1.5.tar.gz', 'about-pp2e.html', 'about-ppr2e.html',
'newdir']

>>> os.listdir('newdir')
['temp1', 'temp2', 'temp3', 'more']
```

This too is done without resorting to shell commands and so is portable to all major Python platforms. The result is not in any particular order (but can be sorted with the list sort method), returns base filenames without their directory path prefixes, and includes names of both files and directories at the listed level.

To compare all three listing techniques, let's run them here side by side on an explicit directory. They differ in some ways but are mostly just variations on a theme—os.popen sorts names and returns end-of-lines, glob.glob accepts a pattern and returns filenames with directory prefixes, and os.listdir takes a simple directory name and returns names without directory prefixes:

```
>>> os.popen('ls C:\PP3rdEd').readlines()
['README.txt\n', 'cdrom\n', 'chapters\n', 'etc\n', 'examples\n',
'examples.tar.gz\n', 'figures\n', 'shots\n']

>>> glob.glob('C:\PP3rdEd\*')
['C:\\PP3rdEd\\examples.tar.gz', 'C:\\PP3rdEd\\README.txt',
'C:\\PP3rdEd\\shots', 'C:\\PP3rdEd\\figures', 'C:\\PP3rdEd\\examples',
'C:\\PP3rdEd\\etc', 'C:\\PP3rdEd\\chapters', 'C:\\PP3rdEd\\cdrom']

>>> os.listdir('C:\PP3rdEd')
['examples.tar.gz', 'README.txt', 'shots', 'figures', 'examples', 'etc',
'chapters', 'cdrom']
```

Of these three, glob and listdir are generally better options if you care about script portability, and listdir seems fastest in recent Python releases (but gauge its performance yourself—implementations may change over time).

Splitting and joining listing results

In the last example, I pointed out that glob returns names with directory paths, whereas listdir gives raw base filenames. For convenient processing, scripts often need to split glob results into base files or expand listdir results into full paths. Such translations are easy if we let the os.path module do all the work for us. For example, a script that intends to copy all files elsewhere will typically need to first split off the base filenames from glob results so that it can add different directory names on the front:

```
>>> dirname = r'C:\PP3rdEd'
>>> for file in glob.glob(dirname + '/*'):
...     head, tail = os.path.split(file)
...     print head, tail, '=>', ('C:\\Other\\' + tail)
...
C:\PP3rdEd examples.tar.gz => C:\Other\examples.tar.gz
C:\PP3rdEd README.txt => C:\Other\README.txt
C:\PP3rdEd shots => C:\Other\shots
C:\PP3rdEd figures => C:\Other\figures
C:\PP3rdEd examples => C:\Other\examples
C:\PP3rdEd etc => C:\Other\etc
C:\PP3rdEd chapters => C:\Other\chapters
C:\PP3rdEd cdrom => C:\Other\cdrom
```

Here, the names after the => represent names that files might be moved to. Conversely, a script that means to process all files in a different directory than the one it runs in will probably need to prepend listdir results with the target directory name before passing filenames on to other tools:

```
>>> for file in os.listdir(dirname):
...     print os.path.join(dirname, file)
...
C:\PP3rdEd\examples.tar.gz
C:\PP3rdEd\README.txt
C:\PP3rdEd\shots
C:\PP3rdEd\figures
C:\PP3rdEd\examples
C:\PP3rdEd\etc
C:\PP3rdEd\chapters
C:\PP3rdEd\cdrom
```

Walking Directory Trees

As you read the prior section, you may have noticed that all of the preceding techniques return the names of files in only a *single* directory. What if you want to apply an operation to every file in every directory and subdirectory in an entire directory *tree*?

For instance, suppose again that we need to find every occurrence of a global name in our Python scripts. This time, though, our scripts are arranged into a module *package*: a directory with nested subdirectories, which may have subdirectories of their own. We could rerun our hypothetical single-directory searcher manually in every directory in the tree, but that's tedious, error prone, and just plain not fun.

Luckily, in Python it's almost as easy to process a directory tree as it is to inspect a single directory. We can either write a recursive routine to traverse the tree, or use one of two tree-walker utilities built into the os module. Such tools can be used to search, copy, compare, and otherwise process arbitrary directory trees on any platform that Python runs on (and that's just about everywhere).

The os.path.walk visitor

To make it easy to apply an operation to all files in a tree hierarchy, Python comes with a utility that scans trees for us and runs a provided function at every directory along the way. The os.path.walk function is called with a directory root, function object, and optional data item, and walks the tree at the directory root and below. At each directory, the function object passed in is called with the optional data item, the name of the current directory, and a list of filenames in that directory (obtained from os.listdir). Typically, the function we provide (often referred to as a *callback* function) scans the filenames list to process files at each directory level in the tree.

That description might sound horribly complex the first time you hear it, but os. path.walk is fairly straightforward once you get the hang of it. In the following code, for example, the lister function is called from os.path.walk at each directory in the tree rooted at .. Along the way, lister simply prints the directory name and all the files at the current level (after prepending the directory name). It's simpler in Python than in English:

```
>>> import os
>>> def lister(dummy, dirname, filesindir):
...     print '[' + dirname + ']'
...     for fname in filesindir:
...         print os.path.join(dirname, fname)          # handle one file
...
>>> os.path.walk('.', lister, None)
[.]
.\about-pp.html
.\python1.5.tar.gz
.\about-pp2e.html
.\about-ppr2e.html
.\newdir
[.\newdir]
.\newdir\temp1
.\newdir\temp2
.\newdir\temp3
.\newdir\more
[.\newdir\more]
.\newdir\more\xxx.txt
.\newdir\more\yyy.txt
```

In other words, we've coded our own custom (and easily changed) recursive directory listing tool in Python. Because this may be something we would like to tweak and reuse elsewhere, let's make it permanently available in a module file, as shown in Example 4-4, now that we've worked out the details interactively.

Example 4-4. PP3E\System\Filetools\lister_walk.py

```
# list file tree with os.path.walk
import sys, os

def lister(dummy, dirName, filesInDir):          # called at each dir
    print '[' + dirName + ']'
    for fname in filesInDir:                      # includes subdir names
        path = os.path.join(dirName, fname)       # add dir name prefix
        if not os.path.isdir(path):               # print simple files only
            print path

if __name__ == '__main__':
    os.path.walk(sys.argv[1], lister, None)       # dir name in cmdline
```

This is the same code except that directory names are filtered out of the filenames list by consulting the `os.path.isdir` test in order to avoid listing them twice (see, it's been tweaked already). When packaged this way, the code can also be run from a shell command line. Here it is being launched from a different directory, with the directory to be listed passed in as a command-line argument:

```
C:\...\PP3E\System\Filetools>python lister_walk.py C:\Temp
[C:\Temp]
C:\Temp\about-pp.html
C:\Temp\python1.5.tar.gz
C:\Temp\about-pp2e.html
C:\Temp\about-ppr2e.html
[C:\Temp\newdir]
C:\Temp\newdir\temp1
C:\Temp\newdir\temp2
C:\Temp\newdir\temp3
[C:\Temp\newdir\more]
C:\Temp\newdir\more\xxx.txt
C:\Temp\newdir\more\yyy.txt
```

The walk paradigm also allows functions to tailor the set of directories visited by changing the file list argument in place. The library manual documents this further, but it's probably more instructive to simply know what walk truly looks like. Here is its actual Python-coded implementation for Windows platforms (at the time of this writing), with comments added to help demystify its operation:

```
def walk(top, func, arg):                    # top is the current dirname
    try:
        names = os.listdir(top)              # get all file/dir names here
    except os.error:                         # they have no path prefix
        return
    func(arg, top, names)                    # run func with names list here
```

```
        exceptions = ('.', '..')
        for name in names:                    # step over the very same list
            if name not in exceptions:        # but skip self/parent names
                name = join(top, name)        # add path prefix to name
                if isdir(name):
                    walk(name, func, arg)     # descend into subdirs here
```

Notice that walk generates filename lists at each level with os.listdir, a call that collects both file and directory names in no particular order and returns them without their directory paths. Also note that walk uses the very same list returned by os.listdir and passed to the function you provide in order to later descend into subdirectories (variable names). Because lists are mutable objects that can be changed in place, if your function modifies the passed-in filenames list, it will impact what walk does next. For example, deleting directory names will prune traversal branches, and sorting the list will order the walk.

The os.walk generator

In recent Python releases, a new directory tree walker has been added which does not require a callback function to be coded. This new call, os.walk, is instead a generator function; when used within a for loop, each time through it yields a tuple containing the current directory name, a list of subdirectories in that directory, and a list of nondirectory files in that directory.

Recall that generators have a .next() method implicitly invoked by for loops and other iteration contexts; each call forces the walker to the next directory in the tree. Essentially, os.walk replaces the os.path.walk callback function with a loop body, and so it may be easier to use (though you'll have to judge that for yourself).

For example, suppose you have a directory tree of files and you want to find all Python source files within it that reference the Tkinter GUI module. The traditional way to accomplish this with os.path.walk requires a callback function run at each level of the tree:

```
>>> import os
>>> def atEachDir(matchlist, dirname, fileshere):
        for filename in fileshere:
            if filename.endswith('.py'):
                pathname = os.path.join(dirname, filename)
                if 'Tkinter' in open(pathname).read():
                    matchlist.append(pathname)

>>> matches = []
>>> os.path.walk(r'D:\PP3E', atEachDir, matches)
>>> matches
['D:\\PP3E\\dev\\examples\\PP3E\\Preview\\peoplegui.py', 'D:\\PP3E\\dev\\examples\\
PP3E\\Preview\\tkinter101.py', 'D:\\PP3E\\dev\\examples\\PP3E\\Preview\\tkinter001.
py', 'D:\\PP3E\\dev\\examples\\PP3E\\Preview\\peoplegui_class.py', 'D:\\PP3E\\dev\\
examples\\PP3E\\Preview\\tkinter102.py', 'D:\\PP3E\\NewExamples\\clock.py', 'D:\\
PP3E\\NewExamples\\calculator.py']
```

This code loops through all the files at each level, looking for files with *.py* at the end of their names and which contain the search string. When a match is found, its full name is appended to the results list object, which is passed in as an argument (we could also just build a list of *.py* files and search each in a for loop after the walk). The equivalent os.walk code is similar, but the callback function's code becomes the body of a for loop, and directory names are filtered out for us:

```
>>> import os
>>> matches = []
>>> for (dirname, dirshere, fileshere) in os.walk(r'D:\PP3E'):
        for filename in fileshere:
            if filename.endswith('.py'):
                pathname = os.path.join(dirname, filename)
                if 'Tkinter' in open(pathname).read( ):
                    matches.append(pathname)

>>> matches
['D:\\PP3E\\dev\\examples\\PP3E\\Preview\\peoplegui.py', 'D:\\PP3E\\dev\\examples\\
PP3E\\Preview\\tkinter101.py', 'D:\\PP3E\\dev\\examples\\PP3E\\Preview\\tkinter001.
py', 'D:\\PP3E\\dev\\examples\\PP3E\\Preview\\peoplegui_class.py', 'D:\\PP3E\\dev\\
examples\\PP3E\\Preview\\tkinter102.py', 'D:\\PP3E\\NewExamples\\clock.py', 'D:\\
PP3E\\NewExamples\\calculator.py']
```

If you want to see what's really going on in the os.walk generator, call its next( ) method manually a few times as the for loop does automatically; each time, you advance to the next subdirectory in the tree:

```
>>> gen = os.walk('D:\PP3E')
>>> gen.next( )
('D:\\PP3E', ['proposal', 'dev', 'NewExamples', 'bkp'], ['prg-python-2.zip'])
>>> gen.next( )
('D:\\PP3E\\proposal', [], ['proposal-programming-python-3e.doc'])
>>> gen.next( )
('D:\\PP3E\\dev', ['examples'], ['ch05.doc', 'ch06.doc', 'ch07.doc', 'ch08.doc',
'ch09.doc', 'ch10.doc', 'ch11.doc', 'ch12.doc', 'ch13.doc', 'ch14.doc', ...more...
```

The os.walk generator has more features than I will demonstrate here. For instance, additional arguments allow you to specify a top-down or bottom-up traversal of the directory tree, and the list of subdirectories in the yielded tuple can be modified in-place to change the traversal in top-down mode, much as for os.path.walk. See the Python library manual for more details.

So why the new call? Is the new os.walk easier to use than the traditional os.path.walk? Perhaps, if you need to distinguish between subdirectories and files in each directory (os.walk gives us two lists rather than one) or can make use of a bottom-up traversal or other features. Otherwise, it's mostly just the trade of a function for a for loop header. You'll have to judge for yourself whether this is more natural or not; we'll use both forms in this book.

Recursive os.listdir traversals

The os.path.walk and os.walk tools do tree traversals for us, but it's sometimes more flexible and hardly any more work to do it ourselves. The following script recodes the directory listing script with a manual *recursive* traversal function (a function that calls itself to repeat its actions). The mylister function in Example 4-5 is almost the same as lister in Example 4-4 but calls os.listdir to generate file paths manually and calls itself recursively to descend into subdirectories.

Example 4-5. PP3E\System\Filetools\lister_recur.py

```
# list files in dir tree by recursion
import sys, os

def mylister(currdir):
    print '[' + currdir + ']'
    for file in os.listdir(currdir):          # list files here
        path = os.path.join(currdir, file)    # add dir path back
        if not os.path.isdir(path):
            print path
        else:
            mylister(path)                     # recur into subdirs

if __name__ == '__main__':
    mylister(sys.argv[1])                      # dir name in cmdline
```

This version is packaged as a script too (this is definitely too much code to type at the interactive prompt); its output is identical when run as a script:

```
C:\...\PP3E\System\Filetools>python lister_recur.py C:\Temp
[C:\Temp]
C:\Temp\about-pp.html
C:\Temp\python1.5.tar.gz
C:\Temp\about-pp2e.html
C:\Temp\about-ppr2e.html
[C:\Temp\newdir]
C:\Temp\newdir\temp1
C:\Temp\newdir\temp2
C:\Temp\newdir\temp3
[C:\Temp\newdir\more]
C:\Temp\newdir\more\xxx.txt
C:\Temp\newdir\more\yyy.txt
```

But this file is just as useful when imported and called elsewhere:

```
C:\temp>python
>>> from PP3E.System.Filetools.lister_recur import mylister
>>> mylister('.')
[.]
.\about-pp.html
.\python1.5.tar.gz
.\about-pp2e.html
.\about-ppr2e.html
[.\newdir]
```

```
.\newdir\temp1
.\newdir\temp2
.\newdir\temp3
[.\newdir\more]
.\newdir\more\xxx.txt
.\newdir\more\yyy.txt
```

We will make better use of most of this section's techniques in later examples in Chapter 7 and in this book at large. For example, scripts for copying and comparing directory trees use the tree-walker techniques listed previously. Watch for these tools in action along the way. If you are interested in directory processing, also see the discussion of Python's old grep module in Chapter 7; it searches files and can be applied to all files in a directory when combined with the glob module, but it simply prints results and does not traverse directory trees by itself.

Rolling Your Own find Module

Another way to go hierarchical is to collect files into a flat list all at once. In the second edition of this book, I included a section on the now-defunct find standard library module, which was used to collect a list of matching filenames in an entire directory tree (much like a Unix find command). Unlike the single-directory tools described earlier, although it returned a flat list, find returned pathnames of matching files nested in subdirectories all the way to the bottom of a tree.

This module is now gone; the os.walk and os.path.walk tools described earlier are recommended as easier-to-use alternatives. On the other hand, it's not completely clear why the standard find module fell into deprecation; it's a useful tool. In fact, I used it often—it is nice to be able to grab a simple linear list of matching files in a single function call and step through it in a for loop. The alternatives still seem a bit more code-y and tougher for beginners to digest.

Not to worry though, because instead of lamenting the loss of a module, I decided to spend 10 minutes whipping up a custom equivalent. In fact, one of the nice things about Python is that it is usually easy to do by hand what a built-in tool does for you; many built-ins are just conveniences. The module in Example 4-6 uses the standard os.path.walk call described earlier to reimplement a find operation for use in Python scripts.

Example 4-6. PP3E\PyTools\find.py

```
#!/usr/bin/python
###########################################################################
# custom version of the now deprecated find module in the standard library:
# import as "PyTools.find"; equivalent to the original, but uses os.path.walk,
# has no support for pruning subdirs in the tree, and is instrumented to be
# runnable as a top-level script; uses tuple unpacking in function arguments;
###########################################################################
```

Example 4-6. PP3E\PyTools\find.py (continued)

```
import fnmatch, os

def find(pattern, startdir=os.curdir):
    matches = []
    os.path.walk(startdir, findvisitor, (matches, pattern))
    matches.sort( )
    return matches

def findvisitor((matches, pattern), thisdir, nameshere):
    for name in nameshere:
        if fnmatch.fnmatch(name, pattern):
            fullpath = os.path.join(thisdir, name)
            matches.append(fullpath)

if __name__ == '__main__':
    import sys
    namepattern, startdir = sys.argv[1], sys.argv[2]
    for name in find(namepattern, startdir): print name
```

There's not much to this file; but calling its find function provides the same utility as the deprecated find standard module and is noticeably easier than rewriting all of this file's code every time you need to perform a find-type search. Because this file is instrumented to be both a script and a library, it can be run or called.

For instance, to process every Python file in the directory tree rooted in the current working directory, I simply run the following command line from a system console window. I'm piping the script's standard output into the more command to page it here, but it can be piped into any processing program that reads its input from the standard input stream:

```
python find.py *.py . | more
```

For more control, run the following sort of Python code from a script or interactive prompt (you can also pass in an explicit start directory if you prefer). In this mode, you can apply any operation to the found files that the Python language provides:

```
from PP3E.PyTools import find
for name in find.find('*.py'):
    ...do something with name...
```

Notice how this avoids the nested loop structure you wind up coding with os.walk and the callback functions you implement for os.path.walk (see the earlier examples), making it seem conceptually simpler. Its only obvious downside is that your script must wait until all matching files have been found and collected; os.walk yields results as it goes, and os.path.walk calls your function along the way.

Here's a more concrete example of our find module at work: the following system command line lists all Python files in directory *D:\PP3E* whose names begin with the letter *c* or *t* (it's being run in the same directory as the *find.py* file). Notice that find returns full directory paths that begin with the start directory specification.

```
C:\Python24>python find.py [ct]*.py D:\PP3E
D:\PP3E\NewExamples\calculator.py
D:\PP3E\NewExamples\clock.py
D:\PP3E\NewExamples\commas.py
D:\PP3E\dev\examples\PP3E\Preview\tkinter001.py
D:\PP3E\dev\examples\PP3E\Preview\tkinter101.py
D:\PP3E\dev\examples\PP3E\Preview\tkinter102.py
```

And here's some Python code that does the same find but also extracts base names
and file sizes for each file found:

```
>>> import os
>>> from find import find
>>> for name in find('[ct]*.py', r'D:\PP3E'):
...     print os.path.basename(name), '=>', os.path.getsize(name)
...
calculator.py => 14101
clock.py => 11000
commas.py => 2508
tkinter001.py => 62
tkinter101.py => 235
tkinter102.py => 421
```

As a more useful example, I use the following simple script to clean out any old output text files located anywhere in the book examples tree. I usually run this script
from the example's root directory. I don't really need the full path to the find module in the import here because it is in the same directory as this script itself; if I ever
move this script, though, the full path will be required:

```
C:\...\PP3E>type PyTools\cleanoutput.py
import os                                     # delete old output files in tree
from PP3E.PyTools.find import find           # only need full path if I'm moved
for filename in find('*.out.txt'):
    print filename
    if raw_input('View?') == 'y':
        print open(filename).read()
    if raw_input('Delete?') == 'y':
        os.remove(filename)

C:\temp\examples>python %X%\PyTools\cleanoutput.py
.\Internet\Cgi-Web\Basics\languages.out.txt
View?
Delete?
.\Internet\Cgi-Web\PyErrata\AdminTools\dbaseindexed.out.txt
View?
Delete?y
```

To achieve such code economy, the custom find module calls os.path.walk to register a function to be called per directory in the tree and simply adds matching filenames to the result list along the way.

New here, though, is the fnmatch module—yet another Python standard library module that performs Unix-like pattern matching against filenames. This module supports common operators in name pattern strings: * (to match any number of characters), ? (to match any single character), and [...] and [!...] (to match any character inside the bracket pairs, or not); other characters match themselves.[*] If you haven't already noticed, the standard library is a fairly amazing collection of tools.

Incidentally, find.find is also roughly equivalent to platform-specific shell commands such as find -print on Unix and Linux, and dir /B /S on DOS and Windows. Since we can usually run such shell commands in a Python script with os. popen, the following does the same work as find.find but is inherently nonportable and must start up a separate program along the way:

```
>>> import os
>>> for line in os.popen('dir /B /S').readlines(): print line,
...
C:\temp\about-pp.html
C:\temp\about-pp2e.html
C:\temp\about-ppr2e.html
C:\temp\newdir
C:\temp\newdir\temp1
C:\temp\newdir\temp2
C:\temp\newdir\more
C:\temp\newdir\more\xxx.txt
```

The equivalent Python metaphors, however, work unchanged across platforms—one of the implicit benefits of writing system utilities in Python:

```
C:\...> python find.py * .

>>> from find import find
>>> for name in find(pattern='*', startdir='.'): print name
```

Finally, if you come across older Python code that fails because there is no standard library find to be found, simply change find-module imports in the source code to, say:

```
from PP3E.PyTools import find
```

rather than:

```
import find
```

The former form will find the custom find module in the book's example package directory tree. And if you are willing to add the *PP3E\PyTools* directory to your PYTHONPATH setting, all original import find statements will continue to work unchanged.

---

[*] Unlike the re module, fnmatch supports only common Unix shell matching operators, not full-blown regular expression patterns; to understand why this matters, see Chapter 18 for more details.

Better still, do nothing at all—most find-based examples in this book automatically pick the alternative by catching import exceptions just in case they are run on a more modern Python and their top-level files aren't located in the *PyTools* directory:

```
try:
    import find
except ImportError:
    from PP3E.PyTools import find
```

The find module may be gone, but it need not be forgotten.

Python Versus csh

If you are familiar with other common shell script languages, it might be useful to see how Python compares. Here is a simple script in a Unix shell language called csh that mails all the files in the current working directory with a suffix of *.py* (i.e., all Python source files) to a hopefully fictitious address:

```
#!/bin/csh
foreach x (*.py)
    echo $x
    mail eric@halfabee.com -s $x < $xend
```

The equivalent Python script looks similar:

```
#!/usr/bin/python
import os, glob
for x in glob.glob('*.py'):
    print x
    os.system('mail eric@halfabee.com -s %s < %s' % (x, x))
```

but is slightly more verbose. Since Python, unlike csh, isn't meant just for shell scripts, system interfaces must be imported and called explicitly. And since Python isn't just a string-processing language, character strings must be enclosed in quotes, as in C.

Although this can add a few extra keystrokes in simple scripts like this, being a general-purpose language makes Python a better tool once we leave the realm of trivial programs. We could, for example, extend the preceding script to do things like transfer files by FTP, pop up a GUI message selector and status bar, fetch messages from an SQL database, and employ COM objects on Windows, all using standard Python tools.

Python scripts also tend to be more portable to other platforms than csh. For instance, if we used the Python SMTP interface to send mail instead of relying on a Unix command-line mail tool, the script would run on any machine with Python and an Internet link (as we'll see in Chapter 14, SMTP only requires sockets). And like C, we don't need $ to evaluate variables; what else would you expect in a free language?

Parallel System Tools

"Telling the Monkeys What to Do"

Most computers spend a lot of time doing nothing. If you start a system monitor tool and watch the CPU utilization, you'll see what I mean—it's rare to see one hit 100 percent, even when you are running multiple programs.[*] There are just too many delays built into software: disk accesses, network traffic, database queries, waiting for users to click a button, and so on. In fact, the majority of a modern CPU's capacity is often spent in an idle state; faster chips help speed up performance demand peaks, but much of their power can go largely unused.

Early on in computing, programmers realized that they could tap into such unused processing power by running more than one program at the same time. By dividing the CPU's attention among a set of tasks, its capacity need not go to waste while any given task is waiting for an external event to occur. The technique is usually called *parallel processing* because many tasks seem to be performed at once, overlapping and parallel in time. It's at the heart of modern operating systems, and it gave rise to the notion of multiple active-window computer interfaces we've all come to take for granted. Even within a single program, dividing processing into tasks that run in parallel can make the overall system faster, at least as measured by the clock on your wall.

Just as important is that modern software systems are expected to be responsive to users regardless of the amount of work they must perform behind the scenes. It's usually unacceptable for a program to stall while busy carrying out a request. Consider an email-browser user interface, for example; when asked to fetch email from a server, the program must download text from a server over a network. If you have

---

[*] To watch on Windows, click the Start button, select Programs → Accessories → System Tools → System Monitor, and monitor Processor Usage. The graph rarely climbed above 50 percent on my laptop machine while writing this (at least until I typed while 1: pass in a Python interactive session—a program with little practical value apart from warming up your laptop on a cold winter's day).

enough email and a slow enough Internet link, that step alone can take minutes to finish. But while the download task proceeds, the program as a whole shouldn't stall—it still must respond to screen redraws, mouse clicks, and so on.

Parallel processing comes to the rescue here too. By performing such long-running tasks in parallel with the rest of the program, the system at large can remain responsive no matter how busy some of its parts may be. Moreover, the parallel processing model is a natural fit for such programs, and others; some tasks are more easily conceptualized and coded as components running as independent, parallel entities.

There are two fundamental ways to get tasks running at the same time in Python— process forks and spawned threads. Functionally, both rely on underlying operating system services to run bits of Python code in parallel. Procedurally, they are very different in terms of interface, portability, and communication. At this writing, process forks are not supported on Windows under standard Python (more on this in the next section), but Python's thread support works on all major platforms. Moreover, the os.spawn family of calls provides additional ways to launch programs in a platform-neutral way that is similar to forks, and the os.popen and os.system calls can be used to portably spawn programs with shell commands.

In this chapter, which is a continuation of our look at system interfaces available to Python programmers, we explore Python's built-in tools for starting tasks in parallel as well as communicating with those tasks. In some sense, we've already started doing so—the os.system and os.popen calls introduced and applied in the prior two chapters are a fairly portable way to spawn and speak with command-line programs too. Here, our emphasis is on introducing more direct techniques—forks, threads, pipes, signals, and other launcher tools. In the next chapter (and in the remainder of this book), we use these techniques in more realistic programs, so be sure you understand the basics here before flipping ahead.

Forking Processes

Forked processes are the traditional way to structure parallel tasks, and they are a fundamental part of the Unix tool set. It's a straightforward way to start an independent program, whether it is different from the calling program or not. Forking is based on the notion of *copying* programs: when a program calls the fork routine, the operating system makes a new copy of that program in memory and starts running that copy in parallel with the original. Some systems don't really copy the original program (it's an expensive operation), but the new copy works as if it were a literal copy.

After a fork operation, the original copy of the program is called the *parent* process, and the copy created by os.fork is called the *child* process. In general, parents can make any number of children, and children can create child processes of their own; all forked processes run independently and in parallel under the operating system's control. It is probably simpler in practice than in theory, though. The Python script in Example 5-1 forks new child processes until you type the letter *q* at the console.

Example 5-1. PP3E\System\Processes\fork1.py

```
# forks child processes until you type 'q'

import os

def child():
    print 'Hello from child',  os.getpid()
    os._exit(0)  # else goes back to parent loop

def parent():
    while 1:
        newpid = os.fork()
        if newpid == 0:
            child()
        else:
            print 'Hello from parent', os.getpid(), newpid
        if raw_input() == 'q': break

parent()
```

Python's process forking tools, available in the os module, are simply thin wrappers over standard forking calls in the C library. To start a new, parallel process, call the os.fork built-in function. Because this function generates a copy of the calling program, it returns a different value in each copy: zero in the child process, and the process ID of the new child in the parent. Programs generally test this result to begin different processing in the child only; this script, for instance, runs the child function in child processes only.[*]

Unfortunately, this won't work on Windows in standard Python today; fork is too much at odds with the Windows model, and a port of this call is still in the works (see also this chapter's sidebar about Cygwin Python—you can fork with Python on Windows under Cygwin, but it's not exactly the same). Because forking is ingrained in the Unix programming model, though, this script works well on Unix, Linux, and modern Macs:

```
[mark@toy]$ python fork1.py
Hello from parent 671 672
Hello from child 672

Hello from parent 671 673
Hello from child 673
```

---

[*] At least in the current Python implementation, calling os.fork in a Python script actually copies the Python interpreter process (if you look at your process list, you'll see two Python entries after a fork). But since the Python interpreter records everything about your running script, it's OK to think of fork as copying your program directly. It really will if Python scripts are ever compiled to binary machine code.

```
Hello from parent 671 674
Hello from child 674
q
```

These messages represent three forked child processes; the unique identifiers of all
the processes involved are fetched and displayed with the os.getpid call. A subtle
point: the child process function is also careful to exit explicitly with an os._exit
call. We'll discuss this call in more detail later in this chapter, but if it's not made,
the child process would live on after the child function returns (remember, it's just a
copy of the original process). The net effect is that the child would go back to the
loop in parent and start forking children of its own (i.e., the parent would have
grandchildren). If you delete the exit call and rerun, you'll likely have to type more
than one q to stop, because multiple processes are running in the parent function.

In Example 5-1, each process exits very soon after it starts, so there's little overlap in
time. Let's do something slightly more sophisticated to better illustrate multiple
forked processes running in parallel. Example 5-2 starts up 10 copies of itself, each
copy counting up to 10 with a one-second delay between iterations. The time.sleep
built-in call simply pauses the calling process for a number of seconds (you can pass
a floating-point value to pause for fractions of seconds).

Example 5-2. PP3E\System\Processes\fork-count.py

```
#############################################################################
# fork basics: start 10 copies of this program running in parallel with
# the original; each copy counts up to 10 on the same stdout stream—forks
# copy process memory, including file descriptors; fork doesn't currently
# work on Windows (without Cygwin): use os.spawnv to start programs on
# Windows instead; spawnv is roughly like a fork+exec combination;
#############################################################################

import os, time

def counter(count):
    for i in range(count):
        time.sleep(1)
        print '[%s] => %s' % (os.getpid( ), i)

for i in range(10):
    pid = os.fork( )
    if pid != 0:
        print 'Process %d spawned' % pid
    else:
        counter(10)
        os._exit(0)

print 'Main process exiting.'
```

When run, this script starts 10 processes immediately and exits. All 10 forked
processes check in with their first count display one second later and every second

---

thereafter. Child processes continue to run, even if the parent process that created them terminates:

```
mark@toy]$ python fork-count.py
Process 846 spawned
Process 847 spawned
Process 848 spawned
Process 849 spawned
Process 850 spawned
Process 851 spawned
Process 852 spawned
Process 853 spawned
Process 854 spawned
Process 855 spawned
Main process exiting.
[mark@toy]$
[846] => 0
[847] => 0
[848] => 0
[849] => 0
[850] => 0
[851] => 0
[852] => 0
[853] => 0
[854] => 0
[855] => 0
[847] => 1
[846] => 1
...more output deleted...
```

The output of all of these processes shows up on the same screen, because all of them share the standard output stream. Technically, a forked process gets a copy of the original process's global memory, including open file descriptors. Because of that, global objects like files start out with the same values in a child process, so all the processes here are tied to the same single stream. But it's important to remember that global memory is copied, not shared; if a child process changes a global object, it changes only its own copy. (As we'll see, this works differently in threads, the topic of the next section.)

The fork/exec Combination

In Examples 5-1 and 5-2, child processes simply ran a function within the Python program and then exited. On Unix-like platforms, forks are often the basis of starting independently running programs that are completely different from the program that performed the fork call. For instance, Example 5-3 forks new processes until we type q again, but child processes run a brand-new program instead of calling a function in the same file.

Forking on Windows with Cygwin

Actually, the os.fork call is present in the Cygwin version of Python on Windows. In other words, even though this call is missing in the standard version of Python for Windows, you can now fork processes on Windows with Python if you install and use Cygwin. However, the Cygwin fork call is not as efficient and does not work exactly the same as a fork on true Unix systems.

Cygwin is a freeware package that includes a library that attempts to provide a Unix-like API for use on Windows machines, along with a set of command-line tools that implement a Unix-like environment. It makes it easier to apply Unix skills and code on Windows computers.

According to its current documentation, though, "Cygwin fork( ) essentially works like a non-copy on write version[s] of fork( ) (like old Unix versions used to do). Because of this it can be a little slow. In most cases, you are better off using the spawn family of calls if possible."

In addition to the fork call, Cygwin provides other Unix tools that would otherwise not be available on all flavors of Windows, including os.mkfifo (discussed later in this chapter). It also comes with a gcc compiler environment for building C extensions for Python on Windows that will be familiar to Unix developers. As long as you're willing to use Cygwin libraries to build your application and power your Python, it's very close to Unix on Windows.

Like all third-party libraries, though, Cygwin adds an extra dependency to your systems. Perhaps more critically, Cygwin currently uses the GNU GPL license, which adds distribution requirements beyond those of standard Python. Unlike using Python itself, shipping a program that uses Cygwin libraries may require that your program's source code be made freely available, unless you purchase a special "buy-out" license to free your program of the GPL's requirements. Note that this is a complex legal issue, and you should study Cygwin's license on your own. Its license does, however, impose more constraints than Python's (Python uses a "BSD"-style license, not the GPL).

Still, Cygwin can be a great way to get Unix-like functionality on Windows without installing a completely different operating system such as Linux—a more complete but generally more complex option. For more details, see *http://cygwin.com* or run a search for Cygwin at Google.com.

See also the standard library's os.spawn family of calls covered later in this chapter for an alternative way to start programs on Unix and Windows that does not require fork and exec calls. To run a simple function call in parallel on Windows (rather than on an external program), also see the section on standard library threads later in this chapter. Both threads and os.spawn calls now work on Windows in standard Python.

Example 5-3. PP3E\System\Processes\fork-exec.py

```
# starts programs until you type 'q'

import os

parm = 0
while 1:
    parm = parm+1
    pid = os.fork()
    if pid == 0:                                             # copy process
        os.execlp('python', 'python', 'child.py', str(parm)) # overlay program
        assert False, 'error starting program'              # shouldn't return
    else:
        print 'Child is', pid
        if raw_input() == 'q': break
```

If you've done much Unix development, the fork/exec combination will probably look familiar. The main thing to notice is the os.execlp call in this code. In a nutshell, this call *overlays* (i.e., replaces) with another process the program that is running in the current process. Because of that, the *combination* of os.fork and os.execlp means start a new process and run a new program in that process—in other words, launch a new program in parallel with the original program.

os.exec call formats

The arguments to os.execlp specify the program to be run by giving command-line arguments used to start the program (i.e., what Python scripts know as sys.argv). If successful, the new program begins running and the call to os.execlp itself never returns (since the original program has been replaced, there's really nothing to return to). If the call does return, an error has occurred, so we code an assert after it that will always raise an exception if reached.

There are a handful of os.exec variants in the Python standard library; some allow us to configure environment variables for the new program, pass command-line arguments in different forms, and so on. All are available on both Unix and Windows, and they replace the calling program (i.e., the Python interpreter). exec comes in eight flavors, which can be a bit confusing unless you generalize:

os.execv(*program, commandlinesequence*)
> The basic "v" exec form is passed an executable program's name, along with a list or tuple of command-line argument strings used to run the executable (that is, the words you would normally type in a shell to start a program).

os.execl(*program, cmdarg1, cmdarg2,... cmdargN*)
> The basic "l" exec form is passed an executable's name, followed by one or more command-line arguments passed as individual function arguments. This is the same as os.execv(*program, (cmdarg1, cmdarg2,...)*).

```
os.execlp
os.execvp
```
> Adding the letter p to the execv and execl names means that Python will locate the executable's directory using your system search-path setting (i.e., PATH).

```
os.execle
os.execve
```
> Adding a letter e to the execv and execl names means an extra, *last* argument is a dictionary containing shell environment variables to send to the program.

```
os.execvpe
os.execlpe
```
> Adding the letters p and e to the basic exec names means to use the search path *and* to accept a shell environment settings dictionary.

So, when the script in Example 5-3 calls os.execlp, individually passed parameters specify a command line for the program to be run on, and the word *python* maps to an executable file according to the underlying system search-path setting environment variable (PATH). It's as if we were running a command of the form python child.py 1 in a shell, but with a different command-line argument on the end each time.

Spawned child program

Just as when typed at a shell, the string of arguments passed to os.execlp by the fork-exec script in Example 5-3 starts another Python program file, as shown in Example 5-4.

Example 5-4. PP3E\System\Processes\child.py

```
import os, sys
print 'Hello from child', os.getpid( ), sys.argv[1]
```

Here is this code in action on Linux. It doesn't look much different from the original *fork1.py*, but it's really running a new *program* in each forked process. The more observant readers may notice that the child process ID displayed is the same in the parent program and the launched *child.py* program; os.execlp simply overlays a program in the same process.

```
[mark@toy]$ python fork-exec.py
Child is 1094
Hello from child 1094 1

Child is 1095
Hello from child 1095 2

Child is 1096
Hello from child 1096 3
q
```

There are other ways to start up programs in Python, including the os.system and os.popen we first met in Chapter 3 (to start shell command lines), and the os.spawnv call we'll meet later in this chapter (to start independent programs on Windows and Unix); we will further explore such process-related topics in more detail later in this chapter. We'll also discuss additional process topics in later chapters of this book. For instance, forks are revisited in Chapter 13 to deal with servers and their *zombies*—i.e., dead processes lurking in system tables after their demise.

Threads

Threads are another way to start activities running at the same time. In short, they run a function call in parallel with the rest of the program. Threads are sometimes called "lightweight processes," because they run in parallel like forked processes, but all of them run within the same single process. While processes are commonly used to start independent programs, threads are commonly used for tasks such as non-blocking input calls and long-running tasks in a GUI. They also provide a natural model for algorithms that can be expressed as independently running tasks. For applications that can benefit from parallel processing, some developers consider threads to offer a number of advantages:

Performance

Because all threads run within the same process, they don't generally incur a big startup cost to copy the process itself. The costs of both copying forked processes and running threads can vary per platform, but threads are usually considered less expensive in terms of performance overhead.

Simplicity

Threads can be noticeably simpler to program too, especially when some of the more complex aspects of processes enter the picture (e.g., process exits, communication schemes, and zombie processes, covered in Chapter 13).

Shared global memory

Also because threads run in a single process, every thread shares the same global memory space of the process. This provides a natural and easy way for threads to communicate—by fetching and setting data in global memory. To the Python programmer, this means that both global scope (module-level) variables and program-wide interpreter components are shared among all threads in a program; if one thread assigns a global variable, its new value will be seen by other threads. Some care must be taken to control access to shared global objects, but to some they seem generally simpler to use than the process communication tools necessary for forked processes, which we'll meet later in this chapter and book (e.g., pipes, streams, signals, sockets, etc.). Like much in programming, this is not a universally shared view, however, so you'll have to weigh the difference for your programs and platforms yourself.

Portability

Perhaps most important is the fact that threads are more portable than forked processes. At this writing, os.fork is not supported by the standard version of Python on Windows, but threads are. If you want to run parallel tasks portably in a Python script today and you are unwilling or unable to install a Unix-like library such as Cygwin on Windows, threads may be your best bet. Python's thread tools automatically account for any platform-specific thread differences, and they provide a consistent interface across all operating systems.

So what's the catch? There are three potential downsides you should be aware of before you start spinning your threads:

Function calls versus programs

First of all, threads are not a way—at least, not a direct way—to start up another *program*. Rather, threads are designed to run a call to a *function* in parallel with the rest of the program. As we saw in the prior section, by contrast, forked processes can either call a function or start a new program. The thread function can run scripts with the execfile function and can start programs with tools such as os.popen; but fundamentally, they are in-program functions.

In practice, this is usually not a limitation. For many applications, parallel functions are sufficiently powerful. For instance, if you want to implement nonblocking input and output and avoid blocking a GUI with long-running tasks, threads do the job; simply spawn a thread to run a function that performs the potentially long-running task. The rest of the program will continue independently.

Thread synchronization and queues

Secondly, the fact that threads share global memory and resources is both good news and bad news—it provides a communication mechanism, but we have to be careful to synchronize a variety of operations. Even operations such as printing are a potential conflict since there is only one sys.stdout per process, which is shared by all threads.

Luckily, the Python Queue module, described in this section, makes this simple: realistic threaded programs are usually structured as one or more producer threads that add data to a queue, along with one or more consumer threads that take the data off the queue and process it. In a typical threaded GUI, for example, producers may download or compute data and place it on the queue; the consumer—the main GUI thread—checks the queue for data periodically with a timer event and displays it in the GUI when it arrives.

The global interpreter lock (GIL)

Finally, as we'll learn in more detail later in this section, Python's implementation of threads means that only one thread is ever running in the Python virtual machine at any point in time. Python threads are true operating system threads, but all threads must acquire a single shared lock when they are ready to run, and each thread may be swapped out after running for a set number of virtual machine instructions.

Because of this structure, Python threads cannot today be distributed across multiple CPUs on a multi-CPU computer. To leverage more than one CPU, you'll simply need to use process forking, not threads (the amount and complexity of code required for both are roughly the same). Moreover, long-running tasks implemented as C extensions can run truly independently if they release the GIL to allow Python threads to run while their task is in progress. Python code, however, cannot truly overlap in time.

The advantage of Python's implementation of threads is performance—when it was attempted, making the virtual machine truly thread safe reportedly slowed all programs by a factor of two on Windows and by an even larger factor on Linux. Even nonthreaded programs ran at half speed.

Despite what you may think after reading the last few introductory paragraphs, threads are remarkably easy to use in Python. In fact, when a program is started it is already running a thread, usually called the "main thread" of the process. To start new, independent threads of execution within a process, we use either the Python thread module to run a function call in a spawned thread or the Python threading module to manage threads with high-level objects. Both modules also provide tools for synchronizing access to shared objects with locks.

The thread Module

Since the basic thread module is a bit simpler than the more advanced threading module covered later in this section, let's look at some of its interfaces first. This module provides a *portable* interface to whatever threading system is available in your platform: its interfaces work the same on Windows, Solaris, SGI, and any system with an installed pthreads POSIX threads implementation (including Linux). Python scripts that use the Python thread module work on all of these platforms without changing their source code.

Let's start off by experimenting with a script that demonstrates the main thread interfaces. The script in Example 5-5 spawns threads until you reply with a "q" at the console; it's similar in spirit to (and a bit simpler than) the script in Example 5-1, but it goes parallel with threads, not with forks.

Example 5-5. PP3E\System\Threads\thread1.py

```
# spawn threads until you type 'q'

import thread

def child(tid):
    print 'Hello from thread', tid

def parent():
    i = 0
    while 1:
```

Example 5-5. PP3E\System\Threads\thread1.py (continued)

```
    i = i+1
    thread.start_new(child, (i,))
    if raw_input() == 'q': break

parent()
```

This script really contains only two thread-specific lines: the import of the `thread` module and the thread creation call. To start a thread, we simply call the `thread.start_new` function, no matter what platform we're programming on.* This call takes a function object and an arguments tuple and starts a new thread to execute a call to the passed function with the passed arguments. It's almost like the built-in `apply` function and newer `function(*args)` call syntax (and, like `apply`, it also accepts an optional keyword arguments dictionary), but in this case, the function call begins running in parallel with the rest of the program.

Operationally speaking, the `thread.start_new` call itself returns immediately with no useful value, and the thread it spawns silently exits when the function being run returns (the return value of the threaded function call is simply ignored). Moreover, if a function run in a thread raises an uncaught exception, a stack trace is printed and the thread exits, but the rest of the program continues.

In practice, though, it's almost trivial to use threads in a Python script. Let's run this program to launch a few threads; we can run it on both Linux and Windows this time, because threads are more portable than process forks:

```
C:\...\PP3E\System\Threads>python thread1.py
Hello from thread 1

Hello from thread 2

Hello from thread 3

Hello from thread 4
q
```

Each message here is printed from a new thread, which exits almost as soon as it is started. To really understand the power of threads running in parallel, we have to do something more long-lived in our threads. The good news is that threads are both easy and fun to play with in Python. Let's mutate the fork-count program of the prior section to use threads. The script in Example 5-6 starts 10 copies of its counter running in parallel threads.

---

* This call is also available as `thread.start_new_thread` for historical reasons. It's possible that one of the two names for the same function may become deprecated in future Python releases, but both appear in this text's examples. As of Python 2.4, both names are still available.

Example 5-6. PP3E\System\Threads\thread-count.py

```
##########################################################################
# thread basics: start 10 copies of a function running in parallel;
# uses time.sleep so that the main thread doesn't die too early--this
# kills all other threads on both Windows and Linux; stdout is shared:
# thread outputs may be intermixed in this version occasionally.
##########################################################################

import thread, time

def counter(myId, count):                    # this function runs in threads
    for i in range(count):
        #time.sleep(1)
        print '[%s] => %s' % (myId, i)

for i in range(10):                          # spawn 10 threads
    thread.start_new(counter, (i, 3))        # each thread loops 3 times

time.sleep(4)
print 'Main thread exiting.'                 # don't exit too early
```

Each parallel copy of the counter function simply counts from zero up to two here. When run on Windows, all 10 threads run at the same time, so their output is intermixed on the standard output stream:

```
C:\...\PP3E\System\Threads>python thread-count.py
...some lines deleted...
[5] => 0
[6] => 0
[7] => 0
[8] => 0
[9] => 0
[3] => 1
[4] => 1
[1] => 0
[5] => 1
[6] => 1
[7] => 1
[8] => 1
[9] => 1
[3] => 2
[4] => 2
[1] => 1
[5] => 2
[6] => 2
[7] => 2
[8] => 2
[9] => 2
[1] => 2
Main thread exiting.
```

In fact, the output of these threads is mixed arbitrarily, at least on Windows. It may even be in a *different* order each time you run this script. Because all 10 threads run as independent entities, the exact ordering of their overlap in time depends on nearly random system state at large at the time they are run.

If you care to make this output a bit more coherent, uncomment the time.sleep(1) call in the counter function (that is, remove the # before it) and rerun the script. If you do, each of the 10 threads now pauses for one second before printing its current count value. Because of the pause, all threads check in at the same time with the same count; you'll actually have a one-second delay before each batch of 10 output lines appears:

```
C:\...\PP3E\System\Threads>python thread-count.py
...some lines deleted...
[7] => 0
[6] => 0                                      pause...
[0] => 1
[1] => 1
[2] => 1
[3] => 1
[5] => 1
[7] => 1
[8] => 1
[9] => 1
[4] => 1
[6] => 1                                      pause...
[0] => 2
[1] => 2
[2] => 2
[3] => 2
[5] => 2
[9] => 2
[7] => 2
[6] => 2
[8] => 2
[4] => 2
Main thread exiting.
```

Even with the sleep synchronization active, though, there's no telling in what order the threads will print their current count. It's random on purpose. The whole point of starting threads is to get work done independently, in parallel.

Notice that this script sleeps for four seconds at the end. It turns out that, at least on my Windows and Linux installs, the main thread cannot exit while any spawned threads are running; if it does, all spawned threads are immediately terminated. Without the sleep here, the spawned threads would die almost immediately after they are started. This may seem ad hoc, but it isn't required on all platforms, and programs are usually structured such that the main thread naturally lives as long as the threads it starts. For instance, a user interface may start an FTP download running in a thread, but the download lives a much shorter life than the user interface itself. Later in this section, we'll see different ways to avoid this sleep using global flags, and we will also meet a "join" utility in a different module that lets us wait for spawned threads to finish explicitly.

Synchronizing access to global objects

One of the nice things about threads is that they automatically come with a cross-task communications mechanism: shared global memory. For instance, because every thread runs in the same process, if one Python thread changes a global variable, the change can be seen by every other thread in the process, main or child. This serves as a simple way for a program's threads to pass information—exit flags, result objects, event indicators, and so on—back and forth to each other.

The downside to this scheme is that our threads must sometimes be careful to avoid changing global objects at the same time. If two threads change an object at once, it's not impossible that one of the two changes will be lost (or worse, will corrupt the state of the shared object completely). The extent to which this becomes an issue varies per application, and sometimes it isn't an issue at all.

But even things that aren't obviously at risk may be at risk. Files and streams, for example, are shared by all threads in a program; if multiple threads write to one stream at the same time, the stream might wind up with interleaved, garbled data. Here's an example: if you edit Example 5-6, comment out the sleep call in counter, and increase the per-thread count parameter from 3 to 100, you might occasionally see the same strange results on Windows that I did:

```
C:\...\PP3E\System\Threads\>python thread-count.py | more
...more deleted...
[5] => 14
[7] => 14
[9] => 14
[3] => 15
[5] => 15
[7] => 15
[9] => 15
[3] => 16 [5] => 16 [7] => 16 [9] => 16


[3] => 17
[5] => 17
[7] => 17
[9] => 17
...more deleted...
```

Because all 10 threads are trying to write to stdout at the same time, once in a while the output of more than one thread winds up on the same line. Such an oddity in this artificial script isn't exactly going to crash the Mars Lander, but it's indicative of the sorts of clashes in time that can occur when our programs go parallel. To be robust, thread programs need to control access to shared global items like this such that only one thread uses it at once.[*]

---

[*] If it's not clear why this should be so, watch for a more detailed explanation of this phenomenon in the section "The Global Interpreter Lock and Threads" near the end of this discussion of threads.

Luckily, Python's thread module comes with its own easy-to-use tools for synchronizing access to shared objects among threads. These tools are based on the concept of a *lock*—to change a shared object, threads *acquire* a lock, make their changes, and then *release* the lock for other threads to grab. Lock objects are allocated and processed with simple and portable calls in the thread module and are automatically mapped to thread locking mechanisms on the underlying platform.

For instance, in Example 5-7, a lock object created by thread.allocate_lock is acquired and released by each thread around the print statement that writes to the shared standard output stream.

Example 5-7. PP3E\System\Threads\thread-count-mutex.py

```
##############################################################
# synchronize access to stdout: because it is shared global,
# thread outputs may be intermixed if not synchronized
##############################################################

import thread, time

def counter(myId, count):
    for i in range(count):
        mutex.acquire()
        #time.sleep(1)
        print '[%s] => %s' % (myId, i)
        mutex.release()

mutex = thread.allocate_lock()
for i in range(10):
    thread.start_new_thread(counter, (i, 3))

time.sleep(6)
print 'Main thread exiting.'
```

Python guarantees that only one thread can acquire a lock at any given time; all other threads that request the lock are blocked until a release call makes it available for acquisition. The net effect of the additional lock calls in this script is that no two threads will ever execute a print statement at the same point in time; the lock ensures mutually exclusive access to the stdout stream. Hence, the output of this script is the same as the original *thread_count.py* except that standard output text is never munged by overlapping prints.

Incidentally, uncommenting the time.sleep call in this version's counter function makes each output line show up one second apart. Because the sleep occurs while a thread holds the mutex lock, all other threads are blocked while the lock holder sleeps, even though time.sleep itself does not block other threads. One thread grabs the mutex lock, sleeps one second, and prints; another thread grabs, sleeps, and prints, and so on. Given 10 threads counting up to three, the program as a whole takes 30 seconds (10 x 3) to finish, with one line appearing per second. Of course, that assumes that the main thread sleeps at least that long too; to see how to remove this assumption, we need to move on to the next section.

Waiting for spawned thread exits

Thread module locks are surprisingly useful. They can form the basis of higher-level synchronization paradigms (e.g., semaphores) and can be used as general thread communication devices.* For example, Example 5-8 uses a global list of locks to know when all child threads have finished.

Example 5-8. PP3E\System\Threads\thread-count-wait1.py

```
###################################################
# uses mutexes to know when threads are done
# in parent/main thread, instead of time.sleep;
# lock stdout to avoid multiple prints on 1 line;
###################################################

import thread

def counter(myId, count):
    for i in range(count):
        stdoutmutex.acquire( )
        print '[%s] => %s' % (myId, i)
        stdoutmutex.release( )
    exitmutexes[myId].acquire( )     # signal main thread

stdoutmutex = thread.allocate_lock( )
exitmutexes = []
for i in range(10):
    exitmutexes.append(thread.allocate_lock( ))
    thread.start_new(counter, (i, 100))

for mutex in exitmutexes:
    while not mutex.locked( ): pass
print 'Main thread exiting.'
```

A lock's locked method can be used to check its state. To make this work, the main thread makes one lock per child and tacks them onto a global exitmutexes list (remember, the threaded function shares global scope with the main thread). On exit, each thread acquires its lock on the list, and the main thread simply watches for all locks to be acquired. This is much more accurate than naïvely sleeping while child threads run in hopes that all will have exited after the sleep.

---

* They cannot, however, be used to directly synchronize processes. Since processes are more independent, they usually require locking mechanisms that are more long-lived and external to programs. Both the os.open call with an open flag of O_EXCL, as well as the less portable fcntl.flock call, allow scripts to lock and unlock files and so are ideal as cross-process locking tools.

But wait, it gets even simpler: since threads share global memory anyhow, we can achieve the same effect with a simple global list of *integers*, not locks. In Example 5-9, the module's namespace (scope) is shared by top-level code and the threaded function, as before. exitmutexes refers to the same list object in the main thread and all threads it spawns. Because of that, changes made in a thread are still noticed in the main thread without resorting to extra locks.

Example 5-9. PP3E\System\Threads\thread-count-wait2.py

```
#####################################################
# uses simple shared global data (not mutexes) to
# know when threads are done in parent/main thread;
#####################################################

import thread
stdoutmutex = thread.allocate_lock()
exitmutexes = [0] * 10

def counter(myId, count):
    for i in range(count):
        stdoutmutex.acquire()
        print '[%s] => %s' % (myId, i)
        stdoutmutex.release()
    exitmutexes[myId] = 1  # signal main thread

for i in range(10):
    thread.start_new(counter, (i, 100))

while 0 in exitmutexes: pass
print 'Main thread exiting.'
```

The main threads of both of the last two scripts fall into busy-wait loops at the end, which might become significant performance drains in tight applications. If so, simply add a time.sleep call in the wait loops to insert a pause between end tests and to free up the CPU for other tasks. Even threads must be good citizens.

Both of the last two counting thread scripts produce roughly the same output as the original *thread_count.py*, albeit without stdout corruption and with different random ordering of output lines. The main difference is that the main thread exits immediately after (and no sooner than!) the spawned child threads:

```
C:\...\PP3E\System\Threads>python thread-count-wait2.py
...more deleted...
[2] => 98
[6] => 97
[0] => 99
[7] => 97
[3] => 98
[8] => 97
[9] => 97
[1] => 99
[4] => 98
```

```
[5] => 98
[2] => 99
[6] => 98
[7] => 98
[3] => 99
[8] => 98
[9] => 98
[4] => 99
[5] => 99
[6] => 99
[7] => 99
[8] => 99
[9] => 99
Main thread exiting.
```

Of course, threads are for much more than counting. We'll put shared global data to more practical use in a later chapter, where it will serve as completion signals from child processing threads transferring data over a network to a main thread controlling a Tkinter GUI user interface display (see Chapter 14). Shared global data among threads also turns out to be the basis of queues, which are discussed later in this section; each thread gets or puts data using the same queue object.

The threading Module

The Python standard library comes with two thread modules—thread, the basic lower-level interface illustrated thus far, and threading, a higher-level interface based on objects. The threading module internally uses the thread module to implement objects that represent threads and common synchronization tools. It is loosely based on a subset of the Java language's threading model, but it differs in ways that only Java programmers would notice.[*] Example 5-10 morphs our counting threads example one last time to demonstrate this new module's interfaces.

Example 5-10. PP3E\System\Threads\thread-classes.py

```
#############################################################################
# uses higher-level Java-like threading module object join method (not
# mutexes or shared global vars) to know when threads are done in main
# parent thread; see library manual for more details on threading;
#############################################################################

import threading

class mythread(threading.Thread):              # subclass Thread object
    def __init__(self, myId, count):
        self.myId  = myId
```

---

[*] But in case this means you, Python's lock and condition variables are distinct objects, not something inherent in all objects, and Python's Thread class doesn't have all the features of Java's. See Python's library manual for further details.

Example 5-10. PP3E\System\Threads\thread-classes.py (continued)

```
        self.count = count
        threading.Thread.__init__(self)
    def run(self):                       # run provides thread logic
        for i in range(self.count):      # still sync stdout access
            stdoutmutex.acquire()
            print '[%s] => %s' % (self.myId, i)
            stdoutmutex.release()

stdoutmutex = threading.Lock()           # same as thread.allocate_lock()
threads = []
for i in range(10):
    thread = mythread(i, 100)            # make/start 10 threads
    thread.start()                       # start run method in a thread
    threads.append(thread)

for thread in threads:
    thread.join()                        # wait for thread exits
print 'Main thread exiting.'
```

The output of this script is the same as that shown for its ancestors earlier (again, randomly distributed). Using the threading module is largely a matter of specializing classes. Threads in this module are implemented with a Thread object, a Python class which we customize per application by providing a run method that defines the thread's action. For example, this script subclasses Thread with its own mythread class; the run method will be executed by the Thread framework in a new thread when we make a mythread and call its start method.

In other words, this script simply provides methods expected by the Thread framework. The advantage of taking this more coding-intensive route is that we get a set of additional thread-related tools from the framework "for free." The Thread.join method used near the end of this script, for instance, waits until the thread exits (by default); we can use this method to prevent the main thread from exiting too early rather than using the time.sleep calls and global locks and variables we relied on in earlier threading examples.

The example script also uses threading.Lock to synchronize stream access (though this name is just a synonym for thread.allocate_lock in the current implementation). The Thread class can also be used to start a simple function without subclassing, though this call form is not noticeably simpler than the basic thread module. For example, the following four code snippets spawn the same sort of thread:

```
# subclass with state
class mythread(threading.Thread):
    def __init__(self, myId, count):
        self.i = i
        threading.Thread.__init__(self)
    def run(self):
        consumer(self.i)
mythread().start()
```

```
# pass action in
thread = threading.Thread(target=(lambda: consumer(i)))
thread.start( )

# same but no lambda wrapper for state
Threading.Thread(target=consumer, args=(i,)).start( )

# basic thread module
thread.start_new_thread(consumer, (i,))
```

Besides Thread and Lock, the threading module also includes higher-level objects for synchronizing access to shared items (e.g., Semaphore, Condition, Event)—many more than we have space to cover here; see the library manual for details.[*]

For more examples of threads and forks in general, see the following sections of this chapter as well as the examples in the GUI and network scripting parts of this book. We will thread GUIs, for instance, to avoid blocking them, and we will thread and fork network servers to avoid denying service to clients.

The Queue Module

You can synchronize your threads' access to shared resources with locks, but you usually don't have to. As mentioned in our introduction to threads, realistically scaled, threaded programs are often structured as a set of producer and consumer threads, which communicate by placing data on, and taking it off of, a shared queue.

The Python Queue module implements this storage device. It provides a standard queue data structure (a fifo, a first-in first-out list, in which items are added on one end and removed from the other), which may contain any type of Python object. However, the queue object is automatically controlled with thread lock acquire and release calls, such that only one thread can modify the queue at any given point in time. Because of this, programs that use a queue for their cross-thread communication will be thread-safe and can usually avoid dealing with locks of their own.

Like the other tools in Python's threading arsenal, queues are surprisingly simple to use. The script in Example 5-11, for instance, spawns two consumer threads that watch for data to appear on the shared queue and four producer threads that place data on the queue periodically after a sleep interval (each of their sleep durations differs to simulate a real, long-running task). Because the queue is assigned to a global variable, it is shared by all of the spawned threads; all of them run in the same process and in the same global scope.

---

[*] Some Python users would probably recommend that you use threading rather than thread in general. Unless you need the more powerful tools in threading, though, the choice is arbitrary. The basic thread module does not impose OOP, and as you can see from the four coding alternatives in this section, it can be simpler. The most general Python rule of thumb applies here as always: *keep it simple, unless it has to be complex*.

Example 5-11. PP3E\System\Threads\xd5 ueuetest.py

```
###################################################################
# producer and consumer threads communicating with a shared queue
###################################################################

numconsumers = 2                    # how many consumers to start
numproducers = 4                    # how many producers to start
nummessages  = 4                    # messages per producer to put

import thread, Queue, time
safeprint = thread.allocate_lock()   # else prints may overlap
dataQueue = Queue.Queue()            # shared global. infinite size

def producer(idnum):
    for msgnum in range(nummessages):
        time.sleep(idnum)
        dataQueue.put('producer %d:%d' % (idnum, msgnum))

def consumer(idnum):
    while 1:
        time.sleep(0.1)
        try:
            data = dataQueue.get(block=False)
        except Queue.Empty:
            pass
        else:
            safeprint.acquire()
            print 'consumer', idnum, 'got =>', data
            safeprint.release()

if __name__ == '__main__':
    for i in range(numconsumers):
        thread.start_new_thread(consumer, (i,))
    for i in range(numproducers):
        thread.start_new_thread(producer, (i,))
    time.sleep(((numproducers-1) * nummessages) + 1)
```

Following is the output of Example 5-11 when run on my Windows XP machine.
Notice that even though the queue automatically coordinates the communication of
data between the threads, this script still must use a lock to manually synchronize
access to the standard output stream. As in prior examples, if the safeprint lock is
not used, the printed lines from one consumer may be intermixed with those of
another. It is not impossible that a consumer may be paused in the middle of a print
operation (in fact, this occurs regularly on my test machine in some test scenarios;
try it on yours to see for yourself).

```
C:\...\PP3E\System\Threads >queuetest.py
consumer 0 got => producer 0:0
consumer 1 got => producer 0:1
consumer 0 got => producer 0:2
consumer 1 got => producer 0:3
consumer 0 got => producer 1:0
```

```
consumer 1 got => producer 1:1
consumer 0 got => producer 2:0
consumer 1 got => producer 1:2
consumer 0 got => producer 3:0
consumer 0 got => producer 1:3
consumer 1 got => producer 2:1
consumer 1 got => producer 2:2
consumer 0 got => producer 3:1
consumer 1 got => producer 2:3
consumer 0 got => producer 3:2
consumer 1 got => producer 3:3
```

Try adjusting the parameters at the top of this script to experiment with different scenarios. A single consumer, for instance, would simulate a GUI's main thread; the output of a single-consumer run is given here. Producers still add to the queue in fairly random fashion, because threads run in parallel with each other and with the consumer.

```
C:\...\PP3E\System\Threads >queuetest.py
consumer 0 got => producer 0:0
consumer 0 got => producer 0:1
consumer 0 got => producer 0:2
consumer 0 got => producer 0:3
consumer 0 got => producer 1:0
consumer 0 got => producer 2:0
consumer 0 got => producer 1:1
consumer 0 got => producer 1:2
consumer 0 got => producer 3:0
consumer 0 got => producer 2:1
consumer 0 got => producer 1:3
consumer 0 got => producer 2:2
consumer 0 got => producer 3:1
consumer 0 got => producer 2:3
consumer 0 got => producer 3:2
consumer 0 got => producer 3:3
```

Queues may be fixed or infinite in size, and get and put calls may or may not block; see the Python library manual for more details on queue interface options.

The Global Interpreter Lock and Threads

Strictly speaking, Python currently uses a *global interpreter lock* (GIL) mechanism, which guarantees that at most, one thread is running code within the Python interpreter at any given point in time. We introduced the GIL at the start of the "Threads" section. In addition, to make sure that each thread gets a chance to run, the interpreter automatically switches its attention between threads at regular intervals (by releasing and acquiring the lock after a number of bytecode instructions) as well as at the start of long-running operations (e.g., on file input/output requests).

This scheme avoids problems that could arise if multiple threads were to update Python system data at the same time. For instance, if two threads were allowed to

GUIs and Threads

We will return to threads and queues and see additional thread and queue examples when we study GUIs in a later part of the book. The PyMailGUI example in Chapter 15, for instance, will make extensive use of thread tools introduced here and developed further in Chapter 11. Although we can't get into code at this point, threads are usually an integral part of most nontrivial GUIs. In fact, many GUIs are a combination of threads, a queue, and a timer-based loop.

Here's why. In the context of a GUI, any operation that can block or take a long time to complete must be spawned off in a thread so that the GUI (the main thread) remains active. Because only the main thread can generally update the display, GUI programs typically take the form of a main GUI thread and one or more long-running producer threads—one for each long-running task being performed. To synchronize their points of interface, all of the threads share data on a global queue. More specifically:

- The *main thread* handles all GUI updates and runs a timer-based loop that wakes up periodically to check for new data on the queue to be displayed on-screen. The `after( )` Tkinter method can be used to schedule queue-check events. All GUI updates occur only in this main thread.

- The *child threads* don't do anything GUI related. They just produce data and put it on the queue to be picked up by the main thread. Alternatively, child threads can place a callback function on the queue, to be picked up and run by the main thread. It's not generally sufficient, however, to simply pass in a GUI update callback function from the main thread to the child thread and run it from there. The function in shared memory will still be executed in the child thread.

Since threads are much more responsive than a timer event loop in the GUI, this scheme both avoids blocking the GUI (producer threads run in parallel with the GUI) and avoids missing incoming events (producer threads run independent of the GUI event loop). The main GUI thread will display the queued results as quickly as it can, in the context of a slower GUI event loop. See also this chapter's discussion of `sys.setcheckinterval` for tweaking the responsiveness of spawned producer threads.

---

simultaneously change an object's reference count, the result may be unpredictable. This scheme can also have subtle consequences. In this chapter's threading examples, for instance, the `stdout` stream is likely corrupted only because each thread's call to write text is a long-running operation that triggers a thread switch within the interpreter. Other threads are then allowed to run and make write requests while a prior write is in progress.

Moreover, even though the GIL prevents more than one Python thread from running at the same time, it is not enough to ensure thread safety in general, and it does not address higher-level synchronization issues at all. For example, in the case that more than one thread might attempt to *update* the same variable at the same time, the threads should generally be given exclusive access to the object with locks. Otherwise, it's not impossible that thread switches will occur in the middle of an update statement's bytecode. Consider this code:

```
import thread, time
count = 0

def adder():
    global count
    count = count + 1     # concurrently update a shared global
    count = count + 1     # thread swapped out in the middle of this

for i in range(100):
    thread.start_new(adder, ())   # start 100 update threads

time.sleep(5)
print count
```

As is, this code fails on Windows due to the way its threads are interleaved (you may get a different result each time, but you usually won't get 200), but it works if lock acquire/release calls are inserted around the addition statements. The reason for the failure is subtle, but eventually, one thread will fetch the current value of count and be swapped out of memory before incrementing it. When this thread resumes, it will be updating a potentially *old* value of count, which other threads may have subsequently changed. All the work done since the thread was suspended will be lost.

Locks are not strictly required for all shared object access, especially if a single thread updates an object inspected by other threads. As a rule of thumb, though, you should generally use locks to synchronize threads whenever update rendezvous are possible instead of relying on the current thread implementation. The following version of the prior code works as expected:

```
import thread, time
count = 0

def adder():
    global count
    lock.acquire()        # only one thread running this at a time
    count = count + 1     # concurrently update a shared global
    count = count + 1
    lock.release()

lock = thread.allocate_lock()
for i in range(100):
    thread.start_new(adder, ())   # start 100 update threads

time.sleep(5)
print count                       # prints 200
```

The thread switch interval

Interestingly, the preceding example also works without locks if the thread-switch check interval is made high enough to allow each thread to finish without being swapped out. The sys.setcheckinterval(N) call sets the frequency with which the interpreter checks for things like thread switches and signal handlers.

This interval defaults to 100, the number of bytecode instructions before a switch. It does not need to be reset for most programs, but it can be used to tune thread performance. Setting higher values means switches happen less often: threads incur less overhead but they are less responsive to events. Setting lower values makes threads more responsive to events but increases thread switch overhead.

Atomic operations

Note that because of the way Python uses the GIL to synchronize threads' access to the virtual machine, whole statements are not generally thread-safe, but each bytecode instruction is. Aa thread will never be suspended in the middle of a bytecode's operation, and generally won't be during the execution of the C code that the bytecode invokes (though some long-running C code tasks release the GIL and allow the thread to be suspended—in fact, this is likely why print statements' output may be intermixed).

Because of this bytecode indivisibility, some Python language operations are thread-safe—also called *atomic*, because they run without interruption—and do not require the use of locks or queues to avoid concurrent update issues. As of this writing, for instance, the following operations are thread-safe (in this listing L, L1, and L2 are lists; D, D1, and D2 are dictionaries; x and y are objects; and i and j are integers):

```
L.append(x)
L1.extend(L2)
x = L[i]
x = L.pop( )
L1[i:j] = L2
L.sort( )
x = y
x.field = y
D[x] = y
D1.update(D2)
D.keys( )
```

The following are not thread-safe. Relying on these rules is a bit of a gamble, though, because they require a deep understanding of Python internals and may vary per release. As a rule of thumb, it may be easier to use locks for all access to global and shared objects than to try to remember which types of access may or may not be safe across multiple threads.

```
i = i+1
L.append(L[-1])
L[i] = L[j]
D[x] = D[x] + 1
```

C API thread considerations

Finally, if you plan to mix Python with C, also see the thread interfaces described in the Python/C API standard manual. In threaded programs, C extensions must release and reacquire the GIL around long-running operations to let other Python threads run during the wait. Specifically, the long-running C extension function should release the lock on entry and reacquire it on exit when resuming Python code.

Also note that even though Python threads cannot truly overlap in time due to the GIL synchronization, C-coded threads can; any number may be running in parallel, as long as they do work outside the scope of the Python virtual machine. In fact, C threads may overlap both with other C threads and with Python language threads run in the virtual machine. Because of this, splitting code off to C libraries is one way that Python applications can still take advantage of multi-CPU machines.

Still, it will usually be easier to leverage such machines by simply writing Python programs that fork processes instead of starting threads. The complexity of process and thread code is similar. For more on C extensions and their threading requirements, see Chapter 22. There, we'll meet a pair of macros that can be used to wrap long-running operations in C coded extensions and that allow other Python threads to run in parallel.

Program Exits

As we've seen, unlike C, there is no "main" function in Python. When we run a program, we simply execute all of the code in the top-level file, from top to bottom (i.e., in the filename we listed in the command line, clicked in a file explorer, and so on). Scripts normally exit when Python falls off the end of the file, but we may also call for program exit explicitly with the built-in sys.exit function:

```
>>> sys.exit(N)          # else exits on end of script, with status N
```

Interestingly, this call really just raises the built-in SystemExit exception. Because of this, we can catch it as usual to intercept early exits and perform cleanup activities; if uncaught, the interpreter exits as usual. For instance:

```
C:\...\PP3E\System>python
>>> import sys
>>> try:
...     sys.exit()             # see also: os._exit, Tk().quit()
... except SystemExit:
...     print 'ignoring exit'
...
ignoring exit
>>>
```

In fact, explicitly raising the built-in SystemExit exception with a Python raise statement is equivalent to calling sys.exit. More realistically, a try block would catch the exit exception raised elsewhere in a program; the script in Example 5-12 exits from within a processing function.

Example 5-12. PP3E\System\Exits\testexit_sys.py

```
def later( ):
    import sys
    print 'Bye sys world'
    sys.exit(42)
    print 'Never reached'

if __name__ == '__main__': later( )
```

Running this program as a script causes it to exit before the interpreter falls off the end of the file. But because sys.exit raises a Python exception, importers of its function can trap and override its exit exception, or specify a finally cleanup block to be run during program exit processing:

```
C:\...\PP3E\System\Exits>python testexit_sys.py
Bye sys world

C:\...\PP3E\System\Exits>python
>>> from testexit_sys import later
>>> try:
...     later( )
... except SystemExit:
...     print 'Ignored...'
...
Bye sys world
Ignored...
>>> try:
...     later( )
... finally:
...     print 'Cleanup'
...
Bye sys world
Cleanup

C:\...\PP3E\System\Exits>
```

os Module Exits

It's possible to exit Python in other ways, too. For instance, within a forked child process on Unix, we typically call the os._exit function rather than sys.exit, threads may exit with a thread.exit call, and Tkinter GUI applications often end by calling something named Tk().quit( ). We'll meet the Tkinter module later in this book, but os and thread exits merit a look here. When os._exit is called, the calling process exits immediately instead of raising an exception that could be trapped and ignored (see Example 5-13).

Example 5-13. PP3E\System\Exits\testexit_os.py

```
def outahere( ):
    import os
    print 'Bye os world'
    os._exit(99)
    print 'Never reached'

if __name__ == '__main__': outahere( )
```

Unlike sys.exit, os._exit is immune to both try/except and try/finally interception:

```
C:\...\PP3E\System\Exits>python testexit_os.py
Bye os world

C:\...\PP3E\System\Exits>python
>>> from testexit_os import outahere
>>> try:
...     outahere( )
... except:
...     print 'Ignored'
...
Bye os world

C:\...\PP3E\System\Exits>python
>>> from testexit_os import outahere
>>> try:
...     outahere( )
... finally:
...     print 'Cleanup'
...
Bye os world
```

Exit Status Codes

Both the sys and os exit calls we just met accept an argument that denotes the exit status code of the process (it's optional in the sys call but required by os). After exit, this code may be interrogated in shells and by programs that ran the script as a child process. On Linux, for example, we ask for the "status" shell variable's value in order to fetch the last program's exit status; by convention, a nonzero status generally indicates that some sort of problem occurred.

```
[mark@toy]$ python testexit_sys.py
Bye sys world
[mark@toy]$ echo $status
42
[mark@toy]$ python testexit_os.py
Bye os world
[mark@toy]$ echo $status
99
```

In a chain of command-line programs, exit statuses could be checked along the way as a simple form of cross-program communication. We can also grab hold of the exit status of a program run by another script. When launching shell commands, it's provided as the return value of an os.system call and the return value of the close method of an os.popen object; when forking programs, the exit status is available through the os.wait and os.waitpid calls in a parent process. Let's look at the case of the shell commands first:

```
[mark@toy]$ python
>>> import os
>>> pipe = os.popen('python testexit_sys.py')
>>> pipe.read( )
'Bye sys world\012'
>>> stat = pipe.close( )                # returns exit code
>>> stat
10752
>>> hex(stat)
'0x2a00'
>>> stat >> 8
42

>>> pipe = os.popen('python testexit_os.py')
>>> stat = pipe.close( )
>>> stat, stat >> 8
(25344, 99)
```

When using os.popen, the exit status, for reasons we won't go into here, is actually packed into specific bit positions of the return value; it's really there, but we need to shift the result right by eight bits to see it. Commands run with os.system send their statuses back through the Python library call:

```
>>> import os
>>> for prog in ('testexit_sys.py', 'testexit_os.py'):
...     stat = os.system('python ' + prog)
...     print prog, stat, stat >> 8
...
Bye sys world
testexit_sys.py 10752 42
Bye os world
testexit_os.py 25344 99
```

Unlike when I wrote the previous edition of this book, exit status works on Windows now too, though it is not encoded in a bit mask as on Linux:

```
>>> import sys
>>> sys.platform
'win32'

>>> import os
>>> stat = os.system('python testexit_sys.py')
Bye sys world
>>> stat
42
```

```
>>> pipe = os.popen('python testexit_sys.py')
>>> print pipe.read( ),
Bye sys world
>>> stat = pipe.close( )
>>> stat
42

>>> os.system('python testexit_os.py')
Bye os world
99

>>> pipe = os.popen('python -u testexit_os.py')
>>> pipe.read(); pipe.close( )
'Bye os world\n'
99
```

Notice the last test in the preceding code. Here, we have to run the os exit script in unbuffered mode with the –u Python command-line flag. Otherwise, the text printed to the standard output stream will not be flushed from its buffer when os._exit is called in this case (by default, standard output is buffered). In practice, flushing buffers, if required, should probably be done in the exiting script itself. More on buffering when we discuss deadlocks later in this chapter.

```
>>> os.popen('python -u testexit_os.py').read( )
'Bye os world\n'
>>> os.popen('python testexit_os.py').read( )
''
```

Process Exit Status

Now, to learn how to get the exit status from forked processes, let's write a simple forking program: the script in Example 5-14 forks child processes and prints child process exit statuses returned by os.wait calls in the parent until a "q" is typed at the console.

Example 5-14. PP3E\System\Exits\testexit_fork.py

```python
############################################################
# fork child processes to watch exit status with os.wait;
# fork works on Linux but not Windows as of Python 1.5.2;
# note: spawned threads share globals, but each forked
# process has its own copy of them--exitstat always the
# same here but will vary if we start threads instead;
############################################################

import os
exitstat = 0

def child( ):                          # could os.exit a script here
    global exitstat                    # change this process's global
    exitstat = exitstat + 1            # exit status to parent's wait
    print 'Hello from child', os.getpid( ), exitstat
```

Example 5-14. PP3E\System\Exits\testexit_fork.py (continued)

```
    os._exit(exitstat)
    print 'never reached'

def parent():
    while 1:
        newpid = os.fork()                  # start a new copy of process
        if newpid == 0:                     # if in copy, run child logic
            child()                         # loop until 'q' console input
        else:
            pid, status = os.wait()
            print 'Parent got', pid, status, (status >> 8)
            if raw_input() == 'q': break

parent()
```

Running this program on Linux (remember, fork still doesn't work on Windows as I write the third edition of this book) produces the following results:

```
[mark@toy]$ python testexit_fork.py
Hello from child 723 1
Parent got 723 256 1

Hello from child 724 1
Parent got 724 256 1

Hello from child 725 1
Parent got 725 256 1
q
```

If you study this output closely, you'll notice that the exit status (the last number printed) is always the same—the number 1. Because forked processes begin life as *copies* of the process that created them, they also have copies of global memory. Because of that, each forked child gets and changes its own exitstat global variable without changing any other process's copy of this variable.

Thread Exits

In contrast, threads run in parallel within the *same* process and share global memory. Each thread in Example 5-15 changes the single shared global variable, exitstat.

Example 5-15. PP3E\System\Exits\testexit_thread.py

```
#############################################################
# spawn threads to watch shared global memory change;
# threads normally exit when the function they run returns,
# but thread.exit() can be called to exit calling thread;
# thread.exit is the same as sys.exit and raising SystemExit;
# threads communicate with possibly locked global vars;
#############################################################
```

Example 5-15. PP3E\System\Exits\testexit_thread.py (continued)

```
import thread
exitstat = 0

def child():
    global exitstat                        # process global names
    exitstat = exitstat + 1                # shared by all threads
    threadid = thread.get_ident()
    print 'Hello from child', threadid, exitstat
    thread.exit()
    print 'never reached'

def parent():
    while 1:
        thread.start_new_thread(child, ())
        if raw_input() == 'q': break

parent()
```

Here is this script in action on Linux; the global exitstat is changed by each thread, because threads share global memory within the process. In fact, this is often how threads communicate in general. Rather than exit status codes, threads assign module-level globals to signal conditions and use thread module locks and queues to synchronize access to shared globals if needed (this script normally should too if it ever does something more realistic, but for this simple demo, it forgoes locks by assuming threads won't overlap):

```
[mark@toy]$ /usr/bin/python testexit_thread.py
Hello from child 1026 1

Hello from child 2050 2

Hello from child 3074 3
q
```

Unlike forks, threads now run in the standard version of Python on Windows too. This program works the same there, but thread identifiers differ; they are arbitrary but unique among active threads and so may be used as dictionary keys to keep per-thread information:

```
C:\...\PP3E\System\Exits>python testexit_thread.py
Hello from child -587879 1

Hello from child -587879 2

Hello from child -587879 3
q
```

Speaking of exits, a thread normally exits silently when the function it runs returns, and the function return value is ignored. Optionally, the thread.exit function can be called to terminate the calling thread explicitly. This call works almost exactly like sys.exit (but takes no return status argument), and it works by raising a SystemExit exception in the calling thread. Because of that, a thread can also prematurely end by calling sys.exit or by directly raising SystemExit. Be sure not to call os._exit within a thread function, though—doing so hangs the entire process on my Linux system and kills every thread in the process on Windows!

When used well, exit status can be used to implement error detection and simple communication protocols in systems composed of command-line scripts. But having said that, I should underscore that most scripts do simply fall off the end of the source to exit, and most thread functions simply return; explicit exit calls are generally employed for exceptional conditions only.

Interprocess Communication

As we saw earlier, when scripts spawn *threads*—tasks that run in parallel within the program—they can naturally communicate by changing and inspecting shared global memory. As we also saw, some care must be taken to use locks to synchronize access to shared objects that can't be updated concurrently, but it's a fairly straightforward communication model.

Things aren't quite as simple when scripts start processes and programs. If we limit the kinds of communications that can happen between programs, many options are available, most of which we've already seen in this and the prior chapters. For example, the following can all be interpreted as cross-program communication devices:

- Command-line arguments
- Standard stream redirections
- Pipes generated by os.popen calls
- Program exit status codes
- Shell environment variables
- Simple files
- Sockets, shared memory, signals, named pipes, and so on

For instance, sending command-line options and writing to input streams lets us pass in program execution parameters; reading program output streams and exit codes gives us a way to grab a result. Because shell variable settings are inherited by spawned programs, they provide another way to pass context in. Pipes made by os.popen and simple files allow even more dynamic communication. Data can be sent between programs at arbitrary times, not only at program start and exit.

Beyond this set, there are other tools in the Python library for performing Inter-Process Communication (IPC). Some vary in portability, and all vary in complexity. For instance, in the Internet scripting part of this text we will meet the Python socket module, which lets us transfer data between programs running on the same computer as well as programs located on remote networked machines.

In this section, we introduce *pipes*—both anonymous and named—as well as *signals*, or cross-program event triggers. Other IPC tools are available to Python programmers (e.g., shared memory; see the mmap module) but are not covered here for lack of space; search the Python manuals and web site for more details on other IPC schemes if you're looking for something more specific.

Pipes

Pipes, another cross-program communication device, are made available in Python with the built-in os.pipe call. Pipes are unidirectional channels that work something like a shared memory buffer, but with an interface resembling a simple file on each of two ends. In typical use, one program writes data on one end of the pipe, and another reads that data on the other end. Each program sees only its end of the pipes and processes it using normal Python file calls.

Pipes are much more within the operating system, though. For instance, calls to read a pipe will normally block the caller until data becomes available (i.e., is sent by the program on the other end) instead of returning an end-of-file indicator. Because of such properties, pipes are also a way to synchronize the execution of independent programs.

Anonymous Pipe Basics

Pipes come in two flavors—*anonymous* and *named*. Named pipes (sometimes called fifos) are represented by a file on your computer. Anonymous pipes exist only within processes, though, and are typically used in conjunction with process *forks* as a way to link parent and spawned child processes within an application; parent and child converse over shared pipe file descriptors. Because named pipes are really external files, the communicating processes need not be related at all (in fact, they can be independently started programs).

Since they are more traditional, let's start with a look at anonymous pipes. To illustrate, the script in Example 5-16 uses the os.fork call to make a copy of the calling process as usual (we met forks earlier in this chapter). After forking, the original parent process and its child copy speak through the two ends of a pipe created with os.pipe prior to the fork. The os.pipe call returns a tuple of two *file descriptors*—the low-level file identifiers we met earlier—representing the input and output sides of the pipe. Because forked child processes get *copies* of their parents' file descriptors, writing to the pipe's output descriptor in the child sends data back to the parent on the pipe created before the child was spawned.

Example 5-16. PP3E\System\Processes\pipe1.py

```python
import os, time

def child(pipeout):
    zzz = 0
    while 1:
        time.sleep(zzz)                          # make parent wait
        os.write(pipeout, 'Spam %03d' % zzz)     # send to parent
        zzz = (zzz+1) % 5                         # goto 0 after 4

def parent():
    pipein, pipeout = os.pipe()                  # make 2-ended pipe
    if os.fork() == 0:                           # copy this process
        child(pipeout)                           # in copy, run child
    else:                                        # in parent, listen to pipe
        while 1:
            line = os.read(pipein, 32)           # blocks until data sent
            print 'Parent %d got "%s" at %s' % (os.getpid(), line, time.time())

parent()
```

If you run this program on Linux (pipe is now available on Windows, but fork is not), the parent process waits for the child to send data on the pipe each time it calls os.read. It's almost as if the child and parent act as client and server here—the parent starts the child and waits for it to initiate communication.[*] Just to tease, the child keeps the parent waiting one second longer between messages with time.sleep calls, until the delay has reached four seconds. When the zzz delay counter hits 005, it rolls back down to 000 and starts again:

```
[mark@toy]$ python pipe1.py
Parent 1292 got "Spam 000" at 968370008.322
Parent 1292 got "Spam 001" at 968370009.319
Parent 1292 got "Spam 002" at 968370011.319
Parent 1292 got "Spam 003" at 968370014.319
Parent 1292 got "Spam 004Spam 000" at 968370018.319
Parent 1292 got "Spam 001" at 968370019.319
Parent 1292 got "Spam 002" at 968370021.319
Parent 1292 got "Spam 003" at 968370024.319
Parent 1292 got "Spam 004Spam 000" at 968370028.319
Parent 1292 got "Spam 001" at 968370029.319
Parent 1292 got "Spam 002" at 968370031.319
Parent 1292 got "Spam 003" at 968370034.319
```

If you look closely, you'll see that when the child's delay counter hits 004, the parent ends up reading two messages from the pipe *at once*; the child wrote two distinct

---

[*] We will clarify the notions of "client" and "server" in the Internet programming part of this book. There, we'll communicate with *sockets* (which are very roughly like bidirectional pipes for networks), but the overall conversation model is similar. Named pipes (fifos), described later, are a better match to the client/server model because they can be accessed by arbitrary, unrelated processes (no forks are required). But as we'll see, the socket port model is generally used by most Internet scripting protocols.

messages, but they were close enough in time to be fetched as a single unit by the parent. Really, the parent blindly asks to read, at most, 32 bytes each time, but it gets back whatever text is available in the pipe (when it becomes available). To distinguish messages better, we can mandate a separator character in the pipe. An end-of-line makes this easy, because we can wrap the pipe descriptor in a file object with os.fdopen and rely on the file object's readline method to scan up through the next \n separator in the pipe. Example 5-17 implements this scheme.

Example 5-17. PP3E\System\Processes\pipe2.py

```
# same as pipe1.py, but wrap pipe input in stdio file object
# to read by line, and close unused pipe fds in both processes

import os, time

def child(pipeout):
    zzz = 0
    while 1:
        time.sleep(zzz)                        # make parent wait
        os.write(pipeout, 'Spam %03d\n' % zzz) # send to parent
        zzz = (zzz+1) % 5                       # roll to 0 at 5

def parent():
    pipein, pipeout = os.pipe()                # make 2-ended pipe
    if os.fork() == 0:                         # in child, write to pipe
        os.close(pipein)                       # close input side here
        child(pipeout)
    else:                                      # in parent, listen to pipe
        os.close(pipeout)                      # close output side here
        pipein = os.fdopen(pipein)             # make stdio input object
        while 1:
            line = pipein.readline()[:-1]      # blocks until data sent
            print 'Parent %d got "%s" at %s' % (os.getpid(), line, time.time())

parent()
```

This version has also been augmented to *close* the unused end of the pipe in each process (e.g., after the fork, the parent process closes its copy of the output side of the pipe written by the child); programs should close unused pipe ends in general. Running with this new version returns a single child message to the parent each time it reads from the pipe, because they are separated with markers when written:

```
[mark@toy]$ python pipe2.py
Parent 1296 got "Spam 000" at 968370066.162
Parent 1296 got "Spam 001" at 968370067.159
Parent 1296 got "Spam 002" at 968370069.159
Parent 1296 got "Spam 003" at 968370072.159
Parent 1296 got "Spam 004" at 968370076.159
Parent 1296 got "Spam 000" at 968370076.161
Parent 1296 got "Spam 001" at 968370077.159
Parent 1296 got "Spam 002" at 968370079.159
Parent 1296 got "Spam 003" at 968370082.159
```

```
Parent 1296 got "Spam 004" at 968370086.159
Parent 1296 got "Spam 000" at 968370086.161
Parent 1296 got "Spam 001" at 968370087.159
Parent 1296 got "Spam 002" at 968370089.159
```

Bidirectional IPC with Pipes

Pipes normally let data flow in only one direction—one side is input, one is output. What if you need your programs to talk back and forth, though? For example, one program might send another a request for information and then wait for that information to be sent back. A single pipe can't generally handle such bidirectional conversations, but two pipes can. One pipe can be used to pass requests to a program and another can be used to ship replies back to the requestor.[*]

The module in Example 5-18 demonstrates one way to apply this idea to link the input and output streams of two programs. Its spawn function forks a new child program and connects the input and output streams of the parent to the output and input streams of the child. That is:

- When the parent reads from its standard input, it is reading text sent to the child's standard output.

- When the parent writes to its standard output, it is sending data to the child's standard input.

The net effect is that the two independent programs communicate by speaking over their standard streams.

Example 5-18. PP3E\System\Processes\pipes.py

```
###########################################################################
# spawn a child process/program, connect my stdin/stdout to child process's
# stdout/stdin--my reads and writes map to output and input streams of the
# spawned program; much like os.popen2 plus parent stream redirection;
###########################################################################

import os, sys

def spawn(prog, *args):                    # pass progname, cmdline args
    stdinFd  = sys.stdin.fileno( )         # get descriptors for streams
    stdoutFd = sys.stdout.fileno( )        # normally stdin=0, stdout=1

    parentStdin, childStdout  = os.pipe( ) # make two IPC pipe channels
```

---

[*] This really does have real-world applications. For instance, I once added a GUI interface to a command-line debugger for a C-like programming language by connecting two processes with pipes. The GUI ran as a separate process that constructed and sent commands to the existing debugger's input stream pipe and parsed the results that showed up in the debugger's output stream pipe. In effect, the GUI acted like a programmer typing commands at a keyboard. By spawning command-line programs with streams attached by pipes, systems can add new interfaces to legacy programs. We'll see a simple example of this sort of structure in Chapter 11.

Example 5-18. PP3E\System\Processes\pipes.py (continued)

```
    childStdin, parentStdout = os.pipe()      # pipe returns (inputfd, outoutfd)
    pid = os.fork()                           # make a copy of this process
    if pid:
        os.close(childStdout)                 # in parent process after fork:
        os.close(childStdin)                  # close child ends in parent
        os.dup2(parentStdin,  stdinFd)        # my sys.stdin copy  = pipe1[0]
        os.dup2(parentStdout, stdoutFd)       # my sys.stdout copy = pipe2[1]
    else:
        os.close(parentStdin)                 # in child process after fork:
        os.close(parentStdout)                # close parent ends in child
        os.dup2(childStdin,  stdinFd)         # my sys.stdin copy  = pipe2[0]
        os.dup2(childStdout, stdoutFd)        # my sys.stdout copy = pipe1[1]
        args = (prog,) + args
        os.execvp(prog, args)                 # new program in this process
        assert False, 'execvp failed!'        # os.exec call never returns here

if __name__ == '__main__':
    mypid = os.getpid()
    spawn('python', 'pipes-testchild.py', 'spam')     # fork child program

    print 'Hello 1 from parent', mypid                # to child's stdin
    sys.stdout.flush()                                # subvert stdio buffering
    reply = raw_input()                               # from child's stdout
    sys.stderr.write('Parent got: "%s"\n' % reply)    # stderr not tied to pipe!

    print 'Hello 2 from parent', mypid
    sys.stdout.flush()
    reply = sys.stdin.readline()
    sys.stderr.write('Parent got: "%s"\n' % reply[:-1])
```

The spawn function in this module does not work on Windows (remember that fork isn't yet available there today). In fact, most of the calls in this module map straight to Unix system calls (and may be arbitrarily terrifying at first glance to non-Unix developers). We've already met some of these (e.g., os.fork), but much of this code depends on Unix concepts we don't have time to address well in this text. But in simple terms, here is a brief summary of the system calls demonstrated in this code:

os.fork

Copies the calling process as usual and returns the child's process ID in the parent process only.

os.execvp

Overlays a new program in the calling process; it's just like the os.execlp used earlier but takes a *tuple* or *list* of command-line argument strings (collected with the *args form in the function header).

os.pipe

Returns a tuple of file descriptors representing the input and output ends of a pipe, as in earlier examples.

```
os.close(fd)
```
Closes the descriptor-based file `fd`.

```
os.dup2(fd1,fd2)
```
Copies all system information associated with the file named by the file descriptor `fd1` to the file named by `fd2`.

In terms of connecting standard streams, `os.dup2` is the real nitty-gritty here. For example, the call `os.dup2(parentStdin,stdinFd)` essentially assigns the parent process's stdin file to the input end of one of the two pipes created; all `stdin` reads will henceforth come from the pipe. By connecting the other end of this pipe to the child process's copy of the `stdout` stream file with `os.dup2(childStdout,stdoutFd)`, text written by the child to its sdtdout winds up being routed through the pipe to the parent's `stdin` stream.

To test this utility, the self-test code at the end of the file spawns the program shown in Example 5-19 in a child process and reads and writes standard streams to converse with it over two pipes.

Example 5-19. PP3E\System\Processes\pipes-testchild.py

```
import os, time, sys
mypid     = os.getpid( )
parentpid = os.getppid( )
sys.stderr.write('Child %d of %d got arg: %s\n' %
                            (mypid, parentpid, sys.argv[1]))

for i in range(2):
    time.sleep(3)               # make parent process wait by sleeping here
    input = raw_input( )        # stdin tied to pipe: comes from parent's stdout
    time.sleep(3)
    reply = 'Child %d got: [%s]' % (mypid, input)
    print reply                 # stdout tied to pipe: goes to parent's stdin
    sys.stdout.flush( )         # make sure it's sent now or else process blocks
```

Here is our test in action on Linux; its output is not incredibly impressive to read, but it represents two programs running independently and shipping data back and forth through a pipe device managed by the operating system. This is even more like a client/server model (if you imagine the child as the server). The text in square brackets in this output went from the parent process to the child and back to the parent again, all through pipes connected to standard streams:

```
[mark@toy]$ python pipes.py
Child 797 of 796 got arg: spam
Parent got: "Child 797 got: [Hello 1 from parent 796]"
Parent got: "Child 797 got: [Hello 2 from parent 796]"
```

Deadlocks, flushes, and unbuffered streams

The two processes of the prior section's example engage in a simple dialog, but it's already enough to illustrate some of the dangers lurking in cross-program communications. First of all, notice that both programs need to write to stderr to display a message; their stdout streams are tied to the other program's input stream. Because processes share file descriptors, stderr is the same in both parent and child, so status messages show up in the same place.

More subtly, note that both parent and child call sys.stdout.flush after they print text to the stdout stream. Input requests on pipes normally block the caller if no data is available, but it seems that this shouldn't be a problem in our example because there are as many writes as there are reads on the other side of the pipe. By default, though, sys.stdout is *buffered*, so the printed text may not actually be transmitted until some time in the future (when the stdio output buffers fill up). In fact, if the flush calls are not made, both processes will get stuck waiting for input from the other—input that is sitting in a buffer and is never flushed out over the pipe. They wind up in a *deadlock* state, both blocked on raw_input calls waiting for events that never occur.

Keep in mind that output buffering is really a function of the system libraries used to access pipes, not of the pipes themselves (pipes do queue up output data, but they never hide it from readers!). In fact, it occurs in this example only because we copy the pipe's information over to sys.stdout, a built-in file object that uses stdio buffering by default. However, such anomalies can also occur when using other cross-process tools, such as the popen2 and popen3 calls introduced in Chapter 3.

In general terms, if your programs engage in a two-way dialog like this, there are at least three ways to avoid buffer-related deadlock problems:

- As demonstrated in this example, manually flushing output pipe streams by calling the file flush method is an easy way to force buffers to be cleared.

- It's possible to use pipes in unbuffered mode. Either use low-level os module calls to read and write pipe descriptors directly, or (on most systems) pass a buffer size argument of zero to os.fdopen to disable stdio buffering in the file object used to wrap the descriptor. For fifos, described in the next section, do the same for open.

- Simply use the -u Python command-line flag to turn off buffering for the sys.stdout stream (or equivalently, set your PYTHONUNBUFFERED environment variable to a nonempty value).

The last technique merits a few more words. Try this: delete all the sys.stdout.flush calls in Example 5-18 and Example 5-19 (the files *pipes.py* and *pipes-testchild.py*) and change the parent's spawn call in *pipes.py* to this (i.e., add a -u command-line argument):

```
spawn('python', '-u', 'pipes-testchild.py', 'spam')
```

Then start the program with a command line like this: python -u pipes.py. It will work as it did with the manual stdout flush calls, because stdout will be operating in unbuffered mode.

We'll revisit the effects of unbuffered output streams in Chapter 11, when we code a GUI that displays the output of a non-GUI program by reading it over a pipe in a thread. Deadlock in general, though, is a bigger problem than we have space to address here; on the other hand, if you know enough that you want to do IPC in Python, you're probably already a veteran of the deadlock wars. See also the sidebar below on the pty module and Pexpect package for related tools.

More on Stream Buffering: pty and Pexpect

On Unix-like platforms, you may also be able to use the Python pty standard library module to force another program's standard output to be unbuffered, especially if it's not a Python program and you cannot change its code.

Technically, default buffering for stdout is determined by whether the underlying file descriptor refers to a terminal. This occurs in the stdio library and cannot be controlled by the spawning program. In general, output to terminals is line buffered, and output to nonterminals (including files, pipes, and sockets) is fully buffered. This policy is used for efficiency.

The pty module essentially fools the spawned program into thinking it is connected to a terminal so that only one line is buffered for stdout. The net effect is that each newline flushes the prior line—typical of interactive programs, and what you need if you wish to grab each piece of the printed output as it is produced.

Note, however, that the pty module is not required for this role when spawning Python scripts with pipes: simply use the -u Python command-line flag or manually call sys.stdout.flush( ) in the spawned program. The pty module is also not available on all Python platforms today.

The Pexpect package, a pure-Python equivalent of the Unix expect program, uses pty to add additional functionality and to handle interactions that bypass standard streams (e.g., password inputs). See the Python library manual for more on pty, and search the Web for Pexpect.

Named Pipes (Fifos)

On some platforms, it is also possible to create a pipe that exists as a file. Such files are called named pipes (or, sometimes, fifos) because they behave just like the pipes created within the previous section's programs but are associated with a real file somewhere on your computer, external to any particular program.

Once a named pipe file is created, processes read and write it using normal file operations. Fifos are unidirectional streams. In typical operation, a server program reads data from the fifo, and one or more client programs write data to it. But a set of two fifos can be used to implement bidirectional communication just as we did for anonymous pipes in the prior section.

Because fifos reside in the filesystem, they are longer-lived than in-process anonymous pipes and can be accessed by programs started independently. The unnamed, in-process pipe examples thus far depend on the fact that file descriptors (including pipes) are copied to child processes' memory. That makes it difficult to use anonymous pipes to connect programs started independently. With fifos, pipes are accessed instead by a filename visible to all programs running on the computer, regardless of any parent/child process relationships.

Because of that, fifos are better suited as general IPC mechanisms for independent client and server programs. For instance, a perpetually running server program may create and listen for requests on a fifo that can be accessed later by arbitrary clients not forked by the server. In a sense, fifos are an alternative to the socket interface we'll meet in the next part of this book, but fifos do not directly support remote network connections, are not available on as many platforms, and are accessed using the standard file interface instead of the more unique socket port numbers and calls we'll study later.

In Python, named pipe files are created with the os.mkfifo call, available today on Unix-like platforms but not on all flavors of Windows (though this call is also available in Cygwin Python on Windows—see the earlier sidebar). This creates only the external file, though; to send and receive data through a fifo, it must be opened and processed as if it were a standard file. Example 5-20 is a derivation of the *pipe2.py* script listed earlier. It is written to use fifos rather than anonymous pipes.

Example 5-20. PP3E\System\Processes\pipefifo.py

```
#####################################################################
# named pipes; os.mkfifo not available on Windows 95/98/XP
# (without Cygwin); no reason to fork here, since fifo file
# pipes are external to processes--shared fds are irrelevent;
#####################################################################

import os, time, sys
fifoname = '/tmp/pipefifo'                       # must open same name

def child():
    pipeout = os.open(fifoname, os.O_WRONLY)      # open fifo pipe file as fd
    zzz = 0
    while 1:
        time.sleep(zzz)
        os.write(pipeout, 'Spam %03d\n' % zzz)
        zzz = (zzz+1) % 5

def parent():
    pipein = open(fifoname, 'r')                  # open fifo as stdio object
    while 1:
        line = pipein.readline()[:-1]            # blocks until data sent
        print 'Parent %d got "%s" at %s' % (os.getpid(), line, time.time())

if __name__ == '__main__':
```

Example 5-20. PP3E\System\Processes\pipefifo.py (continued)

```
if not os.path.exists(fifoname):
    os.mkfifo(fifoname)                # create a named pipe file
if len(sys.argv) == 1:
    parent()                          # run as parent if no args
else:                                 # else run as child process
    child()
```

Because the fifo exists independently of both parent and child, there's no reason to fork here. The child may be started independently of the parent as long as it opens a fifo file by the same name. Here, for instance, on Linux the parent is started in one xterm window and then the child is started in another. Messages start appearing in the parent window only after the child is started and begins writing messages onto the fifo file:

```
[mark@toy]$ python pipefifo.py
Parent 657 got "Spam 000" at 968390065.865
Parent 657 got "Spam 001" at 968390066.865
Parent 657 got "Spam 002" at 968390068.865
Parent 657 got "Spam 003" at 968390071.865
Parent 657 got "Spam 004" at 968390075.865
Parent 657 got "Spam 000" at 968390075.867
Parent 657 got "Spam 001" at 968390076.865
Parent 657 got "Spam 002" at 968390078.865

[mark@toy]$ file /tmp/pipefifo
/tmp/pipefifo: fifo (named pipe)
[mark@toy]$ python pipefifo.py -child
```

Signals

For lack of a better analogy, signals are a way to poke a stick at a process. Programs generate signals to trigger a handler for that signal in another process. The operating system pokes too—some signals are generated on unusual system events and may kill the program if not handled. If this sounds a little like raising exceptions in Python, it should; signals are software-generated events and the cross-process analog of exceptions. Unlike exceptions, though, signals are identified by number, are not stacked, and are really an asynchronous event mechanism outside the scope of the Python interpreter controlled by the operating system.

In order to make signals available to scripts, Python provides a `signal` module that allows Python programs to register Python functions as handlers for signal events. This module is available on both Unix-like platforms and Windows (though the Windows version defines fewer kinds of signals to be caught). To illustrate the basic signal interface, the script in Example 5-21 installs a Python handler function for the signal number passed in as a command-line argument.

Example 5-21. PP3E\System\Processes\signal1.py

```
###########################################################################
# catch signals in Python; pass signal number N as a command-line arg,
# use a "kill -N pid" shell command to send this process a signal;  most
# signal handlers restored by Python after caught (see network scripting
# chapter for SIGCHLD details); on Windows, signal module is available,
# but it defines only a few signal types there, and os.kill is missing;
###########################################################################

import sys, signal, time
def now(): return time.ctime(time.time())        # current time string

def onSignal(signum, stackframe):                # python signal handler
    print 'Got signal', signum, 'at', now()      # most handlers stay in effect

signum = int(sys.argv[1])
signal.signal(signum, onSignal)                  # install signal handler
while 1: signal.pause()                          # wait for signals (or: pass)
```

There are only two `signal` module calls at work here:

`signal.signal`

Takes a signal number and function object and installs that function to handle that signal number when it is raised. Python automatically restores most signal handlers when signals occur, so there is no need to recall this function within the signal handler itself to reregister the handler. That is, except for SIGCHLD, a signal handler remains installed until explicitly reset (e.g., by setting the handler to SIG_DFL to restore default behavior, or to SIG_IGN to ignore the signal). SIGCHLD behavior is platform specific.

`signal.pause`

Makes the process sleep until the next signal is caught. A `time.sleep` call is similar but doesn't work with signals on my Linux box; it generates an interrupted system call error. A busy `while 1: pass` loop here would pause the script too but may squander CPU resources.

Here is what this script looks like running on Linux: a signal number to watch for (12) is passed in on the command line, and the program is made to run in the background with an & shell operator (available in most Unix-like shells):

```
[mark@toy]$ python signal1.py 12 &
[1] 809
[mark@toy]$ ps
  PID TTY        TIME CMD
  578 ttyp1   00:00:00 tcsh
  809 ttyp1   00:00:00 python
  810 ttyp1   00:00:00 ps
[mark@toy]$ kill -12 809
[mark@toy]$ Got signal 12 at Fri Sep  8 00:27:01 2000
kill -12 809
[mark@toy]$ Got signal 12 at Fri Sep  8 00:27:03 2000
```

```
kill -12 809
[mark@toy]$ Got signal 12 at Fri Sep  8 00:27:04 2000

[mark@toy]$ kill -9 809          # signal 9 always kills the process
```

Inputs and outputs are a bit jumbled here because the process prints to the same screen used to type new shell commands. To send the program a signal, the kill shell command takes a signal number and a process ID to be signaled (809); every time a new kill command sends a signal, the process replies with a message generated by a Python signal handler function.

The signal module also exports a signal.alarm function for scheduling a SIGALRM signal to occur at some number of seconds in the future. To trigger and catch timeouts, set the alarm and install a SIGALRM handler as shown in Example 5-22.

Example 5-22. PP3E\System\Processes\signal2.py

```
#############################################################################
# set and catch alarm timeout signals in Python; time.sleep doesn't play
# well with alarm (or signal in general in my Linux PC), so we call
# signal.pause here to do nothing until a signal is received;
#############################################################################

import sys, signal, time
def now(): return time.ctime(time.time( ))

def onSignal(signum, stackframe):                # python signal handler
    print 'Got alarm', signum, 'at', now( )      # most handlers stay in effect

while 1:
    print 'Setting at', now( )
    signal.signal(signal.SIGALRM, onSignal)      # install signal handler
    signal.alarm(5)                              # do signal in 5 seconds
    signal.pause( )                              # wait for signals
```

Running this script on Linux causes its onSignal handler function to be invoked every five seconds:

```
[mark@toy]$ python signal2.py
Setting at Fri Sep  8 00:27:53 2000
Got alarm 14 at Fri Sep  8 00:27:58 2000
Setting at Fri Sep  8 00:27:58 2000
Got alarm 14 at Fri Sep  8 00:28:03 2000
Setting at Fri Sep  8 00:28:03 2000
Got alarm 14 at Fri Sep  8 00:28:08 2000
Setting at Fri Sep  8 00:28:08 2000
```

Generally speaking, signals must be used with cautions not made obvious by the examples we've just seen. For instance, some system calls don't react well to being interrupted by signals, and only the main thread can install signal handlers and respond to signals in a multithreaded program.

When used well, though, signals provide an event-based communication mechanism. They are less powerful than data streams such as pipes, but are sufficient in situations in which you just need to tell a program that something important has occurred and don't need to pass along any details about the event itself. Signals are sometimes also combined with other IPC tools. For example, an initial signal may inform a program that a client wishes to communicate over a named pipe—the equivalent of tapping someone's shoulder to get their attention before speaking. Most platforms reserve one or more SIGUSR signal numbers for user-defined events of this sort. Such an integration structure is sometimes an alternative to running a blocking input call in a spawned thread.

See also the os.kill(pid, sig) call for sending signals to known processes from within a Python script on Unix-like platforms (the required process ID can be obtained from the os.fork call's child process ID return value or from other interfaces). Also watch for the discussion about using signal handlers to clean up zombie processes in the Internet scripting part later in this book.

Other Ways to Start Programs

Suppose, just for a moment, that you've been asked to write a big Python book and you want to provide a way for readers to easily start the book's examples on just about any platform that Python runs on. Books are nice, but it's awfully fun to be able to click on demos right away. That is, you want to write a general and portable launcher program in Python for starting other Python programs. What to do?

In this chapter, we've seen how to portably spawn threads, but these are simply parallel functions, not external programs. We've also learned how to go about starting new, independently running programs, with both the fork/exec combination and with tools for launching shell commands such as os.popen and os.system. Along the way, though, I've also been careful to point out numerous times that the os.fork call doesn't work on Windows today. This constraint may be improved by the time you read this book, but it still is a limitation as I write these words. Moreover, for reasons we'll explore later, the os.popen call is prone to blocking (pausing) its caller in some scenarios and requires a potentially platform-specific command-line string.

Luckily, there are other ways to start programs in the Python standard library, some of which are more platform neutral than others:

- The os.spawnv and os.spawnve calls were originally introduced to launch programs on Windows, much like a fork/exec call combination on Unix-like platforms. Today, these calls work on both Windows and Unix-like systems, and additional variants have been added to parrot os.exec.

- The os.system call can be used on Windows to launch a DOS start command, which opens (i.e., runs) a file independently based on its Windows filename associations, as though it were clicked. os.startfile makes this even simpler in recent Python releases.

- Tools in the Python PyWin32 extensions package provide other, less standardized ways to start programs (e.g., the `WinExec` call).

- Other tools such as the `commands` and `subprocess` modules provide additional options in this domain.

We won't talk about the PyWin32 extensions package in this chapter, but the other tools available in the standard library merit a quick look here.

The os.spawn Calls

The `os.spawn` family of calls execute a program named by a command line in a new process, on both Windows and Unix-like systems. In basic operation, they are similar to the `fork`/`exec` call combination on Unix and can be used as alternatives to the system and popen calls we've already learned. In the following interaction, for instance, we start a Python program with a command line in two traditional ways (the second also reads its output):

```
>>> print open('makewords.py').read()
print 'spam'
print 'eggs'
print 'ham'

>>> os.system('python makewords.py')
spam
eggs
ham
0

>>> result = os.popen('python makewords.py').read()
>>> print result
spam
eggs
ham
```

The equivalent `os.spawn` calls achieve the same effect, with a slightly more complex call signature that provides more control over the way the program is launched:

```
>>> os.spawnv(os.P_WAIT, r'C:\Python24\python', ('python', 'makewords.py'))
spam
eggs
ham
0
>>> os.spawnl(os.P_NOWAIT, r'C:\Python24\python', 'python', 'makewords.py')
1820
>>> spam
eggs
ham
```

The spawn calls are also much like forking programs in Unix. They don't actually copy the calling process (so shared descriptor operations won't work), but they can be used to start a program running completely independent of the calling program,

even on Windows. The script in Example 5-23 makes the similarity to Unix programming patterns more obvious. It launches a program with a fork/exec combination in Linux, or an os.spawnv call on Windows.

Example 5-23. PP3E\System\Processes\spawnv.py

```
############################################################
# start up 10 copies of child.py running in parallel;
# use spawnv to launch a program on Windows (like fork+exec)
# P_OVERLAY replaces, P_DETACH makes child stdout go nowhere
############################################################

import os, sys

for i in range(10):
    if sys.platform[:3] == 'win':
        pypath = sys.executable
        os.spawnv(os.P_NOWAIT, pypath, ('python', 'child.py', str(i)))
    else:
        pid = os.fork()
        if pid != 0:
            print 'Process %d spawned' % pid
        else:
            os.execlp('python', 'python', 'child.py', str(i))
print 'Main process exiting.'
```

To make sense of these examples, you have to understand the arguments being
passed to the spawn calls. In this script, we call os.spawnv with a process mode flag,
the full directory path to the Python interpreter, and a tuple of strings representing
the DOS command line with which to start a new program. The path to the Python
interpreter executable program running a script is available as sys.executable in
recent Python releases. In general, the *process mode* flag is taken from these predefined values:

os.P_NOWAIT *and* os.P_NOWAITO
> The spawn functions will return as soon as the new process has been created,
> with the process ID as the return value. Available on Unix and Windows.

os.P_WAIT
> The spawn functions will not return until the new process has run to completion
> and will return the exit code of the process if the run is successful or "-signal" if
> a signal kills the process. Available on Unix and Windows.

os.P_DETACH *and* os.P_OVERLAY
> P_DETACH is similar to P_NOWAIT, but the new process is detached from the con-
> sole of the calling process. If P_OVERLAY is used, the current program will be
> replaced (much like os.exec). Available on Windows.

In fact, there are eight different calls in the spawn family, which all start a program but
vary slightly in their call signatures. In their names, an "l" means you list arguments

individually, "p" means the executable file is looked up on the system path, and "e" means a dictionary is passed in to provide the shelled environment of the spawned program: the os.spawnve call, for example, works the same way as os.spawnv but accepts an extra fourth dictionary argument to specify a different shell environment for the spawned program (which, by default, inherits all of the parent's settings):

```
os.spawnl(mode, path, ...)
os.spawnle(mode, path, ..., env)
os.spawnlp(mode, file, ...)                # Unix only
os.spawnlpe(mode, file, ..., env)          # Unix only
os.spawnv(mode, path, args)
os.spawnve(mode, path, args, env)
os.spawnvp(mode, file, args)               # Unix only
os.spawnvpe(mode, file, args, env)         # Unix only
```

Because these calls mimic the names and call signatures of the os.exec variants, see the section "The fork/exec Combination," earlier in this chapter, for more details on the differences between these call forms. Unlike the os.exec calls, only half of the os.spawn forms—those without system path checking (and hence without a "p" in their names)—are currently implemented on Windows. All the process mode flags are supported on Windows, but detach and overlay modes are not available on Unix. To see which are present, read the library manual or ask Python:

```
>>> import sys, os
>>> sys.platform
'win32'

>>> [x for x in dir(os) if x.startswith('spawn')]
['spawnl', 'spawnle', 'spawnv', 'spawnve']

>>> [x for x in dir(os) if x.startswith('P_')]
['P_DETACH', 'P_NOWAIT', 'P_NOWAITO', 'P_OVERLAY', 'P_WAIT']
```

Run a few tests or see the Python library manual for more details; things such as standard stream connection policies vary between the P_DETACH and P_NOWAIT modes in subtle ways. Here is the script in Example 5-23 at work on Windows, spawning 10 independent copies of the *child.py* Python program we met earlier in this chapter:

```
C:\...\PP3E\System\Processes>type child.py
import os, sys
print 'Hello from child', os.getpid( ), sys.argv[1]

C:\...\PP3E\System\Processes>python spawnv.py
Hello from child -583587 0
Hello from child -558199 2
Hello from child -586755 1
Hello from child -562171 3
Main process exiting.
Hello from child -581867 6
Hello from child -588651 5
Hello from child -568247 4
```

```
Hello from child -563527 7
Hello from child -543163 9
Hello from child -587083 8
```

Notice that the copies print their output in random order, and the parent program exits before all children do; all of these programs are really running in parallel on Windows. Also observe that the child program's output shows up in the console box where *spawnv.py* was run; when using P_NOWAIT, standard output comes to the parent's console, but it seems to go nowhere when using P_DETACH (which is most likely a feature when spawning GUI programs).

Launching Programs on Windows

The os.system, os.popen, and os.spawn calls can be used to start command lines on Windows just as on Unix-like platforms (but with the handful of caveats mentioned earlier). On Windows, though, the DOS start command combined with os.system provides an easy way for scripts to launch any file on the system, using Windows filename associations. Starting a program file this way makes it run as independently as its starter. Example 5-24 demonstrates these launch techniques.

Example 5-24. PP3E\System\Processes\dosstart.py

```
#######################################################################
# start up 5 copies of child.py running in parallel;
# - on Windows, os.system always blocks its caller,
# - using DOS start command pops up a DOS box (which goes
#   away immediately when the child.py program exits)
# - running child-wait.py with DOS start, 5 independent
#   DOS console windows pop up and stay up (1 per program)
# DOS start command uses registry filename associations to know
# to run Python on the file, as though double-clicked in a Windows
# file explorer GUI (any filename can be started this way);
#######################################################################

import os, sys

for i in range(5):
    #print os.popen('python child.py ' + str(i)).read()[:-1]
    #os.system('python child.py ' + str(i))
    #os.system('start child.py ' + str(i))
    os.system('start child-wait.py ' + str(i))
print 'Main process exiting.'
```

Uncomment one of the lines in this script's for loop to experiment with these schemes on your computer. On mine, when run with either of the first two calls in the loop uncommented, I get the following sort of output—the text printed by five spawned Python programs:

```
C:\...\PP3E\System\Processes>python dosstart.py
Hello from child -582331 0
```

```
Hello from child -547703 1
Hello from child -547703 2
Hello from child -547651 3
Hello from child -547651 4
Main process exiting.
```

The `os.system` call usually blocks its caller until the spawned program exits; reading the output of an `os.popen` call has the same blocking effect (the reader waits for the spawned program's output to be complete). But with either of the last two statements in the loop uncommented, I get output that simply looks like this:

```
C:\...\PP3E\System\Processes>python dosstart.py
Main process exiting.
```

In both cases, I also see five new and completely independent DOS console windows appear on my display; when the third line in the loop is uncommented, all of the DOS boxes go away right after they appear; when the last line in the loop is active, they remain on the screen after the dosstart program exits because the `child-wait` script pauses for input before exiting.

Using the DOS start command

To understand why, first you need to know how the DOS start command works in general. Roughly, a DOS command line of the form `start` *command* works as if *command* were typed in the Windows Run dialog box available in the Start button menu. If *command* is a filename, it is opened exactly as if its name had been double-clicked in the Windows Explorer file selector GUI.

For instance, the following three DOS commands automatically start Internet Explorer on a file named *index.html*, my registered image viewer program on a file named *uk-1.jpg*, and my sound media player program on a file named *sousa.au*. Windows simply opens the file with whatever program is associated to handle filenames of that form. Moreover, all three of these programs run independently of the DOS console box where the command is typed:

```
C:\temp>start c:\stuff\website\public_html\index.html
C:\temp>start c:\stuff\website\public_html\uk-1.jpg
C:\...\PP3E\System\Processes>start ..\..\Internet\Ftp\sousa.au
```

Now, because the `start` command can run any file and command line, there is no reason it cannot also be used to start an independently running Python program:

```
C:\...\PP3E\System\Processes>start child.py 1
```

Because Python is registered to open names ending in *.py* when it is installed, this really does work. The script *child.py* is launched independently of the DOS console window even though we didn't provide the name or path of the Python interpreter program. Because *child.py* simply prints a message and exits, though, the result isn't exactly satisfying: a new DOS window pops up to serve as the script's standard output, and it immediately goes away when the child exits (it's that Windows "flash feature" described earlier!). To do better, add a raw_input call at the bottom of the program file to wait for a key press before exiting:

```
C:\...\PP3E\System\Processes>type child-wait.py
import os, sys
print 'Hello from child', os.getpid( ), sys.argv[1]
raw_input("Press <Enter>")   # don't flash on Windows

C:\...\PP3E\System\Processes>start child-wait.py 2
```

Now the child's DOS window pops up and stays up after the start command has returned. Pressing the Enter key in the pop-up DOS window makes it go away.

Using start in Python scripts

Since we know that Python's os.system and os.popen can be called by a script to run *any* command line that can be typed at a DOS shell prompt, we can also start independently running programs from a Python script by simply running a DOS start command line. For instance:

```
C:\...\PP3E>python
>>> import os
>>>
>>> cmd = r'start c:\stuff\website\public_html\index.html'  # start IE browser
>>> os.system(cmd)                                          # runs independent
0
>>> file = r'gui\gifs\pythonPowered.gif'                # start image viewer
>>> os.system('start ' + file)                          # IE opens .gif for me
0
>>> os.system('start ' + 'Gui/gifs/PythonPowered.gif')  # fwd slashes work too
0
>>> os.system(r'start Internet\Ftp\sousa.au')           # start media player
0
```

The four Python os.system calls here start whatever web-page browser, image viewer, and sound player are registered on your machine to open *.html*, *.gif*, and *.au* files (unless these programs are already running). The launched programs run completely independent of the Python session—when running a DOS start command, os.system does not wait for the spawned program to exit. For instance, Figure 5-1 shows the *.gif* file handler in action on my machine, generated by both the second and the third os.system calls in the preceding code.

Now, since we also know that a Python program can be started from a command line, this yields two ways to launch Python programs:

```
C:\...\PP3E>python
>>> os.system(r'python Gui\TextEditor\textEditor.pyw')   # start and wait
0
>>> os.system(r'start  Gui\TextEditor\textEditor.pyw')   # start, go on
0
```

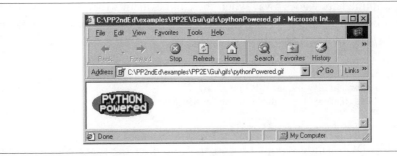

Figure 5-1. Started image viewer (Internet Explorer)

When running a python command, the os.system call waits (blocks) for the command to finish. When running a start command, it does not; the launched Python program (here, PyEdit, a text editor GUI we'll meet in Chapter 12) runs independent of the os.system caller. And finally, that's why the following call in *dosstart.py* generates a new, independent instance of *child-wait.py*:

```
C:\...\PP3E\System\Processes>python
>>> os.system('start child-wait.py 1')
0
```

When run, this call pops up a new, independent DOS console window to serve as the standard input and output streams of the child-wait program. It truly is independent—in fact, it keeps running if we exit both this Python interpreter session and the DOS console box where the command was typed.* An os.popen call can launch a start command too; but since it normally starts commands independently anyhow, the only obvious advantages of start here are the pop-up DOS box and the fact that Python need not be in the system search path setting:

```
>>> file = os.popen('start child-wait.py 1')    # versus: python child-wait...
>>> file.read()
'Hello from child -413849 1\012Press <Enter>'
```

Which scheme to use, then? Using os.system or os.popen to run a python command works fine, but only if your users have added the *python.exe* directory to their system search path setting. Running a DOS start command is often a simpler alternative to both running python commands and calling the os.spawnv function, since filename associations are automatically installed along with Python and os.spawnv requires a full directory path to the Python interpreter program (*python.exe*). On the

---

* And remember, if you want to start a Python GUI program this way and not see the new DOS standard stream console box at all, simply name the script *child-wait.pyw*; the "w" on the end tells the Windows Python port to avoid the DOS box. For DOS jockeys: the start command also allows a few interesting options: /m (run minimized), /max (run maximized), /r (run restored—the default), and /w (don't return until the other program exits—this adds caller blocking if you need it). Type start /? for help. And for any Unix developers peeking over the fence: you can also launch independent programs with os.system—append the & background operator to the command line. The standard library webbrowser module also provides a portable way to pop up an HTML file in a web browser, without requiring Windows registry associations.

other hand, running start commands with os.system calls can fail on Windows for very long command-line strings:

```
>>> os.system('start child-wait.py ' + 'Z'*425)    # OK- 425 Zs in dos pop up
0
>>> os.system('start child-wait.py ' + 'Z'*450)    # fails- msg, not exception
Access is denied.
0
>>> os.popen('python child-wait.py ' + 'Z'*500).read()    # works if PATH set
>>> os.system('python child-wait.py ' + 'Z'*500)          # works if PATH set

>>> pypath = r'C:\program files\python\python.exe'    # this works too
>>> os.spawnv(os.P_NOWAIT, pypath, ('python', 'child-wait.py', 'Z'*500))
```

As a rule of thumb, use one of the os.spawn variants if your commands are (or may be) long. For instance, we'll meet a script in Chapter 6 that launches web browsers to view HTML files; even though a start command applied to an HTML file will automatically start a browser program, this script instead must use os.spawnv to accommodate potentially long directory paths in HTML filenames.

The os.startfile call

One more Windows twist: as mentioned previously in this book, recent Python releases also include an os.startfile call, which is essentially the same as spawning a DOS start command with os.system and works as though the named file were double-clicked. The following calls, for instance, have a similar effect:

```
>>> os.startfile('README.txt')
>>> os.system('start README.txt')
```

Both pop up the *README.txt* file in Notepad on my Windows XP computer. Unlike the second of these calls, though, os.startfile provides no option to wait for the application to close (the DOS start command's /WAIT option does) and no way to retrieve the application's exit status (returned from os.system).

On recent versions of Windows, the following has a similar effect too, because the registry is used at the command line (though this form pauses until the file's viewer is closed—like using start /WAIT):

```
>>> os.system('README.txt')       # 'start' is optional today
```

A subtle thing: under the IDLE GUI in Python 2.4, the os.startfile call also does not pop up an intermediate DOS console window, whereas running a start command with os.system does, both from IDLE's interactive window and from within a script launched in IDLE. This seems to be just an artifact of the IDLE system, though; neither call pops up a DOS console outside of IDLE, whether typed interactively or run by a program that is launched from a system command line or icon click.

If you start a Python script with any of these call forms, what happens also depends upon the name of the file: a *.py* file pops up a console window for os.startfile, but a *.pyw* file will not (exactly as when a file icon is clicked). The os.system call may map the script's output to the interactive session window unless start is used in the command, in which case we get a console pop up again. This is complex and seems like the sort of small nonlanguage detail that may vary over time, so try the variations that you care about on your own to see the DOS pop-up differences among these three call forms

The os.startfile call works only on Windows, because it uses the Windows registry to know how to open the file. If you want to be more platform neutral, consider using os.popen or os.spawnv.

For more information on other Windows-specific program launcher tools, see O'Reilly's *Python Programming on Win32*, by Mark Hammond and Andy Robinson. Other schemes are less standard than those shown here but are given excellent coverage in that text.

Other Program Launch Options

For a slightly higher-level interface for launching shell commands, see also the standard library commands module, a Unix-only module which is roughly just a wrapper around the os.popen call.

In Python 2.4 and later, the subprocess module also allows you to spawn new processes, connect to their input, output, and error streams, and obtain their return codes. This module can be used to replace several older modules and functions, including os.system, os.spawn*, os.popen*, and commands.*. It provides lower-level control over spawned programs and is generally portable, but it can be more complex to code in some cases. Some advanced roles are made simpler by this module, however. For instance, to emulate shell-level command chaining with pipes, the following Python code:

```
from subprocess import Popen
p1 = Popen(["dmesg"], stdout=PIPE)
p2 = Popen(["grep", "hda"], stdin=p1.stdout)
output = p2.communicate( )[0]
```

is equivalent to this Unix shell language command:

```
output=`dmesg | grep hda`
```

A Portable Program-Launch Framework

With all of these different ways to start programs on different platforms, it can be difficult to remember what tools to use in a given situation. Moreover, some of these tools are called in ways that are complicated and thus easy to forget (for me, at least). I write scripts that need to launch Python programs often enough that I eventually wrote a module to try to hide most of the underlying details. While I was at it, I made this module smart enough to automatically pick a launch scheme based on the underlying platform. Laziness is the mother of many a useful module.

Example 5-25 collects in a single module many of the techniques we've met in this chapter. It implements an abstract superclass, LaunchMode, which defines what it means to start a Python program, but it doesn't define how. Instead, its subclasses provide a run method that actually starts a Python program according to a given scheme, and (optionally) define an announce method to display a program's name at startup time.

Example 5-25. PP3E\launchmodes.py

```
###############################################################
# launch Python programs with reusable launcher scheme classes;
# assumes 'python' is on your system path (but see Launcher.py)
###############################################################

import sys, os
pyfile = (sys.platform[:3] == 'win' and 'python.exe') or 'python'

def findPythonExe():
    try:                                    # get path to python
        pypath = sys.executable             # use sys in newer pys
    except AttributeError:                  # else env or search
        try:
            pypath = os.environ['PP3E_PYTHON_FILE']   # run by launcher?
        except KeyError:                              # if so configs env
            from Launcher import which, guessLocation
            pypath = (which(pyfile, trace=False) or
                        guessLocation(pyfile, trace=False))
    return pypath

class LaunchMode:
    def __init__(self, label, command):
        self.what  = label
        self.where = command
    def __call__(self):                      # on call, ex: button press callback
        self.announce(self.what)
        self.run(self.where)                 # subclasses must define run()
    def announce(self, text):                # subclasses may redefine announce()
        print text                           # methods instead of if/elif logic
    def run(self, cmdline):
        assert 0, 'run must be defined'

class System(LaunchMode):                    # run shell commands
    def run(self, cmdline):                  # caveat: blocks caller
        pypath = findPythonExe()
        os.system('%s %s' % (pypath, cmdline))   # unless '&' added on Linux

class Popen(LaunchMode):                      # caveat: blocks caller
    def run(self, cmdline):                   # since pipe closed too soon
        pypath = findPythonExe()
```

Example 5-25. PP3E\launchmodes.py (continued)

```
        os.popen(pypath + ' ' + cmdline)

class Fork(LaunchMode):
    def run(self, cmdline):
        assert hasattr(os, 'fork')              # for Unix systems today
        cmdline = cmdline.split()               # convert string to list
        if os.fork() == 0:                      # start new child process
            pypath = findPythonExe()
            os.execvp(pypath, [pyfile] + cmdline) # run new program in child

class Start(LaunchMode):
    def run(self, cmdline):                     # for Windows only
        assert sys.platform[:3] == 'win'        # runs independent of caller
        os.startfile(cmdline)                   # uses Windows associations

class StartArgs(LaunchMode):
    def run(self, cmdline):                     # for Windows only
        assert sys.platform[:3] == 'win'        # args may require real start
        os.system('start ' + cmdline)          # creates pop-up window

class Spawn(LaunchMode):                         # for Windows or Unix
    def run(self, cmdline):                     # run python in new process
        pypath = findPythonExe()               # runs independent of caller
        os.spawnv(os.P_DETACH, pypath, (pyfile, cmdline)) # P_NOWAIT: dos box

class Top_level(LaunchMode):
    def run(self, cmdline):                     # new window, same process
        assert 0, 'Sorry - mode not yet implemented' # tbd: need GUI class info

if sys.platform[:3] == 'win':
    PortableLauncher = Spawn                    # pick best launcher for platform
else:                                           # need to tweak this code elsewhere
    PortableLauncher = Fork

class QuietPortableLauncher(PortableLauncher):
    def announce(self, text):
        pass

def selftest():
    myfile  = 'launchmodes.py'
    program = 'Gui/TextEditor/textEditor.py ' + myfile      # assume in cwd
    raw_input('default mode...')
    launcher = PortableLauncher('PyEdit', program)
    launcher()                                              # no block

    raw_input('system mode...')
    System('PyEdit', program)()                             # blocks

    raw_input('popen mode...')
    Popen('PyEdit', program)()                              # blocks

    if sys.platform[:3] == 'win':
```

Example 5-25. PP3E\launchmodes.py (continued)

```
        raw_input('DOS start mode...')                        # no block
        StartArgs('PyEdit', os.path.normpath(program))( )

if __name__ == '__main__': selftest( )
```

Near the end of the file, the module picks a default class based on the sys.platform attribute: PortableLauncher is set to a class that uses spawnv on Windows and one that uses the fork/exec combination elsewhere (in recent Pythons, we could probably just use the spawnv scheme on most platforms, but the alternatives in this module are used in additional contexts). If you import this module and always use its PortableLauncher attribute, you can forget many of the platform-specific details enumerated in this chapter.

To run a Python program, simply import the PortableLauncher class, make an instance by passing a label and command line (without a leading "python" word), and then call the instance object as though it were a function. The program is started by a call operation instead of a method so that the classes in this module can be used to generate callback handlers in Tkinter-based GUIs. As we'll see in the upcoming chapters, button-presses in Tkinter invoke a callable object with no arguments; by registering a PortableLauncher instance to handle the press event, we can automatically start a new program from another program's GUI.

When run standalone, this module's selftest function is invoked as usual. On both Windows and Linux, all classes tested start a new Python text editor program (the upcoming PyEdit GUI program again) running independently with its own window. Figure 5-2 shows one in action on Windows; all spawned editors open the *launchmodes.py* source file automatically, because its name is passed to PyEdit as a command-line argument. As coded, both System and Popen block the caller until the editor exits, but PortableLauncher (really, Spawn or Fork) and Start do not:[*]

```
C:\...\PP3E>python launchmodes.py
default mode...
PyEdit
system mode...
PyEdit
popen mode...
PyEdit
DOS start mode...
PyEdit
```

---

[*] This is fairly subtle. Technically, Popen blocks its caller only because the input pipe to the spawned program is closed too early, when the os.popen call's result is garbage collected in Popen.run; os.popen normally does not block (in fact, assigning its result here to a global variable postpones blocking, but only until the next Popen object run frees the prior result). On Linux, adding an & to the end of the constructed command line in the System and Popen.run methods makes these objects no longer block their callers when run. Since the fork/exec, spawnv, and system/start schemes seem at least as good in practice, these Popen block states have not been addressed. Note too that the StartArgs scheme may not generate a DOS console pop-up window in the self-test if the text editor program file's name ends in a *.pyw* extension; starting *.py* program files normally creates the console pop-up box.

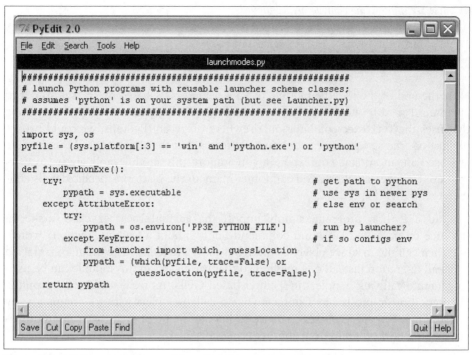

Figure 5-2. PyEdit program spawned from launchmodes

As a more practical application, this file is also used by launcher scripts designed to run examples in this book in a portable fashion. The PyDemos and PyGadgets scripts at the top of this book's examples distribution directory tree (described in the Preface) simply import PortableLauncher and register instances to respond to GUI events. Because of that, these two launcher GUIs run on both Windows and Linux unchanged (Tkinter's portability helps too, of course). The PyGadgets script even customizes PortableLauncher to update a label in a GUI at start time.

```
class Launcher(launchmodes.PortableLauncher):    # use wrapped launcher class
    def announce(self, text):                    # customize to set GUI label
        Info.config(text=text)
```

We'll explore these scripts in Part III (but feel free to peek at the end of Chapter 10 now). Because of this role, the Spawn class in this file uses additional tools to search for the Python executable's path, which is required by os.spawnv. If the sys. executable path string is not available in an older version of Python that you happen to be using, it calls two functions exported by a file named *Launcher.py* to find a suitable Python executable regardless of whether the user has added its directory to his system PATH variable's setting. The idea is to start Python programs, even if Python hasn't been installed in the shell variables on the local machine. Because we're going to meet *Launcher.py* in the next chapter, though, I'm going to postpone further details for now.

Other System Tools

In this and the prior two chapters, we've met most of the commonly used system tools in the Python library. Along the way, we've also learned how to use them to do useful things such as start programs, process directories, and so on. The next two chapters are something of a continuation of this topic. They use the tools we've just met to implement scripts that do useful and more realistic system-level work, so read on for the rest of this story.

Still, other system-related tools in Python appear even later in this text. For instance:

- Sockets (used to communicate with other programs and networks) are introduced in Chapter 13.

- Select calls (used to multiplex among tasks) are also introduced in Chapter 13 as a way to implement servers.

- File locking with os.open and calls in the fcntl module appear in the PyErrata example described at the end of Chapter 17.

- Regular expressions (string pattern matching used by many text processing tools) don't appear until Chapter 21.

Moreover, things like forks and threads are used extensively in the Internet scripting chapters: see the server implementations in Chapter 13 and the FTP and email GUIs in Chapter 14. Along the way, we'll also meet higher-level Python modules such as SocketServer, which implement fork and thread-based server code for us. In fact, most of this chapter's tools will pop up constantly in later examples in this book—about what one would expect of general-purpose, portable libraries.

Last but not necessarily least, I'd like to point out one more time that many additional tools in the Python library don't appear in this book at all. With hundreds of library modules, Python book authors have to pick and choose their topics frugally! As always, be sure to browse the Python library manuals early and often in your Python career.

CHAPTER 6

System Examples: Utilities

"Splits and Joins and Alien Invasions"

This chapter and the next continue our look at the system utilities domain in Python. They present a collection of larger Python scripts that do real systems work—comparing and copying directory trees, splitting files, searching files and directories, testing other programs, configuring program shell environments, launching web browsers, and so on. To make this collection easier to absorb, it's been split into a two-chapter set. This chapter presents assorted Python system utility programs that illustrate typical tasks and techniques in this domain. The next chapter presents larger Python programs that focus on more advanced file and directory tree processing.

Although the main point of these two case-study chapters is to give you a feel for realistic scripts in action, the size of these examples also gives us an opportunity to see Python's support for development paradigms like object-oriented programming (OOP) and reuse at work. It's really only in the context of nontrivial programs such as the ones we'll meet here that such tools begin to bear tangible fruit. These chapters also emphasize the "why" of system tools, not just the "how"; along the way, I'll point out real-world needs met by the examples we'll study, to help you put the details in context.

One note up front: these chapters move quickly, and a few of their examples are largely listed just for independent study. Because all the scripts here are heavily documented and use Python system tools described in the prior two chapters, I won't go through all the code in detail. You should read the source code listings and experiment with these programs on your own computer to get a better feel for how to combine system interfaces to accomplish realistic tasks. All are available in source code form on the book's example's distribution and most work on all major platforms.

I should also mention that these are programs I really use, not examples written just for this book. In fact, they were coded over a period of years and perform widely differing tasks, so there is no obvious common thread to connect the dots here. On the other hand, they help explain why system tools are useful in the first place, demonstrate larger development concepts that simpler examples cannot, and bear collective witness to the simplicity and portability of automating system tasks with Python. Once you've mastered the basics, you'll probably wish you had done so sooner.

Splitting and Joining Files

Like most kids, mine spend a lot of time on the Internet. As far as I can tell, it's the thing to do these days. Among this latest generation, computer geeks and gurus seem to be held in the same sort of esteem that my generation once held rock stars. When kids disappear into their rooms, the chances are good that they are hacking on computers, not mastering guitar riffs. It's probably healthier than some of the diversions of my own misspent youth, but that's a topic for another kind of book.

If you have teenage kids and computers, or know someone who does, you probably know that it's not a bad idea to keep tabs on what those kids do on the Web. Type your favorite four-letter word in almost any web search engine and you'll understand the concern—it's much better stuff than I could get during my teenage career. To sidestep the issue, only a few of the machines in my house have Internet feeds.

While they're on one of these machines, my kids download lots of games. To avoid infecting our Very Important Computers with viruses from public-domain games, though, my kids usually have to download games on a computer with an Internet feed and transfer them to their own computers to install. The problem is that game files are not small; they are usually much too big to fit on a floppy (and burning a CD takes away valuable game-playing time).

If all the machines in my house ran Linux, this would be a nonissue. There are standard command-line programs on Unix for chopping a file into pieces small enough to fit on a floppy (split), and others for putting the pieces back together to re-create the original file (cat). Because we have all sorts of different machines in the house, though, we needed a more portable solution.[*]

Splitting Files Portably

Since all the computers in my house run Python, a simple portable Python script came to the rescue. The Python program in Example 6-1 distributes a single file's contents among a set of part files and stores those part files in a directory.

---

[*] As I'm writing the third edition of this book, I should probably note that some of this background story is now a bit dated. Some six years later, floppies have largely gone the way of the parallel port and the dinosaur. Moreover, burning a CD is no longer as painful as it once was, there are new options today such as large flash memory cards and wireless home networks, and the configuration of my home computers isn't what it once was. For that matter, some of my kids are no longer kids (though they've retained backward compatibility with the past).

Example 6-1. PP3E\System\Filetools\split.py

```
#!/usr/bin/python
###########################################################################
# split a file into a set of parts; join.py puts them back together;
# this is a customizable version of the standard Unix split command-line
# utility; because it is written in Python, it also works on Windows and
# can be easily modified; because it exports a function, its logic can
# also be imported and reused in other applications;
###########################################################################

import sys, os
kilobytes = 1024
megabytes = kilobytes * 1000
chunksize = int(1.4 * megabytes)                    # default: roughly a floppy

def split(fromfile, todir, chunksize=chunksize):
    if not os.path.exists(todir):                   # caller handles errors
        os.mkdir(todir)                             # make dir, read/write parts
    else:
        for fname in os.listdir(todir):             # delete any existing files
            os.remove(os.path.join(todir, fname))
    partnum = 0
    input = open(fromfile, 'rb')                    # use binary mode on Windows
    while 1:                                        # eof=empty string from read
        chunk = input.read(chunksize)              # get next part <= chunksize
        if not chunk: break
        partnum = partnum+1
        filename = os.path.join(todir, ('part%04d' % partnum))
        fileobj = open(filename, 'wb')
        fileobj.write(chunk)
        fileobj.close()                             # or simply open().write()
    input.close()
    assert partnum <= 9999                          # join sort fails if 5 digits
    return partnum

if __name__ == '__main__':
    if len(sys.argv) == 2 and sys.argv[1] == '-help':
        print 'Use: split.py [file-to-split target-dir [chunksize]]'
    else:
        if len(sys.argv) < 3:
            interactive = 1
            fromfile = raw_input('File to be split? ')        # input if clicked
            todir    = raw_input('Directory to store part files? ')
        else:
            interactive = 0
            fromfile, todir = sys.argv[1:3]                   # args in cmdline
            if len(sys.argv) == 4: chunksize = int(sys.argv[3])
        absfrom, absto = map(os.path.abspath, [fromfile, todir])
        print 'Splitting', absfrom, 'to', absto, 'by', chunksize

        try:
            parts = split(fromfile, todir, chunksize)
        except:
```

Example 6-1. PP3E\System\Filetools\split.py (continued)

```
        print 'Error during split:'
        print sys.exc_info()[0], sys.exc_info()[1]
    else:
        print 'Split finished:', parts, 'parts are in', absto
    if interactive: raw_input('Press Enter key') # pause if clicked
```

By default, this script splits the input file into chunks that are roughly the size of a floppy disk—perfect for moving big files between electronically isolated machines. Most importantly, because this is all portable Python code, this script will run on just about any machine, even ones without their own file splitter. All it requires is an installed Python. Here it is at work splitting the Python 1.5.2 self-installer executable on Windows:

```
C:\temp>echo %X%             shorthand shell variable
C:\PP3rdEd\examples\PP3E

C:\temp>ls -l py152.exe
-rwxrwxrwa   1 0        0        5028339 Apr 16  1999 py152.exe

C:\temp>python %X%\System\Filetools\split.py -help
Use: split.py [file-to-split target-dir [chunksize]]

C:\temp>python %X%\System\Filetools\split.py py152.exe pysplit
Splitting C:\temp\py152.exe to C:\temp\pysplit by 1433600
Split finished: 4 parts are in C:\temp\pysplit

C:\temp>ls -l pysplit
total 9821
-rwxrwxrwa   1 0        0        1433600 Sep 12 06:03 part0001
-rwxrwxrwa   1 0        0        1433600 Sep 12 06:03 part0002
-rwxrwxrwa   1 0        0        1433600 Sep 12 06:03 part0003
-rwxrwxrwa   1 0        0         727539 Sep 12 06:03 part0004
```

Each of these four generated part files represents one binary chunk of the file *py152. exe*—aa chunk small enough to fit comfortably on a floppy disk. In fact, if you add the sizes of the generated part files given by the ls command, you'll come up with 5,028,339 bytes—exactly the same as the original file's size. Before we see how to put these files back together again, let's explore a few of the splitter script's finer points.

Operation modes

This script is designed to input its parameters in either *interactive* or *command-line* mode; it checks the number of command-line arguments to find out the mode in which it is being used. In command-line mode, you list the file to be split and the output directory on the command line, and you can optionally override the default part file size with a third command-line argument.

In interactive mode, the script asks for a filename and output directory at the console window with raw_input and pauses for a key press at the end before exiting. This mode is nice when the program file is started by clicking on its icon; on Windows, parameters are typed into a pop-up DOS box that doesn't automatically disappear. The script also shows the absolute paths of its parameters (by running them through os.path.abspath) because they may not be obvious in interactive mode. We'll see examples of other split modes at work in a moment.

Binary file access

This code is careful to open both input and output files in binary mode (rb, wb), because it needs to portably handle things like executables and audio files, not just text. In Chapter 4, we learned that on Windows, text-mode files automatically map \r\n end-of-line sequences to \n on input and map \n to \r\n on output. For true binary data, we really don't want any \r characters in the data to go away when read, and we don't want any superfluous \r characters to be added on output. Binary-mode files suppress this \r mapping when the script is run on Windows and so avoid data corruption.

Manually closing files

This script also goes out of its way to manually close its files. For instance:

```
fileobj  = open(partname, 'wb')
fileobj.write(chunk)
fileobj.close()
```

As we also saw in Chapter 4, these three lines can usually be replaced with this single line:

```
open(partname, 'wb').write(chunk)
```

This shorter form relies on the fact that the current Python implementation automatically closes files for you when file objects are reclaimed (i.e., when they are garbage collected, because there are no more references to the file object). In this line, the file object would be reclaimed immediately, because the open result is temporary in an expression and is never referenced by a longer-lived name. Similarly, the input file is reclaimed when the split function exits.

As I was writing this chapter, though, there was some possibility that this automatic-close behavior may go away in the future. Moreover, the Jython Java-based Python implementation does not reclaim unreferenced objects as immediately as the standard Python. If you care about the Java port, your script may potentially create many files in a short amount of time, and it may run on a machine that has a limit on the number of open files per program and then close manually. The close calls in this script have never been necessary for my purposes, but because the split function in this module is intended to be a general-purpose tool, it accommodates such worst-case scenarios.

Joining Files Portably

Back to moving big files around the house: after downloading a big game program file, my kids generally run the previous splitter script by clicking on its name in Windows Explorer and typing filenames. After a split, they simply copy each part file onto its own floppy, walk the floppies upstairs, and re-create the split output directory on their target computer by copying files off the floppies. Finally, the script in Example 6-2 is clicked or otherwise run to put the parts back together.

Example 6-2. PP3E\System\Filetools\join.py

```
#!/usr/bin/python
###########################################################################
# join all part files in a dir created by split.py, to re-create file.
# This is roughly like a 'cat fromdir/* > tofile' command on unix, but is
# more portable and configurable, and exports the join operation as a
# reusable function.  Relies on sort order of filenames: must be same
# length.  Could extend split/join to pop up Tkinter file selectors.
###########################################################################

import os, sys
readsize = 1024

def join(fromdir, tofile):
    output = open(tofile, 'wb')
    parts  = os.listdir(fromdir)
    parts.sort()
    for filename in parts:
        filepath = os.path.join(fromdir, filename)
        fileobj  = open(filepath, 'rb')
        while 1:
            filebytes = fileobj.read(readsize)
            if not filebytes: break
            output.write(filebytes)
        fileobj.close()
    output.close()

if __name__ == '__main__':
    if len(sys.argv) == 2 and sys.argv[1] == '-help':
        print 'Use: join.py [from-dir-name to-file-name]'
    else:
        if len(sys.argv) != 3:
            interactive = 1
            fromdir = raw_input('Directory containing part files? ')
            tofile  = raw_input('Name of file to be recreated? ')
        else:
            interactive = 0
            fromdir, tofile = sys.argv[1:]
        absfrom, absto = map(os.path.abspath, [fromdir, tofile])
        print 'Joining', absfrom, 'to make', absto

        try:
```

Example 6-2. PP3E\System\Filetools\join.py (continued)

```
        join(fromdir, tofile)
    except:
        print 'Error joining files:'
        print sys.exc_info()[0], sys.exc_info()[1]
    else:
        print 'Join complete: see', absto
    if interactive: raw_input('Press Enter key') # pause if clicked
```

After running the join script, my kids still may need to run something like zip, gzip, or tar to unpack an archive file, unless it's shipped as an executable;* but at least they're much closer to seeing the Starship Enterprise spring into action. Here is a join in progress on Windows, combining the split files we made a moment ago:

```
C:\temp>python %X%\System\Filetools\join.py -help
Use: join.py [from-dir-name to-file-name]

C:\temp>python %X%\System\Filetools\join.py pysplit mypy152.exe
Joining C:\temp\pysplit to make C:\temp\mypy152.exe
Join complete: see C:\temp\mypy152.exe

C:\temp>ls -l mypy152.exe py152.exe
-rwxrwxrwa   1 0        0         5028339 Sep 12 06:05 mypy152.exe
-rwxrwxrwa   1 0        0         5028339 Apr 16  1999 py152.exe

C:\temp>fc /b mypy152.exe py152.exe
Comparing files mypy152.exe and py152.exe
FC: no differences encountered
```

The join script simply uses os.listdir to collect all the part files in a directory created by split, and sorts the filename list to put the parts back together in the correct order. We get back an exact byte-for-byte copy of the original file (proved by the DOS fc command in the code; use cmp on Unix).

Some of this process is still manual, of course (I haven't quite figured out how to script the "walk the floppies upstairs" bit yet), but the split and join scripts make it both quick and simple to move big files around. Because this script is also portable Python code, it runs on any platform to which we care to move split files. For instance, my kids typically download both Windows and Linux games; since this script runs on either platform, they're covered.

---

* It turns out that the zip, gzip, and tar commands can all be replaced with pure Python code today. The gzip module in the Python standard library provides tools for reading and writing compressed gzip files, usually named with a *.gz* filename extension. It can serve as an all-Python equivalent of the standard gzip and gunzip command-line utility programs. This built-in module uses another module called zlib that implements gzip-compatible data compressions. In recent Python releases, the zipfile module can be imported to make and use ZIP format archives (zip is an archive and compression format, gzip is a compression scheme), and the tarfile module allows scripts to read and write tar archives. See the Python library manual for details.

Reading by blocks or files

Before we move on, there are a couple of details worth underscoring in the join script's code. First of all, notice that this script deals with files in binary mode but also reads each part file in blocks of 1 KB each. In fact, the readsize setting here (the size of each block read from an input part file) has no relation to chunksize in *split.py* (the total size of each output part file). As we learned in Chapter 4, this script could instead read each part file all at once:

```
filebytes = open(filepath, 'rb').read()
output.write(filebytes)
```

The downside to this scheme is that it really does load all of a file into memory at once. For example, reading a 1.4 MB part file into memory all at once with the file object read method generates a 1.4 MB string in memory to hold the file's bytes. Since split allows users to specify even larger chunk sizes, the join script plans for the worst and reads in terms of limited-size blocks. To be completely robust, the split script could read its input data in smaller chunks too, but this hasn't become a concern in practice (recall that as your program runs, Python automatically reclaims strings that are no longer referenced, so this isn't as wasteful as it might seem).

Sorting filenames

If you study this script's code closely, you may also notice that the join scheme it uses relies completely on the sort order of filenames in the parts directory. Because it simply calls the list sort method on the filenames list returned by os.listdir, it implicitly requires that filenames have the same length and format when created by split. The splitter uses zero-padding notation in a string formatting expression ('part%04d') to make sure that filenames all have the same number of digits at the end (four), much like this list:

```
>>> list = ['xx008', 'xx010', 'xx006', 'xx009', 'xx011', 'xx111']
>>> list.sort()
>>> list
['xx006', 'xx008', 'xx009', 'xx010', 'xx011', 'xx111']
```

When sorted, the leading zero characters in small numbers guarantee that part files are ordered for joining correctly. Without the leading zeros, join would fail whenever there were more than nine part files, because the first digit would dominate:

```
>>> list = ['xx8', 'xx10', 'xx6', 'xx9', 'xx11', 'xx111']
>>> list.sort()
>>> list
['xx10', 'xx11', 'xx111', 'xx6', 'xx8', 'xx9']
```

Because the list sort method accepts a comparison function as an argument, we could in principle strip off digits in filenames and sort numerically:

```
>>> list = ['xx8', 'xx10', 'xx6', 'xx9', 'xx11', 'xx111']
>>> list.sort(lambda x, y: cmp(int(x[2:]), int(y[2:])))
>>> list
['xx6', 'xx8', 'xx9', 'xx10', 'xx11', 'xx111']
```

But that still implies that all filenames must start with the same length substring, so this doesn't quite remove the file-naming dependency between the split and join scripts. Because these scripts are designed to be two steps of the same process, though, some dependencies between them seem reasonable.

Usage Variations

Let's run a few more experiments with these Python system utilities to demonstrate other usage modes. When run without full command-line arguments, both split and join are smart enough to input their parameters *interactively*. Here they are chopping and gluing the Python self-installer file on Windows again, with parameters typed in the DOS console window:

```
C:\temp>python %X%\System\Filetools\split.py
File to be split? py152.exe
Directory to store part files? splitout
Splitting C:\temp\py152.exe to C:\temp\splitout by 1433600
Split finished: 4 parts are in C:\temp\splitout
Press Enter key

C:\temp>python %X%\System\Filetools\join.py
Directory containing part files? splitout
Name of file to be recreated? newpy152.exe
Joining C:\temp\splitout to make C:\temp\newpy152.exe
Join complete: see C:\temp\newpy152.exe
Press Enter key

C:\temp>fc /B py152.exe newpy152.exe
Comparing files py152.exe and newpy152.exe
FC: no differences encountered
```

When these program files are double-clicked in a file explorer GUI, they work the same way (there are usually no command-line arguments when they are launched this way). In this mode, absolute path displays help clarify where files really are. Remember, the current working directory is the script's home directory when clicked like this, so the name *tempsplit* actually maps to a source code directory; type a full path to make the split files show up somewhere else:

```
[in a pop-up DOS console box when split is clicked]
File to be split? c:\temp\py152.exe
Directory to store part files? tempsplit
Splitting c:\temp\py152.exe to C:\PP3rdEd\examples\PP3E\System\Filetools\
tempsplit by 1433600
Split finished: 4 parts are in C:\PP3rdEd\examples\PP3E\System\Filetools\
tempsplit
Press Enter key

[in a pop-up DOS console box when join is clicked]
Directory containing part files? tempsplit
Name of file to be recreated? c:\temp\morepy152.exe
Joining C:\PP3rdEd\examples\PP3E\System\Filetools\tempsplit to make
c:\temp\morepy152.exe
```

```
Join complete: see c:\temp\morepy152.exe
Press Enter key
```

Because these scripts package their core logic in functions, though, it's just as easy to reuse their code by importing and calling from another Python component:

```
C:\temp>python
>>> from PP3E.System.Filetools.split import split
>>> from PP3E.System.Filetools.join  import join
>>>
>>> numparts = split('py152.exe', 'calldir')
>>> numparts
4
>>> join('calldir', 'callpy152.exe')
>>>
>>> import os
>>> os.system(r'fc /B py152.exe callpy152.exe')
Comparing files py152.exe and callpy152.exe
FC: no differences encountered
0
```

A word about performance: all the split and join tests shown so far process a 5 MB file, but they take at most one second of real wall-clock time to finish on my Windows 98 300 and 650 MHz laptop computers—plenty fast for just about any use I could imagine. (They run even faster after Windows has cached information about the files involved, and they would be even quicker on a more modern computer.) Both scripts run just as fast for other reasonable part file sizes too; here is the splitter chopping up the file into 500,000- and 50,000-byte parts:

```
C:\temp>python %X%\System\Filetools\split.py py152.exe tempsplit 500000
Splitting C:\temp\py152.exe to C:\temp\tempsplit by 500000
Split finished: 11 parts are in C:\temp\tempsplit

C:\temp>ls -l tempsplit
total 9826
-rwxrwxrwa   1 0        0            500000 Sep 12 06:29 part0001
-rwxrwxrwa   1 0        0            500000 Sep 12 06:29 part0002
-rwxrwxrwa   1 0        0            500000 Sep 12 06:29 part0003
-rwxrwxrwa   1 0        0            500000 Sep 12 06:29 part0004
-rwxrwxrwa   1 0        0            500000 Sep 12 06:29 part0005
-rwxrwxrwa   1 0        0            500000 Sep 12 06:29 part0006
-rwxrwxrwa   1 0        0            500000 Sep 12 06:29 part0007
-rwxrwxrwa   1 0        0            500000 Sep 12 06:29 part0008
-rwxrwxrwa   1 0        0            500000 Sep 12 06:29 part0009
-rwxrwxrwa   1 0        0            500000 Sep 12 06:29 part0010
-rwxrwxrwa   1 0        0             28339 Sep 12 06:29 part0011

C:\temp>python %X%\System\Filetools\split.py py152.exe tempsplit 50000
Splitting C:\temp\py152.exe to C:\temp\tempsplit by 50000
Split finished: 101 parts are in C:\temp\tempsplit

C:\temp>ls tempsplit
part0001  part0014  part0027  part0040  part0053  part0066  part0079  part0092
part0002  part0015  part0028  part0041  part0054  part0067  part0080  part0093
```

```
part0003    part0016    part0029    part0042    part0055    part0068    part0081    part0094
part0004    part0017    part0030    part0043    part0056    part0069    part0082    part0095
part0005    part0018    part0031    part0044    part0057    part0070    part0083    part0096
part0006    part0019    part0032    part0045    part0058    part0071    part0084    part0097
part0007    part0020    part0033    part0046    part0059    part0072    part0085    part0098
part0008    part0021    part0034    part0047    part0060    part0073    part0086    part0099
part0009    part0022    part0035    part0048    part0061    part0074    part0087    part0100
part0010    part0023    part0036    part0049    part0062    part0075    part0088    part0101
part0011    part0024    part0037    part0050    part0063    part0076    part0089
part0012    part0025    part0038    part0051    part0064    part0077    part0090
part0013    part0026    part0039    part0052    part0065    part0078    part0091
```

The split can take longer to finish, but only if the part file's size is set small enough to generate thousands of part files; splitting into 1,006 parts works but runs slower (though machines today are quick enough that you probably won't notice):

```
C:\temp>python %X%\System\Filetools\split.py py152.exe tempsplit 5000
Splitting C:\temp\py152.exe to C:\temp\tempsplit by 5000
Split finished: 1006 parts are in C:\temp\tempsplit

C:\temp>python %X%\System\Filetools\join.py tempsplit mypy152.exe
Joining C:\temp\tempsplit to make C:\temp\py152.exe
Join complete: see C:\temp\py152.exe

C:\temp>fc /B py152.exe mypy152.exe
Comparing files py152.exe and mypy152.exe
FC: no differences encountered

C:\temp>ls -l tempsplit
...1,000 lines deleted...
-rwxrwxrwa   1 0        0            5000 Sep 12 06:30 part1001
-rwxrwxrwa   1 0        0            5000 Sep 12 06:30 part1002
-rwxrwxrwa   1 0        0            5000 Sep 12 06:30 part1003
-rwxrwxrwa   1 0        0            5000 Sep 12 06:30 part1004
-rwxrwxrwa   1 0        0            5000 Sep 12 06:30 part1005
-rwxrwxrwa   1 0        0            3339 Sep 12 06:30 part1006
```

Finally, the splitter is also smart enough to create the output directory if it doesn't yet exist and to clear out any old files there if it does exist. Because the joiner combines whatever files exist in the output directory, this is a nice ergonomic touch. If the output directory was not cleared before each split, it would be too easy to forget that a prior run's files are still there. Given that my kids are running these scripts, they need to be as forgiving as possible; your user base may vary, but perhaps not by much.

```
C:\temp>python %X%\System\Filetools\split.py py152.exe tempsplit 700000
Splitting C:\temp\py152.exe to C:\temp\tempsplit by 700000
Split finished: 8 parts are in C:\temp\tempsplit

C:\temp>ls -l tempsplit
total 9827
-rwxrwxrwa   1 0        0          700000 Sep 12 06:32 part0001
-rwxrwxrwa   1 0        0          700000 Sep 12 06:32 part0002
-rwxrwxrwa   1 0        0          700000 Sep 12 06:32 part0003
```

```
...
...only new files here...
...
-rwxrwxrwa  1 0        0        700000 Sep 12 06:32 part0006
-rwxrwxrwa  1 0        0        700000 Sep 12 06:32 part0007
-rwxrwxrwa  1 0        0        128339 Sep 12 06:32 part0008
```

Generating Forward-Link Web Pages

Moving is rarely painless, even in the brave new world of cyberspace. Changing your web site's Internet address can lead to all sorts of confusion. You need to ask known contacts to use the new address, and hope that others will eventually stumble onto it themselves. But if you rely on the Internet, moves are bound to generate at least as much confusion as an address change in the real world.

Unfortunately, such site relocations are often unavoidable. Both Internet Service Providers (ISPs) and server machines come and go over the years. Moreover, some ISPs let their service fall to intolerably low levels; if you are unlucky enough to have signed up with such an ISP, there is not much recourse but to change providers, and that often implies a change of web addresses.[*]

Imagine, though, that you are an O'Reilly author and have published your web site's address in multiple books sold widely all over the world. What do you do when your ISP's service level requires a site change? Notifying the tens or hundreds of thousands of readers out there isn't exactly a practical solution.

Probably the best you can do is to leave forwarding instructions at the old site for some reasonably long period of time—the virtual equivalent of a "We've Moved" sign in a storefront window. On the Web, such a sign can also send visitors to the new site automatically: simply leave a page at the old site containing a hyperlink to the page's address at the new site. With such *forward-link files* in place, visitors to the old addresses will be only one click away from reaching the new ones.

That sounds simple enough. But because visitors might try to directly access the address of *any* file at your old site, you generally need to leave one forward-link file for every old file—HTML pages, images, and so on. If you happen to enjoy doing lots of mindless typing, you could create each forward-link file by hand. But given that my home site contained 140 files at the time I wrote this paragraph, the prospect of running one editor session per file was more than enough motivation for an automated solution.

---

[*] It happens. In fact, most people who spend any substantial amount of time in cyberspace could probably tell a horror story or two. Mine goes like this: I had an account with an ISP that went completely offline for a few weeks in response to a security breach by an ex-employee. Worse, not only was personal email disabled, but queued up messages were permanently lost. If your livelihood depends on email and the Web as much as mine does, you'll appreciate the havoc such an outage can wreak.

Page Template File

Here's what I came up with. First of all, I create a general *page template* text file, shown in Example 6-3, to describe how all the forward-link files should look, with parts to be filled in later.

Example 6-3. PP3E\System\Filetools\template.html

```
<HTML><BODY>
<H1>This page has moved</H1>

<P>This page now lives at this address:

<P><A HREF="http://$server$/$home$/$file$">
http://$server$/$home$/$file$</A>

<P>Please click on the new address to jump to this page, and
update any links accordingly.
</P>

<HR>
<H3><A HREF="ispmove.html">Why the move? - The ISP story</A></H3>

</BODY></HTML>
```

To fully understand this template, you have to know something about HTML, a web page description language that we'll explore in Part IV. But for the purposes of this example, you can ignore most of this file and focus on just the parts surrounded by dollar signs: the strings $server$, $home$, and $file$ are targets to be replaced with real values by global text substitutions. They represent items that vary per site relocation and file.

Page Generator Script

Now, given a page template file, the Python script in Example 6-4 generates all the required forward-link files automatically.

Example 6-4. PP3E\System\Filetools\site-forward.py

```
#############################################################################
# Create forward-link pages for relocating a web site.
# Generates one page for every existing site file; upload the generated
# files to your old web site.  Performance note: the first 2 str.replace
# calls could be moved out of the for loop, but this runs in < 1 second
# on my Win98 machine for 150 site files.  Lib note: the os.listdir call
# can be replaced with: sitefiles = glob.glob(sitefilesdir + os.sep + '*')
# but then the file/directory names must be split up manually with:
# dirname, filename = os.path.split(sitefile);
#############################################################################
```

Example 6-4. PP3E\System\Filetools\site-forward.py (continued)

```
import os
servername   = 'starship.python.net'   # where site is relocating to
homedir      = '~lutz/home'            # where site will be rooted
sitefilesdir = 'public_html'           # where site files live locally
uploaddir    = 'isp-forward'           # where to store forward files
templatename = 'template.html'         # template for generated pages

try:
    os.mkdir(uploaddir)                # make upload dir if needed
except OSError: pass

template  = open(templatename).read()  # load or import template text
sitefiles = os.listdir(sitefilesdir)   # filenames, no directory prefix

count = 0
for filename in sitefiles:
    fwdname = os.path.join(uploaddir, filename)        # or + os.sep + filename
    print 'creating', filename, 'as', fwdname

    filetext = template.replace('$server$', servername)   # insert text
    filetext = filetext.replace('$home$',   homedir)      # and write
    filetext = filetext.replace('$file$',   filename)     # file varies
    open(fwdname, 'w').write(filetext)
    count += 1

print 'Last file =>\n', filetext
print 'Done:', count, 'forward files created.'
```

Notice that the template's text is loaded by reading a *file*; it would work just as well to code it as an imported Python string variable (e.g., a triple-quoted string in a module file). Also observe that all configuration options are assignments at the top of the *script*, not command-line arguments; since they change so seldom, it's convenient to type them just once in the script itself.

But the main thing worth noticing here is that this script doesn't care what the template file looks like at all; it simply performs global substitutions blindly in its text, with a different filename value for each generated file. In fact, we can change the template file any way we like without having to touch the script. Such a division of labor can be used in all sorts of contexts—generating "makefiles," form letters, and so on. In terms of library tools, the generator script does the following:

- Uses os.listdir to step through all the filenames in the site's directory
- Uses the string object's replace method to perform global search-and-replace operations that fill in the $-delimited targets in the template file's text
- Uses os.path.join and built-in file objects to write the resulting text out to a forward-link file of the same name in an output directory

The end result is a mirror image of the original web site directory, containing only forward-link files generated from the page template. As an added bonus, the generator script can be run on just about any Python platform—I can run it on my Windows laptop (where I'm writing this book), on my Zaurus Linux-based PDA (where my web site files are maintained these days), as well as on a Unix server (where I keep a copy of my site). Here it is in action on Windows:

```
C:\Stuff\Website>python %X%\System\Filetools\site-forward.py
creating about-hop1.html as isp-forward\about-hop1.html
creating about-lp-toc.html as isp-forward\about-lp-toc.html
creating about-lp.html as isp-forward\about-lp.html
creating about-pp-japan.html as isp-forward\about-pp-japan.html
...
...more lines deleted...
...
creating whatsold.html as isp-forward\whatsold.html
creating xlate-lp.html as isp-forward\xlate-lp.html
creating about-pp2e.html as isp-forward\about-pp2e.html
creating about-ppr2e.html as isp-forward\about-ppr2e.html
Last file =>
<HTML><BODY>
<H1>This page has moved</H1>

<P>This page now lives at this address:

<P><A HREF="http://starship.python.net/~lutz/home/about-ppr2e.html">
http://starship.python.net/~lutz/home/about-ppr2e.html</A>

<P>Please click on the new address to jump to this page, and
update any links accordingly.
</P>

<HR>
<H3><A HREF="ispmove.html">Why the move? - The ISP story</A></H3>

</BODY></HTML>

Done: 137 forward files created.
```

To verify this script's output, double-click on any of the output files to see what they look like in a web browser (or run a start command in a DOS console on Windows—e.g., start isp-forward\about-ppr2e.html). Figure 6-1 shows what one generated page looks like on my machine.

To complete the process, you still need to install the forward links: upload all the generated files in the output directory to your old site's web directory. If that's too much to do by hand too, be sure to see the FTP site upload scripts in Chapter 14 for an automatic way to do that step with Python as well (*PP3E\Internet\Ftp\uploadflat.py* will do the job). Once you've caught the scripting bug, you'll be amazed at how much manual labor Python can automate.

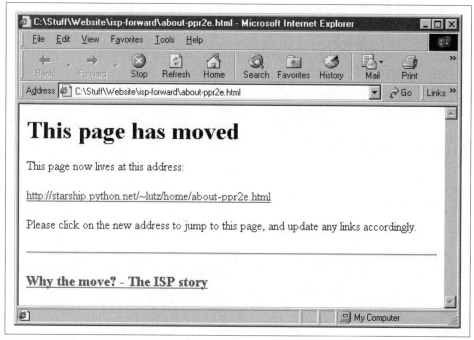

Figure 6-1. Site-forward output file page

A Regression Test Script

As we've seen, Python provides interfaces to a variety of system services, along with tools for adding others. Example 6-5 shows some commonly used services in action. It implements a simple *regression-test* system by running a command-line program with a set of given input files and comparing the output of each run to the prior run's results. This script was adapted from an automated testing system I wrote to catch errors introduced by changes in program source files; in a big system, you might not know when a fix is really a bug in disguise.

Example 6-5. PP3E\System\Filetools\regtest.py

```
#!/usr/local/bin/python
import os, sys, time                    # get system, python services
from glob import glob                   # filename expansion

print 'RegTest start.'
print 'user:', os.environ['USER']       # environment variables
print 'path:', os.getcwd()              # current directory
print 'time:', time.asctime(), '\n'
program = sys.argv[1]                   # two command-line args
testdir = sys.argv[2]

for test in glob(testdir + '/*.in'):    # for all matching input files
```

Example 6-5. PP3E\System\Filetools\regtest.py (continued)

```
    if not os.path.exists('%s.out' % test):
        # no prior results
        os.system('%s < %s > %s.out 2>&1' % (program, test, test))
        print 'GENERATED:', test
    else:
        # backup, run, compare
        os.rename(test + '.out', test + '.out.bkp')
        os.system('%s < %s > %s.out 2>&1' % (program, test, test))
        os.system('diff %s.out %s.out.bkp > %s.diffs' % ((test,)*3) )
        if os.path.getsize(test + '.diffs') == 0:
            print 'PASSED:', test
            os.remove(test + '.diffs')
        else:
            print 'FAILED:', test, '(see %s.diffs)' % test

print 'RegTest done:', time.asctime( )
```

Some of this script is Unix biased. For instance, the 2>&1 syntax to redirect stderr works on Unix but not on all flavors of Windows, and the diff command line spawned is a Unix utility (cmp does similar wok on Windows). You'll need to tweak such code a bit to run this script on certain platforms.

Also, given the improvements to the os module's popen calls as of Python 2.0, these calls have now become a more portable way to redirect streams in such a script and an alternative to shell command redirection syntax (see the subprocess module mentioned near the end of the prior chapter for another way to control process streams).

But this script's basic operation is straightforward: for each filename with an *.in* suffix in the test directory, this script runs the program named on the command line and looks for deviations in its results. This is an easy way to spot changes (called *regressions*) in the behavior of programs spawned from the shell. The real secret of this script's success is in the filenames used to record test information; within a given test directory *testdir*:

- *testdir/test.in* files represent standard input sources for program runs.
- *testdir/test.in.out* files represent the output generated for each input file.
- *testdir/test.in.out.bkp* files are backups of prior *.in.out* result files.
- *testdir/test.in.diffs* files represent regressions; output file differences.

Output and difference files are generated in the test directory with distinct suffixes. For example, if we have an executable program or script called shrubbery and a test directory called *test1* containing a set of *.in* input files, a typical run of the tester might look something like this:

```
% regtest.py shrubbery test1
RegTest start.
user: mark
path: /home/mark/stuff/python/testing
```

```
time: Mon Feb 26 21:13:20 1996

FAILED: test1/t1.in (see test1/t1.in.diffs)
PASSED: test1/t2.in
FAILED: test1/t3.in (see test1/t3.in.diffs)
RegTest done: Mon Feb 26 21:13:27 1996
```

Here, shrubbery is run three times for the three *.in* canned input files, and the results of each run are compared to output generated for these three inputs the last time testing was conducted. Such a Python script might be launched once a day to automatically spot deviations caused by recent source code changes (e.g., from a cron job on Unix).

We've already met system interfaces used by this script; most are fairly standard Unix calls, and they are not very Python specific. In fact, much of what happens when we run this script occurs in programs spawned by os.system calls. This script is really just a *driver*; because it is completely independent of both the program to be tested and the inputs it will read, we can add new test cases on the fly by dropping a new input file in a test directory.

So given that this script just drives other programs with standard Unix-like calls, why use Python here instead of something like C? First, the equivalent program in C would be much longer: it would need to declare variables, handle data structures, and more. In C, all external services exist in a single global scope (the linker's scope); in Python, they are partitioned into module namespaces (os, sys, etc.) to avoid name clashes. And unlike C, the Python code can be run immediately, without compiling and linking; changes can be tested much quicker in Python. Moreover, with just a little extra work, we could make this script run on Windows too. As you can probably tell by now, Python excels when it comes to portability and productivity.

Because of such benefits, automated testing is a very common role for Python scripts. If you are interested in using Python for testing, be sure to see Python's web site (*http://www.python.org*) for other available tools. In particular, the PyUnit (a.k.a. unittest) and doctest standard library modules provide testing frameworks for Python programmers. In a nutshell, here's what each does:

PyUnit
> An object-oriented framework that specifies test cases, expected results, and test suites; subclasses provide test methods that assert result

doctest
> Parses out and reruns tests from an interactive session log that is pasted into a module's docstrings. The logs give both test calls and expected results

See the Python library manual for more details and the Vaults of Parnassus and PyPI web sites for additional testing toolkits in the third-party domain.

Packing and Unpacking Files

Many moons ago (about 10 years), I used machines that had no tools for bundling files into a single package for easy transport. Here is the situation: you have a large set of text files laying around that you need to transfer to another computer. These days, tools like tar are widely available for packaging many files into a single file that can be copied, uploaded, mailed, or otherwise transferred in a single step. As mentioned in an earlier footnote, even Python itself has grown to support zip and tar archives in the standard library (see the zipfile and tarfile modules in the library reference).

Before I managed to install such tools on my PC, though, portable Python scripts served just as well. Example 6-6 copies all of the files listed on the command line to the standard output stream, separated by marker lines.

Example 6-6. PP3E\System\App\Clients\textpack.py

```
#!/usr/local/bin/python
import sys                          # load the system module
marker = ':'*10 + 'textpak=>'      # hopefully unique separator

def pack():
    for name in sys.argv[1:]:      # for all command-line arguments
        input = open(name, 'r')    # open the next input file
        print marker + name        # write a separator line
        print input.read(),        # and write the file's contents

if __name__ == '__main__': pack()  # pack files listed on cmdline
```

The first line in this file is a Python comment (#...), but it also gives the path to the Python interpreter using the Unix executable-script trick discussed in Chapter 3. If we give *textpack.py* executable permission with a Unix chmod command, we can pack files by running this program file directly from a shell console and redirect its standard output stream to the file in which we want the packed archive to show up:

```
C:\...\PP3E\System\App\Clients\test>type spam.txt
SPAM
spam

C:\......\test>python ..\textpack.py spam.txt eggs.txt ham.txt > packed.all

C:\......\test>type packed.all
::::::::::::textpak=>spam.txt
SPAM
spam
::::::::::::textpak=>eggs.txt
EGGS
::::::::::::textpak=>ham.txt
ham
```

Running the program this way creates a single output file called *packed.all*, which contains all three input files, with a header line giving the original file's name before each file's contents. Combining many files into one file in this way makes it easy to transfer in a single step—only one file need be copied to floppy, emailed, and so on. If you have hundreds of files to move, this can be a big win.

After such a file is transferred, though, it must somehow be unpacked on the receiving end to re-create the original files. To do so, we need to scan the combined file line by line, watching for header lines left by the packer to know when a new file's contents begin. Another simple Python script, shown in Example 6-7, does the trick.

Example 6-7. PP3E\System\App\Clients\textunpack.py

```
#!/usr/local/bin/python
import sys
from textpack import marker                     # use common separator key
mlen = len(marker)                              # filenames after markers

for line in sys.stdin.readlines( ):             # for all input lines
    if line[:mlen] != marker:
        print line,                             # write real lines
    else:
        sys.stdout = open(line[mlen:-1], 'w')   # or make new output file
```

We could code this in a function like we did in textpack, but there is little point in doing so here; as written, the script relies on standard streams, not function parameters. Run this in the directory where you want unpacked files to appear, with the packed archive file piped in on the command line as the script's standard input stream:

```
C:\......\test\unpack>python ..\..\textunpack.py < ..\packed.all

C:\......\test\unpack>ls
eggs.txt  ham.txt   spam.txt
```

```
C:\......\test\unpack>type spam.txt
SPAM
Spam
```

Packing Files "++"

So far so good; the textpack and textunpack scripts made it easy to move lots of files around without lots of manual intervention. They are prime examples of what are often called *tactical* scripts—programs you code quickly for a specific task.

But after playing with these and similar scripts for a while, I began to see *commonalities* that almost cried out for reuse. For instance, almost every shell tool I wrote had to scan command-line arguments, redirect streams to a variety of sources, and so on. Further, almost every command-line utility wound up with a different command-line option pattern, because each was written from scratch.

The following few classes are one solution to such problems. They define a *class hierarchy* that is designed for reuse of common shell tool code. Moreover, because of the reuse going on, every program that ties into its hierarchy sports a common look-and-feel in terms of command-line options, environment variable use, and more. As usual with object-oriented systems, once you learn which methods to overload, such a class framework provides a lot of work and consistency for free.

And once you start thinking in such ways, you make the leap to more *strategic* development modes, writing code with broader applicability and reuse in mind. The module in Example 6-8, for instance, adapts the textpack script's logic for integration into this hierarchy.

Example 6-8. PP3E\System\App\Clients\packapp.py

```python
#!/usr/local/bin/python
###################################################
# pack text files into one, separated by marker line;
# % packapp.py -v -o target src src...
# % packapp.py *.txt -o packed1
# >>> apptools.appRun('packapp.py', args...)
# >>> apptools.appCall(PackApp, args...)
###################################################

from textpack import marker
from PP3E.System.App.Kinds.redirect import StreamApp

class PackApp(StreamApp):
    def start(self):
        StreamApp.start(self)
        if not self.args:
            self.exit('packapp.py [-o target]? src src...')
    def run(self):
        for name in self.restargs():
            try:
```

Example 6-8. PP3E\System\App\Clients\packapp.py (continued)

```
                self.message('packing: ' + name)
                self.pack_file(name)
            except:
                self.exit('error processing: ' + name)
    def pack_file(self, name):
        self.setInput(name)
        self.write(marker + name + '\n')
        while 1:
            line = self.readline()
            if not line: break
            self.write(line)

if __name__ == '__main__':  PackApp().main()
```

Here, `PackApp` inherits members and methods that handle:

- Operating system services
- Command-line processing
- Input/output stream redirection

from the `StreamApp` class, imported from another Python module file (listed in Example 6-10). `StreamApp` provides a "read/write" interface to redirected streams and a standard "start/run/stop" script execution protocol. `PackApp` simply redefines the `start` and `run` methods for its own purposes and reads and writes *itself* to access its standard streams. Most low-level system interfaces are hidden by the `StreamApp` class; in OOP terms, we say they are *encapsulated*.

This module can both be run as a program and imported by a client (remember, Python sets a module's name to `__main__` when it's run directly, so it can tell the difference). When run as a program, the last line creates an instance of the `PackApp` class and starts it by calling its `main` method—a method call exported by `StreamApp` to kick off a program run:

```
C:\......\test>python ..\packapp.py -v -o packedapp.all spam.txt eggs.txt ham.txt
PackApp start.
packing: spam.txt
packing: eggs.txt
packing: ham.txt
PackApp done.

C:\......\test>type packedapp.all
:::::::::::textpak=>spam.txt
SPAM
spam
:::::::::::textpak=>eggs.txt
EGGS
:::::::::::textpak=>ham.txt
ham
```

This has the same effect as the *textpack.py* script, but command-line options (-v for verbose mode, -o to name an output file) are inherited from the StreamApp super-class. The unpacker in Example 6-9 looks similar when migrated to the object-oriented framework, because the very notion of running a program has been given a standard structure.

Example 6-9. PP3E\System\App\Clients\unpackapp.py

```
#!/usr/bin/python
###########################################
# unpack a packapp.py output file;
# % unpackapp.py -i packed1 -v
# apptools.appRun('unpackapp.py', args...)
# apptools.appCall(UnpackApp, args...)
###########################################

from textpack import marker
from PP3E.System.App.Kinds.redirect import StreamApp

class UnpackApp(StreamApp):
    def start(self):
        StreamApp.start(self)
        self.endargs()                  # ignore more -o's, etc.
    def run(self):
        mlen = len(marker)
        while True:
            line = self.readline()
            if not line:
                break
            elif line[:mlen] != marker:
                self.write(line)
            else:
                name = line[mlen:].strip()
                self.message('creating: ' + name)
                self.setOutput(name)

if __name__ == '__main__':  UnpackApp().main()
```

This subclass redefines the start and run methods to do the right thing for this script: prepare for and execute a file unpacking operation. All the details of parsing command-line arguments and redirecting standard streams are handled in super-classes:

```
C:\......\test\unpackapp>python ..\..\unpackapp.py -v -i ..\packedapp.all
UnpackApp start.
creating: spam.txt
creating: eggs.txt
creating: ham.txt
UnpackApp done.

C:\......\test\unpackapp>ls
eggs.txt  ham.txt   spam.txt
```

```
C:\......\test\unpackapp>type spam.txt
SPAM
spam
```

Running this script does the same job as the original *textunpack.py*, but we get command-line flags for free (-i specifies the input files). In fact, there are more ways to launch classes in this hierarchy than I have space to show here. A command-line pair, -i -, for instance, makes the script read its input from stdin, as though it were simply piped or redirected in the shell:

```
C:\......\test\unpackapp>type ..\packedapp.all | python ..\..\unpackapp.py -i -
creating: spam.txt
creating: eggs.txt
creating: ham.txt
```

Application Hierarchy Superclasses

This section lists the source code of StreamApp and App—the classes that do all of this extra work on behalf of PackApp and UnpackApp. We don't have space to go through all of this code in detail, so be sure to study these listings on your own for more information. It's all straight Python code.

I should also point out that the classes listed in this section are just the ones used by the object-oriented mutations of the textpack and textunpack scripts. They represent just one branch of an overall application framework class tree, which you can study on this book's examples distribution (browse its directory, *PP3E\System\App*). Other classes in the tree provide command menus, internal string-based file streams, and so on. You'll also find additional clients of the hierarchy that do things like launch other shell tools and scan Unix-style email mailbox files.

StreamApp: adding stream redirection

StreamApp adds a few command-line arguments (-i, -o) and input/output stream redirection to the more general App root class listed later in this section; App, in turn, defines the most general kinds of program behavior, to be inherited in Examples 6-8, 6-9, and 6-10—i.e., in all classes derived from App.

Example 6-10. PP3E\System\App\Kinds\redirect.py

```
###############################################################################
# App subclasses for redirecting standard streams to files
###############################################################################

import sys
from PP3E.System.App.Bases.app import App

###############################################################################
# an app with input/output stream redirection
###############################################################################
```

Example 6-10. PP3E\System\App\Kinds\redirect.py (continued)

```python
class StreamApp(App):
    def __init__(self, ifile='-', ofile='-'):
        App.__init__(self)                            # call superclass init
        self.setInput( ifile or self.name + '.in')    # default i/o filenames
        self.setOutput(ofile or self.name + '.out')   # unless '-i', '-o' args

    def closeApp(self):                               # not __del__
        try:
            if self.input != sys.stdin:               # may be redirected
                self.input.close()                    # if still open
        except: pass
        try:
            if self.output != sys.stdout:             # don't close stdout!
                self.output.close()                   # input/output exist?
        except: pass

    def help(self):
        App.help(self)
        print '-i <input-file |"-"> (default: stdin  or per app)'
        print '-o <output-file|"-"> (default: stdout or per app)'

    def setInput(self, default=None):
        file = self.getarg('-i') or default or '-'
        if file == '-':
            self.input = sys.stdin
            self.input_name = '<stdin>'
        else:
            self.input = open(file, 'r')              # cmdarg | funcarg | stdin
            self.input_name = file                    # cmdarg '-i -' works too

    def setOutput(self, default=None):
        file = self.getarg('-o') or default or '-'
        if file == '-':
            self.output = sys.stdout
            self.output_name = '<stdout>'
        else:
            self.output = open(file, 'w')             # error caught in main()
            self.output_name = file                   # make backups too?

class RedirectApp(StreamApp):
    def __init__(self, ifile=None, ofile=None):
        StreamApp.__init__(self, ifile, ofile)
        self.streams = sys.stdin, sys.stdout
        sys.stdin    = self.input                     # for raw_input, stdin
        sys.stdout   = self.output                    # for print, stdout

    def closeApp(self):                               # not __del__
        StreamApp.closeApp(self)                      # close files?
        sys.stdin, sys.stdout = self.streams          # reset sys files
```

Example 6-10. PP3E\System\App\Kinds\redirect.py (continued)

```
###############################################################################
# to add as a mix-in (or use multiple-inheritance...)
###############################################################################

class RedirectAnyApp:
    def __init__(self, superclass, *args):
        superclass.__init__(self, *args)
        self.super   = superclass
        self.streams = sys.stdin, sys.stdout
        sys.stdin    = self.input                # for raw_input, stdin
        sys.stdout   = self.output               # for print, stdout

    def closeApp(self):
        self.super.closeApp(self)                # do the right thing
        sys.stdin, sys.stdout = self.streams     # reset sys files
```

App: the root class

The top of the hierarchy knows what it means to be a shell application, but not how
to accomplish a particular utility task (those parts are filled in by subclasses). App,
listed in Example 6-11, exports commonly used tools in a standard and simplified
interface and a customizable start/run/stop method protocol that abstracts script
execution. It also turns application objects into file-like objects: when an application
reads itself, for instance, it really reads whatever source its standard input stream has
been assigned to by other superclasses in the tree (such as StreamApp).

Example 6-11. PP3E\System\App\Bases\app.py

```
###############################################################################
# an application class hierarchy, for handling top-level components;
# App is the root class of the App hierarchy, extended in other files;
###############################################################################

import sys, os, traceback
class AppError(Exception): pass                        # errors raised here

class App:                                             # the root class
    def __init__(self, name=None):
        self.name    = name or self.__class__.__name__    # the lowest class
        self.args    = sys.argv[1:]
        self.env     = os.environ
        self.verbose = self.getopt('-v') or self.getenv('VERBOSE')
        self.input   = sys.stdin
        self.output  = sys.stdout
        self.error   = sys.stderr                      # stdout may be piped
    def closeApp(self):                                # not __del__: ref's?
        pass                                           # nothing at this level
    def help(self):
        print self.name, 'command-line arguments:'     # extend in subclass
        print '-v (verbose)'
```

Example 6-11. PP3E\System\App\Bases\app.py (continued)

```python
###############################
# script environment services
###############################

def getopt(self, tag):
    try:                                       # test "-x" command arg
        self.args.remove(tag)                  # not real argv: > 1 App?
        return 1
    except:
        return 0
def getarg(self, tag, default=None):
    try:                                       # get "-x val" command arg
        pos = self.args.index(tag)
        val = self.args[pos+1]
        self.args[pos:pos+2] = []
        return val
    except:
        return default                         # None: missing, no default
def getenv(self, name, default=''):
    try:                                       # get "$x" environment var
        return self.env[name]
    except KeyError:
        return default
def endargs(self):
    if self.args:
        self.message('extra arguments ignored: ' + repr(self.args))
        self.args = []
def restargs(self):
    res, self.args = self.args, []             # no more args/options
    return res
def message(self, text):
    self.error.write(text + '\n')              # stdout may be redirected
def exception(self):
    return tuple(sys.exc_info()[:2])           # the last exception type,data
def exit(self, message='', status=1):
    if message:
        self.message(message)
    sys.exit(status)
def shell(self, command, fork=0, inp=''):
    if self.verbose:
        self.message(command)                              # how about ipc?
    if not fork:
        os.system(command)                                 # run a shell cmd
    elif fork == 1:
        return os.popen(command, 'r').read()               # get its output
    else:                                                  # readlines too?
        pipe = os.popen(command, 'w')
        pipe.write(inp)                                    # send it input
        pipe.close()
```

Example 6-11. PP3E\System\App\Bases\app.py (continued)

```
##################################################
# input/output-stream methods for the app itself;
# redefine in subclasses if not using files, or
# set self.input/output to file-like objects;
##################################################

def read(self, *size):
    return self.input.read(*size)
def readline(self):
    return self.input.readline( )
def readlines(self):
    return self.input.readlines( )
def write(self, text):
    self.output.write(text)
def writelines(self, text):
    self.output.writelines(text)


###################################################
# to run the app
# main( ) is the start/run/stop execution protocol;
###################################################

def main(self):
    res = None
    try:
        self.start( )
        self.run( )
        res = self.stop( )              # optional return val
    except SystemExit:                 # ignore if from exit( )
        pass
    except:
        self.message('uncaught: ' + str(self.exception( )))
        traceback.print_exc( )
    self.closeApp( )
    return res

def start(self):
    if self.verbose: self.message(self.name + ' start.')
def stop(self):
    if self.verbose: self.message(self.name + ' done.')
def run(self):
    raise AppError, 'run must be redefined!'
```

Why use classes here?

Now that I've listed all this code, some readers might naturally want to ask, "So why
go to all this trouble?" Given the amount of *extra* code in the object-oriented version of
these scripts, it's a perfectly valid question. Most of the code listed in Example 6-11 is
general-purpose logic, designed to be used by many applications. Still, that doesn't
explain why the packapp and unpackapp object-oriented scripts are larger than the original equivalent textpack and textunpack non-object-oriented scripts.

The answers will become more apparent after the first few times you *don't* have to write code to achieve a goal, but there are some concrete benefits worth summarizing here:

Encapsulation
> StreamApp clients need not remember all the system interfaces in Python, because StreamApp exports its own unified view. For instance, arguments, streams, and shell variables are split across Python modules (e.g., sys.argv, sys.stdout, os.environ); in these classes, they are all collected in the same single place.

Standardization
> From the shell user's perspective, StreamApp clients all have a common look-and-feel, because they inherit the same interfaces to the outside world from their superclasses (e.g., -i and -v flags).

Maintenance
> As an added benefit of encapsulation, all of the common code in the App and StreamApp superclasses must be debugged only once. Moreover, localizing code in superclasses makes it easier to understand and change in the future. Only one copy of the code implements a system operation, and we're free to change its implementation in the future without breaking code that makes use of it.

Reuse
> Such a framework can provide an extra precoded utility that we would otherwise have to recode in every script we write (command-line argument extraction, for instance). That holds true now and will hold true in the future— services added to the App root class become immediately usable and customizable among all applications derived from this hierarchy.

Utility
> Because file access isn't hardcoded in PackApp and UnpackApp, they can easily take on new behavior just by changing the class they inherit from. Given the right superclass, PackApp and UnpackApp could just as easily read and write to strings or sockets as to text files and standard streams.

Although it's not obvious until you start writing larger class-based systems, code reuse is perhaps the biggest win for class-based programs. For instance, in Chapter 11, we will reuse the object-oriented-based packer and unpacker scripts by invoking them from a menu GUI like so:

```
from PP3E.System.App.Clients.packapp import PackApp
...get dialog inputs, glob filename patterns
app = PackApp(ofile=output)           # run with redirected output
app.args = filenames                  # reset cmdline args list
app.main( )


from PP3E.System.App.Clients.unpackapp import UnpackApp
...get dialog input
```

```
app = UnpackApp(ifile=input)          # run with input from file
app.main( )                           # execute app class
```

Because these classes encapsulate the notion of streams, they can be imported and called, not just run as top-level scripts. Further, their code is reusable in two ways: not only do they export common system interfaces for reuse in subclasses, but they can also be used as software *components*, as in the previous code listing. See the *PP3E\Gui\Shellgui* directory for the full source code of these clients.

Python doesn't impose object-oriented programming, of course, and you can get a lot of work done with simpler functions and scripts. But once you learn how to structure class trees for reuse, going the extra object-oriented mile usually pays off in the long run.

Automated Program Launchers

Suppose, for just a moment, that you wish to ship Python programs to an audience that may be in the very early stages of evolving from computer user to computer programmer. Maybe you are shipping a Python application to nontechnical users, or perhaps you're interested in shipping a set of Python demo programs with a book. Whatever the reason, some of the people who will use your software can't be expected to do anything more than click a mouse. They certainly won't be able to edit their system configuration files to set things such as PATH and PYTHONPATH per your programs' assumptions. Your software will have to configure itself.

Luckily, Python scripts can do that too. In the next three sections, we're going to study three modules that aim to automatically launch programs with minimal assumptions about the environment on the host machine:

Launcher.py
> A library of tools for automatically configuring the shell environment in preparation for launching a Python script. It can be used to set required shell variables—both the PATH system program search path (used to find the "python" executable) and the PYTHONPATH module search path (used to resolve imports within scripts). Because such variable settings made in a parent program are *inherited* by spawned child programs, this interface lets scripts preconfigure search paths for other scripts.

LaunchBrowser.py
> Aims to portably locate and start an Internet browser program on the host machine in order to view a local file or remote web page. It uses tools in *Launcher.py* to search for a reasonable browser to run.

Playfile.py
> Provides tools for opening media files with either a platform-specific player or a general web browser. It can play audio, images, and video, and it uses the Python library's webbrowser and mimetypes modules to do some of its work.

All of these modules are designed to be reusable in any context where you want your software to be user friendly. By searching for files and configuring environments automatically, your users can avoid (or at least postpone) having to learn the intricacies of environment configuration.

Launcher Module Clients

The three modules in this section see action in many of this book's examples. In fact, we've already used some of these tools. The launchmodes script we met at the end of the prior chapter imported Launcher functions to hunt for the local *python.exe* interpreter's path, needed by os.spawnv calls. That script could have assumed that everyone who installs it on their machine will edit its source code to add their own Python location; but the technical know-how required for even that task is already light-years beyond many potential users.* It's much nicer to invest a negligible amount of startup time to locate Python automatically.

The two modules listed in Examples 6-14 and 6-15, together with launchmodes of the prior chapter, also form the core of the *demo-launcher programs* at the top of the examples distribution tree. There's nothing quite like being able to witness programs in action first hand, so I wanted to make it as easy as possible to launch the Python examples in this book. Ideally, they should run straight from the book examples distribution package when clicked, and not require readers to wade through a complex environment installation procedure.

However, many demos perform cross-directory imports and so require the book's module package directories to be installed in PYTHONPATH; it is not enough just to click on some programs' icons at random. Moreover, when first starting out, users can't be assumed to have added the Python executable to their system search path either; the name "python" might not mean anything in the shell.

At least on platforms tested thus far, the following two modules solve such configuration problems. For example, the *Launch_PyDemos.pyw* script in the root directory automatically configures the system and Python execution environments using *Launcher.py* tools, and then spawns *PyDemos2.pyw*, a Tkinter GUI demo interface we'll meet in Chapter 10. PyDemos in turn uses launchmodes to spawn other programs that also inherit the environment settings made at the top. The net effect is that clicking any of the Launch_* scripts starts Python programs even if you haven't touched your environment settings at all.

---

* You gurus and wizards out there will just have to take my word for it. One of the very first things you learn from flying around the world teaching Python to beginners is just how much knowledge developers take for granted. In the first edition of the book *Learning Python*, for example, my coauthor and I directed readers to do things like "open a file in your favorite text editor" and "start up a DOS command console." We had no shortage of email from beginners wondering what in the world we meant.

You still need to install Python if it's not present, of course, but the Python Windows self-installer is a simple point-and-click affair too. Because searches and configuration take extra time, it's still to your advantage to *eventually* configure your environment settings and run programs such as PyDemos directly instead of through the launcher scripts. But there's much to be said for instant gratification when it comes to software.

These tools will show up in other contexts later in this text. For instance, a GUI example in Chapter 11, big_gui, will use a Launcher tool to locate canned Python source-distribution demo programs in arbitrary and unpredictable places on the underlying computer.

The LaunchBrowser script in Example 6-15 also uses Launcher to locate suitable web browsers and is itself used to start Internet demos in the PyDemos and PyGadgets launcher GUIs—that is, Launcher starts PyDemos, which starts LaunchBrowser, which uses Launcher. By optimizing generality, these modules also optimize reusability.

Launching Programs Without Environment Settings

Because the *Launcher.py* file is heavily documented, I won't go over its fine points in narrative here. Instead, I'll just point out that all of its functions are useful by themselves, but the main entry point is the launchBookExamples function near the end; you need to work your way from the bottom of this file up in order to glimpse its larger picture.

The launchBookExamples function uses all the others to configure the environment and then spawn one or more programs to run in that environment. In fact, the top-level demo launcher scripts shown in Examples 6-12 and 6-13 do nothing more than ask this function to spawn GUI demo interface programs we'll meet in Chapter 10 (e.g., *PyDemos2.pyw* and *PyGadgets_bar.pyw*). Because the GUIs are spawned indirectly through this interface, all programs they spawn inherit the environment configurations too.

Example 6-12. PP3E\Launch_PyDemos.pyw

```
#!/bin/env python
##################################################
# PyDemos + environment search/config first
# run this if you haven't set up your paths yet
# you still must install Python first, though
##################################################

import Launcher
Launcher.launchBookExamples(['PyDemos2.pyw'], trace=False)
```

Example 6-13. PP3E\Launch_PyGadgets_bar.pyw

```
#!/bin/env python
##################################################
# PyGadgets_bar + environment search/config first
# run this if you haven't set up your paths yet
# you still must install Python first, though
##################################################

import Launcher
Launcher.launchBookExamples(['PyGadgets_bar.pyw'], trace=False)
```

When run directly, *PyDemos2.pyw* and *PyGadgets_bar.pyw* instead rely on the configuration settings on the underlying machine. In other words, Launcher effectively hides configuration details from the GUI interfaces by enclosing them in a configuration program layer. To understand how, study Example 6-14.

Example 6-14. PP3E\Launcher.py

```
#!/usr/bin/env python
"""

============================================================================
Tools to find files, and run Python demos even if your environment has
not been manually configured yet.  For instance, provided you have already
installed Python, you can launch Tkinter GUI demos directly from the book's
examples distribution tree by double-clicking this file's icon, without
first changing your environment configuration.

Assumes Python has been installed first (double-click on the python self
installer on Windows), and tries to find where Python and the examples
distribution live on your machine.  Sets Python module and system search
paths before running scripts: this only works because env settings are
inherited by spawned programs on both Windows and Linux.

You may want to edit the list of directories searched for speed, and will
probably want to configure your PYTHONPATH eventually to avoid this
search.  This script is friendly to already-configured path settings,
and serves to demo platform-independent directory path processing.
Python programs can always be started under the Windows port by clicking
(or spawning a 'start' DOS command), but many book examples require the
module search path too for cross-directory package imports.
============================================================================
"""

import sys, os
try:
    PyInstallDir = os.path.dirname(sys.executable)
except:
    PyInstallDir = r'C:\Python24'        # for searches, set for older pythons
BookExamplesFile = 'README-PP3E.txt'     # for pythonpath configuration


def which(program, trace=True):
    """
```

Example 6-14. PP3E\Launcher.py (continued)

```
    Look for program in all dirs in the system's search
    path var, PATH; return full path to program if found,
    else None. Doesn't handle aliases on Unix (where we
    could also just run a 'which' shell cmd with os.popen),
    and it might help to also check if the file is really
    an executable with os.stat and the stat module, using
    code like this: os.stat(filename)[stat.ST_MODE] & 0111
    """
    try:
        ospath = os.environ['PATH']
    except:
        ospath = ''  # OK if not set
    systempath = ospath.split(os.pathsep)
    if trace: print 'Looking for', program, 'on', systempath

    for sysdir in systempath:
        filename = os.path.join(sysdir, program)      # adds os.sep between
        if os.path.isfile(filename):                  # exists and is a file?
            if trace: print 'Found', filename
            return filename
        else:
            if trace: print 'Not at', filename
    if trace: print program, 'not on system path'
    return None


def findFirst(thisDir, targetFile, trace=False):
    """
    Search directories at and below thisDir for a file
    or dir named targetFile.  Like find.find in standard
    lib, but no name patterns, follows Unix links, and
    stops at the first file found with a matching name.
    targetFile must be a simple base name, not dir path.
    could also use os.walk or os.path.walk to do this.
    """
    if trace: print 'Scanning', thisDir
    for filename in os.listdir(thisDir):              # skip . and ..
        if filename in [os.curdir, os.pardir]:       # just in case
            continue
        elif filename == targetFile:                 # check name match
            return os.path.join(thisDir, targetFile) # stop at this one
        else:
            pathname = os.path.join(thisDir, filename)   # recur in subdirs
            if os.path.isdir(pathname):                  # stop at 1st match
                below = findFirst(pathname, targetFile, trace)
                if below: return below


def guessLocation(file, isOnWindows=(sys.platform[:3]=='win'), trace=True):
    """
    Try to find directory where file is installed
    by looking in standard places for the platform.
```

Example 6-14. PP3E\Launcher.py (continued)

```
    Change tries lists as needed for your machine.
    """
    cwd = os.getcwd( )                          # directory where py started
    tryhere = cwd + os.sep + file               # or os.path.join(cwd, file)
    if os.path.exists(tryhere):                 # don't search if it is here
        return tryhere                          # findFirst(cwd,file) descends

    if isOnWindows:
        tries = []
        for pydir in [PyInstallDir, r'C:\Program Files\Python']:
            if os.path.exists(pydir):
                tries.append(pydir)
        tries = tries + [cwd, r'C:\Program Files']
        for drive in 'CDEFG':
            tries.append(drive + ':\\')
    else:
        tries = [cwd, os.environ['HOME'], '/usr/bin', '/usr/local/bin']

    for dir in tries:
        if trace: print 'Searching for %s in %s' % (file, dir)
        try:
            match = findFirst(dir, file)
        except OSError:
            if trace: print 'Error while searching', dir     # skip bad drives
        else:
            if match: return match
    if trace: print file, 'not found! - configure your environment manually'
    return None


PP3EpackageRoots = [                            # python module search path
    #'%sPP3E' % os.sep,                          # pass in your own elsewhere
    '']                                         # '' adds examplesDir root


def configPythonPath(examplesDir, packageRoots=PP3EpackageRoots, trace=True):
    """
    Set up the Python module import search-path directory
    list as necessary to run programs in the book examples
    distribution, in case it hasn't been configured already.
    Add examples package root + any nested package roots
    that imports are relative to (just top root currently).

    os.environ assignments call os.putenv internally in 1.5+,
    so these settings will be inherited by spawned programs.
    Python source lib dir and '.' are automatically searched;
    unix|win os.sep is '/' | '\\', os.pathsep is ':' | ';'.
    sys.path is for this process only--must set os.environ.
    adds new dirs to front, in case there are two installs.
    """
    try:
        ospythonpath = os.environ['PYTHONPATH']
```

Example 6-14. PP3E\Launcher.py (continued)

```
    except:
        ospythonpath = '' # OK if not set
    if trace: print 'PYTHONPATH start:\n', ospythonpath

    addList = []
    for root in packageRoots:
        importDir = examplesDir + root
        if importDir in sys.path:
            if trace: print 'Exists', importDir
        else:
            if trace: print 'Adding', importDir
            sys.path.append(importDir)
            addList.append(importDir)

    if addList:
        addString = os.pathsep.join(addList) + os.pathsep
        os.environ['PYTHONPATH'] = addString + ospythonpath
        if trace: print 'PYTHONPATH updated:\n', os.environ['PYTHONPATH']
    else:
        if trace: print 'PYTHONPATH unchanged'


def configSystemPath(pythonDir, trace=True):
    """
    Add python executable dir to system search path if needed
    """
    try:
        ospath = os.environ['PATH']
    except:
        ospath = '' # OK if not set
    if trace: print 'PATH start:\n', ospath

    if ospath.lower().find(pythonDir.lower()) == -1:       # not found?
        os.environ['PATH'] = ospath + os.pathsep + pythonDir  # not case diff
        if trace: print 'PATH updated:\n', os.environ['PATH']
    else:
        if trace: print 'PATH unchanged'


def runCommandLine(pypath, exdir, command, isOnWindows=0, trace=True):
    """
    Run python command as an independent program/process on
    this platform, using pypath as the Python executable,
    and exdir as the installed examples root directory.

    Need full path to Python on Windows, but not on Unix.
    On Windows, an os.system('start ' + command) is similar,
    except that .py files pop up a DOS console box for I/O.
    Could use launchmodes.py too but pypath is already known.
    """
    command = exdir + os.sep + command       # rooted in examples tree
    command = os.path.normpath(command)      # fix up mixed slashes
```

Example 6-14. PP3E\Launcher.py (continued)

```
    os.environ['PP3E_PYTHON_FILE'] = pypath        # export directories for
    os.environ['PP3E_EXAMPLE_DIR'] = exdir         # use in spawned programs

    if trace: print 'Spawning:', command
    if isOnWindows:
        os.spawnv(os.P_DETACH, pypath, ('python', command))
    else:
        cmdargs = [pypath] + command.split( )
        if os.fork( ) == 0:
            os.execv(pypath, cmdargs)              # run prog in child process


def launchBookExamples(commandsToStart, trace=True):
    """
    Toplevel entry point: find python exe and examples dir,
    configure environment, and spawn programs.  Spawned
    programs will inherit any configurations made here.
    """
    isOnWindows = (sys.platform[:3] == 'win')
    pythonFile  = (isOnWindows and 'python.exe') or 'python'
    if trace:
        print os.getcwd( ), os.curdir, os.sep, os.pathsep
        print 'starting on %s...' % sys.platform

    # find python executable: check system path, then guess
    try:
        pypath = sys.executable      # python executable running me
    except:
        # on older pythons
        pypath = which(pythonFile) or guessLocation(pythonFile, isOnWindows)
    assert pypath
    pydir, pyfile = os.path.split(pypath)              # up 1 from file
    if trace:
        print 'Using this Python executable:', pypath
        raw_input('Press <enter> key')

    # find examples root dir: check cwd and others
    expath = guessLocation(BookExamplesFile, isOnWindows)
    assert expath
    updir = expath.split(os.sep)[:-2]                  # up 2 from file
    exdir = os.sep.join(updir)                         # to PP3E pkg parent
    if trace:
        print 'Using this examples root directory:', exdir
        raw_input('Press <enter> key')

    # export python and system paths if needed
    configSystemPath(pydir)
    configPythonPath(exdir)
    if trace:
        print 'Environment configured'
        raw_input('Press <enter> key')
```

Example 6-14. PP3E\Launcher.py (continued)

```
    # spawn programs: inherit configs
    for command in commandsToStart:
        runCommandLine(pypath, os.path.dirname(expath), command, isOnWindows)


if __name__ == '__main__':
    #
    # if no args, spawn all in the list of programs below
    # else rest of cmd line args give single cmd to be spawned
    #
    if len(sys.argv) == 1:
        commandsToStart = [
            'Gui/TextEditor/textEditor.py',           # either slash works
            'Lang/Calculator/calculator.py',          # launcher normalizes path
            'PyDemos2.pyw',
           #'PyGadgets.py',
            'echoEnvironment.pyw'
        ]
    else:
        commandsToStart = [ ' '.join(sys.argv[1:]) ]
    launchBookExamples(commandsToStart)
    if sys.platform[:3] == 'win':
        raw_input('Press Enter') # to read msgs if clicked
```

One way to understand the launcher script is to trace the messages it prints along the way. When run on my Windows test machine for the third edition of this book, I have a PYTHONPATH but have not configured my PATH to include Python. Here is the script's trace output:

```
C:\...\PP3E>Launcher.py
C:\Mark\PP3E-cd\Examples\PP3E . \ ;
starting on win32...
Using this Python executable: C:\Python24\python.exe
Press <enter> key
Using this examples root directory: C:\Mark\PP3E-cd\Examples
Press <enter> key
PATH start:
C:\WINDOWS\system32;...more deleted...;C:\Program Files\MySQL\MySQL Server
4.1\bin
PATH updated:
C:\WINDOWS\system32;...more deleted...;C:\Program Files\MySQL\MySQL Server 4.1\bin;C:
\Python24
PYTHONPATH start:
C:\Mark\PP3E-cd\Examples;C:\Mark\PP2E-cd\Examples
Exists C:\Mark\PP3E-cd\Examples
PYTHONPATH unchanged
Environment configured
Press <enter> key
Spawning: C:\Mark\PP3E-cd\Examples\PP3E\Gui\TextEditor\textEditor.py
Spawning: C:\Mark\PP3E-cd\Examples\PP3E\Lang\Calculator\calculator.py
Spawning: C:\Mark\PP3E-cd\Examples\PP3E\PyDemos2.pyw
Spawning: C:\Mark\PP3E-cd\Examples\PP3E\echoEnvironment.pyw
Press Enter
```

Four programs are spawned with PATH and PYTHONPATH preconfigured according to the location of your Python interpreter program, the location of your examples distribution tree, and the list of required PYTHONPATH entries in the script variable, PP3EpackageRoots.

Just one directory needs to be added to PYTHONPATH for book examples today—the one containing the *PP3E* root directory—since all cross-directory imports are package paths relative to the *PP3E* root. That makes it easier to configure, but the launcher code still supports a list of entries for generality (it may be used for a different tree).

To demonstrate, let's look at some trace outputs obtained with different configurations in the past. When run by itself without a PYTHONPATH setting, the script finds a suitable Python and the examples root directory (by hunting for its README file), uses those results to configure PATH and PYTHONPATH settings if needed and spawns a precoded list of program examples. For example, here is a launch on Windows with an empty PYTHONPATH, a different directory structure, and an older version of Python:

```
C:\temp\examples>set PYTHONPATH=

C:\temp\examples>python Launcher.py
C:\temp\examples . \ ;
starting on win32...
Looking for python.exe on ['C:\\WINDOWS', 'C:\\WINDOWS',
'C:\\WINDOWS\\COMMAND', 'C:\\STUFF\\BIN.MKS', 'C:\\PROGRAM FILES\\PYTHON']
Not at C:\WINDOWS\python.exe
Not at C:\WINDOWS\python.exe
Not at C:\WINDOWS\COMMAND\python.exe
Not at C:\STUFF\BIN.MKS\python.exe
Found C:\PROGRAM FILES\PYTHON\python.exe
Using this Python executable: C:\PROGRAM FILES\PYTHON\python.exe
Press <enter> key
Using this examples root directory: C:\temp\examples
Press <enter> key
PATH start C:\WINDOWS;C:\WINDOWS;C:\WINDOWS\COMMAND;C:\STUFF\BIN.MKS;
C:\PROGRAM FILES\PYTHON
PATH unchanged
PYTHONPATH start:

Adding C:\temp\examples\Part3
Adding C:\temp\examples\Part2
Adding C:\temp\examples\Part2\Gui
Adding C:\temp\examples
PYTHONPATH updated:
C:\temp\examples\Part3;C:\temp\examples\Part2;C:\temp\examples\Part2\Gui;
C:\temp\examples;
Environment configured
Press <enter> key
Spawning: C:\temp\examples\Part2\Gui\TextEditor\textEditor.pyw
Spawning: C:\temp\examples\Part2\Lang\Calculator\calculator.py
Spawning: C:\temp\examples\PyDemos.pyw
Spawning: C:\temp\examples\echoEnvironment.pyw
```

When used by the PyDemos launcher script, Launcher does not pause for key presses along the way (the trace argument is passed in false). Here is the output generated when using the module to launch PyDemos with PYTHONPATH already set to include all the required directories; the script both avoids adding settings redundantly and retains any exiting settings already in your environment (again, this reflects an older tree structure and Python install to demonstrate the search capabilities of the script):

```
C:\PP3rdEd\examples>python Launch_PyDemos.pyw
Looking for python.exe on ['C:\\WINDOWS', 'C:\\WINDOWS',
'C:\\WINDOWS\\COMMAND', 'C:\\STUFF\\BIN.MKS', 'C:\\PROGRAM FILES\\PYTHON']
Not at C:\WINDOWS\python.exe
Not at C:\WINDOWS\python.exe
Not at C:\WINDOWS\COMMAND\python.exe
Not at C:\STUFF\BIN.MKS\python.exe
Found C:\PROGRAM FILES\PYTHON\python.exe
PATH start C:\WINDOWS;C:\WINDOWS;C:\WINDOWS\COMMAND;C:\STUFF\BIN.MKS;
C:\PROGRAM FILES\PYTHON
PATH unchanged
PYTHONPATH start:
C:\PP3rdEd\examples\Part3;C:\PP3rdEd\examples\Part2;C:\PP3rdEd\examples\
Part2\Gui;C:\PP3rdEd\examples
Exists C:\PP3rdEd\examples\Part3
Exists C:\PP3rdEd\examples\Part2
Exists C:\PP3rdEd\examples\Part2\Gui
Exists C:\PP3rdEd\examples
PYTHONPATH unchanged
Spawning: C:\PP3rdEd\examples\PyDemos.pyw
```

And finally, here is the trace output of a launch on my Linux system; because Launcher is written with portable Python code and library calls, environment configuration and directory searches work just as well there:

```
[mark@toy ~/PP3rdEd/examples]$ unsetenv PYTHONPATH
[mark@toy ~/PP3rdEd/examples]$ python Launcher.py
/home/mark/PP3rdEd/examples . / :
starting on linux2...
Looking for python on ['/home/mark/bin', '.', '/usr/bin', '/usr/bin', '/usr/local/
bin', '/usr/X11R6/bin', '/bin', '/usr/X11R6/bin', '/home/mark/
bin', '/usr/X11R6/bin', '/home/mark/bin', '/usr/X11R6/bin']
Not at /home/mark/bin/python
Not at ./python
Found /usr/bin/python
Using this Python executable: /usr/bin/python
Press <enter> key
Using this examples root directory: /home/mark/PP3rdEd/examples
Press <enter> key
PATH start /home/mark/bin:.:/usr/bin:/usr/bin:/usr/local/bin:/usr/X11R6/bin:/bin:/
usr
/X11R6/bin:/home/mark/bin:/usr/X11R6/bin:/home/mark/bin:/usr/X11R6/bin
PATH unchanged
PYTHONPATH start:
```

```
Adding /home/mark/PP3rdEd/examples/Part3
Adding /home/mark/PP3rdEd/examples/Part2
Adding /home/mark/PP3rdEd/examples/Part2/Gui
Adding /home/mark/PP3rdEd/examples
PYTHONPATH updated:
/home/mark/PP3rdEd/examples/Part3:/home/mark/PP3rdEd/examples/Part2:/home/
mark/PP3rdEd/examples/Part2/Gui:/home/mark/PP3rdEd/examples:
Environment configured
Press <enter> key
Spawning: /home/mark/PP3rdEd/examples/Part2/Gui/TextEditor/textEditor.py
Spawning: /home/mark/PP3rdEd/examples/Part2/Lang/Calculator/calculator.py
Spawning: /home/mark/PP3rdEd/examples/PyDemos.pyw
Spawning: /home/mark/PP3rdEd/examples/echoEnvironment.pyw
```

In all but the first of these launches, the Python interpreter was found on the system search path, so no real searches were performed (the Not at lines near the top represent the module's which function, and the first launch used the more recent sys.executable instead of searching). In a moment, we'll also use the launcher's which and guessLocation functions to look for web browsers in a way that kicks off searches in standard install directory trees. Later in the book, we'll use this module in other ways—for instance, to search for demo programs and source code files somewhere on the machine with calls of this form:

```
C:\temp>python
>>> from PP3E.Launcher import guessLocation
>>> guessLocation('hanoi.py')
Searching for hanoi.py in C:\Program Files\Python
Searching for hanoi.py in C:\temp\examples
Searching for hanoi.py in C:\Program Files
Searching for hanoi.py in C:\
'C:\\PP3rdEd\\cdrom\\Python1.5.2\\SourceDistribution\\Unpacked\\Python-1.5.2
\\Demo\\tkinter\\guido\\hanoi.py'

>>> from PP3E.Launcher import findFirst
>>> findFirst('.', 'PyMailGui.py')
'.\\examples\\Internet\\Email\\PyMailGui.py'

>>> findFirst('.', 'peoplecgi.py', True)
Scanning .
Scanning .\PP3E
Scanning .\PP3E\Preview
Scanning .\PP3E\Preview\.idlerc
Scanning .\PP3E\Preview\cgi-bin
'.\\PP3E\\Preview\\cgi-bin\\peoplecgi.py'
```

Such searches aren't necessary if you can rely on an environment variable to give at least part of the path to a file; for instance, paths scripts within the *PP3E* examples tree can be named by joining the PP3EHOME shell variable with the rest of the script's path (assuming the rest of the script's path won't change and that we can rely on that shell variable being set everywhere).

Some scripts may also be able to compose relative paths to other scripts using the sys.path[0] home-directory indicator added for imports (see Chapter 3). But in cases where a file can appear at arbitrary places, searches like those shown previously are sometimes the best scripts can do. The earlier *hanoi.py* program file, for example, can be anywhere on the underlying machine (if present at all); searching is a more user-friendly final alternative than simply giving up.

Launching Web Browsers Portably

Web browsers can do amazing things these days. They can serve as document viewers, remote program launchers, database interfaces, media players, and more. Being able to open a browser on a local or remote page file from within a script opens up all kinds of interesting user-interface possibilities. For instance, a Python system might automatically display its HTML-coded documentation when needed by launching the local web browser on the appropriate page file.* Because most browsers know how to present pictures, audio files, and movie clips, opening a browser on such a file is also a simple way for scripts to deal with multimedia generically.

The next script listed in this chapter is less ambitious than *Launcher.py*, but equally reusable: *LaunchBrowser.py* attempts to provide a portable interface for starting a web browser. Because techniques for launching browsers vary per platform, this script provides an interface that aims to hide the differences from callers. Once launched, the browser runs as an independent program and may be opened to view either a local file or a remote page on the Web.

Here's how it works. Because most web browsers can be started with shell command lines, this script simply builds and launches one as appropriate. For instance, to run a Netscape browser on Linux, a shell command of the form netscape url is run, where url begins with file:// for local files and http:// for live remote-page accesses (this is per URL conventions we'll meet in more detail later in Chapter 16). On Windows, a shell command such as start url achieves the same goal. Here are some platform-specific highlights:

Windows platforms

On Windows, the script either opens browsers with DOS start commands or searches for and runs browsers with the os.spawnv call. On this platform, browsers can usually be opened with simple start commands (e.g., os.system("start xxx.html")). Unfortunately, start relies on the underlying filename associations for web page files on your machine, picks a browser for you per those associations, and has a command-line length limit that this script might exceed for long local file paths or remote page addresses.

---

* For example, the PyDemos demo bar GUI we'll meet in Chapter 10 has buttons that automatically open a browser on web pages related to this book—the publisher's site, the Python home page, my update files, and so on—when clicked.

Because of that, this script falls back on running an explicitly named browser with os.spawnv, if requested or required. To do so, though, it must find the full path to a browser executable. Since it can't assume that users will add it to the PATH system search path (or this script's source code), the script searches for a suitable browser with Launcher module tools in both directories on PATH and in common places where executables are installed on Windows.

Unix-like platforms

On other platforms, the script relies on os.system and the system PATH setting on the underlying machine. It simply runs a command line naming the first browser on a candidates list that it can find on your PATH setting. Because it's much more likely that browsers are in standard search directories on platforms like Unix and Linux (e.g., /usr/bin), the script doesn't look for a browser elsewhere on the machine. Notice the & at the end of the browser command-line run; without it, os.system calls block on Unix-like platforms.

All of this is easily customized (this is Python code, after all), and you may need to add additional logic for other platforms. But on all of my machines, the script makes reasonable assumptions that allow me to largely forget most of the platform-specific bits previously discussed; I just call the same launchBrowser function everywhere. For more details, let's look at Example 6-15.

Example 6-15. PP3E\LaunchBrowser.py

```
#!/bin/env python
###############################################################################
# Launch a web browser to view a web page, portably.  If run in '-live'
# mode, assumes you have an Internet feed and opens page at a remote site.
# Otherwise, assumes the page is a full file pathname on your machine,
# and opens the page file locally.  On Unix/Linux, finds first browser
# on your $PATH.  On Windows, tries DOS "start" command first, or searches
# for the location of a browser on your machine for os.spawnv by checking
# PATH and common Windows executable directories. You may need to tweak
# browser executable name/dirs if this fails. This has only been tested in
# Windows and Linux; you may need to add more code for other machines (mac:
# ic.launcurl(url)?). See also the new standard library webbrowser module.
###############################################################################

import os, sys
from Launcher import which, guessLocation      # file search utilities
useWinStart = False                            # 0=ignore name associations
onWindows   = sys.platform[:3] == 'win'

def launchUnixBrowser(url, verbose=True):           # add your platform if unique
    tries = ['netscape', 'mosaic', 'lynx']         # order your preferences here
    tries = ['firefox'] + tries                    # Firefox rules!
    for program in tries:
        if which(program): break                   # find one that is on $path
    else:
        assert 0, 'Sorry - no browser found'
```

Example 6-15. PP3E\LaunchBrowser.py (continued)

```
        if verbose: print 'Running', program
        os.system('%s %s &' % (program, url))         # or fork+exec; assumes $path

def launchWindowsBrowser(url, verbose=True):
    if useWinStart and len(url) <= 400:               # on Windows: start or spawnv
        try:                                          # spawnv works if cmd too long
            if verbose: print 'Starting'
            os.system('start ' + url)                 # try name associations first
            return                                    # fails if cmdline too long
        except: pass
    browser = None                                    # search for a browser exe
    tries   = ['IEXPLORE.EXE', 'netscape.exe']        # try Explorer, then Netscape
    tries   = ['firefox.exe'] + tries
    for program in tries:
        browser = which(program) or guessLocation(program, 1)
        if browser: break
    assert browser != None, 'Sorry - no browser found'
    if verbose: print 'Spawning', browser
    os.spawnv(os.P_DETACH, browser, (program, url))

def launchBrowser(Mode='-file', Page='index.html', Site=None, verbose=True):
    if Mode == '-live':
        url = 'http://%s/%s' % (Site, Page)           # open page at remote site
    else:
        url = 'file://%s' % Page                      # open page on this machine
    if verbose: print 'Opening', url
    if onWindows:
        launchWindowsBrowser(url, verbose)            # use windows start, spawnv
    else:
        launchUnixBrowser(url, verbose)               # assume $path on Unix, Linux

if __name__ == '__main__':
    # defaults
    Mode = '-file'
    Page = os.getcwd( ) + '/Internet/Web/PyInternetDemos.html'
    Site = 'starship.python.net/~lutz'

    # get command-line args
    helptext = "Usage: LaunchBrowser.py [ -file path | -live path site ]"
    argc = len(sys.argv)
    if argc > 1:  Mode = sys.argv[1]
    if argc > 2:  Page = sys.argv[2]
    if argc > 3:  Site = sys.argv[3]
    if Mode not in ['-live', '-file']:
        print helptext
        sys.exit(1)
    else:
        launchBrowser(Mode, Page, Site)
```

Launching browsers with command lines

This module is designed to be both run and imported. When run by itself on my Windows machine, Firefox starts up. The requested page file is always displayed in a new browser window when os.spawnv is applied but in the currently open browser window (if any) when running a start command:

```
C:\...\PP3E>LaunchBrowser.py
Opening file://C:\Mark\PP3E-cd\Examples\PP3E/Internet/Web/PyInternetDemos.html
Starting
```

The seemingly odd mix of forward and backward slashes in the URL here works fine within the browser; it pops up the window shown in Figure 6-2. Note that this script may be renamed with a *.pyw* extension by the time you fetch its source in order to suppress its pop-up window on Windows; rename back to a *.py* to see its trace outputs.

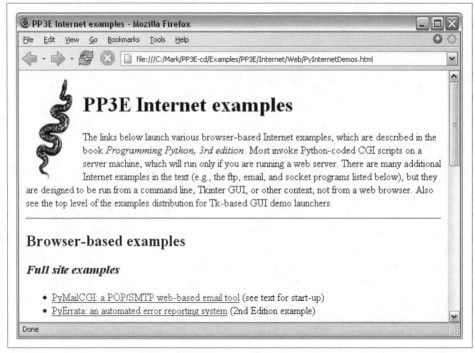

Figure 6-2. Launching a Windows browser on a local file

By default, a start command is spawned; to see the browser search procedure in action on Windows, set the script's useWinStart variable to False (or 0). The script will search for a browser on your PATH settings, and then search in common Windows install directories hardcoded in *Launcher.py*. Here is the search in action on an older machine with Internet Explorer as the first in the list of browsers to try (the PATH on my newer machine is too complex to bear):

```
C:\...\PP3E>python LaunchBrowser.py
                    -file C:\Stuff\Website\public_html\about-pp.html
Opening file://C:\Stuff\Website\public_html\about-pp.html
Looking for IEXPLORE.EXE on ['C:\\WINDOWS', 'C:\\WINDOWS',
'C:\\WINDOWS\\COMMAND', 'C:\\STUFF\\BIN.MKS', 'C:\\PROGRAM FILES\\PYTHON']
Not at C:\WINDOWS\IEXPLORE.EXE
Not at C:\WINDOWS\IEXPLORE.EXE
Not at C:\WINDOWS\COMMAND\IEXPLORE.EXE
Not at C:\STUFF\BIN.MKS\IEXPLORE.EXE
Not at C:\PROGRAM FILES\PYTHON\IEXPLORE.EXE
IEXPLORE.EXE not on system path
Searching for IEXPLORE.EXE in C:\Program Files\Python
Searching for IEXPLORE.EXE in C:\PP3rdEd\examples\PP3E
Searching for IEXPLORE.EXE in C:\Program Files
Spawning C:\Program Files\Internet Explorer\IEXPLORE.EXE
```

If you study these trace message you'll notice that the browser wasn't on the system search path but was eventually located in a local *C:\Program Files* subdirectory; this is just the Launcher module's which and guessLocation functions at work. As run here, the script searches for Internet Explorer first; if that's not to your liking, try changing the script's tries list to make Netscape (or Firefox) first:

```
C:\...\PP3E>python LaunchBrowser.py
Opening file://C:\PP3rdEd\examples\PP3E\Internet\Cgi-Web\PyInternetDemos.html
Looking for netscape.exe on ['C:\\WINDOWS', 'C:\\WINDOWS',
'C:\\WINDOWS\\COMMAND', 'C:\\STUFF\\BIN.MKS', 'C:\\PROGRAM FILES\\PYTHON']
Not at C:\WINDOWS\netscape.exe
Not at C:\WINDOWS\netscape.exe
Not at C:\WINDOWS\COMMAND\netscape.exe
Not at C:\STUFF\BIN.MKS\netscape.exe
Not at C:\PROGRAM FILES\PYTHON\netscape.exe
netscape.exe not on system path
Searching for netscape.exe in C:\Program Files\Python
Searching for netscape.exe in C:\PP3rdEd\examples\PP3E
Searching for netscape.exe in C:\Program Files
Spawning C:\Program Files\Netscape\Communicator\Program\netscape.exe
```

Here, the script eventually found Netscape in a different install directory on the local machine. Besides automatically finding a user's browser for him, this script also aims to be portable. When running this file unchanged on Linux, the local Netscape browser starts if it lives on your PATH; otherwise, others are tried:

```
[mark@toy ~/PP3rdEd/examples/PP3E]$ python LaunchBrowser.py
Opening file:///home/mark/PP3rdEd/examples/PP3E/Internet/Cgi-
Web/PyInternetDemos.html
Looking for netscape on ['/home/mark/bin', '.', '/usr/bin', '/usr/bin',
'/usr/local/bin', '/usr/X11R6/bin', '/bin', '/usr/X11R6/bin', '/home/mark/
bin', '/usr/X11R6/bin', '/home/mark/bin', '/usr/X11R6/bin']
Not at /home/mark/bin/netscape
Not at ./netscape
Found /usr/bin/netscape
Running netscape
[mark@toy ~/PP3rdEd/examples/PP3E]$
```

If you have an Internet connection, you can open pages at *remote* servers too—the next command opens the root page at my site on the *starship.python.net* server, located somewhere on the East Coast the last time I checked:

```
C:\...\PP3E>python LaunchBrowser.py -live ~lutz starship.python.net
Opening http://starship.python.net/~lutz
Starting
```

In Chapter 10, we'll see that this script is also run to start Internet examples in the top-level demo launcher system: the PyDemos script presented in that chapter portably opens local or remote web page files with this button-press callback:

```
[File mode]
    pagepath = os.getcwd() + '/Internet/Web'
    demoButton('PyMailCGI2',
               'Browser-based pop/smtp email interface',
               'LaunchBrowser.pyw -file %s/PyMailCgi/pymailcgi.html' % pagepath,
               pymailcgifiles)

[Live mode]
    site = 'localhost:%s'
    demoButton('PyMailCGI2',
               'Browser-based pop/smtp email interface',
               'LaunchBrowser.pyw -live pymailcgi.html '+ (site % 8000),
               pymailcgifiles)
```

Launching browsers with function calls

Other programs can spawn *LaunchBrowser.py* command lines such as those shown previously with tools such as os.system, as usual; but since the script's core logic is coded in a function, it can just as easily be imported and called:

```
>>> from PP3E.LaunchBrowser import launchBrowser
>>> launchBrowser(Page=r'C:\Mark\WEBSITE\public_html\about-pp.html')
Opening file://C:\Mark\WEBSITE\public_html\about-pp.html
Starting
>>>
```

When called like this, launchBrowser isn't much different than spawning a start command on DOS or a netscape command on Linux, but the Python launchBrowser function is designed to be a portable interface for browser startup across platforms. Python scripts can use this interface to pop up local HTML documents in web browsers; on machines with live Internet links, this call even lets scripts open browsers on remote pages on the Web:

```
>>> launchBrowser(Mode='-live', Page='index.html', Site='www.python.org')
Opening http://www.python.org/index.html
Starting
```

```
>>> launchBrowser(Mode='-live', Page='PyInternetDemos.html',
...                         Site='localhost')
Opening http://localhost/PyInternetDemos.html
Starting
```

On a computer where there is just a dial-up connection, the first call here opens a new Internet Explorer GUI window if needed, dials out through a modem, and fetches the Python home page from *http://www.python.org* on both Windows and Linux—not bad for a single function call. On broadband connections, the page comes up directly. The second call does the same but, using a locally running web server, opens a web demos page we'll explore in Chapter 16.

Viewing multimedia in browsers

I mentioned earlier that browsers are a cheap way to present multimedia. Alas, this sort of thing is best viewed live, so the best I can do is show startup commands here. The next command line and function call, for example, display two GIF images in Internet Explorer on my machine (be sure to use full local pathnames). The result of the first of these is captured in Figure 6-3 (you may have to edit the browser tries list and start-mode flags on your machine to make this work).

```
C:\...\PP3E>python LaunchBrowser.py
        -file C:\Mark\PP3E-cd\Examples\PP3E\Gui\PIL\images\dublin3.jpg

C:\temp>python
>>> from LaunchBrowser import launchBrowser
>>> launchBrowser(Page=r'C:\temp\Examples\PP3E\Gui\gifs\mp_lumberjack.gif')
```

The next command line and call open the *sousa.au* audio file on my machine; the second of these downloads the file from *http://www.rmi.net* first. If all goes as planned, the Monty Python theme song should play on your computer:

```
C:\PP3rdEd\examples>python LaunchBrowser.py
                -file C:\Mark\PP3E-cd\Examples\PP3E\Internet\Ftp\sousa.au
Opening file://C:\PP3E-cd\Examples\PP3E\Internet\Ftp\sousa.au
Starting

>>> launchBrowser(Mode='-live',
...               Site='www.rmi.net',
...               Page='~lutz/sousa.au',
...               verbose=0)
>>>
```

Of course, you could just pass these filenames to a spawned start command or os. startfile call on Windows, or run the appropriate handler program directly with something like os.system. But opening these files in a browser is a more portable

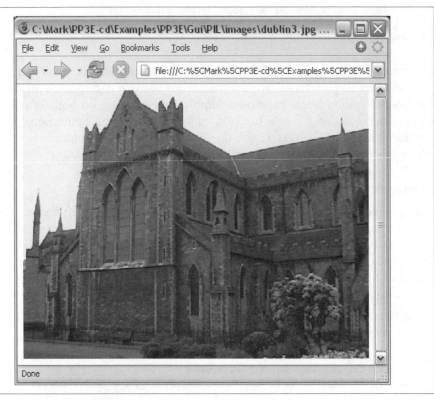

Figure 6-3. Launching a browser on an image file

approach; you don't need to keep track of a set of file-handler programs per platform. Provided your scripts use a portable browser launcher such as LaunchBrowser, you don't even need to keep track of a browser per platform.

That generality is a win unless you wish to do something more specific for certain media types or can't run a web browser. On some PDAs, for instance, you may not be able to open a general web browser on a particular file. In the next section, we'll see how to get more specific when we need to.

Finally, I want to point out that LaunchBrowser reflects browsers that I tend to use. For instance, it tries to find Firefox and then Internet Explorer before Netscape on Windows, and prefers Netscape over Mosaic and Lynx on Linux, but you should feel free to change these choices in your copy of the script. In fact, both LaunchBrowser and Launcher make a few heuristic guesses when searching for files that may not make sense on every computer. Configure as needed.

A Portable Media File Player Tool

Reptilian minds think alike. Roughly one year after I wrote the LaunchBrowser script of the prior section for the second edition of this book, Python sprouted a new standard library module that serves a similar purpose: webbrowser. In this section, we wrap up the chapter with a script that makes use of this new module as well as the Python mimetypes module in order to implement a generic, portable, and extendable media file player.

The Python webbrowser module

Like LaunchBrowser of the prior section, the standard library webbrowser module also attempts to provide a portable interface for launching browsers from scripts. Its implementation is more complex but likely to support more options and platforms than the LaunchBrowser script presented earlier (classic Macintosh browsers, for instance, are directly supported as well). Its interface is straightforward:

```
import webbrowser
webbrowser.open_new('file://' + fullfilename)          # or http://...
```

The preceding code will open the named file in a new web browser window using whatever browser is found on the underlying computer or raise an exception if it cannot. Use the module's open call to reuse an already-open browser window if possible, and use an argument string of the form "http://..." to open a page on a web server. In fact, you can pass in any URL that the browser understands. The following pops up Python's home page in a new browser window, for example:

```
>>> webbrowser.open_new('http://www.python.org')
```

Among other things, this is an easy way to display HTML documents as well as media files, as shown in the prior section. We'll use this module later in this book as a way to display HTML-formatted email messages in the PyMailGUI program in Chapter 15. See the Python library manual for more details. In Chapter 16, we'll also meet a related call, urllib.urlopen, which fetches a web page's text but does not open it in a browser.

To demonstrate the webbrowser module's basic utility, though, let's code another way to open multimedia files. Example 6-16 tries to open a media file on your computer in a somewhat more intelligent way. As a last resort, it always falls back on trying to open the file in a web browser, much like we did in the prior section. Here, though, we first try to run a type-specific player if one is specific in tables, and we use the Python standard library's webbrowser to open a browser instead of using our LaunchBrowser.

The Python mimetypes module

To make this even more useful, we also use the Python mimetypes standard library module to automatically determine the media type from the filename. We get back a type/subtype MIME content-type string if the type can be determined or None if the guess failed:

```
>>> import mimetypes
>>> mimetypes.guess_type('spam.jpg')
('image/jpeg', None)

>>> mimetypes.guess_type('TheBrightSideOfLife.mp3')
('audio/mpeg', None)

>>> mimetypes.guess_type('lifeofbrian.mpg')
('video/mpeg', None)

>>> mimetypes.guess_type('lifeofbrian.xyz')        # unknown type
(None, None)
```

Stripping off the first part of the content-type string gives the file's general media type, which we can use to select a generic player:

```
>>> contype, encoding = mimetypes.guess_type('spam.jpg')
>>> contype.split('/')[0]
'image'
```

A subtle thing: the second item in the tuple returned from the mimetypes guess is an encoding type we won't use here for opening purposes. We still have to pay attention to it, though—if it is not None, it means the file is compressed (gzip or compress), even if we receive a media content type. For example, if the filename is something like *spam.gif.gz*, it's a compressed image that we don't want to try to open directly:

```
>>> mimetypes.guess_type('spam.gz')                # content unknown
(None, 'gzip')

>>> mimetypes.guess_type('spam.gif.gz')            # don't play me!
('image/gif', 'gzip')

>>> mimetypes.guess_type('spam.zip')               # skip archives
('application/zip', None)
```

This module is even smart enough to give us a filename extension for a type:

```
>>> mimetypes.guess_type('sousa.au')
('audio/basic', None)

>>> mimetypes.guess_extension('audio/basic')
'.au'
```

We'll use the mimetypes module again in FTP examples in Chapter 14 to determine transfer type (text or binary), and in our email examples in Chapters 14 and 15 to send, save, and open mail attachments.

In Example 6-16, we use mimetypes to select a table of platform-specific player commands for the media type of the file to be played. That is, we pick a player table for the file's media type, and then pick a command from the player table for the platform. At each step, we give up and run a web browser if there is nothing more specific to be done. The end result is a general and smarter media player tool that you can extend as needed. It will be as portable and specific as the tables you provide to it.

Example 6-16. PP3E\System\Media\playfile.py

```
#!/usr/local/bin/python
###############################################################################
# Try to play an arbitrary media file.  This may not work on your system as is;
# audio files use filters and command lines on Unix, and filename associations
# on Windows via the start command (i.e., whatever you have on your machine to
# run .au files--an audio player, or perhaps a web browser).  Configure and
# extend as needed.  As a last resort, always tries to launch a web browser with
# Python webbrowser module (like LaunchBrowser.py).  See also: Lib/audiodev.py.
# playknownfile assumes you know what sort of media you wish to open; playfile
# tries to determine media type automatically using Python mimetypes module.
###############################################################################

import os, sys

helpmsg = """
Sorry: can't find a media player for '%s' on your system!
Add an entry for your system to the media player dictionary
for this type of file in playfile.py, or play the file manually.
"""

def trace(*args):
    print ' '.join(args)    # with spaces between


###############################################################################
# player techniques: generic and otherwise: extend me
###############################################################################

class MediaTool:
    def __init__(self, runtext=''):
        self.runtext = runtext

class Filter(MediaTool):
    def run(self, mediafile, **options):
        media  = open(mediafile, 'rb')
```

Example 6-16. PP3E\System\Media\playfile.py (continued)

```
            player = os.popen(self.runtext, 'w')          # spawn shell tool
            player.write(media.read())                     # send to its stdin

class Cmdline(MediaTool):
    def run(self, mediafile, **options):
        cmdline = self.runtext % mediafile               # run any cmd line
        os.system(cmdline)                               # use %s for filename

class Winstart(MediaTool):                                # use Windows registry
    def run(self, mediafile, wait=False):                # or os.system('start file')
        if not wait:                                     # allow wait for curr media
            os.startfile(mediafile)
        else:
            os.system('start /WAIT ' + mediafile)

class Webbrowser(MediaTool):
    def run(self, mediafile, **options):                 # open in web browser
        import webbrowser                                # find browser, no wait
        fullpath = os.path.abspath(mediafile)            # file:// needs abs dir
        webbrowser.open_new('file://%s' % fullpath)      # open media file


###############################################################################
# media- and platform-specific policies: change me, or pass one in
###############################################################################


# map platform to player: change me!

audiotools = {
    'sunos5':  Filter('/usr/bin/audioplay'),             # os.popen().write()
    'linux2':  Cmdline('cat %s > /dev/audio'),           # on zaurus, at least
    'sunos4':  Filter('/usr/demo/SOUND/play'),
    'win32':   Winstart()                                # startfile or system
   #'win32':   Cmdline('start %s')
    }

videotools = {
    'linux2':  Cmdline('tkcVideo_c700 %s'),              # zaurus pda
    'win32':   Winstart(),                               # avoid DOS pop up
    }

imagetools = {
    'linux2':  Cmdline('zimager %s/%%s' % os.getcwd()),  # zaurus pda
    'win32':   Winstart(),
    }

# map mimetype of filenames to player tables
```

Example 6-16. PP3E\System\Media\playfile.py (continued)

```
mimetable = {'audio': audiotools,                        # add text: PyEdit?
             'video': videotools,
             'image': imagetools}


###############################################################################
# top-level interfaces
###############################################################################

def trywebbrowser(mediafile, helpmsg=helpmsg):
    """
    try to open a file in a web browser
    """
    trace('trying browser', mediafile)                   # last resort
    try:
        player = Webbrowser()
        player.run(mediafile)
    except:
        print helpmsg % mediafile                        # nothing worked

def playknownfile(mediafile, playertable={}, **options):
    """
    play media file of known type: uses platform-specific
    player objects, or spawns a web browser if nothing for
    this platform; pass in a media-specific player table
    """
    if sys.platform in playertable:
        playertable[sys.platform].run(mediafile, **options)   # specific tool
    else:
        trywebbrowser(mediafile)                         # general scheme

def playfile(mediafile, mimetable=mimetable, **options):
    """
    play media file of any type: uses mimetypes to guess
    media type and map to platform-specific player tables;
    spawn web browser if media type unknown, or has no table
    """
    import mimetypes
    (contenttype, encoding) = mimetypes.guess_type(mediafile)   # check name
    if contenttype == None or encoding is not None:      # can't guess
        contenttype = '?/?'                              # poss .txt.gz
    maintype, subtype = contenttype.split('/', 1)        # 'image/jpeg'
    if maintype in mimetable:
        playknownfile(mediafile, mimetable[maintype], **options)  # try table
    else:
        trywebbrowser(mediafile)                         # other types


###############################################################################
# self-test code
###############################################################################
```

Example 6-16. PP3E\System\Media\playfile.py (continued)

```
if __name__ == '__main__':
    # media type known
    playknownfile('sousa.au', audiotools, wait=True)
    playknownfile('ora-pp2e.jpg', imagetools, wait=True)
    playknownfile('mov10428.mpg', videotools, wait=True)
    playknownfile('img_0276.jpg', imagetools)
    playknownfile('mov10510.mpg', mimetable['video'])

    # media type guessed
    raw_input('Stop players and press Enter')
    playfile('sousa.au', wait=True)                     # default mimetable
    playfile('img_0268.jpg')
    playfile('mov10428.mpg' , mimetable)                # no extra options
    playfile('calendar.html')                           # default web browser
    playfile('wordfile.doc')
    raw_input('Done')                                   # stay open if clicked
```

One coding note: we could also write the `playknownfile` function the following way (this form is more concise, but some future readers of our code might make the case that it is also less explicit and hence less understandable, especially if we code the same way in `playfile` with an empty table default):

```
defaultplayer = Webbrowser( )
player = playertable.get(sys.platform, defaultplayer)
player.run(mediafile, **options)
```

Study this script's code and run it on your own computer to see what happens. As usual, you can test it interactively (use the package path to import from a different directory):

```
>>> from PP3E.System.Media.playfile import playfile
>>> playfile('mov10428.mpg')
```

We'll use this example again as an imported library like this in Chapter 14 to open media files downloaded by FTP. When the script file is run directly, if all goes well, its self-test code at the end opens a number of audio, image, and video files located in the script's directory, using either platform-specific players or a general web browser on your machine. Just for fun, it also opens an HTML file and a Word document to test the web browser code. As is, its player tables are only populated with commands for the machines on which I tested it:

- On my Windows XP computer, the script opens audio and video files in Windows Media Player, images in the Windows standard picture viewer, HTML files in the Firefox web browser, and Word documents in Microsoft Word (more on this in the webbrowser sidebar). This may vary on your machine; Windows ultimately decides which player to run based on what you have registered to open a filename extension. We also wait for some files to play or the viewer to be closed before starting another; Media Player versions 7 and later cannot open multiple instances of the Player and so can handle only one file at a time.

- My Linux test machine for this script was a Zaurus PDA; on that platform, this script opens image and audio files in machine-specific programs, runs audio files by sending them to the /dev/audio device file, and fails on the HTML file (it's not yet configured to use Netfront). On a Zaurus, the script runs command lines, and always pauses until a viewer is closed.

Figure 6-4 shows the script's handiwork on Windows. For other platforms and machines, you will likely have to extend the player dictionaries with platform-specific entries, within this file, or by assigning from outside:

```
import playfile
playfile.audiotools['platformX'] = playfile.Cmdline('...')
playfile.mimetable['newstuff'] = {...}
```

Figure 6-4. Launching media files with specific players

Or you can pass your own player table to the playfile function:

```
from playfile import playfile
myplayers = {...}                              # or start with mimetools.copy()
playfile('Nautyus_Maximus.xyz', myplayers)
```

The MediaTool classes in this file provide general ways to open files, but you may also need to subclass to customize for unique cases. This script also assumes the media file is located on the local machine (even though the webbrowser module supports remote files with "http://" names), and it does not currently allow different players for different MIME subtypes (you may want to handle both "text/plain" and "text/xml" differently).

In fact, this script is really just something of a simple framework that was designed to be extended. As always, hack on; this is Python, after all.

More on the webbrowser Module

In Example 6-16, Microsoft Word is opened directly by webbrowser for the *.doc* file instead of being spawned by, or embedded in, an intermediate web browser. The explanation for this is both subtle and instructive.

Technically, on Windows the current version of the webbrowser module by default uses Netscape if program netscape is on your system PATH setting, and otherwise issues an os.startfile call to open files per your filename associations (and assumes this will launch your web browser—it won't for a Word document!). The net effect is that you may not get a web browser at all.

If you really mean to open a browser regardless of the document type, you can set your BROWSER environment variable to a list of candidate browsers which will be used instead if any one of them is on your PATH or is a command-line string containing a "%s" URL substitution target. If this is not set, the default browser rules of the prior paragraph are used.

In other words, on Windows, if you don't have Netscape and don't set your BROWSER, then using webbrowser.open_new today is similar to using our playfile script's Winstart class, but without a wait option. To force webbrowser to use Firefox, I set my BROWSER as follows (you can make this system-wide via the System settings GUI in Control Pad):

```
...\PP3E\System\Media>set BROWSER=C:\"Program Files"\"Mozilla Firefox"\firefox.
exe %s
...\PP3E\System\Media>playfile.py
```

Once set, Word documents open in Firefox with its standard open dialogs rather than in Word directly. Also, your script also now waits for each browser open call to exit (that is, until the browser window is closed), because os.system is used to start the browser. You should in principle also be able to add Firefox to your PATH and configure webbrowser this way too:

```
...\PP3E\System\Media>set PATH=%PATH%;C:\Program Files\Mozilla Firefox
...\PP3E\System\Media>set BROWSER=firefox.exe
...\PP3E\System\Media>playfile.py
```

This doesn't quite work, though, because webbrowser currently adds single quotes around the URL name for this case, which Firefox does not recognize (webbrowser seems to have a few Unix biases—it also looks for program netscape on Windows, not netscape.exe, and naively splits a command line on spaces in an attempt to extract a program name).

This may be improved but is mostly a moot point on Windows; the default os.startfile is sufficient for most use cases. In fact, we adopted a similar default policy in the LaunchBrowser example we coded in this chapter.

—continued—

The webbrowser module also has lower-level get and register calls to select and name specific browsers, and uses different text and GUI-based default browsers on Unix-like platforms. Moreover, its default browser choices may change over time, especially given the explosive growth of the open source Firefox browser in recent years. See the Python library manual or *webbrowser.py* in the standard library directory for details.

System Examples: Directories

"The Greps of Wrath"

This chapter continues our exploration of systems programming case studies. Here, the focus is on Python scripts that perform more advanced kinds of file and directory processing. The examples in this chapter do system-level tasks such as converting files, comparing and copying directories, and searching files and directories for strings—a task idiomatically known as *grepping*.

Most of the tools these scripts employ were introduced in Chapter 4. Here, the goal is to show these tools in action in the context of more useful and realistic programs. As in the prior chapter, learning about Python programming techniques such as object-oriented programming (OOP) and encapsulation is also a hidden subgoal of most of the examples presented here.

Fixing DOS Line Ends

When I wrote the first edition of this book, I shipped two copies of every example file on the CD-ROM—one with Unix line-end markers and one with DOS markers. The idea was that this would make it easy to view and edit the files on either platform. Readers would simply copy the examples directory tree designed for their platform onto their hard drive and ignore the other one.

If you read Chapter 4, you know the issue here: DOS (and by proxy, Windows) marks line ends in text files with the two characters \r\n (carriage return, line feed), but Unix uses just a single \n. Most modern text editors don't care—they happily display text files encoded in either format. Some tools are less forgiving, though. I still occasionally see the odd \r character when viewing DOS files on Unix, or an entire file in a single line when looking at Unix files on DOS (the Notepad accessory does this on Windows, for example).

Because this is only an occasional annoyance, and because it's easy to forget to keep two distinct example trees in sync, I adopted a different policy as of the book's second edition: we're shipping a single copy of the examples (in DOS format), along with a portable converter tool for changing to and from other line-end formats.

The main obstacle, of course, is how to go about providing a portable and easy-to-use converter—one that runs "out of the box" on almost every computer, without changes or recompiles. Some Unix platforms have commands such as fromdos and dos2unix, but they are not universally available even on Unix. DOS batch files and csh scripts could do the job on Windows and Unix, respectively, but neither solution works on both platforms.

Fortunately, Python does. The scripts presented in Examples 7-1, 7-3, and 7-4 convert end-of-line markers between DOS and Unix formats; they convert a single file, a directory of files, and a directory tree of files. In this section, we briefly look at each script and contrast some of the system tools they apply. Each reuses the prior script's code and becomes progressively more powerful in the process.

The last of these three scripts, Example 7-4, is the portable converter tool I was looking for; it converts line ends in the entire examples tree, in a single step. Because it is pure Python, it also works on *both* DOS and Unix unchanged; as long as Python is installed, it is the only line converter you may ever need to remember.

Converting Line Ends in One File

These three scripts were developed in stages on purpose, so that I could focus on getting line-feed conversions right before worrying about directories and tree walking logic. With that scheme in mind, Example 7-1 addresses just the task of converting lines in a single text file.

Example 7-1. PP3E\PyTools\fixeoln_one.py

```
#############################################################################
# Use: "python fixeoln_one.py [tounix|todos] filename".
# Convert end-of-lines in the single text file whose name is passed in on the
# command line, to the target format (tounix or todos).  The _one, _dir, and
# _all converters reuse the convert function here.  convertEndlines changes
# end-lines only if necessary: lines that are already in the target format
# are left unchanged, so it's OK to convert a file > once with any of the
# 3 fixeoln scripts.  Note: must use binary file open modes for this to work
# on Windows, else default text mode automatically deletes the \r on reads,
# and adds extra \r for each \n on writes; dee PyTools\dumpfile.py raw bytes;
#############################################################################

import os
listonly = False                        # True=show file to be changed, don't rewrite

def convertEndlines(format, fname):     # convert one file
    if not os.path.isfile(fname):       # todos:  \n   => \r\n
```

Example 7-1. PP3E\PyTools\fixeoln_one.py (continued)

```
        print 'Not a text file', fname          # tounix: \r\n => \n
        return                                    # skip directory names

    newlines = []
    changed  = 0
    for line in open(fname, 'rb').readlines():    # use binary i/o modes
        if format == 'todos':                     # else \r lost on Win
            if line[-1:] == '\n' and line[-2:-1] != '\r':
                line = line[:-1] + '\r\n'
                changed = 1
        elif format == 'tounix':                  # avoids IndexError
            if line[-2:] == '\r\n':               # slices are scaled
                line = line[:-2] + '\n'
                changed = 1
        newlines.append(line)

    if changed:
        try:                                       # might be read-only
            print 'Changing', fname
            if not listonly: open(fname, 'wb').writelines(newlines)
        except IOError, why:
            print 'Error writing to file %s: skipped (%s)' % (fname, why)

if __name__ == '__main__':
    import sys
    errmsg = 'Required arguments missing: ["todos"|"tounix"] filename'
    assert (len(sys.argv) == 3 and sys.argv[1] in ['todos', 'tounix']), errmsg
    convertEndlines(sys.argv[1], sys.argv[2])
    print 'Converted', sys.argv[2]
```

This script is fairly straightforward as system utilities go; it relies primarily on the built-in file object's methods. Given a target format flag and filename, it loads the file into a lines list using the readlines method, converts input lines to the target format if needed, and writes the result back to the file with the writelines method if any lines were changed:

```
C:\temp\examples>python %X%\PyTools\fixeoln_one.py tounix PyDemos.pyw
Changing PyDemos.pyw
Converted PyDemos.pyw

C:\temp\examples>python %X%\PyTools\fixeoln_one.py todos PyDemos.pyw
Changing PyDemos.pyw
Converted PyDemos.pyw

C:\temp\examples>fc PyDemos.pyw %X%\PyDemos.pyw
Comparing files PyDemos.pyw and C:\PP3rdEd\examples\PP3E\PyDemos.pyw
FC: no differences encountered

C:\temp\examples>python %X%\PyTools\fixeoln_one.py todos PyDemos.pyw
Converted PyDemos.pyw

C:\temp\examples>python %X%\PyTools\fixeoln_one.py toother nonesuch.txt
```

```
Traceback (innermost last):
  File "C:\PP3rdEd\examples\PP3E\PyTools\fixeoln_one.py", line 45, in ?
    assert (len(sys.argv) == 3 and sys.argv[1] in ['todos', 'tounix']), errmsg
AssertionError: Required arguments missing: ["todos"|"tounix"] filename
```

Here, the first command converts the file to Unix line-end format (tounix), and the second and fourth convert to the DOS convention—all regardless of the platform on which this script is run. To make typical usage easier, converted text is written back to the file *in place*, instead of to a newly created output file. Notice that this script's filename has an _ (underscore) in it, not a - (hyphen); because it is meant to be both run as a script and imported as a library, its filename must translate to a legal Python *variable* name in importers (*fixeoln-one.py* won't work for both roles).

 In all the examples in this chapter that change files in directory trees, the *C:\temp\examples* and *C:\temp\cpexamples* directories used in testing are full copies of the real *PP3E* examples root directory. I don't always show the copy commands used to create these test directories along the way (at least not until we've written our own in Python).

Slinging bytes and verifying results

The fc DOS file-compare command in the preceding interaction confirms the conversions, but to better verify the results of this Python script, I wrote another, shown in Example 7-2.

Example 7-2. PP3E\PyTools\dumpfile.py

```
import sys
bytes = open(sys.argv[1], 'rb').read( )
print '-'*40
print repr(bytes)

print '-'*40
while bytes:
    bytes, chunk = bytes[4:], bytes[:4]        # show four bytes per line
    for c in chunk: print oct(ord(c)), '\t',   # show octal of binary value
    print

print '-'*40
for line in open(sys.argv[1], 'rb').readlines( ):
    print repr(line)
```

To give a clear picture of a file's contents, this script opens a file in binary mode (to suppress automatic line-feed conversions), prints its raw contents (bytes) all at once, displays the octal numeric ASCII codes of it contents four bytes per line, and shows its raw lines. Let's use this to trace conversions. First of all, use a simple text file to make wading through bytes a bit more humane:

```
C:\temp>type test.txt
a
```

```
b
c

C:\temp>python %X%\PyTools\dumpfile.py test.txt
----------------------------------------
'a\r\nb\r\nc\r\n'
----------------------------------------
0141    015     012     0142
015     012     0143    015
012
----------------------------------------
'a\r\n'
'b\r\n'
'c\r\n'
```

The *test.txt* file here is in DOS line-end format; the escape sequence \r\n is simply the DOS line-end marker. Now, converting to Unix format changes all the DOS \r\n markers to a single \n as advertised:

```
C:\temp>python %X%\PyTools\fixeoln_one.py tounix test.txt
Changing test.txt
Converted test.txt

C:\temp>python %X%\PyTools\dumpfile.py test.txt
----------------------------------------
'a\nb\nc\n'
----------------------------------------
0141    012     0142    012
0143    012
----------------------------------------
'a\n'
'b\n'
'c\n'
```

And converting back to DOS restores the original file format:

```
C:\temp>python %X%\PyTools\fixeoln_one.py todos test.txt
Changing test.txt
Converted test.txt

C:\temp>python %X%\PyTools\dumpfile.py test.txt
----------------------------------------
'a\r\nb\r\nc\r\n'
----------------------------------------
0141    015     012     0142
015     012     0143    015
012
----------------------------------------
'a\r\n'
'b\r\n'
'c\r\n'

C:\temp>python %X%\PyTools\fixeoln_one.py todos test.txt     # makes no changes
Converted test.txt
```

Nonintrusive conversions

Notice that no "Changing" message is emitted for the last command just run because no changes were actually made to the file (it was already in DOS format). Because this program is smart enough to avoid converting a line that is already in the target format, it is safe to rerun on a file even if you can't recall what format the file already uses. More naïve conversion logic might be simpler, but it may not be repeatable. For instance, a `replace` string method call can be used to expand a Unix \n to a DOS \r\n, but only once:

```
>>> lines = 'aaa\nbbb\nccc\n'
>>> lines = lines.replace('\n', '\r\n')       # OK: \r added
>>> lines
'aaa\r\nbbb\r\nccc\r\n'
>>> lines = lines.replace('\n', '\r\n')       # bad: double \r
>>> lines
'aaa\r\r\nbbb\r\r\nccc\r\r\n'
```

Such logic could easily trash a file if applied to it twice.* To really understand how the script gets around this problem, though, we need to take a closer look at its use of slices and binary file modes.

Slicing strings out of bounds

This script relies on subtle aspects of string slicing behavior to inspect parts of each line without size checks. For instance:

- The expression `line[-2:]` returns the last two characters at the end of the line (or one or zero characters, if the line isn't at least two characters long).

- A slice such as `line[-2:-1]` returns the second-to-last character (or an empty string if the line is too small to have a second-to-last character).

- The operation `line[:-2]` returns all characters except the last two at the end (or an empty string if there are fewer than three characters).

Because out-of-bounds slices scale slice limits to be inbounds, the script doesn't need to add explicit tests to guarantee that the line is big enough to have end-line characters at the end. For example:

```
>>> 'aaaXY'[-2:], 'XY'[-2:], 'Y'[-2:], ''[-2:]
('XY', 'XY', 'Y', '')

>>> 'aaaXY'[-2:-1], 'XY'[-2:-1], 'Y'[-2:-1], ''[-2:-1]
('X', 'X', '', '')
```

---

* In fact, see the files *old_todos.py*, *old_tounix.py*, and *old_toboth.py* in the *PyTools* directory in the examples distribution for a complete earlier implementation built around `replace`. It was repeatable for to-Unix changes, but not for to-DOS conversion (only the latter may add characters). The `fixeoln` scripts here were developed as a replacement, after I got burned by running to-DOS conversions twice.

```
>>> 'aaaXY'[:-2], 'aaaY'[:-1], 'XY'[:-2], 'Y'[:-1]
('aaa', 'aaa', '', '')
```

If you imagine characters such as \r and \n rather than the X and Y here, you'll understand how the script exploits slice scaling to good effect.

Binary file mode revisited

Because this script aims to be portable to Windows, it also takes care to open files in binary mode, even though they contain text data. As we've seen, when files are opened in text mode on Windows, \r is stripped from \r\n markers on input, and \r is added before \n markers on output. This automatic conversion allows scripts to represent the end-of-line marker as \n on all platforms. Here, though, it would also mean that the script would never see the \r it's looking for to detect a DOS-encoded line because the \r would be dropped before it ever reached the script:

```
>>> open('temp.txt', 'w').writelines(['aaa\n', 'bbb\n'])
>>> open('temp.txt', 'rb').read()
'aaa\r\nbbb\r\n'
>>> open('temp.txt', 'r').read()
'aaa\nbbb\n'
```

Without binary open mode, this can lead to fairly subtle and incorrect behavior on Windows. For example, if files are opened in text mode, converting in todos mode on Windows would actually produce double \r characters: the script might convert the stripped \n to \r\n, which is then expanded on output to \r\r\n!

```
>>> open('temp.txt', 'w').writelines(['aaa\r\n', 'bbb\r\n'])
>>> open('temp.txt', 'rb').read()
'aaa\r\r\nbbb\r\r\n'
```

With binary mode, the script inputs a full \r\n, so no conversion is performed. Binary mode is also required for output on Windows in order to suppress the insertion of \r characters; without it, the tounix conversion would fail on that platform.[*]

If all that is too subtle to bear, just remember to use the b in file open mode strings if your scripts might be run on Windows, and that you mean to process either true binary data or text data as it is actually stored in the file.

Converting Line Ends in One Directory

Armed with a fully debugged single file converter, it's an easy step to add support for converting all files in a single directory. Simply call the single file converter on every

---

[*] But wait, it gets worse. Because of the auto-deletion and insertion of \r characters in Windows text mode, we might simply read and write files in text mode to perform the todos line conversion when run on Windows; the file interface will automatically add the \r on output if it's missing. However, this fails for other usage modes—tounix conversions on Windows (only binary writes can omit the \r), and todos when running on Unix (no \r is inserted). Magic is not always our friend.

Macintosh Line Conversions

As coded, the convertEndlines function does not support classic Macintosh single \r line terminators. It neither converts *to* Macintosh terminators from DOS and Unix format (\r\n and \n to \r), nor converts *from* Macintosh terminators to DOS or Unix format (\r to \r\n or \n). Files in Mac format pass untouched through both the todos and tounix conversions in this script (study the code to see why). I don't use a Mac, but some readers may.

Since adding Mac support would make this code more complex, and since I don't like publishing code in books unless it's been well tested, I'll leave such an extension as an exercise for the Mac Python users in the audience. But for implementation hints, see the *PP3E\PyTools\fixeoln_one_mac.py* file in the book's examples distribution. When run on Windows, it does to-Mac conversions but fails to convert files already in Mac format to Unix or DOS, because the file readlines method does not treat a bare \r as a line break on that platform.

filename returned by a directory listing tool. The script in Example 7-3 uses the glob module we met in Chapter 4 to grab a list of files to convert.

Example 7-3. PP3E\PyTools\fixeoln_dir.py

```
#############################################################################
# Use: "python fixeoln_dir.py [tounix|todos] patterns?".
# convert end-lines in all the text files in the current directory
# (only: does not recurse to subdirectories). Reuses converter in the
# single-file version, file_one.
#############################################################################

import sys, glob
from fixeoln_one import convertEndlines
listonly = 0
patts = ['*.py', '*.pyw', '*.txt', '*.cgi', '*.html',    # text filenames
         '*.c',  '*.cxx', '*.h',   '*.i',   '*.out',      # in this package
         'README*', 'makefile*', 'output*', '*.note']

if __name__ == '__main__':
    errmsg = 'Required first argument missing: "todos" or "tounix"'
    assert (len(sys.argv) >= 2 and sys.argv[1] in ['todos', 'tounix']), errmsg

    if len(sys.argv) > 2:                    # glob anyhow: '*' not applied on DOS
        patts = sys.argv[2:]                 # though not really needed on Linux
    filelists = map(glob.glob, patts)        # name matches in this dir only

    count = 0
    for list in filelists:
        for fname in list:
            if listonly:
                print count+1, '=>', fname
```

Example 7-3. PP3E\PyTools\fixeoln_dir.py (continued)

```
        else:
            convertEndlines(sys.argv[1], fname)
        count += 1

    print 'Visited %d files' % count
```

This module defines a list, patts, containing filename patterns that match all the kinds of text files that appear in the book examples tree; each pattern is passed to the built-in glob.glob call by map to be separately expanded into a list of matching files. That's why there are nested for loops near the end. The outer loop steps through each glob result list, and the inner steps through each name within each list. Try the map call interactively if this doesn't make sense:

```
>>> import glob
>>> map(glob.glob, ['*.py', '*.html'])
[['helloshell.py'], ['about-pp.html', 'about-pp2e.html', 'about-ppr2e.html']]
```

This script requires a convert mode flag on the command line and assumes that it is run in the directory where files to be converted live; cd to the directory to be converted before running this script (or change it to accept a directory name argument too):

```
C:\temp\examples>python %X%\PyTools\fixeoln_dir.py tounix
Changing Launcher.py
Changing Launch_PyGadgets.py
Changing LaunchBrowser.py
...lines deleted...
Changing PyDemos.pyw
Changing PyGadgets_bar.pyw
Changing README-PP3E.txt
Visited 21 files

C:\temp\examples>python %X%\PyTools\fixeoln_dir.py todos
Changing Launcher.py
Changing Launch_PyGadgets.py
Changing LaunchBrowser.py
...lines deleted...
Changing PyDemos.pyw
Changing PyGadgets_bar.pyw
Changing README-PP3E.txt
Visited 21 files

C:\temp\examples>python %X%\PyTools\fixeoln_dir.py todos      # makes no changes
Visited 21 files

C:\temp\examples>fc PyDemos.pyw %X%\PyDemos.pyw
Comparing files PyDemos.pyw and C:\PP3rdEd\examples\PP3E\PyDemos.pyw
FC: no differences encountered
```

Notice that the third command generated no "Changing" messages again. Because the convertEndlines function of the single-file module is reused here to perform the

---

actual updates, this script inherits that function's *repeatability*: it's OK to rerun this script on the same directory any number of times. Only lines that require conversion will be converted. This script also accepts an optional list of filename patterns on the command line in order to override the default patts list of files to be changed:

```
C:\temp\examples>python %X%\PyTools\fixeoln_dir.py tounix *.pyw *.csh
Changing echoEnvironment.pyw
Changing Launch_PyDemos.pyw
Changing Launch_PyGadgets_bar.pyw
Changing PyDemos.pyw
Changing PyGadgets_bar.pyw
Changing cleanall.csh
Changing makeall.csh
Changing package.csh
Changing setup-pp.csh
Changing setup-pp-embed.csh
Changing xferall.linux.csh
Visited 11 files

C:\temp\examples>python %X%\PyTools\fixeoln_dir.py tounix *.pyw *.csh
Visited 11 files
```

Also notice that the single-file script's convertEndlines function performs an initial os.path.isfile test to make sure the passed-in filename represents a *file*, not a directory; when we start globbing with patterns to collect files to convert, it's not impossible that a pattern's expansion might include the name of a directory along with the desired files.

 Unix and Linux users: Unix-like shells automatically glob (i.e., expand) filename pattern operators like * in command lines before they ever reach your script. You generally need to *quote* such patterns to pass them in to scripts verbatim (e.g., "*.py"). The fixeoln_dir script will still work if you don't. Its glob.glob calls will simply find a single matching filename for each already globbed name, and so have no effect:

```
>>>glob.glob('PyDemos.pyw')
['PyDemos.pyw']
```

Patterns are not preglobbed in the DOS shell, though, so the glob.glob calls here are still a good idea in scripts that aspire to be as portable as this one.

Converting Line Ends in an Entire Tree

Finally, Example 7-4 applies what we've already learned to an entire directory tree. It simply runs the file-converter function to every filename produced by tree-walking logic. In fact, this script really just orchestrates calls to the original and already debugged convertEndlines function.

Example 7-4. PP3E\PyTools\fixeoln_all.py

```
#############################################################################
# Use: "python fixeoln_all.py [tounix|todos] patterns?".
# find and convert end-of-lines in all text files at and below the directory
# where this script is run (the dir you are in when you type the command).
# If needed, tries to use the Python find.py library module, else reads the
# output of a Unix-style find command; uses a default filename patterns list
# if patterns argument is absent. This script only changes files that need
# to be changed, so it's safe to run brute force from a root-level dir.
#############################################################################

import os, sys
debug     = False
pyfind    = False        # force py find
listonly  = False        # True=show find results only

def findFiles(patts, debug=debug, pyfind=pyfind):
    try:
        if sys.platform[:3] == 'win' or pyfind:
            print 'Using Python find'
            try:
                import find                    # use python-code find.py
            except ImportError:                # use mine if deprecated!
                from PP3E.PyTools import find   # may get from my dir anyhow
            matches = map(find.find, patts)    # startdir default = '.'
        else:
            print 'Using find executable'
            matches = []
            for patt in patts:
                findcmd = 'find . -name "%s" -print' % patt  # run find command
                lines = os.popen(findcmd).readlines()         # remove endlines
                matches.append(map(str.strip, lines))         # lambda x: x[:-1]
    except:
        assert 0, 'Sorry - cannot find files'
    if debug: print matches
    return matches

if __name__ == '__main__':
    from fixeoln_dir import patts
    from fixeoln_one import convertEndlines

    errmsg = 'Required first argument missing: "todos" or "tounix"'
    assert (len(sys.argv) >= 2 and sys.argv[1] in ['todos', 'tounix']), errmsg

    if len(sys.argv) > 2:            # quote in Unix shell
        patts = sys.argv[2:]        # else tries to expand
    matches = findFiles(patts)

    count = 0
    for matchlist in matches:                # a list of lists
        for fname in matchlist:              # one per pattern
            if listonly:
                print count+1, '=>', fname
```

Example 7-4. PP3E\PyTools\fixeoln_all.py (continued)

```
        else:
            convertEndlines(sys.argv[1], fname)
        count += 1
print 'Visited %d files' % count
```

On Windows, the script uses the portable find.find built-in tool we built in Chapter 4 (the hand-rolled equivalent of Python's original find module)[*] to generate a list of all matching file and directory names in the tree; on other platforms, it resorts to spawning a less portable and perhaps slower find shell command just for illustration purposes.

Once the file pathname lists are compiled, this script simply converts each found file in turn using the single-file converter module's tools. Here is the collection of scripts at work converting the book examples tree on Windows; notice that this script also processes the current working directory (*CWD*; cd to the directory to be converted before typing the command line), and that Python treats forward and backward slashes the same way in the program filename:

```
C:\temp\examples>python %X%/PyTools/fixeoln_all.py tounix
Using Python find
Changing .\LaunchBrowser.py
Changing .\Launch_PyGadgets.py
Changing .\Launcher.py
Changing .\Other\cgimail.py
...lots of lines deleted...
Changing .\EmbExt\Exports\ClassAndMod\output.prog1
Changing .\EmbExt\Exports\output.prog1
Changing .\EmbExt\Regist\output
Visited 1051 files

C:\temp\examples>python %X%/PyTools/fixeoln_all.py todos
Using Python find
Changing .\LaunchBrowser.py
Changing .\Launch_PyGadgets.py
Changing .\Launcher.py
Changing .\Other\cgimail.py
...lots of lines deleted...
Changing .\EmbExt\Exports\ClassAndMod\output.prog1
Changing .\EmbExt\Exports\output.prog1
Changing .\EmbExt\Regist\output
Visited 1051 files

C:\temp\examples>python %X%/PyTools/fixeoln_all.py todos
```

---

[*] Recall that the home directory of a running script is always added to the front of sys.path to give the script import visibility to other files in the script's directory. Because of that, this script would normally load the PP3E\PyTools\find.py module anyhow by just saying import find; it need not specify the full package path in the import. The try handler and full path import are useful here only if this script is moved to a different source directory. Since I move files a lot, I tend to code with self-inflicted worst-case scenarios in mind.

```
Using Python find
Not a text file .\Embed\Inventory\Output
Not a text file .\Embed\Inventory\WithDbase\Output
Visited 1051 files
```

The view from the top

This script and its ancestors are shipped in the book's example distribution as that portable converter tool I was looking for. To convert all example files in the tree to Unix line-terminator format, simply copy the entire *PP3E* examples tree to some "examples" directory on your hard drive and type these two commands in a shell:

```
cd examples/PP3E
python PyTools/fixeoln_all.py tounix
```

Of course, this assumes Python is already installed (see the example distribution's README file for details) but will work on almost every platform in use today. To convert back to DOS, just replace tounix with todos and rerun. I ship this tool with a training CD for Python classes I teach too; to convert those files, we simply type:

```
cd Html\Examples
python ..\..\Tools\fixeoln_all.py tounix
```

Once you get accustomed to the command lines, you can use this in all sorts of contexts. Finally, to make the conversion easier for beginners to run, the top-level examples directory includes *tounix.py* and *todos.py* scripts that can be simply double-clicked in a file explorer GUI; Example 7-5 shows the tounix converter.

Example 7-5. PP3E\tounix.py

```python
#!/usr/local/bin/python
#####################################################################
# Run me to convert all text files to Unix/Linux line-feed format.
# You only need to do this if you see odd '\r' characters at the end
# of lines in text files in this distribution, when they are viewed
# with your text editor (e.g., vi).  This script converts all files
# at and below the examples root, and only converts files that have
# not already been converted (it's OK to run this multiple times).
#
# Since this is a Python script which runs another Python script,
# you must install Python first to run this program; then from your
# system command line (e.g., a xterm window), cd to the directory
# where this script lives, and then type "python tounix.py".  You
# may also be able to simply click on this file's icon in your file
# system explorer, if it knows what '.py' files are.
#####################################################################

import os
prompt = """
This program converts all text files in the book
examples distribution to UNIX line-feed format.
Are you sure you want to do this (y=yes)? """
```

Example 7-5. PP3E\tounix.py (continued)

```
answer = raw_input(prompt)
if answer not in ['y', 'Y', 'yes']:
    print 'Cancelled'
else:
    os.system('python PyTools/fixeoln_all.py tounix')
```

This script addresses the *end user's* perception of usability, but other factors impact *programmer* usability—just as important to systems that will be read or changed by others. For example, the file, directory, and tree converters are coded in separate script files, but there is no law against combining them into a single program that relies on a command-line arguments pattern to know which of the three modes to run. The first argument could be a mode flag, tested by such a program:

```
if   mode == '-one':
    ...
elif mode == '-dir':
    ...
elif mode == '-all:
    ...
```

That seems more confusing than separate files per mode, though; it's usually much easier to botch a complex command line than to type a specific program file's name. It will also make for a confusing mix of global names and one very big piece of code at the bottom of the file. As always, simpler is usually better.

Fixing DOS Filenames

The heart of the prior script was `findFiles`, a function that knows how to portably collect matching file and directory names in an entire tree, given a list of filename patterns. It doesn't do much more than the built-in `find.find` call, but it can be augmented for our own purposes. Because this logic was bundled up in a function, though, it automatically becomes a *reusable* tool.

For example, the next script imports and applies `findFiles`, to collect *all* filenames in a directory tree, by using the filename pattern * (it matches everything). I use this script to fix a legacy problem in the book's examples tree. The names of some files created under MS-DOS were made all uppercase; for example, *spam.py* became *SPAM.PY* somewhere along the way. Because case is significant both in Python and on some platforms, an import statement such as `import spam` will sometimes fail for uppercase filenames.

To repair the damage everywhere in the thousand-file examples tree, I wrote and ran Example 7-6. It works like this: for every filename in the tree, it checks to see whether the name is all uppercase and asks the console user whether the file should be renamed with the `os.rename` call. To make this easy, it also comes up with a reasonable default for most new names—the old one in all-lowercase form.

Example 7-6. PP3E\PyTools\fixnames_all.py

```
###########################################################################
# Use: "python ..\..\PyTools\fixnames_all.py".
# find all files with all uppercase names at and below the current
# directory ('.'); for each, ask the user for a new name to rename the
# file to; used to catch old uppercase filenames created on MS-DOS
# (case matters, when importing Python module files); caveats: this
# may fail on case-sensitive machines if directory names are converted
# before their contents—the original dir name in the paths returned by
# find may no longer exist; the allUpper heuristic also fails for
# odd filenames that are all non-alphabetic (ex: '.');
###########################################################################

import os, string
listonly = False

def allUpper(name):
    for char in name:
        if char in string.lowercase:    # any lowercase letter disqualifies
            return 0                     # else all upper, digit, or special
    return 1

def convertOne(fname):
    fpath, oldfname = os.path.split(fname)
    if allUpper(oldfname):
        prompt = 'Convert dir=%s file=%s? (y|Y)' % (fpath, oldfname)
        if raw_input(prompt) in ['Y', 'y']:
            default  = oldfname.lower()
            newfname = raw_input('Type new file name (enter=%s): ' % default)
            newfname = newfname or default
            newfpath = os.path.join(fpath, newfname)
            os.rename(fname, newfpath)
            print 'Renamed: ', fname
            print 'to:      ', str(newfpath)
            raw_input('Press enter to continue')
            return 1
    return 0

if __name__ == '__main__':
    patts = "*"                          # inspect all filenames
    from fixeoln_all import findFiles    # reuse finder function
    matches = findFiles(patts)

    ccount = vcount = 0
    for matchlist in matches:            # list of lists, one per pattern
        for fname in matchlist:          # fnames are full directory paths
            print vcount+1, '=>', fname  # includes names of directories
            if not listonly:
                ccount += convertOne(fname)
            vcount += 1
    print 'Converted %d files, visited %d' % (ccount, vcount)
```

As before, the findFiles function returns a list of simple filename lists, representing the expansion of all patterns passed in (here, just one result list, for the wildcard pattern *).* For each file and directory name in the result, this script's convertOne function prompts for name changes; an os.path.split and an os.path.join call combination portably tacks the new filename onto the old directory name. Here is a renaming session in progress on Windows:

```
C:\temp\examples>python %X%\PyTools\fixnames_all.py
Using Python find
1 => .\.cshrc
2 => .\LaunchBrowser.out.txt
3 => .\LaunchBrowser.py
...
...more deleted...
...
218 => .\Ai
219 => .\Ai\ExpertSystem
220 => .\Ai\ExpertSystem\TODO
Convert dir=.\Ai\ExpertSystem file=TODO? (y|Y)n
221 => .\Ai\ExpertSystem\__init__.py
222 => .\Ai\ExpertSystem\holmes
223 => .\Ai\ExpertSystem\holmes\README.1ST
Convert dir=.\Ai\ExpertSystem\holmes file=README.1ST? (y|Y)y
Type new file name (enter=readme.1st):
Renamed:  .\Ai\ExpertSystem\holmes\README.1st
to:       .\Ai\ExpertSystem\holmes\readme.1st
Press enter to continue
224 => .\Ai\ExpertSystem\holmes\README.2ND
Convert dir=.\Ai\ExpertSystem\holmes file=README.2ND? (y|Y)y
Type new file name (enter=readme.2nd): readme-more
Renamed:  .\Ai\ExpertSystem\holmes\README.2nd
to:       .\Ai\ExpertSystem\holmes\readme-more
Press enter to continue
...
...more deleted...
...
1471 => .\todos.py
1472 => .\tounix.py
1473 => .\xferall.linux.csh
Converted 2 files, visited 1473
```

This script could simply convert every all-uppercase name to an all-lowercase equivalent automatically, but that's potentially dangerous (some names might require mixed case). Instead, it asks for input during the traversal and shows the results of each renaming operation along the way.

---

* Interestingly, using string '*' for the patterns list works the same way as using list ['*'] here, only because a single-character string is a sequence that contains itself; compare the results of map(find.find, '*') with map(find.find, ['*']) interactively to verify.

Rewriting with os.path.walk

Notice, though, that the pattern-matching power of the find.find call goes completely unused in this script. Because this call must always visit *every* file in the tree, the os.path.walk interface we studied in Chapter 4 would work just as well and avoids any initial pause while a filename list is being collected (that pause is negligible here but may be significant for larger trees). Example 7-7 is an equivalent version of this script that does its tree traversal with the walk callbacks-based model.

Example 7-7. PP3E\PyTools\fixnames_all2.py

```
#############################################################################
# Use: "python ..\..\PyTools\fixnames_all2.py".
# same, but use the os.path.walk interface, not find.find; to make this
# work like the simple find version, puts off visiting directories until
# just before visiting their contents (find.find lists dir names before
# their contents); renaming dirs here can fail on case-sensitive platforms
# too--walk keeps extending paths containing old dir names;
#############################################################################

import os
listonly = False
from fixnames_all import convertOne

def visitname(fname):
    global ccount, vcount
    print vcount+1, '=>', fname
    if not listonly:
        ccount += convertOne(fname)
    vcount += 1

def visitor(myData, directoryName, filesInDirectory):  # called for each dir
    visitname(directoryName)                            # do dir we're in now,
    for fname in filesInDirectory:                      # and non-dir files here
        fpath = os.path.join(directoryName, fname)      # fnames have no dirpath
        if not os.path.isdir(fpath):
            visitname(fpath)

ccount = vcount = 0
os.path.walk('.', visitor, None)
print 'Converted %d files, visited %d' % (ccount, vcount)
```

This version does the same job but visits one extra file (the topmost root directory), and it may visit directories in a different order (os.listdir results are unordered).

Both versions run in similar time for the examples directory tree on my computer.* We'll revisit this script, as well as the fixeoln line-end fixer, in the context of a general tree-walker class hierarchy later in this chapter.

Searching Directory Trees

Engineers love to change things. As I was writing this book, I found it almost *irresistible* to move and rename directories, variables, and shared modules in the book examples tree whenever I thought I'd stumbled onto a more coherent structure. That was fine early on, but as the tree became more intertwined, this became a maintenance nightmare. Things such as program directory paths and module names were hardcoded all over the place—in package import statements, program startup calls, text notes, configuration files, and more.

One way to repair these references, of course, is to edit every file in the directory by hand, searching each for information that has changed. That's so tedious as to be utterly impossible in this book's examples tree, though; as I wrote these words, the examples tree contained 118 directories and 1,342 files! (To count for yourself, run a command-line python PyTools/visitor.py 1 in the *PP3E* examples root directory.) Clearly, I needed a way to automate updates after changes.

Greps and Globs in Shells and Python

There is a standard way to search files for strings on Unix and Linux systems: the command-line program grep and its relatives list all lines in one or more files containing a string or string pattern.† Given that Unix shells expand (i.e., "glob") filename patterns automatically, a command such as grep popen *.py will search a single directory's Python files for the string "popen". Here's such a command in action on Windows (I installed a commercial Unix-like fgrep program on my Windows laptop because I missed it too much there):

```
C:\...\PP3E\System\Filetools>fgrep popen *.py
diffall.py:# - we could also os.popen a diff (unix) or fc (dos)
```

---

* A very subtle thing: both versions of this script might fail on platforms where case matters if they rename directories along the way. If a directory is renamed *before* the contents of that directory have been visited (e. g., a directory *SPAM* renamed to *spam*), then later reference to the directory's contents using the old name (e.g., *SPAM/filename*) will no longer be valid on case-sensitive platforms. This can happen in the find.find version, because directories can and do show up in the result list *before* their contents. It's also a potential with the os.path.walk version, because the prior directory path (with original directory names) keeps being extended at each level of the tree. I use this script only on Windows (DOS), so I haven't been bitten by this in practice. Workarounds—ordering find result lists, walking trees in a bottom-up fashion, making two distinct passes for files and directories, queuing up directory names on a list to be renamed later, or simply not renaming directories at all—are all complex enough to be delegated to the realm of reader experiments (see the newer os.walk walker in Chapter 4 for bottom-up traversal options). As a rule of thumb, changing a tree's names or structure while it is being walked is a risky venture.

† In fact, the act of searching files often goes by the colloquial name "grepping" among developers who have spent any substantial time in the Unix ghetto.

```
dirdiff.py:# - use os.popen('ls...') or glob.glob + os.path.split
dirdiff6.py:    files1 = os.popen('ls %s' % dir1).readlines()
dirdiff6.py:    files2 = os.popen('ls %s' % dir2).readlines()
testdirdiff.py:   expected = expected + os.popen(test % 'dirdiff').read()
testdirdiff.py:      output = output + os.popen(test % script).read()
```

DOS has a command for searching files too—find, not to be confused with the Unix find directory walker command:

```
C:\...\PP3E\System\Filetools>find /N "popen" testdirdiff.py

---------- testdirdiff.py
[8]    expected = expected + os.popen(test % 'dirdiff').read()
[15]       output = output + os.popen(test % script).read()
```

You can do the same within a Python script by running the previously mentioned shell command with os.system or os.popen. Until recently, this could also be done by combining the (now defunct) grep and glob built-in modules. We met the glob module in Chapter 4; it expands a filename pattern into a list of matching filename strings (much like a Unix shell). In the past, the standard library also included a grep module, which acted like a Unix grep command: grep.grep printed lines containing a pattern string among a set of files. When used with glob, the effect was much like that of the fgrep command:

```
>>> from grep import grep
>>> from glob import glob
>>> grep('popen', glob('*.py'))
diffall.py:  16: # - we could also os.popen a diff (unix) or fc (dos)
dirdiff.py:  12: # - use os.popen('ls...') or glob.glob + os.path.split
dirdiff6.py:  19:    files1 = os.popen('ls %s' % dir1).readlines()
dirdiff6.py:  20:    files2 = os.popen('ls %s' % dir2).readlines()
testdirdiff.py:  8:    expected = expected + os.popen(test % 'dirdiff')...
testdirdiff.py: 15:       output = output + os.popen(test % script).read()

>>> import glob, grep
>>> grep.grep('system', glob.glob('*.py'))
dirdiff.py:  16: # - on unix systems we could do something similar by
regtest.py:  18:        os.system('%s < %s > %s.out 2>&1' % (program, ...
regtest.py:  23:        os.system('%s < %s > %s.out 2>&1' % (program, ...
regtest.py:  24:        os.system('diff %s.out %s.out.bkp > %s.diffs' ...
```

Unfortunately, the grep module, much like the original find module discussed at the end of Chapter 4, has been removed from the standard library in the time since I wrote this example for the second edition of this book (it was limited to printing results, and so is less general than other tools). On Unix systems, we can work around its demise by running a grep shell command from within a find shell command. For instance, the following Unix command line:

```
find . -name "*.py" -print -exec fgrep popen {} \;
```

would pinpoint lines and files at and below the current directory that mention popen. If you happen to have a Unix-like find command on every machine you will ever use, this is one way to process directories.

Cleaning up bytecode files

For instance, I used to run the script in Example 7-8 on some of my machines to remove all *.pyc* bytecode files in the examples tree before packaging or upgrading Pythons (it's not impossible that old binary bytecode files are not forward compatible with newer Python releases).

Example 7-8. PP3E\PyTools\cleanpyc.py

```
#############################################################################
# find and delete all "*.pyc" bytecode files at and below the directory
# where this script is run; this assumes a Unix-like find command, and
# so is very nonportable; we could instead use the Python find module,
# or just walk the directory trees with portable Python code; the find
# -exec option can apply a Python script to each file too;
#############################################################################

import os, sys

if sys.platform[:3] == 'win':
    findcmd = r'c:\stuff\bin.mks\find . -name "*.pyc" -print'
else:
    findcmd = 'find . -name "*.pyc" -print'
print findcmd

count = 0
for file in os.popen(findcmd).readlines():          # for all filenames
    count += 1                                      # have \n at the end
    print str(file[:-1])
    os.remove(file[:-1])

print 'Removed %d .pyc files' % count
```

This script uses os.popen to collect the output of a commercial package's find program installed on one of my Windows computers, or else the standard find tool on the Linux side. It's also *completely nonportable* to Windows machines that don't have the commercial Unix-like find program installed, and that includes other computers in my house, not to mention those throughout most of the world at large.

Python scripts can reuse underlying shell tools with os.popen, but by so doing they lose much of the portability advantage of the Python language. The Unix find command is not universally available and is a complex tool by itself (in fact, too complex to cover in this book; see a Unix manpage for more details). As we saw in Chapter 4, spawning a shell command also incurs a performance hit, because it must start a new independent program on your computer.

To avoid some of the portability and performance costs of spawning an underlying find command, I eventually recoded this script to use the find utilities we met and wrote in Chapter 4. The new script is shown in Example 7-9.

Example 7-9. PP3E\PyTools\cleanpyc-py.py

```
#############################################################################
# find and delete all "*.pyc" bytecode files at and below the directory
# where this script is run; this uses a Python find call, and so is
# portable to most machines; run this to delete .pyc's from an old Python
# release; cd to the directory you want to clean before running;
#############################################################################

import os, sys, find              # here, gets PyTools find

count = 0
for file in find.find("*.pyc"):   # for all filenames
    count += 1
    print file
    os.remove(file)

print 'Removed %d .pyc files' % count
```

This works portably, and it avoids external program startup costs. But find is really just a tree searcher that doesn't let you hook into the tree search—if you need to do something unique while traversing a directory tree, you may be better off using a more manual approach. Moreover, find must collect all names before it returns; in very large directory trees, this may introduce significant performance and memory penalties. It's not an issue for my trees, but it could be for yours.

A Python Tree Searcher

To help ease the task of performing global searches on all platforms I might ever use, I coded a Python script to do most of the work for me. Example 7-10 employs the following standard Python tools that we met in the preceding chapters:

- os.path.walk to visit files in a directory
- find string method to search for a string in a text read from a file
- os.path.splitext to skip over files with binary-type extensions
- os.path.join to portably combine a directory path and filename
- os.path.isdir to skip paths that refer to directories, not files

Because it's pure Python code, though, it can be run the same way on both Linux and Windows. In fact, it should work on any computer where Python has been installed. Moreover, because it uses direct system calls, it will likely be faster than using op.popen to spawn a find command that spawns many grep commands.

Example 7-10. PP3E\PyTools\search_all.py

```
#############################################################################
# Use: "python ..\..\PyTools\search_all.py string".
# search all files at and below current directory for a string; uses the
# os.path.walk interface, rather than doing a find to collect names first;
#############################################################################
```

Example 7-10. PP3E\PyTools\search_all.py (continued)

```
import os, sys
listonly = False
skipexts = ['.gif', '.exe', '.pyc', '.o', '.a']        # ignore binary files

def visitfile(fname, searchKey):                       # for each non-dir file
    global fcount, vcount                               # search for string
    print vcount+1, '=>', fname                         # skip protected files
    try:
        if not listonly:
            if os.path.splitext(fname)[1] in skipexts:
                print 'Skipping', fname
            elif open(fname).read().find(searchKey) != -1:
                raw_input('%s has %s' % (fname, searchKey))
                fcount += 1
    except: pass
    vcount += 1

def visitor(myData, directoryName, filesInDirectory):  # called for each dir
    for fname in filesInDirectory:                      # do non-dir files here
        fpath = os.path.join(directoryName, fname)      # fnames have no dirpath
        if not os.path.isdir(fpath):                    # myData is searchKey
            visitfile(fpath, myData)

def searcher(startdir, searchkey):
    global fcount, vcount
    fcount = vcount = 0
    os.path.walk(startdir, visitor, searchkey)

if __name__ == '__main__':
    searcher('.', sys.argv[1])
    print 'Found in %d files, visited %d' % (fcount, vcount)
```

This file also uses the sys.argv command-line list and the __name__ trick for running in two modes. When run standalone, the search key is passed on the command line; when imported, clients call this module's searcher function directly. For example, to search (grep) for all appearances of the directory name "Part2" in the examples tree (an old directory that really did go away!), run a command line like this in a DOS or Unix shell:

```
C:\...\PP3E>python PyTools\search_all.py Part2
1 => .\autoexec.bat
2 => .\cleanall.csh
3 => .\echoEnvironment.pyw
4 => .\Launcher.py
.\Launcher.py has Part2
5 => .\Launcher.pyc
Skipping .\Launcher.pyc
6 => .\Launch_PyGadgets.py
7 => .\Launch_PyDemos.pyw
8 => .\LaunchBrowser.out.txt
.\LaunchBrowser.out.txt has Part2
```

```
9 => .\LaunchBrowser.py
.\LaunchBrowser.py has Part2
...
```
...more lines deleted
```
...
1339 => .\old_Part2\Basics\unpack2b.py
1340 => .\old_Part2\Basics\unpack3.py
1341 => .\old_Part2\Basics\__init__.py
Found in 74 files, visited 1341
```

The script lists each file it checks as it goes, tells you which files it is skipping (names that end in extensions listed in the variable skipexts that imply binary data), and pauses for an Enter key press each time it announces a file containing the search string (bold lines). A solution based on find could not pause this way; although trivial in this example, find doesn't return until the entire tree traversal is finished. The search_all script works the same way when it is *imported* rather than run, but there is no final statistics output line (fcount and vcount live in the module and so would have to be imported to be inspected here):

```
>>> from PP3E.PyTools.search_all import searcher
>>> searcher('.', '-exec')            # find files with string '-exec'
1 => .\autoexec.bat
2 => .\cleanall.csh
3 => .\echoEnvironment.pyw
4 => .\Launcher.py
5 => .\Launcher.pyc
Skipping .\Launcher.pyc
6 => .\Launch_PyGadgets.py
7 => .\Launch_PyDemos.pyw
8 => .\LaunchBrowser.out.txt
9 => .\LaunchBrowser.py
10 => .\Launch_PyGadgets_bar.pyw
11 => .\makeall.csh
12 => .\package.csh
.\package.csh has -exec
```
...more lines deleted...

However launched, this script tracks down all references to a string in an entire directory tree—a name of a changed book examples file, object, or directory, for instance.[*]

---

[*] See the coverage of regular expressions in Chapter 21. The search_all script here searches for a simple string in each file with the string find method, but it would be trivial to extend it to search for a regular expression pattern match instead (roughly, just replace find with a call to a regular expression object's search method). Of course, such a mutation will be much more trivial after we've learned how to do it. Also notice the skipexts list in Example 7-10, which attempts to list all possible binary file types: it would be more general and robust to use the mimetypes logic we met at the end of Chapter 6 in order to guess file content type from its name.

Visitor: Walking Trees Generically

Armed with the portable search_all script from Example 7-10, I was able to better pinpoint files to be edited every time I changed the book examples tree structure. At least initially, in one window I ran search_all to pick out suspicious files and edited each along the way by hand in another window.

Pretty soon, though, this became tedious too. Manually typing filenames into editor commands is no fun, especially when the number of files to edit is large; the search for "Part2" shown earlier returned 74 files, for instance. Since I occasionally have better things to do than manually start 74 editor sessions, I looked for a way to *automatically* run an editor on each suspicious file.

Unfortunately, search_all simply prints results to the screen. Although that text could be intercepted and parsed, a more direct approach that spawns edit sessions during the search may be easier, but may require major changes to the tree search script as currently coded. At this point, two thoughts came to mind.

First, I knew it would be easier in the long run to be able to add features to a general directory searcher as *external components*, not by changing the original script. Because editing files was just one possible extension (what about automating text replacements too?), a more generic, customizable, and reusable search component seemed the way to go.

Second, after writing a few directory walking utilities, it became clear that I was rewriting the same sort of code over and over again. Traversals could be even further simplified by wrapping common details for easier reuse. The os.path.walk tool helps, but its use tends to foster redundant operations (e.g., directory name joins), and its function-object-based interface doesn't quite lend itself to customization the way a class can.

Of course, both goals point to using an object-oriented framework for traversals and searching. Example 7-11 is one concrete realization of these goals. It exports a general FileVisitor class that mostly just wraps os.path.walk for easier use and extension, as well as a generic SearchVisitor class that generalizes the notion of directory searches. By itself, SearchVisitor simply does what search_all did, but it also opens up the search process to customization; bits of its behavior can be modified by overloading its methods in subclasses. Moreover, its core search logic can be reused everywhere we need to search. Simply define a subclass that adds search-specific extensions. As is usual in programming, once you repeat *tactical* tasks often enough, they tend to inspire this kind of *strategic* thinking.

Example 7-11. PP3E\PyTools\visitor.py

```
###########################################################################
# Test: "python ..\..\PyTools\visitor.py testmask [string]".  Uses OOP,
# classes, and subclasses to wrap some of the details of os.path.walk
# usage to walk and search; testmask is an integer bitmask with 1 bit
# per available selftest; see also: visitor_edit/replace/find/fix*/.py
# subclasses, and the fixsitename.py client script in Internet\Cgi-Web;
###########################################################################

import os, sys
listonly = False

class FileVisitor:
    """
    visits all nondirectory files below startDir;
    override visitfile to provide a file handler
    """
    def __init__(self, data=None, listonly=False):
        self.context = data
        self.fcount  = 0
        self.dcount  = 0
        self.listonly = listonly
    def run(self, startDir=os.curdir):                       # default start='.'
        os.path.walk(startDir, self.visitor, None)
    def visitor(self, data, dirName, filesInDir):            # called for each dir
        self.visitdir(dirName)                               # do this dir first
        for fname in filesInDir:                             # do non-dir files
            fpath = os.path.join(dirName, fname)             # fnames have no path
            if not os.path.isdir(fpath):
                self.visitfile(fpath)
    def visitdir(self, dirpath):                             # called for each dir
        self.dcount += 1                                     # override or extend me
        print dirpath, '...'
    def visitfile(self, filepath):                          # called for each file
        self.fcount += 1                                     # override or extend me
        print self.fcount, '=>', filepath                    # default: print name

class SearchVisitor(FileVisitor):
    """
    search files at and below startDir for a string
    """
    skipexts = ['.gif', '.exe', '.pyc', '.o', '.a']         # skip binary files
    def __init__(self, key, listonly=False):
        FileVisitor.__init__(self, key, listonly)
        self.scount = 0
    def visitfile(self, fname):                              # test for a match
        FileVisitor.visitfile(self, fname)
        if not self.listonly:
            if os.path.splitext(fname)[1] in self.skipexts:
                print 'Skipping', fname
            else:
                text = open(fname).read()
                if text.find(self.context) != -1:
```

Example 7-11. PP3E\PyTools\visitor.py (continued)

```
                    self.visitmatch(fname, text)
                    self.scount += 1
    def visitmatch(self, fname, text):                 # process a match
        raw_input('%s has %s' % (fname, self.context))  # override me lower


# self-test logic
dolist   = 1
dosearch = 2      # 3=do list and search
donext   = 4      # when next test added

def selftest(testmask):
    if testmask & dolist:
        visitor = FileVisitor()
        visitor.run('.')
        print 'Visited %d files and %d dirs' % (visitor.fcount, visitor.dcount)

    if testmask & dosearch:
        visitor = SearchVisitor(sys.argv[2], listonly)
        visitor.run('.')
        print 'Found in %d files, visited %d' % (visitor.scount, visitor.fcount)

if __name__ == '__main__':
    selftest(int(sys.argv[1]))     # e.g., 5 = dolist | dorename
```

This module primarily serves to export classes for external use, but it does something useful when run standalone too. If you invoke it as a script with a single argument, 1, it makes and runs a FileVisitor object and prints an exhaustive listing of every file and directory at and below the place you are at when the script is invoked (i.e., ".", the current working directory):

```
C:\temp>python %X%\PyTools\visitor.py 1
. ...
1 => .\autoexec.bat
2 => .\cleanall.csh
3 => .\echoEnvironment.pyw
4 => .\Launcher.py
5 => .\Launcher.pyc
6 => .\Launch_PyGadgets.py
7 => .\Launch_PyDemos.pyw
...more deleted...
479 => .\Gui\Clock\plotterGui.py
480 => .\Gui\Clock\plotterText.py
481 => .\Gui\Clock\plotterText1.py
482 => .\Gui\Clock\__init__.py
.\Gui\gifs ...
483 => .\Gui\gifs\frank.gif
484 => .\Gui\gifs\frank.note
485 => .\Gui\gifs\gilligan.gif
486 => .\Gui\gifs\gilligan.note
...more deleted...
1352 => .\PyTools\visitor_fixnames.py
```

```
1353 => .\PyTools\visitor_find_quiet2.py
1354 => .\PyTools\visitor_find.pyc
1355 => .\PyTools\visitor_find_quiet1.py
1356 => .\PyTools\fixeoln_one.doc.txt
Visited 1356 files and 119 dirs
```

If you instead invoke this script with a 2 as its first argument, it makes and runs a
SearchVisitor object using the second argument as the search key. This form is
equivalent to running the *search_all.py* script we met earlier; it pauses for an Enter
key press after each matching file is reported (lines in bold font here):

```
C:\temp\examples>python %X%\PyTools\visitor.py 2 Part3
. ...
1 => .\autoexec.bat
2 => .\cleanall.csh
.\cleanall.csh has Part3
3 => .\echoEnvironment.pyw
4 => .\Launcher.py
.\Launcher.py has Part3
5 => .\Launcher.pyc
Skipping .\Launcher.pyc
6 => .\Launch_PyGadgets.py
7 => .\Launch_PyDemos.pyw
8 => .\LaunchBrowser.out.txt
9 => .\LaunchBrowser.py
10 => .\Launch_PyGadgets_bar.pyw
11 => .\makeall.csh
.\makeall.csh has Part3
...
...more deleted
...
1353 => .\PyTools\visitor_find_quiet2.py
1354 => .\PyTools\visitor_find.pyc
Skipping .\PyTools\visitor_find.pyc
1355 => .\PyTools\visitor_find_quiet1.py
1356 => .\PyTools\fixeoln_one.doc.txt
Found in 49 files, visited 1356
```

Technically, passing this script a first argument of 3 runs *both* a FileVisitor and a
SearchVisitor (two separate traversals are performed). The first argument is really
used as a bit mask to select one or more supported self-tests; if a test's bit is on in the
binary value of the argument, the test will be run. Because 3 is 011 in binary, it
selects both a search (010) and a listing (001). In a more user-friendly system, we
might want to be more symbolic about that (e.g., check for -search and -list arguments), but bit masks work just as well for this script's scope.

Editing Files in Directory Trees

Now, after genericizing tree traversals and searches, it's an easy step to add automatic file editing in a brand-new, separate component. Example 7-12 defines a new
EditVisitor class that simply customizes the visitmatch method of the

---

Text Editor War and Peace

In case you don't know, the vi setting used in the *visitor_edit.py* script is a Unix text editor; it's available for Windows too but is not standard there. If you run this script, you'll probably want to change its editor setting on your machine. For instance, "emacs" should work on Linux, and "edit" or "notepad" should work on all Windows boxes.

These days, I tend to use an editor I coded in Python (PyEdit), so I'll leave the editor wars to more politically minded readers. In fact, changing the script to assign editor in either of these ways:

```
editor = r'python Gui\TextEditor\textEditorNoConsole.pyw'
editor = r'start  Gui\TextEditor\textEditorNoConsole.pyw'
```

will open the matched file in a pure and portable Python text editor GUI—one coded in Python with the Tkinter interface, which runs on all major GUI platforms and which we'll meet in Chapter 12. If you read about the start command in Chapter 5, you know that the first editor setting pauses the traversal while the editor runs, but the second does not (you'll get as many PyEdit windows as there are matched files).

This may fail, however, for very long file directory names (remember, os.system has a length limit, unlike os.spawnv). Moreover, the path to the *textEditor.pyw* program may vary depending on where you are when you run *visitor_edit.py* (i.e., the CWD). There are four ways around this latter problem:

- Prefixing the script's path string with the value of the PP3EHOME shell variable, fetched with os.environ; with the standard book setup scripts, PP3EHOME gives the absolute root directory, from which the editor script's path can be found
- Prefixing the path with sys.path[0] and a '../' to exploit the fact that the first import directory is always the script's home directory (see Chapter 3)
- Windows shortcuts or Unix links to the editor script from the CWD
- Searching for the script naïvely with Launcher.findFirst or guessLocation, described near the end of Chapter 6

But these are all beyond the scope of a sidebar on text editor politics.

SearchVisitor class to open a text editor on the matched file. Yes, this is the complete program. It needs to do something special only when visiting matched files, and so it needs provide only that behavior; the rest of the traversal and search logic is unchanged and inherited.

Example 7-12. PP3E\PyTools\visitor_edit.py

```
#################################################################
# Use: "python PyTools\visitor_edit.py string".
# add auto-editor startup to SearchVisitor in an external
# component (subclass), not in-place changes; this version
# automatically pops up an editor on each file containing the
```

Example 7-12. PP3E\PyTools\visitor_edit.py (continued)

```
# string as it traverses; you can also use editor='edit' or
# 'notepad' on Windows; 'vi' and 'edit' run in console window;
# editor=r'python Gui\TextEditor\textEditor.py' may work too;
# caveat: we might be able to make this smarter by sending
# a search command to go to the first match in some editors;
##############################################################

import os, sys
from visitor import SearchVisitor
listonly = False

class EditVisitor(SearchVisitor):
    """
    edit files at and below startDir having string
    """
    editor = 'vi'   # ymmv
    def visitmatch(self, fname, text):
        os.system('%s %s' % (self.editor, fname))

if __name__ == '__main__':
    visitor = EditVisitor(sys.argv[1], listonly)
    visitor.run('.')
    print 'Edited %d files, visited %d' % (visitor.scount, visitor.fcount)
```

When we make and run an EditVisitor, a text editor is started with the os.system command-line spawn call, which usually blocks its caller until the spawned program finishes. On my machines, each time this script finds a matched file during the traversal, it starts up the vi text editor within the console window where the script was started; exiting the editor resumes the tree walk.

Let's find and edit some files. When run as a script, we pass this program the search string as a command argument (here, the string -exec is the search key, not an option flag). The root directory is always passed to the run method as ".", the current run directory. Traversal status messages show up in the console as before, but each matched file now automatically pops up in a text editor along the way. Here, the editor is started eight times:

```
C:\...\PP3E>python PyTools\visitor_edit.py -exec
1 => .\autoexec.bat
2 => .\cleanall.csh
3 => .\echoEnvironment.pyw
4 => .\Launcher.py
5 => .\Launcher.pyc
Skipping .\Launcher.pyc
...more deleted...
1340 => .\old_Part2\Basics\unpack2.py
1341 => .\old_Part2\Basics\unpack2b.py
1342 => .\old_Part2\Basics\unpack3.py
1343 => .\old_Part2\Basics\__init__.py
Edited 8 files, visited 1343
```

This, finally, is the exact tool I was looking for to simplify global book examples tree maintenance. After major changes to things such as shared modules and file and directory names, I run this script on the examples root directory with an appropriate search string and edit any files it pops up as needed. I still need to change files by hand in the editor, but that's often safer than blind global replacements.

Global Replacements in Directory Trees

But since I brought it up, given a general tree traversal class, it's easy to code a global search-and-replace subclass too. The FileVisitor subclass in Example 7-13, ReplaceVisitor, customizes the visitfile method to globally replace any appearances of one string with another, in all text files at and below a root directory. It also collects the names of all files that were changed in a list just in case you wish to go through and verify the automatic edits applied (a text editor could be automatically popped up on each changed file, for instance).

Example 7-13. PP3E\PyTools\visitor_replace.py

```
#################################################################
# Use: "python PyTools\visitor_replace.py fromStr toStr".
# does global search-and-replace in all files in a directory
# tree--replaces fromStr with toStr in all text files; this
# is powerful but dangerous!! visitor_edit.py runs an editor
# for you to verify and make changes, and so is much safer;
# use CollectVisitor to simply collect a list of matched files;
#################################################################

import sys
from visitor import SearchVisitor
listonly = False

class ReplaceVisitor(SearchVisitor):
    """
    change fromStr to toStr in files at and below startDir;
    files changed available in obj.changed list after a run
    """
    def __init__(self, fromStr, toStr, listonly=False):
        self.changed = []
        self.toStr   = toStr
        SearchVisitor.__init__(self, fromStr, listonly)
    def visitmatch(self, fname, text):
        fromStr, toStr = self.context, self.toStr
        text = text.replace(fromStr, toStr)
        open(fname, 'w').write(text)
        self.changed.append(fname)

if __name__ == '__main__':
    if raw_input('Are you sure?') == 'y':
        visitor = ReplaceVisitor(sys.argv[1], sys.argv[2], listonly)
        visitor.run(startDir='.')
```

Example 7-13. PP3E\PyTools\visitor_replace.py (continued)

```
print 'Visited %d files' % visitor.fcount
print 'Changed %d files:' % len(visitor.changed)
for fname in visitor.changed: print fname
```

To run this script over a directory tree, go to the directory to be changed and run the following sort of command line with "from" and "to" strings. On my current machine, doing this on a 1,354-file tree and changing 75 files along the way takes roughly six seconds of real clock time when the system isn't particularly busy.

```
C:\temp\examples>python %X%/PyTools/visitor_replace.py Part2 SPAM2
Are you sure?y
. ...
1 => .\autoexec.bat
2 => .\cleanall.csh
3 => .\echoEnvironment.pyw
4 => .\Launcher.py
5 => .\Launcher.pyc
Skipping .\Launcher.pyc
6 => .\Launch_PyGadgets.py
...more deleted...
1351 => .\PyTools\visitor_find_quiet2.py
1352 => .\PyTools\visitor_find.pyc
Skipping .\PyTools\visitor_find.pyc
1353 => .\PyTools\visitor_find_quiet1.py
1354 => .\PyTools\fixeoln_one.doc.txt
Visited 1354 files
Changed 75 files:
.\Launcher.py
.\LaunchBrowser.out.txt
.\LaunchBrowser.py
.\PyDemos.pyw
.\PyGadgets.py
.\README-PP3E.txt
...more deleted...
.\PyTools\search_all.out.txt
.\PyTools\visitor.out.txt
.\PyTools\visitor_edit.py

[to delete, use an empty toStr]
C:\temp\examples>python %X%/PyTools/visitor_replace.py SPAM ""
```

This is both wildly powerful and dangerous. If the string to be replaced can show up in places you didn't anticipate, you might just ruin an entire tree of files by running the ReplaceVisitor object defined here. On the other hand, if the string is something very specific, this object can obviate the need to automatically edit suspicious files. For instance, we will use this approach to automatically change web site addresses in HTML files in Chapter 16; the addresses are likely too specific to show up in other places by chance.

Collecting Matched Files in Trees

The scripts so far search and replace in directory trees, using the same traversal code base (the visitor module). Suppose, though, that you just want to get a Python *list* of files in a directory containing a string. You could run a search and parse the output messages for "found" messages. Much simpler, simply knock off another SearchVisitor subclass to collect the list along the way, as in Example 7-14.

Example 7-14. PP3E\PyTools\visitor_collect.py

```
##################################################################
# Use: "python PyTools\visitor_collect.py searchstring".
# CollectVisitor simply collects a list of matched files, for
# display or later processing (e.g., replacement, auto-editing);
##################################################################

import sys
from visitor import SearchVisitor

class CollectVisitor(SearchVisitor):
    """
    collect names of files containing a string;
    run this and then fetch its obj.matches list
    """
    def __init__(self, searchstr, listonly=False):
        self.matches = []
        SearchVisitor.__init__(self, searchstr, listonly)
    def visitmatch(self, fname, text):
        self.matches.append(fname)

if __name__ == '__main__':
    visitor = CollectVisitor(sys.argv[1])
    visitor.run(startDir='.')
    print 'Found these files:'
    for fname in visitor.matches: print fname
```

CollectVisitor is just a tree search again, with a new kind of specialization—collecting files instead of printing messages. This class is useful from other scripts that mean to collect a matched files list for later processing; it can be run by itself as a script too:

```
C:\...\PP3E>python PyTools\visitor_collect.py -exec
...
...more deleted...
...
1342 => .\old_Part2\Basics\unpack2b.py
1343 => .\old_Part2\Basics\unpack3.py
1344 => .\old_Part2\Basics\__init__.py
Found these files:
.\package.csh
.\README-PP3E.txt
.\readme-old-pp1E.txt
```

```
.\PyTools\cleanpyc.py
.\PyTools\fixeoln_all.py
.\System\Processes\output.txt
.\Internet\Cgi-Web\fixcgi.py
```

Suppressing status messages

Here, the items in the collected list are displayed at the end—all the files containing the string -exec. Notice, though, that traversal status messages are still printed along the way (in fact, I deleted about 1,600 lines of such messages here!). In a tool meant to be called from another script, that may be an undesirable side effect; the calling script's output may be more important than the traversal's.

We could add mode flags to SearchVisitor to turn off status messages, but that makes it more complex. Instead, the following two files show how we might go about collecting matched filenames without letting any traversal messages show up in the console, all without changing the original code base. The first, shown in Example 7-15, simply takes over and copies the search logic, without print statements. It's a bit redundant with SearchVisitor, but only in a few lines of mimicked code.

Example 7-15. PP3E\PyTools\visitor_collect_quiet1.py

```
#############################################################
# Like visitor_collect, but avoid traversal status messages
#############################################################

import os, sys
from visitor import FileVisitor, SearchVisitor

class CollectVisitor(FileVisitor):
    """
    collect names of files containing a string, silently;
    """
    skipexts = SearchVisitor.skipexts
    def __init__(self, searchStr):
        self.matches = []
        self.context = searchStr
    def visitdir(self, dname): pass
    def visitfile(self, fname):
        if (os.path.splitext(fname)[1] not in self.skipexts and
            open(fname).read().find(self.context) != -1):
            self.matches.append(fname)

if __name__ == '__main__':
    visitor = CollectVisitor(sys.argv[1])
    visitor.run(startDir='.')
    print 'Found these files:'
    for fname in visitor.matches: print fname
```

When this class is run, only the contents of the matched filenames list show up at the end; no status messages appear during the traversal. Because of that, this form may be more useful as a general-purpose tool used by other scripts:

```
C:\...\PP3E>python PyTools\visitor_collect_quiet1.py -exec
Found these files:
.\package.csh
.\README-PP3E.txt
.\readme-old-pp1E.txt
.\PyTools\cleanpyc.py
.\PyTools\fixeoln_all.py
.\System\Processes\output.txt
.\Internet\Cgi-Web\fixcgi.py
```

A more interesting and less redundant way to suppress printed text during a traversal is to apply the stream redirection tricks we met in Chapter 3. Example 7-16 sets sys.stdin to a NullOut object that throws away all printed text for the duration of the traversal (its write method does nothing). We could also use the StringIO module we met in Chapter 3 for this purpose, but it's overkill here; we don't need to retain printed text.

The only real complication with this scheme is that there is no good place to insert a restoration of sys.stdout at the end of the traversal; instead, we code the restore in the __del__ destructor method and require clients to delete the visitor to resume printing as usual. An explicitly called method would work just as well, if you prefer less magical interfaces.

Example 7-16. PP3E\PyTools\visitor_collect_quiet2.py

```
#############################################################
# Like visitor_collect, but avoid traversal status messages
#############################################################

import sys
from visitor import SearchVisitor

class NullOut:
    def write(self, line): pass

class CollectVisitor(SearchVisitor):
    """
    collect names of files containing a string, silently
    """
    def __init__(self, searchstr, listonly=False):
        self.matches = []
        self.saveout, sys.stdout = sys.stdout, NullOut()
        SearchVisitor.__init__(self, searchstr, listonly)
    def __del__(self):
        sys.stdout = self.saveout
    def visitmatch(self, fname, text):
        self.matches.append(fname)
```

Example 7-16. PP3E\PyTools\visitor_collect_quiet2.py (continued)

```
if __name__ == '__main__':
    visitor = CollectVisitor(sys.argv[1])
    visitor.run(startDir='.')
    matches = visitor.matches
    del visitor
    print 'Found these files:'
    for fname in matches: print fname
```

When this script is run, output is identical to the prior run—just the matched filenames at the end. Perhaps better still, why not code and debug just one verbose CollectVisitor utility class, and require *clients* to wrap calls to its run method in the redirect.redirect function we wrote in Example 3-10?

```
>>> from PP3E.PyTools.visitor_collect import CollectVisitor
>>> from PP3E.System.Streams.redirect import redirect
>>> walker = CollectVisitor('-exec')              # object to find '-exec'
>>> output = redirect(walker.run, ('.',), '')     # function, args, input
>>> for line in walker.matches: print line        # print items in list
...
.\package.csh
.\README-PP3E.txt
.\readme-old-pp1E.txt
.\PyTools\cleanpyc.py
.\PyTools\fixeoln_all.py
.\System\Processes\output.txt
.\Internet\Cgi-Web\fixcgi.py
```

The redirect call employed here resets standard input and output streams to file-like objects for the duration of *any* function call; because of that, it's a more general way to suppress output than recoding every outputter. Here, it has the effect of intercepting (and hence suppressing) printed messages during a walker.run('.') traversal. They really *are* printed, but show up in the string result of the redirect call, not on the screen:

```
>>> output[:60]
'. ...\n1 => .\\autoexec.bat\n2 => .\\cleanall.csh\n3 => .\\echoEnv'

>>> len(output), len(output.split('\n'))            # bytes, lines
(67609, 1592)

>>> walker.matches
['.\\package.csh', '.\\README-PP3E.txt', '.\\readme-old-pp1E.txt',
 '.\\PyTools\\cleanpyc.py', '.\\PyTools\\fixeoln_all.py',
 '.\\System\\Processes\\output.txt',
 '.\\Internet\\Cgi-Web\\fixcgi.py']
```

Because redirect saves printed text in a string, it may be less appropriate than the two quiet CollectVisitor variants for functions that generate much output. Here, for example, 67,609 bytes of output were queued up in an in-memory string (see the len call results); such a buffer may or may not be significant in most applications.

In more general terms, redirecting sys.stdout to dummy objects as done here is a simple way to turn off outputs (and is the equivalent to the Unix notion of redirecting output to the file */dev/null*—a file that discards everything sent to it). For instance, we'll pull this trick out of the bag again in the context of server-side Internet scripting, to prevent utility status messages from showing up in generated web page output streams.[*]

Recoding Fixers with Visitors

Be warned: once you've written and debugged a class that knows how to do something useful like walking directory trees, it's easy for it to spread throughout your system utility libraries. Of course, that's the whole point of code reuse. For instance, very soon after writing the visitor classes presented in the prior sections, I recoded both the *fixnames_all.py* and the *fixeoln_all.py* directory walker scripts listed earlier in Examples 7-6 and 7-4, respectively, to use visitor rather than proprietary tree-walk logic (they both originally used find.find). Example 7-17 combines the original convertLines function (to fix end-of-lines in a single file) with visitor's tree walker class, to yield an alternative implementation of the line-end converter for directory trees.

Example 7-17. PP3E\PyTools\visitor_fixeoln.py

```
###############################################################
# Use: "python visitor_fixeoln.py todos|tounix".
# recode fixeoln_all.py as a visitor subclass: this version
# uses os.path.walk, not find.find to collect all names first;
# limited but fast: if os.path.splitext(fname)[1] in patts:
###############################################################

import visitor, sys, fnmatch, os
from fixeoln_dir import patts
from fixeoln_one import convertEndlines

class EolnFixer(visitor.FileVisitor):
    def visitfile(self, fullname):                     # match on basename
        basename = os.path.basename(fullname)          # to make result same
        for patt in patts:                             # else visits fewer
            if fnmatch.fnmatch(basename, patt):
                convertEndlines(self.context, fullname)
                self.fcount += 1                       # could break here
                                                       # but results differ
if __name__ == '__main__':
    walker = EolnFixer(sys.argv[1])
```

---

[*] For the impatient: see commonhtml.runsilent in the PyMailCGI system presented in Chapter 17. It's a variation on redirect.redirect that discards output as it is printed (instead of retaining it in a string), returns the return value of the function called (not the output string), and lets exceptions pass via a try/finally statement (instead of catching and reporting them with a try/except). It's still redirection at work, though.

Example 7-17. PP3E\PyTools\visitor_fixeoln.py (continued)

```
walker.run( )
print 'Files matched (converted or not):', walker.fcount
```

As we saw in Chapter 4, the built-in fnmatch module performs Unix shell-like file-name matching; this script uses it to match names to the previous version's filename patterns (simply looking for filename extensions after a "." is simpler, but not as general):

```
C:\temp\examples>python %X%/PyTools/visitor_fixeoln.py tounix

. ...
Changing .\echoEnvironment.pyw
Changing .\Launcher.py
Changing .\Launch_PyGadgets.py
Changing .\Launch_PyDemos.pyw
...more deleted...
Changing .\PyTools\visitor_find.py
Changing .\PyTools\visitor_fixnames.py
Changing .\PyTools\visitor_find_quiet2.py
Changing .\PyTools\visitor_find_quiet1.py
Changing .\PyTools\fixeoln_one.doc.txt
Files matched (converted or not): 1065


C:\temp\examples>python %X%/PyTools/visitor_fixeoln.py tounix
...more deleted...
.\Extend\Swig\Shadow ...
.\ ...
.\EmbExt\Exports ...
.\EmbExt\Exports\ClassAndMod ...
.\EmbExt\Regist ...
.\PyTools ...
Files matched (converted or not): 1065
```

If you run this script and the original *fixeoln_all.py* on the book examples tree, you'll notice that this version visits two fewer matched files. This simply reflects the fact that fixeoln_all also collects and skips over two directory names for its patterns in the find.find result (both called "Output"). In all other ways, this version works the same way even when it could do better; adding a break statement after the convertEndlines call here avoids visiting files that appear redundantly in the original's find results lists.

The second command here takes roughly two-thirds as long as the first to finish on my computer (there are no files to be converted). That's roughly 33 percent faster than the original find.find-based version of this script, but they differ in the amount of output, and benchmarks are usually much subtler than you imagine. Most of the real clock time is likely spent scrolling text in the console, not doing any real directory processing. Since both are plenty fast for their intended purposes, finer-grained performance figures are left as exercises.

The script in Example 7-18 combines the original convertOne function (to rename a single file or directory) with the visitor's tree walker class, to create a directory tree-wide fix for uppercase filenames. Notice that we redefine both file and directory visitation methods here, as we need to rename both.

Example 7-18. PP3E\PyTools\visitor_fixnames.py

```
################################################################
# recode fixnames_all.py name case fixer with the Visitor class
# note: "from fixnames_all import convertOne" doesn't help at
# top level of the fixnames class, since it is assumed to be a
# method and called with extra self argument (an exception);
################################################################

from visitor import FileVisitor

class FixnamesVisitor(FileVisitor):
    """
    check filenames at and below startDir for uppercase
    """
    import fixnames_all
    def __init__(self, listonly=False):
        FileVisitor.__init__(self, listonly=listonly)
        self.ccount = 0
    def rename(self, pathname):
        if not self.listonly:
            convertflag = self.fixnames_all.convertOne(pathname)
            self.ccount += convertflag
    def visitdir(self, dirname):
        FileVisitor.visitdir(self, dirname)
        self.rename(dirname)
    def visitfile(self, filename):
        FileVisitor.visitfile(self, filename)
        self.rename(filename)

if __name__ == '__main__':
    walker = FixnamesVisitor()
    walker.run()
    allnames = walker.fcount + walker.dcount
    print 'Converted %d files, visited %d' % (walker.ccount, allnames)
```

This version is run like the original find.find-based version, fixnames_all, but visits one more name (the top-level root directory), and there is no initial delay while filenames are collected on a list—we're using os.path.walk again, not find.find. It's also close to the original os.path.walk version of this script but is based on a class hierarchy, not direct function callbacks:

```
C:\temp\examples>python %X%/PyTools/visitor_fixnames.py
...more deleted...
303 => .\__init__.py
304 => .\__init__.pyc
305 => .\Ai\ExpertSystem\holmes.tar
```

```
306 => .\Ai\ExpertSystem\TODO
Convert dir=.\Ai\ExpertSystem file=TODO? (y|Y)
307 => .\Ai\ExpertSystem\__init__.py
308 => .\Ai\ExpertSystem\holmes\cnv
309 => .\Ai\ExpertSystem\holmes\README.1ST
Convert dir=.\Ai\ExpertSystem\holmes file=README.1ST? (y|Y)
...more deleted...
1353 => .\PyTools\visitor_find.pyc
1354 => .\PyTools\visitor_find_quiet1.py
1355 => .\PyTools\fixeoln_one.doc.txt
Converted 1 files, visited 1474
```

Both of these fixer scripts work roughly the same way as the originals, but because the directory-walking logic lives in just one file (*visitor.py*), it needs to be debugged only once. Moreover, improvements in that file will automatically be inherited by every directory-processing tool derived from its classes. Even when coding system-level scripts, reuse and reduced redundancy pay off in the end.

Fixing File Permissions in Trees

Just in case the preceding visitor-client sections weren't quite enough to convince you of the power of code reuse, another piece of evidence surfaced very late in this book project. It turns out that copying files off a CD using Windows drag-and-drop sometimes makes them *read only* in the copy. That's less than ideal for the book examples distribution if it is obtained on CD; you must copy the directory tree onto your hard drive to be able to experiment with program changes (naturally, files on CD can't be changed in place). But if you copy with drag-and-drop, you may wind up with a tree of more than 1,000 read-only files.

The book CD use cases described for this and some other examples in this chapter are something of historic artifacts today. As mentioned in the Preface, as of this third edition, the book's examples are made available on the Web instead of on an enclosed CD.

The Web is more pervasive today and allows for much more dynamic updates. However, even though the book CD is a vestige of the past, the examples which were originally coded to manage it still apply to other types of CDs and so are generally useful tools.

Since drag-and-drop is perhaps the most common way to copy off a CD on Windows, I needed a portable and easy-to-use way to undo the read-only setting. Asking readers to make all of these writable by hand would be impolite, to say the least. Writing a full-blown install system seemed like overkill. Providing different fixes for different platforms doubles or triples the complexity of the task.

Much better, the Python script in Example 7-19 can be run in the root of the copied examples directory to repair the damage of a read-only drag-and-drop operation. It specializes the traversal implemented by the `FileVisitor` class again, this time to run an `os.chmod` call on every file and directory visited along the way.

Example 7-19. PP3E\PyTools\fixreadonly-all.py

```python
#!/usr/bin/env python
##############################################################################
# Use: python PyTools\fixreadonly-all.py
# run this script in the top-level examples directory after copying all
# examples off the book's CD-ROM, to make all files writable again--by
# default, copying files off the CD with Windows drag-and-drop (at least)
# may create them as read-only on your hard drive; this script traverses
# entire directory tree at and below the dir it is run in (all subdirs);
##############################################################################

import os
from PP3E.PyTools.visitor import FileVisitor       # os.path.walk wrapper
listonly = False

class FixReadOnly(FileVisitor):
    def __init__(self, listonly=0):
        FileVisitor.__init__(self, listonly=listonly)
    def visitDir(self, dname):
        FileVisitor.visitfile(self, fname)
        if self.listonly:
            return
        os.chmod(dname, 0777)
    def visitfile(self, fname):
        FileVisitor.visitfile(self, fname)
        if self.listonly:
            return
        os.chmod(fname, 0777)

if __name__ == '__main__':
    # don't run auto if clicked
    go = raw_input('This script makes all files writeable; continue?')
    if go != 'y':
        raw_input('Canceled - hit enter key')
    else:
        walker = FixReadOnly(listonly)
        walker.run()
        print 'Visited %d files and %d dirs' % (walker.fcount, walker.dcount)
```

As we saw in Chapter 3, the built-in `os.chmod` call changes the permission settings on an external file (here, to 0777—global read, write, and execute permissions). Because `os.chmod` and the `FileVisitor`'s operations are portable, this same script will work to set permissions in an entire tree on both Windows and Unix-like platforms. Notice that it asks whether you really want to proceed when it first starts up, just in case someone accidentally clicks the file's name in an explorer GUI. Also note that Python must be installed before this script can be run in order to make files writable;

that seems a fair assumption to make about users who are about to change Python scripts.

```
C:\temp\examples>python PyTools\fixreadonly-all.py
This script makes all files writeable; continue?y
. ...
1 => .\autoexec.bat
2 => .\cleanall.csh
3 => .\echoEnvironment.pyw
...more deleted...
1352 => .\PyTools\visitor_find.pyc
1353 => .\PyTools\visitor_find_quiet1.py
1354 => .\PyTools\fixeoln_one.doc.txt
Visited 1354 files and 119 dirs
```

Changing Unix Executable Path Lines

Finally, the following script does something more unique: it uses the visitor classes to replace the "#!" lines at the top of all scripts in a directory tree (this line gives the path to the Python interpreter on Unix-like machines). It's easy to do this with the visitor_replace script of Example 7-13 that we coded earlier. For example, say something like this to replace all #!/usr/bin/python lines with #!\Python24\python:

```
C:\...\PP3E>python PyTools\visitor_replace.py
                #!/usr/bin/python #!\Python24\python
```

Lots of status messages scroll by unless redirected to a file. visitor_replace does a simple global search-and-replace operation on all nonbinary files in an entire directory tree. It's also a bit naïve: it won't change other "#!" line patterns that mention python (e.g., you'll have to run it again to change #!/usr/local/bin/python), and it might change occurrences besides those on a first line. That probably won't matter, but if it does, it's easy to write your own visitor subclass to be more accurate.

When run, the script in Example 7-20 converts all "#!" lines in all script files in an entire tree. It changes every first line that starts with "#!" and names "python" to a line you pass in on the command line or assign in the script, like this:

```
C:\...\PP3E>python PyTools\visitor_poundbang.py #!\MyPython24\python
Are you sure?y
. ...
1 => .\__init__.py
2 => .\PyDemos2.pyw
3 => .\towriteable.py
...
1474 => .\Integrate\Mixed\Exports\ClassAndMod\output.prog1
1475 => .\Integrate\Mixed\Exports\ClassAndMod\setup-class.csh
Visited 1475 files and 133 dirs, changed 190 files
.\towriteable.py
.\Launch_PyGadgets.py
.\Launch_PyDemos.pyw
...
```

```
C:\...\PP3E>type .\Launch_PyGadgets.py
#!\MyPython24\python
##############################################
# PyGadgets + environment search/config first
...
```

This script caught and changed 190 files (more than visitor_replace), so there must be other "#!" line patterns lurking in the examples tree besides #!/usr/bin/python.

Example 7-20. PP3E\PyTools\visitor_poundbang.py

```
#############################################################################
# change all "#!...python" source lines at the top of scripts to either
# commandline arg or changeToDefault, in all files in all dirs at and
# below the dir where run; could skip binary filename extensions too,
# but works ok; this version changes all #! first lines that name python,
# and so is more accurate than a simple visitor_replace.py run;
#############################################################################

"""
Run me like this, to convert all scripts in the book
examples tree, and redirect/save messages to a file:
C:\...\PP3E>python PyTools\visitor_poundbang.py
                        #!\MyPython24\python > out.txt
"""

import sys
from PP3E.PyTools.visitor import FileVisitor    # reuse the walker classes
changeToDefault = '#!\Python24\python'          # used if no cmdline arg

class PoundBangFixer(FileVisitor):
    def __init__(self, changeTo=changeToDefault):
        FileVisitor.__init__(self)
        self.changeTo = changeTo
        self.clist    = []
    def visitfile(self, fullname):
        FileVisitor.visitfile(self, fullname)
        try:
            lines = open(fullname, 'r').readlines()
            if (len(lines) > 0        and
                lines[0][0:2] == '#!' and                # or lines[0].startswith()
                'python' in lines[0]                     # or lines[0].find() != -1
                ):
                lines[0] = self.changeTo + '\n'
                open(fullname, 'w').writelines(lines)
                self.clist.append(fullname)
        except:
            print 'Error translating %s -- skipped' % fullname
            print '...', sys.exc_info()

if __name__ == '__main__':
    if raw_input('Are you sure?') != 'y': sys.exit()
    if len(sys.argv) == 2: changeToDefault = sys.argv[1]
    walker = PoundBangFixer(changeToDefault)
```

Example 7-20. PP3E\PyTools\visitor_poundbang.py (continued)

```
walker.run( )
print 'Visited %d files and %d dirs,' % (walker.fcount, walker.dcount),
print 'changed %d files' % len(walker.clist)
for fname in walker.clist: print fname
```

Summary: Counting Source Lines Four Ways

We've seen a few techniques for scanning directory trees in this book so far. To summarize and contrast, this section briefly lists four scripts that count the number of lines in all program source files in an entire tree. Each script uses a different directory traversal scheme, but returns the same result.

I counted 41,938 source lines of code (SLOC) in the book examples distribution with these scripts, as of November 2001 (for the second edition of this book). Study these scripts' code for more details. They don't count everything (e.g., they skip makefiles), but are comprehensive enough for ballpark figures. Here's the output for the visitor class version when run on the root of the book examples tree; the root of the tree to walk is passed in as a command-line argument, and the last output line is a dictionary that keeps counts for the specific file-type extensions in the tree:

```
C:\temp>python wcall_visitor.py %X%
...lines deleted...
C:\PP2ndEd\examples\PP3E\Integrate\Mixed\Exports\ClassAndMod\cinterface.py
C:\PP2ndEd\examples\PP3E\Integrate\Mixed\Exports\ClassAndMod\main-table.c
Visited 1478 files and 133 dirs
------------------------------------------------------------------------

Files=> 903 Lines=> 41938
{'.c': 46, '.cgi': 24, '.html': 41, '.pyw': 11, '.cxx': 2, '.py': 768,
 '.i': 3,  '.h': 8}
```

The first version, listed in Example 7-21, counts lines using the standard library's os.path.walk call, which we met in Chapter 4 (using os.walk would be similar, but we would replace the callback function with a for loop, and subdirectories and files would be segregated into two lists of names).

Example 7-21. PP3E\PyTools\wcall.py

```
###############################################################
# count lines in all source files in tree; os.path.walk version
###############################################################

import os, sys
allLines = allFiles = 0
allExts  = ['.py', '.pyw', '.cgi', '.html', '.c', '.cxx', '.h', '.i']
allSums = dict.fromkeys(allExts, 0)

def sum(dir, file, ext):
    global allFiles, allLines
    print file
```

Example 7-21. PP3E\PyTools\wcall.py (continued)

```
        fname = os.path.join(dir, file)
        lines = open(fname).readlines( )
        allFiles += 1                              # or all = all + 1
        allLines += len(lines)
        allSums[ext] += 1

def wc(ignore, dir, fileshere):
    for file in fileshere:
        for ext in allExts:
            if file.endswith(ext):                 # or f[-len(e):] == e
                sum(dir, file, ext)
                break

if __name__ == '__main__':
    os.path.walk(sys.argv[1], wc, None)            # cmd arg=root dir
    print '-'*80
    print 'Files=>', allFiles, 'Lines=>', allLines
    print allSums
```

Counting with the find module we wrote at the end of Chapter 4 with Example 7-22 is noticeably simpler, though we must wait for the list of files to be collected.

Example 7-22. PP3E\PyTools\wcall_find.py

```
###################################################################
# count lines in all source files in tree; find file list version
###################################################################

import sys
from wcall import allExts
from PP3E.PyTools.find import find

allLines = allFiles = 0
allSums  = dict.fromkeys(allExts, 0)

def sum(fname, ext):
    global allFiles, allLines
    print fname
    lines = open(fname).readlines( )
    allFiles += 1
    allLines += len(lines)
    allSums[ext] += 1

for file in find('*', sys.argv[1]):
    for ext in allExts:
        if file.endswith(ext):
            sum(file, ext)
            break

print '-'*80
print 'Files=>', allFiles, 'Lines=>', allLines
print allSums
```

The prior script collected all source files in the tree with find and manually checked their extensions; the next script (Example 7-23) uses the pattern-matching capability in find to collect only source files in the result list.

Example 7-23. PP3E\PyTools\wcall_find_patt.py

```
#################################################################
# count lines in all source files in tree; find patterns version
#################################################################

import sys
from wcall import allExts
from PP3E.PyTools.find import find

allLines = allFiles = 0
allSums  = dict.fromkeys(allExts, 0)

def sum(fname, ext):
    global allFiles, allLines
    print fname
    lines = open(fname).readlines()
    allFiles += 1
    allLines += len(lines)
    allSums[ext] += 1

for ext in allExts:
    files = find('*' + ext, sys.argv[1])
    for file in files:
        sum(file, ext)

print '-'*80
print 'Files=>', allFiles, 'Lines=>', allLines
print allSums
```

And finally, Example 7-24 is the SLOC counting logic refactored to use the visitor class framework we wrote in this chapter; OOP adds a bit more code here, but this version is more accurate (if a directory name happens to have a source-like extension, the prior versions will incorrectly tally it). More importantly, by using OOP:

- We get the superclass's walking logic for free, including a directory counter.
- We have a self-contained package of names that supports multiple independent instances and can be used more easily in other contexts.
- We can further customize this operation because it is a class.
- We will automatically inherit any changes made to visitor in the future.

Even in the systems tools domains, strategic thinking can pay off eventually.

Example 7-24. PP3E\PyTools\wcall_visitor.py

```
###################################################################
# count lines in all source files in tree; visitor class version
###################################################################

import sys
from wcall import allExts
from PP3E.PyTools.visitor import FileVisitor

class WcAll(FileVisitor):
    def __init__(self):
        FileVisitor.__init__(self)
        self.allLines = self.allFiles = 0
        self.allSums  = dict.fromkeys(allExts, 0)

    def sum(self, fname, ext):
        print fname
        lines = open(fname).readlines()
        self.allFiles += 1
        self.allLines += len(lines)
        self.allSums[ext] += 1

    def visitfile(self, filepath):
        self.fcount += 1
        for ext in allExts:
            if filepath.endswith(ext):
                self.sum(filepath, ext)
                break

if __name__ == '__main__':
    walker = WcAll()
    walker.run(sys.argv[1])
    print 'Visited %d files and %d dirs' % (walker.fcount, walker.dcount)
    print '-'*80
    print 'Files=>', walker.allFiles, 'Lines=>', walker.allLines
    print walker.allSums
```

Copying Directory Trees

The next three sections conclude this chapter by exploring a handful of additional utilities for processing directories (a.k.a. folders) on your computer with Python. They present directory *copy*, *deletion*, and *comparison* scripts that demonstrate system tools at work. All of these were born of necessity, are generally portable among all Python platforms, and illustrate Python development concepts along the way.

Some of these scripts do something too unique for the visitor module's classes we've been applying in early sections of this chapter, and so require more custom solutions (e.g., we can't remove directories we intend to walk through). Most have platform-specific equivalents too (e.g., drag-and-drop copies), but the Python utilities shown here are portable, easily customized, callable from other scripts, and surprisingly fast.

A Python Tree Copy Script

My CD writer sometimes does weird things. In fact, copies of files with odd names can be totally botched on the CD, even though other files show up in one piece. That's not necessarily a showstopper; if just a few files are trashed in a big CD backup copy, I can always copy the offending files to floppies one at a time. Unfortunately, Windows drag-and-drop copies don't play nicely with such a CD: the copy operation stops and exits the moment the first bad file is encountered. You get only as many files as were copied up to the error, but no more.

In fact, this is not limited to CD copies. I've run into similar problems when trying to back up my laptop's hard drive to another drive—the drag-and-drop copy stops with an error as soon as it reaches a file with a name that is too long to copy (common in saved web pages). The last 45 minutes spent copying is wasted time; frustrating, to say the least!

There may be some magical Windows setting to work around this feature, but I gave up hunting for one as soon as I realized that it would be easier to code a copier in Python. The *cpall.py* script in Example 7-25 is one way to do it. With this script, I control what happens when bad files are found—I can skip over them with Python exception handlers, for instance. Moreover, this tool works with the same interface and effect on other platforms. It seems to me, at least, that a few minutes spent writing a portable and reusable Python script to meet a need is a better investment than looking for solutions that work on only one platform (if at all).

Example 7-25. PP3E\System\Filetools\cpall.py

```
#############################################################################
# Usage: "python cpall.py dirFrom dirTo".
# Recursive copy of a directory tree.  Works like a "cp -r dirFrom/* dirTo"
# Unix command, and assumes that dirFrom and dirTo are both directories.
# Was written to get around fatal error messages under Windows drag-and-drop
# copies (the first bad file ends the entire copy operation immediately),
# but also allows for coding customized copy operations.  May need to
# do more file type checking on Unix: skip links, fifos, etc.
#############################################################################

import os, sys
verbose = 0
dcount = fcount = 0
maxfileload = 500000
blksize = 1024 * 100

def cpfile(pathFrom, pathTo, maxfileload=maxfileload):
    """
```

Example 7-25. PP3E\System\Filetools\cpall.py (continued)

```
        copy file pathFrom to pathTo, byte for byte
        """
        if os.path.getsize(pathFrom) <= maxfileload:
            bytesFrom = open(pathFrom, 'rb').read()      # read small file all at once
            open(pathTo, 'wb').write(bytesFrom)          # need b mode on Windows
        else:
            fileFrom = open(pathFrom, 'rb')              # read big files in chunks
            fileTo   = open(pathTo,   'wb')              # need b mode here too
            while 1:
                bytesFrom = fileFrom.read(blksize)       # get one block, less at end
                if not bytesFrom: break                  # empty after last chunk
                fileTo.write(bytesFrom)

def cpall(dirFrom, dirTo):
    """
    copy contents of dirFrom and below to dirTo
    """
    global dcount, fcount
    for file in os.listdir(dirFrom):                     # for files/dirs here
        pathFrom = os.path.join(dirFrom, file)
        pathTo   = os.path.join(dirTo,   file)           # extend both paths
        if not os.path.isdir(pathFrom):                  # copy simple files
            try:
                if verbose > 1: print 'copying', pathFrom, 'to', pathTo
                cpfile(pathFrom, pathTo)
                fcount = fcount+1
            except:
                print 'Error copying', pathFrom, 'to', pathTo, '--skipped'
                print sys.exc_info()[0], sys.exc_info()[1]
        else:
            if verbose: print 'copying dir', pathFrom, 'to', pathTo
            try:
                os.mkdir(pathTo)                         # make new subdir
                cpall(pathFrom, pathTo)                  # recur into subdirs
                dcount = dcount+1
            except:
                print 'Error creating', pathTo, '--skipped'
                print sys.exc_info()[0], sys.exc_info()[1]

def getargs():
    try:
        dirFrom, dirTo = sys.argv[1:]
    except:
        print 'Use: cpall.py dirFrom dirTo'
    else:
        if not os.path.isdir(dirFrom):
            print 'Error: dirFrom is not a directory'
        elif not os.path.exists(dirTo):
            os.mkdir(dirTo)
            print 'Note: dirTo was created'
            return (dirFrom, dirTo)
        else:
```

Example 7-25. PP3E\System\Filetools\cpall.py (continued)

```
            print 'Warning: dirTo already exists'
            if dirFrom == dirTo or (hasattr(os.path, 'samefile') and
                                    os.path.samefile(dirFrom, dirTo)):
                print 'Error: dirFrom same as dirTo'
            else:
                return (dirFrom, dirTo)

if __name__ == '__main__':
    import time
    dirstuple = getargs()
    if dirstuple:
        print 'Copying...'
        start = time.time()
        cpall(*dirstuple)
        print 'Copied', fcount, 'files,', dcount, 'directories',
        print 'in', time.time() - start, 'seconds'
```

This script implements its own recursive tree traversal logic and keeps track of both the "from" and "to" directory paths as it goes. At every level, it copies over simple files, creates directories in the "to" path, and recurs into subdirectories with "from" and "to" paths extended by one level. There are other ways to code this task (e.g., other cpall variants in the book's examples distribution change the working directory along the way with os.chdir calls), but extending paths on descent works well in practice.

Notice this script's reusable cpfile function—just in case there are multigigabyte files in the tree to be copied, it uses a file's size to decide whether it should be read all at once or in chunks (remember, the file read method without arguments actually loads the entire file into an in-memory string). We choose fairly large file and block sizes, because the more we read at once in Python, the faster our scripts will typically run. This is more efficient than it may sound; strings left behind by prior reads will be garbage collected and reused as we go.

Also note that this script creates the "to" directory if needed, but it assumes that the directory is empty when a copy starts up; be sure to remove the target directory before copying a new tree to its name (more on this in the next section).

Here is a big book examples tree copy in action on Windows; pass in the name of the "from" and "to" directories to kick off the process, redirect the output to a file if there are too many error messages to read all at once (e.g., > output.txt), and run an rm shell command (or similar platform-specific tool) to delete the target directory first if needed:

```
C:\temp>rm -rf cpexamples
```

```
C:\temp>python %X%\system\filetools\cpall.py examples cpexamples
Note: dirTo was created
```

```
Copying...
Copied 1356 files, 118 directories in 2.41999995708 seconds

C:\temp>fc /B examples\System\Filetools\cpall.py
              cpexamples\System\Filetools\cpall.py
Comparing files examples\System\Filetools\cpall.py and
cpexamples\System\Filetools\cpall.py
FC: no differences encountered
```

At the time I wrote this example in 2000, this test run copied a tree of 1,356 files and
118 directories in 2.4 seconds on my 650 MHz Windows 98 laptop (the built-in
time.time call can be used to query the system time in seconds). It runs a bit slower if
some other programs are open on the machine, and may run arbitrarily faster or
slower for you. Still, this is at least as fast as the best drag-and-drop I've timed on
Windows.

So how does this script work around bad files on a CD backup? The secret is that it
catches and ignores file *exceptions*, and it keeps walking. To copy all the files that are
good on a CD, I simply run a command line such as this one:

```
C:\temp>python %X%\system\filetools\cpall_visitor.py
              g:\PP3rdEd\examples\PP3E cpexamples
```

Because the CD is addressed as "G:" on my Windows machine, this is the command-
line equivalent of drag-and-drop copying from an item in the CD's top-level folder,
except that the Python script will recover from errors on the CD and get the rest. On
copy errors, it prints a message to standard output and continues; for big copies,
you'll probably want to redirect the script's output to a file for later inspection.

In general, cpall can be passed any absolute directory path on your machine, even
those that indicate devices such as CDs. To make this go on Linux, try a root directory such as */dev/cdrom* or something similar to address your CD drive.

Recoding Copies with a Visitor-Based Class

When I first wrote the cpall script just discussed, I couldn't see a way that the
visitor class hierarchy we met earlier would help. *Two* directories needed to be traversed in parallel (the original and the copy), and visitor is based on climbing one
tree with os.path.walk. There seemed no easy way to keep track of where the script
was in the copy directory.

The trick I eventually stumbled onto is not to keep track at all. Instead, the script
in Example 7-26 simply replaces the "from" directory path string with the "to"
directory path string, at the front of all directory names and pathnames passed in
from os.path.walk. The results of the string replacements are the paths to which
the original files and directories are to be copied.

Example 7-26. PP3E\System\Filetools\cpall_visitor.py

```
############################################################
# Use: "python cpall_visitor.py fromDir toDir"
# cpall, but with the visitor classes and os.path.walk;
# the trick is to do string replacement of fromDir with
# toDir at the front of all the names walk passes in;
# assumes that the toDir does not exist initially;
############################################################

import os
from PP3E.PyTools.visitor import FileVisitor
from cpall import cpfile, getargs
verbose = True

class CpallVisitor(FileVisitor):
    def __init__(self, fromDir, toDir):
        self.fromDirLen = len(fromDir) + 1
        self.toDir      = toDir
        FileVisitor.__init__(self)
    def visitdir(self, dirpath):
        toPath = os.path.join(self.toDir, dirpath[self.fromDirLen:])
        if verbose: print 'd', dirpath, '=>', toPath
        os.mkdir(toPath)
        self.dcount += 1
    def visitfile(self, filepath):
        toPath = os.path.join(self.toDir, filepath[self.fromDirLen:])
        if verbose: print 'f', filepath, '=>', toPath
        cpfile(filepath, toPath)
        self.fcount += 1

if __name__ == '__main__':
    import sys, time
    fromDir, toDir = sys.argv[1:3]
    if len(sys.argv) > 3: verbose = 0
    print 'Copying...'
    start = time.time()
    walker = CpallVisitor(fromDir, toDir)
    walker.run(startDir=fromDir)
    print 'Copied', walker.fcount, 'files,', walker.dcount, 'directories',
    print 'in', time.time() - start, 'seconds'
```

This version accomplishes roughly the same goal as the original, but it has made a few assumptions to keep code simple. The "to" directory is assumed not to exist initially, and exceptions are not ignored along the way. Here it is copying the book examples tree again on Windows:

```
C:\temp>rm -rf cpexamples

C:\temp>python %X%\system\filetools\cpall_visitor.py
                                    examples cpexamples -quiet
Copying...
Copied 1356 files, 119 directories in 2.09000003338 seconds
```

```
C:\temp>fc /B examples\System\Filetools\cpall.py
            cpexamples\System\Filetools\cpall.py
Comparing files examples\System\Filetools\cpall.py and
cpexamples\System\Filetools\cpall.py
FC: no differences encountered
```

Despite the extra string slicing going on, this version runs just as fast as the original. For tracing purposes, this version also prints all the "from" and "to" copy paths during the traversal unless you pass in a third argument on the command line or set the script's verbose variable to False or 0:

```
C:\temp>python %X%\system\filetools\cpall_visitor.py examples cpexamples
Copying...
d examples => cpexamples\
f examples\autoexec.bat => cpexamples\autoexec.bat
f examples\cleanall.csh => cpexamples\cleanall.csh
...more deleted...
d examples\System => cpexamples\System
f examples\System\System.txt => cpexamples\System\System.txt
f examples\System\more.py => cpexamples\System\more.py
f examples\System\reader.py => cpexamples\System\reader.py
...more deleted...
Copied 1356 files, 119 directories in 2.31000006199 seconds
```

Deleting Directory Trees

Both of the copy scripts in the last section work as planned, but they aren't very forgiving of existing directory trees. That is, they implicitly assume that the "to" target directory either is empty or doesn't exist at all, and they fail badly if that isn't the case. Presumably, you will first somehow delete the target directory on your machine. For my purposes, that was a reasonable assumption to make.

The copiers could be changed to work with existing "to" directories too (e.g., ignore os.mkdir exceptions), but I prefer to start from scratch when copying trees; you never know what old garbage might be lying around in the "to" directory. So when testing the earlier copies, I was careful to run an rm -rf cpexamples command line to recursively delete the entire *cpexamples* directory tree before copying another tree to that name.

Unfortunately, the rm command used to clear the target directory is really a Unix utility that I installed on my PC from a commercial package; it probably won't work on your computer. There are other platform-specific ways to delete directory trees (e.g., deleting a folder's icon in a Windows explorer GUI), but why not do it once in Python for every platform? Example 7-27 deletes every file and directory at and below a passed-in directory's name. Because its logic is packaged as a function, it is also an *importable* utility that can be run from other scripts. Because it is pure Python code, it is a *cross-platform* solution for tree removal.

Example 7-27. PP3E\System\Filetools\rmall.py

```
#!/usr/bin/python
###############################################################
# Use: "python rmall.py directoryPath directoryPath..."
# recursive directory tree deletion: removes all files and
# directories at and below directoryPaths; recurs into subdirs
# and removes parent dir last, because os.rmdir requires that
# directory is empty; like a Unix "rm -rf directoryPath"
###############################################################

import sys, os
fcount = dcount = 0

def rmall(dirPath):                              # delete dirPath and below
    global fcount, dcount
    namesHere = os.listdir(dirPath)
    for name in namesHere:                       # remove all contents first
        path = os.path.join(dirPath, name)
        if not os.path.isdir(path):              # remove simple files
            os.remove(path)
            fcount += 1
        else:                                    # recur to remove subdirs
            rmall(path)
    os.rmdir(dirPath)                            # remove now-empty dirPath
    dcount += 1

if __name__ == '__main__':
    import time
    start = time.time()
    for dname in sys.argv[1:]: rmall(dname)
    tottime = time.time() - start
    print 'Removed %d files and %d dirs in %s secs' % (fcount, dcount, tottime)
```

The great thing about coding this sort of tool in Python is that it can be run with the same command-line interface on any machine where Python is installed. If you don't have an `rm -rf` type command available on your Windows, Unix, or Macintosh computer, simply run the Python `rmall` script instead:

```
C:\temp>python %X%\System\Filetools\cpall.py examples cpexamples
Note: dirTo was created
Copying...
Copied 1379 files, 121 directories in 2.68999993801 seconds

C:\temp>python %X%\System\Filetools\rmall.py cpexamples
Removed 1379 files and 122 dirs in 0.549999952316 secs

C:\temp>ls cpexamples
ls: File or directory "cpexamples" is not found
```

Here, the script traverses and deletes a tree of 1,379 files and 122 directories in about half a second—substantially impressive for a noncompiled programming language, and roughly equivalent to the commercial `rm -rf` program I purchased and installed on my PC.

One subtlety here: this script must be careful to delete the contents of a directory *before* deleting the directory itself—the os.rmdir call mandates that directories must be empty when deleted (and throws an exception if they are not). Because of that, the recursive calls on subdirectories need to happen before the os.mkdir call. Computer scientists would recognize this as a *postorder*, depth-first tree traversal, since we process parent directories after their children. This also makes any traversals based on os.path.walk out of the question: we need to *return* to a parent directory to delete it after visiting its descendents.

To illustrate, let's run interactive os.remove and os.rmdir calls on a *cpexamples* directory containing files or nested directories:

```
>>> os.path.isdir('cpexamples')
1
>>> os.remove('cpexamples')
Traceback (innermost last):
  File "<stdin>", line 1, in ?
OSError: [Errno 2] No such file or directory: 'cpexamples'
>>> os.rmdir('cpexamples')
Traceback (innermost last):
  File "<stdin>", line 1, in ?
OSError: [Errno 13] Permission denied: 'cpexamples'
```

Both calls always fail if the directory is not empty. But now, delete the contents of *cpexamples* in another window and try again:

```
>>> os.path.isdir('cpexamples')
1
>>> os.remove('cpexamples')
Traceback (innermost last):
  File "<stdin>", line 1, in ?
OSError: [Errno 2] No such file or directory: 'cpexamples'
>>> os.rmdir('cpexamples')
>>> os.path.exists('cpexamples')
0
```

The os.remove still fails—it's meant only for deleting nondirectory items—but os.rmdir now works because the directory is empty. The upshot of this is that a tree deletion traversal must generally remove directories "on the way out."

Recoding Deletions for Generality

As coded, the rmall script processes directory names and fails only if it's given names of simple files, but it's trivial to generalize the script to eliminate that restriction. The recoding in Example 7-28 accepts an arbitrary command-line list of file and directory names, deletes simple files, and recursively deletes directories.

Example 7-28. PP3E\System\Filetools\rmall2.py

```
#!/usr/bin/python
###############################################################
# Use: "python rmall2.py fileOrDirPath fileOrDirPath..."
# like rmall.py, alternative coding, files OK on cmd line
###############################################################

import sys, os
fcount = dcount = 0

def rmone(pathName):
    global fcount, dcount
    if not os.path.isdir(pathName):             # remove simple files
        os.remove(pathName)
        fcount += 1
    else:                                       # recur to remove contents
        for name in os.listdir(pathName):
            rmone(os.path.join(pathName, name))
        os.rmdir(pathName)                      # remove now-empty dirPath
        dcount += 1

if __name__ == '__main__':
    import time
    start = time.time()
    for name in sys.argv[1:]: rmone(name)
    tottime = time.time() - start
    print 'Removed %d files and %d dirs in %s secs' % (fcount, dcount, tottime)
```

This shorter version runs the same way, and just as fast, as the original:

```
C:\temp>python %X%\System\Filetools\cpall.py examples cpexamples
Note: dirTo was created
Copying...
Copied 1379 files, 121 directories in 2.52999997139 seconds

C:\temp>python %X%\System\Filetools\rmall2.py cpexamples
Removed 1379 files and 122 dirs in 0.550000071526 secs

C:\temp>ls cpexamples
ls: File or directory "cpexamples" is not found
```

But it can also be used to delete simple files:

```
C:\temp>python %X%\System\Filetools\rmall2.py spam.txt eggs.txt
Removed 2 files and 0 dirs in 0.0600000619888 secs

C:\temp>python %X%\System\Filetools\rmall2.py spam.txt eggs.txt cpexamples
Removed 1381 files and 122 dirs in 0.630000042915 secs
```

As usual, there is more than one way to do it in Python (though you'll have to try hard to find many spurious ways). Notice that these scripts trap no exceptions; in programs designed to blindly delete an entire directory tree, exceptions are all likely to denote truly bad things. We could get fancier and support filename patterns by using the built-in fnmatch module along the way too, but this was beyond the scope

---

of these scripts' goals (for pointers on matching, see Example 7-17 and *find.py* in Chapter 4).

Also note that because the newer os.walk call we met in Chapter 4 provides a *bottom-up* tree search option, it gives another way to delete a tree without recursion (subdirectory triples are returned before their containing directory):[*]

```
# delete everything in the tree rooted at 'top'
import os
for (root, dirs, files) in os.walk(top, topdown=False):
    for name in files:
        os.remove(os.path.join(root, name))
    for name in dirs:
        os.rmdir(os.path.join(root, name))
```

Comparing Directory Trees

Engineers can be a paranoid sort (but you didn't hear that from me). At least I am. It comes from decades of seeing things go terribly wrong, I suppose. When I create a CD backup of my hard drive, for instance, there's still something a bit too magical about the process to trust the CD writer program to do the right thing. Maybe I should, but it's tough to have a lot of faith in tools that occasionally trash files and seem to crash my Windows machine every third Tuesday of the month. When push comes to shove, it's nice to be able to verify that data copied to a backup CD is the same as the original—or at least to spot deviations from the original—as soon as possible. If a backup is ever needed, it will be *really* needed.

Because data CDs are accessible as simple directory trees, we are once again in the realm of tree walkers—to verify a backup CD, we simply need to walk its top-level directory. If our script is general enough, we will also be able to use it to verify other copy operations as well—e.g., downloaded tar files, hard-drive backups, and so on. In fact, the combination of the cpall script we saw earlier and a general tree comparison would provide a portable and scriptable way to copy and verify data sets.

We've already written a generic walker class (the visitor module), but it won't help us here directly: we need to walk *two* directories in parallel and inspect common files along the way. Moreover, walking either one of the two directories won't allow us to spot files and directories that exist only in the other. Something more custom seems in order here.

---

[*] A related concept: see Chapter 14 for examples that delete remote directory trees on an FTP server. They are similar in spirit, but they must get listings and send deletion commands over network sockets by FTP.

Finding Directory Differences

Before we start coding, the first thing we need to clarify is what it means to compare two directory trees. If both trees have exactly the same branch structure and depth, this problem reduces to comparing corresponding files in each tree. In general, though, the trees can have arbitrarily different shapes, depths, and so on.

More generally, the contents of a directory in one tree may have more or fewer entries than the corresponding directory in the other tree. If those differing contents are filenames, there is no corresponding file to compare with; if they are directory names, there is no corresponding branch to descend through. In fact, the only way to detect files and directories that appear in one tree but not the other is to detect differences in each level's directory.

In other words, a tree comparison algorithm will also have to perform *directory* comparisons along the way. Because this is a nested and simpler operation, let's start by coding and debugging a single-directory comparison of filenames in Example 7-29.

Example 7-29. PP3E\System\Filetools\dirdiff.py

```
#!/bin/env python
##############################################################################
# use: python dirdiff.py dir1-path dir2-path
# compare two directories to find files that exist in one but not the other;
# this version uses the os.listdir function and list difference;  note that
# this script only checks filenames, not file contents--see diffall.py for an
# extension that does the latter by comparing .read( ) results;
##############################################################################

import os, sys

def reportdiffs(unique1, unique2, dir1, dir2):
    if not (unique1 or unique2):
        print 'Directory lists are identical'
    else:
        if unique1:
            print 'Files unique to', dir1
            for file in unique1:
                print '...', file
        if unique2:
            print 'Files unique to', dir2
            for file in unique2:
                print '...', file

def unique(seq1, seq2):
    uniques = []                         # return items in seq1 only
    for item in seq1:
        if item not in seq2:
            uniques.append(item)
    return uniques

def comparedirs(dir1, dir2):
```

Example 7-29. PP3E\System\Filetools\dirdiff.py (continued)

```
    print 'Comparing', dir1, 'to', dir2
    files1  = os.listdir(dir1)
    files2  = os.listdir(dir2)
    unique1 = unique(files1, files2)
    unique2 = unique(files2, files1)
    reportdiffs(unique1, unique2, dir1, dir2)
    return not (unique1 or unique2)              # true if no diffs

def getargs():
    try:
        dir1, dir2 = sys.argv[1:]                # 2 command-line args
    except:
        print 'Usage: dirdiff.py dir1 dir2'
        sys.exit(1)
    else:
        return (dir1, dir2)

if __name__ == '__main__':
    dir1, dir2 = getargs()
    comparedirs(dir1, dir2)
```

Given listings of names in two directories, this script simply picks out unique names in the first and unique names in the second, and reports any unique names found as differences (that is, files in one directory but not the other). Its comparedirs function returns a true result if no differences were found, which is useful for detecting differences in callers.

Let's run this script on a few directories; differences are detected and reported as names unique in either passed-in directory pathname. Notice that this is only a *structural* comparison that just checks names in listings, not file contents (we'll add the latter in a moment):

```
C:\temp>python %X%\system\filetools\dirdiff.py examples cpexamples
Comparing examples to cpexamples
Directory lists are identical

C:\temp>python %X%\system\filetools\dirdiff.py
                             examples\PyTools cpexamples\PyTools
Comparing examples\PyTools to cpexamples\PyTools
Files unique to examples\PyTools
... visitor.py

C:\temp>python %X%\system\filetools\dirdiff.py
                             examples\System\Filetools
                             cpexamples\System\Filetools
Comparing examples\System\Filetools to cpexamples\System\Filetools
Files unique to examples\System\Filetools
... dirdiff2.py
Files unique to cpexamples\System\Filetools
... cpall.py
```

The unique function is the heart of this script: it performs a simple list difference operation. Here's how it works apart from the rest of this script's code:

```
>>> L1 = [1, 3, 5, 7, 9]
>>> L2 = [2, 3, 6, 8, 9]
>>> from dirdiff import unique
>>> unique(L1, L2)            # items in L1 but not in L2
[1, 5, 7]
>>> unique(L2, L1)            # items in L2 but not in L1
[2, 6, 8]
```

These two lists have objects 3 and 9 in common; the rest appear only in one of the two. When applied to directories, *unique* items represent tree differences, and *common* items are names of files or subdirectories that merit further comparisons or traversals. There are other ways to code this operation; see the dirdiff variants on the book's examples distribution for a few of them.

In fact, in Python 2.4 and later, we could also use the built-in set object type if we don't care about the order in the results (we'll use our own functions for now to avoid requiring users to upgrade):

```
>>> S1 = set([1, 3, 5, 7, 9])
>>> S2 = set([2, 3, 6, 8, 9])

>>> S1 - S2           # difference: unique
set([1, 5, 7])
>>> S2 - S1
set([8, 2, 6])

>>> S1 & S2           # intersection: common
set([9, 3])
```

Finding Tree Differences

Now all we need is a tree walker that applies dirdiff at each level to pick out unique files and directories, explicitly compares the contents of files in common, and descends through directories in common. Example 7-30 fits the bill.

Example 7-30. PP3E\System\Filetools\diffall.py

```
#############################################################################
# Usage: "python diffall.py dir1 dir2".  recursive tree comparison:
# report unique files that exist in only dir1 or dir2,
# report files of same name in dir1 and dir2 with differing contents,
# report instances of same name but different type in dir1 and dir2,
# and do the same for all subdirectories of the same names in and below
# dir1 and dir2;  summary of diffs appears at end of output, but search
# redirected output for "DIFF" and "unique" strings for further details;
# new: limit reads to 1M for large files, catch same name=file/dir;
#############################################################################
```

Example 7-30. PP3E\System\Filetools\diffall.py (continued)

```
import os, dirdiff
blocksize = 1024 * 1024                    # up to 1M per read

def intersect(seq1, seq2):
    commons = []                           # items in seq1 and seq2
    for item in seq1:                      # or use new set() object
        if item in seq2:
            commons.append(item)
    return commons

def comparedirs(dir1, dir2, diffs, verbose=False):
                                           # compare filename lists
    print '-'*20
    if not dirdiff.comparedirs(dir1, dir2):
        diffs.append('unique files at %s - %s' % (dir1, dir2))

    print 'Comparing contents'
    names1 = os.listdir(dir1)
    names2 = os.listdir(dir2)
    common = intersect(names1, names2)
    missed = common[:]

    # compare contents of files in common
    for name in common:
        path1 = os.path.join(dir1, name)
        path2 = os.path.join(dir2, name)
        if os.path.isfile(path1) and os.path.isfile(path2):
            missed.remove(name)
            file1 = open(path1, 'rb')
            file2 = open(path2, 'rb')
            while True:
                bytes1 = file1.read(blocksize)
                bytes2 = file2.read(blocksize)
                if (not bytes1) and (not bytes2):
                    if verbose: print name, 'matches'
                    break
                if bytes1 != bytes2:
                    diffs.append('files differ at %s - %s' % (path1, path2))
                    print name, 'DIFFERS'
                    break

    # recur to compare directories in common
    for name in common:
        path1 = os.path.join(dir1, name)
        path2 = os.path.join(dir2, name)
        if os.path.isdir(path1) and os.path.isdir(path2):
            missed.remove(name)
            comparedirs(path1, path2, diffs, verbose)

    # same name but not both files or dirs?
    for name in missed:
        diffs.append('files missed at %s - %s: %s' % (dir1, dir2, name))
```

Example 7-30. PP3E\System\Filetools\diffall.py (continued)

```
        print name, 'DIFFERS'


if __name__ == '__main__':
    dir1, dir2 = dirdiff.getargs()
    mydiffs = []
    comparedirs(dir1, dir2, mydiffs, True)      # changes mydiffs in-place
    print '='*40                                # walk, report diffs list
    if not mydiffs:
        print 'No diffs found.'
    else:
        print 'Diffs found:', len(mydiffs)
        for diff in mydiffs: print '-', diff
```

At each directory in the tree, this script simply runs the `dirdiff` tool to detect unique names, and then compares names in common by intersecting directory lists. It uses recursive function calls to traverse the tree and visits subdirectories only after comparing all the files at each level so that the output is more coherent to read (the trace output for subdirectories appears after that for files; it is not intermixed).

Notice the `misses` list, added in the third edition of this book; it's very unlikely, but not impossible, that the same name might be a file in one directory and a subdirectory in the other. Also notice the `blocksize` variable; as in the tree copy script we saw earlier, instead of blindly reading entire files into memory all at once, we limit each read to grab up to 1 MB at a time, just in case any files in the directories are too big to be loaded into available memory. Without this limit, I ran into `MemoryError` exceptions on some machines with a prior version of this script that read both files all at once, like this:

```
        bytes1 = open(path1, 'rb').read()
        bytes2 = open(path2, 'rb').read()
        if bytes1 == bytes2:
            ...match...
        else:
            ...difference...
```

This code was simpler, but is less practical for very large files that can't fit into your available memory space (consider CD and DVD image files, for example). In the new version's loop, the file reads return what is left when there is less than 1 MB present or remaining and return empty strings at end-of-file. Files match if all blocks read are the same, and they reach end-of-file at the same time. On some platforms, you may also want to detect and skip certain kinds of special files in order to be fully general, but these were not in my trees, so they are not in my script.

Running the Script

Since we've already studied the tree-walking tools this script employs, let's jump right into a few example runs. When run on identical trees, status messages scroll during the traversal, and a `No diffs found.` message appears at the end:

```
C:\temp>python %X%\system\filetools\diffall.py examples cpexamples
--------------------
Comparing examples to cpexamples
Directory lists are identical
Comparing contents
--------------------
Comparing examples\old_Part2 to cpexamples\old_Part2
Directory lists are identical
Comparing contents
--------------------
...more lines deleted...
--------------------
Comparing examples\EmbExt\Regist to cpexamples\EmbExt\Regist
Directory lists are identical
Comparing contents
--------------------
Comparing examples\PyTools to cpexamples\PyTools
Directory lists are identical
Comparing contents
========================================
No diffs found.
```

I run this with the verbose flag passed in as `False`; use `True` to watch more status messages fly by. To show how differences are reported, we need to generate a few. Let's run the global search-and-replace script we met earlier in order to change a few files scattered about one of the trees (see—I told you global replacement could trash your files!):

```
C:\temp\examples>python %X%\PyTools\visitor_replace.py -exec SPAM
Are you sure?y
...
1355 => .\PyTools\visitor_find_quiet1.py
1356 => .\PyTools\fixeoln_one.doc.txt
Visited 1356 files
Changed 8 files:
.\package.csh
.\README-PP3E.txt
.\readme-old-pp1E.txt
.\temp
.\remp
.\Internet\Cgi-Web\fixcgi.py
.\System\Processes\output.txt
.\PyTools\cleanpyc.py
```

While we're at it, let's remove a few common files so that directory uniqueness differences show up on the scope too; the following three removal commands will make two directories differ (the last two commands impact the same directory in different trees):

```
C:\temp>rm cpexamples\PyTools\visitor.py
C:\temp>rm cpexamples\System\Filetools\dirdiff2.py
C:\temp>rm examples\System\Filetools\cpall.py
```

Now, rerun the comparison walker to pick out differences and redirect its output report to a file for easy inspection. The following lists just the parts of the output report that identify differences. In typical use, I inspect the summary at the bottom of the report first, and then search for the strings "DIFF" and "unique" in the report's text if I need more information about the differences summarized; this could be more user-friendly, but it does the job for me:

```
C:\temp>python %X%\system\filetools\diffall.py examples cpexamples > diffs
C:\temp>type diffs
--------------------
Comparing examples to cpexamples
Directory lists are identical
Comparing contents
package.csh DIFFERS
README-PP3E.txt DIFFERS
readme-old-pp1E.txt DIFFERS
temp DIFFERS
remp DIFFERS
--------------------
Comparing examples\old_Part2 to cpexamples\old_Part2
Directory lists are identical
Comparing contents
--------------------
...
--------------------
Comparing examples\Internet\Cgi-Web to cpexamples\Internet\Cgi-Web
Directory lists are identical
Comparing contents
fixcgi.py DIFFERS
--------------------
...
--------------------
Comparing examples\System\Filetools to cpexamples\System\Filetools
Files unique to examples\System\Filetools
... dirdiff2.py
Files unique to cpexamples\System\Filetools
... cpall.py
Comparing contents
--------------------
...
--------------------
Comparing examples\System\Processes to cpexamples\System\Processes
Directory lists are identical
Comparing contents
output.txt DIFFERS
--------------------
```

```
...
--------------------
Comparing examples\PyTools to cpexamples\PyTools
Files unique to examples\PyTools
... visitor.py
Comparing contents
cleanpyc.py DIFFERS
========================================
Diffs found: 10
- files differ at examples\package.csh - cpexamples\package.csh
- files differ at examples\README-PP3E.txt - cpexamples\README-PP3E.txt
- files differ at examples\readme-old-pp1E.txt - cpexamples\readme-old-pp1E.txt
- files differ at examples\temp - cpexamples\temp
- files differ at examples\remp - cpexamples\remp
- files differ at examples\Internet\Cgi-Web\fixcgi.py -
          cpexamples\Internet\Cgi-Web\fixcgi.py
- unique files at examples\System\Filetools -
          cpexamples\System\Filetools
- files differ at examples\System\Processes\output.txt -
          cpexamples\System\Processes\output.txt
- unique files at examples\PyTools - cpexamples\PyTools
- files differ at examples\PyTools\cleanpyc.py - cpexamples\PyTools\cleanpyc.py
```

I added line breaks and tabs in a few of these output lines to make them fit on this page, but the report is simple to understand. Ten differences were found—the eight files we changed (trashed) with the replacement script, and the two directories we threw out of sync with the three rm remove commands.

Verifying CD backups

So how does this script placate CD backup paranoia? To double-check my CD writer's work, I run a command such as the following. I can also use a command like this to find out what has been changed since the last backup. Again, since the CD is "G:" on my machine when plugged in, I provide a path rooted there; use a root such as */dev/cdrom* or */mnt/cdrom* on Linux:

```
C:\temp>python %X%\system\filetools\diffall.py
              examples g:\PP3rdEd\examples\PP3E > exdiffs091500

C:\temp>more exdiffs091500
--------------------
Comparing examples to g:\PP3rdEd\examples\PP3E
Files unique to examples
... .cshrc
Comparing contents
tounix.py DIFFERS
--------------------
Comparing examples\old_Part2 to g:\PP3rdEd\examples\PP3E\old_Part2
Directory lists are identical
Comparing contents
--------------------
```
...more

```
visitor_fixeoln.py DIFFERS
visitor_fixnames.py DIFFERS
==========================================
Diffs found: 41
- unique files at examples - g:\PP3rdEd\examples\PP3E
- files differ at examples\tounix.py - g:\PP3rdEd\examples\PP3E\tounix.py
...more
```

The CD spins, the script compares, and a summary of 41 differences appears at the end of the report (in this case, representing changes to the examples tree since the latest backup CD was burned). For an example of a full difference report, see the file *exdiffs091500* in the book's examples distribution. More typically, this is what turns up for most of my example backups; files with a leading "." are not copied to the CD:

```
C:\temp>python %X%\System\Filetools\diffall.py
                 examples g:\PP3rdEd\examples\PP3E

...
---------------------
Comparing examples\Config to g:\PP3rdEd\examples\PP3E\Config
Files unique to examples\Config
... .cshrc
Comparing contents
==========================================
Diffs found: 1
- unique files at examples\Config - g:\PP3rdEd\examples\PP3E\Config
```

And to be *really* sure, I run the following global comparison command against the true book directory to verify the entire book tree backup on CD:

```
C:\>python %X%\System\Filetools\diffall.py PP3rdEd G:\PP3rdEd
---------------------
Comparing PP3rdEd to G:\PP3rdEd
Files unique to G:\PP3rdEd
... examples.tar.gz
Comparing contents
README.txt DIFFERS
---------------------
...more
---------------------
Comparing PP3rdEd\examples\PP3E\Config to G:\PP3rdEd\examples\PP3E\Config
Files unique to PP3rdEd\examples\PP3E\Config
... .cshrc
Comparing contents
---------------------
...more
---------------------
Comparing PP3rdEd\chapters to G:\PP3rdEd\chapters
Directory lists are identical
Comparing contents
ch01-intro.doc DIFFERS
ch04-os3.doc DIFFERS
ch05-gui1.doc DIFFERS
ch06-gui2.doc DIFFERS
---------------------
```

```
...more
==========================================
Diffs found: 11
- unique files at PP3rdEd - G:\PP3rdEd
- files differ at PP3rdEd\README.txt - G:\PP3rdEd\README.txt
...more
```

This particular run indicates that I've changed a README file, four chapter files, and a bunch more since the last backup; if run immediately after making a backup, only the *.cshrc* unique file shows up on diffall radar. This global comparison can take a few minutes. It performs byte-for-byte comparisons of all chapter files and screenshots, the examples tree, and more, but it's an accurate and complete verification. Given that this book tree contained roughly 119 MB of data in 7,300 files and 570 directories the last time I checked, a more manual verification procedure without Python's help would be utterly impossible.

After writing this script, I also started using it to verify full backups of my laptops onto an external hard-drive device. To do so, I run the cpall copy script we met earlier, and then the comparison script here to check results and get a list of files that didn't copy correctly. The last time I did this, this procedure copied and compared 225,000 files and 15,000 directories in 20 GB of space—not the sort of task that lends itself to manual labor!

Here are the magic incantations on my Windows laptop. f:\ is a partition on my external hard drive, and you shouldn't be surprised if each of these commands runs for half an hour or more on currently common hardware. A drag-and-drop copy takes at least as long, assuming it works at all.

```
C:\...\System\Filetools>cpall.py c:\ f:\    > f:\copy-log.txt
C:\...\System\Filetools>diffall.py f:\ c:\ > f:\diff-log.txt
```

Reporting Differences

Finally, it's worth noting that this script still only *detects* differences in the tree but does not give any further details about individual file differences. In fact, it simply loads and compares the binary contents of corresponding files with string comparisons. It's a simple yes/no result.

If and when I need more details about how two reported files actually differ, I either edit the files or run the file-comparison command on the host platform (e.g., fc on Windows/DOS, diff or cmp on Unix and Linux). That's not a portable solution for this last step; but for my purposes, just finding the differences in a 1,300-file tree was much more critical than reporting which lines differ in files flagged in the report.

Of course, since we can always run shell commands in Python, this last step could be automated by spawning a diff or fc command with os.popen as differences are encountered (or after the traversal, by scanning the report summary). The output of these system calls could be displayed verbatim, or parsed for relevant parts.

We also might try to do a bit better here by opening text files in text mode to ignore line-terminator differences, but it's not clear that such differences should be ignored (what if the caller wants to know whether line-end markers have been changed?). For example, after downloading a web site with an FTP script we'll meet in Chapter 14, the diffall script detected a discrepancy between the local copy of a file and the one at the remote server. To probe further, I simply ran some interactive Python code:

```
>>> a = open('lp2e-updates.html', 'rb').read()
>>> b = open(r'C:\Mark\WEBSITE\public_html\lp2e-updates.html', 'rb').read()
>>> a == b
False
```

This verifies that there really is a binary difference in the downloaded and local versions of the file; to see whether it's because a Unix or DOS line-end snuck into the file, try again in text mode so that line ends are all mapped to the standard \n character:

```
>>> a = open('lp2e-updates.html', 'r').read()
>>> b = open(r'C:\Mark\WEBSITE\public_html\lp2e-updates.html', 'r').read()
>>> a == b
True
```

Sure enough; now, to find where the difference is, the following code checks character by character until the first mismatch is found (in binary mode, so we retain the difference):

```
>>> a = open('lp2e-updates.html', 'rb').read()
>>> b = open(r'C:\Mark\WEBSITE\public_html\lp2e-updates.html', 'rb').read()

>>> for (i, (ac, bc)) in enumerate(zip(a, b)):
...     if ac != bc:
...         print i, repr(ac), repr(bc)
...         break
...
37966 '\r' '\n'
```

This means that at byte offset 37,966, there is a \r in the downloaded file, but a \n in the local copy. This line has a DOS line end in one and a Unix line end in the other. To see more, print text around the mismatch:

```
>>> for (i, (ac, bc)) in enumerate(zip(a, b)):
...     if ac != bc:
...         print i, repr(ac), repr(bc)
...         print repr(a[i-20:i+20])
...         print repr(b[i-20:i+20])
...         break
...
37966 '\r' '\n'
're>\r\ndef min(*args):\r\n    tmp = list(arg'
're>\r\ndef min(*args):\n    tmp = list(args'
```

Apparently, I wound up with a Unix line end at one point in the local copy and a DOS line end in the version I downloaded—the combined effect of the text mode used by the download script itself (which translated \n to \r\n) and years of edits on both Linux and Windows PDAs and laptops (I probably coded this change on Linux and copied it to my local Windows copy in binary mode). Code such as this could be integrated into the diffall script to make it more intelligent about text files and difference reporting.

Because Python excels at processing files and strings, it's even possible to go one step further and code a Python equivalent of the fc and diff commands. In fact, much of the work has already been done; the standard library module difflib, new as of Python 2.1, could make this task simple. See the Python library manual for details and usage examples.

We could also be smarter by avoiding the load and compare steps for files that differ in size, and we might use a smaller block size to reduce the script's memory requirements. For most trees, such optimizations are unnecessary; reading multimegabyte files into strings is very fast in Python, and garbage collection reclaims the space as you go.

Since such extensions are beyond both this script's scope and this chapter's size limits, though, they will have to await the attention of a curious reader.

GUI Programming

This part of the book shows you how to apply Python to build portable graphical user interfaces, primarily with Python's standard Tkinter library. The following chapters cover this topic in depth:

Chapter 8, *Graphical User Interfaces*
> This chapter outlines GUI options available to Python developers, and then presents a tutorial that illustrates core Tkinter coding concepts in the context of simple user interfaces.

Chapter 9, *A Tkinter Tour, Part 1*
> This chapter begins a two-part tour of the Tkinter library—its widget set and related tools. This first tour chapter covers simpler library tools and widgets: pop-up windows, various types of buttons, images, and so on. We also meet the Python Imaging Library (PIL) image processing extension here.

Chapter 10, *A Tkinter Tour, Part 2*
> This chapter continues the library tour begun in the prior chapter. It presents the rest of the Tkinter widget library, including menus, text, canvases, scroll bars, grids, and time-based events and animation. This section leads us toward some of the larger examples to follow.

Chapter 11, *GUI Coding Techniques*
> This chapter takes a look at GUI programming techniques: we'll learn how to build menus automatically from object templates, spawn GUIs as separate programs, run long-running tasks in parallel with threads and queues, and more.

Chapter 12, *Complete GUI Programs*
> This chapter pulls the earlier chapters' ideas together to implement a collection of user interfaces. It presents a collection of larger GUIs—clocks, text editors, drawing programs, image viewers, and so on—which also demonstrate general Python programming-in-the-large concepts along the way.

As in the first part of this book, the material presented here is applicable to a wide variety of domains and will be utilized again to build domain-specific user interfaces in later chapters of this book. For instance, the PyMailGUI, PyForm, and PyCalc examples of later chapters will assume that you've covered the basics here.

Graphical User Interfaces

"Here's Looking at You, Kid"

For most software systems, a graphical user interface (GUI) has become an expected part of the package. Even if the GUI acronym is new to you, chances are that you are already familiar with such interfaces—i.e., the windows, buttons, and menus that we use to interact with software programs. In fact, most of what we do on computers today is done with some sort of point-and-click graphical interface. From web browsers to system tools, programs are routinely dressed up with a GUI component to make them more flexible and easier to use.

In this part of the book, we will learn how to make Python scripts sprout such graphical interfaces too, by studying examples of programming with the Tkinter module, a portable GUI library that is a standard part of the Python system. As we'll see, it's easy to program user interfaces in Python scripts thanks to both the simplicity of the language and the power of its GUI libraries. As an added bonus, GUIs programmed in Python with Tkinter are automatically portable to all major computer systems.

GUI Programming Topics

Because GUIs are a major area, I want to say a few more words about this part of the book. To make them easier to absorb, GUI programming topics are split over the next five chapters of this book:

- This chapter begins with a quick Tkinter tutorial to teach coding basics. Interfaces are kept simple here on purpose, so you can master the fundamentals before moving on to the following chapter's interfaces. On the other hand, this chapter covers all the basics: event processing, the pack geometry manager, using inheritance and composition in GUIs, and more. As we'll see, object-oriented programming (OOP) isn't required for Tkinter, but it makes GUIs structured and reusable.

- Chapters 9 and 10 take you on a tour of the Tkinter widget set.* Roughly, Chapter 9 presents simple widgets and Chapter 10 covers more advanced widgets and related tools. Most of the interface devices you're accustomed to seeing—sliders, menus, dialogs, images, and their kin—show up here. These two chapters are not a fully complete Tkinter reference (which could easily fill a large book by itself), but they should be enough to help you get started coding substantial Python GUIs. The examples in these chapters are focused on widgets and Tkinter tools, but Python's support for code reuse is also explored along the way.

- Chapter 11 covers more advanced GUI programming techniques. It includes an exploration of techniques for automating common GUI tasks with Python. Although Tkinter is a full-featured library, a small amount of reusable Python code can make its interfaces even more powerful and easier to use.

- Chapter 12 wraps up by presenting a handful of complete GUI programs that make use of coding and widget techniques presented in the four preceding chapters. We'll learn how to implement text editors, image viewers, clocks, and more.

Because GUIs are actually cross-domain tools, other GUI examples will also show up throughout the remainder of this book. For example, we'll later see email GUIs, calculators, tree viewers, table browsers, and so on. See the end of Chapter 12 for a list of forward pointers to other Tkinter examples in this text.

One point I'd like to make right away: most GUIs are dynamic and interactive interfaces, and the best I can do here is show static screenshots representing selected states in the interactions such programs implement. This really won't do justice to most examples. If you are not working along with the examples already, I encourage you to run the GUI examples in this and later chapters on your own.

On Windows, the standard Python install comes with Tkinter support built in, so all these examples should work immediately. For other systems, Pythons with Tkinter support are readily available as well (see the top-level *README-PP3E.txt* file in the book examples distribution for more details). It's worth whatever extra install details you may need to absorb, though; experimenting with these programs is a great way to learn about both GUI programming and Python itself.

---

* The term "widget set" refers to the objects used to build familiar point-and-click user interface devices—push buttons, sliders, input fields, and so on. Tkinter comes with Python classes that correspond to all the widgets you're accustomed to seeing in graphical displays. Besides widgets, Tkinter also comes with tools for other activities, such as scheduling events to occur, waiting for socket data to arrive, and so on.

Has Anyone Noticed That G-U-I Are the First Three Letters of "GUIDO"?

Python's creator didn't originally set out to build a GUI development tool, but Python's ease of use and rapid turnaround have made this one of its primary roles. From an implementation perspective, GUIs in Python are really just instances of C extensions, and extendibility was one of the main ideas behind Python. When a script builds push buttons and menus, it ultimately talks to a C library; and when a script responds to a user event, a C library ultimately talks back to Python.

But from a practical point of view, GUIs are a critical part of modern systems and an ideal domain for a tool like Python. As we'll see, Python's simple syntax and object-oriented flavor blend well with the GUI model—it's natural to represent each device drawn on a screen as a Python class. Moreover, Python's quick turnaround lets programmers experiment with alternative layouts and behavior rapidly, in ways not possible with traditional development techniques. In fact, you can usually make a change to a Python-based GUI, and observe its effects in a matter of seconds. Don't try this with C or C++.

Python GUI Development Options

Before we start wading into the Tkinter pond, let's begin with some perspective on Python GUI options in general. Because Python has proven to be such a good match for GUI work, this domain has seen much activity in recent years. In fact, although Tkinter is the most widely used GUI toolkit in Python, there are a variety of ways to program user interfaces in Python today. Some are specific to Windows or X Windows,* some are cross-platform solutions, and all have followings and strong points of their own. To be fair to all the alternatives, here is a brief inventory of GUI toolkits available to Python programmers as I write these words:

Tkinter

An open source GUI library and the continuing de facto standard for portable GUI development in Python. Python scripts that use Tkinter to build GUIs run portably on Windows, X Windows (Unix and Linux), and Macintosh (both classic and OS X), and they display a native look-and-feel on each of these. Tkinter makes it easy to build simple and portable GUIs quickly. Moreover, it can be easily augmented with Python code, as well as with larger extension packages such as Pmw (a third-party widget library), Tix (another widget library, and now a standard part of Python), and PIL (an image-processing extension).

---

* In this book, "Windows" refers to the Microsoft Windows interface common on PCs, and "X Windows" refers to the X11 interface most commonly found on Unix and Linux platforms. These two interfaces are generally tied to the Microsoft and Unix platforms, respectively. It's possible to run X Windows on top of a Microsoft operating system and Windows emulators on Unix and Linux, but it's not common.

The underlying Tk library used by Tkinter is a standard in the open source world at large and is also used by the Perl, Ruby, PHP, and Tcl scripting languages, giving it a user base that numbers in the millions. The Python binding to Tk is enhanced by Python's simple object model; Tk widgets become customizable and embeddable objects, not string commands.

Tkinter is mature, robust, widely used, and well documented. It includes roughly 25 basic widget types, plus various dialogs and other tools. Moreover, there is a dedicated book on the subject, plus a large library of published Tkinter and Tk documentation. Perhaps most importantly, because it is based on a library developed for scripting languages, Tkinter is also a relatively lightweight toolkit, and as such it meshes well with a scripting language like Python.

Because of such attributes, Python's Tkinter module ships with Python as a standard library module and is the basis of Python's standard IDLE integrated development environment GUI. In fact, Tkinter is the only GUI toolkit that is part of Python; all others on this list are third-party extensions. The underlying Tk library is also shipped with Python on some platforms (including Windows and most Linux systems).

Although Tkinter is easy to use, its text and canvas widgets are powerful enough to implement web pages, three-dimensional visualization, and animation. PythonWorks, Komodo, and others provide GUI builders for Tkinter, and some Tk tools work for Python too; as we will see, though, Tkinter is usually so easy to code that GUI builders are not widely used.

wxPython

A Python interface for the open source wxWidgets (formerly called wxWindows[*]) library, a portable GUI class framework originally written to be used from the C++ programming language. The wxPython system is an extension module that wraps wxWindows classes. This library is generally considered to excel at building sophisticated interfaces and is probably the second most popular Python GUI toolkit today, behind Tkinter. Today, wxPython code is portable to Windows, Unix-like platforms, and Mac OS X.

Because wxPython is based on a C++ class library, it is generally more complex than Tkinter: it provides more than 200 classes at last count, requires an object-oriented coding style, and has a design reminiscent of MFC. wxPython often expects programmers to write more code, partly because it is a more complex system and partly because it inherits this mindset from its underlying C++ library.

Moreover, wxPython is not as well documented as Tkinter: some of its documentation is oriented toward C++, and there are no books dedicated to

---

[*] Per an article that appeared on slashdot.org in 2004, the name of the underlying wxWidgets library was changed from wxWindows in response to a "polite request" by Microsoft.

wxPython as I write these words. By contrast, Tkinter is covered by one book dedicated to it, large sections of other Python books, and an even larger library of existing literature on the underlying Tk toolkit. (After I wrote this paragraph, a wxPython book was preannounced, but it is still under development and will likely be the only Python-specific wxPython resource available for some time to come.)

On the other hand, in exchange for its added complexity, wxPython provides a powerful toolkit. wxPython comes with a richer set of widgets out of the box than Tkinter, including trees and HTML viewers—things that require extensions such as Pmw or Tix in Tkinter. In addition, some prefer the appearance of the interfaces it renders. BoaConstructor and wxDesigner, among other options, provide a GUI builder that generates wxPython code. Some wxWidgets tools also support Python work. For a quick look at wxPython widgets and code, run the demo that comes with the system.

PyQt

A Python interface to Qt, perhaps the third most widely used GUI toolkit for Python today. PyQt is a full-featured GUI library and runs portably today on Windows, Mac OS X, and Unix and Linux (including the Zaurus Linux-based PDA). Qt is generally more complex, yet more feature rich, than Tkinter as well; it currently contains 300 classes and more than 5,750 functions and methods. Perhaps its most widely cited drawback is that it is not completely open source for commercial use. (Qt 4, announced after this chapter was written, now provides both GPL and commercial license versions on all platforms, including Windows. The GPL version is open source, but also imposes requirements beyond those of the Python BSD-style license; you must, for example, make your source code freely available to end users under the GPL unless you purchase a commercial license instead.) Qt grew up on Linux; the PyQt and PyKDE extension packages provide access to KDE development libraries (PyKDE requires PyQt). The BlackAdder and Qt Designer systems provide a GUI builder for PyQt.

PyGTK

A Python interface to GTK, a portable GUI library originally used as the core of the Gnome window system on Linux. The gnome-python and PyGTK extension packages export Gnome and GTK toolkit calls. At this writing, PyGTK runs portably on Windows and POSIX systems such as Linux and Mac OS X (provided that an X server for Mac OS X has been installed, though a native version is in the works).

Jython

As we will see in Chapter 18, Jython (the system formerly known as JPython) is a Python port for Java, which gives Python scripts seamless access to Java class libraries on the local machine. Because of that, Java GUI libraries such as swing and awt become another way to construct GUIs in Python code run by the JPython system. Such solutions are obviously Java specific and limited in portability to the portability of Java and its libraries. Furthermore, swing is likely the largest and most complex GUI option for Python work. A new package named jTkinter also provides a Tkinter port to Jython using Java's JNI; if installed, Python scripts may also use Tkinter to build GUIs under JPython.

MFC

The Windows PyWin32 extensions package for Python, available at Python's web site, includes wrappers for the Microsoft Foundation Classes (MFC) framework—a development library that includes user interface components. With the Windows extensions, Python programs can construct Windows GUIs using the same MFC calls applied in languages such as Visual C++. Pythonwin, an MFC sample program that implements a Python development GUI, is included with the extensions package. This is a Windows-only solution, but it may be an appealing option for developers with a prior intellectual investment in using the MFC framework from Visual C++.

PythonCard

An open source GUI builder and library built on top of the wxPython toolkit and considered by some to currently be Python's closest equivalent to GUI builders such as those familiar to Visual Basic developers. PythonCard describes itself as a GUI construction kit for building cross-platform desktop applications on Windows, Mac OS X, and Linux, using the Python language.

Dabo

An emerging open source GUI builder also built on wxPython, and a bit more. Dabo is a portable, three-tier, cross-platform application development framework, inspired by Visual FoxPro and written in Python. Its tiers support database access, business logic, and user interface. Its open design is intended to eventually support a variety of databases and multiple user interfaces (wxPython, Tkinter, and even HTML over HTTP).

AnyGui

A toolkit that aims to provide an API that is portable across a variety of underlying toolkits, including Tkinter, wxPython, and Qt. This API takes a lowest-common-denominator approach to achieve its portability. (As of this writing, AnyGui is no longer being actively developed and serves mostly as a proof-of-concept project.)

WPY

An MFC-like GUI library for Python, ported to run on both X Windows for Unix (where it uses Tk) and Windows for PCs (where it uses MFC). WPY scripts run unchanged on each platform, but they use MFC coding styles.

Others

On Macintosh OS X platforms, Python scripts can use the Cocoa library. For Unix-like systems, interfaces to the raw X Windows and Motif libraries also exist for Python; they provide maximum control over the X11 development environment but are an X-only solution.

See the web sites of these toolkits for more details. There are other lesser-known GUI toolkits for Python, and new ones are likely to emerge by the time you read this book (e.g., the IronPython Python port to the .NET Framework on Windows may offer user interface options as well). Moreover, packages like those in this list mutate over time. For an up-to-date list of available tools, see *http://www.python.org* and the Vaults of Parnassus third-party packages site, currently at *http://www.vex.net/ parnassus.**

Tkinter Overview

Of all these GUI options, though, Tkinter is by far the de facto standard way to implement portable user interfaces in Python today, and the focus of this part of the book. The rationale for this approach was explained in Chapter 2; in short, we have elected to present one toolkit in satisfying depth instead of many toolkits in less-than-useful fashion. Most of the Tkinter programming concepts you learn here will translate directly to any other GUI toolkit you choose to utilize.

Tkinter Pragmatics

Perhaps more to the point, though, there are pragmatic reasons that the Python world still gravitates to Tkinter as its de facto standard portable GUI toolkit. Among them, Tkinter's accessibility, portability, availability, documentation, and extensions have made it the most widely used Python GUI solution for many years running:

Accessibility

Tkinter is generally regarded as a *lightweight toolkit* and one of the simplest GUI solutions for Python available today. Unlike larger frameworks, it is easy to get started in Tkinter right away, without first having to grasp a much larger class interaction model. As we'll see, programmers can create simple Tkinter GUIs in a few lines of Python code and scale up to writing industrial-strength GUIs gradually. Although the Tkinter API is basic, additional widgets can be coded in Python or obtained in extension packages such as Pmw and Tix (described later).

---

* In Part IV, we'll also learn how to build basic user interfaces within a web browser, using HTML and Python scripts that run on a server. For now, we'll focus on more traditional GUIs that may or may not be connected to a network.

Portability

A Python script that builds a GUI with Tkinter will run without source code changes on all major windowing platforms today: Microsoft Windows, X Windows (on Unix and Linux), and the classic and new Macintosh. Further, that same script will provide a native look-and-feel to its users on each of these platforms. A Python/Tkinter script looks like a Windows program on Windows; on Unix and Linux, it provides the same interaction but sports an appearance familiar to X Windows users; and on the Mac, it looks like a Mac program should (menu bars fill the entire top of the screen).

Availability

Tkinter is a standard module in the Python library, shipped with the interpreter. If you have Python, you have Tkinter. Moreover, most Python installation packages (including the standard Python self-installer for Windows, and many Linux distributions) come with Tkinter support bundled. Because of that scripts written to use the Tkinter module work immediately on most Python interpreters, without any extra installation steps.* Tkinter is also generally better supported than its alternatives today. Because the underlying Tk library is also used by the Tcl and Perl programming languages, it tends to receive more development time and effort than other toolkits available.

Naturally, other factors such as documentation and extensions are important when using a GUI toolkit too; let's take a quick look at the story Tkinter has to tell on these fronts as well.

Tkinter Documentation

This book explores Tkinter fundamentals and most widgets tools, and it should be enough to get started with substantial GUI development in Python. On the other hand, it is not an exhaustive reference to the Tkinter library. Happily, at least one book dedicated to using Tkinter in Python is now commercially available as I write this paragraph, and others are on the way (see the Python books list at *http://www.python.org* for details). Besides books, you can also now find Tkinter documentation online; a complete set of Tkinter manuals is currently maintained on the Web at *http://www.pythonware.com/library*.

---

* Some Python distributions on Unix-like platforms still come without Tk support bundled, so you may need to add it on your machine. On some Unix and Linux platforms, you may also need to set your Tcl/Tk library shell variables to use Tkinter. See Tkinter resources for install details; you can usually sidestep Tk build details by finding an alternative Python distribution with Tk bundled (e.g., Linux RPMs). At this writing, the version of Python that is shipped as a standard part of Mac OS X systems did not include Tkinter support either (apparently because Tk was not yet ported to that platform's GUI library in time for release). Tkinter support for OS X is available on the Internet as a separate package today, and may be standard on that platform in the near future.

In addition, because the underlying Tk toolkit used by Tkinter is also a de facto standard in the open source scripting community at large, other documentation sources apply. For instance, because Tk has also been adopted by the Tcl and Perl programming languages, Tk-oriented books and documentation written for both of these are directly applicable to Python/Tkinter as well (albeit, with some syntactic mapping).

Frankly, I learned Tkinter by studying Tcl/Tk texts and references—just replace Tcl strings with Python objects and you have additional reference libraries at your disposal (see Table 8-2, the Tk-to-Tkinter conversion guide, at the end of this chapter for help reading Tk documentation). For instance, the *Tcl/Tk Pocket Reference* (O'Reilly), by Paul Raines, can serve as a nice supplement to the Tkinter tutorial material in this part of the book. Moreover, since Tk concepts are familiar to a large body of programmers, Tk support is also readily available on the Net.

Tkinter Extensions

Because Tkinter is so widely used, programmers also have access to precoded Python extensions designed to work with or augment it. For instance:

Pmw

Python Mega Widgets is an extension toolkit for building high-level compound widgets in Python using the Tkinter module. It extends the Tkinter API with a collection of more sophisticated widgets for advanced GUI development and a framework for implementing some of your own. Among the precoded and extensible megawidgets shipped with the package are notebooks, combo boxes, selection widgets, paned widgets, scrolled widgets, dialog windows, button boxes, balloon help, and an interface to the Blt graph widget.

The interface to Pmw megawidgets is similar to that of basic Tkinter widgets, so Python scripts can freely mix Pmw megawidgets with standard Tkinter widgets. Moreover, Pmw is pure Python code, and so requires no C compiler or tools to install. To view its widgets and the corresponding code you use to construct them, run the *demos\All.py* script in the Pmw distribution package. You can find Pmw today at *http://pmw.sourceforge.net*.

Tix

Tix is another collection of advanced widgets, originally written for Tcl/Tk but now available for use in Python/Tkinter programs. This package is now a Python standard library module, called Tix. Like Tk, the underlying Tix library is also shipped today with Python on Windows. In other words, on Windows, if you install Python you also have Tix as a preinstalled library of additional widgets (the Tix library may need to be installed separately on other platforms).

Tix includes many of the same devices as Pmw, including spin boxes, trees, tabbed notebooks, balloon help pop ups, paned windows, and much more. See the Python library manual's entry for the Tix module for more details. For a quick look at its widgets, as well as the Python source code used to program them, run the *tixwidgets.py* demonstration program in the *Demo\tix* directory of the Python source distribution (this directory is not installed by default on Windows—you can find it after fetching and unpacking Python's source code from Python.org).

PIL

The Python Imaging Library (PIL) is an open source extension package that adds image processing tools to Python. Among other things, it provides tools for image thumbnails, transforms, and conversions, and it extends the basic Tkinter image object to add support for displaying many image file types (see the end of Chapter 9 for more details and examples). PIL, for instance, allows Tkinter GUIs to display JPEG images not supported by the base Tkinter toolkit itself. Besides developing PIL, PythonWare is also building GUI development tools for Python and Tkinter programming; visit *http://www.pythonware.com* for more details.

IDLE

The IDLE integrated Python development environment is both written in Python with Tkinter and shipped and installed with the Python package (if you have a recent Python interpreter, you should have IDLE too; on Windows, click the Start button, select the Programs menu, and click the Python entry to find it). IDLE provides syntax-coloring text editors for Python code, point-and-click debugging, and more, and is an example of Tkinter's utility.

Others

Many of the extensions that provide visualization tools for Python are based on the Tkinter library and its canvas widget. See the Vaults of Parnassus web site for more Tkinter extension examples.

If you plan to do any commercial-grade GUI development with Tkinter, you'll probably want to explore extensions such as Pmw, PIL, and Tix after learning Tkinter basics in this text. They can save development time and add pizzazz to your GUIs. See the Python-related web sites mentioned earlier for up-to-date details and links.

Tkinter Structure

From a more nuts-and-bolts perspective, Tkinter is an integration system that implies a somewhat unique program structure. We'll see what this means in terms of code in a moment, but here is a brief introduction to some of the terms and concepts at the core of Python GUI programming.

Strictly speaking, Tkinter is simply the name of Python's interface to Tk—a GUI library originally written for use with the Tcl programming language and developed by Tcl's creator, John Ousterhout. Python's Tkinter module talks to Tk, and the Tk API in turn interfaces with the underlying window system: Microsoft Windows, X Windows on Unix, and whatever system is running on your Macintosh.

Python's Tkinter adds a software layer on top of Tk that allows Python scripts to call out to Tk to build and configure interfaces, and routes control back to Python scripts that handle user-generated events (e.g., mouse clicks). That is, GUI calls are internally routed from Python script, to Tkinter, to Tk; GUI events are routed from Tk, to Tkinter, and back to a Python script. In Part VI, we'll know these transfers by their C integration terms, *extending* and *embedding*.*

Luckily, Python programmers don't normally need to care about all this call routing going on internally; they simply make widgets and register Python functions to handle widget events. Because of the overall structure, though, event handlers are usually known as *callback* handlers, because the GUI library "calls back" to Python code when events occur.

In fact, we'll find that Python/Tkinter programs are entirely *event driven*: they build displays and register handlers for events, and then do nothing but wait for events to occur. During the wait, the Tk GUI library runs an event loop that watches for mouse clicks, keyboard presses, and so on. All application program processing happens in the registered callback handlers in response to events. Further, any information needed across events must be stored in long-lived references such as global variables and class instance attributes. The notion of a traditional linear program control flow doesn't really apply in the GUI domain; you need to think in terms of smaller chunks.

In Python, Tk also becomes object oriented simply because Python is object oriented: the Tkinter layer exports Tk's API as Python classes. With Tkinter, we can either use a simple function-call approach to create widgets and interfaces, or apply object-oriented techniques such as inheritance and composition to customize and extend the base set of Tkinter classes. Larger Tkinter GUIs are generally constructed as trees of linked Tkinter widget objects, and are often implemented as Python classes to provide structure and retain state information between events. As we'll see in this part of the book, a Tkinter GUI coded with classes almost by default becomes a reusable software component.

Climbing the GUI Learning Curve

On to the code; let's start out by quickly stepping through a few small examples that illustrate basic concepts, and show the windows they create on the screen. The examples will become more sophisticated as we move along.

---

* Since I brought it up: Tkinter is structured as a combination of the Python-coded Tkinter module file and an extension module called _tkinter that is written in C. _tkinter interfaces with the Tk library and dispatches callbacks back to Python objects using embedding tools; Tkinter adds a class-based interface on top of _tkinter. You should always import Tkinter (not _tkinter) in your scripts, though; the latter is an implementation module for internal use only (it was oddly named for a reason).

"Hello World" in Four Lines (or Less)

The usual first example for GUI systems is to show how to display a "Hello World" message in a window. As coded in Example 8-1, it's just four lines in Python.

Example 8-1. PP3E\Gui\Intro\gui1.py

```
from Tkinter import Label                          # get a widget object
widget = Label(None, text='Hello GUI world!')      # make one
widget.pack()                                       # arrange it
widget.mainloop()                                   # start event loop
```

This is a complete Python Tkinter GUI program. When this script is run, we get a simple window with a label in the middle; it looks like Figure 8-1 on Windows.

Figure 8-1. "Hello World" (gui1) on Windows

This isn't much to write home about yet; but notice that this is a completely functional, independent window on the computer's display. It can be maximized to take up the entire screen, minimized to hide it in the system bar, and resized. Click on the window's "X" box in the top right to kill the window and exit the program.

The script that builds this window is also fully portable. When this same file is run on Linux it produces a similar window, but it behaves according to the underlying Linux window manager. For instance, Figure 8-2 and Figure 8-3 show this simple script in action on the Linux X Windows system, under the KDE and Gnome window managers, respectively. Even on the same operating system, the same Python code yields a different look-and-feel for different window systems.

Figure 8-2. "Hello World" on Linux with KDE

Figure 8-3. "Hello World" on Linux with Gnome

The same script file would look different still when run on Macintosh and other Unix-like window managers. On all platforms, though, its basic functional behavior will be the same.

Tkinter Coding Basics

The gui1 script is a trivial example, but it illustrates steps common to most Tkinter programs. This Python code does the following:

1. Loads a widget class from the Tkinter module
2. Makes an instance of the imported Label class
3. Packs (arranges) the new Label in its parent widget
4. Calls mainloop to bring up the window and start the Tkinter event loop

The mainloop method called last puts the label on the screen and enters a Tkinter wait state, which watches for user-generated GUI events. Within the mainloop function, Tkinter internally monitors things such as the keyboard and mouse to detect user-generated events. In fact, the Tkinter mainloop function is similar in spirit to the following pseudo-Python code:

```
def mainloop():
    while the main window has not been closed:
        if an event has occurred:
            run the associated event handler function
```

Because of this model, the mainloop call in Example 8-1 never returns to our script while the GUI is displayed on-screen.* When we write larger scripts, the only way we can get anything done after calling mainloop is to register callback handlers to respond to events.

This is called *event-driven programming*, and it is perhaps one of the most unusual aspects of GUIs. GUI programs take the form of a set of event handlers that share saved information rather than of a single main control flow. We'll see how this looks in terms of real code in later examples.

Note that in a script, you really need steps 3 and 4 in the preceding list to open this script's GUI. To display a GUI's window at all, you need to call mainloop; to display widgets within the window, they must be packed (or otherwise arranged) so that the Tkinter geometry manager knows about them. In fact, if you call either mainloop or pack without calling the other, your window won't show up as expected: a mainloop without a pack shows an empty window, and a pack without a mainloop in a script shows nothing since the script never enters an event wait state (try it).

Since the concepts illustrated by this simple script are at the core of most Tkinter programs, let's take a deeper look at some of them before moving on.

---

* Technically, the mainloop call returns to your script only after the Tkinter event loop exits. This normally happens when the GUI's main window is closed, but it may also occur in response to explicit quit method calls that terminate nested event loops but leave open the GUI at large. You'll see why this matters in Chapter 9.

Making Widgets

When widgets are constructed in Tkinter, we can specify how they should be configured. The gui1 script passes two arguments to the Label class constructor:

- The first is a parent-widget object, which we want the new label to be attached to. Here, None means "attach the new Label to the default top-level window of this program." Later, we'll pass real widgets in this position to attach our labels to other container objects.

- The second is a configuration option for the Label, passed as a keyword argument: the text option specifies a text string to appear as the label's message. Most widget constructors accept multiple keyword arguments for specifying a variety of options (color, size, callback handlers, and so on). Most widget configuration options have reasonable defaults per platform, though, and this accounts for much of Tkinter's simplicity. You need to set most options only if you wish to do something custom.

As we'll see, the parent-widget argument is the hook we use to build up complex GUIs as widget trees. Tkinter works on a "what-you-build-is-what-you-get" principle: we construct widget object trees as models of what we want to see on the screen, and then ask the tree to display itself by calling mainloop.

Geometry Managers

The pack widget method called by the gui1 script invokes the packer geometry manager, one of three ways to control how widgets are arranged in a window. Tkinter geometry managers simply arrange one or more widgets within a container (sometimes called a parent or master). Both top-level windows and frames (a special kind of widget we'll meet later) can serve as containers, and containers may be nested inside other containers to build hierarchical displays.

The packer geometry manager uses constraint option settings to automatically position widgets in a window. Scripts supply higher-level instructions (e.g., "attach this widget to the top of its container, and stretch it to fill its space vertically"), not absolute pixel coordinates. Because such constraints are so abstract, the packer provides a powerful and easy-to-use layout system. In fact, you don't even have to specify constraints. If you don't pass any arguments to pack, you get default packing, which attaches the widget to the top side of its container.

We'll visit the packer repeatedly in this chapter and use it in many of the examples in this book. In Chapter 10, we will also meet an alternative grid geometry manager and layout system that arranges widgets within a container in tabular form (i.e., by rows and columns). A third alternative, called the *placer* geometry manager system, is described in Tk documentation but not in this book; it's less popular than the pack and grid managers and can be difficult to use for larger GUIs.

Running GUI Programs

Like all Python code, the module in Example 8-1 can be started in a number of ways: by running it as a top-level program file:

```
C:\...\PP3E\Gui\Intro>python gui1.py
```

by importing it from a Python session or another module file:

```
>>> import gui1
```

by running it as a Unix executable if we add the special #! line at the top:

```
% gui1.py &
```

and in any other way Python programs can be launched on your platform. For instance, the script can also be run by clicking on the file's name in a Windows file explorer, and its code can be typed interactively at the >>> prompt.* It can even be run from a C program by calling the appropriate embedding API function (see Chapter 23 for details).

In other words, there are really no special rules to follow when running GUI Python code. The Tkinter interface (and Tk itself) is linked into the Python interpreter. When a Python program calls GUI functions, they're simply passed to the embedded GUI system behind the scenes. That makes it easy to write command-line tools that pop up windows; they are run the same way as the purely text-based scripts we studied in the prior part of this book.

Avoiding DOS consoles on Windows

Earlier in this book we learned that if a program's name ends in a *.pyw* extension rather than a *.py* extension, the Windows Python port does not pop up a DOS console box to serve as its standard streams when the file is launched by clicking its filename icon. Now that we've finally started making windows of our own, that filename trick will start to become even more useful.

If you just want to see the windows that your script makes no matter how it is launched, be sure to name your GUI scripts with a *.pyw* if they might be run on Windows. For instance, clicking on the file in Example 8-2 in a Windows explorer creates just the window in Figure 8-1.

Example 8-2. PP3E\Gui\Intro\gui1.pyw

...same as gui1.py...

---

* Tip: when typing Tkinter GUI code *interactively*, you may or may not need to call mainloop to display widgets. This is required in the current IDLE interface, but not from a simple interactive session running in a system console window. In either case, control will return to the interactive prompt when you kill the window you created. Note that if you create an explicit main-window widget by calling Tk( ) and attach widgets to it (described later), you must call this again after killing the window; otherwise, the application window will not exist.

You can also avoid the DOS pop up on Windows by running the program with the *pythonw.exe* executable, not *python.exe* (in fact, *.pyw* files are simply registered to be opened by pythonw). On Linux, the *.pyw* doesn't hurt, but it isn't necessary; there is no notion of a streams pop up on Unix-like machines. On the other hand, if your GUI scripts might run on Windows in the future, adding an extra "w" at the end of their names now might save porting effort later. In this book, *.py* filenames are still sometimes used to pop up console windows for viewing printed messages on Windows.

Tkinter Coding Alternatives

As you might expect, there are a variety of ways to code the gui1 example. For instance, if you want to make all your Tkinter imports more explicit in your script, grab the whole module and prefix all of its names with the module's name, as in Example 8-3.

Example 8-3. PP3E\Gui\Intro\gui1b.py—import versus from

```
import Tkinter
widget = Tkinter.Label(None, text='Hello GUI world!')
widget.pack()
widget.mainloop()
```

That will probably get tedious in realistic examples, though—Tkinter exports dozens of widget classes and constants that show up all over Python GUI scripts. In fact, it is usually easier to use a * to import everything from the Tkinter module by name in one shot. This is demonstrated in Example 8-4.

Example 8-4. PP3E\Gui\Intro\gui1c.py—roots, sides, pack in place

```
from Tkinter import *
root = Tk()
Label(root, text='Hello GUI world!').pack(side=TOP)
root.mainloop()
```

The Tkinter module goes out of its way to export only what we really need, so it's one of the few for which the * import form is relatively safe to apply.[*] The TOP constant in the pack call here, for instance, is one of those many names exported by the Tkinter module. It's simply a variable name (TOP="top") preassigned in Tkconstants, a module automatically loaded by Tkinter.

When widgets are packed, we can specify which side of their parent they should be attached to—TOP, BOTTOM, LEFT, or RIGHT. If no side option is sent to pack (as in prior

---

[*] If you study the file *Tkinter.py* in the Python source library, you'll notice that top-level module names not meant for export start with a single underscore. Python never copies over such names when a module is accessed with the * form of the from statement.

examples), a widget is attached to its parent's TOP by default. In general, larger Tkinter GUIs can be constructed as sets of rectangles, attached to the appropriate sides of other, enclosing rectangles. As we'll see later, Tkinter arranges widgets in a rectangle according to both their packing order and their side attachment options. When widgets are gridded, they are assigned row and column numbers instead. None of this will become very meaningful, though, until we have more than one widget in a window, so let's move on.

Notice that this version calls the pack method right away after creating the label, without assigning it a variable. If we don't need to save a widget, we can pack it in place like this to eliminate a statement. We'll use this form when a widget is attached to a larger structure and never again referenced. This can be tricky if you assign the pack result, though, but I'll postpone an explanation of why until we've covered a few more basics.

We also use a Tk widget class instance, instead of None, as the parent here. Tk represents the main ("root") window of the program—the one that starts when the program does. Tk is also used as the default parent widget, both when we don't pass any parent to other widget calls and when we pass the parent as None. In other words, widgets are simply attached to the main program window by default. This script just makes this default behavior explicit by making and passing the Tk object itself. In Chapter 9, we'll see that Toplevel widgets are typically used to generate new pop-up windows that operate independently of the program's main window.

In Tkinter, some widget methods are exported as functions, and this lets us shave Example 8-5 to just three lines of code.

Example 8-5. PP3E\Gui\Intro\gui1d.py—a minimal version

```
from Tkinter import *
Label(text='Hello GUI world!').pack()
mainloop()
```

The Tkinter mainloop can be called with or without a widget (i.e., as a function or method). We didn't pass Label a parent argument in this version either: it simply defaults to None when omitted (which in turn defaults to Tk). But relying on that default is less useful once we start building larger displays. Things such as labels are more typically attached to other widget containers.

Widget Resizing Basics

Top-level windows, such as the one built by all of the coding variants we have seen thus far, can normally be resized by the user; simply drag out the window with your mouse. Figure 8-4 shows how our window looks when it is expanded.

Figure 8-4. Expanding gui1

This isn't very good—the label stays attached to the top of the parent window instead of staying in the middle on expansion—but it's easy to improve on this with a pair of pack options, demonstrated in Example 8-6.

Example 8-6. PP3E\Gui\Intro\gui1e.py—expansion

```
from Tkinter import *
Label(text='Hello GUI world!').pack(expand=YES, fill=BOTH)
mainloop( )
```

When widgets are packed, we can specify whether a widget should expand to take up all available space, and if so, how it should stretch to fill that space. By default, widgets are not expanded when their parent is. But in this script, the names YES and BOTH (imported from the Tkinter module) specify that the label should grow along with its parent, the main window. It does so in Figure 8-5.

Figure 8-5. gui1e with widget resizing

Technically, the packer geometry manager assigns a size to each widget in a display based on what it contains (text string lengths, etc.). By default, a widget can occupy only its allocated space and is no bigger than its assigned size. The expand and fill options let us be more specific about such things:

expand=YES *option*

Asks the packer to expand the allocated space for the widget in general into any unclaimed space in the widget's parent.

fill *option*

Can be used to stretch the widget to occupy all of its allocated space.

Combinations of these two options produce different layout and resizing effects, some of which become meaningful only when there are multiple widgets in a window. For example, using expand without fill centers the widget in the expanded space, and the fill option can specify vertical stretching only (fill=Y), horizontal stretching only (fill=X), or both (fill=BOTH). By providing these constraints and attachment sides for all widgets in a GUI, we can control the layout in fairly precise terms. In later chapters, we'll find that the grid geometry manager uses a different resizing protocol entirely.

All of this can be confusing the first time you hear it, and we'll return to this later. But if you're not sure what an expand and fill combination will do, simply try it out—this is Python, after all. For now, remember that the combination of expand=YES and fill=BOTH is perhaps the most common setting; it means "expand my space allocation to occupy all available space, and stretch me to fill the expanded space in both directions." For our "Hello World" example, the net result is that the label grows as the window is expanded, and so is always centered.

Configuring Widget Options and Window Titles

So far, we've been telling Tkinter what to display on our label by passing its text as a keyword argument in label constructor calls. It turns out that there are two other ways to specify widget configuration options. In Example 8-7, the text option of the label is set after it is constructed, by assigning to the widget's text key. Widget objects overload index operations such that options are also available as mapping keys, much like a dictionary.

Example 8-7. PP3E\Gui\Intro\guif.py—option keys

```
from Tkinter import *
widget = Label( )
widget['text'] = 'Hello GUI world!'
widget.pack(side=TOP)
mainloop( )
```

More commonly, widget options can be set after construction by calling the widget config method, as in Example 8-8.

Example 8-8. PP3E\Gui\Intro\gui1g.py—config and titles

```
from Tkinter import *
root = Tk( )
widget = Label(root)
widget.config(text='Hello GUI world!')
widget.pack(side=TOP, expand=YES, fill=BOTH)
root.title('gui1g.py')
root.mainloop( )
```

The config method (which can also be called by its synonym, configure) can be called at any time after construction to change the appearance of a widget on the fly. For instance, we could call this label's config method again later in the script to change the text that it displays; watch for such dynamic reconfigurations in later examples in this part of the book.

Notice that this version also calls a root.title method; this call sets the label that appears at the top of the window, as pictured in Figure 8-6. In general terms, top-level windows like the Tk root here export window-manager interfaces—i.e., things that have to do with the border around the window, not its contents.

Figure 8-6. gui1g with expansion and a window title

Just for fun, this version also centers the label upon resizes by setting the expand and fill pack options. In fact, this version makes just about everything explicit, and is more representative of how labels are often coded in full-blown interfaces; their parents, expansion policies, and attachments are usually spelled out rather than defaulted.

One More for Old Times' Sake

Finally, if you are a minimalist and you're nostalgic for old Python code, you can also program this "Hello World" example as in Example 8-9.

Example 8-9. PP3E\Gui\Intro\gui1-old.py—dictionary calls

```
from Tkinter import *
Label(None, {'text': 'Hello GUI world!', Pack: {'side': 'top'}}).mainloop()
```

This makes the window in just two lines, albeit gruesome ones! This scheme relies on an old coding style that was widely used until Python 1.3 that passed configuration options in a dictionary instead of keyword arguments.* In this scheme, packer options can be sent as values of the key Pack (a class in the Tkinter module).

---

* In fact, Python's pass-by-name keyword arguments were first introduced to help clean up Tkinter calls such as this one. Internally, keyword arguments really are passed as a dictionary (which can be collected with the **name argument form in a def header), so the two schemes are similar in implementation. But they vary widely in the number of characters you need to type and debug.

The dictionary call scheme still works and you may see it in old Python code, but please don't do this. Use keywords to pass options, and use explicit pack method calls in your Tkinter scripts instead. In fact, the only reason I didn't cut this example completely is that dictionaries can still be useful if you want to compute and pass a set of options dynamically. On the other hand, the built-in apply function (and newer func (*pargs, **kargs) syntax) now also allows you to pass an explicit dictionary of keyword arguments in its third argument slot, so there's no compelling reason to ever use the pre-1.3 Tkinter dictionary call form at all.

Packing Widgets Without Saving Them

In *gui1c.py* (shown in Example 8-4), I started packing labels without assigning them to names. This works, and it is an entirely valid coding style; but because it tends to confuse beginners at first glance, I need to explain why it works in more detail here.

In Tkinter, Python class objects correspond to real objects displayed on a screen; we make the Python object to make a screen object, and we call the Python object's methods to configure that screen object. Because of this correspondence, the lifetime of the Python object must generally correspond to the lifetime of the corresponding object on the screen.

Luckily, Python scripts don't usually have to care about managing object lifetimes. In fact, they do not normally need to maintain a reference to widget objects created along the way at all unless they plan to reconfigure those objects later. For instance, it's common in Tkinter programming to pack a widget immediately after creating it if no further reference to the widget is required:

```
Label(text='hi').pack()                          # OK
```

This expression is evaluated left to right, as usual. It creates a new label and then immediately calls the new object's pack method to arrange it in the display. Notice, though, that the Python Label object is temporary in this expression; because it is not assigned to a name, it would normally be garbage collected (destroyed and reclaimed) by Python immediately after running its pack method.

However, because Tkinter emits Tk calls when objects are constructed, the label will be drawn on the display as expected, even though we haven't held onto the corresponding Python object in our script. In fact, Tkinter internally cross-links widget objects into a long-lived tree used to represent the display, so the Label object made during this statement actually is retained, even if not by our code.[*]

---

[*] Ex-Tcl programmers in the audience may be interested to know that, at least at the time I was writing this footnote, Python not only builds the widget tree internally, but uses it to automatically generate widget pathname strings coded manually in Tcl/Tk (e.g., .panel.row.cmd). Python uses the addresses of widget class objects to fill in the path components and records pathnames in the widget tree. A label attached to a container, for instance, might have an assigned name such as .8220096.8219408 inside Tkinter. You don't have to care, though. Simply make and link widget objects by passing parents, and let Python manage pathname details based on the object tree. See the end of this chapter for more on Tk/Tkinter mappings.

In other words, your scripts don't generally have to care about widget object lifetimes, and it's OK to make widgets and pack them immediately in the same statement. But that does not mean that it's OK to say something like this:

```
widget = Label(text='hi').pack( )              # wrong!
...use widget...
```

This statement almost seems like it should assign a newly packed label to widget, but it does not do this. In fact, it's really a notorious Tkinter beginner's mistake. The widget pack method packs the widget but does not return the widget thus packed. Really, pack returns the Python object None; after such a statement, widget will be a reference to None, and any further widget operations through that name will fail. For instance, the following fails too for the same reason:

```
Label(text='hi').pack().mainloop( )              # wrong!
```

Since pack returns None, asking for its mainloop attribute generates an exception (as it should). If you really want to both pack a widget and retain a reference to it, say this instead:

```
widget = Label(text='hi')              # OK too
widget.pack( )
...use widget...
```

This form is a bit more verbose but is less tricky than packing a widget in the same statement that creates it, and it allows you to hold onto the widget for later processing. On the other hand, scripts that compose layouts often add widgets once and for all when they are created, and never need to reconfigure them later; assigning to long-lived names in such programs is pointless and unnecessary.[*]

Adding Buttons and Callbacks

So far, we've learned how to display messages in labels, and we've met Tkinter core concepts along the way. Labels are nice for teaching the basics, but user interfaces usually need to do a bit more; like actually responding to users. The program in Example 8-10 creates the window in Figure 8-7.

Figure 8-7. A button on the top

---

[*] In Chapter 9, we'll meet two exceptions to this rule. Scripts must manually retain a reference to image objects because the underlying image data is discarded if the Python image object is garbage collected. Tkinter variable class objects temporarily unset an associated Tk variable if reclaimed, but this is uncommon and less harmful.

Example 8-10. PP3E\Gui\Intro\gui2.py

```
import sys
from Tkinter import *
widget = Button(None, text='Hello widget world', command=sys.exit)
widget.pack()
widget.mainloop()
```

Here, instead of making a label, we create an instance of the Tkinter Button class. It's attached to the default top level as before on the default TOP packing side. But the main thing to notice here is the button's configuration arguments: we set an option called command to the sys.exit function.

For buttons, the command option is the place where we specify a callback handler function to be run when the button is later pressed. In effect, we use command to register an action for Tkinter to call when a widget's event occurs. The callback handler used here isn't very interesting: as we learned in an earlier chapter, the built-in sys.exit function simply shuts down the calling program. Here, that means that pressing this button makes the window go away.

Just as for labels, there are other ways to code buttons. Example 8-11 is a version that packs the button in place without assigning it to a name, attaches it to the LEFT side of its parent window explicitly, and specifies root.quit as the callback handler—a standard Tk object method that shuts down the GUI and so ends the program (really, it ends the current mainloop event loop call).

Example 8-11. PP3E\Gui\Intro\gui2b.py

```
from Tkinter import *
root = Tk()
Button(root, text='press', command=root.quit).pack(side=LEFT)
root.mainloop()
```

This version produces the window in Figure 8-8. Because we didn't tell the button to expand into all available space, it does not do so.

Figure 8-8. A button on the left

In both of the last two examples, pressing the button makes the GUI program exit. In older Tkinter code, you may sometimes see the string exit assigned to the command option to make the GUI go away when pressed. This exploits a tool in the underlying Tk library and is less Pythonic than sys.exit or root.quit.

Widget Resizing Revisited: Expansion

Even with a GUI this simple, there are many ways to lay out its appearance with Tkinter's constraint-based pack geometry manager. For example, to center the button in its window, add an expand=YES option to the button's pack method call, and generate a window such as Figure 8-9. This makes the packer allocate all available space to the button but does not stretch the button to fill that space.

Figure 8-9. side=LEFT, expand=YES

If you want the button to be given all available space and to stretch to fill all of its assigned space horizontally, add expand=YES and fill=X keyword arguments to the pack call. This will create the scene in Figure 8-10.

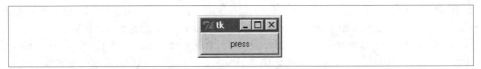

Figure 8-10. side=LEFT, expand=YES, fill=X

This makes the button fill the whole window initially (its allocation is expanded, and it is stretched to fill that allocation). It also makes the button grow as the parent window is resized. As shown in Figure 8-11, the button in this window does expand when its parent expands, but only along the X horizontal axis.

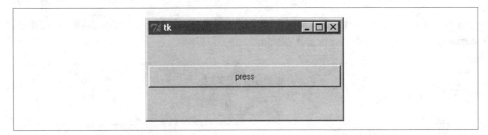

Figure 8-11. Resizing with expand=YES, fill=X

To make the button grow in both directions, specify both expand=YES and fill=BOTH in the pack call; now resizing the window makes the button grow in general, as shown in Figure 8-12. In fact, for a good time, maximize this window to fill the entire screen; you'll get one very big Tkinter button indeed.

Figure 8-12. Resizing with expand=YES, fill=BOTH

In more complex displays, such a button will expand only if all of the widgets it is contained by are set to expand too. Here, the button's only parent is the Tk root window of the program, so parent expandability isn't yet an issue. We will revisit the packer geometry manager when we meet multiple-widget displays later in this tutorial and again when we study the alternative grid call in Chapter 10.

Adding User-Defined Callback Handlers

In the simple button examples in the preceding section, the callback handler was simply an existing function that killed the GUI program. It's not much more work to register callback handlers that do something a bit more useful. Example 8-12 defines a callback handler of its own in Python.

Example 8-12. PP3E\Gui\Intro\gui3.py

```
from Tkinter import *

def quit():                              # a custom callback handler
    print 'Hello, I must be going...'    # kill windows and process
    import sys; sys.exit()

widget = Button(None, text='Hello event world', command=quit)
widget.pack()
widget.mainloop()
```

The window created by this script is shown in Figure 8-13. This script and its GUI are almost identical to the last example. But here, the command option specifies a function we've defined locally. When the button is pressed, Tkinter calls the quit function in this file to handle the event, passing it zero arguments. Inside quit, the print statement types a message on the program's stdout stream, and the GUI process exits as before.

As usual, stdout is normally the window that the program was started from unless it's been redirected to a file. It's a pop-up DOS console if you run this program by clicking it on Windows; add a raw_input call before sys.exit if you have trouble seeing the message before the pop up disappears. Here's what the printed output looks

Figure 8-13. A button that runs a Python function

like back in standard stream world when the button is pressed; it is generated by a Python function called automatically by Tkinter:

```
C:\...\PP3E\Gui\Intro>python gui3.py
Hello, I must be going...


C:\...\PP3E\Gui\Intro>
```

Normally, such messages would be displayed in another window, but we haven't gotten far enough to know just yet. Callback functions usually do more, of course (and may even pop up new windows altogether), but this example illustrates the basics.

In general, callback handlers can be any callable object: functions, anonymous functions generated with lambda expressions, bound methods of class or type instances, or class instances that inherit a __call__ operator overload method. For Button press callbacks, callback handlers always receive no arguments (other than a self, for bound methods); any state information required by the callback handler must be provided in other ways—as global variables, class instance attributes, extra arguments provided by an indirection layer, and so on.

Lambda Callback Handlers

To make the last paragraph a bit more concrete, let's take a quick look at some other ways to code the callback handler in this example. Recall that the Python lambda expression generates a new, unnamed function object when run. If we need extra data passed in to the handler function, we can register lambda expressions to defer the call to the real handler function, and specify the extra data it needs.

Later in this part of the book, we'll see how this can be useful, but to illustrate the basic idea, Example 8-13 shows what this example looks like when recoded to use a lambda instead of a def.

Example 8-13. PP3E\Gui\Intro\gui3b.py

```
from Tkinter import *
from sys import stdout, exit               # lambda generates a function

widget = Button(None,                       # but contains just an expression
            text='Hello event world',
            command=(lambda: stdout.write('Hello lambda world\n') or exit()) )

widget.pack( )
widget.mainloop( )
```

This code is a bit tricky because lambdas can contain only an expression; to emulate the original script, this version uses an or operator to force two expressions to be run, and writes to stdout to mimic a print. More typically, lambdas are used to provide an indirection layer that passes along extra data to a callback handler:

```
def handler(A, B):              # would normallly be called with no args
    use A and B...

X = 42
Button(text='ni', command=(lambda: handler(X, 'spam')))
mainloop( )
```

Although Tkinter invokes command callbacks with no arguments, such a lambda can be used to provide an indirect anonymous function that wraps the real handler call and passes along information that existed when the GUI was first constructed. The call to the real handler is, in effect, deferred, so we can add the extra arguments it requires. Here, the value of global variable X and string 'spam' will be passed to arguments A and B, even though Tkinter itself runs callbacks with no arguments. The net effect is that the lambda serves to map a no-argument function call to one with arguments supplied by the lambda.

If lambda syntax confuses you, remember that a lambda expression such as the one in the preceding code can usually be coded as a simple def statement instead, nested or otherwise. In the following code, the second function does exactly the same work as the prior lambda:

```
def handler(A, B):              # would normally be called with no args
    use A and B...
.
X = 42

def func( ):                    # indirection layer to add arguments
    handler(X, 'spam')

Button(text='ni', command=func)
mainloop( )
```

Notice that the handler function in this code could refer to X directly, because it is a global variable (and would exist by the time the code inside the handler is run). Because of that, we make the handler a one-argument function and pass in just the string 'spam' in the lambda:

```
def handler(A):                 # X is in my global scope, implicitly
    use X and A...

X = 42
Button(text='ni', command=(lambda: handler('spam')))
mainloop( )
```

Arguments are generally preferred to globals, though, because they make external dependencies more explicit, and so make code easier to understand and change. In general, using a lambda to pass extra data with an inline function definition:

```
def handler(name):
    print name

Button(command=(lambda: handler('spam')))
```

is always equivalent to the longer, and arguably less convenient, double-function form:

```
def handler(name):
    print name

def temp():
    handler('spam')

Button(command=temp)
```

To make that more obvious, notice what happens if you code the handler call in the button call without the lambda—it runs immediately when the button is created, not when it is later clicked. That's why we need to wrap the call in an intermediate function:

```
def handler(name):
    print name

Button(command=handler('spam'))    # runs the callback now!
```

Passing in values with default arguments

Although lambda-based callbacks defer calls and allow extra data to be passed in, they also imply some scoping issues that may seem subtle at first glance. Notice that if the button in the example we've been discussing was constructed inside a *function* rather than at the top level of the file, name X would no longer be global but would be in the enclosing function's local scope; it would disappear after the function exits and before the callback event occurs and runs the lambda's code.

Luckily, default argument values can be used to remember the values of variables in the enclosing local scope, even after the enclosing function returns. In the following code, for instance, the default argument name X (on the left side of the X=X default) will remember object 42, because the variable name X (on the right side of the X=X) is evaluated in the enclosing scope, and the generated function is later called without any arguments:

```
def handler(A, B):              # older Pythons: defaults save state
    use A and B...

def makegui():
    X = 42
    Button(text='ni', command=(lambda X=X: handler(X, 'spam')))
```

```
makegui( )                       # lambda function is created here
mainloop( )                      # event happens after makegui returns
```

Since default arguments are evaluated and saved when the lambda runs (not when the function it creates is later called), they are a way to explicitly remember objects that must be accessed again later, during event processing. And because Tkinter calls the lambda with no arguments, all its defaults are used. This was not an issue in the original version of this example because name X lived in the global scope, and the code of the lambda will find it there when it is run. When nested within a function, though, X may have disappeared after the enclosing function exits.

Passing in values with enclosing scope references

Things are a bit simpler today, however. In more recent Python releases that support automatic nested scope lookup (added in release 2.2), defaults are less commonly needed to retain state this way. Rather, lambdas simply defer the call to the actual handler and provide extra handler arguments. Variables from the enclosing scope used by the lambda are *automatically* retained, even after the enclosing function exits.

For instance, the prior code listing can today normally be coded as follows; name X in the handler will be automatically mapped to X in the enclosing scope, and so effectively remember what X was when the button was made:

```
def handler(A, B):               # enclosing scope X automatically retained
    use A and B...

def makegui( ):
    X = 42.
    Button(text='ni', command=(lambda: handler(X, 'spam')))

makegui( )
mainloop( )
```

We'll see this technique put to more concrete use later. When using classes to build your GUI, for instance, the self argument is a local variable in methods and is thus available in the bodies of lambda functions today without passing it in explicitly with defaults:

```
class Gui:
    def handler(self, A, B):
        use self, A and B...
    def makegui(self):
        X = 42.
        Button(text='ni', command=(lambda: self.handler(X, 'spam')))

Gui().makegui( )
mainloop( )
```

When using classes, though, instance attributes provide an alternative way to provide extra state for use in callback handlers. We'll see how in a moment. First, though, we need to take a quick diversion onto Python's scope rules to understand why default arguments are still sometimes necessary to pass values into nested lambda functions.

Enclosing scopes versus defaults

As we saw in the prior section, enclosing scope references can simplify callback handler code in recent Python releases. In fact, it seems as though the new nested scope lookup rules in Python automate and replace the previously manual task of passing in enclosing scope values with defaults.

Well, almost. There is a catch. It turns out that within a lambda (or def), references to names in the enclosing scope are actually resolved when the generated function is *called*, not when it is created. Because of this, when the function is later called, such name references will reflect the latest or final assignments made to the names anywhere in the enclosing scope, which are not necessarily the values they held when the function was made. This holds true even when the callback function is nested only in a module's global scope, not in an enclosing function; in either case, all enclosing scope references are resolved at function call time, not at creation time.

This is subtly different from default argument values, which are evaluated once when the function is *created*, not when it is later called. Because of that, they can be used to remember the values of enclosing scope variables as they were when you made the function. Unlike enclosing scope name references, defaults will not have a different value if the variable later changes in the enclosing scope. (In fact, this is why mutable defaults retain their state between calls—they are created only once, when the function is made.)

This is normally a nonissue, because most enclosing scope references name a variable that is assigned just once in the enclosing scope (the self argument in class methods, for example). But this can lead to coding mistakes if not understood, especially if you create functions within a loop; if those functions reference the loop variable, it will evaluate to the value it was given on the *last* loop iteration in *all* the functions generated. By contrast, if you use defaults instead, each function will remember the *current* value of the loop variable, not the last.

Because of this difference, nested scope references are not always sufficient to remember enclosing scope values, and defaults are sometimes still required today. Let's see what this means in terms of code. Consider the following nested function:

```
def simple():
    spam = 'ni'
    def action():
        print spam        # name maps to enclosing function
    return action

act = simple()            # make and return nested function
act()                     # then call it: prints 'ni'
```

This is the simple case for enclosing scope references, and it works the same way whether the nested function is generated with a def or a lambda. But notice that this still works if we assign the enclosing scope's spam variable *after* the nested function is created:

```
def normal():
    def action():
        return spam        # really, looked up when used
    spam = 'ni'
    return action

act = normal()
print act()                # also prints 'ni'
```

As this implies, the enclosing scope name isn't resolved when the nested function is made—in fact, the name hasn't even been assigned yet in this example. The name is resolved when the nested function is called. The same holds true for lambdas:

```
def weird():
    spam = 42
    return (lambda: spam * 2)    # remembers spam in enclosing scope

act = weird()
print act()      # prints 84
```

So far so good. The spam inside this nested lambda function remembers the value that this variable had in the enclosing scope, even after the enclosing scope exits. This pattern corresponds to a registered GUI callback handler run later on events. But once again, the nested scope reference really isn't being resolved when the lambda is run to create the function; it's being resolved when the generated function is later *called*. To make that more apparent, look at this code:

```
def weird():
    tmp = (lambda: spam * 2)     # remembers spam
    spam = 42                    # even though not set till here
    return tmp

act = weird()
print act()                      # prints 84
```

Here again, the nested function refers to a variable that hasn't even been assigned yet when that function is made. Really, enclosing scope references yield the latest setting made in the enclosing scope, whenever the function is called. Watch what happens in the following code:

```
def weird():
    spam = 42
    handler = (lambda: spam * 2)     # func doesn't save 42 now
    spam = 50
    print handler()                  # prints 100: spam looked up now
    spam = 60
    print handler()                  # prints 120: spam looked up again now

weird()
```

Now, the reference to spam inside the lambda is different each time the generated function is called! In fact, it refers to what the variable was set to *last* in the enclosing scope at the time the nested function is called, because it is resolved at function call time, not at function creation time. In terms of GUIs, this becomes significant most often when you generate callback handlers within loops and try to use enclosing scope references to remember extra data created within the loops. If you're going to make functions within a loop, you have to apply the last example's behavior to the loop variable:

```
def odd():
    funcs = []
    for c in 'abcdefg':
        funcs.append((lambda: c))      # c will be looked up later
    return funcs                       # does not remember current c

for func in odd():
    print func(),                      # print 7 g's, not a,b,c,... !
```

Here, the func list simulates registered GUI callback handlers associated with widgets. This doesn't work the way most people expect it to. The variable c within the nested function will always be g here, the value that the variable was set to on the final iteration of the loop in the enclosing scope. The net effect is that all seven generated lambda functions wind up with the same extra state information when they are later called.

Analogous GUI code that adds information to lambda callback handlers will have similar problems—all buttons created in a loop, for instance, may wind up doing the same thing when clicked! To make this work, we still have to pass values into the nested function with defaults in order to save the current value of the loop variable (not its future value):

```
def odd():
    funcs = []
    for c in 'abcdefg':
        funcs.append((lambda c=c: c))  # force to remember c now
    return funcs                       # defaults eval now

for func in odd():
    print func(),                      # OK: now prints a,b,c,...
```

This works now only because the default, unlike an external scope reference, is evaluated at function *creation* time, not at function call time. It remembers the value that a name in the enclosing scope had when the function was made, not the last assignment made to that name anywhere in the enclosing scope. The same is true even if the function's enclosing scope is a module, not another function; if we don't use the default argument in the following code, the loop variable will resolve to the same value in all seven functions:

```
funcs = []               # enclosing scope is module
for c in 'abcdefg':      # force to remember c now
```

```
        funcs.append((lambda c=c: c))          # else prints 7 g's again

    for func in funcs:
        print func(),                          # OK: prints a,b,c,...
```

The moral of this story is that enclosing scope name references are a replacement for passing values in with defaults, but only as long as the name in the enclosing scope will not change to a value you don't expect after the nested function is created. You cannot generally reference enclosing scope loop variables within a nested function, for example, because they will change as the loop progresses. In most other cases, though, enclosing scope variables will take on only one value in their scope and so can be used freely.

We'll see this phenomenon at work in later examples. For now, remember that enclosing scopes are not a complete replacement for defaults; defaults are still required in some contexts to pass values into callback functions. Also keep in mind that classes are often a better and simpler way to retain extra state for use in callback handlers than are nested functions. Because state is explicit in classes, these scope issues do not apply. The next two sections cover this in detail.

Bound Method Callback Handlers

Class bound methods work particularly well as callback handlers: they record both an instance to send the event to and an associated method to call. For instance, Example 8-14 shows Example 8-12 rewritten to register a bound class method rather than a function or lambda result.

Example 8-14. PP3E\Gui\Intro\gui3c.py

```
from Tkinter import *

class HelloClass:
    def __init__(self):
        widget = Button(None, text='Hello event world', command=self.quit)
        widget.pack()
    def quit(self):
        print 'Hello class method world'    # self.quit is a bound method
        import sys; sys.exit()               # retains the self+quit pair

HelloClass()
mainloop()
```

On a button press, Tkinter calls this class's quit method with no arguments, as usual. But really, it does receive one argument—the original self object—even though Tkinter doesn't pass it explicitly. Because the self.quit bound method retains both self and quit, it's compatible with a simple function call; Python automatically passes the self argument along to the method function. Conversely, registering an unbound method such as HelloClass.quit won't work, because there is no self object to pass along when the event later occurs.

Later, we'll see that class callback handler coding schemes provide a natural place to remember information for use on events; simply assign the information to self instance attributes:

```
class someGuiClass:
    def __init__(self):
        self.X = 42
        self.Y = 'spam'
        Button(text='Hi', command=self.handler)
    def handler(self):
        use self.X, self.Y ...
```

Because the event will be dispatched to this class's method with a reference to the original instance object, self gives access to attributes that retain original data. In effect, the instance's attributes retain state information to be used when events occur.

Callable Class Object Callback Handlers

Because Python class instance objects can also be called if they inherit a __call__ method to intercept the operation, we can pass one of these to serve as a callback handler. Example 8-15 shows a class that provides the required function-like interface.

Example 8-15. PP3E\Gui\Intro\gui3d.py

```
from Tkinter import *

class HelloCallable:
    def __init__(self):                          # __init__ run on object creation
        self.msg = 'Hello __call__ world'
    def __call__(self):
        print self.msg                           # __call__ run later when called
        import sys; sys.exit()                    # class object looks like a function

widget = Button(None, text='Hello event world', command=HelloCallable())
widget.pack()
widget.mainloop()
```

Here, the HelloCallable instance registered with command can be called like a normal function; Python invokes its __call__ method to handle the call operation made in Tkinter on the button press. Notice that self.msg is used to retain information for use on events here; self is the original instance when the special __call__ method is automatically invoked.

All four gui3 variants create the same GUI window but print different messages to stdout when their button is pressed:

```
C:\...\PP3E\Gui\Intro>python gui3.py
Hello, I must be going...
```

```
C:\...\PP3E\Gui\Intro>python gui3b.py
Hello lambda world

C:\...\PP3E\Gui\Intro>python gui3c.py
Hello class method world

C:\...\PP3E\Gui\Intro>python gui3d.py
Hello __call__ world
```

There are good reasons for each callback coding scheme (function, lambda, class method, callable class), but we need to move on to larger examples in order to uncover them in less theoretical terms.

Other Tkinter Callback Protocols

For future reference, also keep in mind that using command options to intercept user-generated button press events is just one way to register callbacks in Tkinter. In fact, there are a variety of ways for Tkinter scripts to catch events:

Button command options

As we've just seen, button press events are intercepted by providing a callable object in widget command options. This is true of other kinds of button-like widgets we'll meet in Chapter 9 (e.g., radio and check buttons, and scales).

Menu command options

In the upcoming Tkinter tour chapters, we'll also find that a command option is used to specify callback handlers for menu selections.

Scroll bar protocols

Scroll bar widgets register handlers with command options too, but they have a unique event protocol that allows them to be cross-linked with the widget they are meant to scroll (e.g., listboxes, text displays, and canvases): moving the scroll bar automatically moves the widget, and vice versa.

General widget bind *methods*

A more general Tkinter event bind method mechanism can be used to register callback handlers for lower-level interface events—key presses, mouse movement and clicks, and so on. Unlike command callbacks, bind callbacks receive an event object argument (an instance of the Tkinter Event class) that gives context about the event—subject widget, screen coordinates, and so on.

Window manager protocols

In addition, scripts can also intercept window manager events (e.g., window close requests) by tapping into the window manager protocol method mechanism available on top-level window objects. Setting a handler for WM_DELETE_WINDOW, for instance, takes over window close buttons.

Scheduled event callbacks

Finally, Tkinter scripts can also register callback handlers to be run in special contexts, such as timer expirations, input data arrival, and event-loop idle states. Scripts can also pause for state-change events related to windows and special variables. We'll meet these event interfaces in more detail near the end of Chapter 10.

Binding Events

Of all the options listed in the prior section, `bind` is the most general, but also perhaps the most complex. We'll study it in more detail later, but to let you sample its flavor now, Example 8-16 uses `bind`, not the `command` keyword, to catch button presses.

Example 8-16. PP3E\Gui\Intro\gui3e.py

```
from Tkinter import *

def hello(event):
    print 'Press twice to exit'          # on single-left click

def quit(event):                         # on double-left click
    print 'Hello, I must be going...'    # event gives widget, x/y, etc.
    import sys; sys.exit( )

widget = Button(None, text='Hello event world')
widget.pack( )
widget.bind('<Button-1>', hello)         # bind left mouse clicks
widget.bind('<Double-1>', quit)          # bind double-left clicks
widget.mainloop( )
```

In fact, this version doesn't specify a `command` option for the button at all. Instead, it binds lower-level callback handlers for both left mouse clicks (`<Button-1>`) and double-left mouse clicks (`<Double-1>`) within the button's display area. The `bind` method accepts a large set of such event identifiers in a variety of formats, which we'll meet in Chapter 9.

When run, this script makes the same window as before (see Figure 8-13). Clicking on the button once prints a message but doesn't exit; you need to double-click on the button now to exit as before. Here is the output after clicking twice and double-clicking once (a double-click fires the single-click callback first):

```
C:\...\PP3E\Gui\Intro>python gui3e.py
Press twice to exit
Press twice to exit
Press twice to exit
Hello, I must be going...
```

Although this script intercepts button clicks manually, the end result is roughly the same; widget-specific protocols such as button command options are really just higher-level interfaces to events you can also catch with bind.

We'll meet bind and all of the other Tkinter event callback handler hooks again in more detail later in this book. First, though, let's focus on building GUIs that are larger than a single button and on other ways to use classes in GUI work.

Adding Multiple Widgets

It's time to start building user interfaces with more than one widget. Example 8-17 makes the window shown in Figure 8-14.

Example 8-17. PP3E\Gui\Intro\gui4.py

```
from Tkinter import *

def greeting():
    print 'Hello stdout world!...'

win = Frame()
win.pack()
Label(win,  text='Hello container world').pack(side=TOP)
Button(win, text='Hello', command=greeting).pack(side=LEFT)
Button(win, text='Quit',  command=win.quit).pack(side=RIGHT)

win.mainloop()
```

Figure 8-14. A multiple-widget window

This example makes a Frame widget (another Tkinter class) and attaches three other widget objects to it, a Label and two Buttons, by passing the Frame as their first argument. In Tkinter terms, we say that the Frame becomes a parent to the other three widgets. Both buttons on this display trigger callbacks:

- Pressing the Hello button triggers the greeting function defined within this file, which prints to stdout again.

- Pressing the Quit button calls the standard Tkinter quit method, inherited by win from the Frame class (Frame.quit has the same effect as the Tk.quit we used earlier).

Here is the stdout text that shows up on Hello button presses, wherever this script's standard streams may be:

```
C:\...\PP3E\Gui\Intro>python gui4.py
Hello stdout world!...
Hello stdout world!...
Hello stdout world!...
Hello stdout world!...
```

The notion of attaching widgets to containers turns out to be at the core of layouts in Tkinter. Before we go into more detail on that topic, though, let's get small.

Widget Resizing Revisited: Clipping

Earlier, we saw how to make widgets expand along with their parent window, by passing expand and fill options to the pack geometry manager. Now that we have a window with more than one widget, I can let you in on one of the more useful secrets in the packer. As a rule, widgets packed first are clipped last when a window is shrunk. That is, the order in which you pack items determines which items will be cut out of the display if it is made too small. Widgets packed later are cut out first. For example, Figure 8-15 shows what happens when the gui4 window is shrunk interactively.

Figure 8-15. gui4 gets small

Try reordering the label and button lines in the script and see what happens when the window shrinks; the first one packed is always the last to go away. For instance, if the label is packed last, Figure 8-16 shows that it is clipped first, even though it is attached to the top: side attachments and packing order both impact the overall layout, but only packing order matters when windows shrink.

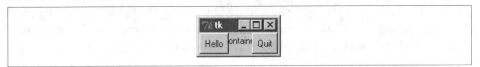

Figure 8-16. Label packed last, clipped first

Tkinter keeps track of the packing order internally to make this work. Scripts can plan ahead for shrinkage by calling pack methods of more important widgets first. For instance, on the upcoming Tkinter tour, we'll meet code that builds menus and toolbars at the top and bottom of the window; to make sure these are lost last as a window is shrunk, they are packed first, before the application components in the middle. Similarly, displays that include scroll bars normally pack them before the items they scroll (e.g., text, lists) so that the scroll bars remain as the window shrinks.

Attaching Widgets to Frames

In larger terms, the critical innovation in this example is its use of frames: Frame widgets are just containers for other widgets, and so give rise to the notion of GUIs as widget hierarchies, or trees. Here, win serves as an enclosing window for the other three widgets. In general, though, by attaching widgets to frames, and frames to other frames, we can build up arbitrary GUI layouts. Simply divide the user interface into a set of increasingly smaller rectangles, implement each as a Tkinter Frame, and attach basic widgets to the frame in the desired screen position.

In this script, when you specify win in the first argument to the Label and Button constructors, Tkinter attaches them to the Frame (they become children of the win parent). win itself is attached to the default top-level window, since we didn't pass a parent to the Frame constructor. When we ask win to run itself (by calling mainloop), Tkinter draws all the widgets in the tree we've built.

The three child widgets also provide pack options now: the side arguments tell which part of the containing frame (i.e., win) to attach the new widget to. The label hooks onto the top, and the buttons attach to the sides. TOP, LEFT, and RIGHT are all preassigned string variables imported from Tkinter. Arranging widgets is a bit subtler than simply giving a side, though, but we need to take a quick detour into packer geometry management details to see why.

Layout: Packing Order and Side Attachments

When a widget tree is displayed, child widgets appear inside their parents and are arranged according to their order of packing and their packing options. Because of this, the order in which widgets are packed not only gives their clipping order, but also determines how their side settings play out in the generated display.

Here's how the packer's layout system works:

1. The packer starts out with an available space cavity that includes the entire parent container (e.g., the whole Frame or top-level window).

2. As each widget is packed on a side, that widget is given the entire requested side in the remaining space cavity, and the space cavity is shrunk.

3. Later pack requests are given an entire side of what is left, after earlier pack requests have shrunk the cavity.

4. After widgets are given cavity space, expand divides any space left, and fill and anchor stretch and position widgets within their assigned space.

For instance, if you recode the gui4 child widget creation logic like this:

```
Button(win, text='Hello', command=greeting).pack(side=LEFT)
Label(win,  text='Hello container world').pack(side=TOP)
Button(win, text='Quit',  command=win.quit).pack(side=RIGHT)
```

you will wind up with the very different display in Figure 8-17, even though you've moved the label code only one line down in the source file (contrast with Figure 8-14).

Figure 8-17. Packing the label second

Despite its side setting, the label does not get the entire top of the window now, and you have to think in terms of *shrinking cavities* to understand why. Because the Hello button is packed first, it is given the entire LEFT side of the Frame. Next, the label is given the entire TOP side of what is left. Finally, the Quit button gets the RIGHT side of the remainder—a rectangle to the right of the Hello button and under the label. When this window shrinks, widgets are clipped in reverse order of their packing: the Quit button disappears first, followed by the label.* In the original version of this example, the label spans the entire top side just because it is the first one packed, not because of its side option.

The Packer's Expand and Fill Revisited

Beyond all of this, the fill option we met earlier can be used to stretch the widget to occupy all the space in the cavity side it has been given, and any cavity space left after all packing is evenly allocated among widgets with the expand=YES we saw before. For example, coding this way creates the window in Figure 8-18:

```
Button(win, text='Hello', command=greeting).pack(side=LEFT, fill=Y)
Label(win,  text='Hello container world').pack(side=TOP)
Button(win, text='Quit', command=win.quit).pack(side=RIGHT, expand=YES, fill=X)
```

To make all of these grow along with their window, though, we also need to make the container frame expandable; widgets expand beyond their initial packer arrangement only if all of their parents expand too:

```
win = Frame()
win.pack(side=TOP, expand=YES, fill=BOTH)
Button(win, text='Hello', command=greeting).pack(side=LEFT, fill=Y)
```

---

* Technically, the packing steps are just rerun again after a window resize. But since this means that there won't be enough space left for widgets packed last when the window shrinks, it is as if widgets packed first are clipped last.

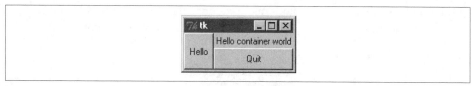

Figure 8-18. Packing with expand and fill options

```
Label(win,  text='Hello container world').pack(side=TOP)
Button(win, text='Quit', command=win.quit).pack(side=RIGHT, expand=YES,fill=X)
```

When this code runs, the Frame is assigned the entire top side of its parent as before (that is, the top parcel of the root window); but because it is now marked to expand into unused space in its parent and to fill that space both ways, it and all of its attached children expand along with the window. Figure 8-19 shows how.

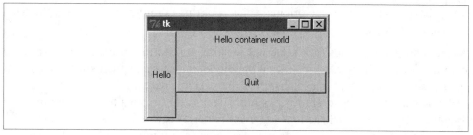

Figure 8-19. gui4 gets big with an expandable frame

Using Anchor to Position Instead of Stretch

And as if that isn't flexible enough, the packer also allows widgets to be positioned within their allocated space with an anchor option, instead of filling that space with a fill. The anchor option accepts Tkinter constants identifying all eight points of the compass (N, NE, NW, S, etc.) and CENTER as its value (e.g., anchor=NW). It instructs the packer to position the widget at the desired position within its allocated space, if the space allocated for the widget is larger than the space needed to display the widget.

The default anchor is CENTER, so widgets show up in the middle of their space (the cavity side they were given) unless they are positioned with anchor or stretched with fill. To demonstrate, change gui4 to use this sort of code:

```
Button(win, text='Hello', command=greeting).pack(side=LEFT, anchor=N)
Label(win,  text='Hello container world').pack(side=TOP)
Button(win, text='Quit',  command=win.quit).pack(side=RIGHT)
```

The only thing new here is that the Hello button is anchored to the north side of its space allocation. Because this button was packed first, it got the entire left side of the parent frame. This is more space than is needed to show the button, so it shows up in the middle of that side by default, as in Figure 8-17 (i.e., anchored to the center). Setting the anchor to N moves it to the top of its side, as shown in Figure 8-20.

Figure 8-20. Anchoring a button to the north

Keep in mind that `fill` and `anchor` are applied after a widget has been allocated cavity side space by its `side`, packing order, and expand extra space request. By playing with packing orders, sides, fills, and anchors, you can generate lots of layout and clipping effects, and you should take a few moments to experiment with alternatives if you haven't already. In the original version of this example, for instance, the label spans the entire top side just because it is the first packed.

As we'll see later, frames can be nested in other frames too in order to make more complex layouts. In fact, because each parent container is a distinct space cavity, this provides a sort of escape mechanism for the packer cavity algorithm: to better control where a set of widgets show up, simply pack them within a nested subframe and attach the frame as a package to a larger container. A row of push buttons, for example, might be easier laid out in a frame of its own than if mixed with other widgets in the display directly.

Finally, also keep in mind that the widget tree created by these examples is really an implicit one; Tkinter internally records the relationships implied by passed parent widget arguments. In OOP terms, this is a composition relationship—the `Frame` contains a `Label` and `Button`s; let's look at inheritance relationships next.

Customizing Widgets with Classes

You don't have to use OOP in Tkinter scripts, but it can definitely help. As we just saw, Tkinter GUIs are built up as class-instance object trees. Here's another way Python's OOP features can be applied to GUI models: specializing widgets by inheritance. Example 8-18 builds the window in Figure 8-21.

Figure 8-21. A button subclass in action

Example 8-18. PP3E\Gui\Intro\gui5.py

```
from Tkinter import *

class HelloButton(Button):
    def __init__(self, parent=None, **config):        # add callback method
        Button.__init__(self, parent, config)          # and pack myself
        self.pack()
        self.config(command=self.callback)
    def callback(self):                                 # default press action
        print 'Goodbye world...'                        # replace in subclasses
        self.quit()

if __name__ == '__main__':
    HelloButton(text='Hello subclass world').mainloop()
```

This example isn't anything special to look at: it just displays a single button that, when pressed, prints a message and exits. But this time, it is a button widget we created on our own. The HelloButton class inherits everything from the Tkinter Button class, but adds a callback method and constructor logic to set the command option to self.callback, a bound method of the instance. When the button is pressed this time, the new widget class's callback method, not a simple function, is invoked.

The **config argument here is assigned unmatched keyword arguments; they're passed along to the Button constructor. We met the config widget method called in HelloButton's constructor earlier; it is just an alternative way to pass configuration options after the fact (instead of passing constructor arguments).

So what's the point of subclassing widgets like this? It allows widgets to be configured by subclassing instead of by passing in options. HelloButton is a true button; we pass in configuration options as usual when one is made. But we can also specify callback handlers by overriding the callback method in subclasses, as shown in Example 8-19.

Example 8-19. PP3E\Gui\Intro\gui5b.py

```
from gui5 import HelloButton

class MyButton(HelloButton):        # subclass HelloButton
    def callback(self):             # redefine press-handler method
        print "Ignoring press!..."

if __name__ == '__main__':
    MyButton(None, text='Hello subclass world').mainloop()
```

Instead of exiting, this MyButton button, when pressed, prints to stdout and stays up. Here is its standard output after being pressed a few times:

```
C:\PP2ndEd\examples\PP3E\Gui\Intro>python gui5b.py
Ignoring press!...
Ignoring press!...
Ignoring press!...
Ignoring press!...
```

Whether it's simpler to customize widgets by subclassing or passing in options is probably a matter of taste. But the point to notice is that Tk becomes truly object oriented in Python, just because Python is object oriented: we can specialize widget classes using normal class-based object-oriented techniques. The next example provides yet another way to arrange for specialization.

Reusable GUI Components with Classes

Larger GUI interfaces are often built up as subclasses of Frame, with callback handlers implemented as methods. This structure gives us a natural place to store information between events: instance attributes record state. It also allows us to both specialize GUIs by overriding their methods in new subclasses, and attach them to larger GUI structures to reuse them as general components. For instance, a GUI text editor implemented as a Frame subclass can be attached to and configured by any number of other GUIs; if done well, we can plug such a text editor into any user interface that needs text editing tools.

We'll meet such a text editor component in Chapter 12. For now, Example 8-20 illustrates the concept in a simple way. The script *gui6.py* produces the window in Figure 8-22.

Figure 8-22. A custom Frame in action

Example 8-20. PP3E\Gui\Intro\gui6.py

```
from Tkinter import *

class Hello(Frame):                             # an extended Frame
    def __init__(self, parent=None):
        Frame.__init__(self, parent)            # do superclass init
        self.pack()
        self.data = 42
        self.make_widgets()                     # attach widgets to self
    def make_widgets(self):
        widget = Button(self, text='Hello frame world!', command=self.message)
        widget.pack(side=LEFT)
    def message(self):
        self.data += 1
        print 'Hello frame world %s!' % self.data

if __name__ == '__main__': Hello().mainloop()
```

This example pops up a single-button window. When pressed, the button triggers the self.message bound method to print to stdout again. Here is the output after pressing this button four times; notice how self.data (a simple counter here) retains its state between presses:

```
C:\...\PP3E\Gui\Intro>python gui6.py
Hello frame world 43!
Hello frame world 44!
Hello frame world 45!
Hello frame world 46!
```

This may seem like a roundabout way to show a Button (we did it in fewer lines in Examples 8-10, 8-11, and 8-12). But the Hello class provides an enclosing organizational structure for building GUIs. In the examples prior to the last section, we made GUIs using a function-like approach: we called widget constructors as though they were functions and hooked widgets together manually by passing in parents to widget construction calls. There was no notion of an enclosing context, apart from the global scope of the module file containing the widget calls. This works for simple GUIs but can make for brittle code when building up larger GUI structures.

But by subclassing Frame as we've done here, the class becomes an enclosing context for the GUI:

- Widgets are added by attaching objects to self, an instance of a Frame container subclass (e.g., Button).
- Callback handlers are registered as bound methods of self, and so are routed back to code in the class (e.g., self.message).
- State information is retained between events by assigning to attributes of self, visible to all callback methods in the class (e.g., self.data).
- It's easy to make multiple copies of such a GUI component, because each class instance is a distinct namespace.
- Classes naturally support customization by inheritance and by composition attachment.

In a sense, entire GUIs become specialized Frame objects with extensions for an application. Classes can also provide protocols for building widgets (e.g., the make_widgets method here), handle standard configuration chores (like setting window manager options), and so on. In short, Frame subclasses provide a simple way to organize collections of other widget-class objects.

Attaching Class Components

Perhaps more importantly, subclasses of Frame are true widgets: they can be further extended and customized by subclassing and can be attached to enclosing widgets. For instance, to attach the entire package of widgets that a class builds to something else, simply create an instance of the class with a real parent widget passed in. To illustrate, running the script in Example 8-21 creates the window shown in Figure 8-23.

Example 8-21. PP3E\Gui\Intro\gui6b.py

```
from sys import exit
from Tkinter import *              # get Tk widget classes
from gui6 import Hello             # get the subframe class

parent = Frame(None)              # make a container widget
parent.pack()
Hello(parent).pack(side=RIGHT)    # attach Hello instead of running it

Button(parent, text='Attach', command=exit).pack(side=LEFT)
parent.mainloop()
```

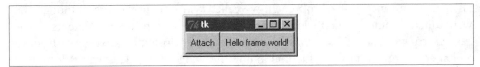

Figure 8-23. An attached class component on the right

This script just adds Hello's button to the right side of parent—a container Frame. In fact, the button on the right in this window represents an embedded component: its button really represents an attached Python class object. Pressing the embedded class's button on the right prints a message as before; pressing the new button exits the GUI by a sys.exit call:

```
C:\...\PP3E\Gui\Intro>python gui6b.py
Hello frame world 43!
Hello frame world 44!
Hello frame world 45!
Hello frame world 46!
```

In more complex GUIs, we might instead attach large Frame subclasses to other container components and develop each independently. For instance, Example 8-22 is yet another specialized Frame itself, but attaches an instance of the original Hello class in a more object-oriented fashion. When run as a top-level program, it creates a window identical to the one shown in Figure 8-23.

Example 8-22. PP3E\Gui\Intro\gui6c.py

```
from Tkinter import *              # get Tk widget classes
from gui6 import Hello             # get the subframe class

class HelloContainer(Frame):
    def __init__(self, parent=None):
        Frame.__init__(self, parent)
        self.pack()
        self.makeWidgets()
    def makeWidgets(self):
        Hello(self).pack(side=RIGHT)      # attach a Hello to me
        Button(self, text='Attach', command=self.quit).pack(side=LEFT)

if __name__ == '__main__': HelloContainer().mainloop()
```

This looks and works exactly like gui6b but registers the added button's callback handler as self.quit, which is just the standard quit widget method this class inherits from Frame. The window this time represents two Python classes at work—the embedded component's widgets on the right (the original Hello button) and the container's widgets on the left.

Naturally, this is a simple example (we attached only a single button here, after all). But in more practical user interfaces, the set of widget class objects attached in this way can be much larger. If you imagine replacing the Hello call in this script with a call to attach an already coded and fully debugged calculator object, you'll begin to better understand the power of this paradigm. If we code all of our GUI components as classes, they automatically become a library of reusable widgets, which we can combine in other applications as often as we like.

Extending Class Components

When GUIs are built with classes, there are a variety of ways to reuse their code in other displays. To extend Hello instead of attaching it, we just override some of its methods in a new subclass (which itself becomes a specialized Frame widget). This technique is shown in Example 8-23.

Example 8-23. PP3E\Gui\Intro\gui6d.py

```
from Tkinter import *
from gui6 import Hello

class HelloExtender(Hello):
    def make_widgets(self):                          # extend method here
        Hello.make_widgets(self)
        Button(self, text='Extend', command=self.quit).pack(side=RIGHT)
    def message(self):
        print 'hello', self.data                     # redefine method here

if __name__ == '__main__': HelloExtender().mainloop()
```

This subclass's make_widgets method here first builds the superclass's widgets and then adds a second Extend button on the right, as shown in Figure 8-24.

Figure 8-24. A customized class's widgets, on the left

Because it redefines the `message` method, pressing the original superclass's button on the left now prints a different string to `stdout` (when searching up from `self`, the `message` attribute is found first in this subclass, not in the superclass):

```
C:\...\PP3E\Gui\Intro>python gui6d.py
hello 42
hello 42
hello 42
hello 42
```

But pressing the new Extend button on the right, which is added by this subclass, exits immediately, since the `quit` method (inherited from `Hello`, which inherits it from `Frame`) is the added button's callback handler. The net effect is that this class customizes the original to add a new button and change `message`'s behavior.

Although this example is simple, it demonstrates a technique that can be powerful in practice: to change a GUI's behavior, we can write a new class that customizes its parts rather than changing the existing GUI code in place. The main code need be debugged only once and customized with subclasses as unique needs arise.

The moral of this story is that Tkinter GUIs can be coded without ever writing a single new class, but using classes to structure your GUI code makes it much more reusable in the long run. If done well, you can both attach already debugged components to new interfaces, and specialize their behavior in new external subclasses as needed for custom requirements. Either way, the initial upfront investment to use classes is bound to save coding time in the end.

Standalone Container Classes

Before we move on, I want to point out that it's possible to reap most of the benefits previously mentioned by creating standalone classes not derived from Tkinter `Frames` or other widgets. For instance, the class in Example 8-24 generates the window shown in Figure 8-25.

Figure 8-25. A standalone class package in action

Example 8-24. PP3E\Gui\Intro\gui7.py

```
from Tkinter import *

class HelloPackage:                              # not a widget subbclass
    def __init__(self, parent=None):
        self.top = Frame(parent)                 # embed a Frame
        self.top.pack()
        self.data = 0
```

Example 8-24. PP3E\Gui\Intro\gui7.py (continued)

```
        self.make_widgets()                    # attach widgets to self.top
    def make_widgets(self):
        Button(self.top, text='Bye', command=self.top.quit).pack(side=LEFT)
        Button(self.top, text='Hye', command=self.message).pack(side=RIGHT)
    def message(self)):
        self.data += 1
        print 'Hello number', self.data

if __name__ == '__main__': HelloPackage().top.mainloop()
```

When run, the Bye button here prints to stdout and Bye closes and exits the GUI, much as before:

```
C:\...\PP3E\Gui\Intro>python gui7.py
Hello number 1
Hello number 2
Hello number 3
Hello number 4
```

Also as before, self.data retains state between events, and callbacks are routed to the self.message method within this class. Unlike before, the HelloPackage class is not itself a kind of Frame widget. In fact, it's not a kind of anything—it serves only as a generator of namespaces for storing away real widget objects and state. Because of that, widgets are attached to a self.top (an embedded Frame), not to self. Moreover, all references to the object as a widget must descend to the embedded frame, as in the top.mainloop call to start the GUI.

This makes for a bit more coding within the class, but it avoids potential name clashes with both attributes added to self by the Tkinter framework and existing Tkinter widget methods. For instance, if you define a config method in your class, it will hide the config call exported by Tkinter. With the standalone class package in this example, you get only the methods and instance attributes that your class defines.

In practice, Tkinter doesn't use very many names, so this is not generally a big concern.* It can happen, of course; but frankly, I've never seen a real Tkinter name clash in widget subclasses in some 13 years of Python coding. Moreover, using standalone classes is not without other downsides. Although they can generally be attached and subclassed as before, they are not quite plug-and-play compatible with real widget

---

* If you study the Tkinter.py module's source code, you'll notice that many of the attribute names it creates start with a single underscore to make them unique from yours; others do not because they are potentially useful outside of the Tkinter implementation (e.g., self.master, self.children). Oddly, at this writing, most of Tkinter still does not use the new Python "pseudoprivate attributes" trick of prefixing attribute names with two leading underscores to automatically add the enclosing class's name and thus localize them to the creating class. If Tkinter is ever rewritten to employ this feature, name clashes will be much less likely in widget subclasses. Most of the attributes of widget classes, though, are methods intended for use in client scripts.

objects. For instance, the configuration calls made in Example 8-21 for the Frame subclass fail in Example 8-25.

Example 8-25. PP3E\Gui\Intro\gui7b.py

```
from Tkinter import *
from gui7 import HelloPackage      # or get from gui7c--__getattr__ added

frm = Frame()
frm.pack()
Label(frm, text='hello').pack()

part = HelloPackage(frm)
part.pack(side=RIGHT)             # fails!--need part.top.pack(side=RIGHT)
frm.mainloop()
```

This won't quite work, because part isn't really a widget. To treat it as such, you must descend to part.top before making GUI configurations and hope that the name top is never changed by the class's developer. In other words, it exposes some of the class's internals. The class could make this better by defining a method that always routes unknown attribute fetches to the embedded Frame, as in Example 8-26.

Example 8-26. PP3E\Gui\Intro\gui7c.py

```
import gui7
from Tkinter import *

class HelloPackage(gui7.HelloPackage):
    def __getattr__(self, name):
        return getattr(self.top, name)      # pass off to a real widget

if __name__ == '__main__': HelloPackage().top.mainloop()
```

But that then requires even more extra coding in standalone package classes. As usual, though, the significance of all these trade-offs varies per application.

The End of the Tutorial

In this chapter, we learned the core concepts of Python/Tkinter programming and met a handful of simple widget objects along the way—e.g., labels, buttons, frames, and the packer geometry manager. We've seen enough to construct simple interfaces, but we have really only scratched the surface of the Tkinter widget set.

In the next two chapters, we will apply what we've learned here to study the rest of the Tkinter library, and we'll learn how to use it to generate the kinds of interfaces you expect to see in realistic GUI programs. As a preview and roadmap, Table 8-1 lists the kinds of widgets we'll meet there in roughly their order of appearance. Note that this table lists only widget classes; along the way, we will also meet a few additional widget-related topics that don't appear in this table.

Table 8-1. Tkinter widget classes

Widget class	Description
Label	A simple message area
Button	A simple labeled push-button widget
Frame	A container for attaching and arranging other widget objects
Toplevel, Tk	A new window managed by the window manager
Message	A multiline label
Entry	A simple single-line text-entry field
Checkbutton	A two-state button widget, typically used for multiple-choice selections
Radiobutton	A two-state button widget, typically used for single-choice selections
Scale	A slider widget with scalable positions
PhotoImage	An image object used for displaying full-color images on other widgets
BitmapImage	An image object used for displaying bitmap images on other widgets
Menu	A set of options associated with a Menubutton or top-level window
Menubutton	A button that opens a Menu of selectable options and submenus
Scrollbar	A control for scrolling other widgets (e.g., listbox, canvas, text)
Listbox	A list of selection names
Text	A multiline text browse/edit widget, with support for fonts, and so on
Canvas	A graphic drawing area, which supports lines, circles, photos, text, and so on

We've already met the Label, Button, and Frame in this chapter's tutorial. To make the remaining topics easier to absorb, they are split over the next two chapters: Chapter 9 covers the first widgets in this table up to but not including Menu, and Chapter 10 presents widgets that are lower in this table.

Besides the widget classes in this table, there are additional classes and tools in the Tkinter library, many of which we'll explore in the following two chapters as well:

Geometry management
　　pack, grid, place

Tkinter linked variables
　　StringVar, IntVar, DoubleVar, BooleanVar

Advanced Tk widgets
　　Spinbox, LabelFrame, PanedWindow

Composite widgets
　　Dialog, ScrolledText, OptionMenu

Scheduled callbacks
　　Widget after, wait, and update methods

Other tools
　　Standard dialogs, clipboard, bind and Event, widget configuration options, custom and modal dialogs, animation techniques

Most Tkinter widgets are familiar user interface devices. Some are remarkably rich in functionality. For instance, the Text class implements a sophisticated multiline text widget that supports fonts, colors, and special effects and is powerful enough to implement a web browser's page display, and the Canvas class provides extensive drawing tools powerful enough for visualization and other image processing applications. Beyond this, Tkinter extensions such as the Pmw and Tix packages described at the start of this chapter add even richer widgets to a GUI programmer's toolbox.

Python/Tkinter for Tcl/Tk Converts

At the start of this chapter, I mentioned that Tkinter is Python's interface to the Tk GUI library, originally written for the Tcl language. To help readers migrating from Tcl to Python and to summarize some of the main topics we met in this chapter, this section contrasts Python's Tk interface with Tcl's. This mapping also helps make Tk references written for other languages more useful to Python developers.

In general terms, Tcl's command-string view of the world differs widely from Python's object-based approach to programming. In terms of Tk programming, though, the syntactic differences are fairly small. Here are some of the main distinctions in Python's Tkinter interface:

Creation
    Widgets are created as class instance objects by calling a widget class.

Masters (parents)
    Parents are previously created objects that are passed to widget-class constructors.

Widget options
    Options are constructor or config keyword arguments or indexed keys.

Operations
    Widget operations (actions) become Tkinter widget class object methods.

Callbacks
    Callback handlers are any callable objects: function, method, lambda, and so on.

Extension
    Widgets are extended using Python class inheritance mechanisms.

Composition
    Interfaces are constructed by attaching objects, not by concatenating names.

Linked variables (next chapter)
    Variables associated with widgets are Tkinter class objects with methods.

In Python, widget creation commands (e.g., button) are Python class names that start with an uppercase letter (e.g., Button), two-word widget operations (e.g., add command) become a single method name with an underscore (e.g., add_command), and the "configure" method can be abbreviated as "config," as in Tcl. In Chapter 9, we will also see that Tkinter "variables" associated with widgets take the form of class instance objects (e.g., StringVar, IntVar) with get and set methods, not simple Python or Tcl variable names. Table 8-2 shows some of the primary language mappings in more concrete terms.

Table 8-2. Tk-to-Tkinter mappings

Operation	Tcl/Tk	Python/Tkinter
Creation	`Frame .panel`	`panel = Frame( )`
Masters	`button .panel.quit`	`quit = Button(panel)`
Options	`button .panel.go -fg black`	`go = Button(panel, fg='black')`
Configure	`.panel.go config -bg red`	`go.config(bg='red')  go['bg'] = 'red'`
Actions	`.popup invoke`	`popup.invoke( )`
Packing	`pack .panel -side left -fill x`	`panel.pack(side=LEFT, fill=X)`

Some of these differences are more than just syntactic, of course. For instance, Python builds an internal widget object tree based on parent arguments passed to widget constructors, without ever requiring concatenated widget pathname strings. Once you've made a widget object, you can use it directly by reference. Tcl coders can hide some dotted pathnames by manually storing them in variables, but that's not quite the same as Python's purely object-based model.

Once you've written a few Python/Tkinter scripts, though, the coding distinctions in the Python object world will probably seem trivial. At the same time, Python's support for object-oriented techniques adds an entirely new component to Tk development; you get the same widgets, plus Python's support for code structure and reuse.

CHAPTER 9

A Tkinter Tour, Part 1

"Widgets and Gadgets and GUIs, Oh My!"

This chapter is a continuation of our look at GUI programming in Python. The previous chapter used simple widgets—buttons, labels, and the like—to demonstrate the fundamentals of Tkinter coding in Python. That was simple by design: it's easier to grasp the big GUI picture if widget interface details don't get in the way. But now that we've seen the basics, this chapter and the next move on to present a tour of more advanced widget objects and tools available in the Tkinter library.

As we'll find, this is where GUI scripting starts getting both practical and fun. In these two chapters, we'll meet classes that build the interface devices you expect to see in real programs—e.g., sliders, check buttons, menus, scrolled lists, dialogs, graphics, and so on. After these chapters, the last GUI chapter moves on to present larger GUIs that utilize the coding techniques and the interfaces shown in all prior GUI chapters. In these two chapters, though, examples are small and self-contained so that we can focus on widget details.

This Chapter's Topics

Technically, we've already used a handful of simple widgets in Chapter 8. So far we've met Label, Button, Frame, and Tk, and studied pack geometry management concepts along the way. Although all of these are basic, they represent Tkinter interfaces in general and can be workhorses in typical GUIs. Frame containers, for instance, are the basis of hierarchical display layout.

In this and the following chapter, we'll explore additional options for widgets we've already seen and move beyond the basics to cover the rest of the Tkinter widget set. Here are some of the widgets and topics we'll explore in this chapter:

- Top-level and Tk widgets
- Message and Entry widgets

- Checkbutton, Radiobutton, and Scale widgets
- Images: PhotoImage and BitmapImage objects
- Dialogs, both standard and custom
- Widget configuration options
- Low-level event binding
- Tkinter variable objects
- Using the Python Imaging Library (PIL) extension for other image types and operations

After this chapter, Chapter 10 concludes the tour by presenting the remainder of the Tkinter library's tool set: menus, text, canvases, animation, and more.

To make this tour interesting, I'll also introduce a few notions of component reuse along the way. For instance, some later examples will be built using components written for prior examples. Although these two tour chapters introduce widget interfaces, this book is really about Python programming in general; as we'll see, Tkinter programming in Python can be much more than simply drawing circles and arrows.

Configuring Widget Appearance

So far, all the buttons and labels in examples have been rendered with a default look-and-feel that is standard for the underlying platform. With my machine's color scheme, that usually means that they're gray on Windows. Tkinter widgets can be made to look arbitrarily different, though, using a handful of widget and packer options.

Because I generally can't resist the temptation to customize widgets in examples, I want to cover this topic early on the tour. Example 9-1 introduces some of the configuration options available in Tkinter.

Example 9-1. PP3E\Gui\Tour\config-label.py

```
from Tkinter import *
root = Tk()
labelfont = ('times', 20, 'bold')                    # family, size, style
widget = Label(root, text='Hello config world')
widget.config(bg='black', fg='yellow')               # yellow text on black label
widget.config(font=labelfont)                        # use a larger font
widget.config(height=3, width=20)                    # initial size: lines,chars
widget.pack(expand=YES, fill=BOTH)
root.mainloop()
```

Remember, we can call a widget's config method to reset its options at any time, instead of passing all of them to the object's constructor. Here, we use it to set options that produce the window in Figure 9-1.

Figure 9-1. A custom label appearance

This may not be completely obvious unless you run this script on a real computer (alas, I can't show it in color here), but the label's text here shows up in yellow on a black background, and with a font that's very different from what we've seen so far. In fact, this script customizes the label in a number of ways:

Color

By setting the bg option of the label widget here, its background is displayed in black; the fg option similarly changes the foreground (text) color of the widget to yellow. These color options work on most Tkinter widgets and accept either a simple color name (e.g., 'blue') or a hexadecimal string. Most of the color names you are familiar with are supported (unless you happen to work for Crayola). You can also pass a hexadecimal color identifier string to these options to be more specific; they start with a # and name a color by its red, green, and blue saturations, with an equal number of bits in the string for each. For instance, '#ff0000' specifies eight bits per color and defines pure red; "f" means four "1" bits in hexadecimal. We'll come back to this hex form when we meet the color selection dialog later in this chapter.

Size

The label is given a preset size in lines high and characters wide by setting its height and width attributes. You can use this setting to make the widget larger than the Tkinter geometry manager would by default.

Font

This script specifies a custom font for the label's text by setting the label's font attribute to a three-item tuple giving the font family, size, and style (here: Times, 20-point, and bold). Font style can be normal, bold, roman, italic, underline, overstrike, or combinations of these (e.g., "bold italic"). Tkinter guarantees that Times, Courier, and Helvetica font family names exist on all platforms, but others may work too (e.g., system gives the system font on Windows). Font settings like this work on all widgets with text, such as labels, buttons, entry fields, listboxes, and Text (the latter of which can display more than one font at once with "tags"). The font option still accepts older X-style font indicators—long strings with dashes and stars—but the new tuple font indicator form is more platform independent.

Layout and expansion

Finally, the label is made generally expandable and stretched by setting the pack expand and fill options we met in the last chapter; the label grows as the window does. If you maximize this window, its black background fills the whole screen and the yellow message is centered in the middle; try it.

In this script, the net effect of all these settings is that this label looks radically different from the ones we've been making so far. It no longer follows the Windows standard look-and-feel, but such conformance isn't always important. Tkinter provides additional ways to customize appearance that are not used by this script:

Border and relief

A bd=N widget option can be used to set border width, and a relief=S option can specify a border style; S can be FLAT, SUNKEN, RAISED, GROOVE, SOLID, or RIDGE—all constants exported by the Tkinter module.

Cursor

A cursor option can be given to change the appearance of the mouse pointer when it moves over the widget. For instance, cursor='gumby' changes the pointer to a Gumby figure (the green kind). Other common cursor names used in this book include watch, pencil, cross, and hand2.

State

Some widgets also support the notion of a state, which impacts their appearance. For example, a state=DISABLED option will generally stipple (gray out) a widget on screen and make it unresponsive; NORMAL does not. Some widgets support a READONLY state as well, which displays normally but is unresponsive to changes.

Padding

Extra space can be added around many widgets (e.g., buttons, labels, and text) with the padx=N and pady=N options. Interestingly, you can set these options both in pack calls (where it adds empty space around the widget in general) and in a widget object itself (where it makes the widget larger).

To illustrate some of these extra settings, Example 9-2 configures the custom button captured in Figure 9-2 and changes the mouse pointer when it is positioned above it.

Figure 9-2. Config button at work

Example 9-2. PP3E\Gui\Tour\config-button.py

```
from Tkinter import *
widget = Button(text='Spam', padx=10, pady=10)
widget.pack(padx=20, pady=20)
widget.config(cursor='gumby')
widget.config(bd=8, relief=RAISED)
widget.config(bg='dark green', fg='white')
widget.config(font=('helvetica', 20, 'underline italic'))
mainloop()
```

To see the effects generated by these two scripts' settings, try out a few changes on your computer. Most widgets can be given a custom appearance in the same way, and we'll see such options used repeatedly in this text. We'll also meet operational configurations, such as focus (for focusing input), and others. In fact, widgets can have dozens of options; most have reasonable defaults that produce a native look-and-feel on each windowing platform, and this is one reason for Tkinter's simplicity. But Tkinter lets you build more custom displays when you want to.

Top-Level Windows

Tkinter GUIs always have a root window, whether you get it by default or create it explicitly by calling the Tk object constructor. This main root window is the one that opens when your program runs, and it is where you generally pack your most important widgets. In addition, Tkinter scripts can create any number of independent windows, generated and popped up on demand, by creating Toplevel widget objects.

Each Toplevel object created produces a new window on the display and automatically adds it to the program's GUI event-loop processing stream (you don't need to call the mainloop method of new windows to activate them). Example 9-3 builds a root and two pop-up windows.

Example 9-3. PP3E\Gui\Tour\toplevel0.py

```
import sys
from Tkinter import Toplevel, Button, Label

win1 = Toplevel()                    # two independent windows
win2 = Toplevel()                    # but part of same process

Button(win1, text='Spam', command=sys.exit).pack()
Button(win2, text='SPAM', command=sys.exit).pack()

Label(text='Popups').pack()          # on default Tk() root window
win1.mainloop()
```

The toplevel0 script gets a root window by default (that's what the Label is attached to, since it doesn't specify a real parent), but it also creates two standalone Toplevel windows that appear and function independently of the root window, as seen in Figure 9-3.

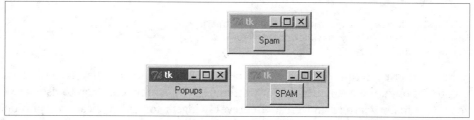

Figure 9-3. Two Toplevel windows and a root window

The two Toplevel windows on the right are full-fledged windows; they can be independently iconified, maximized, and so on. Toplevels are typically used to implement multiple-window displays and pop-up modal and nonmodal dialogs (more on dialogs in the next section). They stay up until they are explicitly destroyed or until the application that created them exits.

It's important to know that although Toplevels are independently active windows, they are not separate processes; if your program exits, all of its windows are erased, including all Toplevel windows it may have created. We'll learn how to work around this rule later by launching independent GUI programs.

Toplevel and Tk Widgets

A Toplevel is roughly like a Frame that is split off into its own window, and has additional methods that allow you to deal with top-level window properties. The Tk widget is roughly like a Toplevel, but it is used to represent the application root window. We got one for free in Example 9-3 because the Label had a default parent; in other scripts, we've made the Tk root more explicit by creating it directly, like this:

```
root = Tk( )
Label(root, text='Popups').pack( )          # on explicit Tk( ) root window
root.mainloop( )
```

In fact, because Tkinter GUIs are built as a hierarchy, you always get a root window by default, whether it is named explicitly, as here, or not. You should generally use the root to display top-level information of some sort; if you don't attach widgets to the root, it shows up as an odd empty window when you run your script. Technically, you can suppress the default root creation logic and make multiple root windows with the Tk widget, as in Example 9-4.

Example 9-4. PP3E\Gui\Tour\toplevel1.py

```
import Tkinter
from Tkinter import Tk, Button
Tkinter.NoDefaultRoot( )
```

Example 9-4. PP3E\Gui\Tour\toplevel1.py (continued)

```
win1 = Tk( )          # two independent root windows
win2 = Tk( )

Button(win1, text='Spam', command=win1.destroy).pack( )
Button(win2, text='SPAM', command=win2.destroy).pack( )
win1.mainloop( )
```

When run, this script displays the two pop-up windows of the screenshot in Figure 9-3 only (there is no third root window). But it's more common to use the Tk root as a main window and create Toplevel widgets for an application's pop-up windows.

Top-Level Window Protocols

Both Tk and Toplevel widgets export extra methods and features tailored for their top-level role, as illustrated in Example 9-5.

Example 9-5. PP3E\Gui\Tour\toplevel2.py

```
###########################################################################
# pop up three new windows, with style
# destroy() kills one window, quit( ) kills all windows and app;  top-level
# windows have title, icon, iconify/deiconify and protocol for wm events;
# there always is an app root window, whether by default or created as an
# explicit Tk() object; all top-level windows are containers, but never
# packed/gridded; Toplevel is like frame, but new window, and can have menu;
###########################################################################

from Tkinter import *
root = Tk( )                                              # explicit root

trees = [('The Larch!',           'light blue'),
         ('The Pine!',            'light green'),
         ('The Giant Redwood!',   'red')]

for (tree, color) in trees:
    win = Toplevel(root)                                  # new window
    win.title('Sing...')                                 # set border
    win.protocol('WM_DELETE_WINDOW', lambda:0)           # ignore close
    win.iconbitmap('py-blue-trans-out.ico')              # not red Tk

    msg = Button(win, text=tree, command=win.destroy)    # kills one win
    msg.pack(expand=YES, fill=BOTH)
    msg.config(padx=10, pady=10, bd=10, relief=RAISED)
    msg.config(bg='black', fg=color, font=('times', 30, 'bold italic'))

root.title('Lumberjack demo')
Label(root, text='Main window', width=30).pack( )
Button(root, text='Quit All', command=root.quit).pack( ) # kills all app
root.mainloop( )
```

This program adds widgets to the Tk root window, immediately pops up three Toplevel windows with attached buttons, and uses special top-level protocols. When run, it generates the scene captured in living black-and-white in Figure 9-4 (the buttons' text shows up blue, green, and red on a color display).

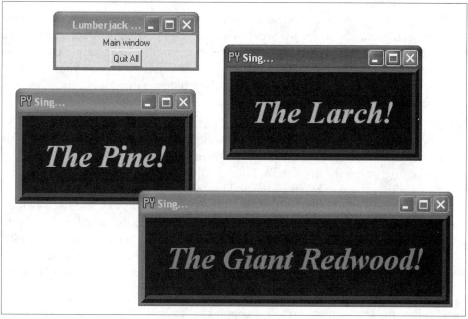

Figure 9-4. Three Toplevel windows with configurations

There are a few operational details worth noticing here, all of which are more obvious if you run this script on your machine:

Intercepting closes: protocol
> Because the window manager close event has been intercepted by this script using the top-level widget protocol method, pressing the X in the top-right corner doesn't do anything in the three Toplevel pop ups. The name string WM_DELETE_WINDOW identifies the close operation. You can use this interface to disallow closes apart from the widgets your script creates. The function created by this script's lambda:0 does nothing but return zero.

Killing one window: destroy
> Pressing the big black buttons in any one of the three pop ups only kills that pop up, because the pop up runs the widget destroy method. The other windows live on, much as you would expect of a pop-up dialog window.

Killing all windows: quit
> To kill all the windows at once and end the GUI application (really, its active mainloop call), the root window's button runs the quit method instead. Pressing the root window's button ends the application.

Window titles: `title`

As introduced in Chapter 8, top-level window widgets (Tk and Toplevel) have a `title` method that lets you change the text displayed on the top border. Here, the window title text is set to the string 'Sing...' to override the default 'tk'.

Window icons: `iconbitmap`

The `iconbitmap` method changes a top-level window's icon. It accepts an icon or bitmap file and uses it for the window's icon graphic when it is both minimized and open. On Windows, pass in the name of a *.ico* file (this example uses one in the current directory); it will replace the normal red "Tk" icon that normally appears in the upper-lefthand corner of the window as well as in the Windows taskbar.

Geometry management

Top-level windows are containers for other widgets, much like a standalone Frame. Unlike frames, though, top-level window widgets are never themselves packed (or gridded, or placed). To embed widgets, this script passes its windows as parent arguments to label and button constructors. It is also possible to fetch the maximum window size (the physical screen display size, as a [width, height] tuple) with the `maxsize()` method, as well as set the initial size of a window with the top-level `geometry("widthhxheight+x+y")` method. It is generally easier and more user-friendly to let Tkinter (or your users) work out window size for you, but display size may be used for tasks such as scaling images (see the discussion on PyPhoto in Chapter 12 for an example).

In addition, top-level window widgets support other kinds of protocols that we will utilize later on in this tour:

State

The `iconify` and `withdraw` top-level window object methods allow scripts to hide and erase a window on the fly; `deiconify` redraws a hidden or erased window. The state method queries or changes a window's state; valid states passed in or returned include `iconic`, `withdrawn`, `zoomed` (full screen on Windows; use geometry elsewhere), and `normal` (large enough for window content). The methods `lift` and `lower` raise and lower a window with respect to its siblings (`lift` is the Tk raise command). See the alarm scripts near the end of Chapter 10 for usage.

Menus

Each top-level window can have its own window menus too; both the Tk and the Toplevel widgets have a menu option used to associate a horizontal menu bar of pull-down option lists. This menu bar looks as it should on each platform on which your scripts are run. We'll explore menus early in Chapter 10.

Most top-level window-manager-related methods can also be named with a "wm_" at the front; for instance, state and protocol can also be called `wm_state` and `wm_protocol`.

Notice that the script in Example 9-3 passes its `Toplevel` constructor calls an explicit parent widget—the Tk root window (that is, `Toplevel(root)`). `Toplevel`s can be associated with a parent just as other widgets can, even though they are not visually embedded in their parents. I coded the script this way to avoid what seems like an odd feature; if coded instead like this:

```
win = Toplevel()                              # new window
```

and if no Tk root yet exists, this call actually generates a default Tk root window to serve as the `Toplevel`'s parent, just like any other widget call without a parent argument. The problem is that this makes the position of the following line crucial:

```
root = Tk()                                   # explicit root
```

If this line shows up above the `Toplevel` calls, it creates the single root window as expected. But if you move this line below the `Toplevel` calls, Tkinter creates a default Tk root window that is different from the one created by the script's explicit Tk call. You wind up with two Tk roots just as in Example 9-5. Move the Tk call below the `Toplevel` calls and rerun it to see what I mean. You'll get a fourth window that is completely empty! As a rule of thumb, to avoid such oddities, make your Tk root windows early on and make them explicit.

All of the top-level protocol interfaces are available only on top-level window widgets, but you can often access them by going through other widgets' master attributes—links to the widget parents. For example, to set the title of a window in which a frame is contained, say something like this:

```
theframe.master.title('Spam demo')     # master is the container window
```

Naturally, you should do so only if you're sure that the frame will be used in only one kind of window. General-purpose attachable components coded as classes, for instance, should leave window property settings to their client applications.

Top-level widgets have additional tools, some of which we may not meet in this book. For instance, under Unix window managers, you can also set the name used on the window's icon (`iconname`). Because some icon options may be useful when scripts run on Unix only, see other Tk and Tkinter resources for more details on this topic. For now, the next scheduled stop on this tour explores one of the more common uses of top-level windows.

Dialogs

Dialogs are windows popped up by a script to provide or request additional information. They come in two flavors, modal and nonmodal:

Modal

These dialogs block the rest of the interface until the dialog window is dismissed; users must reply to the dialog before the program continues.

Nonmodal

These dialogs can remain on-screen indefinitely without interfering with other windows in the interface; they can usually accept inputs at any time.

Regardless of their modality, dialogs are generally implemented with the Toplevel window object we met in the prior section, whether you make the Toplevel or not. There are essentially three ways to present pop-up dialogs to users with Tkinter: by using common dialog calls, by using the now-dated Dialog object, and by creating custom dialog windows with Toplevels and other kinds of widgets. Let's explore the basics of all three schemes.

Standard (Common) Dialogs

Because standard dialog calls are simpler, let's start here first. Tkinter comes with a collection of precoded dialog windows that implement many of the most common pop ups programs generate—file selection dialogs, error and warning pop ups, and question and answer prompts. They are called *standard dialogs* (and sometimes *common dialogs*) because they are part of the Tkinter library, and they use platform-specific library calls to look like they should on each platform. A Tkinter file open dialog, for instance, looks like any other on Windows.

All standard dialog calls are modal (they don't return until the dialog box is dismissed by the user), and they block the program's main window while they are displayed. Scripts can customize these dialogs' windows by passing message text, titles, and the like. Since they are so simple to use, let's jump right into Example 9-6.

Example 9-6. PP3E\Gui\Tour\dlg1.pyw

```
from Tkinter import *
from tkMessageBox import *

def callback():
    if askyesno('Verify', 'Do you really want to quit?'):
        showwarning('Yes', 'Quit not yet implemented')
    else:
        showinfo('No', 'Quit has been cancelled')

errmsg = 'Sorry, no Spam allowed!'
Button(text='Quit', command=callback).pack(fill=X)
Button(text='Spam', command=(lambda: showerror('Spam', errmsg))).pack(fill=X)
mainloop()
```

A lambda anonymous function is used here to wrap the call to showerror so that it is passed two hardcoded arguments (remember, button-press callbacks get no arguments from Tkinter itself). When run, this script creates the main window in Figure 9-5.

Figure 9-5. dlg1 main window: buttons to trigger pop ups

When you press this window's Quit button, the dialog in Figure 9-6 pops up by calling the standard askyesno function in the tkmessagebox module. This looks different on Unix and Macintosh systems, but it looks like you'd expect when run on Windows. This dialog blocks the program until the user clicks one of its buttons; if the dialog's Yes button is clicked (or the Enter key is pressed), the dialog call returns with a true value and the script pops up the standard dialog in Figure 9-7 by calling showwarning.

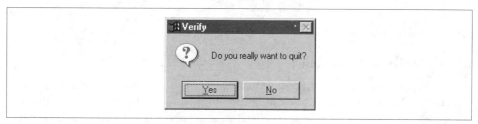

Figure 9-6. dlg1 askyesno dialog (Windows)

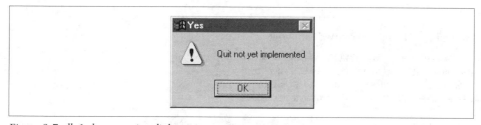

Figure 9-7. dlg1 showwarning dialog

There is nothing the user can do with Figure 9-7's dialog but press OK. If No is clicked in Figure 9-6's quit verification dialog, a showinfo call creates the pop up in Figure 9-8 instead. Finally, if the Spam button is clicked in the main window, the standard dialog captured in Figure 9-9 is generated with the standard showerror call.

All of this makes for a lot of window pop ups, of course, and you need to be careful not to rely on these dialogs too much (it's generally better to use input fields in long-lived windows than to distract the user with pop ups). But where appropriate, such pop ups save coding time and provide a nice, native look-and-feel.

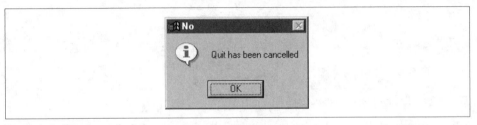

Figure 9-8. dlg1 showinfo dialog

Figure 9-9. dlg1 showerror dialog

A "smart" and reusable Quit button

Let's put some of these canned dialogs to better use. Example 9-7 implements an attachable Quit button that uses standard dialogs to verify the quit request. Because it's a class, it can be attached and reused in any application that needs a verifying Quit button. Because it uses standard dialogs, it looks as it should on each GUI platform.

Example 9-7. PP3E\Gui\Tour\xd5 uitter.py

```
###############################################
# a Quit button that verifies exit requests;
# to reuse, attach an instance to other GUIs
###############################################

from Tkinter import *                          # get widget classes
from tkMessageBox import askokcancel           # get canned std dialog

class Quitter(Frame):                          # subclass our GUI
    def __init__(self, parent=None):           # constructor method
        Frame.__init__(self, parent)
        self.pack()
        widget = Button(self, text='Quit', command=self.quit)
        widget.pack(side=LEFT)
    def quit(self):
        ans = askokcancel('Verify exit', "Really quit?")
        if ans: Frame.quit(self)

if __name__ == '__main__': Quitter().mainloop()
```

This module is mostly meant to be used elsewhere, but it puts up the button it implements when run standalone. Figure 9-10 shows the Quit button itself in the upper left, and the askokcancel verification dialog that pops up when Quit is pressed.

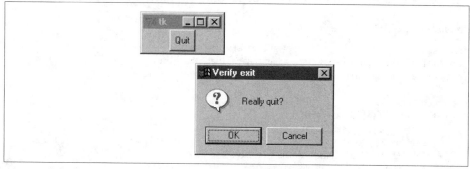

Figure 9-10. Quitter, with askokcancel dialog

If you press OK here, Quitter runs the Frame quit method to end the GUI to which this button is attached (really, the mainloop call). But to really understand how such a spring-loaded button can be useful, we need to move on and study a client GUI in the next section.

A dialog demo launcher bar

So far, we've seen a handful of standard dialogs, but there are quite a few more. Instead of just throwing these up in dull screenshots, though, let's write a Python demo script to generate them on demand. Here's one way to do it. First of all, in Example 9-8 we write a module to define a table that maps a demo name to a standard dialog call (and we use lambda to wrap the call if we need to pass extra arguments to the dialog function).

Example 9-8. PP3E\Gui\Tour\dialogTable.py

```
# define a name:callback demos table

from tkFileDialog    import askopenfilename       # get standard dialogs
from tkColorChooser  import askcolor              # they live in Lib/lib-tk
from tkMessageBox    import askquestion, showerror
from tkSimpleDialog  import askfloat

demos = {
    'Open':  askopenfilename,
    'Color': askcolor,
    'Query': lambda: askquestion('Warning', 'You typed "rm *"\nConfirm?'),
    'Error': lambda: showerror('Error!', "He's dead, Jim"),
    'Input': lambda: askfloat('Entry', 'Enter credit card number')
}
```

I put this table in a module so that it might be reused as the basis of other demo scripts later (dialogs are more fun than printing to stdout). Next, we'll write a Python script, shown in Example 9-9, which simply generates buttons for all of this table's entries—use its keys as button labels and its values as button callback handlers.

Example 9-9. PP3E\Gui\Tour\demoDlg.py

```
from Tkinter import *              # get base widget set
from dialogTable import demos      # button callback handlers
from quitter import Quitter        # attach a quit object to me

class Demo(Frame):
    def __init__(self, parent=None):
        Frame.__init__(self, parent)
        self.pack()
        Label(self, text="Basic demos").pack()
        for (key, value) in demos.items():
            Button(self, text=key, command=value).pack(side=TOP, fill=BOTH)
        Quitter(self).pack(side=TOP, fill=BOTH)

if __name__ == '__main__': Demo().mainloop()
```

This script creates the window shown in Figure 9-11 when run as a standalone program; it's a bar of demo buttons that simply route control back to the values of the table in the module dialogTable when pressed.

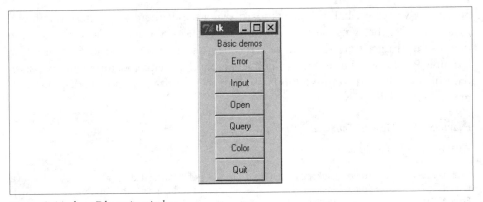

Figure 9-11. demoDlg main window

Notice that because this script is driven by the contents of the dialogTable module's dictionary, we can change the set of demo buttons displayed by changing just dialogTable (we don't need to change any executable code in demoDlg). Also note that the Quit button here is an attached instance of the Quitter class of the prior section—it's at least one bit of code that you never have to write again.

We've already seen some of the dialogs triggered by this demo bar window's other buttons, so I'll just step through the new ones here. Pressing the main window's Query button, for example, generates the standard pop up in Figure 9-12.

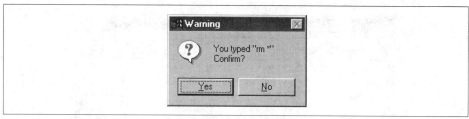

Figure 9-12. demoDlg query, askquestion dialog

This askquestion dialog looks like the askyesno we saw earlier, but actually it returns either string "yes" or "no" (askyesno and askokcancel return 1 or 0, true or false). Pressing the demo bar's Input button generates the standard askfloat dialog box shown in Figure 9-13.

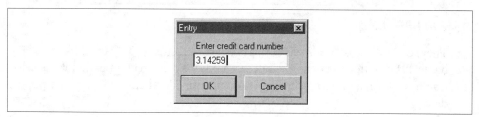

Figure 9-13. demoDlg input, askfloat dialog

This dialog automatically checks the input for valid floating-point syntax before it returns, and is representative of a collection of single-value input dialogs (askinteger and askstring prompt for integer and string inputs too). It returns the input as a floating-point number object (not as a string) when the OK button or Enter key is pressed, or the Python None object if the user clicks Cancel. Its two relatives return the input as integer and string objects instead.

When the demo bar's Open button is pressed, we get the standard file open dialog made by calling askopenfilename and captured in Figure 9-14. This is Windows' look-and-feel; it looks radically different on Linux, but appropriately so.

A similar dialog for selecting a save-as filename is produced by calling asksaveasfilename (see the Text widget section in Chapter 10 for an example). Both file dialogs let the user navigate through the filesystem to select a subject filename, which is returned with its full directory pathname when Open is pressed; an empty string comes back if Cancel is pressed instead. Both also have additional protocols not demonstrated by this example:

- They can be passed a filetypes keyword argument—a set of name patterns used to select files, which appear in the "Files of type" pull down at the bottom of the dialog.

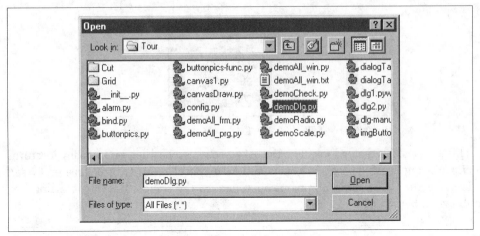

Figure 9-14. demoDlg open, askopenfilename dialog

- They can be passed an `initialdir` (start directory), `initialfile` (for "File name"), `title` (for the dialog window), `defaultextension` (appended if the selection has none), and `parent` (to appear as an embedded child instead of a pop-up dialog).

- They can be made to remember the last directory selected by using exported objects instead of these function calls.

Another common dialog call in the `tkFileDialog` module, `askdirectory`, can be used to pop up a dialog that allows users to choose a directory rather than a file. It presents a tree view that users can navigate to pick the desired directory, and it accepts keyword arguments including `initialdir` and `title`. The corresponding `Directory` object remembers the last directory selected and starts there the next time the dialog is shown.

We'll use most of these interfaces later in the book, especially for the file dialogs in the PyEdit example in Chapter 12, but feel free to flip ahead for more details now. The directory selection dialog will show up in the PyPhoto example in Chapter 12 and the PyMailGUI example in Chapter 15; again, skip ahead for code and screen-shots.

Finally, the demo bar's Color button triggers a standard `askcolor` call, which generates the standard color selection dialog shown in Figure 9-15.

If you press its OK button, it returns a data structure that identifies the selected color, which can be used in all color contexts in Tkinter. It includes RGB values and a hexadecimal color string (e.g., `((160, 160, 160), '#a0a0a0')`). More on how this tuple can be useful in a moment. If you press Cancel, the script gets back a tuple containing two nones (`None`s of the Python variety, that is).

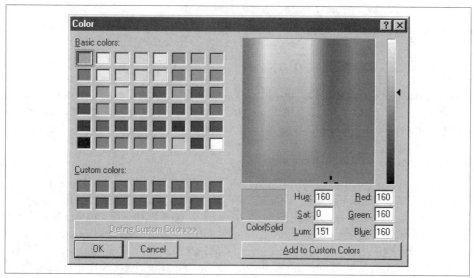

Figure 9-15. demoDlg color, askcolor dialog

Printing dialog results (and passing callback data with lambdas)

The dialog demo launcher bar displays standard dialogs and can be made to display others by simply changing the dialogTable module it imports. As coded, though, it really shows only dialogs; it would also be nice to see their return values so that we know how to use them in scripts. Example 9-10 adds printing of standard dialog results to the stdout standard output stream.

Example 9-10. PP3E\Gui\Tour\demoDlg-print.py

```
#############################################################################
# same, but show return values of dialog calls;  the lambda saves
# data from the local scope to be passed to the handler (button press
# handlers normally get no arguments) and works just like a nested def
# statement of this form: def func(key=key): self.printit(key)
#############################################################################

from Tkinter import *                # get base widget set
from dialogTable import demos        # button callback handlers
from quitter import Quitter          # attach a quit object to me

class Demo(Frame):
    def __init__(self, parent=None):
        Frame.__init__(self, parent)
        self.pack()
        Label(self, text="Basic demos").pack()
        for (key, value) in demos.items():
            func = (lambda key=key: self.printit(key))
            Button(self, text=key, command=func).pack(side=TOP, fill=BOTH)
        Quitter(self).pack(side=TOP, fill=BOTH)
```

Example 9-10. PP3E\Gui\Tour\demoDlg-print.py (continued)

```
    def printit(self, name):
        print name, 'returns =>', demos[name]()      # fetch, call, print

if __name__ == '__main__': Demo().mainloop()
```

This script builds the same main button-bar window, but notice that the callback handler is an anonymous function made with a lambda now, not a direct reference to dialog calls in the imported dialogTable dictionary:

```
    # use enclosing scope lookup
    func = (lambda key=key: self.printit(key))
```

We talked about this in the prior chapter's tutorial, but this is the first time we've actually used lambda like this, so let's get the facts straight. Because button-press callbacks are run with no arguments, if we need to pass extra data to the handler, it must be wrapped in an object that remembers that extra data and passes it along. Here, a button press runs the function generated by the lambda, an indirect call layer that retains information from the enclosing scope. The net effect is that the real handler, printit, receives an extra required name argument giving the demo associated with the button pressed, even though this argument wasn't passed back from Tkinter itself. The lambda remembers and passes on state information.

Notice, though, that this lambda function's body references both self and key in the enclosing method's local scope. In recent Pythons, the reference to self just works because of the enclosing function scope lookup rules, but we need to pass key in explicitly with a default argument or else it will be the same in all the generated lambda functions—the value it has after the last loop iteration. As we learned in Chapter 8, enclosing scope references are resolved when the nested function is called, but defaults are resolved when the nested function is created. Because self won't change after the function is made, we can rely on the scope lookup rules for that name, but not for key.

In earlier Pythons, default arguments were required to pass all values in from enclosing scopes explicitly, using either of these two techniques:

```
    # use simple defaults
    func = (lambda self=self, name=key: self.printit(name))

    # use a bound method default
    func = (lambda handler=self.printit, name=key: handler(name))
```

Today, we can get away with the simpler technique, though we still need a default for the loop variable, and you may still see the default forms in older Python code.

Note that the parentheses around the lambdas are not required here; I add them as a personal style preference just to set the lambda off from its surrounding code (your mileage can vary). Also notice that the lambda does the same work as a nested def statement here; in practice, though, the lambda could appear within the call to

Button itself because it is an expression and it need not be assigned to a name. The following two forms are equivalent:

```
for (key, value) in demos.items():
    func = (lambda key=key: self.printit(key))

for (key, value) in demos.items():
    def func(key=key): self.printit(key)
```

You can also use a callable class object here that retains state as instance attributes (see the tutorial's __call__ example in Chapter 8 for hints). But as a rule of thumb, if you want a lambda's result to use any names from the enclosing scope when later called, either simply name them and let Python save their values for future use, or pass them in with defaults to save the values they have at lambda function creation time. The latter scheme is required only if the required variable may change before the callback occurs.

When run, this script prints dialog return values; here is the output after clicking all the demo buttons in the main window and picking both Cancel/No and OK/Yes buttons in each dialog:

```
C:\...\PP3E\Gui\Tour>python demoDlg-print.py
Error returns => ok
Input returns => None
Input returns => 3.14159
Open returns =>
Open returns => C:/PP2ndEd/examples/PP3E/Gui/Tour/demoDlg-print.py
Query returns => no
Query returns => yes
Color returns => (None, None)
Color returns => ((160, 160, 160), '#a0a0a0')
```

Now that I've shown you these dialog results, I want to next show you how one of them can actually be useful.

Letting users select colors on the fly

The standard color selection dialog isn't just another pretty face—scripts can pass the hexadecimal color string it returns to the bg and fg widget color configuration options we met earlier. That is, bg and fg accept both a color name (e.g., blue) and an askcolor result string that starts with a # (e.g., the #a0a0a0 in the last output line of the prior section).

This adds another dimension of customization to Tkinter GUIs: instead of hardcoding colors in your GUI products, you can provide a button that pops up color selectors that let users choose color preferences on the fly. Simply pass the color string to widget config methods in callback handlers, as in Example 9-11.

Example 9-11. PP3E\Gui\Tour\setcolor.py

```
from Tkinter import *
from tkColorChooser import askcolor

def setBgColor():
    (triple, hexstr) = askcolor()
    if hexstr:
        print hexstr
        push.config(bg=hexstr)

root = Tk()
push = Button(root, text='Set Background Color', command=setBgColor)
push.config(height=3, font=('times', 20, 'bold'))
push.pack(expand=YES, fill=BOTH)
root.mainloop()
```

This script creates the window in Figure 9-16 when launched (its button's background is a sort of green, but you'll have to trust me on this). Pressing the button pops up the color selection dialog shown earlier; the color you pick in that dialog becomes the background color of this button after you press OK.

Figure 9-16. setcolor main window

Color strings are also printed to the stdout stream (the console window); run this on your computer to experiment with available color settings:

```
C:\...\PP3E\Gui\Tour>python setcolor.py
#c27cc5
#5fe28c
#69d8cd
```

Other standard dialog calls

We've seen most of the standard dialogs and will use these pop ups in examples throughout the rest of this book. But for more details on other calls and options available, either consult other Tkinter documentation or browse the source code of the modules used at the top of the dialogTable module; all are simple Python files installed in the *lib-tk* subdirectory of the Python source library on your machine. And keep this demo bar example filed away for future reference; we'll reuse it later in the tour when we meet other button-like widgets.

The Old-Style Dialog Module

In older Python code, you may see dialogs occasionally coded with the standard Dialog module. This is a bit dated now, and it uses an X Windows look-and-feel; but just in case you run across such code in your Python maintenance excursions, Example 9-12 gives you a feel for the interface.

Example 9-12. PP3E\Gui\Tour\dlg-old.py

```
from Tkinter import *
from Dialog import Dialog

class OldDialogDemo(Frame):
    def __init__(self, master=None):
        Frame.__init__(self, master)
        Pack.config(self)  # same as self.pack()
        Button(self, text='Pop1', command=self.dialog1).pack()
        Button(self, text='Pop2', command=self.dialog2).pack()
    def dialog1(self):
        ans = Dialog(self,
                     title   = 'Popup Fun!',
                     text    = 'An example of a popup-dialog '
                               'box, using older "Dialog.py".',
                     bitmap  = 'questhead',
                     default = 0, strings = ('Yes', 'No', 'Cancel'))
        if ans.num == 0: self.dialog2()
    def dialog2(self):
        Dialog(self, title    = 'HAL-9000',
                     text     = "I'm afraid I can't let you do that, Dave...",
                     bitmap   = 'hourglass',
                     default  = 0, strings = ('spam', 'SPAM'))

if __name__ == '__main__': OldDialogDemo().mainloop()
```

If you supply Dialog a tuple of button labels and a message, you get back the index of the button pressed (the leftmost is index zero). Dialog windows are modal: the rest of the application's windows are disabled until the Dialog receives a response from the user. When you press the Pop2 button in the main window created by this script, the second dialog pops up, as shown in Figure 9-17.

Figure 9-17. Old-style dialog

This is running on Windows, and as you can see, it is nothing like what you would expect on that platform for a question dialog. In fact, this dialog generates an X Windows look-and-feel, regardless of the underlying platform. Because of both Dialog's appearance and the extra complexity required to program it, you are probably better off using the standard dialog calls of the prior section instead.

Custom Dialogs

The dialogs we've seen so far have a standard appearance and interaction. They are fine for many purposes, but often we need something a bit more custom. For example, forms that request multiple field inputs (e.g., name, age, shoe size) aren't directly addressed by the common dialog library. We could pop up one single-input dialog in turn for each requested field, but that isn't exactly user friendly.

Custom dialogs support arbitrary interfaces, but they are also the most complicated to program. Even so, there's not much to it—simply create a pop-up window as a Toplevel with attached widgets, and arrange a callback handler to fetch user inputs entered in the dialog (if any) and to destroy the window. To make such a custom dialog modal, we also need to wait for a reply by giving the window input focus, making other windows inactive, and waiting for an event. Example 9-13 illustrates the basics.

Example 9-13. PP3E\Gui\Tour\dlg-custom.py

```
import sys
from Tkinter import *
makemodal = (len(sys.argv) > 1)

def dialog():
    win = Toplevel()                                     # make a new window
    Label(win, text='Hard drive reformatted!').pack()   # add a few widgets
    Button(win, text='OK', command=win.destroy).pack()  # set destroy callback
    if makemodal:
        win.focus_set()          # take over input focus,
        win.grab_set()           # disable other windows while I'm open,
        win.wait_window()        # and wait here until win destroyed
    print 'dialog exit'          # else returns right away

root = Tk()
Button(root, text='popup', command=dialog).pack()
root.mainloop()
```

This script is set up to create a pop-up dialog window in either modal or nonmodal mode, depending on its makemodal global variable. If it is run with no command-line arguments, it picks nonmodal style, captured in Figure 9-18.

The window in the upper right is the root window here; pressing its "popup" button creates a new pop-up dialog window. Because dialogs are nonmodal in this mode,

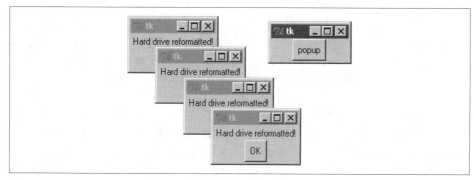

Figure 9-18. Nonmodal custom dialogs at work

the root window remains active after a dialog is popped up. In fact, nonmodal dialogs never block other windows, so you can keep pressing the root's button to generate as many copies of the pop-up window as will fit on your screen. Any or all of the pop ups can be killed by pressing their OK buttons, without killing other windows in this display.

Making custom dialogs modal

Now, when the script is run with a command-line argument (e.g., python dlg-custom.py 1), it makes its pop ups modal instead. Because modal dialogs grab all of the interface's attention, the main window becomes inactive in this mode until the pop up is killed; you can't even click on it to reactivate it while the dialog is open. Because of that, you can never make more than one copy of the pop up on-screen at once, as shown in Figure 9-19.

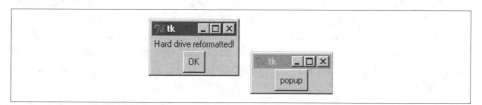

Figure 9-19. A modal custom dialog at work

In fact, the call to the dialog function in this script doesn't return until the dialog window on the left is dismissed by pressing its OK button. The net effect is that modal dialogs impose a function call-like model on an otherwise event-driven programming model; user inputs can be processed right away, not in a callback handler triggered at some arbitrary point in the future.

Forcing such a linear control flow on a GUI takes a bit of extra work, though. The secret to locking other windows and waiting for a reply boils down to three lines of code, which are a general pattern repeated in most custom modal dialogs.

`win.focus_set()`

> Makes the window take over the application's input focus, as if it had been clicked with the mouse to make it the active window. This method is also known by the synonym `focus`, and it's also common to set the focus on an input widget within the dialog (e.g., an `Entry`) rather than on the entire window.

`win.grab_set()`

> Disables all other windows in the application until this one is destroyed. The user cannot interact with other windows in the program while a grab is set.

`win.wait_window()`

> Pauses the caller until the `win` widget is destroyed, but keeps the main event-processing loop (`mainloop`) active during the pause. That means that the GUI at large remains active during the wait; its windows redraw themselves if covered and uncovered, for example. When the window is destroyed with the `destroy` method, it is erased from the screen, the application grab is automatically released, and this method call finally returns.

Because the script waits for a window destroy event, it must also arrange for a callback handler to destroy the window in response to interaction with widgets in the dialog window (the only window active). This example's dialog is simply informational, so its OK button calls the window's `destroy` method. In user-input dialogs, we might instead install an Enter key-press callback handler that fetches data typed into an `Entry` widget and then calls `destroy` (see later in this chapter).

Other ways to be modal

Modal dialogs are typically implemented by waiting for a newly created pop-up window's destroy event, as in this example. But other schemes are viable too. For example, it's possible to create dialog windows ahead of time, and show and hide them as needed with the top-level window's `deiconify` and `withdraw` methods (see the alarm scripts near the end of Chapter 10 for details). Given that window creation speed is generally fast enough as to appear instantaneous today, this is much less common than making and destroying a window from scratch on each interaction.

It's also possible to implement a modal state by waiting for a Tkinter variable to change its value, instead of waiting for a window to be destroyed. See this chapter's discussion of Tkinter variables (which are class objects, not normal Python variables), and the `wait_variable` method discussed near the end of Chapter 10, for more details. This scheme allows a long-lived dialog box's callback handler to signal a state change to a waiting main program, without having to destroy the dialog box.

Finally, if you call the `mainloop` method recursively, the call won't return until the widget `quit` method has been invoked. The `quit` method terminates a `mainloop` call, and so normally ends a GUI program. But it will simply exit a recursive `mainloop` level if one is active. Because of this, modal dialogs can also be written without wait method calls if you are careful. For instance, Example 9-14 works the same way as `dlg-custom`.

Example 9-14. PP3E\Gui\Tour\dlg-recursive.py

```
from Tkinter import *

def dialog( ):
    win = Toplevel( )                              # make a new window
    Label(win, text='Hard drive reformatted!').pack( )   # add a few widgets
    Button(win, text='OK', command=win.quit).pack( )     # set quit callback
    win.protocol('WM_DELETE_WINDOW', win.quit)           # quit on wm close too!

    win.focus_set( )        # take over input focus,
    win.grab_set( )         # disable other windows while I'm open,
    win.mainloop( )         # and start a nested event loop to wait
    win.destroy( )
    print 'dialog exit'

root = Tk( )
Button(root, text='popup', command=dialog).pack( )
root.mainloop( )
```

If you go this route, be sure to call quit rather than destroy in dialog callback handlers (destroy doesn't terminate the mainloop level), and be sure to use protocol to make the window border close button call quit too (or else it won't end the recursive mainloop level call and will generate odd error messages when your program finally exits). Because of this extra complexity, you're probably better off using wait_window or wait_variable, not recursive mainloop calls.

We'll see how to build form-like dialogs with labels and input fields later in this chapter when we meet Entry, and again when we study the grid manager in Chapter 10. For more custom dialog examples, see ShellGui (Chapter 11), PyMailGUI (Chapter 15), PyCalc (Chapter 21), and the nonmodal *form.py* (Chapter 13). Here, we're moving on to learn more about events that will prove to be useful currency at later tour destinations.

Binding Events

We met the bind widget method in the prior chapter, when we used it to catch button presses in the tutorial. Because bind is commonly used in conjunction with other widgets (e.g., to catch return key presses for input boxes), we're going to make a stop early in the tour here as well. Example 9-15 illustrates more bind event protocols.

Example 9-15. PP3E\Gui\Tour\bind.py

```
from Tkinter import *

def showPosEvent(event):
    print 'Widget=%s X=%s Y=%s' % (event.widget, event.x, event.y)

def showAllEvent(event):
    print event
```

Example 9-15. PP3E\Gui\Tour\bind.py (continued)

```
      for attr in dir(event):
          print attr, '=>', getattr(event, attr)

def onKeyPress(event):
    print 'Got key press:', event.char

def onArrowKey(event):
    print 'Got up arrow key press'

def onReturnKey(event):
    print 'Got return key press'

def onLeftClick(event):
    print 'Got left mouse button click:',
    showPosEvent(event)

def onRightClick(event):
    print 'Got right mouse button click:',
    showPosEvent(event)

def onMiddleClick(event):
    print 'Got middle mouse button click:',
    showPosEvent(event)
    showAllEvent(event)

def onLeftDrag(event):
    print 'Got left mouse button drag:',
    showPosEvent(event)

def onDoubleLeftClick(event):
    print 'Got double left mouse click',
    showPosEvent(event)
    tkroot.quit()

tkroot = Tk()
labelfont = ('courier', 20, 'bold')                # family, size, style
widget = Label(tkroot, text='Hello bind world')
widget.config(bg='red', font=labelfont)            # red background, large font
widget.config(height=5, width=20)                  # initial size: lines,chars
widget.pack(expand=YES, fill=BOTH)

widget.bind('<Button-1>',   onLeftClick)           # mouse button clicks
widget.bind('<Button-3>',   onRightClick)
widget.bind('<Button-2>',   onMiddleClick)         # middle=both on some mice
widget.bind('<Double-1>',   onDoubleLeftClick)     # click left twice
widget.bind('<B1-Motion>', onLeftDrag)             # click left and move

widget.bind('<KeyPress>',   onKeyPress)            # all keyboard presses
widget.bind('<Up>',         onArrowKey)            # arrow button pressed
widget.bind('<Return>',     onReturnKey)           # return/enter key pressed
widget.focus()                                     # or bind keypress to tkroot
tkroot.title('Click Me')
tkroot.mainloop()
```

Most of this file consists of callback handler functions triggered when bound events occur. As we learned in Chapter 8, these callbacks receive an event object argument that gives details about the event that fired. Technically, this argument is an instance of the Tkinter Event class, and its details are attributes; most of the callbacks simply trace events by displaying relevant event attributes.

When run, this script makes the window shown in Figure 9-20; it's mostly intended just as a surface for clicking and pressing event triggers.

Figure 9-20. A bind window for the clicking

The black-and-white medium of the book you're holding won't really do justice to this script. When run live, it uses the configuration options shown earlier to make the window show up as black on red, with a large Courier font. You'll have to take my word for it (or run this on your own).

But the main point of this example is to demonstrate other kinds of event binding protocols at work. We saw a script that intercepted left and double-left mouse clicks with the widget bind method earlier; the script here demonstrates other kinds of events that are commonly caught with bind:

<KeyPress>

> To catch the press of a single key on the keyboard, register a handler for the <KeyPress> event identifier; this is a lower-level way to input data in GUI programs than the Entry widget covered in the next section. The key pressed is returned in ASCII form in the event object passed to the callback handler (event.char). Other attributes in the event structure identify the key pressed in lower-level detail. Key presses can be intercepted by the top-level root window widget or by a widget that has been assigned keyboard focus with the focus method used by this script.

<B1-Motion>

> This script also catches mouse motion while a button is held down: the registered <B1-Motion> event handler is called every time the mouse is moved while the left button is pressed, and receives the current X/Y coordinates of the mouse pointer in its event argument (event.x, event.y). Such information can be used to implement object moves, drag-and-drop, pixel-level painting, and so on (e.g., see the PyDraw examples in Chapter 12).

‹Button-3›, ‹Button-2›

This script also catches right and middle mouse button clicks (known as buttons 3 and 2). To make the middle button 2 click work on a two-button mouse, try clicking both buttons at the same time; if that doesn't work, check your mouse setting in your properties interface (the Control Panel on Windows).

‹Return›, ‹Up›

To catch more specific kinds of key presses, this script registers for the Return/Enter and up-arrow key press events; these events would otherwise be routed to the general ‹KeyPress› handler and require event analysis.

Here is what shows up in the stdout output stream after a left click, right click, left click and drag, a few key presses, a Return and up-arrow press, and a final double-left click to exit. When you press the left mouse button and drag it around on the display, you'll get lots of drag event messages; one is printed for every move during the drag (and one Python callback is run for each):

```
C:\...\PP3E\Gui\Tour>python bind.py
Got left mouse button click: Widget=.7871632 X=209 Y=79
Got right mouse button click: Widget=.7871632 X=209 Y=79
Got left mouse button click: Widget=.7871632 X=83 Y=63
Got left mouse button drag: Widget=.7871632 X=83 Y=65
Got left mouse button drag: Widget=.7871632 X=84 Y=66
Got left mouse button drag: Widget=.7871632 X=85 Y=66
Got left mouse button drag: Widget=.7871632 X=85 Y=67
Got left mouse button drag: Widget=.7871632 X=85 Y=68
Got key press: s
Got key press: p
Got key press: a
Got key press: m
Got key press: 1
Got key press: -
Got key press: 2
Got key press: .
Got return key press
Got up arrow key press
Got left mouse button click: Widget=.7871632 X=85 Y=68
Got double left mouse click Widget=.7871632 X=85 Y=68
```

For mouse-related events, callbacks print the X and Y coordinates of the mouse pointer, in the event object passed in. Coordinates are usually measured in pixels from the upper-left corner (0,0), but are relative to the widget being clicked. Here's what is printed for a left, middle, and double-left click. Notice that the middle-click callback dumps the entire argument—all of the Event object's attributes. Different event types set different event attributes; most key presses put something in char, for instance:

```
C:\...\PP3E\Gui\Tour>python bind.py
Got left mouse button click: Widget=.7871632 X=163 Y=18
Got middle mouse button click: Widget=.7871632 X=152 Y=110
<Tkinter.Event instance at 7b3640>
```

```
char => ??
height => 0
keycode => 2
keysym => ??
keysym_num => 2
num => 2
send_event => 0
serial => 14
state => 0
time => 5726238
type => 4
widget => .7871632
width => 0
x => 152
x_root => 156
y => 110
y_root => 133
Got left mouse button click: Widget=.7871632 X=152 Y=110
Got double left mouse click Widget=.7871632 X=152 Y=110
```

Besides the ones illustrated in this example, a Tkinter script can register to catch additional kinds of bindable events. For example:

- `<ButtonRelease>` fires when a button is released (`<ButtonPress>` is run when the button first goes down).

- `<Motion>` is triggered when a mouse pointer is moved.

- `<Enter>` and `<Leave>` handlers intercept mouse entry and exit in a window's display area (useful for automatically highlighting a widget).

- `<Configure>` is invoked when the window is resized, repositioned, and so on (e.g., the event object's width and height give the new window size).

- `<Destroy>` is invoked when the window widget is destroyed (and differs from the protocol mechanism for window manager close button presses).

- `<FocusIn>` and `<FocusOut>` are run as the widget gains and loses focus.

- `<Map>` and `<Unmap>` are run when a window is opened and iconified.

- `<Escape>`, `<BackSpace>`, and `<Tab>` catch other special key presses.

- `<Down>`, `<Left>`, and `<Right>` catch other arrow key presses.

This is not a complete list, and event names can be written with a somewhat sophisticated syntax of their own. For example:

- *Modifiers* can be added to event identifiers to make them even more specific; for instance, `<B1-Motion>` means moving the mouse with the left button pressed, and `<KeyPress-a>` refers to pressing the "a" key only.

- *Synonyms* can be used for some common event names; for instance, `<ButtonPress-1>`, `<Button-1>`, and `<1>` mean a left mouse button press, and `<KeyPress-a>` and `<Key-a>` mean the "a" key. All forms are case sensitive: use `<Key-Escape>`, not `<KEY-ESCAPE>`.

- *Virtual* event identifiers can be defined within double bracket pairs (e.g., <<PasteText>>) to refer to a selection of one or more event sequences.

In the interest of space, though, we'll defer to other Tk and Tkinter reference sources for an exhaustive list of details on this front. Alternatively, changing some of the settings in the example script and rerunning can help clarify some event behavior too; this is Python, after all.

Message and Entry

The Message and Entry widgets allow for display and input of simple text. Both are essentially functional subsets of the Text widget we'll meet later; Text can do everything Message and Entry can, but not vice versa.

Message

The Message widget is simply a place to display text. Although the standard showinfo dialog we met earlier is perhaps a better way to display pop-up messages, Message splits up long strings automatically and flexibly, and can be embedded inside container widgets any time you need to add some read-only text to a display. Moreover, this widget sports more than a dozen configuration options that let you customize its appearance. Example 9-16 and Figure 9-21 illustrate Message basics; see a Tk or Tkinter reference for other options it supports.

Figure 9-21. A Message widget at work

Example 9-16. PP3E\Gui\tour\message.py

```
from Tkinter import *
msg = Message(text="Oh by the way, which one's Pink?")
msg.config(bg='pink', font=('times', 16, 'italic'))
msg.pack()
mainloop()
```

Entry

The Entry widget is a simple, single-line text input field. It is typically used for input fields in form-like dialogs, and anywhere else you need the user to type a value into a field of a larger display. Entry also supports advanced concepts such as scrolling, key bindings for editing, and text selections, but it's simple to use in practice. Example 9-17 builds the input window shown in Figure 9-22.

Figure 9-22. entry1 caught in the act

Example 9-17. PP3E\Gui\tour\entry1.py

```
from Tkinter import *
from quitter import Quitter

def fetch():
    print 'Input => "%s"' % ent.get()                # get text

root = Tk()
ent = Entry(root)
ent.insert(0, 'Type words here')                     # set text
ent.pack(side=TOP, fill=X)                           # grow horiz

ent.focus()                                          # save a click
ent.bind('<Return>', (lambda event: fetch()))        # on enter key
btn = Button(root, text='Fetch', command=fetch)      # and on button
btn.pack(side=LEFT)
Quitter(root).pack(side=RIGHT)
root.mainloop()
```

On startup, the entry1 script fills the input field in this GUI with the text "Type words here" by calling the widget's insert method. Because both the Fetch button and the Enter key are set to trigger the script's fetch callback function, either user event gets and displays the current text in the input field, using the widget's get method:

```
C:\...\PP3E\Gui\Tour>python entry1.py
Input => "Type words here"
Input => "Have a cigar"
```

We met the <Return> event earlier when we studied bind; unlike button presses, these lower-level callbacks get an event argument, so the script uses a lambda wrapper to ignore it. This script also packs the entry field with fill=X to make it expand horizontally with the window (try it out), and it calls the widget focus method to give the entry field input focus when the window first appears. Manually setting the focus like this saves the user from having to click the input field before typing.

Programming Entry widgets

Generally speaking, the values typed into and displayed by Entry widgets are set and fetched with either tied "variable" objects (described later in this chapter) or Entry widget method calls such as this one:

```
ent.insert(0, 'some text')          # set value
value = ent.get()                    # fetch value (a string)
```

The first parameter to the insert method gives the position where the text is to be inserted. Here, "0" means the front because offsets start at zero, and integer 0 and string '0' mean the same thing (Tkinter method arguments are always converted to strings if needed). If the Entry widget might already contain text, you also generally need to delete its contents before setting it to a new value, or else new text will simply be added to the text already present:

```
ent.delete(0, END)                   # first, delete from start to end
ent.insert(0, 'some text')          # then set value
```

The name END here is a preassigned Tkinter constant denoting the end of the widget; we'll revisit it in Chapter 10 when we meet the full-blown and multiple-line Text widget (Entry's more powerful cousin). Since the widget is empty after the deletion, this statement sequence is equivalent to the prior one:

```
ent.delete('0', END)                 # delete from start to end
ent.insert(END, 'some text')        # add at end of empty text
```

Either way, if you don't delete the text first, new text that is inserted is simply added. If you want to see how, try changing the fetch function to look like this; an "x" is added at the beginning and end of the input field on each button or key press:

```
def fetch():
    print 'Input => "%s"' % ent.get()      # get text
    ent.insert(END, 'x')                     # to clear: ent.delete('0', END)
    ent.insert(0, 'x')                       # new text simply added
```

In later examples, we'll also see the Entry widget's state='disabled' option, which makes it read only, as well as its show='*' option, which makes it display each character as a * (useful for password-type inputs). Try this out on your own by changing and running this script, for a quick look. Entry supports other options we'll skip here too; see later examples and other resources for additional details.

Laying out input forms

As mentioned, Entry widgets are often used to get field values in form-like displays. We're going to create such displays often in this book, but to show you how this works in simpler terms, Example 9-18 combines labels and entries to achieve the multiple-input display captured in Figure 9-23.

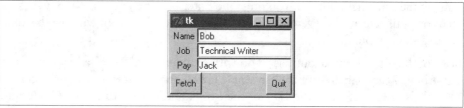

Figure 9-23. entry2 (and entry3) form displays

Example 9-18. PP3E\Gui\Tour\entry2.py

```python
# use Entry widgets directly and lay out by rows

from Tkinter import *
from quitter import Quitter
fields = 'Name', 'Job', 'Pay'

def fetch(entries):
    for entry in entries:
        print 'Input => "%s"' % entry.get()        # get text

def makeform(root, fields):
    entries = []
    for field in fields:
        row = Frame(root)                           # make a new row
        lab = Label(row, width=5, text=field)       # add label, entry
        ent = Entry(row)
        row.pack(side=TOP, fill=X)                  # pack row on top
        lab.pack(side=LEFT)
        ent.pack(side=RIGHT, expand=YES, fill=X)    # grow horizontal
        entries.append(ent)
    return entries

if __name__ == '__main__':
    root = Tk()
    ents = makeform(root, fields)
    root.bind('<Return>', (lambda event: fetch(ents)))
    Button(root, text='Fetch',
                command= (lambda: fetch(ents))).pack(side=LEFT)
    Quitter(root).pack(side=RIGHT)
    root.mainloop()
```

The input fields here are just simple Entry widgets. The script builds an explicit list of these widgets to be used to fetch their values later. Every time you press this window's Fetch button, it grabs the current values in all the input fields and prints them to the standard output stream:

```
C:\...\PP3E\Gui\Tour>python entry2.py
Input => "Bob"
Input => "Technical Writer"
Input => "Jack"
```

You get the same field dump if you press the Enter key anytime this window has the focus on your screen; this event has been bound to the whole root window this time, not to a single input field.

Most of the art in form layout has to do with arranging widgets in a hierarchy. This script builds each label/entry row as a new Frame attached to the window's current TOP; labels are attached to the LEFT of their row, and entries to the RIGHT. Because each row is a distinct Frame, its contents are insulated from other packing going on in this window. The script also arranges for just the entry fields to grow vertically on a resize, as in Figure 9-24.

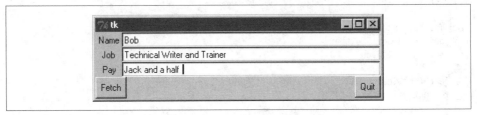

Figure 9-24. entry2 (and entry3) expansion at work

Going modal again

Later on this tour, we'll see how to make similar form layouts with the grid geometry manager. But now that we have a handle on form layout, let's see how to apply the modal dialog techniques we met earlier to a more complex input display.

Example 9-19 uses the prior example's makeform and fetch functions to generate a form and prints its contents, much as before. Here, though, the input fields are attached to a new Toplevel pop-up window created on demand, and an OK button is added to the pop-up window to trigger a window destroy event. As we learned earlier, the wait_window call pauses until the destroy happens.

Example 9-19. PP3E\Gui\Tour\entry2-modal.py

```
# must fetch before destroy with entries

from Tkinter import *
from entry2 import makeform, fetch, fields

def show(entries):
    fetch(entries)                    # must fetch before window destroyed!
    popup.destroy()                   # fails with msgs if stmt order is reversed

def ask():
    global popup
    popup = Toplevel()                # show form in modal dialog window
    ents = makeform(popup, fields)
    Button(popup, text='OK', command=(lambda: show(ents)) ).pack()
    popup.grab_set()
```

Example 9-19. PP3E\Gui\Tour\entry2-modal.py (continued)

```
    popup.focus_set( )
    popup.wait_window( )              # wait for destroy here

root = Tk( )
Button(root, text='Dialog', command=ask).pack( )
root.mainloop( )
```

When you run this code, pressing the button in this program's main window creates the blocking form input dialog in Figure 9-25, as expected.

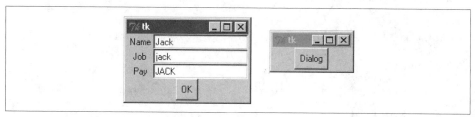

Figure 9-25. entry2-modal (and entry3-modal) displays

But a subtle danger is lurking in this modal dialog code: because it fetches user inputs from Entry widgets embedded in the popped-up display, it must fetch those inputs before destroying the pop-up window in the OK press callback handler. It turns out that a destroy call really does destroy all the child widgets of the window destroyed; trying to fetch values from a destroyed Entry not only doesn't work, but also generates a host of error messages in the console window. Try reversing the statement order in the show function to see for yourself.

To avoid this problem, we can either be careful to fetch before destroying, or use Tkinter variables, the subject of the next section.

Tkinter "variables"

Entry widgets (among others) support the notion of an associated variable; changing the associated variable changes the text displayed in the Entry, and changing the text in the Entry changes the value of the variable. These aren't normal Python variable names, though. Variables tied to widgets are instances of variable classes in the Tkinter module library. These classes are named StringVar, IntVar, DoubleVar, and BooleanVar; you pick one based on the context in which it is to be used. For example, a StringVar class instance can be associated with an Entry field, as demonstrated in Example 9-20.

Example 9-20. PP3E\Gui\Tour\entry3.py

```
# use StringVar variables and lay out by columns

from Tkinter import *
from quitter import Quitter
```

Example 9-20. PP3E\Gui\Tour\entry3.py (continued)

```python
fields = 'Name', 'Job', 'Pay'

def fetch(variables):
    for variable in variables:
        print 'Input => "%s"' % variable.get()      # get from var

def makeform(root, fields):
    form = Frame(root)                               # make outer frame
    left = Frame(form)                               # make two columns
    rite = Frame(form)
    form.pack(fill=X)
    left.pack(side=LEFT)
    rite.pack(side=RIGHT, expand=YES, fill=X)        # grow horizontal

    variables = []
    for field in fields:
        lab = Label(left, width=5, text=field)       # add to columns
        ent = Entry(rite)
        lab.pack(side=TOP)
        ent.pack(side=TOP, fill=X)                   # grow horizontal
        var = StringVar()
        ent.config(textvariable=var)                 # link field to var
        var.set('enter here')
        variables.append(var)
    return variables

if __name__ == '__main__':
    root = Tk()
    vars = makeform(root, fields)
    Button(root, text='Fetch', command=(lambda: fetch(vars))).pack(side=LEFT)
    Quitter(root).pack(side=RIGHT)
    root.bind('<Return>', (lambda event: fetch(vars)))
    root.mainloop()
```

Except for the fact that this script initializes input fields with the string 'enter here', it makes a window identical in appearance and function to that created by the script entry2 (see Figure 9-23). For illustration purposes, the window is laid out differently—as a Frame containing two nested subframes used to build the left and right columns of the form area—but the end result is the same when it is displayed on screen.

The main thing to notice here, though, is the use of StringVar variables. Instead of using a list of Entry widgets to fetch input values, this version keeps a list of StringVar objects that have been associated with the Entry widgets, like this:

```python
ent = Entry(rite)
var = StringVar()
ent.config(textvariable=var)             # link field to var
```

Once you've tied variables in this way, changing and fetching the variable's value:

```python
var.set('text here')
value = var.get()
```

will really change and fetch the corresponding display's input field value.* The variable object get method returns as a string for StringVar, an integer for IntVar, and a floating-point number for DoubleVar.

Of course, we've already seen that it's easy to set and fetch text in Entry fields directly, without adding extra code to use variables. So, why the bother about variable objects? For one thing, it clears up that nasty fetch-after-destroy peril we met in the prior section. Because StringVars live on after the Entry widgets they are tied to have been destroyed, it's OK to fetch input values from them long after a modal dialog has been dismissed, as shown in Example 9-21.

Example 9-21. PP3E\Gui\Tour\entry3-modal.py

```
# can fetch values after destroy with stringvars

from Tkinter import *
from entry3 import makeform, fetch, fields

def show(variables):
    popup.destroy()                    # order doesn't matter here
    fetch(variables)                   # variables live on after window destroyed

def ask():
    global popup
    popup = Toplevel()                 # show form in modal dialog window
    vars = makeform(popup, fields)
    Button(popup, text='OK', command=(lambda: show(vars)) ).pack()
    popup.grab_set()
    popup.focus_set()
    popup.wait_window()                # wait for destroy here

root = Tk()
Button(root, text='Dialog', command=ask).pack()
root.mainloop()
```

This version is the same as the original (shown in Example 9-19 and Figure 9-25), but show now destroys the pop up before inputs are fetched through StringVars in the list created by makeform. In other words, variables are a bit more robust in some contexts because they are not part of a real display tree. For example, they are also associated with check buttons, radio boxes, and scales in order to provide access to current settings and link multiple widgets together. Almost coincidentally, that's the topic of the next section.

---

* In a now-defunct Tkinter release shipped with Python 1.3, you could also set and fetch variable values by calling them like functions, with and without an argument (e.g., var(value) and var( )). Today, you should call variable set and get methods instead. For unknown reasons, the function call form stopped working years ago, but you may still see it in older Python code (and in first editions of at least one O'Reilly Python book).

Checkbutton, Radiobutton, and Scale

This section introduces three widget types: the Checkbutton (a multiple-choice input widget), the Radiobutton (a single-choice device), and the Scale (sometimes known as a "slider"). All are variations on a theme and are somewhat related to simple buttons, so we'll explore them as a group here. To make these widgets more fun to play with, we'll reuse the dialogTable module shown in Example 9-8 to provide callbacks for widget selections (callbacks pop up dialog boxes). Along the way, we'll also use the Tkinter variables we just met to communicate with these widgets' state settings.

Checkbuttons

The Checkbutton and Radiobutton widgets are designed to be associated with Tkinter variables: clicking the button changes the value of the variable, and setting the variable changes the state of the button to which it is linked. In fact, Tkinter variables are central to the operation of these widgets:

- A collection of Checkbuttons implements a multiple-choice interface by assigning each button a variable of its own.
- A collection of Radiobuttons imposes a mutually exclusive single-choice model by giving each button a unique value and the same Tkinter variable.

Both kinds of buttons provide both command and variable options. The command option lets you register a callback to be run immediately on button-press events, much like normal Button widgets. But by associating a Tkinter variable with the variable option, you can also fetch or change widget state at any time by fetching or changing the value of the widget's associated variable.

Since it's a bit simpler than the others, let's start with the Tkinter Checkbutton. Example 9-22 creates the set of five captured in Figure 9-26. To make this more useful, it also adds a button that dumps the current state of all Checkbuttons and attaches an instance of the Quitter button we built earlier in the tour.

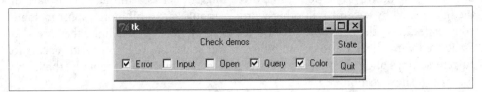

Figure 9-26. demoCheck in action

Example 9-22. PP3E\Gui\Tour\demoCheck.py

```
from Tkinter import *            # get base widget set
from dialogTable import demos    # get canned dialogs
from quitter import Quitter      # attach a quitter object to "me"
```

Example 9-22. PP3E\Gui\Tour\demoCheck.py (continued)

```
class Demo(Frame):
    def __init__(self, parent=None, **args):
        Frame.__init__(self, parent, args)
        self.pack()
        self.tools()
        Label(self, text="Check demos").pack()
        self.vars = []
        for key in demos.keys():
            var = IntVar()
            Checkbutton(self,
                        text=key,
                        variable=var,
                        command=demos[key]).pack(side=LEFT)
            self.vars.append(var)
    def report(self):
        for var in self.vars:
            print var.get(),   # current toggle settings: 1 or 0
        print
    def tools(self):
        frm = Frame(self)
        frm.pack(side=RIGHT)
        Button(frm, text='State', command=self.report).pack(fill=X)
        Quitter(frm).pack(fill=X)

if __name__ == '__main__': Demo().mainloop()
```

In terms of program code, check buttons resemble normal buttons; they are even packed within a container widget. Operationally, though, they are a bit different. As you can probably tell from this figure (and can better tell by running this live), a check button works as a toggle—pressing one changes its state from off to on (from deselected to selected); or from on to off again. When a check button is selected, it has a checked display, and its associated IntVar variable has a value of 1; when deselected, its display is empty, and its IntVar has a value of 0.

To simulate an enclosing application, the State button in this display triggers the script's report method to display the current values of all five toggles on the stdout stream. Here is the output after a few clicks:

```
C:\...\PP3E\Gui\Tour>python demoCheck.py
0 0 0 0 0
1 0 0 0 0
1 0 1 0 0
1 0 1 1 0
1 0 0 1 0
1 0 0 1 1
```

Really, these are the values of the five Tkinter variables associated with the Checkbuttons with variable options, but they give the buttons' values when queried. This script associates IntVar variables with each Checkbutton in this display, since they are 0 or 1 binary indicators. StringVars will work here too, although their get methods would return strings '0' or '1' (not integers), and their initial state would be an empty string (not the integer 0).

This widget's command option lets you register a callback to be run each time the button is pressed. To illustrate, this script registers a standard dialog demo call as a handler for each of the Checkbuttons: pressing a button changes the toggle's state but also pops up one of the dialog windows we visited earlier in this tour.

Interestingly, you can run the report method interactively too. When working this way, widgets pop up as lines are typed, and are fully active, even without calling mainloop:

```
C:\...\PP3E\Gui\Tour>python
>>> from demoCheck import Demo
>>> d = Demo()
>>> d.report()
0 0 0 0 0
>>> d.report()
1 0 0 0 0
>>> d.report()
1 0 0 1 1
```

Check buttons and variables

When I first studied this widget, my initial reaction was: Why do we need Tkinter variables here at all when we can register button-press callbacks? Linked variables may seem superfluous at first glance, but they simplify some GUI chores. Instead of asking you to accept this blindly, though, let me explain why.

Keep in mind that a Checkbutton's command callback will be run on every press, whether the press toggles the check button to a selected or a deselected state. Because of that, if you want to run an action immediately when a check button is pressed, you will generally want to check the button's current value in the callback handler. Because there is no check button "get" method for fetching values, you usually need to interrogate an associated variable to see if the button is on or off.

Moreover, some GUIs simply let users set check buttons without running command callbacks at all and fetch button settings at some later point in the program. In such a scenario, variables serve to automatically keep track of button settings. The demoCheck script's report method represents this latter approach.

Of course, you could manually keep track of each button's state in press callback handlers, too. Example 9-23 keeps its own list of state toggles and updates it manually on command press callbacks.

Example 9-23. PP3E\Gui\Tour\demo-check-manual.py

```
# check buttons, the hard way (without variables)

from Tkinter import *
states = []
```

Example 9-23. PP3E\Gui\Tour\demo-check-manual.py (continued)

```
def onPress(i):                        # keep track of states
    states[i] = not states[i]          # changes 0->1, 1->0

root = Tk()
for i in range(10):
    chk = Checkbutton(root, text=str(i), command=(lambda i=i: onPress(i)) )
    chk.pack(side=LEFT)
    states.append(0)
root.mainloop()
print states                           # show all states on exit
```

The lambda here passes along the pressed button's index in the states list. Otherwise, we would need a separate callback function for each button. Here again, we need to use a default argument to pass the loop variable into the lambda, or the loop variable will be its value on the last loop iteration for all 10 of the generated functions (each press would update the tenth item in the list; see Chapter 8 for background details). When run, this script makes the 10–check button display in Figure 9-27.

Figure 9-27. Manual check button state window

Manually maintained state toggles are updated on every button press and are printed when the GUI exits (technically, when the mainloop call returns):

```
C:\...\PP3E\Gui\Tour>python demo-check-manual.py
[0, 0, 1, 0, 1, 0, 0, 0, 1, 0]
```

This works, and it isn't too horribly difficult to manage manually. But linked Tkinter variables make this task noticeably easier, especially if you don't need to process check button states until some time in the future. This is illustrated in Example 9-24.

Example 9-24. PP3E\Gui\Tour\demo-check-auto.py

```
# check buttons, the easy way

from Tkinter import *
root = Tk()
states = []
for i in range(10):
    var = IntVar()
    chk = Checkbutton(root, text=str(i), variable=var)
    chk.pack(side=LEFT)
    states.append(var)
root.mainloop()                              # let Tkinter keep track
print map((lambda var: var.get()), states)  # show all states on exit
```

This looks and works the same way, but there is no `command` button-press callback handler at all, because toggle state is tracked by Tkinter automatically:

```
C:\...\PP3E\Gui\Tour>python demo-check-auto.py
[0, 0, 1, 0, 0, 0, 1, 0, 0, 0]
```

The point here is that you don't necessarily have to link variables with check buttons, but your GUI life will be simpler if you do. The bound-method `map` call in this code, by the way, is equivalent to both the unbound-method form `map (IntVar.get, states)`, as well as the list comprehension `[var.get( ) for var in states]` (the form that seems clearest to you may very well depend upon your shoe size).

Radio Buttons

Radio buttons are toggles too, but they are generally used in groups: just like the mechanical station selector pushbuttons on radios of times gone by, pressing one `Radiobutton` widget in a group automatically deselects the one pressed last. In other words, at most, only one can be selected at one time. In Tkinter, associating all radio buttons in a group with unique values and the same variable guarantees that, at most, only one can ever be selected at a given time.

Like check buttons and normal buttons, radio buttons support a `command` option for registering a callback to handle presses immediately. Like check buttons, radio buttons also have a `variable` attribute for associating single-selection buttons in a group and fetching the current selection at arbitrary times.

In addition, radio buttons have a `value` attribute that lets you tell Tkinter what value the button's associated variable should have when the button is selected. Because more than one radio button is associated with the same variable, you need to be explicit about each button's value (it's not just a 1 or 0 toggle scenario). Example 9-25 demonstrates radio button basics.

Example 9-25. PP3E\Gui\Tour\demoRadio.py

```
from Tkinter import *              # get base widget set
from dialogTable import demos      # button callback handlers
from quitter import Quitter        # attach a quit object to "me"

class Demo(Frame):
    def __init__(self, parent=None):
        Frame.__init__(self, parent)
        self.pack()
        Label(self, text="Radio demos").pack(side=TOP)
        self.var = StringVar()
        for (key, value) in demos.items( ):
            Radiobutton(self, text=key,
                              command=self.onPress,
                              variable=self.var,
                              value=key).pack(anchor=NW)
        Button(self, text='State', command=self.report).pack(fill=X)
        Quitter(self).pack(fill=X)
```

Example 9-25. PP3E\Gui\Tour\demoRadio.py (continued)

```
    def onPress(self):
        pick = self.var.get( )
        print 'you pressed', pick
        print 'result:', demos[pick]( )
    def report(self):
        print self.var.get( )

if __name__ == '__main__': Demo().mainloop( )
```

Figure 9-28 shows what this script generates when run. Pressing any of this window's radio buttons triggers its command handler, pops up one of the standard dialog boxes we met earlier, and automatically deselects the button previously pressed. Like check buttons, radio buttons are packed; this script packs them to the top to arrange them vertically, and then anchors each on the northwest corner of its allocated space so that they align well.

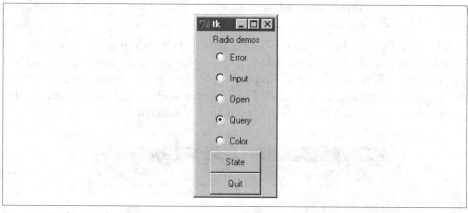

Figure 9-28. demoRadio in action

Like the check button demo script, this one also puts up a State button to run the class's report method and to show the current radio state (the button selected). Unlike the check button demo, this script also prints the return values of dialog demo calls that are run as its buttons are pressed. Here is what the stdout stream looks like after a few presses and state dumps; states are shown in bold:

```
C:\...\PP3E\Gui\Tour>python demoRadio.py
you pressed Input
result: 3.14
Input
you pressed Open
result: C:/PP2ndEd/examples/PP3E/Gui/Tour/demoRadio.py
Open
you pressed Query
result: yes
Query
```

Radio buttons and variables

So, why variables here? For one thing, radio buttons also have no "get" widget method to fetch the selection in the future. More importantly, in radio button groups, the value and variable settings turn out to be the whole basis of single-choice behavior. In fact, to make radio buttons work normally at all, it's crucial that they are all associated with the same Tkinter variable and have distinct value settings. To truly understand why, though, you need to know a bit more about how radio buttons and variables do their stuff.

We've already seen that changing a widget changes its associated Tkinter variable, and vice versa. But it's also true that changing a variable in any way automatically changes every widget it is associated with. In the world of radio buttons, pressing a button sets a shared variable, which in turn impacts other buttons associated with that variable. Assuming that all buttons have distinct values, this works as you expect it to work. When a button press changes the shared variable to the pressed button's value, all other buttons are deselected, simply because the variable has been changed to a value not their own.

This ripple effect is a bit subtle, but it might help to know that within a group of radio buttons sharing the same variable, if you assign a set of buttons the same value, the entire set will be selected if any one of them is pressed. Consider Example 9-26 and Figure 9-29, for instance; because radio buttons 0, 3, 6, and 9 have value 0 (the remainder of division by 3), all are selected if any are selected.

Figure 9-29. Radio buttons gone bad?

Example 9-26. PP3E\Gui\Tour\demo-radio-multi.py

```
# see what happens when some buttons have same value

from Tkinter import *
root = Tk()
var = StringVar()
for i in range(10):
    rad = Radiobutton(root, text=str(i), variable=var, value=str(i % 3))
    rad.pack(side=LEFT)
root.mainloop()
```

If you press 1, 4, or 7 now, all three of these are selected, and any existing selections are cleared (they don't have the value "1"). That's not normally what you want, so be sure to give each button the same variable but a unique value if you want radio buttons to work as expected. In the demoRadio script, for instance, the name of the demo provides a naturally unique value for each button.

Radio buttons without variables

In Example 9-27, too, you could implement a single-selection model without variables, by manually selecting and deselecting widgets in the group, in a callback handler of your own. On each press event, for example, you could issue deselect calls for every widget object in the group and select the one pressed.

Example 9-27. PP3E\Gui\Tour\demo-radio-manual.py

```
# radio buttons, the hard way (without variables)
# note that deselect for radio buttons simply sets the button's
# associated value to a null string, so we either need to still
# give buttons unique values, or use checkbuttons here instead;

from Tkinter import *
state = ''
buttons = []

def onPress(i):
    global state
    state = i
    for btn in buttons:
        btn.deselect()
    buttons[i].select()

root = Tk()
for i in range(10):
    rad = Radiobutton(root, text=str(i),
                            value=str(i), command=(lambda i=i: onPress(i)) )
    rad.pack(side=LEFT)
    buttons.append(rad)
root.mainloop()
print state              # show state on exit
```

This works. It creates a 10–radio button window that looks just like the one in Figure 9-29 but implements a single-choice radio-style interface, with current state available in a global Python variable printed on script exit. By associating Tkinter variables and unique values, though, you can let Tkinter do all this work for you, as shown in Example 9-28.

Example 9-28. PP3E\Gui\Tour\demo-radio-auto.py

```
# radio buttons, the easy way

from Tkinter import *
root = Tk()                     # IntVars work too
var  = IntVar()                 # state = var.get()
for i in range(10):
    rad = Radiobutton(root, text=str(i), value=i, variable=var)
    rad.pack(side=LEFT)
root.mainloop()
print var.get()                 # show state on exit
```

This works the same way, but it is a lot less to type and debug. Notice that this script associates the buttons with an IntVar, the integer type sibling of StringVar; as long as button values are unique, integers work fine for radio buttons too.

Hold onto your variables

One minor word of caution: you should generally hold onto the Tkinter variable object used to link radio buttons for as long as the radio buttons are displayed. Assign it to a module global variable, store it in a long-lived data structure, or save it as an attribute of a long-lived class object as done by demoRadio. Just make sure you retain a reference to it somehow. You will normally fetch state anyhow, so it's unlikely that you'll ever care about what I'm about to tell you.

But in the current Tkinter, variable classes have a __del__ destructor that automatically unsets a generated Tk variable when the Python object is reclaimed (i.e., garbage collected). The upshot is that all of your radio buttons may be deselected if the variable object is collected, at least until the next press resets the Tk variable to a new value. Example 9-29 shows one way to trigger this.

Example 9-29. PP3E\Gui\Tour\demo-radio-clear.py

```
# hold on to your radio variables (an obscure thing, indeed)

from Tkinter import *
root = Tk( )

def radio1( ):                     # local vars are temporary
    #global tmp                     # making it global fixes the problem
    tmp = IntVar( )
    for i in range(10):
        rad = Radiobutton(root, text=str(i), value=i, variable=tmp)
        rad.pack(side=LEFT)
    tmp.set(5)

radio1( )
root.mainloop( )
```

This should come up with button 5 selected initially, but it doesn't. The variable referenced by local tmp is reclaimed on function exit, the Tk variable is unset, and the 5 setting is lost (all buttons come up unselected). These radio buttons work fine, though, once you start pressing them, because that resets the Tk variable. Uncommenting the global statement here makes 5 start out set, as expected.

Of course, this is an atypical example—as coded, there is no way to know which button is pressed, because the variable isn't saved (and command isn't set). In fact, this is so obscure that I'll just refer you to *demo-radio-clear2.py* in the book's examples distribution for an example that works hard to trigger this oddity in other ways. You probably won't care, but you can't say that I didn't warn you if you ever do.

Scales (Sliders)

Scales (sometimes called "sliders") are used to select among a range of numeric values. Moving the scale's position with mouse drags or clicks moves the widget's value among a range of integers and triggers Python callbacks if registered.

Like check buttons and radio buttons, scales have both a command option for registering an event-driven callback handler to be run right away when the scale is moved, and a variable option for associating a Tkinter variable that allows the scale's position to be fetched and set at arbitrary times. You can process scale settings when they are made, or let the user pick a setting for later use.

In addition, scales have a third processing option—get and set methods that scripts may call to access scale values directly without associating variables. Because scale command movement callbacks also get the current scale setting value as an argument, it's often enough just to provide a callback for this widget, without resorting to either linked variables or get/set method calls.

To illustrate the basics, Example 9-30 makes two scales—one horizontal and one vertical—and links them with an associated variable to keep them in sync.

Example 9-30. PP3E\Gui\Tour\demoScale.py

```
from Tkinter import *                    # get base widget set
from dialogTable import demos            # button callback handlers
from quitter import Quitter              # attach a quit frame to me

class Demo(Frame):
    def __init__(self, parent=None):
        Frame.__init__(self, parent)
        self.pack()
        Label(self, text="Scale demos").pack()
        self.var = IntVar()
        Scale(self, label='Pick demo number',
                    command=self.onMove,               # catch moves
                    variable=self.var,                 # reflects position
                    from_=0, to=len(demos)-1).pack()
        Scale(self, label='Pick demo number',
                    command=self.onMove,               # catch moves
                    variable=self.var,                 # reflects position
                    from_=0, to=len(demos)-1,
                    length=200, tickinterval=1,
                    showvalue=YES, orient='horizontal').pack()
        Quitter(self).pack(side=RIGHT)
        Button(self, text="Run demo", command=self.onRun).pack(side=LEFT)
        Button(self, text="State",    command=self.report).pack(side=RIGHT)
    def onMove(self, value):
        print 'in onMove', value
    def onRun(self):
        pos = self.var.get()
        print 'You picked', pos
        pick = demos.keys()[pos]    # map from position to key
```

Example 9-30. PP3E\Gui\Tour\demoScale.py (continued)

```
        print demos[pick]( )
    def report(self):
        print self.var.get( )

if __name__ == '__main__':
    print demos.keys( )
    Demo( ).mainloop( )
```

Besides value access and callback registration, scales have options tailored to the notion of a range of selectable values, most of which are demonstrated in this example's code:

- The label option provides text that appears along with the scale, length specifies an initial size in pixels, and orient specifies an axis.

- The from_ and to options set the scale range's minimum and maximum values (note that from is a Python reserved word, but from_ is not).

- The tickinterval option sets the number of units between marks drawn at regular intervals next to the scale (the default means no marks are drawn).

- The resolution option provides the number of units that the scale's value jumps on each drag or left mouse click event (defaults to 1).

- The showvalue option can be used to show or hide the scale's current value next to its slider bar (the default showvalue=YES means it is drawn).

Note that scales are also packed in their container, just like other Tkinter widgets. Let's see how these ideas translate in practice; Figure 9-30 shows the window you get if you run this script live on Windows (you get a similar one on Unix and Mac machines).

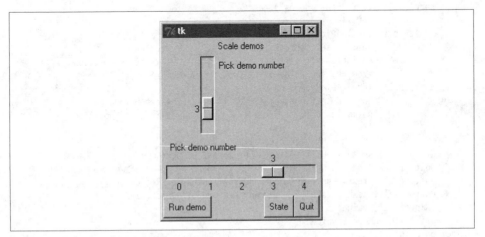

Figure 9-30. demoScale in action

For illustration purposes, this window's State button shows the scales' current values, and "Run demo" runs a standard dialog call as before using the integer value of the scales to index the demos table. The script also registers a command handler that fires every time either of the scales is moved, and prints their new positions. Here is a set of messages sent to stdout after a few moves, demo runs (italic), and state requests (bold):

```
C:\...\PP3E\Gui\Tour>python demoScale.py
['Error', 'Input', 'Open', 'Query', 'Color']
in onMove 0
in onMove 0
in onMove 1
1
in onMove 2
You picked 2
C:/PP2ndEd/examples/PP3E/Gui/Tour/demoScale.py
in onMove 3
3
You picked 3
yes
```

Scales and variables

As you can probably tell, scales offer a variety of ways to process their selections: immediately in move callbacks, or later by fetching current positions with variables or scale method calls. In fact, Tkinter variables aren't needed to program scales at all—simply register movement callbacks, or call the scale get method to fetch scale values on demand, as in the simpler scale example in Example 9-31.

Example 9-31. PP3E\Gui\Tour\demo-scale-simple.py

```
from Tkinter import *
root = Tk()
scl = Scale(root, from_=-100, to=100, tickinterval=50, resolution=10)
scl.pack(expand=YES, fill=Y)
def report(): print scl.get()
Button(root, text='state', command=report).pack(side=RIGHT)
root.mainloop()
```

Figure 9-31 shows two instances of this program running on Windows—one stretched and one not (the scales are packed to grow vertically on resizes). Its scale displays a range from –100 to 100, uses the resolution option to adjust the current position up or down by 10 on every move, and sets the tickinterval option to show values next to the scale in increments of 50. When you press the State button in this script's window, it calls the scale's get method to display the current setting, without variables or callbacks of any kind:

```
C:\...\PP3E\Gui\Tour>python demo-scale-simple.py
0
60
-70
```

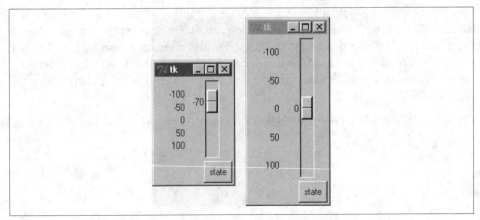

Figure 9-31. A simple scale without variables

Frankly, the only reason Tkinter variables are used in the demoScale script at all is to synchronize scales. To make the demo interesting, this script associates the same Tkinter variable object with both scales. As we learned in the last section, changing a widget changes its variable, but changing a variable also changes all the widgets it is associated with. In the world of sliders, moving the slide updates that variable, which in turn might update other widgets associated with the same variable. Because this script links one variable with two scales, it keeps them automatically in sync: moving one scale moves the other too, because the shared variable is changed in the process and so updates the other scale as a side effect.

Linking scales like this may or may not be typical of your applications (and borders on deep magic), but it's a powerful tool once you get your mind around it. By linking multiple widgets on a display with Tkinter variables, you can keep them automatically in sync, without making manual adjustments in callback handlers. On the other hand, the synchronization could be implemented without a shared variable at all by calling one scale's set method from a move callback handler of the other. I'll leave such a manual mutation as a suggested exercise, though. One person's deep magic might be another's evil hack.

Running GUI Code Three Ways

Now that we've built a handful of similar demo launcher programs, let's write a few top-level scripts to combine them. Because the demos were coded as both reusable classes and scripts, they can be deployed as attached frame components, run in their own top-level windows, and launched as standalone programs. All three options illustrate code reuse in action.

Attaching Frames

To illustrate hierarchical GUI composition on a grander scale than we've seen so far, Example 9-32 arranges to show all four of the dialog launcher bar scripts of this chapter in a single frame. It reuses Examples 9-9, 9-22, 9-25, and 9-30.

Example 9-32. PP3E\Gui\Tour\demoAll-frm.py

```
#####################################################
# 4 demo class components (subframes) on one window;
# there are 5 Quitter buttons on this one window too;
# GUIs can be reused as frames, windows, processes;
#####################################################

from Tkinter import *
from quitter import Quitter
demoModules = ['demoDlg', 'demoCheck', 'demoRadio', 'demoScale']
parts = []

def addComponents(root):
    for demo in demoModules:
        module = __import__(demo)             # import by name string
        part = module.Demo(root)              # attach an instance
        part.config(bd=2, relief=GROOVE)
        part.pack(side=LEFT, fill=BOTH)
        parts.append(part)                    # change list in-place

def dumpState():
    for part in parts:                        # run demo report if any
        print part.__module__ + ':',
        if hasattr(part, 'report'):
            part.report()
        else:
            print 'none'

root = Tk()                                        # default toplevel window
Label(root, text='Multiple Frame demo', bg='white').pack()
Button(root, text='States', command=dumpState).pack(fill=X)
Quitter(root).pack(expand=YES, fill=X)
addComponents(root)
mainloop()
```

Because all four demo launcher bars are coded to attach themselves to parent container widgets, this is easier than you might think: simply pass the same parent widget (here, the root window) to all four demo constructor calls, and pack and configure the demo objects as desired. Figure 9-32 shows this script's graphical result—a single window embedding instances of all four of the dialog demo launcher demos we saw earlier.

Naturally, this example is artificial, but it illustrates the power of composition when applied to building larger GUI displays. If you pretend that each of the four attached

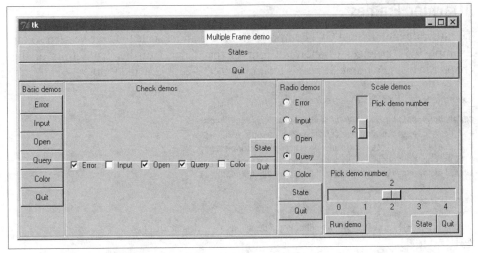

Figure 9-32. demoAll_frm: nested subframes

demo objects was something more useful, like a text editor, calculator, or clock, you'll better appreciate the point of this example.

Besides demo object frames, this composite window also contains no fewer than five instances of the Quitter button we wrote earlier (any one of which can end the GUI), and a States button to dump the current values of all the embedded demo objects at once (it calls each object's report method, if it has one). Here is a sample of the sort of output that shows up in the stdout stream after interacting with widgets on this display; States output is in bold:

```
C:\...\PP3E\Gui\Tour>python demoAll_frm.py
in onMove 0
in onMove 0
demoDlg: none
demoCheck: 0 0 0 0 0
demoRadio:
demoScale: 0
you pressed Input
result: 1.234
demoDlg: none
demoCheck: 1 0 1 1 0
demoRadio: Input
demoScale: 0
you pressed Query
result: yes
in onMove 1
in onMove 2
You picked 2
C:/PP2ndEd/examples/PP3E/Gui/Tour/demoAll_frm.py
demoDlg: none
demoCheck: 1 0 1 1 0
demoRadio: Query
demoScale: 2
```

The only substantially tricky part of this script is its use of Python's built-in `__import__` function to import a module by a name string. Look at the following two lines from the script's addComponents function:

```
module = __import__(demo)          # import module by name string
part = module.Demo(root)           # attach an instance of its Demo
```

This is equivalent to saying something like this:

```
import 'demoDlg'
part = 'demoDlg'.Demo(root)
```

However, the preceding code is not legal Python syntax; the module name in import statements must be a Python variable, not a string. To be generic, addComponents steps through a list of name strings and relies on `__import__` to import and return the module identified by each string. It's as though all of these statements were run:

```
import demoDlg, demoRadio, demoCheck, demoScale
part = demoDlg.Demo(root)
part = demoRadio.Demo(root)
part = demoCheck.Demo(root)
part = demoScale.Demo(root)
```

But because the script uses a list of name strings, it's easier to change the set of demos embedded—simply change the list, not the lines of executable code. Moreover, such data-driven code tends to be more compact, less redundant, and easier to debug and maintain. Incidentally, modules can also be imported from name strings by dynamically constructing and running import statements, like this:

```
for demo in demoModules:
    exec 'from %s import Demo' % demo     # make and run a from
    part = Demo(root)                     # or eval('Demo')(window)
```

The exec statement compiles and runs a Python statement string (here, a from to load a module's Demo class); it works here as if the statement string were pasted into the source code where the exec statement appears. Because it supports any sort of Python statement, this technique is more general than the `__import__` call, but it can also be slower, since it must parse code strings before running them.[*] However, that slowness may not matter in a GUI; users tend to be slower than parsers.

As we saw in Chapter 8, attaching nested frames like this is really just one way to reuse GUI code structured as classes. It's just as easy to customize such interfaces by subclassing rather than embedding. Here, though, we're more interested in deploying an existing widget package than changing it; the next two sections show two other ways to present such packages to users.

---

[*] As we'll see later, exec can also be dangerous if it is running code strings fetched from users or network connections. That's not an issue for the hardcoded strings in this example.

Independent Windows

Once you have a set of component classes, any parent will work—both frames, and brand-new, top-level windows. Example 9-33 attaches instances of all four demo bar objects to their own Toplevel windows, not to the same Frame.

Example 9-33. PP3E\Gui\Tour\demoAll-win.py

```
###################################################
# 4 demo classes in independent top-level windows;
# not processes: when one is quit all others go away
# because all windows run in the same process here
###################################################

from Tkinter import *
demoModules = ['demoDlg', 'demoRadio', 'demoCheck', 'demoScale']

demoObjects = []
for demo in demoModules:
    module = __import__(demo)          # import by name string
    window = Toplevel()                # make a new window
    demo   = module.Demo(window)       # parent is the new window
    demoObjects.append(demo)

def allstates():
    for obj in demoObjects:
        if hasattr(obj, 'report'):
            print obj.__module__,
            obj.report()

Label(text='Multiple Toplevel window demo', bg='white').pack()
Button(text='States', command=allstates).pack(fill=X)
mainloop()
```

We met the Toplevel class earlier; every instance generates a new window on your screen. The net result is captured in Figure 9-33. Each demo runs in an independent window of its own instead of being packed together in a single display.

The main root window of this program appears in the lower left of this screenshot; it provides a States button that runs the report method of each demo object, producing this sort of stdout text:

```
C:\...\PP3E\Gui\Tour>python demoAll_win.py
in onMove 0
in onMove 0
in onMove 1
you pressed Open
result: C:/PP2ndEd/examples/PP3E/Gui/Tour/demoAll_win.txt
demoRadio Open
demoCheck 1 1 0 0 0
demoScale 1
```

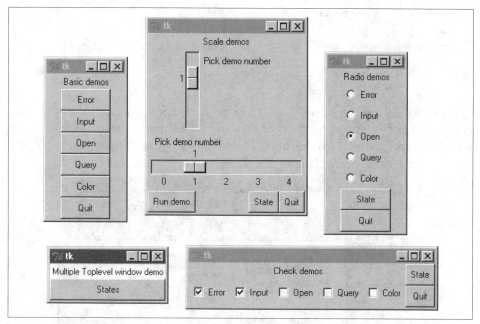

Figure 9-33. demoAll_win: new Toplevel windows

Running Programs

Finally, as we learned earlier in this chapter, Toplevel windows function independently, but they are not really independent programs. Quitting any of the windows created in Example 9-33 quits them all, because all run in the same program process. That's OK in some applications, but not all.

To go truly independent, Example 9-34 spawns each of the four demo launchers as independent programs, using the launchmodes module we wrote at the end of Chapter 5. This works only because the demos were written as both importable classes and runnable scripts. Launching them here makes all their names __main__ when run.

Example 9-34. PP3E\Gui\Tour\demoAll-prg.py

```
#######################################################
# 4 demo classes run as independent program processes;
# if one window is quit now, the others will live on;
# there is no simple way to run all report calls here,
# and some launch schemes drop child program stdout;
#######################################################

from Tkinter import *
demoModules = ['demoDlg', 'demoRadio', 'demoCheck', 'demoScale']
from PP3E.launchmodes import PortableLauncher
```

Example 9-34. PP3E\Gui\Tour\demoAll-prg.py (continued)

```
for demo in demoModules:                          # see Parallel System Tools
    PortableLauncher(demo, demo+'.py')()          # start as top-level programs

Label(text='Multiple program demo', bg='white').pack()
mainloop()
```

As Figure 9-34 shows, the display generated by this script is similar to the prior one; all four demos come up in windows of their own. This time, though, these are truly independent programs: if any one of the five windows here is quit, the others live on.

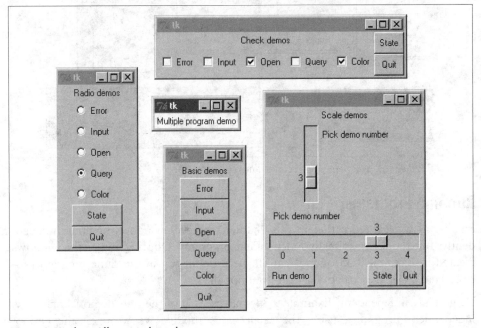

Figure 9-34. demoAll_prg: independent programs

Cross-program communication

Spawning GUIs as programs is the ultimate in code independence, but it makes the lines of communication between components more complex. For instance, because the demos run as programs here, there is no easy way to run all their report methods from the launching script's window pictured in the middle of Figure 9-34. In fact, the States button is gone this time, and we only get `PortableLauncher` messages in `stdout` as the demos start up:

```
C:\...\PP3E\Gui\Tour>python demoAll_prg.py
demoDlg
demoRadio
demoCheck
demoScale
```

On some platforms, messages printed by the demo programs (including their own State buttons) may show up in the original console window where this script is launched; on Windows, the os.spawnv call used to start programs in launchmodes completely disconnects the child program's stdout stream from its parent. Regardless, there is no way to call all demos' report methods at once; they are spawned programs in distinct address spaces, not imported modules.

Of course, we could trigger report methods in the spawned programs with some of the Inter-Process Communication (IPC) mechanisms we met in Chapter 5. For instance:

- The demos could be instrumented to catch a user signal, and could run their report in response.
- They could also watch for request strings sent by the launching program to show up in pipes or fifos; the demoAll launching program would essentially act as a client, and the demo GUIs as servers.
- Independent programs can also converse this way over sockets, a tool we'll meet in depth in Part IV.

Given their event-driven nature, GUI-based programs may need to be augmented with threads, timer-event callbacks, nonblocking input calls, or some combination of such techniques to periodically check for such incoming messages on pipes, fifos, or sockets, and to avoid becoming stuck in wait states (e.g., see the after method call described near the end of the next chapter). We'll explore some of these options in Chapter 11. But since this is well beyond the scope of the current chapter's simple demo programs, I'll leave such cross-program extensions up to more parallel-minded readers for now.

Coding for reusability

A postscript: I coded all the demo launcher bars deployed by the last three examples to demonstrate all the different ways that their widgets can be used. They were not developed with general-purpose reusability in mind; in fact, they're not really useful outside the context of introducing widgets in this book.

That was by design; most Tkinter widgets are easy to use once you learn their interfaces, and Tkinter already provides lots of configuration flexibility by itself. But if I had it in mind to code checkbutton and radiobutton classes to be reused as general library components, they would have to be structured differently:

Extra widgets
> They would not display anything but radio buttons and check buttons. As is, the demos each embed State and Quit buttons for illustration, but there really should be just one Quit per top-level window.

Geometry management

They would allow for different button arrangements and would not pack (or grid) themselves at all. In a true general-purpose reuse scenario, it's often better to leave a component's geometry management up to its caller.

Usage mode limitations

They would either have to export complex interfaces to support all possible Tkinter configuration options and modes, or make some limiting decisions that support one common use only. For instance, these buttons can either run callbacks at press time or provide their state later in the application.

Example 9-35 shows one way to code check button and radio button bars as library components. It encapsulates the notion of associating Tkinter variables and imposes a common usage mode on callers—state fetches rather than press callbacks—to keep the interface simple.

Example 9-35. PP3E\Gui\Tour\buttonbars.py

```
# check and radio button bar classes for apps that fetch state later;
# pass a list of options, call state(), variable details automated

from Tkinter import *

class Checkbar(Frame):
    def __init__(self, parent=None, picks=[], side=LEFT, anchor=W):
        Frame.__init__(self, parent)
        self.vars = []
        for pick in picks:
            var = IntVar()
            chk = Checkbutton(self, text=pick, variable=var)
            chk.pack(side=side, anchor=anchor, expand=YES)
            self.vars.append(var)
    def state(self):
        return [var.get() for var in self.vars]        # or map(lambda, self.vars)

class Radiobar(Frame):
    def __init__(self, parent=None, picks=[], side=LEFT, anchor=W):
        Frame.__init__(self, parent)
        self.var = StringVar()
        for pick in picks:
            rad = Radiobutton(self, text=pick, value=pick, variable=self.var)
            rad.pack(side=side, anchor=anchor, expand=YES)
    def state(self):
        return self.var.get()

if __name__ == '__main__':
    root = Tk()
    lng = Checkbar(root, ['Python', 'C#', 'Java', 'C++'])
    gui = Radiobar(root, ['win', 'x11', 'mac'], side=TOP, anchor=NW)
    tgl = Checkbar(root, ['All'])
    gui.pack(side=LEFT, fill=Y)
    lng.pack(side=TOP,  fill=X)
```

Example 9-35. PP3E\Gui\Tour\buttonbars.py (continued)

```
tgl.pack(side=LEFT)
lng.config(relief=GROOVE, bd=2)
gui.config(relief=RIDGE,  bd=2)
from quitter import Quitter
def allstates(): print gui.state(), lng.state(), tgl.state()
Quitter(root).pack(side=RIGHT)
Button(root, text='Peek', command=allstates).pack(side=RIGHT)
root.mainloop()
```

To reuse these classes in your scripts, import and call them with a list of the options that you want to appear in a bar of check buttons or radio buttons. This module's self-test code at the bottom of the file gives further usage details. It generates Figure 9-35—a top-level window that embeds two Checkbars, one Radiobar, a Quitter button to exit, and a Peek button to show bar states—when this file is run as a program instead of being imported.

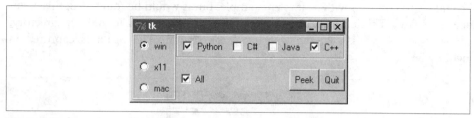

Figure 9-35. buttonbars self-test window

Here's the stdout text you get after pressing Peek—the results of these classes' state methods:

```
x11 [1, 0, 1, 1] [0]
win [1, 0, 0, 1] [1]
```

The two classes in this module demonstrate how easy it is to wrap Tkinter interfaces to make them easier to use; they completely abstract away many of the tricky parts of radio button and check button bars. For instance, you can forget about linked variable details completely if you use such higher-level classes instead; simply make objects with option lists and call their state methods later. If you follow this path to its conclusion, you might just wind up with a higher-level widget library on the order of the Pmw package mentioned in Chapter 8.

On the other hand, these classes are still not universally applicable; if you need to run actions when these buttons are pressed, for instance, you'll need to use other high-level interfaces. Luckily, Python/Tkinter already provides plenty. Later in this book, we'll again use the widget combination and reuse techniques introduced in this section to construct larger GUIs. For now, this first chapter in the widget tour is about to make one last stop—the photo shop.

Images

In Tkinter, graphical images are displayed by creating independent `PhotoImage` or `BitmapImage` objects, and then attaching those image objects to other widgets via image attribute settings. Buttons, labels, canvases, text, and menus can display images by associating prebuilt image objects in this way. To illustrate, Example 9-36 throws a picture up on a button.

Example 9-36. PP3E\Gui\Tour\imgButton.py

```
gifdir = "../gifs/"
from Tkinter import *
win = Tk( )
igm = PhotoImage(file=gifdir+"ora-pp.gif")
Button(win, image=igm).pack( )
win.mainloop( )
```

I could try to come up with a simpler example, but it would be tough—all this script does is make a Tkinter `PhotoImage` object for a GIF file stored in another directory, and associate it with a `Button` widget's image option. The result is captured in Figure 9-36.

Figure 9-36. imgButton in action

`PhotoImage` and its cousin, `BitmapImage`, essentially load graphics files and allow those graphics to be attached to other kinds of widgets. To open a picture file, pass its name to the `file` attribute of these image objects. `Canvas` widgets—general drawing surfaces discussed in more detail later in this tour—can display pictures too; Example 9-37 renders Figure 9-37.

Figure 9-37. An image on canvas

Example 9-37. PP3E\Gui\Tour\imgCanvas.py

```
gifdir = "../gifs/"
from Tkinter import *
win = Tk( )
img = PhotoImage(file=gifdir+"ora-lp.gif")
can = Canvas(win)
can.pack(fill=BOTH)
can.create_image(2, 2, image=img, anchor=NW)          # x, y coordinates
win.mainloop( )
```

Buttons are automatically sized to fit an associated photo, but canvases are not
(because you can add objects to a canvas, as we'll see in Chapter 10). To make a canvas fit the picture, size it according to the `width` and `height` methods of image
objects, as in Example 9-38. This version will make the canvas smaller or larger than
its default size as needed, lets you pass in a photo file's name on the command line,
and can be used as a simple image viewer utility. The visual effect of this script is
captured in Figure 9-38.

Figure 9-38. Sizing the canvas to match the photo

Example 9-38. PP3E\Gui\Tour\imgCanvas2.py

```
gifdir = "../gifs/"
from sys import argv
from Tkinter import *
filename = (len(argv) > 1 and argv[1]) or 'ora-lp.gif'    # name on cmdline?
win = Tk()
img = PhotoImage(file=gifdir+filename)
can = Canvas(win)
can.pack(fill=BOTH)
can.config(width=img.width(), height=img.height())         # size to img size
can.create_image(2, 2, image=img, anchor=NW)
win.mainloop()
```

And that's all there is to it. In Chapter 10, we'll see images show up in a Menu, other Canvas examples, and the image-friendly Text widget. In later chapters, we'll find them in an image slideshow (PyView), in a paint program (PyDraw), on clocks (PyClock), and so on. It's easy to add graphics to GUIs in Python/Tkinter.

Once you start using photos in earnest, though, you're likely to run into two tricky bits which I want to warn you about here:

Supported file types

At present, the PhotoImage widget only supports GIF, PPM, and PGM graphic file formats, and BitmapImage supports X Windows-style *.xbm* bitmap files. This may be expanded in future releases, and you can convert photos in other formats to these supported formats, of course. But as we'll see later in this chapter, it's easy to support additional image types with the PIL open source extension toolkit.

Hold on to your photos

Unlike all other Tkinter widgets, an image is utterly lost if the corresponding Python image object is garbage collected. That means you must retain an explicit reference to image objects for as long as your program needs them (e.g., assign them to a long-lived variable name or data structure component). Python does not automatically keep a reference to the image, even if it is linked to other GUI components for display; moreover, image destructor methods erase the image from memory. We saw earlier that Tkinter variables can behave oddly when reclaimed too, but the effect is much worse and more likely to happen with images. This may change in future Python releases (though there are good reasons for not retaining big image files in memory indefinitely); for now, though, images are a "use it or lose it" widget.

Fun with Buttons and Pictures

I tried to come up with an image demo for this section that was both fun and useful. I settled for the fun part. Example 9-39 displays a button that changes its image at random each time it is pressed.

Example 9-39. PP3E\Gui\Tour\buttonpics-func.py

```
from Tkinter import *                    # get base widget set
from glob import glob                    # filename expansion list
import demoCheck                         # attach checkbutton demo to me
import random                            # pick a picture at random
gifdir = '../gifs/'                      # where to look for GIF files

def draw():
    name, photo = random.choice(images)
    lbl.config(text=name)
    pix.config(image=photo)

root=Tk()
lbl = Label(root,  text="none", bg='blue', fg='red')
pix = Button(root, text="Press me", command=draw, bg='white')
lbl.pack(fill=BOTH)
pix.pack(pady=10)
demoCheck.Demo(root, relief=SUNKEN, bd=2).pack(fill=BOTH)

files = glob(gifdir + "*.gif")                              # GIFs for now
images = map((lambda x: (x, PhotoImage(file=x))), files)    # load and hold
print files
root.mainloop()
```

This code uses a handful of built-in tools from the Python library:

- The Python glob module we met earlier in the book gives a list of all files ending in *.gif* in a directory; in other words, all GIF files stored there.

- The Python random module is used to select a random GIF from files in the directory: random.choice picks and returns an item from a list at random.

- To change the image displayed (and the GIF file's name in a label at the top of the window), the script simply calls the widget config method with new option settings; changing on the fly like this changes the widget's display.

Just for fun, this script also attaches an instance of the demoCheck check button demo bar, which in turn attaches an instance of the Quitter button we wrote earlier. This is an artificial example, of course, but again it demonstrates the power of component class attachment at work.

Notice how this script builds and holds on to all images in its images list. The map here applies a PhotoImage constructor call to every *.gif* file in the photo directory, producing a list of (file,image) tuples that is saved in a global variable (a list comprehension [(x, PhotoImage(file=x)) for x in files] would do the same). Remember, this guarantees that image objects won't be garbage collected as long as the program is running. Figure 9-39 shows this script in action on Windows.

Although it may not be obvious in this grayscale book, the name of the GIF file being displayed is shown in red text in the blue label at the top of this window. This program's window grows and shrinks automatically when larger and smaller GIF files

Figure 9-39. buttonpics in action

are displayed; Figure 9-40 shows it randomly picking a taller photo globbed from the image directory.

Figure 9-40. buttonpics showing a taller photo

And finally, Figure 9-41 captures this script's GUI displaying one of the wider GIFs, selected completely at random from the photo file directory.[*]

While we're playing, let's recode this script as a class in case we ever want to attach or customize it later (it could happen). It's mostly a matter of indenting and adding self before global variable names, as shown in Example 9-40.

---

[*] This particular image appeared as a banner ad on developer-related web sites such as *slashdot.com* when the book *Learning Python* was first published. It generated enough of a backlash from Perl zealots that O'Reilly eventually pulled the ad altogether. Which is why, of course, it appears in this book.

Figure 9-41. buttonpics gets political

Example 9-40. PP3E\Gui\Tour\buttonpics.py

```
from Tkinter import *              # get base widget set
from glob import glob             # filename expansion list
import demoCheck                  # attach check button example to me
import random                     # pick a picture at random
gifdir = '../gifs/'               # default dir to load GIF files

class ButtonPicsDemo(Frame):
    def __init__(self, gifdir=gifdir, parent=None):
        Frame.__init__(self, parent)
        self.pack()
        self.lbl = Label(self,  text="none", bg='blue', fg='red')
        self.pix = Button(self, text="Press me", command=self.draw, bg='white')
        self.lbl.pack(fill=BOTH)
        self.pix.pack(pady=10)
        demoCheck.Demo(self, relief=SUNKEN, bd=2).pack(fill=BOTH)
        files = glob(gifdir + "*.gif")
        self.images = map(lambda x: (x, PhotoImage(file=x)), files)
        print files

    def draw(self):
        name, photo = random.choice(self.images)
        self.lbl.config(text=name)
        self.pix.config(image=photo)

if __name__ == '__main__': ButtonPicsDemo().mainloop()
```

This version works the same way as the original, but it can now be attached to any other GUI where you would like to include such an unreasonably silly button.

Viewing and Processing Images with PIL

As mentioned earlier, Python Tkinter scripts show images by associating independently created image objects with real widget objects. At this writing, Tkinter GUIs can display photo image files in GIF, PPM, and PGM formats by creating a

`PhotoImage` object, as well as X11-style bitmap files (usually suffixed with an *.xbm* extension) by creating a `BitmapImage` object.

This set of supported file formats is limited by the underlying Tk library, not by Tkinter itself, and may expand in the future. But if you want to display files in other formats today (e.g., the popular JPEG format), you can either convert your files to one of the supported formats with an image-processing program, or install the PIL Python extension package mentioned at the start of Chapter 8.

PIL, the Python Imaging Library, is an open source system that supports nearly 30 graphics file formats (including GIF, JPEG, TIFF, and BMP). In addition to allowing your scripts to display a much wider variety of image types than standard Tkinter, PIL also provides tools for image processing, including geometric transforms, thumbnail creation, format conversions, and much more.

PIL Basics

To use its tools, you must first fetch and install the PIL package: see *http://www. pythonware.com* (or search for "PIL" on Google). Then, simply use special `PhotoImage` and `BitmapImage` objects imported from the PIL `ImageTk` module to open files in other graphic formats. These are compatible replacements for the standard Tkinter classes of the same name, and they may be used anywhere Tkinter expects a `PhotoImage` or `BitmapImage` object (i.e., in label, button, canvas, text, and menu object configurations).

That is, replace standard Tkinter code such as this:

```
from Tkinter import *
imgobj = PhotoImage(file=imgdir + "spam.gif")
Button(image=imgobj).pack( )
```

with code of this form:

```
from Tkinter import *
import ImageTk
photoimg = ImageTk.PhotoImage(file=imgdir + "spam.jpg")
Button(image=photoimg).pack( )
```

or with the more verbose equivalent, which comes in handy if you will perform image processing in addition to image display:

```
from Tkinter import *
import Image, ImageTk
imageobj = Image.open(imgdir + "spam.jpeg")
photoimg = ImageTk.PhotoImage(imageobj)
Button(image=photoimg).pack( )
```

In fact, to use PIL for image display, all you really need to do is install it and add a single `from` statement to your code to get its replacement `PhotoImage` object, after loading the original from Tkinter. The rest of your code remains unchanged but will be able to display JPEG and other image types:

```
from Tkinter import *
from ImageTk import PhotoImage                          # <== add this line
imgobj = PhotoImage(file=imgdir + "spam.jpg")
Button(image=imgobj).pack( )
```

PIL installation details vary per platform; on Windows, it is just a matter of down-loading and running a self-installer. PIL code winds up in the Python install direc-tory's Lib\site packages; because this is automatically added to the module import search path, no path configuration is required to use PIL. Simply run the installer and import PIL modules. On other platforms, you might untar or unZIP a fetched source code archive and add PIL directories to the front of your PYTHONPATH setting; see the PIL system's web site for more details.

There is much more to PIL than we have space to cover here. For instance, it also provides image conversion, resizing, and transformation tools, some of which can be run as command-line programs that have nothing to do with GUIs directly. Espe-cially for Tkinter-based programs that display or process images, PIL will likely become a standard component in your software tool set.

See *http://www.pythonware.com* for more information, as well as online PIL and Tkinter documentation sets. To help get you started, though, we'll close out this chapter with a handful of real scripts that use PIL for image display and processing.

Displaying Other Image Types with PIL

In our earlier image examples, we attached widgets to buttons and canvases, but the standard Tkinter toolkit allows images to be added to a variety of widget types, including simple labels, text, and menu entries. Example 9-41, for instance, uses unadorned Tkinter to display a single image by attaching it to a label, in the main application window. The example assumes that images are stored in an *images* sub-directory, and allows the image filename to be passed in as a command-line argu-ment (it defaults to *spam.gif* if no argument is passed). It also prints the image's height and width in pixels to the standard output stream, just to give extra informa-tion.

Example 9-41. PP3E\Gui\PIL\viewer-tk.py

```
#######################################################
# show one image with standard Tkinter photo object
# as is this handles GIF files, but not JPEG images
# image filename listed in command line, or default
# use a Canvas instead of Label for scrolling, etc.
#######################################################

import os, sys
from Tkinter import *                       # use standard Tkinter photo object
                                            # GIF works, but JPEG requires PIL

imgdir  = 'images'
imgfile = 'newmarket-uk-2.gif'
```

Example 9-41. PP3E\Gui\PIL\viewer-tk.py (continued)

```
if len(sys.argv) > 1:                      # cmdline argument given?
    imgfile = sys.argv[1]
imgpath = os.path.join(imgdir, imgfile)

win = Tk( )
win.title(imgfile)
imgobj = PhotoImage(file=imgpath)          # display photo on a Label
Label(win, image=imgobj).pack( )
print imgobj.width(), imgobj.height( )      # show size in pixels before destroyed
win.mainloop( )
```

Figure 9-42 captures this script's display on Windows XP, showing the default GIF image file. Run this from the system console with a filename as a command-line argument to view other files (e.g., *python viewer_tk.py filename.gif*).

Figure 9-42. Tkinter GIF display

Example 9-41 works but only for image types supported by the base Tkinter toolkit. To display other image formats such as JPEG, we need to install PIL and use its replacement PhotoImage object. In terms of code, it's simply a matter of adding one import statement, as illustrated in Example 9-42.

Example 9-42. PP3E\GuiPIL\viewer-pil.py

```
#######################################################
# show one image with PIL photo replacement object
# install PIL first: placed in Lib\site-packages
#######################################################
```

Example 9-42. PP3E\GuiPIL\viewer-pil.py (continued)

```
import os, sys
from Tkinter import *
from ImageTk import PhotoImage        # <== use PIL replacement class
                                      # rest of code unchanged
imgdir  = 'images'
imgfile = 'newmarket-uk-1.jpg'
if len(sys.argv) > 1:
    imgfile = sys.argv[1]
imgpath = os.path.join(imgdir, imgfile)

win = Tk()
win.title(imgfile)
imgobj = PhotoImage(file=imgpath)        # now JPEGs work!
Label(win, image=imgobj).pack()
win.mainloop()
print imgobj.width(), imgobj.height()    # show size in pixels on exit
```

With PIL, our script is now able to display many image types, including the default JPEG image defined in the script and captured in Figure 9-43.

Figure 9-43. Tkinter+PIL JPEG display

Displaying all images in a directory

While we're at it, it's not much extra work to allow viewing all images in a directory, using some of the directory path tools we met in the first part of this book. Example 9-43, for instance, simply opens a new Toplevel pop-up window for each image in a directory (given as a command-line argument, or a default), taking care to skip nonimage files by catching exceptions.

Example 9-43. PP3E\Gui\PIL\viewer-dir.py

```
######################################################
# display all images in a directory in pop-up windows
# GIFs work, but JPEGs will be skipped without PIL
######################################################

import os, sys
from Tkinter import *
from ImageTk import PhotoImage           # <== required for JPEGs and others

imgdir = 'images'
if len(sys.argv) > 1: imgdir = sys.argv[1]
imgfiles = os.listdir(imgdir)            # does not include directory prefix

main = Tk()
main.title('Viewer')
quit = Button(main, text='Quit all', command=main.quit, font=('courier', 25))
quit.pack()
savephotos = []

for imgfile in imgfiles:
    imgpath = os.path.join(imgdir, imgfile)
    win = Toplevel()
    win.title(imgfile)
    try:
        imgobj = PhotoImage(file=imgpath)
        Label(win, image=imgobj).pack()
        print imgpath, imgobj.width(), imgobj.height()      # size in pixels
        savephotos.append(imgobj)                           # keep a reference
    except:
        errmsg = 'skipping %s\n%s' % (imgfile, sys.exc_info()[1])
        Label(win, text=errmsg).pack()

main.mainloop()
```

Run this code on your own to see the windows it generates. If you do, you'll get one main window with a Quit button, plus as many pop-up image view windows as there are images in the directory. This is convenient for a quick look, but not exactly the epitome of user friendliness for large directories—those created by your digital camera, for instance. To do better, let's move on to the next section.

Creating Image Thumbnails with PIL

As mentioned, PIL does more than display images in a GUI; it also comes with tools for resizing, converting, and more. One of the many useful tools it provides is the ability to generate small, "thumbnail" images from originals. Such thumbnails may be displayed in a web page or selection GUI to allow the user to open full-size images on demand.

Example 9-44 is a concrete implementation of this idea—it generates thumbnail images using PIL and displays them on buttons which open the corresponding original image when clicked. The net effect is much like the file explorer GUIs that are now standard on modern operating systems, but by coding this in Python, we're able to control its behavior and to reuse and customize its code in our own applications. As usual, these are some of the primary benefits inherent in open source software in general.

Example 9-44. PP3E\Gui\PIL\viewer_thumbs.py

```
#######################################################
# display all images in a directory as thumbnail image
# buttons that display the full image when clicked;
# requires PIL for JPEGs and thumbnail img creation;
# to do: add scrolling if too many thumbs for window!
#######################################################

import os, sys, math
from Tkinter import *
import Image                       # <== required for thumbs
from ImageTk import PhotoImage     # <== required for JPEG display

def makeThumbs(imgdir, size=(100, 100), subdir='thumbs'):
    """
    get thumbnail images for all images in a directory;
    for each image, create and save a new thumb, or load
    and return an existing thumb; makes thumb dir if needed;
    returns list of (image filename, thumb image object);
    the caller can also run listdir on thumb dir to load;
    on bad file types we may get IOError, or other: overflow
    """
    thumbdir = os.path.join(imgdir, subdir)
    if not os.path.exists(thumbdir):
        os.mkdir(thumbdir)

    thumbs = []
    for imgfile in os.listdir(imgdir):
        thumbpath = os.path.join(thumbdir, imgfile)
        if os.path.exists(thumbpath):
            thumbobj = Image.open(thumbpath)          # use already created
```

Example 9-44. PP3E\Gui\PIL\viewer_thumbs.py (continued)

```
                thumbs.append((imgfile, thumbobj))
        else:
            print 'making', thumbpath
            imgpath = os.path.join(imgdir, imgfile)
            try:
                imgobj = Image.open(imgpath)               # make new thumb
                imgobj.thumbnail(size, Image.ANTIALIAS) # best downsize filter
              imgobj.save(thumbpath)                     # type via ext or passed
                thumbs.append((imgfile, imgobj))
            except:                                        # not always IOError
                print "Skipping: ", imgpath
    return thumbs

class ViewOne(Toplevel):
    """
    open a single image in a pop-up window when created;
    photoimage obj must be saved: erased if reclaimed;
    """
    def __init__(self, imgdir, imgfile):
        Toplevel.__init__(self)
        self.title(imgfile)
        imgpath = os.path.join(imgdir, imgfile)
        imgobj  = PhotoImage(file=imgpath)
        Label(self, image=imgobj).pack()
        print imgpath, imgobj.width(), imgobj.height()   # size in pixels
        self.savephoto = imgobj                          # keep reference on me

def viewer(imgdir, kind=Toplevel, cols=None):
    """
    make thumb links window for an image directory:
    one thumb button per image; use kind=Tk to show
    in main  app window, or Frame container (pack);
    imgfile differs per loop: must save with a default;
    photoimage objs must be saved: erased if reclaimed;
    """
    win = kind()
    win.title('Viewer: ' + imgdir)
    thumbs = makeThumbs(imgdir)
    if not cols:
        cols = int(math.ceil(math.sqrt(len(thumbs))))    # fixed or N x N

    savephotos = []
    while thumbs:
        thumbsrow, thumbs = thumbs[:cols], thumbs[cols:]
        row = Frame(win)
        row.pack(fill=BOTH)
        for (imgfile, imgobj) in thumbsrow:
            photo   = PhotoImage(imgobj)
```

Example 9-44. PP3E\Gui\PIL\viewer_thumbs.py (continued)

```
            link    = Button(row, image=photo)
            handler = lambda savefile=imgfile: ViewOne(imgdir, savefile)
            link.config(command=handler)
            link.pack(side=LEFT, expand=YES)
            savephotos.append(photo)

    Button(win, text='Quit', command=win.quit).pack(fill=X)
    return win, savephotos

if __name__ == '__main__':
    imgdir = (len(sys.argv) > 1 and sys.argv[1]) or 'images'
    main, save = viewer(imgdir, kind=Tk)
    main.mainloop( )
```

Most of the PIL-specific code in this example is in the makeThumbs function. It opens, creates, and saves the thumbnail image, unless one has already been saved (i.e., cached) to a local file. As coded, thumbnail images are saved in the same image format as the original full-size photo.

We also use the PIL ANTIALIAS filter—the best quality for down-sampling (shrinking), and likely the default in the future; this does a better job on low-resolution GIFs. Thumbnail generation is essentially just an in-place resize that preserves the original aspect ratio. We'll defer to PIL documentation for more details on that package's API.

But notice how this code must pass in the imgfile to the generated callback handler with a default argument; as we've learned, because imgfile is a loop variable, all callbacks will have its final loop iteration value if its current value is not saved this way (all buttons would open the same image!). Also notice how we keep a list of references to the photo image objects; as we've also seen, photos are erased when their object is garbage collected, even if they are currently being displayed. To avoid this, we simply generate references in a long-lived list.

Figure 9-44 shows the main thumbnail selection window generated by Example 9-44 when you're viewing the default *images* subdirectory in the examples source tree. As in the previous examples, you can pass in an optional directory name to run the viewer on a directory of your own (for instance, one copied from your digital camera). Clicking on any thumbnail button in the main window opens a corresponding image in an independent pop-up window; Figure 9-45 captures one of these.

Figure 9-44. Simple thumbnail selection GUI

Performance: saving thumbnail files

Before we move on, three variations on the thumbnail viewer are worth considering. The first underscores performance concepts. As is, the viewer saves the generated thumbnail image in a file, so it can be loaded quickly the next time the script is run. This isn't strictly required—Example 9-45, for instance, customizes the thumbnail generation function to generate the thumbnail images in memory, but never save them.

There is no noticeable speed difference for small image collections. If you run these alternatives on larger image collections, though, you'll notice that the original version in Example 9-44 gains a big performance advantage by saving and loading the thumbnails to files; on some tests with many large image files on my machine, the original version usually opens the GUI in roughly 1 second, compared to as much as 5 to 15 seconds for Example 9-45. For thumbnails, loading from files is quicker than recalculation.

Figure 9-45. Thumbnail viewer pop-up image window

Example 9-45. PP3E\Gui\PIL\viewer-thumbs-nosave.py

```
###########################################################
# same, but make thumb images in memory without saving
# to or loading from files -- this seems just as fast
# for small directories, but saving to files makes
# startup much quicker for large image collections;
# saving may also be needed in some apps (e.g., web pages)
###########################################################

import os, sys
import Image
from Tkinter import Tk
import viewer_thumbs

def makeThumbs(imgdir, size=(100, 100), subdir='thumbs'):
    """
    create thumbs in memory but don't cache to files
    """
    thumbs = []
    for imgfile in os.listdir(imgdir):
        imgpath = os.path.join(imgdir, imgfile)
        try:
            imgobj = Image.open(imgpath)          # make new thumb
            imgobj.thumbnail(size)
            thumbs.append((imgfile, imgobj))
        except:
```

Example 9-45. PP3E\Gui\PIL\viewer-thumbs-nosave.py (continued)

```
            print "Skipping: ", imgpath
    return thumbs

if __name__ == '__main__':
    imgdir = (len(sys.argv) > 1 and sys.argv[1]) or 'images'
    viewer_thumbs.makeThumbs = makeThumbs
    main, save = viewer_thumbs.viewer(imgdir, kind=Tk)
    main.mainloop( )
```

Layout: gridding and fixed-size widgets

The next variations on our viewer are purely cosmetic, but they illustrate Tkinter layout concepts. If you look at Figure 9-44 long enough, you'll notice that its layout of thumbnails is not as uniform as it could be. For larger collections, it could become difficult to locate and open specific images. With just a little extra work, we can achieve a more uniform layout by either laying out the thumbnails in a grid, or using uniform fixed-size buttons. Example 9-46 positions buttons in a row/column grid by using the Tkinter grid geometry manager—a topic we will explore in more detail in the next chapter; you should consider some of this code a preview.

Example 9-46. PP3E\Gui\PIL\viewer-thumbs-grid.py

```
#####################################################
# same as viewer_thumbs, but uses the grid geometry
# manager to try to achieve a more uniform layout;
# can generally achieve the same with frames and pack
# if buttons are all fixed and uniform in size;
#####################################################

import sys, math
from Tkinter import *
from ImageTk import PhotoImage
from viewer_thumbs import makeThumbs, ViewOne

def viewer(imgdir, kind=Toplevel, cols=None):
    """
    custom version that uses gridding
    """
    win = kind( )
    win.title('Viewer: ' + imgdir)
    thumbs = makeThumbs(imgdir)
    if not cols:
        cols = int(math.ceil(math.sqrt(len(thumbs))))     # fixed or N x N

    rownum = 0
    savephotos = []
    while thumbs:
        thumbsrow, thumbs = thumbs[:cols], thumbs[cols:]
        colnum = 0
        for (imgfile, imgobj) in thumbsrow:
            photo    = PhotoImage(imgobj)
```

Example 9-46. PP3E\Gui\PIL\viewer-thumbs-grid.py (continued)

```
            link    = Button(win, image=photo)
            handler = lambda savefile=imgfile: ViewOne(imgdir, savefile)
            link.config(command=handler)
            link.grid(row=rownum, column=colnum)
            savephotos.append(photo)
            colnum += 1
        rownum += 1

    Button(win, text='Quit', command=win.quit).grid(columnspan=cols, stick=EW)
    return win, savephotos

if __name__ == '__main__':
    imgdir = (len(sys.argv) > 1 and sys.argv[1]) or 'images'
    main, save = viewer(imgdir, kind=Tk)
    main.mainloop()
```

Figure 9-46 displays the effect of gridding; our buttons line up in rows and columns in a more uniform fashion.

Figure 9-46. Gridded thumbnail selection GUI

We can achieve a layout that is perhaps even more uniform than gridding, by giving each thumbnail button a fixed size. Example 9-47 does the trick. It sets the height and width of each button to match the maximum dimension of the thumbnail icon.

Example 9-47. PP3E\Gui\PIL\viewer-thumbs-fixed.py

```
######################################################
# use fixed size for thumbnails, so align regularly;
# size taken from image object, assume all same max;
# this is essentially what file selection GUIs do;
######################################################

import sys, math
from Tkinter import *
from ImageTk import PhotoImage
from viewer_thumbs import makeThumbs, ViewOne

def viewer(imgdir, kind=Toplevel, cols=None):
    """
    custom version that lays out with fixed-size buttons
    """
    win = kind()
    win.title('Viewer: ' + imgdir)
    thumbs = makeThumbs(imgdir)
    if not cols:
        cols = int(math.ceil(math.sqrt(len(thumbs))))        # fixed or N x N

    savephotos = []
    while thumbs:
        thumbsrow, thumbs = thumbs[:cols], thumbs[cols:]
        row = Frame(win)
        row.pack(fill=BOTH)
        for (imgfile, imgobj) in thumbsrow:
            size    = max(imgobj.size)                        # width, height
            photo   = PhotoImage(imgobj)
            link    = Button(row, image=photo)
            handler = lambda savefile=imgfile: ViewOne(imgdir, savefile)
            link.config(command=handler, width=size, height=size)
            link.pack(side=LEFT, expand=YES)
            savephotos.append(photo)

    Button(win, text='Quit', command=win.quit, bg='beige').pack(fill=X)
    return win, savephotos

if __name__ == '__main__':
    imgdir = (len(sys.argv) > 1 and sys.argv[1]) or 'images'
    main, save = viewer(imgdir, kind=Tk)
    main.mainloop()
```

Figure 9-47 shows the results of applying a fixed size to our buttons; all are the same size now, using a size taken from the images themselves. Naturally, other layout schemes are possible as well; experiment with some of the configuration options in this code on your own to see their effect on the display.

Figure 9-47. Fixed-size thumbnail selection GUI

Scrolling and canvases

The thumbnail viewer scripts presented in this section work well for reasonably sized image directories, and you can use smaller thumbnail size settings for larger image collections. Perhaps the biggest limitation of these programs, though, is that the thumbnail windows they create will become too large to handle (or display at all) if the image directory contains very many files. A directory copied from your camera with more than 100 images, for example, might produce a window too large to fit on your computer's screen.

To do better, we could arrange the thumbnails on a widget that supports scrolling. The open source Pmw package includes a handy scrolled frame that may help. Moreover, the standard Tkinter Canvas widget gives us more control over image displays and supports horizontal and vertical scrolling.

In fact, one final extension to our scripts in the source code directory, *viewer_thumbs_scrolled.py*, does just that—it displays thumbnails in a scrolled canvas and so handles large collections much better. We'll study that extension in conjunction with canvases in the next chapter. And in Chapter 12, we'll apply this technique to a more full-featured image viewing program called PyPhoto, whose main window is captured in Figure 9-48. To learn how these programs do their job, though, we need to move on to the next chapter, and the second half of our widget tour.

Figure 9-48. Scrollable thumbnail selection GUI

A Tkinter Tour, Part 2

"On Today's Menu: Spam, Spam, and Spam"

This chapter is the second in a two-part tour of the Tkinter library. It picks up where Chapter 9 left off and covers some of the more advanced widgets and tools in the Tkinter arsenal. Among the topics presented in this chapter:

- Menu, Menubutton, and OptionMenu widgets
- The Scrollbar widget: for scrolling text, lists, and canvases
- The Listbox widget: a list of multiple selections
- The Text widget: a general text display and editing tool
- The Canvas widget: a general graphical drawing tool
- The grid table-based geometry manager
- Time-based tools: after, update, wait, and threads
- Basic Tkinter animation techniques
- Clipboards, erasing widgets and windows, and so on

By the time you've finished this chapter, you will have seen the bulk of the Tkinter library, and you will have all the information you need to compose larger, portable user interfaces of your own. You'll also be ready to tackle the larger GUI techniques and examples presented in Chapters 11 and 12. As a segue to the next chapter, this one also closes with a look at the PyDemos and PyGadgets launcher toolbars—GUIs used to start larger GUI examples.

Menus

Menus are the pull-down lists you're accustomed to seeing at the top of a window (or the entire display, if you're accustomed to seeing them on a Macintosh). Move the mouse cursor to the menu bar at the top and click on a name (e.g., File), and a list of selectable options pops up under the name you clicked (e.g., Open, Save). The options within a menu might trigger actions, much like clicking on a button; they may also open other "cascading" submenus that list more options, pop up dialog windows, and so on. In Tkinter, there are two kinds of menus you can add to your scripts: top-level window menus and frame-based menus. The former option is better suited to whole windows, but the latter also works as a nested component.

Top-Level Window Menus

In more recent Python releases (using Tk 8.0 and later), you can associate a horizontal menu bar with a top-level window object (e.g., a Tk or Toplevel). On Windows and Unix (X Windows), this menu bar is displayed along the top of the window; on Macintosh, this menu replaces the one shown at the top of the screen when the window is selected. In other words, window menus look like you would expect on whatever underlying platform your script runs upon.

This scheme is based on building trees of Menu widget objects. Simply associate one top-level Menu with the window, add other pull-down Menu objects as cascades of the top-level Menu, and add entries to each of the pull-down objects. Menus are cross-linked with the next higher level, by using parent widget arguments and the Menu widget's add_cascade method. It works like this:

1. Create a topmost Menu as the child of the window widget and configure the window's menu attribute to be the new Menu.
2. For each pull-down object, make a new Menu as the child of the topmost Menu and add the child as a cascade of the topmost Menu using add_cascade.
3. Add menu selections to each pull-down Menu from step 2, using the command options of add_command to register selection callback handlers.
4. Add a cascading submenu by making a new Menu as the child of the Menu the cascade extends and using add_cascade to link the parent to the child.

The end result is a tree of Menu widgets with associated command callback handlers. This is probably simpler in code than in words, though. Example 10-1 makes a main menu with two pull downs, File and Edit; the Edit pull down in turn has a nested submenu of its own.

Example 10-1. PP3E\Gui\Tour\menu_win.py

```
# Tk8.0 style top-level window menus

from Tkinter import *                          # get widget classes
from tkMessageBox import *                     # get standard dialogs

def notdone():
    showerror('Not implemented', 'Not yet available')

def makemenu(win):
    top = Menu(win)                            # win=top-level window
```

Example 10-1. PP3E\Gui\Tour\menu_win.py (continued)

```
    win.config(menu=top)                              # set its menu option

    file = Menu(top)
    file.add_command(label='New...',   command=notdone,  underline=0)
    file.add_command(label='Open...',  command=notdone,  underline=0)
    file.add_command(label='Quit',     command=win.quit, underline=0)
    top.add_cascade(label='File',      menu=file,        underline=0)

    edit = Menu(top, tearoff=0)
    edit.add_command(label='Cut',      command=notdone,  underline=0)
    edit.add_command(label='Paste',    command=notdone,  underline=0)
    edit.add_separator()
    top.add_cascade(label='Edit',      menu=edit,        underline=0)

    submenu = Menu(edit, tearoff=0)
    submenu.add_command(label='Spam',  command=win.quit, underline=0)
    submenu.add_command(label='Eggs',  command=notdone,  underline=0)
    edit.add_cascade(label='Stuff',    menu=submenu,     underline=0)

if __name__ == '__main__':
    root = Tk()                                 # or Toplevel()
    root.title('menu_win')                      # set window-mgr info
    makemenu(root)                              # associate a menu bar
    msg = Label(root, text='Window menu basics')  # add something below
    msg.pack(expand=YES, fill=BOTH)
    msg.config(relief=SUNKEN, width=40, height=7, bg='beige')
    root.mainloop()
```

A lot of code in this file is devoted to setting callbacks and such, so it might help to isolate the bits involved with the menu tree–building process. For the File menu, it's done like this:

```
    top = Menu(win)                            # attach Menu to window
    win.config(menu=top)                       # cross-link window to menu
    file = Menu(top)                           # attach a Menu to top Menu
    top.add_cascade(label='File', menu=file)   # cross-link parent to child
```

Apart from building up the menu object tree, this script also demonstrates some of the most common menu configuration options:

Separator lines

> The script makes a separator in the Edit menu with add_separator; it's just a line used to set off groups of related entries.

Tear-offs

> The script also disables menu tear-offs in the Edit pull down by passing a tearoff=0 widget option to Menu. Tear-offs are dashed lines that appear by default at the top of Tkinter menus and create a new window containing the menu's contents when clicked. They can be a convenient shortcut device (you can click items in the tear-off window right away, without having to navigate through menu trees), but they are not widely used on all platforms.

Keyboard shortcuts

The script uses the `underline` option to make a unique letter in a menu entry a keyboard shortcut. It gives the offset of the shortcut letter in the entry's label string. On Windows, for example, the Quit option in this script's File menu can be selected with the mouse as usual, but also by pressing the Alt key, then "f," and then "q." You don't strictly have to use `underline`—on Windows, the first letter of a pull-down name is a shortcut automatically, and arrow and Enter keys can be used to move through and select pull-down items. But explicit keys can enhance usability in large menus; for instance, the key sequence Alt-E-S-S runs the quit action in this script's nested submenu, without any mouse or arrow key movement.

Let's see what all this translates to in the realm of the pixel. Figure 10-1 shows the window that first appears when this script is run live on Windows; it looks different, but similar, on Unix and Macintosh.

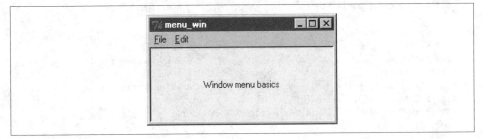

Figure 10-1. menu_win: a top-level window menu bar

Figure 10-2 shows the scene when the File pull down is selected. Notice that Menu widgets are linked, not packed (or gridded)—the geometry manager doesn't really come into play here. If you run this script, you'll also notice that all of its menu entries either quit the program immediately or pop up a "Not Implemented" standard error dialog. This example is about menus, after all, but menu selection callback handlers generally do more useful work in practice.

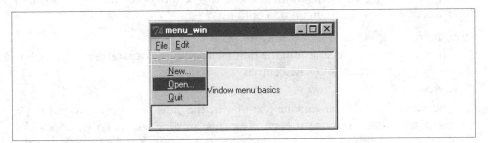

Figure 10-2. The File menu pull down

And finally, Figure 10-3 shows what happens after clicking the File menu's tear-off line and selecting the cascading submenu in the Edit pull down. Cascades can be nested as deep as you like, but your users probably won't be happy if this gets silly.

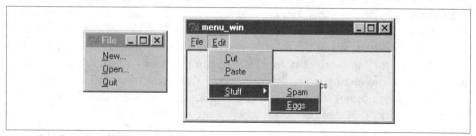

Figure 10-3. A File tear-off and Edit cascade

In Tkinter, every top-level window can have a menu bar, including pop ups that you create with the Toplevel widget. Example 10-2 makes three pop-up windows with the same menu bar as the one we just met; when run, it constructs the scene captured in Figure 10-4.

Example 10-2. PP3E\Gui\Tour\menu_win-multi.py

```
from menu_win import makemenu
from Tkinter import *

root = Tk()
for i in range(3):                       # Three pop-up windows with menus
    win = Toplevel(root)
    makemenu(win)
    Label(win, bg='black', height=5, width=15).pack(expand=YES, fill=BOTH)
Button(root, text="Bye", command=root.quit).pack()
root.mainloop()
```

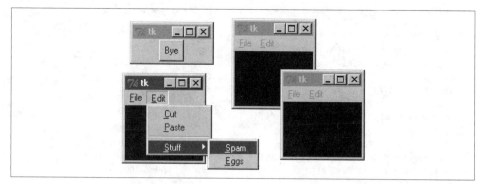

Figure 10-4. Multiple Toplevels with menus

Frame- and Menubutton-Based Menus

Although less commonly used for top-level windows, it's also possible to create a menu bar as a horizontal Frame. Before I show you how, though, let me explain why you should care. Because this frame-based scheme doesn't depend on top-level window protocols, it can also be used to add menus as nested components of larger displays. In other words, it's not just for top-level windows. For example, Chapter 12's PyEdit text editor can be used both as a program and as an attachable component. We'll use window menus to implement PyEdit selections when PyEdit is run as a standalone program, but we'll use frame-based menus when PyEdit is embedded in the PyMail and PyView displays. Both schemes are worth knowing.

Frame-based menus require a few more lines of code, but they aren't much more complex than window menus. To make one, simply pack Menubutton widgets within a Frame container, associate Menu widgets with the Menubuttons, and associate the Frame with the top of a container window. Example 10-3 creates the same menu as Example 10-2, but using the frame-based approach.

Example 10-3. PP3E\Gui\Tour\menu_frm.py

```
# Frame-based menus: for top-levels and components

from Tkinter import *                          # get widget classes
from tkMessageBox import *                     # get standard dialogs

def notdone():
    showerror('Not implemented', 'Not yet available')

def makemenu(parent):
    menubar = Frame(parent)                    # relief=RAISED, bd=2...
    menubar.pack(side=TOP, fill=X)

    fbutton = Menubutton(menubar, text='File', underline=0)
    fbutton.pack(side=LEFT)
    file = Menu(fbutton)
    file.add_command(label='New...',  command=notdone,     underline=0)
    file.add_command(label='Open...', command=notdone,     underline=0)
    file.add_command(label='Quit',    command=parent.quit, underline=0)
    fbutton.config(menu=file)

    ebutton = Menubutton(menubar, text='Edit', underline=0)
    ebutton.pack(side=LEFT)
    edit = Menu(ebutton, tearoff=0)
    edit.add_command(label='Cut',   command=notdone,     underline=0)
    edit.add_command(label='Paste', command=notdone,     underline=0)
    edit.add_separator()
    ebutton.config(menu=edit)

    submenu = Menu(edit, tearoff=0)
    submenu.add_command(label='Spam', command=parent.quit, underline=0)
    submenu.add_command(label='Eggs', command=notdone,     underline=0)
```

Example 10-3. PP3E\Gui\Tour\menu_frm.py (continued)

```
    edit.add_cascade(label='Stuff',   menu=submenu,        underline=0)
    return menubar

if __name__ == '__main__':
    root = Tk()                                    # or TopLevel or Frame
    root.title('menu_frm')                         # set window-mgr info
    makemenu(root)                                 # associate a menu bar
    msg = Label(root, text='Frame menu basics')    # add something below
    msg.pack(expand=YES, fill=BOTH)
    msg.config(relief=SUNKEN, width=40, height=7, bg='beige')
    root.mainloop()
```

Again, let's isolate the linkage logic here to avoid getting distracted by other details. For the File menu case, here is what this boils down to:

```
menubar = Frame(parent)                    # make a Frame for the menubar
fbutton = Menubutton(menubar, text='File')  # attach a Menubutton to Frame
file    = Menu(fbutton)                     # attach a Menu to Menubutton
fbutton.config(menu=file)                   # crosslink button to menu
```

There is an extra Menubutton widget in this scheme, but it's not much more complex than making top-level window menus. Figures 10-5 and 10-6 show this script in action on Windows.

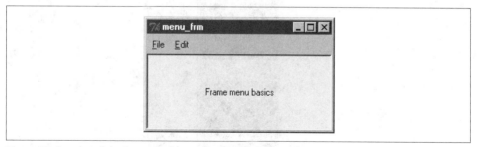

Figure 10-5. menu_frm: Frame and Menubutton menu bar

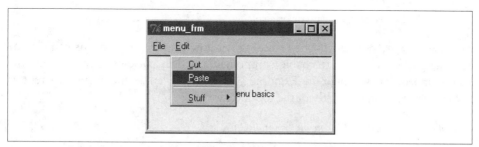

Figure 10-6. With the Edit menu selected

The menu widgets in this script provide a default set of event bindings that automatically pop up menus when selected with a mouse. This doesn't look or behave exactly like the top-level window menu scheme shown earlier, but it is close, can be configured in any way that frames can (i.e., with colors and borders), and will look similar on every platform (though this is probably not a feature).

The biggest advantage of frame-based menu bars, though, is that they can also be attached as nested components in larger displays. Example 10-4 and its resulting interface (Figure 10-7) show how.

Example 10-4. PP3E\Gui\Tour\menu_frm-multi.py

```
from menu_frm import makemenu        # can't use menu_win here--one window
from Tkinter import *                # but can attach frm menus to windows

root = Tk()
for i in range(2):                   # 2 menus nested in one window
    mnu = makemenu(root)
    mnu.config(bd=2, relief=RAISED)
    Label(root, bg='black', height=5, width=15).pack(expand=YES, fill=BOTH)
Button(root, text="Bye", command=root.quit).pack()
root.mainloop()
```

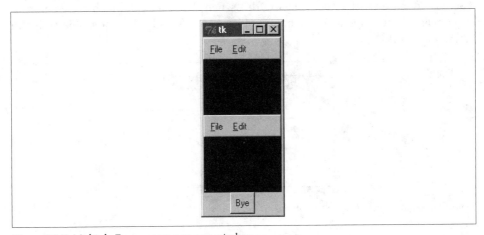

Figure 10-7. Multiple Frame menus on one window

Because they are not tied to the enclosing window, frame-based menus can also be used as part of another attachable component's widget package. For example, the menu-embedding behavior in Example 10-5 works even if the menu's parent is another Frame container and not the top-level window.

Example 10-5. PP3E\Gui\Tour\menu_frm-multi2.py

```
from menu_frm import makemenu        # can't use menu_win here--root=Frame
from Tkinter import *

root = Tk()
for i in range(3):                   # Three menus nested in the containers
    frm = Frame()
```

Example 10-5. PP3E\Gui\Tour\menu_frm-multi2.py (continued)

```
    mnu = makemenu(frm)
    mnu.config(bd=2, relief=RAISED)
    frm.pack(expand=YES, fill=BOTH)
    Label(frm, bg='black', height=5, width=15).pack(expand=YES, fill=BOTH)
Button(root, text="Bye", command=root.quit).pack( )
root.mainloop( )
```

Using Menubuttons and Optionmenus

In fact, menus based on `Menubutton` are even more general than Example 10-3 implies—they can actually show up anywhere on a display that normal buttons can, not just within a menu bar `Frame`. Example 10-6 makes a `Menubutton` pull-down list that simply shows up by itself, attached to the root window; Figure 10-8 shows the GUI it produces.

Example 10-6. PP3E\Gui\Tour\mbutton.py

```
from Tkinter import *
root    = Tk( )
mbutton = Menubutton(root, text='Food')      # the pull-down stands alone
picks   = Menu(mbutton)
mbutton.config(menu=picks)
picks.add_command(label='spam',  command=root.quit)
picks.add_command(label='eggs',  command=root.quit)
picks.add_command(label='bacon', command=root.quit)
mbutton.pack( )
mbutton.config(bg='white', bd=4, relief=RAISED)
root.mainloop( )
```

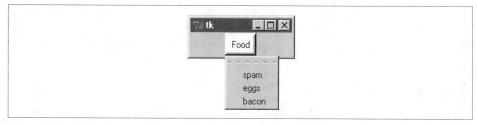

Figure 10-8. A Menubutton all by itself

The related Tkinter `Optionmenu` widget displays an item selected from a pull-down menu. It's roughly like a `Menubutton` plus a display label, and it displays a menu of choices when clicked, but you must link Tkinter variables (described in Chapter 9) to fetch the choice after the fact instead of registering callbacks, and menu entries are passed as arguments in the widget constructor call after the variable.

Example 10-7 illustrates typical `Optionmenu` usage and builds the interface captured in Figure 10-9. Clicking on either of the first two buttons opens a pull-down menu of options; clicking on the third "state" button fetches and prints the current values displayed in the first two.

Example 10-7. PP3E\Gui\Tour\optionmenu.py

```
from Tkinter import *
root = Tk()
var1 = StringVar()
var2 = StringVar()
opt1 = OptionMenu(root, var1, 'spam', 'eggs',  'toast')     # like Menubutton
opt2 = OptionMenu(root, var2, 'ham',  'bacon', 'sausage')   # but shows choice
opt1.pack(fill=X)
opt2.pack(fill=X)
var1.set('spam')
var2.set('ham')
def state(): print var1.get(), var2.get()                    # linked variables
Button(root, command=state, text='state').pack()
root.mainloop()
```

Figure 10-9. An Optionmenu at work

There are other menu-related topics that we'll skip here in the interest of space. For instance, scripts can add entries to system menus and can generate pop-up menus (posted in response to events, without an associated button). Refer to Tk and Tkinter resources for more details on this front.

In addition to simple selections and cascades, menus can also contain disabled entries, check button and radio button selections, and bitmap and photo images. The next section demonstrates how some of these special menu entries are programmed.

Windows with Both Menus and Toolbars

Besides showing a menu at the top, it is common for windows to display a row of buttons at the bottom. This bottom button row is usually called a toolbar, and it often contains shortcuts to items also available in the menus at the top. It's easy to add a toolbar to windows in Tkinter—simply pack buttons (and other kinds of widgets) into a frame, pack the frame on the bottom of the window, and set it to expand horizontally only. This is really just hierarchical GUI layout at work again, but make sure to pack toolbars (and frame-based menu bars) early so that other widgets in the middle of the display are clipped first when the window shrinks.

Example 10-8 shows one way to go about adding a toolbar to a window. It also demonstrates how to add photo images in menu entries (set the image attribute to a PhotoImage object) and how to disable entries and give them a grayed-out appearance (call the menu entryconfig method with the index of the item to disable, starting from 1). Notice that PhotoImage objects are saved as a list; remember, unlike other widgets, these go away if you don't hold on to them.

Example 10-8. PP3E\Gui\Tour\menuDemo.py

```python
#!/usr/local/bin/python
##########################################################################
# Tk8.0 style main window menus
# menu/tool bars packed before middle, fill=X (pack first=clip last);
# adds photo menu entries; see also: add_checkbutton, add_radiobutton
##########################################################################

from Tkinter import *                        # get widget classes
from tkMessageBox import *                    # get standard dialogs

class NewMenuDemo(Frame):                     # an extended frame
    def __init__(self, parent=None):         # attach to top-level?
        Frame.__init__(self, parent)         # do superclass init
        self.pack(expand=YES, fill=BOTH)
        self.createWidgets()                  # attach frames/widgets
        self.master.title("Toolbars and Menus")  # set window-manager info
        self.master.iconname("tkpython")     # label when iconified

    def createWidgets(self):
        self.makeMenuBar()
        self.makeToolBar()
        L = Label(self, text='Menu and Toolbar Demo')
        L.config(relief=SUNKEN, width=40, height=10, bg='white')
        L.pack(expand=YES, fill=BOTH)

    def makeToolBar(self):
        toolbar = Frame(self, cursor='hand2', relief=SUNKEN, bd=2)
        toolbar.pack(side=BOTTOM, fill=X)
        Button(toolbar, text='Quit',  command=self.quit    ).pack(side=RIGHT)
        Button(toolbar, text='Hello', command=self.greeting).pack(side=LEFT)

    def makeMenuBar(self):
        self.menubar = Menu(self.master)
        self.master.config(menu=self.menubar)    # master=top-level window
        self.fileMenu()
        self.editMenu()
        self.imageMenu()

    def fileMenu(self):
        pulldown = Menu(self.menubar)
        pulldown.add_command(label='Open...', command=self.notdone)
        pulldown.add_command(label='Quit',    command=self.quit)
        self.menubar.add_cascade(label='File', underline=0, menu=pulldown)

    def editMenu(self):
        pulldown = Menu(self.menubar)
        pulldown.add_command(label='Paste',  command=self.notdone)
        pulldown.add_command(label='Spam',   command=self.greeting)
```

Example 10-8. PP3E\Gui\Tour\menuDemo.py (continued)

```
        pulldown.add_separator()
        pulldown.add_command(label='Delete',  command=self.greeting)
        pulldown.entryconfig(4, state=DISABLED)
        self.menubar.add_cascade(label='Edit', underline=0, menu=pulldown)

    def imageMenu(self):
        photoFiles = ('guido.gif', 'pythonPowered.gif', 'ppython_sm_ad.gif')
        pulldown = Menu(self.menubar)
        self.photoObjs = []
        for file in photoFiles:
            img = PhotoImage(file='../gifs/' + file)
            pulldown.add_command(image=img, command=self.notdone)
            self.photoObjs.append(img)    # keep a reference
        self.menubar.add_cascade(label='Image', underline=0, menu=pulldown)

    def greeting(self):
        showinfo('greeting', 'Greetings')
    def notdone(self):
        showerror('Not implemented', 'Not yet available')
    def quit(self):
        if askyesno('Verify quit', 'Are you sure you want to quit?'):
            Frame.quit(self)

if __name__ == '__main__': NewMenuDemo().mainloop()  # if I'm run as a script
```

When run, this script generates the scene in Figure 10-10 at first. Figure 10-11 shows this window after being stretched a bit, with its File and Edit menus torn off and its Image menu selected. That's Python creator Guido van Rossum in this script's third menu (wearing his now-deprecated eyeglasses). Run this on your own computer to get a better feel for its behavior.[*]

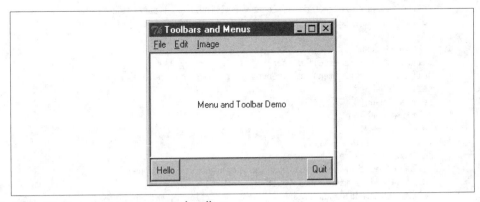

Figure 10-10. menuDemo: menus and toolbars

---

[*] Also note that toolbar items can be pictures too—simply associate small images with toolbar buttons, as shown at the end of Chapter 7.

Figure 10-11. Images and tear-offs on the job

Automating menu construction

Menus are a powerful Tkinter interface device. If you're like me, though, the examples in this section probably seem like a lot of work. Menu construction can be both code intensive and error prone if done by calling Tkinter methods directly. A better approach might automatically build and link up menus from a higher-level description of their contents. In fact, in Chapter 11, we'll meet a tool called GuiMixin that automates the menu construction process, given a data structure that contains all menus desired. As an added bonus, it supports both window and frame-style menus, so it can be used by both standalone programs and nested components. Although it's important to know the underlying calls used to make menus, you don't necessarily have to remember them for long.

Listboxes and Scrollbars

Listbox widgets allow you to display a list of items for selection, and Scrollbars are designed for navigating through the contents of other widgets. Because it is common to use these widgets together, let's study them both at once. Example 10-9 builds both a Listbox and a Scrollbar, as a packaged set.

Example 10-9. PP3E\Gui\Tour\scrolledlist.py

```
from Tkinter import *

class ScrolledList(Frame):
    def __init__(self, options, parent=None):
        Frame.__init__(self, parent)
        self.pack(expand=YES, fill=BOTH)              # make me expandable
        self.makeWidgets(options)
    def handleList(self, event):
```

Example 10-9. PP3E\Gui\Tour\scrolledlist.py (continued)

```
            index = self.listbox.curselection()         # on list double-click
            label = self.listbox.get(index)             # fetch selection text
            self.runCommand(label)                       # and call action here
    def makeWidgets(self, options):                      # or get(ACTIVE)
        sbar = Scrollbar(self)
        list = Listbox(self, relief=SUNKEN)
        sbar.config(command=list.yview)                  # xlink sbar and list
        list.config(yscrollcommand=sbar.set)             # move one moves other
        sbar.pack(side=RIGHT, fill=Y)                    # pack first=clip last
        list.pack(side=LEFT, expand=YES, fill=BOTH)      # list clipped first
        pos = 0
        for label in options:                            # add to listbox
            list.insert(pos, label)                      # or insert(END,label)
            pos += 1
        #list.config(selectmode=SINGLE, setgrid=1)       # select,resize modes
        list.bind('<Double-1>', self.handleList)         # set event handler
        self.listbox = list
    def runCommand(self, selection):                     # redefine me lower
        print 'You selected:', selection

if __name__ == '__main__':
    options = map((lambda x: 'Lumberjack-' + str(x)), range(20))
    #options = [('Lumberjack-%s' % x) for  x in range(20)]
    ScrolledList(options).mainloop()
```

This module can be run standalone to experiment with these widgets, but is also designed to be useful as a library object. By passing in different selection lists to the options argument and redefining the runCommand method in a subclass, the ScrolledList component class defined here can be reused anytime you need to display a scrollable list. With just a little forethought, it's easy to extend the Tkinter library with Python classes.

When run standalone, this script generates the window shown in Figure 10-12. It's a Frame, with a Listbox on its left containing 20 generated entries (the 5th has been clicked), along with an associated Scrollbar on its right for moving through the list. If you move the scroll, the list moves, and vice versa.

Programming Listboxes

Listboxes are straightforward to use, but they are populated and processed in somewhat unique ways compared to the widgets we've seen so far. Many listbox calls accept a passed-in index to refer to an entry in the list. Indexes start at integer 0 and grow higher, but Tkinter also accepts special name strings in place of integer offsets: end to refer to the end of the list, active to denote the line selected, and more. This generally yields more than one way to code listbox calls.

For instance, this script adds items to the listbox in this window by calling its insert method, with successive offsets (starting at zero):

Figure 10-12. scrolledlist at the top

```
list.insert(pos, label)
pos += 1
```

But you can also fill a list by simply adding items at the end without keeping a position counter at all, with either of these statements:

```
list.insert('end', label)    # add at end: no need to count positions
list.insert(END, label)      # END is preset to 'end' inside Tkinter
```

The listbox widget doesn't have anything like the command option we use to register callback handlers for button presses, so you either need to fetch listbox selections while processing other widgets' events (e.g., a button press elsewhere in the GUI) or tap into other event protocols to process user selections. To fetch a selected value, this script binds the <Double-1> left mouse button double-click event to a callback handler method with bind (seen earlier on this tour).

In the double-click handler, this script grabs the selected item out of the listbox with this pair of listbox method calls:

```
index = self.listbox.curselection( )     # get selection index
label = self.listbox.get(index)          # fetch text by its index
```

Here, too, you can code this differently. Either of the following lines has the same effect; they get the contents of the line at index 'active'—the one selected:

```
label = self.listbox.get('active')       # fetch from active index
label = self.listbox.get(ACTIVE)         # ACTIVE='active' in Tkinter
```

For illustration purposes, the class's default runCommand method prints the value selected each time you double-click an entry in the list—as fetched by this script, it comes back as a string reflecting the text in the selected entry:

```
C:\...\PP3E\Gui\Tour>python scrolledlist.py
You selected: Lumberjack-2
You selected: Lumberjack-19
You selected: Lumberjack-4
You selected: Lumberjack-12
```

Listboxes can also be useful input devices even without attached scroll bars; they accept color, font, and relief configuration options. They also support both single and multiple selection modes. The default mode allows only a single item to be selected, but the selectmode argument supports four settings: SINGLE, BROWSE, MULTIPLE, and EXTENDED (the default is BROWSE). Of these, the first two are single selection modes, and the last two allow multiple items to be selected.

These modes vary is subtle ways. For instance, BROWSE is like SINGLE, but it also allows the selection to be dragged. Clicking an item in MULTIPLE mode toggles its state without affecting other selected items. And the EXTENDED mode allows for multiple selections and works like the Windows file explorer GUI—you select one item with a simple click, multiple items with a Ctrl-click combination, and ranges of items with Shift-clicks. Multiple selections can be programmed with code of this sort:

```
listbox = Listbox(window, bg='white', font=('courier', fontsz))
listbox.config(selectmode=EXTENDED)
listbox.bind('<Double-1>', (lambda event: onDoubleClick()))

# get messages selected in listbox
selections = listbox.curselection()          # tuple of digit strs, 0..N-1
selections = [int(x)+1 for x in selections]   # convert to ints, make 1..N
```

When multiple selections are enabled, the curselection method returns a list of digit strings giving the relative numbers of the items selected, or it returns an empty tuple if none is selected. Really, this method always returns a tuple of digit strings, even in single selection mode (we don't care in Example 10-9, because the get method does the right thing for a one-item tuple, when fetching a value out of the listbox).

You can experiment with the selection alternatives on your own by uncommenting the selectmode setting in Example 10-9 and changing its value. You may get an error on double-clicks in multiple selection modes, though, because the get method will be passed a tuple of more than one selection index (print it out to see for yourself). We'll see multiple selections in action in the PyMailGUI example later in this book.

Programming Scroll Bars

The deepest magic in the Example 10-9 script, though, boils down to two lines of code:

```
sbar.config(command=list.yview)        # call list.yview when I move
list.config(yscrollcommand=sbar.set)   # call sbar.set when I move
```

The scroll bar and listbox are effectively cross-linked to each other through these configuration options; their values simply refer to bound widget methods of the other. By linking like this, Tkinter automatically keeps the two widgets in sync with each other as they move. Here's how this works:

- Moving a scroll bar invokes the callback handler registered with its `command` option. Here, `list.yview` refers to a built-in listbox method that adjusts the listbox display proportionally, based on arguments passed to the handler.

- Moving a listbox vertically invokes the callback handler registered with its `yscrollcommand` option. In this script, the `sbar.set` built-in method adjusts a scroll bar proportionally.

In other words, moving one automatically moves the other. It turns out that every scrollable object in Tkinter—`Listbox`, `Entry`, `Text`, and `Canvas`—has built-in `yview` and `xview` methods to process incoming vertical and horizontal scroll callbacks, as well as `yscrollcommand` and `xscrollcommand` options for specifying an associated scroll bar's callback handler to invoke. All scroll bars have a `command` option, to name an associated widget's handler to be called on moves. Internally, Tkinter passes information to all of these methods, and that information specifies their new position (e.g., "go 10 percent down from the top"), but your scripts need never deal with that level of detail.

Because the scroll bar and listbox have been cross-linked in their option settings, moving the scroll bar automatically moves the list, and moving the list automatically moves the scroll bar. To move the scroll bar, either drag the solid part or click on its arrows or empty areas. To move the list, click on the list and move the mouse pointer above or below the listbox without releasing the mouse button. In both cases, the list and scroll bar move in unison. Figure 10-13 shows the scene after moving down a few entries in the list, one way or another.

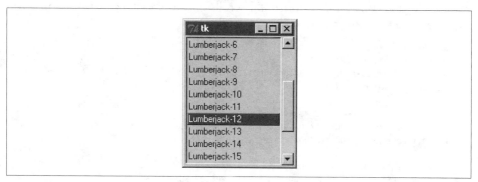

Figure 10-13. scrolledlist in the middle

Packing Scroll Bars

Finally, remember that widgets packed last are always clipped first when a window is shrunk. Because of that, it's important to pack scroll bars in a display as soon as possible so that they are the last to go when the window becomes too small for everything. You can generally make due with less than complete listbox text, but the scroll bar is crucial for navigating through the list. As Figure 10-14 shows, shrinking this script's window cuts out part of the list, but retains the scroll bar.

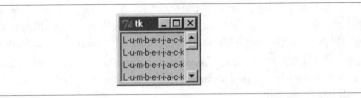

Figure 10-14. scrolledlist gets small

At the same time, you don't generally want a scroll bar to expand with a window, so be sure to pack it with just a fill=Y (or fill=X for a horizontal scroll) and not an expand=YES. Expanding this example's window, for instance, makes the listbox grow along with the window, but it keeps the scroll bar attached to the right and it keeps it the same size.

We'll see both scroll bars and listboxes repeatedly in later examples in this and later chapters (flip ahead to examples for PyEdit, PyForm, PyTree, and ShellGui, later in this chapter, for more). And although the example script in this section captures the fundamentals, I should point out that there is more to both scroll bars and listboxes than meets the eye here.

For example, it's just as easy to add *horizontal* scroll bars to scrollable widgets. They are programmed almost exactly like the vertical one implemented here, but callback handler names start with "x," not "y" (e.g., xscrollcommand), and an orient='horizontal' configuration option is set for the scroll bar object. For example, to add both vertical and horizontal scrolls and to crosslink their motions, you would use the following sort of code:

```
window  = Frame(self)
vscroll = Scrollbar(window)
hscroll = Scrollbar(window, orient='horizontal')
listbox = Listbox(window)

# move listbox when scroll moved
vscroll.config(command=listbox.yview, relief=SUNKEN)
hscroll.config(command=listbox.xview, relief=SUNKEN)

# move scroll when listbox moved
listbox.config(yscrollcommand=vscroll.set, relief=SUNKEN)
listbox.config(xscrollcommand=hscroll.set)
```

See the PyEdit, PyTree, and PyMailGUI programs later in this book for examples of horizontal scroll bars at work. Scroll bars see more kinds of GUI action too—they can be associated with other kinds of widgets in the Tkinter library. For instance, it is common to attach one to the Text widget. This brings us to the next point of interest on this tour.

Text

It's been said that Tkinter's strongest points may be its Text and Canvas widgets. Both provide a remarkable amount of functionality. For instance, the Tkinter Text widget was powerful enough to implement the web pages of Grail, an experimental web browser coded in Python; Text supports complex font-style settings, embedded images, unlimited undo and redo, and much more. The Tkinter Canvas widget, a general-purpose drawing device, allows for efficient free-form graphics and has been the basis of sophisticated image processing and visualization applications.

In Chapter 12, we'll put these two widgets to use to implement text editors (PyEdit), paint programs (PyDraw), clock GUIs (PyClock), and photo slideshows (PyView). For the purposes of this tour chapter, though, let's start out using these widgets in simpler ways. Example 10-10 implements a simple scrolled-text display, which knows how to fill its display with a text string or file.

Example 10-10. PP3E\Gui\Tour\scrolledtext.py

```
# a simple text or file viewer component

print 'PP3E scrolledtext'
from Tkinter import *

class ScrolledText(Frame):
    def __init__(self, parent=None, text='', file=None):
        Frame.__init__(self, parent)
        self.pack(expand=YES, fill=BOTH)             # make me expandable
        self.makewidgets()
        self.settext(text, file)
    def makewidgets(self):
        sbar = Scrollbar(self)
        text = Text(self, relief=SUNKEN)
        sbar.config(command=text.yview)              # xlink sbar and text
        text.config(yscrollcommand=sbar.set)         # move one moves other
        sbar.pack(side=RIGHT, fill=Y)                # pack first=clip last
        text.pack(side=LEFT, expand=YES, fill=BOTH)  # text clipped first
        self.text = text
    def settext(self, text='', file=None):
        if file:
            text = open(file, 'r').read()
        self.text.delete('1.0', END)                 # delete current text
        self.text.insert('1.0', text)                # add at line 1, col 0
        self.text.mark_set(INSERT, '1.0')            # set insert cursor
        self.text.focus()                            # save user a click
    def gettext(self):                               # returns a string
        return self.text.get('1.0', END+'-1c')       # first through last

if __name__ == '__main__':
    root = Tk()
    try:
        st = ScrolledText(file=sys.argv[1])          # filename on cmdline
```

Example 10-10. PP3E\Gui\Tour\scrolledtext.py (continued)

```
except IndexError:
    st = ScrolledText(text='Words\ngo here')      # or not: two lines
def show(event): print repr(st.gettext())         # show as raw string
root.bind('<Key-Escape>', show)                    # esc = dump text
root.mainloop()
```

Like the ScrolledList in Example 10-9, the ScrolledText object in this file is
designed to be a reusable component, but it can also be run standalone to display
text file contents. Also like the last section, this script is careful to pack the scroll
bar first so that it is cut out of the display last as the window shrinks, and arranges for
the embedded Text object to expand in both directions as the window grows. When
run with a filename argument, this script makes the window shown in Figure 10-15;
it embeds a Text widget on the left and a cross-linked Scrollbar on the right.

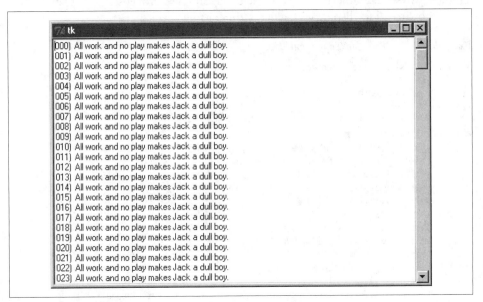

Figure 10-15. scrolledtext in action

Just for fun, I populated the text file displayed in the window with the following
code and command lines (and not just because I happen to live near an infamous
hotel in Colorado):

```
C:\...\PP3E\Gui\Tour>type temp.py
f = open('temp.txt', 'w')
for i in range(250):
    f.write('%03d)  All work and no play makes Jack a dull boy.\n' % i)
f.close()

C:\...\PP3E\Gui\Tour>python temp.py

C:\...\PP3E\Gui\Tour>python scrolledtext.py temp.txt
PP3E scrolledtext
```

To view a file, pass its name on the command line—its text is automatically displayed in the new window. By default, it is shown in a non-fixed-width font, but we'll pass a font option to the Text widget in the next example to change that.

Notice the PP3E scrolledtext message printed when this script runs. Because there is also a *ScrolledText.py* file in the standard Python distribution with a very different interface, the one here identifies itself when run or imported, so you can tell which one you've got. If the standard one ever goes away, import the one listed here for a simple text browser, and adjust configuration calls to include a .text qualifier level (the library version subclasses Text, not Frame).

Programming the Text Widget

To understand how this script works at all, though, we have to detour into a few Text widget details here. Earlier we met the Entry and Message widgets, which address a subset of the Text widget's uses. The Text widget is much richer in both features and interfaces—it supports both input and display of multiple lines of text, editing operations for both programs and interactive users, multiple fonts and colors, and much more. Text objects are created, configured, and packed just like any other widget, but they have properties all their own.

Text is a Python string

Although the Text widget is a powerful tool, its interface seems to boil down to two core concepts. First, the content of a Text widget is represented as a string in Python scripts, and multiple lines are separated with the normal \n line terminator. The string 'Words\ngo here', for instance, represents two lines when stored in or fetched from a Text widget; it would normally have a trailing \n also, but it doesn't have to.

To help illustrate this point, this script binds the Escape key press to fetch and print the entire contents of the Text widget it embeds:

```
C:\...\PP3E\Gui\Tour>python scrolledtext.py
PP3E scrolledtext
'Words\ngo here'
'Always look\non the bright\nside of life\n'
```

When run with arguments, the script stores a file's contents in the Text widget. When run without arguments, the script stuffs a simple literal string into the widget, displayed by the first Escape press output here (recall that \n is the escape sequence for the line terminator character). The second output here happens when pressing Escape in the shrunken window captured in Figure 10-16.

String positions

The second key to understanding Text code has to do with the ways you specify a position in the text string. Like the listbox, Text widgets allow you to specify such a

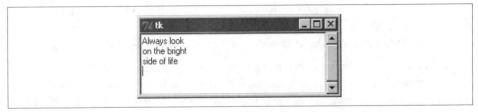

Figure 10-16. scrolledtext gets a positive outlook

position in a variety of ways. In Text, methods that expect a position to be passed in will accept an index, a mark, or a tag reference. Moreover, some special operations are invoked with predefined marks and tags—the insert cursor is mark INSERT, and the current selection is tag SEL.

Text indexes. Because it is a multiple-line widget, Text indexes identify both a line and a column. For instance, consider the interfaces of the basic insert, delete, and fetch text operations used by this script:

```
self.text.insert('1.0', text)          # insert text at the start
self.text.delete('1.0', END)           # delete all current text
return self.text.get('1.0', END+'-1c') # fetch first through last
```

In all of these, the first argument is an absolute index that refers to the start of the text string: string '1.0' means row 1, column (rows are numbered from 1 and columns from 0). An index '2.1' refers to the second character in the second row.

Like the listbox, text indexes can also be symbolic names: the END in the preceding delete call refers to the position just past the last character in the text string (it's a Tkinter variable preset to string 'end'). Similarly, the symbolic index INSERT (really, string 'insert') refers to the position immediately after the insert cursor—the place where characters would appear if typed at the keyboard. Symbolic names such as INSERT can also be called marks, described in a moment.

For added precision, you can add simple arithmetic extensions to index strings. The index expression END+'-1c' in the get call in the previous example, for instance, is really the string 'end-1c' and refers to one character back from END. Because END points to just beyond the last character in the text string, this expression refers to the last character itself. The -1c extension effectively strips the trailing \n that this widget adds to its contents (and may add a blank line if saved in a file).

Similar index string extensions let you name characters ahead (+1c), name lines ahead and behind (+2l, -2l), and specify things such as line ends and word starts around an index (lineend, wordstart). Indexes show up in most Text widget calls.

Text marks. Besides row/column identifier strings, you can also pass positions as names of marks—symbolic names for a position between two characters. Unlike absolute row/column positions, marks are virtual locations that move as new text is inserted or deleted (by your script or your user). A mark always refers to its original location, even if that location shifts to a different row and column over time.

To create a mark, call the text mark_set method with a string name and an index to give its logical location. For instance, this script sets the insert cursor at the start of the text initially, with a call like the first one here:

```
self.text.mark_set(INSERT, '1.0')          # set insert cursor to start
self.text.mark_set('linetwo', '2.0')       # mark current line 2
```

The name INSERT is a predefined special mark that identifies the insert cursor position; setting it changes the insert cursor's location. To make a mark of your own, simply provide a unique name as in the second call here and use it anywhere you need to specify a text position. The mark_unset call deletes marks by name.

Text tags. In addition to absolute indexes and symbolic mark names, the Text widget supports the notion of tags—symbolic names associated with one or more substrings within the Text widget's string. Tags can be used for many things, but they also serve to represent a position anywhere you need one: tagged items are named by their beginning and ending indexes, which can be later passed to position-based calls.

For example, Tkinter provides a built-in tag name, SEL—a Tkinter name preassigned to string 'sel'—which automatically refers to currently selected text. To fetch the text selected (highlighted) with a mouse, run either of these calls:

```
text = self.text.get(SEL_FIRST, SEL_LAST)     # use tags for from/to indexes
text = self.text.get('sel.first', 'sel.last') # strings and constants work
```

The names SEL_FIRST and SEL_LAST are just preassigned variables in the Tkinter module that refer to the strings used in the second line here. The text get method expects two indexes; to fetch text names by a tag, add .first and .last to the tag's name to get its start and end indexes.

To tag a substring, call the Text widget's tag_add method with a tag name string and start and stop positions (text can also be tagged as added in insert calls). To remove a tag from all characters in a range of text, call tag_remove:

```
self.text.tag_add('alltext', '1.0', END)   # tag all text in the widget
self.text.tag_add(SEL, index1, index2)     # select from index1 up to index2
self.text.tag_remove(SEL, '1.0', END)      # remove selection from all text
```

The first line here creates a new tag that names all text in the widget—from start through end positions. The second line adds a range of characters to the built-in SEL selection tag—they are automatically highlighted, because this tag is predefined to configure its members that way. The third line removes all characters in the text string from the SEL tag (all selections are unselected). Note that the tag_remove call just untags text within the named range; to really delete a tag completely, call tag_delete instead.

You can map indexes to tags dynamically too. For example, the text search method returns the row.column index of the first occurrence of a string between start and stop positions. To automatically select the text thus found, simply add its index to the built-in SEL tag:

```
where = self.text.search(target, INSERT, END)   # search from insert cursor
pastit = where + ('+%dc' % len(target))          # index beyond string found
self.text.tag_add(SEL, where, pastit)            # tag and select found string
self.text.focus()                                # select text widget itself
```

If you want only one string to be selected, be sure to first run the tag_remove call listed earlier—this code adds a selection in addition to any selections that already exist (it may generate multiple selections in the display). In general, you can add any number of substrings to a tag to process them as a group.

To summarize: indexes, marks, and tag locations can be used anytime you need a text position. For instance, the text see method scrolls the display to make a position visible; it accepts all three kinds of position specifiers:

```
self.text.see('1.0')          # scroll display to top
self.text.see(INSERT)         # scroll display to insert cursor mark
self.text.see(SEL_FIRST)      # scroll display to selection tag
```

Text tags can also be used in broader ways for formatting and event bindings, but I'll defer those details until the end of this section.

Adding Text-Editing Operations

Example 10-11 puts some of these concepts to work. It adds support for four common text-editing operations—file save, text cut and paste, and string find searching—by subclassing ScolledText to provide additional buttons and methods. The Text widget comes with a set of default keyboard bindings that perform some common editing operations too, but they roughly mimic the Unix Emacs editor and are somewhat obscure; it's more common and user friendly to provide GUI interfaces to editing operations in a GUI text editor.

Example 10-11. PP3E\Gui\Tour\simpleedit.py

```
##########################################################
# add common edit tools to scrolled text by inheritance;
# composition (embedding) would work just as well here;
# this is not robust! see PyEdit for a feature superset;
##########################################################

from Tkinter import *
from tkSimpleDialog import askstring
from tkFileDialog   import asksaveasfilename
from quitter        import Quitter
from scrolledtext   import ScrolledText              # here, not Python's

class SimpleEditor(ScrolledText):                     # see PyEdit for more
```

Example 10-11. PP3E\Gui\Tour\simpleedit.py (continued)

```python
    def __init__(self, parent=None, file=None):
        frm = Frame(parent)
        frm.pack(fill=X)
        Button(frm, text='Save',  command=self.onSave).pack(side=LEFT)
        Button(frm, text='Cut',   command=self.onCut).pack(side=LEFT)
        Button(frm, text='Paste', command=self.onPaste).pack(side=LEFT)
        Button(frm, text='Find',  command=self.onFind).pack(side=LEFT)
        Quitter(frm).pack(side=LEFT)
        ScrolledText.__init__(self, parent, file=file)
        self.text.config(font=('courier', 9, 'normal'))
    def onSave(self):
        filename = asksaveasfilename()
        if filename:
            alltext = self.gettext()                     # first through last
            open(filename, 'w').write(alltext)           # store text in file
    def onCut(self):
        text = self.text.get(SEL_FIRST, SEL_LAST)        # error if no select
        self.text.delete(SEL_FIRST, SEL_LAST)            # should wrap in try
        self.clipboard_clear()
        self.clipboard_append(text)
    def onPaste(self):                                   # add clipboard text
        try:
            text = self.selection_get(selection='CLIPBOARD')
            self.text.insert(INSERT, text)
        except TclError:
            pass                                         # not to be pasted
    def onFind(self):
        target = askstring('SimpleEditor', 'Search String?')
        if target:
            where = self.text.search(target, INSERT, END) # from insert cursor
            if where:                                    # returns an index
                print where
                pastit = where + ('+%dc' % len(target))  # index past target
                #self.text.tag_remove(SEL, '1.0', END)   # remove selection
                self.text.tag_add(SEL, where, pastit)    # select found target
                self.text.mark_set(INSERT, pastit)       # set insert mark
                self.text.see(INSERT)                    # scroll display
                self.text.focus()                        # select text widget

if __name__ == '__main__':
    try:
        SimpleEditor(file=sys.argv[1]).mainloop()    # filename on command line
    except IndexError:
        SimpleEditor().mainloop()                    # or not
```

This, too, was written with one eye toward reuse—the SimpleEditor class it defines could be attached or subclassed by other GUI code. As I'll explain at the end of this section, though, it's not yet as robust as a general-purpose library tool should be. Still, it implements a functional text editor in a small amount of portable code. When run standalone, it brings up the window in Figure 10-17 (shown running in Windows); index positions are printed on stdout after each successful find operation:

```
C:\...\PP3E\Gui\Tour>python simpleedit.py simpleedit.py
PP3E scrolledtext
14.4
24.4
```

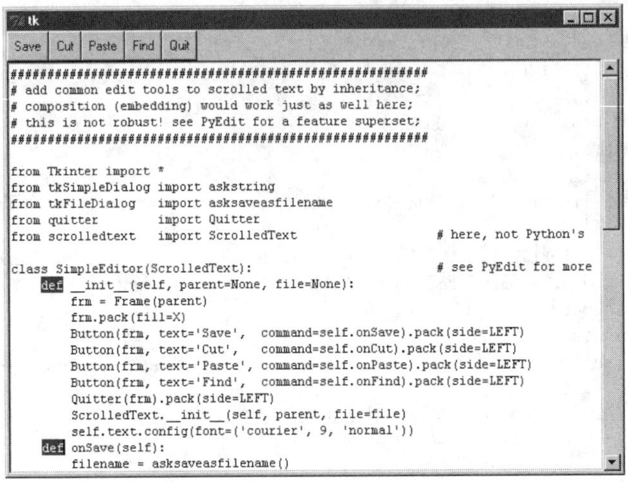

Figure 10-17. simpleedit in action

The save operation pops up the common save dialog that is available in Tkinter and is tailored to look native on each platform. Figure 10-18 shows this dialog in action on Windows. Find operations also pop up a standard dialog box to input a search string (Figure 10-19); in a full-blown editor, you might want to save this string away to repeat the find again (we will, in Chapter 12's PyEdit discussion).

Using the clipboard

Besides Text widget operations, Example 10-11 applies the Tkinter clipboard interfaces in its cut-and-paste functions. Together, these operations allow you to move text within a file (cut in one place, paste in another). The clipboard they use is just a place to store data temporarily—deleted text is placed on the clipboard on a cut, and text is inserted from the clipboard on a paste. If we restrict our focus to this program alone, there really is no reason that the text string cut couldn't simply be stored in a Python instance variable. But the clipboard is actually a much larger concept.

The clipboard used by this script is an interface to a system-wide storage space, shared by all programs on your computer. Because of that, it can be used to transfer data between applications, even ones that know nothing of Tkinter. For instance,

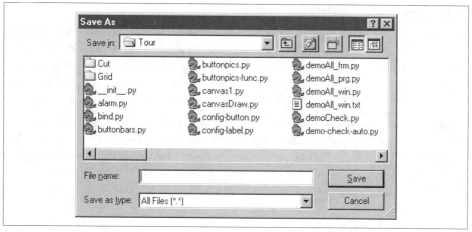

Figure 10-18. Save pop-up dialog on Windows

Figure 10-19. Find pop-up dialog

text cut or copied in a Microsoft Word session can be pasted in a SimpleEditor window, and text cut in SimpleEditor can be pasted in a Microsoft Notepad window (try it). By using the clipboard for cut and paste, SimpleEditor automatically integrates with the window system at large. Moreover, the clipboard is not just for the Text widget—it can also be used to cut and paste graphical objects in the Canvas widget (discussed next).

As used in this script, the basic Tkinter clipboard interface looks like this:

```
self.clipboard_clear()                        # clear the clipboard
self.clipboard_append(text)                   # store a text string on it
text = self.selection_get(selection='CLIPBOARD') # fetch contents, if any
```

All of these calls are available as methods inherited by all Tkinter widget objects because they are global in nature. The CLIPBOARD selection used by this script is available on all platforms (a PRIMARY selection is also available, but is only generally useful on X Windows, so we'll ignore it here). Notice that the clipboard selection_get call throws a TclError exception if it fails; this script simply ignores it and abandons a paste request, but we'll do better later.

Composition versus inheritance

As coded, `SimpleEditor` uses inheritance to extend `ScrolledText` with extra buttons and callback methods. As we've seen, it's also reasonable to attach (embed) GUI objects coded as components, such as `ScrolledText`. The attachment model is usually called composition; some people find it simpler to understand and less prone to name clashes than extension by inheritance.

To give you an idea of the differences between these two approaches, the following sketches the sort of code you would write to attach `ScrolledText` to `SimpleEditor` with changed lines in bold font (see the file *simpleedit-2.py* on the book's examples distribution for a complete composition implementation). It's mostly a matter of passing in the right parents and adding an extra `st` attribute name to get to the Text widget's methods:

```
class SimpleEditor(Frame):
    def __init__(self, parent=None, file=None):
        Frame.__init__(self, parent)
        self.pack()
        frm = Frame(self)
        frm.pack(fill=X)
        Button(frm, text='Save',  command=self.onSave).pack(side=LEFT)
                    ...more...
        Quitter(frm).pack(side=LEFT)
        self.st = ScrolledText(self, file=file)         # attach, not subclass
        self.st.text.config(font=('courier', 9, 'normal'))
    def onSave(self):
        filename = asksaveasfilename()
        if filename:
            alltext = self.st.gettext()                 # go through attribute
            open(filename, 'w').write(alltext)
    def onCut(self):
        text = self.st.text.get(SEL_FIRST, SEL_LAST)
        self.st.text.delete(SEL_FIRST, SEL_LAST)
                    ...more...
```

The window looks identical when such code is run. I'll let you be the judge of whether composition or inheritance is better here. If you code your Python GUI classes right, they will work under either regime.

It's called "Simple" for a reason

Finally, before you change your system registry to make `SimpleEditor` your default text file viewer, I should mention that although it shows the basics, it's something of a stripped-down version of the PyEdit example we'll meet in Chapter 12. In fact, you should study that example now if you're looking for more complete Tkinter text-processing code in general. There, we'll also use more advanced text operations, such as the undo/redo interface, case-insensitive searches, and more. Because the Text widget is so powerful, it's difficult to demonstrate more of its features without the volume of code that is already listed in the PyEdit program.

I should also point out that SimpleEditor not only is limited in function, but also is just plain careless—many boundary cases go unchecked and trigger uncaught exceptions that don't kill the GUI, but are not handled or reported. Even errors that are caught are not reported to the user (e.g., a paste, with nothing to be pasted). Be sure to see the PyEdit example for a more robust and complete implementation of the operations introduced in SimpleEditor.

Advanced Text and Tag Operations

Besides position specifiers, text tags can also be used to apply formatting and behavior to all characters in a substring and all substrings added to a tag. In fact, this is where much of the power of the Text widget lies:

- Tags have formatting attributes for setting color, font, tabs, and line spacing and justification; to apply these to many parts of the text at once, associate them with a tag and apply formatting to the tag with the tag_config method, much like the general config widget we've been using.

- Tags can also have associated event bindings, which let you implement things such as hyperlinks in a Text widget: clicking the text triggers its tag's event handler. Tag bindings are set with a tag_bind method, much like the general widget bind method we've already met.

With tags, it's possible to display multiple configurations within the same Text widget; for instance, you can apply one font to the Text widget at large and other fonts to tagged text. In addition, the Text widget allows you to embed other widgets at an index (they are treated like a single character), as well as images.

Example 10-12 illustrates the basics of all these advanced tools at once and draws the interface captured in Figure 10-20. This script applies formatting and event bindings to three tagged substrings, displays text in two different font and color schemes, and embeds an image and a button. Double-clicking any of the tagged substrings (or the embedded button) with a mouse triggers an event that prints a "Got tag event" message to stdout.

Example 10-12. PP3E\Gui\Tour\texttags.py

```
# demo advanced tag and text interfaces

from Tkinter import *
root = Tk( )
def hello(event): print 'Got tag event'

# make and config a Text
text = Text( )
text.config(font=('courier', 15, 'normal'))              # set font for all
text.config(width=20, height=12)
text.pack(expand=YES, fill=BOTH)
text.insert(END, 'This is\n\nthe meaning\n\nof life.\n\n')   # insert six lines
```

Example 10-12. PP3E\Gui\Tour\texttags.py (continued)

```
# embed windows and photos
btn = Button(text, text='Spam', command=lambda: hello(0))    # embed a button
btn.pack()
text.window_create(END, window=btn)                          # embed a photo
text.insert(END, '\n\n')
img = PhotoImage(file='../gifs/PythonPowered.gif')
text.image_create(END, image=img)

# apply tags to substrings
text.tag_add('demo', '1.5', '1.7')                           # tag 'is'
text.tag_add('demo', '3.0', '3.3')                           # tag 'the'
text.tag_add('demo', '5.3', '5.7')                           # tag 'life'
text.tag_config('demo', background='purple')                 # change colors in tag
text.tag_config('demo', foreground='white')                  # not called bg/fg here
text.tag_config('demo', font=('times', 16, 'underline'))     # change font in tag
text.tag_bind('demo', '<Double-1>', hello)                   # bind events in tag
root.mainloop()
```

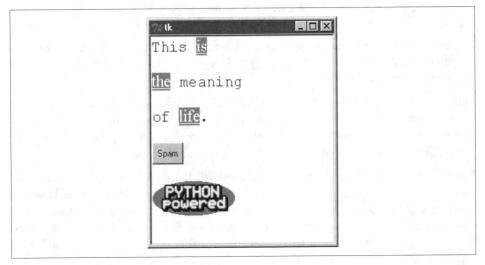

Figure 10-20. Text tags in action

Such embedding and tag tools could ultimately be used to render a web page. In fact, Python's standard htmllib HTML parser module can help automate web page GUI construction. As you can probably tell, though, the Text widget offers more GUI programming options than we have space to list here. For more details on tag and text options, consult other Tk and Tkinter references. Right now, art class is about to begin.

Canvas

When it comes to graphics, the Tkinter Canvas widget is the most free-form device in the library. It's a place to draw shapes, move objects dynamically, and place other kinds of widgets. The canvas is based on a structured graphic object model: everything drawn on a canvas can be processed as an object. You can get down to the pixel-by-pixel level in a canvas, but you can also deal in terms of larger objects such as shapes, photos, and embedded widgets. And the canvas is powerful enough to support everything from simple paint programs to full-scale visualization and animation.

Basic Canvas Operations

Canvases are ubiquitous in much nontrivial GUI work, and we'll see larger canvas examples show up later in this book under the names PyDraw, PyView, PyClock, and PyTree. For now, let's jump right into an example that illustrates the basics. Example 10-13 runs most of the major canvas drawing methods.

Example 10-13. PP3E\Gui\Tour\canvas1.py

```
# demo all basic canvas interfaces
from Tkinter import *

canvas = Canvas(width=300, height=300, bg='white')    # 0,0 is top left corner
canvas.pack(expand=YES, fill=BOTH)                     # increases down, right

canvas.create_line(100, 100, 200, 200)                # fromX, fromY, toX, toY
canvas.create_line(100, 200, 200, 300)                # draw shapes
for i in range(1, 20, 2):
    canvas.create_line(0, i, 50, i)

canvas.create_oval(10, 10, 200, 200, width=2, fill='blue')
canvas.create_arc(200, 200, 300, 100)
canvas.create_rectangle(200, 200, 300, 300, width=5, fill='red')
canvas.create_line(0, 300, 150, 150, width=10, fill='green')

photo=PhotoImage(file='../gifs/guido.gif')
canvas.create_image(250, 0, image=photo, anchor=NW)   # embed a photo

widget = Label(canvas, text='Spam', fg='white', bg='black')
widget.pack()
canvas.create_window(100, 100, window=widget)         # embed a widget
canvas.create_text(100, 280, text='Ham')              # draw some text
mainloop()
```

When run, this script draws the window captured in Figure 10-21. We saw how to place a photo on canvas and size a canvas for a photo earlier on this tour (see Chapter 9). This script also draws shapes, text, and even an embedded Label widget.

Its window gets by on looks alone; in a moment, we'll learn how to add event callbacks that let users interact with drawn items.

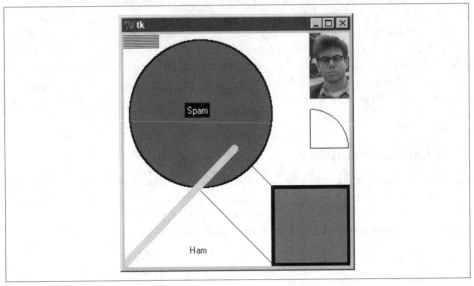

Figure 10-21. canvas1 hardcoded object sketches

Programming the Canvas Widget

Canvases are easy to use, but they rely on a coordinate system, define unique drawing methods, and name objects by identifier or tag. This section introduces these core canvas concepts.

Coordinates

All items drawn on a canvas are distinct objects, but they are not really widgets. If you study the canvas1 script closely, you'll notice that canvases are created and packed (or gridded or placed) within their parent container just like any other widget in Tkinter. But the items drawn on a canvas are not. Shapes, images, and so on, are positioned and moved on the canvas by coordinates, identifiers, and tags. Of these, coordinates are the most fundamental part of the canvas model.

Canvases define an (X,Y) coordinate system for their drawing area; x means the horizontal scale, y means vertical. By default, coordinates are measured in screen pixels (dots), the upper-left corner of the canvas has coordinates (0,0), and x and y coordinates increase to the right and down, respectively. To draw and embed objects within a canvas, you supply one or more (X,Y) coordinate pairs to give absolute canvas locations. This is different from the constraints we've used to pack widgets thus far, but it allows very fine-grained control over graphical layouts, and it supports more free-form interface techniques such as animation.[*]

Object construction

The canvas allows you to draw and display common shapes such as lines, ovals, rectangles, arcs, and polygons. In addition, you can embed text, images, and other kinds of Tkinter widgets such as labels and buttons. The canvas1 script demonstrates all the basic graphic object constructor calls; to each, you pass one or more sets of (X,Y) coordinates to give the new object's location, start point and endpoint, or diagonally opposite corners of a bounding box that encloses the shape:

```
id = canvas.create_line(fromX, fromY, toX, toY)      # line start, stop
id = canvas.create_oval(fromX, fromY, toX, toY)      # two opposite box corners
id = canvas.create_arc( fromX, fromY, toX, toY)      # two opposite oval corners
id = canvas.create_rectangle(fromX, fromY, toX, toY) # two opposite corners
```

Other drawing calls specify just one (X,Y) pair, to give the location of the object's upper-left corner:

```
id = canvas.create_image(250, 0, image=photo, anchor=NW)  # embed a photo
id = canvas.create_window(100, 100, window=widget)        # embed a widget
id = canvas.create_text(100, 280, text='Ham')             # draw some text
```

The canvas also provides a create_polygon method that accepts an arbitrary set of coordinate arguments defining the endpoints of connected lines; it's useful for drawing more arbitrary kinds of shapes composed of straight lines.

In addition to coordinates, most of these drawing calls let you specify common configuration options, such as outline width, fill color, outline color, and so on. Individual object types have unique configuration options all their own too; for instance, lines may specify the shape of an optional arrow, and text, widgets, and images may be anchored to a point of the compass (this looks like the packer's anchor, but really it gives a point on the object that is positioned at the [X,Y] coordinates given in the create call; NW puts the upper-left corner at [X,Y]).

Perhaps the most important thing to notice here, though, is that Tkinter does most of the "grunt" work for you—when drawing graphics, you provide coordinates, and shapes are automatically plotted and rendered in the pixel world. If you've ever done any lower-level graphics work, you'll appreciate the difference.

---

[*] Animation techniques are covered at the end of this tour. Because you can embed other widgets in a canvas's drawing area, their coordinate system also makes them ideal for implementing GUIs that let users design other GUIs by dragging embedded widgets around on the canvas—a useful canvas application we would explore in this book if I had a few hundred pages to spare.

Object identifiers and operations

Although not used by the canvas1 script, every object you put on a canvas has an identifier, returned by the create_ method that draws or embeds the object (what was coded as id in the last section's examples). This identifier can later be passed to other methods that move the object to new coordinates, set its configuration options, delete it from the canvas, raise or lower it among other overlapping objects, and so on.

For instance, the canvas move method accepts both an object identifier and X and Y offsets (not coordinates), and it moves the named object by the offsets given:

```
canvas.move(objectIdOrTag, offsetX, offsetY)    # move object(s) by offset
```

If this happens to move the object off-screen, it is simply clipped (not shown). Other common canvas operations process objects too:

```
canvas.delete(objectIdOrTag)                    # delete object(s) from canvas
canvas.tkraise(objectIdOrTag)                   # raise object(s) to front
canvas.lower(objectIdOrTag)                     # lower object(s) below others
canvas.itemconfig(objectIdOrTag, fill='red')    # fill object(s) with red color
```

Notice the tkraise name—raise by itself is a reserved word in Python. Also note that the itemconfig method is used to configure objects drawn on a canvas after they have been created; use config to set configuration options for the canvas itself. The best thing to notice here, though, is that because Tkinter is based on structured objects, you can process a graphic object all at once; there is no need to erase and redraw each pixel manually to implement a move or a raise.

Canvas object tags

But it gets even better. In addition to object identifiers, you can also perform canvas operations on entire sets of objects at once, by associating them all with a *tag*, a name that you make up and apply to objects on the display. Tagging objects in a Canvas is at least similar in spirit to tagging substrings in the Text widget we studied in the prior section. In general terms, canvas operation methods accept either a single object's identifier or a tag name.

For example, you can move an entire set of drawn objects by associating all with the same tag and passing the tag name to the canvas move method. In fact, this is why move takes offsets, not coordinates—when given a tag, each object associated with the tag is moved by the same (X,Y) offsets; absolute coordinates would make all the tagged objects appear on top of each other instead.

To associate an object with a tag, either specify the tag name in the object drawing call's tag option or call the addtag_withtag(tag, objectIdOrTag) canvas method (or its relatives). For instance:

```
canvas.create_oval(x1, y1, x2, y2, fill='red', tag='bubbles')
canvas.create_oval(x3, y3, x4, y4, fill='red', tag='bubbles')
objectId = canvas.create_oval(x5, y5, x6, y6, fill='red')
```

```
canvas.addtag_withtag('bubbles', objectId)
canvas.move('bubbles', diffx, diffy)
```

This makes three ovals and moves them at the same time by associating them all with the same tag name. Many objects can have the same tag, many tags can refer to the same object, and each tag can be individually configured and processed.

As in Text, Canvas widgets have predefined tag names too: the tag all refers to all objects on the canvas, and current refers to whatever object is under the mouse cursor. Besides asking for an object under the mouse, you can also search for objects with the find_ canvas methods: canvas.find_closest(X,Y), for instance, returns a tuple whose first item is the identifier of the closest object to the supplied coordinates—handy after you've received coordinates in a general mouse-click event callback.

We'll revisit the notion of canvas tags by example later in this chapter (see the animation scripts near the end if you can't wait). Canvases support additional operations and options that we don't have space to cover here (e.g., the canvas postscript method lets you save the canvas in a PostScript file). See later examples in this book, such as PyDraw, for more details, and consult other Tk or Tkinter references for an exhaustive list of canvas object options.

Scrolling Canvases

As demonstrated in Example 10-14, scroll bars can be cross-linked with a canvas using the same protocols we used to add them to listboxes and text earlier, but with a few unique requirements.

Example 10-14. PP3E\Gui\Tour\scrolledcanvas.py

```
from Tkinter import *

class ScrolledCanvas(Frame):
    def __init__(self, parent=None, color='brown'):
        Frame.__init__(self, parent)
        self.pack(expand=YES, fill=BOTH)              # make me expandable
        canv = Canvas(self, bg=color, relief=SUNKEN)
        canv.config(width=300, height=200)            # display area size
        canv.config(scrollregion=(0,0,300, 1000))     # canvas size corners
        canv.config(highlightthickness=0)             # no pixels to border

        sbar = Scrollbar(self)
        sbar.config(command=canv.yview)               # xlink sbar and canv
        canv.config(yscrollcommand=sbar.set)          # move one moves other
        sbar.pack(side=RIGHT, fill=Y)                 # pack first=clip last
        canv.pack(side=LEFT, expand=YES, fill=BOTH)   # canv clipped first

        for i in range(10):
            canv.create_text(150, 50+(i*100), text='spam'+str(i), fill='beige')
        canv.bind('<Double-1>', self.onDoubleClick)   # set event handler
        self.canvas = canv
```

Example 10-14. PP3E\Gui\Tour\scrolledcanvas.py (continued)

```
    def onDoubleClick(self, event):
        print event.x, event.y
        print self.canvas.canvasx(event.x), self.canvas.canvasy(event.y)

if __name__ == '__main__': ScrolledCanvas().mainloop()
```

This script makes the window in Figure 10-22. It is similar to prior scroll examples, but scrolled canvases introduce two kinks:

Scrollable versus viewable sizes

You can specify the size of the displayed view window, but you must specify the size of the scrollable canvas at large. The size of the view window is what is displayed, and it can be changed by the user by resizing. The size of the scrollable canvas will generally be larger—it includes the entire content, of which only part is displayed in the view window. Scrolling moves the view window over the scrollable size canvas.

Viewable to absolute coordinate mapping

In addition, you may need to map between event view area coordinates and overall canvas coordinates if the canvas is larger than its view area. In a scrolling scenario, the canvas will almost always be larger than the part displayed, so mapping is often needed when canvases are scrolled. In some applications, this mapping is not required, because widgets embedded in the canvas respond to users directly (e.g., buttons in the PyPhoto example in Chapter 12). If the user interacts with the canvas directly, though (e.g., in a drawing program), mapping from view coordinates to scrollable size coordinates may be necessary.

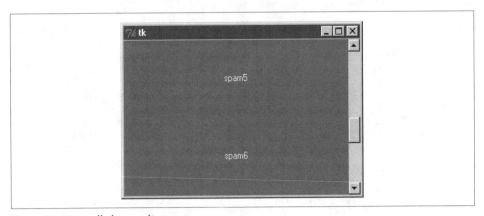

Figure 10-22. scrolledcanvas live

Sizes are given as configuration options. To specify a view area size, use canvas `width` and `height` options. To specify an overall canvas size, give the (X,Y) coordinates of the upper-left and lower-right corners of the canvas in a four-item tuple passed to the `scrollregion` option. If no view area size is given, a default size is used. If no scrollregion is given, it defaults to the view area size; this makes the scroll bar useless, since the view is assumed to hold the entire canvas.

Mapping coordinates is a bit subtler. If the scrollable view area associated with a canvas is smaller than the canvas at large, the (X,Y) coordinates returned in event objects are view area coordinates, not overall canvas coordinates. You'll generally want to scale the event coordinates to canvas coordinates, by passing them to the canvasx and canvasy canvas methods before using them to process objects.

For example, if you run the scrolled canvas script and watch the messages printed on mouse double-clicks, you'll notice that the event coordinates are always relative to the displayed view window, not to the overall canvas:

```
C:\...\PP3E\Gui\Tour>python scrolledcanvas.py
2 0                     event x,y when scrolled to top of canvas
2.0 0.0                 canvas x,y -same, as long as no border pixels
150 106
150.0 106.0
299 197
299.0 197.0
3 2                     event x,y when scrolled to bottom of canvas
3.0 802.0               canvas x,y -y differs radically
296 192
296.0 992.0
152 97                  when scrolled to a midpoint in the canvas
152.0 599.0
16 187
16.0 689.0
```

Here, the mapped canvas X is always the same as the canvas X because the display area and canvas are both set at 300 pixels wide (it would be off by 2 pixels due to automatic borders if not for the script's highlightthickness setting). But notice that the mapped Y is wildly different from the event Y if you click after a vertical scroll. Without scaling, the event's Y incorrectly points to a spot much higher in the canvas.

Most of this book's canvas examples need no such scaling—(0,0) always maps to the upper-left corner of the canvas display in which a mouse click occurs—but just because canvases are not scrolled. See the next section for a canvas with both horizontal and vertical scrolls; the PyTree program later in this book is similar, but it also uses dynamically changed scrollable region sizes when new trees are viewed.

As a rule of thumb, if your canvases scroll, be sure to scale event coordinates to true canvas coordinates in callback handlers that care about positions. Some handlers might not care whether events are bound to individual drawn objects or embedded widgets instead of the canvas at large, but we need to move on to the next two sections to see why.

Scrollable Canvases and Image Thumbnails

At the end of Chapter 9, we looked at a collection of scripts that display thumbnail image links for all photos in a directory. There, we noted that scrolling is a major requirement for large photo collections. Now that we know about scrolling canvases, we can finally put them to work to implement this final extension.

Example 10-15 is a customization of the last chapter's code, which displays thumbnails in a scrollable canvas. See the prior chapter for more details on its operation (including the ImageTk module imported from the required Python Imaging Library [PIL] third-party extension). Here, we are just adding a canvas positioning the thumbnail buttons at absolute coordinates in the canvas, and computing the scrollable size using concepts outlined in the prior section.

Example 10-15. PP3E\Gui\PIL\viewer_thumbs_scrolled.py

```
###############################################################
# image viewer extension: uses fixed size for thumbnails
# for uniform layout, and adds scrolling for large image sets
# by displaying thumbs in a canvas widget with scroll bars;
# requires PIL to view image formats such as JPEG, and reuses
# thumbs maker and single photo viewer in viewer_thumbs.py;
# caveat/to do: this could also scroll popped-up images that
# are too large for the screen, cropped on Windows as is;
# see PyPhoto later in book for a much more complete version;
###############################################################

import sys, math
from Tkinter import *
from ImageTk import PhotoImage
from viewer_thumbs import makeThumbs, ViewOne

def viewer(imgdir, kind=Toplevel, numcols=None, height=300, width=300):
    """
    use fixed-size buttons, scrollable canvas;
    sets scrollable (full) size, and places
    thumbs at abs x,y coordinates in canvas;
    caveat: assumes all thumbs are same size
    """
    win = kind( )
    win.title('Simple viewer: ' + imgdir)
    quit = Button(win, text='Quit', command=win.quit, bg='beige')
    quit.pack(side=BOTTOM, fill=X)

    canvas = Canvas(win, borderwidth=0)
    vbar = Scrollbar(win)
    hbar = Scrollbar(win, orient='horizontal')

    vbar.pack(side=RIGHT,  fill=Y)              # pack canvas after bars
    hbar.pack(side=BOTTOM, fill=X)              # so clipped first
    canvas.pack(side=TOP, fill=BOTH, expand=YES)
```

Example 10-15. PP3E\Gui\PIL\viewer_thumbs_scrolled.py (continued)

```
    vbar.config(command=canvas.yview)              # call on scroll move
    hbar.config(command=canvas.xview)
    canvas.config(yscrollcommand=vbar.set)         # call on canvas move
    canvas.config(xscrollcommand=hbar.set)
    canvas.config(height=height, width=width)      # init viewable area size
                                                   # changes if user resizes
    thumbs = makeThumbs(imgdir)                     # [(imgfile, imgobj)]
    numthumbs = len(thumbs)
    if not numcols:
        numcols = int(math.ceil(math.sqrt(numthumbs)))  # fixed or N x N
    numrows = int(math.ceil(numthumbs / float(numcols)))

    linksize = max(thumbs[0][1].size)              # (width, height)
    fullsize = (0, 0,                              # upper left  X,Y
        (linksize * numcols), (linksize * numrows) )  # lower right X,Y
    canvas.config(scrollregion=fullsize)           # scrollable area size

    rowpos = 0
    savephotos = []
    while thumbs:
        thumbsrow, thumbs = thumbs[:numcols], thumbs[numcols:]
        colpos = 0
        for (imgfile, imgobj) in thumbsrow:
            photo   = PhotoImage(imgobj)
            link    = Button(canvas, image=photo)
            handler = lambda savefile=imgfile: ViewOne(imgdir, savefile)
            link.config(command=handler, width=linksize, height=linksize)
            link.pack(side=LEFT, expand=YES)
            canvas.create_window(colpos, rowpos, anchor=NW,
                    window=link, width=linksize, height=linksize)
            colpos += linksize
            savephotos.append(photo)
        rowpos += linksize
    return win, savephotos

if __name__ == '__main__':
    imgdir = (len(sys.argv) > 1 and sys.argv[1]) or 'images'
    main, save = viewer(imgdir, kind=Tk)
    main.mainloop()
```

To see this program in action, install the PIL extension described at the end of Chapter 9 and launch the script from a command line, passing the name of the image directory to be viewed as a command-line argument:

```
...\PP3E\Gui\PIL>viewer_thumbs_scrolled.py c:\mark\camera\jun1705\DCIM\100CANON
```

As before, clicking on a thumbnail image opens the corresponding image at its full size in a new pop-up window. Figure 10-23 shows the viewer at work on a directory copied from my digital camera.

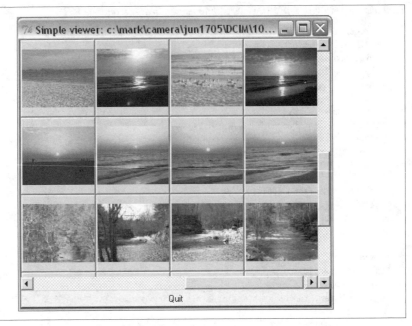

Figure 10-23. Scrolled thumbnail image viewer

Or, simply run the script as is from a command line by clicking its icon or within IDLE—without command-line arguments, it displays the contents of the default *images* subdirectory in the book's source code tree, as captured in Figure 10-24.

Scrolling images too: PyPhoto (ahead)

As is, the scrollable thumbnail viewer in Example 10-15 has a major limitation: images that are larger than the physical screen are simply truncated on Windows when popped up. Moreover, there is no way to resize images once opened, to open other directories, and so on. It's a fairly simplistic demonstration of canvas programming.

In Chapter 12, we'll learn how to do better when we meet the PyPhoto example program. PyPhoto will scroll the full size of images well. In addition, it has tools for a variety of resizing effects, and it supports saving images to files and opening other image directories on the fly. At its core, though, PyPhoto will reuse the techniques of our simple browser here, as well as the thumbnail generation code we wrote in the prior chapter.

For the rest of this story, watch for PyPhoto in Chapter 12 or study the source code of the example program *pyphoto1.py*, in the source directory.

For the purposes of this chapter, notice how in Example 10-15, the thumbnail viewer's actions are associated with embedded button widgets, not with the canvas itself. To see how to implement the latter, let's move on to the next section.

Figure 10-24. Displaying the default images directory

Using Canvas Events

Like Text and Listbox, there is no notion of a single command callback for Canvas. Instead, canvas programs generally use other widgets, as in Example 10-15 and in the earlier section "Scrolling Canvases," or the lower-level bind call to set up handlers for mouse clicks, key presses, and the like. Example 10-16 shows how to bind events for the canvas itself, in order to implement a few of the more common canvas drawing operations.

Example 10-16. PP3E\Gui\Tour\canvasDraw.py

```
#####################################################################
# draw elastic shapes on a canvas on drag, move on right click;
# see canvasDraw_tags*.py for extensions with tags and animation
#####################################################################

from Tkinter import *
trace = 0

class CanvasEventsDemo:
    def __init__(self, parent=None):
        canvas = Canvas(width=300, height=300, bg='beige')
        canvas.pack()
        canvas.bind('<ButtonPress-1>', self.onStart)      # click
        canvas.bind('<B1-Motion>',     self.onGrow)       # and drag
```

Example 10-16. PP3E\Gui\Tour\canvasDraw.py (continued)

```
        canvas.bind('<Double-1>',      self.onClear)     # delete all
        canvas.bind('<ButtonPress-3>', self.onMove)      # move latest
        self.canvas = canvas
        self.drawn  = None
        self.kinds = [canvas.create_oval, canvas.create_rectangle]
    def onStart(self, event):
        self.shape = self.kinds[0]
        self.kinds = self.kinds[1:] + self.kinds[:1]     # start dragout
        self.start = event
        self.drawn = None
    def onGrow(self, event):                             # delete and redraw
        canvas = event.widget
        if self.drawn: canvas.delete(self.drawn)
        objectId = self.shape(self.start.x, self.start.y, event.x, event.y)
        if trace: print objectId
        self.drawn = objectId
    def onClear(self, event):
        event.widget.delete('all')                       # use tag all
    def onMove(self, event):
        if self.drawn:                                   # move to click spot
            if trace: print self.drawn
            canvas = event.widget
            diffX, diffY = (event.x - self.start.x), (event.y - self.start.y)
            canvas.move(self.drawn, diffX, diffY)
            self.start = event

if __name__ == '__main__':
    CanvasEventsDemo()
    mainloop()
```

This script intercepts and processes three mouse-controlled actions:

Clearing the canvas

> To erase everything on the canvas, the script binds the double left-click event to run the canvas's delete method with the all tag—again, a built-in tag that associates every object on the screen. Notice that the Canvas widget clicked is available in the event object passed in to the callback handler (it's also available as self.canvas).

Dragging out object shapes

> Pressing the left mouse button and dragging (moving it while the button is still pressed) creates a rectangle or oval shape as you drag. This is often called dragging out an object—the shape grows and shrinks in an elastic rubber-band fashion as you drag the mouse and winds up with a final size and location given by the point where you release the mouse button.

> To make this work in Tkinter, all you need to do is delete the old shape and draw another as each drag event fires; both delete and draw operations are fast enough to achieve the elastic drag-out effect. Of course, to draw a shape to the current mouse location you need a starting point; to delete before a redraw you

also must remember the last drawn object's identifier. Two events come into play: the initial button press event saves the start coordinates (really, the initial press event object, which contains the start coordinates), and mouse movement events erase and redraw from the start coordinates to the new mouse coordinates and save the new object ID for the next event's erase.

Object moves

When you click the right mouse button (button 3), the script moves the most recently drawn object to the spot you clicked in a single step. The event argument gives the (X,Y) coordinates of the spot clicked, and we subtract the saved starting coordinates of the last drawn object to get the (X,Y) offsets to pass to the canvas move method (again, move does not take positions). Remember to scale event coordinates first if your canvas is scrolled.

The net result creates a window like that shown in Figure 10-25 after user interaction. As you drag out objects, the script alternates between ovals and rectangles; set the script's trace global to watch object identifiers scroll on stdout as new objects are drawn during a drag. This screenshot was taken after a few object drag-outs and moves, but you'd never tell from looking at it; run this example on your own computer to get a better feel for the operations it supports.

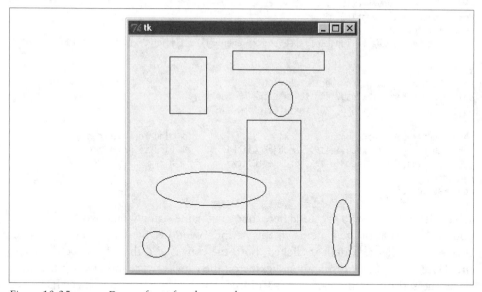

Figure 10-25. canvasDraw after a few drags and moves

Binding events on specific items

Much like we did for the Text widget, it is also possible to bind events for one or more specific objects drawn on a Canvas with its tag_bind method. This call accepts either a tag name string or an object ID in its first argument. For instance, you can register a different callback handler for mouse clicks on every drawn item or on any in a group of drawn and tagged items, rather than for the entire canvas at large. Example 10-17 binds a double-click handler in both the canvas itself and on two specific text items within it, to illustrate the interfaces. It generates Figure 10-26 when run.

Figure 10-26. Canvas-bind window

Example 10-17. PP3E\Gui\Tour\canvas-bind.py

```
from Tkinter import *

def onCanvasClick(event):
    print 'Got canvas click', event.x, event.y, event.widget
def onObjectClick(event):
    print 'Got object click', event.x, event.y, event.widget,
    print event.widget.find_closest(event.x, event.y)   # find text object's ID

root = Tk( )
canv = Canvas(root, width=100, height=100)
obj1 = canv.create_text(50, 30, text='Click me one')
obj2 = canv.create_text(50, 70, text='Click me two')

canv.bind('<Double-1>', onCanvasClick)                   # bind to whole canvas
canv.tag_bind(obj1, '<Double-1>', onObjectClick)         # bind to drawn item
canv.tag_bind(obj2, '<Double-1>', onObjectClick)         # a tag works here too
canv.pack( )
root.mainloop( )
```

Object IDs are passed to tag_bind here, but a tag name string would work too. When you click outside the text items in this script's window, the canvas event handler fires; when either text item is clicked, both the canvas and the text object handlers fire. Here is the stdout result after clicking on the canvas twice and on each text item once; the script uses the canvas find_closest method to fetch the object ID of the particular text item clicked (the one closest to the click spot):

```
C:\...\PP3E\Gui\Tour>python canvas-bind.py
Got canvas click 3 6 .8217952                canvas clicks
Got canvas click 46 52 .8217952
Got object click 51 33 .8217952 (1,)         first text click
Got canvas click 51 33 .8217952
Got object click 55 69 .8217952 (2,)         second text click
Got canvas click 55 69 .8217952
```

We'll revisit the notion of events bound to canvases in the PyDraw example in Chapter 12, where we'll use them to implement a feature-rich paint and motion program. We'll also return to the canvasDraw script later in this chapter, to add tag-based moves and simple animation with time-based tools, so keep this page bookmarked for reference. First, though, let's follow a promising side road to explore another way to lay out widgets within windows.

Grids

So far, we've been arranging widgets in displays by calling their pack methods—an interface to the packer geometry manager in Tkinter. This section introduces grid, the most commonly used alternative to the packer.

As we learned earlier, Tkinter geometry managers work by arranging child widgets within a parent container widget (parents are typically Frames or top-level windows). When we ask a widget to pack or grid itself, we're really asking its parent to place it among its siblings. With pack, we provide constraints and let the geometry manager lay out widgets appropriately. With grid, we arrange widgets in rows and columns in their parent, as though the parent container widget was a table.

Gridding is an entirely distinct geometry management system in Tkinter. In fact, at this writing, pack and grid are mutually exclusive for widgets that have the same parent—within a given parent container, we can either pack widgets or grid them, but we cannot do both. That makes sense, if you realize that geometry managers do their jobs as parents, and a widget can be arranged by only one geometry manager.

At least within one container, though, that means you must pick either grid or pack and stick with it. So why grid, then? In general, grid is handy for laying out form-like displays; arranging input fields in row/column fashion can be at least as easy as laying out the display with nested frames. As we'll see, though, grid doesn't offer substantial code or complexity savings compared to equivalent packer solutions in practice, especially when things like resizability are added to the GUI picture. In other words, the choice between the two layout schemes is largely one of style, not technology.

Grid Basics

Let's start off with the basics; Example 10-18 lays out a table of Labels and Entry fields—widgets we've already met. Here, though, they are arrayed on a grid.

Example 10-18. PP3E\Gui\Tour\Grid\grid1.py

```
from Tkinter import *
colors = ['red', 'green', 'orange', 'white', 'yellow', 'blue']

r = 0
```

Example 10-18. PP3E\Gui\Tour\Grid\grid1.py (continued)

```
for c in colors:
    Label(text=c, relief=RIDGE,  width=25).grid(row=r, column=0)
    Entry(bg=c,   relief=SUNKEN, width=50).grid(row=r, column=1)
    r = r+1

mainloop()
```

When run, this script creates the window shown in Figure 10-27, pictured with data typed into a few of the input fields. Once again, this book won't do justice to the colors displayed on the right, so you'll have to stretch your imagination a little (or run this script on a computer of your own).

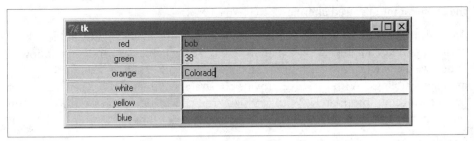

Figure 10-27. The grid geometry manager in pseudoliving color

This is a classic input form layout: labels on the left describe data to type into entry fields on the right. Just for fun, this script displays color names on the left and the entry field of the corresponding color on the right. It achieves its nice table-like layout with the following two lines:

```
    Label(...).grid(row=r, column=0)
    Entry(...).grid(row=r, column=1)
```

From the perspective of the container window, the label is gridded to columns in the current row number (a counter that starts at 0), and the entry is placed in column 1. The upshot is that the grid system lays out all the labels and entries in a two-dimensional table automatically, with evenly sized columns large enough to hold the largest item in each column.

grid Versus pack

Time for some compare-and-contrast: Example 10-19 implements the same sort of colorized input form with both grid and pack, to make it easy to see the differences between the two approaches.

Example 10-19. PP3E\Gui\Tour\Grid\grid2.py

```
# add equivalent pack window

from Tkinter import *
```

Example 10-19. PP3E\Gui\Tour\Grid\grid2.py (continued)

```
colors = ['red', 'green', 'yellow', 'orange', 'blue', 'navy']

def gridbox(parent):
    r = 0
    for c in colors:
        l = Label(parent, text=c, relief=RIDGE,  width=25)
        e = Entry(parent, bg=c,   relief=SUNKEN, width=50)
        l.grid(row=r, column=0)
        e.grid(row=r, column=1)
        r = r+1

def packbox(parent):
    for c in colors:
        f = Frame(parent)
        l = Label(f, text=c, relief=RIDGE,  width=25)
        e = Entry(f, bg=c,   relief=SUNKEN, width=50)
        f.pack(side=TOP)
        l.pack(side=LEFT)
        e.pack(side=RIGHT)

if __name__ == '__main__':
    root = Tk()
    gridbox(Toplevel())
    packbox(Toplevel())
    Button(root, text='Quit', command=root.quit).pack()
    mainloop()
```

The basic label and entry widgets are created the same way by these two functions, but they are arranged in very different ways:

- With pack, we use side options to attach labels and rows on the left and right, and create a Frame for each row (itself attached to the parent's top).

- With grid, we instead assign each widget a row and column position in the implied tabular grid of the parent, using options of the same name.

The difference in the amount of code required for each scheme is roughly a wash: the pack scheme must create a Frame per row, but the grid scheme must keep track of the current row number. Running the script makes the windows in Figure 10-28.

Combining grid and pack

Notice that the prior script passes a brand-new Toplevel to each form constructor function so that the grid and pack versions wind up in distinct top-level windows. Because the two geometry managers are mutually exclusive within a given parent, we have to be careful not to mix them carelessly. For instance, Example 10-20 is able to put both the packed and the gridded widgets on the same window, but only by isolating each in its own Frame container widget.

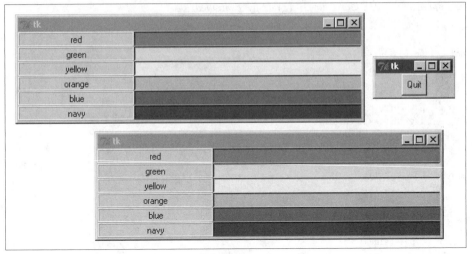

Figure 10-28. Equivalent grid and pack windows

Example 10-20. PP3E\Gui\Tour\Grid\grid2-same.py

```
###################################################################
# can't grid and pack in same parent container (e.g., root window)
# but can mix in same window if done in different parent frames;
###################################################################

from Tkinter import *
from grid2 import gridbox, packbox

root = Tk()

Label(root, text='Grid:').pack()
frm = Frame(root, bd=5, relief=RAISED); frm.pack(padx=5, pady=5)
gridbox(frm)

Label(root, text='Pack:').pack()
frm = Frame(root, bd=5, relief=RAISED); frm.pack(padx=5, pady=5)
packbox(frm)

Button(root, text='Quit', command=root.quit).pack()
mainloop()
```

We get a composite window when this runs with two forms that look identical
(Figure 10-29), but the two nested frames are actually controlled by completely different geometry managers.

On the other hand, the sort of code in Example 10-21 fails badly, because it attempts
to use pack and grid within the same parent—only one geometry manager can be
used on any one parent.

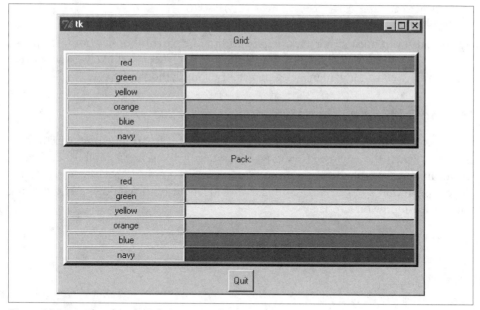

Figure 10-29. grid and pack in the same window

Example 10-21. PP3E\Gui\Tour\Grid\grid2-fails.py

```
###################################################################
# FAILS-- can't grid and pack in same parent (root window)
###################################################################

from Tkinter import *
from grid2 import gridbox, packbox

root = Tk( )
gridbox(root)
packbox(root)
Button(root, text='Quit', command=root.quit).pack( )
mainloop( )
```

This script passes the same parent (the top-level window) to each function in an effort to make both forms appear in one window. It also utterly hangs the Python process on my machine, without ever showing any windows at all (on Windows 98, I had to resort to Ctrl-Alt-Delete to kill it). Geometry manager combinations can be subtle until you get the hang of this; to make this example work, for instance, we simply need to isolate the grid box in a parent container all its own to keep it away from the packing going on in the root window:

```
root = Tk( )
frm = Frame(root)
frm.pack( )                # this works
gridbox(frm)              # gridbox must have its own parent in which to grid
packbox(root)
```

```
    Button(root, text='Quit', command=root.quit).pack( )
    mainloop( )
```

Again, today you must either pack or grid within one parent, but not both. It's possible that this restriction may be lifted in the future, but it seems unlikely given the disparity in the two window manager schemes; try your Python to be sure.

Making Gridded Widgets Expandable

And now, some practical bits: the grids we've seen so far are fixed in size; they do not grow when the enclosing window is resized by a user. Example 10-22 implements an unreasonably patriotic input form with both grid and pack again, but adds the configuration steps needed to make all widgets in both windows expand along with their window on a resize.

Example 10-22. PP3E\Gui\Tour\Grid\grid3.py

```
# add label and resizing

from Tkinter import *
colors = ['red', 'white', 'blue']

def gridbox(root):
    Label(root, text='Grid').grid(columnspan=2)
    r = 1
    for c in colors:
        l = Label(root, text=c, relief=RIDGE,  width=25)
        e = Entry(root, bg=c,   relief=SUNKEN, width=50)
        l.grid(row=r, column=0, sticky=NSEW)
        e.grid(row=r, column=1, sticky=NSEW)
        root.rowconfigure(r, weight=1)
        r = r+1
    root.columnconfigure(0, weight=1)
    root.columnconfigure(1, weight=1)


def packbox(root):
    Label(root, text='Pack').pack( )
    for c in colors:
        f = Frame(root)
        l = Label(f, text=c, relief=RIDGE,  width=25)
        e = Entry(f, bg=c,   relief=SUNKEN, width=50)
        f.pack(side=TOP,   expand=YES, fill=BOTH)
        l.pack(side=LEFT,  expand=YES, fill=BOTH)
        e.pack(side=RIGHT, expand=YES, fill=BOTH)

root = Tk( )
gridbox(Toplevel(root))
packbox(Toplevel(root))
Button(root, text='Quit', command=root.quit).pack( )
mainloop( )
```

When run, this script makes the scene in Figure 10-30. It builds distinct pack and grid windows again, with entry fields on the right colored red, white, and blue (or for readers not working along on a computer: gray, white, and an arguably darker gray).

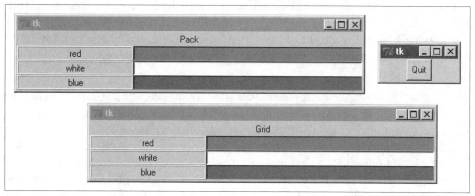

Figure 10-30. grid and pack windows before resizing

This time, though, resizing both windows with mouse drags makes all their embedded labels and entry fields expand along with the parent window, as we see in Figure 10-31.

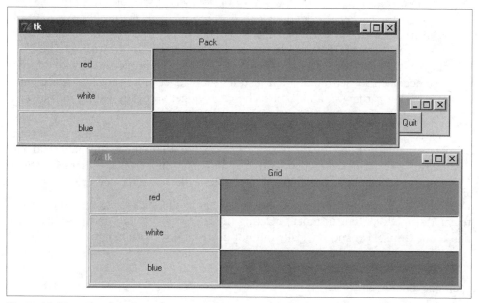

Figure 10-31. grid and pack windows resized

Resizing in grids

Now that I've shown you what these windows do, I need to explain how they do it. We learned earlier how to make widgets expand with pack: we use expand and fill options to increase space allocations and stretch into them. To make expansion work for widgets arranged by grid, we need to use different protocols. Rows and columns must be marked with a weight to make them expandable, and widgets must also be made sticky so that they are stretched within their allocated grid cell:

Heavy rows and columns

> With pack, we make each row expandable by making the corresponding Frame expandable, with expand=YES and fill=BOTH. Gridders must be a bit more specific: to get full expandability, call the grid container's rowconfigure method for each row and its columnconfigure for each column. To both methods, pass a weight option with a value greater than zero to enable rows and columns to expand. Weight defaults to zero (which means no expansion), and the grid container in this script is just the top-level window. Using different weights for different rows and columns makes them grow at proportionally different rates.

Sticky widgets

> With pack, we use fill options to stretch widgets to fill their allocated space horizontally or vertically, and anchor options to position widgets within their allocated space. With grid, the sticky option serves the roles of both fill and anchor in the packer. Gridded widgets can optionally be made sticky on one side of their allocated cell space (such as anchor) or more than one side to make them stretch (such as fill). Widgets can be made sticky in four directions—N, S, E, and W, and concatenations of these letters specify multiple-side stickiness. For instance, a sticky setting of W left justifies the widget in its allocated space (such as a packer anchor=W), and NS stretches the widget vertically within its allocated space (such as a packer fill=Y).

> Widget stickiness hasn't been useful in examples thus far because the layouts were regularly sized (widgets were no smaller than their allocated grid cell space), and resizes weren't supported at all. Here, this script specifies NSEW stickiness to make widgets stretch in all directions with their allocated cells.

Different combinations of row and column weights and sticky settings generate different resize effects. For instance, deleting the columnconfig lines in the grid3 script makes the display expand vertically but not horizontally. Try changing some of these settings yourself to see the sorts of effects they produce.

Spanning columns and rows

There is one other big difference in how the grid3 script configures its windows. Both the grid and the pack windows display a label on the top that spans the entire window. For the packer scheme, we simply make a label attached to the top of the window at large (remember, side defaults to TOP):

```
Label(root, text='Pack').pack()
```

Because this label is attached to the window's top before any row frames are, it appears across the entire window top as expected. But laying out such a label takes a bit more work in the rigid world of grids; the first line of the grid implementation function does it like this:

```
Label(root, text='Grid').grid(columnspan=2)
```

To make a widget span across multiple columns, we pass grid a columnspan option with a spanned-column count. Here, it just specifies that the label at the top of the window should stretch over the entire window—across both the label and the entry columns. To make a widget span across multiple rows, pass a rowspan option instead. The regular layouts of grids can be either an asset or a liability, depending on how regular your user interface will be; these two span settings let you specify exceptions to the rule when needed.

So which geometry manager comes out on top here? When resizing is factored in, as in this script, gridding actually becomes slightly more complex (in fact, gridding requires three extra lines of code here). On the other hand, grid is nice for simple forms, and your grids and packs may vary.

Laying Out Larger Tables with grid

So far, we've been building two-column arrays of labels and input fields. That's typical of input forms, but the Tkinter grid manager is capable of configuring much grander matrixes. For instance, Example 10-23 builds a five-row by four-column array of labels, where each label simply displays its row and column number (row. col). When run, the window in Figure 10-32 appears on-screen.

Example 10-23. PP3E\Gui\Tour\Grid\grid4.py

```
# simple 2D table

from Tkinter import *

for i in range(5):
    for j in range(4):
        l = Label(text='%d.%d' % (i, j), relief=RIDGE)
        l.grid(row=i, column=j, sticky=NSEW)

mainloop( )
```

If you think this is starting to look like it might be a way to program spreadsheets, you may be on to something. Example 10-24 takes this idea a bit further and adds a button that prints the table's current input field values to the stdout stream (usually, to the console window).

Figure 10-32. A 5×4 array of coordinate labels

Example 10-24. PP3E\Gui\Tour\Grid\grid5.py

```python
# 2D table of input fields

from Tkinter import *

rows = []
for i in range(5):
    cols = []
    for j in range(4):
        e = Entry(relief=RIDGE)
        e.grid(row=i, column=j, sticky=NSEW)
        e.insert(END, '%d.%d' % (i, j))
        cols.append(e)
    rows.append(cols)

def onPress():
    for row in rows:
        for col in row:
            print col.get(),
        print

Button(text='Fetch', command=onPress).grid()
mainloop()
```

When run, this script creates the window in Figure 10-33 and saves away all the grid's entry field widgets in a two-dimensional list of lists. When its Fetch button is pressed, the script steps through the saved list of lists of entry widgets, to fetch and display all the current values in the grid. Here is the output of two Fetch presses—one before I made input field changes, and one after:

```
C:\...\PP3E\Gui\Tour\Grid>python grid5.py
0.0 0.1 0.2 0.3
1.0 1.1 1.2 1.3
2.0 2.1 2.2 2.3
3.0 3.1 3.2 3.3
4.0 4.1 4.2 4.3
0.0 0.1 0.2 42
1.0 1.1 1.2 43
2.0 2.1 2.2 44
3.0 3.1 3.2 45
4.0 4.1 4.2 46
```

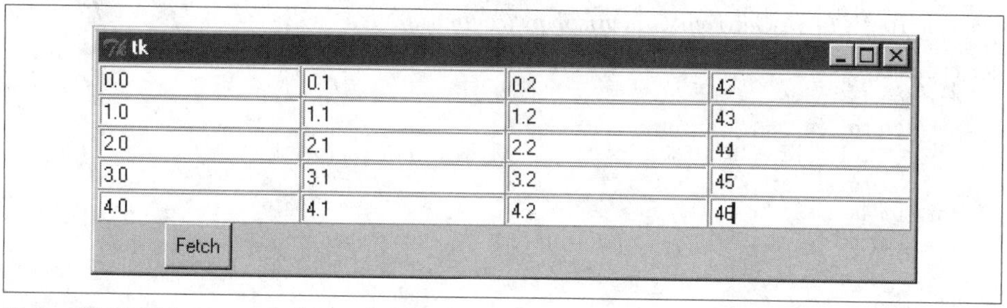

Figure 10-33. A larger grid of input fields

Now that we know how to build and step through arrays of input fields, let's add a few more useful buttons. Example 10-25 adds another row to display column sums and adds buttons to clear all fields to zero and calculate column sums.

Example 10-25. PP3E\Gui\Tour\Grid\grid5b.py

```python
# add column sums, clearing

from Tkinter import *
numrow, numcol = 5, 4

rows = []
for i in range(numrow):
    cols = []
    for j in range(numcol):
        e = Entry(relief=RIDGE)
        e.grid(row=i, column=j, sticky=NSEW)
        e.insert(END, '%d.%d' % (i, j))
        cols.append(e)
    rows.append(cols)

sums = []
for i in range(numcol):
    l = Label(text='?', relief=SUNKEN)
    l.grid(row=numrow, column=i, sticky=NSEW)
    sums.append(l)

def onPrint():
    for row in rows:
        for col in row:
            print col.get(),
        print
    print

def onSum():
    t = [0] * numcol
    for i in range(numcol):
        for j in range(numrow):
            t[i]= t[i] + eval(rows[j][i].get())
    for i in range(numcol):
        sums[i].config(text=str(t[i]))
```

Example 10-25. PP3E\Gui\Tour\Grid\grid5b.py (continued)

```
def onClear( ):
    for row in rows:
        for col in row:
            col.delete('0', END)
            col.insert(END, '0.0')
    for sum in sums:
        sum.config(text='?')

import sys
Button(text='Sum',   command=onSum).grid(row=numrow+1, column=0)
Button(text='Print', command=onPrint).grid(row=numrow+1, column=1)
Button(text='Clear', command=onClear).grid(row=numrow+1, column=2)
Button(text='Quit',  command=sys.exit).grid(row=numrow+1, column=3)
mainloop( )
```

Figure 10-34 shows this script at work summing up four columns of numbers; to get a different size table, change the numrow and numcol variables at the top of the script.

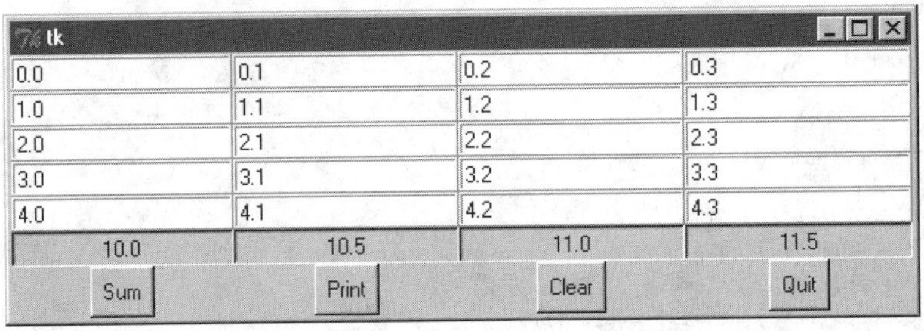

Figure 10-34. Adding column sums

And finally, Example 10-26 is one last extension that is coded as a class for reusability, and adds a button to load the table from a datafile. Datafiles are assumed to be coded as one line per row, with whitespace (spaces or tabs) between each column within a row line. Loading a file of data automatically resizes the table GUI to accommodate the number of columns in the table.

Example 10-26. PP3E\Gui\Tour\Grid\grid5c.py

```
# recode as an embeddable class

from Tkinter import *
from PP3E.Gui.Tour.quitter import Quitter        # reuse, pack, and grid

class SumGrid(Frame):
    def __init__(self, parent=None, numrow=5, numcol=5):
        Frame.__init__(self, parent)
        self.numrow = numrow                       # I am a frame container
        self.numcol = numcol                       # caller packs or grids me
        self.makeWidgets(numrow, numcol)           # else only usable one way
```

Example 10-26. PP3E\Gui\Tour\Grid\grid5c.py (continued)

```python
    def makeWidgets(self, numrow, numcol):
        self.rows = []
        for i in range(numrow):
            cols = []
            for j in range(numcol):
                e = Entry(self, relief=RIDGE)
                e.grid(row=i+1, column=j, sticky=NSEW)
                e.insert(END, '%d.%d' % (i, j))
                cols.append(e)
            self.rows.append(cols)

        self.sums = []
        for i in range(numcol):
            l = Label(self, text='?', relief=SUNKEN)
            l.grid(row=numrow+1, column=i, sticky=NSEW)
            self.sums.append(l)

        Button(self, text='Sum',   command=self.onSum).grid(row=0, column=0)
        Button(self, text='Print', command=self.onPrint).grid(row=0, column=1)
        Button(self, text='Clear', command=self.onClear).grid(row=0, column=2)
        Button(self, text='Load',  command=self.onLoad).grid(row=0, column=3)
        Quitter(self).grid(row=0, column=4)     # fails: Quitter(self).pack( )

    def onPrint(self):
        for row in self.rows:
            for col in row:
                print col.get( ),
            print
        print

    def onSum(self):
        t = [0] * self.numcol
        for i in range(self.numcol):
            for j in range(self.numrow):
                t[i]= t[i] + eval(self.rows[j][i].get( ))
        for i in range(self.numcol):
            self.sums[i].config(text=str(t[i]))

    def onClear(self):
        for row in self.rows:
            for col in row:
                col.delete('0', END)
                col.insert(END, '0.0')
        for sum in self.sums:
            sum.config(text='?')

    def onLoad(self):
        from tkFileDialog import *
        file = askopenfilename( )
        if file:
            for r in self.rows:
                for c in r: c.grid_forget( )
```

Example 10-26. PP3E\Gui\Tour\Grid\grid5c.py (continued)

```
            for s in self.sums:
                s.grid_forget()
            filelines  = open(file, 'r').readlines()
            self.numrow = len(filelines)
            self.numcol = len(filelines[0].split())
            self.makeWidgets(self.numrow, self.numcol)
            row = 0
            for line in filelines:
                fields = line.split()
                for col in range(self.numcol):
                    self.rows[row][col].delete('0', END)
                    self.rows[row][col].insert(END, fields[col])
                row = row+1

if __name__ == '__main__':
    import sys
    root = Tk()
    root.title('Summer Grid')
    if len(sys.argv) != 3:
        SumGrid(root).pack()      # .grid() works here too
    else:
        rows, cols = eval(sys.argv[1]), eval(sys.argv[2])
        SumGrid(root, rows, cols).pack()
    mainloop()
```

Notice that this module's SumGrid class is careful not to either grid or pack itself. In order to be attachable to containers where other widgets are being gridded or packed, it leaves its own geometry management ambiguous and requires callers to pack or grid its instances. It's OK for containers to pick either scheme for their own children because they effectively seal off the pack-or-grid choice. But attachable component classes that aim to be reused under both geometry managers cannot manage themselves because they cannot predict their parent's policy.

This is a fairly long example that doesn't say much else about gridding or widgets in general, so I'll leave most of it as suggested reading and just show what it does. Figure 10-35 shows the initial window created by this script after changing the last column and requesting a sum.

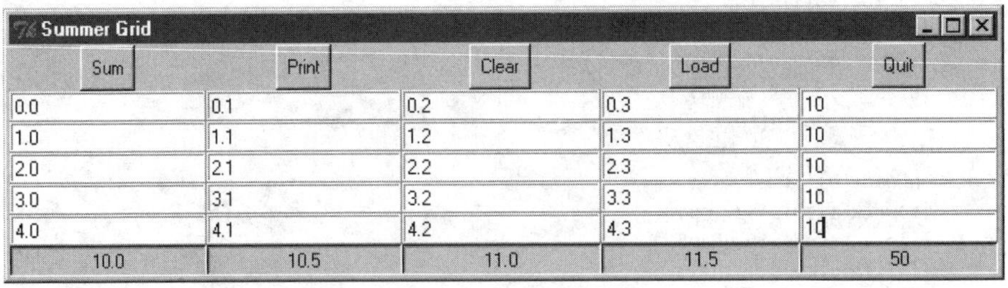

Figure 10-35. Adding datafile loads

By default, the class makes the 5×5 grid here, but we can pass in other dimensions to both the class constructor and the script's command line. When you press the Load button, you get the standard file selection dialog we met earlier on this tour (Figure 10-36).

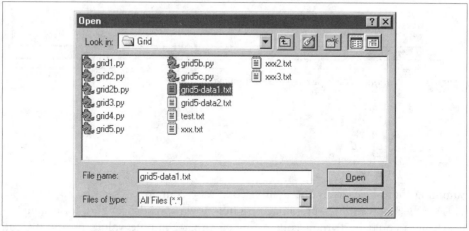

Figure 10-36. Opening a datafile for SumGrid

The datafile *grid-data1.txt* contains seven rows and six columns of data:

```
C:\...\PP3E\Gui\Tour\Grid>type grid5-data1.txt
1 2 3 4 5 6
1 2 3 4 5 6
1 2 3 4 5 6
1 2 3 4 5 6
1 2 3 4 5 6
1 2 3 4 5 6
1 2 3 4 5 6
```

Loading this into our GUI makes the dimensions of the grid change accordingly—the class simply reruns its widget construction logic after erasing all the old entry widgets with the grid_forget method.* Figure 10-37 captures the scene after a file load.

The *grid5-data2.txt* datafile has the same dimensions but contains expressions in two of its columns, not just simple numbers. Because this script converts input field values with the Python eval built-in function, any Python syntax will work in this table's fields, as long as it can be parsed and evaluated within the scope of the onSum method:

```
C:\...\PP3E\Gui\Tour\Grid>type grid5-data2.txt
1 2 3 2*2 5 6
```

---

* grid_forget unmaps gridded widgets and so effectively erases them from the display. Also see the pack_forget widget and window withdraw methods used in the after event "alarm" examples of the next section for other ways to erase and redraw GUI components.

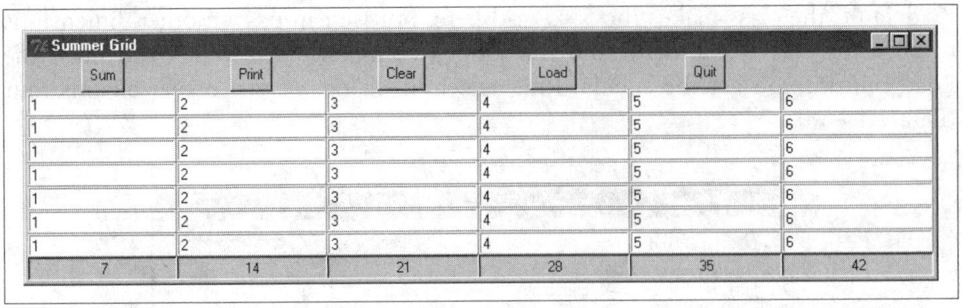

Figure 10-37. Datafile loaded, displayed, and summed

```
1 3-1 3 2<<1 5 6
1 5%3 3 pow(2,2) 5 6
1 2 3 2**2 5 6
1 2 3 [4,3][0] 5 6
1 {'a':2}['a'] 3 len('abcd') 5 6
1 abs(-2) 3 eval('2+2') 5 6
```

Summing these fields runs the Python code they contain, as seen in Figure 10-38. This can be a powerful feature; imagine a full-blown spreadsheet grid, for instance— field values could be Python code "snippets" that compute values on the fly, call functions in modules, and even download current stock quotes over the Internet with tools we'll meet in the next part of this book.

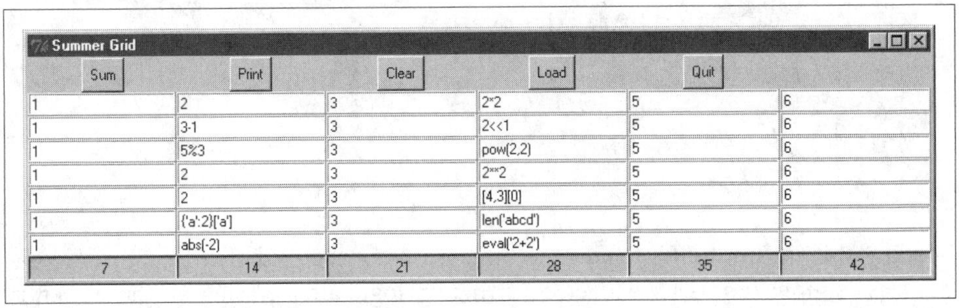

Figure 10-38. Python expressions in the data and table

It's also a potentially dangerous tool—a field might just contain an expression that erases your hard drive! If you're not sure what expressions may do, either don't use eval (convert with more limited built-in functions like int and float instead) or see Chapter 18 for details on the Python rexec restricted-execution mode module.

Of course, this still is nowhere near a true spreadsheet program; further mutations toward that goal are left as exercises. I should also point out that there is more to gridding than we have time to present fully here. For instance, by creating subframes that have grids of their own, we can build up more sophisticated layouts in much the same way as nested frames arranged with the packer. For now, let's move on to one last widget survey topic.

Time Tools, Threads, and Animation

The last stop on our widget tour is the most unique. Tkinter also comes with a handful of tools that have to do with the event-driven programming model, not graphics displayed on a computer screen.

Some GUI applications need to perform background activities periodically. For example, to "blink" a widget's appearance, we'd like to register a callback handler to be invoked at regular time intervals. Similarly, it's not a good idea to let a long-running file operation block other activity in a GUI; if the event loop could be forced to update periodically, the GUI could remain responsive. Tkinter comes with tools for both scheduling such delayed actions and forcing screen updates:

widget.after(*milliseconds, function, *args*)
> This tool schedules the function to be called after a number of milliseconds. function can be any callable Python object: a function, bound method, and so on. This form of the call does not pause the program—the callback function is run later from the normal Tkinter event loop. The *milliseconds* value can be a floating-point number, to specify fractions of a second. This returns an ID that can be passed to after_cancel to cancel the callback. Since this method is so commonly used, I'll say more about it by example in a moment.

widget.after(*milliseconds*)
> This tool pauses the program for a number of milliseconds—for example, an argument of 5,000 pauses for 5 seconds. This is essentially the same as Python's library function, time.sleep, and both calls can be used to add a delay in time-sensitive displays (e.g., animation programs such as PyDraw and the simpler examples ahead).

widget.after_idle(*function, *args*)
> This tool schedules the function to be called when there are no more pending events to process. That is, function becomes an idle handler, which is invoked when the GUI isn't busy doing anything else.

widget.after_cancel(*id*)
> This tool cancels a pending after callback event before it occurs.

widget.update()
> This tool forces Tkinter to process all pending events in the event queue, including geometry resizing and widget updates and redraws. You can call this periodically from a long-running callback handler to refresh the screen and perform any updates to it that your handler has already requested. If you don't, your updates may not appear on-screen until your callback handler exits. In fact, your display may hang completely during long-running handlers if not manually updated (and handlers are not run in threads, as described in the next section); the window won't even redraw itself until the handler returns if covered and uncovered by another. For instance, programs that animate by repeatedly moving an object

and pausing must call for an update before the end of the animation or only the final object position will appear on-screen; worse, the GUI will be completely inactive until the animation callback returns (see the simple animation examples later in this chapter, and see PyDraw in Chapter 12).

`widget.update_idletasks()`

This tool processes any pending idle events. This may sometimes be safer than `after` which has the potential to set up race (looping) conditions in some scenarios. Tk widgets use idle events to display themselves.

`_tkinter.createfilehandler(file, mask, function)`

This tool schedules the function to be called when a file's status changes. The function may be invoked when the file has data for reading, is available for writing, or triggers an exception. The `file` argument is a Python file or socket object (technically, anything with a `fileno()` method) or an integer file descriptor; `mask` is `Tkinter.READABLE` or `Tkinter.WRITABLE` to specify the mode; and the callback function takes two arguments—the file ready to converse, and a mask. File handlers are often used to process pipes or sockets, since normal input/output requests can block the caller.

Because this call is not available on Windows under Tk 8.0—and is still not available on Windows XP under Python 2.4 and Tk 8.4 as I write this third edition—it won't be used in this book. Because it is currently a Unix-only alternative, portable GUIs may be better off using `after` timer loops to poll for data and spawning threads to read data and place it on queues if needed—see Chapter 11 for more details. Threads are a much more general solution to nonblocking data transfers.

`widget.wait_variable(var)`
`widget.wait_window(win)`
`widget.wait_visibility(win)`

These tools pause the caller until a Tkinter variable changes its value, a window is destroyed, or a window becomes visible. All of these enter a local event loop, such that the application's `mainloop` continues to handle events. Note that var is a Tkinter variable object (discussed earlier), not a simple Python variable. To use for modal dialogs, first call `widget.focus()` (to set input focus) and `widget.grab()` (to make a window be the only one active).

We won't go into further details on all of these tools here; see other Tk and Tkinter documentation for more information.

Using Threads with GUIs

Keep in mind that for many programs, Python's thread support that we discussed in Chapter 5 can serve some of the same roles as the Tkinter tools listed in the preceding section. For instance, to avoid blocking a GUI during a long-running file or socket transfer, the transfer can simply be run in a spawned thread, while the rest of the program continues to run normally. Similarly, GUIs that must watch for inputs on pipes or sockets can do so in spawned threads (or `after` callbacks), without blocking the GUI itself. We'll explore GUI threading in more detail in Chapter 11, and we'll meet more realistic threaded GUI programs in Part IV (e.g., PyMailGUI in Chapter 15).

If you do use threads in Tkinter programs, however, only the main thread (the one that built the GUI and started the `mainloop`) can make GUI calls. Things like the `update` method described in the preceding section cannot be called from spawned threads in a GUI program—they'll likely trigger very strange program crashes. This GUI thread story may be improved in future Python and Tkinter releases, but it imposes a few structural and platform-specific constraints today.

For example, because spawned threads cannot perform GUI processing, they must generally communicate with the main thread using global variables, as required by the application. A thread that watches a socket, for instance, might simply set global variables that trigger GUI changes in `after` event callbacks. Note that this is not a Python or Tkinter limitation (it's much lower in the software hierarchy that runs your GUI), and it may go away in the future. In addition, some Tkinter canvas calls may actually be thread safe (see the animation script later in Example 10-32). We'll revisit this limitation later in this book; PyMailGUI, for instance, will collect data produced by threads and stored on a queue.

Using the after Method

The `after` method allows scripts to schedule a callback handler to be run at some time in the future, and we'll use this often, in later examples in this book. For instance, in Chapter 12, we'll meet a clock program that uses `after` to wake up 10 times per second and check for a new time, and we'll use an image slideshow program that uses `after` to schedule the next photo display (see PyClock and PyView). To illustrate the basics of scheduled callbacks, Example 10-27 does something a bit different.

Example 10-27. PP3E\Gui\Tour\alarm.py

```
#!/usr/local/bin/python
from Tkinter import *

class Alarm(Frame):
    def repeater(self):                       # on every N millisecs
        self.bell()                           # beep now
        self.stopper.flash()                  # flash button now
        self.after(self.msecs, self.repeater) # reschedule handler
    def __init__(self, msecs=1000):           # default = 1 second
        Frame.__init__(self)
        self.msecs = msecs
        self.pack()
        stopper = Button(self, text='Stop the beeps!', command=self.quit)
```

Example 10-27. PP3E\Gui\Tour\alarm.py (continued)

```
        stopper.pack( )
        stopper.config(bg='navy', fg='white', bd=8)
        self.stopper = stopper
        self.repeater( )

if __name__ == '__main__': Alarm(msecs=1000).mainloop( )
```

This script builds the window in Figure 10-39 and periodically calls both the button widget's flash method to make the button flash momentarily (it alternates colors quickly) and the Tkinter bell method to call your system's sound interface. The repeater method beeps and flashes once and schedules a callback to be invoked after a specific amount of time with the after method.

Figure 10-39. Stop the beeps!

But after doesn't pause the caller: callbacks are scheduled to occur in the background, while the program performs other processing—technically, as soon as the Tk event loop is able to notice the time rollover. To make this work, repeater calls after each time through, to reschedule the callback. Delayed events are one-shot callbacks; to repeat the event, we need to reschedule.

The net effect is that when this script runs, it starts beeping and flashing once its one-button window pops up. And it keeps beeping and flashing. And beeping. And flashing. Other activities and GUI operations don't affect it. Even if the window is iconified, the beeping continues because Tkinter timer events fire in the background. You need to kill the window or press the button to stop the alarm. By changing the msecs delay, you can make this beep as fast or as slow as your system allows (some platforms can't beep as fast as others). This may or may not be the best demo to launch in a crowded office, but at least you've been warned.

Hiding and redrawing widgets and windows

The button flash method flashes the widget, but it's easy to dynamically change other appearance options of widgets, such as buttons, labels, and text, with the widget config method. For instance, you can also achieve a flash-like effect by manually reversing foreground and background colors with the widget config method in scheduled after callbacks. Just for fun, Example 10-28 specializes the alarm to go a step further.

Example 10-28. PP3E\Gui\Tour\alarm-hide.py

```
from Tkinter import *
import alarm

class Alarm(alarm.Alarm):                        # change alarm callback
    def repeater(self):                          # on every N millisecs
        self.bell()                              # beep now
        if self.shown:
            self.stopper.pack_forget()           # hide or erase button now
        else:
            self.stopper.pack()                  # or reverse colors, flash...
        self.shown = not self.shown              # toggle state for next time
        self.after(self.msecs, self.repeater)    # reschedule handler
    def __init__(self, msecs=1000):              # default = 1 second
        self.shown = 0
        alarm.Alarm.__init__(self, msecs)

if __name__ == '__main__': Alarm(msecs=500).mainloop()
```

When this script is run, the same window appears, but the button is erased or redrawn on alternating timer events. The widget pack_forget method erases (unmaps) a drawn widget, and pack makes it show up again; grid_forget and grid similarly hide and show widgets in a grid. The pack_forget method is useful for dynamically drawing and changing a running GUI. For instance, you can be selective about which components are displayed, and you can build widgets ahead of time and show them only as needed. Here, it just means that users must press the button while it's displayed, or else the noise keeps going.

Example 10-29 goes even further. There are a handful of methods for hiding and unhiding entire top-level windows:

- To hide and unhide the entire window instead of just one widget within it, use the top-level window widget withdraw and deiconify methods. The withdraw method, demonstrated in Example 10-29, completely erases the window and its icon (use iconify if you want the window's icon to appear during a hide).

- The lift method raises a window above all its siblings, or relative to another you pass in (this method is also known as tkraise, but not raise—its name in Tk—because raise is a reserved word in Python).

- The state method returns or changes the window's current state (normal, iconic, zoomed [full screen], or withdrawn).

Experiment with these methods on your own to see how they differ. They are also useful to pop up prebuilt dialog windows dynamically, but are perhaps less practical here.

Example 10-29. PP3E\Gui\Tour\alarm-withdraw.py

```
from Tkinter import *
import alarm

class Alarm(alarm.Alarm):
    def repeater(self):                         # on every N millisecs
        self.bell()                             # beep now
        if self.master.state() == 'normal':     # is window displayed?
            self.master.withdraw()              # hide entire window, no icon
        else:                                   # iconify shrinks to an icon
            self.master.deiconify()             # else redraw entire window
            self.master.lift()                  # and raise above others
        self.after(self.msecs, self.repeater)   # reschedule handler

if __name__ == '__main__': Alarm().mainloop()   # master = default Tk root
```

This works the same, but the entire window appears or disappears on beeps—you have to press it when it's shown. You could add lots of other effects to the alarm. Whether your buttons and windows should flash and disappear, though, probably depends less on Tkinter technology than on your users' patience.

Simple Animation Techniques

Apart from the direct shape moves in the canvasDraw example, all of the GUIs presented so far in this part of the book have been fairly static. This last section shows you how to change that, by adding simple shape movement animations to the canvas drawing example listed in Example 10-16. It also demonstrates the notion of canvas tags—the move operations performed here move all canvas objects associated with a tag at once. All oval shapes move if you press "o," and all rectangles move if you press "r"; as mentioned earlier, canvas operation methods accept both object IDs and tag names.

But the main goal here is to illustrate simple animation techniques using the time-based tools described earlier in this section. There are three basic ways to move objects around a canvas:

- By loops that use time.sleep to pause for fractions of a second between multiple move operations, along with manual update calls. The script moves, sleeps, moves a bit more, and so on. A time.sleep call pauses the caller and so fails to return control to the GUI event loop—any new requests that arrive during a move are deferred. Because of that, canvas.update must be called to redraw the screen after each move, or else updates don't appear until the entire movement loop callback finishes and returns. This is a classic long-running callback scenario; without manual update calls, no new GUI events are handled until the callback returns in this scheme (even window redraws).

- By using the `widget.after` method to schedule multiple move operations to occur every few milliseconds. Because this approach is based upon scheduled events dispatched by Tkinter to your handlers, it allows multiple moves to occur in parallel and doesn't require `canvas.update` calls. You rely on the event loop to run moves, so there's no reason for sleep pauses, and the GUI is not blocked while moves are in progress.

- By using threads to run multiple copies of the `time.sleep` pausing loops of the first approach. Because threads run in parallel, a sleep in any thread blocks neither the GUI nor other motion threads. GUIs should not be updated from spawned threads in general (in fact, calling `canvas.update` from a spawned thread will likely crash the GUI today), but some canvas calls such as `movement` seem to be thread safe in the current implementation.

Of these three schemes, the first yields the smoothest animations but makes other operations sluggish during movement, the second seems to yield slower motion than the others but is safer than using threads in general, and the second and third allow multiple objects to be in motion at the same time.

Using time.sleep loops

The next three sections demonstrate the code structure of all three approaches in turn, with new subclasses of the `canvasDraw` example we met in Example 10-16. Example 10-30 illustrates the first approach.

Example 10-30. PP3E\Gui\Tour\canvasDraw_tags.py

```
###################################################################
# add tagged moves with time.sleep (not widget.after or threads);
# time.sleep does not block the GUI event loop while pausing, but
# screen not redrawn until callback returns or widget.update call;
# the currently running onMove callback gets exclusive attention
# until it returns: others pause if press 'r' or 'o' during move;
###################################################################

from Tkinter import *
import canvasDraw, time

class CanvasEventsDemo(canvasDraw.CanvasEventsDemo):
    def __init__(self, parent=None):
        canvasDraw.CanvasEventsDemo.__init__(self, parent)
        self.canvas.create_text(75, 8, text='Press o and r to move shapes')
        self.canvas.master.bind('<KeyPress-o>', self.onMoveOvals)
        self.canvas.master.bind('<KeyPress-r>', self.onMoveRectangles)
        self.kinds = self.create_oval_tagged, self.create_rectangle_tagged
    def create_oval_tagged(self, x1, y1, x2, y2):
        objectId = self.canvas.create_oval(x1, y1, x2, y2)
        self.canvas.itemconfig(objectId, tag='ovals', fill='blue')
        return objectId
    def create_rectangle_tagged(self, x1, y1, x2, y2):
```

Example 10-30. PP3E\Gui\Tour\canvasDraw_tags.py (continued)

```
        objectId = self.canvas.create_rectangle(x1, y1, x2, y2)
        self.canvas.itemconfig(objectId, tag='rectangles', fill='red')
        return objectId
    def onMoveOvals(self, event):
        print 'moving ovals'
        self.moveInSquares(tag='ovals')            # move all tagged ovals
    def onMoveRectangles(self, event):
        print 'moving rectangles'
        self.moveInSquares(tag='rectangles')
    def moveInSquares(self, tag):                  # 5 reps of 4 times per sec
        for i in range(5):
            for (diffx, diffy) in [(+20, 0), (0, +20), (-20, 0), (0, -20)]:
                self.canvas.move(tag, diffx, diffy)
                self.canvas.update()               # force screen redraw/update
                time.sleep(0.25)                   # pause, but don't block GUI

if __name__ == '__main__':
    CanvasEventsDemo()
    mainloop()
```

All three of the scripts in this section create a window of blue ovals and red rectangles as you drag new shapes out with the left mouse button. The drag-out implementation itself is inherited from the superclass. A right-mouse-button click still moves a single shape immediately, and a double-left click still clears the canvas too—other operations inherited from the original superclass. In fact, all this new script really does is change the object creation calls to add tags and colors here, add a text field, and add bindings and callbacks for motion. Figure 10-40 shows what this subclass's window looks like after dragging out a few shapes to be animated.

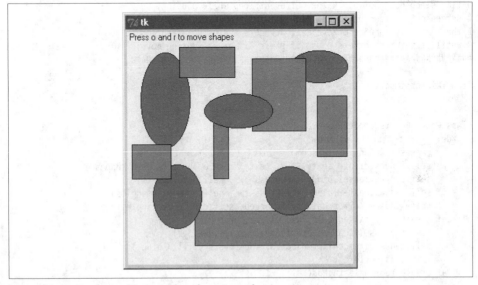

Figure 10-40. Drag-out objects ready to be animated

The "o" and "r" keys are set up to start animation of all the ovals and rectangles you've drawn, respectively. Pressing "o," for example, makes all the blue ovals start moving synchronously. Objects are animated to mark out five squares around their location and to move four times per second. New objects drawn while others are in motion start to move too because they are tagged. You need to run these live to get a feel for the simple animations they implement, of course. (You could try moving this book back and forth and up and down, but it's not quite the same, and might look silly in public places.)

Using widget.after events

The main drawback of this first approach is that only one animation can be going at once: if you press "r" or "o" while a move is in progress, the new request puts the prior movement on hold until it finishes because each move callback handler assumes the only thread of control while it runs. Screen updates are a bit sluggish while moves are in progress too, because they happen only as often as manual update calls are made (try a drag-out or a cover/uncover of the window during a move to see for yourself). Example 10-31 specializes just the moveInSquares method to remove such limitations.

Example 10-31. PP3E\Gui\Tour\canvasDraw_tags_after.py

```
#######################################################################
# similar, but with .after scheduled events, not time.sleep loops;
# because these are scheduled events, this allows both ovals and
# rectangles to be moving at the _same_ time and does not require
# update calls to refresh the GUI (only one time.sleep loop callback
# can be running at once, and blocks others started until it returns);
# the motion gets wild if you press 'o' or 'r' while move in progress,
# though--multiple move updates start firing around the same time;
#######################################################################

from Tkinter import *
import canvasDraw_tags

class CanvasEventsDemo(canvasDraw_tags.CanvasEventsDemo):
    def moveEm(self, tag, moremoves):
        (diffx, diffy), moremoves = moremoves[0], moremoves[1:]
        self.canvas.move(tag, diffx, diffy)
        if moremoves:
            self.canvas.after(250, self.moveEm, tag, moremoves)
    def moveInSquares(self, tag):
        allmoves = [(+20, 0), (0, +20), (-20, 0), (0, -20)] * 5
        self.moveEm(tag, allmoves)

if __name__ == '__main__':
    CanvasEventsDemo()
    mainloop()
```

This version lets you make both ovals and rectangles move at the same time—drag out a few ovals and rectangles, and then press "o" and then "r" right away to make this go. In fact, try pressing both keys a few times; the more you press, the more the objects move, because multiple scheduled events are firing and moving objects from wherever they happen to be positioned. If you drag out a new shape during a move, it starts moving immediately as before.

Using multiple time.sleep loop threads

Running animations in threads can sometimes achieve the same effect; it can be dangerous to update the screen from a spawned thread in general, but it works in this example, at least on Windows. Example 10-32 runs each animation task as an independent and parallel thread. That is, each time you press the "o" or "r" key to start an animation, a new thread is spawned to do the work. This works on Windows, but it failed on Linux at the time of writing this book—the screen is not updated as threads change it, so you won't see any changes until later GUI events.

Example 10-32. PP3E\Gui\Tour\canvasDraw_tags_thread.py

```
#############################################################################
# similar, but run time.sleep loops in parallel with threads, not
# .after events or single active time.sleep loop; because threads run
# in parallel, this also allows ovals and rectangles to be moving at
# the _same_ time and does not require update calls to refresh the GUI:
# in fact, calling .update() can make this _crash_ today, though some
# canvas calls seem to be thread safe or else this wouldn't work at all;
#############################################################################

from Tkinter import *
import canvasDraw_tags
import thread, time

class CanvasEventsDemo(canvasDraw_tags.CanvasEventsDemo):
    def moveEm(self, tag):
        for i in range(5):
            for (diffx, diffy) in [(+20, 0), (0, +20), (-20, 0), (0, -20)]:
                self.canvas.move(tag, diffx, diffy)
                time.sleep(0.25)                        # pause this thread only
    def moveInSquares(self, tag):
        thread.start_new_thread(self.moveEm, (tag,))

if __name__ == '__main__':
    CanvasEventsDemo()
    mainloop()
```

This version lets you move shapes at the same time, just like Example 10-31, but this time it's a reflection of threads running in parallel. In fact, this uses the same scheme as the first time.sleep version. Here, though, there is more than one active thread of control, so move handlers can overlap in time—time.sleep blocks only the calling thread, not the program at large. This seems to work (at least on Windows), but it is usually safer to have your threads do number crunching only and let the main thread (the one that built the GUI) handle any screen updates. It's not impossible that GUI threads may be better supported in later Tkinter releases, so see more recent releases for more details.

Other Animation Concepts: Threads and Toolkits

We'll revisit animation in Chapter 12's PyDraw example; there, all three techniques will be resurrected to move shapes, text, and photos to arbitrary spots on a canvas marked with a mouse click. And, although the canvas widget's absolute coordinate system makes it the workhorse of most nontrivial animations, Tkinter animation in general is limited mostly by your imagination.

Besides canvas-based animations, widget configuration tools support a variety of animation effects. For example, as we saw in the flashing and hiding alarm scripts earlier (see Example 10-28), it is also easy to change the appearance of other kinds of widgets dynamically with after timer-event loops. With timer-based loops, you can periodically flash widgets, completely erase and redraw widgets and windows on the fly, reverse widget colors, and so on.

Furthermore, the techniques for running long-running tasks in parallel threads (which we will study in the next chapter) become more important if animations must remain active while your program waits.

For instance, imagine that your program will spend minutes downloading data from a network, calculating the output of a numeric model, or performing other long-running tasks. If you want your program's GUI to display an animation or otherwise show progress while waiting for the task, you can do so by either altering a widget's appearance or by moving objects in a canvas periodically—simply use the after method to wake up intermittently to modify your GUI as we've seen. A progress bar or counter, for instance, may be updated during after timer-event handling.

In addition, though, the long-running task itself will likely have to be run in a spawned parallel *thread* so that your GUI remains active and performs the animation during the wait. Otherwise, no GUI updates will occur until the task returns control to the GUI. During after timer-event processing, the main GUI thread might check global variables set by the long-running task's thread to determine completion or progress.

Especially if more than one long-running task may be active at the same time, the spawned thread might also communicate with the GUI thread by storing information in a Python Queue object, to be picked up and handled by the GUI during after events. For generality, the Queue might even contain function objects that are run by the GUI to update the display. We will study such techniques in Chapter 11. For now, keep in mind that spawning tasks in threads allows the GUI itself to perform animations and to remain active in general during wait states.

I should also note that the sorts of movement and animation techniques shown in this chapter and the next are suitable for some game-like programs, but not all. For more advanced 3-D animation needs, be sure to also see the support in the PIL extension package for common animation and movie file formats such as FLI and MPEG. Other third-party systems such as OpenGL, Blender, PyGame, and VPython provide even higher-level graphics and animation toolkits; the PyOpenGL system also offers Tk support for GUIs. See the Vaults of Parnassus and PyPI sites for links, or search on Google.com.

As currently implemented, Python is not widely used as the sole implementation language of graphics-intensive game programs, but it can still be used as both a prototyping and a scripting language for such products.* When integrated with 3D graphics libraries, it can serve even broader roles. See *http://www.python.org* for links to other available extensions in this domain.

Finally, be sure to also watch for more on GUIs, threads, and thread communication queues in the next chapter, as well as check out the PyMailGUI example later in this book.

The End of the Tour

And that's a wrap for our tour around the Tkinter library. You have now seen all the core widgets and tools previewed at the end of Chapter 8 (flip back for a summary of territory covered on this tour). For more details, watch for all of the tools introduced here to appear again in the advanced GUI techniques in Chapter 11, the larger GUI examples in Chapter 12, and the remainder of the book at large.

I should point out, though, that this story is not quite complete. Although we've covered the entire basic Tkinter widget arsenal, we've skipped a handful of newer and more advanced widgets introduced to Tkinter recently:

Spinbox
> An Entry used to select among a set or range of values

LabelFrame
> A Frame with a border and title around a group of items

PanedWindow
> A geometry manager widget containing multiple widgets that can be resized by moving separator lines with the mouse

---

* Origin Systems, a major game software development company, used Python in this role to script the animation in some of its games. At last report, its online game product, Ultima Online II, was to be scripted with Python. In fact, many games utilize Python. Civilization IV uses Python as a scripting language, and Temple of Elemental Evil uses Python as well. Eve Online uses Python for scripting and much of the functionality.

Moreover, we haven't even mentioned any of the higher-level widgets available in the popular Pmw and Tix extension packages for Tkinter (described in Chapter 8) or any other third-party packages. For instance, the third-party domain hosts Tree widgets, HTML viewers, font selection dialogs, tables, and much more for Tkinter. See Tkinter, Tk, Tix, and Pmw documentation for more details on additional widgets, and visit the Vaults of Parnassus web site (*http://www.vex.net/parnassus/*) or search Google for other third-party extensions.

Because it is just a Python/Tkinter program, Python's standard IDLE development GUI is another resource—its code includes font dialogs, Tree widgets, and more that you can use in your own applications. See the IDLE source directory on your machine for more details.

I should also mention that there are more widget configuration options than we have met on this tour. Consult Tk and Tkinter resources for options not listed explicitly here. Although other Tkinter tools are analogous to those presented here, the space I have for illustrating additional widgets and options in this book is limited by both my publisher and my fingers.

The PyDemos and PyGadgets Launchers

To close out this chapter, let's explore the implementations of the two GUIs used to run major book examples. The following GUIs, PyDemos and PyGadgets, are simply GUIs for launching other GUI programs. In fact, we've now come to the end of the demo launcher story—both of the programs here interact with modules that we met earlier in Chapters 5 and 6:

launchmodes.py
> Starts independent Python programs portably.

Launcher.py
> Finds programs, and ultimately runs both PyDemos and PyGadgets when used by the self-configuring top-level launcher scripts.

LaunchBrowser.py
> Spawns web browsers.

See Example 5-25 in Chapter 5, and Examples 6-14 and 6-15 in Chapter 6, for the code for these modules. The programs listed here add the GUI components to the program-launching system—they simply provide easy-to-use pushbuttons that spawn most of the larger examples in this text when pressed.

Both of these scripts also assume that they will be run with the current working directory set to their directory (they hardcode paths to other programs relative to that). Either click on their names in a file explorer or run them from a command-line shell after a cd to the top-level *PP3E* examples root directory. These scripts could allow invocations from other directories by prepending the PP3EHOME environment variable's value to program script paths, but they were really designed to be run only out of the *PP3E* root.

PyDemos Launcher Bar

The PyDemos script constructs a bar of buttons that run programs in demonstration mode, not for day-to-day use. I use PyDemos to show off Python programs—it's much easier to press its buttons than to run command lines or fish through a file explorer GUI to find scripts. You should use PyDemos to start and interact with examples presented in this book—all of the buttons on this GUI represent examples we will meet in later chapters.

To make this launcher bar even easier to run, drag it out to your desktop to generate a clickable Windows shortcut (do something similar on other systems). Since this script hardcodes command lines for running programs elsewhere in the examples tree, it is also useful as an index to major book examples. Figure 10-41 shows what PyDemos looks like when run on Windows; it looks slightly different but works the same on Linux.

The source code that constructs this scene is listed in Example 10-33. PyDemos doesn't present much that's new in terms of GUI interface programming; its demoButton function simply attaches a new button to the main window, spring-loaded to spawn a Python program when pressed. To start programs, PyDemos calls an instance of the launchmodes.PortableLauncher object we met at the end of Chapter 5—its role as a Tkinter callback handler here is why a call operation is used to kick off the launched program.

For this third edition of the book, I've also added "code" buttons to the right of each demo's button, which open the source files that implement the associated example. These files open in pop-up versions of the PyEdit text editor that we'll meet in Chapter 12. This version also sets the main window's icon where applicable and attempts to spawn a locally running web server for web-based demos (we'll meet the server in Chapter 16).

As pictured in Figure 10-41, PyDemos also constructs two pop-up windows when buttons at the bottom of the main window are pressed—an Info pop up giving a short description of the last demo spawned, and a Links pop up containing radio buttons that open a local web browser on book-related sites when pressed:

- The Info pop up displays a simple message line and changes its font every second to draw attention to itself; since this can be a bit distracting, the pop up starts out iconified (click the Info button to see or hide it).

- The Links pop up's radio buttons are much like hyperlinks in a web page, but this GUI isn't a browser: when the Links pop up is pressed, the portable LaunchBrowser script we met in Chapter 6 is used to find and start a web browser used to connect to the relevant site, assuming you have an Internet connection.

- A module we'll meet in the next chapter, named windows, is used to give this GUI's windows a blue "PY" icon, instead of the standard red "Tk."

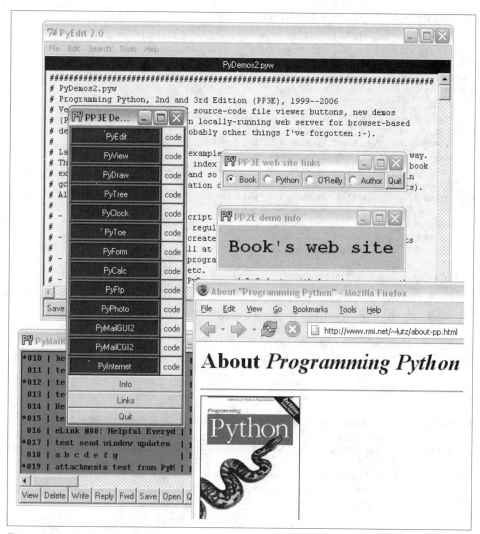

Figure 10-41. PyDemos with its pop ups

PyDemos runs on Windows and Linux, but that's largely due to the inherent portability of both Python and Tkinter. For more details, consult the source, which is
shown in Example 10-33.

Example 10-33. PP3E\PyDemos2.pyw

```
###############################################################################
# PyDemos2.pyw
# Programming Python, 2nd and 3rd Edition (PP3E), 1999--2006
# Version 2.0, March '06: add source-code file viewer buttons, new demos
# (PyPhoto, PyMailGUI2), spawn locally running web server for browser-based
# demos, window icons, and probably other things I've forgotten :-).
#
```

Example 10-33. PP3E\PyDemos2.pyw (continued)

```
# Launch major Python+Tk GUI examples from the book, in a platform-neutral way.
# This file also serves as an index to major program examples, though many book
# examples aren't GUI-based, and so aren't listed here (e.g., see the Cygwin
# gcc makefiles in the Integration directory for C integration code pointers).
# Also see:
#
# - PyGadgets.py, a simpler script for starting programs in non-demo mode
#   that you wish to use on a regular basis
# - PyGadgets_bar.pyw, which creates a button bar for starting all PyGadgets
#   programs on demand, not all at once
# - Launcher.py for starting programs without environment settings--finds
#   Python, sets PYTHONPATH, etc.
# - Launch_*.py for starting PyDemos and PyGadgets with Launcher.py--run these
#   for a quick look
# - LaunchBrowser.py for running example web pages with an automatically
#   located web browser
# - README-PP3E.txt, for general examples information
#
# This program tries to start a locally running web server and web browser
# automatically, for web-based denmos.  Additional program comments
# were moved to file PyDemos.doc.txt
###############################################################################

import sys, time, os, glob, launchmodes
from Tkinter import *

# -live loads root pages from server so CGIs run, -file loads local files
InternetMode = '-live'

###############################################################################
# start building main GUI windows
###############################################################################

from PP3E.Gui.Tools.windows import MainWindow      # a Tk with icon, title, quit
from PP3E.Gui.Tools.windows import PopupWindow      # same but Toplevel, diff quit
Root = MainWindow('PP3E Demos 2.0')

# build message window
Stat = PopupWindow('PP2E demo info')
Stat.protocol('WM_DELETE_WINDOW', lambda:0)         # ignore wm delete

Info = Label(Stat, text = 'Select demo',
                font=('courier', 20, 'italic'), padx=12, pady=12, bg='lightblue')
Info.pack(expand=YES, fill=BOTH)

###############################################################################
# add launcher buttons with callback objects
###############################################################################

from PP3E.Gui.TextEditor.textEditor import TextEditorMainPopup

# demo launcher class
```

Example 10-33. PP3E\PyDemos2.pyw (continued)

```
class Launcher(launchmodes.PortableLauncher):     # use wrapped launcher class
    def announce(self, text):                      # customize to set GUI label
        Info.config(text=text)

def viewer(sources):
    for filename in sources:
        TextEditorMainPopup(Root, filename)        # as pop up in this process

def demoButton(name, what, doit, code):
    rowfrm = Frame(Root)
    rowfrm.pack(side=TOP, expand=YES, fill=BOTH)

    b = Button(rowfrm, bg='navy', fg='white', relief=RIDGE, border=4)
    b.config(text=name, width=20, command=Launcher(what, doit))
    b.pack(side=LEFT, expand=YES, fill=BOTH)

    b = Button(rowfrm, bg='beige', fg='navy')
    b.config(text='code', command=(lambda: viewer(code)))
    b.pack(side=LEFT, fill=BOTH)

# some imported module source files could be determined
# but we can't know where to stop on the import chains

##############################################################################
# Tkinter GUI demos - some use network connections
##############################################################################

demoButton(name='PyEdit',
           what='Text file editor',                              # edit myself
           doit='Gui/TextEditor/textEditor.py PyDemos2.pyw',     # assume in cwd
           code=['Gui/Tools/guimaker.py',                        # show viewer
                 'Gui/TextEditor/textEditor.py'])

demoButton(name='PyView',
           what='Image slideshow, plus note editor',
           doit='Gui/SlideShow/slideShowPlus.py Gui/gifs',
           code=['Gui/Texteditor/textEditor.py',
                 'Gui/SlideShow/slideShowPlus.py',
                 'Gui/SlideShow/slideShow.py'])

demoButton(name='PyDraw',
           what='Draw and move graphics objects',
           doit='Gui/MovingPics/movingpics.py Gui/gifs',
           code=['Gui/MovingPics/movingpics.py'])

demoButton(name='PyTree',
           what='Tree data structure viewer',
           doit='Dstruct/TreeView/treeview.py',
           code=['Dstruct/TreeView/treeview.py',
                 'Dstruct/TreeView/treeview_wrappers.py',
                 'Dstruct/Classics/btree.py',
                 'Lang/Parser/parser2.py'])
```

Example 10-33. PP3E\PyDemos2.pyw (continued)

```
demoButton(name='PyClock',
           what='Analog/digital clocks',
           doit='Gui/Clock/clockStyles.py Gui/gifs',
           code=['Gui/Tools/windows.py',
                 'Gui/Clock/clockStyles.py',
                 'Gui/Clock/clock.py'])


demoButton(name='PyToe',
           what='Tic-tac-toe game (AI)',
           doit='Ai/TicTacToe/tictactoe.py',
           code=['Ai/TicTacToe/tictactoe.py',
                 'Ai/TicTacToe/tictactoe_lists.py'])


demoButton(name='PyForm',                              # view in-memory dict
           what='Persistent table viewer/editor',      # or cwd shelve of class
           doit='Dbase/TableBrowser/formgui.py',       # 0=do not reinit shelve
          #doit='Dbase/TableBrowser/formtable.py  shelve 0 pyformData-1.5.2',
          #doit='Dbase/TableBrowser/formtable.py  shelve 1 pyformData',
           code=['Dbase/TableBrowser/formgui.py',
                 'Dbase/TableBrowser/formtable.py'])


demoButton(name='PyCalc',
           what='Calculator, plus extensions',
           doit='Lang/Calculator/calculator_plusplus.py',
           code=['Lang/Calculator/calculator_plusplus.py',
                 'Lang/Calculator/calculator_plus_ext.py',
                 'Lang/Calculator/calculator_plus_emb.py',
                 'Lang/Calculator/calculator.py'])


demoButton(name='PyFtp',
           what='Python+Tk ftp clients',
           doit='Internet/Ftp/PyFtpGui.pyw',
           code=['Internet/Ftp/PyFtpGui.pyw',
                 'Internet/Ftp/getfilegui.py',
                 'Internet/Ftp/putfilegui.py',
                 'Internet/Ftp/getfile.py',
                 'Internet/Ftp/putfile.py',
                 'Internet/Sockets/form.py'])


# caveat: PyPhoto requires PIL to be installed: show note
demoButton(name='PyPhoto',
           what='PIL thumbnail image viewer',
           doit='Gui/PIL/pyphoto1.py Gui/PIL/images',      # script, image dir
           code=['PyDemos-pil-note.txt',
                 'Gui/PIL/viewer_thumbs.py',
                 'Gui/PIL/pyphoto1.py'])


# get pymailgui source files
locat  = 'Internet/Email'
locat2 = locat + '/PyMailGui'
saved  = '%s/SavedMail/savemany.txt %s/SavedMail/savefew.txt' % (locat2, locat2)
source = glob.glob(locat + '/PyMailGui/*.py') # 9 source files here + __init__
```

Example 10-33. PP3E\PyDemos2.pyw (continued)

```
source+= glob.glob(locat + '/mailtools/*.py') # 4 source files here + __init__

demoButton(name='PyMailGUI2',
           what='Python+Tk pop/smtp email client',          # open on save file
           doit='%s/PyMailGui2.py %s' % (locat2, saved),
           code=(['Gui/Texteditor/textEditor.py',
                  'Gui/Tools/windows.py',
                  'Gui/Tools/threadtools.py'] + source) )


###############################################################################
# web-based demos - PyInternet opens many smaller demos
###############################################################################

# get pymailcgi source files - not incl mailtools!
pymailcgifiles = (['Internet/Web/PyMailCgi/pymailcgi.html'] +
                   glob.glob('Internet/Web/PyMailCgi/cgi-bin/*.py'))  # 11 .py

if InternetMode == '-file':
    pagepath = os.getcwd() + '/Internet/Web'

    demoButton('PyMailCGI2',
               'Browser-based pop/smtp email interface',
               'LaunchBrowser.pyw -file %s/PyMailCgi/pymailcgi.html' % pagepath,
               pymailcgifiles)

    demoButton('PyInternet',
               'Internet-based demo launcher page',
               'LaunchBrowser.pyw -file %s/PyInternetDemos.html' % pagepath,
               ['Internet/Cgi-Web/PyInternetDemos.html'])

else:
    def startLocalWebServers():
        """
        on Windows succeeds silently if server already listening
        on the port; caveat: should only run 1 server per port;
        global per-process flag won't fix: the servers live on
        """
        launchmodes.PortableLauncher('server80',
            'Internet/Web/webserver.py Internet/Web')()
        launchmodes.PortableLauncher('server8000',
            'Internet/Web/webserver.py Internet/Web/PyMailCgi 8000')()

    site = 'localhost:%s'
    startLocalWebServers()  # run webserver on port 80 and 8000 on localhost
    print 'servers started'

    # PyErrata removed in 3rd Ed

    demoButton('PyMailCGI2',
               'Browser-based pop/smtp email interface',
               'LaunchBrowser.pyw -live pymailcgi.html '+ (site % 8000),
               pymailcgifiles)
```

Example 10-33. PP3E\PyDemos2.pyw (continued)

```
    demoButton('PyInternet',
               'Main Internet demos launcher page',
               'LaunchBrowser.pyw -live PyInternetDemos.html ' + (site % 80),
               ['Internet/Web/PyInternetDemos.html'])

#To try: bind mouse entry events to change info text when over a button
#See also: site http://starship.python.net/~lutz/PyInternetDemos.html

##############################################################################
# toggle info message box font once a second
##############################################################################

def refreshMe(info, ncall):
    slant = ['normal', 'italic', 'bold', 'bold italic'][ncall % 4]
    info.config(font=('courier', 20, slant))
    Root.after(1000, (lambda: refreshMe(info, ncall+1)) )

##############################################################################
# unhide/hide status box on info clicks
##############################################################################

Stat.iconify()
def onInfo():
    if Stat.state() == 'iconic':
        Stat.deiconify()
    else:
        Stat.iconify()  # was 'normal'

##############################################################################
# pop up a few web link buttons if connected
##############################################################################

radiovar = StringVar() # use a global

def onLinks():
    popup = PopupWindow('PP3E web site links')
    links = [("Book",
                    'LaunchBrowser.pyw -live about-pp.html www.rmi.net/~lutz'),
             ("Python",
                    'LaunchBrowser.pyw -live index.html www.python.org'),
             ("O'Reilly",
                    'LaunchBrowser.pyw -live index.html www.oreilly.com'),
             ("Author",
                    'LaunchBrowser.pyw -live index.html www.rmi.net/~lutz')]

    for (name, command) in links:
        callback = Launcher((name + "'s web site"), command)
        link = Radiobutton(popup, text=name, command=callback)
```

Example 10-33. PP3E\PyDemos2.pyw (continued)

```
        link.config(relief=GROOVE, variable=radiovar, value=name)
        link.pack(side=LEFT, expand=YES, fill=BOTH)
    Button(popup, text='Quit', command=popup.destroy).pack(expand=YES,fill=BOTH)

    if InternetMode != '-live':
        from tkMessageBox import showwarning
        showwarning('PP3E Demos', 'Web links require an Internet connection')

################################################################################
# finish building main GUI, start event loop
################################################################################

Button(Root, text='Info',  command=onInfo).pack(side=TOP, fill=X)
Button(Root, text='Links', command=onLinks).pack(side=TOP, fill=X)
Button(Root, text='Quit',  command=Root.quit).pack(side=BOTTOM, fill=X)
refreshMe(Info, 0)  # start toggling
Root.mainloop()
```

PyGadgets Launcher Bar

The PyGadgets script runs some of the same programs as PyDemos, but for real, practical use, not as flashy demonstrations. Both scripts use launchmodes to spawn other programs and display bars of launcher buttons, but this one is a bit simpler because its task is more focused. PyGadgets also supports two spawning modes: it can either start a canned list of programs immediately and all at once, or display a GUI for running each program on demand. (Figure 10-42 shows the launch bar GUI made in on-demand mode.)

Because of such differences, PyGadgets takes a more data-driven approach to building the GUI: it stores program names in a list and steps through it as needed, instead of using a sequence of precoded demoButton calls. The set of buttons on the launcher bar GUI in Figure 10-42, for example, depends entirely upon the contents of the programs list.

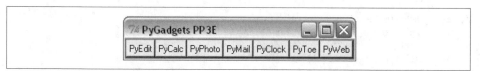

Figure 10-42. PyGadgets launcher bar

The source code behind this GUI is listed in Example 10-34; it's not much because it relies on other modules (launchmodes, LaunchBrowser) to work most of its magic.

PyGadgets is always open on my machines (I have a clickable shortcut to this script on my Windows desktop too). I use it to gain easy access to Python tools that I use on a daily basis—text editors, calculators, email and photo tools, and so on—all of which we'll meet in upcoming chapters.

To customize PyGadgets for your own use, simply import and call its functions with program command-line lists of your own or change the mytools list of spawnable programs near the end of this file. This is Python, after all.

Example 10-34. PP3E\PyGadgets.py

```python
#!/bin/env python
###########################################################################
# Start various examples; run me at system boot time to make them always
# available.  This file is meant for starting programs you actually wish
# to use; see PyDemos for starting Python/Tk demos and more details on
# program start options.  Windows usage note: this is a '.py' file, so you
# get a DOS box console window when it is clicked; the DOS box is used to
# show a startup message (and we sleep 5 seconds to make sure it's visible
# while gadgets start up).  If you don't want the DOS pop up, run with the
# 'pythonw' program (not 'python'), use a '.pyw' suffix, mark with a 'run
# minimized' Windows property, or spawn the file from elsewhere; see PyDemos.
###########################################################################

import sys, time, os, time
from Tkinter import *
from launchmodes import PortableLauncher      # reuse program start class

def runImmediate(mytools):
    # launch gadget programs immediately
    print 'Starting Python/Tk gadgets...'          # msgs to temp stdout screen
    for (name, commandLine) in mytools:
        PortableLauncher(name, commandLine)()      # call now to start now
    print 'One moment please...'                    # \b means a backspace
    if sys.platform[:3] == 'win':
        # on Windows keep stdio console window up for 5 seconds
        for i in range(5): time.sleep(1); print ('\b' + '.'*10),

def runLauncher(mytools):
    # put up a simple launcher bar for later use
    root = Tk()
    root.title('PyGadgets PP3E')
    for (name, commandLine) in mytools:
        b = Button(root, text=name, fg='black', bg='beige', border=2,
                   command=PortableLauncher(name, commandLine))
        b.pack(side=LEFT, expand=YES, fill=BOTH)
    root.mainloop()
```

Example 10-34. PP3E\PyGadgets.py (continued)

```
mytools = [
    ('PyEdit',    'Gui/TextEditor/textEditor.py'),
    ('PyCalc',    'Lang/Calculator/calculator.py'),
    ('PyPhoto',   'Gui/PIL/pyphoto1.py Gui/PIL/images'),
    ('PyMail',    'Internet/Email/PyMailGui/PyMailGui2.py'),
    ('PyClock',   'Gui/Clock/clock.py -size 175 -bg white'
                            ' -picture Gui/gifs/pythonPowered.gif'),
    ('PyToe',     'Ai/TicTacToe/tictactoe.py'
                            ' -mode Minimax -fg white -bg navy'),
    ('PyWeb',     'LaunchBrowser.pyw'
                            ' -live PyInternetDemos.html localhost:80')
]                                    # PyWeb assumes local server started

if __name__ == '__main__':
    prestart, toolbar = 1, 0
    if prestart:
        runImmediate(mytools)
    if toolbar:
        runLauncher(mytools)
```

By default, PyGadgets starts programs immediately when it is run. To run PyGadgets in launcher bar mode instead, Example 10-35 simply imports and calls the appropriate function with an imported program list. Because it is a *.pyw* file, you see only the launcher bar GUI it constructs initially, not a DOS console streams window.

Example 10-35. PP3E\PyGadgets_bar.pyw

```
# run PyGadgets toolbar only, instead of starting all the
# gadgets immediately; filename avoids DOS pop up on Windows

import PyGadgets
PyGadgets.runLauncher(PyGadgets.mytools)
```

This script is the file my desktop shortcut invokes; I prefer to run gadget GUIs on demand. You can also run a script like this at your system's startup to make it always available (and to save a mouse click). For instance:

- On Windows, such a script can be automatically started by adding it to your StartUp folder—click on your system's Start button, select Settings, go to the Taskbar & Start Menu dialog, and click your way through the remaining steps.

- On Linux and Unix, you can automatically start this script by spawning it with a command line in your startup scripts (e.g., your home directory's *.cshrc*, *.profile*, or *.login*) after X Windows has been started.

Whether run via a shortcut, a file explorer click, a typed command line, or other means, the PyGadgets launcher bar at the top of Figure 10-43 appears.

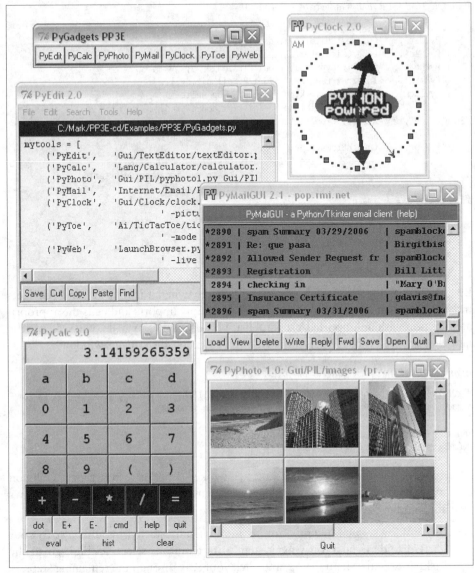

Figure 10-43. PyGadgets launcher bar with gadgets

Of course, the whole point of PyGadgets is to spawn other programs. Pressing on its launcher bar's buttons starts programs like those shown in the rest of Figure 10-43, but if you want to know more about those, you'll have to turn the page and move on to the next chapter.

GUI Coding Techniques

"Building a Better Mouse Trap"

This chapter continues our look at building GUIs with Python and the Tkinter library by presenting a collection of more advanced GUI programming patterns and techniques. In the last three chapters, we explored all the fundamentals of Tkinter itself. Here, our goal is to put them to work to add higher-level structures that will be useful in larger programs. Some of the techniques we will be studying in this chapter are as follows:

- Providing common GUI operations in "mixin" classes
- Building menus and toolbars from data structure templates
- Adding GUI interfaces to command-line tools
- Redirecting input and output streams to GUI widgets
- Reloading GUI callback handlers on the fly
- Wrapping up top-level window interfaces
- Using threads and queues to avoiding blocking in GUIs
- Popping up GUI windows on demand from non-GUI programs
- Adding GUIs as separate programs with sockets and pipes

As with other chapters in this book, this chapter has a dual agenda—not only will we be studying GUI programming, but we'll also be learning more about general Python development concepts such as object-oriented programming (OOP) and code reuse. As we'll see, by coding GUI tools in Python, it's easy to apply them in a wide variety of contexts and programs.

Two notes before we begin: first, be sure to read the code listings in this chapter for details we won't present in the narrative. Second, although small examples that apply in this chapter's techniques will show up along the way, more realistic application will have to await more realistic programs. We'll put these techniques to use in the larger examples in the next chapter and throughout the rest of the book. In fact, we'll be reusing the modules we develop here often, as tools in other programs in this book; reusable software wants to be reused. For now, though, let's do what our species does best and build some tools.

GuiMixin: Common Tool Mixin Classes

If you read the last three chapters, you probably noticed that the code used to construct nontrivial GUIs can become long if we make each widget by hand. Not only do we have to link up all the widgets manually, but we also need to remember and then set dozens of options. If we stick to this strategy, GUI programming often becomes an exercise in typing, or at least in cut-and-paste text editor operations.

Instead of performing each step by hand, a better idea is to wrap or automate as much of the GUI construction process as possible. One approach is to code functions that provide typical widget configurations; for instance, we could define a button function to handle configuration details and support most of the buttons we draw.

Alternatively, we can implement common methods in a class and inherit them everywhere they are needed. Such classes are commonly called *mixin* classes because their methods are "mixed in" with other classes. Mixins serve to package generally useful tools as methods. The concept is almost like importing a module, but mixin classes can access the subject instance, self, to utilize per-instance state and inherited methods. The script in Example 11-1 shows how.

Example 11-1. PP3E\Gui\Tools\guimixin.py

```
###############################################################################
# a "mixin" class for other frames: common methods for canned dialogs,
# spawning programs, simple text viewers, etc; this class must be mixed
# with a Frame (or a subclass derived from Frame) for its quit method
###############################################################################

from Tkinter import *
from tkMessageBox import *
from tkFileDialog import *
from ScrolledText import ScrolledText
from PP3E.launchmodes import PortableLauncher, System

class GuiMixin:
    def infobox(self, title, text, *args):          # use standard dialogs
        return showinfo(title, text)                # *args for bkwd compat
    def errorbox(self, text):
        showerror('Error!', text)
    def question(self, title, text, *args):
        return askyesno(title, text)

    def notdone(self):
        showerror('Not implemented', 'Option not available')
```

Example 11-1. PP3E\Gui\Tools\guimixin.py (continued)

```
    def quit(self):
        ans = self.question('Verify quit', 'Are you sure you want to quit?')
        if ans == 1:
            Frame.quit(self)                          # quit not recursive!
    def help(self):
        self.infobox('RTFM', 'See figure 1...')       # override this better

    def selectOpenFile(self, file="", dir="."):       # use standard dialogs
        return askopenfilename(initialdir=dir, initialfile=file)
    def selectSaveFile(self, file="", dir="."):
        return asksaveasfilename(initialfile=file, initialdir=dir)

    def clone(self):
        new = Toplevel()                     # make a new version of me
        myclass = self.__class__             # instance's (lowest) class object
        myclass(new)                         # attach/run instance to new window

    def spawn(self, pycmdline, wait=0):
        if not wait:
            PortableLauncher(pycmdline, pycmdline)()   # run Python progam
        else:
            System(pycmdline, pycmdline)()             # wait for it to exit

    def browser(self, filename):
        new  = Toplevel()                              # make new window
        text = ScrolledText(new, height=30, width=90)  # Text with scrollbar
        text.config(font=('courier', 10, 'normal'))    # use fixed-width font
        text.pack()
        new.title("Text Viewer")                       # set window mgr attrs
        new.iconname("browser")
        text.insert('0.0', open(filename, 'r').read() ) # insert file's text

if __name__ == '__main__':
    class TestMixin(GuiMixin, Frame):        # standalone test
        def __init__(self, parent=None):
            Frame.__init__(self, parent)
            self.pack()
            Button(self, text='quit',  command=self.quit).pack(fill=X)
            Button(self, text='help',  command=self.help).pack(fill=X)
            Button(self, text='clone', command=self.clone).pack(fill=X)
    TestMixin().mainloop()
```

Although Example 11-1 is geared toward GUIs, it's really about design concepts. The GuiMixin class implements common operations with standard interfaces that are immune to changes in implementation. In fact, the implementations of some of this class's methods did change—between the first and second editions of this book, old-style Dialog calls were replaced with the new Tk standard dialog calls. Because this class's interface hides such details, its clients did not have to be changed to use the new dialog techniques.

As is, `GuiMixin` provides methods for common dialogs, window cloning, program spawning, text file browsing, and so on. We can add more methods to such a mixin later if we find ourselves coding the same methods repeatedly; they will all become available immediately everywhere this class is imported and mixed. Moreover, `GuiMixin`'s methods can be inherited and used as is, or they can be redefined in subclasses.

There are a few things to notice here:

- The `quit` method serves some of the same purpose as the reusable `Quitter` button we used in earlier chapters. Because mixin classes can define a large library of reusable methods, they can be a more powerful way to package reusable components than individual classes. If the mixin is packaged well, we can get a lot more from it than a single button's callback.

- The `clone` method makes a new copy, in a new top-level window, of the most specific class that mixes in a `GuiMixin` (`self.__class__` is the class object that the instance was created from). This opens a new independent copy of the window.

- The `browser` method opens the standard library's `ScrolledText` object in a new window and fills it with the text of a file to be viewed. We wrote our own `ScrolledText` in the previous chapter; you might need to use it here instead, if the standard library's class ever becomes deprecated (please, no wagering).

- The `spawn` method launches a Python program command line as a new process and waits for it to end or not (depending on the `wait` argument). This method is simple, though, because we wrapped launching details in the `launchmodes` module presented at the end of Chapter 5. `GuiMixin` both fosters and practices good code reuse habits.

The `GuiMixin` class is meant to be a library of reusable tool methods and is essentially useless by itself. In fact, it must generally be mixed with a `Frame`-based class to be used: quit assumes it's mixed with a `Frame`, and clone assumes it's mixed with a widget class. To satisfy such constraints, this module's self-test code at the bottom combines `GuiMixin` with a `Frame` widget. Figure 11-1 shows the scene created by the self-test after pressing "clone" twice, and then "help" in one of the three copies.

We'll see this class show up again as a mixin in later examples—that's the whole point of code reuse, after all.

GuiMaker: Automating Menus and Toolbars

The last section's mixin class makes common tasks simpler, but it still doesn't address the complexity of linking up widgets such as menus and toolbars. Of course, if we had access to a GUI layout tool that generates Python code, this would not be an issue. We'd design our widgets interactively, press a button, and fill in the callback handler blanks.

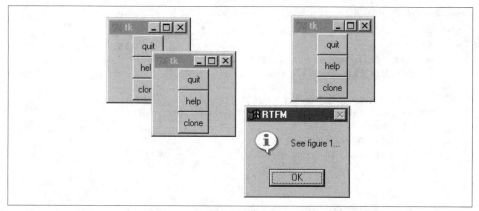

Figure 11-1. GuiMixin self-test code in action

For now, a programming-based approach can work just as well. We'd like to be able to inherit something that does all the grunt work of construction for us, given a template for the menus and toolbars in a window. Here's one way it can be done—using trees of simple objects. The class in Example 11-2 interprets data structure representations of menus and toolbars and builds all the widgets automatically.

Example 11-2. PP3E\Gui\Tools\guimaker.py

```
###############################################################################
# An extended Frame that makes window menus and toolbars automatically.
# Use GuiMakerFrameMenu for embedded components (makes frame-based menus).
# Use GuiMakerWindowMenu for top-level windows (makes Tk8.0 window menus).
# See the self-test code (and PyEdit) for an example layout tree format.
###############################################################################

import sys
from Tkinter import *                       # widget classes
from types    import *                      # type constants

class GuiMaker(Frame):
    menuBar    = []                         # class defaults
    toolBar    = []                         # change per instance in subclasses
    helpButton = 1                          # set these in start() if need self

    def __init__(self, parent=None):
        Frame.__init__(self, parent)
        self.pack(expand=YES, fill=BOTH)    # make frame stretchable
        self.start()                        # for subclass: set menu/toolBar
        self.makeMenuBar()                  # done here: build menu bar
        self.makeToolBar()                  # done here: build toolbar
        self.makeWidgets()                  # for subclass: add middle part

    def makeMenuBar(self):
        """
        make menu bar at the top (Tk8.0 menus below)
```

Example 11-2. PP3E\Gui\Tools\guimaker.py (continued)

```
    expand=no, fill=x so same width on resize
    """

    menubar = Frame(self, relief=RAISED, bd=2)
    menubar.pack(side=TOP, fill=X)

    for (name, key, items) in self.menuBar:
        mbutton  = Menubutton(menubar, text=name, underline=key)
        mbutton.pack(side=LEFT)
        pulldown = Menu(mbutton)
        self.addMenuItems(pulldown, items)
        mbutton.config(menu=pulldown)

    if self.helpButton:
        Button(menubar, text    = 'Help',
                        cursor  = 'gumby',
                        relief  = FLAT,
                        command = self.help).pack(side=RIGHT)

def addMenuItems(self, menu, items):
    for item in items:                          # scan nested items list
        if item == 'separator':                 # string: add separator
            menu.add_separator({})
        elif type(item) == ListType:            # list: disabled item list
            for num in item:
                menu.entryconfig(num, state=DISABLED)
        elif type(item[2]) != ListType:
            menu.add_command(label     = item[0],   # command:
                             underline = item[1],   # add command
                             command   = item[2])   # cmd=callable
        else:
            pullover = Menu(menu)
            self.addMenuItems(pullover, item[2])    # sublist:
            menu.add_cascade(label     = item[0],   # make submenu
                             underline = item[1],   # add cascade
                             menu      = pullover)

def makeToolBar(self):
    """
    make button bar at bottom, if any
    expand=no, fill=x so same width on resize
    """
    if self.toolBar:
        toolbar = Frame(self, cursor='hand2', relief=SUNKEN, bd=2)
        toolbar.pack(side=BOTTOM, fill=X)
        for (name, action, where) in self.toolBar:
            Button(toolbar, text=name, command=action).pack(where)

def makeWidgets(self):
    """
    make 'middle' part last, so menu/toolbar
    is always on top/bottom and clipped last;
    override this default, pack middle any side;
```

Example 11-2. PP3E\Gui\Tools\guimaker.py (continued)

```
        for grid: grid middle part in a packed frame
        """
        name = Label(self,
                     width=40, height=10,
                     relief=SUNKEN, bg='white',
                     text   = self.__class__.__name__,
                     cursor = 'crosshair')
        name.pack(expand=YES, fill=BOTH, side=TOP)

    def help(self):
        """
        override me in subclass
        """
        from tkMessageBox import showinfo
        showinfo('Help', 'Sorry, no help for ' + self.__class__.__name__)

    def start(self): pass   # override me in subclass


###############################################################################
# For Tk 8.0 main window menu bar, instead of a frame
###############################################################################

GuiMakerFrameMenu = GuiMaker              # use this for embedded component menus

class GuiMakerWindowMenu(GuiMaker):      # use this for top-level window menus
    def makeMenuBar(self):
        menubar = Menu(self.master)
        self.master.config(menu=menubar)

        for (name, key, items) in self.menuBar:
            pulldown = Menu(menubar)
            self.addMenuItems(pulldown, items)
            menubar.add_cascade(label=name, underline=key, menu=pulldown)

        if self.helpButton:
            if sys.platform[:3] == 'win':
                menubar.add_command(label='Help', command=self.help)
            else:
                pulldown = Menu(menubar)  # Linux needs real pull down
                pulldown.add_command(label='About', command=self.help)
                menubar.add_cascade(label='Help', menu=pulldown)


###############################################################################
# Self-test when file run standalone: 'python guimaker.py'
###############################################################################

if __name__ == '__main__':
    from guimixin import GuiMixin              # mix in a help method

    menuBar = [
```

Example 11-2. PP3E\Gui\Tools\guimaker.py (continued)

```
        ('File', 0,
            [('Open',  0, lambda:0),        # lambda:0 is a no-op
             ('Quit',  0, sys.exit)]),      # use sys, no self here
        ('Edit', 0,
            [('Cut',    0, lambda:0),
             ('Paste', 0, lambda:0)]) ]
    toolBar = [('Quit', sys.exit, {'side': LEFT})]

    class TestAppFrameMenu(GuiMixin, GuiMakerFrameMenu):
        def start(self):
            self.menuBar = menuBar
            self.toolBar = toolBar
    class TestAppWindowMenu(GuiMixin, GuiMakerWindowMenu):
        def start(self):
            self.menuBar = menuBar
            self.toolBar = toolBar
    class TestAppWindowMenuBasic(GuiMakerWindowMenu):
        def start(self):
            self.menuBar = menuBar
            self.toolBar = toolBar    # guimaker help, not guimixin

    root = Tk()
    TestAppFrameMenu(Toplevel())
    TestAppWindowMenu(Toplevel())
    TestAppWindowMenuBasic(root)
    root.mainloop()
```

To make sense of this module, you have to be familiar with the menu fundamentals introduced in Chapter 10. If you are, though, it's straightforward—the GuiMaker class simply traverses the menu and toolbar structures and builds menu and toolbar widgets along the way. This module's self-test code includes a simple example of the data structures used to lay out menus and toolbars:

Menu bar templates

Lists and nested sublists of (`label, underline, handler`) triples. If a handler is a sublist rather than a function or method, it is assumed to be a cascading submenu.

Toolbar templates

List of (`label, handler, pack-options`) triples. pack-options is coded as a dictionary of options passed on to the widget pack method (it accepts dictionaries, but we could also transform the dictionary into keyword arguments by passing it as a third argument to apply or by using the newer func(*pargs, **kargs) syntax).

Subclass Protocols

In addition to menu and toolbar layouts, clients of this class can also tap into and customize the method and geometry protocols the class implements:

Template attributes

Clients of this class are expected to set menuBar and toolBar attributes some-where in the inheritance chain by the time the start method has finished.

Initialization

The start method can be overridden to construct menu and toolbar templates dynamically (since self is then available); start is also where general initializa-tions should be performed—GuiMixin's __init__ constructor must be run, not overridden.

Adding widgets

The makeWidgets method can be redefined to construct the middle part of the window—the application portion between the menu bar and the toolbar. By default, makeWidgets adds a label in the middle with the name of the most spe-cific class, but this method is expected to be specialized.

Packing protocol

In a specialized makeWidgets method, clients may attach their middle portion's widgets to any side of self (a Frame) since the menu and toolbars have already claimed the container's top and bottom by the time makeWidgets is run. The mid-dle part does not need to be a nested frame if its parts are packed. The menu and toolbars are also automatically packed first so that they are clipped last if the window shrinks.

Gridding protocol

The middle part can contain a grid layout, as long as it is gridded in a nested Frame that is itself packed within the self parent. (Remember that each con-tainer level may use grid or pack, not both, and that self is a Frame with already packed bars by the time makeWidgets is called.) Because the GuiMaker Frame packs itself within its parent, it is not directly embeddable in a container with widgets arranged in a grid, for similar reasons; add an intermediate gridded Frame to use it in this context.

GuiMaker Classes

In return for conforming to GuiMaker protocols and templates, client subclasses get a Frame that knows how to automatically build up its own menus and toolbars from template data structures. If you read the last chapter's menu examples, you probably know that this is a big win in terms of reduced coding requirements. GuiMaker is also clever enough to export interfaces for both menu styles that we met in Chapter 10:

GuiMakerWindowMenu

Implements Tk 8.0–style top-level window menus, useful for menus associated with standalone programs and pop ups.

GuiMakerFrameMenu

Implements alternative Frame/Menubutton-based menus, useful for menus on objects embedded as components of a larger GUI.

Both classes build toolbars, export the same protocols, and expect to find the same template structures; they differ only in the way they process menu templates. In fact, one is simply a subclass of the other with a specialized menu maker method—only top-level menu processing differs between the two styles (a Menu with Menu cascades rather than a Frame with Menubuttons).

GuiMaker Self-Test

Like GuiMixin, when we run Example 11-2 as a top-level program, we trigger the self-test logic at the bottom; Figure 11-2 shows the windows we get. Three windows come up, representing each of the self-test code's TestApp classes. All three have a menu and toolbar with the options specified in the template data structures created in the self-test code: File and Edit menu pull downs, plus a Quit toolbar button and a standard Help menu button. In the screenshot, one window's File menu has been torn off and the Edit menu of another is being pulled down.

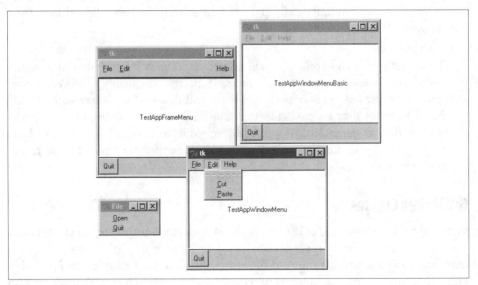

Figure 11-2. GuiMaker self-test at work

Because of the superclass relationships coded, two of the three windows get their help callback handler from GuiMixin; TestAppWindowMenuBasic gets GuiMaker's instead. Notice that the order in which these two classes are mixed can be important: because both GuiMixin and Frame define a quit method, we need to list the class from which we want to get it first in the mixed class's header line due to the left-to-right search rule of multiple inheritance. To select GuiMixin's methods, it should usually be listed before a superclass derived from real widgets.

We'll put GuiMaker to more practical use in instances such as the PyEdit example in Chapter 12. The next module shows another way to use GuiMaker's templates to build up a sophisticated interface.

BigGui: A Client Demo Program

Let's look at a program that makes better use of the two automation classes we just wrote. In the module in Example 11-3, the Hello class inherits from both GuiMixin and GuiMaker. GuiMaker provides the link to the Frame widget, plus the menu/toolbar construction logic. GuiMixin provides extra common-behavior methods. Really, Hello is another kind of extended Frame widget because it is derived from GuiMaker. To get a menu and toolbar for free, it simply follows the protocols defined by GuiMaker—it sets the menuBar and toolBar attributes in its start method, and overrides make-Widgets to put a label in the middle.

Example 11-3. PP3E\Gui\Tools\BigGui\big_gui.py

```
#!/usr/bin/python
#######################################################
# GUI implementation - combines maker, mixin, and this
#######################################################

import sys, os
from Tkinter import *                          # widget classes
from PP3E.Gui.Tools.guimixin import *          # mix-in methods
from PP3E.Gui.Tools.guimaker import *          # frame, plus menu/toolbar builder
from find_demo_dir import findDemoDir          # Python demos search

class Hello(GuiMixin, GuiMakerWindowMenu):     # or GuiMakerFrameMenu
    def start(self):
        self.hellos = 0
        self.master.title("GuiMaker Demo")
        self.master.iconname("GuiMaker")

        self.menuBar = [                        # a tree: 3 pull downs
          ('File', 0,                           # (pull-down)
             [('New...',  0, self.notdone),     # [menu items list]
              ('Open...', 0, self.fileOpen),
              ('Quit',    0, self.quit)]        # label,underline,action
          ),

          ('Edit', 0,
             [('Cut',   -1, self.notdone),      # no underline|action
              ('Paste',-1, self.notdone),       # lambda:0 works too
              'separator',                      # add a separator
              ('Stuff', -1,
                 [('Clone', -1, self.clone),    # cascaded submenu
                  ('More',  -1, self.more)]
```

Example 11-3. PP3E\Gui\Tools\BigGui\big_gui.py (continued)

```
                ),
                ('Delete', -1, lambda:0),
                [5]]                                    # disable 'delete'
            ),

            ('Play', 0,
                [('Hello',    0, self.greeting),
                 ('Popup...',  0, self.dialog),
                 ('Demos', 0,
                     [('Hanoi', 0,
                          lambda:
                          self.spawn(findDemoDir() + '\guido\hanoi.py', wait=0)),
                     ('Pong',  0,
                          lambda:
                          self.spawn(findDemoDir() + '\matt\pong-demo-1.py', wait=0)),
                     ('Other...', -1, self.pickDemo)]
                 )]
            )]

    self.toolBar = [
        ('Quit',  self.quit,     {'side': RIGHT}),        # add 3 buttons
        ('Hello', self.greeting, {'side': LEFT}),
        ('Popup', self.dialog,   {'side': LEFT, 'expand':YES}) ]

def makeWidgets(self):                              # override default
    middle = Label(self, text='Hello maker world!', width=40, height=10,
                cursor='pencil', bg='white', relief=SUNKEN)
    middle.pack(expand=YES, fill=BOTH)

def greeting(self):
    self.hellos += 1
    if self.hellos % 3:
        print "hi"
    else:
        self.infobox("Three", 'HELLO!')    # on every third press

def dialog(self):
    button = self.question('OOPS!',
                        'You typed "rm*" ... continue?',
                        'questhead', ('yes', 'no', 'help'))
    [lambda:0, self.quit, self.help][button]()

def fileOpen(self):
    pick = self.selectOpenFile(file='big_gui.py')
    if pick:
        self.browser(pick)     # browse my source file, or other

def more(self):
    new = Toplevel()
    Label(new,  text='A new non-modal window').pack()
    Button(new, text='Quit', command=self.quit).pack(side=LEFT)
    Button(new, text='More', command=self.more).pack(side=RIGHT)
```

Example 11-3. PP3E\Gui\Tools\BigGui\big_gui.py (continued)

```
    def pickDemo(self):
        pick = self.selectOpenFile(dir=findDemoDir( )+'\guido')
        if pick:
            self.spawn(pick, wait=0)     # spawn any Python program

if __name__ == '__main__': Hello().mainloop( )   # make one, run one
```

This script lays out a fairly large menu and toolbar structure that we'll see in a moment. It also adds callback methods of its own that print stdout messages, pop up text file browsers and new windows, and run other programs. Many of the callbacks don't do much more than run the notDone method inherited from GuiMixin, though; this code is intended mostly as a GuiMaker and GuiMixin demo.

The big_gui script is almost a complete program, but not quite: it relies on a utility module to search for canned demo programs that come packaged with the Python full source distribution. (These demos are not part of this book's examples collection.) The Python source distribution might be unpacked anywhere on the host machine.

Because of that, it's impossible to know where the demo directory is located (if it is present at all). But instead of expecting beginners to change the source code of this script to hardcode a path, the guessLocation tool in the Launcher module we met at the end of Chapter 6 is used to hunt for the demo directory (see Example 11-4). Flip back if you've forgotten how this works (though the beauty of code reuse is that it's often OK to forget).

Example 11-4. PP3E\Gui\Tools\BigGui\find_demo_dir.py

```
#########################################################
# search for demos shipped in Python source distribution;
# PATH and PP3EHOME won't help here, because these demos
# are not part of the standard install or the book's tree
#########################################################

import os, PP3E.Launcher
demoDir  = None
myTryDir = ''

#sourceDir = r'C:\Stuff\Etc\Python-ddj-cd\distributions'
#myTryDir  = sourceDir + r'\Python-1.5.2\Demo\tkinter'

def findDemoDir( ):
    global demoDir
    if not demoDir:                      # only searches on first call
        if os.path.exists(myTryDir):     # use hardcoded dir, or search
            demoDir = myTryDir           # save in global for next call
        else:
            print 'Searching for standard demos on your machine...'
            path = PP3E.Launcher.guessLocation('hanoi.py')
```

Example 11-4. PP3E\Gui\Tools\BigGui\find_demo_dir.py (continued)

```
        if path:
            demoDir = os.sep.join(path.split(os.sep)[:-2])
            print 'Using demo dir:', demoDir
    assert demoDir, 'Where is your demo directory?'
    return demoDir
```

When big_gui is run as a top-level program, it creates a window with four menu pull downs on top, and a three-button toolbar on the bottom, shown in Figure 11-3 along with some of the pop-up windows its callbacks create. The menus have separators, disabled entries, and cascading submenus, all as defined by the menuBar template.

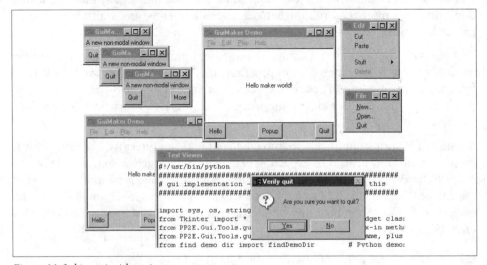

Figure 11-3. big_gui with various pop ups

Figure 11-4 shows this script's window again, after its Play pull down has been used to launch two independently running instances of the *hanoi.py* demo script that is shipped in the Python source distribution and was coded by Python creator, Guido van Rossum. This demo shows a simple animation of solutions to the "Towers of Hanoi" puzzle—a classic recursive problem popular on computer science quizzes (if you never heard of it, I'll spare you the gory details here).

To find this demo, the script searches directory trees on your machine rooted at common places; it was found on mine only by a last-resort traversal of my entire C: hard drive:

```
C:\...\PP3E\Gui\Tools\BigGui>python big_gui.py
Searching for standard demos on your machine...
Searching for hanoi.py in C:\Program Files\Python
Searching for hanoi.py in C:\PP3rdEd\examples\PP3E\Gui\Tools\BigGui
Searching for hanoi.py in C:\Program Files
Searching for hanoi.py in C:\
Using demo dir: C:\PP3rdEd\cdrom\Python1.5.2\SourceDistribution\Unpacked\Python-
```

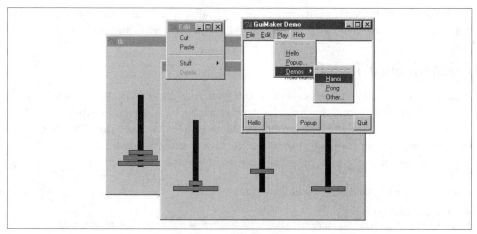

Figure 11-4. big_gui with spawned hanoi demos on the move

```
1.5.2\Demo\tkinter
C:\PP3rdEd\cdrom\Python1.5.2\SourceDistribution\Unpacked\Python-1.5.2\Demo\tkint
er\guido\hanoi.py
```

This search takes about 20 seconds on my 650 MHz Windows laptop, but is done only the first time you select one of these demos—after a successful search, the find_ demo_dir module caches away the directory name in a global variable for immediate retrieval the next time you start a demo. If you want to run demos from other directories (e.g., one of the book demos in the *PP3E* tree), select the Play menu's Other option to pop up a standard file selection dialog instead and navigate to the desired program's file.

Finally, I should note that GuiMaker can be redesigned to use trees of embedded class instances that know how to apply themselves to the Tkinter widget tree being constructed, instead of branching on the types of items in template data structures. In the interest of space, though, we'll banish that extension to the land of suggested exercises in this edition.

ShellGui: GUIs for Command-Line Tools

To better show how things like the GuiMixin class can be of practical use, we need a more realistic application. Here's one: in Chapter 6, we saw simple scripts for packing and unpacking text files. The *packapp.py* script we met there, you'll recall, concatenates multiple text files into a single file, and *unpackapp.py* extracts the original files from the combined file.

We ran these scripts in that chapter with manually typed command lines that weren't the most complex ever devised, but were complicated enough to be easily forgotten. Instead of requiring users of such tools to type cryptic commands at a shell, why not also provide an easy-to-use Tkinter GUI interface for running such programs? While we're at it, why not generalize the whole notion of running command-line tools from a GUI, to make it easy to support future tools too?

A Generic Shell-Tools Display

Examples 11-5 through 11-8 comprise one concrete implementation of these artificially rhetorical musings. Because I wanted this to be a general-purpose tool that could run any command-line program, its design is factored into modules that become more application-specific as we go lower in the software hierarchy. At the top, things are about as generic as they can be, as shown in Example 11-5.

Example 11-5. PP3E\Gui\ShellGui\shellgui.py.py

```
#!/usr/local/bin/python
###############################################################################
# tools launcher; uses guimaker templates, guimixin std quit dialog;
# I am just a class library: run mytools script to display the GUI;
###############################################################################

from Tkinter import *                             # get widgets
from PP3E.Gui.Tools.guimixin import GuiMixin      # get quit, not done
from PP3E.Gui.Tools.guimaker import *             # menu/toolbar builder

class ShellGui(GuiMixin, GuiMakerWindowMenu):     # a frame + maker + mixins
    def start(self):                              # use GuiMaker if component
        self.setMenuBar()
        self.setToolBar()
        self.master.title("Shell Tools Listbox")
        self.master.iconname("Shell Tools")

    def handleList(self, event):                  # on listbox double-click
        label = self.listbox.get(ACTIVE)          # fetch selection text
        self.runCommand(label)                    # and call action here

    def makeWidgets(self):                        # add listbox in middle
        sbar = Scrollbar(self)                    # cross link sbar, list
        list = Listbox(self, bg='white')          # or use Tour.ScrolledList
        sbar.config(command=list.yview)
        list.config(yscrollcommand=sbar.set)
        sbar.pack(side=RIGHT, fill=Y)                    # pack 1st=clip last
        list.pack(side=LEFT, expand=YES, fill=BOTH)      # list clipped first
        for (label, action) in self.fetchCommands():     # add to listbox
            list.insert(END, label)                      # and menu/toolbars
        list.bind('<Double-1>', self.handleList)         # set event handler
        self.listbox = list

    def forToolBar(self, label):                  # put on toolbar?
        return 1                                  # default = all

    def setToolBar(self):
        self.toolBar = []
        for (label, action) in self.fetchCommands():
```

Example 11-5. PP3E\Gui\ShellGui\shellgui.py.py (continued)

```
            if self.forToolBar(label):
                self.toolBar.append((label, action, {'side': LEFT}))
        self.toolBar.append(('Quit', self.quit, {'side': RIGHT}))

    def setMenuBar(self):
        toolEntries  = []
        self.menuBar = [
            ('File',  0, [('Quit', -1, self.quit)]),      # pull-down name
            ('Tools', 0, toolEntries)                     # menu items list
            ]                                             # label,underline,action
        for (label, action) in self.fetchCommands():
            toolEntries.append((label, -1, action))       # add app items to menu


###############################################################################
# delegate to template type-specific subclasses
# which delegate to app tool-set-specific subclasses
###############################################################################

class ListMenuGui(ShellGui):
    def fetchCommands(self):             # subclass: set 'myMenu'
        return self.myMenu               # list of (label, callback)
    def runCommand(self, cmd):
        for (label, action) in self.myMenu:
            if label == cmd: action()

class DictMenuGui(ShellGui):
    def fetchCommands(self):   return self.myMenu.items()
    def runCommand(self, cmd): self.myMenu[cmd]()
```

The ShellGui class in this module knows how to use the GuiMaker and GuiMixin interfaces to construct a selection window that displays tool names in menus, a scrolled list, and a toolbar. It also provides a forToolBar method that you can override and that allows subclasses to specify which tools should and should not be added to the window's toolbar (the toolbar can become crowded in a hurry). However, it is deliberately ignorant about both the names of tools that should be displayed in those places and about the actions to be run when tool names are selected.

Instead, ShellGui relies on the ListMenuGui and DictMenuGui subclasses in this file to provide a list of tool names from a fetchCommands method and dispatch actions by name in a runCommand method. These two subclasses really just serve to interface to application-specific tool sets laid out as lists or dictionaries, though; they are still naïve about what tool names really go up on the GUI. That's by design too—because the tool sets displayed are defined by lower subclasses, we can use ShellGui to display a variety of different tool sets.

Application-Specific Tool Set Classes

To get to the actual tool sets, we need to go one level down. The module in Example 11-6 defines subclasses of the two type-specific ShellGui classes, to provide sets of available tools in both list and dictionary formats (you would normally need only one, but this module is meant for illustration). This is also the module that is actually *run* to kick off the GUI—the shellgui module is a class library only.

Example 11-6. PP3E\Gui\ShellGui\mytools.py

```
#!/usr/local/bin/python
from shellgui import *                # type-specific shell interfaces
from packdlg  import runPackDialog    # dialogs for data entry
from unpkdlg  import runUnpackDialog  # they both run app classes


class TextPak1(ListMenuGui):
    def __init__(self):
        self.myMenu = [('Pack',    runPackDialog),
                       ('Unpack',  runUnpackDialog),   # simple functions
                       ('Mtool',   self.notdone)]      # method from guimixin
        ListMenuGui.__init__(self)

    def forToolBar(self, label):
        return label in ['Pack', 'Unpack']


class TextPak2(DictMenuGui):
    def __init__(self):
        self.myMenu = {'Pack':   runPackDialog,        # or use input here...
                       'Unpack': runUnpackDialog,       # instead of in dialogs
                       'Mtool':  self.notdone}
        DictMenuGui.__init__(self)


if __name__ == '__main__':                             # self-test code...
    from sys import argv                                # 'menugui.py list|^'
    if len(argv) > 1 and argv[1] == 'list':
        print 'list test'
        TextPak1().mainloop()
    else:
        print 'dict test'
        TextPak2().mainloop()
```

The classes in this module are specific to a particular tool set; to display a different set of tool names, simply code and run a new subclass. By separating out application logic into distinct subclasses and modules like this, software can become widely reusable.

Figure 11-5 shows the main ShellGui window created when the mytools script is run with its dictionary-based menu layout class on Windows, along with menu tear-offs so that you can see what they contain. This window's menu and toolbar are built by

GuiMaker, and its Quit and Help buttons and menu selections trigger quit and help methods inherited from GuiMixin through the ShellGui module's superclasses. Are you starting to see why this book preaches code reuse so often?

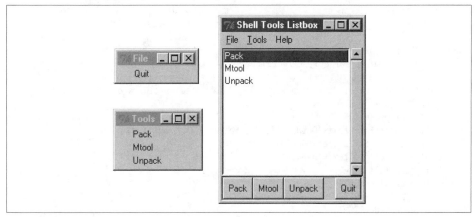

Figure 11-5. mytools items in a ShellGui window

Adding GUI Frontends to Command Lines

The callback actions named within the prior module's classes, though, should normally do something GUI-oriented. Because the original file packing and unpacking scripts live in the world of text-based streams, we need to code wrappers around them that accept input parameters from more GUI-minded users.

The module in Example 11-7 uses the custom modal dialog techniques we studied in Chapter 9 to pop up an input display to collect pack script parameters. Its runPackDialog function is the actual callback handler invoked when tool names are selected in the main ShellGui window.

Example 11-7. PP3E\Gui\ShellGui\packdlg.py

```
# added file select dialogs, empties test; could use grids

from glob import glob                                    # filename expansion
from Tkinter import *                                    # GUI widget stuff
from tkFileDialog import *                               # file selector dialog
from PP3E.System.App.Clients.packapp import PackApp      # use pack class

def runPackDialog():
    s1, s2 = StringVar(), StringVar()        # run class like a function
    PackDialog(s1, s2)                        # pop-up dialog: sets s1/s2
    output, patterns = s1.get(), s2.get()     # whether 'ok' or wm-destroy
    if output != "" and patterns != "":
        patterns = patterns.split()
        filenames = []
        for sublist in map(glob, patterns):    # do expansion manually
```

Example 11-7. PP3E\Gui\ShellGui\packdlg.py (continued)

```
                filenames = filenames + sublist    # Unix does auto on command line
            print 'PackApp:', output, filenames
            app = PackApp(ofile=output)            # run with redirected output
            app.args = filenames                   # reset cmdline args list
            app.main()                             # should show msgs in GUI too

class PackDialog(Toplevel):
    def __init__(self, target1, target2):
        Toplevel.__init__(self)                    # a new top-level window
        self.title('Enter Pack Parameters')        # 2 frames plus a button

        f1 = Frame(self)
        l1 = Label(f1,  text='Output file?', relief=RIDGE, width=15)
        e1 = Entry(f1,  relief=SUNKEN)
        b1 = Button(f1, text='browse...')
        f1.pack(fill=X)
        l1.pack(side=LEFT)
        e1.pack(side=LEFT, expand=YES, fill=X)
        b1.pack(side=RIGHT)
        b1.config(command= (lambda: target1.set(askopenfilename())) )

        f2 = Frame(self)
        l2 = Label(f2,  text='Files to pack?', relief=RIDGE, width=15)
        e2 = Entry(f2,  relief=SUNKEN)
        b2 = Button(f2, text='browse...')
        f2.pack(fill=X)
        l2.pack(side=LEFT)
        e2.pack(side=LEFT, expand=YES, fill=X)
        b2.pack(side=RIGHT)
        b2.config(command=
                (lambda: target2.set(target2.get() +' '+ askopenfilename())) )

        Button(self, text='OK', command=self.destroy).pack()
        e1.config(textvariable=target1)
        e2.config(textvariable=target2)

        self.grab_set()        # make myself modal:
        self.focus_set()       # mouse grab, keyboard focus, wait...
        self.wait_window()     # till destroy; else returns to caller now

if __name__ == '__main__':
    root = Tk()
    Button(root, text='pop', command=runPackDialog).pack(fill=X)
    Button(root, text='bye', command=root.quit).pack(fill=X)
    root.mainloop()
```

When run, this script makes the input form shown in Figure 11-6. Users may either type input and output filenames into the entry fields or press the "browse" buttons to pop up standard file selection dialogs. They can also enter filename patterns—the manual glob.glob call in this script expands filename patterns to match names and filters out nonexistent input filenames. The Unix command line does this pattern expansion automatically when running PackApp from a shell, but Windows does not (see Chapter 4 for more details).

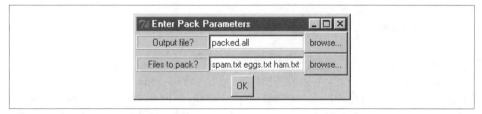

Figure 11-6. The packdlg input form

When the form is filled in and submitted with its OK button, parameters are finally passed to an instance of the PackApp class we wrote in Chapter 6 to do file concatenations. The GUI interface to the unpacking script is simpler because there is only one input field—the name of the packed file to scan. The script in Example 11-8 generates the input form window shown in Figure 11-7.

Example 11-8. PP3E\Gui\ShellGui\unpkdlg.py

```
# added file select dialog, handles cancel better

from Tkinter import *                              # widget classes
from tkFileDialog import *                         # file open dialog
from PP3E.System.App.Clients.unpackapp import UnpackApp   # use unpack class

def runUnpackDialog():
    input = UnpackDialog().input                  # get input from GUI
    if input != '':                               # do non-GUI file stuff
        print 'UnpackApp:', input
        app = UnpackApp(ifile=input)              # run with input from file
        app.main()                                # execute app class

class UnpackDialog(Toplevel):
    def __init__(self):                           # a function would work too
        Toplevel.__init__(self)                   # resizable root box
        self.input = ''                           # a label and an entry
        self.title('Enter Unpack Parameters')
        Label(self, text='input file?', relief=RIDGE, width=11).pack(side=LEFT)
        e = Entry(self, relief=SUNKEN)
        b = Button(self, text='browse...')
        e.bind('<Key-Return>', self.gotit)
        b.config(command=(lambda: e.insert(0, askopenfilename())))
        b.pack(side=RIGHT)
        e.pack(side=LEFT, expand=YES, fill=X)
        self.entry = e
        self.grab_set()                           # make myself modal
        self.focus_set()
        self.wait_window()                        # till I'm destroyed on return->gotit
    def gotit(self, event):                       # on return key: event.widget==Entry
        self.input = self.entry.get()             # fetch text, save in self
```

Example 11-8. PP3E\Gui\ShellGui\unpkdlg.py (continued)

```
        self.destroy()                          # kill window, but instance lives on

if __name__ == "__main__":
    Button(None, text='pop', command=runUnpackDialog).pack()
    mainloop()
```

The "browse" button in Figure 11-7 pops up a file selection dialog just as the packdlg form did. Instead of an OK button, this dialog binds the enter key-press event to kill the window and end the modal wait state pause; on submission, the name of the file is passed to an instance of the UnpackApp class shown in Chapter 6 to perform the actual file scan process.

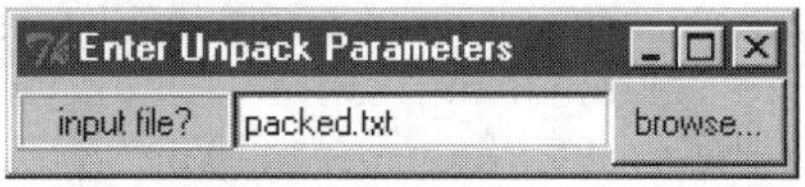

Figure 11-7. The unpkdlg input form

All of this works as advertised—by making command-line tools available in graphical form like this, they become much more attractive to users accustomed to the GUI way of life. Still, two aspects of this design seem prime for improvement.

First, both of the input dialogs use custom code to render a unique appearance, but we could probably simplify them substantially by importing a common form-builder module instead. We met generalized form builder code in Chapters 9 and 10, and we'll meet more later; see the form.py module in Chapter 13 for pointers on genericizing form construction too.

Second, at the point where the user submits input data in either form dialog, we've lost the GUI trail—the GUI is blocked, and messages are routed back to the console. The GUI is technically blocked and will not update itself while the pack and unpack utilities run; although these operations are fast enough for my files as to be negligible, we would probably want to spawn these calls off in threads for very large files to keep the main GUI thread active (more on threads later in this chapter). The console issue is more apparent: PackApp and UnpackApp messages still show up in the stdout console window, not in the GUI:

```
C:\...\PP3E\Gui\ShellGui\test>python ..\mytools.py
dict test
PackApp: packed.all ['spam.txt', 'eggs.txt', 'ham.txt']
packing: spam.txt
packing: eggs.txt
packing: ham.txt
UnpackApp: packed.all
creating: spam.txt
creating: eggs.txt
creating: ham.txt
```

This may be less than ideal for a GUI's users; they may not expect (or even be able to find) the command-line console. We can do better here, by *redirecting* stdout to an object that throws text up in a GUI window as it is received. You'll have to read the next section to see how.

GuiStreams: Redirecting Streams to Widgets

The script in Example 11-9 arranges to map input and output sources to pop-up windows in a GUI application, much as we did with strings in the stream redirection topics in Chapter 3. Although this module is really just a first-cut prototype and needs improvement itself (e.g., each input line request pops up a new input dialog), it demonstrates the concepts in general.

Its GuiOutput and GuiInput objects define methods that allow them to masquerade as files in any interface that expects a real file. As we learned earlier in Chapter 3, this includes standard stream processing tools, such as print and raw_input, and it includes explicit read and write calls. The two top-level interfaces in this module handle common use cases:

- The redirectedGuiFunc function uses this plug-and-play file compatibility to run a function with its standard input and output streams mapped completely to pop-up windows rather than to the console window (or wherever streams would otherwise be mapped in the system shell).
- The redirectedGuiShellCmd function similarly routes the output of a spawned shell command line to a pop-up window. It can be used to display the output of any program in a GUI—including that printed by a Python program.

The module's GuiInput and GuiOutput classes can also be used or customized directly by clients that need more fine-grained control over the process.

Example 11-9. PP3E\Gui\Tools\guiStreams.py

```
#############################################################################
# first-cut implementation of file-like classes that can be used to redirect
# input and output streams to GUI displays; as is, input comes from a common
# dialog pop-up (a single output+input interface or a persistent Entry field
# for input would be better); this also does not properly span lines for read
# requests with a byte count > len(line); see guiStreamsTools.py for more;
#############################################################################

from Tkinter import *
from ScrolledText import ScrolledText
from tkSimpleDialog import askstring

class GuiOutput:
    font = ('courier', 9, 'normal')              # in class for all, self for one
    def __init__(self, parent=None):
        self.text = None
```

Example 11-9. PP3E\Gui\Tools\guiStreams.py (continued)

```
        if parent: self.popupnow(parent)          # pop up now or on first write
    def popupnow(self, parent=None):               # in parent now, Toplevel later
        if self.text: return
        self.text = ScrolledText(parent or Toplevel())
        self.text.config(font=self.font)
        self.text.pack()
    def write(self, text):
        self.popupnow()
        self.text.insert(END, str(text))
        self.text.see(END)
        self.text.update()
    def writelines(self, lines):                   # lines already have '\n'
        for line in lines: self.write(line)        # or map(self.write, lines)

class GuiInput:
    def __init__(self):
        self.buff = ''
    def inputLine(self):
        line = askstring('GuiInput', 'Enter input line + <crlf> (cancel=eof)')
        if line == None:
            return ''                              # pop-up dialog for each line
        else:                                      # cancel button means eof
            return line + '\n'                     # else add end-line marker
    def read(self, bytes=None):
        if not self.buff:
            self.buff = self.inputLine()
        if bytes:                                  # read by byte count
            text = self.buff[:bytes]               # doesn't span lines
            self.buff = self.buff[bytes:]
        else:
            text = ''                              # read all till eof
            line = self.buff
            while line:
                text = text + line
                line = self.inputLine()            # until cancel=eof=''
        return text
    def readline(self):
        text = self.buff or self.inputLine()       # emulate file read methods
        self.buff = ''
        return text
    def readlines(self):
        lines = []                                 # read all lines
        while 1:
            next = self.readline()
            if not next: break
            lines.append(next)
        return lines

def redirectedGuiFunc(func, *pargs, **kargs):
    import sys
    saveStreams = sys.stdin, sys.stdout            # map func streams to pop ups
    sys.stdin   = GuiInput()                       # pops up dialog as needed
```

Example 11-9. PP3E\Gui\Tools\guiStreams.py (continued)

```
        sys.stdout = GuiOutput()                    # new output window per call
        sys.stderr = sys.stdout
        result = func(*pargs, **kargs)              # this is a blocking call
        sys.stdin, sys.stdout = saveStreams
        return result

def redirectedGuiShellCmd(command):
    import os
    input  = os.popen(command, 'r')
    output = GuiOutput()
    def reader(input, output):                      # show a shell command's
        while True:                                 # standard output in a new
            line = input.readline()                 # pop-up text box widget;
            if not line: break                      # the readline call may block
            output.write(line)
    reader(input, output)

if __name__ == '__main__':
    def makeUpper():                                # use standard streams
        while 1:
            try:
                line = raw_input('Line? ')
            except:
                break
            print line.upper()
        print 'end of file'

    def makeLower(input, output):                   # use explicit files
        while 1:
            line = input.readline()
            if not line: break
            output.write(line.lower())
        print 'end of file'

    root = Tk()
    Button(root, text='test streams',
        command=lambda: redirectedGuiFunc(makeUpper)).pack(fill=X)
    Button(root, text='test files  ',
        command=lambda: makeLower(GuiInput(), GuiOutput()) ).pack(fill=X)
    Button(root, text='test popen  ',
        command=lambda: redirectedGuiShellCmd('dir *')).pack(fill=X)
    root.mainloop()
```

As coded here, GuiOutput either attaches a ScrolledText to a parent container or pops up a new top-level window to serve as the container on the first write call. GuiInput pops up a new standard input dialog every time a read request requires a new line of input. Neither one of these policies is ideal for all scenarios (input would be better mapped to a more long-lived widget), but they prove the general point. Figure 11-8 shows the scene generated by this script's self-test code, after capturing the output of a shell dir listing command (on the left) and two interactive loop tests (the one with

"Line?" prompts and uppercase letters represents the makeUpper streams test). An input dialog has just popped up for a new makeLower files test.

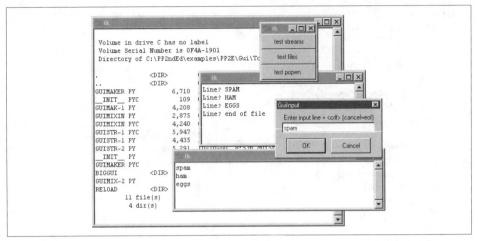

Figure 11-8. guiStreams routing streams to pop-up windows

Before we move on, we should note that this module's calls to a redirected function as well as its loop that reads from a spawned shell command are potentially *blocking*—they won't return to the GUI's event loop until the function or shell command exits. In redirectedGuiShellCmd, for example, the call to input.readline will pause until input is received from the spawned program, rendering the GUI unresponsive. Because the output object runs an update call, the display is still updated during the pause (an update call enters the Tk event loop momentarily). This blocking model is simplistic, though, and might be an issue in a larger GUI. We'll revisit this later in the chapter when we meet threads. For now, the code suits our present purpose.

Using Redirection for the Packing Scripts

Now, to use such redirection tools to map command-line script output back to a GUI, we simply run calls and command lines with the two redirected functions in this module. Example 11-10 shows one way to wrap the packing operation to force its printed output to appear in a pop-up window when generated, instead of in the console.

Example 11-10. PP3E\Gui\ShellGui\packdlg-redirect.py

```
# wrap command-line script in GUI redirection tool to pop p its output

from Tkinter import *
from packdlg import runPackDialog
from PP3E.Gui.Tools.guiStreams import redirectedGuiFunc
```

Example 11-10. PP3E\Gui\ShellGui\packdlg-redirect.py (continued)

```
def runPackDialog_Wrapped( ):
    redirectedGuiFunc(runPackDialog)     # wrap entire callback handler

if __name__ == '__main__':
    root = Tk( )
    Button(root, text='pop', command=runPackDialog_Wrapped).pack(fill=X)
    root.mainloop( )
```

You can run this script directly to test its effect, without bringing up the ShellGui window. Figure 11-9 shows the resulting stdout window after the pack input dialog is dismissed. This window pops up as soon as script output is generated, and it is a bit more GUI user friendly than hunting for messages in a console. You can similarly code the unpack parameters dialog to route its output to a pop-up.* In fact, you can use this technique to route the output of any function call or command line to a pop-up window; as usual, the notion of compatible object interfaces is at the heart of much of Python code's flexibility.

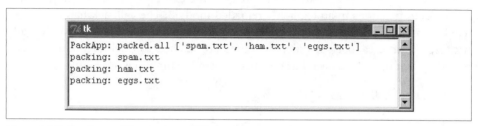

Figure 11-9. Routing script outputs to GUI pop ups

Reloading Callback Handlers Dynamically

Our next GUI-programming technique is all about changing a GUI while it is running—the ultimate in customization. The Python reload function lets you dynamically change and reload a program's modules without stopping the program. For instance, you can bring up a text editor window to change the source code of selected parts of a system while it is running and see those changes show up immediately after reloading the changed module.

This is a powerful feature, especially for developing programs that take a long time to restart. Programs that connect to databases or network servers, initialize large

---

* These two scripts are something of a unique case; because the App superclass they employ saves away standard streams in its own attributes at object creation time, you must kick off the GUI redirection wrapper calls as soon as possible so that App finds the redirected GUI streams in sys when saving them locally. Most other scripts aren't quite as tricky when it comes to internal stream redirections. Trace through the code to see what I mean.

objects, or travel through a long series of steps to retrigger a callback are prime candidates for reload. It can shave substantial time from the development cycle.

The catch for GUIs, though, is that because callback handlers are registered as *object references* rather than module and object names, reloads of callback handler functions are ineffective after the callback has been registered. The Python reload operation works by changing a module object's contents in place. Because Tkinter stores a pointer to the registered handler object directly, though, it is oblivious to any reloads of the module that the handler came from. That is, Tkinter will still reference a module's old objects even after the module is reloaded and changed.

This is a subtle thing, but you really only need to remember that you must do something special to reload callback handler functions dynamically. Not only do you need to explicitly request reloading of the modules that you change, but you must also generally provide an indirection layer that routes callbacks from registered objects to modules so that reloads have impact.

For example, the script in Example 11-11 goes the extra mile to indirectly dispatch callbacks to functions in an explicitly reloaded module. The callback handlers registered with Tkinter are method objects that do nothing but reload and dispatch again. Because the true callback handler functions are fetched through a module object, reloading that module makes the latest versions of the functions accessible.

Example 11-11. PP3E\Gui\Tools\Reload\rad.py

```
from Tkinter import *
import actions                    # get initial callback handlers

class Hello(Frame):
    def __init__(self, master=None):
        Frame.__init__(self, master)
        self.pack()
        self.make_widgets()

    def make_widgets(self):
        Button(self, text='message1', command=self.message1).pack(side=LEFT)
        Button(self, text='message2', command=self.message2).pack(side=RIGHT)

    def message1(self):
        reload(actions)           # need to reload actions module before calling
        actions.message1()        # now new version triggered by pressing button

    def message2(self):
        reload(actions)           # changes to actions.py picked up by reload
        actions.message2(self)    # call the most recent version; pass self

    def method1(self):
        print 'exposed method...'     # called from actions function

Hello().mainloop()
```

When run, this script makes a two-button window that triggers the message1 and message2 methods. Example 11-12 contains the actual callback handler code. Its functions receive a self argument that gives access back to the Hello class object, as though these were real methods. You can change this file any number of times while the rad script's GUI is active; each time you do so, you'll change the behavior of the GUI when a button press occurs.

Example 11-12. PP3E\Gui\Tools\Reload\actions.py

```
# callback handlers: reloaded each time triggered

def message1():                    # change me
    print 'spamSpamSPAM'           # could build a dialog...

def message2(self):
    print 'Ni! Ni!'                # change me
    self.method1()                 # access the 'Hello' instance...
```

Try running rad and editing the messages printed by actions in another window; you should see your new messages printed in the stdout console window each time the GUI's buttons are pressed. This example is deliberately simple to illustrate the concept, but the actions reloaded like this in practice might build pop-up dialogs, new top-level windows, and so on. Reloading the code that creates such windows would also let us dynamically change their appearances.

There are other ways to change a GUI while it's running. For instance, we saw in Chapter 10 that appearances can be altered at any time by calling the widget config method, and widgets can be added and deleted from a display dynamically with methods such as pack_forget and pack (and their grid manager relatives). Furthermore, passing a new command=action option setting to a widget's config method might reset a callback handler to a new action object on the fly; with enough support code, this may be a viable alternative to the indirection scheme used earlier to make reloads more effective in GUIs.

Wrapping Up Top-Level Window Interfaces

Top-level window interfaces were introduced in Chapter 9. This section picks up where that introduction left off and wraps up those interfaces in classes that automate some of the work of building top-level windows—setting titles, finding and displaying window icons, issuing proper close actions based on a window's role, intercepting window manager close button clicks, and so on.

Example 11-13 provides wrapper classes for the most common window types—a main application window, a transient pop-up window, and an embedded GUI component window. These window types vary slightly in terms of their close operations, but most inherit common functionality related to window borders: icons, titles, and close buttons. By creating, mixing in, or subclassing the class for the type of window you wish to make, you'll get all the setup logic for free.

Example 11-13. PP3E\Gui\Tools\windows.py

```
###############################################################################
# classes that encapsulate top-level interfaces;
# allows same GUI to be main, pop-up, or attached;  content classes may inherit
# from these directly, or be mixed together with them per usage mode;  may also
# be called directly without a subclass;  designed to be mixed in after (further
# to the right than) app-specific classes: else, subclass gets methods here
# (destroy, okayToQuit), instead of from app-specific classes--can't redefine.
###############################################################################

import os, glob
from Tkinter      import Tk, Toplevel, Frame, YES, BOTH, RIDGE
from tkMessageBox import showinfo, askyesno


class _window:
    """
    mixin shared by main and pop-up windows
    """
    foundicon = None                                # shared by all inst
    iconpatt  = '*.ico'                             # may be reset
    iconmine  = 'py.ico'

    def configBorders(self, app, kind, iconfile):
        if not iconfile:                            # no icon passed?
            iconfile = self.findIcon()              # try curr,tool dirs
        title = app
        if kind: title += ' - ' + kind
        self.title(title)                           # on window border
        self.iconname(app)                          # when minimized
        if iconfile:
            try:
                self.iconbitmap(iconfile)           # window icon image
            except:                                 # bad py or platform
                pass
        self.protocol('WM_DELETE_WINDOW', self.quit)   # don't close silent

    def findIcon(self):
        if _window.foundicon:                       # already found one?
            return _window.foundicon
        iconfile  = None                            # try curr dir auto
        iconshere = glob.glob(self.iconpatt)        # assume just one
        if iconshere:                               # del icon for red Tk
            iconfile = iconshere[0]
        else:                                       # try tools dir icon
            mymod  = __import__(__name__)           # import self for dir
            path   = __name__.split('.')            # poss a package path
            for mod in path[1:]:                    # follow path to end
                mymod = getattr(mymod, mod)
```

Example 11-13. PP3E\Gui\Tools\windows.py (continued)

```
            mydir  = os.path.dirname(mymod.__file__)
            myicon = os.path.join(mydir, self.iconmine)     # use myicon, not tk
            if os.path.exists(myicon): iconfile = myicon
        _window.foundicon = iconfile                        # don't search again
        return iconfile


class MainWindow(Tk, _window):
    """
    when run in main top-level window
    """
    def __init__(self, app, kind='', iconfile=None):
        Tk.__init__(self)
        self.__app = app
        self.configBorders(app, kind, iconfile)

    def quit(self):
        if self.okayToQuit():                               # threads running?
            if askyesno(self.__app, 'Verify Quit Program?'):
                self.destroy()                              # quit whole app
        else:
            showinfo(self.__app, 'Quit not allowed')        # or in okayToQuit?

    def destroy(self):                                      # exit app silently
        Tk.quit(self)                                       # redef if exit ops

    def okayToQuit(self):                                   # redef me if used
        return True                                         # e.g., thread busy


class PopupWindow(Toplevel, _window):
    """
    when run in secondary pop-up window
    """
    def __init__(self, app, kind='', iconfile=None):
        Toplevel.__init__(self)
        self.__app = app
        self.configBorders(app, kind, iconfile)

    def quit(self):                                         # redef me to change
        if askyesno(self.__app, 'Verify Quit Window?'):     # or call destroy
            self.destroy()                                  # quit this window

    def destroy(self):                                      # close win silently
        Toplevel.destroy(self)                             # redef for close ops


class QuietPopupWindow(PopupWindow):
    def quit(self):
        self.destroy()                                     # don't verify close
```

Example 11-13. PP3E\Gui\Tools\windows.py (continued)

```
class ComponentWindow(Frame):
    """
    when attached to another display
    """
    def __init__(self, parent):                    # if not a frame
        Frame.__init__(self, parent)               # provide container
        self.pack(expand=YES, fill=BOTH)
        self.config(relief=RIDGE, border=2)        # reconfig to change

    def quit(self):
        showinfo('Quit', 'Not supported in attachment mode')

    # destroy from Frame: erase frame silent      # redef for close ops
```

So why not just set an application's icon and title by calling protocol methods directly? For one thing, those are the sorts of details that are easy to forget (you will probably wind up cutting and pasting code much of the time). For another, these classes add higher-level functionality that we might otherwise have to code redundantly. Among other things, the classes arrange for automatic quit verification dialog pop ups and icon file searching. For instance, the window classes always search the current working directory and the directory containing this module for a window icon file, once per process.

By using classes that *encapsulate*—that is, hide—such details, we inherit powerful tools without even having to think about their implementation again in the future. Moreover, by using such classes, we'll give our applications a standard look-and-feel. And if we ever need to change that appearance, we have to change code in only one place, not in every window we generate.

To test this utility module, Example 11-14 exercises its classes in a variety of modes—as mix-in classes, as superclasses, and as calls from nonclass code.

Example 11-14. PP3E\Gui\Tools\windows-test.py

```
# must import windows to test,
# else __name__ is __main__ in findIcon

from Tkinter import Toplevel, Tk, Button, mainloop
from windows import MainWindow, PopupWindow, ComponentWindow

def _selftest():
    from Tkinter import Button, mainloop

    # mixin usage
    class content:
        "same code used as a Tk, Toplevel, and Frame"
        def __init__(self):
            Button(self, text='Larch', command=self.quit).pack()
            Button(self, text='Sing ', command=self.destroy).pack()
```

Example 11-14. PP3E\Gui\Tools\windows-test.py (continued)

```
class contentmix(MainWindow, content):
    def __init__(self):
        MainWindow.__init__(self, 'mixin', 'Main')
        content.__init__(self)
contentmix()

class contentmix(PopupWindow, content):
    def __init__(self):
        PopupWindow.__init__(self, 'mixin', 'Popup')
        content.__init__(self)
prev = contentmix()

class contentmix(ComponentWindow, content):
    def __init__(self):                              # nested frame
        ComponentWindow.__init__(self, prev)         # on prior window
        content.__init__(self)                       # Sing erases frame
contentmix()

# subclass usage
class contentsub(PopupWindow):
    def __init__(self):
        PopupWindow.__init__(self, 'popup', 'subclass')
        Button(self, text='Pine', command=self.quit).pack()
        Button(self, text='Sing', command=self.destroy).pack()
contentsub()

# non-class usage
win = PopupWindow('popup', 'attachment')
Button(win, text='Redwood', command=win.quit).pack()
Button(win, text='Sing   ', command=win.destroy).pack()
mainloop()

if __name__ == '__main__':
    _selftest()
```

When run, the test generates the window in Figure 11-10. All generated windows get a blue "PY" icon automatically, thanks to the search and configuration logic they inherit from the window module's classes. Some of the buttons on the test windows close just the enclosing window, some close the entire applications, some erase an attached window, and others pop up a quit verification dialog. Run this on your own to see what the examples' buttons do.[*]

---

[*] Caveat: in Python 2.4, when setting window `iconbitmask` images, there is a slight pause when opening the window on Windows (during which an empty window flashes briefly for a fraction of a second). No workaround could be found for this, and it may be improved in the future (window icons were first supported on Windows very recently, in Python 2.3). If this startup delay is undesirable, simply delete the *.ico* icon files to force the compiled-in red "Tk" icon to be used; icons can also be set in the C API; see Tk documentation for details.

We'll use these window protocol wrappers in the next chapter's PyClock example, and then again later in Chapter 15 where they'll come in handy to reduce the complexity of the PyMailGUI program. Part of the benefit of doing OOP in Python now is that we can forget the details later.

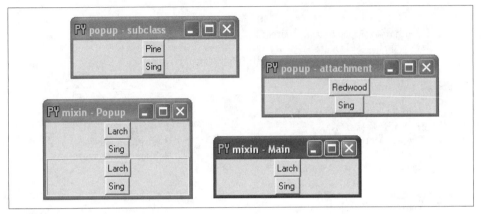

Figure 11-10. windows-test display

GUIs, Threads, and Queues

In Chapter 5, we learned about threads and the queue mechanism that threads typically use to communicate with each other. We also described the application of those ideas to GUIs in the abstract. Now that we've become fully functional GUI programmers, we can finally see what these ideas translate to in terms of code. If you skipped the related material in Chapter 5, you should probably go back and take a look first; we won't be repeating the thread or queue background material here.

The application to GUIs, however, is straightforward. Recall that long-running operations must generally be run in parallel threads, to avoid blocking the GUI from updating itself. In our packing and unpacking examples earlier in this chapter, for instance, we noted that the calls to run the actual file processing should generally run in threads so that the main GUI thread is not blocked until they finish.

In the general case, if a GUI waits for anything to finish, it will be completely unresponsive during the wait—it can't be resized, it can't be minimized, and it won't even redraw itself if it is covered and uncovered by other windows. To avoid being blocked this way, the GUI must run long-running tasks in parallel, usually with threads. That way, the main GUI thread is freed up to update the display while threads do other work.

Because only the main thread should generally update a GUI's display, though, threads you start to handle long-running tasks or to avoid blocking input/output calls cannot update the display with results themselves. Rather, they must place data on a queue (or other mechanism), to be picked up and displayed by the main GUI thread. To make this work, the main thread typically runs a counter loop that periodically checks the thread for new results to be displayed. Spawned threads produce data but know nothing about the GUI; the main GUI thread consumes and displays results but does not generate them.

As a more concrete example, suppose your GUI needs to display telemetry data sent in real time from a satellite over sockets (a network interface we'll meet later). Your program has to be responsive enough to not lose incoming data, but it also cannot get stuck waiting for or processing that data. To achieve both goals, spawn threads that fetch the incoming data and throw it on a queue, to be picked up and displayed periodically by the main GUI thread. With such a separation of labor, the GUI isn't blocked by the satellite, nor vice versa—the GUI itself will run independently of the data streams, but because the data stream threads can run at full speed, they'll be able to pick up incoming data as fast as it's sent. GUI event loops are not generally responsive enough to handle real-time inputs. Without the data stream threads, we might lose incoming telemetry; with them, we'll receive data as it is sent and display it as soon as the GUI's event loop gets around to picking it up off the queue—plenty fast for the real human user to see. If no data is sent, only the spawned threads wait, not the GUI itself.

In other scenarios, threads are required just so that the GUI remains active during long-running tasks. While downloading a reply from a web server, for example, your GUI must be able to redraw itself if covered or resized. Because of that, the download call cannot be a simple function call; it must run in parallel with the rest of your program—typically, as a thread. When the result is fetched, the thread must notify the GUI that data is ready to be displayed; by placing the result on a queue, the notification is simple—the main GUI thread will find it the next time it checks the queue. For example, we'll use threads and queues this way in the PyMailGUI program in Chapter 15, to allow multiple overlapping mail transfers to occur without blocking the GUI itself.

Whether your GUIs interface with satellites, web sites, or something else, this thread-based model turns out to be fairly simple in terms of code. Example 11-15 is the GUI equivalent of the queue-based threaded program we met earlier in Chapter 5. In the context of a GUI, the consumer thread becomes the GUI itself, and producer threads add data to be displayed to the shared queue as it is produced. The main GUI thread uses the Tkinter after method to check the queue for results.

Example 11-15. PP3E\Gui\Tools\xd5 ueuetest-gui.py

```
import thread, Queue, time
dataQueue = Queue.Queue( )      # infinite size

def producer(id):
    for i in range(5):
        time.sleep(0.1)
```

Example 11-15. PP3E\Gui\Tools\xd5 ueuetest-gui.py (continued)

```
        print 'put'
        dataQueue.put('producer %d:%d' % (id, i))

def consumer(root):
    try:
        print 'get'
        data = dataQueue.get(block=False)
    except Queue.Empty:
        pass
    else:
        root.insert('end', 'consumer got: %s\n' % str(data))
        root.see('end')
    root.after(250, lambda: consumer(root))     # 4 times per sec

def makethreads():
    for i in range(4):
        thread.start_new_thread(producer, (i,))

# main Gui thread: spawn batch of worker threads on each mouse click
import ScrolledText
root = ScrolledText.ScrolledText()
root.pack()
root.bind('<Button-1>', lambda event: makethreads())
consumer(root)                          # start queue check loop in main thread
root.mainloop()                         # pop-up window, enter tk event loop
```

When this script is run, the main GUI thread displays the data it grabs off the queue in the ScrolledText window captured in Figure 11-11. A new batch of four producer threads is started each time you left-click in the window, and threads issue "get" and "put" messages to the standard output stream (which isn't synchronized in this example—messages might overlap occasionally). The producer threads issue sleep calls to simulate long-running tasks such as downloading mail, fetching a query result, or waiting for input to show up on a socket (more on sockets later in this chapter).

Example 11-16 takes the model one small step further and migrates it to a class to allow for future customization and reuse. Its operation and output are the same as the prior non-object-oriented version, but the queue is checked more often, and there are no standard output prints.

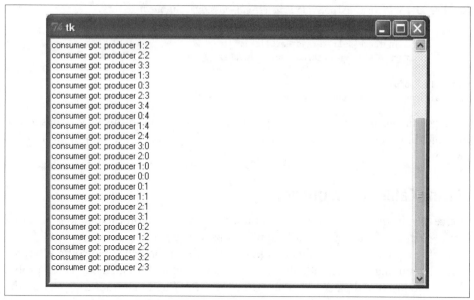

Figure 11-11. Display updated by GUI thread

Example 11-16. PP3E\Gui\Tools\xd5 ueuetest-gui-class.py

```python
import thread, Queue, time
from ScrolledText import ScrolledText

class ThreadGui(ScrolledText):
    threadsPerClick = 4

    def __init__(self, parent=None):
        ScrolledText.__init__(self, parent)
        self.pack()
        self.dataQueue = Queue.Queue()             # infinite size
        self.bind('<Button-1>', self.makethreads)  # on left mouse click
        self.consumer()                            # queue loop in main thread

    def producer(self, id):
        for i in range(5):
            time.sleep(0.1)
            self.dataQueue.put('producer %d:%d' % (id, i))

    def consumer(self):
        try:
            data = self.dataQueue.get(block=False)
        except Queue.Empty:
            pass
        else:
            self.insert('end', 'consumer got: %s\n' % str(data))
            self.see('end')
        self.after(100, self.consumer)     # 10 times per sec
```

Example 11-16. PP3E\Gui\Tools\xd5 ueuetest-gui-class.py (continued)

```
    def makethreads(self, event):
        for i in range(self.threadsPerClick):
            thread.start_new_thread(self.producer, (i,))

root = ThreadGui( )
root.mainloop( )          # pop-up window, enter tk event loop
```

We'll revisit this technique in a more realistic scenario later in this chapter, as a way to avoid blocking a GUI that must read an input stream—the output of another program.

Placing Callbacks on Queues

Notice that in the prior section's examples, the data placed on the queue is always a string. That's sufficient for simple applications where there is just one type of producer. If you may have many different kinds of threads producing many different types of results running at once, though, this can become difficult to manage. You'll probably have to insert and parse out some sort of type information in the string so that the GUI knows how to process it. Imagine an email client, for instance, where multiple sends and receives may overlap in time; if all threads share the same single queue, the information they place on it must somehow designate the sort of event it represents—a downloaded message to display, a successful send completion, and so on.

Luckily, queues support much more than just strings—any type of Python object can be placed on a queue. Perhaps the most general of these is a callable object: by placing a callback function on the queue, a producer thread can tell the GUI how to handle the message in a very direct way. The GUI simply calls the objects it pulls off the queue.

Because Python makes it easy to handle functions and their argument lists in generic fashion, this turns out to be easier than it might sound. Example 11-17, for instance, shows one way to throw callbacks on a queue that we'll be using in Chapter 15 for PyMailGUI. The ThreadCounter class in this module can be used as a shared counter and Boolean flag. The real meat here, though, is the queue interface functions.

This example is mostly just a variation on those of the prior section; we still run a counter loop here to pull items off the queue in the main thread. Here, though, we call the object pulled off the queue, and the producer threads have been generalized to place a success or failure callback on the objects in response to exceptions. Moreover, the actions that run in producer threads receive a progress status function that, when called, simply adds a progress indicator callback to the queue to be dispatched by the main thread. We can use this, for example, to show progress during network downloads.

Example 11-17. PP3E\Gui\Tools\threadtools.py

```
##############################################################################
# system-wide thread interface utilities for GUIs;
# single thread queue and checker timer loop shared by all windows;
# never blocks GUI - just spawns and verifies operations and quits;
# worker threads can overlap with main thread, and other workers;
#
# using a queue of callback functions and arguments is more useful than a
# simple data queue if there can be many kinds of threads running at the
# same time - each kind may have different implied exit actions
#
# because GUI API is not completely thread-safe, instead of calling GUI
# update callbacks directly after thread exit, place them on a shared queue,
# to be run from a timer loop in the main thread, not a child thread; this
# also makes GUI update points less random and unpredictable;
#
# assumes threaded action raises an exception on failure, and has a 'progress'
# callback argument if it supports progress updates;  also assumes that queue
# will contain callback functions for use in a GUI app: requires a widget in
# order to schedule and catch 'after' event loop callbacks;
##############################################################################

# run even if no threads
try:                                    # raise ImportError to
    import thread                       # run with GUI blocking
except ImportError:                     # if threads not available
    class fakeThread:
        def start_new_thread(self, func, args):
            func(*args)
    thread = fakeThread( )

import Queue, sys
threadQueue = Queue.Queue(maxsize=0)              # infinite size


def threadChecker(widget, delayMsecs=100):        # 10x per second
    """
    in main thread: periodically check thread completions queue;
    do implied GUI actions on queue in this main GUI thread;
    one consumer (GUI), multiple producers (load,del,send);
    a simple list may suffice: list.append/pop are atomic;
    one action at a time here: a loop may block GUI temporarily;
    """
    try:
        (callback, args) = threadQueue.get(block=False)
    except Queue.Empty:
        pass
    else:
        callback(*args)
    widget.after(delayMsecs, lambda: threadChecker(widget))


def threaded(action, args, context, onExit, onFail, onProgress):
```

Example 11-17. PP3E\Gui\Tools\threadtools.py (continued)

```
        """
        in a new thread: run action, manage thread queue puts;
        calls added to queue here are dispatched in main thread;
        run action with args now, later run on* calls with context;
        allows action to be ignorant of use as a thread here;
        passing callbacks into thread directly may update GUI in
        thread - passed func in shared memory but called in thread;
        progress callback just adds callback to queue with passed args;
        don't update counters here: not finished till taken off queue
        """
        try:
            if not onProgress:                # wait for action in this thread
                action(*args)                 # assume raises exception if fails
            else:
                progress = (lambda *any: threadQueue.put((onProgress, any+context)))
                action(progress=progress, *args)
        except:
            threadQueue.put((onFail, (sys.exc_info( ),)+context))
        else:
            threadQueue.put((onExit, context))

def startThread(action, args, context, onExit, onFail, onProgress=None):
    thread.start_new_thread(
        threaded, (action, args, context, onExit, onFail, onProgress))


class ThreadCounter:
    """
    a thread-safe counter or flag
    """
    def __init__(self):
        self.count = 0
        self.mutex = thread.allocate_lock( )    # or use Threading.semaphore
    def incr(self):
        self.mutex.acquire( )
        self.count += 1
        self.mutex.release( )
    def decr(self):
        self.mutex.acquire( )
        self.count -= 1
        self.mutex.release( )
    def __len__(self): return self.count        # True/False if used as a flag


if __name__ == '__main__':                       # self-test code when run
    import time, ScrolledText

    def threadaction(id, reps, progress):        # what the thread does
        for i in range(reps):
            time.sleep(1)
            if progress: progress(i)             # progress callback: queued
        if id % 2 == 1: raise Exception          # odd numbered: fail
```

Example 11-17. PP3E\Gui\Tools\threadtools.py (continued)

```
def mainaction(i):                          # code that spawns thread
    myname = 'thread-%s' % i
    startThread(
        action     = threadaction,
        args       = (i, 3),
        context    = (myname,),
        onExit     = threadexit,
        onFail     = threadfail,
        onProgress = threadprogress)

# thread callbacks: dispatched off queue in main thread
def threadexit(myname):
    root.insert('end', '%s\texit\n' % myname)
    root.see('end')
def threadfail(exc_info, myname):
    root.insert('end', '%s\tfail\t%s\n' % (myname, exc_info[0]))
    root.see('end')
def threadprogress(count, myname):
    root.insert('end', '%s\tprog\t%s\n' % (myname, count))
    root.see('end')
    root.update()    # works here: run in main thread

# make enclosing GUI
# spawn batch of worker threads on each mouse click: may overlap
root = ScrolledText.ScrolledText()
root.pack()
threadChecker(root)                         # start thread loop in main thread
root.bind('<Button-1>', lambda event: map(mainaction, range(6)))
root.mainloop()                             # pop-up window, enter tk event loop
```

This module's self-test code demonstrates how this interface is used. On each button click in a ScrolledTest, it starts up six threads, all running the threadaction function. As this threaded function runs, calls to the passed-in progress function place a callback on the queue, which invokes threadprogress in the main thread. When the threaded function exits, the interface layer will place a callback on the queue that will invoke either threadexit or threadfail in the main thread, depending upon whether the threaded function raised an exception. Because all the callbacks placed on the queue are pulled off and run in the main thread's timer loop, this guarantees that GUI updates occur in the main thread only.

Figure 11-12 shows part of the output generated after clicking the example's window once. Its exit, failure, and progress messages are produced by callbacks added to the queue by spawned threads and invoked from the timer loop running in the main thread.

To use this module, you will essentially break a modal operation into thread and post-thread steps, with an optional progress call. Study this code for more details and try to trace through the self-test code. This is a bit complex, and you may have

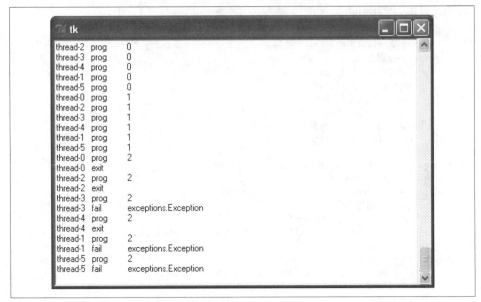

Figure 11-12. Messages from queued callbacks

to make more than one pass over this code. Once you get the hang of this paradigm, though, it provides a general scheme for handling heterogeneous overlapping threads in a uniform way. PyMailGUI, for example, will do very much the same as `mainaction` in the self-test code here, whenever it needs to start a mail transfer.

More Ways to Add GUIs to Non-GUI Code

Sometimes, GUIs pop up quite unexpectedly. Perhaps you haven't learned GUI programming yet; or perhaps you're just pining for non-event-driven days past. But for whatever reason, you may have written a program to interact with a user in an interactive console, only to decide later that interaction in a real GUI would be much nicer. What to do?

Probably the real answer to converting a non-GUI program is to truly convert it—restructure it to initialize widgets on startup, call `mainloop` once to start event processing and display the main window, and move all program logic into callback functions triggered by user actions. Your original program's actions become event handlers, and your original main flow of control becomes a program that builds a main window, calls the GUI's event loop once, and waits.

This is the traditional way to structure a GUI program, and it makes for a coherent user experience; windows pop up on request, instead of showing up at seemingly random times. Until you're ready to bite the bullet and perform such a structural conversion, though, there are other possibilities. For example, in the `ShellGui` section earlier in this chapter, we saw how to add windows to file packing scripts to collect inputs; we also saw how to redirect their outputs to text widgets. This approach works if the non-GUI operation we're wrapping up in a GUI is a single operation; for more dynamic user interaction, other techniques might be needed.

It's possible, for instance, to launch GUI windows from a non-GUI main program, by calling the Tkinter mainloop each time a window must be displayed. It's also possible to take a more grandiose approach and add a completely separate program for the GUI portion of your application. To wrap up this chapter, let's briefly explore each scheme.

Popping up GUI Windows on Demand

If you just want to add a simple GUI user interaction to an existing non-GUI script (e.g., to select files to open or save), it is possible to do so by configuring widgets and calling mainloop from the non-GUI main program when you need to interact with the user. This essentially makes the program GUI capable, but without a persistent main window. The trick is that mainloop doesn't return until the GUI main window is closed by the user (or quit method calls), so you cannot retrieve user inputs from widgets after mainloop returns. To work around this, all you have to do is be sure to save user inputs in a Python object: the object lives on, after the GUI is destroyed. Example 11-18 shows one way to code this idea in Python.

Example 11-18. PP3E\Gui\Tools\mainloopdemo.py

```
###############################################################################
# demo running two distinct mainloop calls;
# each returns after the main window is closed;  save user results on
# Python object: GUI is gone;  GUIs normally configure widgets and then
# run just one mainloop, and have all their logic in callbacks; this
# demo uses mainloop calls to implement two modal user interactions
# from a non-GUI main program; it shows one way to add a GUI component
# to an existing non-GUI script, without restructuring code;
###############################################################################

from Tkinter import *
from tkFileDialog import askopenfilename, asksaveasfilename

class Demo(Frame):
    def __init__(self,parent=None):
        Frame.__init__(self,parent)
        self.pack()
        Label(self, text ="Basic demos").pack()
        Button(self, text='open', command=self.openfile).pack(fill=BOTH)
        Button(self, text='save', command=self.savefile).pack(fill=BOTH)
        self.open_name = self.save_name = ""
    def openfile(self):                          # save user results
        self.open_name = askopenfilename()       # use dialog options here
    def savefile(self):
```

Example 11-18. PP3E\Gui\Tools\mainloopdemo.py (continued)

```
        self.save_name = asksaveasfilename(initialdir='D:\\temp')

if __name__ == "__main__":
    # display window once
    print 'popup1...'
    mydialog = Demo()                # attaches Frame to default Tk()
    mydialog.mainloop()             # display; returns after windows closed
    print mydialog.open_name        # names still on object, though GUI gone
    print mydialog.save_name
    # Non GUI section of the program uses mydialog here

    # display window again
    print 'popup2...'
    mydialog = Demo()               # re-create widgets again
    mydialog.mainloop()             # window pops up again
    print mydialog.open_name        # new values on the object again
    print mydialog.save_name
    # Non GUI section of the program uses mydialog again
    print 'ending...'
```

This program twice builds and displays a simple two-button main window that
launches file selection dialogs, shown in Figure 11-13. Its output, printed as the GUI
windows are closed, looks like this:

```
popup1...
C:/Python23/python.exe
D:/temp/new.txt
popup2...
C:/Python23/dir1/__init__.py
D:/temp/public_html/calendar.html
ending...
```

Figure 11-13. GUI window popped up by non-GUI main program

Notice how this program calls `mainloop` twice, to implement two modal user interactions from an otherwise non-GUI script. It's OK to call `mainloop` more than once, but
this script takes care to re-create the GUI's widgets before each call because they are
destroyed when the previous `mainloop` call exits (widgets are destroyed internally
inside Tk, even though the corresponding Python dialog object still exists). Again,
this can make for an odd user experience compared to a traditional GUI program
structure—windows seem to pop up from nowhere—but it's a quick way to put a
GUI face on a script without reworking its code.

Note that this is different from using nested `mainloop` calls to implement modal dialogs, as we did in Chapter 9. In that mode, the nested `mainloop` call returns when the dialog's `quit` method is called, but we return to the enclosing `mainloop` layer and remain in the realm of event-driven programming. Example 11-18 instead runs `mainloop` two different times, stepping into and out of the event-driven model twice.

Finally, note that this scheme works only if you don't have to run any non-GUI code while the GUI is open, because your script is inactive and blocked while `mainloop` runs. You cannot, for example, apply this technique to use utilities like those in the `guiStreams` module we met earlier in this chapter to route user interaction from non-GUI code to GUI windows. The `GuiInput` and `GuiOutput` classes in that example assume that there is a `mainloop` call running somewhere (they're GUI based, after all). But once you call `mainloop` to pop up these windows, you can't return to your non-GUI code to interact with the user until the GUI is closed and the `mainloop` call returns. The net effect is that these classes can be used only in the context of a fully GUI program.

But really, this is an artificial way to use Tkinter. Example 11-18 works only because the GUI can interact with the user independently, while the `mainloop` call runs; the script is able to surrender control to the Tkinter `mainloop` call and wait for results. That scheme won't work if you must run any non-GUI code while the GUI is open. Because of such constraints, you will generally need a main-window-plus-callbacks model in most GUI programs—callback code runs in response to user interaction while the GUI remains open. That way, your code can run while GUI windows are active. For an example, see earlier in this chapter for the way the non-GUI pack and unpack scripts were run from a GUI so that their results appear in a GUI; technically, these scripts are run in a GUI callback handler so that their output can be routed to a widget.

Adding a GUI As a Separate Program: Sockets

As mentioned earlier, it's also possible to spawn the GUI part of your application as a completely separate program. This is a more advanced technique, but it can make integration simple for some applications because of the loose coupling it implies. It can, for instance, help with the `guiStreams` issues of the prior section, as long as inputs and outputs are communicated to the GUI over Inter-Process Communication (IPC) mechanisms, and the widget `after` method (or similar) is used by the GUI program to detect incoming output to be displayed. The non-GUI script would not be blocked by a `mainloop` call.

More generally, the GUI could be spawned by the non-GUI script as a separate program, where user interaction results can be communicated from the spawned GUI to the script using pipes, sockets, files, or other IPC mechanisms. The advantage to this approach is that it provides a separation of GUI and non-GUI code—the non-GUI script would have to be modified only to spawn and wait for user results to appear from the separate GUI program, but could otherwise be used as is. Moreover, the non-GUI script would not be blocked while an in-process `mainloop` call runs (only the GUI process would run a `mainloop`), and the GUI program could persist after the point at which user inputs are required by the script, leading to fewer pop-up windows.

Examples 11-19 and 11-20 provide a simplistic example of this technique in action. They represent non-GUI and GUI programs that communicate over *sockets*—an IPC and networking device we will explore in the next part of the book. The important point to notice here is the way the programs are linked. When Example 11-19 starts, it spawns the GUI as a separate program; when it prints to standard output, the printed text is sent over a socket connection to the GUI program. Other than the startup and socket creation calls, the non-GUI program knows nothing at all about GUIs.

Example 11-19. PP3E\Gui\Tools\socket-nongui.py

```
import time, sys
from socket import *

# GUI interface
port = 50008                          # I am client: use GUI server port
host = 'localhost'                    # or start me after GUI started
sock = socket(AF_INET, SOCK_STREAM)
sock.connect((host, port))
file = sock.makefile('w', 0)          # file interface wrapper, unbuffered
sys.stdout = file                     # make prints go to sock.send

# non-GUI code
while 1:                              # print data to stdout
    print time.asctime()             # sent to GUI process
    time.sleep(2.0)
```

The GUI part of this exchange is the program in Example 11-20. This script implements a GUI to display the text printed by the non-GUI program, but it knows nothing of that other program's logic. For the display, the GUI program prints to the stream redirection object we met earlier in this chapter; because this program runs a GUI `mainloop` call, this just works. We're also running a timer loop here to detect incoming data on the socket as it arrives, instead of waiting for the non-GUI program to run to completion. Because the socket is set to be nonblocking, input calls don't wait for data to appear, and hence, do not block the GUI.

Example 11-20. PP3E\Gui\Tools\socket-gui.py

```
import sys, os
from socket import *
from Tkinter import Tk
from PP3E.Gui.Tools.guiStreams import GuiOutput

myport = 50008
sockobj = socket(AF_INET, SOCK_STREAM)     # GUI is server, script is client
```

Example 11-20. PP3E\Gui\Tools\socket-gui.py (continued)

```
sockobj.bind(('', myport))              # config server before client
sockobj.listen(5)
os.startfile('socket-nongui.py')        # spawn non-GUI on Windows (os.popen)

conn, addr = sockobj.accept()           # wait for client to connect
sockobj.setblocking(0)                  # use nonblocking socket

def checkdata():
    try:
        print conn.recv(1024),          # if ready, show text in GUI window
    except error:                       # raises socket.error if not ready
        pass                            # or message to sys.__stdout__
    root.after(1000, checkdata)         # check once per second

root = Tk()
sys.stdout = GuiOutput(root)            # socket text is displayed on this
checkdata()
root.mainloop()
```

When both the GUI and the non-GUI processes are running, the GUI picks up a new message over the socket roughly once every two seconds and displays it in the window shown in Figure 11-14. The GUI's timer loop checks for data once per second, but the non-GUI script sends a message every two seconds only due to its `time.sleep` calls.

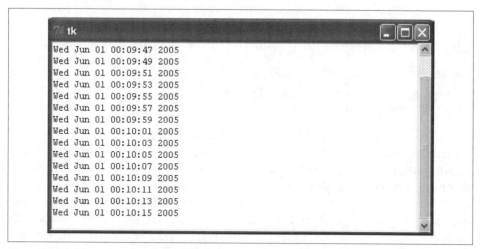

Figure 11-14. Messages printed to a GUI from a non-GUI program

To run this by yourself, start the GUI script—it spawns the non-GUI script and displays a pop-up window that shows the text printed in the socket-nongui script (the date and time). The non-GUI script can keep running linear, procedural code to produce data, because only the socket-GUI program runs an event-driven `mainloop` call.

Although we aren't going to get into enough socket details in this chapter to show how, this example should probably be augmented to detect and handle an end-of-file signal from the spawned program, and then terminate its timer loop. The non-GUI script could also start the GUI instead, but in the socket world, the server's end (the GUI) must be configured to accept connections before the client (the non-GUI) can connect. One way or another, the GUI has to start before the non-GUI connects to it or the non-GUI script will be denied a connection and will fail.

The socket client/server model works well and is a general approach to connecting GUI and non-GUI code, but there are a few coding alternatives worth exploring in the next section before we move on.

Adding a GUI As a Separate Program: Pipes

The net effect of the two programs of the preceding section is similar to a GUI program reading the output of a shell command over a pipe file with os.popen; but as we'll see later, sockets can also link programs running on remote machines across a network. Perhaps subtler and more significant is the fact that without an after timer loop and nonblocking input sources, the GUI may become stuck and unresponsive while waiting for data from the non-GUI program and may not be able to handle more than one data stream.

For instance, consider the guiStreams call we wrote in Example 11-9 to redirect the output of a shell command spawned with os.popen to a GUI window. We could use this with simplistic code like that in Example 11-21 to capture the output of a spawned Python program and display it in a separately running GUI program's window.

Example 11-21. PP3E\Gui\Tools\pipes-gui1.py

```
from PP3E.Gui.Tools.guiStreams import redirectedGuiShellCmd
redirectedGuiShellCmd('python -u pipes-nongui.py')
```

Notice the -u Python command-line flag used here: it forces the spawned program's standard streams to be *unbuffered*, so we get printed text immediately as it is produced, instead of waiting for the spawned program to completely finish. We talked about this option in Chapter 5, when discussing deadlocks and pipes. Recall that print writes to sys.stdout, which is normally buffered. If we don't use the -u flag here and the spawned program doesn't manually call sys.stdout.flush(), we won't see any output in the GUI until the spawned program exits or until its buffers fill up. If the spawned program is a perpetual loop that does not exit, we may be waiting a long time for output to appear on the pipe, and hence, in the GUI.

This approach makes the non-GUI code in Example 11-22 much simpler: it just writes to standard output as usual, and it need not be concerned with creating a socket interface.

Example 11-22. PP3E\Gui\Tools\pipes-nongui.py

```
import time
while 1:                            # non-GUI code
    print time.asctime( )           # sends to GUI process
    time.sleep(2.0)
```

Start the GUI script in Example 11-21: it launches the non-GUI program automatically. This works, but the GUI is odd—we never call `mainloop` ourselves, and we get a default empty top-level window. (In fact, it apparently works at all only because the Tkinter `update` call issued within the redirect function enters the Tk event loop momentarily to process pending events.) To do better, Example 11-23 creates an enclosing GUI and kicks off an event loop manually by the time the shell command is spawned.

Example 11-23. PP3E\Gui\Tools\pipes-gui2.py

```
from Tkinter import *
from PP3E.Gui.Tools.guiStreams import redirectedGuiShellCmd

def launch( ):
    redirectedGuiShellCmd('python -u pipes-nongui.py')

window = Tk( )
Button(window, text='GO!', command=launch).pack( )
window.mainloop( )
```

The -u unbuffered flag is crucial here—without it, you won't see the text output window. The GUI will be blocked in the initial pipe input call indefinitely because the spawned program's standard output will be queued up in an in-memory buffer.

Either way we code this, however, when the GUIs are run they become unresponsive for two seconds at a time while they read data from the `os.popen` pipe—window moves, resizes, redraws, raises, and so on, are delayed for up to two seconds, until the non-GUI program sends data to the GUI to make the pipe read call return. Worse, if you press the "GO!" button twice in the second version of the GUI, only one window updates itself every two seconds, because the GUI is stuck in the second button press callback—it never exits the loop that reads from the pipe until the spawned non-GUI program exits.

Because of such constraints, a separately spawned GUI must generally read a portion of the data at a time to avoid blocking. For instance, in the socket-based scripts of the prior section (Example 11-20), the `after` timer loop allows the GUI to poll for data instead of waiting and display it as it arrives.

Of course, the real issue here is that the `guiStreams` utility is too simplistic; issuing a read call within a GUI is generally prone to blocking. We could try to run the redirect call in a thread—for example, by changing the launch function in Example 11-23 as follows:

```
def launch():
    import thread
    thread.start_new(redirectedGuiShellCmd, ('python -u pipes-nongui.py',))
```

But then we would be updating the GUI from a spawned thread, which, as we've learned, is a generally bad idea. With this change, the GUI hangs on Windows on the first "GO!" button press occasionally, and always hangs eventually if you press the button enough times (in fact, the process must be forcibly killed after it hangs). When it does run, it doesn't help—the text window created in the child thread is still stuck in a read call.

Alternatively, we could try to use the Python select.select call (described in Chapter 13) to implement polling for data on the input pipe; unfortunately, select works only on sockets in Windows today (it also works on pipes and other file descriptors in Unix).

In other contexts, a separately spawned GUI might also use signals to inform the non-GUI program when points of interaction arise, and vice versa (the Python signal module and os.kill call were introduced in Chapter 5). The downside with this approach is that it still requires changes to the non-GUI program to handle the signals.

Named pipes (the fifo files introduced in Chapter 5) are sometimes an alternative to the socket calls of the original Examples 11-19 and 11-20, but sockets work on Windows, and fifos do not (os.mkfifo is not available in Windows XP in 2.4, though it is in Cygwin Python). Even where they do work, we would still need an after timer loop in the GUI to avoid blocking.

We might also use Tkinter's createfilehandler to register a callback to be run when input shows up on the input pipe:

```
def callback(file, mask):
    ...read from file here...

import _tkinter, Tkinter
_tkinter.createfilehandler(file, Tkinter.READABLE, callback)
```

The file handler creation call is also available within Tkinter.tkinter and as a method of a Tk instance object. Unfortunately again, as noted at the end of Chapter 10, this call is not available on Windows and is a Unix-only alternative.

More generally, the GUI process might spawn a thread that reads the socket or pipe and places the data on a queue so that more than one data stream or long-running activity can overlap in time. In fact, the thread techniques we met earlier in this chapter could be used directly in such a role.

Example 11-24 shows how. The main trick this script employs is to split up the input and output parts of the original redirectedGuiShellCmd of the guiStreams module we met earlier in Example 11-9. By so doing, the input portion can be spawned off in a parallel thread and not block the GUI. The main GUI thread uses an after timer loop as usual, to watch for data to be added by the reader thread to a shared queue. Because the main thread doesn't read program output itself, it does not get stuck in wait states.

Example 11-24. PP3E\Gui\Tools\pipes_gui3.py

```
import thread, Queue, os
from Tkinter import Tk
from PP3E.Gui.Tools.guiStreams import GuiOutput
stdoutQueue = Queue.Queue()                          # infinite size

def producer(input):
    while True:
        line = input.readline()                      # OK to block: child thread
        stdoutQueue.put(line)                         # empty at end-of-file
        if not line: break

def consumer(output, root, term='<end>'):
    try:
        line = stdoutQueue.get(block=False)          # main thread: check queue
    except Queue.Empty:                              # 4 times/sec, OK if empty
        pass
    else:
        if not line:                                 # stop loop at end-of-file
            output.write(term)                       # else display next line
            return
        output.write(line)
    root.after(250, lambda: consumer(output, root, term))

def redirectedGuiShellCmd(command, root):
    input  = os.popen(command, 'r')                  # start non-GUI program
    output = GuiOutput(root)
    thread.start_new_thread(producer, (input,))      # start reader thread
    consumer(output, root)

if __name__ == '__main__':
    win = Tk()
    redirectedGuiShellCmd('python -u pipes-nongui.py', win)
    win.mainloop()
```

As usual, we use a queue here to avoid updating the GUI except in the main thread. Note that we didn't need a thread or queue in the prior section's socket example, just because we're able to poll a socket to see whether it has data without blocking; an after timer loop was enough. For a shell-command pipe, though, a thread is an easy way to avoid blocking.

When run, this program's self-test code creates a ScrolledText window that displays the current date and time sent from the *pipes-nongui.py* script in Example 11-22 (its window is identical to Figure 11-14). The window is updated with a new line every two seconds because that's how often the spawned pipes-nongui script prints a message to stdout.

Note how the producer thread calls `readline()` to load just one line at a time. We can't use input calls that consume the entire stream all at once (e.g., `read()`, `readlines()`), because such calls would not return until the program exits and sends end-of-file. The `read(N)` call would work to grab one piece of the output as well, but we assume that the output stream is text here. Also notice that the -u unbuffered stream flag is used here again, to get output as it is produced; without it, output won't show up in the GUI at all because it is buffered in the spawned program (try it yourself).

This is similar in spirit to what we did in Example 11-23. Due to the way its code is structured, though, Example 11-24 has two major advantages:

- Because input calls are spawned off in a thread this time, the GUI is completely responsive. Window moves, resizes, and so forth, happen immediately because the GUI is not blocked while waiting for output from the non-GUI program. Although it is more complex and requires thread support, its lack of blocking makes this `redirectedGuiShellCmd` much more generally useful than the original version we coded earlier.

- Moreover, because this GUI reads the spawned program's standard output, no changes are required in the non-GUI program. Unlike the socket-based example in the prior section, the non-GUI program here needs no knowledge of the GUI that will display its results.

The only downside to this approach compared to the sockets of the prior section is that it does not directly support running the GUI and non-GUI programs on remote machines. As we'll see later, sockets allow data to be passed between programs running on the same machine or across networks. Furthermore, if the GUI must do more than display another program's output, sockets become a more general solution—as we'll learn later, because sockets are bidirectional data streams, they allow data to be passed back and forth between two programs in more arbitrary ways.

Here's another use case: the following code imports the new GUI redirection function as a library component and uses it to create a window that displays four lines of successively longer strings, followed by a final line containing <end>, reflecting the spawned program's exit:

```
>>> print open('spams.py').read()
import time
for i in range(1, 5):
    time.sleep(2)
    print 'spam' * i

>>> from Tkinter import *
>>> from pipes_gui3 import redirectedGuiShellCmd
>>> root = Tk()
>>> redirectedGuiShellCmd('python -u spams.py', root)
```

If the spawned program exits, Example 11-24 detects end-of-file on the pipe and puts the final empty line in the queue; the consumer thread displays an <end> line in the GUI by default when it detects this condition. Here again, the sleep call in the spawned program simulates a long-running task, and we really need the -u unbuffered streams flag—without it, no output appears in the GUI for eight seconds, until the spawned program is completely finished. With it, the GUI receives and displays each line as it is printed, one every two seconds.

This is also, finally, the sort of code you could use to display the output of a non-GUI program in a GUI, without sockets, changes in the original program, or blocking the GUI. Of course, in many cases, if you have to work this hard to add a GUI anyhow, you might as well just make your script a traditional GUI program with a main window and event loop. Furthermore, the GUIs we've coded in this section are limited to displaying another program's output; sometimes the GUI may have to do more. For many programs, though, the general separation of display and program logic provided by the spawned GUI model can be an advantage—it's easier to understand both parts if they are not mixed together.

We'll learn all about sockets in the next part of the book, so you should consider parts of this discussion something of a preview. As we'll see, things start to become more and more interesting when we start combining GUIs, threads, and network sockets. Before we do, though, the next chapter closes out the purely GUI part of this book by applying the widgets and techniques we've learned in more realistically scaled programs.

Complete GUI Programs

"Python, Open Source, and Camaros"

This chapter concludes our look at building GUIs with Python and its standard Tkinter library, by presenting a collection of realistic GUI programs. In the preceding four chapters, we met all the basics of Tkinter programming. We toured the core set of *widgets*—Python classes that generate devices on a computer screen and respond to user events—and we studied a handful of advanced GUI programming techniques. Here, our focus is on putting those widgets and techniques together to create more useful GUIs. We'll study:

PyEdit
> A text editor program

PyPhoto
> A thumbnail photo viewer

PyView
> An image slideshow

PyDraw
> A painting program

PyClock
> A graphical clock

PyToe
> A simple tic-tac-toe game, just for fun[*]

---

[*] All of the larger examples in this book have *Py* at the start of their names. This is by convention in the Python world. If you shop around at *http://www.python.org*, you'll find other free software that follows this pattern too: PyOpenGL (a Python interface to the OpenGL graphics library), PyGame (a Python game development kit), and many more. I'm not sure who started this pattern, but it has turned out to be a more or less subtle way to advertise programming language preferences to the rest of the open source world. Pythonistas are nothing if not PySubtle.

As in Chapters 6 and 7, I've pulled the examples in this chapter from my own library of Python programs that I really use. For instance, the text editor and clock GUIs that we'll meet here are day-to-day workhorses on my machines. Because they are written in Python and Tkinter, they work unchanged on my Windows and Linux machines, and they should work on Macs too.

Since these are pure Python scripts, their future evolution is entirely up to their users—once you get a handle on Tkinter interfaces, changing or augmenting the behavior of such programs by editing their Python code is a snap. Although some of these examples are similar to commercially available programs (e.g., PyEdit is reminiscent of the Windows Notepad accessory), the portability and almost infinite configurability of Python scripts can be a decided advantage.

Examples in Other Chapters

Later in the book, we'll meet other Tkinter GUI programs that put a good face on specific application domains. For instance, the following larger GUI examples show up in later chapters also:

PyMailGUI
> An email client in Chapter 15

PyForm
> A persistent object table viewer in Chapter 19

PyTree
> A tree data structure viewer in Chapter 20

PyCalc
> A calculator widget in Chapter 21

Most of these programs see regular action on my desktop too. Because GUI libraries are general-purpose tools, there are few domains that cannot benefit from an easy-to-use, easy-to-program, and widely portable user interface coded in Python and Tkinter.

Beyond the examples in this book, you can also find higher-level GUI toolkits for Python, such as the Pmw and Tix packages mentioned in Chapter 8. Such systems build upon Tkinter to provide compound components such as notebook tabbed widgets and balloon pop-up help. In the next part of the book, we'll also explore programs that build user interfaces in web browsers, not in Tkinter—a very different way of approaching the user interface experience. But apart from simple web-based interfaces, Tkinter GUIs can be an indispensable feature of almost any Python program you write. The programs in this chapter underscore just how far Python and Tkinter can take you.

This Chapter's Strategy

As for all case-study chapters in this text, this one is largely a learn-by-example exercise; most of the programs here are listed with minimal details. Along the way, I'll point out new Tkinter features that each example introduces, but I'll also assume that you will study the listed source code and its comments for more information. Python's readability becomes a substantial advantage for programmers (and writers of books), especially once we reach the level of complexity demonstrated by programs here.

All of this book's GUI examples are available in source code form in the book's examples distribution. Because I've already shown the interfaces these scripts employ, this section comprises mostly screenshots, program listings, and a few brief words describing some of the most important aspects of these programs. In other words, this is a self-study section: read the source, run the examples on your own computer, and refer to the previous chapters for further details on the code listed here. Some of these programs also are accompanied in the book examples distribution by alternative or experimental implementations not listed here; see the distribution for extra code examples.

Finally, I want to remind you that all of the larger programs listed in the previous sections can be run from the PyDemos and PyGadgets launcher bar GUIs that we met at the end of Chapter 10. Although I will try hard to capture some of their behavior in screenshots here, GUIs are event-driven systems by nature, and there is nothing quite like running one live to sample the flavor of its user interactions. Because of that, the launcher bars are really a supplement to the material in this chapter. They should run on most platforms and are designed to be easy to start (see the top-level *README-PP3E.txt* file for hints). You should go there and start clicking things immediately if you haven't done so already.

PyEdit: A Text Editor Program/Object

In the last few decades, I've typed text into a lot of programs. Most were closed systems (I had to live with whatever decisions their designers made), and many ran on only one platform. The PyEdit program presented in this section does better on both counts: it implements a full-featured, graphical text editor program in roughly 600 lines of portable Python code (including whitespace, comments, and configuration settings). Despite its size, PyEdit was sufficiently powerful and robust to serve as the primary tool used to code most of the examples in this book.

PyEdit supports all the usual mouse and keyboard text-editing operations: cut and paste, search and replace, open and save, undo and redo, and so on. But really, PyEdit is a bit more than just another text editor—it is designed to be used as both a program and a library component, and it can be run in a variety of roles:

Open Source Software and Camaros

Some of the GUI programs in this chapter, as well as the rest of the book, are analogous to utilities found on commonly used operating systems like Windows. For instance, we'll meet calculators, text editors, image viewers, clocks, email clients, and more.

Unlike most utilities, though, these programs are *portable*—because they are written in Python with Tkinter, they will work on all major platforms (Windows, Unix/Linux, and Macs). Perhaps more important, because their source code is available, they can be *scripted*—you can change their appearance or function however you like, just by writing or modifying a little Python code.

An analogy might help underscore the importance of scriptability. There are still a few of us who remember a time when it was completely normal for car owners to work on and repair their own automobiles. I still fondly remember huddling with friends under the hood of a 1970 Camaro in my youth, tweaking and customizing its engine. With a little work, we could make it as fast, flashy, and loud as we liked. Moreover, a break-down in one of those older cars wasn't necessarily the end of the world. There was at least some chance that I could get the car going again on my own.

That's not quite true today. With the introduction of electronic controls and diaboli-cally cramped engine compartments, car owners are usually better off taking their cars back to the dealer or other repair professional for all but the simplest kinds of changes. By and large, cars are no longer user-maintainable products. And if I have a breakdown in my shiny new Jeep, I'm probably going to be completely stuck until an authorized repair person can get around to towing and fixing my ride.

I like to think of the closed and open software models in the same terms. When I use Microsoft-provided programs such as Notepad and Outlook, I'm stuck with both the feature set that a large company dictates, as well as any bugs that it may harbor. But with programmable tools such as PyEdit and PyMailGUI, I can still get under the hood. I can add features, customize the system, and work my way out of any lurking bugs. And I can do so long before the next Microsoft patch or release is available. I'm no longer dependent on a self-interested company to support—or even to continue pro-ducing—the tools I use.

At the end of the day, open source software and Python are as much about *freedom* as they are about cost. Users, not an arbitrarily far-removed company, have the final say. Not everyone wants to work on his own car, of course. On the other hand, software tends to fail much more often than cars, and Python scripting is generally less greasy than auto mechanics.

Standalone mode

As a standalone text-editor program, with or without the name of a file to be edited passed in on the command line. In this mode, PyEdit is roughly like other text-editing utility programs (e.g., Notepad on Windows), but it also provides advanced functions such as running Python program code being edited, changing fonts and colors, and so on. More important, because it is coded in Python, PyEdit is easy to customize, and it runs portably on Windows, X Windows, and Macintosh.

Pop-up mode

Within a new pop-up window, allowing an arbitrary number of copies to appear as pop ups at once in a program. Because state information is stored in class instance attributes, each PyEdit object created operates independently. In this mode and the next, PyEdit serves as a library object for use in other scripts, not as a canned application.

Embedded mode

As an attached component, to provide a text-editing widget for other GUIs. When attached, PyEdit uses a frame-based menu and can optionally disable some of its menu options for an embedded role. For instance, PyView (later in this chapter) uses PyEdit in embedded mode this way to serve as a note editor for photos, and PyMailGUI (in Chapter 15) attaches it to get an email text editor for free.

While such mixed-mode behavior may sound complicated to implement, most of PyEdit's modes are a natural byproduct of coding GUIs with the class-based techniques we've seen in the last three chapters.

Running PyEdit

PyEdit sports lots of features, and the best way to learn how it works is to test-drive it for yourself—you can run it by starting the file *textEditor.pyw*, or from the PyDemos and PyGadgets launcher bars described at the end of Chapter 10 (the launchers themselves live in the top level of the book examples directory tree). To give you a sampling of PyEdit's interfaces, Figure 12-1 shows the main window's default appearance, after opening PyEdit's source code file.

The main part of this window is a Text widget object, and if you read Chapter 10's coverage of this widget, PyEdit text-editing operations will be familiar. It uses text marks, tags, and indexes, and it implements cut-and-paste operations with the system clipboard so that PyEdit can paste data to and from other applications. Both vertical and horizontal scroll bars are cross-linked to the Text widget, to support movement through arbitrary files.

Menus and toolbars

If PyEdit's menu and toolbars look familiar, they should—it builds the main window with minimal code and appropriate clipping and expansion policies, by mixing in the GuiMaker class we coded in the prior chapter. The toolbar at the bottom contains shortcut buttons for operations I tend to use most often; if my preferences

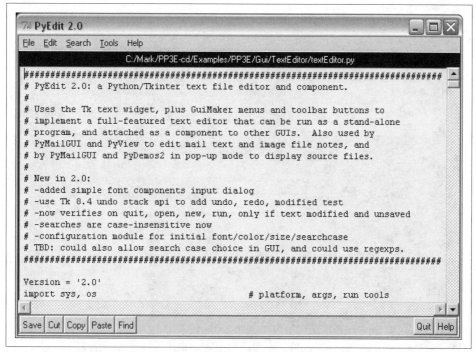

Figure 12-1. PyEdit main window, editing itself

don't match yours, simply change the toolbar list in the source code to show the buttons you want (this is Python, after all).

As usual for Tkinter menus, shortcut key combinations can be used to invoke menu options quickly too—press Alt plus all the underlined keys of entries along the path to the desired action. Menus can also be torn off at their dashed line to provide quick access to menu options in new top-level windows (handy for options without toolbar buttons).

Dialogs

PyEdit pops up a variety of modal and nonmodal dialogs, both standard and custom. Figure 12-2 shows the custom and nonmodal change dialog, along with a standard dialog used to display file statistics.

The main window in Figure 12-2 has been given new foreground and background colors (with the standard color selection dialog), and a new text font has been selected from a canned list in the script that users can change to suit their preferences (this is Python, after all). The standard file open and save selection dialogs in PyEdit use object-based interfaces to remember the last directory visited, so you don't have to navigate there every time.

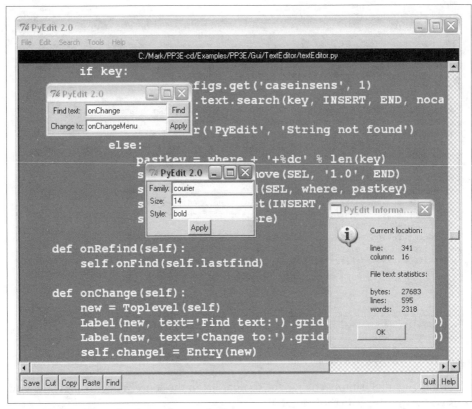

Figure 12-2. PyEdit with colors, a font, and a few pop ups

Running program code

One of the more unique features of PyEdit is that it can actually run Python program
code that you are editing. This isn't as hard as it may sound either—because Python
provides built-ins for compiling and running code strings and for launching programs, PyEdit simply has to make the right calls for this to work. For example, it's
easy to code a simple-minded Python interpreter in Python (though you need a bit
more to handle multiple-line statements), as shown in Example 12-1.

Example 12-1. PP3E\Gui\TextEditor\simpleshell.py

```
namespace= {}
while 1:
    try:
        line = raw_input('>>> ')       # single-line statements only
    except EOFError:
        break
    else:
        exec line in namespace         # or eval() and print result
```

Depending on the user's preference, PyEdit either does something similar to this to run code fetched from the text widget or uses the launchmodes module we wrote at the end of Chapter 5 to run the code's file as an independent program. There are a variety of options in both schemes that you can customize as you like (this is Python, after all). See the onRunCode method for details or simply edit and run some Python code on your own. When edited code is run in nonfile mode, you can view its printed output in PyEdit's console window.

Figure 12-3 shows three independently started instances of PyEdit running with a variety of color schemes, sizes, and fonts. This figure also captures two PyEdit torn-off menus (lower right) and the PyEdit help pop up (upper right). The edit windows' backgrounds are shades of blue, green, and red; use the Tools menu's Pick options to set colors as you like.

Since these three PyEdit sessions are editing Python source-coded text, you can run their contents with the Run Code option in the Tools pull-down menu. Code run from files is spawned independently; the standard streams of code run not from a file (i.e., fetched from the text widget itself) are mapped to the PyEdit session's console window. This isn't an IDE by any means; it's just something I added because I found it to be useful. It's nice to run code you're editing without fishing through directories.

New features in version 2.0

New for this edition of the book is a *font input dialog*—a simple, three-entry, non-modal dialog where you can type the font family, size, and style, instead of picking them from a list of preset options. (You can find more sophisticated Tk font selection dialogs in both the public domain and within the implementation of Python's standard IDLE development GUI—as mentioned earlier, it is itself a Python/Tkinter program.)

Also new in this edition, PyEdit supports unlimited edit undo and redo, as well as an accurate modified check before quit, open, and new actions to prompt for saves (instead of always asking naïvely). The underlying Tk 8.4 library provides an API, which makes this simple—Tk keeps undo and redo stacks automatically. They are enabled with the Text widget's undo configuration option and are accessed with the widget methods edit_undo and edit_redo. Similarly, edit_reset clears the stacks (e.g., after a new file open), and edit_modified checks or sets the automatic text modified flag.

It's also possible to undo cuts and pastes right after you've done them (simply paste back from the clipboard or cut the pasted and selected text), but the new undo/redo operations are more complete and simpler to use. Undo was a suggested exercise in the prior edition of this book, but it has been made almost trivial by the new Tk API.

For usability, this edition's version of PyEdit also allows users to set startup configuration options by assigning variables in a module, textConfig.py. If present, these

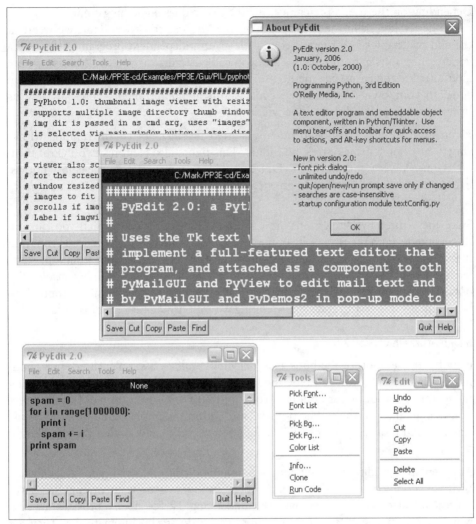

Figure 12-3. Multiple PyEdit sessions at work

assignments give initial values for font, colors, text window size, and search case sensitivity. Fonts and colors can be changed in the menus and windows can be freely resized, so this is largely just a convenience. Also note that this module's settings will be inherited by all instances of PyEdit—even when it is a pop-up window or an embedded component of another application. Client applications should configure per their needs.

PyEdit Source Code

The PyEdit program consists of just a small configuration module and one main source file—a *.py* that can be either run or imported. For use on Windows, there is also a one-line *.pyw* file that just executes the *.py* file's contents with an execfile('textEditor.py') call. The *.pyw* suffix avoids the DOS console streams window pop up when launched on Windows.

Today, *.pyw* files can be both imported and run, like normal *.py* files (they can also be double-clicked, and launched by Python tools such as os.system and os.startfile), so we don't really need a separate file to support both import and console-less run modes. I retained the *.py*, though, in order to see printed text during development and to use PyEdit as a simple IDE—when the run code option is selected, in nonfile mode printed output from code being edited shows up in PyEdit's DOS console window in Windows. Clients will normally import the *.py* file.

First, PyEdit's user configuration module is listed in Example 12-2. As mentioned, this is mostly a convenience, for providing an initial look-and-feel other than the default. PyEdit is coded to work even if this module is missing or contains syntax errors.

Example 12-2. PP3E\Gui\TextEditor\textConfig.py

```
##############################################################
# PyEdit (testEditor.py) user startup configuration module
# comment-out any of these to accept Tk or program defaults
# can also change font/colors from menus, and resize window
##############################################################

# initial font                     # family, size, style
font = ('courier', 9, 'normal')    # e.g., style: 'bold italic'

# initial color                    # default=white, black
bg = 'lightcyan'                   # colorname or RGB hexstr
fg = 'black'                       # e.g., 'powder blue', '#690f96'

# initial size
height = 20                        # Tk default: 24 lines
width  = 80                        # Tk default: 80 characters

# search case-insensitive
caseinsens = 1                     # default=1 (on)
```

Next, Example 12-3 gives the *.pyw* launching file used to suppress a DOS pop up on Windows, but still allow for it when the *.py* file is run directly (to see the output of edited code run in nonfile mode, for example).

Example 12-3. PP3E\Gui\TextEditor\textEditorNoConsole.pyw

```
#########################################################################
# run without a DOS pop up on Windows
# could use just a .pyw for both inports and launch,
# but .py file retained for seeing any printed text
#########################################################################

execfile('textEditor.py')      # as if pasted here (or textEditor.main())
```

And finally, the module in Example 12-4 is PyEdit's implementation. This file may
run directly as a top-level script, or it can be imported from other applications. Its
code is organized by the GUI's main menu options. The main classes used to start
and embed a PyEdit object appear at the end of this file. Study this listing while you
experiment with PyEdit, to learn about its features and techniques.

Example 12-4. PP3E\Gui\TextEditor\textEditor.py

```
#########################################################################
# PyEdit 2.0: a Python/Tkinter text file editor and component.
#
# Uses the Tk text widget, plus GuiMaker menus and toolbar buttons to
# implement a full-featured text editor that can be run as a standalone
# program, and attached as a component to other GUIs.  Also used by
# PyMailGUI and PyView to edit mail text and image file notes, and
# by PyMailGUI and PyDemos2 in pop-up mode to display source files.
#
# New in 2.0:
# -added simple font components input dialog
# -use Tk 8.4 undo stack API to add undo, redo modified test
# -now verifies on quit, open, new, run, only if text modified and unsaved
# -searches are case-insensitive now
# -configuration module for initial font/color/size/searchcase
# TBD: could also allow search case choice in GUI, and could use regexps.
#########################################################################

Version = '2.0'
import sys, os                          # platform, args, run tools
from Tkinter          import *          # base widgets, constants
from tkFileDialog     import Open, SaveAs    # standard dialogs
from tkMessageBox     import showinfo, showerror, askyesno
from tkSimpleDialog   import askstring, askinteger
from tkColorChooser   import askcolor
from PP2E.Gui.Tools.guimaker import *        # Frame + menu/toolbar builders

try:
    import textConfig                   # startup font and colors
    configs = textConfig.__dict__       # work if not on the path or bad
except:
    configs = {}

helptext = """PyEdit version %s
January, 2006
```

Example 12-4. PP3E\Gui\TextEditor\textEditor.py (continued)

```
(1.0: October, 2000)

Programming Python, 3rd Edition
O'Reilly Media, Inc.

A text editor program and embeddable object
component, written in Python/Tkinter.  Use
menu tear-offs and toolbar for quick access
to actions, and Alt-key shortcuts for menus.

New in version %s:
- font pick dialog
- unlimited undo/redo
- quit/open/new/run prompt save only if changed
- searches are case-insensitive
- startup configuration module textConfig.py
"""

START     = '1.0'                      # index of first char: row=1,col=0
SEL_FIRST = SEL + '.first'             # map sel tag to index
SEL_LAST  = SEL + '.last'             # same as 'sel.last'

FontScale = 0                          # use bigger font on Linux
if sys.platform[:3] != 'win':          # and other non-Windows boxes
    FontScale = 3


###############################################################################
# Main class: implements editor GUI, actions
###############################################################################

class TextEditor:                      # mix with menu/toolbar Frame class
    startfiledir = '.'
    ftypes = [('All files',      '*'),          # for file open dialog
              ('Text files',   '.txt'),         # customize in subclass
              ('Python files',  '.py')]         # or set in each instance

    colors = [{'fg':'black',      'bg':'white'},      # color pick list
              {'fg':'yellow',     'bg':'black'},      # first item is default
              {'fg':'white',      'bg':'blue'},       # tailor me as desired
              {'fg':'black',      'bg':'beige'},      # or do PickBg/Fg chooser
              {'fg':'yellow',     'bg':'purple'},
              {'fg':'black',      'bg':'brown'},
              {'fg':'lightgreen', 'bg':'darkgreen'},
              {'fg':'darkblue',   'bg':'orange'},
              {'fg':'orange',     'bg':'darkblue'}]

    fonts  = [('courier',    9+FontScale, 'normal'),  # platform-neutral fonts
              ('courier',   12+FontScale, 'normal'),  # (family, size, style)
              ('courier',   10+FontScale, 'bold'),    # or pop up a listbox
              ('courier',   10+FontScale, 'italic'),  # make bigger on Linux
              ('times',     10+FontScale, 'normal'),  # use 'bold italic' for 2
              ('helvetica', 10+FontScale, 'normal'),  # also 'underline', etc.
```

Example 12-4. PP3E\Gui\TextEditor\textEditor.py (continued)

```
                    ('ariel',      10+FontScale, 'normal'),
                    ('system',     10+FontScale, 'normal'),
                    ('courier',    20+FontScale, 'normal')]

    def __init__(self, loadFirst=''):
        if not isinstance(self, GuiMaker):
            raise TypeError, 'TextEditor needs a GuiMaker mixin'
        self.setFileName(None)
        self.lastfind    = None
        self.openDialog  = None
        self.saveDialog  = None
        self.text.focus()                          # else must click in text
        if loadFirst:
            self.onOpen(loadFirst)

    def start(self):                               # run by GuiMaker.__init__
        self.menuBar = [                           # configure menu/toolbar
            ('File', 0,                            # a GuiMaker menu def tree
                [('Open...',      0, self.onOpen),  # build in method for self
                 ('Save',         0, self.onSave),  # label, shortcut, callback
                 ('Save As...',   5, self.onSaveAs),
                 ('New',          0, self.onNew),
                 'separator',
                 ('Quit...',      0, self.onQuit)]
            ),
            ('Edit', 0,
                [('Undo',         0, self.onUndo),
                 ('Redo',         0, self.onRedo),
                 'separator',
                 ('Cut',          0, self.onCut),
                 ('Copy',         1, self.onCopy),
                 ('Paste',        0, self.onPaste),
                 'separator',
                 ('Delete',       0, self.onDelete),
                 ('Select All',   0, self.onSelectAll)]
            ),
            ('Search', 0,
                [('Goto...',      0, self.onGoto),
                 ('Find...',      0, self.onFind),
                 ('Refind',       0, self.onRefind),
                 ('Change...',    0, self.onChange)]
            ),
            ('Tools', 0,
                [('Pick Font...', 6, self.onPickFont),
                 ('Font List',    0, self.onFontList),
                 'separator',
                 ('Pick Bg...',   3, self.onPickBg),
                 ('Pick Fg...',   0, self.onPickFg),
                 ('Color List',   0, self.onColorList),
                 'separator',
                 ('Info...',      0, self.onInfo),
                 ('Clone',        1, self.onClone),
```

Example 12-4. PP3E\Gui\TextEditor\textEditor.py (continued)

```
                ('Run Code',      0, self.onRunCode)]
        )]
    self.toolBar = [
        ('Save',  self.onSave,    {'side': LEFT}),
        ('Cut',   self.onCut,     {'side': LEFT}),
        ('Copy',  self.onCopy,    {'side': LEFT}),
        ('Paste', self.onPaste,   {'side': LEFT}),
        ('Find',  self.onRefind,  {'side': LEFT}),
        ('Help',  self.help,      {'side': RIGHT}),
        ('Quit',  self.onQuit,    {'side': RIGHT})]

def makeWidgets(self):                          # run by GuiMaker.__init__
    name = Label(self, bg='black', fg='white')  # add below menu, above tool
    name.pack(side=TOP, fill=X)                 # menu/toolbars are packed

    vbar  = Scrollbar(self)
    hbar  = Scrollbar(self, orient='horizontal')
    text  = Text(self, padx=5, wrap='none')
    text.config(undo=1, autoseparators=1)       # 2.0, default is 0, 1

    vbar.pack(side=RIGHT,  fill=Y)
    hbar.pack(side=BOTTOM, fill=X)              # pack text last
    text.pack(side=TOP,    fill=BOTH, expand=YES) # else sbars clipped

    text.config(yscrollcommand=vbar.set)       # call vbar.set on text move
    text.config(xscrollcommand=hbar.set)
    vbar.config(command=text.yview)            # call text.yview on scroll move
    hbar.config(command=text.xview)            # or hbar['command']=text.xview

    # 2.0: apply user configs or defaults
    startfont = configs.get('font', self.fonts[0])
    startbg   = configs.get('bg',   self.colors[0]['bg'])
    startfg   = configs.get('fg',   self.colors[0]['fg'])
    text.config(font=startfont, bg=startbg, fg=startfg)
    if 'height' in configs: text.config(height=configs['height'])
    if 'width'  in configs: text.config(width =configs['width'])
    self.text = text
    self.filelabel = name

##############################################################################
# File menu commands
##############################################################################

def my_askopenfilename(self):        # objects remember last result dir/file
    if not self.openDialog:
        self.openDialog = Open(initialdir=self.startfiledir,
                               filetypes=self.ftypes)
    return self.openDialog.show()

def my_asksaveasfilename(self):      # objects remember last result dir/file
    if not self.saveDialog:
        self.saveDialog = SaveAs(initialdir=self.startfiledir,
```

Example 12-4. PP3E\Gui\TextEditor\textEditor.py (continued)

```
                                filetypes=self.ftypes)
        return self.saveDialog.show( )

    def onOpen(self, loadFirst=''):
        doit = (not self.text_edit_modified( ) or        # 2.0
                askyesno('PyEdit', 'Text has changed: discard changes?'))
        if doit:
            file = loadFirst or self.my_askopenfilename( )
            if file:
                try:
                    text = open(file, 'r').read( )
                except:
                    showerror('PyEdit', 'Could not open file ' + file)
                else:
                    self.setAllText(text)
                    self.setFileName(file)
                    self.text.edit_reset( )        # 2.0: clear undo/redo stks
                    self.text.edit_modified(0)     # 2.0: clear modified flag

    def onSave(self):
        self.onSaveAs(self.currfile)  # may be None

    def onSaveAs(self, forcefile=None):
        file = forcefile or self.my_asksaveasfilename( )
        if file:
            text = self.getAllText( )
            try:
                open(file, 'w').write(text)
            except:
                showerror('PyEdit', 'Could not write file ' + file)
            else:
                self.setFileName(file)              # may be newly created
                self.text.edit_modified(0)          # 2.0: clear modified flag
                                                    # don't clear undo/redo stks
    def onNew(self):
        doit = (not self.text_edit_modified( ) or   # 2.0
                askyesno('PyEdit', 'Text has changed: discard changes?'))
        if doit:
            self.setFileName(None)
            self.clearAllText( )
            self.text.edit_reset( )                 # 2.0: clear undo/redo stks
            self.text.edit_modified(0)              # 2.0: clear modified flag

    def onQuit(self):
        doit = (not self.text_edit_modified( )      # 2.0
                or askyesno('PyEdit',
                            'Text has changed: quit and discard changes?'))
        if doit:
            self.quit( )                            # Frame.quit via GuiMaker

    def text_edit_modified(self):
        """
```

Example 12-4. PP3E\Gui\TextEditor\textEditor.py (continued)

```
      2.0: self.text.edit_modified() broken in Python 2.4:
      do manually for now (seems to be bool result type bug)
      """
      return self.tk.call((self.text._w, 'edit') + ('modified', None))

  ##########################################################################
  # Edit menu commands
  ##########################################################################

  def onUndo(self):                        # 2.0
      try:                                 # tk8.4 keeps undo/redo stacks
          self.text.edit_undo()            # exception if stacks empty
      except TclError:                     # menu tear-offs for quick undo
          showinfo('PyEdit', 'Nothing to undo')

  def onRedo(self):                        # 2.0: redo an undone
      try:
          self.text.edit_redo()
      except TclError:
          showinfo('PyEdit', 'Nothing to redo')

  def onCopy(self):                        # get text selected by mouse, etc.
      if not self.text.tag_ranges(SEL):    # save in cross-app clipboard
          showerror('PyEdit', 'No text selected')
      else:
          text = self.text.get(SEL_FIRST, SEL_LAST)
          self.clipboard_clear()
          self.clipboard_append(text)

  def onDelete(self):                      # delete selected text, no save
      if not self.text.tag_ranges(SEL):
          showerror('PyEdit', 'No text selected')
      else:
          self.text.delete(SEL_FIRST, SEL_LAST)

  def onCut(self):
      if not self.text.tag_ranges(SEL):
          showerror('PyEdit', 'No text selected')
      else:
          self.onCopy()                    # save and delete selected text
          self.onDelete()

  def onPaste(self):
      try:
          text = self.selection_get(selection='CLIPBOARD')
      except TclError:
          showerror('PyEdit', 'Nothing to paste')
          return
      self.text.insert(INSERT, text)       # add at current insert cursor
      self.text.tag_remove(SEL, '1.0', END)
      self.text.tag_add(SEL, INSERT+'-%dc' % len(text), INSERT)
      self.text.see(INSERT)                # select it, so it can be cut
```

Example 12-4. PP3E\Gui\TextEditor\textEditor.py (continued)

```python
    def onSelectAll(self):
        self.text.tag_add(SEL, '1.0', END+'-1c')   # select entire text
        self.text.mark_set(INSERT, '1.0')          # move insert point to top
        self.text.see(INSERT)                      # scroll to top

    ##########################################################################
    # Search menu commands
    ##########################################################################

    def onGoto(self, forceline=None):
        line = forceline or askinteger('PyEdit', 'Enter line number')
        self.text.update()
        self.text.focus()
        if line is not None:
            maxindex = self.text.index(END+'-1c')
            maxline  = int(maxindex.split('.')[0])
            if line > 0 and line <= maxline:
                self.text.mark_set(INSERT, '%d.0' % line)   # goto line
                self.text.tag_remove(SEL, '1.0', END)       # delete selects
                self.text.tag_add(SEL, INSERT, 'insert + 1l') # select line
                self.text.see(INSERT)                       # scroll to line
            else:
                showerror('PyEdit', 'Bad line number')

    def onFind(self, lastkey=None):
        key = lastkey or askstring('PyEdit', 'Enter search string')
        self.text.update()
        self.text.focus()
        self.lastfind = key
        if key:                                            # 2.0: nocase
            nocase = configs.get('caseinsens', 1)          # 2.0: config
            where = self.text.search(key, INSERT, END, nocase=nocase)
            if not where:                                  # don't wrap
                showerror('PyEdit', 'String not found')
            else:
                pastkey = where + '+%dc' % len(key)        # index past key
                self.text.tag_remove(SEL, '1.0', END)      # remove any sel
                self.text.tag_add(SEL, where, pastkey)     # select key
                self.text.mark_set(INSERT, pastkey)        # for next find
                self.text.see(where)                       # scroll display

    def onRefind(self):
        self.onFind(self.lastfind)

    def onChange(self):
        new = Toplevel(self)
        Label(new, text='Find text:').grid(row=0, column=0)
        Label(new, text='Change to:').grid(row=1, column=0)
        self.change1 = Entry(new)
        self.change2 = Entry(new)
        self.change1.grid(row=0, column=1, sticky=EW)
        self.change2.grid(row=1, column=1, sticky=EW)
```

Example 12-4. PP3E\Gui\TextEditor\textEditor.py (continued)

```
        Button(new, text='Find',
               command=self.onDoFind).grid(row=0, column=2, sticky=EW)
        Button(new, text='Apply',
               command=self.onDoChange).grid(row=1, column=2, sticky=EW)
        new.columnconfigure(1, weight=1)      # expandable entries

    def onDoFind(self):
        self.onFind(self.change1.get())                    # Find in change box

    def onDoChange(self):
        if self.text.tag_ranges(SEL):                      # must find first
            self.text.delete(SEL_FIRST, SEL_LAST)          # Apply in change
            self.text.insert(INSERT, self.change2.get())   # deletes if empty
            self.text.see(INSERT)
            self.onFind(self.change1.get())                # goto next appear
            self.text.update()                             # force refresh

    ############################################################################
    # Tools menu commands
    ############################################################################

    def onFontList(self):
        self.fonts.append(self.fonts[0])           # pick next font in list
        del self.fonts[0]                          # resizes the text area
        self.text.config(font=self.fonts[0])

    def onColorList(self):
        self.colors.append(self.colors[0])         # pick next color in list
        del self.colors[0]                         # move current to end
        self.text.config(fg=self.colors[0]['fg'], bg=self.colors[0]['bg'])

    def onPickFg(self):
        self.pickColor('fg')                       # added on 10/02/00
    def onPickBg(self):                            # select arbitrary color
        self.pickColor('bg')                       # in standard color dialog

    def pickColor(self, part):                     # this is too easy
        (triple, hexstr) = askcolor()
        if hexstr:
            self.text.config(**{part: hexstr})

    def onInfo(self):
        text  = self.getAllText()                  # added on 5/3/00 in 15 mins
        bytes = len(text)                          # words uses a simple guess:
        lines = len(text.split('\n'))              # any separated by whitespace
        words = len(text.split())
        index = self.text.index(INSERT)
        where = tuple(index.split('.'))
        showinfo('PyEdit Information',
                 'Current location:\n\n' +
                 'line:\t%s\ncolumn:\t%s\n\n' % where +
                 'File text statistics:\n\n' +
```

Example 12-4. PP3E\Gui\TextEditor\textEditor.py (continued)

```
                    'bytes:\t%d\nlines:\t%d\nwords:\t%d\n' % (bytes, lines, words))

    def onClone(self):
        new = Toplevel()                    # a new edit window in same process
        myclass = self.__class__            # instance's (lowest) class object
        myclass(new)                        # attach/run instance of my class

    def onRunCode(self, parallelmode=True):
        """
        run Python code being edited--not an IDE, but handy;
        tries to run in file's dir, not cwd (may be PP3E root);
        inputs and adds command-line arguments for script files;
        code's stdin/out/err = editor's start window, if any:
        run with a console window to see code's print outputs;
        but parallelmode uses start to open a DOS box for I/O;
        module search path will include '.' dir where started;
        in non-file mode, code's Tk root window is PyEdit win;
        """
        def askcmdargs():
            return askstring('PyEdit', 'Commandline arguments?') or ''

        from PP3E.launchmodes import System, Start, Fork
        filemode = False
        thefile  = str(self.getFileName())
        if os.path.exists(thefile):
            filemode = askyesno('PyEdit', 'Run from file?')
        if not filemode:                                    # run text string
            cmdargs   = askcmdargs()
            namespace = {'__name__': '__main__'}            # run as top-level
            sys.argv  = [thefile] + cmdargs.split()         # could use threads
            exec self.getAllText() + '\n' in namespace      # exceptions ignored
        elif self.text_edit_modified():                     # 2.0: changed test
            showerror('PyEdit', 'Text changed: save before run')
        else:
            cmdargs   = askcmdargs()
            mycwd     = os.getcwd()                          # cwd may be root
            os.chdir(os.path.dirname(thefile) or mycwd)     # cd for filenames
            thecmd    = thefile + ' ' + cmdargs
            if not parallelmode:                            # run as file
                System(thecmd, thecmd)()                    # block editor
            else:
                if sys.platform[:3] == 'win':               # spawn in parallel
                    Start(thecmd, thecmd)()                 # or use os.spawnv
                else:
                    Fork(thecmd, thecmd)()                  # spawn in parallel
            os.chdir(mycwd)

    def onPickFont(self):
        # 2.0 font spec dialog
        new = Toplevel(self)
        Label(new, text='Family:').grid(row=0, column=0)     # nonmodal dialog
        Label(new, text='Size:  ').grid(row=1, column=0)     # see pick list
```

Example 12-4. PP3E\Gui\TextEditor\textEditor.py (continued)

```
        Label(new, text='Style: ').grid(row=2, column=0)      # for valid inputs
        self.font1 = Entry(new)
        self.font2 = Entry(new)
        self.font3 = Entry(new)
        self.font1.insert(0, 'courier')                       # suggested vals
        self.font2.insert(0, '12')
        self.font3.insert(0, 'bold italic')
        self.font1.grid(row=0, column=1, sticky=EW)
        self.font2.grid(row=1, column=1, sticky=EW)
        self.font3.grid(row=2, column=1, sticky=EW)
        Button(new, text='Apply',
               command=self.onDoFont).grid(row=3, columnspan=2)
        new.columnconfigure(1, weight=1)     # expandable entrys

    def onDoFont(self):
        try:
            font = (self.font1.get(), int(self.font2.get()), self.font3.get())
            self.text.config(font=font)
        except:
            showerror('PyEdit', 'Bad font specification')

    ###########################################################################
    # Utilities, useful outside this class
    ###########################################################################

    def isEmpty(self):
        return not self.getAllText()

    def getAllText(self):
        return self.text.get('1.0', END+'-1c')  # extract text as a string
    def setAllText(self, text):
        self.text.delete('1.0', END)            # store text string in widget
        self.text.insert(END, text)             # or '1.0'
        self.text.mark_set(INSERT, '1.0')       # move insert point to top
        self.text.see(INSERT)                   # scroll to top, insert set
    def clearAllText(self):
        self.text.delete('1.0', END)            # clear text in widget

    def getFileName(self):
        return self.currfile
    def setFileName(self, name):                # also: onGoto(linenum)
        self.currfile = name  # for save
        self.filelabel.config(text=str(name))

    def setBg(self, color):
        self.text.config(bg=color)              # to set manually from code
    def setFg(self, color):
        self.text.config(fg=color)              # 'black', hexstring
    def setFont(self, font):
        self.text.config(font=font)             # ('family', size, 'style')

    def setHeight(self, lines):                 # default = 24h x 80w
        self.text.config(height=lines)          # may also be from textCongif.py
```

Example 12-4. PP3E\Gui\TextEditor\textEditor.py (continued)

```
    def setWidth(self, chars):
        self.text.config(width=chars)

    def clearModified(self):
        self.text.edit_modified(0)               # clear modified flag
    def isModified(self):
        return self.text_edit_modified()         # changed since last reset?

    def help(self):
        showinfo('About PyEdit', helptext % ((Version,)*2))


###############################################################################
# ready-to-use editor classes
# mix in a Frame subclass that builds menu/toolbars
###############################################################################

#
# when editor owns the window
#
class TextEditorMain(TextEditor, GuiMakerWindowMenu):   # add menu/toolbar maker
    def __init__(self, parent=None, loadFirst=''):      # when fills whole window
        GuiMaker.__init__(self, parent)                 # use main window menus
        TextEditor.__init__(self, loadFirst)            # self has GuiMaker frame
        self.master.title('PyEdit ' + Version)          # title if standalone
        self.master.iconname('PyEdit')                  # catch wm delete button
        self.master.protocol('WM_DELETE_WINDOW', self.onQuit)


class TextEditorMainPopup(TextEditor, GuiMakerWindowMenu):
    def __init__(self, parent=None, loadFirst='', winTitle=''):
        self.popup = Toplevel(parent)                   # create own window
        GuiMaker.__init__(self, self.popup)             # use main window menus
        TextEditor.__init__(self, loadFirst)
        assert self.master == self.popup
        self.popup.title('PyEdit ' + Version + winTitle)
        self.popup.iconname('PyEdit')
    def quit(self):
        self.popup.destroy()                            # kill this window only


#
# when embedded in another window
#
class TextEditorComponent(TextEditor, GuiMakerFrameMenu):
    def __init__(self, parent=None, loadFirst=''):      # use Frame-based menus
        GuiMaker.__init__(self, parent)                 # all menus, buttons on
        TextEditor.__init__(self, loadFirst)            # GuiMaker must init 1st


class TextEditorComponentMinimal(TextEditor, GuiMakerFrameMenu):
    def __init__(self, parent=None, loadFirst='', deleteFile=1):
        self.deleteFile = deleteFile
        GuiMaker.__init__(self, parent)
        TextEditor.__init__(self, loadFirst)
    def start(self):
        TextEditor.start(self)                          # GuiMaker start call
```

Example 12-4. PP3E\Gui\TextEditor\textEditor.py (continued)

```
        for i in range(len(self.toolBar)):          # delete quit in toolbar
            if self.toolBar[i][0] == 'Quit':        # delete file menu items
                del self.toolBar[i]; break          # or just disable file
        if self.deleteFile:
            for i in range(len(self.menuBar)):
                if self.menuBar[i][0] == 'File':
                    del self.menuBar[i]; break
        else:
            for (name, key, items) in self.menuBar:
                if name == 'File':
                    items.append([1,2,3,4,6])


###############################################################################
# standalone program run
###############################################################################

def testPopup():
    # see PyView and PyMail for component tests
    root = Tk()
    TextEditorMainPopup(root)
    TextEditorMainPopup(root)
    Button(root, text='More', command=TextEditorMainPopup).pack(fill=X)
    Button(root, text='Quit', command=root.quit).pack(fill=X)
    root.mainloop()

def main():                                          # may be typed or clicked
    try:                                             # or associated on Windows
        fname = sys.argv[1]                          # arg = optional filename
    except IndexError:
        fname = None
    TextEditorMain(loadFirst=fname).pack(expand=YES, fill=BOTH)
    mainloop()

if __name__ == '__main__':                           # when run as a script
    #testPopup()
    main()                                           # run .pyw for no DOS box
```

PyPhoto: An Image Viewer and Resizer

In Chapter 10, we wrote a simple thumbnail image viewer that scrolled its thumbnails in a canvas. That program in turn built on techniques and code we developed at the end of Chapter 9 to handle images. In both places, I promised that we'd eventually meet a more full-featured extension of the ideas we deployed.

In this section, we finally wrap up the thumbnail images thread by studying PyPhoto—an enhanced image viewing and resizing program. PyPhoto's basic operation is straightforward: given a directory of image files, PyPhoto displays their thumbnails in a scrollable canvas. When a thumbnail is selected, the corresponding image is displayed full size in a pop-up window.

Unlike our prior viewers, though, PyPhoto is clever enough to scroll (rather than crop) images too large for the physical display. Moreover, PyPhoto introduces the notion of image resizing—it supports mouse and keyboard events that resize the image to one of the display's dimensions and zoom the image in and out. Once images are opened, the resizing logic allows images to be grown or shrunk arbitrarily, which is especially handy for images produced by a digital camera that may be too large to view all at once.

As added touches, PyPhoto also allows the image to be saved in a file (possibly after being resized), and it allows an image directory to be selected and opened in the GUI itself, instead of just as a command-line argument.

Put together, PyPhoto's features make it an image-processing program, albeit one with a currently small set of processing tools. I encourage you to experiment with adding new features of your own; once you get the hang of the Python Imaging Library (PIL) API, the object-oriented nature of PyPhoto makes adding new tools remarkably simple.

Running PyPhoto

In order to run PyPhoto, you'll need to fetch and install the PIL extension package described in Chapter 9. PyPhoto inherits much of its functionality from PIL—PIL is used to support extra image types beyond those handled by standard Tkinter (e.g., JPEG images) and to perform image processing operations such as resizes, thumbnail creation, and saves. PIL is open source like Python, but it is not presently part of the Python standard library. Search the Web for PIL's location (*http://www.pythonware.com* is currently a safe bet).

The best way to get a feel for PyPhoto is to run it live on your own machine to see how images are scrolled and resized. Here, we'll present a few screenshots to give the general flavor of the interaction. You can start PyPhoto by clicking its icon, or you can start it from the command line. When run directly, it opens the *images* subdirectory in its source directory, which contains a handful of photos. When you run it from the command line, you can pass in an initial image directory name as a command-line argument. Figure 12-4 captures the main thumbnail window when run directly.

Internally, PyPhoto is loading or creating thumbnail images before this window appears, using tools coded in Chapter 9. Startup may take a few seconds the first time you open a directory, but it is quick thereafter—PyPhoto caches thumbnails in a local subdirectory so that it can skip the generation step the next time the directory is opened.

Technically, there are three different ways PyPhoto may start up: viewing an explicit directory listed on the command line; viewing the default *images* directory when no command-line argument is given and when *images* is present where the program is

Figure 12-4. PyPhoto main window, default directory

run; or displaying a simple one-button window that allows you to select directories to open on demand, when no initial directory is given or present (see the code's __main__ logic).

PyPhoto also lets you open additional folders in new thumbnail windows, by pressing the D key on your keyboard in either a thumbnail or an image window. Figure 12-5, for instance, captures the pop-up window produced to select a new image folder, and Figure 12-6 shows the result when I select a directory copied from one of my digital cameras. Figure 12-5 is also opened by the one-button window if no initial directory is available.

When a thumbnail is selected, the image is displayed in a canvas, in a new pop-up window. If it's too large for the display, you can scroll through its full size with the window's scroll bars. Figure 12-7 captures one image after its thumbnail is clicked, and Figure 12-8 shows the Save As dialog issued when the S key is pressed in the image window. Any number of thumbnail and image windows can be open at once.

Figure 12-5. PyPhoto open directory dialog (the D key)

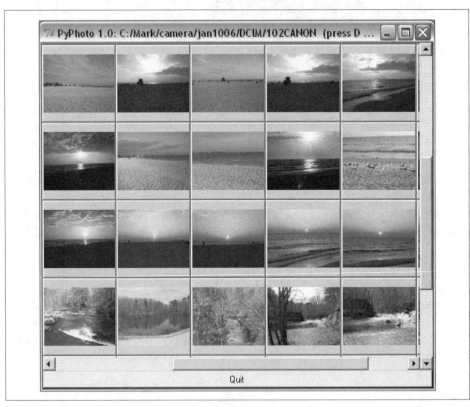

Figure 12-6. PyPhoto thumbnail window, other directory

Figure 12-7. PyPhoto image view window

Beyond the screenshots already shown, this system's interaction is difficult to capture in a static medium such as this book—you're better off test-driving the program live.

For example, clicking the left and right mouse buttons will resize the image to the display's height and width dimensions, respectively, and pressing the I and O keys will zoom the image in and out in 10 percent increments. Both resizing schemes allow you to shrink an image too large to see all at once, as well as expand small photos. They also preserve the original aspect ratio of the photo, by changing its height and width proportionally, while blindly resizing to the display's dimensions would not (height or width may be stretched).

Once resized, images may be saved in files at their current size. PyPhoto is also smart enough to make windows full size on Windows, if an image is larger than the display.

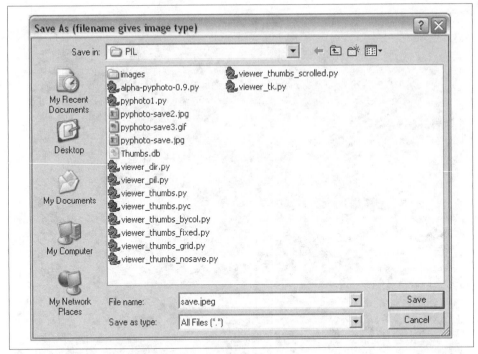

Figure 12-8. PyPhoto Save As dialog (the S key)

PyPhoto Source Code

Because PyPhoto simply extends and reuses techniques and code we met earlier in the book, we'll omit a detailed discussion of its code here. For background, see the discussion of image processing and PIL in Chapter 9, and the coverage of the canvas widget in Chapter 10.

In short, PyPhoto uses canvases in two ways: for thumbnail collections and for opened images. For thumbnails, the same sort of canvas layout code as the thumbnails viewer in Example 10-15 is employed. For images, a canvas is used as well, but the canvas's scrollable (full) size is the image size, and the viewable area size is the minimum of the physical screen size or the size of the image itself. The physical screen size is available from the maxsize( ) method of Toplevel windows. The net effect is that selected images may be scrolled now too, which comes in handy if they are too big for your display (a common case for pictures snapped with newer digital cameras).

In addition, PyPhoto binds keyboard and mouse events to implement resizing and zoom operations. With PIL, this is simple—we save the original PIL image, run its resize method with the new image size, and redraw the image in the canvas. PyPhoto also makes use of file open and save dialog objects, to remember the last directory visited.

PIL supports additional operations, which we could add as new events, but resizing is sufficient for a viewer. PyPhoto does not currently use threads, to avoid becoming blocked for long-running tasks (opening a large directory the first time, for instance). Such enhancements are left as suggested exercises.

PyPhoto is implemented as the single file of Example 12-5, though it gets some utility for free by reusing the thumbnail generation function of the viewer_thumbs module that we originally wrote near the end of Chapter 9 (see Example 9-44).

As you study this file, pay particular attention to the way it *factors* code into reused functions and methods, to avoid redundancy; if we ever need to change the way zooming works, for example, we have just one method to change, not two. Also notice its ScrolledCanvas class—a reusable component that handles the work of linking scroll bars and canvases.

Example 12-5. PP3E\Gui\PIL\pyphoto1.py

```
###############################################################
# PyPhoto 1.0: thumbnail image viewer with resizing and saves;
# supports multiple image directory thumb windows - the initial
# img dir is passed in as cmd arg, uses "images" default, or
# is selected via main window button; later directories are
# opened by pressing "D" in image view or thumbnail windows;
#
# viewer also scrolls popped-up images that are too large
# for the screen; still to do: (1) rearrange thumbnails when
# window resized, based on current window size; (2) resize
# images to fit current window size as an option? (3) avoid
# scrolls if image size is less than window max size: use
# Label if imgwide <= scrwide and imghigh <= scrhigh?
#
# New in 1.0: now does a form of (2) - image is resized to
# one of the display's dimensions if clicked, and zoomed in
# or out in 10% increments on key presses; generalize me;
# caveat: seems to lose quality, pixels after many resizes;
#
# the following scaler adapted from PIL's thumbnail code is
# similar to the screen height scaler here, but only shrinks:
# x, y = imgwide, imghigh
# if x > scrwide: y = max(y * scrwide / x, 1); x = scrwide
# if y > scrhigh: x = max(x * scrhigh / y, 1); y = scrhigh
###############################################################

import sys, math, os
from Tkinter import *
from tkFileDialog import SaveAs, Directory

import Image                              # PIL Image: also in Tkinter
from ImageTk import PhotoImage            # PIL photo widget replacement
from viewer_thumbs import makeThumbs      # developed earlier in book

# remember last dirs across all windows
```

Example 12-5. PP3E\Gui\PIL\pyphoto1.py (continued)

```
saveDialog = SaveAs(title='Save As (filename gives image type)')
openDialog = Directory(title='Select Image Directory To Open')
appname = 'PyPhoto 1.0: '


class ScrolledCanvas(Canvas):
    """
    a canvas in a container that automatically makes
    vertical and horizontal scroll bars for itself
    """
    def __init__(self, container):
        Canvas.__init__(self, container)
        self.config(borderwidth=0)
        vbar = Scrollbar(container)
        hbar = Scrollbar(container, orient='horizontal')

        vbar.pack(side=RIGHT,  fill=Y)               # pack canvas after bars
        hbar.pack(side=BOTTOM, fill=X)               # so clipped first
        self.pack(side=TOP, fill=BOTH, expand=YES)

        vbar.config(command=self.yview)              # call on scroll move
        hbar.config(command=self.xview)
        self.config(yscrollcommand=vbar.set)         # call on canvas move
        self.config(xscrollcommand=hbar.set)


class ViewOne(Toplevel):
    """
    open a single image in a pop-up window when created;
    a class because photoimage obj must be saved, else
    erased if reclaimed; scroll if too big for display;
    on mouse clicks, resizes to window's height or width:
    stretches or shrinks; on I/O keypress, zooms in/out;
    both resizing schemes maintain original aspect ratio;
    code is factored to avoid redundancy here as possible;
    """
    def __init__(self, imgdir, imgfile, forcesize=()):
        Toplevel.__init__(self)
        helptxt = '(click L/R or press I/O to resize, S to save, D to open)'
        self.title(appname + imgfile + '  ' + helptxt)
        imgpath = os.path.join(imgdir, imgfile)
        imgpil  = Image.open(imgpath)
        self.canvas = ScrolledCanvas(self)
        self.drawImage(imgpil, forcesize)
        self.canvas.bind('<Button-1>', self.onSizeToDisplayHeight)
        self.canvas.bind('<Button-3>', self.onSizeToDisplayWidth)
        self.bind('<KeyPress-i>',       self.onZoomIn)
        self.bind('<KeyPress-o>',       self.onZoomOut)
        self.bind('<KeyPress-s>',       self.onSaveImage)
        self.bind('<KeyPress-d>',       onDirectoryOpen)
        self.focus()
```

Example 12-5. PP3E\Gui\PIL\pyphoto1.py (continued)

```
def drawImage(self, imgpil, forcesize=( )):
    imgtk = PhotoImage(image=imgpil)                  # not file=imgpath
    scrwide, scrhigh = forcesize or self.maxsize( )   # wm screen size x,y
    imgwide  = imgtk.width( )                          # size in pixels
    imghigh  = imgtk.height( )                         # same as imgpil.size

    fullsize = (0, 0, imgwide, imghigh)                # scrollable
    viewwide = min(imgwide, scrwide)                   # viewable
    viewhigh = min(imghigh, scrhigh)

    canvas = self.canvas
    canvas.delete('all')                               # clear prior photo
    canvas.config(height=viewhigh, width=viewwide)     # viewable window size
    canvas.config(scrollregion=fullsize)               # scrollable area size
    canvas.create_image(0, 0, image=imgtk, anchor=NW)

    if imgwide <= scrwide and imghigh <= scrhigh:      # too big for display?
        self.state('normal')                           # no: win size per img
    elif sys.platform[:3] == 'win':                    # do windows fullscreen
        self.state('zoomed')                           # others use geometry( )
    self.saveimage = imgpil
    self.savephoto = imgtk                             # keep reference on me
    print (scrwide, scrhigh), imgpil.size

def sizeToDisplaySide(self, scaler):
    # resize to fill one side of the display
    imgpil = self.saveimage
    scrwide, scrhigh = self.maxsize( )                     # wm screen size x,y
    imgwide, imghigh = imgpil.size                         # img size in pixels
    newwide, newhigh = scaler(scrwide, scrhigh, imgwide, imghigh)
    if (newwide * newhigh < imgwide * imghigh):
        filter = Image.ANTIALIAS                           # shrink: antialias
    else:                                                  # grow: bicub sharper
        filter = Image.BICUBIC
    imgnew  = imgpil.resize((newwide, newhigh), filter)
    self.drawImage(imgnew)

def onSizeToDisplayHeight(self, event):
    def scaleHigh(scrwide, scrhigh, imgwide, imghigh):
        newhigh = scrhigh
        newwide = int(scrhigh * (float(imgwide) / imghigh))
        return (newwide, newhigh)
    self.sizeToDisplaySide(scaleHigh)

def onSizeToDisplayWidth(self, event):
    def scaleWide(scrwide, scrhigh, imgwide, imghigh):
        newwide = scrwide
        newhigh = int(scrwide * (float(imghigh) / imgwide))
        return (newwide, newhigh)
    self.sizeToDisplaySide(scaleWide)

def zoom(self, factor):
```

Example 12-5. PP3E\Gui\PIL\pyphoto1.py (continued)

```
        # zoom in or out in increments
        imgpil = self.saveimage
        wide, high = imgpil.size
        if factor < 1.0:                        # antialias best if shrink
            filter = Image.ANTIALIAS            # also nearest, bilinear
        else:
            filter = Image.BICUBIC
        new = imgpil.resize((int(wide * factor), int(high * factor)), filter)
        self.drawImage(new)

    def onZoomIn(self, event, incr=.10):
        self.zoom(1.0 + incr)
    def onZoomOut(self, event, decr=.10):
        self.zoom(1.0 - decr)

    def onSaveImage(self, event):
        # save current image state to file
        filename = saveDialog.show()
        if filename:
            self.saveimage.save(filename)


def onDirectoryOpen(event):
    """
    open a new image directory in new pop up
    available in both thumb and img windows
    """
    dirname = openDialog.show()
    if dirname:
        viewThumbs(dirname, kind=Toplevel)


def viewThumbs(imgdir, kind=Toplevel, numcols=None, height=400, width=500):
    """
    make main or pop-up thumbnail buttons window;
    uses fixed-size buttons, scrollable canvas;
    sets scrollable (full) size, and places
    thumbs at abs x,y coordinates in canvas;
    no longer assumes all thumbs are same size:
    gets max of all (x,y), some may be smaller;
    """
    win = kind()
    helptxt = '(press D to open other)'
    win.title(appname + imgdir + '  ' + helptxt)
    quit = Button(win, text='Quit', command=win.quit, bg='beige')
    quit.pack(side=BOTTOM, fill=X)
    canvas = ScrolledCanvas(win)
    canvas.config(height=height, width=width)   # init viewable window size
                                                # changes if user resizes
    thumbs = makeThumbs(imgdir)                 # [(imgfile, imgobj)]
    numthumbs = len(thumbs)
    if not numcols:
```

Example 12-5. PP3E\Gui\PIL\pyphoto1.py (continued)

```
        numcols = int(math.ceil(math.sqrt(numthumbs)))  # fixed or N x N
    numrows = int(math.ceil(numthumbs / float(numcols)))

    # thumb=(name, obj), thumb.size=(width, height)
    linksize = max([max(thumb[1].size) for thumb in thumbs])
    print linksize
    fullsize = (0, 0,                                    # upper left  X,Y
        (linksize * numcols), (linksize * numrows) )     # lower right X,Y
    canvas.config(scrollregion=fullsize)                 # scrollable area size

    rowpos = 0
    savephotos = []
    while thumbs:
        thumbsrow, thumbs = thumbs[:numcols], thumbs[numcols:]
        colpos = 0
        for (imgfile, imgobj) in thumbsrow:
            photo   = PhotoImage(imgobj)
            link    = Button(canvas, image=photo)
            handler = (lambda savefile=imgfile: ViewOne(imgdir, savefile))
            link.config(command=handler, width=linksize, height=linksize)
            link.pack(side=LEFT, expand=YES)
            canvas.create_window(colpos, rowpos, anchor=NW,
                    window=link, width=linksize, height=linksize)
            colpos += linksize
            savephotos.append(photo)
        rowpos += linksize
    win.bind('<KeyPress-d>', onDirectoryOpen)
    win.savephotos = savephotos
    return win


if __name__ == '__main__':
    """
    open dir = default or cmdline arg
    else show simple window to select
    """
    imgdir = 'images'
    if len(sys.argv) > 1: imgdir = sys.argv[1]
    if os.path.exists(imgdir):
        mainwin = viewThumbs(imgdir, kind=Tk)
    else:
        mainwin = Tk()
        mainwin.title(appname + 'Open')
        handler = lambda: onDirectoryOpen(None)
        Button(mainwin, text='Open Image Directory', command=handler).pack()
    mainwin.mainloop()
```

PyView: An Image and Notes Slideshow

A picture may be worth a thousand words, but it takes considerably fewer to display one with Python. The next program, PyView, implements a simple photo slideshow program in portable Python/Tkinter code. It doesn't have any image processing tools such as PyPhoto's resizing, but it does provide different tools such as image note files, and it can be run without the optional PIL extension.

Running PyView

PyView pulls together many of the topics we studied in Chapter 10: it uses after events to sequence a slideshow, displays image objects in an automatically sized canvas, and so on. Its main window displays a photo on a canvas; users can either open and view a photo directly or start a slideshow mode that picks and displays a random photo from a directory, at regular intervals specified with a scale widget.

By default, PyView slideshows show images in the book's image file directory (though the Open button allows you to load images in arbitrary directories). To view other sets of photos, either pass a directory name in as a first command-line argument or change the default directory name in the script itself. I can't show you a slideshow in action here, but I can show you the main window in general. Figure 12-9 shows the main PyView window's default display.

Figure 12-9. PyView without notes

Though it's not obvious as rendered in this book, the black-on-red label at the top gives the pathname of the photo file displayed. For a good time, move the slider at the bottom all the way over to "0" to specify no delay between photo changes, and then click Start to begin a very fast slideshow. If your computer is at least as fast as mine, photos flip by much too fast to be useful for anything but subliminal advertising. Slideshow photos are loaded on startup to retain references to them (remember, you must hold on to image objects). But the speed with which large GIFs can be thrown up in a window in Python is impressive, if not downright exhilarating.

The GUI's Start button changes to a Stop button during a slideshow (its text attribute is reset with the widget `config` method). Figure 12-10 shows the scene after pressing Stop at an opportune moment.

Figure 12-10. PyView after stopping a slideshow

In addition, each photo can have an associated "notes" text file that is automatically opened along with the image. You can use this feature to record basic information about the photo. Press the Note button to open an additional set of widgets that let you view and change the note file associated with the currently displayed photo. This additional set of widgets should look familiar—the PyEdit text editor of the previous section is attached to PyView to serve as a display and editing widget for photo notes. Figure 12-11 shows PyView with the attached PyEdit note-editing component opened.

This makes for a very big window, usually best view maximized (taking up the entire screen). The main thing to notice, though, is the lower-right corner of this display, above the scale—it's simply an attached PyEdit object, running the very same code listed in the prior section. Because PyEdit is implemented as a GUI class, it can be reused like this in any GUI that needs a text-editing interface. When embedded like this, PyEdit's menus are based on a frame (it doesn't own the window at large), text

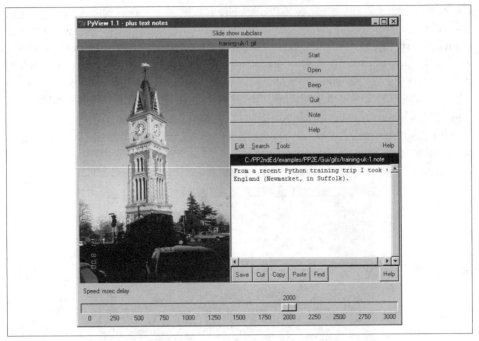

Figure 12-11. PyView with notes

content is stored and fetched directly, and some standalone options are omitted (e.g., the File pull down is gone).

The note file viewer appears only if you press the Note button, and it is erased if you press it again; PyView uses the widget pack and pack_forget methods introduced at the end of Chapter 10 to show and hide the note viewer frame. The window automatically expands to accommodate the note viewer when it is packed and displayed. It is also possible to open the note file in a PyEdit pop-up window, but PyView embeds the editor to retain a direct visual association. Watch for PyEdit to show up embedded within another GUI like this when we meet PyMailGUI in Chapter 15.

A caveat here: out of the box, PyView supports as many photo formats as Tkinter's PhotoImage object does; that's why it looks for GIF files by default. You can improve this by installing the PIL extension to view JPEGs (and many others). But because PIL is an optional extension today, it's not incorporated into this PyView release. See the end of Chapter 9 for more on PIL and image formats.

PyView Source Code

Because the PyView program was implemented in stages, you need to study the union of two files and classes to understand how it truly works. One file implements a class that provides core slideshow functionality; the other implements a class that extends the original class, to add additional features on top of the core behavior.

Let's start with the extension class: Example 12-6 adds a set of features to an imported slideshow base class—note editing, a delay scale and file label, and so on. This is the file that is actually run to start PyView.

Example 12-6. PP3E\Gui\SlideShow\slideShowPlus.py

```
###################################################################
# SlideShowPlus: add note files with an attached PyEdit object,
# a scale for setting the slideshow delay interval, and a label
# that gives the name of the image file currently being displayed;
###################################################################

import os
from Tkinter import *
from PP3E.Gui.TextEditor.textEditor import *
from slideShow import SlideShow
#from slideShow_threads import SlideShow

class SlideShowPlus(SlideShow):
    def __init__(self, parent, picdir, editclass, msecs=2000):
        self.msecs = msecs
        self.editclass = editclass
        SlideShow.__init__(self, parent=parent, picdir=picdir, msecs=msecs)

    def makeWidgets(self):
        self.name = Label(self, text='None', bg='red', relief=RIDGE)
        self.name.pack(fill=X)
        SlideShow.makeWidgets(self)
        Button(self, text='Note', command=self.onNote).pack(fill=X)
        Button(self, text='Help', command=self.onHelp).pack(fill=X)
        s = Scale(label='Speed: msec delay', command=self.onScale,
                  from_=0, to=3000, resolution=50, showvalue=YES,
                  length=400, tickinterval=250, orient='horizontal')
        s.pack(side=BOTTOM, fill=X)
        s.set(self.msecs)
        if self.editclass == TextEditorMain:              # make editor now
            self.editor = self.editclass(self.master)     # need root for menu
        else:
            self.editor = self.editclass(self)            # embedded or pop-up
        self.editor.pack_forget()                         # hide editor initially
        self.editorUp = self.image = None

    def onStart(self):
        SlideShow.onStart(self)
        self.config(cursor='watch')

    def onStop(self):
        SlideShow.onStop(self)
        self.config(cursor='hand2')

    def onOpen(self):
        SlideShow.onOpen(self)
        if self.image:
```

Example 12-6. PP3E\Gui\SlideShow\slideShowPlus.py (continued)

```
            self.name.config(text=os.path.split(self.image[0])[1])
        self.config(cursor='crosshair')
        self.switchNote( )

    def quit(self):
        self.saveNote( )
        SlideShow.quit(self)

    def drawNext(self):
        SlideShow.drawNext(self)
        if self.image:
            self.name.config(text=os.path.split(self.image[0])[1])
        self.loadNote( )

    def onScale(self, value):
        self.msecs = int(value)

    def onNote(self):
        if self.editorUp:                       # if editor already open
            #self.saveNote( )                    # save text, hide editor
            self.editor.pack_forget( )
            self.editorUp = 0
        else:
            self.editor.pack(side=TOP)          # else unhide/pack editor
            self.editorUp = 1                   # and load image note text
            self.loadNote( )

    def switchNote(self):
        if self.editorUp:
            self.saveNote( )                    # save current image's note
            self.loadNote( )                    # load note for new image

    def saveNote(self):
        if self.editorUp:
            currfile = self.editor.getFileName( )    # or self.editor.onSave( )
            currtext = self.editor.getAllText( )     # but text may be empty
            if currfile and currtext:
                try:
                    open(currfile, 'w').write(currtext)
                except:
                    pass # this may be normal if run off cd

    def loadNote(self):
        if self.image and self.editorUp:
            root, ext = os.path.splitext(self.image[0])
            notefile  = root + '.note'
            self.editor.setFileName(notefile)
            try:
                self.editor.setAllText(open(notefile).read( ))
            except:
                self.editor.clearAllText( )
```

Example 12-6. PP3E\Gui\SlideShow\slideShowPlus.py (continued)

```
    def onHelp(self):
        showinfo('About PyView',
                 'PyView version 1.1\nJuly, 1999\n'
                 'An image slide show\nProgramming Python 2E')

if __name__ == '__main__':
    import sys
    picdir = '../gifs'
    if len(sys.argv) >= 2:
        picdir = sys.argv[1]

    editstyle = TextEditorComponentMinimal
    if len(sys.argv) == 3:
        try:
            editstyle = [TextEditorMain,
                         TextEditorMainPopup,
                         TextEditorComponent,
                         TextEditorComponentMinimal][int(sys.argv[2])]
        except: pass

    root = Tk()
    root.title('PyView 1.1 - plus text notes')
    Label(root, text="Slide show subclass").pack()
    SlideShowPlus(parent=root, picdir=picdir, editclass=editstyle)
    root.mainloop()
```

The core functionality extended by SlideShowPlus lives in Example 12-7. This was the initial slideshow implementation; it opens images, displays photos, and cycles through a slideshow. You can run it by itself, but you won't get advanced features such as notes and sliders added by the SlideShowPlus subclass.

Example 12-7. PP3E\Gui\SlideShow\slideShow.py

```
#########################################################################
# SlideShow: a simple photo image slideshow in Python/Tkinter;
# the base feature set coded here can be extended in subclasses;
#########################################################################

from Tkinter import *
from glob import glob
from tkMessageBox import askyesno
from tkFileDialog import askopenfilename
import random
Width, Height = 450, 450

imageTypes = [('Gif files', '.gif'),      # for file open dialog
              ('Ppm files', '.ppm'),      # plus jpg with a Tk patch,
              ('Pgm files', '.pgm'),      # plus bitmaps with BitmapImage
              ('All files', '*')]

class SlideShow(Frame):
    def __init__(self, parent=None, picdir='.', msecs=3000, **args):
```

Example 12-7. PP3E\Gui\SlideShow\slideShow.py (continued)

```
        Frame.__init__(self, parent, args)
        self.makeWidgets()
        self.pack(expand=YES, fill=BOTH)
        self.opens = picdir
        files = []
        for label, ext in imageTypes[:-1]:
            files = files + glob('%s/*%s' % (picdir, ext))
        self.images = map(lambda x: (x, PhotoImage(file=x)), files)
        self.msecs  = msecs
        self.beep   = 1
        self.drawn  = None

    def makeWidgets(self):
        self.canvas = Canvas(self, bg='white', height=Height, width=Width)
        self.canvas.pack(side=LEFT, fill=BOTH, expand=YES)
        self.onoff = Button(self, text='Start', command=self.onStart)
        self.onoff.pack(fill=X)
        Button(self, text='Open', command=self.onOpen).pack(fill=X)
        Button(self, text='Beep', command=self.onBeep).pack(fill=X)
        Button(self, text='Quit', command=self.onQuit).pack(fill=X)

    def onStart(self):
        self.loop = 1
        self.onoff.config(text='Stop', command=self.onStop)
        self.canvas.config(height=Height, width=Width)
        self.onTimer()

    def onStop(self):
        self.loop = 0
        self.onoff.config(text='Start', command=self.onStart)

    def onOpen(self):
        self.onStop()
        name = askopenfilename(initialdir=self.opens, filetypes=imageTypes)
        if name:
            if self.drawn: self.canvas.delete(self.drawn)
            img = PhotoImage(file=name)
            self.canvas.config(height=img.height(), width=img.width())
            self.drawn = self.canvas.create_image(2, 2, image=img, anchor=NW)
            self.image = name, img

    def onQuit(self):
        self.onStop()
        self.update()
        if askyesno('PyView', 'Really quit now?'):
            self.quit()

    def onBeep(self):
        self.beep = self.beep ^ 1

    def onTimer(self):
        if self.loop:
```

Example 12-7. PP3E\Gui\SlideShow\slideShow.py (continued)

```
            self.drawNext( )
            self.after(self.msecs, self.onTimer)

    def drawNext(self):
        if self.drawn: self.canvas.delete(self.drawn)
        name, img  = random.choice(self.images)
        self.drawn = self.canvas.create_image(2, 2, image=img, anchor=NW)
        self.image = name, img
        if self.beep: self.bell( )
        self.canvas.update( )

if __name__ == '__main__':
    import sys
    if len(sys.argv) == 2:
        picdir = sys.argv[1]
    else:
        picdir = '../gifs'
    root = Tk( )
    root.title('PyView 1.0')
    root.iconname('PyView')
    Label(root, text="Python Slide Show Viewer").pack( )
    SlideShow(root, picdir=picdir, bd=3, relief=SUNKEN)
    root.mainloop( )
```

To give you a better idea of what this core base class implements, Figure 12-12 shows what it looks like if run by itself (actually, two copies run by themselves) by a script called slideShow_frames, which is in this book's examples distribution.

Figure 12-12. Two attached SlideShow objects

The simple slideShow_frames scripts attach two instances of SlideShow to a single window—a feat possible only because state information is recorded in class instance variables, not in globals. The slideShow_toplevels script (also in the book's examples distribution) attaches two SlideShows to two top-level pop-up windows instead. In both cases, the slideshows run independently but are based on after events fired from the same single event loop in a single process.

PyDraw: Painting and Moving Graphics

Chapter 10 introduced simple Tkinter animation techniques (see the tour's canvasDraw variants). The PyDraw program listed here builds upon those ideas to implement a more feature-rich painting program in Python. It adds new trails and scribble drawing modes, object and background color fills, embedded photos, and more. In addition, it implements object movement and animation techniques—drawn objects may be moved around the canvas by clicking and dragging, and any drawn object can be gradually moved across the screen to a target location clicked with the mouse.

Running PyDraw

PyDraw is essentially a Tkinter canvas with lots of keyboard and mouse event bindings to allow users to perform common drawing operations. This isn't a professional-grade paint program by any definition, but it's fun to play with. In fact, you really should—it is impossible to capture things such as object motion in the medium afforded by this book. Start PyDraw from the launcher bars (or run the file *movingpics.py* from Example 12-8 directly). Press the ? key to view a help message giving available commands (or read the help string in the code listings).

Figure 12-13 shows PyDraw after a few objects have been drawn on the canvas. To move any object shown here, either click it with the middle mouse button and drag to move it with the mouse cursor, or middle-click the object, and then right-click in the spot you want it to move toward. In the latter case, PyDraw performs an animated (gradual) movement of the object to the target spot. Try this on the picture of Python creator Guido van Rossum, shown near the top of the figure, to start the famous "Moving Guido Demo" (yes, he has a sense of humor too).

Press "p" to insert photos, and use left-button drags to draw shapes. (Note to Windows users: middle-click is usually both mouse buttons at once, but you may need to configure this in your control panel.) In addition to mouse events, there are 17 keypress commands for tailoring sketches that I won't cover here. It takes a while to get the hang of what all the keyboard and mouse commands do; but once you've mastered the bindings, you too can begin generating senseless electronic artwork such as that in Figure 12-14.

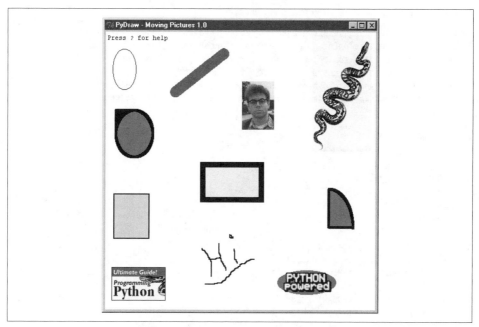

Figure 12-13. PyDraw with draw objects ready to be moved

Figure 12-14. PyDraw after substantial play

PyDraw Source Code

Like PyEdit, PyDraw lives in a single file. Two extensions that customize motion implementations are listed following the main module shown in Example 12-8.

Example 12-8. PP3E\Gui\MovingPics\movingpics.py

```
###########################################################################
# PyDraw: simple canvas paint program and object mover/animator
# uses time.sleep loops to implement object move loops, such that only
# one move can be in progress at once; this is smooth and fast, but see
# the widget.after and thread-based subclasses here for other techniques;
###########################################################################

helpstr = """--PyDraw version 1.0--
Mouse commands:
  Left        = Set target spot
  Left+Move   = Draw new object
  Double Left = Clear all objects
  Right       = Move current object
  Middle      = Select closest object
  Middle+Move = Drag current object

Keyboard commands:
  w=Pick border width  c=Pick color
  u=Pick move unit     s=Pick move delay
  o=Draw ovals         r=Draw rectangles
  l=Draw lines         a=Draw arcs
  d=Delete object      1=Raise object
  2=Lower object       f=Fill object
  b=Fill background    p=Add photo
  z=Save postscript    x=Pick pen modes
  ?=Help               other=clear text
"""

import time, sys
from Tkinter import *
from tkFileDialog import *
from tkMessageBox import *
PicDir = '../gifs'

if sys.platform[:3] == 'win':
    HelpFont = ('courier', 9, 'normal')
else:
    HelpFont = ('courier', 12, 'normal')

pickDelays = [0.01, 0.025, 0.05, 0.10, 0.25, 0.0, 0.001, 0.005]
pickUnits  = [1, 2, 4, 6, 8, 10, 12]
pickWidths = [1, 2, 5, 10, 20]
pickFills  = [None,'white','blue','red','black','yellow','green','purple']
pickPens   = ['elastic', 'scribble', 'trails']

class MovingPics:
    def __init__(self, parent=None):
        canvas = Canvas(parent, width=500, height=500, bg= 'white')
        canvas.pack(expand=YES, fill=BOTH)
        canvas.bind('<ButtonPress-1>',  self.onStart)
        canvas.bind('<B1-Motion>',      self.onGrow)
        canvas.bind('<Double-1>',       self.onClear)
```

Example 12-8. PP3E\Gui\MovingPics\movingpics.py (continued)

```
        canvas.bind('<ButtonPress-3>',  self.onMove)
        canvas.bind('<Button-2>',       self.onSelect)
        canvas.bind('<B2-Motion>',      self.onDrag)
        parent.bind('<KeyPress>',       self.onOptions)
        self.createMethod = Canvas.create_oval
        self.canvas = canvas
        self.moving = []
        self.images = []
        self.object = None
        self.where  = None
        self.scribbleMode = 0
        parent.title('PyDraw - Moving Pictures 1.0')
        parent.protocol('WM_DELETE_WINDOW', self.onQuit)
        self.realquit = parent.quit
        self.textInfo = self.canvas.create_text(
                              5, 5, anchor=NW,
                              font=HelpFont,
                              text='Press ? for help')

    def onStart(self, event):
        self.where  = event
        self.object = None

    def onGrow(self, event):
        canvas = event.widget
        if self.object and pickPens[0] == 'elastic':
            canvas.delete(self.object)
        self.object = self.createMethod(canvas,
                              self.where.x, self.where.y,    # start
                              event.x, event.y,              # stop
                              fill=pickFills[0], width=pickWidths[0])
        if pickPens[0] == 'scribble':
            self.where = event  # from here next time

    def onClear(self, event):
        if self.moving: return       # ok if moving but confusing
        event.widget.delete('all')   # use all tag
        self.images = []
        self.textInfo = self.canvas.create_text(
                              5, 5, anchor=NW,
                              font=HelpFont,
                              text='Press ? for help')

    def plotMoves(self, event):
        diffX = event.x - self.where.x               # plan animated moves
        diffY = event.y - self.where.y               # horizontal then vertical
        reptX = abs(diffX) / pickUnits[0]            # incr per move, number moves
        reptY = abs(diffY) / pickUnits[0]            # from last to event click
        incrX = pickUnits[0] * ((diffX > 0) or -1)
        incrY = pickUnits[0] * ((diffY > 0) or -1)
        return incrX, reptX, incrY, reptY
```

Example 12-8. PP3E\Gui\MovingPics\movingpics.py (continued)

```
def onMove(self, event):
    traceEvent('onMove', event, 0)                # move current object to click
    object = self.object                          # ignore some ops during mv
    if object and object not in self.moving:
        msecs = int(pickDelays[0] * 1000)
        parms = 'Delay=%d msec, Units=%d' % (msecs, pickUnits[0])
        self.setTextInfo(parms)
        self.moving.append(object)
        canvas = event.widget
        incrX, reptX, incrY, reptY = self.plotMoves(event)
        for i in range(reptX):
            canvas.move(object, incrX, 0)
            canvas.update()
            time.sleep(pickDelays[0])
        for i in range(reptY):
            canvas.move(object, 0, incrY)
            canvas.update()                       # update runs other ops
            time.sleep(pickDelays[0])             # sleep until next move
        self.moving.remove(object)
        if self.object == object: self.where  = event

def onSelect(self, event):
    self.where  = event
    self.object = self.canvas.find_closest(event.x, event.y)[0]    # tuple

def onDrag(self, event):
    diffX = event.x - self.where.x                # OK if object in moving
    diffY = event.y - self.where.y                # throws it off course
    self.canvas.move(self.object, diffX, diffY)
    self.where = event

def onOptions(self, event):
    keymap = {
        'w': lambda self: self.changeOption(pickWidths, 'Pen Width'),
        'c': lambda self: self.changeOption(pickFills,  'Color'),
        'u': lambda self: self.changeOption(pickUnits,  'Move Unit'),
        's': lambda self: self.changeOption(pickDelays, 'Move Delay'),
        'x': lambda self: self.changeOption(pickPens,   'Pen Mode'),
        'o': lambda self: self.changeDraw(Canvas.create_oval,      'Oval'),
        'r': lambda self: self.changeDraw(Canvas.create_rectangle, 'Rect'),
        'l': lambda self: self.changeDraw(Canvas.create_line,      'Line'),
        'a': lambda self: self.changeDraw(Canvas.create_arc,       'Arc'),
        'd': MovingPics.deleteObject,
        '1': MovingPics.raiseObject,
        '2': MovingPics.lowerObject,             # if only 1 call pattern
        'f': MovingPics.fillObject,              # use unbound method objects
        'b': MovingPics.fillBackground,          # else lambda passed self
        'p': MovingPics.addPhotoItem,
        'z': MovingPics.savePostscript,
        '?': MovingPics.help}
    try:
        keymap[event.char](self)
```

Example 12-8. PP3E\Gui\MovingPics\movingpics.py (continued)

```
        except KeyError:
            self.setTextInfo('Press ? for help')

    def changeDraw(self, method, name):
        self.createMethod = method              # unbound Canvas method
        self.setTextInfo('Draw Object=' + name)

    def changeOption(self, list, name):
        list.append(list[0])
        del list[0]
        self.setTextInfo('%s=%s' % (name, list[0]))

    def deleteObject(self):
        if self.object != self.textInfo:        # ok if object in moving
            self.canvas.delete(self.object)     # erases but move goes on
            self.object = None

    def raiseObject(self):
        if self.object:                         # ok if moving
            self.canvas.tkraise(self.object)    # raises while moving

    def lowerObject(self):
        if self.object:
            self.canvas.lower(self.object)

    def fillObject(self):
        if self.object:
            type = self.canvas.type(self.object)
            if type == 'image':
                pass
            elif type == 'text':
                self.canvas.itemconfig(self.object, fill=pickFills[0])
            else:
                self.canvas.itemconfig(self.object,
                            fill=pickFills[0], width=pickWidths[0])

    def fillBackground(self):
        self.canvas.config(bg=pickFills[0])

    def addPhotoItem(self):
        if not self.where: return
        filetypes=[('Gif files', '.gif'), ('All files', '*')]
        file = askopenfilename(initialdir=PicDir, filetypes=filetypes)
        if file:
            image = PhotoImage(file=file)                # load image
            self.images.append(image)                   # keep reference
            self.object = self.canvas.create_image(     # add to canvas
                            self.where.x, self.where.y, # at last spot
                            image=image, anchor=NW)

    def savePostscript(self):
        file = asksaveasfilename()
```

Example 12-8. PP3E\Gui\MovingPics\movingpics.py (continued)

```
        if file:
            self.canvas.postscript(file=file)  # save canvas to file

    def help(self):
        self.setTextInfo(helpstr)
        #showinfo('PyDraw', helpstr)

    def setTextInfo(self, text):
        self.canvas.dchars(self.textInfo, 0, END)
        self.canvas.insert(self.textInfo, 0, text)
        self.canvas.tkraise(self.textInfo)

    def onQuit(self):
        if self.moving:
            self.setTextInfo("Can't quit while move in progress")
        else:
            self.realquit()  # std wm delete: err msg if move in progress

def traceEvent(label, event, fullTrace=1):
    print label
    if fullTrace:
        for key in dir(event): print key, '=>', getattr(event, key)

if __name__ == '__main__':
    from sys import argv                       # when this file is executed
    if len(argv) == 2: PicDir = argv[1]        # '..' fails if run elsewhere
    root = Tk( )                               # make, run a MovingPics object
    MovingPics(root)
    root.mainloop( )
```

Just as in Chapter 10's canvasDraw examples, we can add support for moving more than one object at the same time with either after scheduled callback events or threads. Example 12-9 shows a MovingPics subclass that codes the necessary customizations to do parallel moves with after events. Run this file directly to see the difference; I could try to capture the notion of multiple objects in motion with a screenshot, but I would almost certainly fail.

Example 12-9. PP3E\Gui\MovingPics\movingpics_after.py

```
###############################################################################
# PyDraw-after: simple canvas paint program and object mover/animator
# use widget.after scheduled events to implement object move loops, such
# that more than one can be in motion at once without having to use threads;
# this does moves in parallel, but seems to be slower than time.sleep version;
# see also canvasDraw in Tour: builds and passes the incX/incY list at once:
# here, would be allmoves = ([(incrX, 0)] * reptX) + ([(0, incrY)] * reptY)
###############################################################################

from movingpics import *

class MovingPicsAfter(MovingPics):
```

Example 12-9. PP3E\Gui\MovingPics\movingpics_after.py (continued)

```
    def doMoves(self, delay, objectId, incrX, reptX, incrY, reptY):
        if reptX:
            self.canvas.move(objectId, incrX, 0)
            reptX -= 1
        else:
            self.canvas.move(objectId, 0, incrY)
            reptY -= 1
        if not (reptX or reptY):
            self.moving.remove(objectId)
        else:
            self.canvas.after(delay,
                self.doMoves, delay, objectId, incrX, reptX, incrY, reptY)

    def onMove(self, event):
        traceEvent('onMove', event, 0)
        object = self.object                      # move cur obj to click spot
        if object:
            msecs = int(pickDelays[0] * 1000)
            parms = 'Delay=%d msec, Units=%d' % (msecs, pickUnits[0])
            self.setTextInfo(parms)
            self.moving.append(object)
            incrX, reptX, incrY, reptY = self.plotMoves(event)
            self.doMoves(msecs, object, incrX, reptX, incrY, reptY)
            self.where = event

if __name__ == '__main__':
    from sys import argv                          # when this file is executed
    if len(argv) == 2:
        import movingpics                         # not this module's global
        movingpics.PicDir = argv[1]               # and from* doesn't link names
    root = Tk()
    MovingPicsAfter(root)
    root.mainloop()
```

Now, while one or more moves are in progress, you can start another by middle-clicking on another object and right-clicking on the spot to which you want it to move. It starts its journey immediately, even if other objects are in motion. Each object's scheduled after events are added to the same event loop queue and dispatched by Tkinter as soon as possible after a timer expiration. If you run this subclass module directly, you'll probably notice that movement isn't quite as fast or as smooth as in the original, but multiple moves can overlap in time.

Example 12-10 shows how to achieve such parallelism with threads. This process works, but as we learned in Chapters 10 and 11, updating GUIs in spawned threads is generally a dangerous affair. On my machine, the movement that this script implements with threads is a bit jerkier than the original version—a reflection of the overhead incurred for switching the interpreter (and CPU) between multiple threads.

Example 12-10. PP3E\Gui\MovingPics\movingpics_threads.py

```
###################################################################
# use threads to move objects; seems to work on Windows provided
# that canvas.update( ) not called by threads(else exits with fatal
# errors, some objs start moving immediately after drawn, etc.);
# at least some canvas method calls must be thread safe in Tkinter;
# this is less smooth than time.sleep, and is dangerous in general:
# threads are best coded to update global vars, not change GUI;
###################################################################

import thread, time, sys, random
from Tkinter import Tk, mainloop
from movingpics import MovingPics, pickUnits, pickDelays

class MovingPicsThreaded(MovingPics):
    def __init__(self, parent=None):
        MovingPics.__init__(self, parent)
        self.mutex = thread.allocate_lock( )
        import sys
        #sys.setcheckinterval(0) # switch after each vm op- doesn't help

    def onMove(self, event):
        object = self.object
        if object and object not in self.moving:
            msecs = int(pickDelays[0] * 1000)
            parms = 'Delay=%d msec, Units=%d' % (msecs, pickUnits[0])
            self.setTextInfo(parms)
            #self.mutex.acquire( )
            self.moving.append(object)
            #self.mutex.release( )
            thread.start_new_thread(self.doMove, (object, event))

    def doMove(self, object, event):
        canvas = event.widget
        incrX, reptX, incrY, reptY = self.plotMoves(event)
        for i in range(reptX):
            canvas.move(object, incrX, 0)
            # canvas.update( )
            time.sleep(pickDelays[0])            # this can change
        for i in range(reptY):
            canvas.move(object, 0, incrY)
            # canvas.update( )                    # update runs other ops
            time.sleep(pickDelays[0])            # sleep until next move
        #self.mutex.acquire( )
        self.moving.remove(object)
        if self.object == object: self.where = event
        #self.mutex.release( )

if __name__ == '__main__':
    root = Tk( )
    MovingPicsThreaded(root)
    mainloop( )
```

PyClock: An Analog/Digital Clock Widget

One of the first things I always look for when exploring a new computer interface is a clock. Because I spend so much time glued to computers, it's essentially impossible for me to keep track of the time unless it is right there on the screen in front of me (and even then, it's iffy). The next program, PyClock, implements such a clock widget in Python. It's not substantially different from the clock programs that you may be used to seeing on the X Window System. Because it is coded in Python, though, this one is both easily customized and fully portable among Windows, the X Window System, and Macs, like all the code in this chapter. In addition to advanced GUI techniques, this example demonstrates Python `math` and `time` module tools.

A Quick Geometry Lesson

Before I show you PyClock, though, let me provide a little background and a confession. Quick—how do you plot points on a circle? This, along with time formats and events, turns out to be a core concept in clock widget programs. To draw an analog clock face on a canvas widget, you essentially need to be able to sketch a circle—the clock face itself is composed of points on a circle, and the second, minute, and hour hands of the clock are really just lines from a circle's center out to a point on the circle. Digital clocks are simpler to draw, but not much to look at.

Now the confession: when I started writing PyClock, I couldn't answer the last paragraph's opening question. I had utterly forgotten the math needed to sketch out points on a circle (as had most of the professional software developers I queried about this magic formula). It happens. After going unused for a few decades, such knowledge tends to be garbage collected. I finally was able to dust off a few neurons long enough to code the plotting math needed, but it wasn't my finest intellectual hour.[*]

If you are in the same boat, I don't have space to teach geometry in depth here, but I can show you one way to code the point-plotting formulas in Python in simple terms. Before tackling the more complex task of implementing a clock, I wrote the `plotterGui` script shown in Example 12-11 to focus on just the circle-plotting logic.

Its `point` function is where the circle logic lives—it plots the (X,Y) coordinates of a point on the circle, given the relative point number, the total number of points to be placed on the circle, and the circle's radius (the distance from the circle's center to the points drawn upon it). It first calculates the point's angle from the top by dividing 360 by the number of points to be plotted, and then multiplying by the point

---

[*] Lest that make software engineers seem too doltish, I should also note that I have been called on repeatedly to teach Python programming to physicists, all of whom had mathematical training well in advance of my own, and many of whom were still happily abusing FORTRAN common blocks and go-tos. Specialization in modern society can make fools of us all.

number; in case you've forgotten too, it's 360 degrees around the whole circle (e.g., if you plot 4 points on a circle, each is 90 degrees from the last, or 360/4). Python's standard math module gives all the required constants and functions from that point forward—pi, sine, and cosine. The math is really not too obscure if you study this long enough (in conjunction with your old geometry text if necessary). See the book's examples distribution for alternative ways to code the number crunching.

Even if you don't care about the math, though, check out this script's circle function. Given the (X,Y) coordinates of a point on the circle returned by point, it draws a line from the circle's center out to the point and a small rectangle around the point itself—not unlike the hands and points of an analog clock. Canvas tags are used to associate drawn objects for deletion before each plot.

Example 12-11. PP3E\Gui\Clock\plotterGui.py

```python
# plot circles (like I did in high school)

import math, sys
from Tkinter import *

def point(tick, range, radius):
    angle = tick * (360.0 / range)
    radiansPerDegree = math.pi / 180
    pointX = int( round( radius * math.sin(angle * radiansPerDegree) ))
    pointY = int( round( radius * math.cos(angle * radiansPerDegree) ))
    return (pointX, pointY)

def circle(points, radius, centerX, centerY, slow=0):
    canvas.delete('lines')
    canvas.delete('points')
    for i in range(points):
        x, y = point(i+1, points, radius-4)
        scaledX, scaledY = (x + centerX), (centerY - y)
        canvas.create_line(centerX, centerY, scaledX, scaledY, tag='lines')
        canvas.create_rectangle(scaledX-2, scaledY-2,
                                scaledX+2, scaledY+2,
                                        fill='red', tag='points')
        if slow: canvas.update()

def plotter():
    circle(scaleVar.get(), (Width / 2), originX, originY, checkVar.get())

def makewidgets():
    global canvas, scaleVar, checkVar
    canvas = Canvas(width=Width, height=Width)
    canvas.pack(side=TOP)
    scaleVar = IntVar()
    checkVar = IntVar()
    scale = Scale(label='Points on circle', variable=scaleVar, from_=1, to=360)
    scale.pack(side=LEFT)
```

Example 12-11. PP3E\Gui\Clock\plotterGui.py (continued)

```
    Checkbutton(text='Slow mode', variable=checkVar).pack(side=LEFT)
    Button(text='Plot', command=plotter).pack(side=LEFT, padx=50)

if __name__ == '__main__':
    Width = 500                                 # default width, height
    if len(sys.argv) == 2: Width = int(sys.argv[1])   # width cmdline arg?
    originX = originY = Width / 2                # same as circle radius
    makewidgets()                               # on default Tk root
    mainloop()
```

The circle defaults to 500 pixels wide unless you pass a width on the command line. Given a number of points on a circle, this script marks out the circle in clockwise order every time you press Plot, by drawing lines out from the center to small rectangles at points on the circle's shape. Move the slider to plot a different number of points and click the checkbox to make the drawing happen slow enough to notice the clockwise order in which lines and points are drawn (this forces the script to update the display after each line is drawn). Figure 12-15 shows the result for plotting 120 points with the circle width set to 400 on the command line; if you ask for 60 and 12 points on the circle, the relationship to clock faces and hands starts becoming clearer.

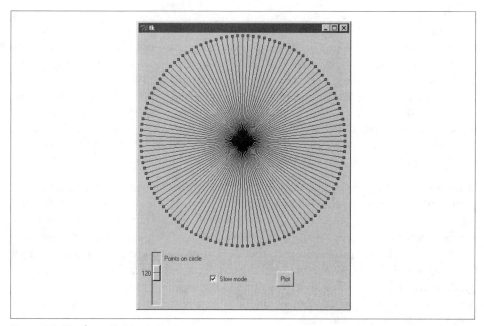

Figure 12-15. plotterGui in action

For more help, this book's examples distribution also includes text-based versions of this plotting script that print circle point coordinates to the stdout stream for review, instead of rendering them in a GUI. See the plotterText scripts in the clock's directory. Here is the sort of output they produce when plotting 4 and 12 points on a circle that is 400 points wide and high; the output format is simply:

```
pointnumber : angle = (Xcoordinate, Ycoordinate)
```

and assumes that the circle is centered at coordinate (0,0):

```
----------
1 : 90.0 = (200, 0)
2 : 180.0 = (0, -200)
3 : 270.0 = (-200, 0)
4 : 360.0 = (0, 200)
----------
1 : 30.0 = (100, 173)
2 : 60.0 = (173, 100)
3 : 90.0 = (200, 0)
4 : 120.0 = (173, -100)
5 : 150.0 = (100, -173)
6 : 180.0 = (0, -200)
7 : 210.0 = (-100, -173)
8 : 240.0 = (-173, -100)
9 : 270.0 = (-200, 0)
10 : 300.0 = (-173, 100)
11 : 330.0 = (-100, 173)
12 : 360.0 = (0, 200)
----------
```

To understand how these points are mapped to a canvas, you first need to know that the width and height of a circle are always the same—the radius × 2. Because Tkinter canvas (X,Y) coordinates start at (0,0) in the upper-left corner, the plotter GUI must offset the circle's center point to coordinates (width/2, width/2)—the origin point from which lines are drawn. For instance, in a 400×400 circle, the canvas center is (200,200). A line to the 90-degree angle point on the right side of the circle runs from (200,200) to (400,200)—the result of adding the (200,0) point coordinates plotted for the radius and angle. A line to the bottom at 180 degrees runs from (200,200) to (200,400) after factoring in the (0,-200) point plotted.

This point-plotting algorithm used by plotterGui, along with a few scaling constants, is at the heart of the PyClock analog display. If this still seems a bit much, I suggest you focus on the PyClock script's *digital* display implementation first; the analog geometry plots are really just extensions of underlying timing mechanisms used for both display modes. In fact, the clock itself is structured as a generic Frame object that *embeds* digital and analog display objects and dispatches time change and resize events to both in the same way. The analog display is an attached Canvas that knows how to draw circles, but the digital object is simply an attached Frame with labels to show time components.

Running PyClock

Apart from the circle geometry bit, the rest of PyClock is straightforward. It simply draws a clock face to represent the current time and uses widget after methods to wake itself up 10 times per second to check whether the system time has rolled over to the next second. On second rollovers, the analog second, minute, and hour hands are redrawn to reflect the new time (or the text of the digital display's labels is changed). In terms of GUI construction, the analog display is etched out on a canvas, redrawn whenever the window is resized, and changes to a digital format upon request.

PyClock also puts Python's standard time module into service to fetch and convert system time information as needed for a clock. In brief, the onTimer method gets system time with time.time, a built-in tool that returns a floating-point number giving seconds since the *epoch*—the point from which your computer counts time. The time.localtime call is then used to convert epoch time into a tuple that contains hour, minute, and second values; see the script and Python library manual for additional time-related call details.

Checking the system time 10 times per second may seem intense, but it guarantees that the second hand ticks when it should, without jerks or skips (after events aren't precisely timed). It is not a significant CPU drain on systems I use.[*] On Linux and

---

[*] Speaking of performance, when I first wrote this example, I ran multiple clocks on all my test machines—from a 650 MHz Pentium III to an "old" 200 MHz Pentium I—without seeing any degraded performance in any running clocks. The PyDemos script, for instance, launches six clocks that run in the same process, and all update smoothly. They probably do on older machines too, but mine have collected too much dust to yield useful metrics.

Windows, PyClock uses negligible processor resource—what it does use is spent largely on screen updates in analog display mode, not on after events. To minimize screen updates, PyClock redraws only clock hands on second rollovers; points on the clock's circle are redrawn only at startup and on window resizes. Figure 12-16 shows the default initial PyClock display format you get when the file *clock.py* is run directly.

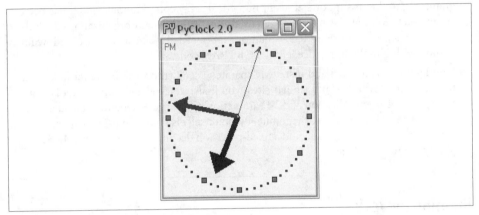

Figure 12-16. PyClock default analog display

The clock hand lines are given arrows at their endpoints with the canvas line object's arrow and arrowshape options. The arrow option can be first, last, none, or both; the arrowshape option takes a tuple giving the length of the arrow touching the line, its overall length, and its width.

Like PyView, PyClock also uses the widget pack_forget and pack methods to dynamically erase and redraw portions of the display on demand (i.e., in response to bound events). Clicking on the clock with a left mouse button changes its display to digital by erasing the analog widgets and drawing the digital interface; you get the simpler display captured in Figure 12-17.

Figure 12-17. PyClock goes digital

This digital display form is useful if you want to conserve real estate on your computer screen and minimize PyClock CPU utilization (it incurs very little screen update overhead). Left-clicking on the clock again changes back to the analog display. The analog and digital displays are both constructed when the script starts, but only one is ever packed at any given time.

A right mouse click on the clock in either display mode shows or hides an attached label that gives the current date in simple text form. Figure 12-18 shows a PyClock running with a digital display, a clicked-on date label, and a centered photo image object.

Figure 12-18. PyClock extended display with an image

The image in the middle of Figure 12-18 is added by passing in a configuration object with appropriate settings to the PyClock object constructor. In fact, almost everything about this display can be customized with attributes in PyClock configuration objects—hand colors, clock tick colors, center photos, and initial size.

Because PyClock's analog display is based upon a manually sketched figure on a canvas, it has to process window *resize* events itself: whenever the window shrinks or expands, the clock face has to be redrawn and scaled for the new window size. To catch screen resizes, the script registers for the <Configure> event with bind; surprisingly, this isn't a top-level window manager event like the Close button. As you expand a PyClock, the clock face gets bigger with the window—try expanding, shrinking, and maximizing the clock window on your computer. Because the clock face is plotted in a square coordinate system, PyClock always expands in equal horizontal and vertical proportions, though; if you simply make the window only wider or taller, the clock is unchanged.

New in this edition and version is a countdown timer feature: press the "s" or "m" key to pop up a simple dialog for entering the number of seconds or minutes for the countdown, respectively. Once the countdown expires, the pop up in Figure 12-19 appears and fills the entire screen on Windows. I sometimes use this in classes I teach to remind myself and my students when it's time to move on (the effect is more striking when this pop up is projected onto an entire wall!).

Finally, like PyEdit, PyClock can be run either standalone or attached to and embedded in other GUIs that need to display the current time. When standalone, the windows module from the last chapter (Example 11-13) is reused here to get a window icon, title, and quit pop up for free. To make it easy to start preconfigured

Figure 12-19. PyClock countdown timer expired

clocks, a utility module called clockStyles provides a set of clock configuration objects you can import, subclass to extend, and pass to the clock constructor; Figure 12-20 shows a few of the preconfigured clock styles and sizes in action, ticking away in sync.

Each of these clocks uses after events to check for system-time rollover 10 times per second. When run as top-level windows in the same process, all receive a timer event from the same event loop. When started as independent programs, each has an event loop of its own. Either way, their second hands sweep in unison each second.

PyClock Source Code

All of the PyClock source code lives in one file, except for the precoded configuration style objects. If you study the code at the bottom of the file shown in Example 12-12, you'll notice that you can either make a clock object with a configuration object passed in or specify configuration options by command-line arguments (in which case, the script simply builds a configuration object for you). More generally, you can run this file directly to start a clock, import and make its objects with configuration objects to get a more custom display, or import and attach its objects

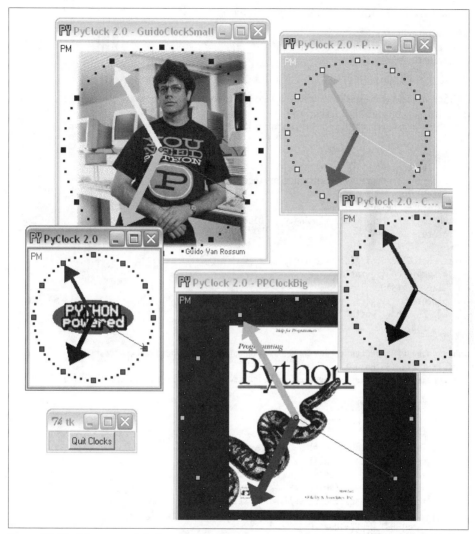

Figure 12-20. A few canned clock styles (Guido's photo reprinted with permission from Dr. Dobb's Journal)

to other GUIs. For instance, PyGadgets in Chapter 10 runs this file with command-line options to tailor the display.

Example 12-12. PP3E\Gui\Clock\clock.py

```
###############################################################################
# PyClock 2.0: a clock GUI, with both analog and digital display modes,
# a pop-up date label, clock face images, resizing, etc.  May be run both
# standalone, or embedded (attached) in other GUIs that need a clock.
# New in 2.0: s/m keys set seconds/minutes timer for pop-up msg; window icon.
###############################################################################
```

Example 12-12. PP3E\Gui\Clock\clock.py (continued)

```python
from Tkinter import *
from tkSimpleDialog import askinteger
import math, time, sys


###############################################################################
# Option configuration classes
###############################################################################


class ClockConfig:
    # defaults--override in instance or subclass
    size = 200                                    # width=height
    bg, fg = 'beige', 'brown'                     # face, tick colors
    hh, mh, sh, cog = 'black', 'navy', 'blue', 'red'  # clock hands, center
    picture = None                                # face photo file

class PhotoClockConfig(ClockConfig):
    # sample configuration
    size    = 320
    picture = '../gifs/ora-pp.gif'
    bg, hh, mh = 'white', 'blue', 'orange'


###############################################################################
# Digital display object
###############################################################################


class DigitalDisplay(Frame):
    def __init__(self, parent, cfg):
        Frame.__init__(self, parent)
        self.hour = Label(self)
        self.mins = Label(self)
        self.secs = Label(self)
        self.ampm = Label(self)
        for label in self.hour, self.mins, self.secs, self.ampm:
            label.config(bd=4, relief=SUNKEN, bg=cfg.bg, fg=cfg.fg)
            label.pack(side=LEFT)

    def onUpdate(self, hour, mins, secs, ampm, cfg):
        mins = str(mins).zfill(2)                          # or '%02d' % x
        self.hour.config(text=str(hour), width=4)
        self.mins.config(text=str(mins), width=4)
        self.secs.config(text=str(secs), width=4)
        self.ampm.config(text=str(ampm), width=4)

    def onResize(self, newWidth, newHeight, cfg):
        pass  # nothing to redraw here
```

Example 12-12. PP3E\Gui\Clock\clock.py (continued)

```
###############################################################################
# Analog display object
###############################################################################

class AnalogDisplay(Canvas):
    def __init__(self, parent, cfg):
        Canvas.__init__(self, parent,
                            width=cfg.size, height=cfg.size, bg=cfg.bg)
        self.drawClockface(cfg)
        self.hourHand = self.minsHand = self.secsHand = self.cog = None

    def drawClockface(self, cfg):                            # on start and resize
        if cfg.picture:                                      # draw ovals, picture
            try:
                self.image = PhotoImage(file=cfg.picture)         # bkground
            except:
                self.image = BitmapImage(file=cfg.picture)        # save ref
            imgx = (cfg.size - self.image.width())  / 2           # center it
            imgy = (cfg.size - self.image.height()) / 2
            self.create_image(imgx+1, imgy+1,  anchor=NW, image=self.image)
        originX =  originY = radius = cfg.size/2
        for i in range(60):
            x, y = self.point(i, 60, radius-6, originX, originY)
            self.create_rectangle(x-1, y-1, x+1, y+1, fill=cfg.fg)  # mins
        for i in range(12):
            x, y = self.point(i, 12, radius-6, originX, originY)
            self.create_rectangle(x-3, y-3, x+3, y+3, fill=cfg.fg)  # hours
        self.ampm = self.create_text(3, 3, anchor=NW, fill=cfg.fg)

    def point(self, tick, units, radius, originX, originY):
        angle = tick * (360.0 / units)
        radiansPerDegree = math.pi / 180
        pointX = int( round( radius * math.sin(angle * radiansPerDegree) ))
        pointY = int( round( radius * math.cos(angle * radiansPerDegree) ))
        return (pointX + originX+1), (originY+1 - pointY)

    def onUpdate(self, hour, mins, secs, ampm, cfg):         # on timer callback
        if self.cog:                                         # redraw hands, cog
            self.delete(self.cog)
            self.delete(self.hourHand)
            self.delete(self.minsHand)
            self.delete(self.secsHand)
        originX = originY = radius = cfg.size/2
        hour = hour + (mins / 60.0)
        hx, hy = self.point(hour, 12, (radius * .80), originX, originY)
        mx, my = self.point(mins, 60, (radius * .90), originX, originY)
        sx, sy = self.point(secs, 60, (radius * .95), originX, originY)
        self.hourHand = self.create_line(originX, originY, hx, hy,
                            width=(cfg.size * .04),
                            arrow='last', arrowshape=(25,25,15), fill=cfg.hh)
        self.minsHand = self.create_line(originX, originY, mx, my,
                            width=(cfg.size * .03),
```

Example 12-12. PP3E\Gui\Clock\clock.py (continued)

```
                             arrow='last', arrowshape=(20,20,10), fill=cfg.mh)
        self.secsHand = self.create_line(originX, originY, sx, sy,
                             width=1,
                             arrow='last', arrowshape=(5,10,5), fill=cfg.sh)
        cogsz = cfg.size * .01
        self.cog = self.create_oval(originX-cogsz, originY+cogsz,
                                     originX+cogsz, originY-cogsz, fill=cfg.cog)
        self.dchars(self.ampm, 0, END)
        self.insert(self.ampm, END, ampm)

    def onResize(self, newWidth, newHeight, cfg):
        newSize = min(newWidth, newHeight)
        #print 'analog onResize', cfg.size+4, newSize
        if newSize != cfg.size+4:
            cfg.size = newSize-4
            self.delete('all')
            self.drawClockface(cfg)   # onUpdate called next


###########################################################################
# Clock composite object
###########################################################################

ChecksPerSec = 10  # second change timer

class Clock(Frame):
    def __init__(self, config=ClockConfig, parent=None):
        Frame.__init__(self, parent)
        self.cfg = config
        self.makeWidgets(parent)                    # children are packed but
        self.labelOn = 0                            # clients pack or grid me
        self.display = self.digitalDisplay
        self.lastSec = self.lastMin = -1
        self.countdownSeconds = 0
        self.onSwitchMode(None)
        self.onTimer()

    def makeWidgets(self, parent):
        self.digitalDisplay = DigitalDisplay(self, self.cfg)
        self.analogDisplay  = AnalogDisplay(self,  self.cfg)
        self.dateLabel      = Label(self, bd=3, bg='red', fg='blue')
        parent.bind('<ButtonPress-1>', self.onSwitchMode)
        parent.bind('<ButtonPress-3>', self.onToggleLabel)
        parent.bind('<Configure>',     self.onResize)
        parent.bind('<KeyPress-s>',    self.onCountdownSec)
        parent.bind('<KeyPress-m>',    self.onCountdownMin)

    def onSwitchMode(self, event):
        self.display.pack_forget()
        if self.display == self.analogDisplay:
            self.display = self.digitalDisplay
        else:
```

Example 12-12. PP3E\Gui\Clock\clock.py (continued)

```
        self.display = self.analogDisplay
        self.display.pack(side=TOP, expand=YES, fill=BOTH)

    def onToggleLabel(self, event):
        self.labelOn += 1
        if self.labelOn % 2:
            self.dateLabel.pack(side=BOTTOM, fill=X)
        else:
            self.dateLabel.pack_forget( )
        self.update( )

    def onResize(self, event):
        if event.widget == self.display:
            self.display.onResize(event.width, event.height, self.cfg)

    def onTimer(self):
        secsSinceEpoch = time.time( )
        timeTuple      = time.localtime(secsSinceEpoch)
        hour, min, sec = timeTuple[3:6]
        if sec != self.lastSec:
            self.lastSec = sec
            ampm = ((hour >= 12) and 'PM') or 'AM'          # 0...23
            hour = (hour % 12) or 12                        # 12..11
            self.display.onUpdate(hour, min, sec, ampm, self.cfg)
            self.dateLabel.config(text=time.ctime(secsSinceEpoch))
            self.countdownSeconds -= 1
            if self.countdownSeconds == 0:
                self.onCountdownExpire( )                   # countdown timer
        self.after(1000 / ChecksPerSec, self.onTimer)  # run N times per second

    def onCountdownSec(self, event):
        secs = askinteger('Countdown', 'Seconds?')
        if secs: self.countdownSeconds = secs

    def onCountdownMin(self, event):
        secs = askinteger('Countdown', 'Minutes')
        if secs: self.countdownSeconds = secs * 60

    def onCountdownExpire(self):
        # caveat: only one active, no progress indicator
        win = Toplevel( )
        msg = Button(win, text='Timer Expired!', command=win.destroy)
        msg.config(font=('courier', 80, 'normal'), fg='white', bg='navy')
        msg.config(padx=10, pady=10)
        msg.pack(expand=YES, fill=BOTH)
        win.lift( )                              # raise above siblings
        if sys.platform[:3] == 'win':            # full screen on Windows
            win.state('zoomed')
```

Example 12-12. PP3E\Gui\Clock\clock.py (continued)

```
###########################################################################
# Standalone clocks
###########################################################################


# b/w compat: manual window borders, passed-in parent
appname = 'PyClock 2.0'

class ClockWindow(Clock):
    def __init__(self, config=ClockConfig, parent=None, name=''):
        Clock.__init__(self, config, parent)
        self.pack(expand=YES, fill=BOTH)
        title = appname
        if name: title = appname + ' - ' + name
        self.master.title(title)                    # master=parent or default
        self.master.protocol('WM_DELETE_WINDOW', self.quit)


# use new custom Tk, Toplevel for icons, etc.
from PP3E.Gui.Tools.windows import PopupWindow, MainWindow

class ClockPopup(PopupWindow):
    def __init__(self, config=ClockConfig, name=''):
        PopupWindow.__init__(self, appname, name)
        clock = Clock(config, self)
        clock.pack(expand=YES, fill=BOTH)

class ClockMain(MainWindow):
    def __init__(self, config=ClockConfig, name=''):
        MainWindow.__init__(self, appname, name)
        clock = Clock(config, self)
        clock.pack(expand=YES, fill=BOTH)


###########################################################################
# Program run
###########################################################################


if __name__ == '__main__':
    def getOptions(config, argv):
        for attr in dir(ClockConfig):               # fill default config obj,
            try:                                    # from "-attr val" cmd args
                ix = argv.index('-' + attr)
            except:
                continue
            else:
                if ix in range(1, len(argv)-1):
                    if type(getattr(ClockConfig, attr)) == type(0):
                        setattr(config, attr, int(argv[ix+1]))
                    else:
                        setattr(config, attr, argv[ix+1])
```

Example 12-12. PP3E\Gui\Clock\clock.py (continued)

```
    #config = PhotoClockConfig( )
    config = ClockConfig( )
    if len(sys.argv) >= 2:
        getOptions(config, sys.argv)          # clock.py -size n -bg 'blue'...
    #myclock = ClockWindow(config, Tk( ))     # parent is Tk root if standalone
    #myclock = ClockPopup(ClockConfig( ), 'popup')
    myclock = ClockMain(config)
    myclock.mainloop( )
```

And finally, Example 12-13 shows the module that is actually run from the PyDemos launcher script—it predefines a handful of clock styles and runs six of them at once, attached to new top-level windows for a demo effect (though one clock per screen is usually enough in practice, even for me).[*]

Example 12-13. PP3E\Gui\Clock\clockStyles.py

```
from clock import *
from Tkinter import mainloop

gifdir = '../gifs/'
if __name__ == '__main__':
    from sys import argv
    if len(argv) > 1:
        gifdir = argv[1] + '/'

class PPClockBig(PhotoClockConfig):
    picture, bg, fg = gifdir + 'ora-pp.gif', 'navy', 'green'

class PPClockSmall(ClockConfig):
    size    = 175
    picture = gifdir + 'ora-pp.gif'
    bg, fg, hh, mh = 'white', 'red', 'blue', 'orange'

class GilliganClock(ClockConfig):
    size    = 550
    picture = gifdir + 'gilligan.gif'
    bg, fg, hh, mh = 'black', 'white', 'green', 'yellow'

class GuidoClock(GilliganClock):
    size = 400
    picture = gifdir + 'guido_ddj.gif'
    bg = 'navy'

class GuidoClockSmall(GuidoClock):
    size, fg = 278, 'black'

class OusterhoutClock(ClockConfig):
```

---

[*] Note that some images named in this script may be missing in the book examples distribution due to copyright concerns. Insert lawyer joke here.

Example 12-13. PP3E\Gui\Clock\clockStyles.py (continued)

```
    size, picture = 200, gifdir + 'ousterhout-new.gif'
    bg, fg, hh    = 'black', 'gold', 'brown'

class GreyClock(ClockConfig):
    bg, fg, hh, mh, sh = 'grey', 'black', 'black', 'black', 'white'

class PinkClock(ClockConfig):
    bg, fg, hh, mh, sh = 'pink', 'yellow', 'purple', 'orange', 'yellow'

class PythonPoweredClock(ClockConfig):
    bg, size, picture = 'white', 175, gifdir + 'pythonPowered.gif'

if __name__ == '__main__':
    for configClass in [
        ClockConfig,
        PPClockBig,
        #PPClockSmall,
        GuidoClockSmall,
        #GilliganClock,
        OusterhoutClock,
        #GreyClock,
        PinkClock,
        PythonPoweredClock
    ]:
        ClockPopup(configClass, configClass.__name__)
    Button(text='Quit Clocks', command='exit').pack()
    mainloop()
```

PyToe: A Tic-Tac-Toe Game Widget

Finally, a bit of fun to close out this chapter; our last example, PyToe, implements an artificially intelligent tic-tac-toe (sometimes called "naughts and crosses") game-playing program in Python. Most readers are probably familiar with this simple game, so I won't dwell on its details. In short, players take turns marking board positions, in an attempt to occupy an entire row, column, or diagonal. The first player to fill such a pattern wins.

In PyToe, board positions are marked with mouse clicks, and one of the players is a Python program. The game board itself is displayed with a simple Tkinter GUI; by default, PyToe builds a 3×3 game board (the standard tic-tac-toe setup), but it can be configured to build and play an arbitrary $N \times N$ game.

When it comes time for the computer to select a move, artificial intelligence (AI) algorithms are used to score potential moves and search a tree of candidate moves and countermoves. This is a fairly simple problem as gaming programs go, and the heuristics used to pick moves are not perfect. Still, PyToe is usually smart enough to spot wins a few moves in advance of the user.

Running PyToe

PyToe's GUI is implemented as a frame of packed labels, with mouse-click bindings on the labels to catch user moves. The label's text is configured with the player's mark after each move, computer or user. The GuiMaker class we coded earlier in the prior chapter is also reused here to add a simple menu bar at the top (but no toolbar is drawn at the button, because PyToe leaves its descriptor empty). By default, the user's mark is "X" and PyToe's is "O." Figure 12-21 shows PyToe on the verge of beating me one of two ways.

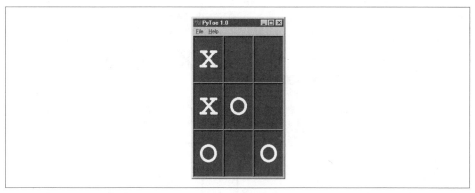

Figure 12-21. PyToe thinking its way to a win

Figure 12-22 shows PyToe's help pop-up dialog, which lists its command-line configuration options. You can specify colors and font sizes for board labels, the player who moves first, the mark of the user ("X" or "O"), the board size (to override the 3×3 default), and the move selection strategy for the computer (e.g., "Minimax" performs a move tree search to spot wins and losses, and "Expert1" and "Expert2" use static scoring heuristics functions).

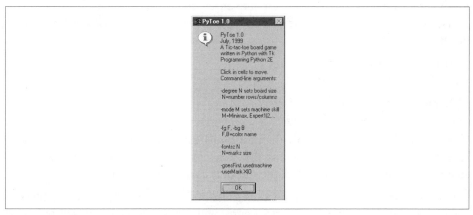

Figure 12-22. PyToe help pop up with options info

The AI gaming techniques used in PyToe are CPU intensive, and some computer move selection schemes take longer than others, but their speed varies mostly with the speed of your computer. Move selection delays are fractions of a second long on my machine for a 3×3 game board, for all "-mode" move-selection strategy options.

Figure 12-23 shows an alternative PyToe configuration just after it beat me. Despite the scenes captured for this book, under some move selection options, I do still win once in awhile. In larger boards and more complex games, PyToe's move selection algorithms become even more useful.

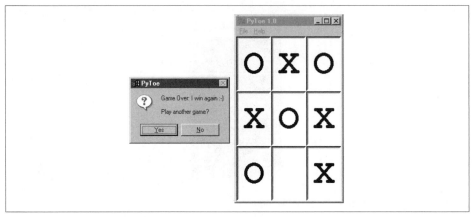

Figure 12-23. An alternative layout

PyToe Source Code (Book Examples Distribution)

PyToe is a big system that assumes some AI background knowledge and doesn't really demonstrate anything new in terms of GUIs. Partly because of that, but mostly because I've already exceeded my page limit for this book, I'm going to refer you to the book's examples distribution for its source code instead of listing it all here. Please see these two files in the examples distribution for PyToe implementation details:

PP3E\Ai\TicTacToe\tictactoe.py
    A top-level wrapper script

PP3E\Ai\TicTacToe\tictactoe_lists.py
    The meat of the implementation

If you do look, though, probably the best hint I can give you is that the data structure used to represent board state is the crux of the matter. That is, if you understand the way boards are modeled, the rest of the code comes naturally.

For instance, the lists-based variant uses a list-of-lists to representation the board's state, along with a simple dictionary of entry widgets for the GUI indexed by board coordinates. Clearing the board after a game is simply a matter of clearing the underlying data structures, as shown in this code excerpt from the examples named earlier:

```
def clearBoard(self):
    for row, col in self.label.keys():
        self.board[row][col] = Empty
        self.label[(row, col)].config(text=' ')
```

Similarly, picking a move, at least in random mode, is simply a matter of picking a nonempty slot in the board array and storing the machine's mark there and in the GUI (degree is the board's size):

```
def machineMove(self):
    row, col = self.pickMove()
    self.board[row][col] = self.machineMark
    self.label[(row, col)].config(text=self.machineMark)

def pickMove(self):
    empties = []
    for row in self.degree:
        for col in self.degree:
            if self.board[row][col] == Empty:
                empties.append((row, col))
    return random.choice(empties)
```

Finally, checking for an end-of-game state boils down to inspecting rows, columns, and diagonals in the two-dimensional list-of-lists board in this scheme:

```
def checkDraw(self, board=None):
    board = board or self.board
    for row in board:
        if Empty in row:
            return 0
    return 1 # none empty: draw or win

def checkWin(self, mark, board=None):
    board = board or self.board
    for row in board:
        if row.count(mark) == self.degree:     # check across
            return 1
    for col in range(self.degree):
        for row in board:                      # check down
            if row[col] != mark:
                break
        else:
            return 1
    for row in range(self.degree):             # check diag1
        col = row                              # row == col
        if board[row][col] != mark: break
    else:
        return 1
    for row in range(self.degree):             # check diag2
        col = (self.degree-1) - row            # row+col = degree-1
        if board[row][col] != mark: break
```

```
        else:
            return 1

    def checkFinish(self):
        if self.checkWin(self.userMark):
            outcome = "You've won!"
        elif self.checkWin(self.machineMark):
            outcome = 'I win again :-)'
        elif self.checkDraw():
            outcome = 'Looks like a draw'
```

Other move-selection code mostly just performs other kinds of analysis on the board data structure or generates new board states to search a tree of moves and countermoves.

You'll also find relatives of these files in the same directory that implements alternative search and move-scoring schemes, different board representations, and so on. For additional background on game scoring and searches in general, consult an AI text. It's fun stuff, but it's too advanced to cover well in this book.

Where to Go from Here

This concludes the GUI section of this book, but this is not an end to the book's GUI coverage. If you want to learn more about GUIs, be sure to see the Tkinter examples that appear later in this book and are described at the start of this chapter. PyMailGUI, PyCalc, PyForm, and PyTree provide additional GUI case studies. In the next section of this book, we'll also learn how to build user interfaces that run in web browsers—a very different concept, but another option for simple interface design.

Keep in mind, too, that even if you don't see a GUI example in this book that looks very close to one you need to program, you've already met all the building blocks. Constructing larger GUIs for your application is really just a matter of laying out hierarchical composites of the widgets presented in this part of the text.

For instance, a complex display might be composed as a collection of radio buttons, listboxes, scales, text fields, menus, and so on—all arranged in frames or grids to achieve the desired appearance. Pop-up top-level windows, as well as independently run GUI programs linked with Inter-Process Communication (IPC) mechanisms, such as pipes, signals, and sockets, can further supplement a complex graphical interface.

Moreover, you can implement larger GUI components as Python classes and attach or extend them anywhere you need a similar interface device (see PyEdit for a prime example). With a little creativity, Tkinter's widget set and Python support a virtually unlimited number of layouts.

Beyond this book, see the documentation and books departments at Python's web site at *http://www.python.org*. I would plug Tkinter-related texts here, but I suspect that the offerings in this department will expand during the shelf life of this book. Finally, if you catch the Tkinter bug, I want to again recommend downloading and experimenting with the packages introduced in Chapter 8—especially Pmw, Tix, and PIL (Tix is a standard part of Python on Windows today). Such extensions add additional tools to the Tkinter arsenal that can make your GUIs more sophisticated, with minimal coding.

Internet Programming

This part of the book explores Python's role as a language for programming Internet-based applications, and its library tools that support this role. Along the way, system and GUI tools presented earlier in the book are put to use as well. Because this is a popular Python domain, chapters here cover all fronts:

Chapter 13, *Network Scripting*

> This chapter introduces Internet concepts, presents Python low-level network communication tools such as sockets and select calls, and illustrates common client/server programming techniques in Python.

Chapter 14, *Client-Side Scripting*

> This chapter shows you how your scripts can use Python to access common client-side network protocols like FTP, email, HTTP, and more. We'll also build email tools here that we'll reuse in later chapters.

Chapter 15, *The PyMailGUI Client*

> This chapter uses the client-side email tools introduced in the prior chapter, as well as the GUI techniques of the prior part, to implement a full-featured email application and to cover larger program concepts.

Chapter 16, *Server-Side Scripting*

> This chapter introduces the basics of Python server-side Common Gateway Interface (CGI) scripts—a kind of program used to implement interactive web sites.

Chapter 17, *The PyMailCGI Server*

> This chapter demonstrates Python web site implementation techniques such as security, by presenting a complete web-based email system. Part of our goal here is to compare and contrast with the client-side PyMailGUI program.

Chapter 18, *Advanced Internet Topics*

> This chapter provides overviews of other Python Internet topics, such as Jython, Zope, PSP, XML parsing, and HTMLgen.

Along the way, we'll also put general programming concepts such as object-oriented programming (OOP) and code refactoring and reuse to work here. As we'll see repeatedly in this part of the book, Python, GUIs, and networking are a powerful combination.

Network Scripting

"Tune In, Log On, and Drop Out"

Over the last decade, the Internet has virtually exploded onto the mainstream stage. It has rapidly grown from a simple communication device used primarily by academics and researchers into a medium that is now nearly as pervasive as the television and telephone. Social observers have likened the Internet's cultural impact to that of the printing press, and technical observers have suggested that all new software development of interest occurs only on the Internet. Naturally, time will be the final arbiter for such claims, but there is little doubt that the Internet is a major force in society, and one of the main application contexts for modern software systems.

The Internet also happens to be one of the primary application domains for the Python programming language. It has been a decade since the first edition of this book was written as well, and in that time the Internet's growth has strongly influenced Python's tool set and roles. Given Python and a computer with a socket-based Internet connection today, we can write Python scripts to read and send email around the world, fetch web pages from remote sites, transfer files by FTP, program interactive web sites, parse HTML and XML files, and much more, simply by using the Internet modules that ship with Python as standard tools.

In fact, companies all over the world do: Google, Yahoo!, Walt Disney, Hewlett-Packard, JPL, and many others rely on Python's standard tools to power their web sites. For example, the Google search engine—widely credited with making the web usable—makes extensive use of Python code. And the BitTorrent peer-to-peer file transfer system—written in Python and already downloaded by tens of millions of users—leverages Python's networking skills to share files among clients and remove server bottlenecks.

Many also build and manage their sites with the Zope web application server, which is itself written and customizable in Python. Others build sites with the Plone content management system, which is built upon Zope and delegates site content to its users. Still others use Python to script Java web applications with Jython (formerly known as JPython)—a system that compiles Python programs to Java bytecode, exports Java libraries for use in Python scripts, and allows Python code to serve as web applets downloaded and run in a browser.

More recently, XML-RPC and SOAP interfaces for Python, such as xmlrpclib and SOAPy, have enabled web service programming; frameworks such as CherryPy, Webware, TurboGears, and Django have emerged as convenient tools for constructing web sites; the new XML package in Python's standard library provides a suite of XML processing tools; and the new IronPython implementation promises to provide seamless .NET/Mono integration for Python code.

As the Internet has grown, so too has Python's role as an Internet tool. Python has proven to be well suited to Internet scripting for some of the very same reasons that make it ideal in other domains. Its modular design and rapid turnaround mix well with the intense demands of Internet development. In this part of the book, we'll find that Python does more than simply support Internet scripts; it also fosters qualities such as productivity and maintainability that are essential to Internet projects of all shapes and sizes.

Internet Scripting Topics

Internet programming entails many topics, so to make the presentation easier to digest, I've split this subject over the next six chapters of this book. This chapter introduces Internet fundamentals and explores sockets, the underlying communications mechanism of the Internet. From there, later chapters move on to discuss the client, the server, web site construction, and more advanced topics.

Each chapter assumes you've read the previous one, but you can generally skip around, especially if you have any experience in the Internet domain. Since these chapters represent a substantial portion of this book at large, the following sections go into a few more details about what we'll be studying.

What we will cover

In conceptual terms, the Internet can roughly be thought of as being composed of multiple functional layers:

Low-level networking layers
Mechanisms such as the TCP/IP transport mechanism, which deal with transferring bytes between machines, but don't care what they mean

Sockets
The programmer's interface to the network, which runs on top of physical networking layers like TCP/IP

Higher-level protocols
Structured communication schemes such as FTP and email, which run on top of sockets and define message formats and standard addresses

Server-side web scripting (CGI)
> Higher-level client/server communication protocols between web browsers and web servers, which also run on top of sockets

Higher-level frameworks and tools
> Third-party systems such as Zope and Jython, which address larger problem domains

In this chapter and in Chapter 14, our main focus is on programming the second and third layers: sockets and higher-level protocols. We'll start this chapter at the bottom, learning about the socket model of network programming. Sockets aren't strictly tied to Internet scripting, but they are presented here because this is their primary role. As we'll see, most of what happens on the Internet happens through sockets, whether you notice or not.

After introducing sockets, the next two chapters make their way up to Python's client-side interfaces to higher-level protocols—things like email and FTP transfers, which run on top of sockets. It turns out that a lot can be done with Python on the client alone, and Chapters 14 and 15 will sample the flavor of Python client-side scripting. The next two chapters then go on to present server-side scripting—programs that run on a server computer and are usually invoked by a web browser. Finally, the last chapter in this part, Chapter 18, briefly introduces even higher-level tools such as Jython and Zope.

Along the way, we will also put to work some of the operating-system and GUI interfaces we studied earlier (e.g., processes, threads, signals, and Tkinter), and we'll investigate some of the design choices and challenges that the Internet presents.

That last statement merits a few more words. Internet scripting, like GUIs, is one of the sexier application domains for Python. As in GUI work, there is an intangible but instant gratification in seeing a Python Internet program ship information all over the world. On the other hand, by its very nature, network programming imposes speed overheads and user interface limitations. Though it may not be a fashionable stance these days, some applications are still better off not being deployed on the Net. In this part of the book, we will take an honest look at the Net's trade-offs as they arise.

The Internet is also considered by many to be something of an ultimate proof of concept for open source tools. Indeed, much of the Net runs on top of a large number of such tools, such as Python, Perl, the Apache web server, the sendmail program, MySQL, and Linux.* Moreover, new tools and technologies for programming the Web sometimes seem to appear faster than developers can absorb them.

---

* In fact, there is even a common acronym for this today: LAMP, for the Linux operating system, the Apache web server, the MySQL database system, and the Python, Perl, and PHP scripting languages. It's possible, and even very common, to put together an entire enterprise-level web server with open source tools. Python users would probably also like to include systems like Zope, Plone, Webware, and CherryPy in this list, but the resulting acronym might be a bit of a stretch.

The good news is that Python's integration focus makes it a natural in such a hetero-geneous world. Today, Python programs can be installed as client-side and server-side tools; used as applets and servlets in Java applications; mixed into distributed object systems like CORBA, SOAP, and XML-RPC; integrated with XML-coded objects; and more. In more general terms, the rationale for using Python in the Inter-net domain is exactly the same as in any other: Python's emphasis on productivity, portability, and integration makes it ideal for writing Internet programs that are open, maintainable, and delivered according to the ever-shrinking schedules in this field.

What we won't cover

Now that I've told you what we will cover in this book, I should also mention what we won't cover. Like Tkinter, the Internet is a vast topic, and this part of the book is mostly an introduction to core concepts and representative tasks, not an exhaustive reference. There are simply too many Python Internet modules to include each in this text, but the examples here should help you understand the library manual entries for modules we don't have time to cover.

I also want to point out that higher-level tools like Jython and Zope are large sys-tems in their own right, and they are best dealt with in more focused documents. Because books on both topics are available, we'll merely scratch their surfaces here. Moreover, this book says almost nothing about lower-level networking layers such as TCP/IP. If you're curious about what happens on the Internet at the bit-and-wire level, consult a good networking text for more details.

Running examples in this part of the book

Internet scripts generally imply execution contexts that earlier examples in this book have not. That is, it usually takes a bit more to run programs that talk over net-works. Here are a few pragmatic notes about this part's examples, up front:

- You don't need to download extra packages to run examples in this part of the book. Except in Chapter 17 and Chapter 18, all of the examples we'll see are based on the standard set of Internet-related modules that come with Python (they are installed in Python's library directory).

- You don't need a state-of-the-art network link or an account on a web server to run most of the examples in this and the following chapters; a PC and dial-up Internet account will usually suffice. We'll study configuration details along the way, but client-side programs are fairly simple to run.

- You don't need an account on a web server machine to run the server-side scripts in later chapters (they can be run by any web browser connected to the Net), but you will need such an account to change these scripts, or a locally run-ning web server.

When a Python script opens an Internet connection (with the socket or protocol modules), Python will happily use whatever Internet link exists on your machine, be that a dedicated T1 line, a DSL line, or a simple modem. For instance, opening a socket on a Windows PC automatically initiates processing to create a dial-up connection to your Internet Service Provider (ISP) if needed (on a Windows laptop without a broadband connection, a modem connection dialog automatically pops up). In other words, if you have a way to connect to the Net, you likely can run programs in this chapter.

Moreover, as long as your machine supports sockets, you probably can run many of the examples here even if you have no Internet connection at all. As we'll see, a machine name localhost or "" (an empty string) usually means the local computer itself. This allows you to test both the client and the server sides of a dialog on the same computer without connecting to the Net. For example, you can run both socket-based clients and servers locally on a Windows PC without ever going out to the Net.

Some later examples assume that a particular kind of server is running on a server machine (e.g., FTP, POP, SMTP), but client-side scripts work on any Internet-aware machine with Python installed. Server-side examples in Chapter 16 and Chapter 17 require more: to develop CGI scripts, you'll need to either have a web server account, or run a web server program locally on your own computer (which is easier than you may think—we'll learn how to code one in Python in Chapter 16). Advanced third-party systems like Jython and Zope must be downloaded separately; we'll peek at some of these briefly in the advanced topics chapter.

Plumbing the Internet

Unless you've been living in a cave for the last decade, you are probably already familiar with the Internet, at least from a user's perspective. Functionally, we use it as a communication and information medium, by exchanging email, browsing web pages, transferring files, and so on. Technically, the Internet consists of many layers of abstraction and devices—from the actual wires used to send bits across the world to the web browser that grabs and renders those bits into text, graphics, and audio on your computer.

In this book, we are primarily concerned with the programmer's interface to the Internet. This too consists of multiple layers: sockets, which are programmable interfaces to the low-level connections between machines, and standard protocols, which add structure to discussions carried out over sockets. Let's briefly look at each of these layers in the abstract before jumping into programming details.

In the Beginning There Was Grail

Besides creating the Python language, Guido van Rossum also wrote a World Wide Web browser in Python, named (appropriately enough) Grail. Grail was partly developed as a demonstration of Python's capabilities. It allows users to browse the Web much like Netscape or Internet Explorer, but it can also be programmed with Grail applets—Python/Tkinter programs downloaded from a server when accessed and run on the client by the browser. Grail applets work much like Java applets in more widespread browsers (more on applets in Chapter 18).

Grail is no longer under development and is mostly used for research purposes today. But Python still reaps the benefits of the Grail project, in the form of a rich set of Internet tools. To write a full-featured web browser, you need to support a wide variety of Internet protocols, and Guido packaged support for all of these as standard library modules that are now shipped with the Python language.

Because of this legacy, Python now includes standard support for Usenet news (NNTP), email processing (POP, SMTP, IMAP), file transfers (FTP), web pages and interactions (HTTP, URLs, HTML, CGI), and other commonly used protocols (Telnet, Gopher, and so on). Python scripts can connect to all of these Internet components by simply importing the associated library module.

Since Grail, additional tools have been added to Python's library for parsing XML files, OpenSSL secure sockets, and more. But much of Python's Internet support can be traced back to the Grail browser—another example of Python's support for code reuse at work. At this writing, you can still find Grail at *http://www.python.org*.

The Socket Layer

In simple terms, sockets are a programmable interface to network connections between computers. They also form the basis, and low-level "plumbing," of the Internet itself: all of the familiar higher-level Net protocols, like FTP, web pages, and email, ultimately occur over sockets. Sockets are also sometimes called communications endpoints because they are the portals through which programs send and receive bytes during a conversation.

Although often used for network conversations, sockets may also be used as a communication mechanism between programs running on the same computer, taking the form of a general Inter-Process Communication (IPC) mechanism. Unlike some IPC devices, sockets are bidirectional data streams: programs may both send and receive data through them.

To programmers, sockets take the form of a handful of calls available in a library. These socket calls know how to send bytes between machines, using lower-level operations such as the TCP network transmission control protocol. At the bottom, TCP knows how to transfer bytes, but it doesn't care what those bytes mean. For the purposes of this text, we will generally ignore how bytes sent to sockets are physically transferred. To understand sockets fully, though, we need to know a bit about how computers are named.

Machine identifiers

Suppose for just a moment that you wish to have a telephone conversation with someone halfway across the world. In the real world, you would probably need either that person's telephone number, or a directory that you could use to look up the number from her name (e.g., a telephone book). The same is true on the Internet: before a script can have a conversation with another computer somewhere in cyberspace, it must first know that other computer's number or name.

Luckily, the Internet defines standard ways to name both a remote machine and a service provided by that machine. Within a script, the computer program to be contacted through a socket is identified by supplying a pair of values—the machine name and a specific port number on that machine:

Machine names
> A machine name may take the form of either a string of numbers separated by dots, called an IP address (e.g., 166.93.218.100), or a more legible form known as a domain name (e.g., *starship.python.net*). Domain names are automatically mapped into their dotted numeric address equivalent when used, by something called a domain name server—a program on the Net that serves the same purpose as your local telephone directory assistance service. As a special case, the machine name localhost, and its equivalent IP address 127.0.0.1, always mean the same local machine; this allows us to refer to servers running locally.

Port numbers
> A port number is simply an agreed-upon numeric identifier for a given conversation. Because computers on the Net can support a variety of services, port numbers are used to name a particular conversation on a given machine. For two machines to talk over the Net, both must associate sockets with the same machine name and port number when initiating network connections. As we'll see, Internet protocols such as email and the Web have standard, reserved port numbers for their connections.

The combination of a machine name and a port number uniquely identifies every dialog on the Net. For instance, an ISP's computer may provide many kinds of services for customers—web pages, Telnet, FTP transfers, email, and so on. Each service on the machine is assigned a unique port number to which requests may be sent. To get web pages from a web server, programs need to specify both the web server's Internet Protocol (IP) or domain name, and the port number on which the server listens for web page requests.

If all of this sounds a bit strange, it may help to think of it in old-fashioned terms. In order to have a telephone conversation with someone within a company, for example, you usually need to dial both the company's phone number and the extension of the person you want to reach. Moreover, if you don't know the company's number, you can probably find it by looking up the company's name in a phone book. It's almost the same on the Net—machine names identify a collection of services (like a company), port numbers identify an individual service within a particular machine (like an extension), and domain names are mapped to IP numbers by domain name servers (like a phone book).

When programs use sockets to communicate in specialized ways with another machine (or with other processes on the same machine), they need to avoid using a port number reserved by a standard protocol—numbers in the range of 0 to 1023—but we first need to discuss protocols to understand why.

The Protocol Layer

Although sockets form the backbone of the Internet, much of the activity that happens on the Net is programmed with protocols,[*] which are higher-level message models that run on top of sockets. In short, Internet protocols define a structured way to talk over sockets. They generally standardize both message formats and socket port numbers:

- *Message formats* provide structure for the bytes exchanged over sockets during conversations.
- *Port numbers* are reserved numeric identifiers for the underlying sockets over which messages are exchanged.

Raw sockets are still commonly used in many systems, but it is perhaps more common (and generally easier) to communicate with one of the standard higher-level Internet protocols.

Port number rules

Technically speaking, socket port numbers can be any 16-bit integer value between 0 and 65,535. However, to make it easier for programs to locate the standard protocols, port numbers in the range of 0 to 1023 are reserved and preassigned to the standard higher-level protocols. Table 13-1 lists the ports reserved for many of the standard protocols; each gets one or more preassigned numbers from the reserved range.

---

[*] Some books also use the term *protocol* to refer to lower-level transport schemes such as TCP. In this book, we use protocol to refer to higher-level structures built on top of sockets; see a networking text if you are curious about what happens at lower levels.

Table 13-1. Port numbers reserved for common protocols

Protocol	Common function	Port number	Python module
HTTP	Web pages	80	`httplib`
NNTP	Usenet news	119	`nntplib`
FTP data default	File transfers	20	`ftplib`
FTP control	File transfers	21	`ftplib`
SMTP	Sending email	25	`smtplib`
POP3	Fetching email	110	`poplib`
IMAP4	Fetching email	143	`imaplib`
Finger	Informational	79	n/a
Telnet	Command lines	23	`telnetlib`
Gopher	Document transfers	70	`gopherlib`

Clients and servers

To socket programmers, the standard protocols mean that port numbers 0 to 1023 are off-limits to scripts, unless they really mean to use one of the higher-level protocols. This is both by standard and by common sense. A Telnet program, for instance, can start a dialog with any Telnet-capable machine by connecting to its port, 23; without preassigned port numbers, each server might install Telnet on a different port. Similarly, web sites listen for page requests from browsers on port 80 by standard; if they did not, you might have to know and type the HTTP port number of every site you visit while surfing the Net.

By defining standard port numbers for services, the Net naturally gives rise to a *client/server* architecture. On one side of a conversation, machines that support standard protocols run a set of perpetually running programs that listen for connection requests on the reserved ports. On the other end of a dialog, other machines contact those programs to use the services they export.

We usually call the perpetually running listener program a *server* and the connecting program a *client*. Let's use the familiar web browsing model as an example. As shown in Table 13-1, the HTTP protocol used by the Web allows clients and servers to talk over sockets on port 80:

Server

> A machine that hosts web sites usually runs a web server program that constantly listens for incoming connection requests, on a socket bound to port 80. Often, the server itself does nothing but watch for requests on its port perpetually; handling requests is delegated to spawned processes or threads.

Clients

> Programs that wish to talk to this server specify the server machine's name and port 80 to initiate a connection. For web servers, typical clients are web browsers like Firefox, Internet Explorer, or Netscape, but any script can open a client-side connection on port 80 to fetch web pages from the server.

In general, many clients may connect to a server over sockets, whether it implements a standard protocol or something more specific to a given application. And in some applications, the notion of client and server is blurred—programs can also pass bytes between each other more as peers than as master and subordinate. An agent in a peer-to-peer file transfer system, for instance, may at various times be both client and server for parts of files transferred.

For the purposes of this book, though, we usually call programs that listen on sockets *servers*, and those that connect *clients*. We also sometimes call the machines that these programs run on *server* and *client* (e.g., a computer on which a web server program runs may be called a *web server machine*, too), but this has more to do with the physical than the functional.

Protocol structures

Functionally, protocols may accomplish a familiar task, like reading email or posting a Usenet newsgroup message, but they ultimately consist of message bytes sent over sockets. The structure of those message bytes varies from protocol to protocol, is hidden by the Python library, and is mostly beyond the scope of this book, but a few general words may help demystify the protocol layer.

Some protocols may define the contents of messages sent over sockets; others may specify the sequence of control messages exchanged during conversations. By defining regular patterns of communication, protocols make communication more robust. They can also minimize deadlock conditions—machines waiting for messages that never arrive.

For example, the FTP protocol prevents deadlock by conversing over two sockets: one for control messages only, and one to transfer file data. An FTP server listens for control messages (e.g., "send me a file") on one port, and transfers file data over another. FTP clients open socket connections to the server machine's control port, send requests, and send or receive file data over a socket connected to a data port on the server machine. FTP also defines standard message structures passed between client and server. The control message used to request a file, for instance, must follow a standard format.

Python's Internet Library Modules

If all of this sounds horribly complex, cheer up: Python's standard protocol modules handle all the details. For example, the Python library's ftplib module manages all the socket and message-level handshaking implied by the FTP protocol. Scripts that import ftplib have access to a much higher-level interface for FTPing files and can be largely ignorant of both the underlying FTP protocol and the sockets over which it runs.[*]

In fact, each supported protocol is represented by a standard Python module file with a name of the form *xxxlib.py*, where *xxx* is replaced by the protocol's name, in lowercase. The last column in Table 13-1 gives the module name for protocol standard modules. For instance, FTP is supported by the module file *ftplib.py*. Moreover, within the protocol modules, the top-level interface object is usually the name of the protocol. So, for instance, to start an FTP session in a Python script, you run import ftplib and pass appropriate parameters in a call to ftplib.FTP( ); for Telnet, create a telnetlib.Telnet( ).

In addition to the protocol implementation modules in Table 13-1, Python's standard library also contains modules for fetching replies from web servers for a web page request (urllib), parsing and handling data once it has been transferred over sockets or protocols (htmllib, the email.* and xml.* packages), and more. Table 13-2 lists some of the more commonly used modules in this category.

Table 13-2. Common Internet-related standard modules

Python modules	Utility
socket	Low-level network communications support (TCP/IP, UDP, etc.)
cgi	Server-side CGI script support: parse input stream, escape HTML text, and so on
urllib	Fetch web pages from their addresses (URLs), escape URL text
httplib, ftplib, nntplib	HTTP (web), FTP (file transfer), and NNTP (news) protocol modules
poplib, imaplib, smtplib	POP, IMAP (mail fetch), and SMTP (mail send) protocol modules
telnetlib, gopherlib	Telnet and Gopher protocol modules
htmllib, sgmllib, xml.*	Parse web page contents (HTML, SGML, and XML documents)
xdrlib	Encode binary data portably (also see the struct and socket modules)
email.*	Parse and compose email messages with headers, attachments, and encodings
rfc822	Parse email-style header lines
mhlib, mailbox	Process complex mail messages and mailboxes
mimetools, mimify	Handle MIME-style message bodies
multifile	Read messages with multiple parts
uu, binhex, base64, binascii, quopri, email.*	Encode and decode binary (or other) data transmitted as text
urlparse	Parse URL string into components
SocketServer	Framework for general Net servers

[*] Since Python is an open source system, you can read the source code of the ftplib module if you are curious about how the underlying protocol actually works. See the *ftplib.py* file in the standard source library directory in your machine. Its code is complex (since it must format messages and manage two sockets), but with the other standard Internet protocol modules, it is a good example of low-level socket programming.

Table 13-2. Common Internet-related standard modules (continued)

Python modules	Utility
BaseHTTPServer	Basic HTTP server implementation
SimpleHTTPServer, CGIHTTPServer	Specific HTTP web server request handler modules

We will meet many of the modules in this table in the next few chapters of this book, but not all of them. The modules demonstrated are representative, but as always, be sure to see Python's standard Library Reference Manual for more complete and up-to-date lists and details.

More on Protocol Standards

If you want the full story on protocols and ports, at this writing you can find a comprehensive list of all ports reserved for protocols, or registered as used by various common systems, by searching the web pages maintained by the Internet Engineering Task Force (IETF) and the Internet Assigned Numbers Authority (IANA). The IETF is the organization responsible for maintaining web protocols and standards. The IANA is the central coordinator for the assignment of unique parameter values for Internet protocols. Another standards body, the W3 (for WWW), also maintains relevant documents. See these web pages for more details:

> *http://www.ietf.org*
> *http://www.iana.org/numbers.html*
> *http://www.iana.org/assignments/port-numbers*
> *http://www.w3.org*

It's not impossible that more recent repositories for standard protocol specifications will arise during this book's shelf life, but the IETF web site will likely be the main authority for some time to come. If you do look, though, be warned that the details are, well, detailed. Because Python's protocol modules hide most of the socket and messaging complexity documented in the protocol standards, you usually don't need to memorize these documents to get web work done with Python.

Socket Programming

Now that we've seen how sockets figure into the Internet picture, let's move on to explore the tools that Python provides for programming sockets with Python scripts. This section shows you how to use the Python socket interface to perform low-level network communications. In later chapters, we will instead use one of the higher-level protocol modules that hide underlying sockets. Python's socket interfaces can be used directly, though, to implement custom network dialogs and to access standard protocols directly.

The basic socket interface in Python is the standard library's socket module. Like the os POSIX module, Python's socket module is just a thin wrapper (interface layer) over the underlying C library's socket calls. Like Python files, it's also object-based—methods of a socket object implemented by this module call out to the corresponding C library's operations after data conversions. For instance, the C library's send and recv function calls become methods of socket objects in Python.

Python's socket module supports socket programming on any machine that supports BSD-style sockets—Windows, Macs, Linux, Unix, and so on—and so provides a portable socket interface. In addition, this module supports all commonly used socket types—TCP/IP, UDP, datagram, and Unix domain—and can be used as both a network interface API and a general IPC mechanism between processes running on the same machine.

Beyond basic data communication tasks, this module also includes a variety of more advanced tools. For instance, it has calls for:

- Converting bytes to a standard network ordering (ntohl, htonl)
- Wrapping socket objects in a file object interface (sockobj.makefile)
- Making socket calls nonblocking (sockbj.setblocking)
- Setting socket timeouts (sockobj.settimeout)

and more. Provided your Python was compiled with Secure Sockets Layer (SSL) support, this module now also supports encrypted transfers with its socket.ssl. This call is used in turn by other standard library modules to support the HTTPS secure web site protocol (httplib, urllib, and urllib2), secure email transfers (poplib and smtplib), and more. We'll meet some of these other modules later in this part of the book, but we won't study all of the socket module's advanced features in this text; see the Python library manual for usage details omitted here.

Socket Basics

Although we won't get into advanced socket use in this chapter, basic socket transfers are remarkably easy to code in Python. To create a connection between machines, Python programs import the socket module, create a socket object, and call the object's methods to establish connections and send and receive data.

Sockets are inherently bidirectional in nature, and socket object methods map directly to socket calls in the C library. For example, the script in Example 13-1 implements a program that simply listens for a connection on a socket, and echoes back over a socket whatever it receives through that socket, adding 'Echo=>' string prefixes.

Example 13-1. PP3E\Internet\Sockets\echo-server.py

```
#######################################################################
# Server side: open a TCP/IP socket on a port, listen for a message from
# a client, and send an echo reply; this is a simple one-shot listen/reply
# conversation per client, but it goes into an infinite loop to listen for
# more clients as long as this server script runs; the client may run on
# a remote machine, or on same computer if it uses 'localhost' for server
#######################################################################

from socket import *                    # get socket constructor and constants
myHost = ''                             # server machine, '' means local host
myPort = 50007                          # listen on a non-reserved port number

sockobj = socket(AF_INET, SOCK_STREAM)  # make a TCP socket object
sockobj.bind((myHost, myPort))          # bind it to server port number
sockobj.listen(5)                       # listen, allow 5 pending connects

while True:                             # listen until process killed
    connection, address = sockobj.accept()  # wait for next client connect
    print 'Server connected by', address    # connection is a new socket
    while True:
        data = connection.recv(1024)    # read next line on client socket
        if not data: break              # send a reply line to the client
        connection.send('Echo=>' + data)  # until eof when socket closed
    connection.close()
```

As mentioned earlier, we usually call programs like this that listen for incoming connections *servers* because they provide a service that can be accessed at a given machine and port on the Internet. Programs that connect to such a server to access its service are generally called *clients*. Example 13-2 shows a simple client implemented in Python.

Example 13-2. PP3E\Internet\Sockets\echo-client.py

```
#######################################################################
# Client side: use sockets to send data to the server, and print server's
# reply to each message line; 'localhost' means that the server is running
# on the same machine as the client, which lets us test client and server
# on one machine;  to test over the Internet, run a server on a remote
# machine, and set serverHost or argv[1] to machine's domain name or IP addr;
# Python sockets are a portable BSD socket interface, with object methods
# for the standard socket calls available in the sytstem's C library;
#######################################################################

import sys
from socket import *                    # portable socket interface plus constants
serverHost = 'localhost'                # server name, or: 'starship.python.net'
serverPort = 50007                      # non-reserved port used by the server

message = ['Hello network world']       # default text to send to server
if len(sys.argv) > 1:
    serverHost = sys.argv[1]            # or server from cmd line arg 1
```

Example 13-2. PP3E\Internet\Sockets\echo-client.py (continued)

```
    if len(sys.argv) > 2:                # or text from cmd line args 2..n
        message = sys.argv[2:]           # one message for each arg listed

sockobj = socket(AF_INET, SOCK_STREAM)    # make a TCP/IP socket object
sockobj.connect((serverHost, serverPort)) # connect to server machine and port

for line in message:
    sockobj.send(line)                    # send line to server over socket
    data = sockobj.recv(1024)             # receive line from server: up to 1k
    print 'Client received:', repr(data)  # make sure it is quoted, was `x`

sockobj.close()                           # close socket to send eof to server
```

Server socket calls

Before we see these programs in action, let's take a minute to explain how this client and server do their stuff. Both are fairly simple examples of socket scripts, but they illustrate the common call patterns of most socket-based programs. In fact, this is boilerplate code: most socket programs generally make the same socket calls that our two scripts do, so let's step through the important points of these scripts line by line.

Programs such as Example 13-1 that provide services for other programs with sockets generally start out by following this sequence of calls:

`sockobj = socket(AF_INET, SOCK_STREAM)`
> Uses the Python socket module to create a TCP socket object. The names `AF_INET` and `SOCK_STREAM` are preassigned variables defined by and imported from the socket module; using them in combination means "create a TCP/IP socket," the standard communication device for the Internet. More specifically, `AF_INET` means the IP address protocol, and `SOCK_STREAM` means the TCP transfer protocol.
>
> If you use other names in this call, you can instead create things like UDP connectionless sockets (use `SOCK_DGRAM` second) and Unix domain sockets on the local machine (use `AF_UNIX` first), but we won't do so in this book. See the Python library manual for details on these and other socket module options. Using other socket types is mostly a matter of using different forms of boilerplate code.

`sockobj.bind((myHost, myPort))`
> Associates the socket object to an address—for IP addresses, we pass a server machine name and port number on that machine. This is where the server identifies the machine and port associated with the socket. In server programs, the hostname is typically an empty string (""), which means the machine that the script runs on and the port is a number outside the range 0 to 1023 (which is reserved for standard protocols, described earlier).
>
> Note that each unique socket dialog you support must have its own port number; if you try to open a socket on a port already in use, Python will raise an

exception. Also notice the nested parentheses in this call—for the AF_INET address protocol socket here, we pass the host/port socket address to bind as a two-item tuple object (pass a string for AF_UNIX). Technically, bind takes a tuple of values appropriate for the type of socket created (but see the next Note box about the older and deprecated convention of passing values to this function as distinct arguments).

sockobj.listen(5)

Starts listening for incoming client connections and allows for a backlog of up to five pending requests. The value passed sets the number of incoming client requests queued by the operating system before new requests are denied (which happens only if a server isn't fast enough to process requests before the queues fill up). A value of 5 is usually enough for most socket-based programs; the value must be at least 1.

At this point, the server is ready to accept connection requests from client programs running on remote machines (or the same machine), and falls into an infinite loop—while True:, or the equivalent while 1: on older Pythons—waiting for them to arrive:

connection, address = sockobj.accept()

Waits for the next client connection request to occur; when it does, the accept call returns a brand-new socket object over which data can be transferred from and to the connected client. Connections are accepted on sockobj, but communication with a client happens on connection, the new socket. This call actually returns a two-item tuple—address is the connecting client's Internet address. We can call accept more than one time, to service multiple client connections; that's why each call returns a new, distinct socket for talking to a particular client.

Once we have a client connection, we fall into another loop to receive data from the client in blocks of 1,024 bytes at a time, and echo each block back to the client:

data = connection.recv(1024)

Reads at most 1,024 more bytes of the next message sent from a client (i.e., coming across the network), and returns it to the script as a string. We get back an empty string when the client has finished—end-of-file is triggered when the client closes its end of the socket.

connection.send('Echo=>' + data)

Sends the latest data block back to the client program, prepending the string 'Echo=>' to it first. The client program can then recv what we send here—the next reply line. Technically this call sends as much data as possible, and returns the number of bytes actually sent. To be fully robust, programs need to resend unsent portions or use connection.sendall to force all bytes to be sent.

connection.close()

Shuts down the connection with this particular client.

After talking with a given client, the server goes back to its infinite loop and waits for the next client connection request.

Client socket calls

On the other hand, client programs like the one shown in Example 13-2 follow simpler call sequences. The main thing to keep in mind is that the client and server must specify the same port number when opening their sockets, and the client must identify the machine on which the server is running (in our scripts, server and client agree to use port number 50007 for their conversation, outside the standard protocol range):

```
sockobj = socket(AF_INET, SOCK_STREAM)
```
Creates a Python socket object in the client program, just like the server.

```
sockobj.connect((serverHost, serverPort))
```
Opens a connection to the machine and port on which the server program is listening for client connections. This is where the client specifies the string name of the service to be contacted. In the client, we can either specify the name of the remote machine as a domain name (e.g., *starship.python.net*) or numeric IP address. We can also give the server name as localhost (or the equivalent IP address 127.0.0.1) to specify that the server program is running on the same machine as the client; that comes in handy for debugging servers without having to connect to the Net. And again, the client's port number must match the server's exactly. Note the nested parentheses again—just as in server bind calls we really pass the server's host/port address to connect in a tuple object.

Once the client establishes a connection to the server, it falls into a loop, sending a message one line at a time and printing whatever the server sends back after each line is sent:

```
sockobj.send(line)
```
Transfers the next message line to the server over the socket.

```
data = sockobj.recv(1024)
```
Reads the next reply line sent by the server program. Technically, this reads up to 1,024 bytes of the next reply message and returns it as a string.

```
sockobj.close( )
```
Closes the connection with the server, sending it the end-of-file signal.

And that's it. The server exchanges one or more lines of text with each client that connects. The operating system takes care of locating remote machines, routing bytes sent between programs across the Internet, and (with TCP) making sure that our messages arrive intact. That involves a lot of processing too—our strings may ultimately travel around the world, crossing phone wires, satellite links, and more along the way. But we can be happily ignorant of what goes on beneath the socket call layer when programming in Python.

In older Python code, you may see the AF_INET server address passed to the server-side bind and client-side connect socket methods as two distinct arguments, instead of as a two-item tuple:

```
soc.bind(host,port)      vs soc.bind((host,port))
soc.connect(host,port)   vs soc.connect((host,port))
```

This two-argument form is now deprecated, and only worked at all due to a shortcoming in earlier Python releases (unfortunately, the Python library manual's socket example used the two-argument form too!). The tuple server address form is preferred and, in a rare Python break with full backward-compatibility, will likely be the only one that will work in future Python releases.

Running socket programs locally

Okay, let's put this client and server to work. There are two ways to run these scripts—on either the same machine or two different machines. To run the client and the server on the same machine, bring up two command-line consoles on your computer, start the server program in one, and run the client repeatedly in the other. The server keeps running and responds to requests made each time you run the client script in the other window.

For instance, here is the text that shows up in the MS-DOS console window where I've started the server script:

```
C:\...\PP3E\Internet\Sockets>python echo-server.py
Server connected by ('127.0.0.1', 1025)
Server connected by ('127.0.0.1', 1026)
Server connected by ('127.0.0.1', 1027)
```

The output here gives the address (machine IP name and port number) of each connecting client. Like most servers, this one runs perpetually, listening for client connection requests. This server receives three, but I have to show you the client window's text for you to understand what this means:

```
C:\...\PP3E\Internet\Sockets>python echo-client.py
Client received: 'Echo=>Hello network world'

C:\...\PP3E\Internet\Sockets>python echo-client.py localhost spam Spam SPAM
Client received: 'Echo=>spam'
Client received: 'Echo=>Spam'
Client received: 'Echo=>SPAM'

C:\...\PP3E\Internet\Sockets>python echo-client.py localhost Shrubbery
Client received: 'Echo=>Shrubbery'
```

Here, I ran the client script three times, while the server script kept running in the other window. Each client connected to the server, sent it a message of one or more lines of text, and read back the server's reply—an echo of each line of text sent from the client. And each time a client is run, a new connection message shows up in the server's window (that's why we got three).

It's important to notice that client and server are running on the same machine here (a Windows PC). The server and client agree on the port number, but they use the machine names "" and localhost, respectively, to refer to the computer on which they are running. In fact, there is no Internet connection to speak of. Sockets also work well as cross-program communications tools on a single machine.

Running socket programs remotely

To make these scripts talk over the Internet rather than on a single machine, we have to do some extra work to run the server on a different computer. First, upload the server's source file to a remote machine where you have an account and a Python. Here's how I do it with FTP; your server name and upload interface details may vary, and there are other ways to copy files to a computer (e.g., email, web page post forms, etc.):[*]

```
C:\...\PP3E\Internet\Sockets>ftp starship.python.net
Connected to starship.python.net.
User (starship.python.net:(none)): lutz
331 Password required for lutz.
Password:
230 User lutz logged in.
ftp> put echo-server.py
200 PORT command successful.
150 Opening ASCII mode data connection for echo-server.py.
226 Transfer complete.
ftp: 1322 bytes sent in 0.06Seconds 22.03Kbytes/sec.
ftp> quit
```

Once you have the server program loaded on the other computer, you need to run it there. Connect to that computer and start the server program. I usually Telnet into my server machine and start the server program as a perpetually running process from the command line.[†] The & syntax in Unix/Linux shells can be used to run the server script in the background; we could also make the server directly executable with a #! line and a chmod command (see Chapter 3 for details). Here is the text that shows up in a Window on my PC that is running a Telnet session connected to the Linux server where I have an account (minus a few deleted informational lines):

```
C:\...\PP3E\Internet\Sockets>telnet starship.python.net
Red Hat Linux release 6.2 (Zoot)
Kernel 2.2.14-5.0smp on a 2-processor i686
```

---

[*] The FTP command is standard on Windows machines and most others. On Windows, simply type it in a DOS console box to connect to an FTP server (or start your favorite FTP program); on Linux, type the FTP command in an xterm window. You'll need to supply your account name and password to connect to a nonanonymous FTP site. For anonymous FTP, use "anonymous" for the username and your email address for the password (anonymous FTP sites are generally limited).

[†] Telnet is a standard command on Windows and Linux machines, too. On Windows, type it at a DOS console prompt or in the Start/Run dialog box (it can also be started via a clickable icon). Telnet usually runs in a window of its own. For some server machines, you'll need to use secure shell rather than Telnet to access a shell prompt.

```
login: lutz
Password:
[lutz@starship lutz]$ python echo-server.py &
[1] 4098
```

Now that the server is listening for connections on the Net, run the client on your local computer multiple times again. This time, the client runs on a different machine than the server, so we pass in the server's domain or IP name as a client command-line argument. The server still uses a machine name of "" because it always listens on whatever machine it runs on. Here is what shows up in the server's Telnet window:

```
[lutz@starship lutz]$ Server connected by ('166.93.68.61', 1037)
Server connected by ('166.93.68.61', 1040)
Server connected by ('166.93.68.61', 1043)
Server connected by ('166.93.68.61', 1050)
```

And here is what appears in the MS-DOS console box where I run the client. A "connected by" message appears in the server Telnet window each time the client script is run in the client window:

```
C:\...\PP3E\Internet\Sockets>python echo-client.py starship.python.net
Client received: 'Echo=>Hello network world'

C:\...\PP3E\Internet\Sockets>python echo-client.py starship.python.net ni Ni NI
Client received: 'Echo=>ni'
Client received: 'Echo=>Ni'
Client received: 'Echo=>NI'

C:\...\PP3E\Internet\Sockets>python echo-client.py starship.python.net Shrubbery
Client received: 'Echo=>Shrubbery'

C:\...\PP3E\Internet\Sockets>ping starship.python.net
Pinging starship.python.net [208.185.174.112] with 32 bytes of data:
Reply from 208.185.174.112: bytes=32 time=311ms TTL=246
ctrl-C
C:\...\PP3E\Internet\Sockets>python echo-client.py 208.185.174.112 Does she?
Client received: 'Echo=>Does'
Client received: 'Echo=>she?'
```

The ping command can be used to get an IP address for a machine's domain name; either machine name form can be used to connect in the client. This output is perhaps a bit understated—a lot is happening under the hood. The client, running on my Windows laptop, connects with and talks to the server program running on a Linux machine perhaps thousands of miles away. It all happens about as fast as when client and server both run on the laptop, and it uses the same library calls; only the server name passed to clients differs.

Socket pragmatics

Before we move on, there are three practical usage details you should know. First, you can run the client and server like this on any two Internet-aware machines where

Python is installed. Of course, to run the client and server on different computers, you need both a live Internet connection and access to another machine on which to run the server. You don't need a big, expensive Internet link, though—a simple modem and dial-up Internet account will do for clients. When sockets are opened, Python is happy to use whatever connectivity you have, be it a dedicated T1 line or a dial-up modem account.

On a laptop PC with just dial-up access, for instance, Windows automatically dials out to your ISP when clients are started or when Telnet server sessions are opened. If a broadband connection is available, that is utilized instead. In this book's examples, server-side programs that run remotely are executed on a machine called *starship.python.net*. If you don't have an account of your own on such a server, simply run client and server examples on the same machine, as shown earlier; all you need then is a computer that allows sockets, and most do.

Second, the socket module generally raises exceptions if you ask for something invalid. For instance, trying to connect to a nonexistent server (or unreachable servers, if you have no Internet link) fails:

```
C:\...\PP3E\Internet\Sockets>python echo-client.py www.nonesuch.com hello
Traceback (innermost last):
  File "echo-client.py", line 24, in ?
    sockobj.connect((serverHost, serverPort))   # connect to server machine...
  File "<string>", line 1, in connect
socket.error: (10061, 'winsock error')
```

Finally, also be sure to kill the server process before restarting it again, or else the port number will still be in use, and you'll get another exception:

```
[lutz@starship uploads]$ ps -x
 PID TTY      STAT   TIME COMMAND
5570 pts/0    S      0:00 -bash
5570 pts/0    S      0:00 -bash
5633 pts/0    S      0:00 python echo-server.py
5634 pts/0    R      0:00 ps -x
[lutz@starship uploads]$ python echo-server.py
Traceback (most recent call last):
  File "echo-server.py", line 14, in ?
    sockobj.bind((myHost, myPort))                # bind it to server port number
socket.error: (98, 'Address already in use')
```

A series of Ctrl-Cs will kill the server on Linux (be sure to type fg to bring it to the foreground first if started with an &):

```
[lutz@starship uploads]$ python echo-server.py
ctrl-c
Traceback (most recent call last):
  File "echo-server.py", line 18, in ?
    connection, address = sockobj.accept()   # wait for next client connect
KeyboardInterrupt
```

A Ctrl-C kill key combination won't kill the server on my Windows machine, however. To kill the perpetually running server process running locally on Windows, you may need to type a Ctrl-Alt-Delete key combination, and then end the Python task by selecting it in the process listbox that appears. Closing the window in which the server is running will also suffice on Windows, but you'll lose that window's command history. You can also usually kill a server on Linux with a `kill -9 pid` shell command if it is running in another window or in the background, but Ctrl-C requires less typing.

Spawning clients in parallel

To see how the server handles the load, let's fire up eight copies of the client script in parallel using the script in Example 13-3 (see the end of Chapter 5 for details on the launchmodes module used here to spawn clients).

Example 13-3. PP3E\Internet\Sockets\testecho.py

```
import sys
from PP3E.launchmodes import QuietPortableLauncher

numclients = 8
def start(cmdline): QuietPortableLauncher(cmdline, cmdline)( )

# start('echo-server.py')            # spawn server locally if not yet started

args = ' '.join(sys.argv[1:])        # pass server name if running remotely
for i in range(numclients):
    start('echo-client.py %s' % args)  # spawn 8? clients to test the server
```

To run this script, pass no arguments to talk to a server listening on port 50007 on the local machine; pass a real machine name to talk to a server running remotely. On Windows, the clients' output is discarded when spawned from this script:

```
C:\...\PP3E\Internet\Sockets>python testecho.py
```

```
C:\...\PP3E\Internet\Sockets>python testecho.py starship.python.net
```

If the spawned clients connect to a server run locally, connection messages show up in the server's window on the local machine:

```
C:\...\PP3E\Internet\Sockets>python echo-server.py
Server connected by ('127.0.0.1', 1283)
Server connected by ('127.0.0.1', 1284)
Server connected by ('127.0.0.1', 1285)
Server connected by ('127.0.0.1', 1286)
Server connected by ('127.0.0.1', 1287)
Server connected by ('127.0.0.1', 1288)
Server connected by ('127.0.0.1', 1289)
Server connected by ('127.0.0.1', 1290)
```

If the server is running remotely, the client connection messages instead appear in the window displaying the Telnet connection to the remote computer:

```
[lutz@starship lutz]$ python echo-server.py
Server connected by ('166.93.68.61', 1301)
Server connected by ('166.93.68.61', 1302)
Server connected by ('166.93.68.61', 1308)
Server connected by ('166.93.68.61', 1309)
Server connected by ('166.93.68.61', 1313)
Server connected by ('166.93.68.61', 1314)
Server connected by ('166.93.68.61', 1307)
Server connected by ('166.93.68.61', 1312)
```

Keep in mind, however, that this works for our simple scripts only because the server doesn't take a long time to respond to each client's requests—it can get back to the top of the server script's outer while loop in time to process the next incoming client. If it could not, we would probably need to change the server to handle each client in parallel, or some might be denied a connection. Technically, client connections would fail after five clients are already waiting for the server's attention, as specified in the server's listen call. We'll see how servers can handle multiple clients robustly in the next section.

Talking to reserved ports

It's also important to know that this client and server engage in a proprietary sort of discussion, and so use the port number 50007 outside the range reserved for standard protocols (0 to 1023). There's nothing preventing a client from opening a socket on one of these special ports, however. For instance, the following client-side code connects to programs listening on the standard email, FTP, and HTTP web server ports on three different server machines:

```
C:\...\PP3E\Internet\Sockets>python
>>> from socket import *
>>> sock = socket(AF_INET, SOCK_STREAM)
>>> sock.connect(('mail.rmi.net', 110))          # talk to RMI POP mail server
>>> print sock.recv(40)
+OK Cubic Circle's v1.31 1998/05/13 POP3
>>> sock.close()

>>> sock = socket(AF_INET, SOCK_STREAM)
>>> sock.connect(('www.python.org', 21))         # talk to Python FTP server
>>> print sock.recv(40)
220 python.org FTP server (Version wu-2.
>>> sock.close()

>>> sock = socket(AF_INET, SOCK_STREAM)
>>> sock.connect(('starship.python.net', 80))    # starship HTTP web server
>>> sock.send('GET /\r\n')                        # fetch root web page
7
>>> sock.recv(60)
'<!DOCTYPE HTML PUBLIC "-//W3C//DTD HTML 3.2 Final//EN">\012<HTM'
```

```
>>> sock.recv(60)
'L>\012 <HEAD>\012  <TITLE>Starship Slowly Recovering</TITLE>\012 </HE'
```

If we know how to interpret the output returned by these ports' servers, we could use raw sockets like this to fetch email, transfer files, and grab web pages and invoke server-side scripts. Fortunately, though, we don't have to worry about all the underlying details—Python's poplib, ftplib, httplib, and urllib modules provide higher-level interfaces for talking to servers on these ports. Other Python protocol modules do the same for other standard ports (e.g., NNTP, Telnet, and so on). We'll meet some of these client-side protocol modules in the next chapter.[*]

By the way, it's all right to open client-side connections on reserved ports like this, but you can't install your own server-side scripts for these ports unless you have special permission:

```
[lutz@starship uploads]$ python
>>> from socket import *
>>> sock = socket(AF_INET, SOCK_STREAM)
>>> sock.bind(('', 80))
Traceback (most recent call last):
  File "<stdin>", line 1, in ?
socket.error: (13, 'Permission denied')
```

Even if run by a user with the required permission, you'll get the different exception we saw earlier if the port is already being used by a real web server. On computers being used as general servers, these ports really are reserved.

Handling Multiple Clients

The echo client and server programs shown previously serve to illustrate socket fundamentals. But the server model suffers from a fairly major flaw: if multiple clients try to connect to the server, and it takes a long time to process a given client's request, the server will fail. More accurately, if the cost of handling a given request prevents the server from returning to the code that checks for new clients in a timely manner, it won't be able to keep up with all the requests, and some clients will eventually be denied connections.

In real-world client/server programs, it's far more typical to code a server so as to avoid blocking new requests while handling a current client's request. Perhaps the easiest way to do so is to service each client's request in parallel—in a new process, in a new thread, or by manually switching (multiplexing) between clients in an event

---

[*] You might be interested to know that the last part of this example, talking to port 80, is exactly what your web browser does as you surf the Web: followed links direct it to download web pages over this port. In fact, this lowly port is the primary basis of the Web. In Chapter 16, we will meet an entire application environment based upon sending formatted data over port 80—CGI server-side scripting. At the bottom, though, the Web is just bytes over sockets, with a user interface. The wizard behind the curtain is not as impressive as he may seem!

loop. This isn't a socket issue per se, and we already learned how to start processes and threads in Chapter 5. But since these schemes are so typical of socket server programming, let's explore all three ways to handle client requests in parallel here.

Forking Servers

The script in Example 13-4 works like the original echo server, but instead forks a new process to handle each new client connection. Because the handleClient function runs in a new process, the dispatcher function can immediately resume its main loop in order to detect and service a new incoming request.

Example 13-4. PP3E\Internet\Sockets\fork-server.py

```
#############################################################################
# Server side: open a socket on a port, listen for a message from a client,
# and send an echo reply; forks a process to handle each client connection;
# child processes share parent's socket descriptors; fork is less portable
# than threads--not yet on Windows, unless Cygwin or similar installed;
#############################################################################

import os, time, sys
from socket import *                       # get socket constructor and constants
myHost = ''                                # server machine, '' means local host
myPort = 50007                             # listen on a non-reserved port number

sockobj = socket(AF_INET, SOCK_STREAM)              # make a TCP socket object
sockobj.bind((myHost, myPort))                      # bind it to server port number
sockobj.listen(5)                                   # allow 5 pending connects

def now():                                          # current time on server
    return time.ctime(time.time())

activeChildren = []
def reapChildren():                                 # reap any dead child processes
    while activeChildren:                           # else may fill up system table
        pid,stat = os.waitpid(0, os.WNOHANG)        # don't hang if no child exited
        if not pid: break
        activeChildren.remove(pid)

def handleClient(connection):                       # child process: reply, exit
    time.sleep(5)                                   # simulate a blocking activity
    while True:                                     # read, write a client socket
        data = connection.recv(1024)               # till eof when socket closed
        if not data: break
        connection.send('Echo=>%s at %s' % (data, now()))
    connection.close()
    os._exit(0)

def dispatcher():                                   # listen until process killed
    while True:                                     # wait for next connection,
        connection, address = sockobj.accept()     # pass to process for service
        print 'Server connected by', address,
```

Example 13-4. PP3E\Internet\Sockets\fork-server.py (continued)

```
    print 'at', now( )
    reapChildren( )                          # clean up exited children now
    childPid = os.fork( )                     # copy this process
    if childPid == 0:                         # if in child process: handle
        handleClient(connection)
    else:                                     # else: go accept next connect
        activeChildren.append(childPid)       # add to active child pid list

dispatcher( )
```

Running the forking server

Parts of this script are a bit tricky, and most of its library calls work only on Unix-like platforms (not Windows). But before we get into too many details, let's start up our server and handle a few client requests. First, notice that to simulate a long-running operation (e.g., database updates, other network traffic), this server adds a five-second time.sleep delay in its client handler function, handleClient. After the delay, the original echo reply action is performed. That means that when we run a server and clients this time, clients won't receive the echo reply until five seconds after they've sent their requests to the server.

To help keep track of requests and replies, the server prints its system time each time a client connect request is received, and adds its system time to the reply. Clients print the reply time sent back from the server, not their own—clocks on the server and client may differ radically, so to compare apples to apples, all times are server times. Because of the simulated delays, we also must usually start each client in its own console window on Windows (on some platforms, clients will hang in a blocked state while waiting for their reply).

But the grander story here is that this script runs one main parent process on the server machine, which does nothing but watch for connections (in dispatcher), plus one child process per active client connection, running in parallel with both the main parent process and the other client processes (in handleClient). In principle, the server can handle any number of clients without bogging down. To test, let's start the server remotely in a Telnet window, and start three clients locally in three distinct console windows:

```
[server telnet window]
[lutz@starship uploads]$ uname -a
Linux starship ...
[lutz@starship uploads]$ python fork-server.py
Server connected by ('38.28.162.194', 1063) at Sun Jun 18 19:37:49 2000
Server connected by ('38.28.162.194', 1064) at Sun Jun 18 19:37:49 2000
Server connected by ('38.28.162.194', 1067) at Sun Jun 18 19:37:50 2000

[client window 1]
C:\...\PP3E\Internet\Sockets>python echo-client.py starship.python.net
Client received: 'Echo=>Hello network world at Sun Jun 18 19:37:54 2000'
```

[client window 2]
```
C:\...\PP3E\Internet\Sockets>python echo-client.py starship.python.net Bruce
Client received: 'Echo=>Bruce at Sun Jun 18 19:37:54 2000'
```

[client window 3]
```
C:\...\PP3E\Internet\Sockets>python echo-client.py starship.python.net The
Meaning of Life
Client received: 'Echo=>The at Sun Jun 18 19:37:55 2000'
Client received: 'Echo=>Meaning at Sun Jun 18 19:37:56 2000'
Client received: 'Echo=>of at Sun Jun 18 19:37:56 2000'
Client received: 'Echo=>Life at Sun Jun 18 19:37:56 2000'
```

Again, all times here are on the server machine. This may be a little confusing because four windows are involved. In English, the test proceeds as follows:

1. The server starts running remotely.

2. All three clients are started and connect to the server at roughly the same time.

3. On the server, the client requests trigger three forked child processes, which all immediately go to sleep for five seconds (to simulate being busy doing something useful).

4. Each client waits until the server replies, which eventually happens five seconds after their initial requests.

In other words, all three clients are serviced at the same time by forked processes, while the main parent process continues listening for new client requests. If clients were not handled in parallel like this, no client could connect until the currently connected client's five-second delay expired.

In a more realistic application, that delay could be fatal if many clients were trying to connect at once—the server would be stuck in the action we're simulating with time. sleep, and not get back to the main loop to accept new client requests. With process forks per request, all clients can be serviced in parallel.

Notice that we're using the same client script here (*echo-client.py*), just a different server; clients simply send and receive data to a machine and port and don't care how their requests are handled on the server. Also note that the server is running remotely on a Linux machine. (As we learned in Chapter 5, the fork call is not supported on Windows in standard Python at the time this book was written.) We can also run this test on a Linux server entirely, with two Telnet windows. It works about the same as when clients are started locally, in a DOS console window, but here "local" means a remote machine you're telnetting to locally:

[one Telnet window]
```
[lutz@starship uploads]$ python fork-server.py &
[1] 3379
Server connected by ('127.0.0.1', 2928) at Sun Jun 18 22:44:50 2000
Server connected by ('127.0.0.1', 2929) at Sun Jun 18 22:45:08 2000
Server connected by ('208.185.174.112', 2930) at Sun Jun 18 22:45:50 2000
```

[another Telnet window, same machine]

```
[lutz@starship uploads]$ python echo-client.py
Client received: 'Echo=>Hello network world at Sun Jun 18 22:44:55 2000'

[lutz@starship uploads]$ python echo-client.py localhost niNiNI
Client received: 'Echo=>niNiNI at Sun Jun 18 22:45:13 2000'

[lutz@starship uploads]$ python echo-client.py starship.python.net Say no More!
Client received: 'Echo=>Say at Sun Jun 18 22:45:55 2000'
Client received: 'Echo=>no at Sun Jun 18 22:45:55 2000'
Client received: 'Echo=>More! at Sun Jun 18 22:45:55 2000'
```

Now let's move on to the tricky bits. This server script is fairly straightforward as forking code goes, but a few comments about some of the library tools it employs are in order.

Forking processes

We met os.fork in Chapter 5, but recall that forked processes are essentially a copy of the process that forks them, and so they inherit file and socket descriptors from their parent process. As a result, the new child process that runs the handleClient function has access to the connection socket created in the parent process. Programs know they are in a forked child process if the fork call returns 0; otherwise, the original parent process gets back the new child's ID.

Exiting from children

In earlier fork examples, child processes usually call one of the exec variants to start a new program in the child process. Here, instead, the child process simply calls a function in the same program and exits with os._exit. It's imperative to call os._exit here—if we did not, each child would live on after handleClient returns, and compete for accepting new client requests.

In fact, without the exit call, we'd wind up with as many perpetual server processes as requests served—remove the exit call and do a ps shell command after running a few clients, and you'll see what I mean. With the call, only the single parent process listens for new requests. os._exit is like sys.exit, but it exits the calling process immediately without cleanup actions. It's normally used only in child processes, and sys.exit is used everywhere else.

Killing the zombies

Note, however, that it's not quite enough to make sure that child processes exit and die. On systems like Linux, parents must also be sure to issue a wait system call to remove the entries for dead child processes from the system's process table. If we don't do this, the child processes will no longer run, but they will consume an entry in the system process table. For long-running servers, these bogus entries may become problematic.

It's common to call such dead-but-listed child processes *zombies*: they continue to use system resources even though they've already passed over to the great operating system beyond. To clean up after child processes are gone, this server keeps a list, activeChildren, of the process IDs of all child processes it spawns. Whenever a new incoming client request is received, the server runs its reapChildren to issue a wait for any dead children by issuing the standard Python os.waitpid(0,os.WNOHANG) call.

The os.waitpid call attempts to wait for a child process to exit and returns its process ID and exit status. With a 0 for its first argument, it waits for any child process. With the WNOHANG parameter for its second, it does nothing if no child process has exited (i.e., it does not block or pause the caller). The net effect is that this call simply asks the operating system for the process ID of any child that has exited. If any have, the process ID returned is removed both from the system process table and from this script's activeChildren list.

To see why all this complexity is needed, comment out the reapChildren call in this script, run it on a server, and then run a few clients. On my Linux server, a ps -f full process listing command shows that all the dead child processes stay in the system process table (show as <defunct>):

```
[lutz@starship uploads]$ ps -f
UID        PID  PPID  C STIME TTY          TIME CMD
lutz      3270  3264  0 22:33 pts/1    00:00:00 -bash
lutz      3311  3270  0 22:37 pts/1    00:00:00 python fork-server.py
lutz      3312  3311  0 22:37 pts/1    00:00:00 [python <defunct>]
lutz      3313  3311  0 22:37 pts/1    00:00:00 [python <defunct>]
lutz      3314  3311  0 22:37 pts/1    00:00:00 [python <defunct>]
lutz      3316  3311  0 22:37 pts/1    00:00:00 [python <defunct>]
lutz      3317  3311  0 22:37 pts/1    00:00:00 [python <defunct>]
lutz      3318  3311  0 22:37 pts/1    00:00:00 [python <defunct>]
lutz      3322  3270  0 22:38 pts/1    00:00:00 ps -f
```

When the reapChildren command is reactivated, dead child zombie entries are cleaned up each time the server gets a new client connection request, by calling the Python os.waitpid function. A few zombies may accumulate if the server is heavily loaded, but they will remain only until the next client connection is received:

```
[lutz@starship uploads]$ ps -f
UID        PID  PPID  C STIME TTY          TIME CMD
lutz      3270  3264  0 22:33 pts/1    00:00:00 -bash
lutz      3340  3270  0 22:41 pts/1    00:00:00 python fork-server.py
lutz      3341  3340  0 22:41 pts/1    00:00:00 [python <defunct>]
lutz      3342  3340  0 22:41 pts/1    00:00:00 [python <defunct>]
lutz      3343  3340  0 22:41 pts/1    00:00:00 [python <defunct>]
lutz      3344  3270  6 22:41 pts/1    00:00:00 ps -f
[lutz@starship uploads]$
Server connected by ('38.28.131.174', 1170) at Sun Jun 18 22:41:43 2000

[lutz@starship uploads]$ ps -f
UID        PID  PPID  C STIME TTY          TIME CMD
lutz      3270  3264  0 22:33 pts/1    00:00:00 -bash
```

```
lutz      3340  3270  0 22:41 pts/1     00:00:00 python fork-server.py
lutz      3345  3340  0 22:41 pts/1     00:00:00 [python <defunct>]
lutz      3346  3270  0 22:41 pts/1     00:00:00 ps -f
```

If you type fast enough, you can actually see a child process morph from a real running program into a zombie. Here, for example, a child spawned to handle a new request (process ID 11785) changes to <defunct> on exit. Its process entry will be removed completely when the next request is received:

```
[lutz@starship uploads]$
Server connected by ('38.28.57.160', 1106) at Mon Jun 19 22:34:39 2000
[lutz@starship uploads]$ ps -f
UID         PID  PPID  C STIME TTY         TIME CMD
lutz      11089 11088  0 21:13 pts/2     00:00:00 -bash
lutz      11780 11089  0 22:34 pts/2     00:00:00 python fork-server.py
lutz      11785 11780  0 22:34 pts/2     00:00:00 python fork-server.py
lutz      11786 11089  0 22:34 pts/2     00:00:00 ps -f

[lutz@starship uploads]$ ps -f
UID         PID  PPID  C STIME TTY         TIME CMD
lutz      11089 11088  0 21:13 pts/2     00:00:00 -bash
lutz      11780 11089  0 22:34 pts/2     00:00:00 python fork-server.py
lutz      11785 11780  0 22:34 pts/2     00:00:00 [python <defunct>]
lutz      11787 11089  0 22:34 pts/2     00:00:00 ps -f
```

Preventing zombies with signal handlers

On some systems, it's also possible to clean up zombie child processes by resetting the signal handler for the SIGCHLD signal raised by the operating system when a child process exits. If a Python script assigns the SIG_IGN (ignore) action as the SIGCHLD signal handler, zombies will be removed automatically and immediately as child processes exit; the parent need not issue wait calls to clean up after them. Because of that, this scheme is a simpler alternative to manually reaping zombies (on platforms where it is supported).

If you've already read Chapter 5, you know that Python's standard signal module lets scripts install handlers for signals—software-generated events. If you haven't read that chapter, here is a brief bit of background to show how this pans out for zombies. The program in Example 13-5 installs a Python-coded signal handler function to respond to whatever signal number you type on the command line.

Example 13-5. PP3E\Internet\Sockets\signal-demo.py

```
#############################################################################
# Demo Python's signal module; pass signal number as a command-line arg,
# use a "kill -N pid" shell command to send this process a signal; e.g.,
# on my Linux machine, SIGUSR1=10, SIGUSR2=12, SIGCHLD=17, and SIGCHLD
# handler stays in effect even if not restored: all other handlers restored
# by Python after caught, but SIGCHLD behavior is left to the platform's
# implementation; signal works on Windows but defines only a few signal
# types; signals are not very portable in general;
```

Example 13-5. PP3E\Internet\Sockets\signal-demo.py (continued)

```
###########################################################################

import sys, signal, time

def now():
    return time.ctime(time.time())

def onSignal(signum, stackframe):                # Python signal handler
    print 'Got signal', signum, 'at', now()      # most handlers stay in effect
    if signum == signal.SIGCHLD:                  # but sigchld handler is not
        print 'sigchld caught'
        #signal.signal(signal.SIGCHLD, onSignal)

signum = int(sys.argv[1])
signal.signal(signum, onSignal)                  # install signal handler
while 1: signal.pause()                          # sleep waiting for signals
```

To run this script, simply put it in the background and send it signals by typing the kill -signal-number process-id shell command line. Process IDs are listed in the PID column of ps command results. Here is this script in action catching signal numbers 10 (reserved for general use) and 9 (the unavoidable terminate signal):

```
[lutz@starship uploads]$ python signal-demo.py 10 &
[1] 11297
[lutz@starship uploads]$ ps -f
UID       PID  PPID  C STIME TTY        TIME CMD
lutz     11089 11088  0 21:13 pts/2    00:00:00 -bash
lutz     11297 11089  0 21:49 pts/2    00:00:00 python signal-demo.py 10
lutz     11298 11089  0 21:49 pts/2    00:00:00 ps -f

[lutz@starship uploads]$ kill -10 11297
Got signal 10 at Mon Jun 19 21:49:27 2000

[lutz@starship uploads]$ kill -10 11297
Got signal 10 at Mon Jun 19 21:49:29 2000

[lutz@starship uploads]$ kill -10 11297
Got signal 10 at Mon Jun 19 21:49:32 2000

[lutz@starship uploads]$ kill -9 11297
[1]+  Killed                  python signal-demo.py 10
```

And here the script catches signal 17, which happens to be SIGCHLD on my Linux server. Signal numbers vary from machine to machine, so you should normally use their names, not their numbers. SIGCHLD behavior may vary per platform as well (see the signal module's library manual entry for more details):

```
[lutz@starship uploads]$ python signal-demo.py 17 &
[1] 11320
[lutz@starship uploads]$ ps -f
UID       PID  PPID  C STIME TTY        TIME CMD
lutz     11089 11088  0 21:13 pts/2    00:00:00 -bash
```

```
lutz      11320 11089  0 21:52 pts/2    00:00:00 python signal-demo.py 17
lutz      11321 11089  0 21:52 pts/2    00:00:00 ps -f

[lutz@starship uploads]$ kill -17 11320
Got signal 17 at Mon Jun 19 21:52:24 2000
[lutz@starship uploads] sigchld caught

[lutz@starship uploads]$ kill -17 11320
Got signal 17 at Mon Jun 19 21:52:27 2000
[lutz@starship uploads]$ sigchld caught
```

Now, to apply all of this to kill zombies, simply set the SIGCHLD signal handler to the SIG_IGN ignore handler action; on systems where this assignment is supported, child processes will be cleaned up when they exit. The forking server variant shown in Example 13-6 uses this trick to manage its children.

Example 13-6. PP3E\Internet\Sockets\fork-server-signal.py

```
#############################################################################
# Same as fork-server.py, but use the Python signal module to avoid keeping
# child zombie processes after they terminate, not an explicit loop before
# each new connection; SIG_IGN means ignore, and may not work with SIG_CHLD
# child exit signal on all platforms; on Linux, socket.accept cannot be
# interrupted with a signal;
#############################################################################

import os, time, sys, signal, signal
from socket import *                        # get socket constructor and constants
myHost = ''                                 # server machine, '' means local host
myPort = 50007                              # listen on a non-reserved port number

sockobj = socket(AF_INET, SOCK_STREAM)              # make a TCP socket object
sockobj.bind((myHost, myPort))                      # bind it to server port number
sockobj.listen(5)                                   # up to 5 pending connects
signal.signal(signal.SIGCHLD, signal.SIG_IGN)       # avoid child zombie processes

def now():                                          # time on server machine
    return time.ctime(time.time())

def handleClient(connection):                       # child process replies, exits
    time.sleep(5)                                   # simulate a blocking activity
    while True:                                     # read, write a client socket
        data = connection.recv(1024)
        if not data: break
        connection.send('Echo=>%s at %s' % (data, now()))
    connection.close()
    os._exit(0)

def dispatcher():                                   # listen until process killed
    while True:                                     # wait for next connection,
        connection, address = sockobj.accept()      # pass to process for service
        print 'Server connected by', address,
        print 'at', now()
```

Example 13-6. PP3E\Internet\Sockets\fork-server-signal.py (continued)

```
        childPid = os.fork( )              # copy this process
        if childPid == 0:                  # if in child process: handle
            handleClient(connection)       # else: go accept next connect

dispatcher( )
```

Where applicable, this technique is:

- Much simpler; we don't need to manually track or reap child processes.
- More accurate; it leaves no zombies temporarily between client requests.

In fact, only one line is dedicated to handling zombies here: the signal.signal call near the top, to set the handler. Unfortunately, this version is also even less portable than using os.fork in the first place, because signals may work slightly differently from platform to platform. For instance, some platforms may not allow SIG_IGN to be used as the SIGCHLD action at all. On Linux systems, though, this simpler forking server variant works like a charm:

```
[lutz@starship uploads]$
Server connected by ('38.28.57.160', 1166) at Mon Jun 19 22:38:29 2000

[lutz@starship uploads]$ ps -f
UID        PID  PPID  C STIME TTY          TIME CMD
lutz     11089 11088  0 21:13 pts/2    00:00:00 -bash
lutz     11827 11089  0 22:37 pts/2    00:00:00 python fork-server-signal.py
lutz     11835 11827  0 22:38 pts/2    00:00:00 python fork-server-signal.py
lutz     11836 11089  0 22:38 pts/2    00:00:00 ps -f

[lutz@starship uploads]$ ps -f
UID        PID  PPID  C STIME TTY          TIME CMD
lutz     11089 11088  0 21:13 pts/2    00:00:00 -bash
lutz     11827 11089  0 22:37 pts/2    00:00:00 python fork-server-signal.py
lutz     11837 11089  0 22:38 pts/2    00:00:00 ps -f
```

Notice that in this version, the child process's entry goes away as soon as it exits, even before a new client request is received; no "defunct" zombie ever appears. More dramatically, if we now start up the script we wrote earlier that spawns eight clients in parallel (*testecho.py*) to talk to this server, all appear on the server while running, but are removed immediately as they exit:

```
[lutz@starship uploads]$ ps -f
UID        PID  PPID  C STIME TTY          TIME CMD
lutz     11089 11088  0 21:13 pts/2    00:00:00 -bash
lutz     11827 11089  0 22:37 pts/2    00:00:00 python fork-server-signal.py
lutz     11839 11827  0 22:39 pts/2    00:00:00 python fork-server-signal.py
lutz     11840 11827  0 22:39 pts/2    00:00:00 python fork-server-signal.py
lutz     11841 11827  0 22:39 pts/2    00:00:00 python fork-server-signal.py
lutz     11842 11827  0 22:39 pts/2    00:00:00 python fork-server-signal.py
lutz     11843 11827  0 22:39 pts/2    00:00:00 python fork-server-signal.py
lutz     11844 11827  0 22:39 pts/2    00:00:00 python fork-server-signal.py
lutz     11845 11827  0 22:39 pts/2    00:00:00 python fork-server-signal.py
```

```
lutz      11846 11827  0 22:39 pts/2    00:00:00 python fork-server-signal.py
lutz      11848 11089  0 22:39 pts/2    00:00:00 ps -f

[lutz@starship uploads]$ ps -f
UID       PID  PPID  C STIME TTY        TIME CMD
lutz      11089 11088  0 21:13 pts/2    00:00:00 -bash
lutz      11827 11089  0 22:37 pts/2    00:00:00 python fork-server-signal.py
lutz      11849 11089  0 22:39 pts/2    00:00:00 ps -f
```

Threading Servers

The forking model just described works well on Unix-like platforms in general, but it suffers from some potentially significant limitations:

Performance

> On some machines, starting a new process can be fairly expensive in terms of time and space resources.

Portability

> Forking processes is a Unix technique; as we just noted, the fork call currently doesn't work on non-Unix platforms such as Windows under standard Python. As we learned in Chapter 5, forks can be used in the Cygwin version of Python on Windows, but they may be inefficient and not exactly the same as Unix forks.

Complexity

> If you think that forking servers can be complicated, you're not alone. As we just saw, forking also brings with it all the shenanigans of managing zombies—cleaning up after child processes that live shorter lives than their parents.

If you read Chapter 5, you know that one solution to all of these dilemmas is to use threads rather than processes. Threads run in parallel and share global (i.e., module and interpreter) memory, but they are usually less expensive to start, and work on both Unix-like machines and Microsoft Windows under standard Python today. Furthermore, some see threads as simpler to program—child threads die silently on exit, without leaving behind zombies to haunt the server.

Example 13-7 is another mutation of the echo server that handles client requests in parallel by running them in threads rather than in processes.

Example 13-7. PP3E\Internet\Sockets\thread-server.py

```
#############################################################################
# Server side: open a socket on a port, listen for a message from a client,
# and send an echo reply; echoes lines until eof when client closes socket;
# spawns a thread to handle each client connection; threads share global
# memory space with main thread; this is more portable than fork: threads
# work on standard Windows systems, but process forks do not;
#############################################################################

import thread, time
from socket import *                    # get socket constructor and constants
```

Example 13-7. PP3E\Internet\Sockets\thread-server.py (continued)

```
myHost = ''                              # server machine, '' means local host
myPort = 50007                           # listen on a non-reserved port number

sockobj = socket(AF_INET, SOCK_STREAM)      # make a TCP socket object
sockobj.bind((myHost, myPort))              # bind it to server port number
sockobj.listen(5)                           # allow up to 5 pending connects

def now():
    return time.ctime(time.time())          # current time on the server

def handleClient(connection):            # in spawned thread: reply
    time.sleep(5)                        # simulate a blocking activity
    while True:                          # read, write a client socket
        data = connection.recv(1024)
        if not data: break
        connection.send('Echo=>%s at %s' % (data, now()))
    connection.close()

def dispatcher():                        # listen until process killed
    while True:                          # wait for next connection,
        connection, address = sockobj.accept()   # pass to thread for service
        print 'Server connected by', address,
        print 'at', now()
        thread.start_new(handleClient, (connection,))

dispatcher()
```

This dispatcher delegates each incoming client connection request to a newly spawned thread running the handleClient function. As a result, this server can process multiple clients at once, and the main dispatcher loop can get quickly back to the top to check for newly arrived requests. The net effect is that new clients won't be denied service due to a busy server.

Functionally, this version is similar to the fork solution (clients are handled in parallel), but it will work on any machine that supports threads, including Windows and Linux. Let's test it on both. First, start the server on a Linux machine and run clients on both Linux and Windows:

[window 1: thread-based server process, server keeps accepting
client connections while threads are servicing prior requests]
[lutz@starship uploads]$ **/usr/bin/python thread-server.py**
Server connected by ('127.0.0.1', 2934) at Sun Jun 18 22:52:52 2000
Server connected by ('38.28.131.174', 1179) at Sun Jun 18 22:53:31 2000
Server connected by ('38.28.131.174', 1182) at Sun Jun 18 22:53:35 2000
Server connected by ('38.28.131.174', 1185) at Sun Jun 18 22:53:37 2000

[window 2: client, but on same server machine]
[lutz@starship uploads]$ **python echo-client.py**
Client received: 'Echo=>Hello network world at Sun Jun 18 22:52:57 2000'

[window 3: remote client, PC]

```
C:\...\PP3E\Internet\Sockets>python echo-client.py starship.python.net
Client received: 'Echo=>Hello network world at Sun Jun 18 22:53:36 2000'

[window 4: client PC]
C:\...\PP3E\Internet\Sockets>python echo-client.py starship.python.net Bruce
Client received: 'Echo=>Bruce at Sun Jun 18 22:53:40 2000'

[window 5: client PC]
C:\...\PP3E\Internet\Sockets>python echo-client.py starship.python.net The
Meaning of Life
Client received: 'Echo=>The at Sun Jun 18 22:53:42 2000'
Client received: 'Echo=>Meaning at Sun Jun 18 22:53:42 2000'
Client received: 'Echo=>of at Sun Jun 18 22:53:42 2000'
Client received: 'Echo=>Life at Sun Jun 18 22:53:42 2000'
```

Because this server uses threads rather than forked processes, we can run it portably on both Linux and a Windows PC. Here it is at work again, running on the same local Windows PC as its clients; again, the main point to notice is that new clients are accepted while prior clients are being processed in parallel with other clients and the main thread (in the five-second sleep delay):

```
[window 1: server, on local PC]
C:\...\PP3E\Internet\Sockets>python thread-server.py
Server connected by ('127.0.0.1', 1186) at Sun Jun 18 23:46:31 2000
Server connected by ('127.0.0.1', 1187) at Sun Jun 18 23:46:33 2000
Server connected by ('127.0.0.1', 1188) at Sun Jun 18 23:46:34 2000

[window 2: client, on local
PC]
C:\...\PP3E\Internet\Sockets>python echo-client.py
Client received: 'Echo=>Hello network world at Sun Jun 18 23:46:36 2000'

[window 3: client]
C:\...\PP3E\Internet\Sockets>python echo-client.py localhost Brian
Client received: 'Echo=>Brian at Sun Jun 18 23:46:38 2000'

[window 4: client]
C:\...\PP3E\Internet\Sockets>python echo-client.py localhost Bright side of Life
Client received: 'Echo=>Bright at Sun Jun 18 23:46:39 2000'
Client received: 'Echo=>side at Sun Jun 18 23:46:39 2000'
Client received: 'Echo=>of at Sun Jun 18 23:46:39 2000'
Client received: 'Echo=>Life at Sun Jun 18 23:46:39 2000'
```

Remember that a thread silently exits when the function it is running returns; unlike the process fork version, we don't call anything like os._exit in the client handler function (and we shouldn't—it may kill all threads in the process!). Because of this, the thread version is not only more portable, but also simpler.

Standard Library Server Classes

Now that I've shown you how to write forking and threading servers to process clients without blocking incoming requests, I should also tell you that there are standard tools in the Python library to make this process easier. In particular, the SocketServer module defines classes that implement all flavors of forking and threading servers that you are likely to be interested in. Simply create the desired kind of imported server object, passing in a handler object with a callback method of your own, as shown in Example 13-8.

Example 13-8. PP3E\Internet\Sockets\class-server.py

```
#############################################################################
# Server side: open a socket on a port, listen for a message from a client,
# and send an echo reply; this version uses the standard library module
# SocketServer to do its work; SocketServer allows us to make a simple
# TCPServer, a ThreadingTCPServer, a ForkingTCPServer, and more, and
# routes each client connect request to a new instance of a passed-in
# request handler object's handle method; SocketServer also supports
# UDP and Unix domain sockets; see the library manual for other usage.
#############################################################################

import SocketServer, time              # get socket server, handler objects
myHost = ''                            # server machine, '' means local host
myPort = 50007                         # listen on a non-reserved port number
def now():
    return time.ctime(time.time())

class MyClientHandler(SocketServer.BaseRequestHandler):
    def handle(self):                        # on each client connect
        print self.client_address, now()     # show this client's address
        time.sleep(5)                        # simulate a blocking activity
        while True:                          # self.request is client socket
            data = self.request.recv(1024)   # read, write a client socket
            if not data: break
            self.request.send('Echo=>%s at %s' % (data, now()))
        self.request.close()

# make a threaded server, listen/handle clients forever
myaddr = (myHost, myPort)
server = SocketServer.ThreadingTCPServer(myaddr, MyClientHandler)
server.serve_forever()
```

This server works the same as the threading server we wrote by hand in the previous section, but instead focuses on service implementation (the customized handle method), not on threading details. It's run the same way, too—here it is processing three clients started by hand, plus eight spawned by the testecho script shown in Example 13-3:

```
[window1: server, serverHost='localhost' in echo-client.py]
C:\...\PP3E\Internet\Sockets>python class-server.py
('127.0.0.1', 1189) Sun Jun 18 23:49:18 2000
('127.0.0.1', 1190) Sun Jun 18 23:49:20 2000
('127.0.0.1', 1191) Sun Jun 18 23:49:22 2000
('127.0.0.1', 1192) Sun Jun 18 23:49:50 2000
('127.0.0.1', 1193) Sun Jun 18 23:49:50 2000
```

```
('127.0.0.1', 1194) Sun Jun 18 23:49:50 2000
('127.0.0.1', 1195) Sun Jun 18 23:49:50 2000
('127.0.0.1', 1196) Sun Jun 18 23:49:50 2000
('127.0.0.1', 1197) Sun Jun 18 23:49:50 2000
('127.0.0.1', 1198) Sun Jun 18 23:49:50 2000
('127.0.0.1', 1199) Sun Jun 18 23:49:50 2000

[window2: client]
C:\...\PP3E\Internet\Sockets>python echo-client.py
Client received: 'Echo=>Hello network world at Sun Jun 18 23:49:23 2000'

[window3: client]
C:\...\PP3E\Internet\Sockets>python echo-client.py localhost Robin
Client received: 'Echo=>Robin at Sun Jun 18 23:49:25 2000'

[window4: client]
C:\...\PP3E\Internet\Sockets>python echo-client.py localhost Brave Sir Robin
Client received: 'Echo=>Brave at Sun Jun 18 23:49:27 2000'
Client received: 'Echo=>Sir at Sun Jun 18 23:49:27 2000'
Client received: 'Echo=>Robin at Sun Jun 18 23:49:27 2000'

C:\...\PP3E\Internet\Sockets>python testecho.py

[window4: contact remote server instead—times skewed]
C:\...\PP3E\Internet\Sockets>python echo-client.py starship.python.net Brave
Sir Robin
Client received: 'Echo=>Brave at Sun Jun 18 23:03:28 2000'
Client received: 'Echo=>Sir at Sun Jun 18 23:03:28 2000'
Client received: 'Echo=>Robin at Sun Jun 18 23:03:29 2000'
```

To build a forking server instead, just use the class name ForkingTCPServer when creating the server object. The SocketServer module has more power than shown by this example; it also supports synchronous (nonparallel) servers, UDP and Unix sockets, and so on. See Python's library manual for more details. Also see the end of Chapter 18 for more on Python server implementation tools.

For more advanced server needs, Python also comes with standard library tools that allow you to implement a full-blown HTTP (web) server that knows how to run server-side CGI scripts in a few lines of Python code. We'll explore those tools in Chapter 16.

Third-Party Server Tools: Twisted

For other server options, see the open source Twisted system (*http://twistedmatrix. com*). Twisted is an asynchronous networking framework written in Python that supports TCP, UDP, multicast, SSL/TLS, serial communication, and more. It supports both clients and servers and includes implementations of a number of commonly used network services such as a web server, an IRC chat server, a mail server, a relational database interface, and an object broker.

Although Twisted supports processes and threads for longer-running actions, it also uses an asynchronous, event-driven model to handle clients, which is similar to the event loop of GUI libraries like Tkinter. In fact, it abstracts an event loop, which multiplexes among open socket connections—coincidentally, the topic of the next section.

Multiplexing Servers with select

So far we've seen how to handle multiple clients at once with both forked processes and spawned threads, and we've looked at a library class that encapsulates both schemes. Under both approaches, all client handlers seem to run in parallel with each other and with the main dispatch loop that continues watching for new incoming requests. Because all of these tasks run in parallel (i.e., at the same time), the server doesn't get blocked when accepting new requests or when processing a long-running client handler.

Technically, though, threads and processes don't really run in parallel, unless you're lucky enough to have a machine with many CPUs. Instead, your operating system performs a juggling act—it divides the computer's processing power among all active tasks. It runs part of one, then part of another, and so on. All the tasks appear to run in parallel, but only because the operating system switches focus between tasks so fast that you don't usually notice. This process of switching between tasks is sometimes called *time-slicing* when done by an operating system; it is more generally known as *multiplexing*.

When we spawn threads and processes, we rely on the operating system to juggle the active tasks, but there's no reason that a Python script can't do so as well. For instance, a script might divide tasks into multiple steps—do a step of one task, then one of another, and so on, until all are completed. The script need only know how to divide its attention among the multiple active tasks to multiplex on its own.

Servers can apply this technique to yield yet another way to handle multiple clients at once, a way that requires neither threads nor forks. By multiplexing client connections and the main dispatcher with the select system call, a single event loop can process clients and accept new ones in parallel (or at least close enough to avoid stalling). Such servers are sometimes called *asynchronous*, because they service clients in spurts, as each becomes ready to communicate. In asynchronous servers, a single main loop run in a single process and thread decides which clients should get a bit of attention each time through. Client requests and the main dispatcher are each given a small slice of the server's attention if they are ready to converse.

Most of the magic behind this server structure is the operating system select call, available in Python's standard select module. Roughly, select is asked to monitor a list of input sources, output sources, and exceptional condition sources and tells us which sources are ready for processing. It can be made to simply poll all the sources to see which are ready; wait for a maximum time period for sources to become ready; or wait indefinitely until one or more sources are ready for processing.

However used, select lets us direct attention to sockets ready to communicate, so as to avoid blocking on calls to ones that are not. That is, when the sources passed to select are sockets, we can be sure that socket calls like accept, recv, and send will not block (pause) the server when applied to objects returned by select. Because of that, a single-loop server that uses select need not get stuck communicating with one client or waiting for new ones while other clients are starved for the server's attention.

A select-based echo server

Let's see how all of this translates into code. The script in Example 13-9 implements another echo server, one that can handle multiple clients without ever starting new processes or threads.

Example 13-9. PP3E\Internet\Sockets\select-server.py

```
#############################################################################
# Server: handle multiple clients in parallel with select. use the select
# module to manually multiplex among a set of sockets: main sockets which
# accept new client connections, and input sockets connected to accepted
# clients; select can take an optional 4th arg--0 to poll, n.m to wait n.m
# seconds, or ommitted to wait till any socket is ready for processing.
#############################################################################

import sys, time
from select import select
from socket import socket, AF_INET, SOCK_STREAM
def now(): return time.ctime(time.time())

myHost = ''                              # server machine, '' means local host
myPort = 50007                          # listen on a non-reserved port number
if len(sys.argv) == 3:                  # allow host/port as cmdline args too
    myHost, myPort = sys.argv[1:]
numPortSocks = 2                        # number of ports for client connects

# make main sockets for accepting new client requests
mainsocks, readsocks, writesocks = [], [], []
for i in range(numPortSocks):
    portsock = socket(AF_INET, SOCK_STREAM)  # make a TCP/IP spocket object
    portsock.bind((myHost, myPort))          # bind it to server port number
    portsock.listen(5)                       # listen, allow 5 pending connects
    mainsocks.append(portsock)               # add to main list to identify
    readsocks.append(portsock)               # add to select inputs list
    myPort += 1                              # bind on consecutive ports

# event loop: listen and multiplex until server process killed
print 'select-server loop starting'
while True:
```

Example 13-9. PP3E\Internet\Sockets\select-server.py (continued)

```
#print readsocks
readables, writeables, exceptions = select(readsocks, writesocks, [])
for sockobj in readables:
    if sockobj in mainsocks:                    # for ready input sockets
        # port socket: accept new client
        newsock, address = sockobj.accept()     # accept should not block
        print 'Connect:', address, id(newsock)  # newsock is a new socket
        readsocks.append(newsock)               # add to select list, wait
    else:
        # client socket: read next line
        data = sockobj.recv(1024)               # recv should not block
        print '\tgot', data, 'on', id(sockobj)
        if not data:                            # if closed by the clients
            sockobj.close()                     # close here and remv from
            readsocks.remove(sockobj)           # del list else reselected
        else:
            # this may block: should really select for writes too
            sockobj.send('Echo=>%s at %s' % (data, now()))
```

The bulk of this script is the big while event loop at the end that calls select to find out which sockets are ready for processing (these include main port sockets on which clients can connect, and open client connections). It then loops over all such ready sockets, accepting connections on main port sockets and reading and echoing input on any client sockets ready for input. Both the accept and recv calls in this code are guaranteed to not block the server process after select returns; as a result, this server can quickly get back to the top of the loop to process newly arrived client requests and already connected clients' inputs. The net effect is that all new requests and clients are serviced in pseudoparallel fashion.

To make this process work, the server appends the connected socket for each client to the readables list passed to select, and simply waits for the socket to show up in the selected inputs list. For illustration purposes, this server also listens for new clients on more than one port—on ports 50007 and 50008, in our examples. Because these main port sockets are also interrogated with select, connection requests on either port can be accepted without blocking either already connected clients or new connection requests appearing on the other port. The select call returns whatever sockets in readables are ready for processing—both main port sockets and sockets connected to clients currently being processed.

Running the select server

Let's run this script locally to see how it does its stuff (the client and server can also be run on different machines, as in prior socket examples). First, we'll assume we've already started this server script in one window, and run a few clients to talk to it. The following code is the interaction in two such client windows running on Windows (MS-DOS consoles). The first client simply runs the echo-client script twice to contact the server, and the second also kicks off the testecho script to spawn eight echo-client programs running in parallel. As before, the server simply echoes back whatever text that client sends. Notice that the second client window really runs a script called echo-client-50008 so as to connect to the second port socket in the server; it's the same as echo-client, with a different port number (alas, the original script wasn't designed to input a port):

```
[client window 1]
C:\...\PP3E\Internet\Sockets>python echo-client.py
Client received: 'Echo=>Hello network world at Sun Aug 13 22:52:01 2000'

C:\...\PP3E\Internet\Sockets>python echo-client.py
Client received: 'Echo=>Hello network world at Sun Aug 13 22:52:03 2000'

[client window 2]
C:\...\PP3E\Internet\Sockets>python echo-client-50008.py localhost Sir Lancelot
Client received: 'Echo=>Sir at Sun Aug 13 22:52:57 2000'
Client received: 'Echo=>Lancelot at Sun Aug 13 22:52:57 2000'

C:\...\PP3E\Internet\Sockets>python testecho.py
```

The next code section is the sort of interaction and output that show up in the window where the server has been started. The first three connections come from echo-client runs; the rest is the result of the eight programs spawned by testecho in the second client window. Notice that for testecho, new client connections and client inputs are multiplexed together. If you study the output closely, you'll see that they overlap in time, because all activity is dispatched by the single event loop in the server.* Also note that the server gets an empty string when the client has closed its socket. We take care to close and delete these sockets at the server right away, or else they would be needlessly reselected again and again, each time through the main loop:

```
[server window]
C:\...\PP3E\Internet\Sockets>python select-server.py
select-server loop starting
Connect: ('127.0.0.1', 1175) 7965520
        got Hello network world on 7965520
        got  on 7965520
Connect: ('127.0.0.1', 1176) 7964288
        got Hello network world on 7964288
        got  on 7964288
Connect: ('127.0.0.1', 1177) 7963920
        got Sir on 7963920
        got Lancelot on 7963920
        got  on 7963920

[testecho results]
Connect: ('127.0.0.1', 1178) 7965216
```

---

* And the trace output on the server will probably look a bit different every time it runs. Clients and new connections are interleaved almost at random due to timing differences on the host machines.

```
        got Hello network world on 7965216
        got  on 7965216
Connect: ('127.0.0.1', 1179) 7963968
Connect: ('127.0.0.1', 1180) 7965424
        got Hello network world on 7963968
Connect: ('127.0.0.1', 1181) 7962976
        got Hello network world on 7965424
        got  on 7963968
        got Hello network world on 7962976
        got  on 7965424
        got  on 7962976
Connect: ('127.0.0.1', 1182) 7963648
        got Hello network world on 7963648
        got  on 7963648
Connect: ('127.0.0.1', 1183) 7966640
        got Hello network world on 7966640
        got  on 7966640
Connect: ('127.0.0.1', 1184) 7966496
        got Hello network world on 7966496
        got  on 7966496
Connect: ('127.0.0.1', 1185) 7965888
        got Hello network world on 7965888
        got  on 7965888
```

A subtle but crucial point: a `time.sleep` call to simulate a long-running task doesn't make sense in the server here—because all clients are handled by the same single loop, sleeping would pause everything (and defeat the whole point of a multiplexing server). Here are a few additional notes before we move on:

select *call details*

Formally, select is called with three lists of selectable objects (input sources, output sources, and exceptional condition sources), plus an optional timeout. The timeout argument may be a real wait expiration value in seconds (use floating-point numbers to express fractions of a second), a zero value to mean simply poll and return immediately, or omitted to mean wait until at least one object is ready (as done in our server script earlier). The call returns a triple of ready objects—subsets of the first three arguments—any or all of which may be empty if the timeout expired before sources became ready.

select *portability*

The select call works only for sockets on Windows, but also works for things like files and pipes on Unix and Macintosh. For servers running over the Internet, of course, the primary devices we are interested in are sockets.

Nonblocking sockets

select lets us be sure that socket calls like accept and recv won't block (pause) the caller, but it's also possible to make Python sockets nonblocking in general. Call the setblocking method of socket objects to set the socket to blocking or nonblocking mode. For example, given a call like sock.setblocking(flag), the socket sock is set to nonblocking mode if the flag is zero, and to blocking mode otherwise. All sockets start out in blocking mode initially, so socket calls may always make the caller wait.

But when in nonblocking mode, a socket.error exception is raised if a recv socket call doesn't find any data, or if a send call can't immediately transfer data. A script can catch this exception to determine whether the socket is ready for processing. In blocking mode, these calls always block until they can proceed. Of course, there may be much more to processing client requests than data transfers (requests may also require long-running computations), so nonblocking sockets don't guarantee that servers won't stall in general. They are simply another way to code multiplexing servers. Like select, they are better suited when client requests can be serviced quickly.

The asyncore *module framework*

If you're interested in using select, you will probably also be interested in checking out the asyncore.py module in the standard Python library. It implements a class-based callback model, where input and output callbacks are dispatched to class methods by a precoded select event loop. As such, it allows servers to be constructed without threads or forks, and is a select-based alternative to the SocketServer threading and forking module we met in the prior sections. We'll discuss this tool again at the end of Chapter 18; see the Python library manual for details and a usage example.

Twisted

The Twisted system, described in the prior section, abstracts away many of the details inherent in an asynchronous server and provides an event-driven model and framework. Twisted's internal event engine is similar in spirit to our select-based server and the asyncore module, but it is regarded as more advanced. Twisted is a third-party system, not a standard library tool.

Choosing a Server Scheme

So when should you use select to build a server, instead of threads or forks? Needs vary per application, of course, but servers based on the select call generally perform very well when client transactions are relatively short and are not CPU-bound. If they are not short, threads or forks may be a better way to split processing among multiple clients. Threads and forks are especially useful if clients require long-running processing above and beyond socket calls. However, combinations are possible too—nothing is stopping a select-based polling loop from using threads, too.

It's important to remember that schemes based on select (and nonblocking sockets) are not completely immune to blocking. In the example earlier, for instance, the send call that echoes text back to a client might block too, and hence stall the entire server. We could work around that blocking potential by using select to make sure that the output operation is ready before we attempt it (e.g., use the writesocks list and add another loop to send replies to ready output sockets), albeit at a noticeable cost in program clarity.

In general, though, if we cannot split up the processing of a client's request in such a way that it can be multiplexed with other requests and not block the server's loop, select may not be the best way to construct the server.

Moreover, select also seems more complex than spawning either processes or threads, because we need to manually transfer control among all tasks (for instance, compare the threaded and select versions of this server, even without write selects). As usual, though, the degree of that complexity varies per application. The *asyncore* standard library module mentioned earlier simplifies some of the tasks of implementing a select-based event-loop socket server.

A Simple Python File Server

Time for something more realistic; let's conclude this chapter by putting some of these socket ideas to work doing something a bit more useful than echoing text back and forth. Example 13-10 implements both the server-side and the client-side logic needed to ship a requested file from server to client machines over a raw socket.

In effect, this script implements a simple file download system. One instance of the script is run on the machine where downloadable files live (the server), and another on the machines you wish to copy files to (the clients). Command-line arguments tell the script which flavor to run and optionally name the server machine and port number over which conversations are to occur. A server instance can respond to any number of client file requests at the port on which it listens, because it serves each in a thread.

Example 13-10. PP3E\Internet\Sockets\getfile.py

```
#############################################################################
# implement client and server-side logic to transfer an arbitrary file from
# server to client over a socket; uses a simple control-info protocol rather
# than separate sockets for control and data (as in ftp), dispatches each
# client request to a handler thread, and loops to transfer the entire file
# by blocks; see ftplib examples for a higher-level transport scheme;
#############################################################################

import sys, os, thread, time
from socket import *
def now(): return time.ctime(time.time())

blksz = 1024
defaultHost = 'localhost'
defaultPort = 50001

helptext = """
Usage...
```

Example 13-10. PP3E\Internet\Sockets\getfile.py (continued)

```
server=> getfile.py  -mode server            [-port nnn] [-host hhh|localhost]
client=> getfile.py [-mode client] -file fff [-port nnn] [-host hhh|localhost]
"""

def parsecommandline():
    dict = {}                       # put in dictionary for easy lookup
    args = sys.argv[1:]             # skip program name at front of args
    while len(args) >= 2:           # example: dict['-mode'] = 'server'
        dict[args[0]] = args[1]
        args = args[2:]
    return dict

def client(host, port, filename):
    sock = socket(AF_INET, SOCK_STREAM)
    sock.connect((host, port))
    sock.send(filename + '\n')                  # send remote name with dir
    dropdir = os.path.split(filename)[1]        # filename at end of dir path
    file = open(dropdir, 'wb')                   # create local file in cwd
    while True:
        data = sock.recv(blksz)                 # get up to 1K at a time
        if not data: break                      # till closed on server side
        file.write(data)                        # store data in local file
    sock.close()
    file.close()
    print 'Client got', filename, 'at', now()

def serverthread(clientsock):
    sockfile = clientsock.makefile('r')         # wrap socket in dup file obj
    filename = sockfile.readline()[:-1]         # get filename up to end-line
    try:
        file = open(filename, 'rb')
        while True:
            bytes = file.read(blksz)            # read/send 1K at a time
            if not bytes: break                 # until file totally sent
            sent = clientsock.send(bytes)
            assert sent == len(bytes)
    except:
        print 'Error downloading file on server:', filename
    clientsock.close()

def server(host, port):
    serversock = socket(AF_INET, SOCK_STREAM)    # listen on TCP/IP socket
    serversock.bind((host, port))                # serve clients in threads
    serversock.listen(5)
    while True:
        clientsock, clientaddr = serversock.accept()
        print 'Server connected by', clientaddr, 'at', now()
        thread.start_new_thread(serverthread, (clientsock,))

def main(args):
    host = args.get('-host', defaultHost)        # use args or defaults
    port = int(args.get('-port', defaultPort))   # is a string in argv
```

Example 13-10. PP3E\Internet\Sockets\getfile.py (continued)

```
    if args.get('-mode') == 'server':          # None if no -mode: client
        if host == 'localhost': host = ''      # else fails remotely
        server(host, port)
    elif args.get('-file'):                     # client mode needs -file
        client(host, port, args['-file'])
    else:
        print helptext

if __name__ == '__main__':
    args = parsecommandline()
    main(args)
```

This script isn't much different from the examples we saw earlier. Depending on the command-line arguments passed, it invokes one of two functions:

- The server function farms out each incoming client request to a thread that transfers the requested file's bytes.

- The client function sends the server a file's name and stores all the bytes it gets back in a local file of the same name.

The most novel feature here is the protocol between client and server: the client starts the conversation by shipping a filename string up to the server, terminated with an end-of-line character, and including the file's directory path in the server. At the server, a spawned thread extracts the requested file's name by reading the client socket, and opens and transfers the requested file back to the client, one chunk of bytes at a time.

Running the File Server and Clients

Since the server uses threads to process clients, we can test both client and server on the same Windows machine. First, let's start a server instance and execute two client instances on the same machine while the server runs:

```
[server window, localhost]
C:\...\PP3E\Internet\Sockets>python getfile.py -mode server
Server connected by ('127.0.0.1', 1089) at Thu Mar 16 11:54:21 2000
Server connected by ('127.0.0.1', 1090) at Thu Mar 16 11:54:37 2000

[client window, localhost]
C:\...\Internet\Sockets>ls
class-server.py    echo.out.txt      testdir            thread-server.py
echo-client.py     fork-server.py    testecho.py
echo-server.py     getfile.py        testechowait.py

C:\...\Internet\Sockets>python getfile.py -file testdir\python15.lib -port 50001
Client got testdir\python15.lib at Thu Mar 16 11:54:21 2000

C:\...\Internet\Sockets>python getfile.py -file testdir\textfile
Client got testdir\textfile at Thu Mar 16 11:54:37 2000
```

Clients run in the directory where you want the downloaded file to appear—the client instance code strips the server directory path when making the local file's name. Here the "download" simply copies the requested files up to the local parent directory (the DOS fc command compares file contents):

```
C:\...\Internet\Sockets>ls
class-server.py    echo.out.txt     python15.lib     testechowait.py
echo-client.py     fork-server.py   testdir          textfile
echo-server.py     getfile.py       testecho.py      thread-server.py

C:\...\Internet\Sockets>fc /B python1.lib testdir\python15.lib
Comparing files python15.lib and testdir\python15.lib
FC: no differences encountered

C:\...\Internet\Sockets>fc /B textfile testdir\textfile
Comparing files textfile and testdir\textfile
FC: no differences encountered
```

As usual, we can run server and clients on different machines as well. Here the script is being used to run a remote server on a Linux machine and a few clients on a local Windows PC (I added line breaks to some of the command lines to make them fit). Notice that client and server machine times are different now—they are fetched from different machines' clocks and so may be arbitrarily skewed:

```
[server Telnet window: first message is the python15.lib request
in client window1]
[lutz@starship lutz]$ python getfile.py -mode server
Server connected by ('166.93.216.248', 1185) at Thu Mar 16 16:02:07 2000
Server connected by ('166.93.216.248', 1187) at Thu Mar 16 16:03:24 2000
Server connected by ('166.93.216.248', 1189) at Thu Mar 16 16:03:52 2000
Server connected by ('166.93.216.248', 1191) at Thu Mar 16 16:04:09 2000
Server connected by ('166.93.216.248', 1193) at Thu Mar 16 16:04:38 2000


[client window 1: started first, runs in thread while other client
requests are made in client window 2, and processed by other threads]
C:\...\Internet\Sockets>python getfile.py -mode client
                        -host starship.python.net
                        -port 50001 -file python15.lib
Client got python15.lib at Thu Mar 16 14:07:37 2000

C:\...\Internet\Sockets>fc /B python15.lib testdir\python15.lib
Comparing files python15.lib and testdir\python15.lib
FC: no differences encountered


[client window 2: requests made while client window 1 request downloading]
C:\...\Internet\Sockets>python getfile.py
                        -host starship.python.net -file textfile
Client got textfile at Thu Mar 16 14:02:29 2000

C:\...\Internet\Sockets>python getfile.py
                        -host starship.python.net -file textfile
```

```
Client got textfile at Thu Mar 16 14:04:11 2000

C:\...\Internet\Sockets>python getfile.py
                       -host starship.python.net -file textfile
Client got textfile at Thu Mar 16 14:04:21 2000

C:\...\Internet\Sockets>python getfile.py
                       -host starship.python.net -file index.html
Client got index.html at Thu Mar 16 14:06:22 2000

C:\...\Internet\Sockets>fc textfile testdir\textfile
Comparing files textfile and testdir\textfile
FC: no differences encountered
```

One subtle security point here: the server instance code is happy to send any server-side file whose pathname is sent from a client, as long as the server is run with a username that has read access to the requested file. If you care about keeping some of your server-side files private, you should add logic to suppress downloads of restricted files. I'll leave this as a suggested exercise here, but I will implement such filename checks in a different getfile download tool in Chapter 16.*

Adding a User-Interface Frontend

You might have noticed that we have been living in the realm of the command line for this entire chapter—our socket clients and servers have been started from simple DOS or Linux shells. Nothing is stopping us from adding a nice point-and-click user interface to some of these scripts, though; GUI and network scripting are not mutually exclusive techniques. In fact, they can be arguably sexy when used together well.

For instance, it would be easy to implement a simple Tkinter GUI frontend to the client-side portion of the getfile script we just met. Such a tool, run on the client machine, may simply pop up a window with Entry widgets for typing the desired filename, server, and so on. Once download parameters have been input, the user interface could either import and call the getfile.client function with appropriate option arguments, or build and run the implied getfile.py command line using tools such as os.system, os.fork, thread, and so on.

Using Frames and command lines

To help make all of this more concrete, let's very quickly explore a few simple scripts that add a Tkinter frontend to the getfile client-side program. All of these

---

* We'll see three more getfile programs before we leave Internet scripting. The next chapter's *getfile.py* fetches a file with the higher-level FTP interface instead of using raw socket calls, and its *http-getfile* scripts fetch files over the HTTP protocol. Later, Example 16-27 presents a server-side *getfile.py* CGI script that transfers file contents over the HTTP port in response to a request made in a web browser client (files are sent as the output of a CGI script). All four of the download schemes presented in this text ultimately use sockets, but only the version here makes that use explicit.

Making Sockets Look Like Files

For illustration purposes, getfile uses the socket object makefile method to wrap the socket in a file-like object. Once so wrapped, the socket can be read and written using normal file methods; getfile uses the file readline call to read the filename line sent by the client.

This isn't strictly required in this example—we could have read this line with the socket recv call too. In general, though, the makefile method comes in handy anytime you need to pass a socket to an interface that expects a file.

For example, the Python pickle module's load and dump methods expect an object with a file-like interface (e.g., read and write methods), but they don't require a physical file. Passing a TCP/IP socket wrapped with the makefile call to the pickler allows us to ship serialized Python objects over the Internet, without having to pickle to strings and ship manually across the socket. See Chapter 19 for more details on object serialization interfaces.

More generally, any component that expects a file-like method protocol will gladly accept a socket wrapped with a socket object makefile call. Such interfaces will also accept strings wrapped with the built-in StringIO module, and any other sort of object that supports the same kinds of method calls as built-in file objects. As always in Python, we code to protocols—object interfaces—not to specific datatypes.

---

examples assume that you are running a server instance of getfile; they merely add a GUI for the client side of the conversation, to fetch a file from the server. The first, in Example 13-11, creates a dialog for inputting server, port, and filename information, and simply constructs the corresponding getfile command line and runs it with os.system.

Example 13-11. PP3E\Internet\Sockets\getfilegui-1.py

```
#########################################################
# launch getfile script client from simple Tkinter GUI;
# could also use os.fork+exec, os.spawnv (see Launcher);
# windows: replace 'python' with 'start' if not on path;
#########################################################

import sys, os
from Tkinter import *
from tkMessageBox import showinfo

def onReturnKey():
    cmdline = ('python getfile.py -mode client -file %s -port %s -host %s' %
                    (content['File'].get(),
                     content['Port'].get(),
                     content['Server'].get()))
    os.system(cmdline)
    showinfo('getfilegui-1', 'Download complete')
```

Example 13-11. PP3E\Internet\Sockets\getfilegui-1.py (continued)

```
box = Frame(Tk( ))
box.pack(expand=YES, fill=X)
lcol, rcol = Frame(box), Frame(box)
lcol.pack(side=LEFT)
rcol.pack(side=RIGHT, expand=Y, fill=X)

labels = ['Server', 'Port', 'File']
content = {}
for label in labels:
    Label(lcol, text=label).pack(side=TOP)
    entry = Entry(rcol)
    entry.pack(side=TOP, expand=YES, fill=X)
    content[label] = entry

box.master.title('getfilegui-1')
box.master.bind('<Return>', (lambda event: onReturnKey( )))
mainloop( )
```

When run, this script creates the input form shown in Figure 13-1. Pressing the Enter key (<Return>) runs a client-side instance of the getfile program; when the generated getfile command line is finished, we get the verification pop up displayed in Figure 13-2.

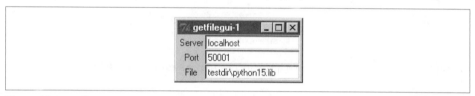

Figure 13-1. getfilegui-1 in action

Figure 13-2. getfilegui-1 verification pop up

Using grids and function calls

The first user-interface script (Example 13-11) uses the pack geometry manager and Frames to lay out the input form, and runs the getfile client as a standalone program. It's just as easy to use the grid manager for layout, and to import and call the client-side logic function instead of running a program. The script in Example 13-12 shows how.

Example 13-12. PP3E\Internet\Sockets\getfilegui-2.py

```
###############################################################
# same, but with grids and import+call, not packs and cmdline;
# direct function calls are usually faster than running files;
###############################################################

import getfile
from Tkinter import *
from tkMessageBox import showinfo

def onSubmit():
    getfile.client(content['Server'].get(),
                   int(content['Port'].get()),
                   content['File'].get())
    showinfo('getfilegui-2', 'Download complete')

box    = Tk()
labels = ['Server', 'Port', 'File']
rownum = 0
content = {}
for label in labels:
    Label(box, text=label).grid(col=0, row=rownum)
    entry = Entry(box)
    entry.grid(col=1, row=rownum, sticky=E+W)
    content[label] = entry
    rownum += 1

box.columnconfigure(0, weight=0)    # make expandable
box.columnconfigure(1, weight=1)
Button(text='Submit', command=onSubmit).grid(row=rownum, column=0, columnspan=2)

box.title('getfilegui-2')
box.bind('<Return>', (lambda event: onSubmit()))
mainloop()
```

This version makes a similar window (Figure 13-3), but adds a button at the bottom that does the same thing as an Enter key press—it runs the getfile client procedure. Generally speaking, importing and calling functions (as done here) is faster than running command lines, especially if done more than once. The getfile script is set up to work either way—as program or function library.

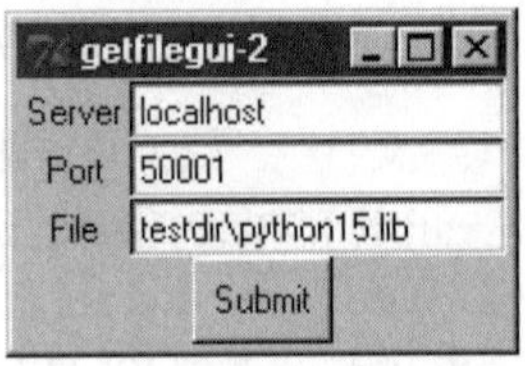

Figure 13-3. getfilegui-2 in action

Using a reusable form-layout class

If you're like me, though, writing all the GUI form layout code in those two scripts can seem a bit tedious, whether you use packing or grids. In fact, it became so tedious to me that I decided to write a general-purpose form-layout class, shown in Example 13-13, which handles most of the GUI layout grunt work.

Example 13-13. PP3E\Internet\Sockets\form.py

```
###########################################################
# a reusable form class, used by getfilegui (and others)
###########################################################

from Tkinter import *
entrysize = 40

class Form:                                             # add non-modal form box
    def __init__(self, labels, parent=None):            # pass field labels list
        box = Frame(parent)
        box.pack(expand=YES, fill=X)
        rows = Frame(box, bd=2, relief=GROOVE)          # box has rows, button
        lcol = Frame(rows)                              # rows has lcol, rcol
        rcol = Frame(rows)                              # button or return key,
        rows.pack(side=TOP, expand=Y, fill=X)           # runs onSubmit method
        lcol.pack(side=LEFT)
        rcol.pack(side=RIGHT, expand=Y, fill=X)
        self.content = {}
        for label in labels:
            Label(lcol, text=label).pack(side=TOP)
            entry = Entry(rcol, width=entrysize)
            entry.pack(side=TOP, expand=YES, fill=X)
            self.content[label] = entry
        Button(box, text='Cancel', command=self.onCancel).pack(side=RIGHT)
        Button(box, text='Submit', command=self.onSubmit).pack(side=RIGHT)
        box.master.bind('<Return>', (lambda event: self.onSubmit()))

    def onSubmit(self):                                 # override this
        for key in self.content.keys():                 # user inputs in
            print key, '\t=>\t', self.content[key].get()   # self.content[k]

    def onCancel(self):                                 # override if need
        Tk().quit()                                     # default is exit

class DynamicForm(Form):
    def __init__(self, labels=None):
        labels = raw_input('Enter field names: ').split()
        Form.__init__(self, labels)
    def onSubmit(self):
        print 'Field values...'
        Form.onSubmit(self)
        self.onCancel()

if __name__ == '__main__':
    import sys
```

Example 13-13. PP3E\Internet\Sockets\form.py (continued)

```
if len(sys.argv) == 1:
    Form(['Name', 'Age', 'Job'])        # precoded fields, stay after submit
else:
    DynamicForm()                        # input fields, go away after submit
mainloop()
```

Running this module standalone triggers its self-test code at the bottom. Without arguments (and when double-clicked in a Windows file explorer), the self-test generates a form with canned input fields captured in Figure 13-4, and displays the fields' values on Enter key presses or Submit button clicks:

```
C:\...\PP3E\Internet\Sockets>python form.py
Job     =>      Educator, Entertainer
Age     =>      38
Name    =>      Bob
```

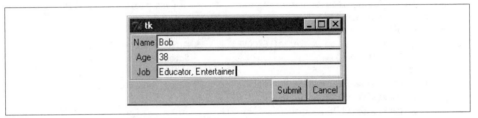

Figure 13-4. Form test, canned fields

With a command-line argument, the form class module's self-test code prompts for an arbitrary set of field names for the form; fields can be constructed as dynamically as we like. Figure 13-5 shows the input form constructed in response to the following console interaction. Field names could be accepted on the command line too, but raw_input works just as well for simple tests like this. In this mode, the GUI goes away after the first submit, because DynamicForm.onSubmit says so.

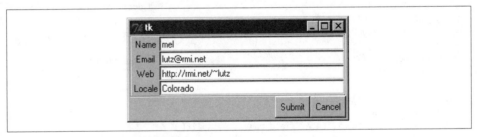

Figure 13-5. Form test, dynamic fields

```
C:\...\PP3E\Internet\Sockets>python form.py -
Enter field names: Name Email Web Locale
Field values...
Email   =>      lutz@rmi.net
Locale  =>      Colorado
```

```
Web       =>      http://rmi.net/~lutz
Name      =>      mel
```

And last but not least, Example 13-14 shows the getfile user interface again, this time constructed with the reusable form layout class. We need to fill in only the form labels list, and provide an onSubmit callback method of our own. All of the work needed to construct the form comes "for free," from the imported and widely reusable Form superclass.

Example 13-14. PP3E\Internet\Sockets\getfilegui.py

```
#################################################################
# launch getfile client with a reusable GUI form class;
# os.chdir to target local dir if input (getfile stores in cwd);
# to do: use threads, show download status and getfile prints;
#################################################################

from form import Form
from Tkinter import Tk, mainloop
from tkMessageBox import showinfo
import getfile, os

class GetfileForm(Form):
    def __init__(self, oneshot=0):
        root = Tk()
        root.title('getfilegui')
        labels = ['Server Name', 'Port Number', 'File Name', 'Local Dir?']
        Form.__init__(self, labels, root)
        self.oneshot = oneshot
    def onSubmit(self):
        Form.onSubmit(self)
        localdir   = self.content['Local Dir?'].get()
        portnumber = self.content['Port Number'].get()
        servername = self.content['Server Name'].get()
        filename   = self.content['File Name'].get()
        if localdir:
            os.chdir(localdir)
        portnumber = int(portnumber)
        getfile.client(servername, portnumber, filename)
        showinfo('getfilegui', 'Download complete')
        if self.oneshot: Tk().quit()  # else stay in last localdir

if __name__ == '__main__':
    GetfileForm()
    mainloop()
```

The form layout class imported here can be used by any program that needs to input form-like data; when used in this script, we get a user interface like that shown in Figure 13-6 under Windows (and similar on other platforms).

Pressing this form's Submit button or the Enter key makes the getfilegui script call the imported getfile.client client-side function as before. This time, though, we also first change to the local directory typed into the form so that the fetched file is stored there (getfile stores in the current working directory, whatever that may be

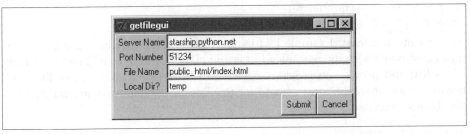

Figure 13-6. getfilegui in action

when it is called). As usual, we can use this interface to connect to servers running locally on the same machine, or remotely. Here is some of the interaction we get for each mode:

```
[talking to a local server]
C:\...\PP3E\Internet\Sockets>python getfilegui.py
Port Number     =>      50001
Local Dir?      =>      temp
Server Name     =>      localhost
File Name       =>      testdir\python15.lib
Client got testdir\python15.lib at Tue Aug 15 22:32:34 2000

[talking to a remote server]
[lutz@starship lutz]$ /usr/bin/python getfile.py -mode server -port 51234
Server connected by ('38.28.130.229', 1111) at Tue Aug 15 21:48:13 2000

C:\...\PP3E\Internet\Sockets>python getfilegui.py
Port Number     =>      51234
Local Dir?      =>      temp
Server Name     =>      starship.python.net
File Name       =>      public_html/index.html
Client got public_html/index.html at Tue Aug 15 22:42:06 2000
```

One caveat worth pointing out here: the GUI is essentially dead while the download is in progress (even screen redraws aren't handled—try covering and uncovering the window and you'll see what I mean). We could make this better by running the download in a thread, but since we'll see how to do that in the next chapter when we explore the FTP protocol, you should consider this problem a preview.

In closing, a few final notes: first, I should point out that the scripts in this chapter use Tkinter techniques we've seen before and won't go into here in the interest of space; be sure to see the GUI chapters in this book for implementation hints.

Keep in mind, too, that these interfaces just add a GUI on top of the existing script to reuse its code; any command-line tool can be easily GUI-ified in this way to make it more appealing and user friendly. In Chapter 15, for example, we'll meet a more useful client-side Tkinter user interface for reading and sending email over sockets (PyMailGUI), which largely just adds a GUI to mail-processing tools. Generally speaking, GUIs can often be added as almost an afterthought to a program. Although the degree of user-interface and core logic separation varies per program, keeping the two distinct makes it easier to focus on each.

And finally, now that I've shown you how to build user interfaces on top of this chapter's getfile, I should also say that they aren't really as useful as they might seem. In particular, getfile clients can talk only to machines that are running a getfile server. In the next chapter, we'll discover another way to download files—FTP—which also runs on sockets but provides a higher-level interface and is available as a standard service on many machines on the Net. We don't generally need to start up a custom server to transfer files over FTP, the way we do with getfile. In fact, the user-interface scripts in this chapter could be easily changed to fetch the desired file with Python's FTP tools, instead of the getfile module. But instead of spilling all the beans here, I'll just say, "Read on."

Using Serial Ports on Windows

Sockets, the main subject of this chapter, are the programmer's interface to network connections in Python scripts. As we've seen, they let us write scripts that converse with computers arbitrarily located on a network, and they form the backbone of the Internet and the Web.

If you're looking for a lower-level way to communicate with devices in general, though, you may also be interested in the topic of Python's serial port interfaces. This isn't quite related to Internet scripting and it applies only on Windows machines, but it's similar enough in spirit and is discussed often enough on the Net to merit a quick look here.

Serial ports are known as COM ports on Windows (not to be confused with the COM object model) and are identified as COM1, COM2, and so on. By using interfaces to these ports, scripts may engage in low-level communication with things like mice, modems, and a wide variety of serial devices. Serial port interfaces are also used to communicate with devices connected over infrared ports (e.g., hand-held computers and remote modems). There are often other higher-level ways to access such devices (e.g., the PyRite package for accessing Palm Pilot databases, or RAS for using modems), but serial port interfaces let scripts tap into raw data streams and implement device protocols of their own.

At this writing, there are at least three ways to send and receive data over serial ports in Python scripts—a public domain C extension package known as pySerial (which works on both Windows and Linux), the proprietary MSComm COM server object interface by Microsoft, and the low-level CreateFile file API call exported by the Python Windows extensions package, available via links at *http://www.python.org*. In addition, there are Python packages for interfacing with USB serial ports; search the Web for pointers.

Unfortunately, there is not enough space to cover any of these in detail in this text. For more information, Mark Hammond and Andy Robinson's book, *Python Programming on Win32* (O'Reilly), includes an entire section dedicated to serial port communication topics. Also be sure to use the search tools at Python's web site for up-to-date details on this front.

CHAPTER 14

Client-Side Scripting

"Socket to Me!"

The preceding chapter introduced Internet fundamentals and explored sockets—the underlying communications mechanism over which bytes flow on the Net. In this chapter, we climb the encapsulation hierarchy one level and shift our focus to Python tools that support the client-side interfaces of common Internet protocols.

We talked about the Internet's higher-level protocols in the abstract at the start of the preceding chapter, and you should probably review that material if you skipped over it the first time around. In short, protocols define the structure of the conversations that take place to accomplish most of the Internet tasks we're all familiar with—reading email, transferring files by FTP, fetching web pages, and so on.

At the most basic level, all of these protocol dialogs happen over sockets using fixed and standard message structures and ports, so in some sense this chapter builds upon the last. But as we'll see, Python's protocol modules hide most of the underlying details—scripts generally need to deal only with simple objects and methods, and Python automates the socket and messaging logic required by the protocol.

In this chapter, we'll concentrate on the FTP and email protocol modules in Python, and we'll peek at a few others along the way (NNTP news, HTTP web pages, and so on). Because it is so prevalent, we will especially focus on email in much of this chapter, as well as in the two to follow—we'll use tools and techniques introduced here in the larger PyMailGUI and PyMailCGI client and server-side programs of Chapters 15 and 17.

All of the tools employed in examples here are in the standard Python library and come with the Python system. All of the examples here are also designed to run on the client side of a network connection—these scripts connect to an already running server to request interaction and can be run from a basic PC or other client device. And as usual, all the code here is also designed to teach us something about Python programming in general—we'll refactor FTP examples and package email code to show object-oriented programming (OOP) in action.

In the next chapter, we'll look at a complete client-side program example before moving on to explore scripts designed to be run on the server side instead. Python programs can also produce pages on a web server, and there is support in the Python world for implementing the server side of things like HTTP, email, and FTP. For now, let's focus on the client.

FTP: Transferring Files over the Net

As we saw in the preceding chapter, sockets see plenty of action on the Net. For instance, the getfile example allowed us to transfer entire files between machines. In practice, though, higher-level protocols are behind much of what happens on the Net. Protocols run on top of sockets, but they hide much of the complexity of the network scripting examples of the prior chapter.

FTP—the File Transfer Protocol—is one of the more commonly used Internet protocols. It defines a higher-level conversation model that is based on exchanging command strings and file contents over sockets. By using FTP, we can accomplish the same task as the prior chapter's getfile script, but the interface is simpler and standard—FTP lets us ask for files from any server machine that supports FTP, without requiring that it run our custom getfile script. FTP also supports more advanced operations such as uploading files to the server, getting remote directory listings, and more.

Really, FTP runs on top of two sockets: one for passing control commands between client and server (port 21), and another for transferring bytes. By using a two-socket model, FTP avoids the possibility of deadlocks (i.e., transfers on the data socket do not block dialogs on the control socket). Ultimately, though, Python's ftplib support module allows us to upload and download files at a remote server machine by FTP, without dealing in raw socket calls or FTP protocol details.

Fetching Files with ftplib

Because the Python FTP interface is so easy to use, let's jump right into a realistic example. The script in Example 14-1 automatically fetches and opens a remote file with Python. More specifically, this Python script does the following:

1. Downloads an image file (by default) from a remote FTP site

2. Opens the downloaded file with a utility we wrote earlier in Example 6-16, in Chapter 6

The download portion will run on any machine with Python and an Internet connection. The opening part works if your *playfile.py* supports your platform; see Chapter 6 for details, and change as needed.

Example 14-1. PP3E\Internet\Ftp\getone.py

```
#!/usr/local/bin/python
################################################################
# A Python script to download and play a media file by FTP.
# Uses ftplib, the ftp protocol handler which uses sockets.
# Ftp runs on 2 sockets (one for data, one for control--on
# ports 20 and 21) and imposes message text formats, but the
# Python ftplib module hides most of this protocol's details.
# Note: change to fetch file from a site you have access to.
################################################################

import os, sys
from getpass import getpass

nonpassive  = False                          # force active mode FTP for server?
filename    = 'lawnlake2-jan-03.jpg'         # file to be downloaded
dirname     = '.'                            # remote directory to fetch from
sitename    = 'ftp.rmi.net'                  # FTP site to contact
userinfo    = ('lutz', getpass('Pswd?'))     # use () for anonymous
if len(sys.argv) > 1: filename = sys.argv[1] # filename on command line?

print 'Connecting...'
from ftplib import FTP                        # socket-based FTP tools
localfile = open(filename, 'wb')             # local file to store download
connection = FTP(sitename)                    # connect to FTP site
connection.login(*userinfo)                   # default is anonymous login
connection.cwd(dirname)                       # xfer 1k at a time to localfile
if nonpassive:                                # force active FTP if server requires
    connection.set_pasv(False)

print 'Downloading...'
connection.retrbinary('RETR ' + filename, localfile.write, 1024)
connection.quit()
localfile.close()

if raw_input('Open file?') in 'Yy':
    from PP3E.System.Media.playfile import playfile
    playfile(filename)
```

Most of the FTP protocol details are encapsulated by the Python `ftplib` module imported here. This script uses some of the simplest interfaces in `ftplib` (we'll see others later in this chapter), but they are representative of the module in general.

To open a connection to a remote (or local) FTP server, create an instance of the `ftplib.FTP` object, passing in the string name (domain or IP style) of the machine you wish to connect to:

```
connection = FTP(sitename)                    # connect to ftp site
```

Assuming this call doesn't throw an exception, the resulting FTP object exports methods that correspond to the usual FTP operations. In fact, Python scripts act much like typical FTP client programs—just replace commands you would normally type or select with method calls:

```
connection.login(*userinfo)          # default is anonymous login
connection.cwd(dirname)              # xfer 1k at a time to localfile
```

Once connected, we log in and change to the remote directory from which we want to fetch a file. The login method allows us to pass in a username and password as additional optional arguments to specify an account login; by default, it performs anonymous FTP. Notice the use of the nonpassive flag in this script:

```
if nonpassive:                       # force active FTP if server requires
    connection.set_pasv(False)
```

If this flag is set to True, the script will transfer the file in active FTP mode rather than the default passive mode. We'll finesse the details of the difference here (it has to do with which end of the dialog chooses port numbers for the transfer), but if you have trouble doing transfers with any of the FTP scripts in this chapter, try using active mode as a first step. In Python 2.1 and later, passive FTP mode is on by default. Now, fetch the file:

```
connection.retrbinary('RETR ' + filename, localfile.write, 1024)
```

Once we're in the target directory, we simply call the retrbinary method to download the target server file in binary mode. The retrbinary call will take a while to complete, since it must download a big file. It gets three arguments:

- An FTP command string; here, the string RETR *filename*, which is the standard format for FTP retrievals.
- A function or method to which Python passes each chunk of the downloaded file's bytes; here, the write method of a newly created and opened local file.
- A size for those chunks of bytes; here, 1,024 bytes are downloaded at a time, but the default is reasonable if this argument is omitted.

Because this script creates a local file named localfile of the same name as the remote file being fetched, and passes its write method to the FTP retrieval method, the remote file's contents will automatically appear in a local, client-side file after the download is finished. Observe how this file is opened in wb binary output mode; if this script is run on Windows, we want to avoid automatically expanding any \n bytes into \r\n byte sequences (that happens automatically on Windows when writing files opened in w text mode).

Finally, we call the FTP quit method to break the connection with the server and manually close the local file to force it to be complete before it is further processed (it's not impossible that parts of the file are still held in buffers before the close call):

```
connection.quit( )
localfile.close( )
```

And that's all there is to it—all the FTP, socket, and networking details are hidden behind the ftplib interface module. Here is this script in action on a Windows machine; after the download, the image file pops up in a Windows picture viewer on my laptop, as captured in Figure 14-1:

```
C:\...\PP3E\Internet\Ftp>python getone.py
Pswd?
Connecting...
Downloading...
Open file?y
```

Notice how the standard Python getpass.getpass is used to ask for an FTP password. Like the raw_input built-in function, this call prompts for and reads a line of text from the console user; unlike raw_input, getpass does not echo typed characters on the screen at all (in fact, on Windows it initially used the low-level direct keyboard interface we met in the stream redirection section of Chapter 3). This is handy for protecting things like passwords from potentially prying eyes. Be careful, though—in the current IDLE GUI, the password is echoed anyhow!

Figure 14-1. Image file downloaded by FTP and opened

Configure this script's initial assignments for a site and file you wish to fetch, and run this on your machine to see the opened file.[*] The thing to notice is that this otherwise typical Python script fetches information from an arbitrarily remote FTP site and machine. Given an Internet link, any information published by an FTP server on the Net can be fetched by and incorporated into Python scripts using interfaces such as these.

Using urllib to FTP Files

In fact, FTP is just one way to transfer information across the Net, and there are more general tools in the Python library to accomplish the prior script's download. Perhaps the most straightforward is the Python urllib module: given an Internet address string—a URL, or Universal Resource Locator—this module opens a connection to the specified server and returns a file-like object ready to be read with normal file object method calls (e.g., read, readline).

We can use such a higher-level interface to download anything with an address on the Web—files published by FTP sites (using URLs that start with "ftp://"); web pages and output of scripts that live on remote servers (using "http://" URLs); local files (using "file://" URLs); Gopher server data; and more. For instance, the script in Example 14-2 does the same as the one in Example 14-1, but it uses the general urllib module to fetch the source distribution file, instead of the protocol-specific ftplib.

Example 14-2. PP3E\Internet\Ftp\getone-urllib.py

```
#!/usr/local/bin/python
#####################################################################
# A Python script to download a file by FTP by its URL string.
# use higher-level urllib instead of ftplib to fetch file;
# urllib supports FTP, HTTP, and gopher protocols, and local files;
# urllib also allows downloads of html pages, images, text, etc.;
# see also Python html/xml parsers for web pages fetched by urllib;
#####################################################################

import os, getpass
import urllib                          # socket-based web tools
filename = 'lawnlake2-jan-03.jpg'      # remote/local filename
password = getpass.getpass('Pswd?')
```

---

[*] In the prior edition of this book, the examples in the first part of this chapter were coded to download files from Python's anonymous FTP site, *ftp.python.org*, so that readers could run them without having to have an FTP account of their own (the examples fetched the Python source distribution, and the *sousa* audio file). Unfortunately, just weeks before the final draft of this edition was wrapped up, that FTP site was shut down permanently, supposedly. If you want to play with the new examples here, you'll need to find a site to transfer to and from, or check whether *ftp.python.org* is available again. HTTP from *www.python.org* still works as before. See the directory *defunct* in the source tree for the original examples.

Example 14-2. PP3E\Internet\Ftp\getone-urllib.py (continued)

```
remoteaddr = 'ftp://lutz:%s@ftp.rmi.net/%s;type=i' % (password, filename)
print 'Downloading', remoteaddr

# this works too:
# urllib.urlretrieve(remoteaddr, filename)

remotefile = urllib.urlopen(remoteaddr)      # returns input file-like object
localfile  = open(filename, 'wb')            # where to store data locally
localfile.write(remotefile.read())
localfile.close()
remotefile.close()
```

Don't sweat the details of the URL string used here; it is fairly complex, and we'll explain its structure and that of URLs in general in Chapter 16. We'll also use `urllib` again in this and later chapters to fetch web pages, format generated URL strings, and get the output of remote scripts on the Web.

Technically speaking, `urllib` supports a variety of Internet protocols (HTTP, FTP, Gopher, and local files). Unlike `ftplib`, `urlib` is generally used for reading remote objects, not for writing or uploading them (though the HTTP and FTP protocols support file uploads). As with `ftplib`, retrievals must generally be run in threads if blocking is a concern. But the basic interface shown in this script is straightforward. The call:

```
remotefile = urllib.urlopen(remoteaddr)      # returns input file-like object
```

contacts the server named in the `remoteaddr` URL string and returns a file-like object connected to its download stream (here, an FTP-based socket). Calling this file's read method pulls down the file's contents, which are written to a local client-side file. An even simpler interface:

```
urllib.urlretrieve(remoteaddr, filename)
```

also does the work of opening a local file and writing the downloaded bytes into it—things we do manually in the script as coded. This comes in handy if we want to download a file, but it is less useful if we want to process its data immediately.

Either way, the end result is the same: the desired server file shows up on the client machine. The output is similar to the original version, but we don't try to automatically open this time (I've changed the password in the URL here to protect the innocent):

```
C:\...\PP3E\Internet\Ftp>getone-urllib.py
Pswd?
Downloading ftp://lutz:password@ftp.rmi.net/lawnlake2-jan-03.jpg;type=i
```

For more `urllib` download examples, see the section on HTTP in this chapter, and the server-side examples in Chapter 16. As we'll see in Chapter 16, in bigger terms, tools like `urllib.urlopen` allow scripts to both download remote files and invoke programs that are located on a remote server machine, and so serves as a useful tool

---

for testing and using web sites in Python scripts. In Chapter 16, we'll also see that urllib includes tools for formatting (escaping) URL strings for safe transmission.

FTP get and put Utilities

When I present the ftplib interfaces in Python classes, students often ask why programmers need to supply the RETR string in the retrieval method. It's a good question—the RETR string is the name of the download command in the FTP protocol, but ftplib is supposed to encapsulate that protocol. As we'll see in a moment, we have to supply an arguably odd STOR string for uploads as well. It's boilerplate code that you accept on faith once you see it, but that begs the question. You could propose a patch to ftplib, but that's not really a good answer for beginning Python students, and it may break existing code (the interface is as it is for a reason).

Perhaps a better answer is that Python makes it easy to extend the standard library modules with higher-level interfaces of our own—with just a few lines of reusable code, we can make the FTP interface look any way we want in Python. For instance, we could, once and for all, write utility modules that wrap the ftplib interfaces to hide the RETR string. If we place these utility modules in a directory on PYTHONPATH, they become just as accessible as ftplib itself, automatically reusable in any Python script we write in the future. Besides removing the RETR string requirement, a wrapper module could also make assumptions that simplify FTP operations into single function calls.

For instance, given a module that encapsulates and simplifies ftplib, our Python fetch-and-play script could be further reduced to the script shown in Example 14-3—essentially just two function calls plus a password prompt.

Example 14-3. PP3E\Internet\Ftp\getone-modular.py

```
#!/usr/local/bin/python
##################################################################
# A Python script to download and play a media file by FTP.
# Uses getfile.py, a utility module which encapsulates FTP step.
##################################################################

import getfile
from getpass import getpass
filename = 'lawnlake2-jan-03.jpg'

# fetch with utility
getfile.getfile(file=filename,
                site='ftp.rmi.net',
                dir ='.',
                user=('lutz', getpass('Pswd?')),
                refetch=True)

# rest is the same
if raw_input('Open file?') in 'Yy':
```

Example 14-3. PP3E\Internet\Ftp\getone-modular.py (continued)

```
from PP3E.System.Media.playfile import playfile
playfile(filename)
```

Besides having a much smaller line count, the meat of this script has been split off into a file for reuse elsewhere. If you ever need to download a file again, simply import an existing function instead of copying code with cut-and-paste editing. Changes in download operations would need to be made in only one file, not everywhere we've copied boilerplate code; getfile.getfile could even be changed to use urllib rather than ftplib without affecting any of its clients. It's good engineering.

Download utility

So just how would we go about writing such an FTP interface wrapper (he asks, rhetorically)? Given the ftplib library module, wrapping downloads of a particular file in a particular directory is straightforward. Connected FTP objects support two download methods:

retrbinary

> This method downloads the requested file in binary mode, sending its bytes in chunks to a supplied function, without line-feed mapping. Typically, the supplied function is a write method of an open local file object, such that the bytes are placed in the local file on the client.

retrlines

> This method downloads the requested file in ASCII text mode, sending each line of text to a supplied function with all end-of-line characters stripped. Typically, the supplied function adds a \n newline (mapped appropriately for the client machine), and writes the line to a local file.

We will meet the retrlines method in a later example; the getfile utility module in Example 14-4 always transfers in binary mode with retrbinary. That is, files are downloaded exactly as they were on the server, byte for byte, with the server's line-feed conventions in text files. You may need to convert line feeds after downloads if they look odd in your text editor—see the converter tools in Chapter 7 for pointers.

Example 14-4. PP3E\Internet\Ftp\getfile.py

```
#!/usr/local/bin/python
##########################################################################
# Fetch an arbitrary file by FTP.  Anonymous FTP unless you pass a
# user=(name, pswd) tuple. Self-test FTPs a test file and site.
##########################################################################

from ftplib  import FTP          # socket-based FTP tools
from os.path import exists       # file existence test

def getfile(file, site, dir, user=(), verbose=True, refetch=False):
    """
```

Example 14-4. PP3E\Internet\Ftp\getfile.py (continued)

```
        fetch a file by ftp from a site/directory
        anonymous or real login, binary transfer
        """
        if exists(file) and not refetch:
            if verbose: print file, 'already fetched'
        else:
            if verbose: print 'Downloading', file
            local = open(file, 'wb')                    # local file of same name
            try:
                remote = FTP(site)                      # connect to FTP site
                remote.login(*user)                     # anonymous=( ) or (name, pswd)
                remote.cwd(dir)
                remote.retrbinary('RETR ' + file, local.write, 1024)
                remote.quit( )
            finally:
                local.close( )                          # close file no matter what
                if verbose: print 'Download done.'      # caller handles exceptions

if __name__ == '__main__':
    from getpass import getpass
    file = 'lawnlake2-jan-03.jpg'
    dir  = '.'
    site = 'ftp.rmi.net'
    user = ('lutz', getpass('Pswd?'))
    getfile(file, site, dir, user)
```

This module is mostly just a repackaging of the FTP code we used to fetch the image file earlier, to make it simpler and reusable. Because it is a callable function, the exported getfile.getfile here tries to be as robust and generally useful as possible, but even a function this small implies some design decisions. Here are a few usage notes:

FTP mode

The getfile function in this script runs in anonymous FTP mode by default, but a two-item tuple containing a username and password string may be passed to the user argument in order to log in to the remote server in nonanonymous mode. To use anonymous FTP, either don't pass the user argument or pass it an empty tuple, ( ). The FTP object login method allows two optional arguments to denote a username and password, and the function(*args) call syntax in Example 14-4 sends it whatever argument tuple you pass to user (it works like the older apply built-in).

Processing modes

If passed, the last two arguments (verbose, refetch) allow us to turn off status messages printed to the stdout stream (perhaps undesirable in a GUI context) and to force downloads to happen even if the file already exists locally (the download overwrites the existing local file).

Exception protocol
> The caller is expected to handle exceptions; this function wraps downloads in a try/finally statement to guarantee that the local output file is closed, but it lets exceptions propagate. If used in a GUI or run from a thread, for instance, exceptions may require special handling unknown in this file.

Self-test
> If run standalone, this file downloads an image file again from my web site as a self-test, but the function will normally be passed FTP filenames, site names, and directory names as well.

File mode
> This script is careful to open the local output file in wb binary mode to suppress end-line mapping, in case it is run on Windows. As we learned in Chapter 4, it's not impossible that true binary datafiles may have bytes whose value is equal to a \n line-feed character; opening in w text mode instead would make these bytes automatically expand to a \r\n two-byte sequence when written locally on Windows. This is only an issue for portability to Windows (mode w works elsewhere). Again, see Chapter 7 for line-feed converter tools.

Directory model
> This function currently uses the same filename to identify both the remote file and the local file where the download should be stored. As such, it should be run in the directory where you want the file to show up; use os.chdir to move to directories if needed. (We could instead assume *filename* is the local file's name, and strip the local directory with os.path.split to get the remote name, or accept two distinct filename arguments—local and remote.)

Also notice that, despite its name, this module is very different from the *getfile.py* script we studied at the end of the sockets material in the preceding chapter. The socket-based getfile implemented client and server-side logic to download a server file to a client machine over raw sockets.

The new getfile here is a client-side tool only. Instead of raw sockets, it uses the simpler FTP protocol to request a file from a server; all socket-level details are hidden in the ftplib module's implementation of the FTP client protocol. Furthermore, the server here is a perpetually running program on the server machine, which listens for and responds to FTP requests on a socket, on the dedicated FTP port (number 21). The net functional effect is that this script requires an FTP server to be running on the machine where the desired file lives, but such a server is much more likely to be available.

Upload utility

While we're at it, let's write a script to upload a single file by FTP to a remote machine. The upload interfaces in the FTP module are symmetric with the download interfaces. Given a connected FTP object, its:

- storbinary method can be used to upload bytes from an open local file object
- storlines method can be used to upload text in ASCII mode from an open local file object

Unlike the download interfaces, both of these methods are passed a file object as a whole, not a file object method (or other function). We will meet the storlines method in a later example. The utility module in Example 14-5 uses storbinary such that the file whose name is passed in is always uploaded verbatim—in binary mode, without line-feed translations for the target machine's conventions. If this script uploads a text file, it will arrive exactly as stored on the machine it came from, client line-feed markers and all.

Example 14-5. PP3E\Internet\Ftp\putfile.py

```
#!/usr/local/bin/python
#############################################################
# Store an arbitrary file by FTP.  Uses anonymous
# ftp unless you pass in a user=(name, pswd) tuple.
#############################################################

import ftplib                    # socket-based FTP tools

def putfile(file, site, dir, user=( ), verbose=True):
    """
    store a file by ftp to a site/directory
    anonymous or real login, binary transfer
    """
    if verbose: print 'Uploading', file
    local  = open(file, 'rb')                # local file of same name
    remote = ftplib.FTP(site)                # connect to FTP site
    remote.login(*user)                      # anonymous or real login
    remote.cwd(dir)
    remote.storbinary('STOR ' + file, local, 1024)
    remote.quit( )
    local.close( )
    if verbose: print 'Upload done.'

if __name__ == '__main__':
    site = 'ftp.rmi.net'
    dir  = '.'
    import sys, getpass
    pswd = getpass.getpass(site + ' pswd?')                # filename on cmdline
    putfile(sys.argv[1], site, dir, user=('lutz', pswd))   # nonanonymous login
```

Notice that for portability, the local file is opened in rb binary mode this time to suppress automatic line-feed character conversions, in case this is run on Windows: if this is binary information, we don't want any bytes that happen to have the value of the \r carriage-return character to mysteriously go away during the transfer.

This script uploads a file you name on the command line as a self-test, but you will normally pass in real remote filename, site name, and directory name strings. Also like the download utility, you may pass a (username, password) tuple to the user argument to trigger nonanonymous FTP mode (anonymous FTP is the default).

Playing the Monty Python theme song

It's time for a bit of fun. Let's use these scripts to transfer a copy of the Monty Python theme song audio file I have at my web site. First, let's write a module that downloads and plays the sample file, as shown in Example 14-6.

Example 14-6. PP3E\Internet\Ftp\sousa.py

```
#!/usr/local/bin/python
##########################################################################
# Usage: sousa.py.  Fetch and play the Monty Python theme song.
# This may not work on your system as is: it requires a machine with
# Internet access, and uses audio filters on Unix and your .au player
# on Windows.  Configure playfile.py as needed for your platform.
##########################################################################

from PP3E.Internet.Ftp.getfile  import getfile
from PP3E.System.Media.playfile import playfile
from getpass import getpass

file = 'sousa.au'                    # default file coordinates
site = 'ftp.rmi.net'                 # Monty Python theme song
dir  = '.'
user = ('lutz', getpass('Pswd?'))

getfile(file, site, dir, user)       # fetch audio file by FTP
playfile(file)                       # send it to audio player

# import os
# os.system('getone.py sousa.au')    # equivalent command line
```

There's not much to this script, because it really just combines two tools we've already coded. We're reusing Example 14-4's getfile to download, and Chapter 6's playfile module (Example 6-16) to play the audio sample after it is downloaded (turn back to that example for more details on the player part of the task). Also notice the last two lines in this file—we can achieve the same effect by passing in the audio filename as a command-line argument to our original script, but it's less direct.

This script will run on any machine with Python, an Internet link, and a recognizable audio player; it works on my Windows laptop with a dial-up or broadband Internet connection, and it plays the music clip in Windows Media Player (if I could insert an audio file hyperlink here to show what it sounds like, I would):

```
C:\...\PP3E\Internet\Ftp>sousa.py
Pswd?
Downloading sousa.au
Download done.
```

```
C:\...\PP3E\Internet\Ftp>sousa.py
Pswd?
sousa.au already fetched
```

The getfile and putfile modules can be used to move the sample file around, too. Both can either be imported by clients that wish to use their functions, or run as top-level programs to trigger self-tests and command-line usage. Let's run these scripts from a command line and the interactive prompt to see how they work. When run standalone, parameters are passed in the command line and the default file settings are used:

```
C:\...\PP3E\Internet\Ftp>putfile.py sousa.py
ftp.rmi.net pswd?
Uploading sousa.py
Upload done.
```

When imported, parameters are passed explicitly to functions:

```
C:\...\PP3E\Internet\Ftp>python
>>> from getfile import getfile
>>> getfile(file='sousa.au', site='ftp.rmi.net', dir='.', user=('lutz', 'XXX'))
sousa.au already fetched

C:\...\PP3E\Internet\Ftp>del sousa.au

C:\...\PP3E\Internet\Ftp>python
>>> from getfile import getfile
>>> getfile(file='sousa.au', site='ftp.rmi.net', dir='.', user=('lutz', 'XXX'))
Downloading sousa.au
Download done.

>>> from PP3E.System.Media.playfile import playfile
>>> playfile('sousa.au')
```

Adding user interfaces

If you read the preceding chapter, you'll recall that it concluded with a quick look at scripts that added a user interface to a socket-based getfile script—one that transferred files over a proprietary socket dialog, instead of over FTP. At the end of that presentation, I mentioned that FTP is a much more generally useful way to move files around because FTP servers are so widely available on the Net. For illustration purposes, Example 14-7 shows a simple mutation of the prior chapter's user interface, implemented as a new subclass of the last chapter's general form builder.

Example 14-7. PP3E\Internet\Ftp\getfilegui.py

```
###############################################################################
# launch FTP getfile function with a reusable form GUI class;  uses os.chdir
# to goto target local dir (getfile currently assumes that filename has no
# local directory path prefix);  runs getfile.getfile in thread to allow more
# than one to be running at once and avoid blocking GUI during downloads;
# this differs from socket-based getfilegui, but reuses Form;  supports both
```

Example 14-7. PP3E\Internet\Ftp\getfilegui.py (continued)

```
# user and anonymous FTP as currently coded; caveats: the password field is
# not displayed as stars here, errors are printed to the console instead of
# shown in the GUI (threads can't touch the GUI on Windows), this isn't 100%
# thread safe (there is a slight delay between os.chdir here and opening the
# local output file in getfile) and we could display both a save-as popup for
# picking the local dir, and a remote dir listing for picking the file to get;
##############################################################################

from Tkinter import Tk, mainloop
from tkMessageBox import showinfo
import getfile, os, sys, thread                # FTP getfile here, not socket
from PP3E.Internet.Sockets.form import Form    # reuse form tool in socket dir

class FtpForm(Form):
    def __init__(self):
        root = Tk()
        root.title(self.title)
        labels = ['Server Name', 'Remote Dir', 'File Name',
                  'Local Dir',   'User Name?', 'Password?']
        Form.__init__(self, labels, root)
        self.mutex = thread.allocate_lock()
        self.threads = 0
    def transfer(self, filename, servername, remotedir, userinfo):
        try:
            self.do_transfer(filename, servername, remotedir, userinfo)
            print '%s of "%s" successful' % (self.mode, filename)
        except:
            print '%s of "%s" has failed:' % (self.mode, filename),
            print sys.exc_info()[0], sys.exc_info()[1]
        self.mutex.acquire()
        self.threads -= 1
        self.mutex.release()
    def onSubmit(self):
        Form.onSubmit(self)
        localdir   = self.content['Local Dir'].get()
        remotedir  = self.content['Remote Dir'].get()
        servername = self.content['Server Name'].get()
        filename   = self.content['File Name'].get()
        username   = self.content['User Name?'].get()
        password   = self.content['Password?'].get()
        userinfo   = ()
        if username and password:
            userinfo = (username, password)
        if localdir:
            os.chdir(localdir)
        self.mutex.acquire()
        self.threads += 1
        self.mutex.release()
        ftpargs = (filename, servername, remotedir, userinfo)
        thread.start_new_thread(self.transfer, ftpargs)
```

Example 14-7. PP3E\Internet\Ftp\getfilegui.py (continued)

```
        showinfo(self.title, '%s of "%s" started' % (self.mode, filename))
    def onCancel(self):
        if self.threads == 0:
            Tk().quit( )
        else:
            showinfo(self.title,
                        'Cannot exit: %d threads running' % self.threads)

class FtpGetfileForm(FtpForm):
    title = 'FtpGetfileGui'
    mode  = 'Download'
    def do_transfer(self, filename, servername, remotedir, userinfo):
        getfile.getfile(filename, servername, remotedir, userinfo, 0, 1)

if __name__ == '__main__':
    FtpGetfileForm( )
    mainloop( )
```

If you flip back to the end of the preceding chapter, you'll find that this version is similar in structure to its counterpart there; in fact, it has the same name (and is distinct only because it lives in a different directory). The class here, though, knows how to use the FTP-based getfile module from earlier in this chapter instead of the socket-based getfile module we met a chapter ago. When run, this version also implements more input fields, as in Figure 14-2.

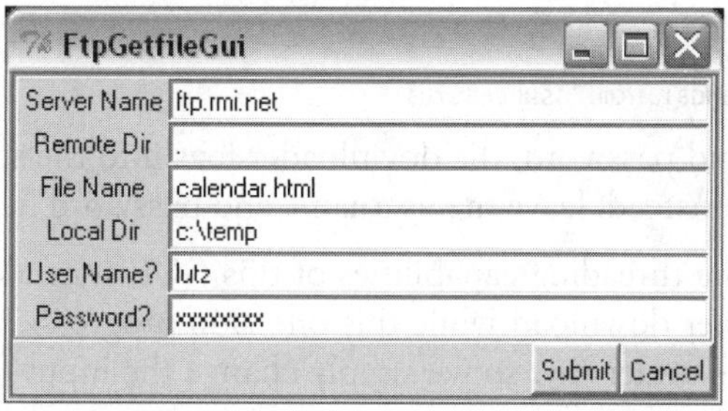

Figure 14-2. FTP getfile input form

Notice that a full file path is entered for the local directory here. Otherwise, the script assumes the current working directory, which changes after each download and can vary depending on where the GUI is launched (e.g., the current directory differs when this script is run by the PyDemos program at the top of the examples tree). When we click this GUI's Submit button (or press the Enter key), the script simply passes the form's input field values as arguments to the getfile.getfile FTP utility function shown earlier in this section. It also posts a pop up to tell us the download has begun (Figure 14-3).

Figure 14-3. FTP getfile info pop up

As currently coded, further download status messages show up in the console window; here are the messages for a successful download, as well as one that failed when I mistyped my password (no, it's not really "xxxxxxxxx"):

```
C:\...\PP3E\Internet\Ftp>getfilegui.py
Server Name    =>    ftp.rmi.net
User Name?     =>    lutz
Local Dir      =>    c:\temp
File Name      =>    calendar.html
Password?      =>    xxxxxxxx
Remote Dir     =>    .
Download of "calendar.html" has failed: ftplib.error_perm 530 Login incorrect.

Server Name    =>    ftp.rmi.net
User Name?     =>    lutz
Local Dir      =>    c:\temp
File Name      =>    calendar.html
Password?      =>    xxxxxxxxx
Remote Dir     =>    .
Download of "calendar.html" successful
```

Given a username and password, the downloader logs into the specified account. To do anonymous FTP instead, leave the username and password fields blank.

Now, to illustrate the threading capabilities of this GUI, start a download of a large file, then start another download while this one is in progress. The GUI stays active while downloads are underway, so we simply change the input fields and press Submit again.

This second download starts and runs in parallel with the first, because each download is run in a thread, and more than one Internet connection can be active at once. In fact, the GUI itself stays active during downloads only because downloads are run in threads; if they were not, even screen redraws wouldn't happen until a download finished.

We discussed threads in Chapter 5, but this script illustrates some practical thread concerns:

- This program takes care to not do anything GUI-related in a download thread. At least in the current release on Windows, only the thread that makes GUIs can process them (this is a Windows rule).

- To avoid killing spawned download threads on some platforms, the GUI must also be careful not to exit while any downloads are in progress. It keeps track of the number of in-progress threads, and just displays a pop up if we try to kill the GUI by pressing the Cancel button while both of these downloads are in progress.

We learned about ways to work around the no-GUI rule for threads in Chapter 11, and we will apply such techniques when we explore the PyMailGUI example in the next chapter. To be portable, though, we can't really close the GUI until the active-thread count falls to zero. Here is the sort of output that appears in the console window when two downloads overlap in time (these particular threads overlapped a long time ago):

```
C:\...\PP3E\Internet\Ftp>python getfilegui.py
User Name?      =>
Server Name     =>      ftp.python.org
Local Dir       =>      c:\temp
Password?       =>
File Name       =>      python1.5.tar.gz
Remote Dir      =>      pub/python/src

User Name?      =>      lutz
Server Name     =>      starship.python.net
Local Dir       =>      c:\temp
Password?       =>      xxxxxx
File Name       =>      about-pp.html
Remote Dir      =>      public_html/home
Download of "about-pp.html" successful
Download of "python1.5.tar.gz" successful
```

This example isn't much more useful than a command line–based tool, of course, but it can be easily modified by changing its Python code, and it provides enough of a GUI to qualify as a simple, first-cut FTP user interface. Moreover, because this GUI runs downloads in Python threads, more than one can be run at the same time from this GUI without having to start or restart a different FTP client tool.

While we're in a GUI mood, let's add a simple interface to the putfile utility too. The script in Example 14-8 creates a dialog that starts uploads in threads. It's almost the same as the getfile GUI we just wrote, so there's nothing new to say. In fact, because get and put operations are so similar from an interface perspective, most of the get form's logic was deliberately factored out into a single generic class (FtpForm), so changes need be made in only a single place. That is, the put GUI here is mostly just a reuse of the get GUI, with distinct output labels and transfer methods. It's in a file by itself to make it easy to launch as a standalone program.

Example 14-8. PP3E\Internet\Ftp\putfilegui.py

```
#############################################################
# launch FTP putfile function with a reusable form GUI class;
# see getfilegui for notes: most of the same caveats apply;
# the get and put forms have been factored into a single
# class such that changes need be made in only one place;
#############################################################

from Tkinter import mainloop
import putfile, getfilegui

class FtpPutfileForm(getfilegui.FtpForm):
    title = 'FtpPutfileGui'
    mode  = 'Upload'
    def do_transfer(self, filename, servername, remotedir, userinfo):
        putfile.putfile(filename, servername, remotedir, userinfo, 0)

if __name__ == '__main__':
    FtpPutfileForm( )
    mainloop( )
```

Running this script looks much like running the download GUI, because it's almost entirely the same code at work. Let's upload some files from the client machine to the server; Figure 14-4 shows the state of the GUI while starting one.

Figure 14-4. FTP putfile input form

And here is the console window output we get when uploading two files in parallel; here again, uploads run in threads, so if we start a new upload before one in progress is finished, they overlap in time:

```
User Name?     =>    lutz
Server Name    =>    starship.python.net
Local Dir      =>    c:\stuff\website\public_html
Password?      =>    xxxxxx
File Name      =>    about-PP3E.html
Remote Dir     =>    public_html
```

```
User Name?      =>      lutz
Server Name     =>      starship.python.net
Local Dir       =>      c:\stuff\website\public_html
Password?       =>      xxxxxx
File Name       =>      about-ppr3e.html
Remote Dir      =>      public_html
Upload of "about-PP3E.html" successful
Upload of "about-ppr2e.html" successful
```

Finally, we can bundle up both GUIs in a single launcher script that knows how to start the get and put interfaces, regardless of which directory we are in when the script is started, and independent of the platform on which it runs. Example 14-9 shows this process.

Example 14-9. PP3E\Internet\Ftp\PyFtpGui.pyw

```
###############################################################
# spawn FTP get and put GUIs no matter what dir I'm run from;
# os.getcwd is not necessarily the place this script lives;
# could also hardcode a path from $PP3EHOME, or guessLocation;
# could also do this but need the DOS pop up for status messages:
# from PP3E.launchmodes import PortableLauncher
# PortableLauncher('getfilegui', '%s/getfilegui.py' % mydir)()
###############################################################

import os, sys
from PP3E.Launcher import findFirst
mydir = os.path.split(findFirst(os.curdir, 'PyFtpGui.pyw'))[0]

if sys.platform[:3] == 'win':
    os.system('start %s/getfilegui.py' % mydir)
    os.system('start %s/putfilegui.py' % mydir)
else:
    os.system('python %s/getfilegui.py &' % mydir)
    os.system('python %s/putfilegui.py &' % mydir)
```

When this script is started, both the get and put GUIs appear as distinct, independently run programs; alternatively, we might attach both forms to a single interface. We could get much fancier than these two interfaces, of course. For instance, we could pop up local file selection dialogs, and we could display widgets that give the status of downloads and uploads in progress. We could even list files available at the remote site in a selectable listbox by requesting remote directory listings over the FTP connection. To learn how to add features like that, though, we need to move on to the next section.

Downloading Web Sites (Mirrors)

Once upon a time, I used Telnet to manage my web site at my Internet Service Provider (ISP).[*] Like most personal web sites, today I maintain mine on my laptop and transfer its files to and from my ISP as needed. Often, this is a simple matter of one or two files, and it can be accomplished with a command-line FTP client. Sometimes, though, I need an easy way to transfer the entire site. Maybe I need to download to detect files that have become out of sync. Occasionally, the changes are so involved that it's easier to upload the entire site in a single step.

Although there are a variety of ways to approach this task, Python can help here, too: by writing Python scripts to automate the upload and download tasks associated with maintaining my web site on my laptop, they provide a portable and mobile solution. Because Python FTP scripts will work on any machine with sockets, they can be run on my laptop and on nearly any other computer where Python is installed. Furthermore, the same scripts used to transfer page files to and from my PC can be used to copy ("mirror") my site to another web server as a backup copy, should my ISP experience an outage.

The following two scripts address these needs. The first, *downloadflat.py*, automatically downloads (i.e., copies) by FTP all the files in a directory at a remote site to a directory on the local machine. I keep the main copy of my web site files on my PC these days, but I use this script in two ways:

- To download my web site to client machines where I want to make edits, I fetch the contents of my web directory of my account on my ISP's machine.

- To mirror my site to my account on another server, I run this script periodically on the target machine if it supports Telnet or secure shell; if it does not, I simply download to one machine and upload from there to the target server.

More generally, this script (shown in Example 14-10) will download a directory full of files to any machine with Python and sockets, from any machine running an FTP server.

Example 14-10. PP3E\Internet\Ftp\mirror\downloadflat.py

```
#!/bin/env python
###########################################################################
# use FTP to copy (download) all files from a single directory at a remote
# site to a directory on the local machine; run me periodically to mirror
# a flat FTP site directory to your ISP account;  set user to 'anonymous'
# to do anonymous FTP; we could use try to skip file failures, but the FTP
```

---

[*] The second edition of this book included a tale of woe here about how my ISP forced its users to wean themselves off Telnet access. This seems like a small issue today. Common practice on the Internet has come far in a short time. Come to think of it, so has Python's presence on the Net. When I first found Python in 1992, it was a set of encoded email messages, which users decoded and concatenated and hoped the result worked. Were we ever that young?

Example 14-10. PP3E\Internet\Ftp\mirror\downloadflat.py (continued)

```
# connection is likely closed if any files fail;  we could also try to
# reconnect with a new FTP instance before each transfer: connects once now;
# if failures, try setting nonpassive for active FTP, or disable firewalls;
# this also depends on a working FTP server, and possibly its load policies.
################################################################################

import os, sys, ftplib
from getpass    import getpass
from mimetypes import guess_type

nonpassive = False                       # passive FTP on by default in 2.1+
remotesite = 'home.rmi.net'              # download from this site
remotedir  = '.'                         # and this dir (e.g., public_html)
remoteuser = 'lutz'
remotepass = getpass('Password for %s on %s: ' % (remoteuser, remotesite))
localdir   = (len(sys.argv) > 1 and sys.argv[1]) or '.'
cleanall   = raw_input('Clean local directory first? ')[:1] in ['y', 'Y']

print 'connecting...'
connection = ftplib.FTP(remotesite)                    # connect to FTP site
connection.login(remoteuser, remotepass)               # login as user/password
connection.cwd(remotedir)                              # cd to directory to copy
if nonpassive:                                         # force active mode FTP
    connection.set_pasv(False)                         # most servers do passive

if cleanall:
    for localname in os.listdir(localdir):             # try to delete all locals
        try:                                           # first to remove old files
            print 'deleting local', localname
            os.remove(os.path.join(localdir, localname))
        except:
            print 'cannot delete local', localname

count = 0                                              # download all remote files
remotefiles = connection.nlst()                        # nlst() gives files list
                                                       # dir()  gives full details

for remotename in remotefiles:
    mimetype, encoding = guess_type(remotename)        # e.g., ('text/plain', 'gzip')
    mimetype = mimetype or '?/?'                       # may be (None, None)
    maintype = mimetype.split('/')[0]                  # .jpg ('image/jpeg', None)

    localpath = os.path.join(localdir, remotename)
    print 'downloading', remotename, 'to', localpath,
    print 'as', maintype, encoding or ''
    if maintype == 'text' and encoding == None:
        # use ascii mode xfer
        localfile = open(localpath, 'w')
        callback  = lambda line: localfile.write(line + '\n')
        connection.retrlines('RETR ' + remotename, callback)
    else:
        # use binary mode xfer
        localfile = open(localpath, 'wb')
```

Example 14-10. PP3E\Internet\Ftp\mirror\downloadflat.py (continued)

```
        connection.retrbinary('RETR ' + remotename, localfile.write)
    localfile.close( )
    count += 1

connection.quit( )
print 'Done:', count, 'files downloaded.'
```

There's not a whole lot that is new to speak of in this script, compared to other FTP examples we've seen thus far. We open a connection with the remote FTP server, log in with a username and password for the desired account (this script never uses anonymous FTP), and go to the desired remote directory. New here, though, are loops to iterate over all the files in local and remote directories, text-based retrievals, and file deletions:

Deleting all local files

This script has a cleanall option, enabled by an interactive prompt. If selected, the script first deletes all the files in the local directory before downloading, to make sure there are no extra files that aren't also on the server (there may be junk here from a prior download). To delete local files, the script calls os.listdir to get a list of filenames in the directory, and os.remove to delete each; see Chapter 4 (or the Python library manual) for more details if you've forgotten what these calls do.

Notice the use of os.path.join to concatenate a directory path and filename according to the host platform's conventions; os.listdir returns filenames without their directory paths, and this script is not necessarily run in the local directory where downloads will be placed. The local directory defaults to the current directory ("."), but can be set differently with a command-line argument to the script.

Fetching all remote files

To grab all the files in a remote directory, we first need a list of their names. The FTP object's nlst method is the remote equivalent of os.listdir: nlist returns a list of the string names of all files in the current remote directory. Once we have this list, we simply step through it in a loop, running FTP retrieval commands for each filename in turn (more on this in a minute).

The nlst method is, more or less, like requesting a directory listing with an ls command in typical interactive FTP programs, but Python automatically splits up the listing's text into a list of filenames. We can pass it a remote directory to be listed; by default it lists the current server directory. A related FTP method, dir, returns the list of line strings produced by an FTP LIST command; its result is like typing a dir command in an FTP session, and its lines contain complete file information, unlike nlst. If you need to know more about all the remote files, parse the result of a dir method call (we'll see how in a later example).

Retrieving: text versus binary

To keep line-ends in sync with the machines that my web files live on, this script distinguishes between binary and text files. It uses the Python mimetypes module to choose between text and binary transfer modes for each file.

We met mimetypes in Chapter 6 near Example 6-16, where we used it to play media files (see the examples and description there for an introduction). Here, mimetypes is used to decide whether a file is text or binary by guessing from its filename extension. For instance, HTML web pages and simple text files are transferred as text with automatic line-end mappings, and images and *tar* archives are transferred in raw binary mode.

Specifically, binary files are pulled down with the retrbinary method we met earlier and a local open mode of wb to suppress line-feed byte mapping—this script may be run on Windows or Unix-like platforms, and we don't want a \n byte embedded in an image to get expanded to \r\n on Windows. We don't use a chunk-size third argument here, though—it defaults to a reasonable size if omitted.

For text files, the script instead uses the retrlines method, passing in a function to be called for each line in the text file downloaded. The text line handler function mostly just writes the line to a local file. But notice that the handler function created by the lambda here also adds a \n line-end character to the end of the line it is passed. Python's retrlines method strips all line-feed characters from lines to sidestep platform differences. By adding a \n, the script is sure to add the proper line-end marker character sequence for the local platform on which this script runs (\n or \r\n). For this automapping of the \n in the script to work, of course, we must also open text output files in w text mode, not in wb—the mapping from \n to \r\n on Windows happens when data is written to the file.

All of this is simpler in action than in words. Here is the command I use to download my entire web site from my ISP server account to my Windows laptop PC, in a single step:

```
C:\Mark\temp\website>c:\...\PP3E\Internet\Ftp\mirror\downloadflat.py
Password for lutz on home.rmi.net:
Clean local directory first? y
connecting...
deleting local 2004-longmont-classes.html
deleting local 2005-longmont-classes.html
deleting local about-hopl.html
deleting local about-lp-toc.html
deleting local about-lp.html
deleting local about-lp2e.html
...
...lines deleted...
...
deleting local dsc00475.jpg
deleting local dsc00506.jpg
downloading 2004-longmont-classes.html to .\2004-longmont-classes.html as text
```

```
downloading 2005-longmont-classes.html to .\2005-longmont-classes.html as text
downloading about-hopl.html to .\about-hopl.html as text
downloading about-lp-toc.html to .\about-lp-toc.html as text
downloading about-lp.html to .\about-lp.html as tex

...
...lines deleted...

...
downloading lp2e-updates.html to .\lp2e-updates.html as text
downloading 109_0137.JPG to .\109_0137.JPG as image
downloading sousa.au to .\sousa.au as audio
downloading sousa.py to .\sousa.py as text
downloading pp2e-cd-dir.txt.gz to .\pp2e-cd-dir.txt.gz as text gzip
downloading wxPython.doc.tgz to .\wxPython.doc.tgz as application gzip
downloading img_0694.jpg to .\img_0694.jpg as image
downloading t250.jpg to .\t250.jpg as image
downloading c3100.gif to .\c3100.gif as image
downloading ipod.gif to .\ipod.gif as image
downloading lp70.jpg to .\lp70.jpg as image
downloading pic23.html to .\pic23.html as text
downloading 2006-longmont-classes.html to .\2006-longmont-classes.html as text
Done: 258 files downloaded.
```

This may take a few moments to complete, depending on your site's size and your connection speed (it's bound by network speed constraints, and it usually takes roughly five minutes on my current laptop and wireless broadband connection). It is much more accurate and easier than downloading files by hand, though. The script simply iterates over all the remote files returned by the nlst method, and downloads each with the FTP protocol (i.e., over sockets) in turn. It uses text transfer mode for names that imply text data, and binary mode for others.

With the script running this way, I make sure the initial assignments in it reflect the machines involved, and then run the script from the local directory where I want the site copy to be stored. Because the target download directory is usually not where the script lives, I need to give Python the full path to the script file. When run on a server in a Telnet session window, for instance, the execution and script directory paths are different, but the script works the same way.

If you elect to delete local files in the download directory, you may also see a batch of "deleting local..." messages scroll by on the screen before any "downloading..." lines appear: this automatically cleans out any garbage lingering from a prior download. And if you botch the input of the remote site password, a Python exception is raised; I sometimes need to run it again (and type more slowly):

```
C:\Mark\temp\website>c:\...\PP3E\Internet\Ftp\mirror\downloadflat.py
Password for lutz on home.rmi.net:
Clean local directory first? y
connecting...
Traceback (most recent call last):
  File "c:\...\PP3E\Internet\Ftp\mirror\downloadflat.py", line 27, in ?
    connection.login(remoteuser, remotepass)        # login as user/pass...
  File "C:\Python24\lib\ftplib.py", line 362, in login
```

```
if resp[0] == '3': resp = self.sendcmd('PASS ' + passwd)
File "C:\Python24\lib\ftplib.py", line 241, in sendcmd
    return self.getresp()
File "C:\Python24\lib\ftplib.py", line 214, in getresp
    raise error_perm, resp
ftplib.error_perm: 530 Login incorrect.
```

It's worth noting that this script is at least partially configured by assignments near the top of the file. In addition, the password and deletion options are given by inter-active inputs, and one command-line argument is allowed—the local directory name to store the downloaded files (it defaults to ".", the directory where the script is run). Command-line arguments could be employed to universally configure all the other download parameters and options, too, but because of Python's simplicity and lack of compile/link steps, changing settings in the text of Python scripts is usually just as easy as typing words on a command line.[*]

Uploading Web Sites

Uploading a full directory is symmetric to downloading: it's mostly a matter of swap-ping the local and remote machines and operations in the program we just met. The script in Example 14-11 uses FTP to copy all files in a directory on the local machine on which it runs, up to a directory on a remote machine.

I really use this script too, most often to upload all of the files maintained on my lap-top PC to my ISP account in one fell swoop. I also sometimes use it to copy my site from my PC to a mirror machine or from the mirror machine back to my ISP. Because this script runs on any computer with Python and sockets, it happily trans-fers a directory from any machine on the Net to any machine running an FTP server. Simply change the initial setting in this module as appropriate for the transfer you have in mind.

Example 14-11. PP3E\Internet\Ftp\mirror\uploadflat.py

```
#!/bin/env python
###############################################################
# use FTP to upload all files from one local dir to a remote site/directory;
# e.g., run me to copy a web/FTP site's files from your PC to your ISP;
# assumes a flat directory upload: uploadall.py does nested directories.
# see downloadflat.py comments for more notes: this script is symmetric.
###############################################################

import os, sys, ftplib
```

[*] To check for version skew after a batch of downloads and uploads, you can run the diffall script we wrote in Chapter 7, Example 7-30. For instance, I find files that have diverged over time due to updates on multiple platforms by comparing the download to a local copy of my web site using a command such as C:\...>c:\ ...\PP3E\System\Filetools\diffall.py . c:\mark\WEBSITE\public_html. See Chapter 7 for more details on this tool.

Example 14-11. PP3E\Internet\Ftp\mirror\uploadflat.py (continued)

```
from getpass import getpass
from mimetypes import guess_type

nonpassive = False                                              # passive FTP by default
remotesite = 'home.rmi.net'                                     # upload to this site
remotedir  = '.'                                                # from machine running on
remoteuser = 'lutz'
remotepass = getpass('Password for %s on %s: ' % (remoteuser, remotesite))
localdir   = (len(sys.argv) > 1 and sys.argv[1]) or '.'
cleanall   = raw_input('Clean remote directory first? ')[:1] in ['y', 'Y']

print 'connecting...'
connection = ftplib.FTP(remotesite)                            # connect to FTP site
connection.login(remoteuser, remotepass)                       # log in as user/password
connection.cwd(remotedir)                                      # cd to directory to copy
if nonpassive:                                                 # force active mode FTP
    connection.set_pasv(False)                                 # most servers do passive

if cleanall:
    for remotename in connection.nlst():                       # try to delete all remotes
        try:                                                   # first to remove old files
            print 'deleting remote', remotename
            connection.delete(remotename)
        except:
            print 'cannot delete remote', remotename

count = 0
localfiles = os.listdir(localdir)                              # upload all local files
                                                              # listdir() strips dir path
                                                              # any failure ends script
for localname in localfiles:
    mimetype, encoding = guess_type(localname)                # e.g., ('text/plain', 'gzip')
    mimetype = mimetype or '?/?'                               # may be (None, None)
    maintype = mimetype.split('/')[0]                         # .jpg ('image/jpeg', None')

    localpath = os.path.join(localdir, localname)
    print 'uploading', localpath, 'to', localname,
    print 'as', maintype, encoding or ''
    if maintype == 'text' and encoding == None:
        # use ascii mode xfer
        localfile = open(localpath, 'r')
        connection.storlines('STOR ' + localname, localfile)
    else:
        # use binary mode xfer
        localfile = open(localpath, 'rb')
        connection.storbinary('STOR ' + localname, localfile)
    localfile.close()
    count += 1

connection.quit()
print 'Done:', count, 'files uploaded.'
```

Similar to the mirror download script, this program illustrates a handful of new FTP interfaces and a set of FTP scripting techniques:

Deleting all remote files

Just like the mirror script, the upload begins by asking whether we want to delete all the files in the remote target directory before copying any files there. This cleanall option is useful if we've deleted files in the local copy of the directory in the client—the deleted files would remain on the server-side copy unless we delete all files there first.

To implement the remote cleanup, this script simply gets a listing of all the files in the remote directory with the FTP nlst method, and deletes each in turn with the FTP delete method. Assuming we have delete permission, the directory will be emptied (file permissions depend on the account we logged into when connecting to the server). We've already moved to the target remote directory when deletions occur, so no directory paths need to be prepended to filenames here. Note that nlst may raise an exception for some servers if the remote directory is empty; we don't catch the exception here, but you can simply not select a cleaning if one fails for you.

Storing all local files

To apply the upload operation to each file in the local directory, we get a list of local filenames with the standard os.listdir call, and take care to prepend the local source directory path to each filename with the os.path.join call. Recall that os.listdir returns filenames without directory paths, and the source directory may not be the same as the script's execution directory if passed on the command line.

Uploading: text versus binary

This script may also be run on both Windows and Unix-like clients, so we need to handle text files specially. Like the mirror download, this script picks text or binary transfer modes by using Python's mimetypes module to guess a file's type from its filename extension; HTML and text files are moved in FTP text mode, for instance. We already met the storbinary FTP object method used to upload files in binary mode—an exact, byte-for-byte copy appears at the remote site.

Text mode transfers work almost identically: the storlines method accepts an FTP command string and a local file (or file-like) object opened in text mode, and simply copies each line in the local file to a same-named file on the remote machine. As usual, if we run this script on Windows, opening the input file in r text mode means that DOS-style \r\n end-of-line sequences are mapped to the \n character as lines are read. When the script is run on Unix and Linux, lines end in a single \n already, so no such mapping occurs. The net effect is that data is read portably, with \n characters to represent end-of-line.

For binary files, we open in rb mode to suppress such automatic mapping everywhere (we don't want bytes in an audio file that happen to have the same value as \r to magically disappear when read on Windows!).[*]

As for the mirror download script, this program simply iterates over all files to be transferred (files in the local directory listing this time), and transfers each in turn—in either text or binary mode, depending on the files' names. Here is the command I use to upload my entire web site from my laptop Windows PC to the remote Unix server at my ISP, in a single step:

```
C:\Mark\temp\website>c:\...\PP3E\Internet\Ftp\mirror\uploadflat.py
Password for lutz on home.rmi.net:
Clean remote directory first? n
connecting...
uploading .\109_0137.JPG to 109_0137.JPG as image
uploading .\2004-longmont-classes.html to 2004-longmont-classes.html as text
uploading .\2005-longmont-classes.html to 2005-longmont-classes.html as text
uploading .\2006-longmont-classes.html to 2006-longmont-classes.html as text
uploading .\about-hopl.html to about-hopl.html as text
...
...lines deleted...
...
uploading .\visitor_poundbang.py to visitor_poundbang.py as text
uploading .\wcall.py to wcall.py as text
uploading .\wcall_find.py to wcall_find.py as text
uploading .\wcall_find_patt.py to wcall_find_patt.py as text
uploading .\wcall_visitor.py to wcall_visitor.py as text
uploading .\whatsnew.html to whatsnew.html as text
uploading .\whatsold.html to whatsold.html as text
uploading .\wxPython.doc.tgz to wxPython.doc.tgz as application gzip
uploading .\xlate-lp.html to xlate-lp.html as text
uploading .\zaurus0.jpg to zaurus0.jpg as image
uploading .\zaurus1.jpg to zaurus1.jpg as image
uploading .\zaurus2.jpg to zaurus2.jpg as image
uploading .\zoo-jan-03.jpg to zoo-jan-03.jpg as image
uploading .\zopeoutline.htm to zopeoutline.htm as text
Done: 258 files uploaded.
```

On my current laptop and wireless broadband connection, this process typically takes seven minutes, depending on server load. As with the download script, I usually run this command from the local directory where my web files are kept, and I pass Python the full path to the script. When I run this on a Linux server, it works in the same way, but the paths to the script and my web files directory differ. If you

---

[*] Technically, Python's storlines method automatically sends all lines to the server with \r\n line-feed sequences, no matter what it receives from the local file readline method (\n or \r\n). Because of that, the most important distinctions for uploads are to use the rb for binary mode and the storlines method for text. Consult the module ftplib.py in the Python source library directory for more details.

elect to clean the remote directory before uploading, you'll get a bunch of "deleting remote..." messages before the "uploading..." lines here, too:*

```
...
deleting remote uk-3.jpg
deleting remote whatsnew.html
deleting remote whatsold.html
deleting remote xlate-lp.html
deleting remote uploadflat.py
deleting remote ora-lp-france.gif
deleting remote LJsuppcover.jpg
deleting remote sonyz505js.gif
deleting remote pic14.html
...
```

Refactoring Uploads and Downloads for Reuse

The directory upload and download scripts of the prior two sections work as advertised and, apart from the new mimetypes logic, were all we wrote in the prior edition of this book. If you look at these two scripts long enough, though, their similarities will pop out at you eventually. In fact, they are largely the same—they use identical code to configure transfer parameters, connect to the FTP server, and determine file type. The exact details have been lost to time, but some of this code was certainly copied from one file to the other.

Although such redundancy isn't a cause for alarm if we never plan on changing these scripts, it can be a killer in software projects in general. When you have two copies of identical bits of code, not only is there a danger of them becoming out of sync over time (you'll lose uniformity in user interface and behavior), but you also effectively double your effort when it comes time to change code that appears in both places. Unless you're a big fan of extra work, avoid redundancy wherever possible.

This redundancy is especially glaring when we look at the complex code that uses mimetypes to determine file types. Repeating magic like this in more than one place is almost always a bad idea—not only do we have to remember how it works every time we need the same utility, but it is a recipe for errors.

Refactoring with functions

As originally coded, our download and upload scripts comprise top-level script code that relies on global variables. Such a structure is difficult to reuse—code runs immediately on imports, and it's difficult to generalize for varying contexts. Worse, it's

---

* Usage note: these scripts are highly dependent on the FTP server functioning properly. For awhile, the upload script occasionally had timeout errors when running over my current broadband connection. These errors went away later, when my ISP fixed or reconfigured their server. If you have failures, try running against a different server; connecting and disconnecting around each transfer may or may not help (some servers limit their number of connections).

difficult to maintain—when you program by cut-and-paste of existing code, you increase the cost of future changes every time you click the Paste button.

To demonstrate how we might do better, Example 14-12 shows one way to *refactor* (reorganize) the download script. By wrapping its parts in functions, they become reusable in other modules, including our upload program.

Example 14-12. PP3E\Internet\Ftp\mirror\downloadflat_modular.py

```python
#!/bin/env python
###############################################################################
# use FTP to copy (download) all files from a remote site and directory
# to a directory on the local machine; this version works the same, but has
# been refactored to wrap up its code in functions that can be reused by the
# uploader, and possibly other programs in the future - else code redundancy,
# which may make the two diverge over time, and can double maintenance costs.
###############################################################################

import os, sys, ftplib
from getpass    import getpass
from mimetypes import guess_type, add_type

defaultSite = 'home.rmi.net'
defaultRdir = '.'
defaultUser = 'lutz'

def configTransfer(site=defaultSite, rdir=defaultRdir, user=defaultUser):
    """
    get upload or download parameters
    uses a class due to the large number
    """
    class cf: pass
    cf.nonpassive = False              # passive FTP on by default in 2.1+
    cf.remotesite = site               # transfer to/from this site
    cf.remotedir  = rdir               # and this dir ('.' means acct root)
    cf.remoteuser = user
    cf.localdir   = (len(sys.argv) > 1 and sys.argv[1]) or '.'
    cf.cleanall   = raw_input('Clean target directory first? ')[:1] in ['y','Y']
    cf.remotepass = getpass(
                  'Password for %s on %s:' % (cf.remoteuser, cf.remotesite))
    return cf

def isTextKind(remotename, trace=True):
    """
    use mimetype to guess if filename means text or binary
    for 'f.html,   guess is ('text/html', None): text
    for 'f.jpeg'   guess is ('image/jpeg', None): binary
    for 'f.txt.gz' guess is ('text/plain', 'gzip'): binary
    for unknowns,  guess may be (None, None): binary
    mimetype can also guess name from type: see PyMailGUI
    """
    add_type('text/x-python-win', '.pyw')                    # not in tables
    mimetype, encoding = guess_type(remotename, strict=False)  # allow extras
```

```
    mimetype    = mimetype or '?/?'                      # type unknown?
    maintype    = mimetype.split('/')[0]                 # get first part
    if trace: print maintype, encoding or ''
    return maintype == 'text' and encoding == None       # not compressed

def connectFtp(cf):
    print 'connecting...'
    connection = ftplib.FTP(cf.remotesite)              # connect to FTP site
    connection.login(cf.remoteuser, cf.remotepass)      # log in as user/password
    connection.cwd(cf.remotedir)                        # cd to directory to xfer
    if cf.nonpassive:                                   # force active mode FTP
        connection.set_pasv(False)                      # most servers do passive
    return connection

def cleanLocals(cf):
    """
    try to delete all locals files first to remove garbage
    """
    if cf.cleanall:
        for localname in os.listdir(cf.localdir):       # local dirlisting
            try:                                        # local file delete
                print 'deleting local', localname
                os.remove(os.path.join(cf.localdir, localname))
            except:
                print 'cannot delete local', localname

def downloadAll(cf, connection):
    """
    download all files from remote site/dir per cf config
    ftp nlst() gives files list, dir() gives full details
    """
    remotefiles = connection.nlst()                     # nlst is remote listing
    for remotename in remotefiles:
        localpath = os.path.join(cf.localdir, remotename)
        print 'downloading', remotename, 'to', localpath, 'as',
        if isTextKind(remotename):
            # use text mode xfer
            localfile = open(localpath, 'w')
            def callback(line): localfile.write(line + '\n')
            connection.retrlines('RETR ' + remotename, callback)
        else:
            # use binary mode xfer
            localfile = open(localpath, 'wb')
            connection.retrbinary('RETR ' + remotename, localfile.write)
        localfile.close()
    connection.quit()
    print 'Done:', len(remotefiles), 'files downloaded.'

if __name__ == '__main__':
    cf = configTransfer()
    conn = connectFtp(cf)
    cleanLocals(cf)             # don't delete if can't connect
    downloadAll(cf, conn)
```

Compare this version with the original. This script, and every other in this section, runs the same as the original flat download and upload programs, so we won't repeat their outputs here. Although we haven't changed its behavior, though, we've modified the script's software structure radically—its code is now a set of *tools* that can be imported and reused in other programs.

The refactored upload program in Example 14-13, for instance, is now noticeably simpler, and the code it shares with the download script only needs to be changed in one place if it ever requires improvement.

Example 14-13. PP3E\Internet\Ftp\mirror\uploadflat_modular.py

```
#!/bin/env python
##############################################################################
# use FTP to upload all files from a local dir to a remote site/directory;
# this version reuses downloader's functions, to avoid code redundancy;
##############################################################################

import os
from downloadflat_modular import configTransfer, connectFtp, isTextKind

def cleanRemotes(cf, connection):
    """
    try to delete all remote files first to remove garbage
    """
    if cf.cleanall:
        for remotename in connection.nlst():          # remote dir listing
            try:                                       # remote file delete
                print 'deleting remote', remotename
                connection.delete(remotename)
            except:
                print 'cannot delete remote', remotename

def uploadAll(cf, connection):
    """
    upload all files to remote site/dir per cf config
    listdir() strips dir path, any failure ends script
    """
    localfiles = os.listdir(cf.localdir)              # listdir is local listing
    for localname in localfiles:
        localpath = os.path.join(cf.localdir, localname)
        print 'uploading', localpath, 'to', localname, 'as',
        if isTextKind(localname):
            # use text mode xfer
            localfile = open(localpath, 'r')
            connection.storlines('STOR ' + localname, localfile)
        else:
            # use binary mode xfer
            localfile = open(localpath, 'rb')
            connection.storbinary('STOR ' + localname, localfile)
        localfile.close()
    connection.quit()
    print 'Done:', len(localfiles), 'files uploaded.'
```

Example 14-13. PP3E\Internet\Ftp\mirror\uploadflat_modular.py (continued)

```
if __name__ == '__main__':
    cf = configTransfer()
    conn = connectFtp(cf)
    cleanRemotes(cf, conn)
    uploadAll(cf, conn)
```

Not only is the upload script simpler now because it reuses common code, but it will also inherit any changes made in the download module. For instance, the isTextKind function was later augmented with code that adds the *.pyw* extension to mimetypes tables (this file type is not recognized by default); because it is a shared function, the change is automatically picked up in the upload program, too.

Refactoring with classes

The function-based approach of the last two examples addresses the redundancy issue, but they are perhaps clumsier than they need to be. For instance, their cf configuration options object provides a namespace that replaces global variables and breaks cross-file dependencies. Once we start making objects to model namespaces, though, Python's OOP support tends to be a more natural structure for our code. As one last twist, Example 14-14 refactors the FTP code one more time in order to leverage Python's class feature.

Example 14-14. PP3E\Internet\Ftp\mirror\ftptools.py

```
#!/bin/env python
##############################################################################
# use FTP to download or upload all files in a single directory from/to a
# remote site and directory;  this version has been refactored to use classes
# and OOP for namespace and a natural structure;  we could also structure this
# as a download superclass, and an upload subclass which redefines the clean
# and transfer methods, but then there is no easy way for another client to
# invoke both an upload and download;  for the uploadall variant and possibly
# others, also make single file upload/download code in orig loops methods;
##############################################################################

import os, sys, ftplib
from getpass    import getpass
from mimetypes import guess_type, add_type

# defaults for all clients
dfltSite = 'home.rmi.net'
dfltRdir = '.'
dfltUser = 'lutz'

class FtpTools:

    # allow these to be redefined
    def getlocaldir(self):
        return (len(sys.argv) > 1 and sys.argv[1]) or '.'
    def getcleanall(self):
```

Example 14-14. PP3E\Internet\Ftp\mirror\ftptools.py (continued)

```
        return raw_input('Clean target dir first?')[:1] in ['y','Y']
    def getpassword(self):
        return getpass(
                'Password for %s on %s:' % (self.remoteuser, self.remotesite))

    def configTransfer(self, site=dfltSite, rdir=dfltRdir, user=dfltUser):
        """
        get upload or download parameters
        from module defaults, args, inputs, cmdline
        anonymous ftp: user='anonymous' pass=emailaddr
        """
        self.nonpassive = False           # passive FTP on by default in 2.1+
        self.remotesite = site            # transfer to/from this site
        self.remotedir  = rdir            # and this dir ('.' means acct root)
        self.remoteuser = user
        self.localdir   = self.getlocaldir()
        self.cleanall   = self.getcleanall()
        self.remotepass = self.getpassword()

    def isTextKind(self, remotename, trace=True):
        """
        use mimetypes to guess if filename means text or binary
        for 'f.html,  guess is ('text/html', None): text
        for 'f.jpeg'  guess is ('image/jpeg', None): binary
        for 'f.txt.gz' guess is ('text/plain', 'gzip'): binary
        for unknowns,  guess may be (None, None): binary
        mimetypes can also guess name from type: see PyMailGUI
        """
        add_type('text/x-python-win', '.pyw')            # not in tables
        mimetype, encoding = guess_type(remotename, strict=False)# allow extras
        mimetype = mimetype or '?/?'                      # type unknown?
        maintype = mimetype.split('/')[0]                # get 1st part
        if trace: print maintype, encoding or ''
        return maintype == 'text' and encoding == None   # not compressed

    def connectFtp(self):
        print 'connecting...'
        connection = ftplib.FTP(self.remotesite)         # connect to FTP site
        connection.login(self.remoteuser, self.remotepass) # log in as user/pswd
        connection.cwd(self.remotedir)                   # cd to dir to xfer
        if self.nonpassive:                              # force active mode
            connection.set_pasv(False)                   # most do passive
        self.connection = connection

    def cleanLocals(self):
        """
        try to delete all local files first to remove garbage
        """
        if self.cleanall:
            for localname in os.listdir(self.localdir):  # local dirlisting
                try:                                     # local file delete
                    print 'deleting local', localname
```

Example 14-14. PP3E\Internet\Ftp\mirror\ftptools.py (continued)

```
                    os.remove(os.path.join(self.localdir, localname))
                except:
                    print 'cannot delete local', localname

    def cleanRemotes(self):
        """
        try to delete all remote files first to remove garbage
        """
        if self.cleanall:
            for remotename in self.connection.nlst():      # remote dir listing
                try:                                         # remote file delete
                    print 'deleting remote', remotename
                    self.connection.delete(remotename)
                except:
                    print 'cannot delete remote', remotename

    def downloadOne(self, remotename, localpath):
        """
        download one file by FTP in text or binary mode
        local name need not be same as remote name
        """
        if self.isTextKind(remotename):
            localfile = open(localpath, 'w')
            def callback(line): localfile.write(line + '\n')
            self.connection.retrlines('RETR '+ remotename, callback)
        else:
            localfile = open(localpath, 'wb')
            self.connection.retrbinary('RETR '+ remotename, localfile.write)
        localfile.close()

    def uploadOne(self, localname, localpath, remotename):
        """
        upload one file by FTP in text or binary mode
        remote name need not be same as local name
        """
        if self.isTextKind(localname):
            localfile = open(localpath, 'r')
            self.connection.storlines('STOR ' + remotename, localfile)
        else:
            localfile = open(localpath, 'rb')
            self.connection.storbinary('STOR ' + remotename, localfile)
        localfile.close()

    def downloadDir(self):
        """
        download all files from remote site/dir per config
        ftp nlst() gives files list, dir() gives full details
        """
        remotefiles = self.connection.nlst()            # nlst is remote listing
        for remotename in remotefiles:
            localpath = os.path.join(self.localdir, remotename)
            print 'downloading', remotename, 'to', localpath, 'as',
```

Example 14-14. PP3E\Internet\Ftp\mirror\ftptools.py (continued)

```
                self.downloadOne(remotename, localpath)
        print 'Done:', len(remotefiles), 'files downloaded.'

    def uploadDir(self):
        """
        upload all files to remote site/dir per config
        listdir() strips dir path, any failure ends script
        """
        localfiles = os.listdir(self.localdir)        # listdir is local listing
        for localname in localfiles:
            localpath = os.path.join(self.localdir, localname)
            print 'uploading', localpath, 'to', localname, 'as',
            self.uploadOne(localname, localpath, localname)
        print 'Done:', len(localfiles), 'files uploaded.'

    def run(self, cleanTarget=lambda:None, transferAct=lambda:None):
        """
        run a complete FTP session
        default clean and transfer are no-ops
        don't delete if can't connect to server
        """
        self.configTransfer()
        self.connectFtp()
        cleanTarget()
        transferAct()
        self.connection.quit()

if __name__ == '__main__':
    ftp = FtpTools()
    xfermode = 'download'
    if len(sys.argv) > 1:
        xfermode = sys.argv.pop(1)    # get+del 2nd arg
    if xfermode == 'download':
        ftp.run(cleanTarget=ftp.cleanLocals,  transferAct=ftp.downloadDir)
    elif xfermode == 'upload':
        ftp.run(cleanTarget=ftp.cleanRemotes, transferAct=ftp.uploadDir)
    else:
        print 'Usage: ftptools.py ["download" | "upload"] [localdir]'
```

In fact, this last mutation combines uploads and downloads into a single file, because they are so closely related. As before, common code is factored into methods to avoid redundancy. New here, the instance object itself becomes a natural namespace for storing configuration options (they become self attributes). Study this example's code for more details of the restructuring applied.

Although this file can still be run as a command-line script (pass in a command-line argument to specify "download" or "upload"), its class is really now a package of FTP tools that can be mixed into other programs and reused. By wrapping its code in a class, it can be easily customized by redefining its methods—its configuration calls, such as getlocaldir, for example, may be redefined in subclasses for custom scenarios.

Perhaps most important, using classes optimizes code reusability. Clients of this file can both upload and download directories by simply subclassing or embedding an instance of this class and calling its methods. To see one example of how, let's move on to the next section.

Uploads and Deletes with Subdirectories

Perhaps the biggest limitation of the web site download and upload scripts we just met is that they assume the site directory is flat (hence their names). That is, both transfer simple files only, and neither handles nested subdirectories within the web directory to be transferred.

For my purposes, that's often a reasonable constraint. I avoid nested subdirectories to keep things simple, and I store my home web site as a simple directory of files. For other sites (including one I keep at another machine), site transfer scripts are easier to use if they also automatically transfer subdirectories along the way.

Uploading local trees

It turns out that supporting directories on uploads is fairly simple—we need to add only a bit of recursion, and remote directory creation calls. The upload script in Example 14-15 extends the version we just saw, to handle uploading all subdirectories nested within the transferred directory. Furthermore, it recursively transfers subdirectories within subdirectories—the entire directory tree contained within the top-level transfer directory is uploaded to the target directory at the remote server.

In terms of its code structure, Example 14-15 is just a customization of the FtpTools class of the prior section—really we're just adding a method for recursive uploads, by subclassing. As one consequence, we get tools such as parameter configuration, content type testing, and connection and upload code for free here; with OOP, some of the work is done before we start.

Example 14-15. PP3E\Internet\Ftp\mirror\uploadall.py

```
#!/bin/env python
#############################################################################
# extend the FtpTools class to upload all files and subdirectories from a
# local dir tree to a remote site/dir; supports nested dirs too, but not
# the cleanall option (that requires parsing FTP listings to detect remote
# dirs: see cleanall.py); to upload subdirectories, uses os.path.isdir(path)
# to see if a local file is really a directory, FTP( ).mkd(path) to make dirs
# on the remote machine (wrapped in a try in case it already exists there),
# and recursion to upload all files/dirs inside the nested subdirectory.
# see also: uploadall-2.py, which doesn't assume the top remotedir exists.
#############################################################################

import os, ftptools

class UploadAll(ftptools.FtpTools):
```

Example 14-15. PP3E\Internet\Ftp\mirror\uploadall.py (continued)

```
    """
    upload an entire tree of subdirectories
    assumes top remote directory exists
    """
    def __init__(self):
        self.fcount = self.dcount = 0

    def getcleanall(self):
        return False   # don't even ask

    def uploadDir(self, localdir):
        """
        for each directory in an entire tree
        upload simple files, recur into subdirectories
        """
        localfiles = os.listdir(localdir)
        for localname in localfiles:
            localpath = os.path.join(localdir, localname)
            print 'uploading', localpath, 'to', localname,
            if not os.path.isdir(localpath):
                self.uploadOne(localname, localpath, localname)
                self.fcount += 1
            else:
                try:
                    self.connection.mkd(localname)
                    print 'directory created'
                except:
                    print 'directory not created'
                self.connection.cwd(localname)          # change remote dir
                self.uploadDir(localpath)               # upload local subdir
                self.connection.cwd('..')               # change back up
                self.dcount += 1
                print 'directory exited'

if __name__ == '__main__':
    ftp = UploadAll()
    ftp.run(transferAct = lambda: ftp.uploadDir(ftp.localdir))
    print 'Done:', ftp.fcount, 'files and', ftp.dcount, 'directories uploaded.'
```

Like the flat upload script, this one can be run on any machine with Python and
sockets and upload to any machine running an FTP server; I run it both on my laptop PC and on other servers by Telnet to upload sites to my ISP.

The crux of the matter in this script is the os.path.isdir test near the top; if this test
detects a directory in the current local directory, we create an identically named directory on the remote machine with connection.mkd and descend into it with connection.
cwd, and recur into the subdirectory on the local machine (we have to use recursive
calls here, because the shape and depth of the tree are arbitrary). Like all FTP object
methods, mkd and cwd methods issue FTP commands to the remote server. When we

exit a local subdirectory, we run a remote cwd('..') to climb to the remote parent directory and continue. The rest of the script is roughly the same as the original.

In the interest of space, I'll leave studying this variant in more depth as a suggested exercise. For more context, see the *experimental\uploadall-2.py* version of this script in the examples distribution; it's similar, but coded so as not to assume that the top-level remote directory already exists.

Here is the sort of output displayed on the console when the upload-all script is run. It's similar to the flat upload (which you might expect, given that it is reusing much of the same code), but notice that it traverses and uploads two nested subdirectories along the way, *.\tempdir* and *.\tempdir\nested*:

```
C:\Mark\temp\website>c:\...\PP3E\Internet\Ftp\mirror\uploadall.py
Password for lutz on home.rmi.net:
connecting...
uploading .\109_0137.JPG to 109_0137.JPG image
uploading .\2004-longmont-classes.html to 2004-longmont-classes.html text
uploading .\2005-longmont-classes.html to 2005-longmont-classes.html text
uploading .\2006-longmont-classes.html to 2006-longmont-classes.html text
...
...lines deleted...
...
uploading .\t615c.jpg to t615c.jpg image
uploading .\talk.html to talk.html text
uploading .\temp.txt to temp.txt text
uploading .\tempdir to tempdir directory created
uploading .\tempdir\index.html to index.html text
uploading .\tempdir\nested to nested directory created
uploading .\tempdir\nested\about-pp.html to about-pp.html text
uploading .\tempdir\nested\calendar.html to calendar.html text
directory exited
uploading .\tempdir\zaurus0.jpg to zaurus0.jpg image
directory exited
uploading .\testicon.jpg to testicon.jpg image
uploading .\testicon_py.html to testicon_py.html text
...
...lines deleted...
...
uploading .\zoo-jan-03.jpg to zoo-jan-03.jpg image
uploading .\zopeoutline.htm to zopeoutline.htm text
Done: 261 files and 2 directories uploaded.
```

As is, the script of Example 14-15 handles only directory tree *uploads*; recursive uploads are generally more useful than recursive downloads if you maintain your web sites on your local PC and upload to a server periodically, as I do. To also *download* (mirror) a web site that has subdirectories, a script must parse the output of a remote listing command to detect remote directories. For the same reason, the recursive upload script was not coded to support the remote directory tree cleanup option of the original—such a feature would require parsing remote listings as well. The next section shows how.

Deleting remote trees

One last example of code reuse at work: when I initially tested the prior section's upload-all script, it contained a bug that caused it to fall into an infinite recursion loop, and keep copying the full site into new subdirectories, over and over, until the FTP server kicked me off (not an intended feature of the program!). In fact, the upload got 13 levels deep before being killed by the server; it effectively locked my site until the mess could be repaired.

To get rid of all the files accidentally uploaded, I quickly wrote the script in Example 14-16 in emergency (really, panic) mode; it deletes all files and nested subdirectories in an entire remote tree. Luckily, this was very easy to do given all the reuse that Example 14-16 inherits from the FtpTools superclass. Here, we just have to define the extension for recursive remote deletions. Even in tactical mode like this, OOP can be a decided advantage.

Example 14-16. PP3E\Internet\Ftp\mirror\cleanall.py

```
#!/bin/env python
##############################################################################
# extend the FtpTools class to delete files and subdirectories from a remote
# directory tree; supports nested directories too;  depends on the dir()
# command output format, which may vary on some servers! - see Python's
# Tools\Scripts\ftpmirror.py for hints;  extend me for remote tree downloads;
##############################################################################

from ftptools import FtpTools

class CleanAll(FtpTools):
    """
    delete an entire remote tree of subdirectories
    """
    def __init__(self):
        self.fcount = self.dcount = 0

    def getlocaldir(self):
        return None  # irrelevent here
    def getcleanall(self):
        return True  # implied here

    def cleanDir(self):
        """
        for each item in current remote directory,
        del simple files, recur into and then del subdirectories
        the dir() ftp call passes each line to a func or method
        """
        lines = []                            # each level has own lines
        self.connection.dir(lines.append)     # list current remote dir
        for line in lines:
            parsed  = line.split()            # split on whitespace
            permiss = parsed[0]               # assume 'drw... ... filename'
            fname   = parsed[-1]
```

Example 14-16. PP3E\Internet\Ftp\mirror\cleanall.py (continued)

```
            if permiss[0] != 'd':                    # simple file: delete
                print 'file', fname
                self.connection.delete(fname)
                self.fcount += 1
            else:                                     # directory: recur, del
                print 'directory', fname
                self.connection.cwd(fname)            # chdir into remote dir
                self.cleanDir()                       # clean subdirectory
                self.connection.cwd('..')             # chdir remote back up
                self.connection.rmd(fname)            # delete empty remote dir
                self.dcount += 1
                print 'directory exited'

if __name__ == '__main__':
    ftp = CleanAll()
    ftp.run(cleanTarget=ftp.cleanDir)
    print 'Done:', ftp.fcount, 'files and', ftp.dcount, 'directories cleaned.'
```

Besides again being recursive in order to handle arbitrarily shaped trees, the main trick employed here is to parse the output of a remote directory listing. The FTP nlst call used earlier gives us a simple list of filenames; here, we use dir to also get file detail lines like these:

```
ftp> dir
...
-rw-r--r--   1 ftp      ftp         10088 Mar 19 19:35 talkmore.html
-rw-r--r--   1 ftp      ftp          8711 Mar 19 19:35 temp.txt
drwxr-xr-x   2 ftp      ftp          4096 Mar 19 20:13 tempdir
-rw-r--r--   1 ftp      ftp          6748 Mar 19 19:35 testicon.jpg
-rw-r--r--   1 ftp      ftp           355 Mar 19 19:35 testicon_py.html
```

This output format is potentially server-specific, so check this on your own server before relying on this script. For my ISP, if the first character of the first item on the line is character "d", the filename at the end of the line names a remote directory (e.g., *tempdir*). To parse, the script simply splits on whitespace to extract parts of a line.

The output of our clean-all script in action follows; it shows up in the system console window where the script is run. This reflects a much larger tree than the one uploaded previously:

```
C:\Mark\temp\website>c:\...\PP3E\Internet\Ftp\mirror\cleanall.py
Password for lutz on home.rmi.net:
connecting...
...
...lines deleted...
...
file t250.jpg
file t615c.jpg
file talk.html
file talkmore.html
directory temp
file 109_0137.JPG
```

```
file 2004-longmont-classes.html
file 2005-longmont-classes.html
file 2006-longmont-classes.html
...
```
...lines deleted...
```
...
directory exited
file testicon.jpg
file testicon_py.html
...
```
...lines deleted...
```
...
file zoo-jan-03.jpg
file zopeoutline.htm
Done: 855 files and 13 directories cleaned.
```

It is possible to extend this remote tree-cleaner to also download a remote tree with subdirectories. We'll leave this final step as a suggested exercise, though, partly because its dependence on the format produced by server directory listings makes it complex to be robust; and partly because this use case is less common for me—in practice, I am more likely to maintain a site on my PC and upload to the server, than to download a tree.

If you do wish to experiment with a recursive download, though, be sure to consult the script *Tools\Scripts\ftpmirror.py* in Python's install or source tree for hints. That script attempts to download a remote directory tree by FTP, and allows for various directory listing formats which we'll skip here in the interest of space. For our purposes, it's time to move on to the next protocol on our tour—Internet email.

Processing Internet Email

Some of the other most common, higher-level Internet protocols have to do with reading and sending email messages: POP and IMAP for fetching email from servers,[*] SMTP for sending new messages, and other formalisms such as rfc822 for specifying email message content and format. You don't normally need to know about such acronyms when using common email tools; but internally, programs like Microsoft Outlook and webmail systems generally talk to POP and SMTP servers to do your bidding.

Like FTP, email ultimately consists of formatted commands and byte streams shipped over sockets and ports (port 110 for POP; 25 for SMTP). But also like FTP, Python has standard library modules to simplify all aspects of email processing:

---

[*] IMAP, or Internet Message Access Protocol, was designed as an alternative to POP, but it is still not as widely available today, and so is not presented in this text. A major commercial provider used for this book's examples only provides POP access to email, for instance. See the Python library manual for IMAP server interface details.

- `poplib` and `imaplib` for fetching email
- `smtplib` for sending email
- The `email` module package for parsing and constructing email

The `email` package also handles tasks such as address parsing and date and time formatting, and additional modules handle more specific tasks (e.g., `mimetypes` to map filenames to and from content types). The module `rfc822` provides an alternative headers parsing tool, but has been deprecated since Python 2.3 (`email` should be used today).

In the next few sections, we explore the POP and SMTP interfaces for fetching and sending email at servers, and the `email` package interfaces for parsing and composing email message text. Other email interfaces in Python are analogous and are documented in the Python library reference manual.

POP: Fetching Email

I admit it: up until just before 2000, I took a lowest-common–denominator approach to email. I preferred to check my messages by Telnetting to my ISP and using a simple command-line email interface. Of course, that's not ideal for mail with attachments, pictures, and the like, but its portability was staggering—because Telnet runs on almost any machine with a network link, I was able to check my mail quickly and easily from anywhere on the planet. Given that I make my living traveling around the world teaching Python classes, this wild accessibility was a big win.

Like web site maintenance, times have changed on this front, too: when my ISP took away Telnet access, they also took away my email access. Luckily, Python came to the rescue—by writing email access scripts in Python, I could still read and send email from any machine in the world that has Python and an Internet connection. Python can be as portable a solution as Telnet, but much more powerful.

Moreover, I can still use these scripts as an alternative to tools suggested by the ISP, such as Microsoft Outlook. Besides not being fond of delegating control to commercial products of large companies, tools like Outlook generally download mail to your PC and delete it from the mail server as soon as you access it by default. This keeps your email box small (and your ISP happy), but it isn't exactly friendly to traveling Python salespeople—once accessed, you cannot reaccess a prior email from any machine except the one to which it was initially downloaded. If you need to see an old email and don't have your PC handy, you're out of luck.

The next two scripts represent one first-cut solution to these portability and single-machine constraints (we'll see others in this and later chapters). The first, *popmail.py*, is a simple mail reader tool, which downloads and prints the contents of each email in an email account. This script is admittedly primitive, but it lets you read your email on any machine with Python and sockets; moreover, it leaves your email intact on the server. The second, *smtpmail.py*, is a one-shot script for writing and sending a new email message.

Later in this chapter, we'll implement an interactive console-based email client (pymail), and later in this book we'll code a full-blown GUI email tool (PyMailGUI) and a web-based email program (PyMailCGI). For now, we'll start with the basics.*

Mail Configuration Module

Before we get to the scripts, let's first take a look at a common module they import and use. The module in Example 14-17 is used to configure email parameters appropriately for a particular user. It's simply a collection of assignments to variables used by mail programs that appear in this book (each major mail client has its own version, to allow content to vary). Isolating these configuration settings in this single module makes it easy to configure the book's email programs for a particular user, without having to edit actual program logic code.

If you want to use any of this book's email programs to do mail processing of your own, be sure to change its assignments to reflect your servers, account usernames, and so on (as shown, they refer to email accounts used for developing this book). Not all scripts use all of these settings; we'll revisit this module in later examples to explain more of them.

Note that to avoid spamming, some ISPs may require that you be connected directly to their systems in order to use their SMTP servers to send mail. For example, when connected directly by dial-up, I can use *smtp.earthlink.net* (my ISP's server), but when connected via broadband, I have to route requests through *smtp.comcast.net* (Comcast is my cable Internet provider). You may need to adjust these settings to match your configuration. Also, some SMTP servers check domain name validity in addresses, and may require an authenticating login step—see the SMTP section later in this chapter for interface details.

Example 14-17. PP3E\Internet\Email\mailconfig.py

```
#############################################################################
# user configuration settings for various email programs (pymail version);
# email scripts get their server names and other email config options from
# this module: change me to reflect your machine names, sig, and preferences;
#############################################################################
```

---

* As I write this third edition, I've also resorted to using my ISP's webmail interface at times. Although webmail is very portable (it runs in any browser), like the client-side Outlook program, it requires me to accept the feature set that it comes with. Worse, when the webmail server goes down, I am basically out of luck (this seems to have a knack for happening at the worst possible times). For such reasons, I still use the Python-coded alternatives of later chapters whenever possible—PyMailGUI on the client and PyMailCGI on the server. PyMailGUI is a webmail interface, too, but it is open to arbitrary customization.

Example 14-17. PP3E\Internet\Email\mailconfig.py (continued)

```
#-------------------------------------------------------------------------------
# (required for load, delete) POP3 email server machine, user
#-------------------------------------------------------------------------------


popservername = 'pop.earthlink.net'      # or pop.rmi.net
popusername   = 'pp3e'                    # pp3e@earthlink.net


#-------------------------------------------------------------------------------
# (required for send) SMTP email server machine name
# see Python smtpd module for a SMTP server class to run locally;
# note: your ISP may require that you be directly connected to their system:
# I can email through Earthlink on dial-up, but cannot via Comcast cable
#-------------------------------------------------------------------------------


smtpservername = 'smtp.comcast.net'      # or 'smtp.mindspring.com', 'localhost'


#-------------------------------------------------------------------------------
# (optional) personal information used by PyMailGUI to fill in edit forms;
# if not set, does not fill in initial form values;
# sig  -- can be a triple-quoted block, ignored if empty string;
# addr -- used for initial value of "From" field if not empty,
# no longer tries to guess From for replies--varying success;
#-------------------------------------------------------------------------------


myaddress   = 'pp3e@earthlink.net'
mysignature = '--Mark Lutz  (http://www.rmi.net/~lutz)'


#-------------------------------------------------------------------------------
# (may be required for send) SMTP user/password if authenticated
# set user to None or '' if no login/authentication is required
# set pswd to name of a file holding your SMTP password, or an
# empty string to force programs to ask (in a console, or GUI)
#-------------------------------------------------------------------------------


smtpuser      = None                     # per your ISP
smtppasswdfile = ''                      # set to '' to be asked


#-------------------------------------------------------------------------------
# (optional) name of local one-line text file with your pop
# password; if empty or file cannot be read, pswd is requested when first
# connecting; pswd not encrypted: leave this empty on shared machines;
#-------------------------------------------------------------------------------


poppasswdfile = r'c:\temp\pymailgui.txt'    # set to '' to be asked


#-------------------------------------------------------------------------------
# (optional) local file where sent messages are saved;
#-------------------------------------------------------------------------------


sentmailfile = r'.\sentmail.txt'            # . means in current working dir


#-------------------------------------------------------------------------------
```

Example 14-17. PP3E\Internet\Email\mailconfig.py (continued)

```
# (optional) local file where pymail saves pop mail;
#-------------------------------------------------------------------------

savemailfile  = r'c:\temp\savemail.txt'        # not used in PyMailGUI: dialog

#end
```

POP Mail Reader Script

On to reading email in Python: the script in Example 14-18 employs Python's standard poplib module, an implementation of the client-side interface to POP—the Post
Office Protocol. POP is a well-defined and widely available way to fetch email from
servers over sockets. This script connects to a POP server to implement a simple yet
portable email download and display tool.

Example 14-18. PP3E\Internet\Email\popmail.py

```
#!/usr/local/bin/python
##############################################################################
# use the Python POP3 mail interface module to view your POP email account
# messages;  this is just a simple listing--see pymail.py for a client with
# more user interaction features, and smtpmail.py for a script which sends
# mail;  POP is used to retrieve mail, and runs on a socket using port number
# 110 on the server machine, but Python's poplib hides all protocol details;
# to send mail, use the smtplib module (or os.popen('mail...').  see also:
# unix mailfile reader in App framework, imaplib module for IMAP alternative
##############################################################################

import poplib, getpass, sys, mailconfig

mailserver = mailconfig.popservername      # ex: 'pop.rmi.net'
mailuser   = mailconfig.popusername        # ex: 'lutz'
mailpasswd = getpass.getpass('Password for %s?' % mailserver)

print 'Connecting...'
server = poplib.POP3(mailserver)
server.user(mailuser)                      # connect, log in to mail server
server.pass_(mailpasswd)                   # pass is a reserved word

try:
    print server.getwelcome()              # print returned greeting message
    msgCount, msgBytes = server.stat()
    print 'There are', msgCount, 'mail messages in', msgBytes, 'bytes'
    print server.list()
    print '-'*80
    raw_input('[Press Enter key]')

    for i in range(msgCount):
        hdr, message, octets = server.retr(i+1)   # octets is byte count
        for line in message: print line           # retrieve, print all mail
        print '-'*80                              # mail box locked till quit
```

Example 14-18. PP3E\Internet\Email\popmail.py (continued)

```
        if i < msgCount - 1:
            raw_input('[Press Enter key]')
finally:                                    # make sure we unlock mbox
    server.quit()                           # else locked till timeout
print 'Bye.'
```

Though primitive, this script illustrates the basics of reading email in Python. To establish a connection to an email server, we start by making an instance of the poplib.POP3 object, passing in the email server machine's name as a string:

```
    server = poplib.POP3(mailserver)
```

If this call doesn't raise an exception, we're connected (by socket) to the POP server listening for requests on POP port number 110 at the machine where our email account lives.

The next thing we need to do before fetching messages is tell the server our username and password; notice that the password method is called pass_. Without the trailing underscore, pass would name a reserved word and trigger a syntax error:

```
    server.user(mailuser)               # connect, log in to mail server
    server.pass_(mailpasswd)            # pass is a reserved word
```

To keep things simple and relatively secure, this script always asks for the account password interactively; the getpass module we met in the FTP section of this chapter is used to input but not display a password string typed by the user.

Once we've told the server our username and password, we're free to fetch mailbox information with the stat method (number messages, total bytes among all messages), and fetch the full text of a particular message with the retr method (pass the message number—they start at 1). The full text includes all headers, followed by a blank line, followed by the mail's text and any attached parts. The retr call sends back a tuple that includes a list of line strings representing the content of the mail:

```
    msgCount, msgBytes = server.stat()
    hdr, message, octets = server.retr(i+1)     # octets is byte count
```

When we're done, we close the email server connection by calling the POP object's quit method:

```
    server.quit()                           # else locked till timeout
```

Notice that this call appears inside the finally clause of a try statement that wraps the bulk of the script. To minimize complications associated with changes, POP servers lock your email inbox between the time you first connect and the time you close your connection (or until an arbitrary, system-defined timeout expires). Because the POP quit method also unlocks the mailbox, it's crucial that we do this before exiting, whether an exception is raised during email processing or not. By wrapping the action in a try/finally statement, we guarantee that the script calls quit on exit to unlock the mailbox to make it accessible to other processes (e.g., delivery of incoming email).

Fetching Messages

Here is the popmail script of Example 14-18 in action, displaying two messages in my account's mailbox on machine *pop.earthlink.net*—the domain name of the mail server machine at earthlink.net, configured in the module `mailconfig`:

```
C:\...\PP3E\Internet\Email>popmail.py
Password for pop.earthlink.net?
Connecting...
+OK NGPopper vEL_6_10 at earthlink.net ready <12517.1139377094@pop-satin.atl.sa.
earthlink.net>
There are 2 mail messages in 1676 bytes
('+OK', ['1 876', '2 800'], 14)
-------------------------------------------------------------------------------

[Press Enter key]
Status:  U
Return-Path: <lumber.jack@thelarch.com>
Received: from sccrmhc13.comcast.net ([63.240.77.83])
        by mx-pinchot.atl.sa.earthlink.net (EarthLink SMTP Server) with SMTP id
1f6HNg7Ex3N134d0
        for <pp3e@earthlink.net>; Wed, 8 Feb 2006 00:23:06 -0500 (EST)
Received: from [192.168.1.117] (c-67-161-147-100.hsd1.co.comcast.net[67.161.147.
100])
          by comcast.net (sccrmhc13) with ESMTP
          id <2006020805230401300nvnlge>; Wed, 8 Feb 2006 05:23:04 +0000
From: lumber.jack@TheLarch.com
To: pp3e@earthlink.net
Subject: I'm a Lumberjack, and I'm Okay
Date: Wed, 08 Feb 2006 05:23:13 -0000
X-Mailer: PyMailGUI 2.1 (Python)
Message-Id: <200602080023.1f6HNg7Ex3N134d0@mx-pinchot.atl.sa.earthlink.net>
X-ELNK-Info: spv=0;
X-ELNK-AV: 0
X-ELNK-Info: sbv=0; sbrc=.0; sbf=00; sbw=000;
X-NAS-Language: English
X-NAS-Bayes: #0: 1.55061E-015; #1: 1
X-NAS-Classification: 0
X-NAS-MessageID: 1469
X-NAS-Validation: {388D038F-95BF-4409-9404-7726720152C4}

I cut down trees, I skip and jump,
I like to press wild flowers...


-------------------------------------------------------------------------------

[Press Enter key]
Status:  U
Return-Path: <pp3e@earthlink.net>
Received: from sccrmhc11.comcast.net ([204.127.200.81])
        by mx-canard.atl.sa.earthlink.net (EarthLink SMTP Server) with SMTP id 1
f6HOh6uy3N136s0
```

```
              for <pp3e@earthlink.net>; Wed, 8 Feb 2006 00:24:09 -0500 (EST)
    Received: from [192.168.1.117] (c-67-161-147-100.hsd1.co.comcast.net[67.161.147.
    100])
              by comcast.net (sccrmhc11) with ESMTP
              id <2006020805235601100dkk93e>; Wed, 8 Feb 2006 05:23:56 +0000
    From: pp3e@earthlink.net
    To: pp3e@earthlink.net
    Subject: testing
    Date: Wed, 08 Feb 2006 05:24:06 -0000
    X-Mailer: PyMailGUI 2.1 (Python)
    Message-Id: <200602080024.1f6HOh6uy3Nl36sO@mx-canard.atl.sa.earthlink.net>
    X-ELNK-Info: spv=0;
    X-ELNK-AV: 0
    X-ELNK-Info: sbv=0; sbrc=.0; sbf=00; sbw=000;
    X-NAS-Classification: 0
    X-NAS-MessageID: 1470
    X-NAS-Validation: {388D038F-95BF-4409-9404-7726720152C4}

    Testing Python mail tools.


    -------------------------------------------------------------------------

    Bye.
```

This interface is about as simple as it could be—after connecting to the server, it prints the complete and raw full text of one message at a time, pausing between each until you press the Enter key. The raw_input built-in is called to wait for the key press between message displays. The pause keeps messages from scrolling off the screen too fast; to make them visually distinct, emails are also separated by lines of dashes.

We could make the display fancier (e.g., we can use the email package to parse headers, bodies, and attachments—watch for examples in this and later chapters), but here we simply display the whole message that was sent. This works well for simple mails like these two, but it can be inconvenient for larger messages with attachments; we'll improve on this in later clients.

If you look closely at the text in these emails, you may notice that the emails were actually sent by another program called PyMailGUI (a program we'll meet in Chapter 15). The X-Mailer header line, if present, typically identifies the sending program. In fact, a variety of extra header lines can be sent in a message's text. The Received: headers, for example, trace the machines that a message passed through on its way to the target mailbox. Because popmail prints the entire raw text of a message, you see all headers here, but you may see only a few by default in end-user–oriented mail GUIs such as Outlook.

The script in Example 14-18 never deletes mail from the server. Mail is simply retrieved and printed and will be shown again the next time you run the script (barring deletion in another tool). To really remove mail permanently, we need to call other methods (e.g., server.dele(msgnum)) but such a capability is best deferred until we develop more interactive mail tools.

Fetching Email at the Interactive Prompt

If you don't mind typing code and reading POP server messages, it's possible to use the Python interactive prompt as a simple email client too. The following session uses two additional interfaces we'll apply in later examples:

conn.list( )
> Returns a list of "message-number message-size" strings.

conn.top(N, 0)
> Retrieves just the header text portion of message number N.

The top call also returns a tuple that includes the list of line strings sent back; its second argument tells the server how many additional lines after the headers to send, if any. If all you need are header details, top can be much quicker than the full text fetch of retr, provided your mail server implements the TOP command (most do).

```
>>> from poplib import POP3
>>> conn = POP3('pop.earthlink.net')
>>> conn.user('pp3e')
'+OK'
>>> conn.pass_('XXXX')
'+OK pp3e has 19 messages (14827231 octets).'
>>> conn.stat( )
(19, 14827231)
>>> conn.list( )
('+OK', ['1 34359', '2 1995', '3 3549', '4 1218', '5 2162', '6 6450837', '7 9666
', '8 178026', '9 841855', '10 289869', '11 2770', '12 2094', '13 2092', '14 305
31', '15 5108864', '16 1032', '17 2729', '18 1850474', '19 13109'], 180)
>>> conn.top(1, 0)
('+OK', ['Status: RO', 'To: pp3e@earthlink.net', 'X-ElinkBul: x+ZDXwyCjyELQIOyCm
...more deleted...
ts, Wireless Security Tips, & More!', 'Content-Type: text/html', ''], 283)
>>> conn.retr(16)
('+OK 1020 octets', ['Status: RO', 'Return-Path: <pp3e@earthlink.net>', 'Receive
...more deleted...
'> Enjoy!', '> ', '', ''], 1140)
>>> conn.quit( )
```

Printing the full text of a message is easy: simply concatenate the line strings returned by retr or top, adding a newline between ('\n'.join(lines) will usually suffice). Parsing email text to extract headers and components is more complex, especially for mails with attached and possibly encoded parts, such as images. As we'll see later in this chapter, the standard library's email package can parse the mail's full or headers text after it has been fetched with poplib (or imaplib).

See the Python library manual for details on other POP module tools. As of Python 2.4, there is also a POP3_SSL class in the poplib module that connects to the server over an

SSL-encrypted socket on port 995 by default (the standard port for POP over SSL). It provides an identical interface, but it uses secure sockets for the conversation where supported by servers.

SMTP: Sending Email

There is a proverb in hackerdom that states that every useful computer program eventually grows complex enough to send email. Whether such wisdom rings true or not in practice, the ability to automatically initiate email from within a program is a powerful tool.

For instance, test systems can automatically email failure reports, user interface programs can ship purchase orders to suppliers by email, and so on. Moreover, a portable Python mail script could be used to send messages from any computer in the world with Python and an Internet connection. Freedom from dependence on mail programs like Outlook is an attractive feature if you happen to make your living traveling around teaching Python on all sorts of computers.

Luckily, sending email from within a Python script is just as easy as reading it. In fact, there are at least four ways to do so:

Calling os.popen *to launch a command-line mail program*
> On some systems, you can send email from a script with a call of the form:
> ```
> os.popen('mail -s "xxx" a@b.c', 'w').write(text)
> ```
> As we saw earlier in the book, the popen tool runs the command-line string passed to its first argument, and returns a file-like object connected to it. If we use an open mode of w, we are connected to the command's standard input stream—here, we write the text of the new mail message to the standard Unix mail command-line program. The net effect is as if we had run mail interactively, but it happens inside a running Python script.

Running the sendmail *program*
> The open source sendmail program offers another way to initiate mail from a program. Assuming it is installed and configured on your system, you can launch it using Python tools like the os.popen call of the previous paragraph.

Using the standard smtplib *Python module*
> Python's standard library comes with support for the client-side interface to SMTP—the Simple Mail Transfer Protocol—a higher-level Internet standard for sending mail over sockets. Like the poplib module we met in the previous section, smtplib hides all the socket and protocol details and can be used to send mail on any machine with Python and a socket-based Internet link.

Fetching and using third-party packages and tools
Other tools in the open source library provide higher-level mail handling packages for Python (accessible from *http://www.python.org*); most build upon one of the prior three techniques.

Of these four options, smtplib is by far the most portable and powerful. Using os.popen to spawn a mail program usually works on Unix-like platforms only, not on Windows (it assumes a command-line mail program), and requires spawning one or more processes along the way. And although the sendmail program is powerful, it is also somewhat Unix-biased, complex, and may not be installed even on all Unix-like machines.

By contrast, the smtplib module works on any machine that has Python and an Internet link, including Unix, Linux, Mac, and Windows. It sends mail over sockets in-process, instead of starting other programs to do the work. Moreover, SMTP affords us much control over the formatting and routing of email.

SMTP Mail Sender Script

Since SMTP is arguably the best option for sending mail from a Python script, let's explore a simple mailing program that illustrates its interfaces. The Python script shown in Example 14-19 is intended to be used from an interactive command line; it reads a new mail message from the user and sends the new mail by SMTP using Python's smtplib module.

Example 14-19. PP3E\Internet\Email\smtpmail.py

```
#!/usr/local/bin/python
#############################################################################
# use the Python SMTP mail interface module to send email messages; this
# is just a simple one-shot send script--see pymail, PyMailGUI, and
# PyMailCGI for clients with more user interaction features; also see
# popmail.py for a script that retrieves mail, and the mailtools pkg
# for attachments and formatting with the newer std lib email package;
#############################################################################

import smtplib, sys, time, mailconfig
mailserver = mailconfig.smtpservername          # ex: starship.python.net

From = raw_input('From? ').strip()              # ex: lutz@rmi.net
To   = raw_input('To?   ').strip()              # ex: python-list@python.org
To   = To.split(';')                            # allow a list of recipients
Subj = raw_input('Subj? ').strip()

# standard headers, followed by blank line, followed by text
date = time.ctime(time.time())
text = ('From: %s\nTo: %s\nDate: %s\nSubject: %s\n\n'
                    % (From, ';'.join(To), date, Subj))

print 'Type message text, end with line=(ctrl + D or Z)'
```

Example 14-19. PP3E\Internet\Email\smtpmail.py (continued)

```
while 1:
    line = sys.stdin.readline( )
    if not line:
        break                        # exit on ctrl-d/z
  # if line[:4] == 'From':
  #     line = '>' + line            # servers escape for us
    text = text + line

print 'Connecting...'
server = smtplib.SMTP(mailserver)             # connect, no log-in step
failed = server.sendmail(From, To, text)
server.quit( )
if failed:                                    # smtplib may raise exceptions
    print 'Failed recipients:', failed        # too, but let them pass here
else:
    print 'No errors.'
print 'Bye.'
```

Most of this script is user interface—it inputs the sender's address ("From"), one or more recipient addresses ("To", separated by ";" if more than one), and a subject line. The sending date is picked up from Python's standard time module, standard header lines are formatted, and the while loop reads message lines until the user types the end-of-file character (Ctrl-Z on Windows, Ctrl-D on Linux).

To be robust, be sure to add a *blank line* between the header lines and the body in the message's text; it's required by the SMTP protocol and some SMTP servers enforce this. Our script conforms by inserting an empty line with \n\n at the end of the string format expression. Later in this chapter, we'll format our messages with the Python email package, which handles such details for us automatically.

The rest of the script is where all the SMTP magic occurs: to send a mail by SMTP, simply run these two sorts of calls:

server = smtplib.SMTP(mailserver)
> Make an instance of the SMTP object, passing in the name of the SMTP server that will dispatch the message first. If this doesn't throw an exception, you're connected to the SMTP server via a socket when the call returns.

failed = server.sendmail(From, To, text)
> Call the SMTP object's sendmail method, passing in the sender address, one or more recipient addresses, and the text of the message itself with as many standard mail header lines as you care to provide.

When you're done, call the object's quit method to disconnect from the server. Notice that, on failure, the sendmail method may either raise an exception or return a list of the recipient addresses that failed; the script handles the latter case but lets exceptions kill the script with a Python error message.

For advanced usage, the call `server.login(user, password)` provides an interface to SMTP servers that require *authentication*; watch for this call to appear in the `mailtools` package example later in this chapter. An additional call, `server.starttls`, puts the SMTP connection in Transport Layer Security (TLS) mode; all commands will be encrypted using the `socket` module's SSL support, and they assume the server supports this mode. See the Python library manual for other calls not covered here.

Sending Messages

Let's ship a few messages across the world. The `smtpmail` script is a one-shot tool: each run allows you to send a single new mail message. Like most of the client-side tools in this chapter, it can be run from any computer with Python and an Internet link. Here it is running on Windows:

```
C:\...\PP3E\Internet\Email>smtpmail.py
From? Eric.the.Half.a.Bee@yahoo.com
To?    pp3e@earthlink.net
Subj? A B C D E F G
Type message text, end with line=(ctrl + D or Z)
Fiddle de dum, Fiddle de dee,
Eric the half a bee.
^Z
Connecting...
No errors.
Bye.
```

This mail is sent to the book's email account address (*pp3e@earthlink.net*), so it ultimately shows up in the inbox at my ISP, but only after being routed through an arbitrary number of machines on the Net, and across arbitrarily distant network links. It's complex at the bottom, but usually, the Internet "just works."

Notice the "From" address, though—it's completely fictitious (as far as I know, at least). It turns out that we can usually provide any "From" address we like because SMTP doesn't check its validity (only its general format is checked). Furthermore, unlike POP, there is usually no notion of a username or password in SMTP, so the sender is more difficult to determine. We need only pass email to any machine with a server listening on the SMTP port, and we don't need an account on that machine. Here, *Eric.the.Half.a.Bee@yahoo.com* works fine as the sender; *Marketing.Geek. From.Hell@spam.com* might work just as well.

It turns out that this behavior is the basis of some of those annoying junk emails that show up in your mailbox without a real sender's address.* Salespeople infected with

---

* We all know by now that such junk mail is usually referred to as spam, but not everyone knows that this name is a reference to a Monty Python skit where people trying to order breakfast at a restaurant were repeatedly drowned out by a group of Vikings singing an increasingly loud chorus of "spam, spam, spam..." (no, really). While spam can be used in many ways, this usage differs from its appearance in this book's examples, and from the name of a much-lauded meat product.

e-millionaire mania will email advertising to all addresses on a list without providing a real "From" address, to cover their tracks.

Normally, of course, you should use the same "To" address in the message and the SMTP call, and provide your real email address as the "From" value (that's the only way people will be able to reply to your message). Moreover, apart from teasing your significant other, sending phony addresses is just plain bad Internet citizenship. Let's run the script again to ship off another mail with more politically correct coordinates:

```
C:\...\PP3E\Internet\Email>python smtpmail.py
From? pp3e@earthlink.net
To?   pp3e@earthlink.net
Subj? testing smtpmail
Type message text, end with line=(ctrl + D or Z)
Lovely Spam! Wonderful Spam!
^Z
Connecting...
No errors.
Bye.
```

At this point, we could run whatever email tool we normally use to access our mail-box to verify the results of these two send operations; the two new emails should show up in our mailbox regardless of which mail client is used to view them. Since we've already written a Python script for reading mail, though, let's put it to use as a verification tool—running the popmail script from the last section reveals our two new messages at the end of the mail list (parts of the output have been trimmed for space here):

```
C:\...\PP3E\Internet\Email>python popmail.py
C:\Mark\PP3E-cd\Examples\PP3E\Internet\Email>popmail.py
Password for pop.earthlink.net?
Connecting...
+OK NGPopper vEL_6_10 at earthlink.net ready <25557.1139379723@pop-borzoi.atl.sa
.earthlink.net>
There are 4 mail messages in 3264 bytes
('+OK', ['1 876', '2 800', '3 818', '4 770'], 28)
--------------------------------------------------------------------------------

[Press Enter key]
--------------------------------------------------------------------------------

...more deleted...

Status:  U
Return-Path: <Eric.the.Half.a.Bee@yahoo.com>
Received: from rwcrmhc12.comcast.net ([216.148.227.152])
        by mx-austrian.atl.sa.earthlink.net (EarthLink SMTP Server) with ESMTP i
d 1f6Iem1pl3Nl34j0
        for <pp3e@earthlink.net>; Wed, 8 Feb 2006 00:51:07 -0500 (EST)
Received: from [192.168.1.117] (c-67-161-147-100.hsd1.co.comcast.net[67.161.147.
100])
        by comcast.net (rwcrmhc12) with ESMTP
```

```
        id <20060208055106m1200t3cj1e>; Wed, 8 Feb 2006 05:51:06 +0000
From: Eric.the.Half.a.Bee@yahoo.com
To: pp3e@earthlink.net
Date: Tue Feb 07 22:51:08 2006
Subject: A B C D E F G
Message-Id: <200602080051.1f6Iem1pl3Nl34jO@mx-austrian.atl.sa.earthlink.net>
...more deleted...

Fiddle de dum, Fiddle de dee,
Eric the half a bee.


---------------------------------------------------------------------------

[Press Enter key]
Status:  U
Return-Path: <pp3e@earthlink.net>
Received: from rwcrmhc11.comcast.net ([204.127.192.81])
        by mx-limpkin.atl.sa.earthlink.net (EarthLink SMTP Server) with SMTP id
1f6IGA3yA3Nl34pO
        for <pp3e@earthlink.net>; Wed, 8 Feb 2006 01:20:16 -0500 (EST)
Received: from [192.168.1.117] (c-67-161-147-62.hsd1.co.comcast.net[67.161.147.6
2])
        by comcast.net (rwcrmhc11) with ESMTP
        id <20060208062000m1100bufjle>; Wed, 8 Feb 2006 06:20:00 +0000
From: pp3e@earthlink.net
To: pp3e@earthlink.net
Date: Tue Feb 07 23:19:51 2006
Subject: testing smtpmail
Message-Id: <200602080120.1f6IGA3yA3Nl34pO@mx-limpkin.atl.sa.earthlink.net>
...more deleted...

Lovely Spam! Wonderful Spam!


---------------------------------------------------------------------------

Bye.
```

Technically, the ISP used for this book's email account in this edition tests to make sure that at least the domain of the email sender's address (the part after "@") is a real, valid domain name, and disallows delivery if not. As mentioned earlier, some servers also require that SMTP senders have a direct connection to their network, and may require an authentication call with username and password (described earlier in this chapter). In the second edition of the book, I used an ISP that let me get away with more nonsense, but this may vary per server; the rules have tightened since then to limit spam.

More Ways to Abuse the Net

The first mail listed at the end of the preceding section was the one we sent with a fictitious address; the second was the more legitimate message. Like "From" addresses, header lines are a bit arbitrary under SMTP. `smtpmail` automatically adds "From:" and "To:" header lines in the message's text with the same addresses as passed to the SMTP interface, but only as a polite convention. Sometimes, though, you can't tell who a mail was sent to, either—to obscure the target audience or to support legitimate email lists, senders may manipulate the contents of headers in the message's text.

For example, if we change `smtpmail` to not automatically generate a "To:" header line with the same address(es) sent to the SMTP interface call, we can manually type a "To:" header that differs from the address we're really sending to—the "To" address list passed into the `smtplib` send call gives the true recipients, but the "To:" header line in the text of the message is what most mail clients will display:

```
C:\...\PP3E\Internet\Email>python smtpmail-noTo.py
From? Eric.the.Half.a.Bee@aol.com
To?    pp3e@earthlink.net
Subj? a b c d e f g
Type message text, end with line=(ctrl + D or Z)
To: nobody.in.particular@marketing.com

Spam; Spam and eggs; Spam, spam, and spam
^Z
Connecting...
No errors.
Bye.
```

In some ways, the "From" and "To" addresses in send method calls and message header lines are similar to addresses on envelopes and letters in envelopes. The former is used for routing, but the latter is what the reader sees. Here, I gave the real "To" address as my mailbox on the earthlink.net server, but then gave a fictitious name in the manually typed "To:" header line; the first address is where it really goes and the second appears in mail clients. If your mail tool picks out the "To:" line, such mails will look odd when viewed.

For instance, when the mail we just sent shows up in my mailbox on *earthlink.net*, it's difficult to tell much about its origin or destination in either Outlook or a Python-coded mail tool we'll meet in the next chapter (see Figure 14-5). And its raw text will show only the machines it has been routed through.

Once again, though, don't do this unless you have good reason. This demonstration is only intended to help you understand mail headers and simple spamming techniques. To write an automatic spam filter that deletes incoming junk mail, for instance, you need to know some of the telltale signs to look for in a message's text.

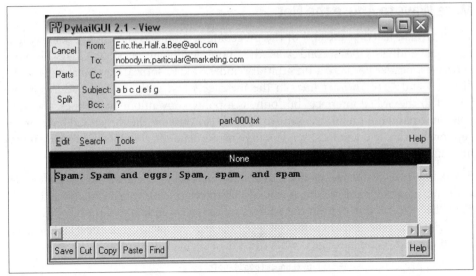

Figure 14-5. Bogus mail in a mail client (PyMailGUI)

Such "To" address juggling may also be useful in the context of legitimate mailing lists—the name of the list appears in the "To:" header when the message is viewed, not the potentially many individual recipients named in the send-mail call. A mail client can simply send a mail to all on the list, but insert the general list name in the "To:" header.

But in other contexts, sending email with bogus "From:" and "To:" lines is equivalent to making anonymous phone calls. Most mailers won't even let you change the "From" line, and they don't distinguish between the "To" address and header line. When you program mail scripts of your own, though, SMTP is wide open in this regard. So be good out there, okay?*

Back to the Big Internet Picture

So where are we in the Internet abstraction model now? Because mail is transferred over sockets (remember sockets?), they are at the root of all of this email fetching and sending. All email read and written ultimately consists of formatted bytes shipped over sockets between computers on the Net. As we've seen, though, the POP and SMTP interfaces in Python hide all the details. Moreover, the scripts we've begun writing even hide the Python interfaces and provide higher-level interactive tools.

---

* Since writing these words for the second edition of this book, spam mail has become quite a bit more sophisticated than simply forging sender and recipient names (as we all know far too well). For more on the subject, see the SpamBayes mail filter written in Python. Also, manipulating recipient names does indeed have practical application for email lists, so the techniques described are not necessarily all bad.

Both popmail and smtpmail provide portable email tools but aren't quite what we'd expect in terms of usability these days. Later in this chapter, we'll use what we've seen thus far to implement a more interactive, console-based mail tool. In the next chapter, we'll also code a Tkinter email GUI, and then we'll go on to build a web-based interface in a later chapter. All of these tools, though, vary primarily in terms of user interface only; each ultimately employs the mail modules we've met here to transfer mail message text over the Internet with sockets.

Sending Email from the Interactive Prompt

Just as for reading mail, we can use the Python interactive prompt as our email sending client too, if we type calls manually:

```
>>> from smtplib import SMTP
>>> conn = SMTP('smtp.comcast.net')
>>> conn.sendmail('pp3e@earthlink.net', ['lutz@rmi.net', 'pp3e@earthlink.net'],
... """From: pp3e@earthlink.net
... To: maillist
... Subject: test smtplib
...
... testing 1 2 3...
... """)
{}
```

This is a bit tricky to get right, though—header lines are governed by standards: the blank line after the subject line is required and significant, for instance. Furthermore, mail formatting gets much more complex as we start writing messages with attachments. In practice, the email package in the standard library is generally used to construct emails, before shipping them off with smtplib. The package lets us build mails by assigning headers and attaching and possibly encoding parts, and creates a correctly formatted mail text. To learn how, let's move on to the next section.

email: Parsing and Composing Mails

The second edition of this book used a handful of standard library modules (rfc822, StringIO, and more) to parse the contents of messages, and simple text processing to compose them. Additionally, that edition included a section on extracting and decoding attached parts of a message using modules such as mhlib, mimetools, and base64.

Those tools are still available, but were, frankly, a bit clumsy and error-prone. Parsing attachments from messages, for example, was tricky, and composing even basic messages was tedious (in fact, an early printing of the prior edition contained a potential bug, because I forgot one \n character in a complex string formatting operation). Adding attachments to sent messages wasn't even attempted, due to the complexity of the formatting involved.

Luckily, things are much simpler today. Since the second edition, Python has sprouted a new email package—a powerful collection of tools that automate most of the work behind parsing and composing email messages. This module gives us an object-based message interface and handles all the textual message structure details, both analyzing and creating it. Not only does this eliminate a whole class of potential bugs, it also promotes more advanced mail processing.

Things like attachments, for instance, become accessible to mere mortals (and authors with limited book real estate). In fact, the entire section on manual attachment parsing and decoding has been deleted in this edition—it's essentially automatic with email. The new package parses and constructs headers and attachments; generates correct email text; decodes and encodes base64, quoted-printable, and uuencoded data; and much more.

We won't cover the email package in its entirety in this book; it is well documented in Python's library manual. Our goal here is to give some example usage code, which you can study in conjunction with the manuals. But to help get you started, let's begin with a quick overview. In a nutshell, the email package is based around the Message object it provides:

Parsing mail

A mail's full text, fetched from poplib or imaplib, is parsed into a new Message object, with an API for accessing its components. In the object, mail headers become dictionary-like keys, and components become a payload that can be walked with a generator interface (more on payloads in a moment).

Creating mail

New mails are composed by creating a Message object, using an API to attach headers and parts, and asking the object for its print representation—a correctly formatted mail message text, ready to be passed to the smtplib module for delivery. Headers are added by key assignment and attachments by method calls.

In other words, the Message object is used both for accessing existing messages and for creating new ones from scratch. In both cases, email can automatically handle details like encodings (e.g., attached binary images can be treated as text with base64 encoding and decoding), content types, and more.

Message Objects

Since the email module's Message object is at the heart of its API, you need a cursory understanding of its form to get started. In short, it is designed to reflect the structure of a formatted email message. Each Message consists of three main pieces of information:

Type

A content type (plain text, HTML text, JPEG image, and so on), encoded as a MIME main type and a subtype. For instance, "text/html" means the main type is text and the subtype is HTML (a web page); "image/jpeg" means a JPEG photo. A "multipart/mixed" type means there are nested parts within the message.

Headers

A dictionary-like mapping interface, with one key per mail header ("From", "To", and so on). This interface supports almost all of the usual dictionary operations, and headers may be fetched or set by normal key indexing.

Content

A payload, which represents the mail's content. This can be either a string for simple messages, or a list of additional Message objects for multipart container messages with attached or alternative parts. For some oddball types, the payload may be a Python None object.

For example, mails with attached images may have a main top-level Message (type multipart/mixed), with three more Message objects in its payload—one for its main text (type text/plain), followed by two of type image for the photos (type image/jpeg). The photo parts may be encoded for transmission as text with base64 or another scheme; the encoding type, as well as the original image filename, are specified in the part's headers.

Similarly, mails that include both simple text and an HTML alternative will have two nested Messages in their payload, of type plain text (text/plain) and HTML text (text/html), along with a main root Message of type multipart/alternative. Your mail client decides which part to display, often based on your preferences.

Simpler messages may have just a root Message of type text/plain or text/html, representing the entire message body. The payload for such mails is a simple string. They may also have no explicitly given type at all, which generally defaults to text/plain. Some single-part messages are text/html, with no text/plain alternative—they require a web browser or other HTML viewer (or a very keen-eyed user).

Other combinations are possible, including some types that are not commonly seen in practice, such as message/delivery status. Most messages have a main text part, though it is not required, and may be nested in a multipart or other construct.

In all cases, these message structures are automatically generated when mail text is parsed, and are created by your method calls when new messages are composed. For instance, when creating messages, the message attach method adds parts for multipart mails, and set_payload sets the entire payload to a string for simple mails.

Message objects also have assorted properties (e.g., the filename of an attachment), and they provide a convenient walk generator method, which returns the next Message in the payload each time through in a for loop. Because the walker yields the root Message object first (i.e., self), this doesn't become a special case this; a non-multipart message is effectively a Message with a single item in its payload—itself.

Ultimately, the Message object structure closely mirrors the way mails are formatted as text. Special header lines in the mail's text give its type (e.g., plain text or multipart), as well as the separator used between the content of nested parts. Since the underlying textual details are automated by the email package—both when parsing and when composing—we won't go into further formatting details here.

If you are interested in seeing how this translates to real emails, a great way to learn mail structure is by inspecting the full raw text of messages displayed by the email clients we'll meet in this book. For more on the Message object, and email in general, consult the email package's entry in Python's library manual. We're skipping details such as its available encoders and MIME object classes here in the interest of space.

Beyond the email package, the Python library includes other tools for mail-related processing. For instance, mimetypes maps a filename to and from a MIME type:

```
mimetypes.guess_type(filename)
```
Maps a filename to a MIME type. Name *spam.txt* maps to text/plan.

```
mimetypes.guess_extension(contype)
```
Maps a MIME type to a filename extension. Type text/html maps to *.html*.

We also used the `mimetypes` module earlier in this chapter to guess FTP transfer modes from filenames (see Example 14-10), as well as in Chapter 6, where we used it to guess a media player for a filename (see the examples there, including *playfile.py*, Example 6-16). For email, these can come in handy when attaching files to a new message (guess_type) and saving parsed attachments that do not provide a filename (guess_extension). In fact, this module's source code is a fairly complete reference to MIME types. See the library manual for more on these tools.

Basic email Interfaces in Action

Although we can't provide an exhaustive reference here, let's step through a simple interactive session to illustrate the fundamentals of email processing. To *compose* the full text of a message—to be delivered with `smtplib`, for instance—make a `Message`, assign headers to its keys, and set its payload to the message body. Converting to a string yields the mail text. This process is substantially simpler and less error-prone than the text operations we used earlier in Example 14-19:

```
>>> from email.Message import Message
>>> m = Message( )
>>> m['from'] = 'Sue Jones <sue@jones.com>'
>>> m['to']   = 'pp3e@earthlink.net'
>>> m.set_payload('The owls are not what they seem...')
>>> s = str(m)
>>> print s
From nobody Sun Jan 22 21:26:53 2006
from: Sue Jones <sue@jones.com>
to: pp3e@earthlink.net

The owls are not what they seem...
```

Parsing a messages text—like the kind you obtain with `poplib`—is similarly simple, and essentially the inverse: we get back a `Message` object from the text, with keys for headers and a payload for the body:

```
>>> from email.Parser import Parser
>>> x = Parser( ).parsestr(s)
>>> x
<email.Message.Message instance at 0x00A7DA30>
>>> x['From']
'Sue Jones <sue@jones.com>'
>>> x.get_payload( )
'The owls are not what they seem...'
>>> x.items( )
[('from', 'Sue Jones <sue@jones.com>'), ('to', 'pp3e@earthlink.net')]
```

This isn't much different from the older `rfc822` module, but as we'll see in a moment, things get more interesting when there is more than one part. For simple messages like this one, the message walk generator treats it as a single-part mail, of type plain text:

```
>>> for part in x.walk():
...     print x.get_content_type()
...     print x.get_payload()
...
text/plain
The owls are not what they seem...
```

Making a mail with *attachments* is a little more work, but not much: we just make a root Message and attach nested Message objects created from the MIME type object that corresponds to the type of data we're attaching. The root message is where we store the main headers of the mail, and we attach parts here, instead of setting the entire payload (the payload is a list now, not a string).

```
>>> from email.MIMEMultipart import MIMEMultipart
>>> from email.MIMEText import MIMEText
>>>
>>> top = MIMEMultipart()
>>> top['from'] = 'Art <arthur@camelot.org>'
>>> top['to']   = 'pp3e@earthlink.net'
>>>
>>> sub1 = MIMEText('nice red uniforms...\n')
>>> sub2 = MIMEText(open('data.txt').read())
>>> sub2.add_header('Content-Disposition', 'attachment', filename='data.txt')
>>> top.attach(sub1)
>>> top.attach(sub2)
```

When we ask for the text, a correctly formatted full mail text is returned, separators and all, ready to be sent with `smtplib`—quite a trick, if you've ever tried this by hand:

```
>>> text = top.as_string()    # same as str() or print
>>> print text
Content-Type: multipart/mixed; boundary="===============0257358049=="
MIME-Version: 1.0
from: Art <arthur@camelot.org>
to: pp3e@earthlink.net

--===============0257358049==
Content-Type: text/plain; charset="us-ascii"
MIME-Version: 1.0
Content-Transfer-Encoding: 7bit

nice red uniforms...

--===============0257358049==
Content-Type: text/plain; charset="us-ascii"
```

```
MIME-Version: 1.0
Content-Transfer-Encoding: 7bit
Content-Disposition: attachment; filename="data.txt"

line1
line2
line3


--===============0257358049==--
```

If we are sent this message and retrieve it via `poplib`, parsing its full text yields a `Message` object just like the one we built to send this. The message `walk` generator allows us to step through each part, fetching their types and payloads:

```
>>> from email.Parser import Parser
>>> msg = Parser().parsestr(text)
>>> msg['from']
'Art <arthur@camelot.org>'

>>> for part in msg.walk():
...     print part.get_content_type()
...     print part.get_payload()
...     print
...
multipart/mixed
[<email.Message.Message instance at 0x00A82058>,        # line-break added
<email.Message.Message instance at 0x00A82260>]

text/plain
nice red uniforms...


text/plain
line1
line2
line3
```

Although this captures the basic flavor of the interface, we need to step up to a larger example to see more of the `email` package's power. The next section takes us on the first of those steps.

pymail: A Console-Based Email Client

Let's put together what we've learned about fetching, sending, parsing, and composing email in a simple but functional command-line console email tool. The script in Example 14-20 implements an interactive email session—users may type commands to read, send, and delete email messages.

Example 14-20. PP3E\Internet\Email\pymail.py

```python
#!/usr/local/bin/python
###########################################################################
# pymail - a simple console email interface client in Python; uses Python
# POP3 mail interface module to view POP email account messages; uses
# email package modules to extract mail message headers (not rfc822);
###########################################################################

import poplib, smtplib, email.Utils
from email.Parser  import Parser
from email.Message import Message

def inputmessage():
    import sys
    From = raw_input('From? ').strip()
    To   = raw_input('To?   ').strip()          # datetime hdr set auto
    To   = To.split(';')
    Subj = raw_input('Subj? ').strip()
    print 'Type message text, end with line="."'
    text = ''
    while True:
        line = sys.stdin.readline()
        if line == '.\n': break
        text += line
    return From, To, Subj, text

def sendmessage():
    From, To, Subj, text = inputmessage()
    msg = Message()
    msg['From']    = From
    msg['To']      = ';'.join(To)
    msg['Subject'] = Subj
    msg['Date']    = email.Utils.formatdate()          # curr datetime, rfc2822
    msg.set_payload(text)
    server = smtplib.SMTP(mailconfig.smtpservername)
    try:
        failed = server.sendmail(From, To, str(msg))   # may also raise exc
    except:
        print 'Error - send failed'
    else:
        if failed: print 'Failed:', failed

def connect(servername, user, passwd):
    print 'Connecting...'
    server = poplib.POP3(servername)
    server.user(user)                    # connect, log in to mail server
    server.pass_(passwd)                 # pass is a reserved word
    print server.getwelcome()            # print returned greeting message
    return server

def loadmessages(servername, user, passwd, loadfrom=1):
    server = connect(servername, user, passwd)
    try:
```

Example 14-20. PP3E\Internet\Email\pymail.py (continued)

```
        print server.list( )
        (msgCount, msgBytes) = server.stat( )
        print 'There are', msgCount, 'mail messages in', msgBytes, 'bytes'
        print 'Retrieving:',
        msgList = []
        for i in range(loadfrom, msgCount+1):              # empty if low >= high
            print i,                                       # fetch mail now
            (hdr, message, octets) = server.retr(i)        # save text on list
            msgList.append('\n'.join(message))             # leave mail on server
        print
    finally:
        server.quit( )                                     # unlock the mail box
    assert len(msgList) == (msgCount - loadfrom) + 1       # msg nums start at 1
    return msgList

def deletemessages(servername, user, passwd, toDelete, verify=1):
    print 'To be deleted:', toDelete
    if verify and raw_input('Delete?')[:1] not in ['y', 'Y']:
        print 'Delete cancelled.'
    else:
        server = connect(servername, user, passwd)
        try:
            print 'Deleting messages from server.'
            for msgnum in toDelete:                        # reconnect to delete mail
                server.dele(msgnum)                        # mbox locked until quit( )
        finally:
            server.quit( )

def showindex(msgList):
    count = 0                                    # show some mail headers
    for msgtext in msgList:
        msghdrs = Parser( ).parsestr(msgtext, headersonly=True)
        count   = count + 1
        print '%d:\t%d bytes' % (count, len(msgtext))
        for hdr in ('From', 'Date', 'Subject'):
            try:
                print '\t%s=>%s' % (hdr, msghdrs[hdr])
            except KeyError:
                print '\t%s=>(unknown)' % hdr
            #print '\n\t%s=>%s' % (hdr, msghdrs.get(hdr, '(unknown)'))
        if count % 5 == 0:
            raw_input('[Press Enter key]')  # pause after each 5

def showmessage(i, msgList):
    if 1 <= i <= len(msgList):
        print '-'*80
        msg = Parser( ).parsestr(msgList[i-1])
        print msg.get_payload( )         # prints payload: string, or [Messages]
        #print msgList[i-1]              # old: prints entire mail--hdrs+text
        print '-'*80                     # to get text only, call file.read( )
    else:                                # after rfc822.Message reads hdr lines
        print 'Bad message number'
```

Example 14-20. PP3E\Internet\Email\pymail.py (continued)

```python
def savemessage(i, mailfile, msgList):
    if 1 <= i <= len(msgList):
        open(mailfile, 'a').write('\n' + msgList[i-1] + '-'*80 + '\n')
    else:
        print 'Bad message number'

def msgnum(command):
    try:
        return int(command.split( )[1])
    except:
        return -1    # assume this is bad

helptext = """
Available commands:
i    - index display
l n? - list all messages (or just message n)
d n? - mark all messages for deletion (or just message n)
s n? - save all messages to a file (or just message n)
m    - compose and send a new mail message
q    - quit pymail
?    - display this help text
"""

def interact(msgList, mailfile):
    showindex(msgList)
    toDelete = []
    while 1:
        try:
            command = raw_input('[Pymail] Action? (i, l, d, s, m, q, ?) ')
        except EOFError:
            command = 'q'

        # quit
        if not command or command == 'q':
            break

        # index
        elif command[0] == 'i':
            showindex(msgList)

        # list
        elif command[0] == 'l':
            if len(command) == 1:
                for i in range(1, len(msgList)+1):
                    showmessage(i, msgList)
            else:
                showmessage(msgnum(command), msgList)

        # save
        elif command[0] == 's':
            if len(command) == 1:
                for i in range(1, len(msgList)+1):
```

Example 14-20. PP3E\Internet\Email\pymail.py (continued)

```
                    savemessage(i, mailfile, msgList)
            else:
                savemessage(msgnum(command), mailfile, msgList)

        # delete
        elif command[0] == 'd':
            if len(command) == 1:
                toDelete = range(1, len(msgList)+1)     # delete all later
            else:
                delnum = msgnum(command)
                if (1 <= delnum <= len(msgList)) and (delnum not in toDelete):
                    toDelete.append(delnum)
                else:
                    print 'Bad message number'

        # mail
        elif command[0] == 'm':                     # send a new mail via SMTP
            sendmessage()
            #execfile('smtpmail.py', {})            # alt: run file in own namespace

        elif command[0] == '?':
            print helptext
        else:
            print 'What? -- type "?" for commands help'
    return toDelete

if __name__ == '__main__':
    import getpass, mailconfig
    mailserver = mailconfig.popservername       # ex: 'starship.python.net'
    mailuser   = mailconfig.popusername         # ex: 'lutz'
    mailfile   = mailconfig.savemailfile        # ex:  r'c:\stuff\savemail'
    mailpswd   = getpass.getpass('Password for %s?' % mailserver)
    print '[Pymail email client]'
    msgList    = loadmessages(mailserver, mailuser, mailpswd)    # load all
    toDelete   = interact(msgList, mailfile)
    if toDelete: deletemessages(mailserver, mailuser, mailpswd, toDelete)
    print 'Bye.'
```

There isn't much new here—just a combination of user-interface logic and tools
we've already met, plus a handful of new techniques:

Loads

This client loads all email from the server into an in-memory Python list only
once, on startup; you must exit and restart to reload newly arrived email.

Saves

On demand, pymail saves the raw text of a selected message into a local file,
whose name you place in the mailconfig module.

Deletions

We finally support on-request deletion of mail from the server here: in pymail, mails are selected for deletion by number, but are still only physically removed from your server on exit, and then only if you verify the operation. By deleting only on exit, we avoid changing mail message numbers during a session—under POP, deleting a mail not at the end of the list decrements the number assigned to all mails following the one deleted. Since mail is cached in memory by pymail, future operations on the numbered messages in memory may be applied to the wrong mail if deletions were done immediately.*

Parsing and composing messages

pymail now displays just the payload of a message on listing commands, not the entire raw text, and the mail index listing only displays selected headers parsed out of each message. Python's email package is used to extract headers and content from a message, as shown in the prior section. Similarly, we use email to compose a message and ask for its string to ship as a mail.

By now, I expect that you know enough Python to read this script for a deeper look, so instead of saying more about its design here, let's jump into an interactive pymail session to see how it works.

Running the pymail Console Client

Let's start up pymail to read and delete email at our mail server and send new messages. pymail runs on any machine with Python and sockets, fetches mail from any email server with a POP interface on which you have an account, and sends mail via the SMTP server you've named in the mailconfig module.

Here it is in action running on my Windows laptop machine; its operation is identical on other machines. First, we start the script, supply a POP password (remember, SMTP servers require no password), and wait for the pymail email list index to appear; as is, this version loads the full text of all mails in the inbox on startup:

```
C:\...\PP3E\Internet\Email>python pymail.py
Password for pop.earthlink.net?
[Pymail email client]
Connecting...
+OK NGPopper vEL_6_10 at earthlink.net ready <27597.1139388190@pop-scotia.atl...
('+OK', ['1 876', '2 800', '3 818', '4 770', '5 819'], 35)
There are 5 mail messages in 4083 bytes
Retrieving: 1 2 3 4 5
```

---

* There will be more on POP message numbers when we study mailtools later in this chapter. Interestingly, the list of message numbers to be deleted need not be sorted; they remain valid for the duration of the delete connection, so deletions earlier in the list don't change numbers of messages later in the list while you are still connected to the POP server. We'll also see that some subtle issues may arise if mails in the server inbox are deleted without pymail's knowledge (e.g., by your ISP or another email client); although very rare, suffice it to say for now that deletions in this script are not guaranteed to be accurate.

```
1:      1019 bytes
        From=>lumber.jack@TheLarch.com
        Date=>Wed, 08 Feb 2006 05:23:13 -0000
        Subject=>I'm a Lumberjack, and I'm Okay
2:      883 bytes
        From=>pp3e@earthlink.net
        Date=>Wed, 08 Feb 2006 05:24:06 -0000
        Subject=>testing
3:      967 bytes
        From=>Eric.the.Half.a.Bee@yahoo.com
        Date=>Tue Feb 07 22:51:08 2006
        Subject=>A B C D E F G
4:      854 bytes
        From=>pp3e@earthlink.net
        Date=>Tue Feb 07 23:19:51 2006
        Subject=>testing smtpmail
5:      968 bytes
        From=>Eric.the.Half.a.Bee@aol.com
        Date=>Tue Feb 07 23:34:23 2006
        Subject=>a b c d e f g
[Press Enter key]
[Pymail] Action? (i, l, d, s, m, q, ?) l 5
-------------------------------------------------------------------------------

Spam; Spam and eggs; Spam, spam, and spam


-------------------------------------------------------------------------------

[Pymail] Action? (i, l, d, s, m, q, ?) l 3
-------------------------------------------------------------------------------

Fiddle de dum, Fiddle de dee,
Eric the half a bee.


-------------------------------------------------------------------------------

[Pymail] Action? (i, l, d, s, m, q, ?)
```

Once pymail downloads your email to a Python list on the local client machine, you type command letters to process it. The l command lists (prints) the contents of a given mail number; here, we used it to list the two emails we wrote with the smtpmail script in the preceding section.

pymail also lets us get command help, delete messages (deletions actually occur at the server on exit from the program), and save messages away in a local text file whose name is listed in the mailconfig module we saw earlier:

```
[Pymail] Action? (i, l, d, s, m, q, ?) ?

Available commands:
i    - index display
```

```
l n?   - list all messages (or just message n)
d n?   - mark all messages for deletion (or just message n)
s n?   - save all messages to a file (or just message n)
m      - compose and send a new mail message
q      - quit pymail
?      - display this help text

[Pymail] Action? (i, l, d, s, m, q, ?) d 1
[Pymail] Action? (i, l, d, s, m, q, ?) s 4
```

Now, let's pick the m mail compose option—pymail inputs the mail parts, builds mail text with email, and ships it off with smtplib. Because the mail is sent by SMTP, you can use arbitrary "From" addresses here; but again, you generally shouldn't do that (unless, of course, you're trying to come up with interesting examples for a book):

```
[Pymail] Action? (i, l, d, s, m, q, ?) m
From? Cardinal@hotmail.com
To?    pp3e@earthlink.net
Subj? Among our weapons are these:
Type message text, end with line="."
Nobody Expects the Spanish Inquisition!
.
 [Pymail] Action? (i, l, d, s, m, q, ?) q
To be deleted: [1]
Delete?y
Connecting...
+OK NGPopper vEL_6_10 at earthlink.net ready <4603.1139389143@pop-satin.atl...
Deleting messages from server.
Bye.
```

As mentioned, deletions really happen only on exit. When we quit pymail with the q command, it tells us which messages are queued for deletion, and verifies the request. Once verified, pymail finally contacts the mail server again and issues POP calls to delete the selected mail messages. Because deletions change message numbers in the server's inbox, postponing deletion until exit simplifies the handling of already loaded email.

Because pymail downloads mail from your server into a local Python list only once at startup, though, we need to start pymail again to refetch mail from the server if we want to see the result of the mail we sent and the deletion we made. Here, our new mail shows up as number 5, and the original mail assigned number 1 is gone:

```
C:\...\PP3E\Internet\Email>pymail.py
Password for pop.earthlink.net?
[Pymail email client]
Connecting...
+OK NGPopper vEL_6_10 at earthlink.net ready <29675.1139389310@pop-satin.atl...
('+OK', ['1 800', '2 818', '3 770', '4 819', '5 841'], 35)
There are 5 mail messages in 4048 bytes
Retrieving: 1 2 3 4 5
1:      883 bytes
        From=>pp3e@earthlink.net
        Date=>Wed, 08 Feb 2006 05:24:06 -0000
```

```
        Subject=>testing
2:      967 bytes
        From=>Eric.the.Half.a.Bee@yahoo.com
        Date=>Tue Feb 07 22:51:08 2006
        Subject=>A B C D E F G
3:      854 bytes
        From=>pp3e@earthlink.net
        Date=>Tue Feb 07 23:19:51 2006
        Subject=>testing smtpmail
4:      968 bytes
        From=>Eric.the.Half.a.Bee@aol.com
        Date=>Tue Feb 07 23:34:23 2006
        Subject=>a b c d e f g
5:      989 bytes
        From=>Cardinal@hotmail.com
        Date=>Wed, 08 Feb 2006 08:58:27 -0000
        Subject=>Among our weapons are these:
[Press Enter key]
[Pymail] Action? (i, l, d, s, m, q, ?) l 5
-------------------------------------------------------------------------------

Nobody Expects the Spanish Inquisition!


-------------------------------------------------------------------------------

[Pymail] Action? (i, l, d, s, m, q, ?) q
Bye.
```

Finally, if you are running this live, you will also find the mail save file on your machine, containing the one message we asked to be saved in the prior session; it's simply the raw text of saved emails, with separator lines. This is both human and machine-readable—in principle, another script could load saved mail from this file into a Python list by calling the string object's `split` method on the file's text with the separator line as a delimiter.

The mailtools Utility Package

The `email` package used by the `pymail` example of the prior section is a collection of powerful tools—in fact, perhaps too powerful to remember completely. At the minimum, some reusable boilerplate code for common use cases can help insulate you from some of its details. To simplify email interfacing for more complex mail clients, and to further demonstrate the use of standard library email tools, I developed the custom utility modules listed in this section—a package called `mailtools`.

`mailtools` is a Python modules package: a directory of code, with one module per tool class, and an initialization module run when the directory is first imported. This package's modules are essentially just a wrapper layer above the standard library's email package, as well as its `poplib` and `smtplib` modules. They make some assumptions about the way `email` is to be used, but they are reasonable and allow us to forget some of the underlying complexity of the standard library tools employed.

In a nutshell, the `mailtools` package provides three classes—to fetch, send, and parse email messages. These classes can be used as *superclasses* to mix in their methods to an application-specific class or to create *standalone* or *embedded* objects that export their methods. We'll see these classes deployed both ways in this text.

One design note worth mentioning up front: none of the code in this package knows anything about the user interface it will be used in (console, GUI, web, or other), or does anything about things like threads; it is just a toolkit. As we'll see, its clients are responsible for deciding how it will be deployed. By focusing on just email processing here, we simplify the code, as well as the programs that will use it.

As a simple example of this package's tools in action, its `selftest.py` module serves as a self-test script. When run, it sends a message from you, to you, which includes the *selftest.py* file as an attachment. It also fetches and displays some mail headers and contents. These interfaces, along with some user-interface magic, will lead us to full-blown email clients and web sites in later chapters.

The next few sections list `mailtools` source code. We won't cover all of this package's code in depth—study its listings for more details, and see its self-test module for a usage example. Also, flip ahead to the three clients that will use it for examples: the modified `pymail2.py` following this listing, the PyMailGUI client in Chapter 15, and the PyMailCGI server in Chapter 17. By sharing and reusing this module, all three systems inherit its utility, as well as any future enhancements.

Initialization File

The module in Example 14-21 implements the initialization logic of the `mailtools` package; as usual, its code is run automatically the first time a script imports through the package's directory. Notice how this file collects the contents of all the nested modules into the directory's namespace with `from *` statements—because `mailtools` began life as a single *.py* file, this provides backward compatibility for existing clients. Since this is the root module, global comments appear here as well.

Example 14-21. PP3E\Internet\Email\mailtools_ _init_ _.py

```
###########################################################################
# interface to mail server transfers, used by pymail, PyMailGUI and PyMailCGI;
# does loads, sends, parsing, composing, and deleting, with attachment parts,
# encoding, etc.;  the parser, fetcher, and sender classes here are designed
# to be mixed-in to subclasses which use their methods, or used as embedded or
# standalone objects;  also has convenience subclasses for silent mode, etc.;
# loads all if pop server doesn't do top;  doesn't handle threads or UI here,
# and allows askPassword to differ per subclass;  progress callback funcs get
# status;  all calls raise exceptions on error--client must handle in GUI/other;
```

Example 14-21. PP3E\Internet\Email\mailtools__init__.py (continued)

```
# this changed from file to package: nested modules imported here for bw compat;
# TBD: in saveparts, should file be opened in text mode for text/ contypes?
# TBD: in walkNamedParts, should we skip oddballs like message/delivery-status?
#############################################################################

# collect modules here, when package dir imported directly
from mailFetcher import *
from mailSender  import *
from mailParser  import *

# export nested modules here, when from mailtools import *
__all__ = 'mailFetcher', 'mailSender', 'mailParser'

# test case moved to selftest.py to allow mailconfig's
# path to be set before importing nested modules above
```

MailTool Class

Example 14-22 contains common superclasses for the other classes in the package. At present, these are used only to enable or disable trace message output (some clients, such as web-based programs, may not want text to be printed to the output stream). Subclasses mix in the silent variant to turn off output.

Example 14-22. PP3E\Internet\Email\mailtools\mailTool.py

```
#############################################################################
# common superclasses: used to turn trace massages on/off
#############################################################################

class MailTool:                        # superclass for all mail tools
    def trace(self, message):          # redef me to disable or log to file
        print message

class SilentMailTool:                  # to mixin instead of subclassing
    def trace(self, message):
        pass
```

MailSender Class

The class used to compose and send messages is coded in Example 14-23. This module provides a convenient interface that combines standard library tools we've already met in this chapter—the email package to compose messages with attachments and encodings, and the smtplib module to send the resulting email text. Attachments are passed in as a list of filenames—MIME types and any required encodings are determined automatically with the module mimetypes. Moreover, date and time strings are automated with an email.Utils call. Study this file's code and comments for more on its operation.

Example 14-23. PP3E\Internet\Email\mailtools\mailSender.py

```
###############################################################################
# send messages, add attachments (see __init__ for docs, test)
###############################################################################

import mailconfig                                    # client's mailconfig
import smtplib, os, mimetypes                        # mime: name to type
import email.Utils, email.Encoders                   # date string, base64
from mailTool import MailTool, SilentMailTool

from email.Message        import Message             # general message
from email.MIMEMultipart  import MIMEMultipart       # type-specific messages
from email.MIMEAudio      import MIMEAudio
from email.MIMEImage      import MIMEImage
from email.MIMEText       import MIMEText
from email.MIMEBase       import MIMEBase

class MailSender(MailTool):
    """
    send mail: format message, interface with SMTP server
    works on any machine with Python+Inet, doesn't use cmdline mail
    a nonauthenticating client: see MailSenderAuth if login required
    """
    def __init__(self, smtpserver=None):
        self.smtpServerName = smtpserver or mailconfig.smtpservername

    def sendMessage(self, From, To, Subj, extrahdrs, bodytext, attaches,
                                    saveMailSeparator=(('='*80)+'PY\n')):
        """
        format,send mail: blocks caller, thread me in a GUI
        bodytext is main text part, attaches is list of filenames
        extrahdrs is list of (name, value) tuples to be added
        raises uncaught exception if send fails for any reason
        saves sent message text in a local file if successful

        assumes that To, Cc, Bcc hdr values are lists of 1 or more already
        stripped addresses (possibly in full name+<addr> format); client
        must split these on delimiters, parse, or use multiline input;
        note that SMTP allows full name+<addr> format in recipients
        """
        if not attaches:
            msg = Message()
            msg.set_payload(bodytext)
        else:
            msg = MIMEMultipart()
            self.addAttachments(msg, bodytext, attaches)

        recip = To
        msg['From']    = From
        msg['To']      = ', '.join(To)              # poss many: addr list
        msg['Subject'] = Subj                       # servers reject ';' sept
        msg['Date']    = email.Utils.formatdate()   # curr datetime, rfc2822 utc
        for name, value in extrahdrs:               # Cc, Bcc, X-Mailer, etc.
```

Example 14-23. PP3E\Internet\Email\mailtools\mailSender.py (continued)

```
        if value:
            if name.lower( ) not in ['cc', 'bcc']:
                msg[name] = value
            else:
                msg[name] = ', '.join(value)      # add commas between
                recip += value                    # some servers reject ['']
        fullText = msg.as_string( )               # generate formatted msg

        # sendmail call raises except if all Tos failed,
        # or returns failed Tos dict for any that failed

        self.trace('Sending to...'+ str(recip))
        self.trace(fullText[:256])
        server = smtplib.SMTP(self.smtpServerName)        # this may fail too
        self.getPassword( )                               # if srvr requires
        self.authenticateServer(server)                   # login in subclass
        try:
            failed = server.sendmail(From, recip, fullText) # except or dict
        finally:
            server.quit( )                                # iff connect OK
        if failed:
            class SomeAddrsFailed(Exception): pass
            raise SomeAddrsFailed('Failed addrs:%s\n' % failed)
        self.saveSentMessage(fullText, saveMailSeparator)
        self.trace('Send exit')

    def addAttachments(self, mainmsg, bodytext, attaches):
        # format a multipart message with attachments
        msg = MIMEText(bodytext)                  # add main text/plain part
        mainmsg.attach(msg)
        for filename in attaches:                 # absolute or relative paths
            if not os.path.isfile(filename):      # skip dirs, etc.
                continue

            # guess content type from file extension, ignore encoding
            contype, encoding = mimetypes.guess_type(filename)
            if contype is None or encoding is not None:  # no guess, compressed?
                contype = 'application/octet-stream'     # use generic default
            self.trace('Adding ' + contype)

            # build sub-Message of appropriate kind
            maintype, subtype = contype.split('/', 1)
            if maintype == 'text':
                data = open(filename, 'r')
                msg  = MIMEText(data.read( ), _subtype=subtype)
                data.close( )
            elif maintype == 'image':
                data = open(filename, 'rb')
                msg  = MIMEImage(data.read( ), _subtype=subtype)
                data.close( )
            elif maintype == 'audio':
                data = open(filename, 'rb')
```

Example 14-23. PP3E\Internet\Email\mailtools\mailSender.py (continued)

```
                    msg  = MIMEAudio(data.read( ), _subtype=subtype)
                    data.close( )
                else:
                    data = open(filename, 'rb')
                    msg  = MIMEBase(maintype, subtype)
                    msg.set_payload(data.read( ))
                    data.close( )                          # make generic type
                    email.Encoders.encode_base64(msg)      # encode using base64

                # set filename and attach to container
                basename = os.path.basename(filename)
                msg.add_header('Content-Disposition',
                                  'attachment', filename=basename)
                mainmsg.attach(msg)

        # text outside mime structure, seen by non-MIME mail readers
        mainmsg.preamble = 'A multi-part MIME format message.\n'
        mainmsg.epilogue = ''  # make sure message ends with a newline

    def saveSentMessage(self, fullText, saveMailSeparator):
        # append sent message to local file if worked
        # client: pass separator used for your app, splits
        # caveat: user may change file at same time (unlikely)
        try:
            sentfile = open(mailconfig.sentmailfile, 'a')
            if fullText[-1] != '\n': fullText += '\n'
            sentfile.write(saveMailSeparator)
            sentfile.write(fullText)
            sentfile.close( )
        except:
            self.trace('Could not save sent message')    # not a show-stopper

    def authenticateServer(self, server):
        pass  # no login required for this server/class

    def getPassword(self):
        pass  # no login required for this server/class


###############################################################################
# specialized subclasses
###############################################################################

class MailSenderAuth(MailSender):
    """
    use for servers that require login authorization;
    client: choose MailSender or MailSenderAuth super
    class based on mailconfig.smtpuser setting (None?)
    """
    def __init__(self, smtpserver=None, smtpuser=None):
        MailSender.__init__(self, smtpserver)
        self.smtpUser = smtpuser or mailconfig.smtpuser
```

Example 14-23. PP3E\Internet\Email\mailtools\mailSender.py (continued)

```
        self.smtpPassword = None

    def authenticateServer(self, server):
        server.login(self.smtpUser, self.smtpPassword)

    def getPassword(self):
        """
        get SMTP auth password if not yet known;
        may be called by superclass auto, or client manual:
        not needed until send, but don't run in GUI thread;
        get from client-side file or subclass method
        """
        if not self.smtpPassword:
            try:
                localfile = open(mailconfig.smtppasswdfile)
                self.smtpPassword = localfile.readline()[:-1]
                self.trace('local file password' + repr(self.smtpPassword))
            except:
                self.smtpPassword = self.askSmtpPassword()

    def askSmtpPassword(self):
        assert False, 'Subclass must define method'

class MailSenderAuthConsole(MailSender):
    def askSmtpPassword(self):
        import getpass
        prompt = 'Password for %s on %s?' % (self.smtpUser, self.smtpServerName)
        return getpass.getpass(prompt)

class SilentMailSender(SilentMailTool, MailSender):
    pass    # replaces trace
```

MailFetcher Class

The class defined in Example 14-24 does the work of interfacing with a POP email server—loading, deleting, and synchronizing.

General usage

This module deals strictly in email text; parsing email after it has been fetched is delegated to a different module in the package. Moreover, this module doesn't cache already loaded information; clients must add their own mail-retention tools if desired. Clients must also provide password input methods or pass one in, if they cannot use the console input subclass here (e.g., GUIs and web-based programs).

The loading and deleting tasks use the standard library poplib module in ways we saw earlier in this chapter, but notice that there are interfaces for fetching just message header text with the TOP action in POP. This can save substantial time if clients need to fetch only basic details for an email index.

This module also supports the notion of progress indicators—for methods that perform multiple downloads or deletions, callers may pass in a function that will be called as each mail is processed. This function will receive the current and total step numbers. It's left up to the caller to render this in a GUI, console, or other user interface.

Inbox synchronization tools

Also notice that Example 14-24 devotes substantial code to detecting synchronization errors between an email list held by a client, and the current state of the inbox at the POP email server. Normally, POP assigns relative message numbers to email in the inbox, and only adds newly arrived emails to the end of the inbox. As a result, relative message numbers from an earlier fetch may usually be used to delete and fetch in the future.

However, although rare, it is not impossible for the server's inbox to change in ways that invalidate previously fetched message numbers. For instance, emails may be deleted in another client, and the server itself may move mails from the inbox to an undeliverable state on download errors (this may vary per ISP). In both cases, email may be removed from the middle of the inbox, throwing some prior relative message numbers out of sync with the server.

This situation can result in fetching the wrong message in an email client—users receive a different message than the one they thought they had selected. Worse, this can make deletions inaccurate—if a mail client uses a relative message number in a delete request, the wrong mail may be deleted if the inbox has changed since the index was fetched.

To assist clients, Example 14-24 includes tools, which match message headers on deletions to ensure accuracy and perform general inbox synchronization tests on demand. These tools can be used only by clients that retain the fetched email list as state information. We'll use these in the PyMailGUI client in Chapter 15. There, deletions use the safe interface, and loads run the synchronization test on demand; on errors, the inbox index is automatically reloaded. For now, see Example 14-24 source code and comments for more details.

Note that the synchronization tests try a variety of matching techniques, but require the complete headers text and, in the worst case, must parse headers and match many header fields. In many cases, the single previously fetched `message-id` header field would be sufficient for matching against messages in the server's inbox. However, because this field is optional and can be forged to have any value, it might not always be a reliable way to identify messages. In other words, a same-valued `message-id` may not suffice to guarantee a match, although it can be used to identify a mismatch; in Example 14-24, the `message-id` is used to rule out a match if either message has one, and they differ in value. This test is performed before falling back on slower parsing and multiple header matches.

Example 14-24. PP3E\Internet\Email\mailtools\mailFetcher.py

```
#############################################################################
# retrieve, delete, match mail from a POP server (see __init__ for docs, test)
#############################################################################

import poplib, mailconfig        # client's mailconfig: script dir or pythonpath
print 'user:', mailconfig.popusername

from mailParser import MailParser              # for headers matching
from mailTool   import MailTool, SilentMailTool  # trace control supers

# index/server msgnum out of synch tests
class DeleteSynchError(Exception): pass        # msg out of synch in del
class TopNotSupported(Exception): pass         # can't run synch test
class MessageSynchError(Exception): pass       # index list out of sync

class MailFetcher(MailTool):
    """
    fetch mail: connect, fetch headers+mails, delete mails
    works on any machine with Python+Inet; subclass me to cache
    implemented with the POP protocol; IMAP requires new class
    """
    def __init__(self, popserver=None, popuser=None, poppswd=None, hastop=True):
        self.popServer   = popserver or mailconfig.popservername
        self.popUser     = popuser   or mailconfig.popusername
        self.srvrHasTop  = hastop
        self.popPassword = poppswd  # ask later if None

    def connect(self):
        self.trace('Connecting...')
        self.getPassword()                     # file, GUI, or console
        server = poplib.POP3(self.popServer)
        server.user(self.popUser)              # connect,login POP server
        server.pass_(self.popPassword)         # pass is a reserved word
        self.trace(server.getwelcome())        # print returned greeting
        return server

    def downloadMessage(self, msgnum):
        """
        load full raw text of one mail msg, given its
        POP relative msgnum; caller must parse content
        """
        self.trace('load '+str(msgnum))
        server = self.connect()
        try:
            resp, msglines, respsz = server.retr(msgnum)
        finally:
            server.quit()
        return '\n'.join(msglines)             # concat lines for parsing

    def downloadAllHeaders(self, progress=None, loadfrom=1):
        """
        get sizes, raw header text only, for all or new msgs
```

Example 14-24. PP3E\Internet\Email\mailtools\mailFetcher.py (continued)

```
        begins loading headers from message number loadfrom
        use loadfrom to load newly arrived mails only
        use downloadMessage to get a full msg text later
        progress is a function called with (count, total);
        returns: [headers text], [mail sizes], loadedfull?
        """
        if not self.srvrHasTop:                      # not all servers support TOP
            return self.downloadAllMsgs(progress)  # naively load full msg text
        else:
            self.trace('loading headers')
            server = self.connect()                     # mbox now locked until quit
            try:
                resp, msginfos, respsz = server.list()   # 'num size' lines list
                msgCount = len(msginfos)                       # alt to srvr.stat[0]
                msginfos = msginfos[loadfrom-1:]          # drop already loadeds
                allsizes = [int(x.split()[1]) for x in msginfos]
                allhdrs  = []
                for msgnum in range(loadfrom, msgCount+1):        # poss empty
                    if progress: progress(msgnum, msgCount)      # callback?
                    resp, hdrlines, respsz = server.top(msgnum, 0)  # hdrs only
                    allhdrs.append('\n'.join(hdrlines))
            finally:
                server.quit()                            # make sure unlock mbox
            assert len(allhdrs) == len(allsizes)
            self.trace('load headers exit')
            return allhdrs, allsizes, False

    def downloadAllMessages(self, progress=None, loadfrom=1):
        """
        load full message text for all msgs from loadfrom..N,
        despite any caching that may be being done in the caller;
        much slower than downloadAllHeaders, if just need hdrs;
        """
        self.trace('loading full messages')
        server = self.connect()
        try:
            (msgCount, msgBytes) = server.stat()          # inbox on server
            allmsgs  = []
            allsizes = []
            for i in range(loadfrom, msgCount+1):          # empty if low >= high
                if progress: progress(i, msgCount)
                (resp, message, respsz) = server.retr(i)  # save text on list
                allmsgs.append('\n'.join(message))        # leave mail on server
                allsizes.append(respsz)                   # diff from len(msg)
        finally:
            server.quit()                                 # unlock the mail box
        assert len(allmsgs) == (msgCount - loadfrom) + 1  # msg nums start at 1
        #assert sum(allsizes) == msgBytes                 # not if loadfrom > 1
        return allmsgs, allsizes, True

    def deleteMessages(self, msgnums, progress=None):
        """
```

Example 14-24. PP3E\Internet\Email\mailtools\mailFetcher.py (continued)

```
        delete multiple msgs off server; assumes email inbox
        unchanged since msgnums were last determined/loaded;
        use if msg headers not available as state information;
        fast, but poss dangerous: see deleteMessagesSafely
        """
        self.trace('deleting mails')
        server = self.connect( )
        try:
            for (ix, msgnum) in enumerate(msgnums):    # don't reconnect for each
                if progress: progress(ix+1, len(msgnums))
                server.dele(msgnum)
        finally:                                       # changes msgnums: reload
            server.quit( )

    def deleteMessagesSafely(self, msgnums, synchHeaders, progress=None):
        """
        delete multiple msgs off server, but use TOP fetches to
        check for a match on each msg's header part before deleting;
        assumes the email server supports the TOP interface of POP,
        else raises TopNotSupported - client may call deleteMessages;

        use if the mail server might change the inbox since the email
        index was last fetched, thereby changing POP relative message
        numbers;  this can happen if email is deleted in a different
        client;  some ISPs may also move a mail from inbox to the
        undeliverable box in response to a failed download;

        synchHeaders must be a list of already loaded mail hdrs text,
        corresponding to selected msgnums (requires state);  raises
        exception if any out of synch with the email server;  inbox is
        locked until quit, so it should not change between TOP check
        and actual delete: synch check must occur here, not in caller;
        may be enough to call checkSynchError+deleteMessages, but check
        each msg here in case deletes and inserts in middle of inbox;
        """
        if not self.srvrHasTop:
            raise TopNotSupported('Safe delete cancelled')

        self.trace('deleting mails safely')
        errmsg  = 'Message %s out of synch with server.\n'
        errmsg += 'Delete terminated at this message.\n'
        errmsg += 'Mail client may require restart or reload.'

        server = self.connect( )                     # locks inbox till quit
        try:                                         # don't reconnect for each
            (msgCount, msgBytes) = server.stat( )    # inbox size on server
            for (ix, msgnum) in enumerate(msgnums):
                if progress: progress(ix+1, len(msgnums))
                if msgnum > msgCount:                          # msgs deleted
                    raise DeleteSynchError(errmsg % msgnum)
                resp, hdrlines, respsz = server.top(msgnum, 0)   # hdrs only
                msghdrs = '\n'.join(hdrlines)
```

Example 14-24. PP3E\Internet\Email\mailtools\mailFetcher.py (continued)

```
                if not self.headersMatch(msghdrs, synchHeaders[msgnum-1]):
                    raise DeleteSynchError(errmsg % msgnum)
                else:
                    server.dele(msgnum)                # safe to delete this msg
        finally:                                       # changes msgnums: reload
            server.quit()                              # unlock inbox on way out

    def checkSynchError(self, synchHeaders):
        """
        check to see if already loaded hdrs text in synchHeaders
        list matches what is on the server, using the TOP command in
        POP to fetch headers text; use if inbox can change due to
        deletes in other client, or automatic action by email server;
        raises except if out of synch, or error while talking to server;

        for speed, only checks last in last: this catches inbox deletes,
        but assumes server won't insert before last (true for incoming
        mails); check inbox size first: smaller if just deletes;  else
        top will differ if deletes and newly arrived messages added at
        end;  result valid only when run: inbox may change after return;
        """
        self.trace('synch check')
        errormsg  = 'Message index out of synch with mail server.\n'
        errormsg += 'Mail client may require restart or reload.'
        server = self.connect()
        try:
            lastmsgnum = len(synchHeaders)                     # 1..N
            (msgCount, msgBytes) = server.stat()              # inbox size
            if lastmsgnum > msgCount:                          # fewer now?
                raise MessageSynchError(errormsg)             # none to cmp
            if self.srvrHasTop:
                resp, hdrlines, respsz = server.top(lastmsgnum, 0)  # hdrs only
                lastmsghdrs = '\n'.join(hdrlines)
                if not self.headersMatch(lastmsghdrs, synchHeaders[-1]):
                    raise MessageSynchError(errormsg)
        finally:
            server.quit()

    def headersMatch(self, hdrtext1, hdrtext2):
        """
        may not be as simple as a string compare: some servers add
        a "Status:" header that changes over time; on one ISP, it
        begins as "Status: U" (unread), and changes to "Status: RO"
        (read, old) after fetched once - throws off synch tests if
        new when index fetched, but have been fetched once before
        delete or last-message check;  "Message-id:" line is unique
        per message in theory, but optional, and can be anything if
        forged; match more common: try first; parsing costly: try last
        """
        # try match by simple string compare
        if hdrtext1 == hdrtext2:
            self.trace('Same headers text')
```

Example 14-24. PP3E\Internet\Email\mailtools\mailFetcher.py (continued)

```
        return True

    # try match without status lines
    split1 = hdrtext1.splitlines()          # s.split('\n'), but no final ''
    split2 = hdrtext2.splitlines()
    strip1 = [line for line in split1 if not line.startswith('Status:')]
    strip2 = [line for line in split2 if not line.startswith('Status:')]
    if strip1 == strip2:
        self.trace('Same without Status')
        return True

    # try mismatch by message-id headers if either has one
    msgid1 = [line for line in split1 if line[:11].lower() == 'message-id:']
    msgid2 = [line for line in split2 if line[:11].lower() == 'message-id:']
    if (msgid1 or msgid2) and (msgid1 != msgid2):
        self.trace('Different Message-Id')
        return False

    # try full hdr parse and common headers if msgid missing or trash
    tryheaders  = ('From', 'To', 'Subject', 'Date')
    tryheaders += ('Cc', 'Return-Path', 'Received')
    msg1 = MailParser().parseHeaders(hdrtext1)
    msg2 = MailParser().parseHeaders(hdrtext2)
    for hdr in tryheaders:                            # poss multiple Received
        if msg1.get_all(hdr) != msg2.get_all(hdr):   # case insens, dflt None
            self.trace('Diff common headers')
            return False

    # all common hdrs match and don't have a diff message-id
    self.trace('Same common headers')
    return True

def getPassword(self):
    """
    get POP password if not yet known
    not required until go to server
    from client-side file or subclass method
    """
    if not self.popPassword:
        try:
            localfile = open(mailconfig.poppasswdfile)
            self.popPassword = localfile.readline()[:-1]
            self.trace('local file password' + repr(self.popPassword))
        except:
            self.popPassword = self.askPopPassword()

def askPopPassword(self):
    assert False, 'Subclass must define method'
```

Example 14-24. PP3E\Internet\Email\mailtools\mailFetcher.py (continued)

```
###########################################################################
# specialized subclasses
###########################################################################

class MailFetcherConsole(MailFetcher):
    def askPopPassword(self):
        import getpass
        prompt = 'Password for %s on %s?' % (self.popUser, self.popServer)
        return getpass.getpass(prompt)

class SilentMailFetcher(SilentMailTool, MailFetcher):
    pass    # replaces trace
```

MailParser Class

Example 14-25 implements the last major class in the mailtools package—given the
text of an email message, its tools parse the mail's content into a message object,
with headers and decoded parts. This module is largely just a wrapper around the
standard library's email package, but it adds convenience tools—finding the main
text part of a message, filename generation for message parts, saving attached parts
to files, and so on. See the code for more information. Also notice the parts walker
here: by coding its search logic in one place, we guarantee that all three clients implement the same traversal.

Example 14-25. PP3E\Internet\Email\mailtools\mailParser.py

```
###########################################################################
# parsing and attachment extract, analyse, save (see __init__ for docs, test)
###########################################################################

import os, mimetypes                             # mime: type to name
import email.Parser
from email.Message import Message
from mailTool import MailTool

class MailParser(MailTool):
    """
    methods for parsing message text, attachments

    subtle thing: Message object payloads are either a simple
    string for non-multipart messages, or a list of Message
    objects if multipart (possibly nested); we don't need to
    distinguish between the two cases here, because the Message
    walk generator always returns self first, and so works fine
    on non-multipart messages too (a single object is walked);

    for simple messages, the message body is always considered
    here to be the sole part of the mail;  for multipart messages,
    the parts list includes the main message text, as well as all
    attachments;  this allows simple messages not of type text to
```

Example 14-25. PP3E\Internet\Email\mailtools\mailParser.py (continued)

```
    be handled like attachments in a UI (e.g., saved, opened);
    Message payload may also be None for some oddball part types;
    """

    def walkNamedParts(self, message):
        """
        generator to avoid repeating part naming logic
        skips multipart headers, makes part filenames
        message is already parsed email.Message object
        doesn't skip oddball types: payload may be None
        """
        for (ix, part) in enumerate(message.walk()):        # walk includes message
            maintype = part.get_content_maintype()          # ix includes multiparts
            if maintype == 'multipart':
                continue                                    # multipart/*: container
            else:
                filename, contype = self.partName(part, ix)
                yield (filename, contype, part)

    def partName(self, part, ix):
        """
        extract filename and content type from message part;
        filename: tries Content-Disposition, then Content-Type
        name param, or generates one based on mimetype guess;
        """
        filename = part.get_filename()                      # filename in msg hdrs?
        contype  = part.get_content_type()                  # lower maintype/subtype
        if not filename:
            filename = part.get_param('name')              # try content-type name
        if not filename:
            if contype == 'text/plain':                     # hardcode plain text ext
                ext = '.txt'                                # else guesses .ksh!
            else:
                ext = mimetypes.guess_extension(contype)
                if not ext: ext = '.bin'                    # use a generic default
            filename = 'part-%03d%s' % (ix, ext)
        return (filename, contype)

    def saveParts(self, savedir, message):
        """
        store all parts of a message as files in a local directory;
        returns [('maintype/subtype', 'filename')] list for use by
        callers, but does not open any parts or attachments here;
        get_payload decodes base64, quoted-printable, uuencoded data;
        mail parser may give us a None payload for oddball types we
        probably should skip over: convert to str here to be safe;
        """
        if not os.path.exists(savedir):
            os.mkdir(savedir)
        partfiles = []
        for (filename, contype, part) in self.walkNamedParts(message):
            fullname = os.path.join(savedir, filename)
```

Example 14-25. PP3E\Internet\Email\mailtools\mailParser.py (continued)

```
            fileobj  = open(fullname, 'wb')             # use binary mode
            content  = part.get_payload(decode=1)        # decode base64,qp,uu
            fileobj.write(str(content))                  # make sure is a str
            fileobj.close()
            partfiles.append((contype, fullname))        # for caller to open
        return partfiles

    def saveOnePart(self, savedir, partname, message):
        """
        ditto, but find and save just one part by name
        """
        if not os.path.exists(savedir):
            os.mkdir(savedir)
        fullname = os.path.join(savedir, partname)
        (contype, content) = self.findOnePart(partname, message)
        open(fullname, 'wb').write(str(content))
        return (contype, fullname)

    def partsList(self, message):
        """
        return a list of filenames for all parts of an
        already parsed message, using same filename logic
        as saveParts, but do not store the part files here
        """
        validParts = self.walkNamedParts(message)
        return [filename for (filename, contype, part) in validParts]

    def findOnePart(self, partname, message):
        """
        find and return part's content, given its name
        intended to be used in conjunction with partsList
        we could also mimetypes.guess_type(partname) here
        we could also avoid this search by saving in dict
        """
        for (filename, contype, part) in self.walkNamedParts(message):
            if filename == partname:
                content = part.get_payload(decode=1)        # base64,qp,uu
                return (contype, content)

    def findMainText(self, message):
        """
        for text-oriented clients, return the first text part;
        for the payload of a simple message, or all parts of
        a multipart message, looks for text/plain, then text/html,
        then text/*, before deducing that there is no text to
        display;  this is a heuristic, but covers most simple,
        multipart/alternative, and multipart/mixed messages;
        content-type defaults to text/plain if not in simple msg;

        handles message nesting at top level by walking instead
        of list scans;  if non-multipart but type is text/html,
        returns the HTML as the text with an HTML type: caller
```

Example 14-25. PP3E\Internet\Email\mailtools\mailParser.py (continued)

```
        may open in web browser;  if nonmultipart and not text,
        no text to display: save/open in UI;  caveat: does not
        try to concatenate multiple inline text/plain parts
        """
        # try to find a plain text
        for part in message.walk( ):                        # walk visits message
            type = part.get_content_type( )                 # if nonmultipart
            if type == 'text/plain':
                return type, part.get_payload(decode=1)      # may be base64,qp,uu

        # try to find an HTML part
        for part in message.walk( ):
            type = part.get_content_type( )
            if type == 'text/html':
                return type, part.get_payload(decode=1)      # caller renders

        # try any other text type, including XML
        for part in message.walk( ):
            if part.get_content_maintype( ) == 'text':
                return part.get_content_type( ), part.get_payload(decode=1)

        # punt: could use first part, but it's not marked as text
        return 'text/plain', '[No text to display]'

    # returned when parses fail
    errorMessage = Message( )
    errorMessage.set_payload('[Unable to parse message - format error]')

    def parseHeaders(self, mailtext):
        """
        parse headers only, return root email.Message object
        stops after headers parsed, even if nothing else follows (top)
        email.Message object is a mapping for mail header fields
        payload of message object is None, not raw body text
        """
        try:
            return email.Parser.Parser( ).parsestr(mailtext, headersonly=True)
        except:
            return self.errorMessage

    def parseMessage(self, fulltext):
        """
        parse entire message, return root email.Message object
        payload of message object is a string if not is_multipart( )
        payload of message object is more Messages if multiple parts
        the call here same as calling email.message_from_string( )
        """
        try:
            return email.Parser.Parser( ).parsestr(fulltext)        # may fail!
        except:
            return self.errorMessage        # or let call handle? can check return
```

Example 14-25. PP3E\Internet\Email\mailtools\mailParser.py (continued)

```
    def parseMessageRaw(self, fulltext):
        """
        parse headers only, return root email.Message object
        stops after headers parsed, for efficiency (not yet used here)
        payload of message object is raw text of mail after headers
        """
        try:
            return email.Parser.HeaderParser().parsestr(fulltext)
        except:
            return self.errorMessage
```

Self-Test Script

The last file in the `mailtools` package, Example 14-26, lists the self-test code for the package. This code is a separate script file, in order to allow for import search path manipulation—it emulates a real client, which is assumed to have a `mailconfig.py` module in its own source directory (this module can vary per client).

Example 14-26. PP3E\Internet\Email\mailtools\selftest.py

```
###########################################################################
# self-test when this file is run as a program
###########################################################################

#
# mailconfig normally comes from the client's source directory or
# sys.path; for testing, get it from Email directory one level up
#
import sys
sys.path.append('..')
import mailconfig
print 'config:', mailconfig.__file__

# get these from __init__
from mailtools import MailFetcherConsole, MailSender, MailSenderAuthConsole

if not mailconfig.smtpuser:
    sender = MailSender()
else:
    sender = MailSenderAuthConsole()

sender.sendMessage(From     = mailconfig.myaddress,
                   To       = [mailconfig.myaddress],
                   Subj     = 'testing 123',
                   extrahdrs = [('X-Mailer', 'mailtools')],
                   bodytext = 'Here is my source code',
                   attaches = ['selftest.py'])

fetcher = MailFetcherConsole()
def status(*args): print args
```

Example 14-26. PP3E\Internet\Email\mailtools\selftest.py (continued)

```
hdrs, sizes, loadedall = fetcher.downloadAllHeaders(status)
for num, hdr in enumerate(hdrs[:5]):
    print hdr
    if raw_input('load mail?') in ['y', 'Y']:
        print fetcher.downloadMessage(num+1), '\n', '-'*70

last5 = len(hdrs)-4
msgs, sizes, loadedall = fetcher.downloadAllMessages(status, loadfrom=last5)
for msg in msgs:
    print msg[:200], '\n', '-'*70
raw_input('Press Enter to exit')
```

Updating the pymail Console Client

Finally, to give a use case for the mailtools module package of the preceding sections, Example 14-27 provides an updated version of the pymail program we met earlier, which uses mailtools to access email instead of older tools. Compare its code to the original pymail in this chapter to see how mailtools is employed here. You'll find that its mail download and send logic is substantially simpler.

Example 14-27. pymail2.py

```
#!/usr/local/bin/python
##########################################################################
# pymail2 - simple console email interface client in Python; this
# version uses the mailtools package, which in turn uses poplib,
# smtplib, and the email package for parsing and composing emails;
# displays first text part of mails, not entire full text;
# fetches just mail headers initially, using the TOP command;
# fetches full text of just email selected to be displayed;
# caches already fetched mails; caveat: no way to refresh index;
# uses standalone mailtools objects - they can also be superclasses;
##########################################################################

mailcache = {}

def fetchmessage(i):
    try:
        fulltext = mailcache[i]
    except KeyError:
        fulltext = fetcher.downloadMessage(i)
        mailcache[i] = fulltext
    return fulltext

def sendmessage():
    from pymail import inputmessage
    From, To, Subj, text = inputmessage()
    sender.sendMessage(From, To, Subj, [], text, attaches=None)

def deletemessages(toDelete, verify=True):
    print 'To be deleted:', toDelete
```

Example 14-27. pymail2.py (continued)

```
    if verify and raw_input('Delete?')[:1] not in ['y', 'Y']:
        print 'Delete cancelled.'
    else:
        print 'Deleting messages from server.'
        fetcher.deleteMessages(toDelete)

def showindex(msgList, msgSizes, chunk=5):
    count = 0
    for (msg, size) in zip(msgList, msgSizes):        # email.Message, int
        count += 1
        print '%d:\t%d bytes' % (count, size)
        for hdr in ('From', 'Date', 'Subject'):
            print '\t%s=>%s' % (hdr, msg.get(hdr, '(unknown)'))
        if count % chunk == 0:
            raw_input('[Press Enter key]')           # pause after each chunk

def showmessage(i, msgList):
    if 1 <= i <= len(msgList):
        fulltext = fetchmessage(i)
        message  = parser.parseMessage(fulltext)
        ctype, maintext = parser.findMainText(message)
        print '-'*80
        print maintext                    # main text part, not entire mail
        print '-'*80                      # and not any attachments after
    else:
        print 'Bad message number'

def savemessage(i, mailfile, msgList):
    if 1 <= i <= len(msgList):
        fulltext = fetchmessage(i)
        open(mailfile, 'a').write('\n' + fulltext + '-'*80 + '\n')
    else:
        print 'Bad message number'

def msgnum(command):
    try:
        return int(command.split( )[1])
    except:
        return -1   # assume this is bad

helptext = """
Available commands:
i    - index display
l n? - list all messages (or just message n)
d n? - mark all messages for deletion (or just message n)
s n? - save all messages to a file (or just message n)
m    - compose and send a new mail message
q    - quit pymail
?    - display this help text
"""

def interact(msgList, msgSizes, mailfile):
```

Example 14-27. pymail2.py (continued)

```
        showindex(msgList, msgSizes)
        toDelete = []
        while 1:
            try:
                command = raw_input('[Pymail] Action? (i, l, d, s, m, q, ?) ')
            except EOFError:
                command = 'q'
            if not command: command = '*'

            if command == 'q':                    # quit
                break

            elif command[0] == 'i':               # index
                showindex(msgList, msgSizes)

            elif command[0] == 'l':               # list
                if len(command) == 1:
                    for i in range(1, len(msgList)+1):
                        showmessage(i, msgList)
                else:
                    showmessage(msgnum(command), msgList)

            elif command[0] == 's':               # save
                if len(command) == 1:
                    for i in range(1, len(msgList)+1):
                        savemessage(i, mailfile, msgList)
                else:
                    savemessage(msgnum(command), mailfile, msgList)

            elif command[0] == 'd':               # mark for deletion later
                if len(command) == 1:
                    toDelete = range(1, len(msgList)+1)
                else:
                    delnum = msgnum(command)
                    if (1 <= delnum <= len(msgList)) and (delnum not in toDelete):
                        toDelete.append(delnum)
                    else:
                        print 'Bad message number'

            elif command[0] == 'm':               # send a new mail via SMTP
                try:
                    sendmessage()
                except:
                    print 'Error - mail not sent'

            elif command[0] == '?':
                print helptext
            else:
                print 'What? -- type "?" for commands help'
        return toDelete

def main():
```

Example 14-27. pymail2.py (continued)

```
    global parser, sender, fetcher
    import mailtools, mailconfig
    mailserver = mailconfig.popservername
    mailuser   = mailconfig.popusername
    mailfile   = mailconfig.savemailfile

    parser     = mailtools.MailParser()
    sender     = mailtools.MailSender()
    fetcher    = mailtools.MailFetcherConsole(mailserver, mailuser)

    def progress(i, max): print i, 'of', max
    hdrsList, msgSizes, ignore = fetcher.downloadAllHeaders(progress)
    msgList = [parser.parseHeaders(hdrtext) for hdrtext in hdrsList]

    print '[Pymail email client]'
    toDelete   = interact(msgList, msgSizes, mailfile)
    if toDelete: deletemessages(toDelete)

if __name__ == '__main__': main()
```

This program is used interactively, the same as the original. In fact, the output is nearly identical, so we won't go into further details. Here's a quick look at this script in action; run this on your own machine to see it firsthand:

```
C:\...\PP3E\Internet\Email>pymail2.py
user: pp3e
loading headers
Connecting...
Password for pp3e on pop.earthlink.net?
+OK NGPopper vEL_6_10 at earthlink.net ready <5870.1139382442@pop-savannah.at...
1 of 5
2 of 5
3 of 5
4 of 5
5 of 5
load headers exit
[Pymail email client]
1:      876 bytes
        From=>lumber.jack@TheLarch.com
        Date=>Wed, 08 Feb 2006 05:23:13 -0000
        Subject=>I'm a Lumberjack, and I'm Okay
2:      800 bytes
        From=>pp3e@earthlink.net
        Date=>Wed, 08 Feb 2006 05:24:06 -0000
        Subject=>testing
3:      818 bytes
        From=>Eric.the.Half.a.Bee@yahoo.com
        Date=>Tue Feb 07 22:51:08 2006
        Subject=>A B C D E F G
4:      770 bytes
        From=>pp3e@earthlink.net
        Date=>Tue Feb 07 23:19:51 2006
```

```
              Subject=>testing smtpmail
    5:        819 bytes
              From=>Eric.the.Half.a.Bee@aol.com
              Date=>Tue Feb 07 23:34:23 2006
              Subject=>a b c d e f g
[Press Enter key]
[Pymail] Action? (i, l, d, s, m, q, ?) l 5
load 5
Connecting...
+OK NGPopper vEL_6_10 at earthlink.net ready <9564.1139382467@pop-savannah.at...
--------------------------------------------------------------------------------

Spam; Spam and eggs; Spam, spam, and spam


--------------------------------------------------------------------------------

[Pymail] Action? (i, l, d, s, m, q, ?) s 1
load 1
Connecting...
+OK NGPopper vEL_6_10 at earthlink.net ready <5266.1139382521@pop-savannah.a...
[Pymail] Action? (i, l, d, s, m, q, ?) m
From? pp3e@earthlink.net
To?   pp3e@earthlink.net
Subj? test pymail2 send
Type message text, end with line=".""
Run away! Run away!
.
Sending to...['pp3e@earthlink.net']
From: pp3e@earthlink.net
To: pp3e@earthlink.net
Subject: test pymail2 send
Date: Wed, 08 Feb 2006 07:09:40 -0000

Run away! Run away!

Send exit
[Pymail] Action? (i, l, d, s, m, q, ?) q
```

As you can see, this version's code eliminates some complexities, such as the manual formatting of composed mail message text. It also does a better job of displaying a mail's text—instead of blindly listing the full mail text (attachments and all), it uses mailtools to fetch the first text part of the message. The messages we're using are too simple to show the difference, but for a mail with attachments, this new version will be more focused about what it displays.

Moreover, because the interface to mail is encapsulated in the mailtools package's modules, if it ever must change, it will only need to be changed in that module, regardless of how many mail clients use its tools. And because this code is shared, if we know it works for one client, we can be sure it will work in another; there is no need to debug new code.

On the other hand, pymail2 doesn't really leverage much of the power of either mailtools or the underlying email package it uses. Things like attachments and inbox synchronization are not handled at all, for example. To see the full scope of the email package, we need to explore a larger email system, such as PyMailGUI or PyMail-CGI. The first of these is the topic of the next chapter, and the second appears in Chapter 17. First, though, let's quickly survey a handful of additional client-side protocol tools.

NNTP: Accessing Newsgroups

So far in this chapter, we have focused on Python's FTP and email processing tools and have met a handful of client-side scripting modules along the way: ftplib, poplib, smtplib, email, mimetools, urllib, and so on. This set is representative of Python's client-side library tools for transferring and processing information over the Internet, but it's not at all complete.

A more or less comprehensive list of Python's Internet-related modules appears at the start of the previous chapter. Among other things, Python also includes client-side support libraries for Internet news, Telnet, HTTP, XML-RPC, and other standard protocols. Most of these are analogous to modules we've already met—they provide an object-based interface that automates the underlying sockets and message structures.

For instance, Python's nntplib module supports the client-side interface to NNTP—the Network News Transfer Protocol—which is used for reading and posting articles to Usenet newsgroups on the Internet. Like other protocols, NNTP runs on top of sockets and merely defines a standard message protocol; like other modules, nntplib hides most of the protocol details and presents an object-based interface to Python scripts.

We won't get into protocol details here, but in brief, NNTP servers store a range of articles on the server machine, usually in a flat-file database. If you have the domain or IP name of a server machine that runs an NNTP server program listening on the NNTP port, you can write scripts that fetch or post articles from any machine that has Python and an Internet connection. For instance, the script in Example 14-28 by default fetches and displays the last 10 articles from Python's Internet newsgroup, *comp.lang.python*, from the *news.rmi.net* NNTP server at my ISP.

Example 14-28. PP3E\Internet\Other\readnews.py

```
#############################################################################
# fetch and print usenet newsgroup posting from comp.lang.python via the
# nntplib module which really runs on top of sockets; nntplib also supports
# posting new messages, etc.; note: posts not deleted after they are read;
#############################################################################
```

Example 14-28. PP3E\Internet\Other\readnews.py (continued)

```
listonly = 0
showhdrs = ['From', 'Subject', 'Date', 'Newsgroups', 'Lines']
try:
    import sys
    servername, groupname, showcount = sys.argv[1:]
    showcount  = int(showcount)
except:
    servername = 'news.rmi.net'
    groupname  = 'comp.lang.python'          # cmd line args or defaults
    showcount  = 10                          # show last showcount posts

# connect to nntp server
print 'Connecting to', servername, 'for', groupname
from nntplib import NNTP
connection = NNTP(servername)
(reply, count, first, last, name) = connection.group(groupname)
print '%s has %s articles: %s-%s' % (name, count, first, last)

# get request headers only
fetchfrom = str(int(last) - (showcount-1))
(reply, subjects) = connection.xhdr('subject', (fetchfrom + '-' + last))

# show headers, get message hdr+body
for (id, subj) in subjects:                  # [-showcount:] if fetch all hdrs
    print 'Article %s [%s]' % (id, subj)
    if not listonly and raw_input('=> Display?') in ['y', 'Y']:
        reply, num, tid, list = connection.head(id)
        for line in list:
            for prefix in showhdrs:
                if line[:len(prefix)] == prefix:
                    print line[:80]; break
        if raw_input('=> Show body?') in ['y', 'Y']:
            reply, num, tid, list = connection.body(id)
            for line in list:
                print line[:80]
    print
print connection.quit()
```

As for FTP and email tools, the script creates an NNTP object and calls its methods to fetch newsgroup information and articles' header and body text. The xhdr method, for example, loads selected headers from a range of messages.

For NNTP servers that require authentication, you may also have to pass a username, a password, and possibly a reader-mode flag to the NNTP call, and you may need to be connected directly to the server's network in order to access it at all (e.g., not connected to an intermediate broadband provider). See the Python Library manual for more on other NNTP parameters and object methods.

When run, this program connects to the server and displays each article's subject line, pausing to ask whether it should fetch and show the article's header information lines (headers listed in the variable showhdrs only) and body text:

```
C:\...\PP3E\Internet\Other>python readnews.py
Connecting to news.rmi.net for comp.lang.python
comp.lang.python has 3376 articles: 30054-33447
Article 33438 [Embedding? file_input and eval_input]
=> Display?

Article 33439 [Embedding? file_input and eval_input]
=> Display?y
From: James Spears <jimsp@ichips.intel.com>
Newsgroups: comp.lang.python
Subject: Embedding? file_input and eval_input
Date: Fri, 11 Aug 2000 10:55:39 -0700
Lines: 34
=> Show body?

Article 33440 [Embedding? file_input and eval_input]
=> Display?

Article 33441 [Embedding? file_input and eval_input]
=> Display?

Article 33442 [Embedding? file_input and eval_input]
=> Display?

Article 33443 [Re: PYTHONPATH]
=> Display?y
Subject: Re: PYTHONPATH
Lines: 13
From: sp00fd <sp00fdNOspSPAM@yahoo.com.invalid>
Newsgroups: comp.lang.python
Date: Fri, 11 Aug 2000 11:06:23 -0700
=> Show body?y
Is this not what you were looking for?

Add to cgi script:
import sys
sys.path.insert(0, "/path/to/dir")
import yourmodule


------------------------------------------------------------
Got questions?  Get answers over the phone at Keen.com.
Up to 100 minutes free!
http://www.keen.com

Article 33444 [Loading new code...]
=> Display?
```

```
Article 33445 [Re: PYTHONPATH]
=> Display?

Article 33446 [Re: Compile snags on AIX & IRIX]
=> Display?

Article 33447 [RE: string.replace() can't replace newline characters???]
=> Display?

205 GoodBye
```

We can also pass this script an explicit server name, newsgroup, and display count on the command line to apply it in different ways. Here is this Python script checking the last few messages in Perl and Linux newsgroups:

```
C:\...\PP3E\Internet\Other>python readnews.py news.rmi.net comp.lang.perl.misc 5
Connecting to news.rmi.net for comp.lang.perl.misc
comp.lang.perl.misc has 5839 articles: 75543-81512
Article 81508 [Re: Simple Argument Passing Question]
=> Display?

Article 81509 [Re: How to Access a hash value?]
=> Display?

Article 81510 [Re: London =?iso-8859-1?Q?=A330-35K?= Perl Programmers Required]
=> Display?

Article 81511 [Re: ODBC question]
=> Display?

Article 81512 [Re: ODBC question]
=> Display?

205 GoodBye


C:\...\PP3E\Internet\Other>python readnews.py news.rmi.net comp.os.linux 4
Connecting to news.rmi.net for comp.os.linux
comp.os.linux has 526 articles: 9015-9606
Article 9603 [Re: Simple question about CD-Writing for Linux]
=> Display?

Article 9604 [Re: How to start the ftp?]
=> Display?

Article 9605 [Re: large file support]
=> Display?

Article 9606 [Re: large file support]
=> Display?y
From: andy@physast.uga.edu (Andreas Schweitzer)
Newsgroups: comp.os.linux.questions,comp.os.linux.admin,comp.os.linux
Subject: Re: large file support
Date: 11 Aug 2000 18:32:12 GMT
```

```
Lines: 19
=> Show body?n

205 GoodBye
```

With a little more work, we could turn this script into a full-blown news interface. For instance, new articles could be posted from within a Python script with code of this form (assuming the local file already contains proper NNTP header lines):

```
# to post, say this (but only if you really want to post!)
connection = NNTP(servername)
localfile = open('filename')     # file has proper headers
connection.post(localfile)       # send text to newsgroup
connection.quit()
```

We might also add a Tkinter-based GUI frontend to this script to make it more usable, but we'll leave such an extension on the suggested exercise heap (see also the PyMailGUI interface's suggested extensions at the end of the next chapter—email and news messages have a similar structure).

HTTP: Accessing Web Sites

Python's standard library (the modules that are installed with the interpreter) also includes client-side support for HTTP—the Hypertext Transfer Protocol—a message structure and port standard used to transfer information on the World Wide Web. In short, this is the protocol that your web browser (e.g., Internet Explorer, Netscape) uses to fetch web pages and run applications on remote servers as you surf the Web. Essentially, it's just bytes sent over port 80.

To really understand HTTP-style transfers, you need to know some of the server-side scripting topics covered in Chapter 16 (e.g., script invocations and Internet address schemes), so this section may be less useful to readers with no such background. Luckily, though, the basic HTTP interfaces in Python are simple enough for a cursory understanding, even at this point in the book, so let's take a brief look here.

Python's standard httplib module automates much of the protocol defined by HTTP and allows scripts to fetch web pages much like web browsers. For instance, the script in Example 14-29 can be used to grab any file from any server machine running an HTTP web server program. As usual, the file (and descriptive header lines) is ultimately transferred as formatted messages over a standard socket port, but most of the complexity is hidden by the httplib module.

Example 14-29. PP3E\Internet\Other\http-getfile.py

```
#####################################################################
# fetch a file from an HTTP (web) server over sockets via httplib;
# the filename param may have a full directory path, and may name a CGI
# script with query parameters on the end to invoke a remote program;
# fetched file data or remote program output could be saved to a local
# file to mimic FTP, or parsed with str.find or the htmllib module;
#####################################################################
```

Example 14-29. PP3E\Internet\Other\http-getfile.py (continued)

```
import sys, httplib
showlines = 6
try:
    servername, filename = sys.argv[1:]           # cmdline args?
except:
    servername, filename = 'starship.python.net', '/index.html'

print servername, filename
server = httplib.HTTP(servername)                 # connect to http site/server
server.putrequest('GET', filename)                # send request and headers
server.putheader('Accept', 'text/html')           # POST requests work here too
server.endheaders()                               # as do CGI script filenames

errcode, errmsh, replyheader = server.getreply()  # read reply info headers
if errcode != 200:                                # 200 means success
    print 'Error sending request', errcode
else:
    file = server.getfile()                       # file obj for data received
    data = file.readlines()
    file.close()                                  # show lines with eoln at end
    for line in data[:showlines]: print line,     # to save, write data to file
```

Desired server names and filenames can be passed on the command line to override hardcoded defaults in the script. You need to know something of the HTTP protocol to make the most sense of this code, but it's fairly straightforward to decipher. When run on the client, this script makes an HTTP object to connect to the server, sends it a GET request along with acceptable reply types, and then reads the server's reply. Much like raw email message text, the HTTP server's reply usually begins with a set of descriptive header lines, followed by the contents of the requested file. The HTTP object's getfile method gives us a file object from which we can read the downloaded data.

Let's fetch a few files with this script. Like all Python client-side scripts, this one works on any machine with Python and an Internet connection (here it runs on a Windows client). Assuming that all goes well, the first few lines of the downloaded file are printed; in a more realistic application, the text we fetch would probably be saved to a local file, parsed with Python's htmllib module, and so on. Without arguments, the script simply fetches the HTML index page at *http://starship.python.org*, a Python community resources site:

```
C:\...\PP3E\Internet\Other>python http-getfile.py
starship.python.net /index.html
<!DOCTYPE html PUBLIC "-//W3C//DTD HTML 4.01 Transitional//EN">
<HTML>
<HEAD>
  <META NAME="GENERATOR" CONTENT="HTMLgen">
  <TITLE>Starship Python -- Python Programming Community</TITLE>
  <LINK REL="SHORTCUT ICON" HREF="http://starship.python.net/favicon.ico">
```

But we can also list a server and file to be fetched on the command line, if we want to be more specific. In the following code, we use the script to fetch files from two different web sites by listing their names on the command lines (I've added line breaks to make these lines fit in this book). Notice that the filename argument can include an arbitrary remote directory path to the desired file, as in the last fetch here:

```
C:\...\PP3E\Internet\Other>python http-getfile.py www.python.org /index.html
www.python.org /index.html
<!DOCTYPE html PUBLIC "-//W3C//DTD HTML 4.01 Transitional//EN"
                      "http://www.w3.org/TR/html4/loose.dtd" >
<?xml-stylesheet href="./css/ht2html.css" type="text/css"?>
<html>
<!-- THIS PAGE IS AUTOMATICALLY GENERATED.  DO NOT EDIT. -->
<!-- Mon Jan 16 13:02:12 2006 -->

C:\...\PP3E\Internet\Other>python http-getfile.py www.python.org index
www.python.org index
Error sending request 404

C:\...\PP3E\Internet\Other>python http-getfile.py www.rmi.net /~lutz
www.rmi.net /~lutz
Error sending request 301

C:\...\PP3E\Internet\Other>python http-getfile.py www.rmi.net
                                                  /~lutz/index.html
www.rmi.net /~lutz/index.html
<HTML>

<HEAD>
<TITLE>Mark Lutz's Home Page</TITLE>
</HEAD>
<BODY BGCOLOR="#f1f1ff">
```

Also notice the second and third attempts in this code: if the request fails, the script receives and displays an HTTP error code from the server (we forgot the leading slash on the second, and the "index.html" on the third—required for this server and interface). With the raw HTTP interfaces, we need to be precise about what we want.

Technically, the string we call `filename` in the script can refer to either a simple static web page file or a server-side program that generates HTML as its output. Those server-side programs are usually called CGI scripts—the topic of Chapters 16 and 17. For now, keep in mind that when `filename` refers to a script, this program can be used to invoke another program that resides on a remote server machine. In that case, we can also specify parameters (called a query string) to be passed to the remote program after a ?.

Here, for instance, we pass a `language=Python` parameter to a CGI script we will meet in Chapter 16 (we're first spawning a locally running HTTP web server coded in Python, using a script we first met in Chapter 2, but will revisit in Chapter 16):

```
In a different window
C:\...\PP3E\Internet\Web>webserver.py
webdir ".", port 80

C:\...\PP3E\Internet\Other>http-getfile.py localhost
                              /cgi-bin/languages.py?language=Python
localhost /cgi-bin/languages.py?language=Python
<TITLE>Languages</TITLE>
<H1>Syntax</H1><HR>
<H3>Python</H3><P><PRE>
 print 'Hello World'
</PRE></P><BR>
<HR>
```

This book has much more to say about HTML, CGI scripts, and the meaning of the
HTTP GET request used in Example 14-29 (along with POST, one of two way to format information sent to an HTTP server) later, so we'll skip additional details here.

Suffice it to say, though, that we could use the HTTP interfaces to write our own web
browsers, and build scripts that use web sites as though they were subroutines. By
sending parameters to remote programs and parsing their results, web sites can take on
the role of simple in-process functions (albeit, much more slowly and indirectly).

Module urllib Revisited

The httplib module we just met provides low-level control for HTTP clients. When
dealing with items available on the Web, though, it's often easier to code downloads
with Python's standard urllib module, introduced in the FTP section earlier in this
chapter. Since this module is another way to talk HTTP, let's expand on its interfaces here.

Recall that given a URL, urllib either downloads the requested object over the Net
to a local file, or gives us a file-like object from which we can read the requested
object's contents. As a result, the script in Example 14-30 does the same work as the
httplib script we just wrote, but requires noticeably less code.

Example 14-30. PP3E\Internet\Other\http-getfile-urllib1.py

```
###################################################################
# fetch a file from an HTTP (web) server over sockets via urllib;
# urllib supports HTTP, FTP, files, etc. via URL address strings;
# for HTTP, the URL can name a file or trigger a remote CGI script;
# see also the urllib example in the FTP section, and the CGI
# script invocation in a later chapter; files can be fetched over
# the net with Python in many ways that vary in complexity and
# server requirements: sockets, FTP, HTTP, urllib, CGI outputs;
# caveat: should run urllib.quote on filename--see later chapters;
###################################################################
```

Example 14-30. PP3E\Internet\Other\http-getfile-urllib1.py (continued)

```
import sys, urllib
showlines = 6
try:
    servername, filename = sys.argv[1:]                # cmdline args?
except:
    servername, filename = 'starship.python.net', '/index.html'

remoteaddr = 'http://%s%s' % (servername, filename)  # can name a CGI script too
print remoteaddr
remotefile = urllib.urlopen(remoteaddr)               # returns input file object
remotedata = remotefile.readlines( )                  # read data directly here
remotefile.close( )
for line in remotedata[:showlines]: print line,
```

Almost all HTTP transfer details are hidden behind the urllib interface here. This version works in almost the same way as the httplib version we wrote first, but it builds and submits an Internet URL address to get its work done (the constructed URL is printed as the script's first output line). As we saw in the FTP section of this chapter, the urllib urlopen function returns a file-like object from which we can read the remote data. But because the constructed URLs begin with "http://" here, the urllib module automatically employs the lower-level HTTP interfaces to download the requested file, not FTP:

```
C:\...\PP3E\Internet\Other>python http-getfile-urllib1.py
http://starship.python.net/index.html
<!DOCTYPE html PUBLIC "-//W3C//DTD HTML 4.01 Transitional//EN">
<HTML>
<HEAD>
  <META NAME="GENERATOR" CONTENT="HTMLgen">
  <TITLE>Starship Python -- Python Programming Community</TITLE>
  <LINK REL="SHORTCUT ICON" HREF="http://starship.python.net/favicon.ico">

C:\...\PP3E\Internet\Other>python http-getfile-urllib1.py www.python.org /index
http://www.python.org/index
<!DOCTYPE html PUBLIC "-//W3C//DTD HTML 4.01 Transitional//EN"
                      "http://www.w3.org/TR/html4/loose.dtd" >
<?xml-stylesheet href="./css/ht2html.css" type="text/css"?>
<html>
<!-- THIS PAGE IS AUTOMATICALLY GENERATED.  DO NOT EDIT. -->
<!-- Mon Jan 16 13:02:12 2006 -->

C:\...\PP3E\Internet\Other>python http-getfile-urllib1.py www.rmi.net /~lutz
http://www.rmi.net/~lutz
<HTML>

<HEAD>
<TITLE>Mark Lutz's Home Page</TITLE>
</HEAD>
<BODY BGCOLOR="#f1f1ff">
```

```
C:\...\PP3E\Internet\Other>python http-getfile-urllib1.py
                                localhost /cgi-bin/languages.py?language=Java
http://localhost/cgi-bin/languages.py?language=Java
<TITLE>Languages</TITLE>
<H1>Syntax</H1><HR>
<H3>Java</H3><P><PRE>
 System.out.println("Hello World");
</PRE></P><BR>
<HR>
```

As before, the filename argument can name a simple file or a program invocation
with optional parameters at the end, as in the last run here. If you read this output
carefully, you'll notice that this script still works if you leave the "index.html" off the
end of a filename (in the third command line); unlike the raw HTTP version of the
preceding section, the URL-based interface is smart enough to do the right thing.

Other urllib Interfaces

One last mutation: the following urllib downloader script uses the slightly higher-
level urlretrieve interface in that module to automatically save the downloaded file
or script output to a local file on the client machine. This interface is handy if we
really mean to store the fetched data (e.g., to mimic the FTP protocol). If we plan on
processing the downloaded data immediately, though, this form may be less convenient than the version we just met: we need to open and read the saved file. Moreover, we need to provide an extra protocol for specifying or extracting a local
filename, as in Example 14-31.

Example 14-31. PP3E\Internet\Other\http-getfile-urllib2.py

```
#####################################################################
# fetch a file from an HTTP (web) server over sockets via urlllib;
# this version uses an interface that saves the fetched data to a
# local file; the local file name is either passed in as a cmdline
# arg or stripped from the URL with urlparse: the filename argument
# may have a directory path at the front and query params at end,
# so os.path.split is not enough (only splits off directory path);
# caveat: should run urllib.quote on filename--see later chapters;
#####################################################################

import sys, os, urllib, urlparse
showlines = 6
try:
    servername, filename = sys.argv[1:3]                 # first 2 cmdline args?
except:
    servername, filename = 'starship.python.net', '/index.html'

remoteaddr = 'http://%s%s' % (servername, filename)      # any address on the Net
if len(sys.argv) == 4:                                    # get result filename
    localname = sys.argv[3]
else:
    (scheme, server, path, parms, query, frag) = urlparse.urlparse(remoteaddr)
```

Example 14-31. PP3E\Internet\Other\http-getfile-urllib2.py (continued)

```
    localname = os.path.split(path)[1]

print remoteaddr, localname
urllib.urlretrieve(remoteaddr, localname)              # can be file or script
remotedata = open(localname).readlines()               # saved to local file
for line in remotedata[:showlines]: print line,
```

Let's run this last variant from a command line. Its basic operation is the same as the last two versions: like the prior one, it builds a URL, and like both of the last two, we can list an explicit target server and file path on the command line:

```
C:\...\PP3E\Internet\Other>python http-getfile-urllib2.py
http://starship.python.net/index.html index.html
<!DOCTYPE html PUBLIC "-//W3C//DTD HTML 4.01 Transitional//EN">
<HTML>
<HEAD>
  <META NAME="GENERATOR" CONTENT="HTMLgen">
  <TITLE>Starship Python -- Python Programming Community</TITLE>
  <LINK REL="SHORTCUT ICON" HREF="http://starship.python.net/favicon.ico">

C:\...\PP3E\Internet\Other>python http-getfile-urllib2.py
                                         www.python.org /index.html
http://www.python.org/index.html index.html
<!DOCTYPE html PUBLIC "-//W3C//DTD HTML 4.01 Transitional//EN"
                     "http://www.w3.org/TR/html4/loose.dtd" >
<?xml-stylesheet href="./css/ht2html.css" type="text/css"?>
<html>
<!-- THIS PAGE IS AUTOMATICALLY GENERATED.  DO NOT EDIT. -->
<!-- Mon Jan 16 13:02:12 2006 -->
```

Because this version uses an urllib interface that automatically saves the downloaded data in a local file, it's similar to FTP downloads in spirit. But this script must also somehow come up with a local filename for storing the data. You can either let the script strip and use the base filename from the constructed URL, or explicitly pass a local filename as a last command-line argument. In the prior run, for instance, the downloaded web page is stored in the local file *index.html* in the current working directory—the base filename stripped from the URL (the script prints the URL and local filename as its first output line). In the next run, the local filename is passed explicitly as *python-org-index.html*:

```
C:\...\PP3E\Internet\Other>python http-getfile-urllib2.py www.python.org
                                     /index.html python-org-index.html
http://www.python.org/index.html python-org-index.html
<!DOCTYPE html PUBLIC "-//W3C//DTD HTML 4.01 Transitional//EN"
                     "http://www.w3.org/TR/html4/loose.dtd" >
<?xml-stylesheet href="./css/ht2html.css" type="text/css"?>
<html>
<!-- THIS PAGE IS AUTOMATICALLY GENERATED.  DO NOT EDIT. -->
<!-- Mon Jan 16 13:02:12 2006 -->
```

```
C:\...\PP3E\Internet\Other>python http-getfile-urllib2.py www.rmi.net
                                    /~lutz/home/index.html
http://www.rmi.net/~lutz/index.html index.html
<HTML>

<HEAD>
<TITLE>Mark Lutz's Home Page</TITLE>
</HEAD>
<BODY BGCOLOR="#f1f1ff">

C:\...\PP3E\Internet\Other>python http-getfile-urllib2.py www.rmi.net
                                    /~lutz/home/about-pp.html
http://www.rmi.net/~lutz/about-pp.html about-pp.html
<HTML>

<HEAD>
<TITLE>About "Programming Python"</TITLE>
</HEAD>
```

What follows is a listing showing this third version being used to trigger a remote program. As before, if you don't give the local filename explicitly, the script strips the base filename out of the filename argument. That's not always easy or appropriate for program invocations—the filename can contain both a remote directory path at the front, and query parameters at the end for a remote program invocation.

Given a script invocation URL and no explicit output filename, the script extracts the base filename in the middle by using first the standard urlparse module to pull out the file path, and then os.path.split to strip off the directory path. However, the resulting filename is a remote script's name, and it may or may not be an appropriate place to store the data locally. In the first run that follows, for example, the script's output goes in a local file called *languages.py*, the script name in the middle of the URL; in the second, we instead name the output *CxxSyntax.html* explicitly to suppress filename extraction:

```
C:\...\PP3E\Internet\Other>python http-getfile-urllib2.py localhost
                              /cgi-bin/languages.py?language=Scheme
http://localhost/cgi-bin/languages.py?language=Scheme languages.py
<TITLE>Languages</TITLE>
<H1>Syntax</H1><HR>
<H3>Scheme</H3><P><PRE>
 (display "Hello World") (newline)
</PRE></P><BR>
<HR>

C:\...\PP3E\Internet\Other>python http-getfile-urllib2.py localhost
                            /cgi-bin/languages.py?language=C++ CxxSyntax.html
http://localhost/cgi-bin/languages.py?language=C++ CxxSyntax.html
<TITLE>Languages</TITLE>
<H1>Syntax</H1><HR>
<H3>C  </H3><P><PRE>
Sorry--I don't know that language
</PRE></P><BR>
<HR>
```

The remote script returns a not-found message when passed "C++" in the last command here. It turns out that "+" is a special character in URL strings (meaning a space), and to be robust, both of the `urllib` scripts we've just written should really run the filename string through something called `urllib.quote`, a tool that escapes special characters for transmission. We will talk about this in depth in Chapter 16, so consider this a preview for now. But to make this invocation work, we need to use special sequences in the constructed URL. Here's how to do it by hand:

```
C:\...\PP3E\Internet\Other>python http-getfile-urllib2.py  localhost
              /cgi-bin/languages.py?language=C%2b%2b CxxSyntax.html
http://localhost/cgi-bin/languages.py?language=C%2b%2b CxxSyntax.html
<TITLE>Languages</TITLE>
<H1>Syntax</H1><HR>
<H3>C++</H3><P><PRE>
 cout &lt;&lt; "Hello World" &lt;&lt; endl;
</PRE></P><BR>
<HR>
```

The odd `%2b` strings in this command line are not entirely magical: the escaping required for URLs can be seen by running standard Python tools manually (this is what these scripts should do automatically to handle all possible cases well):

```
C:\...\PP3E\Internet\Other>python
>>> import urllib
>>> urllib.quote('C++')
'C%2b%2b'
```

Again, don't work too hard at understanding these last few commands; we will revisit URLs and URL escapes in Chapter 16, while exploring server-side scripting in Python. I will also explain there why the C++ result came back with other oddities like `&lt;&lt;`—HTML escapes for <<, generated by the tool `cgi.escape` in the script on the server that produces the reply:

```
>>> import cgi
>>> cgi.escape('<<')
'&lt;&lt;'
```

Also in Chapter 16, we'll meet `urllib` support for proxies, and the support for client-side *cookies* in the newer `urllib2` standard library module. We'll discuss the related HTTPS concept in Chapter 17—HTTP transmissions over secure sockets, supported by `urllib` and `urllib2` if SSL support is compiled into your Python.

Other Client-Side Scripting Options

In this chapter, we focused on client-side interfaces to standard protocols that run over sockets, but client-side programming can take other forms, too. For instance, in Chapter 18, we will meet client-side options such as the *Jython* system, a compiler that supports Python-coded Java applets—general-purpose programs downloaded from a server and run locally on the client when accessed or referenced by a URL.

We'll also introduce the notion of Python code embedded in the HTML that defines a web page and is run on clients, and we will peek at Python tools for processing XML—structured text that may be used as the language of client/server dialogs in protocols such as XML-RPC, supported by Python's `xmlrpclib` standard library module.

In deference to time and space, though, we won't go into further details on these and other client-side tools here. If you are interested in using Python to script clients, you should take a few minutes to become familiar with the list of Internet tools documented in the Python library reference manual. All work on similar principles, but have slightly distinct interfaces.

In Chapter 16, we'll hop the fence to the other side of the Internet world and explore scripts that run on server machines. Such programs give rise to the grander notion of applications that live entirely on the Web and are launched by web browsers. As we take this leap in structure, keep in mind that the tools we met in this and the preceding chapter are often sufficient to implement all the distributed processing that many applications require, and they can work in harmony with scripts that run on a server. To completely understand the Web world-view, though, we need to explore the server realm, too.

Before we get there, though, the next chapter puts concepts we've learned here to work by presenting a complete client-side program—a full-blown mail client GUI, which ties together many of the tools we've learned and coded. Among other things, this example will help us understand the trade-offs between the client-solutions we've met here, and the server-side solutions we'll study later in this part of the book.

The PyMailGUI Client

"Use the Source, Luke"

The preceding chapter introduced Python's client-side Internet tool set—the standard library modules available for email, FTP, network news, and more, from within a Python script. This chapter picks up where the last one left off and presents a complete client-side example—PyMailGUI, a Python program that sends, receives, composes, and parses Internet email messages.

Although the end result is a working program that you can actually use for your email, this chapter also has a few additional agendas worth noting before we get started:

Client-side scripting

For one thing, PyMailGUI implements a full-featured GUI that runs on your machine, and communicates with your mail servers when necessary. As such, it is a network client program that further illustrates some of the preceding chapter's topics, and it will help us contrast server-side solutions introduced in the next chapter.

Code reuse

Additionally, PyMailGUI ties together a number of the utility modules we've been writing in the book so far, and demonstrates the power of code reuse in the process—it uses a thread module to allow mail transfers to overlap in time, a set of mail modules to process message content and route it across networks, a window protocol module to handle icons, and so on. Moreover, it inherits the power of tools in the Python standard library, such as the email package; message construction and parsing, for example, is trivial here.

Programming in the large

And finally, because PyMailGUI is a relatively large-scale program (at least as Python programs go), it shows by example some of the code structuring techniques that come in handy once we leave the realm of the small. Object-oriented programming (OOP) and modular design work well here to divide the system in smaller, self-contained units.

Ultimately, though, PyMailGUI serves to illustrate just how far the combination of GUIs, networking, and Python can take us. Like all Python programs, this system is *scriptable*—once you've learned its general structure, you can easily change it to work as you like, by modifying its source code. And like all Python programs, this one is *portable* across platforms—you can run it on any system with Python and a network connection, without having to change its code. Such advantages become automatic when your software is coded in an open source, portable, and readable language like Python.

Source Code Modules

This chapter is something of a self-study exercise. Because PyMailGUI is fairly large and mostly applies concepts we've already learned, we won't go into much detail about its actual code. Instead, it is listed for you to read on your own. I encourage you to study the source and comments and to run this program on your own to get a feel for its operation. Also, be sure to refer back to the modules we introduced earlier in the book and are reusing here, to gain a full understanding of the system. For reference, here are the major examples that will see new action in this chapter:

Example 14-21: PP3E.Internet.Email.mailtools (package)
　　Server sends and receives, parsing, construction (Chapter 14)

Example 11-17: PP3E.Gui.Tools.threadtools.py
　　Thread queue management for GUI callbacks (Chapter 11)

Example 11-13: PP3E.Gui.Tools.windows.py
　　Border configuration for top-level window (Chapter 11)

Example 12-4: PP3E.Gui.TextEditor.textEditor.py
　　Text widget used in mail view windows, and in some pop ups (Chapter 12)

Some of these modules in turn use additional examples we coded earlier, but that are not imported by PyMailGUI itself (textEditor, for instance, uses guimaker to create its windows and toolbar). We'll also be coding new modules here. The following new modules are intended to be useful in other programs:

utilities.py
　　Various pop-up windows, written for general use

messagecache.py
　　A cache that keeps track of mail already loaded

wraplines.py
　　A utility for wrapping long lines of messages

mailconfig.py
　　User configuration parameters—server names, fonts, and so on (augmented here)

Finally, the following are new modules coded in this chapter and are specific to the PyMailGUI program:

SharedNames.py
> Program-wide globals used by multiple files

ViewWindows.py
> The implementation of View, Write, Reply, and Forward message view windows

ListWindows.py
> The implementation of mail-server and local-file message list windows

PyMailGuiHelp2.py
> User-oriented help text, opened by the main window's bar button

PyMailGui2.py
> The main, top-level file of the program, run to launch the main window

All told, PythonMailGUI comprises the nine new modules in the preceding two lists and is composed of some 2,200 lines of source code (including comments, whitespace, and 530 lines of help text). This doesn't include the four other book examples in the previous list that are reused in PyMailGUI, which themselves constitute 1,600 additional lines.* This is the largest example we'll see in this book, but you shouldn't be deterred by its size. Because it uses modular and OOP techniques, the code is simpler than you may think:

- Python's modules allow us to divide the system into files that have a cohesive purpose, with minimal coupling between them—code is easier to locate and understand if your modules have a logical, self-contained structure.
- Python's OOP support allows us to factor code for reuse, and avoid redundancy—as you'll see, code is customized, not repeated, and the classes we will code reflect the actual components of the GUI to make them easy to follow.

For instance, the implementation of mail list windows is easy to read and change, because it has been factored into a common shared superclass, which is customized by subclasses for mail-server and save-file lists; since these are mostly just variations on a theme, most of the code appears in just one place. Similarly, the code that implements the message view window is a superclass shared by write, reply, and forward composition windows; subclasses simply tailor it for writing rather than viewing.

Although we'll deploy these techniques in the context of a mail processing program here, such techniques will apply to any nontrivial program you'll write in Python.

---

* And remember: you would have to multiply these line counts by a factor of four or five to get the equivalent in a language like C or C++. If you've done much programming, you probably recognize that the fact that we can implement a fairly full-featured mail processing program in roughly 2,000 lines of code speaks volumes about the power of the Python language and its libraries. For comparison, the original version of this program from the second edition of this book was just 725 lines in 3 new modules, but also was very limited—it did not support PyMailGUI2's attachments, thread overlap, local mail files, and so on.

To help get you started, the `PyMailGuiHelp2.py` module listed last in this chapter includes a help text string that describes how this program is used, as well as its major features. Experimenting with the system, while referring to its code, is probably the best and quickest way to uncover its secrets.

Why PyMailGUI?

PyMailGUI is a Python program that implements a client-side email processing user interface with the standard Tkinter GUI toolkit. It is presented both as an instance of Python Internet scripting and as a realistically scaled example that ties together other tools we've already seen, such as threads and Tkinter GUIs.

Like the `pymail` console-based program we wrote in Chapter 14, PyMailGUI runs entirely on your local computer. Your email is fetched from and sent to remote mail servers over sockets, but the program and its user interface run locally. As a result, PyMailGUI is called an email client: like `pymail`, it employs Python's client-side tools to talk to mail servers from the local machine. Unlike `pymail`, though, PyMailGUI is a full-featured user interface: email operations are performed with point-and-click operations and advanced mail processing such as attachments and save files is supported.

Like many examples presented in this text, PyMailGUI is a practical, useful program. In fact, I run it on all kinds of machines to check my email while traveling around the world teaching Python classes. Although PyMailGUI won't put Microsoft Outlook out of business anytime soon, it has two key pragmatic features that have nothing to do with email itself: portability and scriptability, which are attractive features in their own right and they merit a few additional words here.

It's portable

PyMailGUI runs on any machine with sockets and a Python with Tkinter installed. Because email is transferred with the Python libraries, any Internet connection that supports Post Office Protocol (POP) and Simple Mail Transfer Protocol (SMTP) access will do. Moreover, because the user interface is coded with Tkinter, PyMailGUI should work, unchanged, on Windows, the X Window System (Unix, Linux), and the Macintosh (classic and OS X).

Microsoft Outlook may be a more feature-rich package, but it has to be run on Windows, and more specifically, on a single Windows machine. Because it generally deletes email from a server as it is downloaded and stores it on the client, you cannot run Outlook on multiple machines without spreading your email across all those machines. By contrast, PyMailGUI saves and deletes email only on request, and so it is a bit friendlier to people who check their email in an ad hoc fashion on arbitrary computers.

It's scriptable

PyMailGUI can become anything you want it to be because it is fully program-mable. In fact, this is the real killer feature of PyMailGUI and of open source software like Python in general—because you have full access to PyMailGUI's source code, you are in complete control of where it evolves from here. You have nowhere near as much control over commercial, closed products like Outlook; you generally get whatever a large company decided you need, along with what-ever bugs that company might have introduced.

As a Python script, PyMailGUI is a much more flexible tool. For instance, we can change its layout, disable features, and add completely new functionality quickly by changing its Python source code. Don't like the mail-list display? Change a few lines of code to customize it. Want to save and delete your mail automatically as it is loaded? Add some more code and buttons. Tired of seeing junk mail? Add a few lines of text processing code to the load function to filter spam. These are just a few examples. The point is that because PyMailGUI is written in a high-level, easy-to-maintain scripting language, such customizations are relatively simple, and might even be fun.

At the end of the day, because of such features, this is a realistic Python program that I actually *use*—both as a primary email tool and as a fallback option when my ISP's webmail system goes down (which, as I mentioned in the prior chapter, has a way of happening at the worst possible times).* Python scripting is an enabling skill to have.

It's also worth mentioning that PyMailGUI achieves its portability and scriptability, and implements a full-featured email interface along the way, in roughly 2,200 lines of program code. It may not have all the bells and whistles of some commercial prod-ucts, but the fact that it gets as close as it does in so few lines of code is a testament to the power of both the Python language and its libraries.

Running PyMailGUI

Of course, to script PyMailGUI on your own, you'll need to be able to run it. PyMailGUI requires only a computer with some sort of Internet connectivity (a PC with a broadband or dial-up account will do) and an installed Python with the Tkinter extension enabled. The Windows port of Python has this capability, so Win-dows PC users should be able to run this program immediately by clicking its icon.

Two notes on running the system: first, you'll want to change the file *mailconfig.py* in the program's source directory to reflect your account's parameters, if you wish to send or receive mail from a live server; more on this as we interact with the system.

---

* In fact, my ISP's webmail send system went down the very day I had to submit this edition of the book to my publisher! No worries—I fired up PyMailGUI and used it to send the book as attachment files through a different server. In a sense, this book submitted itself.

Second, you can still experiment with the system without a live Internet connection—for a quick look at message view windows, use the main window's Open buttons to open saved-mail files stored in the program's *SavedMail* directory. In fact, the PyDemos launcher script at the top of the book's examples directory forces PyMailGUI to open saved-mail files by passing filenames on the command line.

Presentation Strategy

PyMailGUI is easily the largest program in this book, but it doesn't introduce many library interfaces that we haven't already seen in this book. For instance:

- The PyMailGUI interface is built with Python's Tkinter, using the familiar list-boxes, buttons, and text widgets we met earlier.
- Python's email package is applied to pull-out headers, text, and attachments of messages, and to compose the same.
- Python's POP and SMTP library modules are used to fetch, send, and delete mail over sockets.
- Python threads, if installed in your Python interpreter, are put to work to avoid blocking during potentially overlapping, long-running mail operations.

We're also going to reuse the TextEditor object we wrote in Chapter 12 to view and compose messages, the mailtools package's tools we wrote in Chapter 14 to load and delete mail from the server, and the mailconfig module strategy introduced in Chapter 14 to support end-user settings. PyMailGUI is largely an exercise in combining existing tools.

On the other hand, because this program is so long, we won't exhaustively document all of its code. Instead, we'll begin by describing how PyMailGUI works from an end user's perspective—a brief demo of its windows in action. After that, we'll list the system's new source code modules without many additional comments, for further study.

Like most of the longer case studies in this book, this section assumes that you already know enough Python to make sense of the code on your own. If you've been reading this book linearly, you should also know enough about Tkinter, threads, and mail interfaces to understand the library tools applied here. If you get stuck, you may wish to brush up on the presentation of these topics earlier in the book.

New in This Edition

The 2.1 version of PyMailGUI presented in this third edition of the book is a complete rewrite of the 1.0 version of the prior edition. The main script in the second edition's version was only some 500 lines long, and was really something of a toy or prototype, written mostly to serve as a book example. In this edition, PyMailGUI is a much more realistic and full-featured program that can be used for day-to-day email processing. It has grown to 2,200 source lines (3,800 including related modules that are reused). Among its new weapons are these:

- MIME multipart mails with attachments may be both viewed and composed.
- Mail transfers are no longer blocking, and may overlap in time.
- Mail may be saved and processed offline from a local file.
- Message parts may now be opened automatically within the GUI.
- Multiple messages may be selected for processing in list windows.
- Initial downloads fetch mail headers only; full mails are fetched on request.
- View window headers and list window columns are configurable.
- Deletions are performed immediately, not delayed until program exit.
- Most server transfers report their progress in the GUI.
- Long lines are intelligently wrapped in viewed and quoted text.
- Fonts and colors in list and view windows may be configured by the user.
- Authenticating SMTP mail-send servers that require login are supported.
- Sent messages are saved in a local file, which may be opened in the GUI.
- View windows intelligently pick a main text part to be displayed.
- Already fetched mail headers and full mails are cached for speed.
- Date strings and addresses in composed mails are formatted properly.
- View windows now have quick-access buttons for attachments/parts (2.1).
- Inbox out-of-sync errors are detected on deletes, and on index and mail loads (2.1).
- Save-mail file loads and deletes are threaded, to avoid pauses for large files (2.1).

The last three items on this list were added in version 2.1; the rest were part of the 2.0 rewrite. Some of these changes were made simple by growth in standard library tools (e.g., support for attachments is straightforward with the new email package), but most represent changes in PyMailGUI itself. There have also been a few genuine fixes: addresses are parsed more accurately, and date and time formats in sent mails are now standards conforming, because these tasks use new tools in the email package.

Although there is still room for improvement (see the list at the end of this chapter), the program provides a full-featured interface, represents the most substantial example in this book, and serves to demonstrate a realistic application of the Python language. As its users often attest, Python may be fun to work with, but it's also useful for writing practical and nontrivial software.

A PyMailGUI Demo

PyMailGUI is a multiwindow interface. It consists of the following:

- A main mail-server list window opened initially, for online mail processing
- One or more mail save-file list windows for offline mail processing
- One or more mail-view windows for viewing and editing messages
- Text editor windows for displaying the system's source code
- Nonblocking busy state pop-up dialogs
- Assorted pop-up dialogs for opened message parts, help, and more

Operationally, PyMailGUI runs as a set of parallel threads, which may overlap in time: one for each active server transfer, and one for each active offline save file load or deletion. PyMailGUI supports mail save files, automatic saves of sent messages, configurable fonts and colors, viewing and adding attachments, main message text extraction, and much more.

To make this case study easier to understand, let's begin by seeing what PyMailGUI actually does—its user interaction and email processing functionality—before jumping into the Python code that implements that behavior. As you read this part, feel free to jump ahead to the code listings that appear after the screenshots, but be sure to read this section too; this is where some subtleties of PyMailGUI's design are explained. After this section, you are invited to study the system's Python source code listings on your own for a better and more complete explanation than can be crafted in English.

Getting Started

PyMailGUI is a Python/Tkinter program, run by executing its top-level script file, *PyMailGui.py*. Like other Python programs, PyMailGUI can be started from the system command line by clicking on its filename icon in a file explorer interface, or by pressing its button in the PyDemos or PyGadgets launcher bar. However it is started, the first window PyMailGUI presents is shown in Figure 15-1. Notice the "PY" window icon: this is the handiwork of window protocol tools we wrote earlier in this book.

This is the PyMailGUI main window—every operation starts here. It consists of:

- A help button (the bar at the top)
- A clickable email list area for fetched emails (the middle section)
- A button bar at the bottom for processing messages selected in the list area

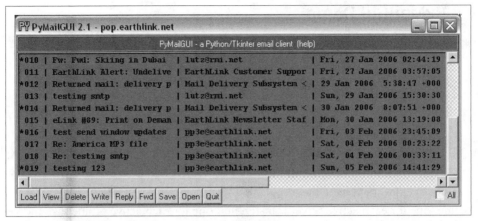

Figure 15-1. PyMailGUI main server list window

In normal operation, users load their email, select an email from the list area by clicking on it, and press a button at the bottom to process it. No mail messages are shown initially; we need to first load them with the Load button—a simple password input dialog is displayed, a busy dialog appears that counts down message headers being loaded to give a status indication, and the index is filled with messages ready to be selected.

PyMailGUI's list windows, such as the one in Figure 15-1, display mail header details in fixed-width columns, up to a maximum size. Mails with attachments are prefixed with a "*" in mail index list windows, and fonts and colors in PyMailGUI windows may be customized by the user in the `mailconfig` configuration file. You can't tell in this black-and-white book, but by default, mail index lists are Indian red, view windows are a shade of purple, pop-up PyEdit windows are light cyan, and help is steel blue; you can change most of these as you like (see Example 9-11 for help with color definition strings).

List windows allow multiple messages to be selected at once—the action selected at the bottom of the window is applied to all selected mails. For instance, to view many mails, select them all and press View; each will be fetched and displayed in its own view window. Use Ctrl-Click and Shift-Click to select more than one (the standard Windows multiple selection operations apply—try it).

Before we go any further, though, let's press the help bar at the top of the list window in Figure 15-1 to see what sort of help is available; Figure 15-2 shows the help window popup that appears.

The main part of this window is simply a block of text in a scrolled-text widget, along with two buttons at the bottom. The entire help text is coded as a single triple-quoted string in the Python program. We could get fancier and spawn a web browser

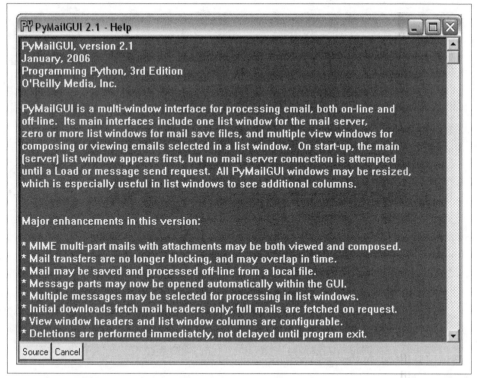

Figure 15-2. PyMailGUI help popup

to view HTML-formatted help, but simple text does the job here.* The Cancel button makes this nonmodal (i.e., nonblocking) window go away; more interestingly, the Source button pops up PyEdit text editor viewer windows for all the source files of PyMailGUI's implementation; Figure 15-3 captures one of these (there are many—this is intended as a demonstration, not as a development environment). Not every program shows you its source code, but PyMailGUI follows Python's open source motif.

When a message is selected in the mail list window, PyMailGUI downloads its full text (if it has not yet been downloaded in this session), and an email viewer window appears, as captured in Figure 15-4. View windows are built in response to actions in list windows; this is described next.

---

* The standard library's webbrowser module would help for HTML-based help. Actually, the help display started life even less fancy: it originally displayed help text in a standard information box pop up, generated by the Tkinter showinfo call used earlier in the book. This worked fine on Windows (at least with a small amount of help text), but it failed on Linux because of a default line-length limit in information pop-up boxes; lines were broken so badly as to be illegible.

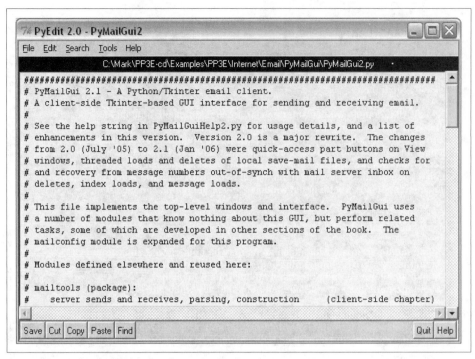

Figure 15-3. PyMailGUI source code viewer window

- The top portion consists of action buttons ("Parts" to list all message parts, "Split" to save and open parts using a selected directory, and "Cancel" to remove this nonmodal window) along with a section for displaying email header lines ("From:", "To:", and so on).

- In the middle, a row of quick-access buttons for opening message parts, including attachments, appears. When clicked, PyMailGUI opens known and generally safe parts according to their type (media types may open in a web browser, text parts in PyEdit, Windows document types per the Windows Registry, and so on).

- The bulk of this window is just another reuse of the TextEditor class object we wrote in Chapter 12 for the PyEdit program—PyMailGUI simply attaches an instance of TextEditor to every view and compose window in order to get a full-featured text editor component for free. In fact, much on this window is implemented by TextEditor, not by PyMailGUI.

For instance, if we pick the Tools menu of the text portion of this window and select its Info entry, we get the standard PyEdit TextEditor object's file text statistics box—the same popup we'd get in the standalone PyEdit text editor and in the PyView image view programs we wrote in Chapter 12 (see Figure 15-5).

In fact, this is the third reuse of TextEditor in this book: PyEdit, PyView, and now PyMailGUI all present the same text-editing interface to users, simply because they all use the same TextEditor object and code. PyMailGUI both attaches instances of this class for mail viewing and editing, and pops up instances for source-code viewing. For mail views, PyMailGUI customizes text fonts and colors per its own configuration module.

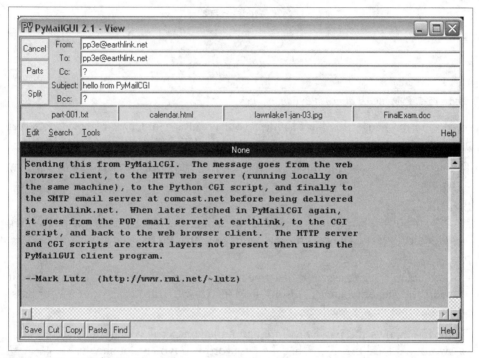

Figure 15-4. PyMailGUI view window

To display email, PyMailGUI inserts its text into an attached TextEditor object; to compose email, PyMailGUI presents a TextEditor and later fetches all its text to ship over the Net. Besides the obvious simplification here, this code reuse makes it easy to pick up improvements and fixes—any changes in the TextEditor object are automatically inherited by PyMailGUI, PyView, and PyEdit. In the current version, for instance, PyMailGUI supports edit undo and redo, just because PyEdit now does, too.

Loading Mail

Now, let's go back to the PyMailGUI main server list window, and click the Load button to retrieve incoming email over the POP protocol. PyMailGUI's load function gets account parameters from the mailconfig module listed later in this chapter,

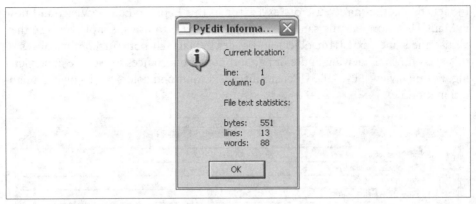

Figure 15-5. PyMailGUI attached PyEdit info box

so be sure to change this file to reflect your email account parameters (i.e., server names and usernames) if you wish to use PyMailGUI to read your own email.

The account password parameter merits a few extra words. In PyMailGUI, it may come from one of two places:

Local file
> If you put the name of a local file containing the password in the `mailconfig` module, PyMailGUI loads the password from that file as needed.

Popup dialog
> If you don't put a password filename in `mailconfig` (or if PyMailGUI can't load it from the file for whatever reason), PyMailGUI will instead ask you for your password anytime it is needed.

Figure 15-6 shows the password input prompt you get if you haven't stored your password in a local file. Note that the password you type is not shown—a `show='*'` option for the `Entry` field used in this popup tells Tkinter to echo typed characters as stars (this option is similar in spirit to both the `getpass` console input module we met earlier in the prior chapter, and an HTML `type=password` option we'll meet in a later chapter). Once entered, the password lives only in memory on your machine; PyMailGUI itself doesn't store it anywhere in a permanent way.

Also notice that the local file password option requires you to store your password unencrypted in a file on the local client computer. This is convenient (you don't need to retype a password every time you check email), but it is not generally a good idea on a machine you share with others; leave this setting blank in `mailconfig` if you prefer to always enter your password in a popup.

Once PyMailGUI fetches your mail parameters and somehow obtains your password, it will next attempt to pull down the header text of all your incoming email from your inbox on your POP email server. On subsequent loads, only newly arrived mails are loaded, if any.

Figure 15-6. PyMailGUI password input dialog

To save time, PyMailGUI fetches message header text only to populate the list window. The full text of messages is fetched later only when a message is selected for viewing or processing, and then only if the full text has not yet been fetched during this session. PyMailGUI reuses the load-mail tools in the `mailtools` module of Chapter 14 to fetch message header text, which in turn uses Python's standard `poplib` module to retrieve your email.

Threading Model

Ultimately, mail fetches run over sockets on relatively slow networks. While the download is in progress, the rest of the GUI remains active—you may compose and send other mails at the same time, for instance. To show its progress, the nonblocking dialog of Figure 15-7 is displayed when the mail index is being fetched.

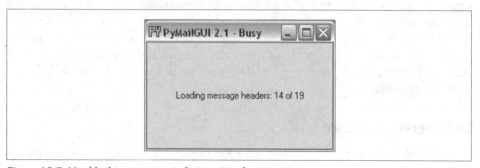

Figure 15-7. Nonblocking progress indicator: Load

In general, all server transfers display such dialogs. Figure 15-8 shows the busy dialog displayed while a full text download of five selected and uncached mails is in progress, in response to a View action. After this download finishes, all five pop up in view windows.

Such server transfers, and other long-running operations, are run in threads to avoid blocking the GUI. They do not disable other actions from running in parallel, as long as those actions would not conflict with a currently running thread. Multiple mail fetches and sends can overlap in time, for instance, and can run in parallel with the GUI itself—the GUI responds to moves, redraws, and resizes during the transfers.

On systems without threads, PyMailGUI instead goes into a blocked state during such long-running operations (it stubs out the thread-spawn operation to perform a simple function call). Because the GUI is essentially dead without threads, covering

Figure 15-8. Nonblocking progress indicator: View

and uncovering the GUI during a mail load on such platforms will erase or otherwise distort its contents. Threads are enabled by default on most platforms that Python run (including Windows), so you probably won't see such oddness on your machine.

One implementation note: as we learned earlier in this book, only the thread that creates windows should generally update them. As a result, PyMailGUI takes care to not do anything related to the user interface within threads that load, send, or delete email. Instead, the main GUI thread continues responding to user interface events and updates, and uses a timer-based event to watch a queue for exit callbacks to be added by threads, using thread tools implemented earlier in the book. Upon receipt, the GUI thread pulls the callback off the queue and dispatches it to modify the GUI (e.g., to display a fetched message, update the mail index list, or close an email composition window).

Load Server Interface

Because the load operation is really a socket operation, PyMailGUI automatically connects to your email server using whatever connectivity exists on the machine on which it is run. For instance, if you connect to the Net over a modem and you're not already connected, Windows automatically pops up the standard connection dialog. On a broadband connection, the interface to your email server is normally automatic.

After PyMailGUI finishes loading your email, it populates the main window's scrolled listbox with all of the messages on your email server and automatically scrolls to the most recently received message. Figure 15-9 shows what the main window looks like after resizing; the text area in the middle grows and shrinks with the window.

Technically, the Load button fetches all your mail's header text the first time it is pressed, but it fetches only newly arrived email headers on later presses. PyMailGUI keeps track of the last email loaded, and requests only higher email numbers on later loads. Already loaded mail is kept in memory, in a Python list, to avoid the cost of downloading it again. PyMailGUI does not delete email from your server when it is loaded; if you really want to not see an email on a later load, you must explicitly delete it.

Entries in the main list show just enough to give the user an idea of what the message contains—each entry gives the concatenation of portions of the message's "Subject:", "From:", "Date:", and other header lines, separated by | characters and prefixed with the message's POP number (e.g., there are 19 emails in this list). Columns are aligned by determining the maximum size needed for any entry, up to a fixed maximum, and the set of headers displayed can be configured in the mailconfig module. Use the horizontal scroll or expand the window to see additional header details.

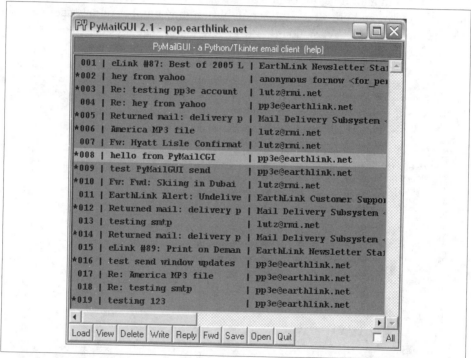

Figure 15-9. PyMailGUI main window resized

As we've seen, a lot of magic happens when downloading email—the client (the machine on which PyMailGUI runs) must connect to the server (your email account machine) over a socket and transfer bytes over arbitrary Internet links. If things go wrong, PyMailGUI pops up standard error dialog boxes to let you know what happened. For example, if you typed an incorrect username or password for your account (in the mailconfig module or in the password pop up), you'll see the message in Figure 15-10. The details displayed here are just the Python exception type and exception data.

Figure 15-10. PyMailGUI invalid password error box

Offline Processing with Save and Open

To save mails in a local file for offline processing, select the desired messages in any mail list window and press the Save action button (any number of messages may be selected for saving). A standard file-selection dialog appears, like that in Figure 15-11, and the mails are saved to the end of the chosen text file.

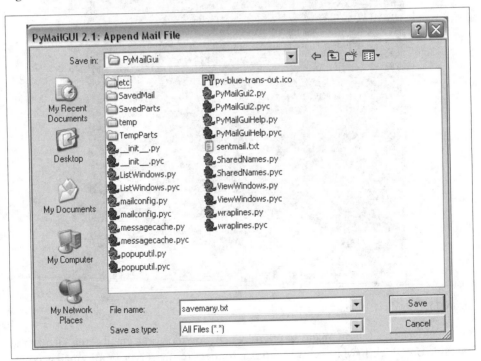

Figure 15-11. Save mail selection dialog

To view saved emails later, select the Open action at the bottom of any list window and pick your save file in the selection dialog. A new mail index list window appears for the save file and it is filled with your saved messages eventually—there may be a slight delay for large save files, because of the work involved. PyMailGUI runs file loads and deletions in threads to avoid blocking the rest of the GUI; these threads can overlap with operations on other open save-mail files, server transfer threads, and the GUI at large.

While a mail save file is being loaded in a parallel thread, its window title is set to "Loading..." as a status indication; the rest of the GUI remains active during the load (you can fetch and delete server messages, view mails in other files, write new messages, and so on). The window title changes to the loaded file's name after the load is finished. Once filled, a message index appears in the save file's window, like the one captured in Figure 15-12 (this window also has three mails selected for processing).

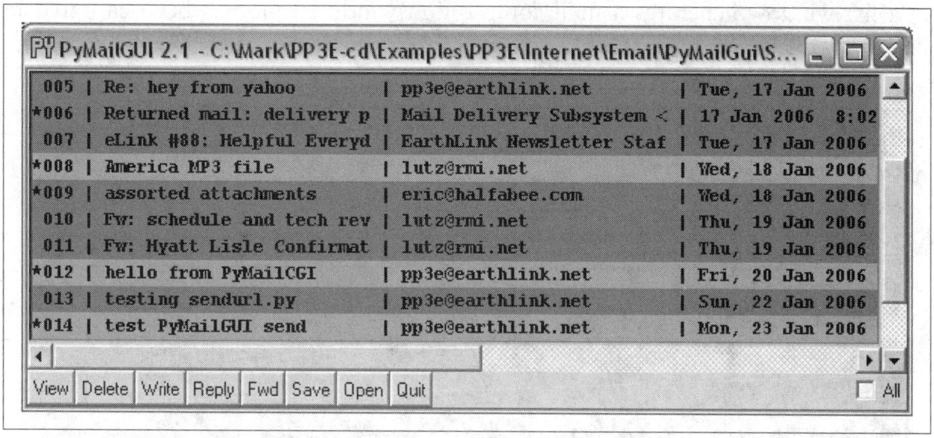

Figure 15-12. List window for mail save file, multiple selections

In general, there may be one server mail list window and any number of save-mail file list windows open at any time. Save-mail file list windows like that in Figure 15-12 can be opened at any time, even before fetching any mail from the server. They are identical to the server's inbox list window, but there is no help bar and no Load action button, and all other action buttons are mapped to the save file, not to the server.

For example, View opens the selected message in a normal mail view window identical to that in Figure 15-4, but the mail originates from the local file. Similarly, Delete removes the message from the save file, instead of from the server's inbox. Deletions from save-mail files are also run in a thread, to avoid blocking the rest of the GUI— the window title changes to "Deleting..." during the delete as a status indicator. Status indicators for loads and deletions in the server inbox window use popups instead, because the wait is longer and there is progress to display (see Figure 15-7).

Technically, saves always append raw message text to the chosen file; the file is opened in 'a' mode, which creates the file if needed, and writes at its end. The Save and Open operations are also smart enough to remember the last directory you selected; the file dialogs begin navigation there the next time you press Save or Open.

You may also save mails from a saved file's window—use Save and Delete to move mails from file to file. In addition, saving to a file whose window is open for viewing automatically updates that file's list window in the GUI. This is also true for the automatically written sent-mail save file, described in the next section.

Sending Email and Attachments

Once we've loaded email from the server or opened a local save file, we can process our messages with the action buttons at the bottom of list windows. We can also send new emails at any time, even before a load or open. Pressing the Write button in a list window generates a mail composition window; one has been captured in Figure 15-13.

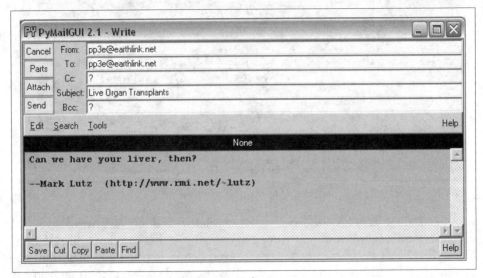

Figure 15-13. PyMailGUI write-mail compose window

This window is much like the message view window we saw in Figure 15-4, except there are no quick-access part buttons in the middle (this window is a new mail). It has fields for entering header line details, and an attached TextEditor object for writing the body of the new email.

For write operations, PyMailGUI automatically fills the "From:" line and inserts a signature text line ("--Mark..."), from your mailconfig module settings. You can change these to any text you like in the GUI, but the defaults are filled in automatically from your mailconfig. When the mail is sent, an email.Utils call handles date and time formatting in the mailtools module in Chapter 14.

There is also a new set of action buttons in the upper left here: Cancel closes the window (if verified), and Send delivers the mail—when you press the Send button, the text you typed into the body of this window is mailed to the addresses you typed into the "To:", "Cc:", and "Bcc:" lines, using Python's `smtplib` module. PyMailGUI adds the header fields you type as mail header lines in the sent message. To send to more than one address, separate them with a ";" character in header fields. In this mail, I fill in the "To:" header with my own email address in order to send the message to myself for illustration purposes.

Also in compose windows, the Attach button issues a file selection dialog for attaching a file to your message, as in Figure 15-14. The Parts button pops up a dialog displaying files already attached, like that in Figure 15-15. When your message is sent, the text in the edit portion of the window is sent as the main message text, and any attached part files are sent as attachments properly encoded according to their type.

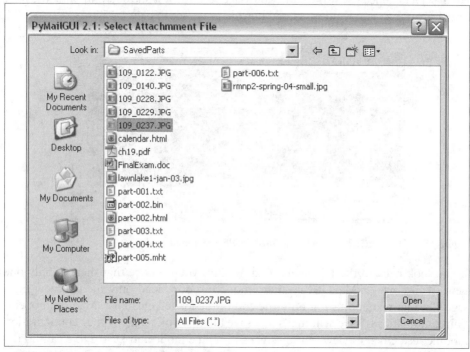

Figure 15-14. Attachment file dialog for Attach

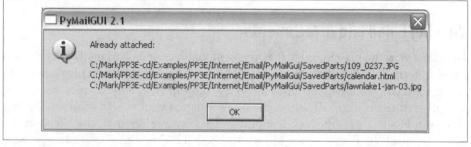

Figure 15-15. Attached parts list dialog for Parts

As we've seen, smtplib ultimately sends bytes to a server over a socket. Since this can be a long-running operation, PyMailGUI delegates this operation to a spawned thread, too. While the send thread runs, a nonblocking wait window appears and the entire GUI stays alive; redraw and move events are handled in the main program thread while the send thread talks to the SMTP server, and the user may perform other tasks in parallel.

You'll get an error popup if Python cannot send a message to any of the target recipients for any reason, and the mail composition window will pop up so that you may try again or save its text for later use. If you don't get an error popup, everything worked correctly, and your mail will show up in the recipients' mailboxes on their email servers. Since I sent the earlier message to myself, it shows up in mine the next time I press the main window's Load button, as we see in Figure 15-16.

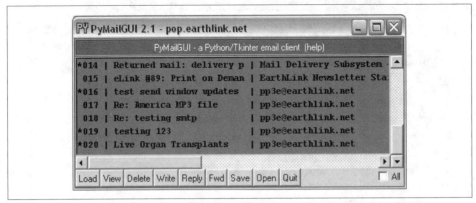

Figure 15-16. PyMailGUI main window after, loading sent mail

If you look back to the last main window shot, you'll notice that there is only one new email now—PyMailGUI is smart enough to download only the one new massage's header text and tack it onto the end of the loaded email list. Mail send operations automatically save sent mails in a save file that you name in your configuration module; use Open to view sent messages in offline mode and Delete to clean up the sent mail file if it grows too large (you can also Save from the sent-mail file to another file).

Viewing Email and Attachments

Now let's view the mail message that was sent and received. PyMailGUI lets us view email in formatted or raw mode. First, highlight (single-click) the mail you want to see in the main window, and press the View button. After the full message text is downloaded (unless it is already cached), a formatted mail viewer window like that shown in Figure 15-17 appears. If multiple messages are selected, the View button will download all that are not already cached (i.e., that have not already been fetched) and will pop up a view window for each. Like all long-running operations, full message downloads are run in parallel threads to avoid blocking.

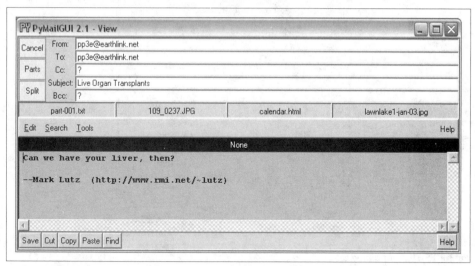

Figure 15-17. PyMailGUI view incoming mail window

Python's email module is used to parse out header lines from the raw text of the email message; their text is placed in the fields in the top right of the window. The message's main text is fetched from its body and stuffed into a new TextEditor object for display (it is also displayed in a web browser automatically if it is HTML text). PyMailGUI uses heuristics to extract the main text of the message to display, if there is one; it does not blindly show the entire raw text of the mail.

Any other parts of the message attached are displayed and opened with quick-access buttons in the middle. They are also listed by the Parts popup dialog, and they can be saved and opened all at once with Split. Figure 15-18 shows this window's Parts list popup, and Figure 15-19 displays this window's Split dialog in action.

Figure 15-18. Parts dialog listing all message parts

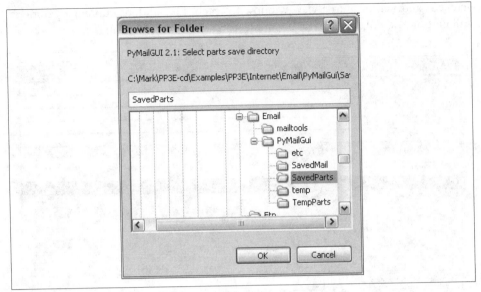

Figure 15-19. Split dialog selection

When the Split dialog in Figure 15-19 is submitted, all message parts are saved to the directory you select, and known parts are automatically opened. Individual parts are also automatically opened by the row of quick-access buttons labeled with the part's filename in the middle of the view window, after being saved to a temporary directory.

For instance, Figure 15-20 shows one of the image parts open on my Windows laptop, in a standard image viewer on that platform; other platforms may open this in a web browser instead. Click the image filename's quick-access button in Figure 15-17 to view it immediately, or run Split to open all parts at once.

By this point, the photo attachment displayed in Figure 15-20 has really gotten around: it has been encoded, attached, and sent, and then fetched, parsed, and decoded. Along the way, it has moved through multiple machines—from the client to the SMTP server, to the POP server, and back to the client.

In terms of user interaction, we attached the image to the email in Figure 15-13 using the dialog in Figure 15-14 before we sent the email. To access it later, we selected the email for viewing in Figure 15-16 and clicked on its quick-access button in Figure 15-17. PyMailGUI encoded it in base64 form, inserted it in the email's text, and later extracted and decoded it to get the original photo. With Python email tools, this just works.

Note that the main message text counts as a mail part, too—when selected, it opens in a PyEdit window, like that captured in Figure 15-21, from which it can be processed and saved (you can also save the main mail text with the Save button in the View window itself). The main part is included, because not all mails have a text

Figure 15-20. PyMailGUI opening image parts in a viewer or browser

part. For messages that have only HTML for their main text part, PyMailGUI displays the HTML text in its window, and opens a web browser to view the mail with its HTML formatting.

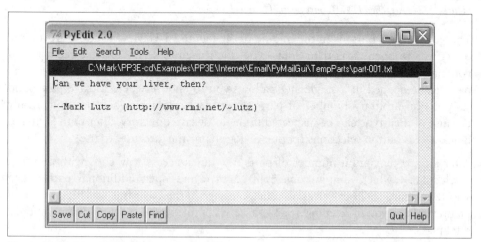

Figure 15-21. Main text part opened in PyEdit

PyMailGUI also opens HTML and XML parts in a web browser and uses the Windows Registry to open well-known Windows document types. For example, .doc, .xls, and .pdf files usually open, respectively, in Word, Excel, and Adobe Reader. Figure 15-22 captures the response to the *calendar.html* quick-access part button in Figure 15-17 on my Windows laptop (Firefox is my default web browser).

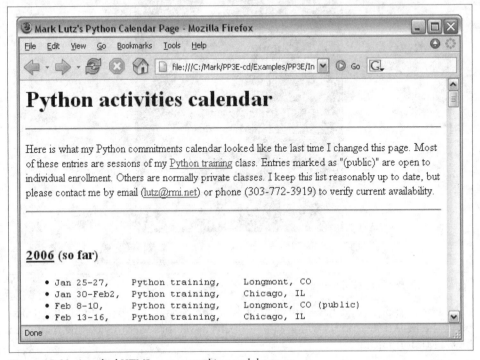

Figure 15-22. Attached HTML part opened in a web browser

The quick-access buttons in the middle of the Figure 15-17 view window are a more direct way to open parts than Split—you don't need to select a save directory, and you can open just the part you want to view. The Split button, though, allows all parts to be opened in a single step; allows you to choose where to save parts; and supports an arbitrary number of parts. Files that cannot be opened automatically because of their type can be inspected in the local save directory, after both Split and quick-access button selections (popup dialogs name the directory to use).

After a fixed maximum number of parts, the quick-access row ends with a button labeled "...", which simply runs Split to save and open additional parts when selected. Figure 15-23 captures one such message in the GUI; this was message 10 in Figure 15-9, if you're keeping track—a very complex mail, with 5 photos and 12 total parts.

Like much of PyMailGUI's behavior, the maximum number of part buttons to display in view windows can be configured in the mailconfig.py user settings module.

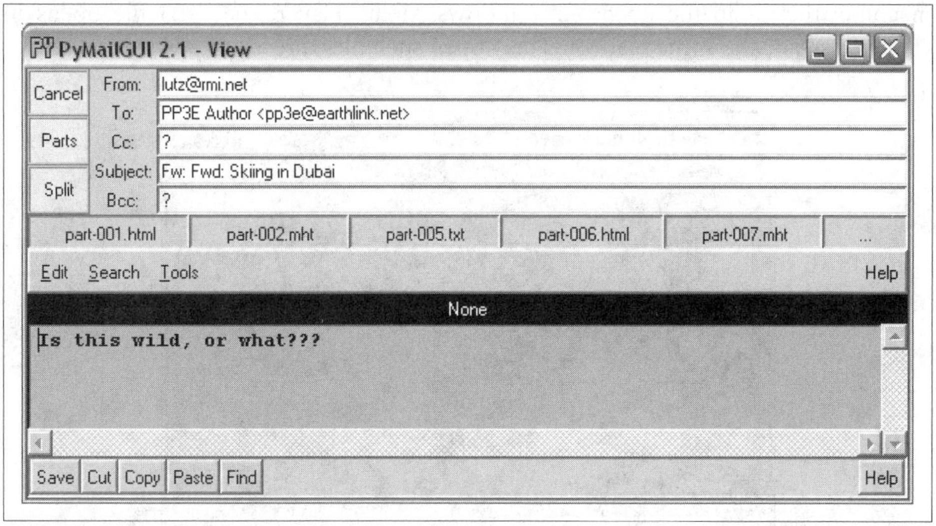

Figure 15-23. View window for a mail with many parts

That setting specified five buttons in Figure 15-23. Figure 15-24 shows a different mail with many attachments being viewed; the part buttons setting has been changed to a maximum of eight (this mail has seven parts). The setting can be higher, but at some point the buttons may become unreadable (use Split instead).

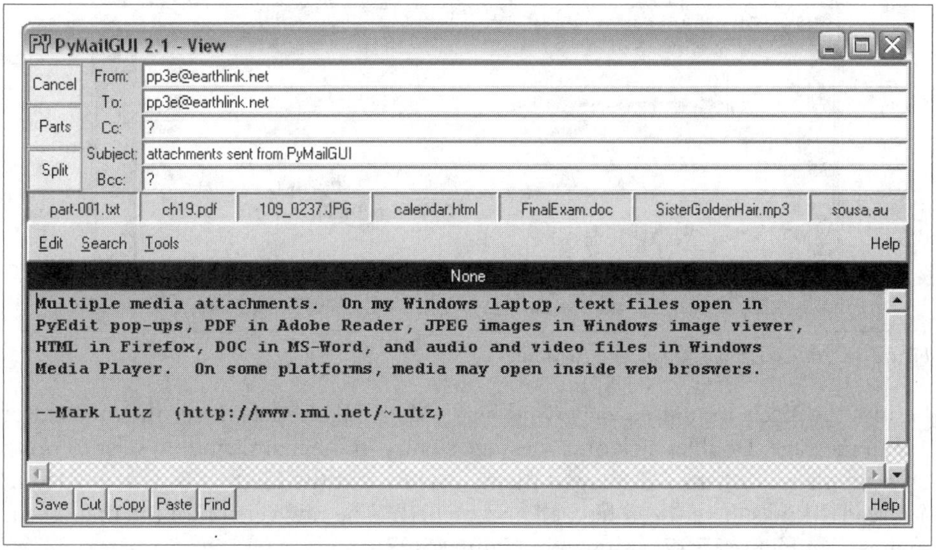

Figure 15-24. View window with part buttons setting increased

Figures 15-25 and 15-26 show what happens when the *sousa.au* and *ch19.pdf* buttons in Figure 15-24 are pressed on my Windows laptop. The results vary per machine; the audio file opens in Windows Media Player, the MP3 file opens in iTunes instead, and some platforms may open such files directly in a web browser.

Figure 15-25. An audio part opened by PyMailGUI

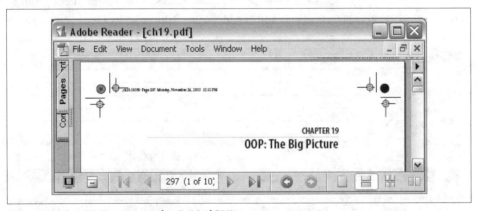

Figure 15-26. A PDF part opened in PyMailGUI

Besides the nicely formatted view window, PyMailGUI also lets us see the raw text of a mail message. Double-click on a message's entry in the main window's list to bring up a simple unformatted display of the mail's raw text (its full text is downloaded in a thread if it hasn't yet been fetched and cached). The raw version of the mail I sent to myself in Figure 15-17 is shown in Figure 15-27.

This raw text display can be useful to see special mail headers not shown in the formatted view. For instance, the optional "X-Mailer:" header in the raw text display identifies the program that transmitted a message; PyMailGUI adds it automatically,

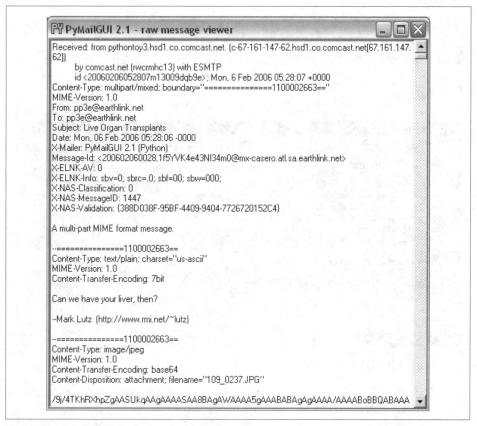

Figure 15-27. PyMailGUI raw mail text view window

along with standard headers like "From:" and "To:". Other headers are added as the mail is transmitted: the "Received:" headers name machines that the message was routed through on its way to our email server, and "Content-Type:" is added and parsed by Python's email package.

And really, the raw text form is all there is to an email message—it's what is transferred from machine to machine when mail is sent. The nicely formatted display of the GUI's view windows simply parses out and decodes components from the mail's raw text with standard Python tools, and places them in the associated fields of the display.

Email Replies and Forwards

Besides allowing users to read and write email, PyMailGUI also lets users forward and reply to incoming email sent from others. To reply to an email, select its entry in the main window's list and click the Reply button. If I reply to the mail I just sent to myself (arguably narcissistic, but demonstrative), the mail composition window shown in Figure 15-28 appears.

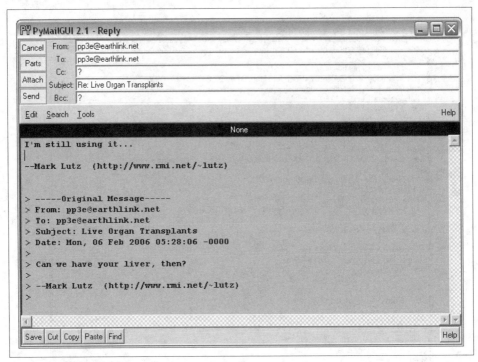

Figure 15-28. PyMailGUI reply compose window

This window is identical in format to the one we saw for the Write operation, except that PyMailGUI fills in some parts automatically:

- The "From" line is set to your email address in your `mailconfig` module.

- The "To:" line is initialized to the original message's "From" address (we're replying to the original sender, after all). An `email.Utils` call processes the "To:".

- The "Subject:" line is set to the original message's subject line, prepended with a "Re:", the standard follow-up subject line form (unless it already has one).

- The body of the reply is initialized with the signature line in `mailconfig`, along with the original message's text. The original message text is quoted with > characters and is prepended with a few header lines extracted from the original message to give some context.

Luckily, all of this is much easier than it may sound. Python's standard `email` module extracts all of the original message's header lines, and a single string `replace` method call does the work of adding the > quotes to the original message body. I simply type what I wish to say in reply (the initial paragraph in the mail's text area) and press the Send button to route the reply message to the mailbox on my mail server again. Physically sending the reply works the same as sending a brand-new message—the mail is routed to your SMTP server in a spawned send-mail thread, and the send-mail wait popup appears while the thread runs.

Forwarding a message is similar to replying: select the message in the main window, press the Fwd button, and fill in the fields and text area of the popped-up composition window. Figure 15-29 shows the window created to forward the mail we originally wrote and received.

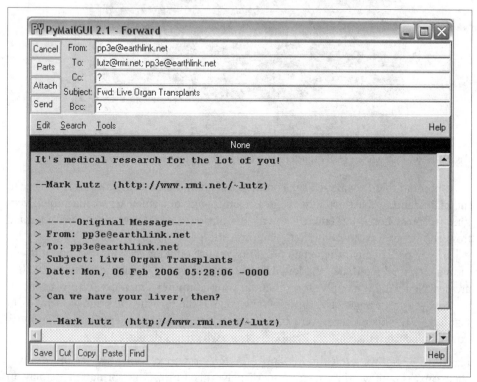

Figure 15-29. PyMailGUI forward compose window

Much like with replies, "From:" is filled from `mailconfig`, the original text is automatically quoted in the message body again, and the subject line is preset to the original message's subject, prepended with the string "Fwd:". I have to fill in the "To:" line manually, though, because this is not a direct reply (it doesn't necessarily go back to the original sender).

Notice that I'm forwarding this message to two different addresses; multiple recipient addresses are separated with a semicolon (;) in the "To:", "Cc:", and "Bcc:" header fields. The Send button in this window fires the forwarded message off to all addresses listed in these headers.

I've now written a new message, replied to it, and forwarded it. The reply and forward were sent to my email address, too; if we press the main window's Load button again, the reply and forward messages should show up in the main window's list. In Figure 15-30, they appear as messages 22 and 21 (the order they appear in may depend on timing issues at your server).

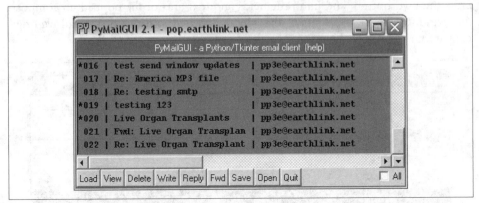

Figure 15-30. PyMailGUI mail list after sends and load

Keep in mind that PyMailGUI runs on the local computer, but the messages you see in the main window's list actually live in a mailbox on your email server machine. Every time we press Load, PyMailGUI downloads but does not delete newly arrived email from the server to your computer. The three messages we just wrote (20 through 22) will also appear in any other email program you use on your account (e.g., in Outlook, or in a web mail interface). PyMailGUI does not automatically delete messages as they are downloaded, but simply stores them in your computer's memory for processing. If we now select message 21 and press View, we see the forward message we sent, as in Figure 15-31. This message went from my machine to a remote email server and was downloaded from there into a Python list from which it is displayed.

Figure 15-32 shows what the forward message's raw text looks like; again, double-click on a main window's entry to display this form. The formatted display in Figure 15-31 simply extracts bits and pieces out of the text shown in the raw display form.

Deleting Email

So far, we've covered every action button on list windows except for Delete and the All checkbox. The All checkbox simply toggles from selecting all messages at once or deselecting all (View, Delete, Reply, Fwd, and Save action buttons apply to all currently selected messages). PyMailGUI also lets us delete messages from the server permanently, so that we won't see them the next time we access our inbox.

Delete operations are kicked off the same way as Views and Saves; just press the Delete button instead. In typical operation, I eventually delete email I'm not interested in, and save and delete emails that are important. We met Save earlier in this demo.

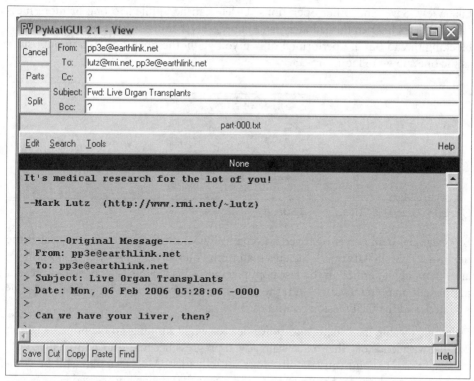

Figure 15-31. PyMailGUI view forwarded mail

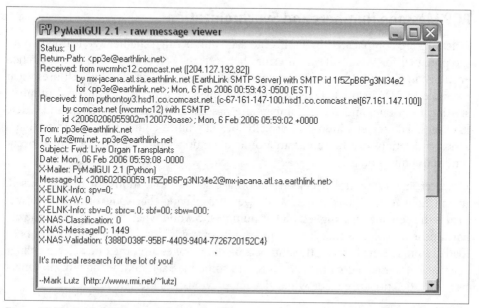

Figure 15-32. PyMailGUI view forwarded mail, raw

Like View, Save, and other operations, Delete can be applied to one or more messages. Deletes happen immediately, and like all server transfers they are run in a nonblocking thread but are performed only if you verify the operation in a popup, such as the one shown in Figure 15-33.

Figure 15-33. PyMailGUI delete verification on quit

By design, no mail is ever removed automatically: you will see the same messages the next time PyMailGUI runs. It deletes mail from your server only when you ask it to, and then only if verified in the last popup shown (this is your last chance to prevent permanent mail removal). After the deletions are performed, the mail index is updated, and the GUI session continues.

Deletions disable mail loads and other deletes while running and cannot be run in parallel with loads or other deletes already in progress because they may change POP message numbers and thus modify the mail index list. Messages may still be composed during a deletion, however, and offline save files may be processed.

POP Message Numbers and Synchronization

Deletions are complicated by POP's message-numbering scheme. We learned about the potential for synchronization errors between the server's inbox and the fetched email list in Chapter 14, when studying the mailtools package PyMailGUI uses (near Example 14-21). In brief, POP assigns each message a relative sequential number, starting from one, and these numbers are passed to the server to fetch and delete messages. The server's inbox is normally locked while a connection is held so that a series of deletions can be run as an atomic operation; no other inbox changes occur until the connection is closed.

However, message number changes also have some implications for the GUI itself. It's all right if new mail arrives while we're displaying the result of a prior download—the new mail is assigned higher numbers, beyond what is displayed on the client. But if we delete a message in the middle of a mailbox after the index has been loaded from the mail server, the numbers of all messages after the one deleted change (they are decremented by one). As a result, some message numbers might no longer be valid if deletions are made while viewing previously loaded email.

To work around this, PyMailGUI adjusts all the displayed numbers after a Delete by simply removing the entries for deleted mails from its index list and mail cache. However, this adjustment is not enough to keep the GUI in sync with the server's inbox if the inbox is modified at a time other than after the end, by deletions in another email client (even in another PyMailGUI session) or by deletions performed by the mail server itself (e.g., messages determined to be undeliverable and automatically removed from the inbox).

To handle these cases, PyMailGUI uses the safe deletion and synchronization tests in mailtools. That module uses mail header matching to detect mail list and server inbox synchronization errors. For instance, if another email client has deleted a message prior to the one to be deleted by PyMailGUI, mailtools catches the problem and cancels the deletion, and an error popup like the one in Figure 15-34 is displayed.

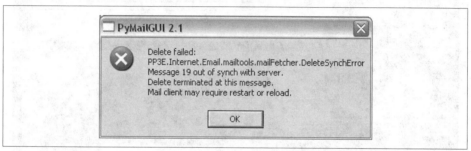

Figure 15-34. Safe deletion test detection of inbox difference

Similarly, index loads and message fetches run a synchronization test in mailtools, as well. Figure 15-35 captures the error generated if a message has been deleted in another client since we last loaded the server index window.

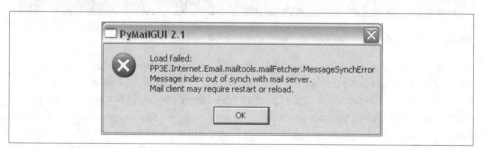

Figure 15-35. Synchronization error on after delete in another client

In both error cases, the inbox is automatically reloaded by PyMailGUI immediately after the error popup is dismissed. This scheme ensures that PyMailGUI won't delete or display the wrong message, in the rare case that the server's inbox is changed without its knowledge. See mailtools in Chapter 14 for more on synchronization tests.

Multiple Windows and Status Messages

Note that PyMailGUI is really meant to be a multiple-window interface—a detail not made obvious by the earlier screenshots. For example, Figure 15-36 shows PyMailGUI with the main server list window, two save-file list windows, two message view windows, and help. All these windows are nonmodal; that is, they are all active and independent, and do not block other windows from being selected. This interface looks slightly different on Linux and the Mac, but it has the same functionality.

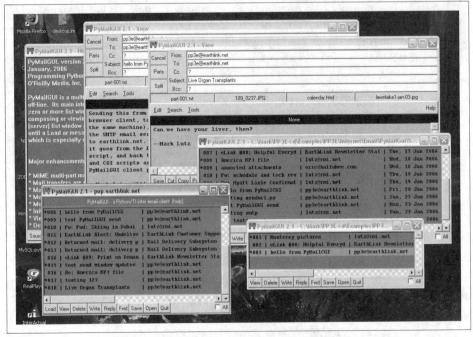

Figure 15-36. PyMailGUI multiple windows and text editors

In general, you can have any number of mail view or compose windows up at once, and cut and paste between them. This matters, because PyMailGUI must take care to make sure that each window has a distinct text-editor object. If the text-editor object were a global, or used globals internally, you'd likely see the same text in each window (and the Send operations might wind up sending text from another window). To avoid this, PyMailGUI creates and attaches a new TextEditor instance to each view and compose window it creates, and associates the new editor with the Send button's callback handler to make sure we get the right text.

Finally, PyMailGUI prints a variety of status messages as it runs, but you see them only if you launch the program from the system command-line console window (e.g., a DOS box on Windows or an xterm on Linux), or by double-clicking on its filename icon (its main script is a *.py*, not a *.pyw*). On Windows, you won't see these messages when PyMailGUI is started from another program, such as the PyDemos or PyGadgets launcher bar GUIs. These status messages print server information, show mail loading status, and trace the load, store, and delete threads that are spawned along the way. If you want PyMailGUI to be more verbose, launch it from a command line and watch:

```
C:\...\PP3E\Internet\Email\PyMailGui>PyMailGui2.py
user: pp3e
loading headers
Connecting...
+OK NGPopper vEL_6_10 at earthlink.net ready<7044.1139211610@poptawny.atl.sa.
earthlink.net>
load headers exit
synch check
Connecting...
+OK NGPopper vEL_6_10 at earthlink.net ready <22399.1139211626@pop-tawny.atl.sa.
earthlink.net>
Same headers text
load 16
Connecting...
+OK NGPopper vEL_6_10 at earthlink.net ready <27558.1139211627@pop-tawny.atl.sa.
earthlink.net>
Sending to...['pp3e@earthlink.net']
From: pp3e@earthlink.net
To: pp3e@earthlink.net
Subject: Fwd: Re: America MP3 file
Date: Mon, 06 Feb 2006 07:41:05 -0000
X-Mailer: PyMailGUI 2.1 (Python)

--Mark Lutz  (http://www.rmi.net/~lutz)

> -----Original Message-----
> From: pp3e@earthlink.net
>
Send exit
```

You can also double-click on the *PyMailGui.py* filename in your file explorer GUI and monitor the popped-up DOS console box on Windows. Console messages are mostly intended for debugging, but they can also be used to help understand the system's operation.

For more details on using PyMailGUI, see its help display, or read the help string in the module PyMailGuiHelp.py, listed in Example 15-9 in the next section.

PyMailGUI Implementation

Last but not least, we get to the code. PyMailGUI consists of the nine new modules listed at the start of this chapter; the source code for these modules is listed in this section.

Code Reuse

Besides the code here, PyMailGUI also gets a lot of mileage out of reusing modules we wrote earlier and won't repeat here: mailtools for mail loads, composition, parsing, and delete operations; threadtools for managing server and local file access threads; the GUI section's TextEditor for displaying and editing mail message text; and so on.

In addition, standard Python modules and packages such as poplib, smtplib, and email hide most of the details of pushing bytes around the Net and extracting and building message components. As usual, the Tkinter standard library module also implements GUI components in a portable fashion.

Code Structure

As mentioned earlier, PyMailGUI applies code factoring and OOP to leverage code reuse. For instance, list view windows are implemented as a common superclass that codes most actions, along with one subclass for the server inbox list window and one for local save-file list windows. The subclasses customize the common superclass for their specific mail media.

This design reflects the operation of the GUI itself—server list windows load mail over POP, and save-file list windows load from local files. The basic operation of list window layout and actions, though, is similar for both and is shared in the common superclass to avoid redundancy and simplify the code. Message view windows are similarly factored: a common view window superclass is reused and customized for write, reply, and forward view windows.

To make the code easier to follow, it is divided into two main modules that reflect the structure of the GUI—one for the implementation of list window actions and one for view window actions. If you are looking for the implementation of a button that appears in a mail view or edit window, for instance, see the view window module and search for a method whose name begins with the word *on*—the convention used for callback handler methods. Button text can also be located in name/callback tables used to build the windows. Actions initiated on list windows are coded in the list window module instead.

In addition, the message cache is split off into an object and module of its own, and potentially reusable tools are coded in importable modules (e.g., line wrapping and utility popups). PyMailGUI also includes a main module that defines startup window classes, a module that contains the help text as a string, and the mailconfig user settings module (a version specific to PyMailGUI is used here).

The next few sections list all of PyMailGUI's code for you to study; as you read, refer back to the demo earlier in this chapter and run the program live to map its behavior back to its code. PyMailGUI also includes a __init__.py file so that it can be used as a package—some of its modules may be useful in other programs. The __init__.py is empty in this package, so we omit it here.

PyMailGui2: The Main Module

Example 15-1 defines the file run to start PyMailGUI. It implements top-level list windows in the system—combinations of PyMailGUI's application logic and the window protocol superclasses we wrote earlier in the text. The latter of these define window titles, icons, and close behavior.

The main documentation is also in this module, as well as command-line logic—the program accepts the names of one or more save-mail files on the command line, and automatically opens them when the GUI starts up. This is used by the PyDemos launcher, for example.

Example 15-1. PP3E\Internet\Email\PyMailGui\PyMailGui2.py

```
###############################################################################
# PyMailGui 2.1 - A Python/Tkinter email client.
# A client-side Tkinter-based GUI interface for sending and receiving email.
#
# See the help string in PyMailGuiHelp2.py for usage details, and a list of
# enhancements in this version.  Version 2.0 is a major rewrite.  The changes
# from 2.0 (July '05) to 2.1 (Jan '06) were quick-access part buttons on View
# windows, threaded loads and deletes of local save-mail files, and checks for
# and recovery from message numbers out-of-synch with mail server inbox on
# deletes, index loads, and message loads.
#
# This file implements the top-level windows and interface.  PyMailGui uses
# a number of modules that know nothing about this GUI, but perform related
# tasks, some of which are developed in other sections of the book.  The
# mailconfig module is expanded for this program.
#
# Modules defined elsewhere and reused here:
#
# mailtools (package):
#     server sends and receives, parsing, construction     (client-side chapter)
# threadtools.py
#     thread queue manangement for GUI callbacks           (GUI tools chapter)
# windows.py
#     border configuration for top-level windows           (GUI tools chapter)
# textEditor.py
#     text widget used in mail view windows, some pop ups   (GUI programs chapter)
#
# Generally useful modules defined here:
#
# popuputil.py
#    help and busy windows, for general use
# messagecache.py
#    a cache that keeps track of mail already loaded
# wraplines.py
```

Example 15-1. PP3E\Internet\Email\PyMailGui\PyMailGui2.py (continued)

```
#     utility for wrapping long lines of messages
# mailconfig.py
#     user configuration parameters: server names, fonts, etc.
#
# Program-specific modules defined here:
#
# SharedNames.py
#     objects shared between window classes and main file
# ViewWindows.py
#     implementation of view, write, reply, forward windows
# ListWindows.py
#     implementation of mail-server and local-file list windows
# PyMailGuiHelp.py
#     user-visible help text, opened by main window bar
# PyMailGui2.py
#     main, top-level file (run this), with main window types
#############################################################################


import mailconfig, sys
from SharedNames import appname, windows
from ListWindows import PyMailServer, PyMailFile



#############################################################################
# Top-level window classes
# View, Write, Reply, Forward, Help, BusyBox all inherit from PopupWindow
# directly: only usage;  askpassword calls PopupWindow and attaches;  order
# matters here!--PyMail classes redef some method defaults in the Window
# classes, like destroy and okayToExit: must be leftmost;  to use
# PyMailFileWindow standalone, imitate logic in PyMailCommon.onOpenMailFile;
#############################################################################


# uses icon file in cwd or default in tools dir
srvrname = mailconfig.popservername or 'Server'

class PyMailServerWindow(PyMailServer, windows.MainWindow):
    def __init__(self):
        windows.MainWindow.__init__(self, appname, srvrname)
        PyMailServer.__init__(self)

class PyMailServerPopup(PyMailServer, windows.PopupWindow):
    def __init__(self):
        windows.PopupWindow.__init__(self, appname, srvrnane)
        PyMailServer.__init__(self)

class PyMailServerComponent(PyMailServer, windows.ComponentWindow):
    def __init__(self):
        windows.ComponentWindow.__init__(self)
        PyMailServer.__init__(self)

class PyMailFileWindow(PyMailFile, windows.PopupWindow):
    def __init__(self, filename):
```

Example 15-1. PP3E\Internet\Email\PyMailGui\PyMailGui2.py (continued)

```
        windows.PopupWindow.__init__(self, appname, filename)
        PyMailFile.__init__(self, filename)


###############################################################################
# when run as a top-level program: create main mail-server list window
###############################################################################

if __name__ == '__main__':
    rootwin = PyMailServerWindow()                # open server window
    if sys.argv > 1:
        for savename in sys.argv[1:]:
            rootwin.onOpenMailFile(savename)      # open save file windows (demo)
        rootwin.lift()                            # save files loaded in threads
    rootwin.mainloop()
```

SharedNames: Program-Wide Globals

The module in Example 15-2 implements a shared, system-wide namespace that collects resources used in most modules in the system, and defines global objects that
span files. This allows other files to avoid redundantly repeating common imports,
and encapsulates the locations of package imports; it is the only file that must be
updated if paths change in the future. Using globals can make programs harder to
understand in general (the source of some names is not as clear), but it is reasonable
if all such names are collected in a single expected module such as this one (because
there is only one place to search for unknown names).

Example 15-2. PP3E\Internet\Email\PyMailGui\SharedNames.py

```
###############################################################################
# objects shared by all window classes and main file: program-wide globals
###############################################################################

# used in all window, icon titles
appname   = 'PyMailGUI 2.1'

# used for list save, open, delete; also for sent messages file
saveMailSeparator = 'PyMailGUI' + ('-'*60) + 'PyMailGUI\n'

# currently viewed mail save files; also for sent-mail file
openSaveFiles      = {}                    # 1 window per file,{name:win}

# standard library services
import sys, os, email, webbrowser
from Tkinter        import *
from tkFileDialog   import SaveAs, Open, Directory
from tkMessageBox   import showinfo, showerror, askyesno

# reuse book examples
from PP3E.Gui.Tools        import windows       # window border, exit protocols
from PP3E.Gui.Tools        import threadtools   # thread callback queue checker
```

Example 15-2. PP3E\Internet\Email\PyMailGui\SharedNames.py (continued)

```
from PP3E.Internet.Email import mailtools     # load,send,parse,build utilities
from PP3E.Gui.TextEditor import textEditor    # component and pop up

# modules defined here
import mailconfig                             # user params: servers, fonts, etc.
import popuputil                              # help, busy, passwd pop-up windows
import wraplines                              # wrap long message lines
import messagecache                           # remember already loaded mail
import PyMailGuiHelp                          # user documentation

def printStack(exc_info):
    # debugging: show exception and stack traceback on stdout
    print exc_info[0]
    print exc_info[1]
    import traceback
    traceback.print_tb(exc_info[2], file=sys.stdout)

# thread busy counters for threads run by this GUI
# sendingBusy shared by all send windows, used by main window quit

loadingHdrsBusy = threadtools.ThreadCounter()    # only 1
deletingBusy    = threadtools.ThreadCounter()    # only 1
loadingMsgsBusy = threadtools.ThreadCounter()    # poss many
sendingBusy     = threadtools.ThreadCounter()    # poss many
```

ListWindows: Message List Windows

The code in Example 15-3 implements mail index list windows—for the server inbox window and for one or more local save-mail file windows. These two types of windows look and behave largely the same, and in fact share most of their code in common in a superclass. The window subclasses mostly just customize the superclass to map mail Load and Delete calls to the server or a local file.

List windows are created on program startup (the initial server window, and possible save-file windows for command-line options), as well as in response to Open button actions in existing list windows (save-file list windows). See the Open button's callback in this example for initiation code.

Notice that the basic mail processing operations in the mailtools package from Chapter 14 are mixed into PyMailGUI in a variety of ways. The list window classes in Example 15-3 inherit from the mailtools mail parser class, but the server list window class embeds an instance of the message cache object, which in turn inherits from the mailtools mail fetcher. The mailtools mail sender class is inherited by message view write windows, not list windows; view windows also inherit from the mail parser.

This is a fairly large file; in principle it could be split into three files, one for each class, but these classes are so closely related that it is handy to have their code in a single file for edits. Really, this is one class, with two minor extensions.

Example 15-3. PP3E\Internet\Email\PyMailGui\ListWindows.py

```
###############################################################################
# Implementation of mail-server and save-file message list main windows:
# one class per kind.  Code is factored here for reuse: server and file
# list windows are customized versions of the PyMailCommon list window class;
# the server window maps actions to mail transferred from a server, and the
# file window applies actions to a local file.  List windows create View,
# Write, Reply, and Forward windows on user actions.  The server list window
# is the main window opened on program startup by the top-level file;  file
# list windows are opened on demand via server and file list window "Open".
# Msgnums may be temporarily out of sync with server if POP inbox changes.
#
# Changes here in 2.1:
# -now checks on deletes and loads to see if msg nums in sync with server
# -added up to N attachment direct-access buttons on view windows
# -threaded save-mail file loads, to avoid N-second pause for big files
# -also threads save-mail file deletes so file write doesn't pause GUI
# TBD:
# -save-mail file saves still not threaded: may pause GUI briefly, but
#  uncommon - unlike load and delete, save/send only appends the local file.
# -implementation of local save-mail files as text files with separators
#  is mostly a prototype: it loads all full mails into memory, and so limits
#  the practical size of these files; better alternative: use 2 DBM keyed
#  access files for hdrs and fulltext, plus a list to map keys to position;
#  in this scheme save-mail files become directories, no longer readable.
###############################################################################

from SharedNames import *      # program-wide global objects
from ViewWindows import ViewWindow, WriteWindow, ReplyWindow, ForwardWindow


###############################################################################
# main frame - general structure for both file and server message lists
###############################################################################


class PyMailCommon(mailtools.MailParser):
    """
    a widget package, with main mail listbox
    mixed in with a Tk, Toplevel, or Frame
    must be customized with actions() and other
    creates view and write windows: MailSenders
    """
    # class attrs shared by all list windows
    threadLoopStarted = False                    # started by first window

    # all windows use same dialogs: remember last dirs
    openDialog = Open(title=appname + ': Open Mail File')
```

Example 15-3. PP3E\Internet\Email\PyMailGui\ListWindows.py (continued)

```
    saveDialog = SaveAs(title=appname + ': Append Mail File')

def __init__(self):
    self.makeWidgets()                          # draw my contents: list,tools
    if not PyMailCommon.threadLoopStarted:      # server,file can both thread
        PyMailCommon.threadLoopStarted = True   # start thread exit check loop
        threadtools.threadChecker(self)         # just one for all windows

def makeWidgets(self):
    # add all/none checkbtn at bottom
    tools = Frame(self)
    tools.pack(side=BOTTOM, fill=X)
    self.allModeVar = IntVar()
    chk = Checkbutton(tools, text="All")
    chk.config(variable=self.allModeVar, command=self.onCheckAll)
    chk.pack(side=RIGHT)

    # add main buttons at bottom
    for (title, callback) in self.actions():
        Button(tools, text=title, command=callback).pack(side=LEFT, fill=X)

    # add multiselect listbox with scrollbars
    mails    = Frame(self)
    vscroll  = Scrollbar(mails)
    hscroll  = Scrollbar(mails, orient='horizontal')
    fontsz   = (sys.platform[:3] == 'win' and 8) or 10       # defaults
    listbg   = mailconfig.listbg   or 'white'
    listfg   = mailconfig.listfg   or 'black'
    listfont = mailconfig.listfont or ('courier', fontsz, 'normal')
    listbox  = Listbox(mails, bg=listbg, fg=listfg, font=listfont)
    listbox.config(selectmode=EXTENDED)
    listbox.bind('<Double-1>', (lambda event: self.onViewRawMail()))

    # crosslink listbox and scrollbars
    vscroll.config(command=listbox.yview, relief=SUNKEN)
    hscroll.config(command=listbox.xview, relief=SUNKEN)
    listbox.config(yscrollcommand=vscroll.set, relief=SUNKEN)
    listbox.config(xscrollcommand=hscroll.set)

    # pack last = clip first
    mails.pack(side=TOP, expand=YES, fill=BOTH)
    vscroll.pack(side=RIGHT,  fill=BOTH)
    hscroll.pack(side=BOTTOM, fill=BOTH)
    listbox.pack(side=LEFT, expand=YES, fill=BOTH)
    self.listBox = listbox

################
# event handlers
################

def onCheckAll(self):
    # all or none click
```

Example 15-3. PP3E\Internet\Email\PyMailGui\ListWindows.py (continued)

```
        if self.allModeVar.get():
            self.listBox.select_set(0, END)
        else:
            self.listBox.select_clear(0, END)

    def onViewRawMail(self):
        # possibly threaded: view selected messages - raw text headers, body
        msgnums = self.verifySelectedMsgs()
        if msgnums:
            self.getMessages(msgnums, after=lambda: self.contViewRaw(msgnums))

    def contViewRaw(self, msgnums):
        for msgnum in msgnums:                          # could be a nested def
            fulltext = self.getMessage(msgnum)          # put in ScrolledText
            from ScrolledText import ScrolledText       # don't need full TextEditor
            window  = windows.QuietPopupWindow(appname, 'raw message viewer')
            browser = ScrolledText(window)
            browser.insert('0.0', fulltext)
            browser.pack(expand=YES, fill=BOTH)

    def onViewFormatMail(self):
        """
        possibly threaded: view selected messages - pop up formatted display
        not threaded if in savefile list, or messages are already loaded
        the after action runs only if getMessages prefetch allowed and worked
        """
        msgnums = self.verifySelectedMsgs()
        if msgnums:
            self.getMessages(msgnums, after=lambda: self.contViewFmt(msgnums))

    def contViewFmt(self, msgnums):
        for msgnum in msgnums:
            fulltext = self.getMessage(msgnum)
            message  = self.parseMessage(fulltext)
            type, content = self.findMainText(message)
            content  = wraplines.wrapText1(content, mailconfig.wrapsz)
            ViewWindow(headermap  = message,
                       showtext    = content,
                       origmessage = message)

            # non-multipart, content-type text/HTML (rude but true!)
            # can also be opened manually from Split or part button
            # if non-multipart, other: must open part manually with
            # Split or part button; no verify if mailconfig says so;

            if type == 'text/html':
                if ((not mailconfig.verifyHTMLTextOpen) or
                    askyesno(appname, 'Open message text in browser?')):
                    try:
                        from tempfile import gettempdir # or a Tk HTML viewer?
                        tempname = os.path.join(gettempdir(), 'pymailgui.html')
                        open(tempname, 'w').write(content)
```

Example 15-3. PP3E\Internet\Email\PyMailGui\ListWindows.py (continued)

```
                    webbrowser.open_new('file://' + tempname)
            except:
                show_error(appname, 'Cannot open in browser')

    def onWriteMail(self):
        # compose new email
        starttext = '\n'                          # use auto signature text
        if mailconfig.mysignature:
            starttext += '%s\n' % mailconfig.mysignature
        WriteWindow(starttext = starttext,
                    headermap = {'From': mailconfig.myaddress})

    def onReplyMail(self):
        # possibly threaded: reply to selected emails
        msgnums = self.verifySelectedMsgs()
        if msgnums:
            self.getMessages(msgnums, after=lambda: self.contReply(msgnums))

    def contReply(self, msgnums):
        for msgnum in msgnums:
            # drop attachments, quote with '>', add signature
            fulltext = self.getMessage(msgnum)
            message  = self.parseMessage(fulltext)          # may fail: error obj
            maintext = self.findMainText(message)[1]
            maintext = wraplines.wrapText1(maintext, mailconfig.wrapsz-2)   # >
            maintext = self.quoteOrigText(maintext, message)
            if mailconfig.mysignature:
                maintext = ('\n%s\n' % mailconfig.mysignature) + maintext

            # preset initial to/from values from mail or config
            # don't use original To for From: may be many or listname
            # To keeps name+<addr> format unless any ';' present: separator
            # ideally, send should fully parse instead of splitting on ';'
            # send changes ';' to ',' required by servers; ',' common in name

            origfrom = message.get('From', '')
            ToPair   = email.Utils.parseaddr(origfrom)      # 1st (name, addr)
            ToStr    = email.Utils.formataddr(ToPair)       # ignore Reply-to
            From     = mailconfig.myaddress                 # don't try 'To'
            Subj     = message.get('Subject', '(no subject)')
            if not Subj.startswith('Re:'):
                Subj = 'Re: ' + Subj
            if ';' not in ToStr:                            # uses separator?
                To = ToStr                                  # use name+addr
            else:
                To = ToPair[1]                              # use just addr
            ReplyWindow(starttext = maintext,
                        headermap = {'From': From, 'To': To, 'Subject': Subj})

    def onFwdMail(self):
        # possibly threaded: forward selected emails
        msgnums = self.verifySelectedMsgs()
```

Example 15-3. PP3E\Internet\Email\PyMailGui\ListWindows.py (continued)

```
        if msgnums:
            self.getMessages(msgnums, after=lambda: self.contFwd(msgnums))

    def contFwd(self, msgnums):
        for msgnum in msgnums:
            # drop attachments, quote with '>', add signature
            fulltext = self.getMessage(msgnum)
            message  = self.parseMessage(fulltext)
            maintext = self.findMainText(message)[1]
            maintext = wraplines.wrapText1(maintext, mailconfig.wrapsz-2)
            maintext = self.quoteOrigText(maintext, message)
            if mailconfig.mysignature:
                maintext = ('\n%s\n' % mailconfig.mysignature) + maintext

            # initial from value from config, not mail
            From = mailconfig.myaddress
            Subj = message.get('Subject', '(no subject)')
            if not Subj.startswith('Fwd: '):
                Subj = 'Fwd: ' + Subj
            ForwardWindow(starttext = maintext,
                          headermap = {'From': From, 'Subject': Subj})

    def onSaveMailFile(self):
        """
        save selected emails for offline viewing
        disabled if target file load/delete is in progress
        disabled by getMessages if self is a busy file too
        contSave not threaded: disables all other actions
        """
        msgnums = self.selectedMsgs()
        if not msgnums:
            showerror(appname, 'No message selected')
        else:
            # caveat: dialog warns about replacing file
            filename = self.saveDialog.show()             # shared class attr
            if filename:                                  # don't verify num msgs
                filename = os.path.abspath(filename)      # normalize / to \
                self.getMessages(msgnums,
                        after=lambda: self.contSave(msgnums, filename))

    def contSave(self, msgnums, filename):
        # test busy now, after poss srvr msgs load
        if (filename in openSaveFiles.keys() and          # viewing this file?
            openSaveFiles[filename].openFileBusy):        # load/del occurring?
            showerror(appname, 'Target file busy - cannot save')
        else:
            try:
                fulltextlist = []
                mailfile = open(filename, 'a')            # caveat:not threaded
                for msgnum in msgnums:                    # < 1sec for N megs
                    fulltext = self.getMessage(msgnum)    # but poss many msgs
                    if fulltext[-1] != '\n': fulltext += '\n'
```

Example 15-3. PP3E\Internet\Email\PyMailGui\ListWindows.py (continued)

```
                        mailfile.write(saveMailSeparator)
                        mailfile.write(fulltext)
                        fulltextlist.append(fulltext)
                    mailfile.close()
                except:
                    showerror(appname, 'Error during save')
                    printStack(sys.exc_info())
                else:                                       # why .keys(): EIBTI
                    if filename in openSaveFiles.keys():    # viewing this file?
                        window = openSaveFiles[filename]    # update list, raise
                        window.addSavedMails(fulltextlist)  # avoid file reload
                        #window.loadMailFileThread()        # this was very slow

    def onOpenMailFile(self, filename=None):
        # process saved mail offline
        filename = filename or self.openDialog.show()       # shared class attr
        if filename:
            filename = os.path.abspath(filename)            # match on full name
            if openSaveFiles.has_key(filename):             # only 1 win per file
                openSaveFiles[filename].lift()              # raise file's window
                showinfo(appname, 'File already open')      # else deletes odd
            else:
                from PyMailGui2 import PyMailFileWindow      # avoid duplicate win
                popup = PyMailFileWindow(filename)          # new list window
                openSaveFiles[filename] = popup             # removed in quit
                popup.loadMailFileThread()                  # try load in thread

    def onDeleteMail(self):
        # delete selected mails from server or file
        msgnums = self.selectedMsgs()                       # subclass: fillIndex
        if not msgnums:                                     # always verify here
            showerror(appname, 'No message selected')
        else:
            if askyesno(appname, 'Verify delete %d mails?' % len(msgnums)):
                self.doDelete(msgnums)


    #################
    # utility methods
    #################

    def selectedMsgs(self):
        # get messages selected in main listbox
        selections = self.listBox.curselection()  # tuple of digit strs, 0..N-1
        return [int(x)+1 for x in selections]      # convert to ints, make 1..N

    warningLimit = 15
    def verifySelectedMsgs(self):
        msgnums = self.selectedMsgs()
        if not msgnums:
            showerror(appname, 'No message selected')
        else:
            numselects = len(msgnums)
```

Example 15-3. PP3E\Internet\Email\PyMailGui\ListWindows.py (continued)

```
            if numselects > self.warningLimit:
                if not askyesno(appname, 'Open %d selections?' % numselects):
                    msgnums = []
        return msgnums

    def fillIndex(self, maxhdrsize=25):
        # fill all of main listbox
        hdrmaps  = self.headersMaps()                    # may be empty
        showhdrs = ('Subject', 'From', 'Date', 'To')     # default hdrs to show
        if hasattr(mailconfig, 'listheaders'):           # mailconfig customizes
            showhdrs = mailconfig.listheaders or showhdrs

        # compute max field sizes <= hdrsize
        maxsize = {}
        for key in showhdrs:
            allLens = [len(msg.get(key, '')) for msg in hdrmaps]
            if not allLens: allLens = [1]
            maxsize[key] = min(maxhdrsize, max(allLens))

        # populate listbox with fixed-width left-justified fields
        self.listBox.delete(0, END)                      # show multiparts with *
        for (ix, msg) in enumerate(hdrmaps):             # via content-type hdr
            msgtype = msg.get_content_maintype()         # no is_multipart yet
            msgline = (msgtype == 'multipart' and '*') or ' '
            msgline += '%03d' % (ix+1)
            for key in showhdrs:
                mysize  = maxsize[key]
                keytext = msg.get(key, ' ')
                msgline += ' | %-*s' % (mysize, keytext[:mysize])
            msgline += '| %.1fK' % (self.mailSize(ix+1) / 1024.0)
            self.listBox.insert(END, msgline)
        self.listBox.see(END)          # show most recent mail=last line

    def quoteOrigText(self, maintext, message):
        quoted   = '\n-----Original Message-----\n'
        for hdr in ('From', 'To', 'Subject', 'Date'):
            quoted += '%s: %s\n' % (hdr, message.get(hdr, '?'))
        quoted   = quoted + '\n' + maintext
        quoted   = '\n' + quoted.replace('\n', '\n> ')
        return quoted


#########################
# subclass requirements
#########################

    def getMessages(self, msgnums, after):           # used by view,save,reply,fwd
        after()                                       # redef if cache, thread test

    # plus okayToQuit?, any unique actions
    def getMessage(self, msgnum): assert False        # used by many: full mail text
    def headersMaps(self): assert False               # fillIndex: hdr mappings list
```

Example 15-3. PP3E\Internet\Email\PyMailGui\ListWindows.py (continued)

```
        def mailSize(self, msgnum): assert False    # fillIndex: size of msgnum
        def doDelete(self): assert False            # onDeleteMail: delete button



################################################################################
# main window - when viewing messages in local save file (or sent-mail file)
################################################################################


class PyMailFile(PyMailCommon):
    """
    customize for viewing saved-mail file offline
    a Tk, Toplevel, or Frame, with main mail listbox
    opens and deletes run in threads for large files

    save and send not threaded, because only append to
    file; save is disabled if source or target file busy
    with load/delete; save disables load, delete, save
    just because it is not run in a thread (blocks GUI);

    TBD: may need thread and O/S file locks if saves ever
    do run in threads: saves could disable other threads
    with openFileBusy, but file may not be open in GUI;
    file locks not sufficient, because GUI updated too;
    TBD: appends to sent-mail file may require O/S locks:
    as is, user gets error pop up if sent during load/del;
    """
    def actions(self):
        return [ ('View',   self.onViewFormatMail),
                 ('Delete', self.onDeleteMail),
                 ('Write',  self.onWriteMail),
                 ('Reply',  self.onReplyMail),
                 ('Fwd',    self.onFwdMail),
                 ('Save',   self.onSaveMailFile),
                 ('Open',   self.onOpenMailFile),
                 ('Quit',   self.quit) ]

    def __init__(self, filename):
        # caller: do loadMailFileThread next
        PyMailCommon.__init__(self)
        self.filename = filename
        self.openFileBusy = threadtools.ThreadCounter()    # one per window

    def loadMailFileThread(self):
        """
        Load or reload file and update window index list;
        called on Open, startup, and possibly on Send if
        sent-mail file appended is currently open;  there
        is always a bogus first item after the text split;
        alt: [self.parseHeaders(m) for m in self.msglist];
        could pop up a busy dialog, but quick for small files;
```

Example 15-3. PP3E\Internet\Email\PyMailGui\ListWindows.py (continued)

```
        2.1: this is now threaded--else runs < 1sec for N meg
        files, but can pause GUI N seconds if very large file;
        Save now uses addSavedMails to append msg lists for
        speed, not this reload;  still called from Send just
        because msg text unavailable - requires refactoring;
        delete threaded too: prevent open and delete overlap;
        """
        if self.openFileBusy:
            # don't allow parallel open/delete changes
            errmsg = 'Cannot load, file is busy:\n"%s"' % self.filename
            showerror(appname, errmsg)
        else:
            #self.listBox.insert(END, 'loading...')      # error if user clicks
            savetitle = self.title()                     # set by window class
            self.title(appname + ' - ' + 'Loading...')
            self.openFileBusy.incr()
            threadtools.startThread(
                action   = self.loadMailFile,
                args     = (),
                context  = (savetitle,),
                onExit   = self.onLoadMailFileExit,
                onFail   = self.onLoadMailFileFail)

    def loadMailFile(self):
        # run in a thread while GUI is active
        # open, read, parser may all raise excs
        allmsgs = open(self.filename).read()
        self.msglist = allmsgs.split(saveMailSeparator)[1:]      # full text
        self.hdrlist = map(self.parseHeaders, self.msglist)      # msg objects

    def onLoadMailFileExit(self, savetitle):
        # on thread success
        self.title(savetitle)         # reset window title to filename
        self.fillIndex()              # updates GUI: do in main thread
        self.lift()                   # raise my window
        self.openFileBusy.decr()

    def onLoadMailFileFail(self, exc_info, savetitle):
        # on thread exception
        showerror(appname, 'Error opening "%s"\n%s\n%s' %
                          ((self.filename,) + exc_info[:2]))
        printStack(exc_info)
        self.destroy()                # always close my window?
        self.openFileBusy.decr()      # not needed if destroy

    def addSavedMails(self, fulltextlist):
        """
        optimization: extend loaded file lists for mails
        newly saved to this window's file; in past called
        loadMailThread to reload entire file on save - slow;
        must be called in main GUI thread only: updates GUI;
        sends still reloads sent file if open: no msg text;
```

Example 15-3. PP3E\Internet\Email\PyMailGui\ListWindows.py (continued)

```
        """
        self.msglist.extend(fulltextlist)
        self.hdrlist.extend(map(self.parseHeaders, fulltextlist))
        self.fillIndex()
        self.lift()

    def doDelete(self, msgnums):
        """
        simple-minded, but sufficient: rewrite all
        nondeleted mails to file; can't just delete
        from self.msglist in-place: changes item indexes;
        Py2.3 enumerate(L) same as zip(range(len(L)), L)
        2.1: now threaded, else N sec pause for large files
        """
        if self.openFileBusy:
            # dont allow parallel open/delete changes
            errmsg = 'Cannot delete, file is busy:\n"%s"' % self.filename
            showerror(appname, errmsg)
        else:
            savetitle = self.title()
            self.title(appname + ' - ' + 'Deleting...')
            self.openFileBusy.incr()
            threadtools.startThread(
                action  = self.deleteMailFile,
                args    = (msgnums,),
                context = (savetitle,),
                onExit  = self.onDeleteMailFileExit,
                onFail  = self.onDeleteMailFileFail)

    def deleteMailFile(self, msgnums):
        # run in a thread while GUI active
        indexed = enumerate(self.msglist)
        keepers = [msg for (ix, msg) in indexed if ix+1 not in msgnums]
        allmsgs = saveMailSeparator.join([''] + keepers)
        open(self.filename, 'w').write(allmsgs)
        self.msglist = keepers
        self.hdrlist = map(self.parseHeaders, self.msglist)

    def onDeleteMailFileExit(self, savetitle):
        self.title(savetitle)
        self.fillIndex()                    # updates GUI: do in main thread
        self.lift()                         # reset my title, raise my window
        self.openFileBusy.decr()

    def onDeleteMailFileFail(self, exc_info, savetitle):
        showerror(appname, 'Error deleting "%s"\n%s\n%s' %
                        ((self.filename,) +  exc_info[:2]))
        printStack(exc_info)
        self.destroy()                      # always close my window?
        self.openFileBusy.decr()            # not needed if destroy
```

Example 15-3. PP3E\Internet\Email\PyMailGui\ListWindows.py (continued)

```python
    def getMessages(self, msgnums, after):
        """
        used by view,save,reply,fwd: file load and delete
        threads may change the msg and hdr lists, so disable
        all other operations that depend on them to be safe;
        this test is for self: saves also test target file;
        """
        if self.openFileBusy:
            errmsg = 'Cannot fetch, file is busy:\n"%s"' % self.filename
            showerror(appname, errmsg)
        else:
            after()                          # mail already loaded

    def getMessage(self, msgnum):
        return self.msglist[msgnum-1]        # full text of 1 mail

    def headersMaps(self):
        return self.hdrlist                  # email.Message objects

    def mailSize(self, msgnum):
        return len(self.msglist[msgnum-1])

    def quit(self):
        # don't destroy during update: fillIndex next
        if self.openFileBusy:
            showerror(appname, 'Cannot quit during load or delete')
        else:
            if askyesno(appname, 'Verify Quit Window?'):
                # delete file from open list
                del openSaveFiles[self.filename]
                Toplevel.destroy(self)


###############################################################################
# main window - when viewing messages on the mail server
###############################################################################


class PyMailServer(PyMailCommon):
    """
    customize for viewing mail still on server
    a Tk, Toplevel, or Frame, with main mail listbox
    maps load, fetch, delete actions to server inbox
    embeds a MessageCache, which is a MailFetcher
    """
    def actions(self):
        return [ ('Load',   self.onLoadServer),
                 ('View',   self.onViewFormatMail),
                 ('Delete', self.onDeleteMail),
                 ('Write',  self.onWriteMail),
                 ('Reply',  self.onReplyMail),
                 ('Fwd',    self.onFwdMail),
```

Example 15-3. PP3E\Internet\Email\PyMailGui\ListWindows.py (continued)

```
                        ('Save',   self.onSaveMailFile),
                        ('Open',   self.onOpenMailFile),
                        ('Quit',   self.quit) ]

    def __init__(self):
        PyMailCommon.__init__(self)
        self.cache = messagecache.GuiMessageCache()   # embedded, not inherited
       #self.listBox.insert(END, 'Press Load to fetch mail')

    def makeWidgets(self):                             # help bar: main win only
        self.addHelp()
        PyMailCommon.makeWidgets(self)

    def addHelp(self):
        msg = 'PyMailGUI - a Python/Tkinter email client  (help)'
        title = Button(self, text=msg)
        title.config(bg='steelblue', fg='white', relief=RIDGE)
        title.config(command=self.onShowHelp)
        title.pack(fill=X)

    def onShowHelp(self):
        """
        load,show text block string
        could use HTML and web browser module here too
        but that adds an external dependency
        """
        from PyMailGuiHelp import helptext
        popuputil.HelpPopup(appname, helptext, showsource=self.onShowMySource)

    def onShowMySource(self, showAsMail=False):
        # display my sourcecode file, plus imported modules here & elsewhere
        import PyMailGui2, ListWindows, ViewWindows, SharedNames
        from PP3E.Internet.Email.mailtools import (    # mailtools now a pkg
             mailSender, mailFetcher, mailParser)      # can't use * in def
        mymods = (
             PyMailGui2, ListWindows, ViewWindows, SharedNames,
             PyMailGuiHelp, popuputil, messagecache, wraplines,
             mailtools, mailFetcher, mailSender, mailParser,
             mailconfig, threadtools, windows, textEditor)
        for mod in mymods:
             source = mod.__file__
             if source.endswith('.pyc'):
                 source = source[:-4] + '.py'          # assume in same dir, .py
             if showAsMail:
                 # this is a bit cheesey...
                 code   = open(source).read()
                 user   = mailconfig.myaddress
                 hdrmap = {'From': appname, 'To': user, 'Subject': mod.__name__}
                 ViewWindow(showtext=code,
                            headermap=hdrmap,
                            origmessage=email.Message.Message())
             else:
```

Example 15-3. PP3E\Internet\Email\PyMailGui\ListWindows.py (continued)

```
                    # more useful text editor
                    wintitle = ' - ' + mod.__name__
                    textEditor.TextEditorMainPopup(self, source, wintitle)

    def onLoadServer(self, forceReload=False):
        """
        threaded: load or reload mail headers list on request
        Exit,Fail,Progress run by threadChecker after callback via queue
        may overlap with sends, disables all but send
        could overlap with loadingmsgs, but may change msg cache list
        forceReload on delete/synch fail, else loads recent arrivals only;
        2.1: cache.loadHeaders may do quick check to see if msgnums
        in synch with server, if we are loading just newly arrived hdrs;
        """
        if loadingHdrsBusy or deletingBusy or loadingMsgsBusy:
            showerror(appname, 'Cannot load headers during load or delete')
        else:
            loadingHdrsBusy.incr()
            self.cache.setPopPassword(appname) # don't update GUI in the thread!
            popup = popuputil.BusyBoxNowait(appname, 'Loading message headers')
            threadtools.startThread(
                action      = self.cache.loadHeaders,
                args        = (forceReload,),
                context     = (popup,),
                onExit      = self.onLoadHdrsExit,
                onFail      = self.onLoadHdrsFail,
                onProgress  = self.onLoadHdrsProgress)

    def onLoadHdrsExit(self, popup):
        self.fillIndex()
        popup.quit()
        self.lift()
        loadingHdrsBusy.decr()

    def onLoadHdrsFail(self, exc_info, popup):
        popup.quit()
        showerror(appname, 'Load failed: \n%s\n\n%s' % exc_info[:2])
        printStack(exc_info)                       # send stack trace to stdout
        loadingHdrsBusy.decr()
        if exc_info[0] == mailtools.MessageSynchError:    # synch inbox/index
            self.onLoadServer(forceReload=True)            # new thread: reload
        else:
            self.cache.popPassword = None          # force re-input next time

    def onLoadHdrsProgress(self, i, n, popup):
        popup.changeText('%d of %d' % (i, n))

    def doDelete(self, msgnumlist):
        """
        threaded: delete from server now - changes msg nums;
        may overlap with sends only, disables all except sends;
        2.1: cache.deleteMessages now checks TOP result to see
```

Example 15-3. PP3E\Internet\Email\PyMailGui\ListWindows.py (continued)

```
        if headers match selected mails, in case msgnums out of
        synch with mail server: poss if mail deleted by other client,
        or server deletes inbox mail automatically - some ISPs may
        move a mail from inbox to undeliverable on load failure;
        """
        if loadingHdrsBusy or deletingBusy or loadingMsgsBusy:
            showerror(appname, 'Cannot delete during load or delete')
        else:
            deletingBusy.incr()
            popup = popuputil.BusyBoxNowait(appname, 'Deleting selected mails')
            threadtools.startThread(
                action    = self.cache.deleteMessages,
                args      = (msgnumlist,),
                context   = (popup,),
                onExit    = self.onDeleteExit,
                onFail    = self.onDeleteFail,
                onProgress = self.onDeleteProgress)

    def onDeleteExit(self, popup):
        self.fillIndex()                    # no need to reload from server
        popup.quit()                        # refill index with updated cache
        self.lift()                         # raise index window, release lock
        deletingBusy.decr()

    def onDeleteFail(self, exc_info, popup):
        popup.quit()
        showerror(appname, 'Delete failed: \n%s\n%s' % exc_info[:2])
        printStack(exc_info)
        deletingBusy.decr()                     # delete or synch check failure
        self.onLoadServer(forceReload=True)  # new thread: some msgnums changed

    def onDeleteProgress(self, i, n, popup):
        popup.changeText('%d of %d' % (i, n))

    def getMessages(self, msgnums, after):
        """
        threaded: prefetch all selected messages into cache now
        used by save, view, reply, and forward to prefill cache
        may overlap with other loadmsgs and sends, disables delete
        only runs "after" action if the fetch allowed and successful;
        2.1: cache.getMessages tests if index in synch with server,
        but we only test if we have to go to server, not if cached;
        """
        if loadingHdrsBusy or deletingBusy:
            showerror(appname, 'Cannot fetch message during load or delete')
        else:
            toLoad = [num for num in msgnums if not self.cache.isLoaded(num)]
            if not toLoad:
                after()          # all already loaded
                return           # process now, no wait pop up
            else:
                loadingMsgsBusy.incr()
```

Example 15-3. PP3E\Internet\Email\PyMailGui\ListWindows.py (continued)

```
                    from popuputil import BusyBoxNowait
                    popup = BusyBoxNowait(appname, 'Fetching message contents')
                    threadtools.startThread(
                        action    = self.cache.getMessages,
                        args      = (toLoad,),
                        context   = (after, popup),
                        onExit    = self.onLoadMsgsExit,
                        onFail    = self.onLoadMsgsFail,
                        onProgress = self.onLoadMsgsProgress)

    def onLoadMsgsExit(self, after, popup):
        popup.quit()
        after()
        loadingMsgsBusy.decr()     # allow others after afterExit done

    def onLoadMsgsFail(self, exc_info, after, popup):
        popup.quit()
        showerror(appname, 'Fetch failed: \n%s\n%s' % exc_info[:2])
        printStack(exc_info)
        loadingMsgsBusy.decr()
        if exc_info[0] == mailtools.MessageSynchError:   # synch inbox/index
            self.onLoadServer(forceReload=True)          # new thread: reload

    def onLoadMsgsProgress(self, i, n, after, popup):
        popup.changeText('%d of %d' % (i, n))

    def getMessage(self, msgnum):
        return self.cache.getMessage(msgnum)             # full mail text

    def headersMaps(self):
        return map(self.parseHeaders, self.cache.allHdrs()) # email.Message objs

    def mailSize(self, msgnum):
        return self.cache.getSize(msgnum)

    def okayToQuit(self):
        # any threads still running?
        filesbusy = [win for win in openSaveFiles.values() if win.openFileBusy]
        busy = loadingHdrsBusy or deletingBusy or sendingBusy or loadingMsgsBusy
        busy = busy or filesbusy
        return not busy
```

ViewWindows: Message View Windows

Example 15-4 lists the implementation of mail view and edit windows. These windows are created in response to actions in list windows—View, Write, Reply, and Forward buttons. See the callbacks for these actions in the list window module of Example 15-3 for view window initiation calls.

As in the prior module (Example 15-3), this file is really one common class and a handful of customizations. The mail view window is nearly identical to the mail edit window, used for Write, Reply, and Forward requests. Consequently, this example defines the common appearance and behavior in the view window superclass, and extends it by subclassing for edit windows.

Replies and forwards are hardly different from the write window here, because their details (e.g., From: and To: addresses, and quoted message text) are worked out in the list window implementation before an edit window is created.

Example 15-4. PP3E\Internet\Email\PyMailGui\ViewWindows.py

```
###############################################################################
# Implementation of View, Write, Reply, Forward windows: one class per kind.
# Code is factored here for reuse: a Write window is a customized View window,
# and Reply and Forward are custom Write windows.  Windows defined in this
# file are created by the list windows, in response to user actions.  Caveat:
# the 'split' pop ups for opening parts/attachments feel a bit nonintuitive.
# 2.1: this caveat was addressed, by adding quick-access attachment buttons.
# TBD: could avoid verifying quits unless text area modified (like PyEdit2.0),
# but these windows are larger, and would not catch headers already changed.
# TBD: should Open dialog in write windows be program-wide? (per-window now).
###############################################################################

from SharedNames import *      # program-wide global objects


###############################################################################
# message view window - also a superclass of write, reply, forward
###############################################################################


class ViewWindow(windows.PopupWindow, mailtools.MailParser):
    """
    a custom Toplevel, with embedded TextEditor
    inherits saveParts,partsList from mailtools.MailParser
    """
    # class attributes
    modelabel      = 'View'                    # used in window titles
    from mailconfig import okayToOpenParts     # open any attachments at all?
    from mailconfig import verifyPartOpens     # ask before open each part?
    from mailconfig import maxPartButtons      # show up to this many + '...'
    tempPartDir    = 'TempParts'               # where 1 selected part saved

    # all view windows use same dialog: remembers last dir
    partsDialog = Directory(title=appname + ': Select parts save directory')

    def __init__(self, headermap, showtext, origmessage=None):
        """
        header map is origmessage, or custom hdr dict for writing;
        showtext is main text part of the message: parsed or custom;
        origmessage is parsed email.Message for view mail windows
        """
        windows.PopupWindow.__init__(self, appname, self.modelabel)
        self.origMessage = origmessage
```

Example 15-4. PP3E\Internet\Email\PyMailGui\ViewWindows.py (continued)

```
        self.makeWidgets(headermap, showtext)

    def makeWidgets(self, headermap, showtext):
        """
        add headers, actions, attachments, text editor
        """
        actionsframe = self.makeHeaders(headermap)
        if self.origMessage and self.okayToOpenParts:
            self.makePartButtons()
        self.editor  = textEditor.TextEditorComponentMinimal(self)
        myactions    = self.actionButtons()
        for (label, callback) in myactions:
            b = Button(actionsframe, text=label, command=callback)
            b.config(bg='beige', relief=RIDGE, bd=2)
            b.pack(side=TOP, expand=YES, fill=BOTH)

        # body text, pack last=clip first
        self.editor.pack(side=BOTTOM)               # may be multiple editors
        self.editor.setAllText(showtext)            # each has own content
        lines = len(showtext.splitlines())
        lines = min(lines + 3, mailconfig.viewheight or 20)
        self.editor.setHeight(lines)                # else height=24, width=80
        self.editor.setWidth(80)                    # or from PyEdit textConfig
        if mailconfig.viewbg:
            self.editor.setBg(mailconfig.viewbg)    # colors, font in mailconfig
        if mailconfig.viewfg:
            self.editor.setFg(mailconfig.viewfg)
        if mailconfig.viewfont:                     # also via editor Tools menu
            self.editor.setFont(mailconfig.viewfont)

    def makeHeaders(self, headermap):
        """
        add header entry fields, return action buttons frame
        """
        top    = Frame(self); top.pack    (side=TOP,   fill=X)
        left   = Frame(top);  left.pack   (side=LEFT,  expand=NO,  fill=BOTH)
        middle = Frame(top);  middle.pack (side=LEFT,  expand=NO,  fill=NONE)
        right  = Frame(top);  right.pack  (side=RIGHT, expand=YES, fill=BOTH)

        # headers set may be extended in mailconfig (Bcc)
        self.userHdrs = ()
        showhdrs = ('From', 'To', 'Cc', 'Subject')
        if hasattr(mailconfig, 'viewheaders') and mailconfig.viewheaders:
            self.userHdrs = mailconfig.viewheaders
            showhdrs += self.userHdrs

        self.hdrFields = []
        for header in showhdrs:
            lab = Label(middle, text=header+':', justify=LEFT)
            ent = Entry(right)
            lab.pack(side=TOP, expand=YES, fill=X)
            ent.pack(side=TOP, expand=YES, fill=X)
```

Example 15-4. PP3E\Internet\Email\PyMailGui\ViewWindows.py (continued)

```
            ent.insert('0', headermap.get(header, '?'))
            self.hdrFields.append(ent)              # order matters in onSend
        return left

    def actionButtons(self):                        # must be method for self
        return [('Cancel', self.destroy),           # close view window silently
                ('Parts',  self.onParts),           # multiparts list or the body
                ('Split',  self.onSplit)]

    def makePartButtons(self):
        """
        add up to N buttons that open attachments/parts
        when clicked; alternative to Parts/Split (2.1);
        okay that temp dir is shared by all open messages:
        part file not saved till later selected and opened;
        partname=partname is required in lambda in Py2.4;
        caveat: we could try to skip the main text part;
        """
        def makeButton(parent, text, callback):
            link = Button(parent, text=text, command=callback, relief=SUNKEN)
            if mailconfig.partfg: link.config(fg=mailconfig.partfg)
            if mailconfig.partbg: link.config(bg=mailconfig.partbg)
            link.pack(side=LEFT, fill=X, expand=YES)

        parts = Frame(self)
        parts.pack(side=TOP, expand=NO, fill=X)
        for (count, partname) in enumerate(self.partsList(self.origMessage)):
            if count == self.maxPartButtons:
                makeButton(parts, '...', self.onSplit)
                break
            openpart = (lambda partname=partname: self.onOnePart(partname))
            makeButton(parts, partname, openpart)

    def onOnePart(self, partname):
        """
        locate selected part for button and save and open
        okay if multiple mails open: resaves each time selected
        we could probably just use web browser directly here
        caveat: tempPartDir is relative to cwd - poss anywhere
        caveat: tempPartDir is never cleaned up: might be large,
        could use tempfile module like HTML main text part code;
        """
        try:
            savedir  = self.tempPartDir
            message  = self.origMessage
            (contype, savepath) = self.saveOnePart(savedir, partname, message)
        except:
            showerror(appname, 'Error while writing part file')
            printStack(sys.exc_info())
        else:
            self.openParts([(contype, os.path.abspath(savepath))])
```

Example 15-4. PP3E\Internet\Email\PyMailGui\ViewWindows.py (continued)

```
    def onParts(self):
        """
        show message part/attachments in pop-up window;
        uses same file naming scheme as save on Split;
        if non-multipart, single part = full body text
        """
        partnames = self.partsList(self.origMessage)
        msg = '\n'.join(['Message parts:\n'] + partnames)
        showinfo(appname, msg)

    def onSplit(self):
        """
        pop up save dir dialog and save all parts/attachments there;
        if desired, pop up HTML and multimedia parts in web browser,
        text in TextEditor, and well-known doc types on windows;
        could show parts in View windows where embedded text editor
        would provide a save button, but most are not readable text;
        """
        savedir = self.partsDialog.show()          # class attr: at prior dir
        if savedir:                                # tk dir chooser, not file
            try:
                partfiles = self.saveParts(savedir, self.origMessage)
            except:
                showerror(appname, 'Error while writing part files')
                printStack(sys.exc_info())
            else:
                if self.okayToOpenParts: self.openParts(partfiles)

    def askOpen(self, appname, prompt):
        if not self.verifyPartOpens:
            return True
        else:
            return askyesno(appname, prompt)   # pop-up dialog

    def openParts(self, partfiles):
        """
        auto-open well known and safe file types, but
        only if verified by the user in a pop up; other
        types must be opened manually from save dir;
        caveat: punts for type application/octet-stream
        even if safe filename extension such as .html;
        caveat: image/audio/video could use playfile.py;
        """
        for (contype, fullfilename) in partfiles:
            maintype  = contype.split('/')[0]                    # left side
            extension = os.path.splitext(fullfilename)[1]        # or [-4:]
            basename  = os.path.basename(fullfilename)           # strip dir

            # HTML and XML text, web pages, some media
            if contype  in ['text/html', 'text/xml']:
                if self.askOpen(appname, 'Open "%s" in browser?' % basename):
                    try:
```

Example 15-4. PP3E\Internet\Email\PyMailGui\ViewWindows.py (continued)

```
                        webbrowser.open_new('file://' + fullfilename)
                except:
                        showerror(appname, 'Browser failed: using editor')
                        textEditor.TextEditorMainPopup(self, fullfilename)

            # text/plain, text/x-python, etc.
            elif maintype == 'text':
                if self.askOpen(appname, 'Open text part "%s"?' % basename):
                    textEditor.TextEditorMainPopup(self, fullfilename)

            # multimedia types: Windows opens mediaplayer, imageviewer, etc.
            elif maintype in ['image', 'audio', 'video']:
                if self.askOpen(appname, 'Open media part "%s"?' % basename):
                    try:
                        webbrowser.open_new('file://' + fullfilename)
                    except:
                        showerror(appname, 'Error opening browser')

            # common Windows documents: Word, Adobe, Excel, archives, etc.
            elif (sys.platform[:3] == 'win' and
                  maintype == 'application' and
                  extension in ['.doc', '.pdf', '.xls', '.zip','.tar', '.wmv']):
                    if self.askOpen(appname, 'Open part "%s"?' % basename):
                        os.startfile(fullfilename)

            else:  # punt!
                msg = 'Cannot open part: "%s"\nOpen manually in: "%s"'
                msg = msg % (basename, os.path.dirname(fullfilename))
                showinfo(appname, msg)


###############################################################################
# message edit windows - write, reply, forward
###############################################################################


if mailconfig.smtpuser:                             # user set in mailconfig?
    MailSenderClass = mailtools.MailSenderAuth      # login/password required
else:
    MailSenderClass = mailtools.MailSender


class WriteWindow(ViewWindow, MailSenderClass):
    """
    customize view display for composing new mail
    inherits sendMessage from mailtools.MailSender
    """

    modelabel = 'Write'

    def __init__(self, headermap, starttext):
        ViewWindow.__init__(self, headermap, starttext)
        MailSenderClass.__init__(self)
```

Example 15-4. PP3E\Internet\Email\PyMailGui\ViewWindows.py (continued)

```
        self.attaches   = []                    # each win has own open dialog
        self.openDialog = None                  # dialog remembers last dir

    def actionButtons(self):
        return [('Cancel', self.quit),          # need method to use self
                ('Parts',  self.onParts),       # PopupWindow verifies cancel
                ('Attach', self.onAttach),
                ('Send  ', self.onSend)]

    def onParts(self):
        # caveat: deletes not currently supported
        if not self.attaches:
            showinfo(appname, 'Nothing attached')
        else:
            msg = '\n'.join(['Already attached:\n'] + self.attaches)
            showinfo(appname, msg)

    def onAttach(self):
        """
        attach a file to the mail: name added
        here will be added as a part on Send;
        """
        if not self.openDialog:
            self.openDialog = Open(title=appname + ': Select Attachment File')
        filename = self.openDialog.show()       # remember prior dir
        if filename:
            self.attaches.append(filename)      # to be opened in send method

    def onSend(self):
        """
        threaded: mail edit window send button press
        may overlap with any other thread, disables none but quit
        Exit,Fail run by threadChecker via queue in after callback
        caveat: no progress here, because send mail call is atomic
        assumes multiple recipient addrs are separated with ';'

        caveat: should parse To,Cc,Bcc instead of splitting on ';',
        or use a multiline input widgets instead of simple entry;
        as is, reply logic and GUI user must avoid embedded ';'
        characters in addresses - very unlikely but not impossible;
        mailtools module saves sent message text in a local file
        """
        fieldvalues = [entry.get() for entry in self.hdrFields]
        From, To, Cc, Subj = fieldvalues[:4]
        extraHdrs  = [('Cc', Cc), ('X-Mailer', appname + ' (Python)')]
        extraHdrs += zip(self.userHdrs, fieldvalues[4:])
        bodytext = self.editor.getAllText()

        # split multiple recipient lists, fix empty fields
        Tos = To.split(';')                                    # split to list
        Tos = [addr.strip() for addr in Tos]                   # spaces around
        for (ix, (name, value)) in enumerate(extraHdrs):
```

Example 15-4. PP3E\Internet\Email\PyMailGui\ViewWindows.py (continued)

```
            if value:                                        # ignored if ''
                if value == '?':                             # ? not replaced
                    extraHdrs[ix] = (name, '')
                elif name.lower() in ['cc', 'bcc']:
                    values = value.split(';')
                    extraHdrs[ix] = (name, [addr.strip() for addr in values])

        # withdraw to disallow send during send
        # caveat: withdraw not foolproof- user may deiconify
        self.withdraw()
        self.getPassword()          # if needed; don't run pop up in send thread!
        popup = popuputil.BusyBoxNowait(appname, 'Sending message')
        sendingBusy.incr()
        threadtools.startThread(
            action  = self.sendMessage,
            args    = (From, Tos, Subj, extraHdrs, bodytext, self.attaches,
                                                    saveMailSeparator),
            context = (popup,),
            onExit  = self.onSendExit,
            onFail  = self.onSendFail)

    def onSendExit(self, popup):
        # erase wait window, erase view window, decr send count
        # sendMessage call auto saves sent message in local file
        # can't use window.addSavedMails: mail text unavailable
        popup.quit()
        self.destroy()
        sendingBusy.decr()

        # poss \ when opened, / in mailconfig
        sentname = os.path.abspath(mailconfig.sentmailfile)  # also expands '.'
        if sentname in openSaveFiles.keys():                 # sent file open?
            window = openSaveFiles[sentname]                 # update list,raise
            window.loadMailFileThread()

    def onSendFail(self, exc_info, popup):
        # pop-up error, keep msg window to save or retry, redraw actions frame
        popup.quit()
        self.deiconify()
        self.lift()
        showerror(appname, 'Send failed: \n%s\n%s' % exc_info[:2])
        printStack(exc_info)
        self.smtpPassword = None         # try again
        sendingBusy.decr()

    def askSmtpPassword(self):
        """
        get password if needed from GUI here, in main thread
        caveat: may try this again in thread if no input first
        time, so goes into a loop until input is provided; see
        pop paswd input logic for a nonlooping alternative
        """
```

Example 15-4. PP3E\Internet\Email\PyMailGui\ViewWindows.py (continued)

```
        password = ''
        while not password:
            prompt = ('Password for %s on %s?' %
                        (self.smtpUser, self.smtpServerName))
            password = popuputil.askPasswordWindow(appname, prompt)
        return password


class ReplyWindow(WriteWindow):
    """
    customize write display for replying
    text and headers set up by list window
    """
    modelabel = 'Reply'


class ForwardWindow(WriteWindow):
    """
    customize reply display for forwarding
    text and headers set up by list window
    """
    modelabel = 'Forward'
```

messagecache: Message Cache Manager

The class in Example 15-5 implements a cache for already loaded messages. Its logic
is split off into this file in order to avoid complicating list window implementations.
The server list window creates and embeds an instance of this class to interface with
the mail server, and to keep track of already loaded mail headers and full text.

Example 15-5. PP3E\Internet\Email\PyMailGui\messagecache.py

```
###############################################################################
# manage message and header loads and context, but not GUI
# a MailFetcher, with a list of already loaded headers and messages
# the caller must handle any required threading or GUI interfaces
###############################################################################

from PP3E.Internet.Email import mailtools
from popuputil import askPasswordWindow


class MessageInfo:
    """
    an item in the mail cache list
    """
    def __init__(self, hdrtext, size):
        self.hdrtext  = hdrtext        # fulltext is cached msg
        self.fullsize = size           # hdrtext is just the hdrs
        self.fulltext = None           # fulltext=hdrtext if no TOP
```

Example 15-5. PP3E\Internet\Email\PyMailGui\messagecache.py (continued)

```
class MessageCache(mailtools.MailFetcher):
    """
    keep track of already loaded headers and messages
    inherits server transfer methods from MailFetcher
    useful in other apps: no GUI or thread assumptions
    """
    def __init__(self):
        mailtools.MailFetcher.__init__(self)
        self.msglist = []

    def loadHeaders(self, forceReloads, progress=None):
        """
        three cases to handle here: the initial full load,
        load newly arrived, and forced reload after delete;
        don't refetch viewed msgs if hdrs list same or extended;
        retains cached msgs after a delete unless delete fails;
        2.1: does quick check to see if msgnums still in sync
        """
        if forceReloads:
            loadfrom = 1
            self.msglist = []                       # msg nums have changed
        else:
            loadfrom = len(self.msglist)+1          # continue from last load

        # only if loading newly arrived
        if loadfrom != 1:
            self.checkSynchError(self.allHdrs())    # raises except if bad

        # get all or newly arrived msgs
        reply = self.downloadAllHeaders(progress, loadfrom)
        headersList, msgSizes, loadedFull = reply

        for (hdrs, size) in zip(headersList, msgSizes):
            newmsg = MessageInfo(hdrs, size)
            if loadedFull:                          # zip result may be empty
                newmsg.fulltext = hdrs               # got full msg if no 'top'
            self.msglist.append(newmsg)

    def getMessage(self, msgnum):                   # get raw msg text
        if not self.msglist[msgnum-1].fulltext:     # add to cache if fetched
            fulltext = self.downloadMessage(msgnum)  # harmless if threaded
            self.msglist[msgnum-1].fulltext = fulltext
        return self.msglist[msgnum-1].fulltext

    def getMessages(self, msgnums, progress=None):
        """
        prefetch full raw text of multiple messages, in thread;
        2.1: does quick check to see if msgnums still in sync;
        we can't get here unless the index list already loaded;
        """
        self.checkSynchError(self.allHdrs())        # raises except if bad
```

Example 15-5. PP3E\Internet\Email\PyMailGui\messagecache.py (continued)

```
            nummsgs = len(msgnums)                        # adds messages to cache
            for (ix, msgnum) in enumerate(msgnums):       # some poss already there
                if progress: progress(ix+1, nummsgs)      # only connects if needed
                self.getMessage(msgnum)                    # but may connect > once

    def getSize(self, msgnum):                            # encapsulate cache struct
        return self.msglist[msgnum-1].fullsize           # it changed once already!

    def isLoaded(self, msgnum):
        return self.msglist[msgnum-1].fulltext

    def allHdrs(self):
        return [msg.hdrtext for msg in self.msglist]

    def deleteMessages(self, msgnums, progress=None):
        """
        if delete of all msgnums works, remove deleted entries
        from mail cache, but don't reload either the headers list
        or already viewed mails text: cache list will reflect the
        changed msg nums on server;  if delete fails for any reason,
        caller should forceably reload all hdrs next, because _some_
        server msg nums may have changed, in unpredictable ways;
        2.1: this now checks msg hdrs to detect out of synch msg
        numbers, if TOP supported by mail server; runs in thread
        """
        try:
            self.deleteMessagesSafely(msgnums, self.allHdrs(), progress)
        except mailtools.TopNotSupported:
            mailtools.MailFetcher.deleteMessages(self, msgnums, progress)

        # no errors: update index list
        indexed = enumerate(self.msglist)
        self.msglist = [msg for (ix, msg) in indexed if ix+1 not in msgnums]


class GuiMessageCache(MessageCache):
    """
    add any GUI-specific calls here so cache usable in non-GUI apps
    """

    def setPopPassword(self, appname):
        """
        get password from GUI here, in main thread
        forceably called from GUI to avoid pop ups in threads
        """
        if not self.popPassword:
            prompt = 'Password for %s on %s?' % (self.popUser, self.popServer)
            self.popPassword = askPasswordWindow(appname, prompt)

    def askPopPassword(self):
        """
        but don't use GUI pop up here: I am run in a thread!
```

Example 15-5. PP3E\Internet\Email\PyMailGui\messagecache.py (continued)

```
        when tried pop up in thread, caused GUI to hang;
        may be called by MailFetcher superclass, but only
        if passwd is still empty string due to dialog close
        """
        return self.popPassword
```

popuputil: General-Purpose GUI Pop Ups

Example 15-6 implements a handful of utility pop-up windows in a module, in case
they ever prove useful in other programs. Note that the same windows utility module is imported here, to give a common look-and-feel to the popups (icons, titles, and
so on).

Example 15-6. PP3E\Internet\Email\PyMailGui\popuputil.py

```
###########################################################################
# utility windows - may be useful in other programs
###########################################################################

from Tkinter import *
from PP3E.Gui.Tools.windows import PopupWindow


class HelpPopup(PopupWindow):
    """
    custom Toplevel that shows help text as scrolled text
    source button runs a passed-in callback handler
    alternative: use HTML file and webbrowser module
    """
    myfont = 'system'   # customizable

    def __init__(self, appname, helptext, iconfile=None, showsource=lambda:0):
        PopupWindow.__init__(self, appname, 'Help', iconfile)
        from ScrolledText import ScrolledText      # a nonmodal dialog
        bar  = Frame(self)                          # pack first=clip last
        bar.pack(side=BOTTOM, fill=X)
        code = Button(bar, bg='beige', text="Source", command=showsource)
        quit = Button(bar, bg='beige', text="Cancel", command=self.destroy)
        code.pack(pady=1, side=LEFT)
        quit.pack(pady=1, side=LEFT)
        text = ScrolledText(self)                   # add Text + scrollbar
        text.config(font=self.myfont,  width=70)    # too big for showinfo
        text.config(bg='steelblue', fg='white')     # erase on btn or return
        text.insert('0.0', helptext)
        text.pack(expand=YES, fill=BOTH)
        self.bind("<Return>", (lambda event: self.destroy()))


def askPasswordWindow(appname, prompt):
    """
    modal dialog to input password string
```

Example 15-6. PP3E\Internet\Email\PyMailGui\popuputil.py (continued)

```
        getpass.getpass uses stdin, not GUI
        tkSimpleDialog.askstring echos input
        """
        win = PopupWindow(appname, 'Prompt')              # a configured Toplevel
        Label(win, text=prompt).pack(side=LEFT)
        entvar = StringVar(win)
        ent = Entry(win, textvariable=entvar, show='*')   # display * for input
        ent.pack(side=RIGHT, expand=YES, fill=X)
        ent.bind('<Return>', lambda event: win.destroy())
        ent.focus_set(); win.grab_set(); win.wait_window()
        win.update()                                       # update forces redraw
        return entvar.get()                                # ent widget is now gone


class BusyBoxWait(PopupWindow):
    """
    pop up blocking wait message box: thread waits
    main GUI event thread stays alive during wait
    but GUI is inoperable during this wait state;
    uses quit redef here because lower, not leftmost;
    """
    def __init__(self, appname, message):
        PopupWindow.__init__(self, appname, 'Busy')
        self.protocol('WM_DELETE_WINDOW', lambda:0)        # ignore deletes
        label = Label(self, text=message + '...')          # win.quit() to erase
        label.config(height=10, width=40, cursor='watch')  # busy cursor
        label.pack()
        self.makeModal()
        self.message, self.label = message, label
    def makeModal(self):
        self.focus_set()                                   # grab application
        self.grab_set()                                    # wait for threadexit
    def changeText(self, newtext):
        self.label.config(text=self.message + ': ' + newtext)
    def quit(self):
        self.destroy()                                     # don't verify quit


class BusyBoxNowait(BusyBoxWait):
    """
    pop up nonblocking wait window
    call changeText to show progress, quit to close
    """
    def makeModal(self):
        pass


if __name__ == '__main__':
    HelpPopup('spam', 'See figure 1...\n')
    print askPasswordWindow('spam', 'enter password')
    raw_input('Enter to exit')
```

wraplines: Line Split Tools

The module in Example 15-7 implements general tools for wrapping long lines, at either a fixed column or the first delimiter at or before a fixed column. PyMailGUI uses this file's `wrapText1` function for text in view, reply, and forward windows, but this code is potentially useful in other programs. Run the file as a script to watch its self-test code at work, and study its functions to see its text-processing logic.

Example 15-7. PP3E\Internet\Email\PyMailGui\wraplines.py

```
###########################################################################
# split lines on fixed columns or at delimiters before a column
# see also: related but different textwrap standard library module (2.3+)
###########################################################################

defaultsize = 80

def wrapLinesSimple(lineslist, size=defaultsize):
    "split at fixed position size"
    wraplines = []
    for line in lineslist:
        while True:
            wraplines.append(line[:size])         # OK if len < size
            line = line[size:]                    # split without analysis
            if not line: break
    return wraplines

def wrapLinesSmart(lineslist, size=defaultsize, delimiters='.,:\t '):
    "wrap at first delimiter left of size"
    wraplines = []
    for line in lineslist:
        while True:
            if len(line) <= size:
                wraplines += [line]
                break
            else:
                for look in range(size-1, size/2, -1):
                    if line[look] in delimiters:
                        front, line = line[:look+1], line[look+1:]
                        break
                else:
                    front, line = line[:size], line[size:]
                wraplines += [front]
    return wraplines


###########################################################################
# common use case utilities
###########################################################################

def wrapText1(text, size=defaultsize):           # better for line-based txt: mail
    "when text read all at once"                 # keeps original line brks struct
    lines = text.split('\n')                      # split on newlines
```

Example 15-7. PP3E\Internet\Email\PyMailGui\wraplines.py (continued)

```
    lines = wrapLinesSmart(lines, size)    # wrap lines on delimiters
    return '\n'.join(lines)                # put back together

def wrapText2(text, size=defaultsize):     # more uniform across lines
    "same, but treat as one long line"     # but loses original line struct
    text  = text.replace('\n', ' ')        # drop newlines if any
    lines = wrapLinesSmart([text], size)   # wrap single line on delimiters
    return lines                           # caller puts back together

def wrapText3(text, size=defaultsize):
    "same, but put back together"
    lines = wrapText2(text, size)          # wrap as single long line
    return '\n'.join(lines) + '\n'         # make one string with newlines

def wrapLines1(lines, size=defaultsize):
    "when newline included at end"
    lines = [line[:-1] for line in lines]  # strip off newlines (or .rstrip)
    lines = wrapLinesSmart(lines, size)    # wrap on delimiters
    return [(line + '\n') for line in lines]  # put them back

def wrapLines2(lines, size=defaultsize):   # more uniform across lines
    "same, but concat as one long line"    # but loses original structure
    text  = ''.join(lines)                 # put together as 1 line
    lines = wrapText2(text)                # wrap on delimiters
    return [(line + '\n') for line in lines]  # put newlines on ends


###############################################################################
# self-test
###############################################################################

if __name__ == '__main__':
    lines = ['spam ham ' * 20 + 'spam,ni' * 20,
             'spam ham ' * 20,
             'spam,ni'   * 20,
             'spam ham.ni' * 20,
             '',
             'spam'*80,
             ' ',
             'spam ham eggs']
    print 'all', '-'*30
    for line in lines: print repr(line)
    print 'simple', '-'*30
    for line in wrapLinesSimple(lines): print repr(line)
    print 'smart', '-'*30
    for line in wrapLinesSmart(lines): print repr(line)

    print 'single1', '-'*30
    for line in wrapLinesSimple([lines[0]], 60): print repr(line)
    print 'single2', '-'*30
    for line in wrapLinesSmart([lines[0]], 60): print repr(line)
    print 'combined text', '-'*30
    for line in wrapLines2(lines): print repr(line)
```

Example 15-7. PP3E\Internet\Email\PyMailGui\wraplines.py (continued)

```
print 'combined lines', '-'*30
print wrapText1('\n'.join(lines))

assert ''.join(lines) == ''.join(wrapLinesSimple(lines, 60))
assert ''.join(lines) == ''.join(wrapLinesSmart(lines, 60))
print len(''.join(lines)),
print len(''.join(wrapLinesSimple(lines))),
print len(''.join(wrapLinesSmart(lines))),
print len(''.join(wrapLinesSmart(lines, 60))),
raw_input('Press enter')
```

mailconfig: User Configurations

In Example 15-8, PyMailGUI's `mailconfig` user settings module is listed. This program has its own version of this module because many of its settings are unique for PyMailGUI. To use the program for reading your own email, set its initial variables to reflect your POP and SMTP server names and login parameters. The variables in this module also allow the user to tailor the appearance and operation of the program without finding and editing actual program logic.

Example 15-8. PP3E\Internet\Email\PyMailGui\mailconfig.py

```
##############################################################################
# PyMailGUI user configuration settings.
# Email scripts get their server names and other email config options from
# this module: change me to reflect your machine names, sig, and preferences.
# Warning: PyMailGUI won't run without most variables here: make a backup copy!
# Notes: could get some settings from the command line too, and a configure
# dialog would be better, but this common module file suffices for now.
##############################################################################


#-----------------------------------------------------------------------------
# (required for load, delete) POP3 email server machine, user
#-----------------------------------------------------------------------------

# popservername = '?Please set your mailconfig.py attributes?'

#popservername = 'pop.rmi.net'          # or starship.python.net, 'localhost'
#popusername   = 'lutz'                 # password fetched or asked when run

#popservername = 'pop.mindspring.com'   # yes, I have a few email accounts
#popusername   = 'lutz4'

#popservername = 'pop.yahoo.com'
#popusername   = 'for_personal_mail'

popservername = 'pop.earthlink.net'     # pp3e@earthlink.net
popusername   = 'pp3e'
```

Example 15-8. PP3E\Internet\Email\PyMailGui\mailconfig.py (continued)

```
#-------------------------------------------------------------------------------
# (required for send) SMTP email server machine name
# see Python smtpd module for a SMTP server class to run locally;
# note: your ISP may require that you be directly connected to their system:
# I can email through Earthlink on dial up, but cannot via Comcast cable
#-------------------------------------------------------------------------------

smtpservername = 'smtp.comcast.net'     # or 'smtp.mindspring.com', 'localhost'

#-------------------------------------------------------------------------------
# (may be required for send) SMTP user/password if authenticated
# set user to None or '' if no login/authentication is required
# set pswd to name of a file holding your SMTP password, or an
# empty string to force programs to ask (in a console, or GUI)
#-------------------------------------------------------------------------------

smtpuser  = None                        # per your ISP
smtppasswdfile = ''                     # set to '' to be asked

#-------------------------------------------------------------------------------
# (optional) PyMailGUI: name of local one-line text file with your POP
# password; if empty or file cannot be read, pswd is requested when first
# connecting; pswd not encrypted: leave this empty on shared machines;
# PyMailCGI always asks for pswd (runs on a possibly remote server);
#-------------------------------------------------------------------------------

poppasswdfile = r'c:\temp\pymailgui.txt'     # set to '' to be asked

#-------------------------------------------------------------------------------
# (optional) personal information used by PyMailGUI to fill in edit forms;
# if not set, does not fill in initial form values;
# sig  -- can be a triple-quoted block, ignored if empty string;
# addr -- used for initial value of "From" field if not empty,
# no longer tries to guess From for replies--varying success;
#-------------------------------------------------------------------------------

myaddress   = 'pp3e@earthlink.net'                  # lutz@rmi.net
mysignature = '--Mark Lutz  (http://www.rmi.net/~lutz)'

#-------------------------------------------------------------------------------
# (optional) local file where sent messages are saved;
# PyMailGUI 'Open' button allows this file to be opened and viewed
# don't use '.' form if may be run from another dir: e.g., pp3e demos
#-------------------------------------------------------------------------------

#sentmailfile  = r'.\sentmail.txt'                # . means in current working dir

#sourcedir    = r'C:\Mark\PP3E-cd\Examples\PP3E\Internet\Email\PyMailGui\'
#sentmailfile = sourcedir + 'sentmail.txt'

# determine auto from one of my source files
import wraplines, os
mysourcedir  = os.path.dirname(os.path.abspath(wraplines.__file__))
```

Example 15-8. PP3E\Internet\Email\PyMailGui\mailconfig.py (continued)

```
sentmailfile = os.path.join(mysourcedir, 'sentmail.txt')


#-----------------------------------------------------------------------------
# (optional) local file where pymail saves POP mail;
# PyMailGUI instead asks for a name with a pop-up dialog
#-----------------------------------------------------------------------------

savemailfile  = r'c:\temp\savemail.txt'       # not used in PyMailGUI: dialog


#-----------------------------------------------------------------------------
# (optional) customize headers displayed in PyMailGUI list and view windows;
# listheaders replaces default, viewheaders extends it; both must be tuple of
# strings, or None to use default hdrs;
#-----------------------------------------------------------------------------

listheaders = ('Subject', 'From', 'Date', 'To', 'X-Mailer')
viewheaders = ('Bcc',)


#-----------------------------------------------------------------------------
# (optional) PyMailGUI fonts and colors for text server/file message list
# windows, message content view windows, and view window attachment buttons;
# use ('family', size, 'style') for font; 'colorname' or hexstr '#RRGGBB' for
# color (background, foreground);  None means use defaults;  font/color of
# view windows can also be set interactively with texteditor's Tools menu;
#-----------------------------------------------------------------------------

listbg  = 'indianred'          # None, 'white', '#RRGGBB' (see setcolor example)
listfg  = 'black'
listfont = ('courier', 9, 'bold')       # None, ('courier', 12, 'bold italic')
                                        # use fixed-width font for list columns

viewbg   = '#dbbedc'
viewfg   = 'black'
viewfont = ('courier', 10, 'bold')
viewheight = 24                         # max lines for height when opened

partfg  = None
partbg  = None

# see Tk color names: aquamarine paleturqoise powderblue goldenrod burgundy ....

#listbg = listfg = listfont = None
#viewbg = viewfg = viewfont = viewheight = None       # to use defaults
#partbg = partfg = None


#-----------------------------------------------------------------------------
# (optional) column at which mail's original text should be wrapped for view,
# reply, and forward;  wraps at first delimiter to left of this position;
# composed text is not auto-wrapped: user or recipient's mail tool must wrap
# new text if desired; to disable wrapping, set this to a high value (1024?);
#-----------------------------------------------------------------------------

wrapsz = 100
```

Example 15-8. PP3E\Internet\Email\PyMailGui\mailconfig.py (continued)

```
#-----------------------------------------------------------------------------
# (optional) control how PyMailGUI opens mail parts in the GUI;
# for view window Split actions and attachment quick-access buttons;
# if not okayToOpenParts, quick-access part buttons will not appear in
# the GUI, and Split saves parts in a directory but does not open them;
# verifyPartOpens used by both Split action and quick-access buttons:
# all known-type parts open automatically on Split if this set to False;
# verifyHTMLTextOpen used by web browser open of HTML main text part:
#-----------------------------------------------------------------------------

okayToOpenParts     = True      # open any parts/attachments at all?
verifyPartOpens     = False     # ask permission before opening each part?
verifyHTMLTextOpen  = False     # if main text part is HTML, ask before open?


#-----------------------------------------------------------------------------
# (optional) the maximum number of quick-access mail part buttons to show
# in the middle of view windows; after this many, a "..." button will be
# displayed, which runs the "Split" action to extract additional parts;
#-----------------------------------------------------------------------------

maxPartButtons = 8              # how many part buttons in view windows

#end
```

PyMailGuiHelp: User Help Text

Finally, Example 15-9 lists the module that defines the text displayed in PyMailGUI's help popup as one triple-quoted string. Read this here or live within the program to learn more about how PyMailGUI's interface operates (click the help bar at the top of the server list window to open the help display). It is included because it explains some properties of PyMailGUI not introduced by the demo earlier in this chapter.

This text may be more usefully formatted as HTML with section links and popped up in a web browser, but we take a lowest-common–denominator approach here to minimize external dependencies—we don't want help to fail if no browser can be located, and we don't want to maintain both text and HTML versions. Other schemes are possible (e.g., converting HTML to text as a fallback by parsing), but they are left as suggested improvements.

Example 15-9. PP3E\Internet\PyMailGui2\PyMailGuiHelp.py

```
######################################################################
# PyMailGUI help text string, in this separate module only to avoid
# distracting from executable code.  As coded, we throw up this text
# in a simple scrollable text box; in the future, we might instead
# use an HTML file opened with a browser (use webbrowser module, or
# run a "netscape help.html" or DOS "start help.html" with os.system);
# that would add an external dependency, unless text on browser fail;
######################################################################
```

Example 15-9. PP3E\Internet\PyMailGui2\PyMailGuiHelp.py (continued)

```
# used to have to be narrow for Linux info box pop ups;
# now uses scrolledtext with buttons instead;

helptext = """PyMailGUI, version 2.1
January, 2006
Programming Python, 3rd Edition
O'Reilly Media, Inc.

PyMailGUI is a multiwindow interface for processing email, both online and
offline.  Its main interfaces include one list window for the mail server,
zero or more list windows for mail save files, and multiple view windows for
composing or viewing emails selected in a list window.  On startup, the main
(server) list window appears first, but no mail server connection is attempted
until a Load or message send request.  All PyMailGUI windows may be resized,
which is especially useful in list windows to see additional columns.


Major enhancements in this version:

* MIME multipart mails with attachments may be both viewed and composed.
* Mail transfers are no longer blocking, and may overlap in time.
* Mail may be saved and processed offline from a local file.
* Message parts may now be opened automatically within the GUI.
* Multiple messages may be selected for processing in list windows.
* Initial downloads fetch mail headers only; full mails are fetched on request.
* View window headers and list window columns are configurable.
* Deletions are performed immediately, not delayed until program exit.
* Most server transfers report their progress in the GUI.
* Long lines are intelligently wrapped in viewed and quoted text.
* Fonts and colors in list and view windows may be configured by the user.
* Authenticating SMTP mail-send servers that require login are supported.
* Sent messages are saved in a local file, which may be opened in the GUI.
* View windows intelligently pick a main text part to be displayed.
* Already fetched mail headers and full mails are cached for speed.
* Date strings and addresses in composed mails are formatted properly.
* (2.1) View windows now have quick-access buttons for attachments/parts.
* (2.1) Inbox out-of-synch errors detected on deletes, and index and mail loads.
* (2.1) Save-file loads and deletes threaded, to avoid pauses for large files.


Note: To use PyMailGUI to read and write email of your own, you must change
the POP and SMTP server names and login details in the file mailconfig.py,
located in PyMailGUI's source-code directory.  See section 10 for details.

Contents:
1)  LIST WINDOW ACTIONS
2)  VIEW WINDOW ACTIONS
3)  OFFLINE PROCESSING
4)  VIEWING TEXT AND ATTACHMENTS
5)  SENDING TEXT AND ATTACHMENTS
6)  MAIL TRANSFER OVERLAP
7)  MAIL DELETION
```

Example 15-9. PP3E\Internet\PyMailGui2\PyMailGuiHelp.py (continued)

```
8)  INBOX MESSAGE NUMBER SYNCHRONIZATION
9)  LOADING EMAIL
10) THE mailconfig CONFIGURATION MODULE
11) DEPENDENCIES
12) MISCELLANEOUS HINTS



1) LIST WINDOW ACTIONS

Click list window buttons to process email:

- Load:\t fetch all (or new) mail headers from POP server inbox
- View:\t display selected emails nicely formatted
- Delete:\t delete selected emails from server or save file
- Write:\t compose a new email message, send by SMTP
- Reply:\t compose replies to selected emails, send by SMTP
- Fwd:\t compose forwards of selected emails, send by SMTP
- Save:\t write all selected emails to a chosen save file
- Open:\t load emails from an offline save file into new list window
- Quit:\t exit program (server list), close window (file list)

Double-click on an email in a list window's listbox to view the mail's raw text,
including any mail headers not shown by the View button.  List windows opened
for mail save files support all of the above except Load.  After the initial
Load, Load only fetches newly arrived message headers.  To forceably reload all
mails from the server, restart PyMailGUI.  There is reload button, because full
reloads are only required on rare deletion and inbox synchronization errors
(described ahead), and reloads are initiated automatically in these cases.

Click on emails in the main window's listbox to select them.  Click the "All"
checkbox to select all or no emails at once.  More than one email may be
selected at the same time: View, Delete, Reply, Fwd, and Save buttons are
applied to all currently selected emails, in both server and save-file list
windows.  Use Ctrl+click to select multiple mails, Shift+click to select all
from prior selecion, or click+move to drag the selection out.

In 2.1, most of the actions in the server List window automatically run a
quick-check to detect inbox out-of-synch errors with the server.  If a synch
error pop up appears, a full index reload will be automatically run; there
is no need to stop and restart PyMailGUI (see ahead in this help).



2) VIEW WINDOW ACTIONS

Action buttons in message view windows (View):

- Cancel:\t closes the message view window
- Parts:\t lists all message parts, including attachments
- Split:\t extracts, saves, and possibly opens message parts
```

Example 15-9. PP3E\Internet\PyMailGui2\PyMailGuiHelp.py (continued)

Actions in message compose windows (Write, Reply, Fwd):

- Cancel:\t closes the message window, discarding its content
- Parts:\t lists files already attached to mail being edited
- Attach:\t adds a file as an attachment to a mail being edited
- Send:\t sends the message to all its recipients

Parts and Split buttons appear in all View windows; for simple messages, the sole part is the message body. Message reply, forward, and delete requests are made in the list windows, not message view windows. Deletions do not erase open view windows.

New in 2.1: View windows also have up to a fixed maximum number of quick access buttons for attached message parts. They are alternatives to Split. After the maximum number, a '...' button is added, which simply runs Split. The maximum number of part buttons to display per view window can be set in the mailconfig.py user settings module (described ahead).

3) OFFLINE PROCESSING

To process email offline: Load from the server, Save to a local file, and later select Open to open a save file's list window in either the server List window or another save file's List window. Open creates a new List window for the file, or raises its window if the file is already open.

A save file's list window allows all main window actions listed above, except for Load. For example, saved messages can be viewed, deleted, replied to, or forwarded, from the file's list window. Operations are mapped to the local mail save file, instead of the server's inbox.   Saved messages may also be saved: to move mails from one save file to another, Save and then Delete from the source file's window.

You do not need to connect to a server to process save files offline: click the Open button in the main list window. In a save-file list window, a Quit erases that window only; a Delete removes the message from the local save file, not from a server. Save-file list windows are automatically updated when new mails are saved to the corresponding file anywhere in the GUI. The sent-mail file may also be opened and processed as a normal save-mail file, with Open.

Save buttons in list windows save the full message text (including its headers, and a message separator). To save just the main text part of a message, either use the Save button in the TextEditor at the bottom of a view or edit window, or select the "Split" action button. To save attachments, see the next section.

New in 2.1: local save-file Open and Delete requests are threaded to avoid blocking the GUI during loads and deletes of large files. Because of this, a loaded file's index may not appear in its List window immediately. Similarly, when new mails are saved or messages are sent, there may be a delay before the corresponding local file's List window is updated, if it is currently open.

Example 15-9. PP3E\Internet\PyMailGui2\PyMailGuiHelp.py (continued)

As a status indication, the window's title changes to "Loading..." on loads
and "Deleting..." during deletes, and is reset to the file's name after the thread
exits (the server window uses pop ups for status indication, because the delay
is longer, and there is progress to display). Eventually, either the index will
appear and its window raised, or an error message will pop up. Save-file loads
and deletes are not allowed to overlap with each other for a given file, but
may overlap with server transfers and operations on other open files.

Note: save-file Save operations are still not threaded, and may pause the GUI
momentarily when saving very many large mails. This is normaly not noticeable,
because unlike Open and Delete, saves simply append to the save-file, and do
not reload its content. To avoid pauses completely, though, don't save very
many large mails in a single operation.

Also note: the current implementation loads the entire save-mail file into
memory when opened. Because of this, save-mail files are limited in size,
depending upon your computer. To avoid consuming too much memory, you
should try to keep your save files relatively small (at the least, smaller
than your computer's available memory). As a rule of thumb, organize your
saved mails by categories into many small files, instead of a few large files.

4) VIEWING TEXT AND ATTACHMENTS

PyMailGUI's view windows use a text-oriented display. When a mail is viewed,
its main text is displayed in the View window. This text is taken from the
entire body of a simple message, or the first text part of a multipart MIME
message. To extract the main message text, PyMailGUI looks for plain text,
then HTML, and then text of any other kind. If no such text content is found,
nothing is displayed in the view window, but parts may be opened manually with
the "Split" button (and quick-access part buttons in 2.1, described below).

If the body of a simple message is HTML type, or a HTML part is used as the
main message text, a web browser is popped up as an alternative display for
the main message text, if verified by the user (the mailconfig module can be
used to bypass the verification; see ahead). This is equivalent to opening
the HTML part with the "Split" button, but is initiated automatically for the
main message text's HTML. If a simple message is something other than text
or HTML, its content must be openened manually with Split.

When viewing mails, messages with multipart attachments are prefixed with
a "*" in list windows. "Parts" and "Split" buttons appear in all View windows.
Message parts are defined as follows:

- For simple messages, the message body is considered to be the sole
  part of the message.

- For multipart messages, the message parts list includes the main
  message text, as well as all attachments.

In both cases, message parts may be saved and opened with the "Split" button.

Example 15-9. PP3E\Internet\PyMailGui2\PyMailGuiHelp.py (continued)

For simple messages, the message body may be saved with Split, as well as the Save button in the view window's text editor. To process multipart messages:

- Use "Parts" to display the names of all message parts, including any attachments, in a pop-up dialog.

- Use "Split" to view message parts: all mail parts are first saved to a selected directory, and any well-known and generally safe part files are opened automatically, but only if verified by the user.

- See also the note below about 2.1 quick access buttons, for an alternative to the Parts/Split interface on View windows.

For "Split", select a local directory to save parts to. After the save, text parts open in the TextEditor GUI, HTML and multimedia types open in a web browser, and common Windows document types (e.g., .doc and .xls files) open via the Windows registry entry for the filename extension. For safety, unknown types and executable program parts are never run automatically; even Python programs are displayed as source text only (save the code to run manually).

Web browsers on some platforms may open multimedia types (image, audio, video) in specific content handler programs (e.g., MediaPlayer, image viewers). No other types of attachments are ever opened, and attachments are never opened without user verification (or mailconfig.py authorization in 2.1, described below). Browse the parts save directory to open other parts manually.

To avoid scrolling for very long lines (sometimes sent by HTML-based mailers), the main text part of a message is automatically wrapped for easy viewing. Long lines are split up at the first delimiter found before a fixed column, when viewed, replied, or forwarded. The wrapping column may be configured or disabled in the mailconfig module (see ahead). Text lines are never automatically wrapped when sent; users or recipients should manage line length in composed mails.

New in 2.1: View windows also have up to a fixed maximum number of quick-access buttons for attached message parts. They are alternatives to Split: selecting an attachment's button automatically extracts, saves, and opens that single attachment directly, without Split directory and pop-up dialogs (a temporary directory is used). The maximum number of part buttons to display per view window can be set in the mailconfig.py user settings module (described ahead). For mails with more than the maximum number of attachments, a '...' button is added which simply runs Split to save and open any additional attachments.

Also in 2.1, two settings in the mailconfig.py module (see section 10) can be used to control how PyMailGUI opens parts in the GUI:

- okayToOpenParts: controls whether part opens are allowed at all
- verifyPartOpens: controls whether to ask before each part is opened.

Both are used for View window Split actions and part quick-access buttons. If okayToOpenParts is False, quick-access part buttons will not appear in the GUI, and Split saves parts in a directory but does not open them. verifyPartOpens

Example 15-9. PP3E\Internet\PyMailGui2\PyMailGuiHelp.py (continued)

is used by both Split and quick-access part buttons: if False, part buttons
open parts immediately, and Split opens all known-type parts automatically
after they are saved (unknown types and executables are never opened).

An additional setting in this module, verifyHTMLTextOpen, controls verification
of opening a web browser on a HTML main text part of a message; if False, the
web browser is opened without prompts. This is a separate setting from
verifyPartOpens, because this is more automatic than part opens, and some
HTML main text parts may have dubious content (e.g., images, ads).

5) SENDING TEXT AND ATTACHMENTS

When composing new mails, the view window's "Attach" button adds selected files
as attachments, to be sent with the email's main text when the View window's
"Send" is clicked. Attachment files may be of any type; they are selected in
a pop-up dialog, but are not loaded until Send. The view window's "Parts"
button displays attachments already added.

The main text of the message (in the view window editor) is sent as a simple
message if there are no attachments, or as the first part of a multipart MIME
message if there are. In both cases, the main message text is always sent as
plain text. HTML files may be attached to the message, but there is no support
for text-or-HTML multipart alternative format for the main text, nor for
sending the main text as HTML only. Not all clients can handle HTML, and
PyMailGUI's text-based view windows have no HTML editing tools.

Multipart nesting is never applied: composed mails are always either a simple
body, or a linear list of parts containing the main message text and attachment
files.

For mail replies and forwards, headers are given intial values, the main
message text (described in the prior section) is wrapped and quoted with '>'
prefixes, and any attachments in the original message are stripped. Only
new attachments added are sent with the message.

To send to multiple addresses, separate each recipient's address in To and Cc
fields with semicolons. For instance:
      tim@oreily.com; "Smith, Bob" <bob@bob.com>; john@nasa.gov
Note that because these fields are split on semicolons without full parsing,
a recipient's address should not embed a ';'. For replies, this is handled
automatically: the To field is prefilled with the original message's From,
using either the original name and address, or just the address if the name
contains a ';' (a rare case). Cc and Bcc headers fields are ignored if they
contain just the initial "?" when sent.

Successfully sent messages are saved in a local file whose name you list in the
mailconfig.py module. Sent mails are saved if the variable "sentmailfile" is
set to a valid filename; set to an empty string to disable saves. This file
may be opened using the Open button of the GUI's list windows, and its content
may be viewed, processed, deleted, saved, and so on within the GUI, just like a

Example 15-9. PP3E\Internet\PyMailGui2\PyMailGuiHelp.py (continued)

manually saved mail file. Also like manually saved mail files, the sent-file
list window is automatically updated whenever a new message is sent, if it is
open (there is no need to close and reopen to see new sends). If this file
grows too large to open, you can delete its content with Delete, after possibly
saving sent mails you wish to keep to another file with Save.

Note that some ISPs may require that you be connected to their systems in order
to use their SMTP servers (sending through your dial-up ISP's server while
connected to a broadband provider may not work--try the SMTP server at your
broadband provider instead), and some SMTP servers may require authentication
(set the "smtpuser" variable in the mailconfig.py module to force authentication
logins on sends). See also the Python library module smtpd for SMTP server
tools; in principle, you could run your own SMTP server locally on 'localhost'.

6) MAIL TRANSFER OVERLAP

PyMailGUI runs mail server transfers (loads, sends, and deletes) in threads, to
avoid blocking the GUI. Transfers never block the GUI's windows, and windows
do not generally block other windows. Users can view, create, and process mails
while server transfers are in progress. The transfers run in the background,
while the GUI remains active.

PyMailGUI also allows mail transfer threads to overlap in time. In particular,
new emails may be written and sent while a load or send is in progress, and mail
loads may overlap with sends and other mail loads already in progress. For
example, while waiting for a download of mail headers or a large message, you
can open a new Write window, compose a message, and send it; the send will
overlap with the load currently in progress. You may also load another mail,
while the load of a large mail is in progress.

While mail transfers are in progress, pop-up windows display their current
progress as a message counter. When sending a message, the original edit
View window is popped back up automatically on Send failures, to save or retry.
Because delete operations may change POP message numbers on the server, this
operation disables other deletions and loads while in progress.

Offline mail save-file loads and deletes are also threaded: these threads may
overlap in time with server transfers, and with operations on other open save
files. Saves are disabled if the source or target file is busy with a load
or save operation. Quit is never allowed while any thread is busy.

7) MAIL DELETION

Mail is not removed from POP servers on Load requests, but only on explicit
"Delete" button deletion requests, if verified by the user. Delete requests
are run immediately, upon user verification.

Example 15-9. PP3E\Internet\PyMailGui2\PyMailGuiHelp.py (continued)

To delete your mail from a server and process offline: in the server list
window select the All checkbutton, Save to a local file, and then Delete to
delete all mails from the server; use Open to open the save file later to view
and process saved mail.

When deleting from the server window, the mail list (and any already viewed
message text) is not reloaded from server, if the delete was successful. If
the delete fails, all email must be reloaded, because some POP message numbers
may have changed; the reload occurs automatically. Delete in a file list
window deletes from the loal file only.

As of version 2.1, PyMailGUI automatically matches messages selected for
deletion with their headers on the mail server, to ensure that the correct
mail is deleted. If the mail index is out of synch with the server, mails
that do not match the server are not deleted, since their POP message numbers
are no longer accurate. In this event, an error is displayed, and a full reload
of the mail index list is automatically performed; you do not need to stop and
restart PyMailGUI to reload the index list. This can slow deletions (it adds
roughly one second per deleted mail on the test machine used), but prevents
the wrong mail from being deleted. See the POP message number synchronization
errors description in the next section.

8) INBOX MESSAGE NUMBER SYNCHRONIZATION

PyMailGUI does header matching in order to ensure that deletions only delete
the correct messages, and periodically detect synchronization errors with the
server. If a synchronization error message appears, the operation is cancelled,
and a full index reload from the server is automatically performed. You need
not stop and restart PyMailGUI and reload the index, but must reattempt the
operation after the reload.

The POP email protocol assigns emails a relative message number, reflecting
their position in your inbox. In the server List window, PyMailGUI loads its
mail index list on demand from the server, and assumes it reflects the content
of your inbox from that point on. A message's position in the index list is
used as its POP relative message number for later loads and deletes.

This normally works well, since newly arrived emails are added to the end
of the inbox. However, the message numbers of the index list can become out
of synch with the server in two ways:

A) Because delete operations change POP relative message numbers in the inbox,
deleting messages in another email client (even another PyMailGUI instance)
while the PyMailGUI server list window is open can invalidate PyMailGUI's
message index numbers. In this case, the index list window may be arbitrarily
out of synch with the inbox on the server.

B) It is also possible that your ISP may automatically delete emails from
your inbox at any time, making PyMailGUI's email list out of synch with message

Example 15-9. PP3E\Internet\PyMailGui2\PyMailGuiHelp.py (continued)

numbers on the mail server. For example, some ISPs may automatically move an
email from the inbox to the undeliverable box, in response to a fetch failure.
If this happens, PyMailGUI's message numbers will be off by one, according to
the server's inbox.

To accommodate such cases, PyMailGUI 2.1 always matches messages to be deleted
against the server's inbox, by comparing already fetched headers text with the
headers text returned for the same message number; the delete only occurs if
the two match. In addition, PyMailGUI runs a quick check for out-of-synch
errors by comparing headers for just the last message in the index, whenever
the index list is updated, and whenever full messages are fetched.

This header matching adds a slight overhead to deletes, index loads, and mail
fetches, but guarantees that deletes will not remove the wrong message, and
ensures that the message you receive corresponds to the item selected in the
server index List window. The synch test overhead is one second or less on
test machines used - it requires 1 POP server connect and an inbox size and
(possibly) header text fetch.

In general, you still shouldn't delete messages in PyMailGUI while running a
different email client, or that client's message numbers may become confused
unless it has simlar synchronization tests. If you receive a synch error
pop up on deletes or loads, PyMailGUI automatically begins a full reload of
the mail index list displayed in the server List window.

9) LOADING EMAIL

To save time, Load requests only fetch mail headers, not entire messages.
View operations fetch the entire message, unless it has been previously viewed
(already loaded messages are cached). Multiple message downloads may overlap
in time, and may overlap with message editing and sends.

In addition, after the initial load, new Load requests only fetch headers of
newly arrived messages. All headers must be refetched after a delete failure,
however, due to possibly changed POP message numbers.

PyMailGUI only is connected to a mail server while a load, send, or delete
operation is in progress. It does not connect at all unless one of these
operations is attempted, and disconnects as soon as the operation finishes.
You do not need any Internet connectivity to run PyMailGUI unless you attempt
one of these operations. In addition, you may disconnect from the Internet
when they are not in progress, without having to stop the GUI--the program
will reconnect on the next transfer operation.

Note: if your POP mail server does support the TOP command for fetching mail
headers (most do), see variable "srvrHasTop" in the mailtools.py module to
force full message downloads.

Also note that, although PyMailGUI only fetches message headers initially if
your email server supports TOP, this can still take some time for very large

Example 15-9. PP3E\Internet\PyMailGui2\PyMailGuiHelp.py (continued)

inboxes; as a rule of thumb, use save-mail files and deletions to keep your
inbox small.

10) THE mailconfig CONFIGURATION MODULE

Change the mailconfig.py module file in PyMailGUI's home directory on your
own machine to reflect your email server names, username, email address, and
optional mail signature line added to all composed mails.

Most settings in this module are optional, or have reasonable preset defaults.
However, you must minimally set this module's "smtpservername" variable to send
mail, and its "popservername" and "popusername" to load mail from a server.
These are simple Python variables assigned to strings in this file. See the
module file and its embedded comments for details.

The mailconfig module's "listheaders" attribute can also be set to a tuple of
string header field name, to customize the set of headers displayed in list
windows; mail size is always displayed last. Similarly mailconfig's
"viewheaders" attribute can extend the set of headers shown in a View window
(though From, To, Cc, and Subject fields are always shown). List windows
display message headers in fixed-width columns.

Variables in the mailconfig module also can be used to tailor the font used in
list windows ("fontsz"), the column at which viewed and quoted text is
automatically wrapped ("wrapsz"), colors and fonts in various windows, the
local file where sent messages are saved, the opening of mail parts, and more;
see the file's source code for more details.

Note: use caution when changing this file, as PyMailGUI may not run at all if
some of its variables are missing. You may wish to make a backup copy before
editing it in case you need to restore its defaults. A future version of this
system may have a configuration dialog which generates this module's code.

11) DEPENDENCIES

This client-side program currently requires Python and Tkinter. It uses Python
threads, if installed, to avoid blocking the GUI. Sending and loading email
from a server requires an Internet connection. Requires Python 2.3 or later,
and uses the Python "email" standard library module to parse and compose mail
text. Reuses a number of modules located in the PP3E examples tree.

12) MISCELLANEOUS HINTS

- Use ';' between multiple addresses in "To" and "Cc" headers.
- Passwords are requested if needed, and not stored by PyMailGUI.
- You may list your password in a file named in mailconfig.py.

Example 15-9. PP3E\Internet\PyMailGui2\PyMailGuiHelp.py (continued)

```
- Reply and Fwd automatically quote the original mail text.
- Save pops up a dialog for selecting a file to hold saved mails.
- Save always appends to the save file, rather than erasing it.
- Delete does not reload message headers, unless it fails.
- Delete checks your inbox to make sure the correct mail is deleted.
- Fetches detect inbox changes and automatically reload index list.
- Open and save dialogs always remember the prior directory.
- To print emails, "Save" to a text file and print with other tools.
- Click this window's Source button to view its source-code files.
- Watch http://www.rmi.net/~lutz for updates and patches
- This is an Open Source system: change its code as you like.
- See the SpamBayes system for a spam filter for incoming email.
"""

if __name__ == '__main__':
    print helptext                    # to stdout if run alone
    raw_input('Press Enter key')      # pause in DOS console pop ups
```

Ideas for Improvement

Although I use PyMailGUI on a regular basis as is, there is always room for improvement to software, and this system is no exception. If you wish to experiment with its code, here are a few suggested projects:

- Mail list windows could be sorted by columns on demand. This may require a more sophisticated list window structure.

- The implementation of save-mail files limits their size by loading them into memory all at once; a DBM keyed-access implementation may work around this constraint. See the list windows module comments for ideas.

- Hyperlink URLs within messages could be highlighted visually and made to spawn a web browser automatically when clicked by using the launcher tools we met in the GUI and system parts of this book (Tkinter's text widget supports links directly).

- Because Internet newsgroup posts are similar in structure to emails (header lines plus body text; see the nntplib example in Chapter 14), this script could in principle be extended to display both email messages and news articles. Classifying such a mutation as clever generalization or diabolical hack is left as an exercise in itself.

- The help text has grown large in this version: this might be better implemented as HTML, and displayed in a web browser, with simple text as a fallback option. In fact, we might extract the simple text from the HTML, to avoid redundant copies.

- Saves and Split writes could also be threaded for worst-case scenarios. For pointers on making Saves parallel, see the comments in the file class of ListWindows.py; there may be some subtle issues that require both thread locks and general file locking for potentially concurrent updates.

- There is currently no way to delete an attachment once it has been added in compose windows. This might be supported by adding quick-access part buttons to compose windows, too, which could verify and delete the part when clicked.

- We could add an automatic spam filter for mails fetched, in addition to any provided at the email server or ISP.

- Mail text is editable in message view windows, even though a new mail is not being composed. This is deliberate—users can annotate the message's text and save it in a text file with the Save button at the bottom of the window. This might be confusing, though, and is redundant (we can also edit and save by clicking on the main text's quick-access part button). Removing edit tools would require extending PyEdit.

- We could also add support for mail lists, allowing users to associate multiple email addresses with a saved list name. On sends to a list name, the mail would be sent to all on the list (the "To:" addresses passed to smtplib), but the email list could be used for the email's "To:" header line).

And so on—because this software is open source, it is also necessarily open-ended. Suggested exercises in this category are delegated to your imagination.

This concludes our tour of Python client-side programming. In the next chapter, we'll hop the fence to the other side of the Internet world and explore scripts that run on server machines. Such programs give rise to the grander notion of applications that live entirely on the Web and are launched by web browsers. As we take this leap in structure, keep in mind that the tools we met in this and the previous chapter are often sufficient to implement all the distributed processing that many applications require, and they can work in harmony with scripts that run on a server. To completely understand the Web world view, though, we need to explore the server realm, too.

Server-Side Scripting

"Oh What a Tangled Web We Weave"

This chapter is the fourth part of our look at Python Internet programming. In the last three chapters, we explored sockets and basic client-side programming interfaces such as FTP and email. In this chapter, our main focus will be on writing server-side scripts in Python—a type of program usually referred to as *CGI scripts*. Server-side scripting and its derivatives are at the heart of much of the interaction that happens on the Web.

As we'll see, Python is an ideal language for writing scripts to implement and customize web sites, due to both its ease of use and its library support. In the following chapter, we will use the basics we learn in this chapter to implement a full-blown web site. After that, we will wrap up this part of the book with a chapter that looks at other Internet-related topics and technologies. Here, our goal is to understand the fundamentals of server-side scripting, before exploring systems that build upon that basic model.

What's a Server-Side CGI Script?

Simply put, CGI scripts implement much of the interaction you typically experience on the Web. They are a standard and widely used mechanism for programming web-based systems and web site interaction. There are other ways to add interactive behavior to web sites with Python, including client-side solutions (e.g., Jython applets and Active Scripting), as well as server-side technologies that build on the basic CGI model (e.g., Python Server Pages, and the Zope, Webware, CherryPy, and Django frameworks). We will discuss such alternatives in Chapter 18.

But by and large, CGI server-side scripts are used to program much of the activity on the Web. They are perhaps the most primitive approach to implementing web sites, and they do not by themselves offer the tools that are often built into larger frameworks. CGI scripts, however, are in many ways the simplest technique for server-side scripting. As a result, they are an ideal way to get started with programming on the server side of the Web. Especially for simpler sites that do not require enterprise-level tools, CGI is sufficient, and can be augmented with additional libraries as needed.

The Script Behind the Curtain

Formally speaking, CGI scripts are programs that run on a server machine and adhere to the Common Gateway Interface—a model for browser/server communications, from which CGI scripts take their name. CGI is an application protocol that web servers use to transfer input data and results between web browsers and server-side scripts. Perhaps a more useful way to understand CGI, though, is in terms of the interaction it implies.

Most people take this interaction for granted when browsing the Web and pressing buttons in web pages, but a lot is going on behind the scenes of every transaction on the Web. From the perspective of a user, it's a fairly familiar and simple process:

Submission

When you visit a web site to purchase a product or submit information online, you generally fill in a form in your web browser, press a button to submit your information, and begin waiting for a reply.

Response

Assuming all is well with both your Internet connection and the computer you are contacting, you eventually get a reply in the form of a new web page. It may be a simple acknowledgment (e.g., "Thanks for your order") or a new form that must be filled out and submitted again.

And, believe it or not, that simple model is what makes most of the Web hum. But internally, it's a bit more complex. In fact, a subtle client/server socket-based architecture is at work—your web browser running on your computer is the *client*, and the computer you contact over the Web is the *server*. Let's examine the interaction scenario again, with all the gory details that users usually never see:

Submission

When you fill out a form page in a web browser and press a submission button, behind the scenes your web browser sends your information across the Internet to the server machine specified as its receiver. The server machine is usually a remote computer that lives somewhere else in both cyberspace and reality. It is named in the URL accessed—the Internet address string that appears at the top of your browser. The target server and file can be named in a URL you type explicitly, but more typically they are specified in the HTML that defines the submission page itself—either in a hyperlink or in the "action" tag of the input form's HTML.

However the server is specified, the browser running on your computer ultimately sends your information to the server as bytes over a socket, using techniques we saw in the last three chapters. On the server machine, a program called an *HTTP server* runs perpetually, listening on a socket for incoming connection requests and data from browsers and other clients, usually on port number 80.

Processing

When your information shows up at the server machine, the HTTP server program notices it first and decides how to handle the request. If the requested URL names a simple *web page* (e.g., a URL ending in *.html*), the HTTP server opens the named HTML file on the server machine and sends its text back to the browser over a socket. On the client, the browser reads the HTML and uses it to construct the next page you see.

But if the URL requested by the browser names an *executable program* instead (e.g., a URL ending in *.cgi* or *.py*), the HTTP server starts the named program on the server machine to process the request and redirects the incoming browser data to the spawned program's stdin input stream, environment variables, and command-line arguments. That program started by the server is usually a CGI script—a program run on the remote server machine somewhere in cyberspace, usually not on your computer. The CGI script is responsible for handling the request from this point on; it may store your information in a database, charge your credit card, and so on.

Response

Ultimately, the CGI script prints HTML, along with a few header lines, to generate a new response page in your browser. When a CGI script is started, the HTTP server takes care to connect the script's stdout standard output stream to a socket that the browser is listening to. As a result, HTML code printed by the CGI script is sent over the Internet, back to your browser, to produce a new page. The HTML printed back by the CGI script works just as if it had been stored and read from an HTML file; it can define a simple response page or a brand-new form coded to collect additional information.

In other words, CGI scripts are something like *callback handlers* for requests generated by web browsers that require a program to be run dynamically. They are automatically run on the server machine in response to actions in a browser. Although CGI scripts ultimately receive and send standard structured messages over sockets, CGI is more like a higher-level procedural convention for sending and receiving information between a browser and a server.

Writing CGI Scripts in Python

If all of this sounds complicated, relax—Python, as well as the resident HTTP server, automates most of the tricky bits. CGI scripts are written as fairly autonomous programs, and they assume that startup tasks have already been accomplished. The HTTP web server program, not the CGI script, implements the server side of the HTTP protocol itself. Moreover, Python's library modules automatically dissect information sent up from the browser and give it to the CGI script in an easily digested form. The upshot is that CGI scripts may focus on application details like processing input data and producing a result page.

As mentioned earlier, in the context of CGI scripts, the stdin and stdout streams are automatically tied to sockets connected to the browser. In addition, the HTTP server passes some browser information to the CGI script in the form of shell environment variables, and possibly command-line arguments. To CGI programmers, that means:

- *Input* data sent from the browser to the server shows up as a stream of bytes in the stdin input stream, along with shell environment variables.
- *Output* is sent back from the server to the client by simply printing properly formatted HTML to the stdout output stream.

The most complex parts of this scheme include parsing all the input information sent up from the browser and formatting information in the reply sent back. Happily, Python's standard library largely automates both tasks:

Input

With the Python cgi module, input typed into a web browser form or appended to a URL string shows up as values in a dictionary-like object in Python CGI scripts. Python parses the data itself and gives us an object with one *key:value* pair per input sent by the browser that is fully independent of transmission style (roughly, by form or URL).

Output

The cgi module also has tools for automatically escaping strings so that they are legal to use in HTML (e.g., replacing embedded <, >, and & characters with HTML escape codes). Module urllib provides other tools for formatting text inserted into generated URL strings (e.g., adding %XX and + escapes).

We'll study both of these interfaces in detail later in this chapter. For now, keep in mind that although any language can be used to write CGI scripts, Python's standard modules and language attributes make it a snap.

Perhaps less happily, CGI scripts are also intimately tied to the syntax of HTML, since they must generate it to create a reply page. In fact, it can be said that Python CGI scripts embed HTML, which is an entirely distinct language in its own right.[*] As we'll also see, the fact that CGI scripts create a user interface by printing HTML syntax means that we have to take special care with the text we insert into a web page's code (e.g., escaping HTML operators). Worse, CGI scripts require at least a cursory knowledge of HTML forms, since that is where the inputs and target script's address are typically specified.

This book won't teach HTML in depth; if you find yourself puzzled by some of the arcane syntax of the HTML generated by scripts here, you should glance at an HTML introduction, such as *HTML and XHTML: The Definitive Guide*. Also keep in mind that higher-level tools and frameworks can sometimes hide the details of HTML generation from Python programmers; with the HTMLgen extension we'll meet in Chapter 18, for instance, it's possible to deal in Python objects, not HTML syntax.

Running Server-Side Examples

Like GUIs, web-based systems are highly interactive, and the best way to get a feel for some of these examples is to test-drive them live. Before we get into some code, let's get set up to run the examples we're going to see.

Running CGI-based programs requires three pieces of software:

- The client, to submit requests: a browser or script
- The web server that receives the request
- The CGI script, which is run by the server to process the request

---

[*] In Chapter 18, we'll see other systems that take the opposite route—embedding Python code or calls in HTML. The server-side templating languages in Zope, PSP, ActiveX Scripting, and other web frameworks use this method. Because Python is embedded, these systems must run special servers to evaluate the embedded tags. Because Python CGI scripts embed HTML in Python instead, they can be run as standalone programs directly, though they must be launched by a CGI-capable web server.

We'll be writing CGI scripts as we move along, and any web browser can be used as a client (e.g., Firefox or Internet Explorer). As we'll see later, Python's urllib module can also serve as a web client in scripts we write. The only missing piece here is the intermediate web server.

Web Server Options

There are a variety of approaches to running web servers. For example, the open source Apache system provides a complete, production-grade web server, and its mod_python extension discussed later runs Python scripts quickly. Provided you are willing to install and configure, it is a complete solution, which you can run on a machine of your own. Apache usage is beyond our present scope here, though.

If you have access to an account on a web server machine that runs Python, you can also install the HTML and script files we'll see there. For the second edition of this book, for instance, all the web examples were uploaded to an account I had on the "starship" Python server, and were accessed with URLs of this form:

```
http://starship.python.net/~lutz/PyInternetDemos.html
```

If you go this route, replace starship.python.net/~lutz with the names of your own server and account directory path. The downside of using a remote server account is that changing code is more involved—you will have to either work on the server machine itself, or transfer code back and forth on changes. Moreover, you need access to such a server in the first place, and server configuration details can vary widely. On the starship machine, for example, Python CGI scripts were required to have a *.cgi* filename extension, executable permission, and the Unix #! line at the top to point the shell to Python.

Running a Local Web Server

To keep things simple, this edition is taking a different approach. All the examples will be run using a simple web server coded in Python itself. Moreover, the web server will be run on the same, local machine as the web browser client. This way, all you have to do to run the server-side examples is start the web server script, and use "localhost" as the server name in all the URLs you will submit or code (see Chapter 13 if you've forgotten why this name means the local machine). For example, to view a web page, use a URL of this form in the address field of your web browser:

```
http://localhost/tutor0.html
```

This also avoids some of the complexity of per-server differences, and it makes changing the code simple—it can be edited on the local machine directly.

For this book's examples, we'll use the web server in Example 16-1. This is essentially the same script introduced in Chapter 2, augmented slightly to allow the working directory and port number to be passed in as command-line arguments (we'll also run this in the root directory of a larger example in the next chapter).

More subtly, here we also add the *cgi-bin* subdirectory to the module import search path, to mimic the current working directory when scripts are run independently on other platforms (on Windows, they are run in the same process as this server, and the server classes do not change to the CGI's directory). This last point can make a difference if a CGI script must import an application's modules from its own directory—its container directory must be on the module search path, regardless of how it was started.

We won't go into details on all the modules and classes Example 16-1 uses here; see the Python library manual. But as described in Chapter 2, this script implements an HTTP web server, which:

- Listens for incoming socket requests from clients on the machine it is run on, and the port number specified in the script or command line (which defaults to 80, that standard HTTP port)
- Serves up HTML pages from the *webdir* directory specified in the script or command line (which defaults to the directory it is launched from)
- Runs Python CGI scripts that are located in the *cgi-bin* (or *htbin*) subdirectory of the *webdir* directory, with a *.py* filename extension

See Chapter 2 for additional background on this web server's operation.

Example 16-1. PP3E\Internet\Web\webserver.py

```
##########################################################################
# implement HTTP web server in Python which knows how to serve HTML
# pages and run server-side CGI scripts;  serves files/scripts from
# the current working dir and port 80, unless command-line args;
# Python scripts must be stored in webdir\cgi-bin or webdir\htbin;
# more than one of these may be running on the same machine to serve
# from different directories, as long as they listen on different ports;
##########################################################################

webdir = '.'    # where your HTML files and cgi-bin script directory live
port   = 80     # http://servername/ if 80, else use http://servername:xxxx/

import os, sys
from BaseHTTPServer import HTTPServer
from CGIHTTPServer  import CGIHTTPRequestHandler

if len(sys.argv) > 1: webdir = sys.argv[1]              # command-line args
if len(sys.argv) > 2: port   = int(sys.argv[2])        # else default ., 80
print 'webdir "%s", port %s' % (webdir, port)

# hack for Windows: os.environ not propagated
# to subprocess by os.popen2, force in-process
if sys.platform[:3] == 'win':
```

Example 16-1. PP3E\Internet\Web\webserver.py (continued)

```
    CGIHTTPRequestHandler.have_popen2 = False
    CGIHTTPRequestHandler.have_popen3 = False        # emulate path after fork
    sys.path.append('cgi-bin')                       # else only adds my dir

os.chdir(webdir)                                     # run in HTML root dir
srvraddr = ("", port)                                # my hostname, portnumber
srvrobj  = HTTPServer(srvraddr, CGIHTTPRequestHandler)
srvrobj.serve_forever()                              # serve clients till exit
```

To start the server to run this chapter's examples, simply run this script from the directory the script's file is located in, with no command-line arguments. For instance, from a DOS command line:

```
C:\...\PP3E\Internet\Web>webserver.py
webdir ".", port 80
```

On Windows, you can simply click its icon and keep the console window open, or launch it from a DOS command prompt. On Unix it can be run from a command line in the background, or in its own terminal window.

By default, while running locally this way, the script serves up HTML pages requested on "localhost" from the directory it lives in or is launched from, and runs Python CGI scripts from the *cgi-bin* subdirectory located there; change its webdir variable or pass in a command-line argument to point it to a different directory. Because of this structure, in the examples distribution HTML files are in the same directory as the web server script, and CGI scripts are located in the *cgi-bin* subdirectory. In other words, to visit web pages and run scripts, we'll be using URLs of these forms, respectively:

```
http://localhost/somepage.html
http://localhost/cgi-bin/somescript.py
```

Both map to the directory that contains the web server script (*PP3E\Internet\Web*) by default. Again, to run the examples on a different server of your own, simply replace the "localhost" and "localhost/cgi-bin" parts of these addresses with your server and directory path details (more on URLs later in this chapter).

The server in Example 16-1 is by no means a production-grade web server, but it can be used to experiment with this book's examples and is viable as way to test your CGI scripts locally before deploying them on a real remote server. If you wish to install and run the examples under a different web server, you'll want to extrapolate the examples for your context. Things like server names and pathnames in URLs, as well as CGI script filename extensions and other conventions, can vary widely; consult your server's documentation for more details. For this chapter and the next, we'll assume that you have the *webserver.py* script running locally.

The Server-Side Examples Root Page

To confirm that you are set up to run the examples, start the web server script in Example 16-1 and type the following URL in the address field at the top of your web browser:

```
http://localhost/PyInternetDemos.html
```

This address loads a launcher page with links to this chapter's example files (see the examples distribution for this page's HTML source code). The launcher page itself appears as in Figure 16-1, shown running under the open source Firefox web browser (it looks similar in other browsers). Each major example has a link on this page, which runs when clicked.

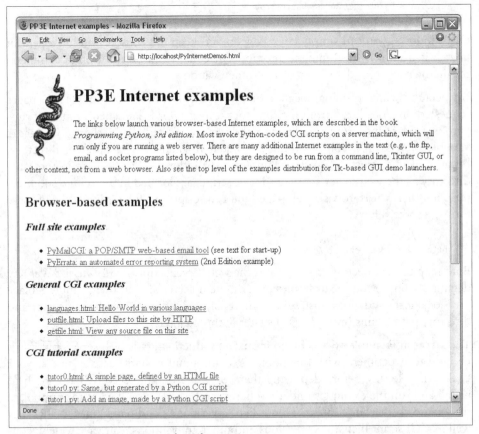

Figure 16-1. The PyInternetDemos launcher page

It's possible to open some of the examples by clicking on their HTML file directly in your system's file explorer GUI. However, the CGI scripts ultimately invoked by some of the example links must be run by a web server. If you browse such pages directly, your browser will likely display the scripts' source code, instead of running it. To run scripts too, be sure to open the HTML pages by typing their "localhost" URL address into your browser's address field.

Eventually, you probably will want to start using a more powerful web server, so we will study additional CGI installation details later in this chapter, and explore a few custom server options at the end of Chapter 18. Such details can be safely skipped or skimmed if you will not be installing on another server right away. For now, we'll run locally.

Viewing Server-Side Examples and Output

The source code of examples in this part of the book is listed in the text and included in the book's examples distribution. In all cases, if you wish to view the source code of an HTML file, or the HTML generated by a Python CGI script, you can also simply select your browser's View Source menu option while the corresponding web page is displayed.

Keep in mind, though, that your browser's View Source option lets you see the *output* of a server-side script after it has run, but not the source code of the script itself. There is no automatic way to view the Python source code of the CGI scripts themselves, short of finding them in this book or in its examples distribution.

To address this issue, later in this chapter we'll also write a CGI-based program called getfile, which allows the source code of any file on this book's web site (HTML, CGI script, and so on) to be downloaded and viewed. Simply type the desired file's name into a web page form referenced by the *getfile.html* link on the Internet demos launcher page, or add it to the end of an explicitly typed URL as a parameter like the following; replace tutor5.py at the end with the name of script whose code you wish to view:

```
http://localhost/cgi-bin/getfile.py?filename=cgi-bin/tutor5.py
```

In response, the server will ship back the text of the named file to your browser. This process requires explicit interface steps, though, and much more knowledge of URLs than we've gained thus far; to learn how and why this magic line works, let's move on to the next section.

Climbing the CGI Learning Curve

Now that we've looked at setup issues, it's time to get into concrete programming details. This section is a tutorial that introduces CGI coding one step at a time— from simple, noninteractive scripts to larger programs that utilize all the common web page user input devices (what we called widgets in the Tkinter GUI chapters in Part III).

Along the way, we'll also explore the core ideas behind server-side scripting. We'll move slowly at first, to learn all the basics; the next chapter will use the ideas presented here to build up larger and more realistic web site examples. For now, let's work through a simple CGI tutorial, with just enough HTML thrown in to write basic server-side scripts.

A First Web Page

As mentioned, CGI scripts are intimately bound up with HTML, so let's start with a simple HTML page. The file *tutor0.html*, shown in Example 16-2, defines a bona fide, fully functional web page—a text file containing HTML code, which specifies the structure and contents of a simple web page.

Example 16-2. PP3E\Internet\Web\tutor0.html

```
<HTML>
<TITLE>HTML 101</TITLE>
<BODY>
<H1>A First HTML page</H1>
<P>Hello, HTML World!</P>
</BODY></HTML>
```

If you point your favorite web browser to the Internet address of this file, you should see a page like that shown in Figure 16-2. This figure shows the Firefox browser at work on the address *http://localhost/tutor0.html* (type this into your browser's address field), and it assumes that the local web browser described in the prior section is running; other browsers render the page similarly. Since this is a static HTML file, you'll get the same result if you simply click on the file's icon on most platforms.

Figure 16-2. A simple web page from an HTML file

To truly understand how this little file does its work, you need to know something about HTML syntax, Internet addresses, and file permission rules. Let's take a quick first look at each of these topics before we move on to the next example.

HTML basics

I promised that I wouldn't teach much HTML in this book, but you need to know enough to make sense of examples. In short, HTML is a descriptive markup language, based on *tags*—items enclosed in <> pairs. Some tags stand alone (e.g., <HR> specifies a horizontal rule). Others appear in begin/end pairs in which the end tag includes an extra slash.

For instance, to specify the text of a level-one header line, we write HTML code of the form <H1>*text*</H1>; the text between the tags shows up on the web page. Some tags also allow us to specify options. For example, a tag pair like <A href="*address*"> *text*</A> specifies a *hyperlink*: pressing the link's text in the page directs the browser to access the Internet address (URL) listed in the href option.

It's important to keep in mind that HTML is used only to describe pages: your web browser reads it and translates its description to a web page with headers, paragraphs, links, and the like. Notably absent are both *layout information*—the browser is responsible for arranging components on the page—and syntax for *programming logic*—there are no if statements, loops, and so on. Also, Python code is nowhere to be found in Example 16-2; raw HTML is strictly for defining pages, not for coding programs or specifying all user interface details.

HTML's lack of user interface control and programmability is both a strength and a weakness. It's well suited to describing pages and simple user interfaces at a high level. The browser, not you, handles physically laying out the page on your screen. On the other hand, HTML does not directly support full-blown GUIs and requires us to introduce CGI scripts (and other technologies) to web sites, in order to add dynamic programmability to otherwise static HTML.

Internet addresses (URLs)

Once you write an HTML file, you need to put it somewhere a web browser can reference it. If you are using the locally running Python web server described earlier, this becomes trivial: use a URL of the form *http://localhost/file.html* to access web pages, and *http://localhost/cgi-bin/file.py* to name CGI scripts. This is implied by the fact that the web server script serves pages and scripts from the directory in which it is.

On other servers, URLs may be more complex. Like all HTML files, *tutor0.html* must be stored in a directory on the server machine, from which the resident web server program allows browsers to fetch pages. For example, on the server used for the second edition of this book, the page's file must be stored in or below the *public_html* directory of my personal home directory—that is, somewhere in the directory tree rooted at */home/lutz/public_html*. The complete Unix pathname of this file on the server is:

```
/home/lutz/public_html/tutor0.html
```

This path is different from its *PP3E\Internet\Web* location in the book's examples distribution, as given in the example file listing's title. When referencing this file on the client, though, you must specify its Internet address, sometimes called a URL, instead. The following URL was used to load the remote page from the server:

```
http://starship.python.net/~lutz/tutor0.html
```

The server maps this URL to the Unix pathname automatically. In general, URL strings like this one are composed as the concatenation of multiple parts:

Protocol name: http

The protocol part of this URL tells the browser to communicate with the HTTP (i.e., web) server program on the server machine, using the HTTP message protocol. URLs used in browsers can also name different protocols—for example, *ftp://* to reference a file managed by the FTP protocol and server, *file://* to reference a file on the local machine, *telnet* to start a Telnet client session, and so on.

Server machine name and port: starship.python.net

A URL also names the target server machine's domain name or Internet Protocol (IP) address following the protocol type. Here, we list the domain name of the server machine where the examples are installed; the machine name listed is used to open a socket to talk to the server. As usual, a machine name of *localhost* (or the equivalent IP address *127.0.0.1*) here means the server is running on the same machine as the client.

Optionally, this part of the URL may also explicitly give the socket port on which the server is listening for connections, following a colon (e.g., *starship. python.net:8000*, or *127.0.0.1:80*). For HTTP, the socket is usually connected to port number 80, so this is the default if the port is omitted. See Chapter 13 if you need a refresher on machine names and ports.

File path: ~lutz/tutor0.html

Finally, the URL gives the path to the desired file on the remote machine. The HTTP web server automatically translates the URL's file path to the file's true pathname: on the starship server, *~lutz* is automatically translated to the *public_ html* directory in my home directory. When using the Python-coded web server script in Example 16-1, files are mapped to the server's current working directory instead. URLs typically map to such files, but they can reference other sorts of items as well, and may name an executable CGI script to be run when accessed.

Query parameters (used in later examples)

URLs may also be followed by additional input parameters for CGI programs. When used, they are introduced by a ? and are typically separated by & characters. For instance, a string of the form ?name=bob&job=hacker at the end of a URL passes parameters named name and job to the CGI script named earlier in the URL, with values bob and hacker, respectively. As we'll discuss later in this chapter when we explore escaping rules, the parameters may sometimes be separated by ; characters instead, as in ?name=bob;job=hacker, though this form is less common.

These values are sometimes called URL *query string parameters* and are treated the same as form inputs by scripts. Technically speaking, query parameters may have other structures (e.g., unnamed values separated by +), but we will ignore additional options in this text; more on both parameters and input forms later in this tutorial.

To make sure we have a handle on URL syntax, let's pick apart another example that we will be using later in this chapter. In the following HTTP protocol URL:

```
http://localhost:80/cgi-bin/languages.py?language=All
```

the components uniquely identify a server script to be run as follows:

- The server name localhost means the web server is running on the same machine as the client; as explained earlier, this is the configuration we're using for our examples.

- Port number 80 gives the socket port on which the web server is listening for connections (port 80 is the default if this part is omitted, so we will usually omit it).

- The file path cgi-bin/languages.py gives the location of the file to be run on the server machine, within the directory where the server looks for referenced files.

- The query string ?language=All provides an input parameter to the referenced script languages.py, as an alternative to user input in form fields (described later).

Although this covers most URLs you're likely to encounter in the wild, the full format of URLs is slightly richer:

```
protocol://networklocation/path;parameters?querystring#fragment
```

For instance, the fragment part may name a section within a page (e.g., #part1). Moreover, each part can have formats of their own, and some are not used in all protocols. The ;parameters part is omitted for HTTP, for instance (it gives an explicit file type for FTP), and the networklocation part may also specify optional user login parameters for some protocol schemes (its full format is user:password@host:port for FTP and Telnet, but just host:port for HTTP). We used a complex FTP URL in Chapter 14, for example, which included a username and password, as well as a binary file type (the server may guess if no type is given):

```
ftp://lutz:password@ftp.rmi.net/filename;type=i
```

We'll ignore additional URL formatting rules here. If you're interested in more details, you might start by reading the urlparse module's entry in Python's library manual, as well as its source code in the Python standard library. You may also notice that a URL you type to access a page looks a bit different after the page is fetched (spaces become + characters, % characters are added, and so on). This is simply because browsers must also generally follow URL escaping (i.e., translation) conventions, which we'll explore later in this chapter.

Using minimal URLs

Because browsers remember the prior page's Internet address, URLs embedded in HTML files can often omit the protocol and server names, as well as the file's directory path. If missing, the browser simply uses these components' values from the last page's address. This minimal syntax works for URLs embedded in hyperlinks and for form actions (we'll meet forms later in this tutorial). For example, within a page that was fetched from the directory *dirpath* on the server *www.server.com*, minimal hyperlinks and form actions such as:

```
<A HREF="more.html">
<FORM ACTION="next.py"  ...>
```

are treated exactly as if we had specified a complete URL with explicit server and path components, like the following:

```
<A HREF="http://www.server.com/dirpath/more.html">
<FORM ACTION="http://www.server.com/dirpath/next.py"  ...>
```

The first minimal URL refers to the file *more.html* on the same server and in the same directory from which the page containing this hyperlink was fetched; it is expanded to a complete URL within the browser. URLs can also employ Unix-style relative path syntax in the file path component. A hyperlink tag like <A HREF="../spam.gif">, for instance, names a GIF file on the server machine and parent directory of the file that contains this link's URL.

Why all the fuss about shorter URLs? Besides extending the life of your keyboard and eyesight, the main advantage of such minimal URLs is that they don't need to be changed if you ever move your pages to a new directory or server—the server and path are inferred when the page is used; they are not hardcoded into its HTML. The flipside of this can be fairly painful: examples that do include explicit site names and pathnames in URLs embedded within HTML code cannot be copied to other servers without source code changes. Scripts and special HTML tags can help here, but editing source code can be error-prone.

The downside of minimal URLs is that they don't trigger automatic Internet connections when followed offline. This becomes apparent only when you load pages from local files on your computer. For example, we can generally open HTML pages without connecting to the Internet at all by pointing a web browser to a page's file that lives on the local machine (e.g., by clicking on its file icon). When browsing a page locally like this, following a fully specified URL makes the browser automatically connect to the Internet to fetch the referenced page or script. Minimal URLs, though, are opened on the local machine again; usually, the browser simply displays the referenced page or script's source code.

The net effect is that minimal URLs are more portable, but they tend to work better when running all pages live on the Internet. To make them easier to work with, the examples in this book will often omit the server and path components in URLs they contain. In this book, to derive a page or script's true URL from a minimal URL, imagine that the string:

```
http://localhost/
```

appears before the filename given by the URL. Your browser will, even if you don't.

HTML file permission constraints

One install pointer before we move on: if you want to use a different server and machine, it may be necessary on some platforms to grant web page files and their directories world-readable permission. That's because they are loaded by arbitrary people over the Web (often by someone named "nobody," who we'll introduce in a moment).

An appropriate chmod command can be used to change permissions on Unix-like machines. For instance, a chmod 755 *filename* shell command usually suffices; it makes *filename* readable and executable by everyone, and writable by you only.* These directory and file permission details are typical, but they can vary from server to server. Be sure to find out about the local server's conventions if you upload HTML files to a remote site.

A First CGI Script

The HTML file we saw in the prior section is just that—an HTML file, not a CGI script. When referenced by a browser, the remote web server simply sends back the file's text to produce a new page in the browser. To illustrate the nature of CGI scripts, let's recode the example as a Python CGI program, as shown in Example 16-3.

Example 16-3. PP3E\Internet\Web\cgi-bin\tutor0.py

```
#!/usr/bin/python
######################################################
# runs on the server, prints HTML to create a new page;
# url=http://localhost/cgi-bin/tutor0.py
######################################################

print "Content-type: text/html\n"
print "<TITLE>CGI 101</TITLE>"
```

---

* These are not necessarily magic numbers. On Unix machines, mode 755 is a bit mask. The first 7 simply means that you (the file's owner) can read, write, and execute the file (7 in binary is 111—each bit enables an access mode). The two 5s (binary 101) say that everyone else (your group and others) can read and execute (but not write) the file. See your system's manpage on the chmod command for more details.

Example 16-3. PP3E\Internet\Web\cgi-bin\tutor0.py (continued)

```
print "<H1>A First CGI script</H1>"
print "<P>Hello, CGI World!</P>"
```

This file, *tutor0.py*, makes the same sort of page as Example 16-2 if you point your browser at it—simply replace *.html* with *.py* in the URL, and add the *cgi-bin* subdirectory name to the path to yield its address, *http://localhost/cgi-bin/tutor0.py*.

But this time it's a very different kind of animal—it is an *executable program* that is run on the server in response to your access request. It's also a completely legal Python program, in which the page's HTML is printed dynamically, instead of being precoded in a static file. In fact, little is CGI-specific about this Python program; if run from the system command line, it simply prints HTML instead of generating a browser page:

```
C:\...\PP3E\Internet\Web\cgi-bin>python tutor0.py
Content-type: text/html

<TITLE>CGI 101</TITLE>
<H1>A First CGI script</H1>
<P>Hello, CGI World!</P>
```

When run by the HTTP server program on a web server machine, however, the standard output stream is tied to a socket read by the browser on the client machine. In this context, all the output is sent across the Internet to your browser. As such, it must be formatted per the browser's expectations.

In particular, when the script's output reaches your browser, the first printed line is interpreted as a header, describing the text that follows. There can be more than one header line in the printed response, but there must always be a blank line between the headers and the start of the HTML code (or other data).

In this script, the first header line tells the browser that the rest of the transmission is HTML text (*text/html*), and the newline character (\n) at the end of the first print statement generates an extra line feed in addition to the one that the print statement generates itself. The net effect is to insert a blank line after the header line. The rest of this program's output is standard HTML and is used by the browser to generate a web page on a client, exactly as if the HTML lived in a static HTML file on the server.[*]

CGI scripts are accessed just like HTML files: you either type the full URL of this script into your browser's address field, or click on the *tutor0.py* link line in the

---

[*] Notice that the script does not generate the enclosing <HEAD> and <BODY> tags included in the static HTML file of the prior section. As mentioned in Chapter 2, strictly speaking, it should—HTML without such tags is technically invalid. But because all commonly used browsers simply ignore the omission, we'll take some liberties with HTML syntax in this book. If you need to care about such things, consult HTML references for more formal details.

examples root page of Figure 16-1 (which follows a minimal hyperlink that resolves to the script's full URL). Figure 16-3 shows the result page generated if you point your browser at this script.

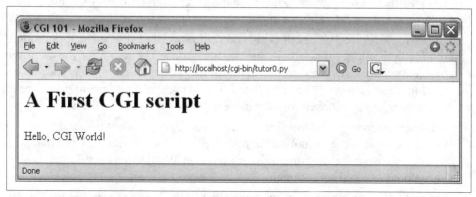

Figure 16-3. A simple web page from a CGI script

Installing CGI scripts

If you are running the local web server described at the start of this chapter, no extra installation steps are required to make this example work, and you can safely skip most of this section. If you want to put CGI scripts on another server, though, there are a few pragmatic details you may need to know about. This section provides a brief overview of common CGI configuration details for reference.

Like HTML files, CGI scripts are simple text files that you can either create on your local machine and upload to the server by FTP, or write with a text editor running directly on the server machine (perhaps using a Telnet client). However, because CGI scripts are run as programs, they have some unique installation requirements that differ from simple HTML files. In particular, they usually must be stored and named specially, and they must be configured as programs that are executable by arbitrary users. Depending on your needs, CGI scripts also may require help finding imported modules and may need to be converted to the server platform's text file format after being uploaded. Let's look at each install constraint in more depth:

Directory and filename conventions

First, CGI scripts need to be placed in a directory that your web server recognizes as a program directory, and they need to be given a name that your server recognizes as a CGI script. In the local web server we're using in this chapter, scripts need to be placed in a special *cgi-bin* subdirectory and be named with a *.py* extension. On the server used for this book's second edition, CGI scripts instead were stored in the user's *public_html* directory just like HTML files, but they required a filename ending in a *.cgi*, not a *.py*. Some servers may allow other suffixes and program directories; this varies widely and can sometimes be configured per server or per user.

Execution conventions

Because they must be executed by the web server on behalf of arbitrary users on the Web, CGI script files may also need to be given executable file permissions to mark them as programs, and be made executable by others. Again, a shell command chmod 0755 *filename* does the trick on most servers.

Under some servers, CGI scripts also need the special #! line at the top, to identify the Python interpreter that runs the file's code. The text after the #! in the first line simply gives the directory path to the Python executable on your server machine. See Chapter 3 for more details on this special first line, and be sure to check your server's conventions for more details on non-Unix platforms.

Some servers may expect this line, even outside Unix. Most of the CGI scripts in this book include the #! line just in case they will ever be run on Unix-like platforms; under our locally running web server on Windows, this first line is simply ignored as a Python comment.

One subtlety worth noting: as we saw earlier in the book, the special first line in executable text files can normally contain either a hardcoded path to the Python interpreter (e.g., *#!/usr/bin/python*) or an invocation of the env program (e.g., *#!/usr/bin/env python*), which deduces where Python lives from environment variable settings (i.e., your $PATH). The env trick is less useful in CGI scripts, though, because their environment settings are those of the user "nobody" (not your own), as explained in the next paragraph.

Module search path configuration (optional)

Some HTTP servers may run CGI scripts with the username "nobody" for security reasons (this limits the user's access to the server machine). That's why files you publish on the Web must have special permission settings that make them accessible to other users. It also means that some CGI scripts can't rely on the Python module search path to be configured in any particular way. As we've seen, the module path is normally initialized from the user's PYTHONPATH setting and .pth files, plus defaults. But because CGI scripts are run by the user "nobody," PYTHONPATH may be arbitrary when a CGI script runs.

Before you puzzle over this too hard, you should know that this is often not a concern in practice. Because Python usually searches the current directory for imported modules by default, this is not an issue if all of your scripts and any modules and packages they use are stored in your web directory. But if the module lives elsewhere, you may need to modify the sys.path list in your scripts to adjust the search path manually before imports—for instance, with sys.path.append(*dirname*) calls, index assignments, and so on.

End-of-line conventions (optional)

On some Unix (and Linux) servers, you might also have to make sure that your script text files follow the Unix end-of-line convention (\n), not DOS (\r\n). This isn't an issue if you edit and debug right on the server (or on another Unix machine) or FTP files one by one in text mode. But if you edit and upload your scripts from a PC to a Unix server in a *tar* file (or in FTP binary mode), you may need to convert end-of-lines after the upload. For instance, the server that was used for the second edition of this text returns a default error page for scripts whose end-of-lines are in DOS format. See Chapter 7 for automated end-of-line converter scripts.

Unbuffered output streams (optional)

Under some servers, the print statement may buffer its output. If you have a long-running CGI script, to avoid making the user wait to see results, you may wish to manually flush your printed text (call sys.stdout.flush( )) or run your Python scripts in unbuffered mode. Recall from Chapter 5 that you can make streams unbuffered by running with the -u command-line flag or by setting your PYTHONUNBUFFERED environment variable to a nonempty value.

To use -u in the CGI world, try using a first line like #!/usr/bin/python –u. In typical usage, output buffering is not usually a factor. On some servers and clients, this may be a resolution for empty reply pages, or premature end-of-script header errors—the client may time out before the buffered output stream is sent (though more commonly, these cases reflect genuine program errors in your script).

This installation process may sound a bit complex at first glance, but much of it is server-dependent, and it's not bad once you've worked through it on your own. It's only a concern at install time and can usually be automated to some extent with Python scripts run on the server. To summarize, most Python CGI scripts are text files of Python code, which:

- Are named according to your web server's conventions (e.g., *file.py*)
- Are stored in a directory recognized by your web server (e.g., *cgi-bin/*)
- Are given executable file permissions if required (e.g., chmod 755 file.py)
- May require the special #!pythonpath line at the top for some servers
- Configure sys.path only if needed to see modules in other directories
- Use Unix end-of-line conventions, if your server rejects DOS format
- Flush output buffers if required, or to send portions of the reply periodically

Even if you must use a server machine configured by someone else, most of the machine's conventions should be easy to root out during a normal debugging cycle. As usual, you should consult the conventions for any machine to which you plan to copy these example files.

Finding Python on remote servers

One last install pointer: even though Python doesn't have to be installed on any *clients* in the context of a server-side web application, it does have to exist on the *server* machine where your CGI scripts are expected to run. If you're running your own server with either the *webserver.py* script we met earlier, or an open source server such as Apache, this is a nonissue.

But if you are using a web server that you did not configure yourself, you must be sure that Python lives on that machine. Moreover, you need to find where it is on that machine so that you can specify its path in the #! line at the top of your script. If you are not sure if or where Python lives on your server machine, here are some tips:

- Especially on Unix systems, you should first assume that Python lives in a standard place (e.g., */usr/local/bin/python*): type python in a shell window and see if it works. Chances are that Python already lives on such machines. If you have Telnet access on your server, a Unix find command starting at */usr* may help.

- If your server runs Linux, you're probably set to go. Python ships as a standard part of Linux distributions these days, and many web sites and Internet Service Providers (ISPs) run the Linux operating system; at such sites, Python probably already lives at */usr/bin/python*.

- In other environments where you cannot control the server machine yourself, it may be harder to obtain access to an already installed Python. If so, you can relocate your site to a server that does have Python installed, talk your ISP into installing Python on the machine you're trying to use, or install Python on the server machine yourself.

If your ISP is unsympathetic to your need for Python and you are willing to relocate your site to one that is, you can find lists of Python-friendly ISPs by searching *http://www.python.org*. And if you choose to install Python on your server machine yourself, be sure to check out the *freeze* tool shipped with the Python source distribution (in the *Tools* directory). With *freeze*, you can create a single executable program file that contains the entire Python interpreter, as well as all the standard library modules. Such a frozen interpreter can be uploaded to your web account by FTP in a single step, and it won't require a full-blown Python installation on the server. Also see the public domain Installer and Py2Exe systems, which can similarly produce a frozen Python binary.

Adding Pictures and Generating Tables

Let's get back to writing server-side code. As anyone who's ever surfed the Web knows, web pages usually consist of more than simple text. Example 16-4 is a Python CGI script that prints an <IMG> HTML tag in its output to produce a graphic image in the client browser. This example isn't very Python-specific, but note that just as for simple HTML files, the image file (*ppsmall.gif*, one level up from the script file) lives on and is downloaded from the server machine when the browser interprets the output of this script to render the reply page.

Example 16-4. PP3E\Internet\Web\cgi-bin\tutor1.py

```
#!/usr/bin/python

text = """Content-type: text/html

<TITLE>CGI 101</TITLE>
<H1>A Second CGI script</H1>
<HR>
<P>Hello, CGI World!</P>
<IMG src="../ppsmall.gif" BORDER=1 ALT=[image]>
<HR>
"""

print text
```

Notice the use of the triple-quoted string block here; the entire HTML string is sent to the browser in one fell swoop, with the print statement at the end. Be sure that the blank line between the Content-type header and the first HTML is truly blank in the string (it may fail in some browsers if you have any spaces or tabs on that line). If both client and server are functional, a page that looks like Figure 16-4 will be generated when this script is referenced and run.

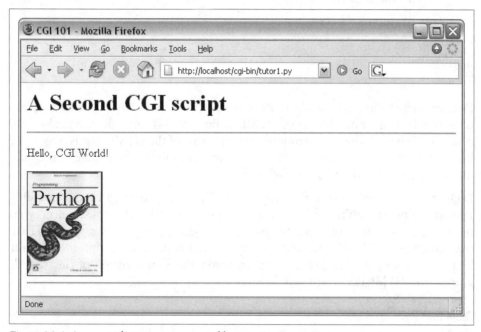

Figure 16-4. A page with an image generated by tutor1.py

So far, our CGI scripts have been putting out canned HTML that could have just as easily been stored in an HTML file. But because CGI scripts are executable programs, they can also be used to generate HTML on the fly, dynamically—even, possibly, in response to a particular set of user inputs sent to the script. That's the whole purpose of CGI scripts, after all. Let's start using this to better advantage now, and write a Python script that builds up response HTML programmatically, listed in Example 16-5.

Example 16-5. PP3E\Internet\Web\cgi-bin\tutor2.py

```
#!/usr/bin/python

print """Content-type: text/html

<TITLE>CGI 101</TITLE>
<H1>A Third CGI script</H1>
<HR>
<P>Hello, CGI World!</P>

<table border=1>
"""

for i in range(5):
    print "<tr>"
    for j in range(4):
        print "<td>%d.%d</td>" % (i, j)
    print "</tr>"

print """
</table>
<HR>
"""
```

Despite all the tags, this really is Python code—the *tutor2.py* script uses triple-quoted strings to embed blocks of HTML again. But this time, the script also uses nested Python for loops to dynamically generate part of the HTML that is sent to the browser. Specifically, it emits HTML to lay out a two-dimensional table in the middle of a page, as shown in Figure 16-5.

Each row in the table displays a "row.column" pair, as generated by the executing Python script. If you're curious how the generated HTML looks, select your browser's View Source option after you've accessed this page. It's a single HTML page composed of the HTML generated by the first print in the script, then the for loops, and finally the last print. In other words, the concatenation of this script's output is an HTML document with headers.

Table tags

The script in Example 16-5 generates HTML table tags. Again, we're not out to learn HTML here, but we'll take a quick look just so that you can make sense of this book's examples. Tables are declared by the text between <table> and </table> tags in HTML. Typically, a table's text in turn declares the contents of each table row between <tr> and </tr> tags and each column within a row between <td> and </td>

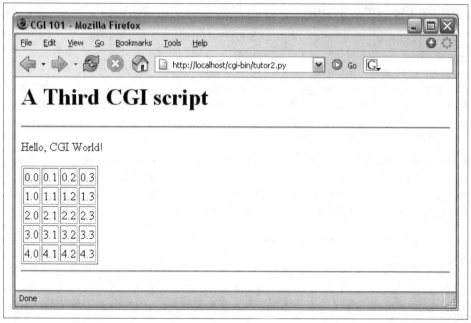

Figure 16-5. A page with a table generated by tutor2.py

tags. The loops in our script build up HTML to declare five rows of four columns each by printing the appropriate tags, with the current row and column number as column values.

For instance, here is part of the script's output, defining the first two rows (to see the full output, run the script standalone from a system command line, or select your browser's View Source option):

```
<table border=1>
<tr>
<td>0.0</td>
<td>0.1</td>
<td>0.2</td>
<td>0.3</td>
</tr>
<tr>
<td>1.0</td>
<td>1.1</td>
<td>1.2</td>
<td>1.3</td>
</tr>
. . .
</table>
```

Other table tags and options let us specify a row title (<th>), layout borders, and so on. We'll use more table syntax to lay out forms in a uniform fashion later in this tutorial.

Adding User Interaction

CGI scripts are great at generating HTML on the fly like this, but they are also commonly used to implement interaction with a user typing at a web browser. As described earlier in this chapter, web interactions usually involve a two-step process and two distinct web pages: you fill out an input form page and press Submit, and a reply page eventually comes back. In between, a CGI script processes the form input.

Submission page

That description sounds simple enough, but the process of collecting user inputs requires an understanding of a special HTML tag, `<form>`. Let's look at the implementation of a simple web interaction to see forms at work. First, we need to define a form page for the user to fill out, as shown in Example 16-6.

Example 16-6. PP3E\Internet\Web\tutor3.html

```
<html>
<title>CGI 101</title>
<body>
<H1>A first user interaction: forms</H1>
<hr>
<form method=POST action="http://localhost/cgi-bin/tutor3.py">
    <P><B>Enter your name:</B>
    <P><input type=text name=user>
    <P><input type=submit>
</form>
</body></html>
```

tutor3.html is a simple HTML file, not a CGI script (though its contents could be printed from a script as well). When this file is accessed, all the text between its `<form>` and `</form>` tags generates the input fields and Submit button shown in Figure 16-6.

More on form tags

We won't go into all the details behind coding HTML forms, but a few highlights are worth underscoring. The following occurs within a form's HTML code:

Form handler action

The form's action option gives the URL of a CGI script that will be invoked to process submitted form data. This is the link from a form to its handler program—in this case, a program called *tutor3.py* in the *cgi-bin* subdirectory of the locally running server's working directory. The action option is the equivalent of command options in Tkinter buttons—it's where a callback handler (here, a remote handler script) is registered to the browser and server.

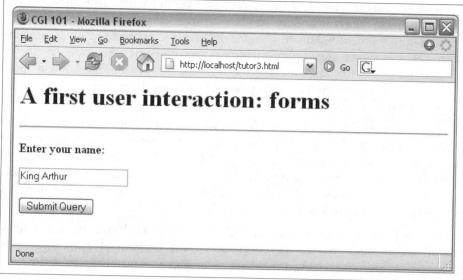

Figure 16-6. A simple form page generated by tutor3.html

Input fields

Input controls are specified with nested <input> tags. In this example, input tags have two key options. The *type* option accepts values such as text for text fields and submit for a Submit button (which sends data to the server and is labeled "Submit Query" by default). The *name* option is the hook used to identify the entered value by key, once all the form data reaches the server. For instance, the server-side CGI script we'll see in a moment uses the string user as a key to get the data typed into this form's text field.

As we'll see in later examples, other input tag options can specify initial values (value=X), display-only mode (readonly), and so on. As we'll also see later, other input *type* option values may transmit hidden data that embeds state information in pages (type=hidden), reinitializes fields (type=reset), or makes multiple-choice buttons (type=checkbox).

Submission method: get *and* post

Forms also include a method option to specify the encoding style to be used to send data over a socket to the target server machine. Here, we use the post style, which contacts the server and then ships it a stream of user input data in a separate transmission over the socket.

An alternative get style ships input information to the server in a single transmission step by appending user inputs to the query string at the end of the URL used to invoke the script, usually after a ? character. Query parameters were introduced earlier when we met URLs; we will put them to use later in this section.

With get, inputs typically show up on the server in environment variables or as arguments in the command line used to start the script. With post, they must be read from standard input and decoded. Because the get method appends inputs to URLs, it allows users to bookmark actions with parameters for later submission (e.g., a link to a retail site, together with the name of a particular item); post is very generally meant for sending data that is to be submitted once (e.g., comment text).

The get method is usually considered more efficient, but it may be subject to length limits in the operating system and is less secure (parameters may be recorded in server logs, for instance). post can handle larger inputs and may be more secure in some scenarios, but it requires an extra transmission. Luckily, Python's cgi module transparently handles either encoding style, so our CGI scripts don't need to know or care which is used.

Notice that the action URL in this example's form spells out the full address for illustration. Because the browser remembers where the enclosing HTML page came from, it works the same with just the script's filename, as shown in Example 16-7.

Example 16-7. PP3E\Internet\Web\tutor3-minimal.html

```
<html>
<title>CGI 101</title>
<body>
<H1>A first user interaction: forms</H1>
<hr>
<form method=POST action="cgi-bin/tutor3.py">
    <P><B>Enter your name:</B>
    <P><input type=text name=user>
    <P><input type=submit>
</form>
</body></html>
```

It may help to remember that URLs embedded in form action tags and hyperlinks are directions to the browser first, not to the script. The *tutor3.py* script itself doesn't care which URL form is used to trigger it—minimal or complete. In fact, all parts of a URL through the script filename (and up to URL query parameters) are used in the conversation between browser and HTTP server, before a CGI script is ever spawned. As long as the browser knows which server to contact, the URL will work.

On the other hand, URLs submitted outside of a page (e.g., typed into a browser's address field or sent to Python's urllib module) usually must be completely specified, because there is no notion of a prior page.

Response script

So far, we've created only a static page with an input field. But the Submit button on this page is loaded to work magic. When pressed, it triggers the possibly remote program whose URL is listed in the form's action option, and passes this program the input data typed by the user, according to the form's method encoding style option. On the server, a Python script is started to handle the form's input data while the user waits for a reply on the client, as shown in Example 16-8.

Example 16-8. PP3E\Internet\Web\cgi-bin\tutor3.py

```
#!/usr/bin/python
#######################################################
# runs on the server, reads form input, prints HTML;
# url=http://server-name/cgi-bin/tutor3.py
#######################################################

import cgi
form = cgi.FieldStorage()               # parse form data
print "Content-type: text/html"         # plus blank line

html = """
<TITLE>tutor3.py</TITLE>
<H1>Greetings</H1>
<HR>
<P>%s</P>
<HR>"""

if not form.has_key('user'):
    print html % "Who are you?"
else:
    print html % ("Hello, %s." % form['user'].value)
```

As before, this Python CGI script prints HTML to generate a response page in the client's browser. But this script does a bit more: it also uses the standard cgi module to parse the input data entered by the user on the prior web page (see Figure 16-6).

Luckily, this is automatic in Python: a call to the standard library cgi module's FieldStorage class automatically does all the work of extracting form data from the input stream and environment variables, regardless of how that data was passed—in a post style stream or in get style parameters appended to the URL. Inputs sent in both styles look the same to Python scripts.

Scripts should call cgi.FieldStorage only once and before accessing any field values. When it is called, we get back an object that looks like a dictionary—user input fields from the form (or URL) show up as values of keys in this object. For example, in the script, form['user'] is an object whose value attribute is a string containing the text typed into the form's text field. If you flip back to the form page's HTML, you'll notice that the input field's name option was user—the name in the form's HTML has become a key we use to fetch the input's value from a dictionary. The object returned by FieldStorage supports other dictionary operations, too—for instance, the has_key method may be used to check whether a field is present in the input data.

Before exiting, this script prints HTML to produce a result page that echoes back what the user typed into the form. Two string-formatting expressions (%) are used to insert the input text into a reply string, and the reply string into the triple-quoted HTML string block. The body of the script's output looks like this:

```
<TITLE>tutor3.py</TITLE>
<H1>Greetings</H1>
<HR>
<P>Hello, King Arthur.</P>
<HR>
```

In a browser, the output is rendered into a page like the one in Figure 16-7.

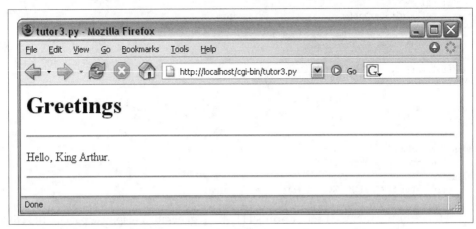

Figure 16-7. tutor3.py result for parameters in a form

Passing parameters in URLs

Notice that the URL address of the script that generated this page shows up at the top of the browser. We didn't type this URL itself—it came from the action tag of the prior page's form HTML. However, nothing is stopping us from typing the script's URL explicitly in our browser's address field to invoke the script, just as we did for our earlier CGI script and HTML file examples.

But there's a catch here: where does the input field's value come from if there is no form page? That is, if we type the CGI script's URL ourselves, how does the input field get filled in? Earlier, when we talked about URL formats, I mentioned that the get encoding scheme tacks input parameters onto the end of URLs. When we type script addresses explicitly, we can also append input values on the end of URLs, where they serve the same purpose as <input> fields in forms. Moreover, the Python cgi module makes URL and form inputs look identical to scripts.

For instance, we can skip filling out the input form page completely, and directly invoke our *tutor3.py* script by visiting a URL of this form (type this in your browser's address field):

```
http://localhost/cgi-bin/tutor3.py?user=Brian
```

In this URL, a value for the input named user is specified explicitly, as if the user had filled out the input page. When called this way, the only constraint is that the parameter name user must match the name expected by the script (and hardcoded in the form's HTML). We use just one parameter here, but in general, URL parameters are typically introduced with a ? and are followed by one or more name=value assignments, separated by & characters if there is more than one. Figure 16-8 shows the response page we get after typing a URL with explicit inputs.

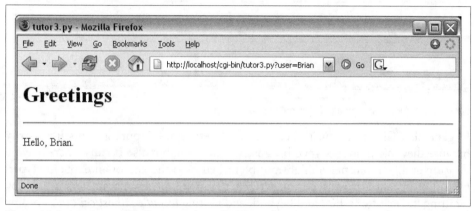

Figure 16-8. tutor3.py result for parameters in a URL

In fact, HTML forms that specify the get encoding style also cause inputs to be added to URLs this way. Try changing Example 16-6 to use method=GET, and submit the form—the name input in the form shows up as a query parameter in the reply page address field, just like the URL we manually entered in Figure 16-8. Forms can use the post or get style. Manually typed URLs with parameters use get.

Generally, any CGI script can be invoked either by filling out and submitting a form page or by passing inputs at the end of a URL. Although hand-coding parameters in URLs can become difficult for scripts that expect many complex parameters, other programs can automate the construction process.

When CGI scripts are invoked with explicit input parameters this way, it's not too difficult to see their similarity to *functions*, albeit ones that live remotely on the Net. Passing data to scripts in URLs is similar to keyword arguments in Python functions, both operationally and syntactically. In fact, in Chapter 18 we will meet a system called Zope that makes the relationship between URLs and Python function calls even more literal (URLs become more direct function calls).

Incidentally, if you clear out the name input field in the form input page (i.e., make it empty) and press Submit, the user name field becomes empty. More accurately, the browser may not send this field along with the form data at all, even though it is listed in the form layout HTML. The CGI script detects such a missing field with the dictionary has_key method and produces the page captured in Figure 16-9 in response.

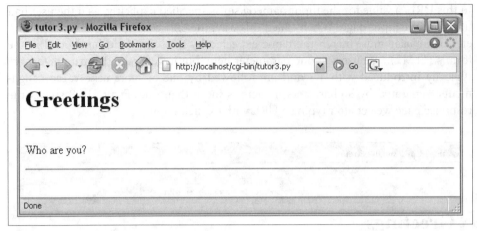

Figure 16-9. An empty name field producing an error page

In general, CGI scripts must check to see whether any inputs are missing, partly because they might not be typed by a user in the form, but also because there may be no form at all—input fields might not be tacked onto the end of an explicitly typed URL. For instance, if we type the script's URL without any parameters at all—by omitting the text from the ? and beyond, and visiting *http://localhost/cgi-bin/tutor3.py* with an explicitly entered URL—we get this same error response page. Since we can invoke any CGI through a form or URL, scripts must anticipate both scenarios.

Testing outside browsers with the module urllib

Once we understand how to send inputs to forms as query string parameters at the end of URLs like this, the Python urllib module we met in Chapters 2 and 14 becomes even more useful. Recall that this module allows us to fetch the reply generated for any URL address. When the URL names a simple HTML file, we simply download its contents. But when it names a CGI script, the effect is to run the remote script and fetch its output.

For example, we can trigger the script in Example 16-8 directly, without either going through the *tutor3.html* web page or typing a URL in a browser's address field:

```
C:\Python24>python
>>> from urllib import urlopen
>>> reply = urlopen('http://localhost/cgi-bin/tutor3.py?user=Brian').read()
>>> print reply
<TITLE>tutor3.py</TITLE>
<H1>Greetings</H1>
<HR>
<P>Hello, Brian.</P>
<HR>

>>> url  = 'http://localhost/cgi-bin/tutor3.py'
>>> conn = urlopen(url)
```

```
>>> reply = conn.read( )
>>> print reply
<TITLE>tutor3.py</TITLE>
<H1>Greetings</H1>
<HR>
<P>Who are you?</P>
<HR>
```

Recall from Chapter 14 that `urllib.urlopen` gives us a file object connected to the generated reply stream. Reading this file's output returns the HTML that would normally be intercepted by a web browser and rendered into a reply page.

When fetched directly, the HTML reply can be parsed with Python text processing tools (e.g., string methods like `split` and `find`, the `re` pattern-matching module, or the `htmllib` HTML parsing module). Extracting text from the reply this way is sometimes informally called *screen scraping*—a way to use web site content in other programs. Screen scraping is an alternative to more complex web services frameworks, though a brittle one: small changes in the page's format can often break scrapers that rely on it. The reply text can also be simply inspected—`urllib` allows us to test CGI scripts from the Python interactive prompt or other scripts, instead of a browser.

More generally, this technique allows us to use a server-side script as a sort of function call. For instance, a client-side GUI can call the CGI script and parse the generated reply page. Similarly, a CGI script that updates a database may be invoked programmatically with `urllib`, outside the context of an input form page. This also opens the door to automated regression testing of CGI scripts—we can invoke scripts on any remote machine, and compare their reply text to the expected output.[*] We'll see `urllib` in action again in later examples.

Before we move on, here are a few advanced `urllib` usage notes. First, this module also supports proxies, alternative transmission modes, and more. For instance, proxies are supported transparently with environment variables or system settings, or by passing in an extra argument. Moreover, although it normally doesn't make a difference to Python scripts, it is possible to send parameters in both the get and the put submission modes described earlier with `urllib`. The get mode, with parameters in the query string at the end of a URL as shown in the prior listing, is used by default. To invoke post, pass parameters in as a separate argument:

```
>>> from urllib import urlopen, urlencode
>>> params = urlencode({'user': 'Brian'})
>>> params
'user=Brian'
>>>
>>> print urlopen('http://localhost/cgi-bin/tutor3.py', params).read( )
<TITLE>tutor3.py</TITLE>
```

---

[*] If your job description includes extensive testing of server-side scripts, you may also want to explore Twill, a relatively new Python-based system that provides a little language for scripting the client-side interface to web applications. Search the Web for details.

```
<H1>Greetings</H1>
<HR>
<P>Hello, Brian.</P>
<HR>
```

Finally, if your web application depends on client-side cookies (discussed later), see also the newer module, urllib2. This module provides the same file-like urlopen interface for opening and reading from a URL, but it uses the cookielib module to automatically store cookies locally, and later return them to the server. It also supports redirection, authentication, and more; both URL modules also support secure HTTP transmissions. See the Python library manual for details. We'll explore both cookies and urllib2 later in this chapter, and introduce secure HTTP in the next.

Using Tables to Lay Out Forms

Now let's move on to something a bit more realistic. In most CGI applications, input pages are composed of multiple fields. When there is more than one, input labels and fields are typically laid out in a table, to give the form a well-structured appearance. The HTML file in Example 16-9 defines a form with two input fields.

Example 16-9. PP3E\Internet\Web\tutor4.html

```
<html>
<title>CGI 101</title>
<body>
<H1>A second user interaction: tables</H1>
<hr>
<form method=POST action="cgi-bin/tutor4.py">
  <table>
    <TR>
      <TH align=right>Enter your name:
      <TD><input type=text name=user>
    <TR>
      <TH align=right>Enter your age:
      <TD><input type=text name=age>
    <TR>
      <TD colspan=2 align=center>
      <input type=submit value="Send">
  </table>
</form>
</body></html>
```

The <TH> tag defines a column like <TD>, but also tags it as a header column, which generally means it is rendered in a bold font. By placing the input fields and labels in a table like this, we get an input page like that shown in Figure 16-10. Labels and inputs are automatically lined up vertically in columns, much as they were by the Tkinter GUI geometry managers we met earlier in this book.

When this form's Submit button (labeled "Send" by the page's HTML) is pressed, it causes the script in Example 16-10 to be executed on the server machine, with the inputs typed by the user.

Figure 16-10. A form laid out with table tags

Example 16-10. PP3E\Internet\Web\cgi-bin\tutor4.py

```python
#!/usr/bin/python
#######################################################
# runs on the server, reads form input, prints HTML;
# URL http://server-name/cgi-bin/tutor4.py
#######################################################

import cgi, sys
sys.stderr = sys.stdout                # errors to browser
form = cgi.FieldStorage()              # parse form data
print "Content-type: text/html\n"      # plus blank line

# class dummy:
#     def __init__(self, s): self.value = s
# form = {'user': dummy('bob'), 'age':dummy('10')}

html = """
<TITLE>tutor4.py</TITLE>
<H1>Greetings</H1>
<HR>
<H4>%s</H4>
<H4>%s</H4>
<H4>%s</H4>
<HR>"""

if not form.has_key('user'):
    line1 = "Who are you?"
else:
    line1 = "Hello, %s." % form['user'].value

line2 = "You're talking to a %s server." % sys.platform

line3 = ""
if form.has_key('age'):
```

Example 16-10. PP3E\Internet\Web\cgi-bin\tutor4.py (continued)

```
    try:
        line3 = "Your age squared is %d!" % (int(form['age'].value) ** 2)
    except:
        line3 = "Sorry, I can't compute %s ** 2." % form['age'].value

print html % (line1, line2, line3)
```

The table layout comes from the HTML file, not from this Python CGI script. In fact, this script doesn't do much new—it uses string formatting to plug input values into the response page's HTML triple-quoted template string as before, this time with one line per input field. When this script is run by submitting the input form page, its output produces the new reply page shown in Figure 16-11.

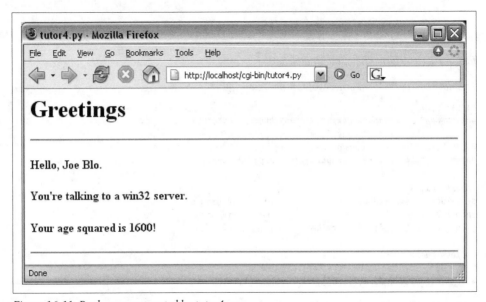

Figure 16-11. Reply page generated by tutor4.py

As usual, we can pass parameters to this CGI script at the end of a URL, too. Figure 16-12 shows the page we get when passing a user and age explicitly in this URL:

```
http://localhost/cgi-bin/tutor4.py?user=Joe+Blow&age=30
```

Notice that we have two parameters after the ? this time; we separate them with &. Also note that we've specified a blank space in the user value with +. This is a common URL encoding convention. On the server side, the + is automatically replaced with a space again. It's also part of the standard escape rule for URL strings, which we'll revisit later.

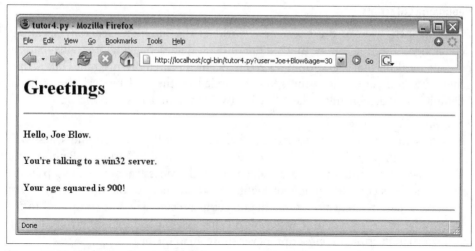

Figure 16-12. Reply page from tutor4.py for parameters in URL

Although Example 16-10 doesn't introduce much that is new about CGI itself, it does highlight a few new coding tricks worth noting, especially regarding CGI script debugging and security. Let's take a quick look.

Converting strings in CGI scripts

Just for fun, the script echoes back the name of the server platform by fetching sys.platform along with the square of the age input field. Notice that the age input's value must be converted to an integer with the built-in int function; in the CGI world, all inputs arrive as strings. We could also convert to an integer with the built-in eval function. Conversion (and other) errors are trapped gracefully in a try statement to yield an error line, instead of letting our script die.

> You should never use eval to convert strings that were sent over the Internet, like the age field in this example, unless you can be absolutely sure that the string does not contain even potentially malicious code. For instance, if this example were available on the general Internet, it's not impossible that someone could type a value into the age field (or append an age parameter to the URL) with a value like os.system('rm *'). Given the appropriate context and process permissions, when passed to eval, such a string might delete all the files in your server script directory!
>
> Unless you run CGI scripts in processes with limited permissions and machine access, strings read off the Web can be dangerous to run as code in CGI scripting. You should never pass them to dynamic coding tools like eval and exec, or to tools that run arbitrary shell commands such as os.popen and os.system, unless you can be sure that they are safe. Always use simpler tools for numeric conversion like int and float, which recognize only numbers.

Debugging CGI scripts

Errors happen, even in the brave new world of the Internet. Generally speaking, debugging CGI scripts can be much more difficult than debugging programs that run on your local machine. Not only do errors occur on a remote machine, but scripts generally won't run without the context implied by the CGI model. The script in Example 16-10 demonstrates the following two common debugging tricks:

Error message trapping

This script assigns `sys.stderr` to `sys.stdout` so that Python error messages wind up being displayed in the response page in the browser. Normally, Python error messages are written to `stderr`, which generally causes them to show up in the web server's console window or logfile. To route them to the browser, we must make `stderr` reference the same file object as `stdout` (which is connected to the browser in CGI scripts). If we don't do this assignment, Python errors, including program errors in our script, never show up in the browser.

Test case mock-up

The `dummy` class definition, commented out in this final version, was used to debug the script before it was installed on the Net. Besides not seeing `stderr` messages by default, CGI scripts also assume an enclosing context that does not exist if they are tested outside the CGI environment. For instance, if run from the system command line, this script has no form input data. Uncomment this code to test from the system command line. The `dummy` class masquerades as a parsed form field object, and `form` is assigned a dictionary containing two form field objects. The net effect is that `form` will be plug-and-play compatible with the result of a `cgi.FieldStorage` call. As usual in Python, object interfaces, not datatypes, are all we must adhere to.

Here are a few general tips for debugging your server-side CGI scripts:

Run the script from the command line

It probably won't generate HTML as is, but running it standalone will detect any syntax errors in your code. Recall that a Python command line can run source code files regardless of their extension: for example, `python somescript.cgi` works fine.

Assign `sys.stderr` to `sys.stdout` as early as possible in your script

This will generally make the text of Python error messages and stack dumps appear in your client browser when accessing the script, instead of the web server's console window or logs. Short of wading through server logs, or manual exception handling, this may be the only way to see the text of error messages after your script aborts.

Mock up inputs to simulate the enclosing CGI context

For instance, define classes that mimic the CGI inputs interface (as done with the `dummy` class in this script) so that you can view the script's output for various test cases by running it from the system command line.* Setting environment variables to mimic form or URL inputs sometimes helps too (we'll see how later in this chapter).

Call utilities to display CGI context in the browser

The CGI module includes utility functions that send a formatted dump of CGI environment variables and input values to the browser, to view in a reply page. For instance, `cgi.print_form(form)` prints all the input parameters sent from the client, and `cgi.test()` prints environment variables, the form, the directory, and more. Sometimes this is enough to resolve connection or input problems. We'll use some of these in the mailer case study in the next chapter.

Show exceptions you catch, print tracebacks

If you catch an exception that Python raises, the Python error message won't be printed to `stderr` (that is normal behavior). In such cases, it's up to your script to display the exception's name and value in the response page; exception details are available in the built-in `sys` module, from `sys.exc_info()`. In addition, Python's `traceback` module can be used to manually generate stack traces on your reply page for errors; tracebacks show source-code lines active when an exception occurred. We'll use this later in the error page in PyMailCGI (Chapter 17).

Add debugging prints

You can always insert tracing `print` statements in your code, just as in normal Python programs. Be sure you print the content-type header line first, though, or your prints may not show up on the reply page. In the worst case, you can also generate debugging and trace messages by opening and writing to a local text file on the server; provided you access that file later, this avoids having to format the trace messages according to HTML reply stream conventions.

Run it live

Of course, once your script is at least half working, your best bet is likely to start running it live on the server, with real inputs coming from a browser. Running a server locally on your machine, as we're doing in this chapter, can help by making changes go faster as you test.

Adding Common Input Devices

So far, we've been typing inputs into text fields. HTML forms support a handful of input controls (what we'd call widgets in the traditional GUI world) for collecting user inputs. Let's look at a CGI program that shows all the common input controls

---

* This technique isn't unique to CGI scripts, by the way. In Chapter 15, we'll meet systems that embed Python code inside HTML. There is no good way to test such code outside the context of the enclosing system without extracting the embedded Python code (perhaps by using the `htmllib` HTML parser that comes with Python) and running it with a passed-in mock-up of the API that it will eventually use.

at once. As usual, we define both an HTML file to lay out the form page and a Python CGI script to process its inputs and generate a response. The HTML file is presented in Example 16-11.

Example 16-11. PP3E\Internet\Web\cgi-bin\tutor5a.html

```
<HTML><TITLE>CGI 101</TITLE>
<BODY>
<H1>Common input devices</H1>
<HR>
<FORM method=POST action="cgi-bin/tutor5.py">
  <H3>Please complete the following form and click Send</H3>
  <P><TABLE>
    <TR>
      <TH align=right>Name:
      <TD><input type=text name=name>
    <TR>
      <TH align=right>Shoe size:
      <TD><table>
      <td><input type=radio name=shoesize value=small>Small
      <td><input type=radio name=shoesize value=medium>Medium
      <td><input type=radio name=shoesize value=large>Large
      </table>
    <TR>
      <TH align=right>Occupation:
      <TD><select name=job>
        <option>Developer
        <option>Manager
        <option>Student
        <option>Evangelist
        <option>Other
      </select>
    <TR>
      <TH align=right>Political affiliations:
      <TD><table>
      <td><input type=checkbox name=language value=Python>Pythonista
      <td><input type=checkbox name=language value=Perl>Perlmonger
      <td><input type=checkbox name=language value=Tcl>Tcler
      </table>
    <TR>
      <TH align=right>Comments:
      <TD><textarea name=comment cols=30 rows=2>Enter text here</textarea>
    <TR>
      <TD colspan=2 align=center>
      <input type=submit value="Send">
  </TABLE>
</FORM>
<HR>
</BODY></HTML>
```

When rendered by a browser, the page in Figure 16-13 appears.

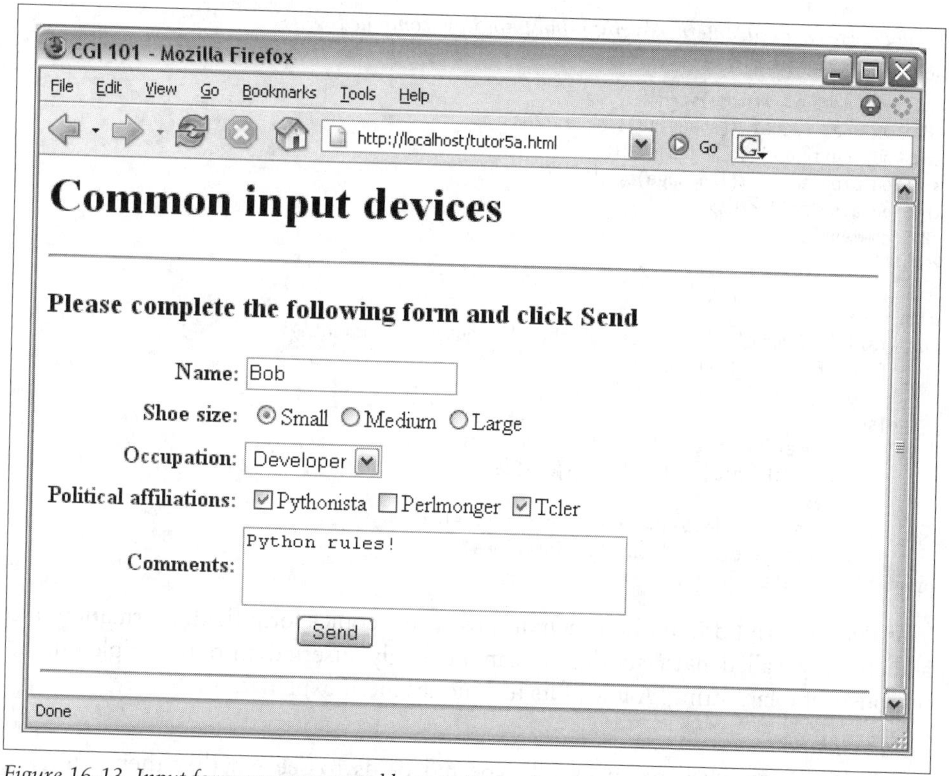

Figure 16-13. Input form page generated by tutor5a.html

This page contains a simple text field as before, but it also has radio buttons, a pull-down selection list, a set of multiple-choice checkbuttons, and a multiple-line text input area. All have a name option in the HTML file, which identifies their selected value in the data sent from client to server. When we fill out this form and click the Send submit button, the script in Example 16-12 runs on the server to process all the input data typed or selected in the form.

Example 16-12. PP3E\Internet\Web\cgi-bin\tutor5.py

```
#!/usr/bin/python
#####################################################
# runs on the server, reads form input, prints HTML
#####################################################

import cgi, sys
form = cgi.FieldStorage()              # parse form data
print "Content-type: text/html"        # plus blank line

html = """
<TITLE>tutor5.py</TITLE>
<H1>Greetings</H1>
```

Example 16-12. PP3E\Internet\Web\cgi-bin\tutor5.py (continued)

```
<HR>
<H4>Your name is %(name)s</H4>
<H4>You wear rather %(shoesize)s shoes</H4>
<H4>Your current job: %(job)s</H4>
<H4>You program in %(language)s</H4>
<H4>You also said:</H4>
<P>%(comment)s</P>
<HR>"""


data = {}
for field in ('name', 'shoesize', 'job', 'language', 'comment'):
    if not form.has_key(field):
        data[field] = '(unknown)'
    else:
        if type(form[field]) != list:
            data[field] = form[field].value
        else:
            values = [x.value for x in form[field]]
            data[field] = ' and '.join(values)
print html % data
```

This Python script doesn't do much; it mostly just copies form field information into a dictionary called data so that it can be easily inserted into the triple-quoted response template string. A few of its techniques merit explanation:

Field validation

As usual, we need to check all expected fields to see whether they really are present in the input data, using the dictionary has_key method. Any or all of the input fields may be missing if they weren't entered on the form or appended to an explicit URL.

String formatting

We're using dictionary key references in the format string this time—recall that %(name)s means pull out the value for the key name in the data dictionary and perform a to-string conversion on its value.

Multiple-choice fields

We're also testing the type of all the expected fields' values to see whether they arrive as a list rather than the usual string. Values of multiple-choice input controls, like the language choice field in this input page, are returned from cgi.FieldStorage as a list of objects with value attributes, rather than a simple single object with a value.

This script copies simple field values to the dictionary verbatim, but it uses a list comprehension to collect the value fields of multiple-choice selections, and the string join method to construct a single string with an and inserted between each selection value (e.g., Python and Tcl). The script's list comprehension is equivalent to the call map(lambda x: x.value, form[field]).*

When the form page is filled out and submitted, the script creates the response shown in Figure 16-14—essentially just a formatted echo of what was sent.

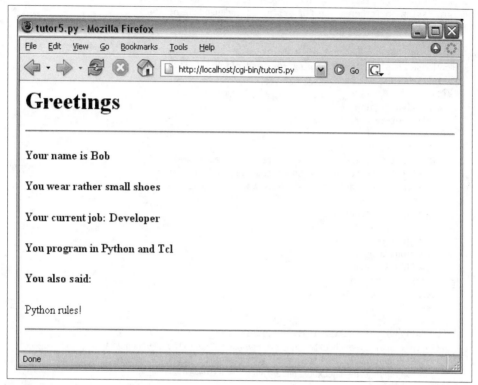

Figure 16-14. Response page created by tutor5.py (1)

Changing Input Layouts

Suppose that you've written a system like that in the prior section, and your users, clients, and significant other start complaining that the input form is difficult to read. Don't worry. Because the CGI model naturally separates the *user interface* (the HTML input page definition) from the *processing logic* (the CGI script), it's completely painless to change the form's layout. Simply modify the HTML file; there's no need to change the CGI code at all. For instance, Example 16-13 contains a new definition of the input that uses tables a bit differently to provide a nicer layout with borders.

---

* Two forward references are worth noting here. Besides simple strings and lists, later we'll see a third type of form input object, returned for fields that specify file uploads. The script in this example should really also escape the echoed text inserted into the HTML reply to be robust, lest it contain HTML operators. We will discuss escapes in detail later.

Example 16-13. PP3E\Internet\Web\tutor5b.html

```
<HTML><TITLE>CGI 101</TITLE>
<BODY>
<H1>Common input devices: alternative layout</H1>
<P>Use the same tutor5.py server side script, but change the
layout of the form itself.  Notice the separation of user interface
and processing logic here; the CGI script is independent of the
HTML used to interact with the user/client.</P><HR>

<FORM method=POST action="cgi-bin/tutor5.py">
  <H3>Please complete the following form and click Submit</H3>
  <P><TABLE border cellpadding=3>
    <TR>
      <TH align=right>Name:
      <TD><input type=text name=name>
    <TR>
      <TH align=right>Shoe size:
      <TD><input type=radio name=shoesize value=small>Small
          <input type=radio name=shoesize value=medium>Medium
          <input type=radio name=shoesize value=large>Large
    <TR>
      <TH align=right>Occupation:
      <TD><select name=job>
        <option>Developer
        <option>Manager
        <option>Student
        <option>Evangelist
        <option>Other
      </select>
    <TR>
      <TH align=right>Political affiliations:
      <TD><P><input type=checkbox name=language value=Python>Pythonista
          <P><input type=checkbox name=language value=Perl>Perlmonger
          <P><input type=checkbox name=language value=Tcl>Tcler
    <TR>
      <TH align=right>Comments:
      <TD><textarea name=comment cols=30 rows=2>Enter spam here</textarea>
    <TR>
      <TD colspan=2 align=center>
      <input type=submit value="Submit">
      <input type=reset  value="Reset">
  </TABLE>
</FORM>
</BODY></HTML>
```

When we visit this alternative page with a browser, we get the interface shown in Figure 16-15.

Now, before you go blind trying to detect the differences in this and the prior HTML file, I should note that the HTML differences that produce this page are much less important than the fact that the action fields in these two pages' forms reference

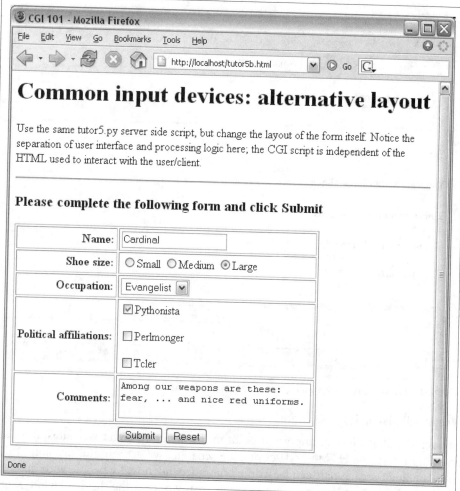

Figure 16-15. Form page created by tutor5b.html

identical URLs. Pressing this version's Submit button triggers the exact same and totally unchanged Python CGI script again, *tutor5.py* (Example 16-12).

That is, scripts are completely independent of both the transmission mode (URL query parameters of form fields) and the layout of the user interface used to send them information. Changes in the response page require changing the script, of course, because the HTML of the reply page is still embedded in the CGI script. But we can change the input page's HTML as much as we like without affecting the server-side Python code. Figure 16-16 shows the response page produced by the script this time around.

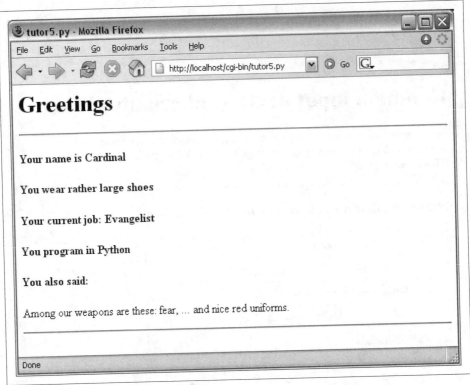

Figure 16-16. Response page created by tutor5.py (2)

Keeping display and logic separate

In fact, this illustrates an important point in the design of larger web sites: if we are careful to keep the HTML and script code separate, we get a useful division of display and logic—each part can be worked on independently, by people with different skill sets. Web page designers, for example, can work on the display layout, while programmers can code business logic.

Although this section's example is fairly small, it already benefits from this separation for the input page. In some cases, the separation is harder to accomplish, because our example scripts embed the HTML of reply pages. With just a little more work, though, we can usually split the reply HTML off into separate files that can also be developed independently of the script's logic. The html string in *tutor5.py* (Example 16-12), for instance, might be stored in a text file and loaded by the script when run.

In larger systems, tools such as server-side HTML templating languages help make the division of display and logic even easier to achieve. The Zope and Python Server Pages examples we'll meet in Chapter 18, for instance, promote the separation of display and logic by providing reply page description languages that are expanded to include portions generated by separate Python program logic. In a sense, server-side templating languages embed Python in HTML—the opposite of CGI scripts that embed HTML in Python—and may provide a cleaner division of labor, provided the Python code is separate components. See Chapter 18 for more details. Similar techniques can be used for separation of layout and login in the GUIs we studied earlier in this book, but they also usually require larger frameworks or models to achieve.

Passing Parameters in Hardcoded URLs

Earlier, we passed parameters to CGI scripts by listing them at the end of a URL typed into the browser's address field—in the query string parameters part of the URL, after the ?. But there's nothing sacred about the browser's address field. In particular, nothing is stopping us from using the same URL syntax in hyperlinks that we hardcode or generate in web page definitions.

For example, the web page from Example 16-14 defines three hyperlinks (the text between the <A> and </A> tags), which trigger our original *tutor5.py* script again (Example 16-12), but with three different precoded sets of parameters.

Example 16-14. PP3E\Internet\Web\tutor5c.html

```
<HTML><TITLE>CGI 101</TITLE>
<BODY>
<H1>Common input devices: URL parameters</H1>

<P>This demo invokes the tutor5.py server-side script again,
but hardcodes input data to the end of the script's URL,
within a simple hyperlink (instead of packaging up a form's
inputs).  Click your browser's "show page source" button
to view the links associated with each list item below.

<P>This is really more about CGI than Python, but notice that
Python's cgi module handles both this form of input (which is
also produced by GET form actions), as well as POST-ed forms;
they look the same to the Python CGI script.  In other words,
cgi module users are independent of the method used to submit
data.

<P>Also notice that URLs with appended input values like this
can be generated as part of the page output by another CGI script,
to direct a next user click to the right place and context; together
with type 'hidden' input fields, they provide one way to
save state between clicks.
</P><HR>

<UL>
<LI><A href="cgi-bin/tutor5.py?name=Bob&shoesize=small">Send Bob, small</A>
<LI><A href="cgi-bin/tutor5.py?name=Tom&language=Python">Send Tom, Python</A>

<LI><A href="http://localhost/cgi-bin/tutor5.py?job=Evangelist&comment=spam">
```

Example 16-14. PP3E\Internet\Web\tutor5c.html (continued)

```
Send Evangelist, spam</A>
</UL>

<HR></BODY></HTML>
```

This static HTML file defines three hyperlinks—the first two are minimal and the third is fully specified, but all work similarly (again, the target script doesn't care). When we visit this file's URL, we see the page shown in Figure 16-17. It's mostly just a page for launching canned calls to the CGI script.

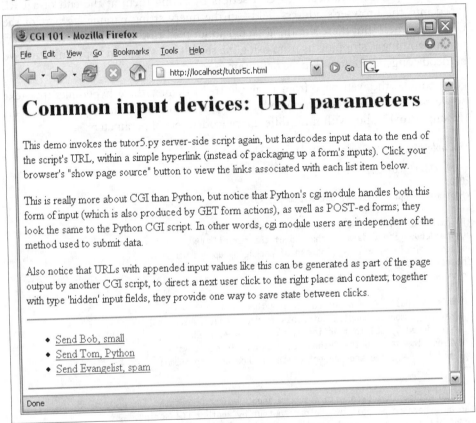

Figure 16-17. Hyperlinks page created by tutor5c.html

Clicking on this page's second link creates the response page in Figure 16-18. This link invokes the CGI script, with the name parameter set to "Tom" and the language parameter set to "Python," simply because those parameters and values are hard-coded in the URL listed in the HTML for the second hyperlink. As such, hyperlinks with parameters like this are sometimes known as *stateful* links—they automatically direct the next script's operation. The net effect is exactly as if we had manually typed the line shown at the top of the browser in Figure 16-18.

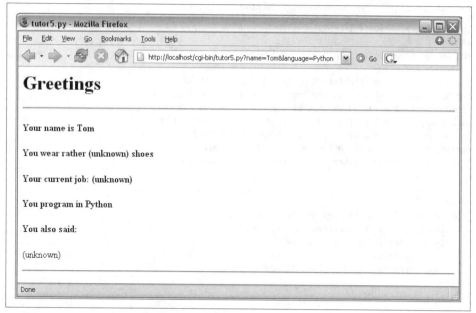

Figure 16-18. Response page created by tutor5.py (3)

Notice that many fields are missing here; the *tutor5.py* script is smart enough to detect and handle missing fields and generate an unknown message in the reply page. It's also worth pointing out that we're reusing the Python CGI script again. The script itself is completely independent of both the user interface format of the submission page, as well as the technique used to invoke it—from a submitted form or a hardcoded URL with query parameters. By separating such user interface details from processing logic, CGI scripts become reusable software components, at least within the context of the CGI environment.

The query parameters in the URLs embedded in Example 16-14 were hardcoded in the page's HTML. But such URLs can also be generated automatically by a CGI script as part of a reply page in order to provide inputs to the script that implements a next step in user interaction. They are a simple way for web-based applications to "remember" things for the duration of a session. Hidden form fields, up next, serve some of the same purposes.

Passing Parameters in Hidden Form Fields

Similar in spirit to the prior section, inputs for scripts can also be hardcoded in a page's HTML as hidden input fields. Such fields are not displayed in the page, but are transmitted back to the server when the form is submitted. Example 16-15, for instance, allows a job field to be entered, but fills in name and language parameters automatically as hidden input fields.

Example 16-15. PP3E\Internet\Web\tutor5d.html

```
<HTML><TITLE>CGI 101</TITLE>
<BODY>
<H1>Common input devices: hidden form fields</H1>

<P>This demo invokes the tutor5.py server-side script again,
but hardcodes input data in the form itself as hidden input
fields, instead of as parameters at the end of URL hyperlinks.
As before, the text of this form, including the hidden fields,
can be generated as part of the page output by another CGI
script, to pass data on to the next script on submit; hidden
form fields provide another way to save state between pages.
</P><HR><p>

<form>
<form method=post action="cgi-bin/tutor5.py">
    <input type=hidden name=name     value=Sue>
    <input type=hidden name=language value=Python>
    <input type=text   name=job      value="Enter job">
    <input type=submit value="Submit Sue">
</form>
</p><HR></BODY></HTML>
```

When Example 16-15 is opened in a browser, we get the input page in Figure 16-19.

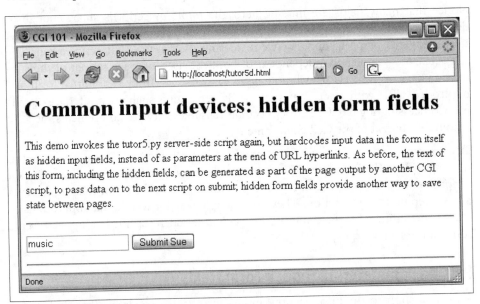

Figure 16-19. tutor5d.html input form page

When submitting, we trigger our original *tutor5.py* script once again (Example 16-12), but some of the inputs have been provided for us as hidden fields. The reply page is captured in Figure 16-20.

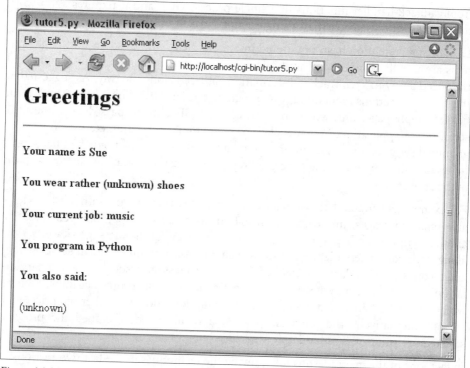

Figure 16-20. Response page created by tutor5.py (4)

Here again, we've hardcoded and embedded the inputs in the page's HTML, but such fields can also be generated on the fly as part of the reply from a CGI script. When they are, they serve as inputs for the next page, and so are a sort of memory. To fully understand how and why this is necessary, we need to next take a short diversion into state retention alternatives.

Saving State Information in CGI Scripts

One of the most unusual aspects of the basic CGI model, and one of its starkest contrasts to the GUI programming techniques we studied in the prior part of this book, is that CGI scripts are *stateless*—each is a standalone program, normally run autonomously, with no knowledge of any other scripts that may run before or after. There is no notion of things such as global variables or objects that outlive a single step of interaction and retain context. Each script begins from scratch, with no memory of where the prior left off.

This makes web servers simple and robust—a buggy CGI script won't interfere with the server process. In fact, a flaw in a CGI script generally affects only the single page it implements, not the entire web-based application. But this is a very different model from callback-handler functions in a single process GUI, and it requires extra work to remember things longer than a single script's execution.

Lack of state retention hasn't mattered in our simple examples so far, but larger systems are usually composed of multiple user interaction steps and many scripts, and they need a way to keep track of information gathered along the way. As suggested in the last two sections, generating query parameters on URL links and hidden form fields in reply pages are two simple ways for a CGI script to pass data to the next script in the application. When clicked or submitted, such parameters send preprogrammed selection or session information back to another server-side handler script. In a sense, the content of the generated reply page itself becomes the memory space of the application.

For example, a site that lets you read your email may present you with a list of viewable email messages, implemented in HTML as a list of hyperlinks generated by another script. Each hyperlink might include the name of the message viewer script, along with parameters identifying the selected message number, email server name, and so on—as much data as is needed to fetch the message associated with a particular link. A retail site may instead serve up a generated list of product links, each of which triggers a hardcoded hyperlink containing the product number, its price, and so on. Alternatively, the purchase page at a retail site may embed the product selected in a prior page as hidden form fields.

In fact, one of the main reasons for showing the techniques in the last two sections is that we're going to use them extensively in the larger case study in the next chapter. For example, we'll use generated stateful URLs with query parameters to implement lists of dynamically generated selections that "know" what to do when clicked. Hidden form fields will also be deployed to pass user login data to the next page's script. From a more general perspective, both techniques are ways to retain state information between pages—they can be used to direct the action of the next script to be run.

Generating URL parameters and hidden form fields works well for retaining state information across pages during a single session of interaction. Some scenarios require more, though. For instance, what if we want to remember a user's login name from session to session? Or what if we need to keep track of pages at our site visited by a user in the past? Because such information must be longer lived than the pages of a single session of interaction, query parameters and hidden form fields won't suffice.

In general, there are a variety of ways to pass or retain state information between CGI script executions and across sessions of interaction:

URL query parameters
     Session state embedded in pages

Hidden form fields
     Session state embedded in pages

Cookies

> Smaller information stored on the client that may span sessions

Server-side databases

> Larger information that might span sessions

CGI model extensions

> Persistent processes, session management, and so on

We'll explore most of these in later examples, but since this is a core idea in server-side scripting, let's take a brief look at each of these in turn.

URL Query Parameters

We met these earlier in this chapter: hardcoded URL parameters in dynamically generated hyperlinks embedded in reply web pages. By including both a processing script name and input to it, such links direct the operation of the next page when selected. The parameters are transmitted from client to server automatically, as part of a GET-style request.

Coding query parameters is straightforward—print the correctly formatted URL to standard output from your CGI script as part of the reply page (albeit following some escaping conventions we'll meet later in this chapter):

```
script = "onViewListLink.py"
user = 'bob'
mnum = 66
pswd = 'xxx'
site = 'pop.rmi.net'
print ('<a href="%s?user=%s&pswd=%s&mnum=%d&site=%s">View %s</a>'
            % (script, user, pswd, mnum, site, mnum))
```

The resulting URL will have enough information to direct the next script when clicked:

```
<a href="onViewListLink.py
    ?user=bob&pswd=xxx&mnum=66&site=pop.rmi.net">View 66</a>
```

Query parameters serve as memory, and they pass information between pages. As such, they are useful for retaining state across the pages of a single session of interaction. Since each generated URL may have different attached parameters, this scheme can provide context per user-selectable action. Each link in a list of selectable alternatives, for example, may have a different implied action coded as a different parameter value. Moreover, users can bookmark a link with parameters, in order to return to a specific state in an interaction.

Because their state retention is lost when the page is abandoned, though, they are not useful for remembering state from session to session. Moreover, the data appended as URL query parameters is generally visible to users and may appear in server log-files; in some applications, it may have to be manually encrypted to avoid display or forgery.

Hidden Form Input Fields

We met these in the prior section as well: hidden form input fields that are attached to form data and are embedded in reply web pages, but are not displayed on web pages. When the form is submitted, all the hidden fields are transmitted to the next script along with any real inputs, to serve as context. The net effect provides context for an entire input form, not a particular hyperlink. An already entered username, password, or selection, for instance, can be implied by the values of hidden fields in subsequently generated pages.

In terms of code, hidden fields are generated by server-side scripts as part of the reply page's HTML, and are later returned by the client with all of the form's input data:

```
print '<form method=post action="%s/onViewSubmit.py">' % urlroot
print '<input type=hidden name=mnum value="%s">' % msgnum
print '<input type=hidden name=user value="%s">' % user
print '<input type=hidden name=site value="%s">' % site
print '<input type=hidden name=pswd value="%s">' % pswd
```

Like query parameters, hidden form fields can also serve as a sort of memory, retaining state information from page to page. Also like query parameters, because this kind of memory is embedded in the page itself, hidden fields are useful for state retention among the pages of a single session of interaction, but not for data that spans multiple sessions.

And like both query parameters and cookies (up next), hidden form fields may be visible to users—their values are displayed if the page's source HTML code is displayed. As a result, hidden form fields are not secure; encryption of the embedded data may again be required in some contexts to avoid display on the client, or forgery in form submissions.

HTTP "Cookies"

Cookies, an extension to the HTTP protocol underlying the web model, are a way for server-side applications to directly store information on the client computer. Because this information is not embedded in the HTML of web pages, it outlives the pages of a single session. As such, cookies are ideal for remembering things that must span sessions.

Things like usernames and preferences, for example, are prime cookie candidates—they will be available the next time the client visits our site. However, because cookies may have space limitations, are seen by some as intrusive, and can be disabled by users on the client, they are not always well suited to general data storage needs. They are often best used for small pieces of noncritical cross-session state information.

Operationally, HTTP cookies are strings of information stored on the client machine and transferred between client and server in HTTP message headers. Server-side scripts generate HTTP headers to request that a cookie be stored on the client as part of the script's reply stream. Later, the client web browser generates HTTP headers that send back all the cookies matching the server and page being contacted. In effect, cookie data is embedded in the data streams much like query parameters and form fields, but is contained in HTTP headers, not in a page's HTML. Moreover, cookie data can be stored permanently on the client, and so outlives both pages and interactive sessions.

For web application developers, Python's standard library includes tools that simplify the task of sending and receiving: cookielib does cookie handling for HTTP clients that talk to web servers, and the module Cookie simplifies the task of creating and receiving cookies on the server. Moreover, the module urllib2 has support for opening URLs with automatic cookie handling.

Creating a cookie

Web browsers such as Firefox and Internet Explorer generally handle the client side of this protocol, storing and sending cookie data. For the purpose of this chapter, we are mainly interested in cookie processing on the server. Cookies are created by sending special HTTP headers at the start of the reply stream:

```
Content-type: text/html
Set-Cookie: foo=bar;

<HTML>...
```

The full format of a cookie's header is as follows:

```
Set-Cookie: name=value; expires=date; path=pathname; domain=domainname; secure
```

The domain defaults to the hostname of the server that set the cookie, and the path defaults to the path of the document or script that set the cookie—these are later matched by the client to know when to send a cookie's value back to the server. In Python, cookie creation is simple; the following in a CGI script stores a last-visited time cookie:

```
import Cookie, time
cook = Cookie.SimpleCookie()
cook["visited"] = str(time.time())    # a dictionary
print cook.output()                   # "Set-Cookie: visited=1137268854.98;"
print 'Content-type: text/html\n'
```

The SimpleCookie call here creates a dictionary-like cookie object whose keys are strings (the names of the cookies), and whose values are "Morsel" objects (describing the cookie's value). Morsels in turn are also dictionary-like objects with one key per cookie property—path and domain, expires to give the cookie an expiration date (the default is the duration of the browser session), and so on. Morsels also have attributes—for instance, key and value give the name and value of the cookie, respectively. Assigning a string to a cookie key automatically creates a Morsel from the string, and the cookie object's output method returns a string suitable for use as an HTTP header (printing the object directly has the same effect, due to its __str__ operator overloading). Here is a more comprehensive example of the interface in action:

```
>>> import Cookie, time
>>> cooks = Cookie.SimpleCookie()
>>> cooks['visited']  = time.asctime()
>>> cooks['username'] = 'Bob'
>>> cooks['username']['path'] = '/myscript'
>>> cooks['visited'].value
'Sun Jan 15 11:31:24 2006'
>>> print cooks['visited']
Set-Cookie: visited="Sun Jan 15 11:31:24 2006";
>>> print cooks
Set-Cookie: username=Bob; Path=/myscript;
Set-Cookie: visited="Sun Jan 15 11:31:24 2006";
```

Receiving a cookie

Now, when the client visits the page again in the future, the cookie's data is sent back from the browser to the server in HTTP headers again, in the form "Cookie: name1=value1; name2=value2 ...". For example:

```
Cookie: visited=1137268854.98
```

Roughly, the browser client returns all cookies that match the requested server's domain name and path. In the CGI script on the server, the environment variable HTTP_COOKIE contains the raw cookie data headers string uploaded from the client; it can be extracted in Python as follows:

```
import os, Cookie
cooks = Cookie.SimpleCookie(os.environ.get("HTTP_COOKIE"))
vcook = cooks.get("visited")     # a Morsel dictionary
if vcook != None:
    time = vcook.value
```

Here, the SimpleCookie constructor call automatically parses the passed-in cookie data string into a dictionary of Morsel objects; as usual, the dictionary get method returns a default None if a key is absent, and we use the Morsel object's value attribute to extract the cookie's value string if sent.

Using cookies in CGI scripts

To help put these pieces together, Example 16-16 lists a CGI script that stores a client-side cookie when first visited, and receives and displays it on subsequent visits.

Example 16-16. PP3E\Internet\Web\cgi-bin\cookies.py

```
#####################################################
# create or use a client-side cookie storing username;
# there is no input form data to parse in this example
#####################################################
```

Example 16-16. PP3E\Internet\Web\cgi-bin\cookies.py (continued)

```
import Cookie, os
cookstr  = os.environ.get("HTTP_COOKIE")
cookies  = Cookie.SimpleCookie(cookstr)
usercook = cookies.get("user")                          # fetch if sent

if usercook == None:                                    # create first time
    cookies = Cookie.SimpleCookie( )                    # print Set-cookie hdr
    cookies['user']  = 'Brian'
    print cookies
    greeting = '<p>His name shall be... %s</p>' % cookies['user']
else:
    greeting = '<p>Welcome back, %s</p>' % usercook.value

print "Content-type: text/html\n"                       # plus blank line now
print greeting
```

Assuming you are running this chapter's local web server from Example 16-1, you can invoke this script with a URL such as *http://localhost/cgi-bin/cookies.py* (type this in your browser's address field, or submit it interactively with the module urllib2). The first time you visit the script, the script sets the cookie within its reply's headers, and you'll see a reply page with this message:

```
His name shall be... Set-Cookie: user=Brian;
```

Thereafter, revisiting the script's URL (use your browser's reload button) produces a reply page with this message:

```
Welcome back, Brian
```

This is because the client is sending the previously stored cookie value back to the script, at least until you kill and restart your web browser—the default expiration of a cookie is the end of a browsing session. In a realistic program, this sort of structure might be used by the login page of a web application; a user would need to enter his name only once per browser session.

Handling cookies with the module urllib2

As mentioned earlier, the urllib2 module provides an interface similar to urllib for reading the reply from a URL, but it uses the cookielib module to also support storing and sending cookies on the client. For example, to use it to test the last section's script, we simply need to enable the cookie-handler class:

```
>>> import urllib2
>>> opener = urllib2.build_opener(urllib2.HTTPCookieProcessor( ))
>>> urllib2.install_opener(opener)
>>>
>>> reply = urllib2.urlopen('http://localhost/cgi-bin/cookies.py').read( )
>>> print reply
<p>His name shall be... Set-Cookie: user=Brian;</p>

>>> reply = urllib2.urlopen('http://localhost/cgi-bin/cookies.py').read( )
```

```
>>> print reply
<p>Welcome back, Brian</p>

>>> reply = urllib2.urlopen('http://localhost/cgi-bin/cookies.py').read()
>>> print reply
<p>Welcome back, Brian</p>
```

This works because urllib2 mimics the cookie behavior of a web browser on the client. Just as in a browser, the cookie is deleted if you exit Python and start a new session to rerun this code. See the library manual for more on this module's interfaces.

Although easy to use, cookies have potential downsides. For one, they may be subject to size limitations (4 KB per cookie, 300 total, and 20 per domain are one common limit). For another, users can disable cookies in most browsers, making them less suited to critical data. Some even see them as intrusive, because they can be abused to track user behavior. Many sites simply require cookies to be turned on, finessing the issue completely. Finally, because they are transmitted over the network between client and server, they are still only as secure as the transmission stream itself; this may be an issue for sensitive data if the page is not using secure HTTP transmissions between client and server. We'll explore secure cookies and server concepts in the next chapter.

For more details on the cookie modules and the cookie protocol in general, see Python's library manual, and search the Web for resources.

Server-Side Databases

For more industrial-strength state retention, Python scripts can employ full-blown database solutions in the server. We will study these options in depth in Chapter 19 of this book. Python scripts have access to a variety of server-side data stores, including flat files, persistent object pickles and shelves, object-oriented databases such as ZODB, and relational SQL-based databases such as MySQL, PostgreSQL, and Oracle. Besides data storage, such systems may provide advanced tools such as transaction commits and rollbacks, concurrent update synchronization, and more.

Full-blown databases are the ultimate storage solution. They can be used to represent state both between the pages of a single session (by tagging the data with generated per-session keys) and across multiple sessions (by storing data under per-user keys).

Given a user's login name, for example, CGI scripts can fetch all of the context we have gathered in the past about that user from the server-side database. Server-side databases are ideal for storing more complex cross-session information; a shopping cart application, for instance, can record items added in the past in a server-side database.

Databases outlive both pages and sessions. Because data is kept explicitly, there is no need to embed it within the query parameters or hidden form fields of reply pages.

Because the data is kept on the server, there is no need to store it on the client in cookies. And because such schemes employ general-purpose databases, they are not subject to the size constraints or optional nature of cookies.

In exchange for their added utility, full-blown databases require more in terms of installation, administration, and coding. As we'll see in Chapter 19, luckily the extra coding part of that trade-off is remarkably simple in Python. Moreover, Python's database interfaces may be used in any application, web-based or otherwise.

Extensions to the CGI Model

Finally, there are more advanced protocols and frameworks for retaining state on the server, which we won't cover in this book. For instance, the Zope web application framework, discussed briefly in Chapter 18, provides a product interface, which allows for the construction of web-based objects that are automatically persistent.

Other schemes, such as FastCGI, as well as server-specific extensions such as mod_python for Apache, may attempt to work around the autonomous, one-shot nature of CGI scripts, or otherwise extend the basic CGI model to support long-lived memory stores. For instance:

- FastCGI allows web applications to run as persistent processes, which receive input data from and send reply streams to the HTTP web server over Inter-Process Communication (IPC) mechanisms such as sockets. This differs from normal CGI, which communicates inputs and outputs with environment variables, standard streams, and command-line arguments, and assumes scripts run to completion on each request. Because a FastCGI process may outlive a single page, it can retain state information from page to page, and avoids startup performance costs.

- mod_python extends the open source Apache web server by embedding the Python interpreter within Apache. Python code is executed directly within the Apache server, eliminating the need to spawn external processes. This package also supports the concept of sessions, which can be used to store data between pages. Session data is locked for concurrent access and can be stored in files or in memory, depending on whether Apache is running in multiprocess or multi-threaded mode. mod_python also includes web development tools, such as the Python Server Pages templating language for HTML generation (described later in this book).

Such models are not universally supported, though, and may come with some added cost in complexity—for example, to synchronize access to persistent data with locks. Moreover, a failure in a FastCGI-style web application impacts the entire application, not just a single page, and things like memory leaks become much more costly. For more on persistent CGI models, and support in Python for things such as FastCGI, search the Web or consult web-specific resources.

Combining Techniques

Naturally, these techniques may be combined to achieve a variety of memory strategies, both for interaction sessions and for more permanent storage needs. For example:

- A web application may use cookies to store a per-user or per-session key on the client, and later use that key to index into a server-side database to retrieve the user's or session's full state information.

- Even for short-lived session information, URL query parameters or hidden form fields may similarly be used to pass a key identifying the session from page to page, to be used by the next script to index a server-side database.

- Moreover, URL query parameters and hidden fields may be generated for temporary state memory that spans pages, even though cookies and databases are used for retention that must span sessions.

The choice of appropriate technique is driven by the application's storage needs. Although not as straightforward as the in-memory variables and objects of single process GUI programs running on a client, with a little creativity, CGI script state retention is entirely possible.

The Hello World Selector

Let's get back to writing some code again. It's time for something a bit more useful than the examples we've seen so far (well, more entertaining, at least). This section presents a program that displays the basic syntax required by various programming languages to print the string "Hello World," the classic language benchmark.

To keep it simple, this example assumes that the string is printed to the standard output stream in the selected language, not to a GUI or web page. It also gives just the output command itself, not the complete programs. The Python version happens to be a complete program, but we won't hold that against its competitors here.

Structurally, the first cut of this example consists of a main page HTML file, along with a Python-coded CGI script that is invoked by a form in the main HTML page. Because no state or database data is stored between user clicks, this is still a fairly simple example. In fact, the main HTML page implemented by Example 16-17 is mostly just one big pull-down selection list within a form.

Example 16-17. PP3E\Internet\Web\languages.html

```
<html><title>Languages</title>
<body>
<h1>Hello World selector</h1>

<P>This demo shows how to display a "hello world" message in various
programming languages' syntax.  To keep this simple, only the output command
is shown (it takes more code to make a complete program in some of these
```

Example 16-17. PP3E\Internet\Web\languages.html (continued)

languages), and only text-based solutions are given (no GUI or HTML construction logic is included). This page is a simple HTML file; the one you see after pressing the button below is generated by a Python CGI script which runs on the server. Pointers:

```
<UL>
<LI>To see this page's HTML, use the 'View Source' command in your browser.
<LI>To view the Python CGI script on the server,
    <A HREF="cgi-bin/languages-src.py">click here</A> or
    <A HREF="cgi-bin/getfile.py?filename=cgi-bin/languages.py">here</A>.
<LI>To see an alternative version that generates this page dynamically,
    <A HREF="cgi-bin/languages2.py">click here</A>.
</UL></P>


<hr>
<form method=POST action="cgi-bin/languages.py">
    <P><B>Select a programming language:</B>
    <P><select name=language>
        <option>All
        <option>Python
        <option>Perl
        <option>Tcl
        <option>Scheme
        <option>SmallTalk
        <option>Java
        <option>C
        <option>C++
        <option>Basic
        <option>Fortran
        <option>Pascal
        <option>Other
    </select>
    <P><input type=Submit>
</form>


</body></html>
```

For the moment, let's ignore some of the hyperlinks near the middle of this file; they introduce bigger concepts like file transfers and maintainability that we will explore in the next two sections. When visited with a browser, this HTML file is downloaded to the client and is rendered into the new browser page shown in Figure 16-21.

That widget above the Submit button is a pull-down selection list that lets you choose one of the <option> tag values in the HTML file. As usual, selecting one of these language names and pressing the Submit button at the bottom (or pressing your Enter key) sends the selected language name to an instance of the server-side CGI script program named in the form's action option. Example 16-18 contains the Python script that is run by the web server upon submission.

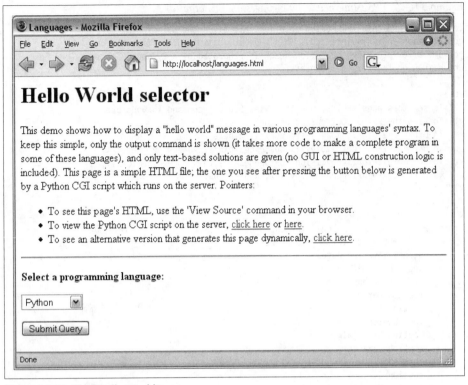

Figure 16-21. The "Hello World" main page

Example 16-18. PP3E\Internet\Web\cgi-bin\languages.py

```
#!/usr/bin/python
##########################################################################
# show hello world syntax for input language name; note that it uses r'...'
# raw strings so that '\n' in the table are left intact, and cgi.escape()
# on the string so that things like '<<' don't confuse browsers--they are
# translated to valid HTML code; any language name can arrive at this script,
# since explicit URLs "http://servername/cgi-bin/languages.py?language=Cobol"
# can be typed in a web browser or sent by a script (e.g., urllib.urlopen).
# caveats: the languages list appears in both the CGI and HTML files—could
# import from single file if selection list generated by a CGI script too;
##########################################################################

debugme  = False                        # True=test from cmd line
inputkey = 'language'                    # input parameter name

hellos = {
    'Python':    r" print 'Hello World'                ",
    'Perl':      r' print "Hello World\n";             ',
    'Tcl':       r' puts "Hello World"                 ',
    'Scheme':    r' (display "Hello World") (newline) ',
    'SmallTalk': r" 'Hello World' print.               ",
    'Java':      r' System.out.println("Hello World"); ',
```

Example 16-18. PP3E\Internet\Web\cgi-bin\languages.py (continued)

```
    'C':          r' printf("Hello World\n");        ',
    'C++':        r' cout << "Hello World" << endl;   ',
    'Basic':      r' 10 PRINT "Hello World"           ',
    'Fortran':    r" print *, 'Hello World'           ",
    'Pascal':     r" WriteLn('Hello World');          "
}

class dummy:                                        # mocked-up input obj
    def __init__(self, str): self.value = str

import cgi, sys
if debugme:
    form = {inputkey: dummy(sys.argv[1])}          # name on cmd line
else:
    form = cgi.FieldStorage()                       # parse real inputs

print 'Content-type: text/html\n'                   # adds blank line
print '<TITLE>Languages</TITLE>'
print '<H1>Syntax</H1><HR>'

def showHello(form):                                # HTML for one language
    choice = form[inputkey].value
    print '<H3>%s</H3><P><PRE>' % choice
    try:
        print cgi.escape(hellos[choice])
    except KeyError:
        print "Sorry--I don't know that language"
    print '</PRE></P><BR>'

if not form.has_key(inputkey) or form[inputkey].value == 'All':
    for lang in hellos.keys():
        mock = {inputkey: dummy(lang)}
        showHello(mock)
else:
    showHello(form)
print '<HR>'
```

And as usual, this script prints HTML code to the standard output stream to produce a response page in the client's browser. Not much is new to speak of in this script, but it employs a few techniques that merit special focus:

Raw strings and quotes

Notice the use of *raw strings* (string constants preceded by an "r" character) in the language syntax dictionary. Recall that raw strings retain \ backslash characters in the string literally, instead of interpreting them as string escape-code introductions. Without them, the \n newline character sequences in some of the language's code snippets would be interpreted by Python as line feeds, instead of being printed in the HTML reply as \n. The code also uses double quotes for strings that embed an unescaped single-quote character, per Python's normal string rules.

Escaping text embedded in HTML and URLs

This script takes care to format the text of each language's code snippet with the `cgi.escape` utility function. This standard Python utility automatically translates characters that are special in HTML into HTML escape code sequences, so that they are not treated as HTML operators by browsers. Formally, `cgi.escape` translates characters to escape code sequences, according to the standard HTML convention: <, >, and & become <, >, and &. If you pass a second true argument, the double-quote character (") is translated to ".

For example, the << left-shift operator in the C++ entry is translated to <<—a pair of HTML escape codes. Because printing each code snippet effectively embeds it in the HTML response stream, we must escape any special HTML characters it contains. HTML parsers (including Python's standard `htmllib` module) translate escape codes back to the original characters when a page is rendered.

More generally, because CGI is based upon the notion of passing formatted strings across the Net, escaping special characters is a ubiquitous operation. CGI scripts almost always need to escape text generated as part of the reply to be safe. For instance, if we send back arbitrary text input from a user or read from a data source on the server, we usually can't be sure whether it will contain HTML characters, so we must escape it just in case.

In later examples, we'll also find that characters inserted into URL address strings generated by our scripts may need to be escaped as well. A literal & in a URL is special, for example, and must be escaped if it appears embedded in text we insert into a URL. However, URL syntax reserves different special characters than HTML code, and so different escaping conventions and tools must be used. As we'll see later in this chapter, `cgi.escape` implements escape translations in HTML code, but `urllib.quote` (and its relatives) escapes characters in URL strings.

Mocking up form inputs

Here again, form inputs are "mocked up" (simulated), both for debugging and for responding to a request for all languages in the table. If the script's global debugme variable is set to a true value, for instance, the script creates a dictionary that is plug-and-play compatible with the result of a `cgi.FieldStorage` call—its "languages" key references an instance of the dummy mock-up class. This class in turn creates an object that has the same interface as the contents of a `cgi.FieldStorage` result—it makes an object with a value attribute set to a passed-in string.

The net effect is that we can test this script by running it from the system command line: the generated dictionary fools the script into thinking it was invoked by a browser over the Net. Similarly, if the requested language name is "All," the script iterates over all entries in the languages table, making a mocked-up form dictionary for each (as though the user had requested each language in turn).

This lets us reuse the existing showHello logic to display each language's code in a single page. As always in Python, object interfaces and protocols are what we usually code for, not specific datatypes. The showHello function will happily process any object that responds to the syntax form['language'].value.* Notice that we could achieve similar results with a default argument in showHello, albeit at the cost of introducing a special case in its code.

Now let's get back to interacting with this program. If we select a particular language, our CGI script generates an HTML reply of the following sort (along with the required content-type header and blank line). Use your browser's View Source option to see this:

```
<TITLE>Languages</TITLE>
<H1>Syntax</H1><HR>
<H3>Scheme</H3><P><PRE>
 (display "Hello World") (newline)
</PRE></P><BR>
<HR>
```

Program code is marked with a <PRE> tag to specify preformatted text (the browser won't reformat it like a normal text paragraph). This reply code shows what we get when we pick Scheme. Figure 16-22 shows the page served up by the script after selecting Python in the pull-down selection list.

Figure 16-22. Response page created by languages.py

---

* If you are reading closely, you might notice that this is the second time we've used mock-ups in this chapter (see the earlier *tutor4.cgi* example). If you find this technique generally useful, it would probably make sense to put the dummy class, along with a function for populating a form dictionary on demand, into a module so that it can be reused. In fact, we will do that in the next section. Even for two-line classes like this, typing the same code the third time around will do much to convince you of the power of code reuse.

Our script also accepts a language name of "All" and interprets it as a request to display the syntax for every language it knows about. For example, here is the HTML that is generated if we set the global variable debugme to True and run from the system command line with a single argument, All. This output is the same as what is printed to the client's web browser in response to an "All" selection:[*]

```
C:\...\PP3E\Internet\Web\cgi-bin>python languages.py All
Content-type: text/html

<TITLE>Languages</TITLE>
<H1>Syntax</H1><HR>
<H3>C</H3><P><PRE>
 printf("Hello World\n");
</PRE></P><BR>
<H3>Java</H3><P><PRE>
 System.out.println("Hello World");
</PRE></P><BR>
<H3>Python</H3><P><PRE>
 print 'Hello World'
</PRE></P><BR>
<H3>Pascal</H3><P><PRE>
 WriteLn('Hello World');
</PRE></P><BR>
<H3>C++</H3><P><PRE>
 cout &lt;&lt; "Hello World" &lt;&lt; endl;
</PRE></P><BR>
<H3>Perl</H3><P><PRE>
 print "Hello World\n";
</PRE></P><BR>
<H3>Fortran</H3><P><PRE>
 print *, 'Hello World'
</PRE></P><BR>
<H3>Tcl</H3><P><PRE>
 puts "Hello World"
</PRE></P><BR>
<H3>Basic</H3><P><PRE>
 10 PRINT "Hello World"
</PRE></P><BR>
<H3>Scheme</H3><P><PRE>
 (display "Hello World") (newline)
</PRE></P><BR>
<H3>SmallTalk</H3><P><PRE>
 'Hello World' print.
</PRE></P><BR>
<HR>
```

---

[*] Interestingly, we also get the "All" reply if debugme is set to False when we run the script from the command line. Instead of throwing an exception, the cgi.FieldStorage call returns an empty dictionary if called outside the CGI environment, so the test for a missing key kicks in. It's likely safer to not rely on this behavior, however.

Each language is represented here with the same code pattern—the showHello function is called for each table entry, along with a mocked-up form object. Notice the way that C++ code is escaped for embedding inside the HTML stream; this is the cgi.escape call's handiwork. Your web browser translates the < escapes to < characters when the page is rendered. When viewed with a browser, the "All" response page is rendered as shown in Figure 16-23.

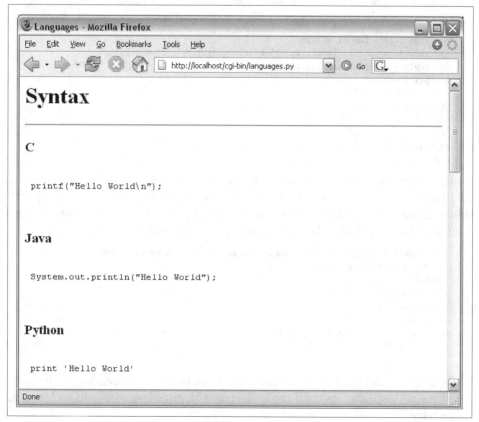

Figure 16-23. Response page for "All" languages choice

Checking for Missing and Invalid Inputs

So far, we've been triggering the CGI script by selecting a language name from the pull-down list in the main HTML page. In this context, we can be fairly sure that the script will receive valid inputs. Notice, though, that there is nothing to prevent a client from passing the requested language name at the end of the CGI script's URL as an explicit query parameter, instead of using the HTML page form. For instance, a URL of the following kind typed into a browser's address field or submitted with the module urllib:

```
http://localhost/cgi-bin/languages.py?language=Python
```

yields the same "Python" response page shown in Figure 16-22. However, because it's always possible for a user to bypass the HTML file and use an explicit URL, a user could invoke our script with an unknown language name, one that is not in the HTML file's pull-down list (and so not in our script's table). In fact, the script might be triggered with no language input at all if someone explicitly submits its URL with no language parameter (or no parameter value) at the end. Such an erroneous URL could be entered into a browser's address field, or be sent by another script using the urllib module techniques described earlier in this chapter:

```
>>> from urllib import urlopen
>>> request = 'http://localhost/cgi-bin/languages.py?language=Python'
>>> reply = urlopen(request).read( )
>>> print reply
<TITLE>Languages</TITLE>
<H1>Syntax</H1><HR>
<H3>Python</H3><P><PRE>
 print 'Hello World'
</PRE></P><BR>
<HR>
```

To be robust, the script checks for both cases explicitly, as all CGI scripts generally should. For instance, here is the HTML generated in response to a request for the fictitious language GuiDO (you can also see this by selecting your browser's View Source option, after typing the URL manually into your browser's address field):

```
>>> request = 'http://localhost/cgi-bin/languages.py?language=GuiDO'
>>> reply = urlopen(request).read( )
>>> print reply
<TITLE>Languages</TITLE>
<H1>Syntax</H1><HR>
<H3>GuiDO</H3><P><PRE>
Sorry--I don't know that language
</PRE></P><BR>
<HR>
```

If the script doesn't receive any language name input, it simply defaults to the "All" case (this can also be triggered if the URL ends with just ?language= and no language name value):

```
>>> reply = urlopen('http://localhost/cgi-bin/languages.py').read( )
>>> print reply
<TITLE>Languages</TITLE>
<H1>Syntax</H1><HR>
<H3>C</H3><P><PRE>
 printf("Hello World\n");
</PRE></P><BR>
<H3>Java</H3><P><PRE>
 System.out.println("Hello World");
</PRE></P><BR>
<H3>Python</H3><P><PRE>
 print 'Hello World'
...more...
```

If we didn't detect these cases, chances are that our script would silently die on a Python exception and leave the user with a mostly useless half-complete page or with a default error page (we didn't assign stderr to stdout here, so no Python error message would be displayed). Figure 16-24 shows the page generated if the script is invoked with an explicit URL like this:

```
http://localhost/cgi-bin/languages.py?language=COBOL
```

To test this error case interactively, the pull-down list includes an "Other" name, which produces a similar error page reply. Adding code to the script's table for the COBOL "Hello World" program is left as an exercise for the reader.

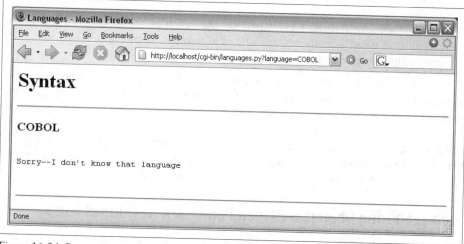

Figure 16-24. Response page for unknown language

Refactoring Code for Maintainability

Let's step back from coding details for just a moment to gain some design perspective. As we've seen, Python code, by and large, automatically lends itself to systems that are easy to read and maintain; it has a simple syntax that cuts much of the clutter of other tools. On the other hand, coding styles and program design can often affect maintainability as much as syntax. For example, the "Hello World" selector pages of the preceding section work as advertised and were very easy and fast to throw together. But as currently coded, the languages selector suffers from substantial maintainability flaws.

Imagine, for instance, that you actually take me up on that challenge posed at the end of the last section, and attempt to add another entry for COBOL. If you add COBOL to the CGI script's table, you're only half done: the list of supported languages lives redundantly in two places—in the HTML for the main page as well as in the script's syntax dictionary. Changing one does not change the other. More generally, there are a handful of ways that this program might fail the scrutiny of a rigorous code review. These are described next.

Selection list

> As just mentioned, the list of languages supported by this program lives in two places: the HTML file and the CGI script's table.

Field name

> The field name of the input parameter, language, is hardcoded into both files as well. You might remember to change it in the other if you change it in one, but you might not.

Form mock-ups

> We've redundantly coded classes to mock-up form field inputs twice in this chapter already; the "dummy" class here is clearly a mechanism worth reusing.

HTML code

> HTML embedded in and generated by the script is sprinkled throughout the program in print statements, making it difficult to implement broad web page layout changes or delegate web page design to nonprogrammers.

This is a short example, of course, but issues of redundancy and reuse become more acute as your scripts grow larger. As a rule of thumb, if you find yourself changing multiple source files to modify a single behavior, or if you notice that you've taken to writing programs by cut-and-paste copying of existing code, it's probably time to think about more rational program structures. To illustrate coding styles and practices that are friendlier to maintainers, let's rewrite (that is, refactor) this example to fix all of these weaknesses in a single mutation.

Step 1: Sharing Objects Between Pages—A New Input Form

We can remove the first two maintenance problems listed earlier with a simple transformation; the trick is to generate the main page dynamically, from an executable script, rather than from a precoded HTML file. Within a script, we can import the input field name and selection list values from a common Python module file, shared by the main and reply page generation scripts. Changing the selection list or field name in the common module changes both clients automatically. First, we move shared objects to a common module file, as shown in Example 16-19.

Example 16-19. PP3E\Internet\Web\cgi-bin\languages2common.py

```
#####################################################
# common objects shared by main and reply page scripts;
# need change only this file to add a new language.
#####################################################

inputkey = 'language'                          # input parameter name

hellos = {
    'Python':    r" print 'Hello World'                ",
    'Perl':      r' print "Hello World\n";             ',
    'Tcl':       r' puts "Hello World"                 ',
    'Scheme':    r' (display "Hello World") (newline) ',
    'SmallTalk': r" 'Hello World' print.              ",
```

Example 16-19. PP3E\Internet\Web\cgi-bin\languages2common.py (continued)

```
    'Java':      r' System.out.println("Hello World"); ',
    'C':         r' printf("Hello World\n");           ',
    'C++':       r' cout << "Hello World" << endl;     ',
    'Basic':     r' 10 PRINT "Hello World"             ',
    'Fortran':   r" print *, 'Hello World'             ",
    'Pascal':    r" WriteLn('Hello World');            "
}
```

The module `languages2common` contains all the data that needs to agree between pages: the field name as well as the syntax dictionary. The `hellos` syntax dictionary isn't quite HTML code, but its keys list can be used to generate HTML for the selection list on the main page dynamically.

Notice that this module is stored in the same *cgi-bin* directory as the CGI scripts that will use it; this makes import search paths simple—the module will be found in the script's current working directory, without path configuration. In general, external references in CGI scripts are resolved as follows:

- Module *imports* will be relative to the CGI script's current working directory (*cgi-bin*), plus any custom path setting in place when the script runs.

- When using *minimal URLs*, referenced pages and scripts in links and form actions within generated HTML are relative to the prior page's location as usual. For a CGI script, such minimal URLs are relative to the location of the generating script itself.

- *Filenames* referenced in query parameters and passed into scripts are normally relative to the directory containing the CGI script (*cgi-bin*). However, on some platforms and servers they may be relative to the web server's directory instead—see the note at the end of this section. For our local web server, the latter case applies.

Next, in Example 16-20, we recode the main page as an executable script, and populate the response HTML with values imported from the common module file in the previous example.

Example 16-20. PP3E\Internet\Web\cgi-bin\languages2.py

```
#!/usr/bin/python
###############################################################
# generate HTML for main page dynamically from an executable
# Python script, not a precoded HTML file; this lets us
# import the expected input field name and the selection table
# values from a common Python module file; changes in either
# now only have to be made in one place, the Python module file;
###############################################################

REPLY = """Content-type: text/html

<html><title>Languages2</title>
<body>
```

Example 16-20. PP3E\Internet\Web\cgi-bin\languages2.py (continued)

```
<h1>Hello World selector</h1>
<P>Similar to file <a href="../languages.html">languages.html</a>, but
this page is dynamically generated by a Python CGI script, using
selection list and input field names imported from a common Python
module on the server. Only the common module must be maintained as
new languages are added, because it is shared with the reply script.

To see the code that generates this page and the reply, click
<a href="getfile.py?filename=cgi-bin/languages2.py">here</a>,
<a href="getfile.py?filename=cgi-bin/languages2reply.py">here</a>,
<a href="getfile.py?filename=cgi-bin/languages2common.py">here</a>, and
<a href="getfile.py?filename=cgi-bin/formMockup.py">here</a>.</P>
<hr>
<form method=POST action="languages2reply.py">
    <P><B>Select a programming language:</B>
    <P><select name=%s>
        <option>All
        %s
        <option>Other
    </select>
    <P><input type=Submit>
</form>
</body></html>
"""


from languages2common import hellos, inputkey

options = []
for lang in hellos.keys():                  # we could sort this too
    options.append('<option>' + lang)       # wrap table keys in HTML code
options = '\n\t'.join(options)
print REPLY % (inputkey, options)           # field name and values from module
```

Again, ignore the getfile hyperlinks in this file for now; we'll learn what they mean in a later section. You should notice, though, that the HTML page definition becomes a printed Python string here (named REPLY), with %s format targets where we plug in values imported from the common module. It's otherwise similar to the original HTML file's code; when we visit this script's URL, we get a similar page, shown in Figure 16-25. But this time, the page is generated by running a script on the server that populates the pull-down selection list from the keys list of the common syntax table. Use your browser's View Source option to see the HTML generated; it's nearly identical to the HTML file in Example 16-17.

One maintenance note here: the content of the REPLY HTML code template string in Example 16-20 could be loaded from an external text file so that it could be worked on independently of the Python program logic. In general, though, external text files are no more easily changed than Python scripts. In fact, Python scripts *are* text files, and this is a major feature of the language—it's easy to change the Python scripts of an installed system onsite, without recompile or relink steps. However, external HTML files could be checked out separately in a source-control system, if this matters in your environment.

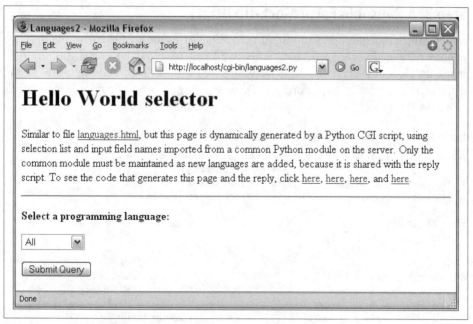

Figure 16-25. Alternative main page made by languages2.py

A subtle issue worth mentioning: on Windows, the locally running web server of Example 16-1 that we're using in this chapter runs CGI scripts in the same process as the web server. Unfortunately, it fails to temporarily change to the home directory of a CGI script it runs, and this cannot be easily customized by subclassing. As a result, just on platforms where the server runs CGI scripts in-process, filenames passed as parameters to scripts are relative to the web server's current working directory (which is one level up from the scripts' *cgi-bin* directory).

This seems like a flaw in the Python CGI server classes, because behavior will differ on other platforms. When CGI scripts are launched elsewhere, they run in the directory in which they are located, such that filename parameters will be relative to *cgi-bin*, the current working directory. This is also why we augmented Example 16-1 to insert the *cgi-bin* directory on sys.path: this step emulates the current working directory path setting on platforms where scripts are separate processes. This applies only to module imports, though, not to relative file paths.

If you use Example 16-1 on a platform where CGI scripts are run in separate processes, or if the Python web server classes are ever fixed to change to the CGI script's home directory, the filename query parameters in Example 16-20 will need to be changed to omit the *cgi-bin* component. Of course, for other servers, URL paths may be arbitrarily different from those you see in this book anyhow.

Step 2: A Reusable Form Mock-Up Utility

Moving the languages table and input field name to a module file solves the first two maintenance problems we noted. But if we want to avoid writing a dummy field mock-up class in every CGI script we write, we need to do something more. Again, it's merely a matter of exploiting the Python module's affinity for code reuse: let's move the dummy class to a utility module, as in Example 16-21.

Example 16-21. PP3E\Internet\Web\cgi-bin\formMockup.py

```
#############################################################
# Tools for simulating the result of a cgi.FieldStorage()
# call; useful for testing CGI scripts outside the Web
#############################################################

class FieldMockup:                              # mocked-up input object
    def __init__(self, str):
        self.value = str

def formMockup(**kwargs):                        # pass field=value args
    mockup = {}                                  # multichoice: [value,...]
    for (key, value) in kwargs.items():
        if type(value) != list:                  # simple fields have .value
            mockup[key] = FieldMockup(str(value))
        else:                                    # multichoice have list
            mockup[key] = []                     # to do: file upload fields
            for pick in value:
                mockup[key].append(FieldMockup(pick))
    return mockup

def selftest():
    # use this form if fields can be hardcoded
    form = formMockup(name='Bob', job='hacker', food=['Spam', 'eggs', 'ham'])
    print form['name'].value
    print form['job'].value
    for item in form['food']:
        print item.value,
    # use real dict if keys are in variables or computed
    print
    form = {'name':FieldMockup('Brian'), 'age':FieldMockup(38)}
    for key in form.keys():
        print form[key].value

if __name__ == '__main__': selftest()
```

When we place our mock-up class in the module `formMockup.py`, it automatically becomes a reusable tool and may be imported by any script we care to write.[*] For

---

[*] Assuming, of course, that this module can be found on the Python module search path when those scripts are run. See the CGI search path discussion earlier in this chapter. Since Python searches the current directory for imported modules by default, this always works without `sys.path` changes if all of our files are in our main web directory. For other applications, we may need to add this directory to `PYTHONPATH`, or use package (directory path) imports.

readability, the dummy field simulation class has been renamed `FieldMockup` here. For convenience, we've also added a `formMockup` utility function that builds up an entire form dictionary from passed-in keyword arguments. Assuming you can hardcode the names of the form to be faked, the mock-up can be created in a single call. This module includes a self-test function invoked when the file is run from the command line, which demonstrates how its exports are used. Here is its test output, generated by making and querying two form mock-up objects:

```
C:\...\PP3E\Internet\Web\cgi-bin>python formMockup.py
Bob
hacker
Spam eggs ham
38
Brian
```

Since the mock-up now lives in a module, we can reuse it anytime we want to test a CGI script offline. To illustrate, the script in Example 16-22 is a rewrite of the *tutor5.py* example we saw earlier, using the form mock-up utility to simulate field inputs. If we had planned ahead, we could have tested the script like this without even needing to connect to the Net.

Example 16-22. PP3E\Internet\Web\cgi-bin\tutor5_mockup.py

```
#!/usr/bin/python
###################################################################
# run tutor5 logic with formMockup instead of cgi.FieldStorage()
# to test: python tutor5_mockup.py > temp.html, and open temp.html
###################################################################

from formMockup import formMockup
form = formMockup(name='Bob',
                  shoesize='Small',
                  language=['Python', 'C++', 'HTML'],
                  comment='ni, Ni, NI')

# rest same as original, less form assignment
```

Running this script from a simple command line shows us what the HTML response stream will look like:

```
C:\...\PP3E\Internet\Web\cgi-bin>python tutor5_mockup.py
Content-type: text/html

<TITLE>tutor5.py</TITLE>
<H1>Greetings</H1>
<HR>
<H4>Your name is Bob</H4>
<H4>You wear rather Small shoes</H4>
<H4>Your current job: (unknown)</H4>
<H4>You program in Python and C++ and HTML</H4>
<H4>You also said:</H4>
<P>ni, Ni, NI</P>
<HR>
```

Running it live yields the page in Figure 16-26. Field inputs are hardcoded, similar in spirit to the *tutor5* extension that embedded input parameters at the end of hyperlink URLs. Here, they come from form mock-up objects created in the reply script that cannot be changed without editing the script. Because Python code runs immediately, though, modifying a Python script during the debug cycle goes as quickly as you can type.

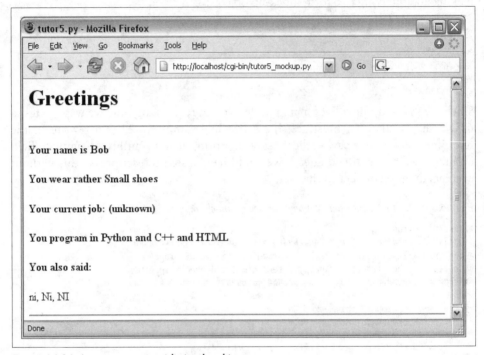

Figure 16-26. A response page with simulated inputs

Step 3: Putting It All Together—A New Reply Script

There's one last step on our path to software maintenance nirvana: we must recode the reply page script itself to import data that was factored out to the common module and import the reusable form mock-up module's tools. While we're at it, we move code into functions (in case we ever put things in this file that we'd like to import in another script), and all HTML code to triple-quoted string blocks. The result is Example 16-23. Changing HTML is generally easier when it has been isolated in single strings like this, instead of being sprinkled throughout a program.

Example 16-23. PP3E\Internet\Web\cgi-bin\languages2reply.py

```
#!/usr/bin/python
##########################################################
# for easier maintenance, use HTML template strings, get
# the language table and input key from common module file,
```

Example 16-23. PP3E\Internet\Web\cgi-bin\languages2reply.py (continued)

```
# and get reusable form field mockup utilities module.
##########################################################

import cgi, sys
from formMockup import FieldMockup              # input field simulator
from languages2common import hellos, inputkey   # get common table, name
debugme = False

hdrhtml = """Content-type: text/html\n
<TITLE>Languages</TITLE>
<H1>Syntax</H1><HR>"""

langhtml = """
<H3>%s</H3><P><PRE>
%s
</PRE></P><BR>"""

def showHello(form):                            # HTML for one language
    choice = form[inputkey].value               # escape lang name too
    try:
        print langhtml % (cgi.escape(choice),
                          cgi.escape(hellos[choice]))
    except KeyError:
        print langhtml % (cgi.escape(choice),
                       "Sorry--I don't know that language")

def main():
    if debugme:
        form = {inputkey: FieldMockup(sys.argv[1])}  # name on cmd line
    else:
        form = cgi.FieldStorage()               # parse real inputs

    print hdrhtml
    if not form.has_key(inputkey) or form[inputkey].value == 'All':
        for lang in hellos.keys():
            mock = {inputkey: FieldMockup(lang)}
            showHello(mock)
    else:
        showHello(form)
    print '<HR>'

if __name__ == '__main__': main()
```

When global debugme is set to True, the script can be tested offline from a simple command line as before:

```
C:\...\PP3E\Internet\Web\cgi-bin>python languages2reply.py Python
Content-type: text/html

<TITLE>Languages</TITLE>
<H1>Syntax</H1><HR>
```

```
<H3>Python</H3><P><PRE>
 print 'Hello World'
</PRE></P><BR>
<HR>
```

When run online, we get the same reply pages we saw for the original version of this example (we won't repeat them here again). This transformation changed the program's architecture, not its user interface.

Most of the code changes in this version of the reply script are straightforward. If you test-drive these pages, the only differences you'll find are the URLs at the top of your browser (they're different files, after all), extra blank lines in the generated HTML (ignored by the browser), and a potentially different ordering of language names in the main page's pull-down selection list.

This selection list ordering difference arises because this version relies on the order of the Python dictionary's keys list, not on a hardcoded list in an HTML file. Dictionaries, you'll recall, arbitrarily order entries for fast fetches; if you want the selection list to be more predictable, simply sort the keys list before iterating over it using the list sort method, or the sorted function introduced in Python 2.4:

```
for lang in sorted(hellos):          # dict iterator instead of .keys()
    mock = {inputkey: FieldMockup(lang)}
```

More on HTML and URL Escapes

Perhaps the subtlest change in the last section's rewrite is that, for robustness, this version's reply script (Example 16-23) also calls cgi.escape for the language *name*, not just for the language's code snippet. This wasn't required in *languages2.py* (Example 16-20) for the known language names in our selection list table. However, it is not impossible that someone could pass the script a language name with an embedded HTML character as a query parameter. For example, a URL such as:

```
http://localhost/cgi-bin/languages2reply.py?language=a<b
```

embeds a < in the language name parameter (the name is a<b). When submitted, this version uses cgi.escape to properly translate the < for use in the reply HTML, according to the standard HTML escape conventions discussed earlier:

```
<TITLE>Languages</TITLE>
<H1>Syntax</H1><HR>

<H3>a&lt;b</H3><P><PRE>
Sorry--I don't know that language
</PRE></P><BR>
<HR>
```

The original version doesn't escape the language name, such that the embedded <b is interpreted as an HTML tag (which may make the rest of the page render in bold font!). As you can probably tell by now, text escapes are pervasive in CGI scripting—

If you know what you're doing, you can also test CGI scripts from the command line on some platforms by setting the same environment variables that HTTP servers set, and then launching your script. For example, we might be able to pretend to be a web server by storing input parameters in the QUERY_STRING environment variable, using the same syntax we employ at the end of a URL string after the ?:

```
$ setenv QUERY_STRING "name=Mel&job=trainer,+writer"
$ python tutor5.py
Content-type: text/html

<TITLE>tutor5.py<?TITLE>
<H1>Greetings</H1>
<HR>
<H4>Your name is Mel</H4>
<H4>You wear rather (unknown) shoes</H4>
<H4>Your current job: trainer, writer</H4>
<H4>You program in (unknown)</H4>
<H4>You also said:</H4>
<P>(unknown)</P>
<HR>
```

Here, we mimic the effects of a GET style form submission or explicit URL. HTTP servers place the query string (parameters) in the shell variable QUERY_STRING. Python's cgi module finds them there as though they were sent by a browser. POST-style inputs can be simulated with shell variables too, but it's more complex—so much so that you may be better off not bothering to learn how. In fact, it may be more robust in general to mock up inputs with Python objects (e.g., as in *formMockup.py*). But some CGI scripts may have additional environment or testing constraints that merit unique treatment.

even text that you may think is safe must generally be escaped before being inserted into the HTML code in the reply stream.

Because the Web is a text-based medium that combines multiple language syntaxes, multiple formatting rules may apply: one for URLs and another for HTML. We met HTML escapes earlier in this chapter; URLs, and combinations of HTML and URLs, merit a few additional words.

URL Escape Code Conventions

Notice that in the prior section, although it's wrong to embed an unescaped < in the HTML code reply, it's perfectly all right to include it literally in the URL string used to trigger the reply. In fact, HTML and URLs define completely different characters as special. For instance, although & must be escaped as &amp inside HTML code, we have to use other escaping schemes to code a literal & within a URL string (where it normally separates parameters). To pass a language name like a&b to our script, we have to type the following URL:

```
http://localhost/cgi-bin/languages2reply.py?language=a%26b
```

Here, %26 represents &—the & is replaced with a % followed by the hexadecimal value (0x26) of its ASCII code value (38). Similarly, as we suggested at the end of Chapter 14, to name C++ as a query parameter in an explicit URL, + must be escaped as %2b:

```
http://localhost/cgi-bin/languages2reply.py?language=C%2b%2b
```

Sending C++ unescaped will not work, because + is special in URL syntax—it represents a space. By URL standards, most nonalphanumeric characters are supposed to be translated to such escape sequences, and spaces are replaced by + signs. Technically, this convention is known as the *application/x-www-form-urlencoded* query string format, and it's part of the magic behind those bizarre URLs you often see at the top of your browser as you surf the Web.

Python HTML and URL Escape Tools

If you're like me, you probably don't have the hexadecimal value of the ASCII code for & committed to memory (though Python's hex(ord(c)) can help). Luckily, Python provides tools that automatically implement URL escapes, just as cgi.escape does for HTML escapes. The main thing to keep in mind is that HTML code and URL strings are written with entirely different syntax, and so employ distinct escaping conventions. Web users don't generally care, unless they need to type complex URLs explicitly—browsers handle most escape code details internally. But if you write scripts that must generate HTML or URLs, you need to be careful to escape characters that are reserved in either syntax.

Because HTML and URLs have different syntaxes, Python provides two distinct sets of tools for escaping their text. In the standard Python library:

- cgi.escape escapes text to be embedded in HTML.
- urllib.quote and quote_plus escape text to be embedded in URLs.

The urllib module also has tools for undoing URL escapes (unquote, unquote_plus), but HTML escapes are undone during HTML parsing at large (e.g., by Python's htmllib module). To illustrate the two escape conventions and tools, let's apply each tool set to a few simple examples.

Escaping HTML Code

As we saw earlier, cgi.escape translates code for inclusion within HTML. We normally call this utility from a CGI script, but it's just as easy to explore its behavior interactively:

```
>>> import cgi
>>> cgi.escape('a < b > c & d "spam"', 1)
'a &lt; b &gt; c &amp; d &quot;spam&quot;'

>>> s = cgi.escape("1<2 <b>hello</b>")
>>> s
'1&lt;2 &lt;b&gt;hello&lt;/b&gt;'
```

Python's cgi module automatically converts characters that are special in HTML syntax according to the HTML convention. It translates <, >, &, and with an extra true argument, ", into escape sequences of the form &X;, where the X is a mnemonic that denotes the original character. For instance, < stands for the "less than" operator (<) and & denotes a literal ampersand (&).

There is no *unescaping* tool in the CGI module, because HTML escape code sequences are recognized within the context of an HTML parser, like the one used by your web browser when a page is downloaded. Python comes with a full HTML parser, too, in the form of the standard module htmllib, which imports and specializes tools in the module sgmllib (HTML is a kind of SGML syntax). We won't go into details on the HTML parsing tools here (see the library manual for details), but to illustrate how escape codes are eventually undone, here is the SGML module at work reading back the last output from earlier:

```
>>> from sgmllib import TestSGMLParser
>>> p = TestSGMLParser(1)
>>> s
'1&lt;2 &lt;b&gt;hello&lt;/b&gt;'
>>> for c in s:
...     p.feed(c)
...
>>> p.close()
data: '1<2 <b>hello</b>'
```

Escaping URLs

By contrast, URLs reserve other characters as special and must adhere to different escape conventions. As a result, we use different Python library tools to escape URLs for transmission. Python's urllib module provides two tools that do the translation work for us: quote, which implements the standard %XX hexadecimal URL escape code sequences for most nonalphanumeric characters, and quote_plus, which additionally translates spaces to + signs. The urllib module also provides functions for unescaping quoted characters in a URL string: unquote undoes %XX escapes, and unquote_plus also changes plus signs back to spaces. Here is the module at work, at the interactive prompt:

```
>>> import urllib
>>> urllib.quote("a & b #! c")
'a%20%26%20b%20%23%21%20c'

>>> urllib.quote_plus("C:\stuff\spam.txt")
```

```
'C%3a%5cstuff%5cspam.txt'

>>> x = urllib.quote_plus("a & b #! c")
>>> x
'a+%26+b+%23%21+c'

>>> urllib.unquote_plus(x)
'a & b #! c'
```

URL escape sequences embed the hexadecimal values of nonsafe characters following a % sign (usually, their ASCII codes). In `urllib`, nonsafe characters are usually taken to include everything except letters, digits, and a handful of safe special characters (any of `_`, `,`, `.`, `-`,), and `/` by default). You can also specify a string of safe characters as an extra argument to the quote calls to customize the translations; the argument defaults to `/`, but passing an empty string forces `/` to be escaped:

```
>>> urllib.quote_plus("uploads/index.txt")
'uploads/index.txt'
```

```
>>> urllib.quote_plus("uploads/index.txt", '')
'uploads%2findex.txt'
```

Note that Python's `cgi` module also translates URL escape sequences back to their original characters and changes + signs to spaces during the process of extracting input information. Internally, `cgi.FieldStorage` automatically calls `urllib.unquote` if needed to parse and unescape parameters passed at the end of URLs (most of the translation happens in `cgi.parse_qs`). The upshot is that CGI scripts get back the original, unescaped URL strings, and don't need to unquote values on their own. As we've seen, CGI scripts don't even need to know that inputs came from a URL at all.

Escaping URLs Embedded in HTML Code

But what do we do for URLs inside HTML? That is, how do we escape when we generate and embed text inside a URL, which is itself embedded inside generated HTML code? Some of our earlier examples used hardcoded URLs with appended input parameters inside <A HREF> hyperlink tags; the file *languages2.py*, for instance, prints HTML that includes a URL:

```
<a href="getfile.py?filename=cgi-bin/languages2.py">
```

Because the URL here is embedded in HTML, it must at least be escaped according to HTML conventions (e.g., any < characters must become <), and any spaces should be translated to + signs per URL conventions. A `cgi.escape(url)` call followed by the string `url.replace(" ", "+")` would take us this far, and would probably suffice for most cases.

That approach is not quite enough in general, though, because HTML escaping conventions are not the same as URL conventions. To robustly escape URLs embedded in HTML code, you should instead call `urllib.quote_plus` on the URL string, or at least most of its components, before adding it to the HTML text. The escaped result also satisfies HTML escape conventions, because `urllib` translates more characters than `cgi.escape`, and the % in URL escapes is not special to HTML.

HTML and URL conflicts: &

But there is one more very subtle (and thankfully rare) wrinkle: you may also have to be careful with & characters in URL strings that are embedded in HTML code (e.g., within `<A>` hyperlink tags). The & symbol is both a query parameter separator in URLs (`?a=1&b=2`) and the start of escape codes in HTML (`&lt;`). Consequently, there is a potential for collision if a query parameter name happens to be the same as an HTML escape sequence code. The query parameter name `amp`, for instance, that shows up as `&amp=1` in parameters two and beyond on the URL may be treated as an HTML escape by some HTML parsers, and translated to `&=1`.

Even if parts of the URL string are URL-escaped, when more than one parameter is separated by a &, the & separator might also have to be escaped as `&amp;` according to HTML conventions. To see why, consider the following HTML hyperlink tag with query parameter names `name`, `job`, `amp`, `sect`, and `lt`:

```
<A HREF="file.py?name=a&job=b&amp=c&sect=d&lt=e">hello</a>
```

When rendered in most browsers tested, this URL link winds up looking incorrectly like this (the S character is really a non-ASCII section marker):

```
file.py?name=a&job=b&=cS=d<=e
```

The first two parameters are retained as expected (`name=a`, `job=b`), because `name` is not preceded with an & and `&job` is not recognized as a valid HTML character escape code. However, the `&amp`, `&sect`, and `&lt` parts are interpreted as special characters, because they do name valid HTML escape codes.

Avoiding conflicts

To make this work as expected, the & separators should be escaped if your parameter names may clash with an HTML escape code:

```
<A HREF="file.py?name=a&amp;job=b&amp;amp=c&amp;sect=d&amp;lt=e">hello</a>
```

Browsers render this fully escaped link as expected:

```
file.py?name=a&job=b&amp=c&sect=d&lt=e
```

Because of this conflict between HTML and URL syntax, most server tools (including Python's `cgi` module) also allow a semicolon to be used as a separator instead of &; the following link, for example, works the same as the fully escaped URL, but does not require an extra HTML escaping step (at least not for the ;):

```
file.py?name=a;job=b;amp=c;sect=d;lt=e
```

To test this for yourself, put these links in an HTML file, open the file in your browser using its *http://localhost/badlink.html* URL, and view the links when followed. The HTML file in Example 16-24 will suffice.

Example 16-24. PP3E\Internet\Web\badlink.html

```
<HTML><BODY>

<p><A HREF=
"cgi-bin/badlink.py?name=a&job=b&amp;c&sect=d&lt;e">unescaped</a>

<p><A HREF=
"cgi-bin/badlink.py?name=a&amp;job=b&amp;amp;c&amp;sect=d&amp;lt;e">escaped</a>

<p><A HREF=
"cgi-bin/badlink.py?name=a;job=b;amp=c;sect=d;lt=e">alternative</a>

</BODY></HTML>
```

When these links are clicked, they invoke the simple CGI script in Example 16-25. This script displays the inputs sent from the client on the standard error stream to avoid any additional translations (for our locally running web server in Example 16-1, this routes the printed text to the server's console window).

Example 16-25. PP3E\Internet\Web\cgi-bin\badlink.py

```
import cgi, sys
form = cgi.FieldStorage()
for name in form.keys():
    print >> sys.stderr, name, '=>', form[name].value
```

When the "escaped" second link in the HTML page is followed by the Firefox web browser, we get back the correct parameters set on the server as a result of the HTML escaping employed, as seen in the web server's console window:

```
..."GET /cgi-bin/badlink.py?name=a&job=b&amp;c&sect=d&lt;e HTTP/1.1" 200 -
name => a
job => b
amp => c
sect => d
lt => e
```

But the accidental HTML escapes cause serious issues for the first "unescaped" link—the client's HTML parser translates these in unintended ways:

```
..."GET /cgi-bin/badlink.py?name=a&job=b&=c%A7=d%3C=e HTTP/1.1" 200 -
name => a
job => b
 => c&#186;=d<=e
```

The third "alternative" link produces the same output as the "escaped link," because ; doesn't cause collisions HTML, like & does. We get the intended set of parameter names:

```
..."GET /cgi-bin/badlink.py?name=a;job=b;amp=c;sect=d;lt=e HTTP/1.1" 200 -
name => a
job => b
amp => c
sect => d
lt => e
```

The moral of this story is that unless you can be sure that the names of all but the leftmost URL query parameters embedded in HTML are not the same as the name of any HTML character escape code like amp, you should generally either use a semicolon as a separator if supported by your tools, or run the entire URL through cgi.escape after escaping its parameter names and values with urllib.quote_plus:

```
>>> import cgi
>>> cgi.escape('file.py?name=a&job=b&amp=c&sect=d&lt=e')
'file.py?name=a&amp;job=b&amp;amp=c&amp;sect=d&amp;lt=e'
```

Having said that, I should add that some examples in this book do not escape & URL separators embedded within HTML simply because their URL parameter names are known not to conflict with HTML escapes. In fact, this concern is likely to be very rare in practice, since your program usually controls the set of parameter names it expects. This is not, however, the most general solution, especially if parameter names may be driven by a dynamic database; when in doubt, escape much and often.

"Always Look on the Bright Side of Life"

Lest the HTML and URL formatting rules sound too clumsy (and send you screaming into the night), note that the HTML and URL escaping conventions are imposed by the Internet itself, not by Python. (As we've seen, Python has a different mechanism for escaping special characters in string constants with backslashes.) These rules stem from the fact that the Web is based on the notion of shipping formatted text strings around the planet, and almost surely influenced by the tendency of different interest groups to develop very different notations.

You can take heart, though, in the fact that you often don't need to think in such cryptic terms; when you do, Python automates the translation process with library tools. Just keep in mind that any script that generates HTML or URLs dynamically probably needs to call Python's escaping tools to be robust. We'll see both the HTML and the URL escape tool sets employed frequently in later examples in this chapter and the next. In Chapter 18, we'll also meet systems such as Zope that aim to get rid of some of the low-level complexities that CGI scripters face. And as usual in programming, there is no substitute for brains; amazing technologies like the Internet come at a cost in complexity.

Transferring Files to Clients and Servers

It's time to explain a bit of HTML code we've been keeping in the shadows. Did you notice those hyperlinks on the language selector example's main page for showing the CGI script's source code? Normally, we can't see such script source code, because accessing a CGI script makes it execute (we can see only its HTML output, generated to make the new page). The script in Example 16-26, referenced by a hyperlink in the main language.html page, works around that by opening the source file and sending its text as part of the HTML response. The text is marked with <PRE> as preformatted text, and is escaped for transmission inside HTML with cgi.escape.

Example 16-26. PP3E\Internet\Web\cgi-bin\languages-src.py

```
#!/usr/bin/python
###############################################################
# Display languages.py script code without running it.
###############################################################

import cgi
filename = 'cgi-bin/languages.py'

print "Content-type: text/html\n"          # wrap up in HTML
print "<TITLE>Languages</TITLE>"
print "<H1>Source code: '%s'</H1>" % filename
print '<HR><PRE>'
print cgi.escape(open(filename).read( ))
print '</PRE><HR>'
```

Here again, the filename is relative to the server's directory for our web server on Windows (see the prior note, and delete the cgi-bin portion of its path on other platforms). When we visit this script on the Web via the hyperlink or a manually typed URL, the script delivers a response to the client that includes the text of the CGI script source file. It appears as in Figure 16-27.

Note that here, too, it's crucial to format the text of the file with cgi.escape, because it is embedded in the HTML code of the reply. If we don't, any characters in the text that mean something in HTML code are interpreted as HTML tags. For example, the C++ < operator character within this file's text may yield bizarre results if not properly escaped. The cgi.escape utility converts it to the standard sequence < for safe embedding.

Displaying Arbitrary Server Files on the Client

Almost immediately after writing the languages source code viewer script in the preceding example, it occurred to me that it wouldn't be much more work, and would be much more useful, to write a generic version—one that could use a passed-in filename to display *any* file on the site. It's a straightforward mutation on the server side; we merely need to allow a filename to be passed in as an input. The *getfile.py*

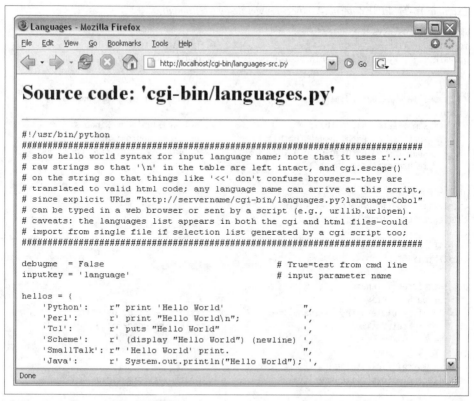

Figure 16-27. Source code viewer page

Python script in Example 16-27 implements this generalization. It assumes the file-name is either typed into a web page form or appended to the end of the URL as a parameter. Remember that Python's cgi module handles both cases transparently, so there is no code in this script that notices any difference.

Example 16-27. PP3E\Internet\Web\cgi-bin\getfile.py

```
#!/usr/bin/python
###################################################################
# Display any CGI (or other) server-side file without running it.
# The filename can be passed in a URL param or form field; e.g.,
# http://servername/cgi-bin/getfile.py?filename=cgi-bin/somefile.py.
# Users can cut-and-paste or "View Source" to save file locally.
# On IE, running the text/plain version (formatted=0) sometimes
# pops up Notepad, but end-of-lines are not always in DOS format;
# Netscape shows the text correctly in the browser page instead.
# Sending the file in text/HTML mode works on both browsers--text
# is displayed in the browser response page correctly. We also
# check the filename here to try to avoid showing private files;
# this may or may not prevent access to such files in general:
# don't install this script if you can't otherwise secure source!
###################################################################
```

Example 16-27. PP3E\Internet\Web\cgi-bin\getfile.py (continued)

```
import cgi, os, sys
formatted = True                                # True=wrap text in HTML
privates  = ['PyMailCgi/cgi-bin/secret.py']     # don't show these

try:
    samefile = os.path.samefile                 # checks device, inode numbers
except:
    def samefile(path1, path2):                 # not available on Windows
        apath1 = os.path.abspath(path1).lower()  # do close approximation
        apath2 = os.path.abspath(path2).lower()  # normalizes path, same case
        return apath1 == apath2

html = """
<html><title>Getfile response</title>
<h1>Source code for: '%s'</h1>
<hr>
<pre>%s</pre>
<hr></html>"""

def restricted(filename):
    for path in privates:
        if samefile(path, filename):            # unify all paths by os.stat
            return True                         # else returns None=false

try:
    form = cgi.FieldStorage()
    filename = form['filename'].value           # URL param or form field
except:
    filename = 'getfile.py'                     # else default filename

try:
    assert not restricted(filename)             # load unless private
    filetext = open(filename).read()
except AssertionError:
    filetext = '(File access denied)'
except:
    filetext = '(Error opening file: %s)' % sys.exc_info()[1]

if not formatted:
    print "Content-type: text/plain\n"          # send plain text
    print filetext                              # works on NS, not IE
else:
    print "Content-type: text/html\n"           # wrap up in HTML
    print html % (filename, cgi.escape(filetext))
```

This Python server-side script simply extracts the filename from the parsed CGI inputs object, and reads and prints the text of the file to send it to the client browser. Depending on the formatted global variable setting, it sends the file in either plain text mode (using text/plain in the response header) or wrapped up in an HTML page definition (text/html).

Both modes (and others) work in general under most browsers, but Internet Explorer doesn't handle the plain text mode as gracefully as Netscape does—during testing, it popped up the Notepad text editor to view the downloaded text, but end-of-line characters in Unix format made the file appear as one long line. (Netscape instead displays the text correctly in the body of the response web page itself.) HTML display mode works more portably with current browsers. More on this script's restricted file logic in a moment.

Let's launch this script by typing its URL at the top of a browser, along with a desired filename appended after the script's name. Figure 16-28 shows the page we get by visiting this URL:

```
http://localhost/cgi-bin/getfile.py?filename=cgi-bin/languages-src.py
```

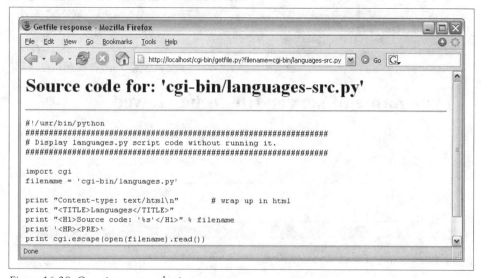

Figure 16-28. Generic source code viewer page

The body of this page shows the text of the server-side file whose name we passed at the end of the URL; once it arrives, we can view its text, cut-and-paste to save it in a file on the client, and so on. In fact, now that we have this generalized source code viewer, we could replace the hyperlink to the script *languages-src.py* in *language.html*, with a URL of this form:

```
http://localhost/cgi-bin/getfile.py?filename=cgi-bin/languages.py
```

For illustration purposes, the main HTML page in Example 16-17 has links to the original source code display script as well as to this URL (less the server name). Really, URLs like these are direct calls (albeit across the Web) to our Python script, with filename parameters passed explicitly. As we've seen, parameters passed in URLs are treated the same as field inputs in forms; for convenience, let's also write a simple web page that allows the desired file to be typed directly into a form, as shown in Example 16-28.

Example 16-28. PP3E\Internet\Web\getfile.html

```
<html><title>Getfile: download page</title>
<body>
<form method=get action="cgi-bin/getfile.py">
  <h1>Type name of server file to be viewed</h1>
  <p><input type=text size=50 name=filename>
  <p><input type=submit value=Download>
</form>
<hr><a href="cgi-bin/getfile.py?filename=cgi-bin/getfile.py">View script code</a>
</body></html>
```

Figure 16-29 shows the page we receive when we visit this file's URL. We need to type only the filename in this page, not the full CGI script address.

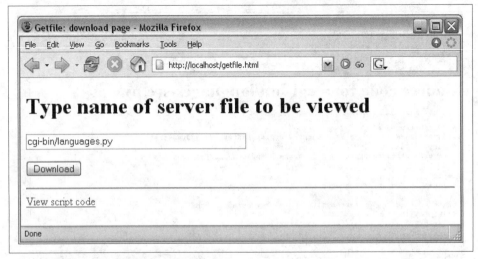

Figure 16-29. Source code viewer selection page

When we press this page's Download button to submit the form, the filename is transmitted to the server, and we get back the same page as before, when the filename was appended to the URL (see Figure 16-28). In fact, the filename *will* be appended to the URL here, too; the get method in the form's HTML instructs the browser to append the filename to the URL, exactly as if we had done so manually. It shows up at the end of the URL in the response page's address field, even though we really typed it into a form.*

---

* You may notice one difference in the response pages produced by the form and an explicitly typed URL: for the form, the value of the "filename" parameter at the end of the URL in the response may contain URL escape codes for some characters in the file path you typed. Browsers automatically translate some non-ASCII characters into URL escapes (just like urllib.quote). URL escapes were discussed earlier in this chapter; we'll see an example of this automatic browser escaping at work in an upcoming screenshot.

Handling private files and errors

As long as CGI scripts have permission to open the desired server-side file, this script can be used to view and locally save *any* file on the server. For instance, Figure 16-30 shows the page we're served after asking for the file path *PyMailCgi/pymailcgi.html*—an HTML text file in another application's subdirectory, nested within the parent directory of this script (we explore PyMailCGI in the next chapter). Users can specify both relative and absolute paths to reach a file—any path syntax the server understands will do.

Figure 16-30. Viewing files with relative paths

More generally, this script will display any file path for which the username under which the CGI script runs has read access. On some servers, this is often the user "nobody"—a predefined username with limited permissions. Just about every server-side file used in web applications will be accessible, though, or else they couldn't be referenced from browsers in the first place. When running our local web server, every file on the computer can be inspected: `C:\Mark\WEBSITE\public_html\index.html` works fine when entered in the form of Figure 16-29 on my laptop, for example.

That makes for a flexible tool, but it's also potentially dangerous if you are running a server on a remote machine. What if we don't want users to be able to view some files on the server? For example, in the next chapter, we will implement an encryption module for email account passwords. On our server, it is in fact addressable as `PyMailCgi/cgi-bin/secret.py`. Allowing users to view that module's source code would make encrypted passwords shipped over the Net much more vulnerable to cracking.

To minimize this potential, the `getfile` script keeps a list, `privates`, of restricted filenames, and uses the `os.path.samefile` built-in to check whether a requested filename path points to one of the names on `privates`. The `samefile` call checks to see whether the `os.stat` built-in returns the same identifying information (device and inode numbers) for both file paths. As a result, pathnames that look different syntactically but reference the same file are treated as identical. For example, on the server used for this book's second edition, the following paths to the encryptor module were different strings, but yielded a true result from os.path.samefile:

```
../PyMailCgi/secret.py
/home/crew/lutz/public_html/PyMailCgi/secret.py
```

Unfortunately, the os.path.samefile call is supported on Unix, Linux, and Macs, but not on Windows. To emulate its behavior in Windows, we expand file paths to be absolute, convert to a common case, and compare:

```
>>> os.getcwd()
'C:\\PP3E-cd\\Examples\\PP3E\\Internet\\Web'
>>>
>>> x = os.path.abspath('../Web/PYMailCgi/cgi-bin/secret.py').lower()
>>> y = os.path.abspath('PyMailCgi/cgi-bin/secret.py').lower()
>>> z = os.path.abspath('./PYMailCGI/cgi-bin/../cgi-bin/SECRET.py').lower()
>>> x
'c:\\pp3e-cd\\examples\\pp3e\\internet\\web\\pymailcgi\\cgi-bin\\secret.py'
>>> y
'c:\\pp3e-cd\\examples\\pp3e\\internet\\web\\pymailcgi\\cgi-bin\\secret.py'
>>> z
'c:\\pp3e-cd\\examples\\pp3e\\internet\\web\\pymailcgi\\cgi-bin\\secret.py'
>>> x == y, y == Z
(True, True)
```

Accessing any of the three paths expanded here generates an error page like that in Figure 16-31.

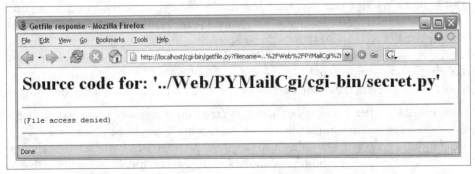

Figure 16-31. Accessing private files

Notice that bona fide file errors are handled differently. Permission problems and attempts to access nonexistent files, for example, are trapped by a different exception handler clause, and they display the exception's message—fetched using Python's sys.exc_info—to give additional context. Figure 16-32 shows one such error page.

As a general rule of thumb, file-processing exceptions should always be reported in detail, especially during script debugging. If we catch such exceptions in our scripts, it's up to us to display the details (assigning sys.stderr to sys.stdout won't help if

Figure 16-32. File errors display

Python doesn't print an error message). The current exception's type, data, and traceback objects are always available in the sys module for manual display.

Do not install the *getfile.py* script if you truly wish to keep your files private! The private files list check it uses attempts to prevent the encryption module from being viewed directly with this script, but it may or may not handle all possible attempts, especially on Windows. This book isn't about security, so we won't go into further details here, except to say that on the Internet, a little paranoia is a Good Thing. Especially for systems installed on the general Internet at large, you should assume that the worst case scenario might eventually happen.

Uploading Client Files to the Server

The getfile script lets us view server files on the client, but in some sense, it is a general-purpose file download tool. Although not as direct as fetching a file by FTP or over raw sockets, it serves similar purposes. Users of the script can either cut-and-paste the displayed code right off the web page or use their browser's View Source option to view and cut.

But what about going the other way—uploading a file from the client machine to the server? For instance, suppose you are writing a web-based email system, and you need a way to allow users to upload mail attachments. This is not an entirely hypothetical scenario; we will actually implement this idea in the next chapter, when we develop PyMailCGI.

As we saw in Chapter 14, uploads are easy enough to accomplish with a client-side script that uses Python's FTP support module. Yet such a solution doesn't really apply in the context of a web browser; we can't usually ask all of our program's clients to start up a Python FTP script in another window to accomplish an upload. Moreover, there is no simple way for the server-side script to request the upload explicitly, unless an FTP server happens to be running on the client machine (not at all the usual case). Users can email files separately, but this can be inconvenient, especially for email attachments.

So is there no way to write a web-based program that lets its users upload files to a common server? In fact, there is, though it has more to do with HTML than with Python itself. HTML <input> tags also support a type=file option, which produces an input field, along with a button that pops up a file-selection dialog. The name of the client-side file to be uploaded can either be typed into the control or selected with the popup dialog. The HTML page file in Example 16-29 defines a page that allows any client-side file to be selected and uploaded to the server-side script named in the form's action option.

Example 16-29. PP3E\Internet\Web\putfile.html

```
<html><title>Putfile: upload page</title>
<body>
<form enctype="multipart/form-data"
      method=post
      action="cgi-bin/putfile.py">
  <h1>Select client file to be uploaded</h1>
  <p><input type=file size=50 name=clientfile>
  <p><input type=submit value=Upload>
</form>
<hr><a href="cgi-bin/getfile.py?filename=cgi-bin/putfile.py">View script code</a>
</body></html>
```

One constraint worth noting: forms that use file type inputs must also specify a multipart/form-data encoding type and the post submission method, as shown in this file; get-style URLs don't work for uploading files (adding their contents to the end of the URL doesn't make sense). When we visit this HTML file, the page shown in Figure 16-33 is delivered. Pressing its Browse button opens a file-selection dialog, while Upload sends the file.

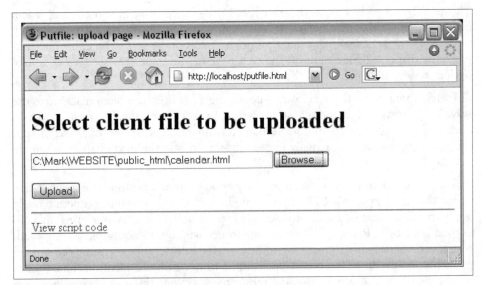

Figure 16-33. File upload selection page

On the client side, when we press this page's Upload button, the browser opens and reads the selected file and packages its contents with the rest of the form's input fields (if any). When this information reaches the server, the Python script named in the form action tag is run as always, as listed in Example 16-30.

Example 16-30. PP3E\Internet\Web\cgi-bin\putfile.py

```python
#!/usr/bin/python
######################################################
# extract file uploaded by HTTP from web browser;
# users visit putfile.html to get the upload form
# page, which then triggers this script on server;
# note: this is very powerful, and very dangerous:
# you will usually want to check the filename, etc.
# this may only work if file or dir is writable;
# a Unix 'chmod 777 uploads' command may suffice;
# file pathnames may arrive in client's path format;
######################################################

import cgi, os, sys
import posixpath, ntpath, macpath      # for client paths
debugmode   = False                    # True=print form info
loadtextauto = False                   # True=read file at once
uploaddir   = './uploads'              # dir to store files

sys.stderr = sys.stdout                # show error msgs
form = cgi.FieldStorage()              # parse form data
print "Content-type: text/html\n"      # with blank line
if debugmode: cgi.print_form(form)     # print form fields

# html templates

html = """
<html><title>Putfile response page</title>
<body>
<h1>Putfile response page</h1>
%s
</html>"""

goodhtml = html % """
<p>Your file, '%s', has been saved on the server as '%s'.
<p>An echo of the file's contents received and saved appears below.
</p><hr>
<p><pre>%s</pre>
</p><hr>
"""

# process form data

def splitpath(origpath):                        # get file at end
```

Example 16-30. PP3E\Internet\Web\cgi-bin\putfile.py (continued)

```
    for pathmodule in [posixpath, ntpath, macpath]:  # try all clients
        basename = pathmodule.split(origpath)[1]     # may be any server
        if basename != origpath:
            return basename                          # lets spaces pass
    return origpath                                  # failed or no dirs

def saveonserver(fileinfo):                          # use file input form data
    basename = splitpath(fileinfo.filename)          # name without dir path
    srvrname = os.path.join(uploaddir, basename)     # store in a dir if set
    if loadtextauto:
        filetext = fileinfo.value                    # reads text into string
        open(srvrname, 'wb').write(filetext)         # save in server file
    else:
        srvrfile = open(srvrname, 'wb')              # else read line by line
        numlines, filetext = 0, ''                   # e.g., for huge files
        while 1:
            line = fileinfo.file.readline()
            if not line: break
            srvrfile.write(line)
            filetext = filetext + line
            numlines = numlines + 1
        filetext = ('[Lines=%d]\n' % numlines) + filetext
    os.chmod(srvrname, 0666)    # make writable: owned by 'nobody'
    return filetext, srvrname

def main():
    if not form.has_key('clientfile'):
        print html % "Error: no file was received"
    elif not form['clientfile'].filename:
        print html % "Error: filename is missing"
    else:
        fileinfo = form['clientfile']
        try:
            filetext, srvrname = saveonserver(fileinfo)
        except:
            errmsg = '<h2>Error</h2><p>%s<p>%s' % tuple(sys.exc_info()[:2])
            print html % errmsg
        else:
            print goodhtml % (cgi.escape(fileinfo.filename),
                              cgi.escape(srvrname),
                              cgi.escape(filetext))
main()
```

Within this script, the Python-specific interfaces for handling uploaded files are employed. They aren't very new, really; the file comes into the script as an entry in the parsed form object returned by cgi.FieldStorage, as usual; its key is clientfile, the input control's name in the HTML page's code.

This time, though, the entry has additional attributes for the file's name on the client. Moreover, accessing the value attribute of an uploaded file input object will automatically read the file's contents all at once into a string on the server. For very large files, we can instead read line by line (or in chunks of bytes) to avoid overflowing memory space. For illustration purposes, the script implements either scheme: based on the setting of the loadtextauto global variable, it either asks for the file contents as a string, or reads it line by line.[*] In general, the CGI module gives us back objects with the following attributes for file upload controls:

filename
> The name of the file as specified on the client

file
> A file object from which the uploaded file's contents can be read

value
> The contents of the uploaded file (read from the file on demand)

Additional attributes are not used by our script. Files represent a third input field object; as we've also seen, the value attribute is a *string* for simple input fields, and we may receive a *list* of objects for multiple-selection controls.

For uploads to be saved on the server, CGI scripts (run by the user "nobody" on some servers) must have write access to the enclosing directory if the file doesn't yet exist, or to the file itself if it does. To help isolate uploads, the script stores all uploads in whatever server directory is named in the uploaddir global. On one Linux server, I had to give this directory a mode of 777 (universal read/write/execute permissions) with chmod to make uploads work in general. This is a nonissue with the local web server used in this chapter, but your mileage may vary; be sure to check permissions if this script fails.

The script also calls os.chmod to set the permission on the server file such that it can be read and written by everyone. If it is created anew by an upload, the file's owner will be "nobody" on some servers, which means anyone out in cyberspace can view and upload the file. On one Linux server, though, the file will also be writable only by the user "nobody" by default, which might be inconvenient when it comes time to change that file outside the Web (the degree of pain can vary per operation).

---

[*] Internally, Python's cgi module stores uploaded files in temporary files automatically; reading them in our script simply reads from that temporary file. If they are very large, though, they may be too long to store as a single string in memory all at once.

Isolating client-side file uploads by placing them in a single directory on the server helps minimize security risks: existing files can't be over-written arbitrarily. But it may require you to copy files on the server after they are uploaded, and it still doesn't prevent all security risks—mischievous clients can still upload huge files, which we would need to trap with additional logic not present in this script as is. Such traps may be needed only in scripts open to the Internet at large.

If both client and server do their parts, the CGI script presents us with the response page shown in Figure 16-34, after it has stored the contents of the client file in a new or existing file on the server. For verification, the response gives the client and server file paths, as well as an echo of the uploaded file with a line count (in line-by-line reader mode).

Figure 16-34. Putfile response page

Incidentally, we can also verify the upload with the getfile program we wrote in the prior section. Simply access the selection page to type the pathname of the file on the server, as shown in Figure 16-35.

If the file upload is successful, the resulting viewer page we will obtain looks like Figure 16-36. Since the user "nobody" (CGI scripts) was able to write the file, "nobody" should be able to view it as well.

Notice the URL in this page's address field—the browser translated the / character we typed into the selection page to a %2F hexadecimal escape code before adding it to the end of the URL as a parameter. We met URL escape codes like this earlier in this

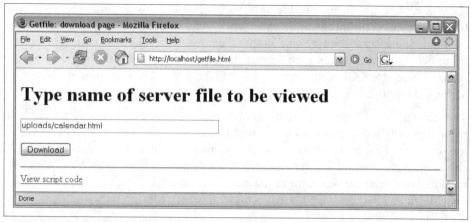

Figure 16-35. Verifying putfile with getfile—selection

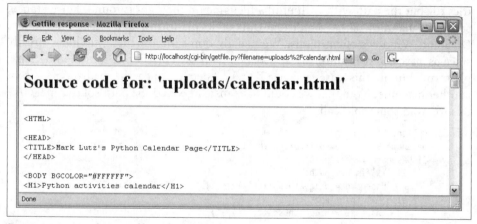

Figure 16-36. Verifying putfile with getfile—response

chapter. In this case, the browser did the translation for us, but the end result is as if we had manually called one of the urllib quoting functions on the file path string.

Technically, the %2F escape code here represents the standard URL translation for non-ASCII characters, under the default encoding scheme browsers employ. Spaces are usually translated to + characters as well. We can often get away without manually translating most non-ASCII characters when sending paths explicitly (in typed URLs). But as we saw earlier, we sometimes need to be careful to escape characters (e.g., &) that have special meaning within URL strings with urllib tools.

Handling client path formats

In the end, the *putfile.py* script stores the uploaded file on the server within a hard-coded *uploaddir* directory, under the filename at the end of the file's path on the client (i.e., less its client-side directory path). Notice, though, that the splitpath function in this script needs to do extra work to extract the base name of the file on the right. Some browsers may send up the filename in the directory path format used on the *client* machine; this path format may not be the same as that used on the server where the CGI script runs. This can vary per browser, but it should be addressed for portability.

The standard way to split up paths, os.path.split, knows how to extract the base name, but only recognizes path separator characters used on the platform on which it is running. That is, if we run this CGI script on a Unix machine, os.path.split chops up paths around a / separator. If a user uploads from a DOS or Windows machine, however, the separator in the passed filename is \, not /. Browsers running on a Macintosh may send a path that is more different still.

To handle client paths generically, this script imports platform-specific, path-processing modules from the Python library for each client it wishes to support, and tries to split the path with each until a filename on the right is found. For instance, posixpath handles paths sent from Unix-style platforms, and ntpath recognizes DOS and Windows client paths. We usually don't import these modules directly since os.path.split is automatically loaded with the correct one for the underlying platform, but in this case, we need to be specific since the path comes from another machine. Note that we could have instead coded the path splitter logic like this to avoid some split calls:

```
def splitpath(origpath):                                    # get name at end
    basename = os.path.split(origpath)[1]                   # try server paths
    if basename == origpath:                                # didn't change it?
        if '\\' in origpath:
            basename = origpath.split('\\')[-1]             # try DOS clients
        elif '/' in origpath:
            basename = origpath.split('/')[-1]              # try Unix clients
    return basename
```

But this alternative version may fail for some path formats (e.g., DOS paths with a drive but no backslashes). As is, both options waste time if the filename is already a base name (i.e., has no directory paths on the left), but we need to allow for the more complex cases generically.

This upload script works as planned, but a few caveats are worth pointing out before we close the book on this example:

- Firstly, putfile doesn't do anything about cross-platform incompatibilities in filenames themselves. For instance, spaces in a filename shipped from a DOS client are not translated to nonspace characters; they will wind up as spaces in the server-side file's name, which may be legal but are difficult to process in some scenarios.

- Secondly, reading line by line means that this CGI script is biased toward uploading text files, not binary datafiles. It uses a wb output open mode to retain the binary content of the uploaded file, but it assumes the data is text in other places, including the reply page. See Chapter 4 for more about binary file modes.

If you run into any of these limitations, you will have crossed over into the domain of suggested exercises.

More Than One Way to Push Bits over the Net

Finally, let's discuss some context. We've seen three getfile scripts at this point in the book. The one in this chapter is different from the other two we wrote in earlier chapters, but it accomplishes a similar goal:

- This chapter's getfile is a server-side CGI script that displays files over the HTTP protocol (on port 80).
- In Chapter 13, we built a client- and server-side getfile to transfer with raw sockets (on port 50001).
- In Chapter 14, we implemented a client-side getfile to ship over FTP (on port 21).

CGI Downloads: Forcing the Issue

In Example 16-27, we wrote a script named *getfile.py*, a Python CGI program designed to display any public server-side file, within a web browser (or other recipient) on the requesting client machine. It uses a Content type of text/plain or text/html to make the requested file's text show up properly inside a browser. In the description, we compared *getfile.py* to a generalized CGI download tool, when augmented with cut-and-paste or save-as interactions.

While real, *getfile.py* was intended to mostly be a file display tool only, not a CGI download demo. If you want to truly and directly download a file by CGI (instead of displaying it in a browser or opening it with an application), you can usually force the browser to pop up a Save As dialog for the file on the client by supplying the appropriate Content-type line in the CGI reply.

Browsers decide what to do with a file using either the file's suffix (e.g., *xxx.jpg* is interpreted as an image), or the Content-type line (e.g., text/html is HTML code). By using various MIME header line settings, you can make the datatype unknown and effectively render the browser clueless about data handling. For instance, a Content type of application/octet-stream in the CGI reply generally triggers the standard Save As dialog box in a browser.

This strategy is sometimes frowned on, though, because it leaves the true nature of the file's data ambiguous—it's usually better to let the user/client decide how to handle downloaded data, rather than force the Save As behavior. It also has very little to do with Python; for more details, consult a CGI-specific text, or try a web search on "CGI download".

Really, the getfile CGI script in this chapter simply displays files only, but it can be considered a download tool when augmented with cut-and-paste operations in a web browser. Moreover, the CGI- and HTTP-based putfile script here is also different from the FTP-based putfile in Chapter 14, but it can be considered an alternative to both socket and FTP uploads.

The point to notice is that there are a variety of ways to ship files around the Internet—sockets, FTP, and HTTP (web pages) can move files between computers. Technically speaking, we can transfer files with other techniques and protocols too—Post Office Protocol (POP) email, Network News Transfer Protocol (NNTP) news, Telnet, and so on.

Each technique has unique properties but does similar work in the end: moving bits over the Net. All ultimately run over sockets on a particular port, but protocols like FTP add additional structure to the socket layer, and application models like CGI add both structure and programmability.

In the next chapter, we're going to use what we've learned here to build a substantial application that runs entirely on the Web—PyMailCGI, a web-based email tool, which allows us to send and view emails in a browser, process email attachments such as images and audio files, and more. At the end of the day, though, it's mostly just bytes over sockets, with a user interface.

## CHAPTER 17

The PyMailCGI Server

"Things to Do When Visiting Chicago"

This chapter is the fifth in our survey of Python Internet programming, and it continues Chapter 16's discussion. There, we explored the fundamentals of server-side Common Gateway Interface (CGI) scripting in Python. Armed with that knowledge, this chapter moves on to a larger case study that underscores advanced CGI topics.

This chapter presents PyMailCGI—a web site for reading and sending email that illustrates security concepts, hidden form fields, URL generation, and more. Because this system is similar in spirit to the PyMailGUI program we studied in Chapter 15, this example also serves as a comparison of web and nonweb applications. This case study is based on CGI scripting, but it implements a complete web site that does something more useful than Chapter 16's examples.

As usual, in this book, this chapter splits its focus between application-level details and Python programming concepts. Because this is a fairly large case study, it illustrates system design concepts that are important in actual projects. It also says more about CGI scripts in general. PyMailCGI expands on the notions of state retention and security concerns and encryption.

The system presented here is neither particularly flashy nor feature rich as web sites go (in fact, the initial cut of PyMailCGI was thrown together during a layover at Chicago's O'Hare airport). Alas, you will find neither dancing bears nor blinking lights at this site. On the other hand, it was written to serve a real purpose, speaks more to us about CGI scripting, and hints at just how far Python server-side programs can take us. In Chapter 18, we will explore higher-level systems and tools that build upon ideas we will apply here. For now, let's have some fun with Python on the Web.

The PyMailCGI Web Site

In Chapter 15, we built a program called PyMailGUI that implements a complete Python+Tkinter email client GUI (if you didn't read that chapter, you may want to take a quick glance at it now). Here, we're going to do something of the same, but on the Web: the system presented in this section, PyMailCGI, is a collection of CGI scripts that implement a simple web-based interface for sending and reading email in any browser. In effect, it is a simple *webmail* system—though not as powerful as what may be available from your Internet Service Provider (ISP), its scriptability gives you control over its operation and future evolution.

Our goal in studying this system is partly to learn a few more CGI tricks, partly to learn a bit about designing larger Python systems in general, and partly to underscore the trade-offs between systems implemented for the Web (the PyMailCGI server) and systems written to run locally (the PyMailGUI client). This chapter hints at some of these trade-offs along the way and returns to explore them in more depth after the presentation of this system.

Implementation Overview

At the top level, PyMailCGI allows users to view incoming email with the Post Office Protocol (POP) interface and to send new mail by Simple Mail Transfer Protocol (SMTP). Users also have the option of replying to, forwarding, or deleting an incoming email while viewing it. As implemented, anyone can send email from a PyMailCGI site, but to view your email, you generally have to install PyMailCGI on your own computer or web server account, with your own mail server information (due to security concerns described later).

Viewing and sending email sounds simple enough, and we've already coded this a few times in this book. But the required interaction involves a number of distinct web pages, each requiring a CGI script or HTML file of its own. In fact, PyMailCGI is a fairly linear system—in the most complex user interaction scenario, there are six states (and hence six web pages) from start to finish. Because each page is usually generated by a distinct file in the CGI world, that also implies six source files.

Technically, PyMailCGI could also be described as a state machine, though very little state is transferred from state to state. Scripts pass user and message information to the next script in hidden form fields and query parameters, but there are no client-side cookies or server-side databases in the current version. Still, along the way we'll encounter situations where more advanced state retention tools could be an advantage.

To help keep track of how all of PyMailCGI's source files fit into the overall system, I jotted down the file in Example 17-1 before starting any real programming. It informally sketches the user's flow through the system and the files invoked along the way. You can certainly use more formal notations to describe the flow of control and information through states such as web pages (e.g., dataflow diagrams), but for this simple example, this file gets the job done.

Example 17-1. PP3E\Internet\Web\PyMailCgi\pageflow.txt

```
file or script                          creates
--------------                          -------

[pymailcgi.html]                        Root window
 => [onRootViewLink.py]                 Pop password window
    => [onViewPswdSubmit.py]            List window (loads all pop mail)
       => [onViewListLink.py]           View Window + pick=del|reply|fwd (fetch)
          => [onViewPageAction.py]      Edit window, or delete+confirm (del)
             => [onEditPageSend.py]     Confirmation (sends smtp mail)
                => back to root

 => [onRootSendLink.py]                 Edit Window
    => [onEditPageSend.py]              Confirmation (sends smtp mail)
       => back to root
```

This file simply lists all the source files in the system, using => and indentation to denote the scripts they trigger.

For instance, links on the pymailcgi.html root page invoke *onRootViewLink.py* and *onRootSendLink.py*, both executable scripts. The script *onRootViewLink.py* generates a password page, whose Submit button in turn triggers *onViewPswdSubmit.py*, and so on. Notice that both the view and the send actions can wind up triggering *onEditPageSend.py* to send a new mail; view operations get there after the user chooses to reply to or forward an incoming mail.

In a system such as this, CGI scripts make little sense in isolation, so it's a good idea to keep the overall page flow in mind; refer to this file if you get lost. For additional context, Figure 17-1 shows the overall contents of this site, viewed as directory listings on Windows in a DOS command prompt window.

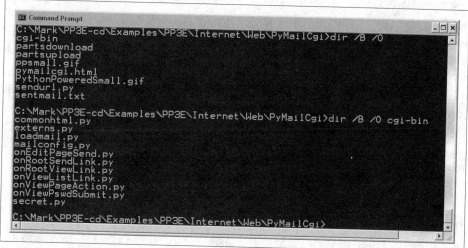

Figure 17-1. PyMailCGI contents

To install this site, all the files you see here are uploaded to a *PyMailCgi* subdirectory of your web directory on your server's machine. Besides the page-flow HTML and CGI script files invoked by user interaction, PyMailCGI uses a handful of utility modules:

commonhtml.py
> Is a library of HTML tools.

externs.py
> Isolates access to modules imported from other places.

loadmail.py
> Encapsulates mailbox fetches for future expansion.

secret.py
> Implements configurable password encryption.

PyMailCGI also reuses parts of the mailtools module package and mailconfig.py module we wrote in Chapter 14. The former of these is accessible to imports from the *PP3E* package root, and the latter is copied to the *PyMailCgi* directory so that it can differ between PyMailGUI and PyMailCGI. The externs.py module is intended to hide these modules' actual locations, in case the install structure varies on some machines.

In fact, this system demonstrates the powers of *code reuse* in a practical way. In this third edition, it gets a great deal of logic for free from the new mailtools package of Chapter 14—message loading, sending, deleting, parsing, composing, and attachments—even though that package's modules were originally develop for the PyMailGUI program. When it came time to update PyMailCGI six months later, tools for handling complex things such as attachments and message text searches were already in place. See Example 14-21 in Chapter 14 for mailtools source code.

As usual, PyMailCGI also uses a variety of standard library modules: smtplib, poplib, email.*, cgi, urllib, and the like. Thanks to the reuse of both custom and standard library code, this system achieves much in a minimal amount of code. All told, PyMail-CGI consists of just 835 lines of new code, including whitespace and comments.

The compares favorably to the 2,200 lines of the PyMailGUI client, but most of this difference owes to the limited functionality in PyMailCGI—there are no local save files, no transfer thread overlap, no message caching, no inbox synchronization tests, no multiple-message selections, and so on. Still, PyMailCGI's code factoring and reuse of existing modules allow it to implement much in a surprisingly small amount of code.

New in This Edition

In this third edition, PyMailCGI has been upgraded to use the new mailtools module package of Chapter 14, employ the PyCrypto package for passwords if it is installed, support viewing and sending message attachments, and run more efficiently.

We'll meet these new features along the way, but the last two of these merit a few words upfront. Attachments are supported in a simplistic but usable fashion and use existing `mailtools` package code for much of their operation:

- For *viewing* attachments, message parts are split off the message and saved in local files on the server. Message view pages are then augmented with hyperlinks pointing to the temporary files; when clicked, they open in whatever way your web browser opens the selected part's file type.

- For *sending* attachments, we use the HTML upload techniques presented near the end of Chapter 16. Mail edit pages now have file-upload controls, to allow a maximum of three attachments. Selected files are uploaded to the server by the browser with the rest of the page as usual, saved in temporary files on the server, and added to the outgoing mail.

Both schemes would fail for multiple simultaneous users, but since PyMailCGI's configuration file scheme (described later in this chapter) already limits it to a single username, this is a reasonable constraint. The links to temporary files generated for attachment viewing also apply only to the last message selected, but this works if the page flow is followed normally. Improving this for a multiuser scenario, as well as adding additional features such as PyMailGUI's local file save and open options, are left as exercises.

For efficiency, this version of PyMailCGI also avoids repeated exhaustive mail downloads. In the prior version, the full text of all messages in an inbox was downloaded every time you visited the list page, and every time you selected a single message to view. In this version, the list page downloads only the header text portion of each message, and only a single message's full text is downloaded when one is selected for viewing.

Even so, the list page's headers-only download can be slow if you have many messages in your inbox (I have more than a thousand in one of mine). A better solution would somehow cache mails to limit reloads, at least for the duration of a browser session. For example, we might load headers of only newly arrived messages, and cache headers of mails already fetched, as done in the PyMailGUI client we met in Chapter 16.

Due to the lack of state retention in CGI scripts, though, this would require some sort of server-side database. We might, for instance, store already fetched message headers under a generated key that identifies the session (e.g., with process number and time) and pass that key between pages as a cookie, hidden form field, or URL query parameter. Each page would use the key to fetch cached mail stored directly on the web server, instead of loading it from the email server again. Presumably, loading from a local cache file would be faster than loading from a network connection to the mail server. This would make for an interesting exercise too, if you wish to extend this system on your own, but it would also result in more pages than this chapter has to spend (frankly, I ran out of real estate in this chapter before I ran out of potential enhancements).

Carry-On Software

PyMailCGI works as planned and illustrates more CGI and email concepts, but I want to point out a few caveats upfront. The application was initially written during a two-hour layover in Chicago's O'Hare airport (though debugging took a few hours more). I wrote it to meet a specific need—to be able to read and send email from any web browser while traveling around the world teaching Python classes. I didn't design it to be aesthetically pleasing to others and didn't spend much time focusing on its efficiency.

I also kept this example intentionally simple for this book. For example, PyMailCGI doesn't provide nearly as many features as the PyMailGUI program in Chapter 15, and it reloads email more than it probably should. Because of this, its performance can be very poor if you keep your inbox large.

In fact, this system almost cries out for more advanced state retention options. As is, user and message details are passed in generated pages as hidden fields and query parameters, but we could avoid reloading mail by also using the server-side database techniques described in Chapter 16. Such extensions might eventually bring PyMailCGI up to the functionality of PyMailGUI, albeit at some cost in code complexity.

In other words, you should consider this system a work in progress; it's not yet software worth selling. On the other hand, it does what it was intended to do, and you can customize it by tweaking its Python source code—something that can't be said of all software sold.

Presentation Overview

Much of the "action" in PyMailCGI is encapsulated in shared utility modules (especially one called commonhtml.py). The CGI scripts that implement user interaction don't do much by themselves. This architecture was chosen deliberately, to make scripts simple, avoid code redundancy, and implement a common look-and-feel in shared code. But it means you must jump between files to understand how the whole system works.

To make this example easier to digest, we're going to explore its code in two chunks: page scripts first, and then the utility modules. First, we'll study screenshots of the major web pages served up by the system and the HTML files and top-level Python CGI scripts used to generate them. We begin by following a send mail interaction, and then trace how existing email is read, and then processed. Most implementation details will be presented in these sections, but be sure to flip ahead to the utility modules listed later to understand what the scripts are really doing.

I should also point out that this is a fairly complex system, and I won't describe it in exhaustive detail; as in the PyMailGUI chapter (Chapter 15), be sure to read the source code along the way for details not made explicit in the narrative. All of the system's source code appears in this chapter (as well as in the book's examples distribution package), and we will study its key concepts here. But as usual with case studies in this book, I assume that you can read Python code by now and that you will consult the example's source code for more details. Because Python's syntax is so close to executable, pseudocode systems are sometimes better described in Python than in English, once you have the overall design in mind.

Running This Chapter's Examples

The HTML pages and CGI scripts of PyMailCGI can be installed on any web server to which you have access. To keep things simple for this book, though, we're going to use the same policy as in Chapter 16—we'll be running the Python-coded *webserver.py* script from Example 16-1 locally, on the same machine as the web browser client. As we learned at the start of the prior chapter, that means we'll be using the server domain name "localhost" (or the equivalent IP address, "127.0.0.1") to access this system's pages in our browser, as well as in the urllib module.

Start this server script on your own machine to test-drive the program. Ultimately, this system must generally contact a mail server over the Internet to fetch or send messages, but the web page server will be running locally on your computer.

One minor twist here: PyMailCGI's code is located in a directory of its own, one level down from the *webserver.py* script. Because of that, we'll start the web server here with an explicit directory and port number in the command line used to launch it:

```
C:\...\PP3E\Internet\Web>webserver.py PyMailCgi 8000
```

Type this sort of command into a command prompt window on Windows or into your system shell prompt on Unix-like platforms. When run this way, the server will listen for URL requests on machine "localhost" and socket port number 8000. It will serve up pages from the *PyMailCgi* subdirectory one level below the script's location, and it will run CGI scripts located in the *PyMailCgi/cgi-bin* directory below that. This works because the script changes its current working directory to the one you name when it starts up.

Subtle point: because we specify a unique port number on the command line this way, it's OK if you simultaneously run another instance of the script to serve up the prior chapter's examples one directory up; that instance will accept connections on port 80, and our new instance will handle requests on port 8000. In fact, you can contact either server from the same browser by specifying the desired server's port number. If you have two instances of the server running in the two different chapters' directories, to access pages and scripts of the prior chapter, use a URL of this form:

```
http://localhost/languages.html
http://localhost/cgi-bin/languages.py?language=All
```

And to run this chapter's pages and scripts, simply use URLs of this form:

```
http://localhost:8000/pymailcgi.html
http://localhost:8000/cgi-bin/onRootSendLink.py
```

You'll see that the HTTP and CGI log messages appear in the window of the server you're contacting. For more background on why this works as it does, see the introduction to network socket addresses in Chapter 13 and the discussion of URLs in Chapter 16.

As in Chapter 16, if you do install this example's code on a different server, simply replace the "localhost:8000/cgi-bin" part of the URLs we'll use here, with your server's name, port, and path details. In practice, a system such as PyMailCGI would be much more useful if it were installed on a remote server, to allow mail processing from any web client.[*]

As with PyMailGUI, also note that you'll have to edit the mailconfig.py module's settings, if you wish to use this system to read your own email. As provided, the email server information is not useful to readers; more on this in a moment.

The Root Page

Let's start off by implementing a main page for this example. The file shown in Example 17-2 is primarily used to publish links to the Send and View functions' pages. It is coded as a static HTML file, because there is nothing to generate on the fly here.

Example 17-2. PP3E\Internet\Web\PyMailCgi\pymailcgi.html

```
<HTML>
<TITLE>PyMailCGI Main Page</TITLE>
<BODY>
<H1 align=center>PyMailCGI</H1>
<H2 align=center>A POP/SMTP Web Email Interface</H2>
<P align=center><I>Version 2.0, January 2006</I></P>

<table>

<tr><td><hr>
<h2>Actions</h2>
<P>
<UL>
```

---

[*] One downside to running a local *webserver.py* script that I noticed during development for this chapter is that on platforms where CGI scripts are run in the same process as the server (including Windows, with the code's workaround), you'll need to stop and restart the server every time you change an imported module. Otherwise, a subsequent import in a CGI script will have no effect: the module has already been imported in the process. This is not an issue on platforms that run the CGI as a separate, new process. The Windows workaround in the code is probably temporary; it is likely that CGIs will eventually be able to be run in separate processes there too.

Example 17-2. PP3E\Internet\Web\PyMailCgi\pymailcgi.html (continued)

```
<LI><a href="cgi-bin/onRootViewLink.py">View, Reply, Forward, Delete POP mail</a>
<LI><a href="cgi-bin/onRootSendLink.py">Send a new email message by SMTP</a>
</UL></P>

<tr><td><hr>
<h2>Overview</h2>
<P>
<A href="http://rmi.net/~lutz/about-pp.html">
<IMG src="ppsmall.gif" align=left
alt="[Book Cover]" border=1 hspace=10></A>
This site implements a simple web-browser interface to POP/SMTP email
accounts.  Anyone can send email with this interface, but for security
reasons, you cannot view email unless you install the scripts with your
own email account information, in your own server account directory.
PyMailCgi is implemented as a number of Python-coded CGI scripts that run on
a server machine (not your local computer), and generate HTML to interact
with the client/browser.  See the book <I>Programming Python, 3rd Edition</I>
for more details.</P>

<tr><td><hr>
<h2>Notes</h2>
<P>Caveats: PyMailCgi 1.0 was initially written during a 2-hour layover at
Chicago's O'Hare airport.  This release is not nearly as fast or complete
as PyMailGUI (e.g., each click requires an Internet transaction, there
is no save operation or multithreading, and there is no caching of email
headers or already-viewed messages).  On the other hand, PyMailCgi runs on
any web broswer, whether you have Python (and Tk) installed on your machine
or not.

<P>Also note that if you use these scripts to read your own email, PyMailCgi
does not guarantee security for your account password. See the notes in the
View action page as well as the book for more information on security policies.

<p><I><U>New in Version 2</U></I>: PyMailCGI now supports viewing and sending
Email attachments for a single user, and avoids some of the prior version's
exhaustive mail downloads. It only fetches message headers for the list page,
and only downloads the full text of the single message selected for viewing.

<p>Also see:

<UL>
<li>The <I>PyMailGUI</I> program in the Internet directory, which
        implements a more complete client-side Python+Tk email GUI
<li>The <I>pymail.py</I> program in the Email directory, which
        provides a simple console command-line email interface
<li>The Python imaplib module which supports the IMAP email protocol
        instead of POP
</UL></P>
</table><hr>

<A href="http://www.python.org">
<IMG SRC="PythonPoweredSmall.gif" ALIGN=left
```

Example 17-2. PP3E\Internet\Web\PyMailCgi\pymailcgi.html (continued)

```
ALT="[Python Logo]" border=0 hspace=15></A>
<A href="http://www.rmi.net/~lutz/about-pp.html">[Book]</a>
<A href="http://www.oreilly.com">[O'Reilly]</a>
</BODY></HTML>
```

The file *pymailcgi.html* is the system's root page and lives in a *PyMailCgi* subdirectory dedicated to this application (and helps keep its files separate from other examples). To access this system, start your locally running web server described earlier in this chapter and point your browser to the following URL (or do the right thing for whatever other web server you may be using):

> *http://localhost:8000/pymailcgi.html*

If you do, the server will ship back a page such as that shown in Figure 17-2, shown rendered in the open source Firefox web browser client.

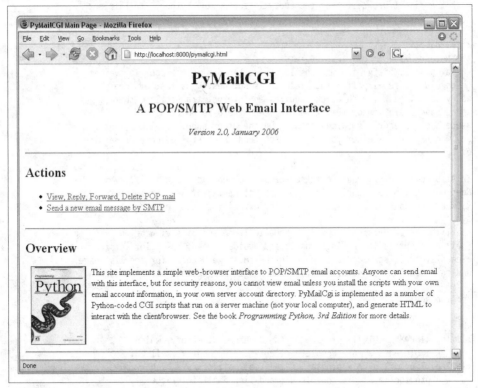

Figure 17-2. PyMailCGI main page

Configuring PyMailCGI

Now, before you click on the "View…" link in Figure 17-2, expecting to read your own email, I should point out that by default, PyMailCGI allows anybody to send email from this page with the Send link (as we learned earlier, there are no passwords in SMTP). It does not, however, allow arbitrary users on the Web to read their email accounts without typing an explicit and unsafe URL or doing a bit of installation and configuration.

This is on purpose, and it has to do with security constraints; as we'll see later, PyMailCGI is written such that it never associates your email username and password together without encryption. This isn't an issue if your web server is running locally, of course, but this policy is in place in case you ever run this system remotely across the Web.

By default, then, this page is set up to read the email account shown in this book—address *pp3e@earthlink.net*—and requires that account's POP password to do so. Since you probably can't guess the password (and wouldn't find its email helpful if you could), PyMailCGI is not incredibly useful as shipped. To use it to read your email instead, you'll want to change its *mailconfig.py* mail configuration file to reflect your mail account's details. We'll see this file later; for now, the examples here will use the book's POP email account; it works the same way, regardless of which account it accesses.

Sending Mail by SMTP

PyMailCGI supports two main functions, as links on the root page: composing and sending new mail to others and viewing incoming mail. The View function leads to pages that let users reply to, forward, and delete existing email. Since the Send function is the simplest, let's start with its pages and scripts first.

The Message Composition Page

The Send function steps users through two pages: one to edit a message and one to confirm delivery. When you click on the Send link on the main page in Figure 17-2 the Python CGI script in Example 17-3 runs on the web server.

Example 17-3. PP3E\Internet\Web\PyMailCgi\cgi-bin\onRootSendLink.py

```
#!/usr/bin/python
# On 'send' click in main root window

import commonhtml
from externs import mailconfig

commonhtml.editpage(kind='Write', headers={'From': mailconfig.myaddress})
```

No, this file wasn't truncated; there's not much to see in this script because all the action has been encapsulated in the commonhtml and externs modules. All that we can tell here is that the script calls something named editpage to generate a reply, passing in something called myaddress for its "From" header.

That's by design—by hiding details in shared utility modules we make top-level scripts such as this much easier to read and write, avoid code redundancy, and achieve a common look-and-feel to all our pages. There are no inputs to this script either; when run, it produces a page for composing a new message, as shown in Figure 17-3.

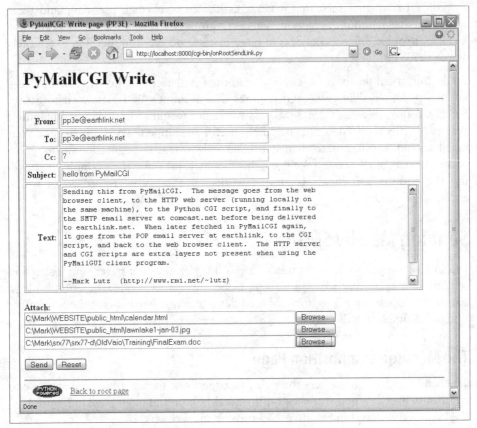

Figure 17-3. PyMailCGI send (write) page

Most of the composition page is self-explanatory—fill in headers and the main text of the message (a "From" header and standard signature line are initialized from settings in the `mailconfig` module, discussed further ahead). The Browse buttons open file selector dialogs, for picking an attachment. This interface looks very different from the PyMailGUI client program in Chapter 15, but it is functionally very similar. Also notice the top and bottom of this page—for reasons explained in the next section, they are going to look the same in all the pages of our system.

The Send Mail Script

As usual, the HTML of the edit page in Figure 17-3 names its handler script. When we click its Send button, Example 17-4 runs on the server to process our inputs and send the mail message.

Example 17-4. PP3E\Internet\Web\PyMailCgi\cgi-bin\onEditPageSend.py

```
#!/usr/bin/python
###############################################################
# On submit in edit window--finish a write, reply, or forward;
# in 2.0, we reuse the send tools in mailtools to construct
# and send the message, instead of older manual string scheme;
# we also now inherit attachment composition from that module;
###############################################################

import cgi, sys, commonhtml, os
from externs import mailtools

def saveAttachments(form, maxattach=3, savedir='partsupload'):
    """
    save uploaded attach files in local files on
    server from which mailtools will add to mail
    """
    partnames = []
    for i in range(1, maxattach+1):
        fieldname = 'attach%d' % i
        if form.has_key(fieldname) and form[fieldname].filename:
            fileinfo = form[fieldname]                    # sent and filled?
            filedata = fileinfo.value                     # read into string
            filename = fileinfo.filename                  # client's pathname
            if '\\' in filename:
                basename = filename.split('\\')[-1]       # try DOS clients
            elif '/' in filename:
                basename = filename.split('/')[-1]        # try Unix clients
            else:
                basename = filename                       # assume dir stripped
            pathname = os.path.join(savedir, basename)
            open(pathname, 'wb').write(filedata)
            os.chmod(pathname, 0666)                      # need for some srvrs
            partnames.append(pathname)                    # list of local paths
    return partnames                                      # gets type from name

#commonhtml.dumpstatepage(0)
form = cgi.FieldStorage()                     # parse form input data
attaches = saveAttachments(form)              # cgi.print_form(form) to see

# server name from module or get-style URL
smtpservername = commonhtml.getstandardsmtpfields(form)

# parms assumed to be in form or URL here
from commonhtml import getfield         # fetch value attributes
From = getfield(form, 'From')           # empty fields may not be sent
```

```
To   = getfield(form, 'To')
Cc   = getfield(form, 'Cc')
Subj = getfield(form, 'Subject')
text = getfield(form, 'text')
if Cc == '?': Cc = ''

# tools reused from PyMailGUI
Tos = [addr.strip() for addr in To.split(';')]          # multiple recip lists
Ccs = (Cc and [addr.strip() for addr in Cc.split(';')]) or ''
extraHdrs = [('Cc', Ccs), ('X-Mailer', 'PyMailCGI2')]

sender = mailtools.SilentMailSender(smtpservername)
try:
    sender.sendMessage(From, Tos, Subj, extraHdrs, text, attaches)
except:
    commonhtml.errorpage('Send mail error')
else:
    commonhtml.confirmationpage('Send mail')
```

This script gets mail header and text input information from the edit page's form (or from query parameters in an explicit URL) and sends the message off using Python's standard smtplib module, courtesy of the mailtools package. We studied mailtools in Chapter 14, so I won't say much more about it now. Note, though, that because we are reusing its send call, sent mail is automatically saved in a "sentmail.txt" file on the server; there are no tools for viewing this in PyMailCGI itself, but it serves as a log.

New in this version, the saveAttachments function grabs any part files sent from the browser and stores them in temporary local files on the server from which they will be added to the mail when sent. We covered CGI upload in detail at the end of Chapter 16; see that discussion for more on how the code here works. The business of attaching the files to the mail is automatic in mailtools.

A utility in commonhtml ultimately fetches the name of the SMTP server to receive the message from either the mailconfig module or the script's inputs (in a form field or URL query parameter). If all goes well, we're presented with a generated confirmation page, as captured in Figure 17-4.

As we'll see, this send mail script is also used to deliver *reply* and *forward* messages for incoming POP mail. The user interface for those operations is slightly different for composing new email from scratch, but as in PyMailGUI, the submission handler logic has been factored into the same, shared code—replies and forwards are really just mail send operations with quoted text and preset header fields.

Notice that there are no usernames or passwords to be found here; as we saw in Chapter 14, SMTP usually requires only a server that listens on the SMTP port, not a user account or password. As we also saw in that chapter, SMTP send operations that fail either raise a Python exception (e.g., if the server host can't be reached) or

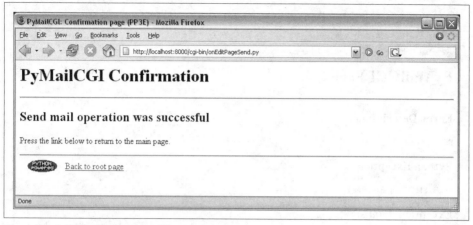

Figure 17-4. PyMailCGI send confirmation page

return a dictionary of failed recipients; our `mailtools` package modules insulate us from these details by always raising an exception in either case.

Error Pages

If there is a problem during mail delivery, we get an error page such as the one shown in Figure 17-5. This page reflects a failed recipient and includes a stack trace generated by the standard library's `traceback` module. On an actual exception, the Python error message and extra details would be displayed.

It's also worth pointing out that the `commonhtml` module encapsulates the generation of both the confirmation and the error pages so that all such pages look the same in PyMailCGI no matter where and when they are produced. Logic that generates the mail edit page in `commonhtml` is reused by the reply and forward actions too (but with different mail headers).

Common Look-and-Feel

In fact, `commonhtml` makes all pages look similar—it also provides common page *header* (top) and *footer* (bottom) generation functions, which are used everywhere in the system. You may have already noticed that all the pages so far follow the same pattern: they start with a title and horizontal rule, have something unique in the middle, and end with another rule, followed by a Python icon and link at the bottom. This *common look-and-feel* is the product of shared code in `commonhtml`; it generates everything but the middle section for every page in the system (except the root page, a static HTML file).

Most important, if we ever change the header and footer format functions in the `commonhtml` module, all our page's headers and footers will automatically be updated.

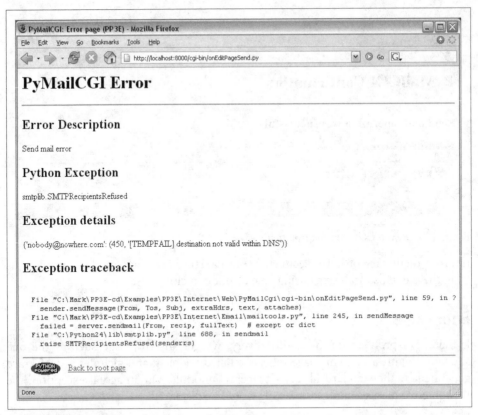

PyMailCGI Error

Error Description

Send mail error

Python Exception

smtplib.SMTPRecipientsRefused

Exception details

('nobody@nowhere.com': (450, '[TEMPFAIL] destination not valid within DNS'))

Exception traceback

```
File "C:\Mark\PP3E-cd\Examples\PP3E\Internet\Web\PyMailCgi\cgi-bin\onEditPageSend.py", line 59, in ?
  sender.sendMessage(From, Tos, Subj, extraHdrs, text, attaches)
File "C:\Mark\PP3E-cd\Examples\PP3E\Internet\Email\mailtools.py", line 245, in sendMessage
  failed = server.sendmail(From, recip, fullText)  # except or dict
File "C:\Python24\lib\smtplib.py", line 688, in sendmail
  raise SMTPRecipientsRefused(senderrs)
```

Back to root page

Figure 17-5. PyMailCGI send error page

If you are interested in seeing how this encapsulated logic works right now, flip ahead to Example 17-14. We'll explore its code after we study the rest of the mail site's pages.

Using the Send Mail Script Outside a Browser

I initially wrote the send script to be used only within PyMailCGI using values typed into the mail edit form. But as we've seen, inputs can be sent in either form fields or URL query parameters. Because the send mail script checks for inputs in CGI inputs before importing from the mailconfig module, it's also possible to call this script outside the edit page to send email—for instance, explicitly typing a URL of this nature into your browser's address field (but all on one line and with no intervening spaces):

```
http://localhost:8000/cgi-bin/
              onEditPageSend.py?site=smtp.rmi.net&
                        From=lutz@rmi.net&
                        To=lutz@rmi.net&
                        Subject=test+url&
                        text=Hello+Mark;this+is+Mark
```

will indeed send an email message as specified by the input parameters at the end. That URL string is a lot to type into a browser's address field, of course, but it might be useful if generated automatically by another script. As we saw in Chapters 14 and 16, the module urllib can then be used to submit such a URL string to the server from within a Python program. Example 17-5 shows one way to automate this.

Example 17-5. PP3E\Internet\Web\PyMailCgi\sendurl.py

```
##################################################################
# Send email by building a URL like this from inputs:
# http://servername/pathname/
#             onEditPageSend.py?site=smtp.rmi.net&
#                              From=lutz@rmi.net&
#                              To=lutz@rmi.net&
#                              Subject=test+url&
#                              text=Hello+Mark;this+is+Mark
##################################################################

from urllib import quote_plus, urlopen

url = 'http://localhost:8000/cgi-bin/onEditPageSend.py'
url = url + '?site=%s'    % quote_plus(raw_input('Site>'))
url = url + '&From=%s'    % quote_plus(raw_input('From>'))
url = url + '&To=%s'      % quote_plus(raw_input('To  >'))
url = url + '&Subject=%s' % quote_plus(raw_input('Subj>'))
url = url + '&text=%s'    % quote_plus(raw_input('text>'))        # or input loop

print 'Reply html:'
print urlopen(url).read()      # confirmation or error page HTML
```

Running this script from the system command line is yet another way to send an email message—this time, by contacting our CGI script on a web server machine to do all the work. The script *sendurl.py* runs on any machine with Python and sockets, lets us input mail parameters interactively, and invokes another Python script that lives on a possibly remote machine. It prints HTML returned by our CGI script:

```
C:\...\PP3E\Internet\Web\PyMailCgi>sendurl.py
Site>smtp.comcast.net
From>pp3e@earthlink.net
To  >pp3e@earthlink.net
Subj>testing sendurl.py
text>But sir, it's only wafer-thin...
Reply html:
<html><head><title>PyMailCGI: Confirmation page (PP3E)</title></head>
<body bgcolor="#FFFFFF"><h1>PyMailCGI Confirmation</h1><hr>
<h2>Send mail operation was successful</h2>
<p>Press the link below to return to the main page.</p>
</p><hr><a href="http://www.python.org">
<img src="../PythonPoweredSmall.gif"
align=left alt="[Python Logo]" border=0 hspace=15></a>
<a href="../pymailcgi.html">Back to root page</a>
</body></html>
```

The HTML reply printed by this script would normally be rendered into a new web page if caught by a browser. Such cryptic output might be less than ideal, but you could easily search the reply string for its components to determine the result (e.g., using the string find method or an in membership test to look for "successful"), parse out its components with Python's standard htmllib or re module, and so on. The resulting mail message—viewed, for variety, with Chapter 15's PyMailGUI program—shows up in this book's email account as seen in Figure 17-6 (it's a single text-part message).

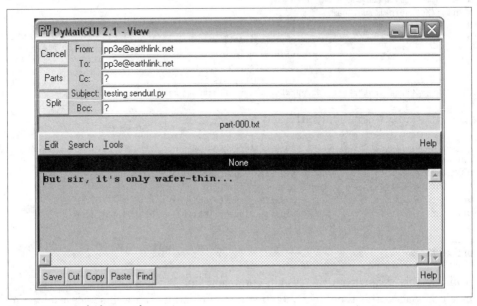

Figure 17-6. sendurl.py result

Of course, there are other, less remote ways to send email from a client machine. For instance, the Python smtplib module (used by mailtools) itself depends only upon the client and SMTP server connections being operational, whereas this script also depends on the web server machine and CGI script (requests go from client to web server to CGI script to SMTP server). Because our CGI script supports general URLs, though, it can do more than a mailto: HTML tag and can be invoked with urllib outside the context of a running web browser. For instance, as discussed in Chapter 16, scripts like *sendurl.py* can be used to invoke and *test* server-side programs.

Reading POP Email

So far, we've stepped through the path the system follows to *send* new mail. Let's now see what happens when we try to *view* incoming POP mail.

The POP Password Page

If you flip back to the main page in Figure 17-2, you'll see a View link; pressing it triggers the script in Example 17-6 to run on the server.

Example 17-6. PP3E\Internet\Web\PyMailCgi\cgi-bin\onRootViewLink.py

```
#!/usr/bin/python
###############################################################
# on view link click on main/root HTML page
# this could almost be an HTML file because there are likely
# no input params yet, but I wanted to use standard header/
# footer functions and display the site/usernames which must
# be fetched;  On submission, doesn't send the user along with
# password here, and only ever sends both as URL params or
# hidden fields after the password has been encrypted by a
# user-uploadable encryption module; put HTML in commonhtml?
###############################################################

# page template

pswdhtml = """
<form method=post action=%sonViewPswdSubmit.py>
<p>
Please enter POP account password below, for user "%s" and site "%s".
<p><input name=pswd type=password>
<input type=submit value="Submit"></form></p>

<hr><p><i>Security note</i>: The password you enter above will be transmitted
over the Internet to the server machine, but is not displayed, is never
transmitted in combination with a username unless it is encrypted, and is
never stored anywhere: not on the server (it is only passed along as hidden
fields in subsequent pages), and not on the client (no cookies are generated).
This is still not guaranteed to be totally safe; use your browser's back button
to back out of PyMailCgi at any time.</p>
"""

# generate the password input page

import commonhtml                                          # usual parms case:
user, pswd, site = commonhtml.getstandardpopfields({})     # from module here,
commonhtml.pageheader(kind='POP password input')           # from html|url later
print pswdhtml % (commonhtml.urlroot, user, site)
commonhtml.pagefooter()
```

This script is almost all embedded HTML: the triple-quoted `pswdhtml` string is printed, with string formatting to insert values, in a single step. But because we need to fetch the username and server name to display on the generated page, this is coded as an executable script, not as a static HTML file. The module `commonhtml` either loads usernames and server names from script inputs (e.g., appended as query parameters to the script's URL) or imports them from the `mailconfig` file; either way, we don't want to hardcode them into this script or its HTML, so a simple HTML file won't do.

Since this is a script, we can also use the commonhtml page header and footer routines to render the generated reply page with a common look-and-feel, as shown in Figure 17-7.

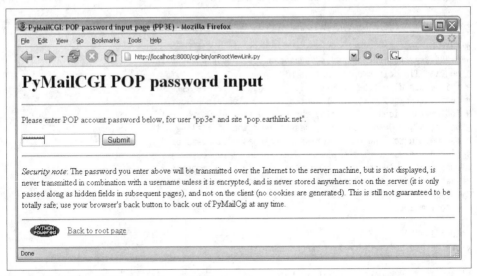

Figure 17-7. PyMailCGI view password login page

At this page, the user is expected to enter the password for the POP email account of the user and server displayed. Notice that the actual password isn't displayed; the input field's HTML specifies type=password, which works just like a normal text field, but shows typed input as stars. (See also the pymail program in Chapter 14 for doing this at a console and PyMailGUI in Chapter 15 for doing this in a GUI.)

The Mail Selection List Page

After you fill out the last page's password field and press its Submit button, the password is shipped off to the script shown in Example 17-7.

Example 17-7. PP3E\Internet\Web\PyMailCgi\cgi-bin\onViewPswdSubmit.py

```
#!/usr/bin/python
###########################################################
# On submit in POP password input window--make view list;
# in 2.0 we only fetch mail headers here, and fetch 1 full
# message later upon request; we still fetch all headers
# each time the index page is made: caching requires a db;
###########################################################

import cgi
import loadmail, commonhtml
from    externs import mailtools
from    secret  import encode        # user-defined encoder module
```

```
MaxHdr = 35                          # max length of email hdrs in list

# only pswd comes from page here, rest usually in module
formdata = cgi.FieldStorage()
mailuser, mailpswd, mailsite = commonhtml.getstandardpopfields(formdata)

try:
    newmails = loadmail.loadmailhdrs(mailsite, mailuser, mailpswd)
    mailnum  = 1
    maillist = []
    for mail in newmails:                          # list of hdr text
        msginfo = []
        hdrs = mailtools.MailParser().parseHeaders(mail)    # email.Message
        for key in ('Subject', 'From', 'Date'):
            msginfo.append(hdrs.get(key, '?')[:MaxHdr])
        msginfo = ' | '.join(msginfo)
        maillist.append((msginfo, commonhtml.urlroot + 'onViewListLink.py',
                            {'mnum': mailnum,
                             'user': mailuser,           # data params
                             'pswd': encode(mailpswd),   # pass in URL
                             'site': mailsite}))          # not inputs
        mailnum += 1
    commonhtml.listpage(maillist, 'mail selection list')
except:
    commonhtml.errorpage('Error loading mail index')
```

This script's main purpose is to generate a selection list page for the user's email account, using the password typed into the prior page (or passed in a URL). As usual with encapsulation, most of the details are hidden in other files:

loadmail.loadmailhdrs

> Reuses the mailtools module package from Chapter 14 to fetch email with the POP protocol; we need a message count and mail headers here to display an index list. In this version, the software fetches only mail header text to save time, not full mail messages (provided your server supports the TOP command of the POP interface—if not, see mailconfig to disable this).

commonhtml.listpage

> Generates HTML to display a passed-in list of tuples (text, URL, parameter-dictionary) as a list of hyperlinks in the reply page; parameter values show up as query parameters at the end of URLs in the response.

The maillist list built here is used to create the body of the next page—a clickable email message selection list. Each generated hyperlink in the list page references a constructed URL that contains enough information for the next script to fetch and display a particular email message. As we learned in the last chapter, this is a simple kind of state retention between pages and scripts.

If all goes well, the mail selection list page HTML generated by this script is rendered as in Figure 17-8. If your inbox is as large as some of mine, you'll probably need to scroll down to see the end of this page. This page follows the common look-and-feel for all PyMailCGI pages, thanks to `commonhtml`.

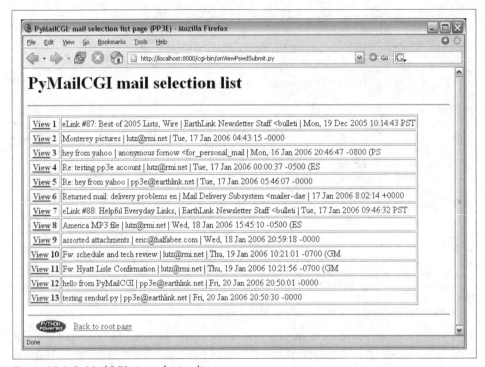

Figure 17-8. PyMailCGI view selection list page, top

If the script can't access your email account (e.g., because you typed the wrong password), its `try` statement handler instead produces a commonly formatted error page. Figure 17-9 shows one that gives the Python exception and details as part of the reply after a genuine exception is caught; as usual, the exception details are fetched from `sys.exc_info`, and Python's `traceback` module is used to generate a stack trace.

Passing State Information in URL Link Parameters

The central mechanism at work in Example 17-7 is the generation of URLs that embed message numbers and mail account information. Clicking on any of the View links in the selection list triggers another script, which uses information in the link's URL parameters to fetch and display the selected email. As mentioned in Chapter 16, because the list's links are effectively programmed to "know" how to load a particular message, they effectively remember what to do next. Figure 17-10 shows part of the HTML generated by this script (use your web browser View Source option to see this for yourself).

Did you get all that? You may not be able to read generated HTML like this, but your browser can. For the sake of readers afflicted with human-parsing limitations, here is

Figure 17-9. PyMailCGI login error page

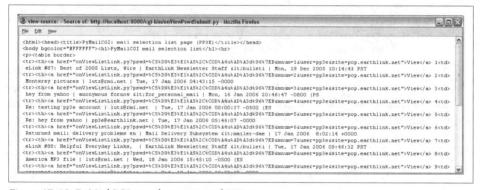

Figure 17-10. PyMailCGI view list, generated HTML

what one of those link lines looks like, reformatted with line breaks and spaces to make it easier to understand:

```
<tr><th><a href="onViewListLink.py?
              pswd=%C5%D9%E3%E1%A5%2C%C0D%A4u%AD%A3d%96%7EB&
```

```
mnum=8&
user=pp3e&
site=pop.earthlink.net">View</a> 8
<td>America MP3 file | lutz@rmi.net | Wed, 18 Jan 2006 15:45:10 -0500 (ES
```

PyMailCGI generates relative minimal URLs (server and pathname values come from the prior page, unless set in commonhtml). Clicking on the word *View* in the hyperlink rendered from this HTML code triggers the onViewListLink script as usual, passing it all the parameters embedded at the end of the URL: the POP username, the POP message number of the message associated with this link, and the POP password and site information. These values will be available in the object returned by cgi. FieldStorage in the next script run. Note that the mnum POP message number parameter differs in each link because each opens a different message when clicked and that the text after <td> comes from message headers extracted by the mailtools package, using the email package.

The commonhtml module escapes all of the link parameters with the urllib module, not cgi.escape, because they are part of a URL. This is obvious only in the pswd password parameter—its value has been encrypted, but urllib additionally escapes non-safe characters in the encrypted string per URL convention (that's where all the %xx characters come from). It's OK if the encryptor yields odd—even nonprintable—characters because URL encoding makes them legible for transmission. When the password reaches the next script, cgi.FieldStorage undoes URL escape sequences, leaving the encrypted password string without % escapes.

It's instructive to see how commonhtml builds up the stateful link parameters. Earlier, we learned how to use the urllib.quote_plus call to escape a string for inclusion in URLs:

```
>>> import urllib
>>> urllib.quote_plus("There's bugger all down here on Earth")
'There%27s+bugger+all+down+here+on+Earth'
```

The module commonhtml, though, calls the higher-level urllib.urlencode function, which translates a dictionary of *name:value* pairs into a complete URL query parameter string, ready to add after a ? marker in a URL. For instance, here is urlencode in action at the interactive prompt:

```
>>> parmdict = {'user': 'Brian',
...             'pswd': '#!/spam',
...             'text': 'Say no more, squire!'}

>>> urllib.urlencode(parmdict)
'pswd=%23%21/spam&user=Brian&text=Say+no+more,+squire%21'

>>> "%s?%s" % ("http://scriptname.py", urllib.urlencode(parmdict))
'http://scriptname.py?pswd=%23%21/spam&user=Brian&text=Say+no+more,+squire%21'
```

Internally, urlencode passes each name and value in the dictionary to the built-in str function (to make sure they are strings), and then runs each one through urllib.quote_plus as they are added to the result. The CGI script builds up a list of similar dictionaries and passes it to commonhtml to be formatted into a selection list page.*

In broader terms, generating URLs with parameters like this is one way to pass state information to the next script (along with cookies, hidden form input fields, and server databases, discussed in Chapter 16). Without such state information, users would have to reenter the username, password, and site name on every page they visit along the way.

Incidentally, the list generated by this script is not radically different in functionality from what we built in the PyMailGUI program in Chapter 15, though the two differ cosmetically. Figure 17-11 shows this strictly client-side GUI's view on the same email list displayed in Figure 17-8.

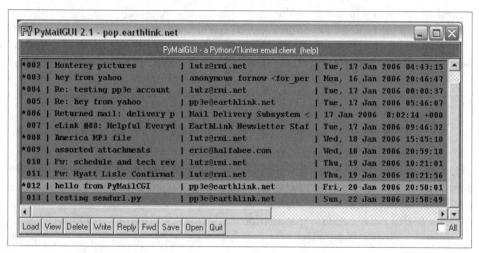

Figure 17-11. PyMailGUI displaying the same view list

However, PyMailGUI uses the Tkinter GUI library to build up a user interface instead of sending HTML to a browser. It also runs entirely on the client and downloads mail from the POP server directly to the client machine over sockets on demand. Because it retains memory for the duration of the session, PyMailGUI can easily minimize mail server access. After the initial header load, it needs to load only newly arrived email headers on load requests. Moreover, it can update its email index in-memory on deletions instead of reloading anew from the server, and it has enough state to perform safe deletions of messages that check for server inbox

---

* Technically, again, you should generally escape & separators in generated URL links by running the URL through cgi.escape, if any parameter's name could be the same as that of an HTML character escape code (e.g., &amp=high). See Chapter 16 for more details; they aren't escaped here because there are no clashes between URL and HTML.

matches. PyMailGUI also remembers emails you've already viewed—they need not be reloaded again while the program runs.

In contrast, PyMailCGI runs on the web server machine and simply displays mail text on the client's browser—mail is downloaded from the POP server machine to the web server, where CGI scripts are run. Due to the autonomous nature of CGI scripts, PyMailCGI by itself has no automatic memory that spans pages and may need to reload headers and already viewed messages during a single session. These architecture differences have some important ramifications, which we'll discuss later in this chapter.

Security Protocols

In `onViewPswdSubmit`'s source code (Example 17-7), notice that password inputs are passed to an encode function as they are added to the parameters dictionary; hence they show up encrypted in hyperlinked URLs. They are also URL encoded for transmission (with % escapes) and are later decoded and decrypted within other scripts as needed to access the POP account. The password encryption step, encode, is at the heart of PyMailCGI's security policy.

In Python today, the standard library's socket module supports Secure Sockets Layer (SSL), if the required library is built into your Python. SSL automatically encrypts transmitted data to make it safe to pass over the Net. Unfortunately, for reasons we'll discuss when we reach the secret.py module later in this chapter (see Example 17-13), this wasn't a universal solution for PyMailCGI's password data. (In short, the web server we're using doesn't directly support its end of a secure HTTP encrypted dialog.) Because of that, an alternative scheme was devised to minimize the chance that email account information could be stolen off the Net in transit.

Here's how it works. When this script is invoked by the password input page's form, it gets only one input parameter: the password typed into the form. The username is imported from a `mailconfig` module installed on the server; it is not transmitted together with the unencrypted password (that could be intercepted).

To pass the POP username and password to the next page as state information, this script adds them to the end of the mail selection list URLs, but only after the password has been encrypted by `secret.encode`—a function in a module that lives on the server and may vary in every location that PyMailCGI is installed. In fact, PyMailCGI was written to not have to know about the password encryptor at all; because the encoder is a separate module, you can provide any flavor you like. Unless you also publish your encoder module, the encoded password shipped with the username won't be of much help to snoopers.

The upshot is that normally, PyMailCGI never sends or receives both username and password values together in a single transaction, unless the password is encrypted with an encryptor of your choice. This limits its utility somewhat (since only a single account username can be installed on the server), but the alternative of popping up two pages—one for password entry and one for user—seems even less friendly. In general, if you want to read your mail with the system as coded, you have to install its files on your server, edit its *mailconfig.py* to reflect your account details, and change its `secret.py` encryptor as desired.

Reading mail with direct URLs

One exception: since any CGI script can be invoked with parameters in an explicit URL instead of form field values, and since `commonhtml` tries to fetch inputs from the form object before importing them from `mailconfig`, it is possible for any person to use this script to check his mail without installing and configuring a copy of PyMail-CGI. For example, a URL such as the following typed into your browser's address field or submitted with tools such as `urllib` (but without the line break used to make it fit here):

```
http://localhost:8000/cgi-bin/
    onViewPswdSubmit.py?user=pp3e&pswd=guess&site=pop.earthlink.net
```

will actually load email into a selection list page such as that in Figure 17-8, using whatever user, password, and mail site names are appended to the URL. From the selection list, you may then view, reply, forward, and delete email.

Notice that at this point in the interaction, the password you send in a URL of this form is *not* encrypted. Later scripts expect that the password inputs will be sent encrypted, though, which makes it more difficult to use them with explicit URLs (you would need to match the encrypted form produced by the secret module on the server). Passwords are encrypted as they are added to links in the reply page's selection list, and they remain encrypted in URLs and hidden form fields thereafter.

 But you shouldn't use a URL like this, unless you don't care about exposing your email password. Sending your unencrypted mail user ID and password strings across the Net in a URL such as this is unsafe and open to snoopers. In fact, it's like giving away your email—anyone who intercepts this URL, or views it in a server logfile will have complete access to your email account. It is made even more treacherous by the fact that this URL format appears in a book that will be distributed all around the world.

If you care about security and want to use PyMailCGI on a remote server, install it on your server and configure `mailconfig` and `secret`. That should at least guarantee that both your user and password information will never be transmitted unencrypted in a single transaction. This scheme may still not be foolproof, so be careful out there. Without secure HTTP and sockets, the Internet is a "use at your own risk" medium.

The Message View Page

Back to our page flow; at this point, we are still viewing the message selection list in Figure 17-8. When we click on one of its generated hyperlinks, the stateful URL invokes the script in Example 17-8 on the server, sending the selected message number and mail account information (user, password, and site) as parameters on the end of the script's URL.

Example 17-8. PP3E\Internet\Web\PyMailCgi\cgi-bin\onViewListLink.py

```python
#!/usr/bin/python
############################################################
# On user click of message link in main selection list;
# cgi.FieldStorage undoes any urllib escapes in the link's
# input parameters (%xx and '+' for spaces already undone);
# in 2.0 we only fetch 1 mail here, not entire list again!
# in 2.0 we also find mail's main text part intelligently
# instead of blindly displaying full text (poss attachments),
# and generate links to attachment files saved on the server;
# saved attachment files only work for 1 user and 1 message;
# most 2.0 enhancements inherited from the mailtools package;
############################################################

import cgi
import commonhtml, secret
from externs import mailtools
#commonhtml.dumpstatepage(0)

def saveAttachments(message, parser, savedir='partsdownload'):
    """
    save fetched email's parts to files on
    server to be viewed in user's web browser
    """
    import os
    if not os.path.exists(savedir):            # in CGI script's cwd on server
        os.mkdir(savedir)                      # will open per your browser
    for filename in os.listdir(savedir):       # clean up last message: temp!
        dirpath = os.path.join(savedir, filename)
        os.remove(dirpath)
    typesAndNames = parser.saveParts(savedir, message)
    filenames = [fname for (ctype, fname) in typesAndNames]
    for filename in filenames:
        os.chmod(filename, 0666)               # some srvrs may need read/write
    return filenames

form = cgi.FieldStorage()
user, pswd, site = commonhtml.getstandardpopfields(form)
pswd = secret.decode(pswd)

try:
    msgnum  = form['mnum'].value                          # from URL link
    parser  = mailtools.MailParser()
    fetcher = mailtools.SilentMailFetcher(site, user, pswd)
```

Example 17-8. PP3E\Internet\Web\PyMailCgi\cgi-bin\onViewListLink.py (continued)

```
    fulltext = fetcher.downloadMessage(int(msgnum))          # don't eval!
    message  = parser.parseMessage(fulltext)                 # email.Message
    parts    = saveAttachments(message, parser)              # for URL links
    mtype, content = parser.findMainText(message)            # first txt part
    commonhtml.viewpage(msgnum, message, content, form, parts) # encoded pswd
except:
    commonhtml.errorpage('Error loading message')
```

Again, much of the work here happens in the commonhtml module, listed later in this section (see Example 17-14). This script adds logic to decode the input password (using the configurable secret encryption module) and extract the selected mail's headers and text using the mailtools module package from Chapter 14 again. The full text of the selected message is ultimately fetched and parsed by mailtools, using the standard library's poplib module and email package. Although we'll have to refetch this message if viewed again, this version does not grab all mails to get just the one selected.[*]

Also new in this version, the saveAttachments function in this script splits off the parts of a fetched message and stores them in a directory on the web server machine. This was discussed earlier in this chapter—the view page is then augmented with URL links that point at the saved part files. Your web browser will open them according to their filenames. All the work of part extraction and naming is inherited from mailtools. Part files are kept temporarily; they are deleted when the next message is fetched. They are also currently stored in a single directory and so apply to only a single user.

If the message can be loaded and parsed successfully, the result page, shown in Figure 17-12, allows us to view, but not edit, the mail's text. The function commonhtml.viewpage generates a "read-only" HTML option for all the text widgets in this page.

View pages like this have a pull-down action selection list near the bottom; if you want to do more, use this list to pick an action (Reply, Forward, or Delete) and click on the Next button to proceed to the next screen. If you're just in a browsing frame of mind, click the "Back to root page" link at the bottom to return to the main page, or use your browser's Back button to return to the selection list page.

Figure 17-12 show the mail we sent earlier in this chapter, being viewed (we sent it to ourselves). Notice its "Parts:" links—when clicked, they trigger URLs that open the temporary part files on the server, according to your browser's rules for the file type. For instance, clicking in the "doc" file will likely open it in Microsoft Word on Win-

---

[*] Notice that the message number arrives as a string and must be converted to an integer in order to be used to fetch the message. But we're careful not to convert with eval here, since this is a string passed over the Net and could have arrived embedded at the end of an arbitrary URL (remember that earlier warning?).

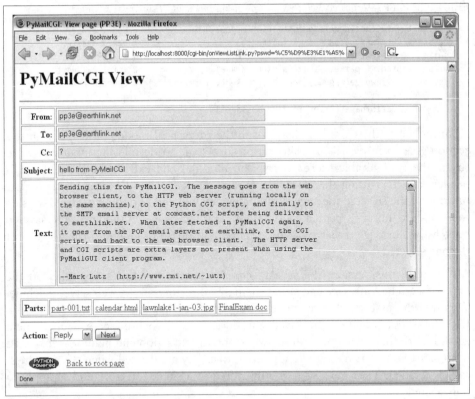

Figure 17-12. PyMailCGI view page

dows; selecting the "jpg" link will open it either in a local image viewer or within the browser itself, as captured in Figure 17-13.

Passing State Information in HTML Hidden Input Fields

What you don't see on the view page in Figure 17-12 is just as important as what you do see. We need to defer to Example 17-14 for coding details, but something new is going on here. The original message number, as well as the POP user and (still encrypted) password information sent to this script as part of the stateful link's URL, wind up being copied into the HTML used to create this view page, as the values of hidden input fields in the form. The hidden field generation code in commonhtml looks like this:

```
print '<form method=post action="%s/onViewPageAction.py">' % urlroot
print '<input type=hidden name=mnum value="%s">' % msgnum
print '<input type=hidden name=user value="%s">' % user    # from page|url
print '<input type=hidden name=site value="%s">' % site    # for deletes
print '<input type=hidden name=pswd value="%s">' % pswd    # pswd encoded
```

Figure 17-13. Attached part file link display

As we've learned, much like parameters in generated hyperlink URLs, hidden fields in a page's HTML allow us to embed state information inside this web page itself. Unless you view that page's source, you can't see this state information because hidden fields are never displayed. But when this form's Submit button is clicked, hidden field values are automatically transmitted to the next script along with the visible fields on the form.

Figure 17-14 shows part of the source code generated for another message's view page; the hidden input fields used to pass selected mail state information are embedded near the top.

The net effect is that hidden input fields in HTML, just like parameters at the end of generated URLs, act like temporary storage areas and retain state between pages and user interaction steps. Both are the Web's equivalent to programming language variables. They come in handy anytime your application needs to remember something between pages.

```
view-source: - Source of: http://localhost:8000/cgi-bin/onViewListLink.py?pswd=%C5%D9...

File   Edit   View

<html><head><title>PyMailCGI: View page (PP3E)</title></head>
<body bgcolor="#FFFFFF"><h1>PyMailCGI View</h1><hr>
<form method=post action="onViewPageAction.py">
<input type=hidden name=mnum value="9">
<input type=hidden name=user value="pp3e">
<input type=hidden name=site value="pop.earthlink.net">
<input type=hidden name=pswd value="ÅÙãá¥,ÀD¤u£d-~B">
<table border cellpadding=3>
<tr><th align=right>From:
    <td><input type=text
    name=From value="eric@halfabee.com" readonly size=60>
<tr><th align=right>To:
    <td><input type=text
    name=To value="pp3e@earthlink.net" readonly size=60>
<tr><th align=right>Cc:
    <td><input type=text
    name=Cc value="?" readonly size=60>
<tr><th align=right>Subject:
    <td><input type=text
    name=Subject value="assorted attachments" readonly size=60>
<tr><th align=right>Text:
<td><textarea name=text cols=80 rows=10 readonly>
Sent from PyMailCGI web site; let's see what
the clients do...

--Eric


</textarea></table>
<hr><table border cellpadding=3><tr><th>Parts:
<td><a href=../partsdownload/part-001.txt>part-001.txt</a>
<td><a href=../partsdownload/calendar.html>calendar.html</a>
<td><a href=../partsdownload/lawnlake1-jan-03.jpg>lawnlake1-jan-03.jpg</a>
<td><a href=../partsdownload/FinalExam.doc>FinalExam.doc</a>
</table><hr>
```

Figure 17-14. PyMailCGI view page, generated HTML

Hidden fields are especially useful if you cannot invoke the next script from a generated URL hyperlink with parameters. For instance, the next action in our script is a form submit button (Next), not a hyperlink, so hidden fields are used to pass state. As before, without these hidden fields, users would need to reenter POP account details somewhere on the view page if they were needed by the next script (in our example, they are required if the next action is Delete).

Escaping Mail Text and Passwords in HTML

Notice that everything you see on the message view page in Figure 17-14 is escaped with cgi.escape. Header fields and the text of the mail itself might contain characters that are special to HTML and must be translated as usual. For instance, because some mailers allow you to send messages in HTML format, it's possible that an email's text could contain a </textarea> tag, which would throw the reply page hopelessly out of sync if not escaped.

One subtlety here: HTML escapes are important only when text is sent to the browser initially (by the CGI script). If that text is later sent out again to another script (e.g., by sending a reply mail), the text will be back in its original, nonescaped format when received again on the server. The browser parses out escape codes and does not put them back again when uploading form data, so we don't need to undo escapes later. For example, here is part of the escaped text area sent to a browser during a Reply transaction (use your browser's View Source option to see this live):

```
<tr><th align=right>Text:
<td><textarea name=text cols=80 rows=10 readonly>
more stuff

--Mark Lutz  (http://rmi.net/~lutz)  [PyMailCgi 2.0]


&gt; -----Original Message-----
&gt; From: lutz@rmi.net
&gt; To: lutz@rmi.net
&gt; Date: Tue May  2 18:28:41 2000
&gt;
&gt; &lt;table&gt;&lt;textarea&gt;
&gt; &lt;/textarea&gt;&lt;/table&gt;
&gt; --Mark Lutz  (http://rmi.net/~lutz)  [PyMailCgi 2.0]
&gt;
&gt;
&gt; &gt; -----Original Message-----
```

After this reply is delivered, its text looks as it did before escapes (and exactly as it appeared to the user in the message edit web page):

```
more stuff

--Mark Lutz  (http://rmi.net/~lutz)  [PyMailCgi 2.0]


> -----Original Message-----
> From: lutz@rmi.net
> To: lutz@rmi.net
> Date: Tue May  2 18:28:41 2000
>
> <table><textarea>
> </textarea></table>
> --Mark Lutz  (http://rmi.net/~lutz)  [PyMailCgi 2.0]
>
>
> > -----Original Message-----
```

Did you notice the odd characters in the hidden password field of the generated HTML screenshot (Figure 17-14)? It turns out that the POP password is still encrypted when placed in hidden fields of the HTML. For security, they have to be. Values of a page's hidden fields can be seen with a browser's View Source option, and it's not impossible that the text of this page could be intercepted off the Net.

The password is no longer URL encoded when put in the hidden field, however, even though it was when it appeared at the end of the smart link URL. Depending on your encryption module, the password might now contain nonprintable characters when generated as a hidden field value here; the browser doesn't care, as long as the field is run through cgi.escape like everything else added to the HTML reply stream. The commonhtml module is careful to route all text and headers through cgi.escape as the view page is constructed.

As a comparison, Figure 17-15 shows what the mail message captured in Figure 17-12 looks like when viewed in PyMailGUI, the client-side Tkinter-based email tool from Chapter 15. In that program, message parts are listed with the Parts button and are extracted, saved, and opened with the Split button; we also get quick-access buttons to parts and attachments just below the message headers. The net effect is similar.

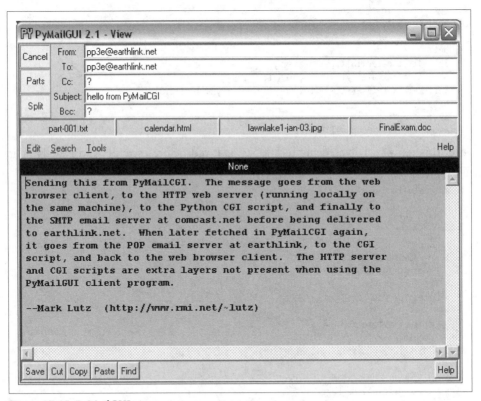

Figure 17-15. PyMailGUI viewer, same message

PyMailGUI doesn't need to care about things such as passing state in URLs or hidden fields (it saves state in Python in-process variables) or escaping HTML and URL strings (there are no browsers, and no network transmission steps once mail is downloaded). It also doesn't have to rely on temporary server file links to give access to message parts—the message is retained in memory attached to a window object and lives on between interactions. PyMailGUI does require Python to be installed on the client, but we'll return to that in a few pages.

Processing Fetched Mail

At this point in our PyMailCGI web interaction, we are viewing an email message (Figure 17-12) that was chosen from the selection list page. On the message view page, selecting an action from the pull-down list and clicking the Next button invokes the script in Example 17-9 on the server to perform a reply, forward, or delete operation for the selected message.

Example 17-9. PP3E\Internet\Web\PyMailCgi\cgi-bin\onViewPageAction.py

```python
#!/usr/bin/python
###########################################################################
# On submit in mail view window, action selected=(fwd, reply, delete)
# in 2.0, we reuse the mailtools delete logic orig coded for PyMailGUI
###########################################################################

import cgi, commonhtml, secret
from    externs import mailtools, mailconfig
from    commonhtml import getfield

def quotetext(form):
    """
    note that headers come from the prior page's form here,
    not from parsing the mail message again; that means that
    commonhtml.viewpage must pass along date as a hidden field
    """
    quoted = '\n-----Original Message-----\n'
    for hdr in ('From', 'To', 'Date'):
        quoted = quoted + '%s: %s\n' % (hdr, getfield(form, hdr))
    quoted = quoted + '\n' +  getfield(form, 'text')
    quoted = '\n' + quoted.replace('\n', '\n> ')
    return quoted

form = cgi.FieldStorage()  # parse form or URL data
user, pswd, site = commonhtml.getstandardpopfields(form)
pswd = secret.decode(pswd)

try:
    if form['action'].value    == 'Reply':
        headers = {'From':    mailconfig.myaddress,
                   'To':      getfield(form, 'From'),
                   'Cc':      mailconfig.myaddress,
                   'Subject': 'Re: ' + getfield(form, 'Subject')}
        commonhtml.editpage('Reply', headers, quotetext(form))

    elif form['action'].value == 'Forward':
        headers = {'From':    mailconfig.myaddress,
```

```
                    'To':      '',
                    'Cc':      mailconfig.myaddress,
                    'Subject': 'Fwd: ' + getfield(form, 'Subject')}
        commonhtml.editpage('Forward', headers, quotetext(form))

    elif form['action'].value == 'Delete':      # mnum field is required here
        msgnum  = int(form['mnum'].value)       # but not eval(): may be code
        fetcher = mailtools.SilentMailFetcher(site, user, pswd)
        fetcher.deleteMessages([msgnum])
        commonhtml.confirmationpage('Delete')

    else:
        assert False, 'Invalid view action requested'
except:
    commonhtml.errorpage('Cannot process view action')
```

This script receives all information about the selected message as form input field data (some hidden and encrypted, some not) along with the selected action's name. The next step in the interaction depends upon the action selected:

Reply and Forward actions

Generate a message edit page with the original message's lines automatically quoted with a leading >.

Delete actions

Trigger immediate deletion of the email being viewed, using a tool imported from the `mailtools` module package from Chapter 14.

All these actions use data passed in from the prior page's form, but only the Delete action cares about the POP username and password and must decode the password received (it arrives here from hidden form input fields generated in the prior page's HTML).

Reply and Forward

If you select Reply as the next action, the message edit page in Figure 17-16 is generated by the script. Text on this page is editable, and pressing this page's Send button again triggers the send mail script we saw in Example 17-4. If all goes well, we'll receive the same confirmation page we got earlier when writing new mail from scratch (Figure 17-4).

Forward operations are virtually the same, except for a few email header differences. All of this busy-ness comes "for free," because Reply and Forward pages are generated by calling `commonhtml.editpage`, the same utility used to create a new mail composition page. Here, we simply pass preformatted header line strings to the utility (e.g., replies add "Re:" to the subject text). We applied the same sort of reuse trick in PyMailGUI, but in a different context. In PyMailCGI, one script handles three pages; in PyMailGUI, one superclass and callback method handles three buttons, but the architecture is similar in spirit.

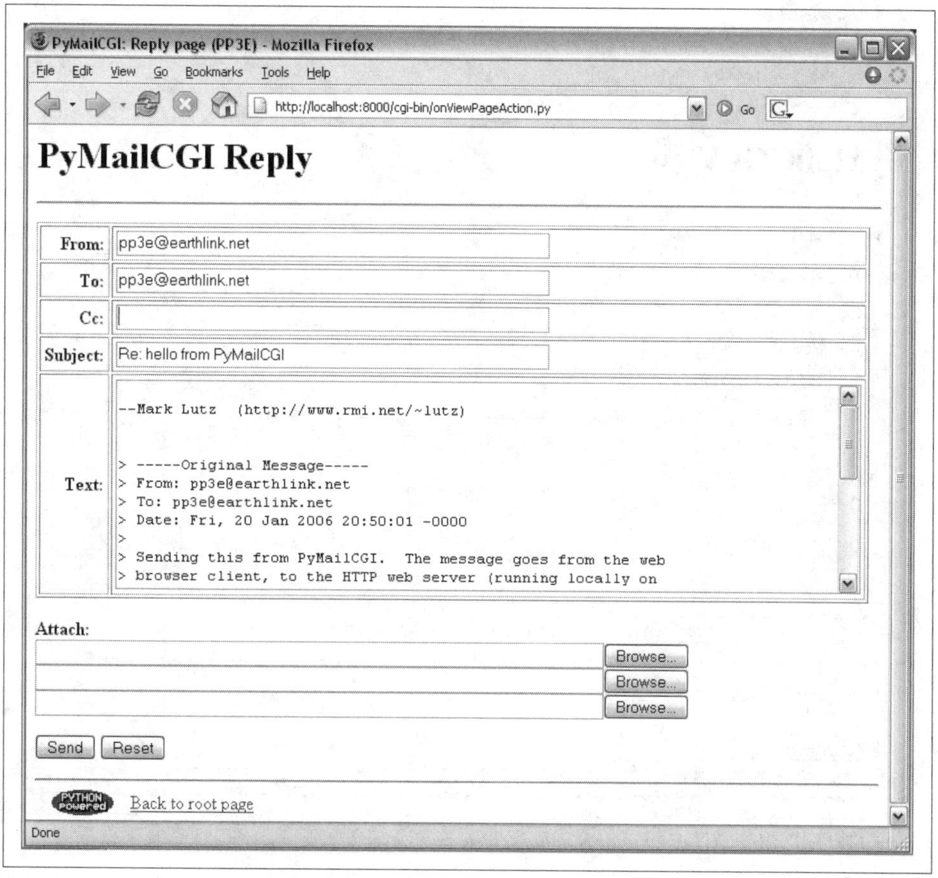

Figure 17-16. PyMailCGI reply page

Delete

Selecting the Delete action on a message view page and pressing Next will cause the `onViewPageAction` script to immediately delete the message being viewed. Deletions are performed by calling a reusable delete utility function coded in Chapter 14's `mailtools` package. In the prior version, the call to the utility was wrapped in a `commonhtml.runsilent` call that prevents `print` statements in the utility from showing up in the HTML reply stream (they are just status messages, not HTML code). In this version, we get the same capability from the "Silent" classes in `mailtools`. Figure 17-17 shows a Delete operation in action.

As mentioned, Delete is the only action that uses the POP account information (user, password, and site) that was passed in from hidden fields on the prior message view page. By contrast, the Reply and Forward actions format an edit page, which ultimately sends a message to the SMTP server; no POP information is needed or passed.

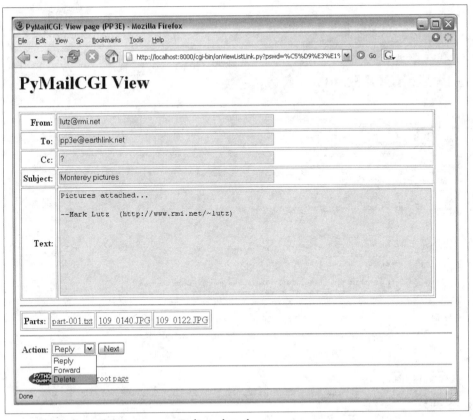

Figure 17-17. PyMailCGI view page, Delete selected

But at this point in the interaction, the POP password has racked up more than a few frequent flyer miles. In fact, it may have crossed phone lines, satellite links, and continents on its journey from machine to machine. Let's trace through the journey:

1. Input (client): the password starts life by being typed into the login page on the client (or being embedded in an explicit URL), unencrypted. If typed into the input form in a web browser, each character is displayed as a star (*).

2. Fetch index (client to CGI server to POP server): it is next passed from the client to the CGI script on the server, which sends it on to your POP server in order to load a mail index. The client sends only the password, unencrypted.

3. List page URLs (CGI server to client): to direct the next script's behavior, the password is embedded in the mail selection list web page itself as hyperlink URL query parameters, encrypted and URL encoded.

4. Fetch message (client to CGI server to POP server): when an email is selected from the list, the password is sent to the next script within the script's URL; the CGI script decrypts it and passes it on to the POP server to fetch the selected message.

5. View page fields (CGI server to client): to direct the next script's behavior, the password is embedded in the view page itself as HTML hidden input fields, encrypted and HTML escaped.

6. Delete message (client to CGI server to POP server): finally, the password is again passed from client to CGI server, this time as hidden form field values; the CGI script decrypts it and passes it to the POP server to delete.

Along the way, scripts have passed the password between pages as both a URL query parameter and an HTML hidden input field; either way, they have always passed its encrypted string and have never passed an unencrypted password and username together in any transaction. Upon a Delete request, the password must be decoded here using the secret module before passing it to the POP server. If the script can access the POP server again and delete the selected message, another confirmation page appears, as shown in Figure 17-18 (there is currently no verification for the delete, so be careful).

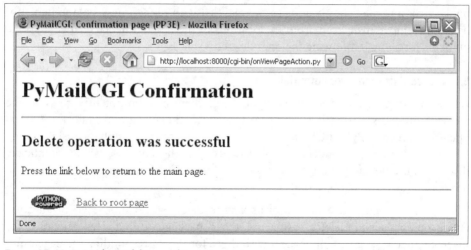

Figure 17-18. PyMailCGI delete confirmation

One subtlety is for replies and forwards, the onViewPageAction mail action script builds up a >-quoted representation of the original message, with original "From:", "To:", and "Date:" header lines prepended to the mail's original text. Notice, though, that the original message's headers are fetched from the CGI form input, not by reparsing the original mail (the mail is not readily available at this point). In other words, the script gets mail header values from the form input fields of the view page. Because there is no "Date" field on the view page, the original message's date is also passed along to the action script as a hidden input field to avoid reloading the message. Try tracing through the code in this chapter's listings to see whether you can follow dates from page to page.

Deletions and POP Message Numbers

Note that you probably *should* click the "Back to root page" link in Figure 17-18 after a successful deletion—don't use your browser's Back button to return to the message selection list at this point because the delete has changed the relative numbers of some messages in the list. The PyMailGUI client program worked around this problem by automatically updating its in-memory message cache and refreshing the index list on deletions, but PyMailCGI doesn't currently have a way to mark older pages as obsolete.

If your browser reruns server-side scripts as you press your Back button, you'll regenerate and hence refresh the list anyhow. If your browser displays cached pages as you go back, though, you might see the deleted message still present in the list. Worse, clicking on a view link in an old selection list page may not bring up the message you think it should, if it appears in the list after a message that was deleted.

This is a property of POP email in general, which we have discussed before in this book: incoming mail simply adds to the mail list with higher message numbers, but deletions remove mail from arbitrary locations in the list and hence change message numbers for all mail following the ones deleted.

Inbox synchronization error potential

As we saw in Chapter 15, even the PyMailGUI client has the potential to get some message numbers wrong if mail is deleted by another program while the GUI is open—in a second PyMailGUI instance, for example, or in a simultaneously running PyMailCGI server session. This can also occur if the email server automatically deletes a message after the mail list has been loaded—for instance, moving it from inbox to undeliverable on errors.

This is why PyMailGUI went out of its way to detect server inbox synchronization errors on loads and deletes, using `mailtools` package utilities. Its deletions, for instance, match saved email headers with those for the corresponding message number in the server's inbox, to ensure accuracy. Unfortunately, without additional state information, PyMailCGI cannot detect such errors: it has no email list to compare against when messages are viewed or deleted, only the message number in a link or hidden form field.

In the worst case, PyMailCGI cannot guarantee that deletes remove the intended mail—it's unlikely but not impossible that a mail earlier in the list may have been deleted between the time message numbers were fetched and a mail is deleted at the server. Without extra state information on the server, PyMailCGI cannot use the safe deletion or synchronization error checks in the `mailtools` modules to check whether subject message numbers are still valid.

To guarantee safe deletes, PyMailCGI would require state retention, which maps message numbers passed in pages to saved mail headers fetched when the numbers were last determined, or a broader policy, which sidesteps the issue completely. The next three sections outline suggested improvements and potential exercises.

Passing header text in hidden input fields (PyMailCGI_2.1)

Perhaps the simplest way to guarantee accurate deletions is to embed the displayed message's full header text in the message view page itself, as hidden form fields, using the following:

onViewListLink.py

> Embeds the header text in hidden form fields, escaped per HTML conventions with cgi.escape (with its quote argument set to True to translate any nested quotes in the header text).

onViewPageAction.py

> Retrieves the embedded header text from the form's input fields, and passes it along to the safe deletion call in mailtools for header matching.

This would be a small code change, but it might require an extra headers fetch in the first of these scripts (it currently loads the full mail text), and it would require building a phony list to represent all mail's headers (we would have headers for and delete only one mail here). Alternatively, the header text could be extracted from the fetched full mail text, by splitting on the blank line that separates headers and message body text.

Moreover, this would increase the size of the data transmitted both from client and server—mail header text is commonly greater than 1 KB in size, and it may be larger. This is a small amount of extra data in modern terms, but it's possible that this may run up against size limitations in some client or server systems.

And really, this scheme is incomplete. It addresses only deletion accuracy and does nothing about other synchronization errors in general. For example, the system still may fetch and display the wrong message from a message list page, after deletions of mails earlier in the inbox. In fact, this technique guarantees only that the message displayed in a view window will be the one deleted for that view window's delete action. It does not ensure that the mail displayed or deleted in the view window corresponds to the selection made by the user in the mail index list.

More specifically, because this scheme embeds headers in the HTML of view windows, its header matching on deletion is useful only if messages earlier in the inbox are deleted elsewhere *after* a mail has already been opened for viewing. If the inbox is changed elsewhere *before* a mail is opened in a view window, the wrong mail may be fetched from the index page. In that event, this scheme avoids deleting a mail other than the one displayed in a view window, but it assumes the user will catch the mistake and avoid deleting if the wrong mail is loaded from the index page. Though such cases are rare, this behavior is less than user friendly.

Even though it is incomplete, this change does at least avoid deleting the wrong email if the server's inbox changes while a message is being viewed—the mail displayed will be the only one deleted. A working but tentative implementation of this scheme is implemented in the following directory of the book's examples distribution:

```
PP3E\Internet\Web\dev\PyMailCGI_2.1
```

It works under the Firefox web browser and requires just more than 10 lines of code changes among 3 source files, listed here (search for "#EXPERIMENTAL" to find the changes made in the source files yourself):

```
# onViewListLink.py
    . . .
    hdrstext = fulltext.split('\n\n')[0]              # use blank line
    commonhtml.viewpage(                              # encodes passwd
            msgnum, message, content, form, hdrstext, parts)


# commonhtml.py
    . . .
    def viewpage(msgnum, headers, text, form, hdrstext, parts=[]):
        . . .
        # delete needs hdrs text for inbox sync tests: can be multi-K large
        hdrstext = cgi.escape(hdrstext, quote=True)   # escape '"' too
        print '<input type=hidden name=Hdrstext value="%s">' % hdrstext


# onViewPageAction.py
    . . .
    fetcher = mailtools.SilentMailFetcher(site, user, pswd)
    #fetcher.deleteMessages([msgnum])
    hdrstext = getfield(form, 'Hdrstext') + '\n'      # get \n from top
    hdrstext = hdrstext.replace('\r\n', '\n')         # only one msg hdr
    dummyhdrslist = [None] * msgnum                   # in hidden field
    dummyhdrslist[msgnum-1] = hdrstext
    fetcher.deleteMessagesSafely([msgnum], dummyhdrslist) # exc on sync err
    commonhtml.confirmationpage('Delete')
```

To run this version locally, run the webserver script from Example 16-1 (in Chapter 16) with the dev subdirectory name, and a unique port number if you want to run both the original and the experimental versions. For instance:

```
C:\...\PP3E\Internet\Web>webserver.py dev\PyMailCGI_2.1 9000     command line
http://localhost:9000/pymailcgi.html                            web browser URL
```

Although this version works on browsers tested, it is considered tentative (and was not used for this chapter) because it is an incomplete solution. In those rare cases where the server's inbox changes in ways that invalidate message numbers after server fetches, this version avoids inaccurate deletions, but index lists may still become out of sync. Messages fetches may still be inaccurate.

Note that in most cases, the message-id header would be sufficient for matching against mails to be deleted in the inbox, and it might be all that is required to pass from page to page. However, because this field is optional and can be forged to have any value, this might not always be a reliable way to identify matched messages; full header matching is necessary to be robust. See the discussion of `mailtools` in Chapter 14 for more details.

Server-side files for headers

The main limitation of the prior section's technique is that it addressed only deletions of already fetched emails. To catch other kinds of inbox synchronization errors, we would have to also record headers fetched when the index list page was constructed.

Since the index list page uses URL query parameters to record state, adding large header texts as an additional parameter on the URLs is not likely a viable option. In principle, the header text of all mails in the list could be embedded in the index page as a single hidden field, but this might add prohibitive size and transmission overheads.

As a more complete approach, each time the mail index list page is generated in `onViewPswdSubmit.py`, fetched headers of all messages could be saved in a flat file on the server, with a generated unique name (possibly from time, process ID, and username). That file's name could be passed along with message numbers in pages as an extra hidden field or query parameter.

On deletions, the header's filename could be used by `onViewPageAction.py` to load the saved headers from the flat file, to be passed to the safe delete call in `mailtools`. On fetches, the header file could also be used for general synchronization tests to avoid loading and displaying the wrong mail. Some sort of aging scheme would be required to delete the header save files eventually (the index page script might clean up old files), and we might also have to consider multiuser issues.

This scheme essentially uses server-side files to emulate PyMailGUI's in-process memory, though it is complicated by the fact that users may back up in their browser—deleting from view pages fetched with earlier list pages, attempting to refetch from an earlier list page and so on. In general, it may be necessary to analyze all possible forward and backward flows through pages (it is essentially a state machine). Header save files might also be used to detect synchronization errors on fetches and may be removed on deletions to effectively disable actions in prior page states, though header matching may suffice to ensure deletion accuracy.

Delete on load

Alternatively, mail clients could delete all email off the server as soon as it is downloaded, such that deletions wouldn't impact POP identifiers (Microsoft Outlook may use this scheme by default, for instance). However, this requires additional mechanisms for storing deleted email persistently for later access, and it means you can view fetched mail only on the machine to which it was downloaded. Since both PyMailGUI and PyMailCGI are intended to be used on a variety of machines, mail is kept on the POP server by default.

Because of the current lack of inbox synchronization error checks in PyMailCGI, you should not delete mails with it in an important account, unless you employ one of the solution schemes described, or you use other tools to save mails to be deleted before deletion. Adding state retention to ensure general inbox synchronization may make an interesting exercise, but would also add more code than we have space for here, especially if generalized for multiple simultaneous site users.

Utility Modules

This section presents the source code of the utility modules imported and used by the page scripts shown earlier. As installed, all of these modules live in the same directory as the CGI scripts, to make imports simple—they are found in the current working directory. There aren't any new screenshots to see here because these are utilities, not CGI scripts. Moreover, these modules aren't all that useful to study in isolation and are included here primarily to be referenced as you go through the CGI scripts' code. See earlier in this chapter for additional details not repeated here.

External Components and Configuration

When running PyMailCGI out of its own directory in the book examples distribution tree, it relies on a number of external modules that are potentially located elsewhere. Because all of these are accessible from the *PP3E* package root, they can be imported with dotted-path names as usual, relative to the root. In case this setup ever changes, though, the module in Example 17-10 encapsulates the location of all external dependencies; if they ever move, this is the only file that must be changed.

Example 17-10. PP3E\Internet\Web\PyMailCgi\externs.py

```
###########################################################################
# Isolate all imports of modules that live outside of the PyMailCgi
# directory, so that their location must only be changed here if moved;
# we use a custom version of mailconfig.py here: a pymailgui2 subset
###########################################################################

#from  PP3E.Internet.Email.PyMailGui import mailconfig

import mailconfig
from  PP3E.Internet.Email import mailtools  # PP3E/.. must be on your PYTHONPATH
```

This module simply preimports all external names needed by PyMailCGI into its own namespace. See Chapter 15 for the content of the mailconfig module; as a reference, Example 17-11 lists part of its content again. This version of PyMailCGI has its own copy of this module, to allow it to differ from PyMailGUI. See Chapter 14 for the mailtools package modules' source code.

Example 17-11. PP3E\Internet\Email\mailconfig.py

```
##################################################################
# user configuration settings for various email programs (PyMailCGI version);
# email scripts get their server names and other email config options from
# this module: change me to reflect your machine names, sig, and preferences;
##################################################################

#-----------------------------------------------------------------
# (required for load, delete) POP3 email server machine, user
#-----------------------------------------------------------------

popservername = 'pop.earthlink.net'     # or starship.python.net, 'localhost'
popusername   = 'pp3e'                   # password fetched or asked when run

#-----------------------------------------------------------------
# (required for send) SMTP email server machine name
# see Python smtpd module for a SMTP server class to run locally
# note: your ISP may require that you be directly connected to their system:
# I can email through Earthlink on dial up, but cannot via Comcast cable
#-----------------------------------------------------------------

smtpservername = 'smtp.comcast.net'     # or 'smtp.mindspring.com', 'localhost'

#-----------------------------------------------------------------
# (optional) personal information used by PyMailGUI to fill in edit forms;
# if not set, does not fill in initial form values;
# sig  -- can be a triple-quoted block, ignored if empty string;
# addr -- used for initial value of "From" field if not empty,
# no longer tries to guess From for replies--varying success;
#-----------------------------------------------------------------

myaddress   = 'pp3e@earthlink.net'
mysignature = '--Mark Lutz  (http://www.rmi.net/~lutz)'

#-----------------------------------------------------------------
# (optional) local file where sent messages are saved;
# PyMailGUI 'Open' button allows this file to be opened and viewed
#-----------------------------------------------------------------

sentmailfile  = r'.\sentmail.txt'          # . means in current working dir
```

POP Mail Interface

The loadmail utility module in Example 17-12 depends on external files and encapsulates access to mail on the remote POP server machine. It currently exports one function, loadmailhdrs, which returns a list of the header text (only) of all mail in the specified POP account; callers are unaware of whether this mail is fetched over the Net, lives in memory, or is loaded from a persistent storage medium on the CGI server machine. That is by design—loadmail changes won't impact its clients. It is mostly a hook for future expansion.

Example 17-12. PP3E\Internet\Web\PyMailCgi\loadmail.py

```
######################################################################
# mail list loader; future--change me to save mail list between
# CGI script runs, to avoid reloading all mail each time; this
# won't impact clients that use the interfaces here if done well;
# for now, to keep this simple, reloads all mail for each list page;
# 2.0: we now only load message headers (via TOP), not full msg,
# but still fetch all hdrs for each index list--in-memory caches
# don't work in a stateless CGI script, and require a real db;
######################################################################

from commonhtml import runsilent      # suppress print's (no verbose flag)
from externs    import mailtools      # shared with PyMailGUI


# load all mail from number 1 up
# this may trigger an exception

import sys
def progress(*args):  # not used
    sys.stderr.write(str(args) + '\n')

def loadmailhdrs(mailserver, mailuser, mailpswd):
    fetcher = mailtools.SilentMailFetcher(mailserver, mailuser, mailpswd)
    hdrs, sizes, full = fetcher.downloadAllHeaders()      # get list of hdr text
    return hdrs
```

It's not much to look at—just an interface and calls to other modules. The mailtools.SilentMailFetcher class (reused here from Chapter 14) uses the Python poplib module to fetch mail over sockets. The silent class prevents mailtools print statements from going to the HTML reply stream (although any exceptions are allowed to propagate there normally).

In this version, loadmail loads just the header text portions of all incoming email to generate the selection list page. However, it still reloads headers every time you refetch the selection list page. As mentioned earlier, this scheme is better than the prior version, but it can still be slow if you have lots of email sitting on your server. Server-side database techniques, combined with a scheme for invalidating message lists on deletions and new receipts, might alleviate some of this bottleneck. Because the interface exported by loadmail would likely not need to change to introduce a caching mechanism, clients of this module would still work.

POP Password Encryption

We discussed PyMailCGI's security protocols in the abstract earlier in this chapter. Here, we look at their concrete implementation. PyMailCGI passes user and password state information from page to page using hidden form fields and URL query parameters embedded in HTML reply pages. We studied these techniques in the prior chapter. Such data is transmitted as simple text over network sockets—within the HTML reply stream from the server, and as parameters in the request from the client. As such, it is subject to security issues.

This isn't a concern if you are running a local web server on your machine, as all our examples do. The data is being shipped back and forth between two programs running on your computer, and it is not accessible to the outside world. If you want to install PyMailCGI on a remote web server machine, though, this can be an issue. Because this data is sensitive, we'd ideally like some way to hide it in transit and prevent it from being viewed in server logs.

In the second edition of this book, we developed a custom encryption module using the standard library's rotor encryption module. This module was used to encrypt data inserted into the server's reply stream, and then to later decrypt it when it was returned as a parameter from the client. Unfortunately, in Python 2.4, the rotor module is no longer available in the standard library; it was withdrawn due to security concerns. This seems a somewhat extreme measure (rotor was adequate for simpler applications), but rotor is no longer a usable solution in recent releases.

There are a variety of general approaches to encrypting information transferred back and forth between client and server. Unfortunately again, none is easily implemented for this chapter's example, none is universally applicable, and most involve tools or techniques that are well beyond the scope and size constraints of this text. The sections that follow contain a brief rundown of some of the common techniques in this domain.

Manual data encryption: rotor (defunct)

In principle, CGI scripts can manually encrypt any sensitive data they insert into reply streams, as PyMailCGI did in this book's second edition. With the removal of the rotor module, though, Python 2.4's standard library has no encryption tools for this task. Moreover, using the original rotor module's code is not advisable from a maintenance perspective and would not be straightforward, since it was coded in the C language (it's not a simple matter of copying a *.py* file from a prior release). Unless you are using an older version of Python, rotor is not a real option.

Mostly for historical interest and comparison today, this module was used as follows. It was based on an Enigma-style encryption scheme: we make a new rotor object with a key (and optionally, a rotor count) and call methods to encrypt and decrypt:

```
>>> import rotor
>>> r = rotor.newrotor('pymailcgi')      # (key, [,numrotors])
>>> r.encrypt('abc123')                  # may return nonprintable chars
' \323an\021\224'

>>> x = r.encrypt('spam123')             # result is same len as input
>>> x
'* _\344\011pY'
```

```
>>> len(x)
7
>>> r.decrypt(x)
'spam123'
```

Notice that the same rotor object can encrypt multiple strings, that the result may contain nonprintable characters (printed as \ascii escape codes when displayed), and that the result is always the same length as the original string. Most important, a string encrypted with rotor can be decrypted in a different process (e.g., in a later CGI script) if we re-create the rotor object:

```
>>> import rotor
>>> r = rotor.newrotor('pymailcgi')      # can be decrypted in new process
>>> r.decrypt('* _\344\011pY')           # use "\ascii" escapes for two chars
'spam123'
```

Our secret module by default simply used rotor to encrypt and did no additional encoding of its own. It relies on URL encoding when the password is embedded in a URL parameter and on HTML escaping when the password is embedded in hidden form fields. For URLs, the following sorts of calls occur:

```
>>> from secret import encode, decode
>>> x = encode('abc$#<>&+')             # CGI scripts do this
>>> x
' \323a\016\317\326\023\0163'


>>> import urllib                        # urllib.urlencode does this
>>> y = urllib.quote_plus(x)
>>> y
'+%d3a%0e%cf%d6%13%0e3'


>>> a = urllib.unquote_plus(y)           # cgi.FieldStorage does this
>>> a
' \323a\016\317\326\023\0163'


>>> decode(a)                            # CGI scripts do this
'abc$#<>&+'
```

Although rotor itself is not a widely viable option today, these same techniques can be used with other encryption schemes.

Manual data encryption: PyCrypto

A variety of encryption tools are available in the third-party public domain, including the popular Python Cryptography Toolkit, also known as PyCrypto. This package adds built-in modules for private and public key algorithms such as AES, DES, IDEA, and RSA encryption, provides a Python module for reading and decrypting PGP files, and much more. Here is an example of using AES encryption, run after installing PyCrypto on my machine with a Windows self-installer:

```
>>> from Crypto.Cipher import AES
>>> AES.block_size
16
```

```
>>> mykey    = 'pymailcgi'.ljust(16, '-')       # key must be 16, 24, or 32 bytes
>>> mykey
'pymailcgi-------'
>>>
>>> password   = 'Already got one.'             # length must be multiple of 16
>>> aesobj1    = AES.new(mykey, AES.MODE_ECB)
>>> cyphertext = aesobj1.encrypt(password)
>>> cyphertext
'\xfez\x95\xb7\x07_"\xd4\xb6\xe3r\x07g~X]'
>>>
>>> aesobj2    = AES.new(mykey, AES.MODE_ECB)
>>> aesobj2.decrypt(cyphertext)
'Already got one.'
```

This interface is similar to that of the original rotor module, but it uses better encryption algorithms. AES is a popular private key encryption algorithm. It requires a fixed length key and a data string to have a length that is a multiple of 16 bytes.

Unfortunately, this is not part of standard Python, may be subject to U.S. export controls in binary form at this writing, and is too large and complex a topic for us to address in this text. This makes it less than universally applicable; at the least, shipping its binary installer with this book's examples package may require legal expertise. And since data encryption is a core requirement of PyMailCGI, this seems too strong an external dependency.

Still, if you are able to install and learn PyCrypto, this can be a powerful solution. For more details, see PyCrypto on the Web; at this writing, its web site lives at *http://www.amk.ca/python/code/crypto*.

Secure HTTP transmissions

Provided you are using a server that supports secure HTTP, you can simply write HTML and delegate the encryption to the web server and browser. As long as both ends of the transmission support this protocol, it is probably the ultimate encrypting solution. In fact, it is used by most e-commerce sites on the Web today.

Secure HTTP (HTTPS) is designated in URLs by using the protocol name *https://* rather than *http://*. Under HTTPS, data is still sent with the usual HTTP protocol, but it is encrypted with SSL. HTTPS is supported by most web browsers and can be configured in most web servers, including Apache and the *webserver.py* script that we are running locally in this chapter. If SSL support is compiled into your Python, Python sockets support it, and the client-side modules urllib and urllib2 we met in Chapter 16 support HTTPS.

Unfortunately, enabling secure HTTP in a web server requires more configuration and background knowledge than we can cover here, and it requires installing tools outside the standard Python release. If you want to explore this issue further, at this writing a coding recipe is available on the ActiveState Programmer Network (ASPN) web site (*http://aspn.activestate.com/ASPN*), which demonstrates how to set up a simple Python HTTPS server that supports SSL secure communications. It extends the BaseHTTPServer standard library module our *webserver.py* script uses, to support the SSL protocol. However, it requires the OpenSSL and pyOpenSSL third-party packages, generation of an SSL certificate, and subclasses of the standard library's server classes.

For more details on HTTPS, search the Web. For more on the ASPN coding recipe, try a web search on "Python secure HTTP" to locate it. It is not impossible that some of the HTTPS extensions for Python's standard web server classes may make their way into the Python standard library in the future.

Secure cookies

It's possible to replace the form fields and query parameter PyMailCGI currently generates, with client-side cookies marked as secure. Such cookies are automatically encrypted when sent. Unfortunately again, marking a cookie as secure simply means that it can be transmitted only if the communications channel with the host is secure. It does not provide any additional encryption. Because of this, this option really just begs the question; it still requires an HTTPS server.

The secret.py module

As you can probably tell, web security is a larger topic than we have time to address here. Because of that, the secret.py module in Example 17-13 finesses the issue, by trying a variety of approaches in turn:

- If you are able to fetch and install the third-party PyCrypto system described earlier, the module will use that package's AES tools to manually encrypt password data when transmitted together with a username.

- If not, it will try rotor next (if you happen to be using a prior version of Python, or otherwise install rotor in the version of Python that you're using).

- And finally, it falls back on a very simplistic default character code shuffling scheme, which you can replace with one of your own if you install this program on the Internet at large.

Function definitions nested in if statements are used to generate the selected encryption scheme's functions. See Example 17-13 for more details.

Example 17-13. PP3E\Internet\Web\PyMailCgi\secret.py

```
###########################################################################
# PyMailCGI encodes the POP password whenever it is sent to/from client over
# the Net with a username, as hidden text fields or explicit URL params; uses
# encode/decode functions in this module to encrypt the pswd--upload your own
# version of this module to use a different encryption mechanism or key; pymail
# doesn't save the password on the server, and doesn't echo pswd as typed,
# but this isn't 100% safe--this module file itself might be vulnerable;
###########################################################################
```

Example 17-13. PP3E\Internet\Web\PyMailCgi\secret.py (continued)

```
import sys, time
dayofweek = time.localtime(time.time( ))[6]      # for custom schemes
forceReadablePassword = False


###################################################################
# string encoding schemes
###################################################################

if not forceReadablePassword:
    ##########################################################
    # don't do anything by default: the urllib.quote or
    # cgi.escape calls in commonhtml.py will escape the
    # password as needed to embed in URL or HTML; the
    # cgi module undoes escapes automatically for us;
    ##########################################################

    def stringify(old):    return old
    def unstringify(old): return old

else:
    ##########################################################
    # convert encoded string to/from a string of digit chars,
    # to avoid problems with some special/nonprintable chars,
    # but still leave the result semi-readable (but encrypted);
    # some browsers had problems with escaped ampersands, etc.;
    ##########################################################

    separator = '-'

    def stringify(old):
        new = ''
        for char in old:
            ascii = str(ord(char))
            new   = new + separator + ascii      # '-ascii-ascii-ascii'
        return new

    def unstringify(old):
        new = ''
        for ascii in old.split(separator)[1:]:
            new = new + chr(int(ascii))
        return new


###################################################################
# encryption schemes: try PyCrypto, then rotor, then simple/custom scheme
###################################################################

useCrypto = useRotor = True
try:
    import Crypto
except:
    useCrypto = False
    try:
```

Example 17-13. PP3E\Internet\Web\PyMailCgi\secret.py (continued)

```
        import rotor
    except:
        useRotor = False

if useCrypto:
    #######################################################
    # use third-party pycrypto package's AES algorithm
    # assumes pswd has no '\0' on the right: used to pad
    # change the private key here if you install this
    #######################################################

    sys.stderr.write('using PyCrypto\n')
    from Crypto.Cipher import AES
    mykey = 'pymailcgi2'.ljust(16, '-')          # key must be 16, 24, or 32 bytes

    def do_encode(pswd):
        over = len(pswd) % 16
        if over: pswd += '\0' * (16-over)        # pad: len must be multiple of 16
        aesobj = AES.new(mykey, AES.MODE_ECB)
        return aesobj.encrypt(pswd)

    def do_decode(pswd):
        aesobj = AES.new(mykey, AES.MODE_ECB)
        pswd   = aesobj.decrypt(pswd)
        return pswd.rstrip('\0')

elif useRotor:
    #######################################################
    # use the standard lib's rotor module to encode pswd
    # this does a better job of encryption than code above
    # unfortunately, it is no longer available in Py 2.4
    #######################################################

    sys.stderr.write('using rotor\n')
    import rotor
    mykey = 'pymailcgi2'

    def do_encode(pswd):
        robj = rotor.newrotor(mykey)             # use enigma encryption
        return robj.encrypt(pswd)

    def do_decode(pswd):
        robj = rotor.newrotor(mykey)
        return robj.decrypt(pswd)

else:
    #######################################################
    # use our own custom scheme as a last resort
    # shuffle characters in some reversible fashion
    # caveat: very simple -- replace with one of your own
    #######################################################
```

Example 17-13. PP3E\Internet\Web\PyMailCgi\secret.py (continued)

```
    sys.stderr.write('using simple\n')
    adder = 1

    def do_encode(pswd):
        pswd = 'b' + pswd + '46'
        res = ''
        for char in pswd:
            res = res + chr(ord(char) + adder)      # inc each ASCII code
        return str(res)

    def do_decode(pswd):
        pswd = pswd[1:-3]
        res = ''
        for char in pswd:
            res = res + chr(ord(char) - adder)
        return res


###############################################################################
# top-level entry points
###############################################################################

def encode(pswd):
    return stringify(do_encode(pswd))          # encrypt plus string encode

def decode(pswd):
    return do_decode(unstringify(pswd))
```

In addition to encryption, this module also implements an encoding method for already encrypted strings, which transforms them to and from printable characters. By default, the encoding functions do nothing, and the system relies on straight URL or HTML encoding of the encrypted string. An optional encoding scheme translates the encrypted string to a string of ASCII code digits separated by dashes. Either encoding method makes nonprintable characters in the encrypted string printable.

To illustrate, let's test this module's tools interactively. For this test, we set forceReadablePassword to True. The top-level entry points encode and decode into printable characters:

```
>>> from secret import *
using PyCrypto
>>> data = encode('spam@123+')
>>> data
'-47-248-2-170-107-242-175-18-227-249-53-130-14-140-163-107'
>>> decode(data)
'spam@123+'
```

But there are actually two steps to this—encryption and printable encoding:

```
>>> raw = do_encode('spam@123+')
>>> raw
'/\xf8\x02\xaak\xf2\xaf\x12\xe3\xf95\x82\x0e\x8c\xa3k'
>>> text = stringify(raw)
```

```
>>> text
'-47-248-2-170-107-242-175-18-227-249-53-130-14-140-163-107'
>>> len(raw), len(text)
(16, 58)
```

Here's what the encoding looks like without the extra printable encoding:

```
>>> raw = do_encode('spam@123+')
>>> raw
'/\xf8\x02\xaak\xf2\xaf\x12\xe3\xf95\x82\x0e\x8c\xa3k'
>>> do_decode(raw)
'spam@123+'
```

Rolling your own encryptor

As is, PyMailCGI avoids ever passing the POP account username and password across the Net together in a single transaction, unless the password is encrypted according to the module secret.py on the server. This module can be different everywhere PyMailCGI is installed, and it can be uploaded anew in the future—encrypted passwords aren't persistent and live only for the duration of one mail-processing interaction session. Provided you don't publish your encryption code or its private keys, your data will be as secure as the custom encryption module you provide on your own server.

If you wish to use this system on the general Internet, you'll want to tailor this code. Ideally, you'll install PyCrypto and change the private key string. Barring that, replace Example 17-13 with a custom encryption coding scheme of your own or deploy one of the general techniques mentioned earlier such as an HTTPS-capable web server. In any event, this software makes no guarantees; the security of your password is ultimately up to you to ensure. For additional information on security tools and techniques, search the Web and consult books geared exclusively toward web-programming techniques.

 Because the encryption schemes used by PyMailCGI are reversible, it is possible to reconstruct my email account's password if you happen to see its encrypted form in a screenshot, unless the private key listed in secret.py was different when the tests shown were run. To sidestep this issue, the email account used in all of this book's examples is temporary and will be deleted by the time you read these words. Please use an email account of your own to test-drive the system.

Common Utilities Module

The file *commonhtml.py*, shown in Example 17-14, is the Grand Central Station of this application—its code is used and reused by just about every other file in the system. Most of it is self-explanatory, and we've already met most of its core idea earlier, in conjunction with the CGI scripts that use it.

I haven't talked about its *debugging* support, though. Notice that this module assigns sys.stderr to sys.stdout, in an attempt to force the text of Python error messages to show up in the client's browser (remember, uncaught exceptions print details to sys.stderr). That works sometimes in PyMailCGI, but not always—the error text shows up in a web page only if a page_header call has already printed a response preamble. If you want to see all error messages, make sure you call page_header (or print Content-type: lines manually) before any other processing. This module also defines functions that dump raw CGI environment information to the browser (dumpstatepage), and that wrap calls to functions that print status messages so that their output isn't added to the HTML stream (runsilent).

I'll leave the discovery of any remaining magic in the code in Example 17-14 up to you, the reader. You are hereby admonished to go forth and read, refer, and reuse.

Example 17-14. PP3E\Internet\Web\PyMailCgi\commonhtml.py

```python
#!/usr/bin/python
###############################################################################
# generate standard page header, list, and footer HTML; isolates HTML
# generation-related details in this file; text printed here goes over a
# socket to the client, to create parts of a new web page in the web browser;
# uses one print per line, instead of string blocks; uses urllib to escape
# parms in URL links auto from a dict, but cgi.escape to put them in HTML
# hidden fields; some of the tools here are useful outside pymailcgi; could
# also return HTML generated here instead of  printing it, so it could be
# included in other pages; could also structure as a single CGI script that
# gets and tests a next action name as a hidden form field; caveat: this
# system works, but was largely written during a two-hour layover at the
# Chicago O'Hare airport: there is room for improvement and optimization;
###############################################################################

import cgi, urllib, sys, os
sys.stderr = sys.stdout            # show error messages in browser
from externs import mailconfig     # from a package somewhere on server

# my cgi address root
#urlroot = 'http://starship.python.net/~lutz/PyMailCgi/'
#urlroot = 'http://localhost:8000/cgi-bin/'

urlroot  = ''   # use minimal, relative paths

def pageheader(app='PyMailCGI', color='#FFFFFF', kind='main', info=''):
    print 'Content-type: text/html\n'
    print '<html><head><title>%s: %s page (PP3E)</title></head>' % (app, kind)
    print '<body bgcolor="%s"><h1>%s %s</h1><hr>' % (color, app, (info or kind))

def pagefooter(root='pymailcgi.html'):
    print '</p><hr><a href="http://www.python.org">'
    print '<img src="../PythonPoweredSmall.gif" '
    print 'align=left alt="[Python Logo]" border=0 hspace=15></a>'
    print '<a href="../%s">Back to root page</a>' % root
```

Example 17-14. PP3E\Internet\Web\PyMailCgi\commonhtml.py (continued)

```python
    print '</body></html>'

def formatlink(cgiurl, parmdict):
    """
    make "%url?key=val&key=val" query link from a dictionary;
    escapes str() of all key and val with %xx, changes ' ' to +
    note that URL escapes are different from HTML (cgi.escape)
    """
    parmtext = urllib.urlencode(parmdict)         # calls urllib.quote_plus
    return '%s?%s' % (cgiurl, parmtext)           # urllib does all the work

def pagelistsimple(linklist):                     # show simple ordered list
    print '<ol>'
    for (text, cgiurl, parmdict) in linklist:
        link = formatlink(cgiurl, parmdict)
        text = cgi.escape(text)
        print '<li><a href="%s">\n    %s</a>' % (link, text)
    print '</ol>'

def pagelisttable(linklist):                      # show list in a table
    print '<p><table border>'                     # escape text to be safe
    count = 1
    for (text, cgiurl, parmdict) in linklist:
        link = formatlink(cgiurl, parmdict)
        text = cgi.escape(text)
        print '<tr><th><a href="%s">View</a> %d<td>\n %s' % (link, count, text)
        count = count+1
    print '</table>'

def listpage(linkslist, kind='selection list'):
    pageheader(kind=kind)
    pagelisttable(linkslist)          # [(/text', 'cgiurl', {'parm':'value'})]
    pagefooter()

def messagearea(headers, text, extra=''):
    print '<table border cellpadding=3>'
    for hdr in ('From', 'To', 'Cc', 'Subject'):
        val = headers.get(hdr, '?')
        val = cgi.escape(val, quote=1)
        print '<tr><th align=right>%s:' % hdr
        print '    <td><input type=text '
        print '    name=%s value="%s" %s size=60>' % (hdr, val, extra)
    print '<tr><th align=right>Text:'
    print '<td><textarea name=text cols=80 rows=10 %s>' % extra
    print '%s\n</textarea></table>' % (cgi.escape(text) or '?')  # if has </>s

def viewattachmentlinks(partnames):
    """
    create hyperlinks to locally saved part/attachment files
    when clicked, user's web browser will handle opening
    assumes just one user, only valid while viewing 1 msg
    """
```

Example 17-14. PP3E\Internet\Web\PyMailCgi\commonhtml.py (continued)

```
    print '<hr><table border cellpadding=3><tr><th>Parts:'
    for filename in partnames:
        basename = os.path.basename(filename)
        filename = filename.replace('\\', '/') # Windows hack
        print '<td><a href=../%s>%s</a>' % (filename, basename)
    print '</table><hr>'

def viewpage(msgnum, headers, text, form, parts=[]):
    """
    on View + select (generated link click)
    very subtle thing: at this point, pswd was URL encoded in the
    link, and then unencoded by CGI input parser; it's being embedded
    in HTML here, so we use cgi.escape; this usually sends nonprintable
    chars in the hidden field's HTML, but works on ie and ns anyhow:
    in url:  ?user=lutz&mnum=3&pswd=%8cg%c2P%1e%fO%5b%c5J%1c%f3&...
    in html: <input type=hidden name=pswd value="...nonprintables..">
    could urllib.quote the html field here too, but must urllib.unquote
    in next script (which precludes passing the inputs in a URL instead
    of the form); can also fall back on numeric string fmt in secret.py
    """
    pageheader(kind='View')
    user, pswd, site = map(cgi.escape, getstandardpopfields(form))
    print '<form method=post action="%sonViewPageAction.py">' % urlroot
    print '<input type=hidden name=mnum value="%s">' % msgnum
    print '<input type=hidden name=user value="%s">' % user      # from page|url
    print '<input type=hidden name=site value="%s">' % site      # for deletes
    print '<input type=hidden name=pswd value="%s">' % pswd      # pswd encoded
    messagearea(headers, text, 'readonly')
    if parts: viewattachmentlinks(parts)

    # onViewPageAction.quotetext needs date passed in page
    print '<input type=hidden name=Date value="%s">' % headers.get('Date','?')
    print '<table><tr><th align=right>Action:'
    print '<td><select name=action>'
    print '   <option>Reply<option>Forward<option>Delete</select>'
    print '<input type=submit value="Next">'
    print '</table></form>'                       # no 'reset' needed here
    pagefooter()

def sendattachmentwidgets(maxattach=3):
    print '<p><b>Attach:</b><br>'
    for i in range(1, maxattach+1):
        print '<input size=80 type=file name=attach%d><br>' % i
    print '</p>'

def editpage(kind, headers={}, text=''):
    # on Send, View+select+Reply, View+select+Fwd
    pageheader(kind=kind)
    print '<p><form enctype="multipart/form-data" method=post',
    print 'action="%sonEditPageSend.py">' % urlroot
    if mailconfig.mysignature:
        text = '\n%s\n%s' % (mailconfig.mysignature, text)
```

Example 17-14. PP3E\Internet\Web\PyMailCgi\commonhtml.py (continued)

```
    messagearea(headers, text)
    sendattachmentwidgets()
    print '<input type=submit value="Send">'
    print '<input type=reset  value="Reset">'
    print '</form>'
    pagefooter()

def errorpage(message, stacktrace=True):
    pageheader(kind='Error')                          # was sys.exc_type/exc_value
    exc_type, exc_value, exc_tb = sys.exc_info()
    print '<h2>Error Description</h2><p>', message
    print '<h2>Python Exception</h2><p>',  cgi.escape(str(exc_type))
    print '<h2>Exception details</h2><p>', cgi.escape(str(exc_value))
    if stacktrace:
        print '<h2>Exception traceback</h2><p><pre>'
        import traceback
        traceback.print_tb(exc_tb, None, sys.stdout)
        print '</pre>'
    pagefooter()

def confirmationpage(kind):
    pageheader(kind='Confirmation')
    print '<h2>%s operation was successful</h2>' % kind
    print '<p>Press the link below to return to the main page.</p>'
    pagefooter()

def getfield(form, field, default=''):
    # emulate dictionary get method
    return (form.has_key(field) and form[field].value) or default

def getstandardpopfields(form):
    """
    fields can arrive missing or '' or with a real value
    hardcoded in a URL; default to mailconfig settings
    """
    return (getfield(form, 'user', mailconfig.popusername),
            getfield(form, 'pswd', '?'),
            getfield(form, 'site', mailconfig.popservername))

def getstandardsmtpfields(form):
    return  getfield(form, 'site', mailconfig.smtpservername)

def runsilent(func, args):
    """
    run a function without writing stdout
    ex: suppress print's in imported tools
    else they go to the client/browser
    """
    class Silent:
        def write(self, line): pass
    save_stdout = sys.stdout
    sys.stdout  = Silent()                             # send print to dummy object
```

Example 17-14. PP3E\Internet\Web\PyMailCgi\commonhtml.py (continued)

```
    try:
        result = func(*args)              # which has a write method
    finally:                              # try to return func result
        sys.stdout = save_stdout          # but always restore stdout
    return result

def dumpstatepage(exhaustive=0):
    """
    for debugging: call me at top of a CGI to
    generate a new page with CGI state details
    """
    if exhaustive:
        cgi.test()
    else:                                 # show page with form, environ, etc.
        pageheader(kind='state dump')
        form = cgi.FieldStorage()
        cgi.print_form(form)              # show just form fields names/values
        pagefooter()
    sys.exit()

def selftest(showastable=False):
    links = [                             # make phony web page
                                          # [(text, url, {parms})]
        ('text1', urlroot + 'page1.cgi', {'a':1}),
        ('text2', urlroot + 'page1.cgi', {'a':2, 'b':'3'}),
        ('text3', urlroot + 'page2.cgi', {'x':'a b', 'y':'a<b&c', 'z':'?'}),
        ('te<>4', urlroot + 'page2.cgi', {'<x>':'', 'y':'<a>', 'z':None})]
    pageheader(kind='View')
    if showastable:
        pagelisttable(links)
    else:
        pagelistsimple(links)
    pagefooter()

if __name__ == '__main__':
    selftest(len(sys.argv) > 1)           # when run, not imported
                                          # HTML goes to stdout
```

CGI Script Trade-Offs

As shown in this chapter, PyMailCGI is still something of a system in the making,
but it does work as advertised: when it is installed on a remote server machine, by
pointing a browser at the main page's URL, I can check and send email from anywhere I happen to be, as long as I can find a machine with a web browser. In fact,
any machine and browser will do: Python doesn't even have to be installed, and I
don't need POP or SMTP access on the client machine itself. That's not the case with
the PyMailGUI client-side program we wrote in Chapter 15. This property is especially useful in organizations that allow web access, but restrict more direct protocols such as POP email.

But before we all jump on the collective Internet bandwagon and utterly abandon traditional APIs such as Tkinter, a few words of larger context may be in order. Besides illustrating larger CGI applications in general, this example was chosen to underscore some of the trade-offs you run into when building applications to run on the Web. PyMailGUI and PyMailCGI do roughly the same things but are radically different in implementation:

PyMailGUI
This is a traditional user-interface program: it runs entirely on the local machine, calls out to an in-process GUI API library to implement interfaces, and talks to the Internet through sockets only when it has to (e.g., to load or send email on demand). User requests are routed immediately to callback handler method functions running locally and in-process, with shared variables that automatically retain state between requests. As mentioned, because its memory is retained between events, PyMailGUI can cache messages in memory—it loads email headers and selected mails only once, fetches newly arrived message headers only on future loads, and has enough information to perform general inbox synchronization checks. On deletions, PyMailGUI can simply refresh its memory cache of loaded headers without having to reload from the server. Moreover, because PyMailGUI runs as a single process on the local machine, it can leverage tools such as multithreading to allow mail transfers to overlap in time (you can send while a load is in progress), and it can more easily support extra functionality such as local mail file saves and opens.

PyMailCGI
This, like all CGI systems, consists of scripts that reside and run on a server machine and generate HTML to interact with a user's web browser on the client machine. It runs only in the context of a web browser or other HTML-aware client, and it handles user requests by running CGI scripts on the web server. Without manually managed state retention techniques such as a server-side database system, there is no equivalent to the persistent memory of PyMailGUI—each request handler runs autonomously, with no memory except that which is explicitly passed along by prior states as hidden form fields, URL query parameters, and so on. Because of that, PyMailCGI currently must reload all email headers whenever it needs to display the selection list, naïvely reloads messages already fetched earlier in the session, and cannot perform general inbox synchronization tests. This can be improved by more advanced state-retention schemes, but none is as straightforward as the persistent in-process memory of PyMailGUI.

On a basic level, both systems use the Python POP and SMTP modules to fetch and send email through sockets. But the implementation alternatives they represent have some critical ramifications that you should know about when considering delivering systems on the Web:

Performance costs

Networks are slower than CPUs. As implemented, PyMailCGI isn't nearly as fast or as complete as PyMailGUI. In PyMailCGI, every time the user clicks a Submit button, the request goes across the network. More specifically, every user request incurs a network transfer overhead, every callback handler may take the form of a newly spawned process or thread on some servers, parameters come in as text strings that must be parsed out, and the lack of state information on the server between pages means that either mail needs to be reloaded often, or relatively slow state retention options must be employed.

In contrast, user clicks in PyMailGUI trigger in-process function calls rather than network traffic and program executions, and state is easily saved as Python in-process variables. Even with an ultra-fast Internet connection, a server-side CGI system is slower than a client-side program. To be fair, some Tkinter operations are sent to the underlying Tcl library as strings too, which must be parsed. This may change in time, but the contrast here is with CGI scripts versus GUI libraries in general. Function calls will probably always beat network transfers.

Some of these bottlenecks may be designed away at the cost of extra program complexity. For instance, some web servers use threads and process pools to minimize process creation for CGI scripts. Moreover, as we've seen, some state information can be manually passed along from page to page in hidden form fields, generated URL parameters, and client-side cookies, and state can be saved between pages in a concurrently accessible database to minimize mail reloads. But there's no getting past the fact that routing events and data over a network to scripts is slower than calling a Python function directly.

Complexity costs

HTML isn't pretty. Because PyMailCGI must generate HTML to interact with the user in a web browser, it is also more complex (or at least, less readable) than PyMailGUI. In some sense, CGI scripts embed HTML code in Python. Because the end result of this is a mixture of two very different languages, creating an interface with HTML in a CGI script can be much less straightforward than making calls to a GUI API such as Tkinter.

Witness, for example, all the care we've taken to escape HTML and URLs in this chapter's examples; such constraints are grounded in the nature of HTML. Furthermore, changing the system to retain loaded-mail list state in a database between pages would introduce further complexities to the CGI-based solution. And secure HTTP would eliminate the manual encryption complexity but would introduce new server configuration complexity.

Functionality costs

HTML *can say only so much.* HTML is a portable way to specify simple pages and forms, but it is poor to useless when it comes to describing more complex user interfaces. Because CGI scripts create user interfaces by writing HTML back to a browser, they are highly limited in terms of user-interface constructs. For example, consider implementing an image processing and animation program as CGI scripts: HTML doesn't easily apply once we leave the domain of fill-out forms and simple interactions.

It is possible to generate graphics in CGI scripts. They may be created and stored in temporary files on the server, with per-session filenames referenced in image tags in the generated HTML reply. For browsers that support the notion, graphic images may also be in-lined in HTML image tags, encoded in base64 format or similar. Either technique is substantially more complex than using an image in the Tkinter GUI library, though. Moreover, responsive animation and drawing applications are beyond the scope of a protocol such as CGI, which requires a network transaction per interaction. The interactive drawing and animation scripts we wrote at the end of Chapter 10, for example, could not be implemented as normal server-side scripts.

This is precisely the limitation that Java applets were designed to address—programs that are stored on a server but are pulled down to run on a client on demand and are given access to a full-featured GUI API for creating richer user interfaces. Nevertheless, strictly server-side programs are inherently limited by the constraints of HTML.

Beyond HTML's limitations, client-side programs such as PyMailGUI also have access to tools such as multithreading which are difficult to emulate in a CGI-based application (threads spawned by a CGI script cannot outlive the CGI script itself, or augment its reply once sent). Persistent process models for web applications such as FastCGI, discussed in Chapter 16, may provide options here, but the picture is not as clear-cut as on the client.

Although web developers make noble efforts at emulating client-side capabilities, such efforts add additional complexity, can stretch the server-side programming model nearly to its breaking point, and account for much of the plethora of divergent web techniques.

Portability benefits

All you need is a browser on clients. Because PyMailCGI runs over the Web, it can be run on any machine with a web browser, whether that machine has Python and Tkinter installed or not. That is, Python needs to be installed on only one computer—the web server machine where the scripts actually live and run. This is probably the most compelling benefit to the web application model.

As long as you know that the users of your system have an Internet browser, installation is simple. You still need Python on the server, but that's easier to guarantee.

Python and Tkinter, you will recall, are very portable too—they run on all major window systems (X, Windows, Mac)—but to run a client-side Python/Tkinter program such as PyMailGUI, you need Python and Tkinter on the client machine itself. Not so with an application built as CGI scripts: they will work on Macintosh, Linux, Windows, and any other machine that can somehow render HTML web pages. In this sense, HTML becomes a sort of portable GUI API language in CGI scripts, interpreted by your web browser. You don't even need the source code or bytecode for the CGI scripts themselves—they run on a remote server that exists somewhere else on the Net, not on the machine running the browser.

Execution requirements

But you do need a browser. That is, the very nature of web-enabled systems can render them useless in some environments. Despite the pervasiveness of the Internet, many applications still run in settings that don't have web browsers or Internet access. Consider, for instance, embedded systems, real-time systems, and secure government applications. While an *intranet* (a local network without external connections) can sometimes make web applications feasible in some such environments, I have worked at more than one company whose client sites had no web browsers to speak of. On the other hand, such clients may be more open to installing systems like Python on local machines, as opposed to supporting an internal or external network.

Administration requirements

You really need a server too. You can't write CGI-based systems at all without access to a web sever. Further, keeping programs on a centralized server creates some fairly critical administrative overheads. Simply put, in a pure client/server architecture, clients are simpler, but the server becomes a critical path resource and a potential performance bottleneck. If the centralized server goes down, you, your employees, and your customers may be knocked out of commission. Moreover, if enough clients use a shared server at the same time, the speed costs of web-based systems become even more pronounced. In production systems, advanced techniques such as load balancing and fail-over servers help, but they add new requirements.

In fact, one could make the argument that moving toward a web server architecture is akin to stepping backward in time—to the time of centralized mainframes and dumb terminals. Whichever way we step, offloading and distributing processing to client machines at least partially avoids this processing bottleneck.

Other Approaches

So what's the best way to build applications for the Internet—as client-side programs that talk to the Net, or as server-side programs that live and breathe on the Net? Naturally, there is no one answer to that question, since it depends upon each application's unique constraints. Moreover, there are more possible answers to it than we have proposed here.

For instance, some systems attempt to separate logic from display so much as to make the choice almost irrelevant—by completely encapsulating display details, a single program can, in principle, render its user interface as either a traditional GUI or an HTML-based web page. Due to the vastly different architectures, though, this ideal is difficult to achieve and does not address larger disparities between the client and server platforms. Issues such as state retention and network interfaces are much more significant than generation of windows and controls, and may impact code more.

Other systems may try to achieve similar goals by abstracting the display representation—a common XML representation, for instance, might lend itself to both a GUI and an HTML rendering. Again, this addresses only the rendering of the display, not the fundamental architectural differences of client- and server-side approaches.

Although the client and server do imply trade-offs, many of the common CGI drawbacks already have common proposed solutions. For example:

Client-side solutions

> Client- and server-side programs can be mixed in many ways. For instance, applet programs live on a server but are downloaded to and run as client-side programs with access to rich GUI libraries (more on applets when we discuss Jython in Chapter 18).

> Other technologies, such as embedding JavaScript or Python directly in HTML code, also support client-side execution and richer GUI possibilities. Such scripts live in HTML on the server but run on the client when downloaded and access browser components through an exposed object model to customize pages (this is introduced near the end of Chapter 18).

> The Dynamic HTML (DHTML) extensions provide yet another client-side scripting option for changing web pages after they have been constructed. And the newly emerging AJAX model offers additional ways to add interactivity to web pages. All of these client-side technologies add extra complexities all their own, but they ease some of the limitations imposed by straight HTML.

State retention solutions

> We discussed general state retention options is detail in the prior chapter, and we will study full-scale database systems for Python in Chapter 19. Some web application servers (e.g., Zope, described in Chapter 18) naturally support state

retention between pages by providing concurrently accessible object databases. Some of these systems have a real underlying database component (e.g., Oracle and MySQL); others may use flat files or Python persistent shelves with appropriate locking.

Scripts can also pass state information around in hidden form fields and generated URL parameters, as done in PyMailCGI, or they can store it on the client machine itself using the standard cookie protocol. As we learned in Chapter 16, cookies are strings of information that are stored on the client upon request from the server, and that are transferred back to the server when a page is revisited (data is sent back and forth in HTTP header lines). Cookies are more complex than program variables and are somewhat controversial, but they can offload some simple state retention tasks.

Alternative models such as FastCGI and mod_python offer additional persistence options—where supported, FastCGI applications may retain context in long-lived processes, and mod_python provides session data within Apache.

HTML generation solutions

Third-party extensions can also take some of the complexity out of embedding HTML in Python CGI scripts, albeit at some cost to execution speed. For instance, the HTMLgen system described in Chapter 18 lets programs build pages as trees of Python objects that "know" how to produce HTML. Other frameworks prove an object-based interface to reply-stream generation (e.g., a reply object with methods). When a system like this is employed, Python scripts deal only with objects, not with the syntax of HTML itself.

Other systems such as PHP, Python Server Pages, Zope's DTML and ZPT, and Active Server Pages (some of which are described in the next chapter) provide server-side templating languages, which allow scripting language code to be embedded in HTML and executed on the server, to dynamically generate or determine part of the HTML that is sent back to a client in response to requests. The net result more cleanly insulates Python code from the complexity of HTML code and promotes the separation of display format and business logic.

Clearly, Internet technology does come with some compromises, and it is still evolving rapidly. It is nevertheless an appropriate delivery context for many, though not all, applications. As with every design choice, you must be the judge. While delivering systems on the Web may have some costs in terms of performance, functionality, and complexity, it is likely that the significance of those overheads may diminish with time. Some of the tools we'll meet in the next chapter are aimed at this very goal.

Suggested Reading: The PyErrata System

Now that I've told you all the reasons you might not want to design systems for the Web, I'm going to completely contradict myself and refer you to a system that almost requires a web-based implementation. The second edition of this book included a chapter that presented the PyErrata web site—a Python program that lets arbitrary people on arbitrary machines submit book comments and bug reports (usually called errata) over the Web, using just a web browser.

Due to space concerns, that chapter has been cut from this edition's printed form. However, we're making its original content available as optional, supplemental reading. You can find this example's code, as well as the original chapter's file, in the directory *PP3E\Internet\Web\PyErrata* of the book examples distribution tree (see the Preface for more on the examples distribution).

PyErrata is in some ways simpler than the PyMailCGI case study presented in this chapter. From a user's perspective, PyErrata is more hierarchical than linear: user interactions are shorter and spawn fewer pages. There is also little state retention in the web pages themselves in PyErrata—URL parameters pass state in only one isolated case, and no hidden form fields are generated.

On the other hand, PyErrata introduces an entirely new dimension: persistent data storage. State (error and comment reports) is stored permanently by this system on the server, either in flat pickle files or in a shelve-based database. Both raise the specter of concurrent updates, since any number of users out in cyberspace may be accessing the site at the same time, so PyErrata also introduces file-locking techniques along the way.

I no longer maintain the web site described by this extra chapter, and the material itself is slightly out of date in some ways (e.g., the os.open call is preferred for file locking now, and I would probably use a different data storage system today, such as ZODB). But it provides an additional Python web site case study, and it more closely reflects web sites that must store information on the server.

## CHAPTER 18

Advanced Internet Topics

"Surfing on the Shoulders of Giants"

This chapter concludes our look at Python Internet programming by exploring a handful of Internet-related topics and packages. We've covered many Internet topics in the previous five chapters—socket basics, client- and server-side scripting tools, and programming full-blown email clients and web sites with Python. Yet we still haven't seen many of Python's standard library Internet modules in action. Moreover, there is a rich collection of third-party extensions for scripting the Web with Python that we have not touched on at all.

In this chapter, we explore a grab bag of additional Internet-related tools and third-party extensions of interest to Python Internet developers. Along the way, we meet larger Internet systems including Zope, HTMLgen, Jython, PSP, and Windows Active Scripting. We also study standard Python tools useful to Internet programmers, including Python's XML support, COM interfaces, and techniques for implementing servers. In addition to their practical uses, these systems demonstrate just how much can be achieved by wedding a powerful object-oriented scripting language such as Python to the Web.

Before we start, a disclaimer: none of these topics is presented in much detail here, and undoubtedly some interesting Internet systems will not be covered at all. Moreover, the Internet evolves at lightning speed, and new tools and techniques are certain to emerge after this edition is published; indeed, most of the systems in this chapter appeared *after* this book was first written, and the years to come promise to be just as prolific. As always, the standard moving-target caveat applies: read the Python library manual's Internet section for details we've skipped and stay in touch with the Python community at *http://www.python.org* for information about extensions not covered due to a lack of space or a lack of clairvoyance.

Zope: A Web Application Framework

Zope is an open source web application server and toolkit, written in and customizable with Python. It is a server-side technology that allows web designers to implement sites and applications by publishing Python object hierarchies on the Web. With Zope, programmers can focus on writing objects and can let Zope handle most of the underlying Hypertext Transfer Protocol (HTTP) and Common Gateway Interface (CGI) details. In short, Zope is a popular and easy way to build enterprise-level web sites, whose basic structure is object oriented and whose dynamic content is scripted in Python.

Sometimes compared to commercial web toolkits such as ColdFusion, Zope is made freely available over the Internet and enjoys a large and very active development community. Indeed, many attendees at recent Python conferences were attracted by Zope, which has its own conference tracks. The use of Zope has spread so quickly that many Pythonistas have looked to it as a Python *killer application*—a system so good that it naturally pushes Python into the development spotlight.*

Although useful by itself, Zope is also the basis of the popular Plone content management system—a way to build web sites that delegate content responsibilities to content producers, thus reducing the webmaster bottleneck. Under Plone, users may extend web site content using a workflow model. Plone is built on top of Zope and is something of a prepackaged and highly customizable Zope site (in fact, Plone sites are generally customized in the Zope ZMI user interface). Because Zope is in turn based on Python, both Plone and Zope are Python-based systems.

If you are interested in implementing more complex web sites than the form-based interactions we've seen in the preceding two chapters, you should investigate Zope. Once its learning curve is mastered, it can obviate many of the tasks that web scripters wrestle with on a daily basis. Zope offers a higher-level way of developing sites for the Web, above and beyond raw CGI scripting.

Zope Overview

Zope began life as a set of tools (part of which was named "Bobo") placed in the public domain by Digital Creations (now known as Zope Corporation). Since then, it has grown into a large system with many components, a growing body of add-ons (called "products" in Zope parlance), and a fairly steep learning curve. If you take the time to learn the Zope way of thinking about a web site, though, building and

---

* Over the years, observers have also pointed to other systems as possible Python "killer applications," including Grail, Python's COM support on Windows, and Jython. I hope they're all correct, and I fully expect new killers to arise after this edition is published. At the time of this writing, the IronPython implementation for .NET, Python's role in systems such as Google and BitTorrent, and other developments in the Python world seem to be helping drive the buzz too.

reusing site objects in Zope is quick and avoids much of the complexity in lower-level techniques such as CGI.

Due to the scope of this system, we can't do it any sort of justice in this book. See Zope- and Plone-specific texts for more on these systems. However, because Zope is a popular Python-based application, and because it is a prime example of Python use on the Internet, a quick overview is in order here.

Zope hierarchy model

The key to understanding Zope is its hierarchical site model—in a nutshell, Zope web sites are constructed as a hierarchy of objects, which reflect site content and acquire attributes from high objects in the web site tree. Every object in a Zope web site is ultimately a Python object, and Zope uses inheritance and acquisition (a containment relationship) to allow behavior to be shared among site objects.

The effect is much like the code reuse possible with Python's own class inheritance model. For instance, all pages in a web site tree can acquire and reuse common header and footer objects higher in the tree, to implement a common look-and-feel. Similarly, methods in the tree have implied context much like the "self" argument in Python classes, and they may be applied in the context of other tree objects—a directory lister, for instance, can be run on any folder in the tree.

Just as important, every object in a Zope web site tree may be addressed and viewed by its direct URL. Zope maps a URL path to the folder structure of the web site. Executable script code, for example, may be either invoked by other code in the web site or called directly through the Web by its URL.

Zope scripting

In Zope-based sites, Python code provides dynamic interaction in a variety of forms, including:

Expressions
  Inline Python expressions, useful for trivial number and string manipulations, passing parameters to script and method calls, and so on

Scripts
  Small function-like blocks of code designed for simple tasks that run in a limited secure context, useful for math and text processing, error checking, and so on

External methods
  Modules with registered functions and arbitrary code, useful for full-blown programming tasks such as image processing, XML parsing, FTP, database, and so on

Products
  Classes that extend Zope with new stateful and persistent objects that can be added to web sites, useful for address books, photo albums, and so on

As we'll see, Python code in a Zope web site may generally be invoked by URL or from other objects in the web site, including Zope's templating languages. The combination of Python code and templating objects provides for both logic and presentation—the presentation languages run Python code to process requests and create parts of the reply.

Zope components

Besides its scriptability, Zope features a variety of components, some of which are designed for enterprise-level sites and many of which would be difficult to implement from scratch in CGI scripting:

- An object request broker that maps URLs to Python objects or code on the server (the ZPublisher ORB)
- An over-the-web-site development paradigm, in which sites are designed and managed from any web browser (the ZMI user interface)
- Two server-side templating languages, which are evaluated and expanded on the server, to render an HTML reply stream (DTML and ZPT/TAL)
- An object-oriented database, for storing site content objects (ZODB, described in Chapter 19)
- Enterprise-level tools such as transaction rollback and server load-balancing tools (ZEO, and more)

Some of its components underscore Zope's object-based model. For instance:

Zope Object Request Broker (ORB)
> At the heart of Zope, the ZPublisher ORB dispatches incoming HTTP requests to Python objects and returns results to the requestor, working as a perpetually running middleman between the HTTP CGI world and your Python objects. The Zope ORB is described further in the next section.

HTML document templates
> Zope provides a simple way to define web pages as templates, with values automatically inserted from Python objects and calls. Templates allow an object's HTML representation to be defined independently of the object's implementation, and they allow for a strong separation of display format and business logic. For instance, values of attributes in a class instance object may be automatically plugged into a template's text by name. Template coders need not be Python coders, and vice versa.

Object database (ZODB)
> To record data persistently, Zope comes with a full object-oriented database system for storing Python objects, called ZODB. The Zope object database is based on the Python `pickle` serialization module that we'll meet in the next part of this book, but it adds support for transactions, write-through to disk on in-memory object attribute changes, concurrent access, and more. The database takes the

form of a persistent dictionary of persistent objects where objects are stored and retrieved by key, much as they are with Python's standard shelve module. However, classes must subclass an imported `Persistent` superclass to take full advantage of the system. Zope automatically starts and commits transactions at the start and end of HTTP requests. Because ZODB is a separate component that is also useful in nonweb applications, we will study it in detail in the next part of this book.

Zope also includes a security model, the ZServer web server, the ZClasses system for development of components, and more. Zope ships its components integrated into a whole system, but many parts can be used on their own as well. For instance, Zope's ZODB object database can be used in arbitrary Python applications by itself.

Zope Object Publishing

If you're like me, the concept of publishing objects on the Web may be a bit vague at first glance, but it's fairly simple in Zope. The Zope ORB automatically maps URLs requested by HTTP into calls on Python objects. Consider the Python module and function in Example 18-1.

Example 18-1. PP3E\Internet\Other\Zope\messages.py

```
"A Python module published on the Web by Zope"

def greeting(size='brief', topic='zope'):
    "a published Python function"
    return 'A %s %s introduction' % (size, topic)
```

This is normal Python code, of course, and apart from its documentation, it says nothing about Zope, CGI, or the Internet at large. We may call the function it defines from the interactive prompt as usual:

```
C:\...\PP3E\Internet\Other\Zope>python
>>> import messages
>>> messages.greeting()
'A brief zope introduction'

>>> messages.greeting(size='short')
'A short zope introduction'

>>> messages.greeting(size='tiny', topic='ORB')
'A tiny ORB introduction'
```

But if we place this module file in the appropriate directory on a server machine running Zope and register it to Zope as part of our site, it automatically becomes visible on the Web. That is, the function becomes a *published object*—it can be invoked through a URL, and its return value becomes a response page.

For instance, if our web site and Zope are installed on a server called `myserver.net`, and the module in Example 18-1 is placed in a Zope folder called "messages" at the top of our web site's object tree, the following URLs are equivalent to the three earlier calls:

```
http://www.myserver.net/messages/greeting
http://www.myserver.net/messages/greeting?size=short
http://www.myserver.net/messages/greeting?size=tiny&topic=ORB
```

When our function is accessed as a URL over the Web this way, the Zope ORB performs two feats of magic:

- The URL is automatically translated into a call to the Python function. The first part of the URL after the directory path (messages) names the Zope site folder (which happens to be the same as the module name but doesn't have to be); the second part (greeting) names a function or other callable object within that module; and any parameters after the ? become keyword arguments passed to the named function. URL query parameters are matched to argument names in the called Python object.

- After the function runs, its return value automatically appears in a new page in your web browser. Zope does all the work of formatting the result as a valid HTTP response.

In other words, URLs in Zope become *remote function calls*, not just script invocations. The functions (and methods) called by accessing URLs are coded in Python and may live at arbitrary places on the Net. It's as if the Internet itself becomes Python namespaces, with one namespace per server and site.

Zope is a server-side technology based on *objects*, not text streams; the main advantage of this scheme is that the details of CGI input and output are handled by Zope, while programmers focus on writing domain objects, not on text generation. When our function is accessed with a URL, Zope automatically finds the referenced object, translates incoming parameters to function call arguments, runs the function, and uses its return value to generate an HTTP response. In general, a URL like:

```
http://servername/folderpath/object1/object2/method?arg1=val1&arg2=val2
```

is mapped by the Zope ORB running on `servername` into a call to a Python object in a Python module file of the form:

```
folderpath.object1.object2.method(arg1=val1, arg2=val2)
```

The return value is formatted into an HTML response page sent back to the client requestor (typically a browser). By using longer paths, programs can publish complete hierarchies of objects; Zope simply uses Python's generic object-access protocols to fetch objects along the path.

As usual, a URL like those listed here can appear as the text of a hyperlink, typed manually into a web browser, or used in an HTTP request generated by a program (e.g., using Python's `urllib` module in a client-side script). Parameters are listed at the end of these URLs directly, but if you post information to this URL with a form instead, it works the same way:

```
<form action="http://www.myserver.net/messages/greeting" method=POST>
    Size:  <input type=text name=size>
    Topic: <input type=text name=topic value=zope>
    <input type=submit>
</form>
```

Here, the action tag references our function's URL again; when the user fills out this form and presses its Submit button, inputs from the form sent by the browser magically show up as arguments to the function again. These inputs are typed by the user, not hardcoded at the end of a URL, but our published function doesn't need to care. In fact, Zope recognizes a variety of parameter sources and translates them all into Python function or method arguments: form inputs, parameters at the end of URLs, HTTP headers and cookies, CGI environment variables, and more.

Although this example describes an external method in Zope, the same concepts apply, whether the referenced object is Python code in a module, or a method implemented within Zope using a page templating language. In fact, under Zope, every component becomes an object in the web site's object tree and can be addressed by direct URL or can be invoked from other program components in the tree.

A Zope External Method

As a more complete example, and to illustrate some of the last section's concepts, consider the module in Example 18-2.

Example 18-2. PP3E\Internet\Other\Zope\webtools.py

```
"""
fetch a web page or FTP file, escape it for embedding in HTML;
functions here become Zope external methods and may be invoked
by URLs or other Zope objects, but can be used outside Zope too
"""

import urllib, ftplib, StringIO, cgi

def fetchWebPage(self, url, sizelimit=None):
    """
    fetch reply from a web page URL
    will also work for ftp:// URLs, script parameters
    """
    site = urllib.urlopen(url)
    text = site.read( )
    if not sizelimit: sizelimit = len(text)
    return cgi.escape(text[:sizelimit])

def fetchFtpFile(self, host, directory, file, userinfo=( ), sizelimit=None):
    """
    fetch a file from an FTP site
```

Example 18-2. PP3E\Internet\Other\Zope\webtools.py (continued)

```
    assume binary mode, anonymous"
    """
    buff = StringIO.StringIO()
    site = ftplib.FTP(host)
    site.login(*userinfo)
    site.cwd(directory)
    site.retrbinary('RETR ' + file, buff.write)
    site.quit()
    text = buff.getvalue()
    if not sizelimit: sizelimit = len(text)
    return cgi.escape(text[:sizelimit])

def selftest():
    X = '-'*40
    import getpass
    login = raw_input('user?'), getpass.getpass('pswd?')
    print fetchWebPage(None, 'http://www.python.org', 193), X
    print fetchFtpFile(None, 'home.rmi.net', '.', 'mytrain.html', login, 72), X
    print fetchWebPage(None, 'http://www.rmi.net/~lutz/mytrain.html', 72), X

if __name__ == '__main__': selftest()
```

The self argument here, if included, can be used to access other objects in the Zope web site tree context (roughly, the URL parent). However, nothing else is Zope specific in this code. In fact, when run standalone without Zope, its self-test code fetches two web pages by HTTP, and one by FTP, using tools we met in Chapter 14:

```
C:\...\PP3E\Internet\Other\Zope>webtools.py
user?lutz
pswd?
&lt;!DOCTYPE html PUBLIC "-//W3C//DTD HTML 4.01 Transitional//EN"
                     "http://www.w3.org/TR/html4/loose.dtd" &gt;
&lt;?xml-stylesheet href="./css/ht2html.css" type="text/css"?&gt;
&lt;html&gt;
----------------------------------------
&lt;HTML&gt;

&lt;HEAD&gt;
&lt;TITLE&gt;Mark Lutz's Python Training Page&lt;/TITLE&gt;
&lt;/HEAD&gt;
----------------------------------------
&lt;HTML&gt;

&lt;HEAD&gt;
&lt;TITLE&gt;Mark Lutz's Python Training Page&lt;/TITLE&gt;
&lt;/HEAD&gt;
----------------------------------------
```

Now, to make the code in Example 18-2 part of a Zope web site as an external method:

---

1. Create, copy, or move the module in the Zope Extensions directory. On Windows, put it in *C:\Zope-Instance\Extensions*.

2. Add its functions as "External Method" objects to your web site in the Zope ZMI (e.g., add it to the "/" root folder to make it visible across the entire site). To add both functions in the module, add two external methods.

Once added in the ZMI interface, the functions are external method objects in the web site tree and will be acquired (roughly, inherited) by objects lower in the tree, as well as by paths in URLs that name the methods to operate on the path context. The end result will be that the two functions in Example 18-2 will become callable through the Web via URLs and from other Zope objects such as DTML template language code and other Python code.

Figure 18-1 shows one of the two functions being added in the Zope ZMI—the web-based interface used to build sites.

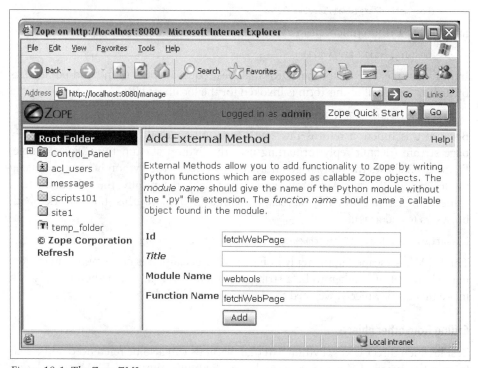

Figure 18-1. The Zope ZMI

The Zope site tree built in the ZMI is separate from the filesystem where the external method's module lives; here, we're adding the method to the root of the Zope site tree (the "/" folder). In Zope, your entire site is designed and maintained in the ZMI interface, and every object added in the ZMI becomes a persistent Python object in the ZODB database used to store your site. However, some components, such as external method module files, also live on the filesystem; as such, they have access to the machine at large.

Calling through the Web

Once added to the site tree, your methods are callable through the Web, using URLs that name the Zope server's hostname and port, any nested folder paths, the name of the external method as registered to Zope in the ZMI, and URL query parameters to provide inputs. Here is a URL that runs the web page fetch function in the module directly; Zope listens for HTTP requests on port number 8080 by default and is running on the local machine ("localhost") here:

```
http://localhost:8080/fetchWebPage?url=http://www.rmi.net/~lutz
```

As mentioned, Zope uses information entered in the ZMI to map URLs that reference external methods of the form:

```
server/method?arg1=va11&arg2=val2
```

into calls to Python functions in Python modules on the server of the following form:

```
method(arg1=val1, arg2=val2)
```

In our example, the ZPublisher ORB matches request inputs to method parameters by name, and a call of this form is invoked for the localhost URL:

```
webtools.fetchWebPage(url='http://www.rmi.net/~lutz')
```

Because this function returns raw text, Zope automatically renders it in the reply page stream (default reply formatting uses the Python str function). For example, Figure 18-2 shows the reply page returned by Zope for the Python home page, using the following URL in a web browser's address field (technically, the url parameter's value string should probably be escaped with urllib.quote_plus, but it works in all browsers tested as is):

```
http://localhost:8080/fetchWebPage?url=http://www.python.org
```

The HTML is escaped in the reply in Figure 18-2 because it is not wrapped in enclosing HTML yet; it is taken to be a string when fetched from the method directly. To make this display nicely, we need to move on to the next section.

Calling from other objects

Besides such direct URLs, Python external methods can also be referenced and called from other types of Zope objects, including Python scripts and DTML templating language code. When referenced, Zope finds the method object by acquisition (web site tree search); calls the Python function in the module file, passing in any arguments; and renders and inserts the returned result into the HTML reply stream.

For instance, the following Zope Python script, fetchscript, is a Script object added in the ZMI to the site's /scripts101 folder (it can also be uploaded to the ZMI from an external file). The script becomes a persistent object in the ZODB database used by

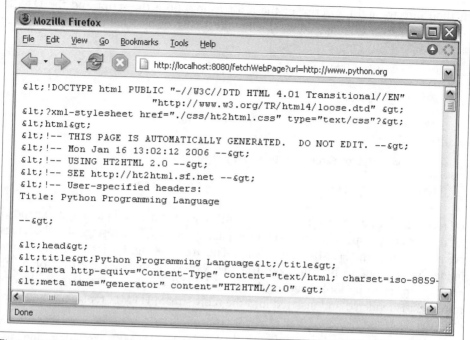

Figure 18-2. Python home page fetched by a Zope external method

Zope; it is not stored in the *Extensions* directory in the filesystem. Assuming this is stored lower in the site tree than the external method, when run, it locates and invokes the code in Example 18-2:

```
# called from DTML or URL, calls external method
# gets external method in "/" by acquisition context
# uses FTP, returned string inserted into HTML reply

site = 'home.rmi.net'
directory = '.'
login = ('lutz', 'XXXXXXXX')
reply = context.fetchFtpFile(context, site, directory, 'mytrain.html', login,72)
return reply
```

Zope Python scripts are small bits of Python code, designed for running calculations that are too complex for templating languages such as DTML, but are not complex enough to warrant an external method or other construct. Scripts generally perform simple numeric or string manipulations. Unlike external methods, scripts run in a limited secure environment and are stored in the Zope site tree. In scripts, the context variable gives access to the Zope acquisition context in which the script is being run, and other variables give access to request inputs and reply output interfaces.

Similarly, the following DTML templating language method object, named fetchdtml and created in the same */scripts101* ZMI web site folder, invokes both the external method directly and the script of the prior listing. Both the script and the DTML objects themselves become addressable by direct URL or by other objects in the web site tree.

```
<dtml-var standard_html_header>

<h2>External Method call (urllib)</h2>
<pre>
<dtml-var expr="fetchWebPage('http://www.python.org')[:277]">
</pre>

<h2>Python script to External Method call (ftplib)</h2>
<pre>
<dtml-var fetchscript>
</pre>
```

DTLM combines normal HTML with DTML tags that are evaluated and expanded on the server by Zope when the enclosing page is fetched. The results of DTML tags are inserted into the HTML reply stream. The dtml-var tag, for instance, can name inline Python code to be run (expr=) in the context of the web site tree, or name another object to be looked up in the tree and called—the expression or object's result text is rendered and inserted into the reply stream HTML, replacing the entire dtml-var tag.

The object called from a dtml-var tag can be another DTML templating language object, a Python script or external method object, or other object types such as images. For example, the standard_html_header in this code references another DTML method object higher in the object tree, which in turn references an image object in the tree; by listing this in each page lower in the tree, it provides a common page header.

Figure 18-3 captures the reply generated when we visit the DTML code in a web browser—the original Python external method is run twice along the way. This page is addressed by the following URL; replace the last component of this URL with fetchscript to access the Python script by direct URL (it is also run by the DTML method):

```
http://localhost:8080/scripts101/fetchdtml
```

In a sense, DTML embeds Python in HTML—it runs Python code in response to tags embedded in the reply page. This is essentially the opposite of the CGI scripts we met earlier which embed HTML in Python, and it is similar to the ASP and PSP systems we'll meet later in this chapter.

More important, DTML, as well as Zope's other templating language, ZPT (TAL), encourages separation of presentation and business logic. DTML presents the results of Python method and script invocations in HTML, but it doesn't know about their operation. The Python code of the script and external method objects referenced by DTML implements more complex programming tasks, but it doesn't know about

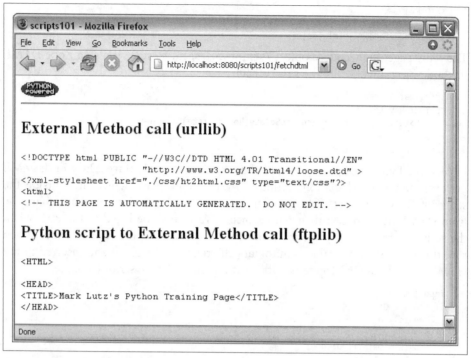

Figure 18-3. Running DTML code that calls Python methods

display formatting of the context in which it may be used. Where appropriate, the display and logic components can be implemented by different specialists.

A Simple Zope Interactive Web Site

As a final example, consider the following Zope-based web site. It consists of three Zope objects, all created and edited in the ZMI: an input page, a reply page, and a Python script used for calculations. Its input page form references the reply page object, and the reply page calls a Python script from a DTML expression.

The input page is a DTML method object, created and stored as the Zope tree object /scripts101/salaryInput in the ZMI. Its form input parameters are automatically converted to float and integer objects by Zope:

```
<dtml-var standard_html_header>

<form action="salaryResult" method=POST>
<h2>Enter job data:</h2>
<table>
  <tr><td>Hours worked: <td><input name="hours:float"><br>
  <tr><td>Pay per hour: <td><input name="rate:int"><br>
</table><br>
<input type="submit" value="Compute"><br>
```

```
    </form>

    <dtml-var standard_html_footer>
```

The reply page, the web tree object /scripts101/salaryResult, is also a Zope DTML method object, invoked by the salaryInput page:

```
    <dtml-var standard_html_header>
    <p>Your pay this week:
        <b><dtml-var expr="calculateSalary(hours, rate)">
    </p>
    <dtml-var standard_html_footer>
```

Finally, the Python script object, added as /scripts101/calculateSalary in the ZMI, performs numeric calculations required by the reply page, which are outside the scope of DTML display code. Input parameters to this script come automatically from DTML namespaces; their names (hours, rate) may be listed in the ZMI when the script is created or by special comments at the start of the script's code. When run, this script's return value is automatically rendered by Zope and inserted in the HTML reply stream, replacing the dtml-var tag that calls the script by name.

```
    import math
    if hours < 0:
        hours = 0
    else:
        hours = math.floor(hours)
    return hours * rate
```

As before, this fosters a separation of presentation and business logic: the DTML salaryResult presents the result of Python calculateSalary, but the DTML code doesn't know about salary calculation and the Python code doesn't know about presentation. Ideally, the two parts can be worked on independently, by people with different skill sets.

This separation is especially striking when compared with classic CGI scripts, which embed and mix HTML reply code with Python code—in the Zope model, salaryResult display is independent of the Python calculateSalary logic. In practice, more complex pages may require additional formatting logic in the templating language code (e.g., loops and tests), but the general separation still applies.

Figure 18-4 captures this site's input page (it can also be displayed with the View tab in the ZMI) at the URL *http://localhost:8080/scripts101/salaryInput*.

Figure 18-5 shows the reply page returned when the input page is submitted. The reply page reflects the DTML code that presents the result returned by the Python script.

We can also call the calculateSalary Python script directly by its URL, though we have to take care to convert the input arguments to their expected datatypes by using type codes after their names—Zope uses these to perform from-string conversions before the values are passed into the called object. We use these in the input fields of

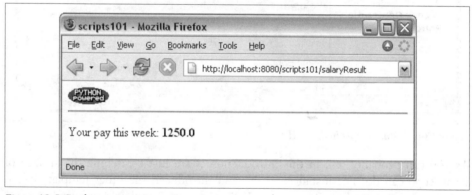

Figure 18-4. Input page

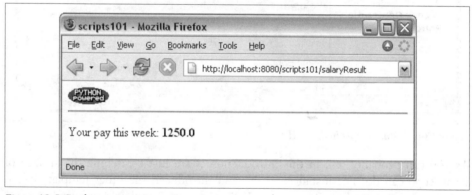

Figure 18-5. Reply page

salaryInput as well. Alternatively, we could restructure the script to convert from strings to the expected types itself by using the REQUEST inputs object rather than declared parameters. As is, the following URL produces a page that displays just the text "5200.0"—the default str rendering of the returned Python floating-point number:

```
http://localhost:8080/scripts101/calculateSalary?hours:float=65&rate:int=80
```

The salaryResult DTML page object can be called directly by a similar URL (replace the Python script's name), though the reply is a complete web page produced by the DTML code.

In fact, as seen in Figure 18-6, the Python script can also be tested within the ZMI itself—click the test tab, and input the parameters manually. Objects can be tested this way in the ZMI, without having to type the corresponding URL in another browser window.

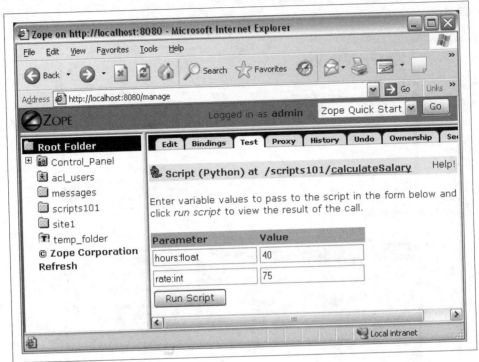

Figure 18-6. Testing scripts in the ZMI

As you can probably tell, in this introduction we're just scratching the surface of what Zope can do. For instance, we haven't introduced the other templating language in Zope, Zope Page Templates (ZPT), coded in Template Attribute Language (TAL). ZPT is an alternative way to describe presentation based on attributes of normal HTML tags, rather than embedded DTML tags. As such, ZPT code may be more easily handled by some HTML editors when edited outside the context of Zope.

Moreover, published functions and methods can use the Zope object database to save state permanently; there are more advanced Python constructs in Zope, including Zope products; URLs can provide method context using reference paths in ways we have not mentioned here; and Zope provides additional tools such as debugging support, precoded HTTP servers for use with the ORB, and finer-grained control over responses to URL requestors.

For all things Zope, visit *http://www.zope.org*. There, you'll find up-to-date releases, as well as documentation ranging from tutorials to references to full-blown Zope example sites.

 During the lifespan of the second edition of this book, Python creator Guido van Rossum and his PythonLabs team of core Python developers were located at the Zope Corporation, home of the Zope framework introduced here. As I write this third edition, Guido has just been hired by Google, but many of the original PythonLabs team members are still at Zope.

HTMLgen: Web Pages from Objects

One of the things that makes basic CGI scripts complex is their inherent dependence on HTML: they must embed and generate legal HTML code to build user interfaces. These tasks might be easier if the syntax of HTML were somehow removed from CGI scripts and handled by an external tool.

HTMLgen is a third-party Python tool designed to fill this need. With it, programs build web pages by constructing trees of Python objects that represent the desired page and "know" how to format themselves as HTML. Once constructed, the program asks the top of the Python object tree to generate HTML for itself, and out comes a complete, legally formatted HTML web page.

Programs that use HTMLgen to generate pages need never deal with the syntax of HTML; instead, they can use the higher-level object model provided by HTMLgen and trust it to do the formatting step. HTMLgen may be used in any context where you need to generate HTML. It is especially suited for HTML that is generated periodically from static data, but it can also be used for HTML creation in CGI scripts (though its use in the CGI context incurs some extra speed costs). For instance, HTMLgen would be ideal if you run a nightly job to generate web pages from database contents. HTMLgen can also be used to generate documents that don't live on the Web at all; the HTML code it produces works just as well when viewed offline.

A Brief HTMLgen Tutorial

We can't investigate HTMLgen in depth here, but let's look at a few simple examples to sample the flavor of the system. HTMLgen is shipped as a collection of Python modules that must be installed on your machine; once it's installed and its directory is added to your module search path, simply import objects from the HTMLgen module corresponding to the tag you wish to generate, and make instances:

```
C:\Stuff\HTMLgen\HTMLgen>python
>>> from HTMLgen import *
>>> p = Paragraph("Making pages from objects is easy\n")
>>> p
```

```
<HTMLgen.Paragraph instance at 7dbb00>
>>> print p
<P>Making pages from objects is easy
</P>
```

Here, we make an `HTMLgen.Paragraph` object (a class instance), passing in the text to be formatted. All HTMLgen objects implement `__str__` methods and can emit legal HTML code for themselves. When we print the `Paragraph` object, it emits an HTML paragraph construct. HTMLgen objects also define append methods, which do the right thing for the object type; `Paragraphs` simply add appended text to the end of the text block:

```
>>> p.append("Special < characters > are & escaped")
>>> print p
<P>Making pages from objects is easy
Special &lt; characters &gt; are &amp; escaped</P>
```

Notice that HTMLgen escaped the special characters (e.g., < means <) so that they are legal HTML; you don't need to worry about writing either HTML or escape codes yourself. HTMLgen has one class for each HTML tag; here is the List object at work, creating an ordered list:

```
>>> choices = ['python', 'tcl', 'perl']
>>> print List(choices)
<UL>
<LI>python
<LI>tcl
<LI>perl
</UL>
```

In general, HTMLgen is smart about interpreting data structures that you pass to it. For instance, embedded sequences are automatically mapped to the HTML code for displaying nested lists:

```
>>> choices = ['tools', ['python', 'c++'], 'food', ['spam', 'eggs']]
>>> l = List(choices)
>>> print l
<UL>
<LI>tools
    <UL>
    <LI>python
    <LI>c++
    </UL>
<LI>food
    <UL>
    <LI>spam
    <LI>eggs
    </UL>
</UL>
```

Hyperlinks are just as easy. Simply make and print an `Href` object with the link target and text. The text argument can be replaced by an image, as we'll see later in Example 18-4.

```
>>> h = Href('http://www.python.org', 'python')
>>> print h
<A HREF="http://www.python.org">python</A>
```

To generate HTML for complete pages, we create one of the HTML document objects, append its component objects, and print the document object. HTMLgen emits a complete page's code, ready to be viewed in a browser:

```
>>> d = SimpleDocument(title='My doc')
>>> p = Paragraph('Web pages made easy')
>>> d.append(p)
>>> d.append(h)
>>> print d
<!DOCTYPE HTML PUBLIC "-//W3C//DTD HTML 3.2//EN">
<HTML>

<!-- This file generated using Python HTMLgen module. -->
<HEAD>
  <META NAME="GENERATOR" CONTENT="HTMLgen 2.2.2">
        <TITLE>My doc</TITLE>
</HEAD>
<BODY>
<P>Web pages made easy</P>

<A HREF="http://www.python.org">python</A>

</BODY> </HTML>
```

There are other kinds of document classes, including a SeriesDocument that implements a standard layout for pages in a series. SimpleDocument is simple indeed: it's essentially a container for other components, and it generates the appropriate wrapper HTML code. HTMLgen also provides classes such as Table, Form, and so on— one for each kind of HTML construct.

Naturally, you ordinarily use HTMLgen from within a script, so you can capture the generated HTML in a file or send it over an Internet connection in the context of a CGI application (remember, printed text goes to the browser in the CGI script environment). The script in Example 18-3 does roughly what we just did interactively, but it saves the printed text in a file.

Example 18-3. PP3E\Internet\Other\HTMLgen\htmlgen101.py

```
import sys
from HTMLgen import *

p = Paragraph('Making pages from objects is easy.\n')
p.append('Special < characters > are & escaped')

choices = ['tools', ['python', 'c++'], 'food', ['spam', 'eggs']]
l = List(choices)

s = SimpleDocument(title="HTMLgen 101")
s.append(Heading(1, 'Basic tags'))
s.append(p)
```

Example 18-3. PP3E\Internet\Other\HTMLgen\htmlgen101.py (continued)

```
s.append(1)
s.append(HR( ))
s.append(Href('http://www.python.org', 'Python home page'))

if len(sys.argv) == 1:
    print s                      # send HTML to sys.stdout or real file
else:
    open(sys.argv[1], 'w').write(str(s))
```

This script also uses the HR object to format a horizontal line, and it uses Heading to insert a header line. It either prints HTML to the standard output stream (if no arguments are listed) or writes HTML to an explicitly named file; the str built-in function invokes object __str__ methods just as print does. Run this script from the system command line to make a file, using one of the following:

```
C:\...\PP3E\Internet\Other\HTMLgen>python htmlgen101.py > htmlgen101.html
C:\...\PP3E\Internet\Other\HTMLgen>python htmlgen101.py htmlgen101.html
```

Either way, the script's output is a legal HTML page file, which you can view in your favorite browser by typing the output filename in the address field or by clicking on the file in your file explorer. Either way, it will look a lot like Figure 18-7.

Figure 18-7. Viewing htmlgen101.py output in a browser

See the file *htmlgen101.html* in the examples distribution if you wish to inspect the HTML generated to describe this page directly (it looks much like the prior document's output). Example 18-4 shows another script that does something less hard-coded: it constructs a web page to display its own source code.

Example 18-4. PP3E\Internet\Other\HTMLgen\htmlgen101-b.py

```
import sys
from HTMLgen import *
d = SimpleDocument(title="HTMLgen 101 B")

# show this script
text = open('htmlgen101-b.py', 'r').read()
d.append(Heading(1, 'Source code'))
d.append(Paragraph( PRE(text) ))

# add GIF and links
site  = 'http://www.python.org'
gif   = 'PythonPoweredSmall.gif'
image = Image(gif, alt='picture', align='left', hspace=10, border=0)

d.append(HR())
d.append(Href(site, image))
d.append(Href(site, 'Python home page'))

if len(sys.argv) == 1:
    print d
else:
    open(sys.argv[1], 'w').write(str(d))
```

We use the PRE object here to specify preformatted text, and the Image object to generate code to display a GIF file on the generated page. Notice that HTML tag options such as alt and align are specified as keyword arguments when making HTMLgen objects. Running this script and pointing a browser at its output yields the page shown in Figure 18-8; the image at the bottom is also a hyperlink because it was embedded inside an Href object.

And that, along with a few nice, advanced features, is all there is to using HTMLgen. Once you become familiar with it, you can construct web pages by writing Python code, without ever needing to manually type HTML tags again. Of course, you still must write code with HTMLgen instead of using a drag-and-drop page layout tool, but that code is incredibly simple and supports the addition of more complex programming logic where needed to construct pages dynamically.

In fact, now that you're familiar with HTMLgen, you'll see that many of the HTML files shown earlier in this book could have been simplified by recoding them to use HTMLgen instead of direct HTML code. The earlier CGI scripts could have used HTMLgen as well, albeit with additional speed overheads—printing text directly is faster than generating it from object trees, though perhaps not significantly so (CGI scripts are generally bound to network speeds, not to CPU speed).

HTMLgen is open source software, but it is not a standard part of Python and must therefore be installed separately. Search the Web to locate HTMLgen's current home and version. Once installed, simply add the HTMLgen path to your PYTHONPATH variable setting to gain access to its modules if required (or copy its directory to your

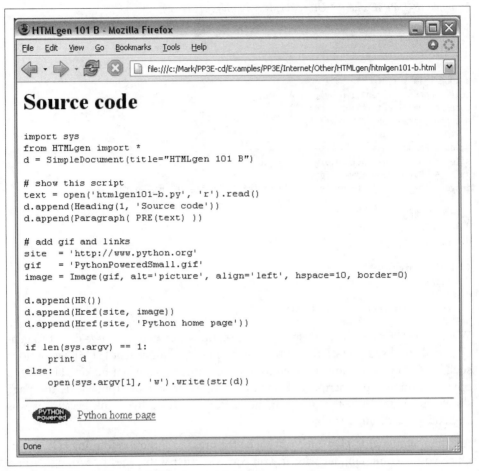

Figure 18-8. Viewing htmlgen101-b.py output in a browser

autosearched *Lib\site-packages* folder). For more about HTMLgen, see the package itself—its *html* subdirectory includes the HTMLgen manual in HTML format.

Jython: Python for Java

Jython (formerly known as JPython) is an entirely distinct implementation of the Python programming language that allows programmers to use Python as an easy-to-use scripting component in Java-based applications. The effect is much the same as deploying standard Python as a scripting language for C and C++ libraries.

In short, Jython makes Python code look like Java and consequently offers a variety of technology options inherited from the Java world. With Jython, Python code may be run as client-side applets in web browsers, as server-side scripts, and in a variety of other roles. Jython is distinct from other systems mentioned in this section in terms of its scope: while it is based on the core Python language we've seen in this book, it actually replaces the underlying implementation of that language rather than augmenting it.*

This section briefly explores Jython and highlights some of the reasons you may or may not want to use it instead of the standard Python implementation. Although Jython is primarily of interest to programmers writing Java-based applications, it underscores integration possibilities and language definition issues that merit the attention of Python users. Because Jython is Java-centric, you need to know something about Java development to make the most sense of Jython, and this book doesn't pretend to teach that in the next few pages. For more details, interested readers should consult other materials, including Jython documentation at *http://www.jython.org*.

 The Java version of Python is now called Jython. Although you are likely to still see it called by its new Jython name on the Net these days (and in this book), its original "JPython" title may still appear in older documentation (it was renamed some years ago for copyright reasons).

A Quick Introduction to Jython

Functionally speaking, Jython is a collection of Java classes that run Python code. It consists of a Python compiler, written in Java, that translates Python scripts to Java bytecode so they can be executed by a *Java Virtual Machine*—the runtime component that executes Java programs and is used by major web browsers. Moreover, Jython automatically exposes all Java class libraries for use in Python scripts. In a nutshell, here's what comes with the Jython system:

Python-to-Java-bytecode compiler

Jython always compiles Python source code into Java bytecode and passes it to a Java Virtual Machine (JVM) runtime engine to be executed. A command-line compiler program, jythonc, is also able to translate Python source code files into Java *.class* and *.jar* files, which can then be used as Java applets, beans, servlets, and so on. To the JVM, Python code run through Jython looks the same as Java code. Besides making Python code work on a JVM, Jython code also inherits all aspects of the Java runtime system, including Java's garbage collection and security models. jythonc imposes Java source file class rules as well.

---

* Jython was the second complete implementation of the Python language. By contrast, the standard, original implementation of Python is sometimes now referred to as CPython, because it is implemented in ANSI C. Among other things, the Jython implementation is driving a clearer definition of the Python language itself, independent of a particular implementation's effects. The newer IronPython Python implementation for Microsoft's C#/.NET environment (mentioned later in this chapter in the sidebar "The IronPython C# Python Compiler") is a third Python implementation, and like Jython, it is also helping to form a definition of what it means to be Python.

Access to Java class libraries (extending)

Jython uses Java's *reflection API* (runtime type information) to expose all available Java class libraries to Python scripts. That is, Python programs written for the Jython system can call out to any resident Java class automatically, simply by importing it. The Python-to-Java interface is completely automatic and remarkably seamless—Java class libraries appear as though they are coded in Python. Import statements in Jython scripts may refer to either Jython modules or Java class libraries. For instance, when a Jython script imports java.awt, it gains access to all the tools available in the awt library. Jython internally creates a "dummy" Python module object to serve as an interface to awt at import time. This dummy module consists of hooks for dispatching calls from Jython code to Java class methods and automatically converting datatypes between Java and Python representations as needed. To Jython scripts, Java class libraries look and feel exactly like normal Python modules (albeit with interfaces defined by the Java world).

Unified object model

Jython objects are actually Java objects internally. In fact, Jython implements Python types as instances of a Java PyObject class. For instance, in Jython, the number 123 is an instance of the PyInteger Java class, and you can specify things like [].__class__, since all objects are class instances (this works in standard C Python today as well). That makes data mapping between languages simple. Java can process Python objects automatically, because they are Java objects. Jython automatically converts types between languages according to a standard type map as needed to call out to Java libraries, and it selects among overloaded Java method signatures.

API for running Python from Java (embedding)

Jython also provides interfaces that allow Java programs to execute Jython code. As for embedding in C and C++, this allows Java applications to be customized by bits of dynamically written Jython code. For instance, Jython ships with a Java PythonInterpreter class, which allows Java programs to create objects that function as Python namespaces for running Python code. Each PythonInterpreter object is roughly a Python module, with methods such as exec (a string of Python code), execfile (a Python filename), and get and set methods for assigning Python global variables. Because Python objects are really instances of a Java PyObject class, an enclosing Java layer can access and process data created by Python code naturally.

Interactive Python command line

Like the standard Python implementation, Jython comes with an interactive command line that runs code immediately after it is typed. Jython's jython program is equivalent to the python executable we've been using in this book; without arguments, it starts an interactive session. Among other things, this allows Jython programmers to import and test class components actually written in Java. This ability alone is compelling enough to interest many Java programmers.

Interface automations

Java libraries are somewhat easier to use in Jython code than in Java. That's because Jython automates some of the coding steps Java implies. For instance, *callback handlers* for Java GUI libraries may be simple Python functions even though Java coders need to provide methods in fully specified classes (Java does not have first-class function objects). Jython also makes Java class *data members* accessible as both Python attribute names (*object.name*) and object constructor keyword arguments (*name=value*); such Python syntax is translated into calls to getName and setName accessor methods in Java classes. We'll see these automation tricks in action in the following examples. You don't have to use any of these (and they may confuse Java programmers at first glance), but they further simplify coding in Jython and give Java class libraries a more Python-like flavor.

The net effect of all this is that Jython allows us to write Python programs that can run on any Java-aware machine—in particular, in the context of most web browsers. More important, because Python programs are translated into Java bytecode, Jython provides an incredibly seamless and natural integration between the two languages. Both walk and talk in terms of the Java model, so calls across language boundaries are trivial. With Jython's approach, it's even possible to subclass a Java class in Python, and vice versa.

Why Jython?

So why go to all this trouble to mix Python into Java environments? The most obvious answer is that Jython makes Java components easier to use: Jython scripts are typically a fraction of the size of their Java equivalents, and are much less complex. More generally, the answer is really the same as it is for C and C++ environments. Python, as an easy-to-use, object-oriented scripting language, naturally complements the Java programming language.

By now, it is clear to most people that Java is too complex to serve as a scripting or rapid-development tool. But this is exactly where Python excels; by adding Python to the mix with Jython, we add a scripting component to Java systems, exactly as we do when integrating Python with C or C++. For instance, we can use Jython to quickly prototype Java systems, test Java classes interactively, and open up Java systems for end-user customization. In general, adding Python to Java development can significantly boost programmer productivity, just as it does for C and C++ systems.

A Simple Jython Example

Once a Python program is compiled with Jython, it is all Java: the program is translated to Java bytecode, it uses Java classes to do its work, and there is no Python left except for the original source code. Because the compiler tool itself is also written in Java, Jython is sometimes called "100 percent pure Java." That label may be more

Jython Versus the Python C API

Functionally, Jython is primarily an integration system: it allows us to mix Python with Java components. We also study ways to integrate Python with C and C++ components in a later part of this book. It's worth noting that we need different techniques to integrate Python with Java (such as the Jython compiler), because Java is a somewhat closed system: it prefers an all-Java mix. The C and C++ integration tools are generally less restrictive in terms of language assumptions, and any C-compatible language components will do. Java's strictness is partly due to its security goals, but the net effect is to foster integration techniques that are specific to Java alone.

On the other hand, because Java exposes runtime type information through its reflection API, Jython can largely automate the conversions and dispatching needed to access Java components from Python scripts; Python code simply imports and calls Java components. When mixing Python with C or C++, we must provide a "glue" code layer that integrates the two languages explicitly. Some of this can be automated (with the SWIG system we'll meet later in this text). No glue code is required in Jython, however, because Jython's (and Java's) developers have done all the linkage work already, in a generic fashion. It is also possible to mix in C/C++ components with Java via its native call interface (JNI), but this can be cumbersome and may cancel out Java's reported portability and security benefits.

profound to marketers than programmers, though, because Jython scripts are still written using standard Python syntax, use Python datatypes, and import many of Python's standard library modules. For instance, Example 18-5 is a legal Jython program, derived from an example originally written by Guido van Rossum.

Example 18-5. PP3E\Internet\Other\Jython\jycalc.py

```
##########################################################################
# implement a simple calculator in Jython; evaluation runs a full
# expression all at once using the Python eval() built-in--Jython's
# source-code compiler is present at runtime, as in standard Python
##########################################################################

from java import awt              # get access to Java class libraries
from pawt import swing            # they look like Python modules here

labels = ['0', '1', '2', '+',    # labels for calculator buttons
          '3', '4', '5', '-',    # will be used for a 4x4 grid
          '6', '7', '8', '*',
          '9', '.', '=', '/' ]

keys = swing.JPanel(awt.GridLayout(4, 4))   # do Java class library magic
display = swing.JTextField()                 # Python data auto-mapped to Java

def push(event):                             # callback for regular keys
    display.replaceSelection(event.actionCommand)
```

Example 18-5. PP3E\Internet\Other\Jython\jycalc.py (continued)

```
def enter(event):                          # callback for the '=' key
    display.text = str(eval(display.text))  # use Python eval() to run expr
    display.selectAll()

for label in labels:                       # build up button widget grid
    key = swing.JButton(label)             # on press, invoke Python funcs
    if label == '=':
        key.actionPerformed = enter
    else:
        key.actionPerformed = push
    keys.add(key)

panel = swing.JPanel(awt.BorderLayout())   # make a swing panel
panel.add("North", display)                # text plus key grid in middle
panel.add("Center", keys)
swing.test(panel)                          # start in a GUI viewer
```

The first thing you should notice is that this is genuine Python code—Jython scripts use the same core language that we've been using all along in this book. That's good news, both because Python is such an easy language to use and because you don't need to learn a new, proprietary scripting language to use Jython. It also means that all of Python's high-level language syntax and tools are available. For example, in this script, the Python eval built-in function is used to parse and evaluate constructed expressions all at once, saving us from having to write an expression evaluator from scratch.

Interface Automation Tricks

The previous calculator example also illustrates two interface automations performed by Jython: function callback and attribute mappings. Java programmers may have already noticed that this example doesn't use classes. Like standard Python and unlike Java, Jython supports but does not impose object-oriented programming (OOP). Simple Python functions work fine as *callback handlers*. In Example 18-5, assigning key.actionPerformed to a Python function object has the same effect as registering an instance of a class that defines a callback handler method:

```
def push(event):
    ...
key = swing.JButton(label)
key.actionPerformed = push
```

This is noticeably simpler than the more Java-like:

```
class handler(awt.event.ActionListener):
    def actionPerformed(self, event):
        ...
key = swing.JButton(label)
key.addActionListener(handler())
```

Jython automatically maps Python functions to the Java class method callback model. Java programmers may now be wondering why we can assign to something named key.actionPerformed in the first place. Jython's second magic feat is to make Java data members look like simple *object attributes* in Python code. In abstract terms, Jython code of the form:

```
X = Object(argument)
X.property = value + X.property
```

is equivalent to the more traditional and complex Java style:

```
X = Object(argument)
X.setProperty(value + X.getProperty())
```

That is, Jython automatically maps attribute assignments and references to Java accessor method calls by inspecting Java class signatures (and possibly Java Bean-Info files if used). Moreover, properties can be assigned with *keyword arguments* in object constructor calls, such that:

```
X = Object(argument, property=value)
```

is equivalent to both this more traditional form:

```
X = Object(argument)
X.setProperty(value)
```

as well as the following, which relies on attribute name mapping:

```
X = Object(argument)
X.property = value
```

We can combine both callback and property automation for an even simpler version of the callback code snippet:

```
def push(event):
    ...
key = swing.JButton(label, actionPerformed=push)
```

You don't need to use these automation tricks, but again, they make Jython scripts simpler, which is most of the point behind mixing Python with Java.

Writing Java Applets in Jython

I would be remiss if I didn't include a brief example of Jython code that more directly masquerades as a Java *applet*: code that lives on a server machine but is downloaded to and run on the client machine when its Internet address is referenced. Most of the magic behind this is subclassing the appropriate Java class in a Jython script, demonstrated in Example 18-6.

Example 18-6. PP3E\Internet\Other\Jython\jyapplet.py

```
#####################################
# a simple Java applet coded in Python
#####################################
```

Example 18-6. PP3E\Internet\Other\Jython\jyapplet.py (continued)

```
from java.applet import Applet                    # get Java superclass

class Hello(Applet):
    def paint(self, gc):                          # on paint callback
        gc.drawString("Hello applet world", 20, 30)   # draw text message

if __name__ == '__main__':                        # if run standalone
    import pawt                                    # get Java awt lib
    pawt.test(Hello())                            # run under awt loop
```

The Python class in this code inherits all the necessary applet protocol from the standard Java Applet superclass, so there is not much new to see here. Under Jython, Python classes can always subclass Java classes, because Python objects really are Java objects when compiled and run. The Python-coded paint method in this script will be automatically run from the Java AWT event loop as needed; it simply uses the passed-in gc user-interface handle object to draw a text message.

If we use Jython's jythonc command-line tool to compile this into a Java *.class* file and properly store that file on a web server, it can then be used exactly like applets written in Java. Because most web browsers include a JVM, this means that such Python scripts may be used as client-side programs that create sophisticated user-interface devices within the browser, and so on.

Jython Trade-Offs

Depending on your background, the potentially less good news about Jython is that even though the calculator and applet scripts discussed here are straight Python code, the libraries they use are different from what we've seen so far. In fact, the library calls employed are radically different. The calculator, for example, relies primarily on imported Java class libraries, not on standard Python libraries. You need to understand Java's awt and swing libraries to make sense of its code, and this *library skew* between language implementations becomes more acute as programs grow larger. The applet example is even more Java bound: it depends both on Java user-interface libraries and on Java applet protocols.

If you are already familiar with Java libraries, this isn't an issue at all, of course. But because most of the work performed by realistic programs is done by using libraries, the fact that most Jython code relies on very different libraries makes compatibility with standard Python less potent than it may seem at first glance. To put that more strongly, apart from simple core language examples, many Jython programs won't run on the standard Python interpreter, and many standard Python programs won't work under Jython.

Generally, Jython presents a number of trade-offs. I want to point out upfront that Jython is indeed an excellent Java scripting tool—arguably the best one available, and most of its trade-offs are probably of little or no concern to Java developers. For instance, if you are coming to Jython from the Java world, the fact that Java libraries are at the heart of Jython scripts may be more asset than downside. But if you are presented with a choice between the standard and Java-based Python language implementations, some of Jython's implications are worth knowing about:

Jython is not fully compatible with the standard Python language

At this writing, Jython is not yet totally compatible with the standard Python language, as defined by the original C implementation. In subtle ways, the core Python language itself works differently in Jython. The list of incompatibilities (viewable at *http://www.jython.org*) will likely shrink over time but will probably never go away completely. Moreover, new language features are likely to show up later in Jython than in the standard C-based implementation.

Jython requires programmers to learn Java development too

Language syntax is only one aspect of programming. The library skew mentioned previously is just one example of Jython's dependence on the Java system. Not only do you need to learn Java libraries to get real work done in Jython, but you also must come to grips with the Java programming environment in general.

Most standard Python libraries have been ported to Jython, and others are being adopted regularly. But major Python tools such as Tkinter GUIs may show up late or never in Jython (and instead are replaced with Java tools).* In addition, many core Python library features cannot be supported in Jython, because they would violate Java's security constraints. For example, some tools in the os module may never become available in Jython.

Jython applies only where a JVM is installed or shipped

You need the Java runtime to run Jython code. This may sound like a nonissue given the pervasiveness of the Internet, but I have worked in more than one company for which delivering applications to be run on JVMs was not an option. Simply put, there was no JVM to be found at the customer's site. In such scenarios, Jython is either not an option, or it will require you to ship a JVM with your application just to run your compiled Jython code.

Shipping the standard Python system with your products is completely free; shipping a JVM may imply licensing and fee issues (though open source options do now exist). On some platforms, finding a JVM to use for development might be an issue as well; see *http://www.jython.org* for current JVM compatibility issues.

Jython doesn't support Python extension modules written in C or C++

At present, no C or C++ extension modules written to work with the C Python implementation will work with Jython. This is a major impediment to deploying

---

* But see the note at the end of the later section "Grail: A Python-Based Web Browser"; a port of Tkinter for Jython known a jTkinter is available. Search the Web for details.

Jython outside the scope of applications run in a browser. To date, the Python user community has developed thousands of extensions written for C Python, and these constitute much of the substance of the Python development world.

Jython's current alternative is to instead expose Java class libraries and ask programmers to write new extensions in Java. But this dismisses a vast library of prior and future Python art. In principle, C extensions could be supported by Java's native call interface, but it is complex and can negate Java portability and security.

Jython is noticeably slower than C Python

Today, Python code generally runs slower under the Jython implementation. How much slower depends on what you test, which JVM you use to run your test, whether a Just-in-Time (JIT) compiler is available, and which tester you cite. Posted benchmarks have run the gamut from 1.7 times slower than C Python, to 10 times slower, and up to 100 times slower. Regardless of the exact number, the extra layer of logic Jython requires to map Python to the Java execution model adds speed overheads to an already slow JVM and makes it unlikely that Jython will ever be as fast as the C Python implementation.

Given that C Python is already slower than compiled languages such as C, the additional slowness of Jython makes it less useful outside the realm of Java scripting. Furthermore, the Swing GUI library used by Jython scripts is powerful, but generally is considered to be the slowest and largest of all Python GUI options. Given that Python's Tkinter library is a portable and standard GUI solution, Java's proprietary user-interface tools by themselves are probably not reason enough to use the Jython implementation.

Jython is less robust than C Python

Jython is generally considered to be buggier than the standard C implementation of the language. This is certainly due to its younger age and smaller user base, and it varies from JVM to JVM, but you are more likely to hit snags in Jython. In contrast, C Python has been amazingly bug-free since its introduction in 1990.

Jython may be less portable than C Python

It's also worth noting that the core Python language is far more portable than Java (despite marketing statements to the contrary). Because of that, deploying standard Python code with the Java-based Jython implementation may actually *lessen* its portability. Naturally, this depends on the set of extensions you use, but standard Python runs today on everything from handheld PDAs, iPods, and cell phones to PCs, Cray supercomputers, and IBM mainframes.

Some incompatibilities between Jython and standard Python can be very subtle. For instance, Jython inherits all of the Java runtime engine's behavior, including Java security constraints and garbage collection. Java garbage collection is not based on standard Python's reference count scheme, and therefore can automatically collect cyclic objects.* It also means that some common Python programming idioms won't work. For example, it's typical in Python to code file-processing loops in this form:

```
for filename in bigfilenamelist:
    text = open(filename).read( )
    dostuffwith(text)
```

That works because files are automatically closed when garbage collected in standard Python, and we can be sure that the file object returned by the open call will be immediately garbage collected (it's temporary, so there are no more references as soon as we call read). This won't work in Jython, though, because we can't be sure when the temporary file object will be reclaimed. To avoid running out of file descriptors, we usually need to code this differently for Jython:

```
for filename in bigfilenamelist:
    file = open(filename)
    text = file.read( )
    dostuffwith(text)
    file.close( )
```

You may face a similar implementation mismatch if you assume that output files are immediately closed: open(name,'w').write(bytes) collects and closes the temporary file object and hence flushes the bytes out to the file under the standard C implementation of Python only, and Jython instead collects the file object at some arbitrary time in the future.

Picking Your Python

Because of concerns such as those just mentioned, the Jython implementation of the Python language is probably best used only in contexts where Java integration or web-browser interoperability is an important design goal. You should always be the judge, of course, but the standard C implementation seems better suited to most other Python applications. Still, that leaves a very substantial domain to Jython— almost all Java systems and programmers can benefit from adding Jython to their tool sets.

Jython allows programmers to write programs that use Java class libraries in a fraction of the code and complexity required by Java-coded equivalents. Hence, Jython excels as an extension language for Java-based systems, especially those that will run in the context of web browsers. Because Java is a standard component of most web browsers, Jython scripts will often run automatically without extra install steps on client machines. Furthermore, even Java-coded applications that have nothing to do with the Web can benefit from Jython's ease of use; its seamless integration with Java class libraries makes Jython arguably the best Java scripting and testing tool available today.

---

* But as of Python 2.0, its garbage collector can now collect cyclic objects too. See the 2.0 release notes and the gc standard library module in Python's library manual.

For most other applications, though, the standard Python implementation, possibly integrated with C and C++ components, is probably a better design choice. The resulting system will likely run faster, cost less to ship, have access to all Python extension modules, be more robust and portable, and be more easily maintained by people familiar with standard Python.

On the other hand, I want to point out again that the trade-offs listed here are mostly written from the Python perspective; if you are a Java developer looking for a scripting tool for Java-based systems, many of these detriments may be of minor concern. And to be fair, some of Jython's problems may be addressed in future releases; for instance, its speed will probably improve over time. Yet even as it exists today, Jython clearly makes an ideal extension-language solution for Java-based applications, and it offers a much more complete Java scripting solution than those currently available for other scripting languages.[*]

For more details, consult the Jython home page, currently maintained at *http://www. jython.org*. You will also find commercially published books about Jython as well; search the Web for pointers. See also the sidebar "The IronPython C# Python Compiler," later in this chapter, about the new Python implementation for the C#/.NET environment on Windows (and its Mono open source equivalent). Though still emerging, it seems likely that there will be three Pythons to choose from very soon and perhaps more in the future. All will likely implement the same core Python language we've used in this text, but they may emphasize alternative integration schemes, application domains, development environments, and so on.

Grail: A Python-Based Web Browser

I briefly mentioned the Grail browser near the start of Chapter 13. Many of Python's Internet tools date back to and reuse the work that went into Grail, a full-blown Internet web browser that:

- Is written entirely in Python
- Uses the Tkinter GUI API to implement its user interface and render pages
- Downloads and runs Python/Tkinter scripts as client-side applets

As mentioned earlier, Grail was something of a proof of concept for using Python to code large-scale Internet applications. It implements all the usual Internet protocols and works much like common browsers such as Netscape and Internet Explorer. Grail pages are implemented with the Tkinter text widgets that we met in Part III of this book.

---

[*] Other scripting languages have addressed Java integration by reimplementing a JVM in the underlying scripting language or by integrating their original C implementations with Java using the Java native call interface. Neither approach is anywhere near as seamless and powerful as generating real Java bytecode.

More interestingly, the Grail browser allows applets to be written in Python. Grail applets are simply bits of Python code that live on a server but are run on a client. If an HTML document references a Python class and file that live on a server machine, Grail automatically downloads the Python code over a socket and runs it on the client machine, passing it information about the browser's user interface. The downloaded Python code may use the passed-in browser context information to customize the user interface, add new kinds of widgets to it, and perform arbitrary client-side processing on the local machine. Roughly speaking, Python applets in Grail serve the same purposes as Java applets in common Internet browsers: they perform client-side tasks that are too complex or slow to implement with other technologies such as server-side CGI scripts and generated HTML.

A Simple Grail Applet Example

Writing Grail applets is remarkably straightforward. In fact, applets are really just Python/Tkinter programs; with a few exceptions, they don't need to "know" about Grail at all. Let's look at a short example; the code in Example 18-7 simply adds a button to the browser, which changes its appearance each time it's pressed (its bitmap is reconfigured in the button callback handler).

There are two components to this page definition: an HTML file and the Python applet code it references. As usual, the *grail.html* HTML file that follows describes how to format the web page when the HTML's URL address is selected in a browser. But here, the APP tag also specifies a Python applet (class) to be run by the browser. By default, the Python module is assumed to have the same name as the class and must be stored in the same location (URL directory) as the HTML file that references it. Additional APP tag options can override the applet's default location.

Example 18-7. PP3E\Internet\Other\Grail\grail.html

```
<HEAD>
<TITLE>Grail Applet Test Page</TITLE>
</HEAD>
<BODY>
<H1>Test an Applet Here!</H1>
Click this button!
<APP CLASS=Question>
</BODY>
```

The applet file referenced by the HTML is a Python script that adds widgets to the Tkinter-based Grail browser. Applets are simply classes in Python modules. When the APP tag is encountered in the HTML, the Grail browser downloads the Question.py source code module (Example 18-8) and makes an instance of its Question class, passing in the browser widget as the master (parent). The master is the hook that lets applets attach new widgets to the browser itself; applets extend the GUI constructed by the HTML in this way.

Example 18-8. PP3E\Internet\Other\Grail\Question.py

```
# Python applet file: Question.py
# in the same location (URL) as the HTML file
# that references it; adds widgets to browser;

from Tkinter import *

class Question:                          # run by Grail?
    def __init__(self, parent):          # parent=browser
        self.button = Button(parent,
                             bitmap='question',
                             command=self.action)
        self.button.pack()

    def action(self):
        if self.button['bitmap'] == 'question':
            self.button.config(bitmap='questhead')
        else:
            self.button.config(bitmap='question')

if __name__ == '__main__':
    root = Tk()                          # run standalone?
    button = Question(root)              # parent=Tk: top-level
    root.mainloop()
```

Notice that nothing in this class is Grail or Internet specific; in fact, it can be run (and tested) standalone as a Python/Tkinter program—try it. When run by Grail (with the browser/page object as the master), the button appears as part of the web page instead. Either way, its bitmap changes on each press.

In effect, Grail applets are simply Python modules that are linked into HTML pages by using the APP tag. The Grail browser downloads the source code identified by an APP tag and runs it locally on the client during the process of creating the new page. New widgets added to the page (like the button here) may run Python callbacks on the client later, when activated by the user.

Applets interact with users by creating one or more arbitrary Tkinter widgets. Of course, the previous example is artificial, but notice that the button's callback handler could do anything we can program in Python: updating persistent information, popping up new user interaction dialogs, calling C extensions, using Python's networking tools, and so on.

Having said all that, I should add that Grail is no longer formally maintained, and it is now used primarily for research purposes (Guido never intended for Grail to put Netscape or Microsoft out of business). You can still find the Grail for free with a web search, and you can use it for surfing the Web or experimenting with alternative web browser concepts, but it is not the active project it was a few years ago.

If you want to code web browser applets in Python, the more common approach today is to use the Jython system described previously. Embedding Python code in

HTML with the Active Scripting extension described later in this chapter is yet another way to integrate client-side code.

The Missing rexec Section

In the second edition of this book, this chapter included a section on the rexec restricted execution mode module in the standard library. This module allowed for safe execution of program code obtained from unknown sources.

For instance, expressions input in GUIs and code typed into web form fields cannot generally be given access to all machine resources—a malicious user might use this as a way to impact your computer. By default, such code has only as much machine access as the permissions of the running Python process allow. The rexec module went beyond this, to make system libraries and system-related functions such as open restricted; Python code could essentially approve or disapprove access to such tools on a case-by-case basis.

Since the second edition of this book, the rexec module (and a relative, bastion) have been shown to have vulnerabilities. In fact, the Python 2.4 manuals claim that they have been removed in Python 2.3. These modules may still be imported in 2.4, but they raise an exception whenever their code is used, with a message that they are unsafe in 2.2 and 2.3. This makes them unusable.

Unfortunately, there is still no replacement for rexec at the time of this writing. It seems likely that rexec will either be replaced or be upgraded in the future; see Python documentation for developments on this front.

As mentioned often in this text, for now be sure to convert strings to numbers with limited tools such as int and float, instead of with tools that treat strings as program code, such as eval and exec. If this is not sufficient, untrusted code must generally be run in a restricted process, and possibly be scanned for unsafe constructs. Security is a complex issue; in fact, one clever reader also pointed out a vulnerability in an example in this deleted section!

See also the discussion of Windows Active Scripting later in this chapter—because that support depended on rexec to run code embedded in web pages in a secure environment, it no longer is provided. Without language support for a secure sandbox, embedded code would have complete access to the underlying client machine. Until a rexec replacement emerges, Active Scripting has been withdrawn. This may be a temporary state, but it is impossible to predict.

XML Processing Tools

Python ships with XML parsing support in its standard library and plays host to a vigorous XML special-interest group. *XML* (eXtended Markup Language) is a tag-based markup language for describing many kinds of structured data. Among other things, it has been adopted in roles such as a standard database and Internet content representation by many companies. As an object-oriented scripting language, Python mixes remarkably well with XML's core notion of structured document interchange.

XML is based upon a tag syntax familiar to web page writers. Python's standard library xml module package includes tools for parsing XML, in both the SAX and the DOM parsing models. In short, SAX parsers provide a subclass with methods called during the parsing operation, and DOM parsers are given access to an object tree representing the (usually) already parsed document. SAX parsers are essentially state machines and must record details as the parse progresses; DOM parsers walk object trees using loops, attributes, and methods defined by the DOM standard.

Beyond these parsing tools, Python also ships with an xmlrpclib to support the XML-RPC protocol (remote procedure calls that transmit objects encoded as XML over HTTP), as well as a standard HTML parser, htmllib, that works on similar principles and is based upon the sgmllib SGML parser module. The third-party domain has even more XML-related tools; some of these are maintained separately from Python to allow for more flexible release schedules.

A Brief Introduction to XML Parsing

XML processing is a large, evolving topic, and it is mostly beyond the scope of this book. For an example of a simple XML parsing task, though, consider the XML file in Example 18-9. This file defines a handful of O'Reilly Python books—ISBN numbers as attributes, and titles and authors as nested tags.

Example 18-9. PP3E\Internet\Other\XML\books.xml

```
<catalog>
  <book isbn="0-596-00128-2">
    <title>Python &amp; XML</title>
    <author>Jones, Drake</author>
  </book>
  <book isbn="0-596-00085-5">
    <title>Programming Python</title>
    <author>Lutz</author>
  </book>
  <book isbn="0-596-00281-5">
    <title>Learning Python</title>
    <author>Lutz, Ascher</author>
  </book>
  <book isbn="0-596-00797-3">
    <title>Python Cookbook</title>
    <author>Martelli, Ravenscroft, Ascher</author>
  </book>
  <!-- imagine more entries here -->
</catalog>
```

Now, suppose we wish to parse this XML code, extracting just the ISBN numbers and titles for each book defined, and stuffing the details into a dictionary indexed by ISBN number. Python's XML parsing tools let us do this in an accurate way. Example 18-10, for instance, defines a SAX-based parsing procedure: its class implements callback methods that will be called during the parse.

Example 18-10. PP3E\Internet\Other\XML\bookhandler.py

```
###################################
# SAX is a callback-based API
# for intercepting parser events
###################################

import xml.sax.handler

class BookHandler(xml.sax.handler.ContentHandler):
    def __init__(self):                        # handle XML parser events
        self.inTitle = 0                       # a state machine model
        self.mapping = {}

    def startElement(self, name, attributes):
        if name == "book":                     # on start book tag
            self.buffer = ""                   # save ISBN for dict key
            self.isbn = attributes["isbn"]
        elif name == "title":                  # on start title tag
            self.inTitle = 1                   # save title text to follow

    def characters(self, data):
        if self.inTitle:                       # on text within tag
            self.buffer += data                # save text if in title

    def endElement(self, name):
        if name == "title":                    # on end title tag
            self.inTitle = 0                   # store title text in dict
            self.mapping[self.isbn] = self.buffer
```

The SAX model is efficient, but it is potentially confusing at first glance, because the class must keep track of where the parse currently is using state information. For example, when the title tag is first detected, we set a state flag and initialize a buffer; as each character within the title tag is parsed, we append it to the buffer until the ending portion of the title tag is encountered. The net effect saves the title tag's content as a string.

To kick off the parse, we make a parser, set its handler to the class in Example 18-10, and start the parse; as Python scans the XML file our class's methods are called automatically as components are encountered:

```
C:\...\PP3E\Internet\Other\XML>python
>>> import xml.sax
>>> import bookhandler
```

```
>>> import pprint
>>>
>>> parser = xml.sax.make_parser()
>>> handler = bookhandler.BookHandler()
>>> parser.setContentHandler(handler)
>>> parser.parse('books.xml')
>>>
>>> pprint.pprint(handler.mapping)
{u'0-596-00085-5': u'Programming Python',
 u'0-596-00128-2': u'Python & XML',
 u'0-596-00281-5': u'Learning Python',
 u'0-596-00797-3': u'Python Cookbook'}
```

When the parse is completed, we use the Python pprint ("pretty printer") module to display the result—the mapping dictionary object attached to our handler. Beginning with Python 2.3 the Expat parser is included with Python as the underlying parsing engine that drives the events intercepted by our class.

DOM parsing is perhaps simpler to understand—we simply traverse a tree of objects after the parse—but it might be less efficient for large documents, if the document is parsed all at once ahead of time. DOM also supports random access to document parts via tree fetches; in SAX, we are limited to a single linear parse. Example 18-11 is a DOM-based equivalent to the SAX parser listed earlier.

Example 18-11. PP3E\Internet\Other\XML\dombook.py

```
#####################################
# DOM gives the whole document to the
# application as a traversable object
#####################################

import pprint
import xml.dom.minidom
from xml.dom.minidom import Node

doc = xml.dom.minidom.parse("books.xml")       # load doc into object
                                               # usually parsed up front
mapping = {}
for node in doc.getElementsByTagName("book"):  # traverse DOM object
  isbn = node.getAttribute("isbn")             # via DOM object API
  L = node.getElementsByTagName("title")
  for node2 in L:
    title = ""
    for node3 in node2.childNodes:
      if node3.nodeType == Node.TEXT_NODE:
        title += node3.data
    mapping[isbn] = title

# mapping now has the same value as in the SAX example
pprint.pprint(mapping)
```

The output of this script is the same as what we generated interactively for the SAX parser; here, though, it is built up by walking the document object tree after the parse has finished using method calls and attributes defined by the cross-language DOM standard specification:

```
C:\...\PP3E\Internet\Other\XML>dombook.py
{u'0-596-00085-5': u'Programming Python',
 u'0-596-00128-2': u'Python & XML',
 u'0-596-00281-5': u'Learning Python',
 u'0-596-00797-3': u'Python Cookbook'}
```

Naturally, there is much more to Python's XML support than these simple examples imply. In deference to space, though, here are pointers to XML resources in lieu of additional examples:

Standard library

First, be sure to consult the Python library manual for more on the standard library's XML support tools. See the entries for xml.sax and xml.dom for more on this section's examples.

ElementTree

The popular ElementTree extension provides easy-to-use tools for parsing, changing, and generating XML documents. It represents documents as a tree of Python objects (in the spirit of HTMLgen described earlier in this chapter). As of this writing, ElementTree (and a fast C implementation of it) is still a third-party package, but its core components were scheduled to be incorporated into the standard library of Python 2.5 in six months, as the package xml.etree. See the 2.5 library manual for details.

PyXML SIG tools

You can also find Python XML tools and documentation at the XML Special Interest Group (SIG) web page at *http://www.python.org* (click on the SIGs link near the top). This SIG is dedicated to wedding XML technologies with Python, and it publishes a free XML tools package distribution called PyXML. That package contains tools not yet part of the standard Python distribution. Much of the standard library's XML support originated in PyXML, though that package still contains tools not present in Python itself.

Third-party tools

You can also find free, third-party Python support tools for XML on the Web by following links at the XML SIGs web page. Of special interest, the 4Suite package from Fourthought provides integrated tools for XML processing, including open technologies such as DOM, SAX, RDF, XSLT, XInclude, XPointer, XLink, and XPath.

Documentation

O'Reilly offers a book dedicated to the subject of XML processing in Python, *Python & XML*, written by Christopher A. Jones and Fred L. Drake, Jr.

As usual, be sure to check Python's web site or your favorite web search engine for more recent developments on this front.

Windows Web Scripting Extensions

Although this book doesn't cover the Windows-specific extensions available for Python in detail, a quick look at Internet scripting tools available to Windows programmers is in order here. On Windows, Python can be used as a scripting language for both the Active Scripting and the Active Server Pages systems, which provide client- and server-side control of HTML-based applications. More generally, Python programs can also take the role of COM and DCOM clients and servers on Windows. The .NET framework provides additional options for Python programmers.

This section is largely Microsoft specific—if you are interested in portability, other systems in this chapter may address your needs better (see Jython's client-side applets, PSP's server-side scripting support, and Zope's server-side object publishing model). On the other hand, if portability isn't a concern, the following techniques provide powerful ways to script both sides of a web conversation with Python.

Active Scripting: Client-Side Embedding

Active Scripting—sometimes known as ActiveX Scripting, or just ActiveX—is a technology that allows scripting languages to communicate with hosting applications. The hosting application provides an application-specific *object model API*, which exposes objects and functions for use in the scripting language programs.

In one of its more common roles, Active Scripting provides support that allows scripting language code embedded in HTML pages to communicate with the local web browser through an automatically exposed object model API. Internet Explorer, for instance, utilizes Active Scripting to export things such as global functions and user-interface objects, for use in scripts embedded in HTML that are run on the client. With Active Scripting, Python code may be embedded in a web page's HTML between special tags; such code is executed on the client machine and serves the same roles as embedded JavaScript and VBScript.

Unfortunately, support for client-side Active Scripting with Python under Internet Explorer no longer works as I write this update using Python 2.4. It relied on the rexec module to implement security for embedded code. As mentioned earlier in this chapter, in the sidebar "The Missing rexec Section," that module was withdrawn due to vulnerabilities. Without it, the Windows extensions have no way to ensure that code embedded in web pages won't do damage on the client—the code would have full access to the client machine, including all its files and data.

Instead of leaving this security hole open, Active Scripting on the client has been disabled, and Python code embedded in HTML will no longer run under Internet Explorer. I've kept a brief overview of its workings in this book, though, because this may be a temporary regression; it might be reenabled in the future if a rexec replacement arises. Moreover, its use in restricted intranets may still be reasonable (though you'll have to modify the Windows extensions code to turn it back on).

Despite the Internet Explorer regression, Python still works as a scripting engine inside trusted hosts, including the Windows Scripting Host, and ASP. In addition, JavaScript or VBScript coded embedded in web pages can still invoke Python-coded COM components on the client. At present, though, Python code embedded in web pages cannot be run on the client directly, and the section you are reading is included for historic or future interest. Check up-to-date resources to see whether Active Scripting under Internet Explorer on the client has been turned back on by the time you read these words.

Active Scripting basics

Embedding Python in client-side HTML works only on machines where Python is installed and Internet Explorer is configured to know about the Python language. Because of that, this technology doesn't apply to most of the browsers in cyberspace today. On the other hand, if you can configure the machines on which a system is to be delivered, this is a nonissue.

Before we get into a Python example, let's look at the way standard browser installations handle other languages embedded in HTML. By default, Internet Explorer knows about JavaScript (really, Microsoft's Jscript implementation of it) and VBScript (a Visual Basic derivative), so you can embed both of those languages in any delivery scenario. For instance, the HTML file in Example 18-12 embeds JavaScript code, the default Internet Explorer scripting language on my PC.

Example 18-12. PP3E\Internet\Other\Win\activescript-js.html

```
<HTML>
<BODY>
<H1>Embedded code demo: JavaScript</H1>
<SCRIPT>
```

Example 18-12. PP3E\Internet\Other\Win\activescript-js.html (continued)

```
// pop up 3 alert boxes while this page is
// being constructed on client side by IE;
// JavaScript is the default script language,
// and alert is an automatically exposed name

function message(i) {
    if (i == 2) {
        alert("Finished!");
    }
    else {
        alert("A JavaScript-generated alert => " + i);
    }
}

for (count = 0; count < 3; count += 1) {
    message(count);
}

</SCRIPT>
</BODY></HTML>
```

All the text between the <SCRIPT> and </SCRIPT> tags in this file is JavaScript code. Don't worry about its syntax—this book isn't about JavaScript. The important thing to know is how this code is used by the browser.

When a browser detects a block of code like this while building up a new page, it strips out the code, locates the appropriate interpreter, tells the interpreter about global object names, and passes the code to the interpreter for execution. The global names become variables in the embedded code and provide links to browser context. For instance, the name alert in the code block refers to a global function that creates a message box. Other global names refer to objects that give access to the browser's user interface: window objects, document objects, and so on.

You can run this HTML file on the local machine by clicking on its name in a file explorer. It can also be stored on a remote server and accessed via its URL in a browser. Whichever way you start it, three pop-up alert boxes created by the embedded code appear during page construction. Figure 18-9 shows one under Internet Explorer.

Embedding Python in HTML

So how about putting Python code in that page, then? Alas, we need to do a bit more first. Although Internet Explorer is language neutral in principle, it does support some languages better than others, at least today. Moreover, other browsers may be more rigid and may not support the Active Scripting concept at all.

To make the Python version work, you must do more than simply installing Python on your PC. You must also install the PyWin32 package separately and run its tools

Figure 18-9. Internet Explorer running embedded JavaScript code

to register Python to Internet Explorer. The PyWin32 package includes the win32com extensions for Python, plus the *PythonWin* IDE (a GUI for editing and running Python programs, written with the MFC interfaces in PyWin32) and many other Windows-specific tools not covered in this book.

In the past, registering Python for use in Internet Explorer was either an automatic side-effect of installing PyWin32 or was achieved by running a script located in the Windows extension's code in Lib\site-packages of the Python install tree, named *win32comext\axscript\client\pyscript.py*. Because this package changes over time, though, see its documentation for current registration details.

Once you've registered Python with Internet Explorer, Python code embedded in HTML works just like our JavaScript example—Internet Explorer presets Python global names to expose its object model and passes the embedded code to your Python interpreter for execution. Example 18-13 shows our alerts example again, programmed with embedded Python code.

Example 18-13. PP3E\Internet\Other\Win\activescript-py.html

```
<HTML>
<BODY>
<H1>Embedded code demo: Python</H1>
<SCRIPT Language=Python>

# do the same but with Python, if configured;
# embedded Python code shows three alert boxes
# as page is loaded; any Python code works here,
# and uses auto-imported global funcs and objects
```

Example 18-13. PP3E\Internet\Other\Win\activescript-py.html (continued)

```
def message(i):
    if i == 2:
        alert("Finished!")
    else:
        alert("A Python-generated alert => %d" % i)

for count in range(3): message(count)

</SCRIPT>
</BODY></HTML>
```

Figure 18-10 shows one of the three pop ups you should see when you open this file in Internet Explorer after installing PyWin32 and registering Python to Internet Explorer. Note that the first time you access this page, Internet Explorer may need to load Python, which could induce an apparent delay on slower machines; later accesses generally start up much faster because Python has already been loaded.

Figure 18-10. Internet Explorer running embedded Python code (currently disabled)

With a simple configuration step, Python code can be embedded in HTML and be made to run under Internet Explorer, just like JavaScript and VBScript. Although this works on only some browsers and platforms, for many applications, the portability constraint is acceptable. Active Scripting is a straightforward way to add client-side Python scripting for web browsers, especially when you can control the target delivery environment. For instance, machines running on an intranet within a company may have well-known configurations. In such scenarios, Active Scripting lets developers apply all the power of Python in their client-side scripts.

Active Server Pages: Server-Side Embedding

Active Server Pages (ASPs) use a similar model: Python code is embedded in the HTML that defines a web page. But ASP is a *server-side* technology—embedded Python code runs on the server machine and uses an object-based API to dynamically generate portions of the HTML that is ultimately sent back to the client-side browser. As we saw in the last two chapters, Python server-side CGI scripts embed and generate HTML, and they deal with raw inputs and output streams. By contrast, server-side ASP scripts are embedded in HTML and use a higher-level object model to get their work done.

Just like client-side Active Scripting, ASP requires you to install Python and the Python Windows PyWin32 extensions package. But because ASP runs embedded code on the server, you need to configure Python only on one machine. Like CGI scripts in general, this generally makes Python ASP scripting much more widely applicable, as you don't need Python support on every client. Moreover, because you control the content of the embedded code on your server, this is a secure configuration. Unlike CGI scripts, however, ASP requires you to run Microsoft's Internet Information Server (IIS) today.

A short ASP example

We can't discuss ASP in any real detail here, but here's an example of what an ASP file looks like when Python code is embedded:

```
<HTML><BODY>
<SCRIPT RunAt=Server Language=Python>
#
# code here is run at the server
#
</SCRIPT>
</BODY></HTML>
```

As before, code may be embedded inside SCRIPT tag pairs. This time, we tell ASP to run the code at the server with the RunAt option; if omitted, the code and its tags are passed through to the client and are run by Internet Explorer (if configured properly). ASP also recognizes code enclosed in <% and %> delimiters and allows a language to be specified for the entire page. This form is handier if there are multiple chunks of code in a page, as shown in Example 18-14.

Example 18-14. PP3E\Internet\Other\Win\asp-py.asp

```
<HTML><BODY>
<%@ Language=Python %>

<%
#
```

Example 18-14. PP3E\Internet\Other\Win\asp-py.asp (continued)

```
# Python code here, using global names Request (input), Response (output), etc.
#
Response.Write("Hello ASP World from URL %s" %
                    Request.ServerVariables("PATH_INFO"))
%>
</BODY></HTML>
```

However the code is marked, ASP executes it on the server after passing in a handful of named objects that the code may use to access input, output, and server context. For instance, the automatically imported Request and Response objects give access to input and output context. The code here calls a Response.Write method to send text back to the browser on the client (much like a print statement in a simple Python CGI script), as well as Request.ServerVariables to access environment variable information.

To make this script run live, you'll need to place it in the proper directory on a server machine running IIS with ASP support, after installing and registering Python. Although this is a simple example, the full power of the Python language is at your disposal when it is embedded like this. By combining Python-generated content with HTML formatting, this yields a natural way to generate pages dynamically and separate logic from display. It's similar in spirit to the more platform-neutral Zope DTML idea we saw earlier, and the PSP pages we'll meet later.

The COM Connection

At their core, both Internet Explorer and IIS are based on the COM (Component Object Model) integration system—they implement their object APIs with standard COM interfaces and look to the rest of the world like any other COM object. From a broader perspective, Python can be used as both a scripting and an implementation language for any COM object. Although the COM mechanism used to run Python code embedded within HTML is automated and hidden, it can also be employed explicitly to make Python programs take the role of both COM clients and COM servers. COM is a general integration technology and is not strictly tied to Internet scripting, but a brief introduction here might help demystify some of the Active Scripting magic behind HTML embedding.

A brief introduction to COM

COM is a Microsoft technology for language-neutral component integration. It is sometimes marketed as ActiveX, partially derived from a system called Object Linking and Embedding (OLE), and it is the technological heart of the Active Scripting system we met earlier.* COM also sports a distributed extension known as DCOM that allows communicating objects to be run on remote machines. Implementing DCOM often simply involves running through Windows registry configuration steps to associate servers with machines on which they run.

Operationally, COM defines a standard way for objects implemented in arbitrary languages to talk to each other, using a published object model. For example, COM components can be written in and used by programs written in Visual Basic, Visual C++, Delphi, PowerBuilder, and Python. Because the COM indirection layer hides the differences among all the languages involved, it's possible for Visual Basic to use an object implemented in Python, and vice versa.

Moreover, many software packages register COM interfaces to support end-user scripting. For instance, Microsoft Excel publishes an object model that allows any COM-aware scripting language to start Excel and programmatically access spreadsheet data. Similarly, Microsoft Word can be scripted through COM to automatically manipulate documents. COM's language neutrality means that programs written in any programming language with a COM interface, including Visual Basic and Python, can be used to automate Excel and Word processing.

Of most relevance to this chapter, Active Scripting also provides COM objects that allow scripts embedded in HTML to communicate with Microsoft's Internet Explorer (on the client) and IIS (on the server). Both systems register their object models with Windows such that they can be invoked from any COM-aware language. For example, when Internet Explorer extracts and executes Python code embedded in HTML, some Python variable names are automatically preset to COM object components that give access to Internet Explorer context and tools (e.g., alert in Example 18-13). Calls to such components from Python code are automatically routed through COM back to Internet Explorer.

Python COM clients

With the PyWin32 Python extension package installed, though, we can also write Python programs that serve as registered COM servers and clients, even if they have nothing to do with the Internet at all. For example, the Python program in Example 18-15 acts as a client to the Microsoft Word COM object.

---

* Roughly, OLE was a precursor to COM, and Active Scripting is just a technology that defines COM interfaces for activities such as passing objects to arbitrary programming language interpreters by name. Active Scripting is not much more than COM itself with a few extensions, but acronym and buzzword overload seem to run rampant in the Windows development world. To further muddy the waters, .NET is essentially a successor to COM.

Example 18-15. PP3E\Internet\Other\Win\comclient.py

```
######################################################################
# a COM client coded in Python: talk to MS-Word via its COM object
# model; uses either dynamic dispatch (runtime lookup/binding),
# or the static and faster type-library dispatch if makepy.py has
# been run; install the Windows PyWin32 extensions package to use
# this interface; Word runs hidden unless Visible is set to 1 (and
# Visible lets you watch, but impacts interactive Word sessions);
######################################################################

from sys import argv
docdir = 'C:\\temp\\'
if len(argv) == 2: docdir = argv[1]            # ex: comclient.py a:\

from win32com.client import Dispatch            # early or late binding
word  = Dispatch('Word.Application')            # connect/start Word
word.Visible = 1                                # else Word runs hidden

# create and save new doc file
newdoc = word.Documents.Add()
spot   = newdoc.Range(0,0)                      # call Word methods
spot.InsertBefore('Hello COM client world!')
newdoc.SaveAs(docdir + 'pycom.doc')            # insert some text
newdoc.SaveAs(docdir + 'copy.doc')             # save in doc file
newdoc.Close()

# open and change a doc file
olddoc = word.Documents.Open(docdir + 'copy.doc')
finder = word.Selection.Find
finder.text = 'COM'
finder.Execute()
word.Selection.TypeText('Automation')
olddoc.Close()

# and so on: see Word's COM interface specs
```

This particular script starts Microsoft Word—known as Word.Application to script-ing clients—if needed, and converses with it through COM. That is, calls in this script are automatically routed from Python to Microsoft Word and back. This code relies heavily on calls exported by Word, which are not described in this book. Armed with documentation for Word's object API, though, we could use such calls to write Python scripts that automate document updates, insert and replace text, create and print documents, and so on.

For instance, Figure 18-11 shows the two Word *.doc* files generated when the previous script is run on Windows: both are new files, and one is a copy of the other with a text replacement applied. The interaction that occurs while the script runs is more interesting. Because Word's Visible attribute is set to 1, you can actually *watch* Word inserting and replacing text, saving files, and so on, in response to calls in the script. (Alas, I couldn't quite figure out how to paste a movie clip in this book.)

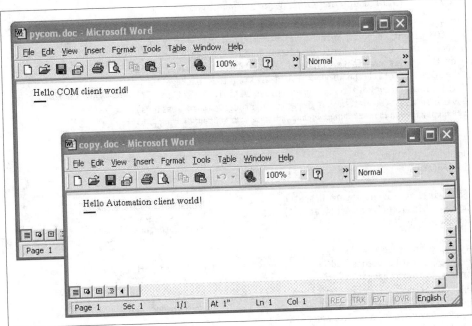

Figure 18-11. Word files generated by Python COM client

In general, Python COM client calls may be dispatched either dynamically by run-time look-ups in the Windows registry, or statically using type libraries created by a Python utility script. These dispatch modes are sometimes called *late* and *early* dispatch binding, respectively. See PyWin32 documentation for more details.

Luckily, we don't need to know which scheme will be used when we write client scripts. The Dispatch call used in Example 18-15 to connect to Word is smart enough to use static binding if server type libraries exist or to use dynamic binding if they do not. To force dynamic binding and ignore any generated type libraries, replace the first line with this:

```
from win32com.client.dynamic import Dispatch     # always late binding
```

However calls are dispatched, the Python COM interface performs all the work of locating the named server, looking up and calling the desired methods or attributes, and converting Python datatypes according to a standard type map as needed. In the context of Active Scripting, the underlying COM model works the same way, but the server is something like Internet Explorer or IIS (not Word), the set of available calls differs, and some Python variables are preassigned to COM server objects. The notions of "client" and "server" can become somewhat blurred in these scenarios, but the net result is similar.

Python COM servers

Python scripts can also be deployed as COM *servers* and can provide methods and attributes that are accessible to any COM-aware programming language or system. This topic is too complex to cover in depth here too, but exporting a Python object to COM is mostly just a matter of providing a set of class attributes to identify the server and utilizing the proper win32com registration utility calls. Example 18-16 is a simple COM server coded in Python as a class.

Example 18-16. PP3E\Internet\Other\Win\comserver.py

```
################################################################
# a COM server coded in Python; the _reg_ class attributes
# give registry parameters, and others list methods and attrs;
# for this to work, you must install Python and the PyWin32
# package, this module file must live on your Python path,
# and the server must be registered to COM (see code at end);
# run pythoncom.CreateGuid( ) to make your own _reg_clsid_ key;
################################################################

import sys
from   win32com.server.exception import COMException     # what to raise
import win32com.server.util                              # server tools
globhellos = 0

class MyServer:

    # COM info settings
    _reg_clsid_      = '{1BA63CC0-7CF8-11D4-98D8-BB74DD3DDE3C}'
    _reg_desc_       = 'Example Python Server'
    _reg_progid_     = 'PythonServers.MyServer'           # external name
    _reg_class_spec_ = 'comserver.MyServer'               # internal name
    _public_methods_ = ['Hello', 'Square']
    _public_attrs_   = ['version']

    # Python methods
    def __init__(self):
        self.version = 1.0
        self.hellos  = 0
    def Square(self, arg):                                # exported methods
        return arg ** 2
    def Hello(self):                                      # global variables
        global globhellos                                 # retain state, but
        globhellos  += 1                                  # self vars don't
        self.hellos += 1
        return 'Hello COM server world [%d, %d]' % (globhellos, self.hellos)

# registration functions
def Register(pyclass=MyServer):
    from win32com.server.register import UseCommandLine
    UseCommandLine(pyclass)
def Unregister(classid=MyServer._reg_clsid_):
    from win32com.server.register import UnregisterServer
```

Example 18-16. PP3E\Internet\Other\Win\comserver.py (continued)

```
    UnregisterServer(classid)

if __name__ == '__main__':      # register server if file run or clicked
    Register()                  # unregisters if --unregister cmd-line arg
```

As usual, this Python file must be placed in a directory in Python's module search path before it can be used by a COM client. Besides the server class itself, the file includes code at the bottom to automatically register and unregister the server to COM when the file is run:

- To *register* a server, simply call the UseCommandLine function in the win32com. server.register package and pass in the Python server class. This function uses all the special class attribute settings to make the server known to COM. The file is set to automatically call the registration tools if it is run by itself (e.g., when clicked in a file explorer).

- To *unregister* a server, simply pass an --unregister argument on the command line when running this file. When run this way, the script automatically calls UseCommandLine again to unregister the server; as its name implies, this function inspects command-line arguments and knows to do the right thing when --unregister is passed. You can also unregister servers explicitly with the UnregisterServer call demonstrated near the end of this script, though this is less commonly used.

Perhaps the more interesting part of this code, though, is the special class attribute assignments at the start of the Python class. These class annotations can provide server registry settings (the _reg_ attributes), accessibility constraints (the _public_ names), and more. Such attributes are specific to the Python COM framework, and their purpose is to configure the server.

For example, the _reg_class_spec_ is simply the Python module and class names separated by a period. If it is set, the resident Python interpreter uses this attribute to import the module and create an instance of the Python class it defines, when accessed by a client.[*]

Other attributes may be used to identify the server in the Windows registry. The _reg_clsid_ attribute, for instance, gives a globally unique identifier (GUID) for the server and should vary in every COM server you write. In other words, don't use the value in this script. Instead, do what I did to make this ID, and paste the result returned on your machine into your script:

```
C:\...>python
>>> import pythoncom
```

---

[*] But note that the _reg_class_spec_ attribute is no longer strictly needed and not specifying it avoids a number of PYTHONPATH issues. Because such settings are prone to change, you should always consult the latest Windows extensions package reference manuals for details on this and other class annotation attributes.

```
>>> pythoncom.CreateGuid()
IID('{1BA63CC0-7CF8-11D4-98D8-BB74DD3DDE3C}')
```

GUIDs are generated by running a tool shipped with the Windows extensions package; simply import and call the `pythoncom.CreateGuid` function and insert the returned text in the script. Windows uses the ID stamped into your network card to come up with a complex ID that is likely to be unique across servers and machines. The more symbolic program ID string, `_reg_progid_`, can be used by clients to name servers too, but it is not as likely to be unique.

The rest of the server class is simply pure-Python methods, which implement the exported behavior of the server; that is, things to be called or fetched from clients. Once this Python server is annotated, coded, and registered, it can be used in any COM-aware language. For instance, programs written in Visual Basic, C++, Delphi, and Python may access its public methods and attributes through COM; of course, other Python programs can also simply import this module, but the point of COM is to open up components for even wider reuse.

Using the Python server from a Python client. Let's put this Python COM server to work. The Python script in Example 18-17 tests the server in Example 18-16 in two ways: first by simply importing and calling it directly, and then by employing Python's client-side COM interfaces that were shown earlier to invoke it less directly. When going through COM, the `PythonServers.MyServer` symbolic program ID we gave the server (by setting the class attribute `_reg_progid_`) can be used to connect to this server from any language—including Python.

Example 18-17. PP3E\Internet\Other\Win\comserver-test.py

```
######################################################################
# test the Python-coded COM server from Python two ways
######################################################################

def testViaPython():
    from comserver import MyServer          # test without COM
    object = MyServer()                     # use Python class name
    print object.Hello()                    # works as for any class
    print object.Square(8)
    print object.version

def testViaCom():
    from win32com.client import Dispatch
    server = Dispatch('PythonServers.MyServer')   # test via client-side COM
    print server.Hello()                          # use Windows registry name
    print server.Square(12)                       # call public methods
    print server.version
                                                  # access attributes
if __name__ == '__main__':
    testViaPython()
    testViaCom()                            # test module, server
    testViaCom()                            # COM object retains state
```

If we've properly configured and registered the Python COM server, we can talk to it by running this Python test script. In the following, we run the server and client files from an MS-DOS console box (though they can usually be run by mouse clicks as well). The first command runs the server file by itself to register the server to COM; the second executes the test script to exercise the server both as an imported module (testViaPython) and as a server accessed through COM (testViaCom):

```
C:\Python24>python d:\PP3E\Internet\Other\Win\comserver.py
Registered: PythonServers.MyServer

C:\Python24>python d:\PP3E\Internet\Other\Win\comserver-test.py
Hello COM server world [1, 1]
64
1.0
Hello COM server world [2, 1]
144
1.0
Hello COM server world [3, 1]
144
1.0

C:\Python24>python d:\PP3E\Internet\Other\Win\comserver.py --unregister
Unregistered: PythonServers.MyServer
```

Notice the two numbers at the end of the Hello output lines: they reflect current values of a global variable and a server instance attribute. Global variables in the server's module retain state as long as the server module is loaded; by contrast, each COM Dispatch (and Python class) call makes a new instance of the server class, and hence new instance attributes. The third command unregisters the server in COM, as a cleanup step. Interestingly, once the server has been unregistered, it's no longer usable, at least not through COM (this output has been truncated to fit here):

```
C:\Python24>python d:\PP3E\Internet\Other\Win\comserver-test.py
Hello COM server world [1, 1]
64
1.0
Traceback (innermost last):
  File "comserver-test.py", line 21, in ?
    testViaCom()                                    # COM object retains
  File "comserver-test.py", line 14, in testViaCom
    server = Dispatch('PythonServers.MyServer')     # use Windows register
  ...more deleted...
pywintypes.com_error: (-2147221005, 'Invalid class string', None, None)
```

Using the Python server from a Visual Basic client. The *comserver-test.py* script just listed demonstrates how to use a Python COM server from a Python COM client. Once we've created and registered a Python COM server, though, it's available to any language that sports a COM interface. For instance, Visual Basic code can run the Python methods in Example 18-16 just as well. Example 18-18 shows the sort of code we write to access the Python server from Visual Basic. Clients coded in other languages (e.g., Delphi or Visual C++) are analogous, but syntax and instantiation calls vary.

Example 18-18. PP3E\Internet\Other\Win\comserver-test.bas

```
Sub runpyserver( )
    ' use python server from vb client
    ' alt-f8 in word to start macro editor
    Set server = CreateObject("PythonServers.MyServer")
    hello1 = server.hello( )
    square = server.square(32)
    pyattr = server.Version
    hello2 = server.hello( )
    sep = Chr(10)
    Result = hello1 & sep & square & sep & pyattr & sep & hello2
    MsgBox Result
End Sub
```

The real trick, if you're not a Windows developer, is how to run this code. Because Visual Basic is embedded in Microsoft Office products such as Word, one approach is to test this code in the context of those systems. Try this: start Word, and then press Alt and F8 together, and you'll wind up in the Word macro dialog. There, enter a new macro name, and then press Create, and you'll find yourself in a development interface where you can paste and run the VB code just shown.

Running the Visual Basic code in this context produces the Word pop-up box in Figure 18-12, showing the results of Visual Basic calls to our Python COM server, initiated by Word. Global variable and instance attribute values at the end of both Hello reply messages are the same this time, because we make only one instance of the Python server class: in Visual Basic, by calling CreateObject, with the program ID of the desired server.

Figure 18-12. Visual Basic client running Python COM server in Word

If your client code runs but generates a COM error, make sure that the PyWin32 package has been installed, that the Python server module file is in a directory on Python's import search path, and that the server file has been run by itself to register the server with COM. If none of that helps, you're probably already beyond the scope of this text. Please see additional Windows programming resources for more details.

Using the Python server with client-side Active Scripting. Another way to kick off the Visual Basic client code is to embed it in a web page and rely on Internet Explorer to strip it out and launch it for us. In fact, even though Python cannot currently be embedded in a page's HTML directly (see the note in the earlier section "Active Scripting: Client-Side Embedding"), it is OK to embed code which runs a registered Python COM component indirectly. Example 18-19, for instance, embeds similar Visual Basic code in a web page; when this file is opened by Internet Explorer, it runs our Python COM server from Example 18-16 again, producing the page and pop up in Figure 18-13.

Example 18-19. PP3E\Internet\Other\Win\comserver-test.bas

```
<HTML><BODY>
<P>Run Python COM server from VBScript embedded in HTML via IE</P>
<SCRIPT Language=VBScript>

Sub runpyserver( )
    ' use python server from vb client
    ' alt-f8 in word to start macro editor
    Set server = CreateObject("PythonServers.MyServer")
    hello1 = server.hello( )
    square = server.square(9)
    pyattr = server.Version
    hello2 = server.hello( )
    sep = Chr(10)
    Result = hello1 & sep & square & sep & pyattr & sep & hello2
    MsgBox Result
End Sub

runpyserver( )

</SCRIPT>
</BODY></HTML>
```

Trace through the calls on your own to see what is happening. An incredible amount of routing is going on here—from Internet Explorer to Visual Basic to Python and back, and a control flow spanning three systems and HTML and Python files—but with COM, it simply works. This structure opens the door to arbitrary client-side scripting from web pages with Python. Because Python COM components invoked from web pages must be manually and explicitly registered on the client, it is secure.

The bigger COM picture: DCOM

So what does writing Python COM servers have to do with the Internet motif of this chapter? After all, Python code embedded in HTML simply plays the role of COM client Internet Explorer or IIS systems that usually run locally. Besides showing how such systems work their magic, I've presented this topic here because COM, at least in its grander world view, is also about communicating over networks.

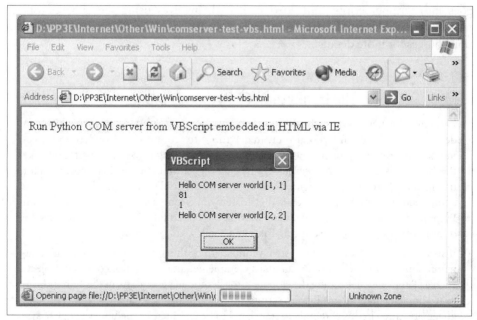

Figure 18-13. Internet Explorer running VBScript running Python COM server

Although we can't get into details in this text, COM's *distributed* extensions, DCOM, make it possible to implement Python-coded COM servers to run on machines that are arbitrarily remote from clients. Although largely transparent to clients, COM object calls like those in the preceding client scripts may imply network transfers of arguments and results. In such a configuration, COM may be used as a general client/server implementation model and an alternative to technologies such as Remote Procedure Calls (RPC).

For some applications, this distributed object approach may even be a viable alternative to Python's other client- and server-side scripting tools we've studied in this part of the book. Moreover, even when not distributed, COM is an alternative to the lower-level Python/C integration techniques we'll meet later in this book.

Once its learning curve is scaled, COM is a straightforward way to integrate arbitrary components and provides a standardized way to script and reuse systems. However, COM also implies a level of dispatch indirection overhead and is a Windows-only solution at this writing. Because of that, it is generally not as fast or as portable as some of the other client/server and C integration schemes discussed in this book. The relevance of such trade-offs varies per application.

As you can probably surmise, there is much more to the Windows scripting story than we cover here. If you are interested in more details, O'Reilly's *Python Programming on Win32* (by Mark Hammond and Andy Robinson) provides an in-depth presentation of these and other Windows development topics. Much of the effort that goes into writing scripts embedded in HTML involves using the exposed object model APIs, which are deliberately skipped in this book; see Windows documentation sources for more details.

The IronPython C# Python Compiler

Late-breaking news: as this third edition was being developed, Microsoft hired Python developer Jim Huginin (who also created Jython) to work on his IronPython implementation. IronPython is a new, independent Python language implementation, like the Jython system described earlier in this chapter, but it compiles Python scripts for use in the Microsoft C# language environment and .NET Framework—a software component system based on XML that fosters cross-language interoperability. IronPython will also work on the Mono open source version of .NET. As such, it opens the door to other Python web-scripting roles and modes.

If successful, this new compiler system promises to be the third complete Python implementation (with Jython and the standard C implementation, and not counting projects such as PyPy) and an exciting development for Python in general. As in the Jython Java-based implementation, IronPython scripts are coded using the standard Python core language presented in this text and are translated to be executed by the underlying C# system. Moreover, .NET interfaces are automatically integrated for use in Python scripts: Python classes may freely use, subclass, and act as .NET components.

Also like Jython, this new alternative implementation of Python has a specific target audience and will likely prove to be of most interest to developers concerned with C# and .NET/Mono Framework integration. However, initial performance results suggest that IronPython may compete favorably with standard C Python, since it can leverage all the work done on .NET Just-in-Time (JIT) compilers. Search the Web for up-to-date details on IronPython.

An earlier version of .NET integration, Python.NET, has similar goals, but it uses the normal Python runtime engine to allow standard Python to use .NET classes. Be sure to watch Python web forums for more developments on this front.

Python Server Pages

Python Server Pages (PSP) is a server-side templating technology that embeds Python code inside HTML. PSP is a Python-based answer to other server-side embedded scripting approaches.

The PSP scripting engine works much like Microsoft's ASP (described earlier) and Sun's Java Server Pages (JSP) specification. At the risk of pushing the acronym tolerance envelope, PSP has also been compared to PHP, a server-side scripting language embedded in HTML.

All of these systems, including PSP, embed scripts within HTML and run them on the server to generate portions of the response stream sent back to the browser on the client. Scripts interact with an exposed object model API to get their work done, which gives access to input and output components. PSP is portable to a wide variety of platforms (ASP applications run on Microsoft platforms).

PSP uses Python as its scripting language—by all accounts, this is a vastly more appropriate choice for scripting web sites than the Java language used in JSP. Since Python code is embedded under PSP, scripts have access to the large number of Python tools and add-ons from within PSP.

We can't cover PSP in detail here; but for a quick look, Example 18-20 illustrates the structure of PSP.

Example 18-20. PP3E\Internet\Other\PSP\hello.psp

```
$[
# Generate a simple message page with the client's IP address
]$
<HTML><HEAD>
<TITLE>Hello PSP World</TITLE>
</HEAD>
<BODY>
$[include banner.psp]$
<H1>Hello PSP World</H1>
<BR>
$[
Response.write("Hello from PSP, %s." % (Request.server["REMOTE_ADDR"]) )
]$
<BR>
</BODY></HTML>
```

A page like this would be installed on a PSP-aware server machine and referenced by a URL from a browser. PSP uses $[and]$ delimiters to enclose Python code embedded in HTML; anything outside these pairs is simply sent to the client browser, and code within these markers is executed. The first code block here is a Python comment (note the # character); the second is an include statement that simply inserts another PSP file's contents.

The third piece of embedded code is more useful. As in Active Scripting technologies, Python code embedded in HTML uses an exposed object API to interact with the execution context—in this case, the Response object is used to write output to the client's browser (much like a print in a CGI script), and Request is used to access HTTP headers for the request. The Request object also has a params dictionary containing GET and POST input parameters, as well as a cookies dictionary holding cookie information stored on the client by a PSP application.

Notice that the previous example could just as easily have been implemented with a Python CGI script using a Python print statement, but PSP's full benefit becomes clearer in large pages that embed and execute much more complex Python code to produce a response.

Under PSP, Python code is embedded in HTML—essentially the opposite of the CGI examples we met earlier, which embed HTML code in Python. PSP is also similar to the Zope DTML server-side templating language we met earlier; though Zope's embedded tags can do more than run Python code (they can also run acquired objects in the site tree, including other templating code objects). Zope encourages separation of HTML display and Python logic code by making the two distinct objects; in PSP, programmers can achieve similar effects by splitting complex logic off into imported modules.

For more details about PSP, visit its web site, currently located at *http://www.webwareforpython.org*, but search *http://www.python.org* or Google for other links if this one changes over time.

PSP in Webware and mod_python

At the time of this writing, implementations of PSP are also now available as components of the Webware suite of tools, as well as the mod_python Apache extension, both described later in this chapter. In both, the inclusion syntax varies slightly from the original PSP implementation: these systems delimit embedded Python code using the tokens <% and %> for statement blocks to be executed, and using <%= and %> for expressions that must render as strings and whose values are inserted into the reply stream, as in Example 18-21.

Example 18-21. PP3E\Internet\Other\PSP\webware.psp

```
<html>
<body>
<%
import time
%>
<h1>The current time is <%= time.asctime( ) %> </h1>

<% for i in range(5):
        res.write("<b>This is number" + str(i) + "</b><br>") %>
</body>
</html>
```

To use such PSP code, create a standard HTML page that embeds the special PSP tags that your page requires. Save this file with an extension of *.psp* and place it in a directory that is served by Webware or mod_python. When a request is received for this page, the server will dynamically compile the code to serve requests for that page. The embedded Python code is run on the server when the page is accessed by a client, to generate parts of the reply.

For more information, see PSP, Webware, and mod_python documentation. Although they are largely just variations on a theme, the various PSP implementations diverge in additional ways and are richer than we have space to cover here.

Rolling Your Own Servers in Python

Most of the Internet modules we looked at in the last few chapters deal with client-side interfaces such as FTP and Post Office Protocol (POP), or special server-side protocols such as CGI that hide the underlying server itself. If you want to build servers in Python by hand, you can do so either manually or by using higher-level tools.

Standard Library Socket Servers

We explored the sort of code needed to build servers manually in Chapter 13. Python programs typically implement servers either by using raw socket calls with threads, forks, or selects to handle clients in parallel, or by using the standard library SocketServer module. As we learned earlier, this module supports TCP and UDP sockets, in threading and forking flavors; you provide a class method invoked to communicate with clients.

Whether clients are handled manually or with Python classes, to serve requests made in terms of higher-level protocols such as FTP, the Network News Transfer Protocol (NNTP), and HTTP, you must listen on the protocol's port and add appropriate code to handle the protocol's message conventions. If you go this route, the client-side protocol modules in Python's standard library can help you understand the message conventions used.

You may also be able to uncover protocol server examples in the *Demos* and *Tools* directories of the Python source distribution and on the Net at large (search *http://www.python.org* or do a general web search). See prior chapters for more details on writing socket-based servers. Also see the asyncore module described ahead for an asynchronous server class in the standard library based on the select system call instead of on threads or forks.

Standard Library Web Servers

As an even higher-level interface, Python also comes with the standard precoded HTTP web protocol server implementations we met in Chapter 16 and employed in Chapter 17. This support takes the form of three standard modules. BaseHTTPServer implements the server itself; this class is derived from the standard SocketServer. TCPServer class. SimpleHTTPServer and CGIHTTPServer implement standard handlers for incoming HTTP requests; the former handles simple web page file requests, while the latter also runs referenced CGI scripts on the server machine by forking processes.

Refer to Example 16-1 for a simple script that uses these modules to implement a web server in Python. Run that script on your server machine to start handling web page requests. This assumes that you have appropriate permissions to run such a script, of course; see the Python library manual for more details on precoded HTTP server and request handler modules.

Once you have your server running, you can access it in any web browser or by using either the Python httplib module, which implements the client side of the HTTP protocol, or the Python urllib module, which provides a file-like interface to data fetched from a named URL address (see the urllib examples in Chapters 14, 16, and 17, use a URL of the form "http://..." to access HTTP documents, and use "*http:// localhost/...*" if the server is running on the same machine as the client).

Third-Party Solutions

Beyond Python's standard library, the public domain also offers many ways to build servers in Python, including the Twisted system described in Chapter 13 and mentioned in the next section. Open source systems such as Apache provide additional options.

And Other Cool Stuff

The Web and the Internet it runs on are large, dynamic domains, and we haven't done justice to all the available tools they offer to Python programmers. To wrap up, the following is a list of some of the more popular, full-featured, and Python-friendly web tools that are freely available on the Net. This list is incomplete and is prone to change over time too, but by way of introduction, here are some of the things Python people use today:

Medusa, asyncore
> The Medusa system is an architecture for building long-running, high-performance network servers in Python, and it is used in several mission-critical systems. Beginning in Python 1.5.2, the core of Medusa became standard in Python, in the form of the asyncore and asynchat library modules. These standard modules may be used by themselves to build high-performance network servers, based on an asynchronous, multiplexing, and single-process model. They use an event loop built using the select system call presented in Chapter 13 of this book to provide concurrency without spawning threads or processes, and are well suited to handling short-lived transactions. See the Python library for details. The complete Medusa system (not shipped with Python) also provides precoded HTTP and FTP servers; it is free for noncommercial use, and it requires a license otherwise.

Twisted

The Twisted system was introduced in Chapter 13. In short, it is an asynchronous, event-driven, networking framework written in Python, with support for a large number of network protocols and with precoded implementations of common network servers. See *http://twistedmatrix.com/trac* or search on Google for details.

Zope

We met Zope earlier in this chapter. If you are doing server-side work, be sure to consider the Zope open source web application server. Zope provides a full-featured web framework that implements an object model that is well beyond standard server-side CGI scripting. The Zope world has also developed full-blown servers (e.g., ZServer). See the earlier Zope section in this chapter, and *http://www.zope.org*.

Other web site frameworks

For an alternative to Zope, also see the popular CherryPy, Webware, Quixote, and other systems.

CherryPy

Bills itself as a Pythonic object-oriented web development framework, which allows developers to build web applications like any other object-oriented Python program, with little or no knowledge of the underlying protocols. As such, it yields smaller source code developed in less time.

Webware

A suite of Python components for developing object-oriented, web-based applications. The suite uses well-known design patterns and includes features such as a fast application server, servlets, the PSP templating system described earlier in this chapter, an object-relational mapping, and a CGI wrapper.

Quixote

Describes itself as a package that supports web application development by Python programmers. In Quixote, the templating language is a small extension of Python itself—the aim is to make web page assembly take maximal advantage of the Python programmer's existing skills.

Django

A relatively new arrival on the Python web framework scene and billed as a high-level Python web framework that encourages rapid development and clean, pragmatic design. It includes a dynamic database access API, its own server-side templating language, and more.

TurboGears

Also a new arrival in the Python web framework space, this an integrated collection of web development tools: MochiKit (a JavaScript library), Kid (a template system), CherryPy (for web input/output), and SQLObject (for accessing databases as you would normal Python classes).

Plone

A Zope-based web site builder, which provides a workflow model (called a content management system) that allows content producers to add their content to a site. By allowing users to add web content, it removes the typical site administrator bottleneck and supports more collaborative sites. Plone is a prepackaged instance of a Zope-based web site, which may be customized both in and with Zope tools.

You can find additional web frameworks available for Python in the public domain, and more may appear over time. In fact, this may be something of an *embarrassment of riches*—at this writing, there is no de facto standard web framework in the Python world, though a small set is likely to emerge as front-runners over time.

Mailman

If you are looking for email list support, be sure to explore the GNU mailing list manager, otherwise known as Mailman. Written in Python, Mailman provides a robust, quick, and feature-rich email discussion list tool. Mailman allows users to subscribe over the Web, supports web-based administration, and provides mail-to-news gateways and integrated spam prevention (spam of the junk mail variety, that is). At this time, *http://www.list.org* is the place to find more Mailman details.

Apache

For server-side scripting, you may be interested in the highly configurable Apache open source web server. Apache is one of the dominant servers used on the Web today, despite its free nature. Among many other things, it supports running Python server-side scripts in a variety of modes; see the site *http://www. apache.org* for details on Apache itself.

mod_python

We introduced mod_python in Chapter 16, in conjunction with server-side state retention options. This package embeds Python within the Apache open source web server, with a substantial boost in performance and added flexibility. Python code may be executed directly in Apache, eliminating the need for spawning processes. In addition, mod_python supports cross-page session data, access to Apache APIs, its own implementation of the PSP server-side reply templating language described in this chapter, and more. See Chapter 16, as well as the mod_python web site, for more details (search on Google.com for an up-to-date link).

CORBA

CORBA is an architecture for distributed programming, in which components communicate across a network, by routing calls through an Object Request Broker (ORB). It is similar in spirit to the distributed flavor of the COM system shown earlier in this chapter, but it is both language and platform neutral.

Python support for CORBA is available in the third-party `ILU`, `fnorb`, and `OmniORB` packages.

XML-RPC, SOAP

XML-RPC is a technology that provides remote procedural calls to components over networks, by routing requests over the HTTP protocol and shipping data back and forth, packaged as XML text. Python's `xmlrpclib` handles the client side of this protocol, and its `SimpleXMLRPCServer` provides tools for the server side. SOAP is a similar but larger system, targeted at the implementation of web services—reusable software components that run on the Web. The third-party SOAPy and PySOAP packages provide Python interfaces for this protocol.

MoinMoin

A powerful and popular Wiki system written in Python, which supports flexible web page content that can be changed by its user community.

Beyond this list there a dozens of additional Internet-related systems and technologies, but we'll omit further examples and descriptions here in the interest of space. Be sure to watch *http://www.python.org* for new developments on the server front, as well as late-breaking advances in Python web-scripting techniques in general.

## PART V

Tools and Techniques

This part of the book presents a collection of additional Python application topics. Most of the tools presented along the way can be used in a wide variety of application domains. You'll find the following chapters here:

Chapter 19, *Databases and Persistence*

> This chapter covers commonly used and advanced Python techniques for storing information between program executions—DBM files, object pickling (serialization), object shelves, the ZODB object database, and Python's SQL database interfaces. MySQL is used for the SQL examples, but the API is portable to other systems.

Chapter 20, *Data Structures*

> This chapter explores techniques for implementing more advanced data structures in Python—stacks, sets, binary search trees, graphs, and the like. In Python, these take the form of object implementations.

Chapter 21, *Text and Language*

> This chapter addresses Python tools and techniques for parsing text-based information—string splits and joins, regular expression matching, recursive descent parsing, and more advanced language-based topics.

This is the last pure Python part of the book, and it makes heavy use of tools presented earlier in the text, especially the Tkinter GUI library. For instance, a tree browser (PyTree) is used to illustrate various object structures, a form browser (PyForm) helps make database concepts more concrete, and a calculator GUI (PyCalc) serves to demonstrate language processing and code reuse concepts.

## CHAPTER 19

Databases and Persistence

"Give Me an Order of Persistence, but Hold the Pickles"

So far in this book, we've used Python in the system programming, GUI develop-ment, and Internet scripting domains—three of Python's most common applica-tions, and representative of its use as an application programming language at large. In the next three chapters, we're going to take a quick look at other major Python programming topics: persistent data, data structure techniques, and text- and language-processing tools. None of these is covered exhaustively (each could easily fill a book alone), but we'll sample Python in action in these domains and highlight their core concepts. If any of these chapters spark your interest, additional resources are readily available in the Python world.

Persistence Options in Python

In this chapter, our focus is on *persistent* data—the kind that outlives a program that creates it. That's not true by default for objects a script constructs; things like lists, dictionaries, and even class instance objects live in your computer's memory and are lost as soon as the script ends. To make data live longer, we need to do something special. In Python programming, there are today at least six traditional ways to save information in between program executions:

Flat files
> Storing text and bytes

DBM keyed files
> Keyed access to strings

Pickled objects
> Serializing Python objects to files and streams

Shelve files
> Storing pickled Python objects in DBM keyed files

ZODB object databases
> Storing Python objects in persistent dictionaries

SQL relational databases
> Table-based systems that support queries

In some sense, Python's interfaces to network-based object transmission protocols such as SOAP, XML-RPC, and CORBA also offer persistence options, but they are beyond the scope of this chapter. Here, our interest is in techniques that allow a program to store its data directly and, usually, on the local machine. Although some database servers may operate on a physically remote machine on a network, this is largely transparent to most of the techniques we'll study here.

We studied Python's simple (or "flat") file interfaces in earnest in Chapter 4, and we have been using them ever since. Python provides standard access to both the stdio filesystem (through the built-in open function), as well as lower-level descriptor-based files (with the built-in os module). For simple data storage tasks, these are all that many scripts need. To save for use in a future program run, simply write data out to a newly opened file on your computer and read it back from that file later. As we've seen, for more advanced tasks, Python also supports other file-like interfaces such as pipes, fifos, and sockets.

Since we've already explored flat files, I won't say more about them here. The rest of this chapter introduces the remaining topics on the preceding list. At the end, we'll also meet a GUI program for browsing the contents of things such as shelves and DBM files. Before that, though, we need to learn what manner of beast these are.

DBM Files

Flat files are handy for simple persistence tasks, but they are generally geared toward a sequential processing mode. Although it is possible to jump around to arbitrary locations with seek calls, flat files don't provide much structure to data beyond the notion of bytes and text lines.

DBM files, a standard tool in the Python library for database management, improve on that by providing key-based access to stored text strings. They implement a random-access, single-key view on stored data. For instance, information related to objects can be stored in a DBM file using a unique key per object and later can be fetched back directly with the same key. DBM files are implemented by a variety of underlying modules (including one coded in Python), but if you have Python, you have a DBM.

Using DBM Files

Although DBM filesystems have to do a bit of work to map chunks of stored data to keys for fast retrieval (technically, they generally use a technique called *hashing* to store data in files), your scripts don't need to care about the action going on behind the scenes. In fact, DBM is one of the easiest ways to save information in Python—DBM files behave so much like in-memory dictionaries that you may forget you're actually dealing with a file. For instance, given a DBM file object:

- Indexing by key fetches data from the file.
- Assigning to an index stores data in the file.

DBM file objects also support common dictionary methods such as keys-list fetches and tests and key deletions. The DBM library itself is hidden behind this simple model. Since it is so simple, let's jump right into an interactive example that creates a DBM file and shows how the interface works:

```
% python
>>> import anydbm                          # get interface: dbm, gdbm, ndbm,..
>>> file = anydbm.open('movie', 'c')       # make a DBM file called 'movie'
>>> file['Batman'] = 'Pow!'                # store a string under key 'Batman'
>>> file.keys()                            # get the file's key directory
['Batman']
>>> file['Batman']                         # fetch value for key 'Batman'
'Pow!'

>>> who  = ['Robin', 'Cat-woman', 'Joker']
>>> what = ['Bang!', 'Splat!', 'Wham!']
>>> for i in range(len(who)):
...     file[who[i]] = what[i]             # add 3 more "records"
...
>>> file.keys()
['Joker', 'Robin', 'Cat-woman', 'Batman']
>>> len(file), file.has_key('Robin'), file['Joker']
(4, 1, 'Wham!')
>>> file.close()                           # close sometimes required
```

Internally, importing anydbm automatically loads whatever DBM interface is available in your Python interpreter, and opening the new DBM file creates one or more external files with names that start with the string 'movie' (more on the details in a moment). But after the import and open, a DBM file is virtually indistinguishable from a dictionary. In effect, the object called file here can be thought of as a dictionary mapped to an external file called movie.

Unlike normal dictionaries, though, the contents of file are retained between Python program runs. If we come back later and restart Python, our dictionary is still available. DBM files are like dictionaries that must be opened:

```
% python
>>> import anydbm
>>> file = anydbm.open('movie', 'c')       # open existing DBM file
>>> file['Batman']
'Pow!'

>>> file.keys()                            # keys gives an index list
['Joker', 'Robin', 'Cat-woman', 'Batman']
```

```
>>> for key in file.keys(): print key, file[key]
...
Joker Wham!
Robin Bang!
Cat-woman Splat!
Batman Pow!

>>> file['Batman'] = 'Ka-Boom!'          # change Batman slot
>>> del file['Robin']                    # delete the Robin entry
>>> file.close()                         # close it after changes
```

Apart from having to import the interface and open and close the DBM file, Python programs don't have to know anything about DBM itself. DBM modules achieve this integration by overloading the indexing operations and routing them to more primitive library tools. But you'd never know that from looking at this Python code—DBM files look like normal Python dictionaries, stored on external files. Changes made to them are retained indefinitely:

```
% python
>>> import anydbm                        # open DBM file again
>>> file = anydbm.open('movie', 'c')
>>> for key in file.keys(): print key, file[key]
...
Joker Wham!
Cat-woman Splat!
Batman Ka-Boom!
```

As you can see, this is about as simple as it can be. Table 19-1 lists the most commonly used DBM file operations. Once such a file is opened, it is processed just as though it were an in-memory Python dictionary. Items are fetched by indexing the file object by key and are stored by assigning to a key.

Table 19-1. DBM file operations

Python code	Action	Description
import anydbm	Import	Get dbm, gdbm, and so on...whatever is installed
file = anydbm.open('filename', 'c')	Open	Create or open an existing DBM file
file['key'] = 'value'	Store	Create or change the entry for key
value = file['key']	Fetch	Load the value for the entry key
count = len(file)	Size	Return the number of entries stored
index = file.keys()	Index	Fetch the stored keys list
found = file.has_key('key')	Query	See if there's an entry for key
del file['key']	Delete	Remove the entry for key
file.close()	Close	Manual close, not always needed

Despite the dictionary-like interface, DBM files really do map to one or more external files. For instance, the underlying gdbm interface writes two files, *movie.dir* and *movie.pag*, when a GDBM file called movie is made. If your Python was built with a different underlying keyed-file interface, different external files might show up on your computer.

Technically, the module anydbm is really an interface to whatever DBM-like filesystem you have available in your Python. When creating a new file, anydbm today tries to load the dbhash, gdbm, and dbm keyed-file interface modules; Pythons without any of these automatically fall back on an all-Python implementation called dumbdbm. When opening an already existing DBM file, anydbm tries to determine the system that created it with the whichdb module instead. You normally don't need to care about any of this, though (unless you delete the files your DBM creates).

Note that DBM files may or may not need to be explicitly closed, per the last entry in Table 19-1. Some DBM files don't require a close call, but some depend on it to flush changes out to disk. On such systems, your file may be corrupted if you omit the close call. Unfortunately, the default DBM as of the 1.5.2 Windows Python port, dbhash (a.k.a. bsddb), is one of the DBM systems that requires a close call to avoid data loss. As a rule of thumb, always close your DBM files explicitly after making changes and before your program exits, to avoid potential problems. This rule extends by proxy to shelves, which is a topic we'll meet later in this chapter.

> In Python versions 1.5.2 and later, be sure to also pass a string 'c' as a second argument when calling anydbm.open, to force Python to create the file if it does not yet exist, and to simply open it otherwise. This used to be the default behavior but is no longer. You do not need the 'c' argument when opening shelves discussed ahead—they still use an "open or create" mode by default if passed no open mode argument. Other open mode strings can be passed to anydbm (e.g., n to always create the file and r for read-only—the new default); see the library reference manuals for more details.

Pickled Objects

Probably the biggest limitation of DBM keyed files is in what they can store: data stored under a key must be a simple text string. If you want to store Python objects in a DBM file, you can sometimes manually convert them to and from strings on writes and reads (e.g., with str and eval calls), but this takes you only so far. For arbitrarily complex Python objects such as class instances and nested data structures, you need something more. Class instance objects, for example, cannot be later re-created from their standard string representations. Custom to-string conversions are error prone and not general.

The Python pickle module, a standard part of the Python system, provides the conversion step needed. It converts nearly arbitrary Python in-memory objects to and from a single linear string format, suitable for storing in flat files, shipping across network sockets between trusted sources, and so on. This conversion from object to string is often called *serialization*—arbitrary data structures in memory are mapped to a serial string form.

The string representation used for objects is also sometimes referred to as a byte stream, due to its linear format. It retains all the content and references structure of the original in-memory object. When the object is later re-created from its byte string, it will be a new in-memory object identical in structure and value to the original, though located at a different memory address. The re-created object is effectively a copy of the original.

Pickling works on almost any Python datatype—numbers, lists, dictionaries, class instances, nested structures, and more—and so is a general way to store data. Because pickles contain native Python objects, there is almost no database API to be found; the objects stored are processed with normal Python syntax when they are later retrieved.

Using Object Pickling

Pickling may sound complicated the first time you encounter it, but the good news is that Python hides all the complexity of object-to-string conversion. In fact, the pickle module's interfaces are incredibly simple to use. For example, to pickle an object into a serialized string, we can either make a pickler and call its methods or use convenience functions in the module to achieve the same effect:

`P = pickle.Pickler(file)`
> Make a new pickler for pickling to an open output file object `file`.

`P.dump(object)`
> Write an object onto the pickler's file/stream.

`pickle.dump(object, file)`
> Same as the last two calls combined: pickle an object onto an open file.

`string = pickle.dumps(object)`
> Return the pickled representation of `object` as a character string.

Unpickling from a serialized string back to the original object is similar—both object and convenience function interfaces are available:

`U = pickle.Unpickler(file)`
> Make an unpickler for unpickling from an open input file object `file`.

`object = U.load( )`
> Read an object from the unpickler's file/stream.

`object = pickle.load(file)`
> Same as the last two calls combined: unpickle an object from an open file.

`object = pickle.loads(string)`
> Read an object from a character string rather than a file.

`Pickler` and `Unpickler` are exported classes. In all of the preceding cases, `file` is either an open file object or any object that implements the same attributes as file objects:

- `Pickler` calls the file's `write` method with a string argument.
- `Unpickler` calls the file's `read` method with a byte count, and `readline` without arguments.

Any object that provides these attributes can be passed in to the `file` parameters. In particular, `file` can be an instance of a Python class that provides the read/write methods (i.e., the expected file-like *interface*). This lets you map pickled streams to in-memory objects with classes, for arbitrary use. For instance, the `StringIO` standard library module discussed in Chapter 3 provides classes that map file calls to and from in-memory strings.

This hook also lets you ship Python objects across a network, by providing sockets wrapped to look like files in pickle calls at the sender, and unpickle calls at the receiver (see the sidebar "Making Sockets Look Like Files," in Chapter 13, for more details). In fact, for some, pickling Python objects across a trusted network serves as a simpler alternative to network transport protocols such as SOAP and XML-RPC; provided that Python is on both ends of the communication (pickled objects are represented with a Python-specific format, not with XML text).

Picking in Action

In more typical use, to pickle an object to a flat file, we just open the file in write mode and call the `dump` function:

```
% python
>>> table = {'a': [1, 2, 3],
             'b': ['spam', 'eggs'],
             'c': {'name':'bob'}}
>>>
>>> import pickle
>>> mydb  = open('dbase', 'w')
>>> pickle.dump(table, mydb)
```

Notice the nesting in the object pickled here—the pickler handles arbitrary structures. To unpickle later in another session or program run, simply reopen the file and call `load`:

```
% python
>>> import pickle
>>> mydb  = open('dbase', 'r')
>>> table = pickle.load(mydb)
>>> table
{'b': ['spam', 'eggs'], 'a': [1, 2, 3], 'c': {'name': 'bob'}}
```

The object you get back from unpickling has the same value and reference structure as the original, but it is located at a different address in memory. This is true whether the object is unpickled in the same or a future process. In Python-speak, the unpick-led object is == but is not is:

```
% python
>>> import pickle
>>> f = open('temp', 'w')
>>> x = ['Hello', ('pickle', 'world')]        # list with nested tuple
>>> pickle.dump(x, f)
>>> f.close()                                 # close to flush changes
>>>
>>> f = open('temp', 'r')
>>> y = pickle.load(f)
>>> y
['Hello', ('pickle', 'world')]
>>>
>>> x == y, x is y
(True, False)
```

To make this process simpler still, the module in Example 19-1 wraps pickling and unpickling calls in functions that also open the files where the serialized form of the object is stored.

Example 19-1. PP3E\Dbase\filepickle.py

```
import pickle

def saveDbase(filename, object):
    file = open(filename, 'w')
    pickle.dump(object, file)        # pickle to file
    file.close()                     # any file-like object will do

def loadDbase(filename):
    file = open(filename, 'r')
    object = pickle.load(file)       # unpickle from file
    file.close()                     # re-creates object in memory
    return object
```

To store and fetch now, simply call these module functions; here they are in action managing a fairly complex structure with multiple references to the same nested object—the nested list called L at first is stored only once in the file:

```
C:\...\PP3E\Dbase>python
>>> from filepickle import *
>>> L = [0]
>>> D = {'x':0, 'y':L}
>>> table = {'A':L, 'B':D}           # L appears twice
>>> saveDbase('myfile', table)       # serialize to file

C:\...\PP3E\Dbase>python
>>> from filepickle import *
>>> table = loadDbase('myfile')      # reload/unpickle
>>> table
{'B': {'x': 0, 'y': [0]}, 'A': [0]}
>>> table['A'][0] = 1                # change shared object
```

```
>>> saveDbase('myfile', table)            # rewrite to the file

C:\...\PP3E\Dbase>python
>>> from filepickle import *
>>> print loadDbase('myfile')             # both L's updated as expected
{'B': {'x': 0, 'y': [1]}, 'A': [1]}
```

Besides built-in types like the lists, tuples, and dictionaries of the examples so far, *class instances* may also be pickled to file-like objects. This provides a natural way to associate behavior with stored data (class methods process instance attributes) and provides a simple migration path (class changes made in module files are automatically picked up by stored instances). Here's a brief interactive demonstration:

```
>>> class Rec:
        def __init__(self, hours):
            self.hours = hours
        def pay(self, rate=50):
            return self.hours * rate

>>> bob = Rec(40)
>>> import pickle
>>> pickle.dump(bob, open('bobrec', 'w'))
>>>
>>> rec = pickle.load(open('bobrec'))
>>> rec.hours
40
>>> rec.pay( )
2000
```

We'll explore how this works in more detail in conjunction with shelves later in this chapter—as we'll see, although the pickle module can be used directly, it is also the underlying translation engine in both shelves and ZODB databases.

In fact, Python can pickle just about anything, except for:

- Compiled code objects; functions and classes record just their names in pickles, to allow for later reimport and automatic acquisition of changes made in module files.

- Instances of classes that do not follow class importability rules (more on this at the end of the section "Shelve Files," later in this chapter).

- Instances of some built-in and user-defined types that are coded in C or depend upon transient operating system states (e.g., open file objects cannot be pickled).

A PicklingError is raised if an object cannot be pickled.

Pickler Protocols and cPickle

In recent Python releases, the pickler introduced the notion of *protocols*—storage formats for pickled data. Specify the desired protocol by passing an extra parameter to the pickling calls (but not to unpickling calls: the protocol is automatically determined from the pickled data):

```
pickle.dump(object, file, protocol)
```

Pickled data may be created in either text or binary protocols. By default, the storage protocol is text (also known as protocol 0). In text mode, the files used to store pickled objects may be opened in text mode as in the earlier examples, and the pickled data is printable ASCII text, which can be read (it's essentially instructions for a stack machine).

The alternative protocols (protocols 1 and 2) store the pickled data in binary format and require that files be opened in binary mode (e.g., rb, wb). Protocol 1 is the original binary format; protocol 2, added in Python 2.3, has improved support for pickling of new-style classes. Binary format is slightly more efficient, but it cannot be inspected. An older option to pickling calls, the bin argument, has been subsumed by using a pickling protocol higher than 0. The pickle module also provides a HIGHEST_PROTOCOL variable that can be passed in to automatically select the maximum value.

One note: if you use the default text protocol, make sure you open pickle files in text mode later. On some platforms, opening text data in binary mode may cause unpickling errors due to line-end formats on Windows:

```
>>> f = open('temp', 'w')                # text mode file on Windows
>>> pickle.dump(('ex', 'parrot'), f)     # use default text protocol
>>> f.close()
>>>
>>> pickle.load(open('temp', 'r'))       # OK in text mode
('ex', 'parrot')
>>> pickle.load(open('temp', 'rb'))      # fails in binary
Traceback (most recent call last):
  File "<pyshell#337>", line 1, in -toplevel-
    pickle.load(open('temp', 'rb'))
...lines deleted...
ValueError: insecure string pickle
```

One way to sidestep this potential issue is to always use binary mode for your files, even for the text pickle protocol. Since you must open files in binary mode for the binary pickler protocols anyhow (higher than the default 0), this isn't a bad habit to get into:

```
>>> f = open('temp', 'wb')               # create in binary mode
>>> pickle.dump(('ex', 'parrot'), f)     # use text protocol
>>> f.close()
>>>
>>> pickle.load(open('temp', 'rb'))
('ex', 'parrot')
>>> pickle.load(open('temp', 'r'))
('ex', 'parrot')
```

Refer to Python's library manual for more information on the pickler. Also check out marshal, a module that serializes an object too, but can handle only simple object types. pickle is more general than marshal and is normally preferred.

And while you are flipping (or clicking) through that manual, be sure to also see the entries for the cPickle module—a reimplementation of pickle coded in C for faster performance. You can explicitly import cPickle for a substantial speed boost; its chief limitation is that you cannot subclass its versions of Pickle and Unpickle because they are functions, not classes (this is not required by most programs). The pickle and cPickle modules use compatible data formats, so they may be used interchangeably.

If it is available in your Python, the shelve module automatically chooses the cPickle module for faster serialization, instead of pickle. I haven't explained shelve yet, but I will now.

Shelve Files

Pickling allows you to store arbitrary objects on files and file-like objects, but it's still a fairly unstructured medium; it doesn't directly support easy access to members of collections of pickled objects. Higher-level structures can be added, but they are not inherent:

- You can sometimes craft your own higher-level pickle file organizations with the underlying filesystem (e.g., you can store each pickled object in a file whose name uniquely identifies the object), but such an organization is not part of pickling itself and must be manually managed.

- You can also store arbitrarily large dictionaries in a pickled file and index them by key after they are loaded back into memory, but this will load the entire dictionary all at once when unpickled, not just the entry you are interested in.

Shelves provide structure to collections of pickled objects that removes some of these constraints. They are a type of file that stores arbitrary Python objects by key for later retrieval, and they are a standard part of the Python system. Really, they are not much of a new topic—shelves are simply a combination of DBM files and object pickling:

- To store an in-memory object by key, the shelve module first serializes the object to a string with the pickle module, and then it stores that string in a DBM file by key with the anydbm module.

- To fetch an object back by key, the shelve module first loads the object's serialized string by key from a DBM file with the anydbm module, and then converts it back to the original in-memory object with the pickle module.

Because shelve uses pickle internally, it can store any object that pickle can: strings, numbers, lists, dictionaries, cyclic objects, class instances, and more.

Using Shelves

In other words, shelve is just a go-between; it serializes and deserializes objects so that they can be placed in DBM files. The net effect is that shelves let you store nearly arbitrary Python objects on a file by key and fetch them back later with the same key.

Your scripts never see all of this interfacing, though. Like DBM files, shelves provide an interface that looks like a dictionary that must be opened. In fact, a shelve is simply a persistent dictionary of persistent Python objects—the shelve dictionary's content is automatically mapped to a file on your computer so that it is retained between program runs. This is quite a trick, but it's simpler to your code than it may sound. To gain access to a shelve, import the module and open your file:

```
import shelve
dbase = shelve.open("mydbase")
```

Internally, Python opens a DBM file with the name *mydbase*, or creates it if it does not yet exist. Assigning to a shelve key stores an object:

```
dbase['key'] = object
```

Internally, this assignment converts the object to a serialized byte stream and stores it by key on a DBM file. Indexing a shelve fetches a stored object:

```
value = dbase['key']
```

Internally, this index operation loads a string by key from a DBM file and unpickles it into an in-memory object that is the same as the object originally stored. Most dictionary operations are supported here too:

```
len(dbase)       # number of items stored
dbase.keys()     # stored item key index
```

And except for a few fine points, that's really all there is to using a shelve. Shelves are processed with normal Python dictionary syntax, so there is no new database API to learn. Moreover, objects stored and fetched from shelves are normal Python objects; they do not need to be instances of special classes or types to be stored away. That is, Python's persistence system is external to the persistent objects themselves. Table 19-2 summarizes these and other commonly used shelve operations.

Table 19-2. Shelve file operations

Python code	Action	Description
`import shelve`	Import	Get dbm, gdbm, and so on...whatever is installed
`file = shelve.open('filename')`	Open	Create or open an existing DBM file
`file['key'] = anyvalue`	Store	Create or change the entry for key
`value = file['key']`	Fetch	Load the value for the entry key
`count = len(file)`	Size	Return the number of entries stored
`index = file.keys()`	Index	Fetch the stored keys list

Table 19-2. Shelve file operations (continued)

Python code	Action	Description
found = file.has_key('key')	Query	See if there's an entry for key
del file['key']	Delete	Remove the entry for key
file.close()	Close	Manual close, not always needed

Because shelves export a dictionary-like interface too, this table is almost identical to the DBM operation table. Here, though, the module name anydbm is replaced by shelve, open calls do not require a second c argument, and stored values can be nearly arbitrary kinds of objects, not just strings. You still should close shelves explicitly after making changes to be safe, though; shelves use anydbm internally, and some underlying DBMs require closes to avoid data loss or damage.

Storing Built-In Object Types in Shelves

Let's run an interactive session to experiment with shelve interfaces. As mentioned, shelves are essentially just persistent dictionaries of objects, which you open and close:

```
% python
>>> import shelve
>>> dbase = shelve.open("mydbase")
>>> object1 = ['The', 'bright', ('side', 'of'), ['life']]
>>> object2 = {'name': 'Brian', 'age': 33, 'motto': object1}
>>> dbase['brian']  = object2
>>> dbase['knight'] = {'name': 'Knight', 'motto': 'Ni!'}
>>> dbase.close()
```

Here, we open a shelve and store two fairly complex dictionary and list data structures away permanently by simply assigning them to shelve keys. Because shelve uses pickle internally, almost anything goes here—the trees of nested objects are automatically serialized into strings for storage. To fetch them back, just reopen the shelve and index:

```
% python
>>> import shelve
>>> dbase = shelve.open("mydbase")
>>> len(dbase)                          # entries
2

>>> dbase.keys()                        # index
['knight', 'brian']

>>> dbase['knight']                     # fetch
{'motto': 'Ni!', 'name': 'Knight'}

>>> for row in dbase.keys():
...     print row, '=>'
...     for field in dbase[row].keys():
```

```
...            print ' ', field, '=', dbase[row][field]
...
knight =>
    motto = Ni!
    name = Knight
brian =>
    motto = ['The', 'bright', ('side', 'of'), ['life']]
    age = 33
    name = Brian
```

The nested loops at the end of this session step through nested dictionaries—the outer scans the shelve and the inner scans the objects stored in the shelve. The crucial point to notice is that we're using normal Python syntax, both to store and to fetch these persistent objects, as well as to process them after loading.

Storing Class Instances in Shelves

One of the more useful kinds of objects to store in a shelve is a class instance. Because its attributes record state and its inherited methods define behavior, persistent class objects effectively serve the roles of both database records and database-processing programs. We can also use the underlying pickle module to serialize instances to flat files and other file-like objects (e.g., trusted network sockets), but the higher-level shelve module also gives us a convenient keyed-access storage medium. For instance, consider the simple class shown in Example 19-2, which is used to model people.

Example 19-2. PP3E\Dbase\person.py (version 1)

```
# a person object: fields + behavior

class Person:
    def __init__(self, name, job, pay=0):
        self.name = name
        self.job  = job
        self.pay  = pay              # real instance data
    def tax(self):
        return self.pay * 0.25       # computed on call
    def info(self):
        return self.name, self.job, self.pay, self.tax()
```

Nothing about this class suggests it will be used for database records—it can be imported and used independent of external storage. It's easy to use it for a database, though: we can make some persistent objects from this class by simply creating instances as usual, and then storing them by key on an opened shelve:

```
C:\...\PP3E\Dbase>python
>>> from person import Person
>>> bob   = Person('bob', 'psychologist', 70000)
>>> emily = Person('emily', 'teacher', 40000)
>>>
```

```
>>> import shelve
>>> dbase = shelve.open('cast')          # make new shelve
>>> for obj in (bob, emily):             # store objects
>>>     dbase[obj.name] = obj            # use name for key
>>> dbase.close( )                       # need for bsddb
```

Here we used the instance objects' name attribute as their key in the shelve database. When we come back and fetch these objects in a later Python session or script, they are re-created in memory as they were when they were stored:

```
C:\...\PP3E\Dbase>python
>>> import shelve
>>> dbase = shelve.open('cast')          # reopen shelve
>>>
>>> dbase.keys( )                        # both objects are here
['emily', 'bob']
>>> print dbase['emily']
<person.Person instance at 799940>
>>>
>>> print dbase['bob'].tax( )            # call: bob's tax
17500.0
```

Notice that calling Bob's tax method works even though we didn't import the Person class here. Python is smart enough to link this object back to its original class when unpickled, such that all the original methods are available through fetched objects.

Changing Classes of Objects Stored in Shelves

Technically, Python reimports a class to re-create its stored instances as they are fetched and unpickled. Here's how this works:

Store

> When Python pickles a class instance to store it in a shelve, it saves the instance's attributes plus a reference to the instance's class. In effect, pickled class instances in the prior example record the self attributes assigned in the class. Really, Python serializes and stores the instance's __dict__ attribute dictionary along with enough source file information to be able to locate the class's module later.

Fetch

> When Python unpickles a class instance fetched from a shelve, it re-creates the instance object in memory by reimporting the class, assigning the saved attribute dictionary to a new empty instance, and linking the instance back to the class.

The key point in this is that the class and stored instance data are separate. The class itself is not stored with its instances, but is instead located in the Python source file and reimported later when instances are fetched.

The upshot is that by modifying external classes in module files, we can change the way stored objects' data is interpreted and used without actually having to change those stored objects. It's as if the class is a program that processes stored records.

To illustrate, suppose the Person class from the previous section was changed to the source code in Example 19-3.

Example 19-3. PP3E\Dbase\person.py (version 2)

```
# a person object: fields + behavior
# change: the tax method is now a computed attribute

class Person:
    def __init__(self, name, job, pay=0):
        self.name = name
        self.job  = job
        self.pay  = pay                # real instance data
    def __getattr__(self, attr):       # on person.attr
        if attr == 'tax':
            return self.pay * 0.30     # computed on access
        else:
            raise AttributeError       # other unknown names
    def info(self):
        return self.name, self.job, self.pay, self.tax
```

This revision has a new tax rate (30 percent), introduces a __getattr__ qualification overload method, and deletes the original tax method. Tax attribute references are intercepted and computed when accessed:

```
C:\...\PP3E\Dbase>python
>>> import shelve
>>> dbase = shelve.open('cast')       # reopen shelve
>>>
>>> print dbase.keys()                # both objects are here
['emily', 'bob']
>>> print dbase['emily']
<person.Person instance at 79aea0>
>>>
>>> print dbase['bob'].tax            # no need to call tax()
21000.0
```

Because the class has changed, tax is now simply qualified, not called. In addition, because the tax rate was changed in the class, Bob pays more this time around. Of course, this example is artificial, but when used well, this separation of classes and persistent instances can eliminate many traditional database update programs. In most cases, you can simply change the class, not each stored instance, for new behavior.

Shelve Constraints

Although shelves are generally straightforward to use, there are a few rough edges worth knowing about.

Keys must be strings

First, although they can store arbitrary objects, keys must still be strings. The following fails, unless you convert the integer 42 to the string 42 manually first:

```
dbase[42] = value       # fails, but str(42) will work
```

This is different from in-memory dictionaries, which allow any immutable object to be used as a key, and derives from the shelve's use of DBM files internally.

Objects are unique only within a key

Although the shelve module is smart enough to detect multiple occurrences of a nested object and re-create only one copy when fetched, this holds true only within a given slot:

```
dbase[key] = [object, object]    # OK: only one copy stored and fetched

dbase[key1] = object
dbase[key2] = object             # bad?: two copies of object in the shelve
```

When key1 and key2 are fetched, they reference independent copies of the original shared object; if that object is mutable, changes from one won't be reflected in the other. This really stems from the fact the each key assignment runs an independent pickle operation—the pickler detects repeated objects but only within each pickle call. This may or may not be a concern in your practice, and it can be avoided with extra support logic, but an object can be duplicated if it spans keys.

Updates must treat shelves as fetch-modify-store mappings

Because objects fetched from a shelve don't know that they came from a shelve, operations that change components of a fetched object change only the in-memory copy, not the data on a shelve:

```
dbase[key].attr = value    # shelve unchanged
```

To really change an object stored on a shelve, fetch it into memory, change its parts, and then write it back to the shelve as a whole by key assignment:

```
object = dbase[key]        # fetch it
object.attr = value        # modify it
dbase[key] = object        # store back-shelve changed
```

Concurrent updates are not directly supported

The shelve module does not currently support simultaneous updates. Simultaneous readers are OK, but writers must be given exclusive access to the shelve. You can trash a shelve if multiple processes write to it at the same time, which is a common potential in things such as Common Gateway Interface (CGI) server-side scripts. If your shelves may be hit by multiple processes, be sure to wrap updates in calls to the fcntl.flock or os.open built-ins to lock files and provide exclusive access.

Underlying DBM format portability

With shelves, the files created by an underlying DBM system used to store your persistent objects are not necessarily compatible with all possible DBM implementations or Pythons. For instance, a file generated by gdbm on Linux, or by the BSD library on Windows, may not be readable by a Python with other DBM modules installed.

Technically, when a DBM file (or by proxy, a shelve) is created, the anydbm module tries to import all possible DBM system modules in a predefined order and uses the first that it finds. When anydmb later opens an existing file, it attempts to determine which DBM system created it by inspecting the files(s) using the module whichdb. Because the BSD system is tried first at file creation time and is available on both Windows and many Unix-like systems, your DBM file is portable as long as your Pythons support BSD on both platforms. If the system used to create a DBM file is not available on the underlying platform, though, the DBM file cannot be used.

If DBM file portability is a concern, make sure that all the Pythons that will read your data use compatible DBM modules. If that is not an option, use the pickle module directly and flat files for storage, or use the ZODB system we'll meet later in this chapter.

Pickled Class Constraints

In addition to these shelve constraints, storing class instances in a shelve adds a set of additional rules you need to be aware of. Really, these are imposed by the pickle module, not by shelve, so be sure to follow these if you store class objects with pickle directly too:

Classes must be importable

The Python pickler stores instance attributes only when pickling an instance object, and it reimports the class later to re-create the instance. Because of that, the classes of stored objects must be importable when objects are unpickled— they must be coded unnested at the top level of a module file that is accessible on the module import search path at load time (e.g., named in PYTHONPATH or in a *.pth* file).

Further, they must be associated with a real module when instances are pickled, not with a top-level script (with the module name __main__), unless they will only ever be used in the top-level script. You need to be careful about moving class modules after instances are stored. When an instance is unpickled, Python must find its class's module on the module search using the original module name (including any package path prefixes) and fetch the class from that module using the original class name. If the module or class has been moved or renamed, it might not be found.

In applications where pickled objects are shipped over network sockets, it's possible to deal with this constraint by shipping the text of the class along with stored instances; recipients may simply store the class in a local module file on the import search path prior to unpickling received instances. Where this is inconvenient, simpler objects such as lists and dictionaries with nesting may be transferred instead.

Class changes must be backward compatible
Although Python lets you change a class while instances of it are stored on a shelve, those changes must be backward compatible with the objects already stored. For instance, you cannot change the class to expect an attribute not associated with already stored persistent instances unless you first manually update those stored instances or provide extra conversion protocols on the class.

Other pickle module constraints
Shelves also inherit the pickling systems' nonclass limitations. As discussed earlier, some types of objects (e.g., open files and sockets) cannot be pickled, and thus cannot be stored in a shelve.

In a prior Python release, persistent object classes also had to either use constructors with no arguments or provide defaults for all constructor arguments (much like the notion of a C++ copy constructor). This constraint was dropped as of Python 1.5.2—classes with nondefaulted constructor arguments now work fine in the pickling system.[*]

Other Shelve Limitations

Finally, although shelves store objects persistently, they are not really object-oriented database systems. Such systems also implement features such as automatic write-through on changes, transaction commits and rollbacks, safe concurrent updates, and object decomposition and delayed ("lazy") component fetches based on generated object ID. Parts of larger objects are loaded into memory only as they are accessed. It's possible to extend shelves to support such features manually, but you don't need to—the ZODB system provides an implementation of a more complete object-oriented database system. It is constructed on top of Python's built-in pickling persistence support, but it offers additional features for advanced data stores. For more on ZODB, let's move on to the next section.

---

[*] Subtle thing: internally, Python now avoids calling the class to re-create a pickled instance and instead simply makes a class object generically, inserts instance attributes, and sets the instance's __class__ pointer to the original class directly. This avoids the need for defaults, but it also means that the class __init__ constructors that are no longer called as objects are unpickled, unless you provide extra methods to force the call. See the library manual for more details, and see the pickle module's source code (*pickle.py* in the source library) if you're curious about how this works. Better yet, see the formtable module listed ahead in this chapter—it does something very similar with __class__ links to build an instance object from a class and dictionary of attributes, without calling the class's __init__ constructor. This makes constructor argument defaults unnecessary in classes used for records browsed by PyForm, but it's the same idea.

The ZODB Object-Oriented Database

ZODB, the Zope Object Database, is a full-featured and Python-specific object-oriented database system. ZODB can be thought of as a more powerful alternative to Python's shelves. It allows you to store nearly arbitrary Python objects persistently by key, like shelves, but it adds a set of additional features in exchange for a small amount of extra interface code.

ZODB is an open source, third-party add-on for Python. It was originally developed as the database mechanism for web sites developed with the Zope system described in Chapter 18, but it is now available as a standalone package. It's useful outside the context of Zope as a general database management system in any domain.

Although ZODB does not support SQL queries, objects stored in ZODB can leverage the full power of the Python language. Moreover, in some applications, stored data is more naturally represented as a structured Python object. Table-based relational systems often must represent such data as parts scattered across multiple tables, associated with keys and joins.

Using a ZODB database is very similar to Python's standard library shelves, described in the prior section. Just like shelves, ZODB uses the Python pickling system to implement a persistent dictionary of persistent Python objects.

In fact, there is almost no database interface to be found—objects are made persistent simply by assigning them to keys of the root ZODB dictionary object, or embedding them in objects stored in the database root. And as in a shelve, records take the form of native Python objects, processed with normal Python syntax and tools.

Unlike shelves, ZODB adds features critical to some types of programs:

Concurrent updates
> You don't need to manually lock files to avoid data corruption if there are potentially many concurrent writers, the way you would for shelves.

Transaction commit and rollback
> If your program crashes, your changes are not retained unless you explicitly commit them to the database.

Automatic updates for some types of in-memory object changes
> Objects in ZODB derived from a persistence superclass are smart enough to know the database must be updated when an attribute is assigned.

Automatic caching of objects
> Objects are cached in memory for efficiency and are automatically removed from the cache when they haven't been used.

Platform-independent storage

> Because ZODB stores your database in a single flat file with large-file support, it is immune to the potential size constraints and DBM filesystem format differences of shelves. As we saw earlier in this chapter, a shelve created on Windows using BSD-DB may not be accessible to a script running with gdbm on Linux.

Because of such advantages, ZODB is probably worth your attention if you need to store Python objects in a database persistently, in a production environment. The only significant price you'll pay for using ZODB is a small amount of extra code:

- Accessing the database requires a small amount of extra boilerplate code to interface with ZODB—it's not a simple open call.

- Classes are derived from a persistence superclass if you want them to take advantage of automatic updates on changes—persistent classes are generally not completely independent of the database as in shelves, though they can be.

Considering the extra functionality ZODB provides beyond shelves, these trade-offs are usually more than justified for many applications.

A ZODB Tutorial

To sample the flavor of ZODB, let's work through a quick interactive tutorial. We'll illustrate common use here, but we won't cover the API exhaustively; as usual, search the Web for more details on ZODB.

Installing ZODB

The first thing we need to do is install ZODB on top of Python. ZODB is an open source package, but it is not a standard part of Python today; it must be fetched and installed separately. To find ZODB, either run a web search on its name or visit *http://www.zope.org*. Apart from Python itself, the ZODB package is the only component you must install to use ZODB databases.

ZODB is available in both source and self-installer forms. On Windows, ZODB is available as a self-installing executable, which installs itself in the standard *site-packages* subdirectory of the Python standard library (specifically, it installs itself in *C:\Python24\site-packages* on Windows under Python 2.4). Because that directory is automatically added to your module search path, no path configuration is needed to import ZODB's modules once they are installed.

Moreover, much like Python's standard pickle and shelve tools, basic ZODB does not require that a perpetually running server be started in order to access your database. Technically speaking, ZODB itself supports safe concurrent updates among multiple threads, as long as each thread maintains its own connection to the database. ZEO, an additional component that ships with ZODB, supports concurrent updates among multiple processes in a client/server context.

The ZEO distributed object server

More generally, ZEO, for Zope Enterprise Objects, adds a distributed object architecture to applications requiring high performance and scalability. To understand how, you have to understand the architecture of ZODB itself. ZODB works by routing object requests to a storage interface object, which in turn handles physical storage tasks. Commonly used storage interface objects allow for file, BerkeleyDB, and even relational database storage media. By delegating physical medium tasks to storage interface objects, ZODB is independent of the underlying storage medium.

Essentially, ZEO replaces the standard file-storage interface object used by clients with one that routes requests across a network to a ZEO storage server. The ZEO storage server acts as a frontend to physical storage, synchronizing data access among multiple clients and allowing for more flexible configurations. For instance, this indirection layer allows for distributing load across multiple machines, storage redundancy, and more. Although not every application requires ZEO, it provides advanced enterprise-level support when needed.

ZEO itself consists of a TCP/IP socket server and the new storage interface object used by clients. The ZEO server may run on the same or a remote machine. Upon receipt, the server passes requests on to a regular storage interface object of its own, such as simple local file storage. On changes, the ZEO server sends invalidation messages to all connected clients, to update their object caches. Furthermore, ZODB avoids file locking by issuing conflict errors to force retries. As one consequence, ZODB/ZEO-based databases may be more efficient for reads than updates (the common case for web-based applications). Internally, the ZEO server is built with the Python standard library's asyncore module, which implements a socket event loop based on the select system call, much as we did in Chapter 13.

In the interest of space, we'll finesse further ZODB and ZEO details here; see other resources for more details on ZEO and ZODB's concurrent updates model. To most programs, ZODB is surprisingly easy to use; let's turn to some real code next.

Creating a ZODB database

Once you've installed ZODB, its interface takes the form of packages and modules to your code. Let's create a first database to see how this works:

```
...\PP3E\Database\ZODBscripts\>python
>>> from ZODB import FileStorage, DB
>>> storage = FileStorage.FileStorage(r'C:\Mark\temp\mydb.fs')
>>> db = DB(storage)
>>> connection = db.open()
>>> root = connection.root()
```

This is mostly standard code for connecting to a ZODB database: we import its tools, create a FileStorage and a DB from it, and then open the database and create the *root object*. The root object is the persistent dictionary in which objects are stored. `FileStorage` is an object that maps the database to a flat file. Other storage interface options, such as relational database-based storage, are also possible. When using the ZEO server configuration discussed earlier, programs import a `ClientStorage` interface object from the ZEO package instead, but the rest of the code is the same.

Now that we have a database, let's add a few objects to it. Almost any Python object will do, including tuples, lists, dictionaries, class instances, and nested combinations thereof. Simply assign your objects to a key in the database root object to make them persistent:

```
>>> object1 = (1, 'spam', 4, 'YOU')
>>> object2 = [[1, 2, 3], [4, 5, 6]]
>>> object2.append([7, 8, 9])
>>> object2
[[1, 2, 3], [4, 5, 6], [7, 8, 9]]
>>>
>>> object3 = {'name': ['Bob', 'Doe'],
                'age':  42,
                'job':  ('dev', 'mgr')}
>>>
>>> root['mystr']   = 'spam' * 3
>>> root['mytuple'] = object1
>>> root['mylist']  = object2
>>> root['mydict']  = object3
>>> root['mylist']
[[1, 2, 3], [4, 5, 6], [7, 8, 9]]
```

Because ZODB supports transaction rollbacks, you must commit your changes to the database to make them permanent. Ultimately, this transfers the pickled representation of your objects to the underlying file storage medium—here, three files that include the name of the file we gave when opening:

```
>>> import transaction
>>> transaction.commit()
>>> storage.close()

...\PP3E\Database\ZODBscripts>dir /B c:\mark\temp\mydb*
mydb.fs
mydb.fs.index
mydb.fs.tmp
```

Without the final commit in this session, none of the changes we made would be saved. This is what we want in general—if a program aborts in the middle of an update task, none of the partially complete work it has done is retained.

Fetching and changing

OK; we've made a few objects persistent in our ZODB. Pulling them back in another session or program is just as straightforward: reopen the database as before and index the root to fetch objects back into memory. The database root supports dictionary interfaces—it may be indexed, has dictionary methods and a length, and so on:

```
...\PP3E\Database\ZODBscripts\>python
>>> from ZODB import FileStorage, DB
>>> storage = FileStorage.FileStorage(r'C:\Mark\temp\mydb.fs')
>>> db = DB(storage)
>>> connection = db.open()
>>> root = connection.root()                    # connect
>>>
>>> print len(root), root.keys()                # size, index
4 ['mylist', 'mystr', 'mytuple', 'mydict']
>>>
>>> print root['mylist']                        # fetch objects
[[1, 2, 3], [4, 5, 6], [7, 8, 9]]
>>> print root['mydict']
{'job': ('dev', 'mgr'), 'age': 42, 'name': ['Bob', 'Doe']}

>>> root['mydict']['name'][-1]                   # Bob's last name
'Doe'
```

Because the database root looks just like a dictionary, we can process it with normal dictionary code—stepping through the keys list to scan record by record, for instance:

```
>>> for key in root.keys():
        print key.ljust(10), '=>', root[key]

mylist      => [[1, 2, 3], [4, 5, 6], [7, 8, 9]]
mystr       => spamspamspam
mytuple     => (1, 'spam', 4, 'YOU')
mydict      => {'job': ('dev', 'mgr'), 'age': 42, 'name': ['Bob', 'Doe']}
```

Now, let's change a few of our stored persistent objects. When changing ZODB persistent class instances, in-memory attribute changes are automatically written back to the database. Other types of changes, such as in-place appends and key assignments, still require reassignment to the original key to force the change to be written to disk (built-in list and dictionary objects do not know that they are persistent):

```
>>> rec = root['mylist']
>>> rec.append([10, 11, 12])          # change in memory
>>> root['mylist'] = rec              # write back to db
>>>
>>> rec = root['mydict']
>>> rec['age'] += 1                   # change in memory
>>> rec['job'] = None
>>> root['mydict'] = rec              # write back to db

>>> import transaction
>>> transaction.commit()
>>> storage.close()
```

As usual, we commit our work before exiting Python or all our changes would be lost. One more interactive session serves to verify that we've updated the database objects; there is no need to commit this time because we aren't making any changes:

```
...\PP3E\Database\ZODBscripts\>python
>>> from ZODB import FileStorage, DB
>>> storage = FileStorage.FileStorage(r'C:\Mark\temp\mydb.fs')
>>> db = DB(storage)
>>> connection = db.open( )
>>> root = connection.root( )
>>>
>>> print root['mylist']
[[1, 2, 3], [4, 5, 6], [7, 8, 9], [10, 11, 12]]
>>>
>>> print  root['mydict']
{'job': None, 'age': 43, 'name': ['Bob', 'Doe']}
>>>
>>> print  root['mydict']['age']
43
```

We are essentially using Python as an interactive object database query language here; to make use of classes and scripts, let's move on to the next section.

Using Classes with ZODB

So far, we've been storing built-in object types such as lists and dictionaries in our ZODB databases. Such objects can handle rich information structures, especially when they are nested—a dictionary with nested lists and dictionaries, for example, can represent complex information. As for shelves, though, class instances open up more possibilities—they can also participate in inheritance hierarchies, and they naturally support record processing behavior in the form of class method functions.

Classes used with ZODB can either be standalone, as in shelves, or derived from the ZODB Persistent class. The latter scheme provides objects with a set of precoded utility, including the ability to automatically write instance attribute changes out to the database storage—no manual reassignment to root keys is required. To see how this works, let's get started by defining the class in Example 19-4: an object that records information about a bookmark in a hypothetical web site application.

Example 19-4. PP3E\Database\ZODBscripts\zodb-class-make.py

```
#############################################################################
# define persistent class, store instances in a ZODB database;
# import, call addobjects elsewhere: pickled class cannot be in __main__
#############################################################################

import time
mydbfile = 'data/class.fs'                      # where database is stored
from persistent import Persistent

class BookMark(Persistent):                     # inherit ZODB features
```

Example 19-4. PP3E\Database\ZODBscripts\zodb-class-make.py (continued)

```
    def __init__(self, title, url):
        self.hits = 0
        self.updateBookmark(self, url)
    def updateBookmark(self, title, url):
        self.title = title              # change attrs updates db
        self.url = url                  # no need to reassign to key
        self.modtime = time.asctime()

def connectdb(dbfile):
    from ZODB import FileStorage, DB
    storage = FileStorage.FileStorage(dbfile)   # automate connect protocol
    db = DB(storage)                             # caller must still commit
    connection = db.open()
    root = connection.root()
    return root, storage

def addobjects():
    root, storage = connectdb(mydbfile)
    root['ora']  = BookMark('Oreilly', 'http://www.oreilly.com')
    root['pp3e'] = BookMark('PP3E',    'http://www.rmi.net/~lutz/about-pp.html')
    import transaction
    transaction.commit()
    storage.close()
```

Notice how this class is no longer standalone—it inherits from a ZODB superclass. In fact, unlike shelve classes, it cannot be tested or used outside the context of a ZODB database. In exchange, updates to instance attributes are automatically written back to the database file. Also note how we've put connection logic in a function for reuse; this avoids repeating login code redundantly, but the caller is still responsible for keeping track of the root and storage objects and for committing changes on exit (we'll see how to hide these details better in the next section). To test, let's make a few database objects interactively:

```
...\PP3E\Database\ZODBscripts>python
>>> from zodb_class_make import addobjects
>>> addobjects()

...\PP3E\Database\ZODBscripts>dir /B data
class.fs
class.fs.index
class.fs.tmp
```

We don't generally want to run the creation code in the top level of our process because then those classes would always have to be in the module __main__ (the name of the top-level file or the interactive prompt) each time the objects are fetched. Recall that this is a constraint of Python's pickling system discussed earlier, which underlies ZODB—classes must be reimported, and hence, located in a file in a directory on the module search path This might work if we load the class name into all our top-level scripts, with from statements, but it can be inconvenient in general. To avoid the issue, define your classes in an imported module file, and not in the main top-level script.

To test database updates, Example 19-5 reads back our two stored objects and changes them—any change that updates an instance attribute in memory is automatically written through to the database file.

Example 19-5. PP3E\Database\ZODBscripts\zodb-class-read.py

```
###########################################################################
# read, update class instances in db; changing immutables like
# lists and dictionaries in-place does not update the db automatically
###########################################################################

mydbfile = 'data/class.fs'
from zodb_class_make import connectdb
root, storage = connectdb(mydbfile)

# this updates db: attrs changed in method
print 'pp3e url:', root['pp3e'].url
print 'pp3e mod:', root['pp3e'].modtime
root['pp3e'].updateBookmark('PP3E', 'www.rmi.net/~lutz/about-pp3e.html')

# this updates too: attr changed here
ora = root['ora']
print 'ora hits:', ora.hits
ora.hits += 1

# commit changes made
import transaction
transaction.commit()
storage.close()
```

Run this script a few times to watch the objects in your database change: the URL and modification time of one is updated, and the hit counter is modified on the other:

```
...\PP3E\Database\ZODBscripts\>python zodb-class-read.py
pp3e url: http://www.rmi.net/~lutz/about-pp.html
pp3e mod: Mon Dec 05 09:11:44 2005
ora hits: 0

...\PP3E\Database\ZODBscripts>python zodb-class-read.py
pp3e url: www.rmi.net/~lutz/about-pp3e.html
pp3e mod: Mon Dec 05 09:12:12 2005
ora hits: 1

...\PP3E\Database\ZODBscripts>python zodb-class-read.py
pp3e url: www.rmi.net/~lutz/about-pp3e.html
pp3e mod: Mon Dec 05 09:12:24 2005
ora hits: 2
```

And because these are Python objects, we can always inspect, modify, and add
records interactively (be sure to also import the class to make and add a new
instance):

```
...\PP3E\Database\ZODBscripts>c:\python24\python
>>> from zodb_class_make import connectdb, mydbfile
>>> root, storage = connectdb(mydbfile)
>>> len(root)
2
>>> root.keys()
['pp3e', 'ora']
>>> root['ora'].hits
3
>>> root['pp3e'].url
'www.rmi.net/~lutz/about-pp3e.html'
>>> root['ora'].hits += 1
>>> import transaction
>>> transaction.commit()
>>> storage.close()

...\PP3E\Database\ZODBscripts>c:\python24\python
>>> from zodb_class_make import connectdb, mydbfile
>>> root, storage = connectdb(mydbfile)
>>> root['ora'].hits
4
```

A ZODB People Database

As a final ZODB example, let's do something a bit more realistic. If you read the
sneak preview in Chapter 2, you'll recall that we used shelves there to record information about people. In this section, we bring that idea back to life, recoded to use
ZODB instead.

By now, we've written the usual ZODB file storage database connection logic enough
times to warrant packaging it as a reusable tool. We used a function to wrap it up in
Example 19-4, but we can go a step further with object-oriented programming
(OOP). As a first step, let's wrap this up for reuse as a component—the class in
Example 19-6 handles the connection task, automatically logging in on construction
and automatically committing changes on close. For convenience, it also embeds the
database root object and delegates attribute fetches and index accesses back to the
root.

The net effect is that this object behaves like an automatically opened and committed database root—it provides the same interface, but adds convenience code for
common use cases. You can reuse this class for any file-based ZODB database you
wish to process (just pass in your filename), and you have to change only this single
copy of the connection logic if it ever has to be updated.

Example 19-6. PP3E\Database\ZODBscripts\zodbtools.py

```
class FileDB:
    "automate zodb connect and close protocols"
    def __init__(self, filename):
        from ZODB import FileStorage, DB
        self.storage = FileStorage.FileStorage(filename)
        db = DB(self.storage)
        connection = db.open()
        self.root = connection.root()
    def commit(self):
        import transaction
        transaction.commit()                  # get_transaction() deprecated
    def close(self):
        self.commit()
        self.storage.close()
    def __getitem__(self, key):
        return self.root[key]                 # map indexing to db root
    def __setitem__(self, key, val):
        self.root[key] = val                  # map key assignment to root
    def __getattr__(self, attr):
        return getattr(self.root, attr)       # keys, items, values
```

Next, the class in Example 19-7 defines the objects we'll store in our database. They are pickled as usual, but they are written out to a ZODB database, not to a shelve file. Note how this class is no longer standalone, as in our earlier shelve examples—it inherits from the ZODB Persistent class, and thus will automatically notify ZODB of changes when its instance attributes are changed. Also notice the __str__ operator overloading method here, to give a custom display format for our objects.

Example 19-7. PP3E\Database\ZODBscripts\person.py

```
#######################################################################
# define persistent object classes; this must be in an imported
# file on your path, not in __main__ per Python pickling rules
# unless will only ever be used in module __main__ in the future;
# attribute assignments, in class or otherwise, update database;
# for mutable object changes, set object's _p_changed to true to
# auto update, or manually reassign to database key after changes;
#######################################################################

from persistent import Persistent           # new module name in 3.3

class Person(Persistent):
    def __init__(self, name, job=None, rate=0):
        self.name = name
        self.job  = job
        self.rate = rate
    def changeRate(self, newrate):
        self.rate = newrate                  # auto updates database
    def calcPay(self, hours=40):
        return self.rate * hours
    def __str__(self):
```

Example 19-7. PP3E\Database\ZODBscripts\person.py (continued)

```
        myclass = self.__class__.__name__
        format = '<%s:\t name=%s, job=%s, rate=%d, pay=%d>'
        values = (myclass, self.name, self.job, self.rate, self.calcPay())
        return format % values

class Engineer(Person):
    def calcPay(self):
        return self.rate / 52    # yearly salary
```

Finally, Example 19-8 tests our Person class, by creating the database and updating objects. As usual for Python's pickling system, we store the class in an imported module, not in this main, top-level script file. Otherwise, it could be reimported by Python only when class instance objects are reloaded, if it is still a part of the module __main__).

Example 19-8. PP3E\Database\ZODBscripts\person-test.py

```
###############################################################################
# test persistence classes in person.py; this runs as __main__, so the
# classes cannot be defined in this file: class's module must be importable
# when obj fetched; can also test from interactive prompt: also is __main__
###############################################################################

from zodbtools import FileDB                  # extended db root
from person import Person, Engineer            # application objects
filename = 'people.fs'                         # external storage

import sys
if len(sys.argv) == 1:                         # no args: create test records
    db = FileDB(filename)                      # db is root object
    db['bob'] = Person('bob', 'devel', 30)     # stores in db
    db['sue'] = Person('sue', 'music', 40)
    tom = Engineer('tom', 'devel', 60000)
    db['tom'] = tom
    db.close()                                 # close commits changes

else:                                          # arg: change tom, sue each run
    db = FileDB(filename)
    print db['bob'].name, db.keys()
    print db['sue']
    db['sue'].changeRate(db['sue'].rate + 10)  # updates db
    tom = db['tom']
    print tom
    tom.changeRate(tom.rate + 5000)            # updates db
    tom.name += '.spam'                        # updates db
    db.close()
```

When run with no command-line arguments, the test script initialized the database with two class instances: two Persons, and one Engineer. When run with any argument, it updates the existing database records, adding 10 to Sue's pay rate and modifying Tom's rate and name:

```
...\PP3E\Database\ZODBscripts>python person-test.py

...\PP3E\Database\ZODBscripts>python person-test.py -
bob ['bob', 'sue', 'tom']
<Person:        name=sue, job=music, rate=40, pay=1600>
<Engineer:      name=tom, job=devel, rate=60000, pay=1153>

...\PP3E\Database\ZODBscripts>python person-test.py -
bob ['bob', 'sue', 'tom']
<Person:        name=sue, job=music, rate=50, pay=2000>
<Engineer:      name=tom.spam, job=devel, rate=65000, pay=1250>

...\PP3E\Database\ZODBscripts>python person-test.py -
bob ['bob', 'sue', 'tom']
<Person:        name=sue, job=music, rate=60, pay=2400>
<Engineer:      name=tom.spam.spam, job=devel, rate=70000, pay=1346>
```

Notice how the changeRate method updates Sue—there is no need to reassign the updated record back to the original key as we have to do for shelves, because ZODB Persistent class instances are smart enough to write attribute changes to the database automatically on commits. Internally, ZODB's persistent superclasses use normal Python operator overloading to intercept attribute changes and mark the object as changed.

However, direct in-place changes to mutable objects (e.g., appending to a built-in list) are not noticed by ZODB and require setting the object's _p_changed, or manual reassignment to the original key, to write changes through. ZODB also provides custom versions of some built-in mutable object types (e.g., PersistentMapping), which write changes through automatically.

ZODB Resources

There are additional ZODB concepts and components that we have not covered and do not have space to discuss in detail in this book. For instance, because ZODB stores objects with Python's pickle module, all of that module's constraints discussed earlier in this chapter apply. Moreover, we have not touched on administrative requirements. Because the FileStorage interface works by appending changes to the file, for example, it requires periodically running a utility to pack the database by removing old object revisions.

For more about ZODB, search for ZODB and Zope resources on the Web. Here, let's move on to see how Python programs can make use of a very different sort of database interface—relational databases and SQL.

SQL Database Interfaces

The shelve module and ZODB package of the prior sections are powerful tools. Both allow scripts to throw nearly arbitrary Python objects on a keyed-access file and load them back later—in a single step for shelves and with a small amount of administrative code for ZODB. Especially for applications that record highly structured data, object databases can be convenient and efficient—there is no need to split and later join together the parts of large objects, and stored data is processed with normal Python syntax because it is normal Python objects.

Shelves and ZODB aren't relational database systems, though; objects (records) are accessed with a single key, and there is no notion of SQL queries. Shelves, for instance, are essentially databases with a single index and no other query-processing support. Although it's possible to build a multiple-index interface to store data with multiple shelves, it's not a trivial task and requires manually coded extensions.

ZODB supports some types of searching beyond shelve (e.g., its cataloging feature), and persistent objects may be traversed with all the power of the Python language. However, neither shelves nor ZODB object-oriented databases provide the full generality of SQL queries. Moreover, especially for data that has a naturally tabular structure, relational databases may sometimes be a better fit.

For programs that can benefit from the power of SQL, Python also supports relational database systems. Relational databases are not necessarily mutually exclusive with the object persistence topics we studied earlier in this chapter—it is possible, for example, to store the serialized string representation of a Python object produced by pickling in a relational database. ZODB also supports the notion of mapping an object database to a relational storage medium.

The databases we'll meet in this section, though, are structured and processed in very different ways:

- They store data in related tables of columns (rather than in persistent dictionaries of arbitrarily structured persistent Python objects).
- They support the SQL query language for accessing data and exploiting relationships among it (instead of Python object traversals).

For some applications, the end result can be a potent combination. Moreover, some SQL-based database systems provide industrial-strength persistence support.

Today, there are freely available interfaces that let Python scripts utilize all common relational database systems, both free and commercial: MySQL, Oracle, Sybase, Informix, InterBase, PostgreSQL (Postgres), SQLite,[*] ODBC, and more. In addition, the Python community has defined a database API specification that works portably with a variety of underlying database packages. Scripts written for this API can be migrated to different database vendor packages, with minimal or no source code changes.

---

[*] Late-breaking news: Python 2.5 will likely include support for the SQLite relational database system as part of its standard library. For more on the cutting edge, see also the popular SQLObject third-party Object Relational Manage, which grafts an object interface onto your database, with tables as classes, rows as instances, and columns as attributes.

SQL Interface Overview

Like ZODB, and unlike the pickle and shelve persistence modules presented earlier, SQL databases are optional extensions that are not part of Python itself. Moreover, you need to know SQL to fully understand their interfaces. Because we don't have space to teach SQL in this text, this section gives a brief overview of the API; please consult other SQL references and the database API resources mentioned in the next section for more details.

The good news is that you can access SQL databases from Python, through a straightforward and portable model. The Python database API specification defines an interface for communicating with underlying database systems from Python scripts. Vendor-specific database interfaces for Python may or may not conform to this API completely, but all database extensions for Python seem minor variations on a theme. SQL databases in Python are grounded on a few concepts:

Connection objects
> Represent a connection to a database, are the interface to rollback and commit operations, and generate cursor objects.

Cursor objects
> Represent an SQL statement submitted as a string and can be used to step through SQL statement results.

Query results of SQL select *statements*
> Are returned to scripts as Python sequences of sequences (e.g., a list of tuples), representing database tables of rows. Within these row sequences, column field values are normal Python objects such as strings, integers, and floats (e.g., [('bob',38), ('emily',37)]). Column values may also be special types that encapsulate things such as date and time, and database NULL values are returned as the Python None object.

Beyond this, the API defines a standard set of database exception types, special database type object constructors, and informational calls.

For instance, to establish a database connection under the Python API–compliant Oracle interface available from Digital Creations, install the extension and Oracle, and then run a line of this form:

```
connobj = Connect("user/password@system")
```

The string argument's contents may vary per database and vendor, but they generally contain what you provide to log in to your database system. Once you have a connection object, there a variety of things you can do with it, including:

```
connobj.close( )              close connection now (not at object __del__ time)
connobj.commit( )             commit any pending transactions to the database
connobj.rollback( )           roll database back to start of pending transactions
connobj.callproce(proc, params)   fetch stored procedure's code
connobj.getSource(proc)       fetch stored procedure's code
```

But one of the most useful things to do with a connection object is to generate a cursor object:

```
cursobj = connobj.cursor()      return a new cursor object for running SQL
```

Cursor objects have a set of methods too (e.g., close to close the cursor before its destructor runs), but the most important may be this one:

```
cursobj.execute(sqlstring [, parameters])   run SQL query or command string
```

Parameters are passed in as a sequence or mapping of values, and are substituted into the SQL statement string according to the interface module's replacement target conventions. The execute method can be used to run a variety of SQL statement strings:

- DDL definition statements (e.g., CREATE TABLE)
- DML modification statements (e.g., UPDATE or INSERT)
- DQL query statements (e.g., SELECT)

After running an SQL statement, the cursor's rowcount attribute gives the number of rows changed (for DML) or fetched (for DQL); execute also returns the number of rows affected or fetched in the most vendor interfaces. For DQL query statements, you must call one of the fetch methods to complete the operation:

```
tuple       = cursobj.fetchone()       fetch next row of a query result
listoftuple = cursobj.fetchmany([size])   fetch next set of rows of query result
listoftuple = cursobj.fetchall()       fetch all remaining rows of the result
```

And once you've received fetch method results, table information is processed using normal Python sequence operations (e.g., you can step through the tuples in a fetchall result list with a simple for loop). Most Python database interfaces also allow you to provide values to be passed to SQL statement strings, by providing targets and a tuple of parameters. For instance:

```
query = 'SELECT name, shoesize FROM spam WHERE job = ? AND age = ?'
cursobj.execute(query, (value1, value2))
results = cursobj.fetchall()
for row in results: ...
```

In this event, the database interface utilizes prepared statements (an optimization and convenience) and correctly passes the parameters to the database regardless of their Python types. The notation used to code targets in the query string may vary in some database interfaces (e.g., :p1 and :p2 rather than the two ?s used by the Oracle interface); in any event, this is not the same as Python's % string formatting operator.

Finally, if your database supports stored procedures, you can generally call them with the callproc method or by passing an SQL CALL or EXEC statement string to the execute method. callproc may generate a result table retrieved with a fetch variant, and returns a modified copy of the input sequence—input parameters are left untouched, and output and input/output parameters are replaced with possibly new values. Additional API features, including support for database blobs, is described in the API's documentation. For now, let's move on to do some real SQL processing in Python.

An SQL Database API Tutorial

We don't have space to provide an exhaustive reference for the database API in this book. To sample the flavor of the interface, though, let's step through a few simple examples. We'll use the MySQL database system for this tutorial. Thanks to Python's portable database API, other popular database packages such as Postgre-SQL, SQLite, and Oracle are used almost identically, but the initial call to log in to the database will generally require different argument values.

The MySQL system

With a reported 8 million installations and support for more than 20 platforms, MySQL is by most accounts the most popular open source relational database system today. It is a powerful, fast, and full-featured SQL database system that serves as the storage mechanism for many of the sites you may visit on the Web.

MySQL consists of a database server, as well as a collection of clients. Technically, its SQL engine is a multithreaded server, which uses some of the same threaded socket server techniques we met in Chapter 13. It listens for requests on a socket and port, can be run either on a remote machine or on your local computer, and handles clients in parallel threads for efficiency and responsiveness.

On Windows, the MySQL server may be run automatically as a Windows service, so it is always available; on Unix-like machines, it runs as a perpetual demon process. In either case, the server can accept requests over a network or simply run on your machine to provide access to locally stored databases. Ultimately, your databases take the form of a set of files, stored in the server's "data" directory and represented as B-tree disk tables. MySQL handles concurrent updates by automatically locking tables when they are written by client conversation threads.

The MySQL server is available both as a separate program for use in a client/server networked environment, and as a library that can be linked into standalone applications. Clients can submit queries to the server over a TCP/IP socket on any platform; as usual with sockets, use the machine name "localhost" if the server is running locally. Besides sockets, the database server also supports connections using named pipes on Windows NT–based platforms (NT, 2000, XP, and so on); Unix domain socket files on Unix; shared memory on Windows; as well as ODBC, JDBC, and ADO.NET.

For our purposes, the main thing to note is that the standard MySQL interface for Python is compliant with the current version of the database API (2.0). Because of that, most of the code we'll see here will also work unchanged on other database systems, as long as their interfaces also support the portable database API. If you use the

PostgreSQL database, for instance, the PyGreSQL open source Python extension provides DB-API 2.0–compliant interfaces that largely work the same way.

Installation

Before we can start coding, we need to install both MySQL itself, as well as the Python MySQL interface module. The MySQL system implements a language-neutral database server; the Python interface module maps calls in our script to the database server's interfaces. This is a straightforward process, but here are a few quick notes:

MySQL

At this writing, MySQL can be found on the Web at *http://dev.mysql.com*. It's available in two flavors—a community version, which is open source (under the GNU license), as well as a commercial version, which is not free, but is relatively inexpensive and removes the restrictions of the GNU license (you won't have to make all your source code available, for instance). See the MySQL web site for more on which version may be right for you; the open source package was used for this book. MySQL installs itself today in *C:\Program Files\MySQL* on Windows. It includes the database server program, command-line tools, and more.

Python MySQL interface

The primary DB API–compliant MySQL interface for Python was `mysql-python` when I wrote this (but run a web search on "Python MySQL" for current information). You may also find links to this package at the *http://www.python.org* page for the database Special Interest Group (SIG), as well as at the Vaults of Parnassus site. Both `mysql-python`, as well as MySQL itself, are simple self-installing executables on Windows. On Windows, like most third-party packages, the Python MySQL interface shows up in the Python install tree, in the *site-packages* subdirectory of the standard library: *C:\Python24\Lib\site-packages\MySQLdb*. As usual, because this directory is automatically added to the module import search path, no path configuration is required.

Getting started

Time to write some code; this isn't a book on either MySQL or the SQL language, so we'll defer to other resources for details on the commands we'll be running here (O'Reilly has a suite of books on both topics). In fact, the databases we'll use are tiny, and the commands we'll use are deliberately simple as SQL goes—you'll want to extrapolate from what you see here to the more realistic tasks you face. This section is just a brief look at how to use the Python language in conjunction with an SQL database.

The basic SQL interface in Python is very simple, though. In fact, it's hardly object-oriented at all—queries and other database commands are sent as strings of SQL. If you know SQL, you already have most of what you need in Python.

The first thing we want to do is open a connection to the database and create a table for storing records:

```
% python
>>> import MySQLdb
>>> conn = MySQLdb.connect(host='localhost', user='root', passwd='python')
```

We start out by importing the Python MySQL interface here—it's a package directory called MySQLdb to our scripts that looks like a simple module. Next we create a connection object, passing in the items our database requires for a login—here, the name of the machine the server is running on, along with a user and password. This first API tends to vary per database system, because each has unique login requirements. After you've connected, though, the rest of the API is largely the same for any database.

As usual, the server name "localhost" means the local computer, but this could also be any TCP/IP server name if we're using a database on a remote machine. You normally would log in with a username created by your database administrator, but we'll use "root" here to keep this simple (the root user is created automatically when MySQL is installed, and I gave it a password of "python" during installation).

Making databases and tables

Next, make a cursor for submitting SQL statements to the database server:

```
>>> curs = conn.cursor( )
>>> curs.execute('create database peopledb')
1L
>>> curs.execute('use peopledb')
0L
>>> tblcmd = 'create table people (name char(30), job char(10), pay int(4))'
>>> curs.execute(tblcmd)
0L
```

The first command here makes a database called *peopledb*. We can make more than one—for instance, one for test and one for production, or one per developer—but most SQL statements are relative to a particular database. We can tell the server which database to use with the use SQL statement or by passing in a db keyword argument when calling connect to make the initial connection. In MySQL, we can also qualify table names with their databases in SQL statements (database.table), but it's usually more convenient to select the database and make it implied.

Finally, the last command creates the table called "people" within the *peopledb* database; the name, job, and pay information specifies the columns in this table, as well as their datatypes using a "type(size)" syntax—two strings and an integer. Datatypes can be more sophisticated than ours, but we'll ignore such details here (see SQL references).

Adding records

So far, we've logged in and created a database and table. Now let's start a new Python session and create some records. There are three basic statement-based approaches we can use here: inserting one row at a time, or inserting multiple rows with a single call statement or a Python loop. Here is the simple case:

```
% python
>>> import MySQLdb
>>> conn = MySQLdb.connect(host='localhost', db='peopledb',
...                        user='root', passwd='python')
>>> curs = conn.cursor()
>>> curs.execute('insert people values (%s, %s, %s)', ('Bob', 'dev', 5000))
1L
>>> curs.rowcount
1L
>>> MySQLdb.paramstyle
'format'
```

Create a cursor object to submit SQL statements to the database server as before. The SQL insert command adds a single row to the table. After an execute call, the cursor's rowcount attribute gives the number of rows produced or affected by the last statement run. This is also available as the return value of an execute call in the MySQL module, but this is not defined in the database API specification (in other words, don't depend on it if you want your database scripts to work on other database systems).

Parameters to substitute into the SQL statement string are passed in as a sequence (e.g., list or tuple). Notice the module's paramstyle—this tells us what style it uses for substitution targets in the statement string. Here, format means this module accepts string formatting-style targets; %s means a string-based substitution, just as in Python % string expressions. Other database modules might use styles such as qmark (a ? target), or numeric indexes or mapping keys (see the DB API for details).

To insert multiple rows with a single statement, use the executemany method and a sequence of row sequences (e.g., a list of lists). This call is like calling execute once for each row sequence in the argument, and in fact may be implemented as such; database interfaces may use database-specific techniques to make this run quicker, though:

```
>>> curs.executemany('insert people values (%s, %s, %s)',
...            [ ('Sue', 'mus', '70000'),
...              ('Ann', 'mus', '60000')])
2L
>>> curs.rowcount
2L
```

We inserted two rows at once in the last statement. It's hardly any more work to achieve the same result by inserting one row at a time with a Python loop:

```
>>> rows = [['Tom', 'mgr', 100000],
...         ['Kim', 'adm', 30000],
```

```
...              ['pat', 'dev', 90000]]
>>> for row in rows:
...     curs.execute('insert people values (%s , %s, %s)', row)
...
1L
1L
1L
>>> conn.commit( )
```

Blending Python and SQL like this starts to open up all sorts of interesting possibilities. Notice the last command; we always need to call the connection's commit method to write our changes out to the database. Otherwise, when the connection is closed, our changes will be lost. In fact, if you quit Python without calling the commit method, none of your inserts will be retained.

Technically, the connection object automatically calls its rollback method to back out changes that have not yet been committed, when it is closed (which happens manually when its close method is called or automatically when the connection object is about to be garbage-collected). For database systems that don't support transaction commit and rollback operations, these calls may do nothing.

Running queries

OK, we've now added six records to our database table. Let's run an SQL query to see how we did:

```
>>> curs.execute('select * from people')
6L
>>> curs.fetchall( )
(('Bob', 'dev', 5000L), ('Sue', 'mus', 70000L), ('Ann', 'mus', 60000L), ('Tom',
'mgr', 100000L), ('Kim', 'adm', 30000L), ('pat', 'dev', 90000L))
```

Run an SQL select statement with a cursor object to grab all rows and call the cursor's fetchall to retrieve them. They come back to our script as a sequence of sequences. In this module, it's a tuple of tuples—the outer tuple represents the result table, the nested tuples are that table's rows, and the nested tuple's contents are the column data. Because it's all Python data, once we get the query result, we process it with normal Python code. For example, to make the display a bit more coherent, loop through the query result:

```
>>> curs.execute('select * from people')
6L
>>> for row in curs.fetchall( ):
...     print row
...
('Bob', 'dev', 5000L)
('Sue', 'mus', 70000L)
('Ann', 'mus', 60000L)
('Tom', 'mgr', 100000L)
('Kim', 'adm', 30000L)
('pat', 'dev', 90000L)
```

Tuple unpacking comes in handy in loops here too, to pick out column values as we go; here's a simple formatted display of two of the columns' values:

```
>>> curs.execute('select * from people')
6L
>>> for (name, job, pay) in curs.fetchall():
...     print name, ':', pay
...
Bob : 5000
Sue : 70000
Ann : 60000
Tom : 100000
Kim : 30000
pat : 90000
```

Because the query result is a sequence, we can use Python's powerful sequence tools to process it. For instance, to select just the name column values, we can run a more specific SQL query and get a tuple of tuples:

```
>>> curs.execute('select name from people')
6L
>>> names = curs.fetchall()
>>> names
(('Bob',), ('Sue',), ('Ann',), ('Tom',), ('Kim',), ('pat',))
```

Or we can use a Python list comprehension to pick out the fields we want—by using Python code, we have more control over the data's content and format:

```
>>> curs.execute('select * from people')
6L
>>> names = [rec[0] for rec in curs.fetchall()]
>>> names
['Bob', 'Sue', 'Ann', 'Tom', 'Kim', 'pat']
```

The fetchall call we've used so far fetches the entire query result table all at once, as a single sequence (an empty sequence comes back, if the result is empty). That's convenient, but it may be slow enough to block the caller temporarily for large result tables or generate substantial network traffic if the server is running remotely. To avoid such a bottleneck, we can also grab just one row, or a bunch of rows, at a time with fetchone and fetchmany. The fetchone call returns the next result row or a None false value at the end of the table:

```
>>> curs.execute('select * from people')
6L
>>> while True:
...     row = curs.fetchone()
...     if not row: break
...     print row
...
('Bob', 'dev', 5000L)
('Sue', 'mus', 70000L)
('Ann', 'mus', 60000L)
('Tom', 'mgr', 100000L)
('Kim', 'adm', 30000L)
('pat', 'dev', 90000L)
```

The `fetchmany` call returns a sequence of rows from the result, but not the entire table; you can specify how many rows to grab each time with a parameter or fall back on the setting of the cursor's arraysize attribute. Each call gets at most that many more rows from the result or an empty sequence at the end of the table:

```
>>> curs.execute('select * from people')
6L
>>> while True:
...     rows = curs.fetchmany()             # size=N optional argument
...     if not rows: break
...     for row in rows:
...         print row
...
('Bob', 'dev', 5000L)
('Sue', 'mus', 70000L)
('Ann', 'mus', 60000L)
('Tom', 'mgr', 100000L)
('Kim', 'adm', 30000L)
('pat', 'dev', 90000L)
```

For this module at least, the result table is exhausted after a `fetchone` or `fetchmany` returns a False, though `fetchall` continues to return the whole table. The DB API says that `fetchall` returns "all (remaining) rows," so you may want to call execute anyhow to regenerate results before fetching, for portability:

```
>>> curs.fetchone()
>>> curs.fetchmany()
()
>>> curs.fetchall()
(('Bob', 'dev', 5000L), ('Sue', 'mus', 70000L), ('Ann', 'mus', 60000L), ('Tom',
'mgr', 100000L), ('Kim', 'adm', 30000L), ('pat', 'dev', 90000L))
```

Naturally, we can do more than fetch an entire table; the full power of the SQL language is at your disposal in Python:

```
>>> curs.execute('select name, job from people where pay > 60000')
3L
>>> curs.fetchall()
(('Sue', 'mus'), ('Tom', 'mgr'), ('pat', 'dev'))
```

The last query fetches names and pay fields for people who earn more than $60,000. The next is similar, but passes in the selection value as a parameter and orders the result table:

```
>>> query = 'select name, job from people where pay >= %s order by name'
>>> curs.execute(query, [60000])
4L
>>> for row in curs.fetchall(): print row
...
('Ann', 'mus')
('pat', 'dev')
('Sue', 'mus')
('Tom', 'mgr')
```

Running updates

Cursor objects also are used to submit SQL update statements to the database server—updates, deletes, and inserts. We've already seen the insert statement at work. Let's start a new session to perform some other kinds of updates:

```
% python
>>> import MySQLdb
>>> conn = MySQLdb.connect(host='localhost', user='root', passwd='python')
>>> curs = conn.cursor()
>>> curs.execute('use peopledb')
>>> curs.execute('select * from people')
6L
>>> curs.fetchall()
(('Bob', 'dev', 5000L), ('Sue', 'mus', 70000L), ('Ann', 'mus', 60000L), ('Tom',
'mgr', 100000L), ('Kim', 'adm', 30000L), ('pat', 'dev', 90000L))
```

The SQL update statement changes records—the following changes three records' pay column values to 65000 (Bob, Ann, and Kim), because their pay was no more than $60,000. As usual, the cursor's rowcount gives the number of records changed:

```
>>> curs.execute('update people set pay=%s where pay <= %s', [65000, 60000])
3L
>>> curs.rowcount
3L
>>> curs.execute('select * from people')
6L
>>> curs.fetchall()
(('Bob', 'dev', 65000L), ('Sue', 'mus', 70000L), ('Ann', 'mus', 65000L), ('Tom',
 'mgr', 100000L), ('Kim', 'adm', 65000L), ('pat', 'dev', 90000L))
```

The SQL delete statement removes records, optionally according to a condition (to delete all records, omit the condition). In the following, we delete Bob's record, as well as any record with a pay that is at least $90,000:

```
>>> curs.execute('delete from people where name = %s', ['Bob'])
1L
>>> curs.execute('delete from people where pay >= %s',(90000,))
2L
>>> curs.execute('select * from people')
3L
>>> curs.fetchall()
(('Sue', 'mus', 70000L), ('Ann', 'mus', 65000L), ('Kim', 'adm', 65000L))

>>> conn.commit()
```

Finally, remember to commit your changes to the database before exiting Python, assuming you wish to keep them. Without a commit, a connection rollback or close call, as well as the connection's _ _del_ _ deletion method, will back out uncommitted changes. Connection objects are automatically closed if they are still open when they are garbage-collected, which in turn triggers a _ _del_ _ and a rollback; garbage collection happens automatically on program exit, if not sooner.

Building Record Dictionaries

Now that we've seen the basics in action, let's move on and apply them to a few large tasks. The SQL API defines query results to be sequences of sequences. One of the more common features that people seem to miss from the API is the ability to get records back as something more structured—a dictionary or class instance, for example, with keys or attributes giving column names. Because this is Python, it's easy to code this kind of transformation, and the API already gives us the tools we need.

Using table descriptions

For example, after a query execute call, the DB API specifies that the cursor's description attribute gives the names and types of the columns in the result table (we're continuing with the database in the state in which we left it in the prior section):

```
>>> curs.execute('select * from people')
3L
>>> curs.description
(('name', 254, 3, 30, 30, 0, 1), ('job', 254, 3, 10, 10, 0, 1), ('pay', 3, 5, 4,
 4, 0, 1))
>>> curs.fetchall()
(('Sue', 'mus', 70000L), ('Ann', 'mus', 65000L), ('Kim', 'adm', 65000L))
```

Formally, the description is a sequence of column-description sequences, each of the following form (see the DB API for more on the meaning of the type code slot—it maps to objects at the top level of the MySQLdb module):

```
(name, type_code, display_size, internal_size, precision, scale, null_ok)
```

Now, we can use this metadata anytime we want to label the columns—for instance, in a formatted records display:

```
>>> colnames = [desc[0] for desc in curs.description]
>>> colnames
['name', 'job', 'pay']

>>> for row in curs.fetchall():
...     for name, value in zip(colnames, row):
...         print name, '\t=>', value
...     print
...
name    => Sue
job     => mus
pay     => 70000

name    => Ann
job     => mus
pay     => 65000

name    => Kim
job     => adm
pay     => 65000
```

Notice how a tab character is used to try to make this output align; a better approach might be to determine the maximum field name length (we'll see how in a later example).

Record dictionaries

It's a minor extension of our formatted display code to create a dictionary for each record, with field names for keys—we just need to fill in the dictionary as we go:

```
>>> curs.execute('select * from people')
3L
>>> colnames = [desc[0] for desc in curs.description]
>>> rowdicts = []
>>> for row in curs.fetchall():
...     newdict = {}
...     for name, val in zip(colnames, row):
...         newdict[name] = val
...     rowdicts.append(newdict)
...
>>> for row in rowdicts: print row
...
{'pay': 70000L, 'job': 'mus', 'name': 'Sue'}
{'pay': 65000L, 'job': 'mus', 'name': 'Ann'}
{'pay': 65000L, 'job': 'adm', 'name': 'Kim'}
```

Because this is Python, though, there are more powerful ways to build up these record dictionaries. For instance, the dictionary constructor call accepts the zipped name/value pairs to fill out the dictionaries for us:

```
>>> curs.execute('select * from people')
3L
>>> colnames = [desc[0] for desc in curs.description]
>>> rowdicts = []
>>> for row in curs.fetchall():
...     rowdicts.append( dict(zip(colnames, row)) )
...
>>> rowdicts[0]
{'pay': 70000L, 'job': 'mus', 'name': 'Sue'}
```

And finally, a list comprehension will do the job of collecting the dictionaries into a list—not only is this less to type, but it probably runs quicker than the original version:

```
>>> curs.execute('select * from people')
3L
>>> colnames = [desc[0] for desc in curs.description]
>>> rowdicts = [dict(zip(colnames, row)) for row in curs.fetchall()]

>>> rowdicts[0]
{'pay': 70000L, 'job': 'mus', 'name': 'Sue'}
```

One of the things we lose when moving to dictionaries is record field order—if you look back at the raw result of fetchall, you'll notice that record fields are in the name, job, and pay order in which they were stored. Our dictionary's fields come back in the pseudorandom order of Python mappings. As long as we fetch fields by key, this is irrelevant to our script. Tables still maintain their order, and dictionary construction works fine because the description result tuple is in the same order as the fields in row tuples returned by queries.

We'll leave the task of translating record tuples into class instances as a suggested exercise, except for the small hint that we can access fields as attributes rather than as keys, by simply creating an empty class instance and assigning to attributes with the Python setattr function. Classes would also provide a natural place to code inheritable tools such as standard display methods.

Automating with scripts and modules

Up to this point, we've essentially used Python as a command-line SQL client—our queries have been typed and run interactively. All the kinds of code we've run, though, can be used as the basis of database access in script files. Working interactively requires retyping things such as logic calls, which can become tedious. With scripts, we can automate our work.

To demonstrate, let's make the last section's prior example into a utility module— Example 19-9 is a reusable module that knows how to translate the result of a query from row tuples to row dictionaries.

Example 19-9. PP3E\Database\SQLscripts\makedicts.py

```
###############################################################################
# convert list of row tuples to list of row dicts with field name keys
# this is not a command-line utility: hardcoded self-test if run
###############################################################################

def makedicts(cursor, query, params=()):
    cursor.execute(query, params)
    colnames = [desc[0] for desc in cursor.description]
    rowdicts = [dict(zip(colnames, row)) for row in cursor.fetchall()]
    return rowdicts

if __name__ == '__main__':    # self test
    import MySQLdb
    conn = MySQLdb.connect(host='localhost', user='root', passwd='python')
    cursor = conn.cursor()
    cursor.execute('use peopledb')
    query  = 'select name, pay from people where pay < %s'
    lowpay = makedicts(cursor, query, [70000])
    for rec in lowpay: print rec
```

As usual, we can run this file from the system command line as a script to invoke its self-test code:

```
...\PP3E\Database\SQLscripts>makedicts.py
{'pay': 65000L, 'name': 'Ann'}
{'pay': 65000L, 'name': 'Kim'}
```

Or we can import it as a module and call its function from another context, like the interactive prompt. Because it is a module, it has become a reusable database tool:

```
...\PP3E\Database\SQLscripts>python
>>> from makedicts import makedicts
>>> from MySQLdb import connect
>>> conn = connect(host='localhost', user='root',passwd='python', db='peopledb')
>>> curs = conn.cursor()
>>> curs.execute('select * from people')
3L
>>> curs.fetchall()
(('Sue', 'mus', 70000L), ('Ann', 'mus', 65000L), ('Kim', 'adm', 65000L))

>>> rows = makedicts(curs, "select name from people where job = 'mus'")
>>> rows
[{'name': 'Sue'}, {'name': 'Ann'}]
```

Our utility handles arbitrarily complex queries—they are simply passed through the DB API to the database server. The order by clause here sorts the result on the name field:

```
>>> query = 'select name, pay from people where job = %s order by name'
>>> musicians = makedicts(curs, query, ['mus'])
>>> for row in musicians: print row
...
{'pay': 65000L, 'name': 'Ann'}
{'pay': 70000L, 'name': 'Sue'}
```

Tying the Pieces Together

So far, we've learned how to makes databases and tables, insert records into tables, query table contents, and extract column names. For reference, and to show how these techniques are combined, Example 19-10 collects them into a single script.

Example 19-10. PP3E\Database\SQLscripts\testdb.py

```
from MySQLdb import Connect
conn = Connect(host='localhost', user='root', passwd='python')
curs = conn.cursor()
try:
    curs.execute('drop database testpeopledb')
except:
    pass  # did not exist

curs.execute('create database testpeopledb')
curs.execute('use testpeopledb')
curs.execute('create table people (name char(30), job char(10), pay int(4))')

curs.execute('insert people values (%s, %s, %s)', ('Bob', 'dev', 50000))
curs.execute('insert people values (%s, %s, %s)', ('Sue', 'dev', 60000))

curs.execute('select * from people')
for row in curs.fetchall():
    print row
```

Example 19-10. PP3E\Database\SQLscripts\testdb.py (continued)

```
curs.execute('select * from people')
colnames = [desc[0] for desc in curs.description]
while True:
    print '-' * 30
    row = curs.fetchone( )
    if not row: break
    for (name, value) in zip(colnames, row):
        print '%s => %s' % (name, value)

conn.commit( )    # save inserted records
```

Refer to prior sections in this tutorial if any of the code in this script is unclear. When run, it creates a two-record database and lists its content to the standard output stream:

```
('Bob', 'dev', 50000L)
('Sue', 'dev', 60000L)
------------------------------
name => Bob
job => dev
pay => 50000
------------------------------
name => Sue
job => dev
pay => 60000
------------------------------
```

As is, this example is really just meant to demonstrate the database API. It hard-codes database names, and it re-creates the database from scratch each time. We could turn this code into generally useful tools by refactoring it into reusable parts, as we'll see later in this section. First, though, let's explore techniques for getting data into our databases.

Loading Database Tables from Files

One of the nice things about using Python in the database domain is that you can combine the power of the SQL query language, with the power of the Python general-purpose programming language. They naturally compliment each other.

Loading with SQL and Python

Suppose, for example, that you want to load a database table from a flat file, where each line in the file represents a database row, with individual field values separated by commas. Examples 19-11 and 19-12 list two such datafiles we're going to be using here.

Example 19-11. PP3E\Database\SQLscripts\data.txt

```
bob,devel,50000
sue,music,60000
ann,devel,40000
tim,admin,30000
kim,devel,60000
```

Example 19-12. PP3E\Database\SQLscripts\data2.txt

```
bob,developer,80000
sue,music,90000
ann,manager,80000
```

Now, MySQL has a handy SQL statement for loading such a table quickly. Its load data statement parses and loads data from a text file, located on either the client or the server machine. In the following, the first command deletes all records in the table, and we're using the fact that Python automatically concatenates adjacent string literals to split the SQL statement over multiple lines:

```
>>> curs.execute('delete from people')            # all records
3L
>>> curs.execute(
...      "load data local infile 'data.txt' "
...             "into table people fields terminated by ','")
5L
>>> curs.execute('select * from people')
5L
>>> for row in curs.fetchall(): print row
...
('bob', 'devel', 50000L)
('sue', 'music', 60000L)
('ann', 'devel', 40000L)
('tim', 'admin', 30000L)
('kim', 'devel', 60000L)

>>> conn.commit()
```

This works as expected. What if you might someday wish to use your script on a system without this SQL statement, though? Perhaps you just need to do something more custom than this MySQL statement allows. Not to worry—a small amount of simple Python code can easily accomplish the same result (some irrelevant output lines are omitted here):

```
>>> curs.execute('delete from people')
>>> file = open('data.txt')
>>> rows = [line.split(',') for line in file]
>>> for rec in rows:
...      curs.execute('insert people values (%s, %s, %s)', rec)
...
>>> curs.execute('select * from people')
>>> for rec in curs.fetchall(): print rec
...
('bob', 'devel', 50000L)
```

```
('sue', 'music', 60000L)
('ann', 'devel', 40000L)
('tim', 'admin', 30000L)
('kim', 'devel', 60000L)
```

This code makes use of a list comprehension to collect string split results for all lines in the file, and file iterators to step through the file line by line. Its Python loop does the same work as the MySQL load statement, and it will work on more database types. We can get the same result from an executemany DB API call shown earlier as well, but the Python for loop here has the potential to be more general.

Python versus SQL

In fact, you have the entire Python language at your disposal for processing database results, and a little Python can often duplicate or go beyond SQL syntax. For instance, SQL has special aggregate function syntax for computing things such as sums and averages:

```
>>> curs.execute("select sum(pay), avg(pay) from people where job = 'devel'")
1L
>>> curs.fetchall()
((150000.0, 50000.0),)
```

By shifting the processing to Python, we can sometimes simplify and do more than SQL's syntax allows (albeit sacrificing any query performance optimizations the database may perform). Computing pay sums and averages with Python can be accomplished with a simple loop:

```
>>> curs.execute("select name, pay from people where job = 'devel'")
3L
>>> result = curs.fetchall()
>>> result
(('bob', 50000L), ('ann', 40000L), ('kim', 60000L))

>>> tot = 0
>>> for (name, pay) in result: tot += pay
...
>>> print 'total:', tot, 'average:', tot / len(result)
total: 150000 average: 50000
```

Or we can use more advanced tools such as comprehensions and generator expressions to calculate sums, averages, maximums, and the like:

```
>>> print sum(rec[1] for rec in result)         # 2.4 generator expr
150000
>>> print sum(rec[1] for rec in result) / len(result)
50000
>>> print max(rec[1] for rec in result)
60000
```

The Python approach is more general, but it doesn't buy us much until things become more complex. For example, here are a few more advanced comprehensions that collect the names of people whose pay is above and below the average in the query result set:

```
>>> avg = sum(rec[1] for rec in result) / len(result)
>>> print [rec[0] for rec in result if rec[1] > avg]
['kim']
>>> print [rec[0] for rec in result if rec[1] < avg]
['ann']
```

We may be able to do some of these kinds of tasks with more advanced SQL techniques such as nested queries, but we eventually reach a complexity threshold where Python's general-purpose nature makes it attractive. For comparison, here is the equivalent SQL:

```
>>> query = ("select name from people where job = 'devel' and "
...                "pay > (select avg(pay) from people where job = 'devel')")
>>> curs.execute(query)
1L
>>> curs.fetchall()
(('kim',),)
>>>
>>> query = ("select name from people where job = 'devel' and "
...                "pay < (select avg(pay) from people where job = 'devel')")
>>> curs.execute(query)
1L
>>> curs.fetchall()
(('ann',),)
```

This isn't the most complex SQL you're likely to meet, but beyond this point, SQL can become more involved. Moreover, unlike Python, SQL is limited to database-specific tasks by design. Imagine a query that compares a column's values to data fetched off the Web, or from a user in a GUI—simple with Python's Internet and GUI support, but well beyond the scope of a special-purpose language such as SQL. By combining Python and SQL, you get the best of both and can choose which is best suited to your goals.

With Python, you also have access to utilities you've already coded: your database tool set is arbitrarily extensible with functions, modules, and classes. To illustrate, here are some of the same operations coded in a more mnemonic fashion with the dictionary-record module we wrote earlier:

```
>>> from makedicts import makedicts
>>> recs = makedicts(curs, "select * from people where job = 'devel'")
>>> print len(recs), recs[0]
3 {'pay': 50000L, 'job': 'devel', 'name': 'bob'}

>>> print [rec['name'] for rec in recs]
['bob', 'ann', 'kim']
>>> print sum(rec['pay'] for rec in recs)
150000

>>> avg = sum(rec['pay'] for rec in recs) / len(recs)
```

```
>>> print [rec['name'] for rec in recs if rec['pay'] > avg]
['kim']
>>> print [rec['name'] for rec in recs if rec['pay'] >= avg]
['bob', 'kim']
```

For more advanced database extensions, see the SQL-related tools available for Python in the third-party domain. The Vaults of Parnassus web site, for example, hosts packages that add an OOP flavor to the DB API.

SQL Utility Scripts

At this point in our SQL DB API tour, we've started to stretch the interactive prompt to its breaking point—we wind up retyping the same boilerplate code again every time we start a session and every time we run a test. Moreover, the code we're writing is substantial enough to be reused in other programs. Let's wrap up by transforming our code into reusable scripts that automate tasks and support reuse.

To illustrate more of the power of the Python/SQL mix, this section presents a handful of utility scripts that perform common tasks—the sorts of things you'd otherwise have to recode often during development. As an added bonus, most of these files are both command-line utilities and modules of functions that can be imported and called from other programs. Most of the scripts in this section also allow a database name to be passed in on the command line; this allows us to use different databases for different purposes during development—changes in one won't impact others.

Table load scripts

Let's take a quick look at code first, before seeing it in action; feel free to skip ahead to correlate the code here with its behavior. As a first step, Example 19-13 shows a simple way to script-ify the table-loading logic of the prior section.

Example 19-13. PP3E\Database\SQLscripts\loaddb1.py

```
###############################################################################
# load table from comma-delimited text file; equivalent to executing this SQL:
# "load data local infile 'data.txt' into table people fields terminated by ','"
###############################################################################

import MySQLdb
conn = MySQLdb.connect(host='localhost', user='root', passwd='python')
curs = conn.cursor()
curs.execute('use peopledb')

file = open('data.txt')
rows = [line.split(',') for line in file]
for rec in rows:
    curs.execute('insert people values (%s, %s, %s)', rec)

conn.commit()          # commit changes now, if db supports transactions
conn.close()           # close, __del__ call rollback if changes not committed yet
```

As is, Example 19-13 is a top-level script geared toward one particular case. It's hardly any extra work to generalize this into a function that can be imported and used in a variety of scenarios, as in Example 19-14.

Notice the way this code uses two list comprehensions to build a string of record values for the insert statement (see its comments for the transforms applied). We could use an executemany call as we did earlier, but we want to be general and avoid hardcoding the fields template.

This file also defines a login function to automate the initial connection calls—after retyping this 4-command sequence 10 times, it seemed a prime candidate for a function. In addition, this reduces code redundancy; in the future, things like username and host need to be changed in only a single location, as long as the login function is used everywhere. (For an alternative approach to such automation that might encapsulate the connection object, see the class we coded for ZODB connections in the prior section.)

Example 19-14. PP3E\Database\SQLscripts\loaddb.py

```
###########################################################################
# like loaddb1, but insert more than one row at once, and reusable function
# command-line usage: loaddb.py dbname? datafile? (tablename is implied)
###########################################################################

tablename = 'people'    # generalize me

def login(host='localhost', user='root', passwd='python', db=None):
    import MySQLdb
    conn = MySQLdb.connect(host=host, user=user, passwd=passwd)
    curs = conn.cursor()
    if db: curs.execute('use ' + db)
    return conn, curs

def loaddb(cursor, table, datafile='data.txt', conn=None):
    file = open(datafile)                       # x,x,x\nx,x,x\n
    rows = [line.split(',') for line in file]   # [ [x,x,x], [x,x,x] ]
    rows = [str(tuple(rec)) for rec in rows]    # [ "(x,x,x)", "(x,x,x)" ]
    rows = ', '.join(rows)                       # "(x,x,x), (x,x,x)"
    curs.execute('insert ' + table + ' values ' + rows)
    print curs.rowcount, 'rows loaded'
    if conn: conn.commit()

if __name__ == '__main__':
    import sys
    database, datafile = 'peopledb', 'data.txt'
    if len(sys.argv) > 1: database = sys.argv[1]
    if len(sys.argv) > 2: datafile = sys.argv[2]
    conn, curs = login(db=database)
    loaddb(curs, tablename, datafile, conn)
```

Table display script

Once we load data, we probably will want to display it. Example 19-15 allows us to display results as we go—it prints an entire table with either a simple display (which could be parsed by other tools), or a formatted display (generated with the dictionary-record utility we wrote earlier). Notice how it computes the maximum field-name size for alignment with a generator expression; the size is passed in to a string formatting expression by specifying an asterisk (*) for the field size in the format string.

Example 19-15. PP3E\Database\SQLscripts\dumpdb.py

```
#############################################################################
# display table contents as raw tuples, or formatted with field names
# command-line usage: dumpdb.py dbname? [-] (dash for formatted display)
#############################################################################

def showformat(recs, sept=('-' * 40)):
    print len(recs), 'records'
    print sept
    for rec in recs:
        maxkey = max(len(key) for key in rec)          # max key len
        for key in rec:                                # or: \t align
            print '%-*s => %s' % (maxkey, key, rec[key])   # -ljust, *len
        print sept

def dumpdb(cursor, table, format=True):
    if not format:
        cursor.execute('select * from ' + table)
        while True:
            rec = cursor.fetchone()
            if not rec: break
            print rec
    else:
        from makedicts import makedicts
        recs = makedicts(cursor, 'select * from ' + table)
        showformat(recs)

if __name__ == '__main__':
    import sys
    dbname, format = 'peopledb', False
    cmdargs = sys.argv[1:]
    if '-' in cmdargs:                      # format if '-' in cmdline args
        format = True                       # dbname if other cmdline arg
        cmdargs.remove('-')
    if cmdargs:
        dbname = cmdargs[0]

    from loaddb import login
    conn, curs = login(db=dbname)
    dumpdb(curs, 'people', format)
```

While we're at it, let's code some utility scripts to initialize and erase the database, so we do not have to type these by hand at the interactive prompt again every time we want to start from scratch. Example 19-16 completely deletes and re-creates the database, to reset it to an initial state (we did this manually at the start of the tutorial).

Example 19-16. PP3E\Database\SQLscripts\makedb.py

```
###########################################################################
# physically delete and re-create db files in mysql's data\ directory
# usage: makedb.py dbname? (tablename is implied)
###########################################################################

import sys
dbname = (len(sys.argv) > 1 and sys.argv[1]) or 'peopledb'

if raw_input('Are you sure?') not in ('y', 'Y', 'yes'):
    sys.exit()

from loaddb import login
conn, curs = login(db=None)
try:
    curs.execute('drop database ' + dbname)
except:
    print 'database did not exist'

curs.execute('create database ' + dbname)          # also: 'drop table tablename'
curs.execute('use ' + dbname)
curs.execute('create table people (name char(30), job char(10), pay int(4))')
conn.commit()   # this seems optional
print 'made', dbname
```

The clear script in Example 19-17 deletes all rows in the table, instead of dropping and re-creating them entirely. For testing purposes, either approach is usually sufficient.

Example 19-17. PP3E\Database\SQLscripts\cleardb.py

```
###########################################################################
# delete all rows in table, but don't drop the table or database it is in
# usage: cleardb.py dbname? (tablename is implied)
###########################################################################

import sys
if raw_input('Are you sure?') not in ('y', 'Y', 'yes'):
    sys.exit()
dbname = 'peopledb'                           # cleardb.py
if len(sys.argv) > 1: dbname = sys.argv[1]    # cleardb.py testdb

from loaddb import login
conn, curs = login(db=dbname)
curs.execute('delete from people')
conn.commit()                                 # else rows not really deleted
print curs.rowcount, 'records deleted'        # conn closed by its __del__
```

Finally, Example 19-18 provides a command-line tool that runs a query and prints its result table in formatted style. There's not much to this script; because we've automated most of its tasks already, this is largely just a combination of existing tools. Such is the power of code reuse in Python.

Example 19-18. PP3E\Database\SQLscripts\xd5 uerydb.py

```
###############################################################################
# run a query string, display formatted result table
# example: querydb.py testdb "select name, job from people where pay > 50000"
###############################################################################

import sys
database, query = 'peopledb', 'select * from people'
if len(sys.argv) > 1: database = sys.argv[1]
if len(sys.argv) > 2: query = sys.argv[2]

from makedicts import makedicts
from dumpdb     import showformat
from loaddb     import login

conn, curs = login(db=database)
rows = makedicts(curs, query)
showformat(rows)
```

Using the scripts

Last but not least, here is a log of a session that makes use of these scripts in command-line mode, to illustrate their operation. Most of the files also have functions that can be imported and called from a different program; the scripts simply map command-line arguments to the functions' arguments when run standalone. The first thing we do is initialize a testing database and load its table from a text file:

```
...\PP3E\Database\SQLscripts>makedb.py testdb
Are you sure?y
database did not exist
made testdb

...\PP3E\Database\SQLscripts>loaddb.py testdb data2.txt
3 rows loaded
```

Next, let's check our work with the dump utility (use a - argument to force a formatted display):

```
...\PP3E\Database\SQLscripts>dumpdb.py testdb
('bob', 'developer', 80000L)
('sue', 'music', 90000L)
('ann', 'manager', 80000L)

...\PP3E\Database\SQLscripts>dumpdb.py testdb -
3 records
----------------------------------------
pay  => 80000
```

```
job  => developer
name => bob
-----------------------------------------
pay  => 90000
job  => music
name => sue
-----------------------------------------
pay  => 80000
job  => manager
name => ann
-----------------------------------------
```

The dump script is an exhaustive display; to be more specific about which records to view, use the query script and pass in a query string on the command line (the command line is wrapped here to fit in this book):

```
...\PP3E\Database\SQLscripts>querydb.py testdb "select name, job from people where
pay = 80000"
2 records
-----------------------------------------
job  => developer
name => bob
-----------------------------------------
job  => manager
name => ann
-----------------------------------------

...\PP3E\Database\SQLscripts>querydb.py testdb "select * from people where name =
'sue'"
1 records
-----------------------------------------
pay  => 90000
job  => music
name => sue
-----------------------------------------
```

Now, let's erase and start again with a new data set file. The clear script erases all records but doesn't reinitialize the database completely:

```
...\PP3E\Database\SQLscripts>cleardb.py testdb
Are you sure?y
3 records deleted

...\PP3E\Database\SQLscripts>dumpdb.py testdb -
0 records
-----------------------------------------

...\PP3E\Database\SQLscripts>loaddb.py testdb data.txt
5 rows loaded

...\PP3E\Database\SQLscripts>dumpdb.py testdb
('bob', 'devel', 50000L)
('sue', 'music', 60000L)
('ann', 'devel', 40000L)
```

```
('tim', 'admin', 30000L)
('kim', 'devel', 60000L)
```

In closing, here are three queries in action on this new data set: they fetch developers' jobs that pay above an amount and record with a given pay sorted on a field. We could run these at the Python interactive prompt, of course, but we're getting a lot of setup and boilerplate code for free here.

```
...\PP3E\Database\SQLscripts>querydb.py testdb "select name from people where job =
'devel'"
3 records
----------------------------------------
name => bob
----------------------------------------
name => ann
----------------------------------------
name => kim
----------------------------------------

...\PP3E\Database\SQLscripts>querydb.py testdb "select job from people where pay >=
60000"
2 records
----------------------------------------
job => music
----------------------------------------
job => devel
----------------------------------------

...\PP3E\Database\SQLscripts>querydb.py testdb "select * from people where pay >=
60000 order by job"
2 records
----------------------------------------
pay  => 60000
job  => devel
name => kim
----------------------------------------
pay  => 60000
job  => music
name => sue
----------------------------------------
```

Before we move on, a few caveats are worth noting. The scripts in this section illustrate the benefits of code reuse, accomplish their purpose (which was partly demonstrating the SQL API), and serve as a model for canned database utilities. But they are not as general or powerful as they could be. As is, these scripts allow you to pass in the database name but not much more. For example, we could allow the table name to be passed in on the command line too, support sorting options in the dump script, and so on.

Although we could generalize to support more options, at some point we may need to revert to typing SQL commands in a client—part of the reason SQL is a language is because it must support so much generality. Further extensions to these scripts are left as exercises. Change this code as you like; it's Python, after all.

SQL Resources

Although the examples we've seen in this section are simple, their techniques scale up to much more realistic databases and contexts. The web sites we studied in the prior part of the book, for instance, can make use of systems such as MySQL to store page state information as well as long-lived client information. Because MySQL supports both large databases and concurrent updates, it's a natural for web site implementation.

There is more to database interfaces than we've seen, but additional API documentation is readily available on the Web. To find the full database API specification, search the Web for "Python Database API" at Google.com (or at a similar site). You'll find the formal API definition—really just a text file describing PEP number 249 (the Python Enhancement Proposal under which the API was hashed out).

Perhaps the best resource for additional information about database extensions today is the home page of the Python database SIG. Go to *http://www.python.org*, click on the SIGs link near the top, and navigate to the database group's page (or go straight to *http://www.python.org/sigs/db-sig*, the page's current address at the time of this writing). There, you'll find API documentation (this is where it is officially maintained), links to database-vendor-specific extension modules, and more.

While you're at Python.org, be sure to also explore the Gadfly database package—a Python-specific SQL-based database extension, which sports wide portability, socket connections for client/server modes, and more. Gadfly loads data into memory, so it is currently somewhat limited in scope. On the other hand, it is ideal for prototyping database applications—you can postpone cutting a check to a vendor until it's time to scale up for deployment. Moreover, Gadfly is suitable by itself for a variety of applications; not every system needs large data stores, but many can benefit from the power of SQL. And as always, see the Vaults of Parnassus and PyPI web sites for related third-party tools and extensions.

PyForm: A Persistent Object Viewer

Instead of going into additional database interface details that are freely available at Python.org, I'm going to close out this chapter by showing you one way to combine the GUI technology we met earlier in the text with the persistence techniques introduced in this chapter. This section presents PyForm, a Tkinter GUI designed to let you browse and edit tables of records:

- Tables browsed are shelves, DBM files, in-memory dictionaries, or any other object that looks and feels like a dictionary.

- Records within tables browsed can be class instances, simple dictionaries, strings, or any other object that can be translated to and from a dictionary.

Although this example is about GUIs and persistence, it also illustrates Python design techniques. To keep its implementation both simple and type-independent, the PyForm GUI is coded to expect tables to look like dictionaries of dictionaries. To support a variety of table and record types, PyForm relies on separate wrapper classes to translate tables and records to the expected protocol:

- At the top table level, the translation is easy—shelves, DBM files, and in-memory dictionaries all have the same key-based interface.

- At the nested record level, the GUI is coded to assume that stored items have a dictionary-like interface too, but classes intercept dictionary operations to make records compatible with the PyForm protocol. Records stored as strings are converted to and from the dictionary objects on fetches and stores; records stored as class instances are translated to and from attribute dictionaries. More specialized translations can be added in new table wrapper classes.

The net effect is that PyForm can be used to browse and edit a wide variety of table types, despite its dictionary interface expectations. When PyForm browses shelves and DBM files, table changes made within the GUI are persistent—they are saved in the underlying files. When used to browse a shelve of class instances, PyForm essentially becomes a GUI frontend to a simple object database that is built using standard Python persistence tools.

Processing Shelves with Code

Before we get to the GUI, though, let's see why you'd want one in the first place. To experiment with shelves in general, I first coded a canned test datafile. The script in Example 19-19 hardcodes a dictionary used to populate databases (cast), as well as a class used to populate shelves of class instances (Actor).

Example 19-19. PP3E\Dbase\testdata.py

```
# definitions for testing shelves, dbm, and formgui

cast = {
    'rob':   {'name': ('Rob', 'P'),   'job': 'writer', 'spouse': 'Laura'},
    'buddy': {'name': ('Buddy', 'S'), 'job': 'writer', 'spouse': 'Pickles'},
    'sally': {'name': ('Sally', 'R'), 'job': 'writer'},
    'laura': {'name': ('Laura', 'P'), 'spouse': 'Rob',   'kids':1},
    'milly': {'name': ('Milly', '?'), 'spouse': 'Jerry', 'kids':2},
    'mel':   {'name': ('Mel', 'C'),   'job': 'producer'},
    'alan':  {'name': ('Alan', 'B'),  'job': 'comedian'}
}

class Actor:                                    # unnested file-level class
    def __init__(self, name=(), job=''):        # no need for arg defaults,
        self.name = name                        # for new pickler or formgui
        self.job  = job
    def __setattr__(self, attr, value):         # on setattr(): validate
```

Example 19-19. PP3E\Dbase\testdata.py (continued)

```
        if attr == 'kids' and value > 10:          # but set it regardless
            print 'validation error: kids =', value
        if attr == 'name' and type(value) != type(()):
            print 'validation error: name type =', type(value)
        self.__dict__[attr] = value                # don't trigger __setattr__
```

The cast object here is intended to represent a table of records (it's really a dictionary of dictionaries when written out in Python syntax like this). Now, given this test data, it's easy to populate a shelve with cast dictionaries. Simply open a shelve and copy over cast, key for key, as shown in Example 19-20.

Example 19-20. PP3E\Dbase\castinit.py

```
import shelve
from testdata import cast
db = shelve.open('data/castfile')        # create a new shelve
for key in cast.keys():
    db[key] = cast[key]                  # store dictionaries in shelve
```

Once you've done that, it's almost as easy to verify your work with a script that prints the contents of the shelve, as shown in Example 19-21.

Example 19-21. PP3E\Dbase\castdump.py

```
import shelve
db = shelve.open('data/castfile')        # reopen shelve
for key in db.keys():                    # show each key,value
    print key, db[key]
```

Here are these two scripts in action, populating and displaying a shelve of dictionaries:

```
...\PP3E\Dbase>python castinit.py
...\PP3E\Dbase>python castdump.py
alan {'job': 'comedian', 'name': ('Alan', 'B')}
mel {'job': 'producer', 'name': ('Mel', 'C')}
buddy {'spouse': 'Pickles', 'job': 'writer', 'name': ('Buddy', 'S')}
sally {'job': 'writer', 'name': ('Sally', 'R')}
rob {'spouse': 'Laura', 'job': 'writer', 'name': ('Rob', 'P')}
milly {'spouse': 'Jerry', 'name': ('Milly', '?'), 'kids': 2}
laura {'spouse': 'Rob', 'name': ('Laura', 'P'), 'kids': 1}
```

So far, so good; but here is where you reach the limitations of manual shelve processing: to modify a shelve you need much more general tools. You could write little Python scripts that each perform very specific updates. Or you might even get by for awhile typing such update commands by hand in the interactive interpreter:

```
>>> import shelve
>>> db  = shelve.open('data/castfile')
>>> rec = db['rob']
>>> rec['job'] = 'hacker'
>>> db['rob'] = rec
```

For all but the most trivial databases, though, this will get tedious in a hurry—especially for a system's end users. What you'd really like is a GUI that lets you view and edit shelves arbitrarily, and that can be started up easily from other programs and scripts, as shown in Example 19-22.

Example 19-22. PP3E\Dbase\castview.py

```
import shelve
from TableBrowser.formgui import FormGui    # after initcast
db = shelve.open('data/castfile')           # reopen shelve file
FormGui(db).mainloop()                       # browse existing shelve-of-dicts
```

To make this particular script work, we need to move on to the next section.

Adding a Graphical Interface

The path traced in the last section really is what led me to write PyForm, a GUI tool for editing arbitrary tables of records. When those tables are shelves and DBM files, the data PyForm displays is persistent; it lives beyond the GUI's lifetime. Because of that, PyForm can be seen as a simple database browser.

We've already met all the GUI interfaces PyForm uses earlier in this book, so I won't go into all of its implementation details here (see the chapters in Part III for background details). Before we see the code at all, though, let's see what it does. Figure 19-1 shows PyForm in action on Windows, browsing a shelve of persistent instance objects, created from the testdata module's Actor class. It looks slightly different but works the same on Linux and Macs.

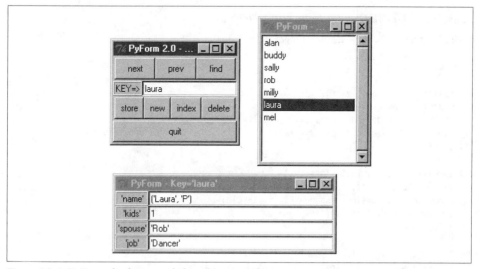

Figure 19-1. PyForm displaying a shelve of Actor objects

PyForm uses a three-window interface to the table being browsed; all windows are packed for proper window expansion and clipping, as set by the rules we studied earlier in this book. The window in the upper left of Figure 19-1 is the main window, created when PyForm starts; it has buttons for navigating through a table, finding items by key, and updating, creating, and deleting records (more useful when browsing tables that persist between runs). The table (dictionary) key of the record currently displayed shows up in the input field in the middle of this window.

The "index" button pops up the listbox window in the upper right, and selecting a record in either window at the top creates the form window at the bottom. The form window is used both to display a record and to edit it—if you change field values and press "store," the record is updated. Pressing "new" clears the form for input of new values (fill in the Key=> field and press "store" to save the new record).

Field values are typed with Python syntax, so strings are quoted (more on this later). When browsing a table with records that contain different sets of field names, PyForm erases and redraws the form window for new field sets as new records are selected. To avoid seeing the window re-created, use the same format for all records within a given table.

PyForm GUI Implementation

On to the code; the first thing I did when writing PyForm was to code utility functions to hide some of the details of widget creation. By making a few simplifying assumptions (e.g., packing protocol), the module in Example 19-23 helps keep some GUI coding details out of the rest of the PyForm implementation.

Example 19-23. PP3E\Dbase\TableBrowser\guitools.py

```
# added extras for entry width, calcgui font/color

from Tkinter import *

def frame(root, side, **extras):
    widget = Frame(root)
    widget.pack(side=side, expand=YES, fill=BOTH)
    if extras: widget.config(**extras)                    # or apply(f, (), {})
    return widget

def label(root, side, text, **extras):
    widget = Label(root, text=text, relief=RIDGE)
    widget.pack(side=side, expand=YES, fill=BOTH)
    if extras: widget.config(**extras)
    return widget

def button(root, side, text, command, **extras):
    widget = Button(root, text=text, command=command)
    widget.pack(side=side, expand=YES, fill=BOTH)
    if extras: widget.config(**extras)
```

Example 19-23. PP3E\Dbase\TableBrowser\guitools.py (continued)

```
    return widget

def entry(root, side, linkvar, **extras):
    widget = Entry(root, relief=SUNKEN, textvariable=linkvar)
    widget.pack(side=side, expand=YES, fill=BOTH)
    if extras: widget.config(**extras)
    return widget
```

Armed with this utility module, the file in Example 19-24 implements the rest of the PyForm GUI. It uses the GuiMixin module we wrote in Chapter 11, for simple access to standard pop-up dialogs. It's also coded as a class that can be specialized in subclasses or attached to a larger GUI. I run PyForm as a standalone program. Attaching its FormGui class really attaches its main window only, but it can be used to provide a precoded table browser widget for other GUIs.

This file's FormGui class creates the GUI shown in Figure 19-1 and responds to user interaction in all three of the interface's windows. Because we've already covered all the GUI tools that PyForm uses, you should study this module's source code listing for additional implementation details. Notice, though, that this file knows almost nothing about the table being browsed, other than that it looks and feels like a dictionary of dictionaries. To understand how PyForm supports browsing things such as shelves of class instances, you will need to look elsewhere (or at least wait for the next module).

Example 19-24. PP3E\Dbase\TableBrowser\formgui.py

```
#!/usr/local/bin/python
#############################################################################
# PyForm: a persistent table viewer GUI. Uses guimixin for std dialogs.
# Assumes the browsed table has a dictionary-of-dictionary interface, and
# relies on table wrapper classes to convert other structures as needed.
# Store an initial record with dbinit script to start a dbase from scratch.
# Caveat: doesn't do object method calls, shows complex field values poorly.
#############################################################################

from Tkinter   import *                       # Tk widgets
from guitools import frame, label, button, entry    # widget builders
from PP3E.Gui.Tools.guimixin import GuiMixin  # common methods

class FormGui(GuiMixin, Frame):
    def __init__(self, mapping):              # an extended frame
        Frame.__init__(self)                  # on default top-level
        self.pack(expand=YES, fill=BOTH)      # all parts expandable
        self.master.title('PyForm 2.0 - Table browser')
        self.master.iconname("PyForm")
        self.makeMainBox()
        self.table    = mapping               # a dict, dbm, shelve, Table,..
        self.index    = mapping.keys()        # list of table keys
        self.cursor   = -1                    # current index position
        self.currslots = []                   # current form's (key,text)s
```

Example 19-24. PP3E\Dbase\TableBrowser\formgui.py (continued)

```
        self.currform  = None                   # current form window
        self.listbox   = None                   # index listbox window

    def makeMainBox(self):
        frm = frame(self, TOP)
        frm.config(bd=2)
        button(frm, LEFT, 'next',  self.onNext)     # next in list
        button(frm, LEFT, 'prev',  self.onPrev)     # backup in list
        button(frm, LEFT, 'find',  self.onFind)     # find from key
        frm = frame(self, TOP)
        self.keytext = StringVar()                  # current record's key
        label(frm, LEFT, 'KEY=>')                   # change before 'find'
        entry(frm, LEFT,  self.keytext)
        frm = frame(self, TOP)
        frm.config(bd=2)
        button(frm,  LEFT, 'store',  self.onStore)    # updated entry data
        button(frm,  LEFT, 'new',    self.onNew)      # clear fields
        button(frm,  LEFT, 'index',  self.onMakeList) # show key list
        button(frm,  LEFT, 'delete', self.onDelete)   # show key list
        button(self, BOTTOM,'quit',    self.quit)     # from guimixin

    def onPrev(self):
        if self.cursor <= 0:
            self.infobox('Backup', "Front of table")
        else:
            self.cursor -= 1
            self.display()

    def onNext(self):
        if self.cursor >= len(self.index)-1:
            self.infobox('Advance', "End of table")
        else:
            self.cursor += 1
            self.display()

    def sameKeys(self, record):               # can we reuse the same form?
        keys1 = record.keys()                 # or map(lambda x:x[0], list)
        keys2 = [x[0] for x in self.currslots]
        keys1.sort(); keys2.sort()            # keys list order differs
        return keys1 == keys2                 # if insertion-order differs

    def display(self):
        key = self.index[self.cursor]          # show record at index cursor
        self.keytext.set(key)                  # change key in main box
        record = self.table[key]               # in dict, dbm, shelf, class
        if self.sameKeys(record):
            self.currform.title('PyForm - Key=' + repr(key))
            for (field, text) in self.currslots:
                text.set(repr(record[field]))  # same fields? reuse form
        else:                                  # repr(x) works like expr `x`
            if self.currform:
                self.currform.destroy()          # different fields?
```

Example 19-24. PP3E\Dbase\TableBrowser\formgui.py (continued)

```
            new = Toplevel()                               # replace current box
            new.title('PyForm - Key=' + repr(key)) # new resizable window
            new.iconname("pform")
            left  = frame(new, LEFT)
            right = frame(new, RIGHT)
            self.currslots = []                            # list of (field, entry)
            for field in record.keys():
                label(left, TOP, repr(field))              # key,value to strings
                text = StringVar()                         # we could sort keys here
                text.set( repr(record[field]) )
                entry(right, TOP, text, width=40)
                self.currslots.append((field, text))
            self.currform = new
            new.protocol('WM_DELETE_WINDOW', lambda:0)   # ignore destroy's
        self.selectlist()                                  # update listbox

    def onStore(self):
        if not self.currform: return
        key = self.keytext.get()
        if key in self.index:
            record = self.table[key]                       # change existing record
        else:                                              # not: self.table[key][field]=
            record = {}                                    # create a new record
            self.index.append(key)                         # add to index and listbox
            if self.listbox:
                self.listbox.insert(END, key)              # or at len(self.index)-1
        for (field, text) in self.currslots:
            try:                                           # fill out dictionary rec
                record[field] = eval(text.get())          # convert back from string
            except:
                self.errorbox('Bad data: "%s" = "%s"' % (field, text.get()))
                record[field] = None
        self.table[key] = record                           # add to dict, dbm, shelf,...
        self.onFind(key)                                   # readback: set cursor,listbox

    def onNew(self):
        if not self.currform: return                       # clear input form and key
        self.keytext.set('?%d' % len(self.index))          # default key unless typed
        for (field, text) in self.currslots:               # clear key/fields for entry
            text.set('')
        self.currform.title('Key: ?')

    def onFind(self, key=None):
        target = key or self.keytext.get()                 # passed in, or entered
        try:
            self.cursor = self.index.index(target)         # find label in keys list
            self.display()
        except:
            self.infobox('Not found', "Key doesn't exist", 'info')

    def onDelete(self):
        if not self.currform or not self.index: return
```

Example 19-24. PP3E\Dbase\TableBrowser\formgui.py (continued)

```
        currkey = self.index[self.cursor]              # table, index, listbox
        del self.table[currkey]                        # like "list[i:i+1] = []"
        del self.index[self.cursor:self.cursor+1]
        if self.listbox:
            self.listbox.delete(self.cursor)           # delete from listbox
        if self.cursor < len(self.index):
            self.display()                             # show next record if any
        elif self.cursor > 0:
            self.cursor = self.cursor-1                # show prior if delete end
            self.display()
        else:                                          # leave box if delete last
            self.onNew()

    def onList(self,evnt):
        if not self.index: return                      # on listbox double-click
        index = self.listbox.curselection()            # fetch selected key text
        label = self.listbox.get(index)                # or use listbox.get(ACTIVE)
        self.onFind(label)                             # and call method here

    def onMakeList(self):
        if self.listbox: return                        # already up?
        new = Toplevel()                               # new resizable window
        new.title("PyForm - Key Index")                # select keys from a listbox
        new.iconname("pindex")
        frm   = frame(new, TOP)
        scroll = Scrollbar(frm)
        list  = Listbox(frm, bg='white')
        scroll.config(command=list.yview, relief=SUNKEN)
        list.config(yscrollcommand=scroll.set, relief=SUNKEN)
        scroll.pack(side=RIGHT, fill=BOTH)
        list.pack(side=LEFT, expand=YES, fill=BOTH)    # pack last, clip first
        for key in self.index:                         # add to list-box
            list.insert(END, key)                      # or: sort list first
        list.config(selectmode=SINGLE, setgrid=1)      # select,resize modes
        list.bind('<Double-1>', self.onList)           # on double-clicks
        self.listbox = list
        if self.index and self.cursor >= 0:            # highlight position
            self.selectlist()
        new.protocol('WM_DELETE_WINDOW', lambda:0)     # ignore destroy's

    def selectlist(self):                              # listbox tracks cursor
        if self.listbox:
            self.listbox.select_clear(0, self.listbox.size())
            self.listbox.select_set(self.cursor)

if __name__ == '__main__':
    from PP3E.Dbase.testdata import cast              # self-test code
    for k in cast.keys(): print k, cast[k]            # view in-memory dict-of-dicts
    FormGui(cast).mainloop()
    for k in cast.keys(): print k, cast[k]            # show modified table on exit
```

The file's self-test code starts up the PyForm GUI to browse the in-memory dictionary of dictionaries called "cast" in the testdata module listed earlier. To start PyForm, you simply make and run the FormGui class object this file defines, passing in the table to be browsed. Here are the messages that show up in stdout after running this file and editing a few entries displayed in the GUI; the dictionary is displayed on GUI startup and exit:

```
...\PP3E\Dbase\TableBrowser>python formgui.py
alan {'job': 'comedian', 'name': ('Alan', 'B')}
sally {'job': 'writer', 'name': ('Sally', 'R')}
rob {'spouse': 'Laura', 'job': 'writer', 'name': ('Rob', 'P')}
mel {'job': 'producer', 'name': ('Mel', 'C')}
milly {'spouse': 'Jerry', 'name': ('Milly', '?'), 'kids': 2}
buddy {'spouse': 'Pickles', 'job': 'writer', 'name': ('Buddy', 'S')}
laura {'spouse': 'Rob', 'name': ('Laura', 'P'), 'kids': 1}

alan {'job': 'comedian', 'name': ('Alan', 'B')}
jerry {'spouse': 'Milly', 'name': 'Jerry', 'kids': 0}
sally {'job': 'writer', 'name': ('Sally', 'R')}
rob {'spouse': 'Laura', 'job': 'writer', 'name': ('Rob', 'P')}
mel {'job': 'producer', 'name': ('Mel', 'C')}
milly {'spouse': 'Jerry', 'name': ('Milly', '?'), 'kids': 2}
buddy {'spouse': 'Pickles', 'job': 'writer', 'name': ('Buddy', 'S')}
laura {'name': ('Laura', 'P'), 'kids': 3, 'spouse': 'bob'}
```

The last line represents a change made in the GUI. Since this is an in-memory table, changes made in the GUI are not retained (dictionaries are not persistent by themselves). To see how to use the PyForm GUI on persistent stores such as DBM files and shelves, we need to move on to the next topic.

PyForm Table Wrappers

The following file defines generic classes that "wrap" (interface with) various kinds of tables for use in PyForm. It's what makes PyForm useful for a variety of table types.

The prior module was coded to handle GUI chores, and it assumes that tables expose a dictionary-of-dictionaries interface. Conversely, this next module knows nothing about the GUI but provides the translations necessary to browse nondictionary objects in PyForm. In fact, this module doesn't even import Tkinter at all—it deals strictly in object protocol conversions and nothing else. Because PyForm's implementation is divided into functionally distinct modules like this, it's easier to focus on each module's task in isolation.

Here is the hook between the two modules: for special kinds of tables, PyForm's FormGui is passed an instance of the Table class coded here. The Table class intercepts table index fetch and assignment operations and uses an embedded record wrapper class to convert records to and from dictionary format as needed.

For example, because DBM files can store only strings, Table converts real dictionaries to and from their printable string representation on table stores and fetches. For class instances, Table extracts the object's __dict__ attribute dictionary on fetches and copies a dictionary's fields to attributes of a newly generated class instance on stores.* The end result is that the GUI thinks the table is all dictionaries, even if it is really something very different here.

While you study this module's listing, shown in Example 19-25, notice that there is nothing here about the record formats of any particular database. In fact, there was none in the GUI-related formgui module either. Because neither module cares about the structure of fields used for database records, both can be used to browse arbitrary records.

Example 19-25. PP3E\Dbase\formtable.py

```
###########################################################################
# PyForm table wrapper classes and tests
# Because PyForm assumes a dictionary-of-dictionary interface, this module
# converts strings and class instance records to and from dicts.  PyForm
# contains the table mapping--Table is not a PyForm subclass.  Note that
# some of the wrapper classes may be useful outside PyForm--DmbOfString can
# wrap a dbm containing arbitrary datatypes.  Run the dbinit scripts to
# start a new database from scratch, and run the dbview script to browse
# a database other than the one tested here.  No longer requires classes to
# have defaults in constructor args, and auto picks up record class from the
# first one fetched if not passed in to class-record wrapper.  Caveat: still
# assumes that all instances in a table are instances of the same class.
###########################################################################


###########################################################################
# records within tables
###########################################################################

class DictionaryRecord:
    def todict(self, value):
        return value                    # to dictionary: no need to convert
    def fromdict(self, value):
        return value                    # from dictionary: no need to convert

class StringRecord:
    def todict(self, value):
        return eval(value)              # convert string to dictionary (or any)
    def fromdict(self, value):
        return str(value)               # convert dictionary (or any) to string
```

---

* Subtle thing revisited: like the new pickle module, PyForm tries to generate a new class instance on store operations by simply setting a generic instance object's __class__ pointer to the original class; only if this fails does PyForm fall back on calling the class with no arguments (in which case the class must have defaults for any constructor arguments other than self). Assignment to __class__ can fail in restricted execution mode. See the class InstanceRecord in the source listing for further details.

Example 19-25. PP3E\Dbase\formtable.py (continued)

```
class InstanceRecord:
    def __init__(self, Class=None):     # need class object to make instances
        self.Class = Class
    def todict(self, value):            # convert instance to attr dictionary
        if not self.Class:              # get class from obj if not yet known
            self.Class = value.__class__
        return value.__dict__
    def fromdict(self, value):          # convert attr dictionary to instance
        try:
            class Dummy: pass                       # try what new pickle does
            instance = Dummy( )                     # fails in restricted mode
            instance.__class__ = self.Class
        except:                                     # else call class, no args
            instance = self.Class( )                # init args need defaults
        for attr in value.keys( ):
            setattr(instance, attr, value[attr])    # set instance attributes
        return instance                             # may run Class.__setattr__


###############################################################################
# table containing records
###############################################################################

class Table:
    def __init__(self, mapping, converter):     # table object, record converter
        self.table  = mapping                   # wrap arbitrary table mapping
        self.record = converter                 # wrap arbitrary record types

    def storeItems(self, items):                # initialize from dictionary
        for key in items.keys( ):               # do __setitem__ to xlate, store
            self[key] = items[key]

    def printItems(self):                       # print wrapped mapping
        for key in self.keys( ):                # do self.keys to get table keys
            print key, self[key]                # do __getitem__ to fetch, xlate

    def __getitem__(self, key):                 # on tbl[key] index fetch
        rawval = self.table[key]                # fetch from table mapping
        return self.record.todict(rawval)       # translate to dictionary

    def __setitem__(self, key, value):          # on tbl[key]=val index assign
        rawval = self.record.fromdict(value)    # translate from dictionary
        self.table[key] = rawval                # store in table mapping

    def __delitem__(self, key):                 # delete from table mapping
        del self.table[key]

    def keys(self):                             # get table mapping keys index
        return self.table.keys( )

    def close(self):
        if hasattr(self.table, 'close'):        # call table close if has one
            self.table.close( )                 # may need for shelves, dbm
```

Example 19-25. PP3E\Dbase\formtable.py (continued)

```
###########################################################################
# table/record combinations
###########################################################################

import shelve, anydbm

def ShelveOfInstance(filename, Class=None):
    return Table(shelve.open(filename), InstanceRecord(Class))
def ShelveOfDictionary(filename):
    return Table(shelve.open(filename), DictionaryRecord())
def ShelveOfString(filename):
    return Table(shelve.open(filename), StringRecord())

def DbmOfString(filename):
    return Table(anydbm.open(filename, 'c'), StringRecord())

def DictOfInstance(dict, Class=None):
    return Table(dict, InstanceRecord(Class))
def DictOfDictionary(dict):
    return Table(dict, DictionaryRecord())
def DictOfString(filename):
    return Table(dict, StringRecord())

ObjectOfInstance   = DictOfInstance         # other mapping objects
ObjectOfDictionary = DictOfDictionary       # classes that look like dicts
ObjectOfString     = DictOfString


###########################################################################
# test common applications
###########################################################################

if __name__ == '__main__':
    from sys import argv
    from formgui import FormGui                 # get dict-based GUI
    from PP3E.Dbase.testdata import Actor, cast # get class, dict-of-dicts

    TestType  = 'shelve'                        # shelve, dbm, dict
    TestInit  = 0                               # init file on startup?
    TestFile  = '../data/shelve1'               # external filename
    if len(argv) > 1: TestType = argv[1]
    if len(argv) > 2: TestInit = int(argv[2])
    if len(argv) > 3: TestFile = argv[3]

    if TestType == 'shelve':                    # Python formtbl.py shelve?
        print 'shelve-of-instance test'
        table = ShelveOfInstance(TestFile, Actor) # wrap shelf in Table object
        if TestInit:
            table.storeItems(cast)              # Python formtbl.py shelve 1
        FormGui(table).mainloop()
        table.close()
        ShelveOfInstance(TestFile).printItems()   # class picked up on fetch
```

Example 19-25. PP3E\Dbase\formtable.py (continued)

```
    elif TestType == 'dbm':                      # Python formtbl.py dbm
        print 'dbm-of-dictstring test'
        table = DbmOfString(TestFile)            # wrap dbm in Table object
        if TestInit:
            table.storeItems(cast)               # Python formtbl.py dbm 1
        FormGui(table).mainloop()
        table.close()
        DbmOfString(TestFile).printItems()       # dump new table contents
```

Besides the Table and record-wrapper classes, the module defines generator functions (e.g., ShelveOfInstance) that create a Table for all reasonable table and record combinations. Not all combinations are valid—DBM files, for example, can contain only dictionaries coded as strings because class instances don't easily map to the string value format expected by DBM. However, these classes are flexible enough to allow additional Table configurations to be introduced.

The only thing that is GUI related about this file at all is its self-test code at the end. When run as a script, this module starts a PyForm GUI to browse and edit either a shelve of persistent Actor class instances or a DBM file of dictionaries, by passing in the right kind of Table object. The GUI looks like the one we saw in Figure 19-1 earlier; when run without arguments, the self-test code lets you browse a shelve of class instances:

```
    ...\PP3E\Dbase\TableBrowser>python formtable.py
    shelve-of-instance test
    ...display of contents on exit...
```

Because PyForm displays a shelve this time, any changes you make are retained after the GUI exits. To reinitialize the shelve from the cast dictionary in testdata, pass a second argument of 1 (0 means don't reinitialize the shelve). To override the script's default shelve filename, pass a different name as a third argument:

```
    ...\PP3E\Dbase\TableBrowser>python formtable.py shelve 1
    ...\PP3E\Dbase\TableBrowser>python formtable.py shelve 0 ../data/shelve1
```

To instead test PyForm on a DBM file of dictionaries mapped to strings, pass a dbm in the first command-line argument; the next two arguments work the same:

```
    ...\PP3E\Dbase\TableBrowser>python formtable.py dbm 1 ..\data\dbm1
    dbm-of-dictstring test
    ...display of contents on exit...
```

Finally, because these self-tests ultimately process concrete shelve and DBM files, you can manually open and inspect their contents using normal library calls. Here is what they look like when opened in an interactive session:

```
    ...\PP3E\Dbase\data>ls
    dbm1          myfile          shelve1

    ...\PP3E\Dbase\data>python
    >>> import shelve
```

```
>>> db = shelve.open('shelve1')
>>> db.keys()
['alan', 'buddy', 'sally', 'rob', 'milly', 'laura', 'mel']
>>> db['laura']
<PP3E.Dbase.testdata.Actor instance at 799850>

>>> import anydbm
>>> db = anydbm.open('dbm1')
>>> db.keys()
['alan', 'mel', 'buddy', 'sally', 'rob', 'milly', 'laura']
>>> db['laura']
"{'name': ('Laura', 'P'), 'kids': 2, 'spouse': 'Rob'}"
```

The shelve file contains real Actor class instance objects, and the DBM file holds dictionaries converted to strings. Both formats are retained in these files between GUI runs and are converted back to dictionaries for later redisplay.[*]

PyForm Creation and View Utility Scripts

The formtable module's self-test code proves that it works, but it is limited to canned test-case files and classes. What about using PyForm for other kinds of databases that store more useful kinds of data?

Luckily, both the formgui and the formtable modules are written to be generic—they are independent of a particular database's record format. Because of that, it's easy to point PyForm to databases of your own; simply import and run the FormGui object with the (possibly wrapped) table you wish to browse.

The required startup calls are not too complex, and you could type them at the interactive prompt every time you want to browse a database; but it's usually easier to store them in scripts so that they can be reused. The script in Example 19-26, for example, can be run to open PyForm on *any* shelve containing records stored in class instance or dictionary format.

Example 19-26. PP3E\Dbase\dbview.py

```
#################################################################
# view any existing shelve directly; this is more general than a
# "formtable.py shelve 1 filename" cmdline--only works for Actor;
# pass in a filename (and mode) to use this to browse any shelve:
# formtable auto picks up class from the first instance fetched;
# run dbinit1 to (re)initialize dbase shelve with a template.
#################################################################
```

---

[*] Note that DBM files of dictionaries use str and eval to convert to and from strings, but could also simply store the pickled representations of record dictionaries in DBM files instead using pickle. But since this is exactly what a shelve of dictionaries does, the str/eval scheme was chosen for illustration purposes here. Suggested exercise: add a new PickleRecord record class based upon the pickle module's loads and dumps functions described earlier in this chapter and compare its performance to StringRecord. See also the pickle file database structure in Chapter 14; its directory scheme with one flat-file per record could be used to implement a "table" here too, with appropriate Table subclassing.

Example 19-26. PP3E\Dbase\dbview.py (continued)

```
from sys import argv
from formtable import *
from formgui import FormGui

mode = 'class'
file = '../data/mydbase-' + mode
if len(argv) > 1: file = argv[1]                # dbview.py file? mode??
if len(argv) > 2: mode = argv[2]

if mode == 'dict':
    table = ShelveOfDictionary(file)            # view dictionaries
else:
    table = ShelveOfInstance(file)              # view class objects

FormGui(table).mainloop()
table.close()                                   # close needed for some dbm
```

The only catch here is that PyForm doesn't handle completely *empty* tables very well; there is no way to add new records within the GUI unless a record is already present. That is, PyForm has no record layout design tool; its "new" button simply clears an existing input form.

Because of that, to start a new database from scratch, you need to add an initial record that gives PyForm the field layout. Again, this requires only a few lines of code that could be typed interactively, but why not instead put it in generalized scripts for reuse? The file in Example 19-27 shows one way to go about initializing a PyForm database with a first empty record.

Example 19-27. PP3E\Dbase\dbinit1.py

```
#######################################################################
# store a first record in a new shelve to give initial fields list;
# PyForm GUI requires an existing record before you can add records;
# delete the '?' key template record after real records are added;
# change mode, file, template to use this for other kinds of data;
# if you populate shelves from other datafiles you don't need this;
# see dbinit2 for object-based version, and dbview to browse shelves.
#######################################################################

import os
from sys import argv
mode = 'class'
file = '../data/mydbase-' + mode
if len(argv) > 1: file = argv[1]                # dbinit1.py file? mode??
if len(argv) > 2: mode = argv[2]
try:
    os.remove(file)                             # delete if present
except: pass

if mode == 'dict':
    template = {'name': None, 'age': None, 'job': None}   # start dict shelve
```

Example 19-27. PP3E\Dbase\dbinit1.py (continued)

```
else:
    from PP3E.Dbase.person import Person          # one arg defaulted
    template = Person(None, None)                 # start object shelve

import shelve
dbase = shelve.open(file)                         # create it now
dbase['?empty?'] = template
dbase.close()
```

Now, simply change some of this script's settings or pass in command-line arguments to generate a new shelve-based database for use in PyForm. You can substitute any fields list or class name in this script to maintain a simple object database with PyForm that keeps track of real-world information (we'll see two such databases in action in a moment).

The empty record created by this script shows up with the key ?empty? when you first browse the database in PyForm with dbview; replace it with a first real record using the PyForm store key, and you are in business. As long as you don't change the database's shelve outside of the GUI, all of its records will have the same fields format, as defined in the initialization script.

But notice that the dbinit1 script goes straight to the shelve file to store the first record; that's fine today, but it might break if PyForm is ever changed to do something more custom with its stored data representation. Perhaps a better way to populate tables outside the GUI is to use the Table wrapper classes it employs. The following alternative script, for instance, initializes a PyForm database with generated Table objects, not direct shelve operations (see Example 19-28).

Example 19-28. PP3E\Dbase\dbinit2.py

```
###############################################################
# this works too--based on Table objects not manual shelve ops;
# store a first record in shelve, as required by PyForm GUI.
###############################################################

from formtable import *
import sys, os

mode = 'dict'
file = '../data/mydbase-' + mode
if len(sys.argv) > 1: file = sys.argv[1]
if len(sys.argv) > 2: mode = sys.argv[2]
try:
    os.remove(file)
except: pass

if mode == 'dict':
    table    = ShelveOfDictionary(file)
    template = {'name': None, 'shoesize': None, 'language': 'Python'}
else:
```

Example 19-28. PP3E\Dbase\dbinit2.py (continued)

```
from PP3E.Dbase.person import Person
table    = ShelveOfInstance(file, Person)
template = Person(None, None).__dict__
```

```
table.storeItems({'?empty?': template})
table.close( )
```

Creating and browsing custom databases

Let's put the prior section's scripts to work to initialize and edit a couple of custom databases. Figure 19-2 shows one being browsed after initializing the database with a script and adding a handful of real records within the GUI.

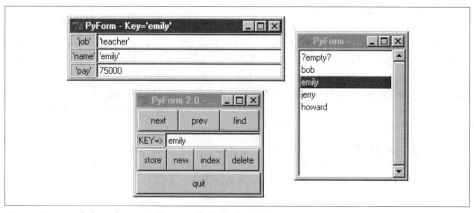

Figure 19-2. A shelve of Person objects (dbinit1, dbview)

The listbox here shows the record I added to the shelve within the GUI. I ran the following commands to initialize the database with a starter record and to open it in PyForm to add records (that is, Person class instances):

```
...\PP3E\Dbase\TableBrowser>python dbinit1.py
```

```
...\PP3E\Dbase\TableBrowser>python dbview.py
```

You can tweak the class name or fields dictionary in the dbinit scripts to initialize records for any sort of database you care to maintain with PyForm; use dictionaries if you don't want to represent persistent objects with classes (but classes let you add other sorts of behavior as methods not visible under PyForm). Be sure to use a distinct filename for each database; the initial ?empty? record can be deleted as soon as you add a real entry (later, simply select an entry from the listbox and press "new" to clear the form for input of a new record's values).

The data displayed in the GUI represents a true shelve of persistent Person class instance objects—changes and additions made in the GUI will be retained for the next time you view this shelve with PyForm. If you like to type, though, you can still open the shelve directly to check PyForm's work:

```
...\PP3E\Dbase\data>ls
mydbase-class  myfile          shelve1

...\PP3E\Dbase\data>python
>>> import shelve
>>> db = shelve.open('mydbase-class')
>>> db.keys()
['emily', 'jerry', '?empty?', 'bob', 'howard']
>>> db['bob']
<PP3E.Dbase.person.Person instance at 798d70>
>>> db['emily'].job
'teacher'
>>> db['bob'].tax
30000.0
```

Notice that bob is an instance of the Person class we met earlier in this chapter (see the section "Shelve Files"). Assuming that the person module is still the version that introduced a __getattr__ method, asking for a shelved object's tax attribute computes a value on the fly because this really invokes a class method. Also note that this works even though Person was never imported here—Python loads the class internally when re-creating its shelved instances.

You can just as easily base a PyForm-compatible database on an internal dictionary structure, instead of on classes. Figure 19-3 shows one being browse after being initialized with a script and populated with the GUI.

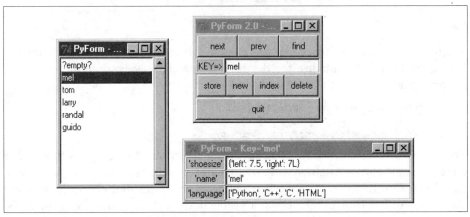

Figure 19-3. A shelve of dictionaries (dbinit2, dbview)

Besides its different internal format, this database has a different record structure (its record's field names differ from the last example), and it is stored in a shelve file of its own. Here are the commands I used to initialize and edit this database:

```
...\PP3E\Dbase\TableBrowser>python dbinit2.py ../data/mydbase-dict dict

...\PP3E\Dbase\TableBrowser>python dbview.py ../data/mydbase-dict dict
```

After adding a few records (that is, dictionaries) to the shelve, you can either view them again in PyForm or open the shelve manually to verify PyForm's work:

```
...\PP3E\Dbase\data>ls
mydbase-class  mydbase-dict  myfile       shelve1

...\PP3E\Dbase\data>python
>>> db = shelve.open('mydbase-dict')
>>> db.keys()
['tom', 'guido', '?empty?', 'larry', 'randal', 'mel']
>>> db['guido']
{'shoesize': 42, 'name': 'benevolent dictator', 'language': 'Python'}
>>> db['mel']['shoesize']
{'left': 7.5, 'right': 7L}
```

This time, shelve entries are really dictionaries, not instances of a class or converted strings. PyForm doesn't care, though—because all tables are wrapped to conform to PyForm's interface, both formats look the same when browsed in the GUI.

Data as Code

Notice that the shoesize and language fields in the screenshot in Figure 19-3 really are a dictionary and a list. You can type any Python expression syntax into this GUI's form fields to give values (that's why strings are quoted there).

PyForm uses the Python built-in repr function to convert value objects for display (repr(x) is like the older `x` expression and is similar to str(x) but yields an as-code display that adds quotes around strings). To convert from a string back to value objects, PyForm uses the Python eval function to parse and evaluate the code typed into fields. The key entry/display field in the main window does not add or accept quotes around the key string because keys must still be strings in things such as shelves (even though fields can be arbitrary types).

As we've seen at various points in this book, eval (and its statement cousin, exec) is powerful but dangerous—you never know when a user might type something that removes files, hangs the system, emails your boss, and so on. If you can't be sure that field values won't contain harmful code (whether malicious or otherwise), use the rexec restricted execution mode tools we met in Chapter 18 to evaluate strings. Alternatively, you can simply limit the kinds of expressions allowed and evaluate them with simpler tools (e.g., int, str) or store all data as strings.

Browsing Other Kinds of Objects with PyForm

Although PyForm expects to find a dictionary-of-dictionary interface (protocol) in the tables it browses, a surprising number of objects fit this mold because dictionaries are so pervasive in Python object internals. In fact, PyForm can be used to browse things that have nothing to do with the notion of database tables of records at all, as long as they can be made to conform to the protocol.

For instance, the Python sys.modules table we met in Chapter 3 is a built-in dictionary of loaded module objects. With an appropriate wrapper class to make modules look like dictionaries, there's no reason we can't browse the in-memory sys.modules with PyForm too, as shown in Example 19-29.

Example 19-29. PP3E\Dbase\TableBrowser\viewsysmod.py

```
# view the sys.modules table in FormGui

class modrec:
    def todict(self, value):
        return value.__dict__       # not dir(value): need dict
    def fromdict(self, value):
        assert 0, 'Module updates not supported'

import sys
from formgui import FormGui
from formtable import Table
FormGui(Table(sys.modules, modrec())).mainloop()
```

This script defines a class to pull out a module's __dict__ attribute dictionary (formtable's InstanceRecord won't do, because it also looks for a __class__). The rest of it simply passes sys.modules to PyForm (FormGui) wrapped in a Table object; the result appears in Figure 19-4.

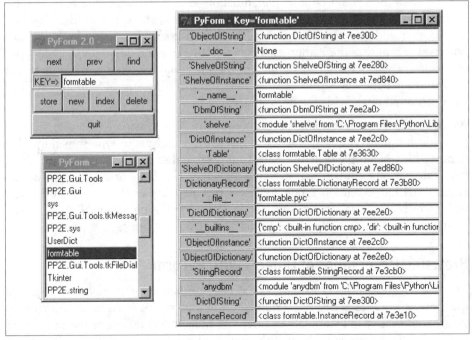

Figure 19-4. FormGui browsing sys.modules (viewsysmod)

With similar record and table wrappers, all sorts of objects could be viewed in PyForm. As usual in Python, all that matters is that they provide a compatible interface.

Browsing Other Kinds of Databases with PyForm

In fact, with just a little creativity, we could also write table wrappers that allow the PyForm GUI to view objects in ZODB databases and records in SQL databases—third-party systems we studied earlier in this chapter:

- ZODB should be simple: it is an access-by-key storage medium with a dictionary-like interface similar to shelves. We would need to provide a close method that commits changes, though, since the table wrapper protocol expects one.

- SQL databases would be more challenging, since they are composed of tables of rows, not objects stored under unique keys. We could, however, define a column to be the unique key values for records in a table and run SQL queries to fetch by key on indexing.

In deference to space, we'll leave the second of these extensions as a suggested exercise. The first is straightforward: Example 19-30 launches the PyForm GUI to browse the ZODB people database we used as an example earlier in this chapter. This script works—it allows you to use the GUI to browse and update persistent class instances stored in a ZODB object database—but it suffers from some innate limitations in the GUI's design.

As coded, PyForm doesn't support instances of more than one class in the database, and it has no way to call class methods. More subtly, PyForm assumes that instances either are created from a class with no nondefault constructor arguments or support _ _class_ _ attribute assignments (its code tries both schemes to re-create the instance from its dictionary-based representation). The former of these constraints was not coded in the original class, and the latter did not work for classes derived from ZODB persistence classes when this script was tested.

Because of these constraints, the test script in Example 19-30 uses an empty class to initialize the database: since methods and derived subclasses aren't yet supported, classes in PyForm are little more than flat attribute namespaces. As currently coded, PyForm does not leverage the full power of Python classes—any methods they contain may still be called by code outside the context of the PyForm GUI, but they have no purpose within it. We'll explore some of these design issues in more detail in the next section.

Perhaps just as remarkable as its flaws, though, is the fact that PyForm can be used on a ZODB database at all—by encapsulating the database behind a common object interface, it supports any conforming object.

Example 19-30. PP3E\Database\ZODBscripts\viewzodb.py

```
##########################################################
# view the person ZODB database in PyForm's FormGui;
# FileDB maps indexing to db root, close does commit;
# caveat 1: FormGui doesn't yet allow mixed class types;
# caveat 2: FormGui has no way to call class methods;
# caveat 3: Persistent subclasses don't allow __class__
# to be set: must have defaults for all __init__ args;
# Person here works only if always defined in __main__;
##########################################################

import sys
filename = 'data/people-simple.fs'
from zodbtools import FileDB
from PP3E.Dbase.TableBrowser.formgui   import FormGui
from PP3E.Dbase.TableBrowser.formtable import Table, InstanceRecord

class Person: pass
initrecs = {'bob': dict(name='bob', job='devel', pay=30),
            'sue': dict(name='sue', job='music', pay=40)}

dbtable = Table(FileDB(filename), InstanceRecord(Person))
if len(sys.argv) > 1:
    for key in dbtable.keys():
        del dbtable[key]                # "viewzodb.py -" inits db
    dbtable.storeItems(initrecs)        # "viewzodb.py" browses db

FormGui(dbtable).mainloop()
dbtable.printItems()
dbtable.close()
```

Run this code on your machine to see its windows—they are exactly like those we've seen before, but the records browsed are objects that reside in a ZODB database instead of a shelve.

PyForm Limitations

Although the `sys.modules` and ZODB viewer scripts of the last two sections work, they highlight a few limitations of PyForm's current design:

Two levels only

PyForm is set up to handle a two-dimensional table/record-mapping structure only. You can't descend further into fields shown in the form, large data structures in fields print as long strings, and complex objects such as nested modules, classes, and functions that contain attributes of their own simply show their default print representation. We could add object viewers to inspect nested objects interactively, but they might be complex to code.

No big forms

PyForm is not equipped to handle a large number of record fields—if you select the os module's entry in the index listbox in Figure 19-4, you'll get a huge form that is likely too big to even fit on your screen (the os module has lots and lots of attributes; it goes off my screen after about 40). We could fix this with a scroll bar, but it's unlikely that records in the databases that PyForm was designed to view will have many dozens of fields.

Data attributes only

PyForm displays record attribute values, but it does not support calling method functions of objects being browsed and cannot display dynamically computed attributes (e.g., the tax attribute in Person objects). Since some class methods require arguments to be passed, an additional interface would be necessary; required arguments could be extracted from the method function itself (hint: see built-in function and code attributes such as function.func_code.co_argcount).

One class per table

PyForm currently assumes all instances in a table are of the same class, even though that's not a requirement for shelves in general.

New style classes with __slots__ don't work

As coded, PyForm may not currently support some instances of new style classes. In particular, new style classes with a __slots__ attribute may not have a __dict__ namespace dictionary and so will not work in PyForm (slots save the space normally taken by the instance __dict__, and may be fetched quicker).

This same restriction currently exists in the Python pickle module, though—a class that defines __slots__ without defining __getstate__ (called to return a state to pickle) cannot be pickled—so this is not an additional constraint imposed by the GUI. Supporting __slots__ in addition to __dict__ may be possible, but we leave this as an exercise (this may require a class tree climb to collect all __slot__ lists in all superclasses, or inspecting the result of a dir call).

Wrapping protocol alternatives

In some cases, it may be possible to avoid the to/from dictionary conversion for class instances browsed. The trick would be to wrap records rather than tables. This would almost allow us to get rid of the Table wrapper class completely for this use case—the GUI could browse either a shelve of instances or a shelve of dictionaries directly, with no conversions. It would not, however, handle other use cases (e.g., DBM files of evaluated strings), and it might turn out to be more complex than the current general dictionary-based scheme, due to extra-special cases.

The last item in the preceding list is a subtle design point, and it merits some addition explanation. PyForm current overloads *table* index fetch and assignment, and the GUI internally uses dictionaries to represent records. Fetches assume a dictionary-like object comes back, and stores make a new dictionary object (or use the current one), fill it out, and pass it off to the Table wrapper for conversion to the table's underlying record implementation. When browsing tables of instances, the fetch conversion is trivial (we use the instance's __dict__ directly), but stores must create and fill out a new instance.

It would be almost as easy to overload *record* field index fetch and assignment instead, to avoid converting dictionaries to instances, and possibly avoid the Table wrapper layer. In this scheme, records held in PyForm might be whatever object the table stores (not necessarily dictionaries), and each record field fetch or assignment in PyForm would be routed back to record wrapper classes.

For example, by wrapping instance records in a class that maps dictionary field indexing to class attributes with __getitem__ and __setitem__ overload methods, the GUI might browse actual class instance objects. These two overload methods would simply call the getattr and setattr built-in functions to access the attribute corresponding to the key by string name, and the keys call in the GUI used to extract field names could be mapped by the record wrapper to the instance __dict__.

The trickiest part of this scheme is that the GUI would have to know how to make a new empty record before filling its fields—this would likely require that the GUI have knowledge of the concrete type of the record (dictionary or instance, as well as the class if it is an instance) or use of a Table wrapper with a customizable method for creating a new empty record. By building and filling dictionaries, the GUI currently finesses this issue completely and delegates it to the customized table and record wrappers.

There are also a few substantial downsides to this approach. For one, PyForm could not browse any instance object unless it inherits from the record wrapper class or is wrapped up in one automatically by a Table interface class on fetches and stores. For another, Table also has some additional interfaces not provided by shelves, which we have to code elsewhere. This scheme might also preclude use of indexing overload methods in the record class itself, though the GUI itself does not support such operations anyhow.

Most significantly, this model would not transparently handle other use cases, such as string-based records. Cases requiring conversion with eval and str, for instance, would not fit the new model at all—DBM files that map whole records to strings might require complex special case logic to handle field-at-a-time requests or fall back to converting from and to dictionaries on fetches and stores, as is currently done.

Because of such exceptions, we would probably wind up with a Table wrapper anyhow, unless we limit the GUI's use cases. Generating a new empty record just by itself varies so much per record kind that we need a class hierarchy to customize the operation. In the end, it may be easier to use dictionaries in all cases and convert from that where needed, as PyForm currently does.

In other words, there is room for improvement if you care to experiment. On the other hand, extensions in this domain are somewhat open-ended, so we'll leave them as suggested exercises. PyForm was designed to view mappings of mappings and was never meant to be a general Python object viewer.

But as a simple GUI for tables of persistent objects, it meets its design goals as planned. Python's shelves and classes make such systems both easy to code and powerful to use. Complex data can be stored and fetched in a single step, as well as augmented with methods that provide dynamic record behavior. As an added bonus, by programming such programs in Python and Tkinter, they are automatically portable among all major GUI platforms. When you mix Python persistence and GUIs, you get a lot of features "for free."

## CHAPTER 20

Data Structures

"Roses Are Red, Violets Are Blue; Lists Are Mutable, and So Is Set Foo"

Data structures are a central theme in most programs, whether you know it or not. It may not always be obvious because Python provides a set of built-in types that make it easy to deal with structured data: lists, strings, tuples, dictionaries, and the like. For simple systems, these types are usually enough. Technically, dictionaries make many of the classical searching algorithms unnecessary in Python, and lists replace much of the work you'd do to support collections in lower-level languages. Both are so easy to use, though, that you generally never give them a second thought.

But for advanced applications, we may need to add more sophisticated types of our own to handle extra requirements. In this chapter, we'll explore a handful of advanced data structure implementations in Python: sets, stacks, graphs, and so on. As we'll see, data structures take the form of new object types in Python, integrated into the language's type model. That is, objects we code in Python become full-fledged datatypes—to the scripts that use them, they can look and feel just like built-in lists, numbers, and dictionaries.

Although the examples in this chapter illustrate advanced programming techniques, they also underscore Python's support for writing reusable software. By coding object implementations with classes, modules, and other Python tools, they naturally become generally useful components, which may be used in any program that imports them. In effect, we will be building libraries of data structure classes, whether we plan for it or not.

In addition, although the examples in this chapter are pure Python code, we will also be building a path toward the next part of the book here. From the most general perspective, new Python objects can be implemented in either Python or an integrated language such as C. In particular, pay attention to the stack objects implemented in the first section of this chapter; they will later be reimplemented in C to gauge both the benefits and the complexity of C migration.

Implementing Stacks

Stacks are a common and straightforward data structure, used in a variety of applications: language processing, graph searches, and so on. In short, stacks are a last-in-first-out collection of objects—the last item added to the collection is always the next one to be removed. Clients use stacks by:

- Pushing items onto the top
- Popping items off the top

Depending on client requirements, there may also be tools for such tasks as testing whether the stack is empty, fetching the top item without popping it, iterating over a stack's items, testing for item membership, and so on.

In Python, a simple list is often adequate for implementing a stack: because we can change lists in place, we can add and delete items from either the beginning (left) or the end (right). Table 20-1 summarizes various built-in operations available for implementing stack-like behavior with Python lists, depending on whether the stack "top" is the first or the last node in the list. In this table, the string 'c' is the top item on the stack.

Table 20-1. Stacks as lists

Operation	Top is end-of-list	Top is front-of-list	Top is front-of-list
New	stack=['a','b','c']	stack=['c','b','a']	stack=['c','b','a']
Push	stack.append('d')	stack.insert(0,'d')	stack[0:0] = ['d']
Pop	x = stack[-1];	x = stack[0];	x = stack[0];
	del stack[-1]	del stack[:1]	stack[:1] = []

Other coding schemes are possible as well. For instance, Python 1.5 introduced a list pop method designed to be used in conjunction with append to implement stacks— for example, to push run list.append(value) and to pop run x=list.pop(). By default, the pop method is equivalent to fetching, and then deleting the last item at offset −1 (and is equivalent to the two statements in the last row in column 1 of Table 20-1). With an argument, pop deletes and returns the item at that offset— list.pop(0) is the same as the table's last rows in columns 2 and 3. And del stack[0] is yet another way to delete the first item in a list-based stack.

This list arrangement works and will be relatively fast. But it also binds stack-based programs to the stack representation chosen: all stack operations will be hardcoded. If we later want to change how a stack is represented or extend its basic operations, we're stuck. Every stack-based program will have to be updated.

For instance, to add logic that monitors the number of stack operations a program performs, we'd have to add code around each hardcoded stack operation. In a large system, this operation may be nontrivial. As we'll see in the next part of the book, we may also decide to move stacks to a C-based implementation, if they prove to be a performance bottleneck. As a general rule, hardcoded operations on built-in data structures don't support future migrations as well as we'd sometimes like.

Built-in types such as lists are actually class-like objects in Python that we can subclass to customize. Unless we anticipate future changes and make instances of a subclass, though, we still have a maintenance issue if we use built-in list operations and ever want to extend what they do in the future (more on subclassing built-in types later in this chapter).

A Stack Module

Perhaps a better approach is to *encapsulate*—that is, wrap up—stack implementations behind interfaces, using Python's code reuse tools. As long as clients stick to using the interfaces, we're free to change the interfaces' implementations arbitrarily without having to change every place they are called. Let's begin by implementing a stack as a module containing a Python list, plus functions to operate on it (see Example 20-1).

Example 20-1. PP3E\Dstruct\Basic\stack1.py

```
stack = []                                  # on first import
class error(Exception): pass                # local excs, stack1.error

def push(obj):
    global stack                            # use 'global' to change
    stack = [obj] + stack                   # add item to the front

def pop():
    global stack
    if not stack:
        raise error, 'stack underflow'      # raise local error
    top, stack = stack[0], stack[1:]        # remove item at front
    return top

def top():
    if not stack:                           # raise local error
        raise error, 'stack underflow'      # or let IndexError occur
    return stack[0]

def empty():        return not stack        # is the stack []?
def member(obj):    return obj in stack     # item in stack?
def item(offset):   return stack[offset]    # index the stack
def length():       return len(stack)       # number entries
def dump():         print '<Stack:%s>' % stack
```

This module creates a list object (stack) and exports functions to manage access to it. The stack is declared global in functions that change it, but not in those that just reference it. The module also defines an error object (error) that can be used to catch exceptions raised locally in this module. Some stack errors are built-in exceptions: the method item triggers IndexError for out-of-bounds indexes.

Most of the stack's functions just delegate the operation to the embedded list used to represent the stack. In fact, the module is really just a wrapper around a Python list. But this extra layer of interface logic makes clients independent of the actual implementation of the stack. So, we're able to change the stack later without impacting its clients.

As usual, one of the best ways to understand such code is to see it in action. Here's an interactive session that illustrates the module's interfaces:

```
C:\...\PP3E\Dstruct\Basic>python
>>> import stack1
>>> stack1.push('spam')
>>> stack1.push(123)
>>> stack1.top()
123
>>> stack1.stack
[123, 'spam']
>>> stack1.pop()
123
>>> stack1.dump()
<Stack:['spam']>
>>> stack1.pop()
'spam'
>>> stack1.empty()
1
>>> for c in 'spam': stack1.push(c)
...
>>> while not stack1.empty():
...     print stack1.pop(),
...
m a p s
>>>
>>> stack1.pop()
Traceback (most recent call last):
  File "<stdin>", line 1, in ?
  File "stack1.py", line 11, in pop
    raise error, 'stack underflow'        # raise local error
stack1.error: stack underflow
```

Other operations are analogous, but the main thing to notice here is that all stack operations are module *functions*. For instance, it's possible to iterate over the stack, but we need to use counter-loops and indexing function calls (item). Nothing is preventing clients from accessing (and changing) stack1.stack directly, but doing so defeats the purpose of interfaces like this one.

A Stack Class

Perhaps the biggest drawback of the module-based stack is that it supports only a single stack object. All clients of the stack module effectively share the same stack. Sometimes we want this feature: a stack can serve as a shared-memory object for multiple modules. But to implement a true stack datatype, we need to use classes.

To illustrate, let's define a full-featured stack *class*. The Stack class shown in Example 20-2 defines a new datatype with a variety of behaviors. Like the module, the class uses a Python list to hold stacked objects. But this time, each instance gets its own list. The class defines both "real" methods, and specially named methods that implement common type operations. Comments in the code describe special methods.

Example 20-2. PP3E\Dstruct\Basic\stack2.py

```python
class error(Exception): pass            # when imported: local exception

class Stack:
    def __init__(self, start=[]):       # self is the instance object
        self.stack = []                 # start is any sequence: stack..
        for x in start: self.push(x)
        self.reverse()                  # undo push's order reversal

    def push(self, obj):                # methods: like module + self
        self.stack = [obj] + self.stack # top is front of list

    def pop(self):
        if not self.stack: raise error, 'underflow'
        top, self.stack = self.stack[0], self.stack[1:]
        return top

    def top(self):
        if not self.stack: raise error, 'underflow'
        return self.stack[0]

    def empty(self):
        return not self.stack           # instance.empty()

    # overloads
    def __repr__(self):
        return '[Stack:%s]' % self.stack    # print, backquotes,..
    def __cmp__(self, other):
        return cmp(self.stack, other.stack) # '==', '>', '<=', '!=',..
    def __len__(self):
        return len(self.stack)          # len(instance), not instance
    def __add__(self, other):
        return Stack(self.stack + other.stack)  # instance1 + instance2
    def __mul__(self, reps):
        return Stack(self.stack * reps) # instance * reps
    def __getitem__(self, offset):
        return self.stack[offset]       # instance[offset], in, for
```

Example 20-2. PP3E\Dstruct\Basic\stack2.py (continued)

```
    def __getslice__(self, low, high):
        return Stack(self.stack[low : high])      # instance[low:high]
    def __getattr__(self, name):
        return getattr(self.stack, name)          # instance.sort()/reverse()/..
```

Now distinct instances are created by calling the Stack class like a function. In most respects, the Stack class implements operations exactly like the stack module in Example 20-1. But here, access to the stack is qualified by self, the subject instance object. Each instance has its own stack attribute, which refers to the instance's own list. Furthermore, instance stacks are created and initialized in the __init__ constructor method, not when the module is imported. Let's make a couple of stacks to see how all this works in practice:

```
>>> from stack2 import Stack
>>> x = Stack()                    # make a stack object, push items
>>> x.push('spam')
>>> x.push(123)
>>> x                              # __repr__ prints a stack
[Stack:[123, 'spam']]

>>> y = Stack()                    # two distinct stack objects
>>> y.push(3.1415)                 # they do not share content
>>> y.push(x.pop())
>>> x, y
([Stack:['spam']], [Stack:[123, 3.1415]])


>>> z = Stack()                    # third distinct stack object
>>> for c in 'spam': z.push(c)
...
>>> while z: print z.pop(),        # __len__ tests stack truth
...
m a p s

>>> z = x + y                      # __add__ handles stack +
>>> z                              # holds three different types
[Stack:['spam', 123, 3.1415]]
>>> for item in z: print item,     # __getitem__ does for
...
spam 123 3.1415
```

Like lists and dictionaries, Stack defines both methods and operators for manipulating instances by attribute qualification and expressions. Additionally, it defines the __getattr__ metaclass method to intercept references to attributes not defined in the class and to route them to the wrapped list object (to support list methods: sort, append, reverse, and so on). Many of the module's operations become operators in the class. Table 20-2 shows the equivalence of module and class operations (columns 1 and 2) and gives the class method that comes into play for each (column 3).

Table 20-2. Module/class operation comparison

Module operations	Class operations	Class method
module.empty( )	not instance	__len__
module.member(x)	x in instance	__getitem__
module.item(i)	instance[i]	__getitem__
module.length( )	len(instance)	__len__
module.dump( )	print instance	__repr__
range( ) *counter loops*	for x in instance	__getitem__
manual loop logic	instance + instance	__add__
module.stack.reverse( )	instance.reverse( )	__getattr__
module.push/pop/top	instance.push/pop/top	push/pop/top

In effect, classes let us extend Python's set of built-in types with reusable types implemented in Python modules. Class-based types may be used just like built-in types: depending on which operation methods they define, classes can implement numbers, mappings, and sequences, and may or may not be mutable. Class-based types may also fall somewhere in between these categories.

Customization: Performance Monitors

So far we've seen how classes support multiple instances and integrate better with Python's object model by defining operator methods. One of the other main reasons for using classes is to allow for future extensions and customizations. By implementing stacks with a class, we can later add subclasses that specialize the implementation for new demands.

For instance, suppose we've started using the Stack class in Example 20-2, but we start running into performance problems. One way to isolate bottlenecks is to instrument data structures with logic that keeps track of usage statistics, which we can analyze after running client applications. Because Stack is a class, we can add such logic in a new subclass without affecting the original stack module (or its clients). The subclass in Example 20-3 extends Stack to keep track of overall push/pop usage frequencies and to record the maximum size of each instance.

Example 20-3. PP3E\Dstruct\Basic\stacklog.py

```
from stack2 import Stack              # extends imported Stack

class StackLog(Stack):                # count pushes/pops, max-size
    pushes = pops = 0                 # shared/static class members
    def __init__(self, start=[]):     # could also be module vars
        self.maxlen = 0
        Stack.__init__(self, start)
```

Example 20-3. PP3E\Dstruct\Basic\stacklog.py (continued)

```
    def push(self, object):
        Stack.push(self, object)                    # do real push
        StackLog.pushes += 1                         # overall stats
        self.maxlen = max(self.maxlen, len(self))    # per-instance stats

    def pop(self):
        StackLog.pops += 1                           # overall counts
        return Stack.pop(self)                       # not 'self.pops': instance

    def stats(self):
        return self.maxlen, self.pushes, self.pops   # get counts from instance
```

This subclass works the same as the original Stack; it just adds monitoring logic. The new stats method is used to get a statistics tuple through an instance:

```
>>> from stacklog import StackLog
>>> x = StackLog()
>>> y = StackLog()                            # make two stack objects
>>> for i in range(3): x.push(i)             # and push object on them
...
>>> for c in 'spam':   y.push(c)
...
>>> x, y                                       # run inherited __repr__
([Stack:[2, 1, 0]], [Stack:['m', 'a', 'p', 's']])
>>> x.stats(), y.stats()
((3, 7, 0), (4, 7, 0))
>>>
>>> y.pop(), x.pop()
('m', 2)
>>> x.stats(), y.stats()
((3, 7, 2), (4, 7, 2))                        # my maxlen, all pushes, all pops
```

Notice the use of *class* attributes to record overall pushes and pops, and *instance* attributes for per-instance maximum length. By hanging attributes on different objects, we can expand or narrow their scopes.

Optimization: Tuple Tree Stacks

One of the nice things about wrapping objects up in classes is that you are free to change the underlying implementation without breaking the rest of your program. Optimizations can be added in the future, for instance, with minimal impact; the interface is unchanged, even if the internals are. There are a variety of ways to implement stacks, some more efficient than others. So far, our stacks have used slicing and concatenation to implement pushing and popping. This method is relatively inefficient: both operations make copies of the wrapped list object. For large stacks, this practice can add a significant time penalty.

One way to speed up such code is to change the underlying data structure completely. For example, we can store the stacked objects in a binary tree of tuples: each item may be recorded as a pair, (object, tree), where object is the stacked item and tree is either another tuple pair giving the rest of the stack or None to designate an empty stack. A stack of items [1,2,3,4] would be internally stored as a tuple tree (1,(2,(3,(4,None)))).

This tuple-based representation is similar to the notion of "cons-cells" in Lisp-family languages: the object on the left is the car, and the rest of the tree on the right is the cdr. Because we add or remove only a top tuple to push and pop items, this structure avoids copying the entire stack. For large stacks, the benefit might be significant. The next class, shown in Example 20-4, implements these ideas.

Example 20-4. PP3E\Dstruct\Basic\stack3.py

```
class Stack:
    def __init__(self, start=[]):          # init from any sequence
        self.stack = None                  # even other (fast)stacks
        for i in range(-len(start), 0):
            self.push(start[-i - 1])       # push in reverse order

    def push(self, node):                  # grow tree 'up/left'
        self.stack = node, self.stack      # new root tuple: (node, tree)

    def pop(self):
        node, self.stack = self.stack      # remove root tuple
        return node                        # TypeError if empty

    def empty(self):
        return not self.stack              # is it 'None'?

    def __len__(self):                     # on: len, not
        len, tree = 0, self.stack
        while tree:
            len, tree = len+1, tree[1]     # visit right subtrees
        return len

    def __getitem__(self, index):          # on: x[i], in, for
        len, tree = 0, self.stack
        while len < index and tree:        # visit/count nodes
            len, tree = len+1, tree[1]
        if tree:
            return tree[0]                 # IndexError if out-of-bounds
        else: raise IndexError             # so 'in' and 'for' stop

    def __repr__(self): return '[FastStack:' + repr(self.stack) + ']'
```

This class's __getitem__ method handles indexing, in tests, and for loop iteration as before, but this version has to traverse a tree to find a node by index. Notice that this isn't a subclass of the original Stack class. Since nearly every operation is implemented differently here, inheritance won't really help. But clients that restrict themselves to the operations that are common to both classes can still use them interchangeably—they just need to import a stack class from a different module to switch implementations. Here's a session with this stack version; as long as we stick to pushing, popping, indexing, and iterating, this version is essentially indistinguishable from the original:

```
>>> from stack3 import Stack
>>> x = Stack()
>>> y = Stack()
>>> for c in 'spam': x.push(c)
...
>>> for i in range(3): y.push(i)
...
>>> x
[FastStack:('m', ('a', ('p', ('s', None))))]
>>> y
[FastStack:(2, (1, (0, None)))]

>>> len(x), x[2], x[-1]
(4, 'p', 'm')
>>> x.pop()
'm'
>>> x
[FastStack:('a', ('p', ('s', None)))]
>>>
>>> while y: print y.pop(),
...
2 1 0
```

Optimization: In-Place List Modifications

Perhaps a better way to speed up the stack object, though, is to fall back on the mutability of Python's list object. Because lists can be changed in place, they can be modified more quickly than any of the prior examples. In-place change operations such as append are prone to complications when a list is referenced from more than one place. But because the list inside the stack object isn't meant to be used directly, we're probably safe.

The module in Example 20-5 shows one way to implement a stack with in-place changes; some operator overloading methods have been dropped to keep this simple. The new Python pop method it uses is equivalent to indexing and deleting the item at offset −1 (top is end-of-list here).

Example 20-5. PP3E\Dstruct\Basic\stack4.py

```
class error(Exception): pass          # when imported: local exception

class Stack:
    def __init__(self, start=[]):     # self is the instance object
        self.stack = []               # start is any sequence: stack...
        for x in start: self.push(x)

    def push(self, obj):              # methods: like module + self
```

Example 20-5. PP3E\Dstruct\Basic\stack4.py (continued)

```
        self.stack.append(obj)                  # top is end of list

    def pop(self):
        if not self.stack: raise error, 'underflow'
        return self.stack.pop()                 # like fetch and delete stack[-1]

    def top(self):
        if not self.stack: raise error, 'underflow'
        return self.stack[-1]

    def empty(self):
        return not self.stack                   # instance.empty()

    def __len__(self):
        return len(self.stack)                  # len(instance), not instance

    def __getitem__(self, offset):
        return self.stack[offset]               # instance[offset], in, for

    def __repr__(self): return '[Stack:%s]' % self.stack
```

This version works like the original in module stack2 too; just replace stack2 with stack4 in the previous interaction to get a feel for its operation. The only obvious difference is that stack items are in reverse when printed (i.e., the top is the end):

```
>>> from stack4 import Stack
>>> x = Stack()
>>> x.push('spam')
>>> x.push(123)
>>> x
[Stack:['spam', 123]]
>>>
>>> y = Stack()
>>> y.push(3.1415)
>>> y.push(x.pop())
>>> x, y
([Stack:['spam']], [Stack:[3.1415, 123]])
>>> y.top()
123
```

Timing the Improvements

The in-place changes stack object probably runs faster than both the original and the tuple-tree versions, but the only way to really be sure how much faster is to time the alternative implementations. Since this could be something we'll want to do more than once, let's first define a general module for timing functions in Python. In Example 20-6, the built-in time module provides a clock function that we can use to get the current CPU time in floating-point seconds, and the function timer.test simply calls a function reps times and returns the number of elapsed seconds by subtracting stop from start CPU times.

Example 20-6. PP3E\Dstruct\Basic\timer.py

```
def test(reps, func, *args):
    import time
    start = time.clock()              # current CPU time in float seconds
    for i in xrange(reps):            # call function reps times
        func(*args)                   # discard any return value
    return time.clock() - start       # stop time - start time
```

Next, we define a test driver script (see Example 20-7). It expects three command-line arguments: the number of pushes, pops, and indexing operations to perform (we'll vary these arguments to test different scenarios). When run at the top level, the script creates 200 instances of the original and optimized stack classes and performs the specified number of operations on each stack.* Pushes and pops change the stack; indexing just accesses it.

Example 20-7. PP3E\Dstruct\Basic\stacktime.py

```
import stack2          # list-based stacks: [x]+y
import stack3          # tuple-tree stacks: (x,y)
import stack4          # in-place stacks:   y.append(x)
import timer           # general function timer function

rept = 200
from sys import argv
pushes, pops, items = eval(argv[1]), eval(argv[2]), eval(argv[3])

def stackops(stackClass):
    #print stackClass.__module__
    x = stackClass('spam')                    # make a stack object
    for i in range(pushes): x.push(i)         # exercise its methods
    for i in range(items):  t = x[i]
    for i in range(pops):   x.pop()

print 'stack2:', timer.test(rept, stackops, stack2.Stack)  # pass class to test
print 'stack3:', timer.test(rept, stackops, stack3.Stack)  # rept*(push+pop+ix)
print 'stack4:', timer.test(rept, stackops, stack4.Stack)
```

Results under Python 1.5.2

Here are some of the timings reported by the test driver script. The three outputs represent the measured run times in seconds for the original, tuple, and in-place stacks. For each stack type, the first test creates 200 stack objects and performs roughly 120,000 stack operations (200 repetitions × (200 pushes + 200 indexes + 200 pops)) in the test duration times listed. These results were obtained on a 650 MHz Pentium III Windows machine and a Python 1.5.2 install:

```
C:\...\PP3E\Dstruct\Basic>python stacktime.py 200 200 200
stack2: 1.67890008213
```

---

* If you have a copy of the first edition of this book lying around, you might notice that I had to scale all test factors way up to get even close to the run times I noticed before. Both Python and chips have gotten a lot faster in five years.

```
stack3: 7.70020952413
stack4: 0.694291724635

C:\...\PP3E\Dstruct\Basic>python stacktime.py 200 50 200
stack2: 1.06876246669
stack3: 7.48964866994
stack4: 0.477584270605

C:\...\PP3E\Dstruct\Basic>python stacktime.py 200 200 50
stack2: 1.34536448817
stack3: 0.795615917129
stack4: 0.57297976835

C:\...\PP3E\Dstruct\Basic>python stacktime.py 200 200 0

stack2: 1.33500477715
stack3: 0.300776077373
stack4: 0.533050336077
```

If you look closely enough, you'll notice that the results show that the tuple-based stack (stack3) performs better when we do more pushing and popping, but worse if we do much indexing. Indexing lists is extremely fast for built-in lists (stack2 and stack4), but very slow for tuple trees—the Python class must traverse the tree manually.

The in-place change stacks (stack4) are almost always fastest, unless no indexing is done at all—tuples won by a hair in the last test case. When there is no indexing (the last test), the tuple and in-place change stacks are roughly four and three times quicker than the simple list-based stack, respectively. Since pushes and pops are most of what clients would do to a stack, tuples are a contender, despite their poor indexing performance.

Of course, we're talking about fractions of a second after many tens of thousands of operations; in many applications, your users probably won't care either way. If you access a stack millions of times in your program, though, this difference may accumulate to a significant amount of time.

Results under Python 2.4

Performance results like those of the prior section are prone to change from release to release in Python, because ongoing optimization work always finds its way into the interpreter over time. For the third edition of this book, I reran the tests of the prior section on a machine that was roughly twice as fast (1.2 GHz), and under Python 2.4. The results are very different, though relatively similar:

```
C:\...\PP3E\Dstruct\Basic>python stacktime.py 200 200 200
stack2: 0.383535616957
stack3: 1.74261840541
stack4: 0.160929391864

C:\...\PP3E\Dstruct\Basic>python stacktime.py 200 50 200
stack2: 0.320245170825
```

```
stack3:  1.70567264834
stack4:  0.121246694761

C:\...\PP3E\Dstruct\Basic>python stacktime.py 200 200 50
stack2:  0.335854417251
stack3:  0.208287086767
stack4:  0.124496549142

C:\...\PP3E\Dstruct\Basic>python stacktime.py 200 200 0
stack2:  0.353687130627
stack3:  0.0953431232182
stack4:  0.110205067963
```

This time, if you study the results long enough, you'll notice that the relative performance of stack2 (simple lists) and stack4 (in-place list changes) is roughly the same—the in-place list stack is usually about three times quicker again, regardless of the amount of indexing going on (which makes sense, given that the two list-based stacks index at the same speed). And as before, in the last test when there is no indexing as is common for stacks, the tuple-based stack3 still performs best of all three: roughly four times better than simple lists, and slightly better than in-place lists.

The results, though, seem to reflect the fact that all of the stack code has been optimized in Python itself since this book's prior edition. All three stacks are roughly four times faster today, likely reflecting a 2X boost in hardware, plus a 2X boost in Python itself. In this case, the relative performance results are similar; but in other cases, such optimizations may invalidate conclusions derived from tests run under previous Python releases.[*]

The short story here is that you must collect timing data for your code, on your machine, and under your version of Python. All three factors can skew results arbitrarily. In the next section, we'll see a more dramatic version impact on the relative performance of set alternatives, and we'll learn how to use the Python profiler to collect performance data in a more generic fashion.

Implementing Sets

Another commonly used data structure is the *set*, a collection of objects that support operations such as:

Intersection
> Make a new set with all items in common.

Union
> Make a new set with all items in either operand.

Membership
> Test whether an item exists in a set.

---

[*] Trust me on this. I once made a sweeping statement in another book about map and list comprehensions being twice as fast as for loops, only to be made wrong by a later Python release that optimized the others much more than map, except in select use cases. Performance measurement in Python is an ongoing task.

And there are others, depending on the intended use. Sets come in handy for dealing with more abstract group combinations. For instance, given a set of engineers and a set of writers, you can pick out individuals who do both activities by intersecting the two sets. A union of such sets would contain either type of individual, but would include any given individual only once.

Python lists, tuples, and strings come close to the notion of a set: the in operator tests membership, for iterates, and so on. Here, we add operations not directly supported by Python sequences. The idea is that we're *extending* built-in types for unique requirements.

Set Functions

As before, let's first start out with a function-based set manager. But this time, instead of managing a shared set object in a module, let's define functions to implement set operations on passed-in Python sequences (see Example 20-8).

Example 20-8. PP3E\Dstruct\Basic\inter.py

```
def intersect(seq1, seq2):
    res = []                        # start with an empty list
    for x in seq1:                  # scan the first sequence
        if x in seq2:
            res.append(x)           # add common items to the end
    return res

def union(seq1, seq2):
    res = list(seq1)                # make a copy of seq1
    for x in seq2:                  # add new items in seq2
        if not x in res:
            res.append(x)
    return res
```

These functions work on any type of sequence—lists strings, tuples, and other objects that conform to the sequence protocols expected by these functions (for loops, in membership tests). In fact, we can even use them on mixed object types: the last two commands in the following code compute the intersection and union of a list and a tuple. As usual in Python, the object *interface* is what matters, not the specific types:

```
C:\...\PP3E\Dstruct\Basic>python
>>> from inter import *
>>> s1 = "SPAM"
>>> s2 = "SCAM"
>>> intersect(s1, s2), union(s1, s2)
(['S', 'A', 'M'], ['S', 'P', 'A', 'M', 'C'])
>>> intersect([1,2,3], (1,4))
[1]
>>> union([1,2,3], (1,4))
[1, 2, 3, 4]
```

Notice that the result is always a list here, regardless of the type of sequences passed in. We could work around this by converting types or by using a class to sidestep this issue (and we will in a moment). But type conversions aren't clear-cut if the operands are mixed-type sequences. Which type do we convert to?

Supporting multiple operands

If we're going to use the intersect and union functions as general tools, one useful extension is support for multiple arguments (i.e., more than two). The functions in Example 20-9 use Python's variable-length argument lists feature to compute the intersection and union of arbitrarily many operands.

Example 20-9. PP3E\Dstruct\Basic\inter2.py

```
def intersect(*args):
    res = []
    for x in args[0]:                      # scan the first list
        for other in args[1:]:             # for all other arguments
            if x not in other: break       # this item in each one?
        else:
            res.append(x)                  # add common items to the end
    return res

def union(*args):
    res = []
    for seq in args:                       # for all sequence-arguments
        for x in seq:                      # for all nodes in argument
            if not x in res:
                res.append(x)              # add new items to result
    return res
```

The multioperand functions work on sequences in the same way as the original functions, but they support three or more operands. Notice that the last two examples in the following session work on lists with embedded compound objects: the in tests used by the intersect and union functions apply equality testing to sequence nodes recursively, as deep as necessary to determine collection comparison results:

```
C:\...\PP3E\Dstruct\Basic>python
>>> from inter2 import *
>>> s1, s2, s3 = 'SPAM', 'SLAM', 'SCAM'
>>> intersect(s1, s2)
['S', 'A', 'M']
>>> intersect(s1, s2, s3)
['S', 'A', 'M']
>>> intersect(s1, s2, s3, 'HAM')
['A', 'M']

>>> union(s1, s2), union(s1, s2, s3)
(['S', 'P', 'A', 'M', 'L'], ['S', 'P', 'A', 'M', 'L', 'C'])
>>> intersect([1,2,3], (1,4), range(5))
[1]
```

```
>>> s1 = (9, (3.14, 1), "bye", [1,2], "mello")
>>> s2 = [[1,2], "hello", (3.14, 0), 9]
>>> intersect(s1, s2)
[9, [1, 2]]
>>> union(s1, s2)
[9, (3.14, 1), 'bye', [1, 2], 'mello', 'hello', (3.14, 0)]
```

Set Classes

The set functions can operate on a variety of sequences, but they aren't as friendly as true objects. Among other things, your scripts need to keep track of the sequences passed into these functions manually. Classes can do better: the class in Example 20-10 implements a set object that can hold any type of object. Like the stack classes, it's essentially a wrapper around a Python list with extra set operations.

Example 20-10. PP3E\Dstruct\Basic\set.py

```
class Set:
    def __init__(self, value = []):      # on object creation
        self.data = []                    # manages a local list
        self.concat(value)

    def intersect(self, other):           # other is any sequence type
        res = []                          # self is the instance subject
        for x in self.data:
            if x in other:
                res.append(x)
        return Set(res)                   # return a new Set

    def union(self, other):
        res = self.data[:]                # make a copy of my list
        for x in other:
            if not x in res:
                res.append(x)
        return Set(res)

    def concat(self, value):              # value: a list, string, Set...
        for x in value:                   # filters out duplicates
            if not x in self.data:
                self.data.append(x)

    def __len__(self):          return len(self.data)
    def __getitem__(self, key): return self.data[key]
    def __and__(self, other):   return self.intersect(other)
    def __or__(self, other):    return self.union(other)
    def __repr__(self):         return '<Set:' + repr(self.data) + '>'
```

The Set class is used like the Stack class we saw earlier in this chapter: we make instances and apply sequence operators plus unique set operations to them. Intersection and union can be called as methods, or by using the & and | operators normally used for built-in integer objects. Because we can string operators in expressions now (e.g., x & y & z), there is no obvious need to support multiple operands in intersect/union methods here. As with all objects, we can either use the Set class within a program or test it interactively as follows:

```
>>> from set import Set
>>> users1 = Set(['Bob', 'Emily', 'Howard', 'Peeper'])
>>> users2 = Set(['Jerry', 'Howard', 'Carol'])
>>> users3 = Set(['Emily', 'Carol'])
>>> users1 & users2
<Set:['Howard']>
>>> users1 | users2
<Set:['Bob', 'Emily', 'Howard', 'Peeper', 'Jerry', 'Carol']>
>>> users1 | users2 & users3
<Set:['Bob', 'Emily', 'Howard', 'Peeper', 'Carol']>
>>> (users1 | users2) & users3
<Set:['Emily', 'Carol']>
>>> users1.data
['Bob', 'Emily', 'Howard', 'Peeper']
```

Optimization: Moving Sets to Dictionaries

Once you start using the Set class, the first problem you might encounter is its performance: its nested for loops and in scans become exponentially slow. That slowness may or may not be significant in your applications, but library classes should generally be coded as efficiently as possible.

One way to optimize set performance is by changing the implementation to use dictionaries rather than lists, for storing sets internally—items may be stored as the keys of a dictionary whose values are all None. Because lookup time is constant and short for dictionaries, the in list scans of the original set may be replaced with direct dictionary fetches in this scheme. In traditional terms, moving sets to dictionaries replaces slow linear searches with fast hash table fetches. A computer scientist would explain this by saying that the repeated nested scanning of the list-based intersection is an *exponential* algorithm in terms of its complexity, but dictionaries can be *linear*.

The module in Example 20-11 implements this idea. Its class is a subclass of the original set, and it redefines the methods that deal with the internal representation but inherits others. The inherited & and | methods trigger the new intersect and union methods here, and the inherited len method works on dictionaries as is. As long as Set clients are not dependent on the order of items in a set, they can switch to this version directly by just changing the name of the module from which Set is imported; the class name is the same.

Example 20-11. PP3E\Dstruct\Basic\fastset.py

```
import set

                                    # fastset.Set extends set.Set
class Set(set.Set):
    def __init__(self, value = []):
```

Example 20-11. PP3E\Dstruct\Basic\fastset.py (continued)

```
        self.data = {}                      # manages a local dictionary
        self.concat(value)                  # hashing: linear search times

    def intersect(self, other):
        res = {}
        for x in other:                     # other: a sequence or Set
            if self.data.has_key(x):        # use hash-table lookup (or "in")
                res[x] = None
        return Set(res.keys())              # a new dictionary-based Set

    def union(self, other):
        res = {}                            # other: a sequence or Set
        for x in other:                     # scan each set just once
            res[x] = None
        for x in self.data.keys():          # '&' and '|' come back here
            res[x] = None                   # so they make new fastset's
        return Set(res.keys())

    def concat(self, value):
        for x in value: self.data[x] = None

    # inherit and, or, len
    def __getitem__(self, key):  return self.data.keys()[key]
    def __repr__(self):          return '<Set:' + repr(self.data.keys()) + '>'
```

This works about the same as the previous version:

```
>>> from fastset import Set
>>> users1 = Set(['Bob', 'Emily', 'Howard', 'Peeper'])
>>> users2 = Set(['Jerry', 'Howard', 'Carol'])
>>> users3 = Set(['Emily', 'Carol'])
>>> users1 & users2
<Set:['Howard']>
>>> users1 | users2
<Set:['Emily', 'Howard', 'Jerry', 'Carol', 'Peeper', 'Bob']>
>>> users1 | users2 & users3
<Set:['Emily', 'Howard', 'Carol', 'Peeper', 'Bob']>
>>> (users1 | users2) & users3
<Set:['Emily', 'Carol']>
>>> users1.data
{'Emily': None, 'Bob': None, 'Peeper': None, 'Howard': None}
```

The main functional difference in this version is the *order* of items in the set: because dictionaries are randomly ordered, this set's order will differ from the original. For instance, you can store compound objects in sets, but the order of items varies in this version:

```
>>> import set, fastset
>>> a = set.Set([(1,2), (3,4), (5,6)])
>>> b = set.Set([(3,4), (7,8)])
>>> a & b
<Set:[(3, 4)]>
>>> a | b
```

```
<Set:[(1, 2), (3, 4), (5, 6), (7, 8)]>

>>> a = fastset.Set([(1,2), (3,4), (5,6)])
>>> b = fastset.Set([(3,4), (7,8)])
>>> a & b
<Set:[(3, 4)]>
>>> a | b
<Set:[(3, 4), (1, 2), (7, 8), (5, 6)]>
>>> b | a
<Set:[(3, 4), (5, 6), (1, 2), (7, 8)]>
```

Sets aren't supposed to be ordered anyhow, so this isn't a showstopper. A deviation that might matter, though, is that this version cannot be used to store *unhashable* (that is, immutable) objects. This stems from the fact that dictionary keys must be immutable. Because values are stored in keys, dictionary sets can contain only things such as tuples, strings, numbers, and class objects with immutable signatures. Mutable objects such as lists and dictionaries won't work directly. For example, the following call:

```
fastset.Set([[1,2],[3,4]])
```

raises an exception with this dictionary-based set, but it works with the original set class. Tuples do work here as set items because they are immutable; Python computes hash values and tests key equality as expected.

Timing the results under Python 2.4

So how did we do on the optimization front? Example 20-12 contains a script to compare set class performance. It reuses the timer module of Example 20-6 used earlier to test stacks.

Example 20-12. PP3E\Dstruct\Basic\settime.py

```
import timer, sys
import set, fastset

def setops(Class):
    a = Class(range(50))          # a 50-integer set
    b = Class(range(20))          # a 20-integer set
    c = Class(range(10))
    d = Class(range(5))
    for i in range(5):
        t = a & b & c & d         # 3 intersections
        t = a | b | c | d         # 3 unions

if __name__ == '__main__':
    rept = int(sys.argv[1])
    print 'set =>   ', timer.test(rept, setops, set.Set)
    print 'fastset =>', timer.test(rept, setops, fastset.Set)
```

The setops function makes four sets and combines them with intersection and union operators five times. A command-line argument controls the number of times this whole process is repeated. More accurately, each call to setops makes 34 Set instances (4 + [5 × (3 + 3)]) and runs the intersect and union methods 15 times each (5 × 3) in the for loop's body. The performance improvement is equally dramatic this time around, on a 1.2 GHz machine:

```
C:\...\PP3E\Dstruct\Basic>python settime.py 50
set =>    0.605568584834
fastset => 0.10293794323

C:\...\PP3E\Dstruct\Basic>python settime.py 100
set =>    1.21189676342
fastset => 0.207752661302

C:\...\PP3E\Dstruct\Basic>python settime.py 200
set =>    2.47468966028
fastset => 0.415944763929
```

These results will vary per machine, and they may vary per Python release. But at least for this test case, the dictionary-based set implementation (fastest) is roughly *six times* faster than the simple list-based set (set). In fact, this sixfold speedup is probably sufficient. Python dictionaries are already optimized hash tables that you might be hard-pressed to improve on. Unless there is evidence that dictionary-based sets are still too slow, our work here is probably done.

Timing results under Python 1.5.2: version skew

For detail-minded readers, the prior section's sixfold speedup results listed in this edition of the book were timed with Python 2.4 on a 1.2 GHz machine. Surprisingly, in the second edition, under an older Python (1.5.2) and slower machine (650 MHz), all list-based set results were roughly twice as slow as today, but the dictionary-based set was roughly four times slower (e.g., 1.54 and 0.44 seconds for dictionaries and lists at 50 iterations). In relative terms, the net effect is that dictionary sets went from being approximately three times faster than list sets to being six times faster today.

That is, machine speed doubled, but in addition, the dictionary code grew twice as quickly as before, relative to list-based sets. This larger jump reflects optimizations in Python itself. As you can see, version skew is an important consideration when analyzing performance; in this case, dictionaries are twice the performance boost they were a few years earlier.

Using the Python profiler

Timing code sections helps, but the ultimate way to isolate bottlenecks is profiling. The Python profiler provides another way to gather performance data besides timing sections of code as done in this chapter so far. Because the profiler tracks all function calls, it provides much more information in a single blow. As such, it's a more powerful way to isolate bottlenecks in slow programs—after profiling, you should have a good idea of where to focus your optimization efforts.

The profiler ships with Python as the standard library module called profile, and it provides a variety of interfaces for measuring code performance. It is structured and used much like the pdb command-line debugger: import the profile module and call its functions with a code string to measure performance. The simplest profiling interface is its profile.run(statementstring) function. When invoked, the profiler runs the code string, collects statistics during the run, and issues a report on the screen when the statement completes. See it in action profiling a 100-iteration call to the set test function of the previous section's Example 20-12, for the list-based sets of Example 20-10 (hint: profile an import statement to profile an entire file):

```
>>> import settime, timer, set
>>> import profile
>>> profile.run('timer.test(100, settime.setops, set.Set)')

        675906 function calls in 6.328 CPU seconds

   Ordered by: standard name

   ncalls  tottime  percall  cumtime  percall filename:lineno(function)
   118500    0.434    0.000    0.434    0.000 :0(append)
        2    0.000    0.000    0.000    0.000 :0(clock)
      500    0.003    0.000    0.003    0.000 :0(range)
        1    0.004    0.004    0.004    0.004 :0(setprofile)
        1    0.000    0.000    6.323    6.323 <string>:1(?)
        0    0.000             0.000          profile:0(profiler)
        1    0.000    0.000    6.328    6.328 profile:0(timer.test(100,...more...))
     1500    0.133    0.000    0.951    0.001 set.py:13(union)
     3400    0.029    0.000    1.011    0.000 set.py:2(__init__)
     3400    0.621    0.000    0.982    0.000 set.py:20(concat)
   544000    2.032    0.000    2.032    0.000 set.py:26(__getitem__)
     1500    0.014    0.000    5.226    0.003 set.py:27(__and__)
     1500    0.013    0.000    0.964    0.001 set.py:28(__or__)
     1500    3.009    0.002    5.212    0.003 set.py:6(intersect)
      100    0.033    0.000    6.321    0.063 settime.py:4(setops)
        1    0.002    0.002    6.323    6.323 timer.py:1(test)
```

The report's format is straightforward and well documented in the Python library manual. By default, it lists the number of calls and times spent in each function invoked during the run. When the profiler is enabled, each interpreter event is routed to a Python handler. This gives an accurate picture of performance, but it tends to make the program being profiled run much slower than normal. In fact, the call profiled runs five times slower in this case under Python 2.4 and the 1.2 GHz test machine (6 seconds versus 1.2 seconds when not profiled).

On the other hand, the profiler's report helps you isolate which functions to recode and possibly migrate to the C language. In the preceding listing, for instance, we can see that the intersect function (and the corresponding __and__ operator method) is the main drag on performance; it takes roughly five-sixths of the total execution time. Indexing (__getitem__) is a close second, most likely because it occurs so often with the repeated scans used by intersection. Union, on the other hand, is fairly quick from a relative perspective.

Here is a profile of the dictionary-based set implementation of Example 20-11 for comparison; the code runs five times slower under the profiler again (1 second versus 0.2 seconds), though the relative speed of the list and dictionary-based set code is the same when both are profiled (6 seconds versus 1 second, the same sixfold difference we noticed before):

```
>>> import settime, timer, fastset
>>> import profile
>>> profile.run('timer.test(100, settime.setops, fastset.Set)')

        111406 function calls in 1.049 CPU seconds

   Ordered by: standard name

   ncalls  tottime  percall  cumtime  percall filename:lineno(function)
        2    0.000    0.000    0.000    0.000 :0(clock)
    17500    0.065    0.000    0.065    0.000 :0(has_key)
    42500    0.166    0.000    0.166    0.000 :0(keys)
      500    0.003    0.000    0.003    0.000 :0(range)
        1    0.000    0.000    0.000    0.000 :0(setprofile)
        1    0.000    0.000    1.049    1.049 <string>:1(?)
     1500    0.159    0.000    0.439    0.000 fastset.py:15(union)
     3400    0.052    0.000    0.052    0.000 fastset.py:23(concat)
    38000    0.299    0.000    0.445    0.000 fastset.py:27(__getitem__)
     3400    0.030    0.000    0.082    0.000 fastset.py:4(__init__)
     1500    0.208    0.000    0.533    0.000 fastset.py:8(intersect)
        0    0.000             0.000          profile:0(profiler)
        1    0.000    0.000    1.049    1.049 profile:0(timer.test(100, ...more...))
     1500    0.014    0.000    0.548    0.000 set.py:27(__and__)
     1500    0.015    0.000    0.454    0.000 set.py:28(__or__)
      100    0.035    0.000    1.048    0.010 settime.py:4(setops)
        1    0.001    0.001    1.049    1.049 timer.py:1(test)
```

This time, there is no obvious culprit behind the total execution time: intersection and union take roughly the same amount of time, and indexing is not much of a factor. Ultimately, the real difference is the exponential algorithm of list-based set intersection versus the linear nature of the dictionary-base algorithms, and this factor outweighs the choice of programming language used to implement the objects. Recoding in Python first is the best bet, since an exponential algorithm would be just as slow if implemented in C.

Optimizing fastset by Coding Techniques (or Not)

As coded, there seems to be a bottleneck in the fastset class: each time we call a dictionary's keys method, Python makes a new list to hold the result. This can happen repeatedly during intersections and unions. If you are interested in trying to optimize this further, see the following files in the book's examples distribution:

- *PP3E\Dstruct\Basic\fastset2.py*
- *PP3E\Dstruct\Basic\fastset3.py*

I wrote these to try to speed up sets further, but failed miserably. It turns out that adding extra code to try to shave operations usually negates the speedup you obtain. There may be faster codings, but the biggest win here was likely in changing the underlying data structure to dictionaries, not in minor code tweaks.

As a rule of thumb, your intuition about performance is almost always wrong in a dynamic language such as Python: the algorithm is usually the real culprit behind performance problems, not the coding style or even the implementation language. By removing the combinatorial list scanning algorithm of the original set class, the Python implementation became dramatically faster.

In fact, moving the original set class to C without fixing the algorithm would not have addressed the real performance problem. Coding tricks don't usually help as much either, and they make your programs difficult to understand. In Python, it's almost always best to code for readability first and optimize later if needed. Despite its simplicity, `fastset` is fast indeed.

Adding Relational Algebra to Sets (External)

If you are interested in studying additional set-like operations coded in Python, see the following files in this book's examples distribution:

PP3E\Dstruct\Basic\rset.py
> RSet implementation

PP3E\Dstruct\Basic\reltest.py
> Test script for RSet

The RSet subclass defined in *rset.py* adds basic relational algebra operations for sets of dictionaries. It assumes the items in sets are mappings (rows), with one entry per column (field). RSet inherits all the original Set operations (iteration, intersection, union, & and | operators, uniqueness filtering, and so on), and adds new operations as methods:

Select
> Return a set of nodes that have a field equal to a given value.

Bagof
> Collect set nodes that satisfy an expression string.

Find
> Select tuples according to a comparison, field, and value.

Match
> Find nodes in two sets with the same values for common fields.

Product
> Compute a Cartesian product: concatenate tuples from two sets.

Join
> Combine tuples from two sets that have the same value for a field.

Project
> Extract named fields from the tuples in a table.

Difference
> Remove one set's tuples from another.

Alternative implementations of set *difference* operations can also be found in the *diff. py* file in the same examples distribution directory.

Subclassing Built-In Types

There is one more twist in the stack and set story, before we move on to some more classical data structures. In recent Python releases, it is also possible to subclass built-in datatypes such as lists and dictionaries, in order to extend them. That is, because datatypes now look and feel just like customizable classes, we can code unique datatypes that are extensions of built-ins, with subclasses that inherit built-in tool sets. For instance, here are our stack and set objects coded in the prior sections, revised as customized lists (the set union method has been simplified slightly here to remove a redundant loop):

```python
class Stack(list):
    "a list with extra methods"
    def top(self):
        return self[-1]

    def push(self, item):
        list.append(self, item)

    def pop(self):
        if not self:
            return None              # avoid exception
        else:
            return list.pop(self)

class Set(list):
    " a list with extra methods and operators"
    def __init__(self, value=[]):      # on object creation
        list.__init__(self)
        self.concat(value)

    def intersect(self, other):        # other is any sequence type
        res = []                       # self is the instance subject
        for x in self:
            if x in other:
                res.append(x)
        return Set(res)                # return a new Set

    def union(self, other):
        res = Set(self)                # new set with a copy of my list
        res.concat(other)              # insert uniques from other
        return res
```

```
    def concat(self, value):            # value: a list, string, Set...
        for x in value:                 # filters out duplicates
            if not x in self:
                self.append(x)

    # len, getitem, iter inherited, use list repr
    def __and__(self, other):   return self.intersect(other)
    def __or__(self, other):    return self.union(other)
    def __str__(self):          return '<Set:' + repr(self) + '>'

class FastSet(dict):
    pass    # this doesn't simplify much
```

The stack and set implemented in this code are essentially like those we saw earlier, but instead of embedding and managing a list, these objects really are customized lists. They add a few additional methods, but they inherit all of the list object's functionality.

This can reduce the amount of wrapper code required, but it can also expose functionality that might not be appropriate in some cases. In the following self-test code, for example, we're able to sort and insert into stacks and reverse a set, because we've inherited these methods from the list object. In most cases, such operations don't make sense for the data structures in question, and the wrapper class approach of the prior sections may still be preferred:

```
def selfTest():
    # normal use cases
    stk = Stack()
    print stk
    for c in 'spam': stk.push(c)
    print stk, stk.top()
    while stk: print stk, stk.pop()
    print stk, stk.pop()

    print
    set = Set('spam')
    print set, 'p' in set
    print set & Set('slim')
    print set | 'slim'
    print Set('slim') | Set('spam')

    # downside? these work too
    print
    stk = Stack('spam')
    print stk
    stk.insert(1, 'X')      # should only access top
    print stk
    stk.sort()              # stack not usually sorted
    print stk

    set = Set('spam')
    set.reverse()           # order should not matter
    print set, set[1]
```

```
if __name__ == '__main__':
    selfTest()
```

When run, this module produces the following results on standard output; we're able to treat the stack and set objects like lists, whether we should or not:

```
[]
['s', 'p', 'a', 'm'] m
['s', 'p', 'a', 'm'] m
['s', 'p', 'a'] a
['s', 'p'] p
['s'] s
[] None

<Set:['s', 'p', 'a', 'm']> True
<Set:['s', 'm']>
<Set:['s', 'p', 'a', 'm', 'l', 'i']>
<Set:['s', 'l', 'i', 'm', 'p', 'a']>

['s', 'p', 'a', 'm']
['s', 'X', 'p', 'a', 'm']
['X', 'a', 'm', 'p', 's']
<Set:['m', 'a', 'p', 's']> a
```

Subclassing built-in types has other applications, which may be more useful than those demonstrated by the preceding code. Consider a queue, or ordered dictionary, for example. The queue could take the form of a list subclass with get and put methods to insert on one end and delete from the other; the dictionary could be coded as a dictionary subclass with an extra list of keys that is sorted on insertion or request. Similarly, the built-in Python bool Boolean datatype is implemented as a subclass that customizes the integer int with a specialized display format (True is like integer 1, but it prints itself as the word *True*).

You can also use type subclassing to alter the way built-in types behave; a list subclass could map indexes 1..N to built-in indexes 0..N–1, for instance:

```
# map 1..N to 0..N-1, by calling back to built-in version

class MyList(list):
    def __getitem__(self, offset):
        print '(indexing %s at %s)' % (self, offset)
        return list.__getitem__(self, offset - 1)

if __name__ == '__main__':
    print list('abc')
    x = MyList('abc')            # __init__ inherited from list
    print x                      # __repr__ inherited from list
    print x[1]                   # MyList.__getitem__
    print x[3]                   # customizes list superclass method
    x.append('spam'); print x    # attributes from list superclass
    x.reverse();      print x

% python typesubclass.py
```

```
['a', 'b', 'c']
['a', 'b', 'c']
(indexing ['a', 'b', 'c'] at 1)
a
(indexing ['a', 'b', 'c'] at 3)
c
['a', 'b', 'c', 'spam']
['spam', 'c', 'b', 'a']
```

This works, but it is probably not a good idea in general. It would likely confuse its users—they will expect Python's standard 0..N–1 indexing, unless they are familiar with the custom class. As a rule of thumb, type subclasses should probably adhere to the interface of the built-in types they customize.

Binary Search Trees

Binary trees are a data structure that impose an order on inserted nodes: items less than a node are stored in the left subtree, and items greater than a node are inserted in the right. At the bottom, the subtrees are empty. Because of this structure, binary trees naturally support quick, recursive traversals—at least ideally, every time you follow a link to a subtree, you divide the search space in half.[*]

Binary trees are named for the implied branch-like structure of their subtree links. Typically, their nodes are implemented as a triple of values: (LeftSubtree, NodeValue, RightSubtree). Beyond that, there is fairly wide latitude in the tree implementation. Here we'll use a class-based approach:

- BinaryTree is a header object, which initializes and manages the actual tree.
- EmptyNode is the empty object, shared at all empty subtrees (at the bottom).
- BinaryNode objects are nonempty tree nodes with a value and two subtrees.

Instead of coding distinct search functions, binary trees are constructed with "smart" objects (class instances) that know how to handle insert/lookup and printing requests and pass them to subtree objects. In fact, this is another example of the object-oriented programming (OOP) composition relationship in action: tree nodes embed other tree nodes and pass search requests off to the embedded subtrees. A single empty class instance is shared by all empty subtrees in a binary tree, and inserts replace an EmptyNode with a BinaryNode at the bottom (see Example 20-13).

---

[*] If you're looking for a more graphical image of binary trees, skip ahead to the PyTree examples at the end of this chapter, or simply run PyTree on your own machine.

The New Built-In Set Datatype

Python has a way of conspiring to make my book examples obsolete over time. Beginning in version 2.4, the language sprouted a new built-in set datatype, which implements much of the set functionality that we coded in the set examples of this chapter (and more). It is implemented with some of the same algorithms we used, but it is available on all Pythons today.

Built-in set usage is straightforward: set objects are created by calling the new built-in set function, passing in an iterable/sequence for the initial components of the set (sets are also available in 2.3, but the set creation call must be imported from a module):

```
>>> x = set('abcde')
>>> y = set('bdxyz')
>>> x
set(['a', 'c', 'b', 'e', 'd'])

>>> 'e' in x                    # membership
True
>>> x - y                       # difference
set(['a', 'c', 'e'])
>>> x | y                       # union
set(['a', 'c', 'b', 'e', 'd', 'y', 'x', 'z'])
>>> x & y                       # intersection
set(['b', 'd'])
```

Interestingly, just like the dictionary-based optimized set we coded, built-in sets are unordered and require that all set components be hashable (immutable). In fact, their current implementation is based on wrapped dictionaries. Making a set with a dictionary of items works, but only because set uses the dictionary iterator, which returns the next key on each iteration (it ignores key values):

```
>>> x = set(['spam', 'ham', 'eggs'])    # list of immutables
>>> x
set(['eggs', 'ham', 'spam'])

>>> x = set([['spam', 'ham'], ['eggs']])
Traceback (most recent call last):
  File "<pyshell#30>", line 1, in -toplevel-
    x = set([['spam', 'ham'], ['eggs']])
TypeError: list objects are unhashable

>>> x = set({'spam':[1, 1], 'ham': [2, 2], 'eggs':[3, 3]})
>>> x
set(['eggs', 'ham', 'spam'])
```

—continued—

Built-in sets also support operations such as superset testing, and they come in two flavors: mutable and frozen (and thus hashable, for sets of sets). For more details, see the set type in the built-in types section of the Python library manual.

The set examples in this chapter are still useful as demonstrations of general data structure coding techniques, but they are not strictly required for set functionality in Python today. In fact, this is how Python tends to evolve over time: operations that are coded manually often enough wind up becoming built-in tools. I can't predict Python evolution, of course, but with any luck at all, the 10th edition of this book might be just a pamphlet.

Example 20-13. PP3E\Dstruct\Classics\btree.py

```
class BinaryTree:
    def __init__(self):        self.tree = EmptyNode( )
    def __repr__(self):        return repr(self.tree)
    def lookup(self, value): return self.tree.lookup(value)
    def insert(self, value): self.tree = self.tree.insert(value)

class EmptyNode:
    def __repr__(self):
        return '*'
    def lookup(self, value):                      # fail at the bottom
        return 0
    def insert(self, value):
        return BinaryNode(self, value, self)      # add new node at bottom

class BinaryNode:
    def __init__(self, left, value, right):
        self.data, self.left, self.right  =  value, left, right
    def lookup(self, value):
        if self.data == value:
            return 1
        elif self.data > value:
            return self.left.lookup(value)              # look in left
        else:
            return self.right.lookup(value)             # look in right
    def insert(self, value):
        if self.data > value:
            self.left = self.left.insert(value)         # grow in left
        elif self.data < value:
            self.right = self.right.insert(value)       # grow in right
        return self
    def __repr__(self):
        return ('( %s, %s, %s )' %
                (repr(self.left), repr(self.data), repr(self.right)))
```

As usual, BinaryTree can contain objects of any type that support the expected interface protocol—here, > and < comparisons. This includes class instances with the __cmp__ method. Let's experiment with this module's interfaces. The following code stuffs five integers into a new tree, and then searches for values 0...9:

```
C:\...\PP3E\Dstruct\Classics>python
>>> from btree import BinaryTree
>>> x = BinaryTree()
>>> for i in [3,1,9,2,7]:  x.insert(i)
...
>>> for i in range(10):  print (i, x.lookup(i)),
...
(0, 0) (1, 1) (2, 1) (3, 1) (4, 0) (5, 0) (6, 0) (7, 1) (8, 0) (9, 1)
```

To watch this tree grow, add a print statement after each insert. Tree nodes print themselves as triples, and empty nodes print as *. The result reflects tree nesting:

```
>>> y = BinaryTree()
>>> y
*
>>> for i in [3,1,9,2,7]:
...     y.insert(i); print y
...
( *, 3, * )
( ( *, 1, * ), 3, * )
( ( *, 1, * ), 3, ( *, 9, * ) )
( ( *, 1, ( *, 2, * ) ), 3, ( *, 9, * ) )
( ( *, 1, ( *, 2, * ) ), 3, ( ( *, 7, * ), 9, * ) )
```

At the end of this chapter, we'll see another way to visualize trees in a GUI (which means you're invited to flip ahead now). Node values in this tree object can be any comparable Python object—for instance, here is a tree of strings:

```
>>> z = BinaryTree()
>>> for c in 'badce':  z.insert(c)
...
>>> z
( ( *, 'a', * ), 'b', ( ( *, 'c', * ), 'd', ( *, 'e', * ) ) )
>>> z = BinaryTree()
>>> for c in 'abcde':  z.insert(c)
...
>>> z
( *, 'a', ( *, 'b', ( *, 'c', ( *, 'd', ( *, 'e', * ) ) ) ) )
```

Notice the last result here: if items inserted into a binary tree are already ordered, you wind up with a *linear* structure and lose the search-space partitioning magic of binary trees (the tree grows in right branches only). This is a worst-case scenario, and binary trees generally do a good job of dividing values in practice. But if you are interested in pursuing this topic further, see a data structures text for tree-balancing techniques that automatically keep the tree as dense as possible.

Also note that to keep the code simple, these trees store a value only and lookups return a 1 or (true or false). In practice, you sometimes may want to store both a key and an associated value (or even more) at each tree node. Example 20-14 shows what such a tree object looks like, for any prospective lumberjacks in the audience.

Example 20-14. PP3E\Dstruct\Classics\btree-keys.py

```
class KeyedBinaryTree:
    def __init__(self):          self.tree = EmptyNode()
    def __repr__(self):          return repr(self.tree)
    def lookup(self, key):       return self.tree.lookup(key)
    def insert(self, key, val):  self.tree = self.tree.insert(key, val)

class EmptyNode:
    def __repr__(self):
        return '*'
    def lookup(self, key):                              # fail at the bottom
        return None
    def insert(self, key, val):
        return BinaryNode(self, key, val, self)         # add node at bottom

class BinaryNode:
    def __init__(self, left, key, val, right):
        self.key,  self.val   = key, val
        self.left, self.right = left, right
    def lookup(self, key):
        if self.key == key:
            return self.val
        elif self.key > key:
            return self.left.lookup(key)                # look in left
        else:
            return self.right.lookup(key)               # look in right
    def insert(self, key, val):
        if self.key == key:
            self.val = val
        elif self.key > key:
            self.left = self.left.insert(key, val)      # grow in left
        elif self.key < key:
            self.right = self.right.insert(key, val)    # grow in right
        return self
    def __repr__(self):
        return ('( %s, %s=%s, %s )' %
        (repr(self.left), repr(self.key), repr(self.val), repr(self.right)))

if __name__ == '__main__':
    t = KeyedBinaryTree()
    for (key, val) in [('bbb', 1), ('aaa', 2), ('ccc', 3)]:
        t.insert(key, val)
    print t
    print t.lookup('aaa'), t.lookup('ccc')
    t.insert('ddd', 4)
    t.insert('aaa', 5)                          # changes key's value
    print t
```

Here is this script's self-test code at work; nodes simply have more content this time around:

```
C:\...\PP3E\Dstruct\Classics>python btree-keys.py
( ( *, 'aaa'=2, * ), 'bbb'=1, ( *, 'ccc'=3, * ) )
```

```
          2 3
          ( ( *, 'aaa'=5, * ), 'bbb'=1, ( *, 'ccc'=3, ( *, 'ddd'=4, * ) ) )
```

Graph Searching

Many problems can be represented as a graph, which is a set of states with transitions ("arcs") that lead from one state to another. For example, planning a route for a trip is really a graph search problem in disguise—the states are places you'd like to visit, and the arcs are the transportation links between them.

This section presents simple Python programs that search through a directed, cyclic graph to find the paths between a start state and a goal. Graphs can be more general than trees because links may point at arbitrary nodes—even ones already searched (hence the word *cyclic*).

The graph used to test searchers in this section is sketched in Figure 20-1. Arrows at the end of arcs indicate valid paths (e.g., *A* leads to *B*, *E*, and *G*). The search algorithms will traverse this graph in a depth-first fashion, and they will trap cycles in order to avoid looping. If you pretend that this is a map, where nodes represent cities and arcs represent roads, this example will probably seem a bit more meaningful.

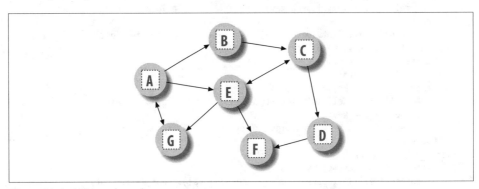

Figure 20-1. A directed graph

The first thing we need to do is choose a way to represent this graph in a Python script. One approach is to use built-in datatypes and searcher functions. The file in Example 20-15 builds the test graph as a simple dictionary: each state is a dictionary key, with a list of keys of nodes it leads to (i.e., its arcs). This file also defines a function that we'll use to run a few searches in the graph.

Example 20-15. PP3E\Dstruct\Classics\gtestfunc.py

```
Graph = {'A':  ['B', 'E', 'G'],
         'B':  ['C'],                        # a directed, cyclic graph
         'C':  ['D', 'E'],                   # stored as a dictionary
         'D':  ['F'],                        # 'key' leads-to [nodes]
         'E':  ['C', 'F', 'G'],
```

Example 20-15. PP3E\Dstruct\Classics\gtestfunc.py (continued)

```
        'F':  [ ],
        'G':  ['A']  }

def tests(searcher):                        # test searcher function
    print searcher('E', 'D', Graph)         # find all paths from 'E' to 'D'
    for x in ['AG', 'GF', 'BA', 'DA']:
        print x, searcher(x[0], x[1], Graph)
```

Now, let's code two modules that implement the actual search algorithms. They are
both independent of the graph to be searched (it is passed in as an argument). The
first searcher, in Example 20-16, uses *recursion* to walk through the graph.

Example 20-16. PP3E\Dstruct\Classics\gsearch1.py

```
# find all paths from start to goal in graph

def search(start, goal, graph):
    solns = []
    generate([start], goal, solns, graph)       # collect paths
    solns.sort( lambda x, y: cmp(len(x), len(y)) )   # sort by path length
    return solns

def generate(path, goal, solns, graph):
    state = path[-1]
    if state == goal:                           # found goal here
        solns.append(path)                      # change solns in-place
    else:                                       # check all arcs here
        for arc in graph[state]:                # skip cycles on path
            if arc not in path:
                generate(path + [arc], goal, solns, graph)

if __name__ == '__main__':
    import gtestfunc
    gtestfunc.tests(search)
```

The second searcher, in Example 20-17, uses an explicit *stack* of paths to be expanded
using the tuple-tree stack representation we explored earlier in this chapter.

Example 20-17. PP3E\Dstruct\Classics\gsearch2.py

```
# use paths stack instead of recursion

def search(start, goal, graph):
    solns = generate(([start], []), goal, graph)
    solns.sort( lambda x, y: cmp(len(x), len(y)) )
    return solns

def generate(paths, goal, graph):               # returns solns list
    solns = []                                  # use a tuple-stack
    while paths:
        front, paths = paths                    # pop the top path
        state = front[-1]
```

Example 20-17. PP3E\Dstruct\Classics\gsearch2.py (continued)

```
        if state == goal:
            solns.append(front)                  # goal on this path
        else:
            for arc in graph[state]:             # add all extensions
                if arc not in front:
                    paths = (front + [arc]), paths
    return solns

if __name__ == '__main__':
    import gtestfunc
    gtestfunc.tests(search)
```

To avoid cycles, both searchers keep track of nodes visited along a path. If an extension is already on the current path, it is a loop. The resulting solutions list is sorted by increasing lengths using the list sort method and the built-in cmp comparison function. To test the searcher modules, simply run them; their self-test code calls the canned search test in the gtestfunc module:

```
C:\...\PP3E\Dstruct\Classics>python gsearch1.py
[['E', 'C', 'D'], ['E', 'G', 'A', 'B', 'C', 'D']]
AG [['A', 'G'], ['A', 'E', 'G'], ['A', 'B', 'C', 'E', 'G']]
GF [['G', 'A', 'E', 'F'], ['G', 'A', 'B', 'C', 'D', 'F'],
    ['G', 'A', 'B', 'C', 'E', 'F'], ['G', 'A', 'E', 'C', 'D', 'F']]
BA [['B', 'C', 'E', 'G', 'A']]
DA []

C:\...\PP3E\Dstruct\Classics>python gsearch2.py
[['E', 'C', 'D'], ['E', 'G', 'A', 'B', 'C', 'D']]
AG [['A', 'G'], ['A', 'E', 'G'], ['A', 'B', 'C', 'E', 'G']]
GF [['G', 'A', 'E', 'F'], ['G', 'A', 'E', 'C', 'D', 'F'],
    ['G', 'A', 'B', 'C', 'E', 'F'], ['G', 'A', 'B', 'C', 'D', 'F']]
BA [['B', 'C', 'E', 'G', 'A']]
DA []
```

This output shows lists of possible paths through the test graph; I added two line breaks to make it more readable. Notice that both searchers find the same paths in all tests, but the order in which they find those solutions may differ. The gsearch2 order depends on how and when extensions are added to its path's stack.

Moving Graphs to Classes

Using dictionaries to represent graphs is efficient: connected nodes are located by a fast hashing operation. But depending on the application, other representations might make more sense. For instance, classes can be used to model nodes in a network too, much like the binary tree example earlier. As classes, nodes may contain content useful for more sophisticated searches. To illustrate, Example 20-18 shows an alternative coding for our graph searcher; its algorithm is closest to gsearch1.

Example 20-18. PP3E\Dstruct\Classics\graph.py

```
# build graph with objects that know how to search

class Graph:
    def __init__(self, label, extra=None):
        self.name = label                              # nodes=inst objects
        self.data = extra                              # graph=linked objs
        self.arcs = []

    def __repr__(self):
        return self.name

    def search(self, goal):
        Graph.solns = []
        self.generate([self], goal)
        Graph.solns.sort(lambda x,y: cmp(len(x), len(y)))
        return Graph.solns

    def generate(self, path, goal):
        if self == goal:                               # class == tests addr
            Graph.solns.append(path)                   # or self.solns: same
        else:
            for arc in self.arcs:
                if arc not in path:
                    arc.generate(path + [arc], goal)

if __name__ == '__main__':
    import gtestobj1
    gtestobj1.tests(Graph)
```

In this version, graphs are represented as a network of embedded class instance objects. Each node in the graph contains a list of the node objects it leads to (arcs), which it knows how to search. The generate method walks through the objects in the graph. But this time, links are directly available on each node's arcs list; there is no need to index (or pass) a dictionary to find linked objects.

To test, the module in Example 20-19 builds the test graph again, this time using linked instances of the Graph class. Notice the use of exec in the self-test code: it executes dynamically constructed strings to do the work of seven assignment statements (A=Graph('A'), B=Graph('B'), and so on).

Example 20-19. PP3E\Dstruct\Classics\gtestobj1.py

```
def tests(Graph):
    for name in "ABCDEFG":                             # make objects first
        exec "%s = Graph('%s')" % (name, name)         # label=variable-name

    A.arcs = [B, E, G]
    B.arcs = [C]                       # now configure their links:
    C.arcs = [D, E]                    # embedded class-instance list
    D.arcs = [F]
    E.arcs = [C, F, G]
```

Example 20-19. PP3E\Dstruct\Classics\gtestobj1.py (continued)

```
    G.arcs = [A]

    A.search(G)
    for (start, stop) in [(E,D), (A,G), (G,F), (B,A), (D,A)]:
        print start.search(stop)
```

Run this test by running the graph module to pass in a graph class, like this:

```
C:\...\PP3E\Dstruct\Classics>python graph.py
[[E, C, D], [E, G, A, B, C, D]]
[[A, G], [A, E, G], [A, B, C, E, G]]
[[G, A, E, F], [G, A, B, C, D, F], [G, A, B, C, E, F], [G, A, E, C, D, F]]
[[B, C, E, G, A]]
[]
```

The results are the same as for the functions, but node name labels are not quoted: nodes on path lists here are Graph instances, and this class's __repr__ scheme suppresses quotes. Example 20-20 is one last graph test before we move on; sketch the nodes and arcs on paper if you have more trouble following the paths than Python.

Example 20-20. PP3E\Dstruct\Classics\gtestobj2.py

```
from graph import Graph

S = Graph('s')
P = Graph('p')        # a graph of spam
A = Graph('a')        # make node objects
M = Graph('m')

S.arcs = [P, M]       # S leads to P and M
P.arcs = [S, M, A]    # arcs: embedded objects
A.arcs = [M]
print S.search(M)     # find all paths from S to M
```

This test finds three paths in its graph between nodes S and M. If you'd like to see more Python graph code, check out the files in the directory *MoreGraphs* in this book's examples distribution. These are roughly the same as the ones listed here, but they add user interaction as each solution is found. In addition, we've really only scratched the surface of this domain here; see other books for additional topics (e.g., breadth- and best-first search):

```
C:\...\PP3E\Dstruct\Classics>python gtestobj2.py
[[s, m], [s, p, m], [s, p, a, m]]
```

Reversing Sequences

Reversal of collections is another typical operation. We can code it either recursively or iteratively in Python, and as functions or class methods. Example 20-21 is a first attempt at two simple reversal functions.

Example 20-21. PP3E\Dstruct\Classics\rev1.py

```
def reverse(list):                  # recursive
    if list == []:
        return []
    else:
        return reverse(list[1:]) + list[:1]

def ireverse(list):                 # iterative
    res = []
    for x in list: res = [x] + res
    return res
```

Both reversal functions work correctly on lists. But if we try reversing nonlist sequences (strings, tuples, and so on) we're in trouble: the `ireverse` function always returns a list for the result regardless of the type of sequence passed:

```
>>> ireverse("spam")
['m', 'a', 'p', 's']
```

Much worse, the recursive reverse version won't work at all for nonlists—it gets stuck in an infinite loop. The reason is subtle: when reverse reaches the empty string (""), it's not equal to the empty list ([]), so the else clause is selected. But slicing an empty sequence returns another empty sequence (indexes are scaled): the else clause recurs again with an empty sequence, without raising an exception. The net effect is that this function gets stuck in a loop, calling itself over and over again until Python runs out of memory.

The versions in Example 20-22 fix both problems by using generic sequence handling techniques:

- reverse uses the not operator to detect the end of the sequence and returns the empty sequence itself, rather than an empty list constant. Since the empty sequence is the type of the original argument, the + operation always builds the correct type sequence as the recursion unfolds.

- ireverse makes use of the fact that slicing a sequence returns a sequence of the same type. It first initializes the result to the slice [:0], a new, empty slice of the argument's type. Later, it uses slicing to extract one-node sequences to add to the result's front, instead of a list constant.

Example 20-22. PP3E\Dstruct\Classics\rev2.py

```
def reverse(list):
    if not list:                            # empty? (not always [])
        return list                         # the same sequence type
    else:
        return reverse(list[1:]) + list[:1] # add front item on the end

def ireverse(list):
    res = list[:0]                          # empty, of same type
    for i in range(len(list)):
        res = list[i:i+1] + res             # add each item to front
    return res
```

These functions work on any sequence, and they return a new sequence of the same type as the sequence passed in. If we pass in a string, we get a new string as the result. In fact, they reverse any sequence object that responds to slicing, concatenation, and len—even instances of Python classes and C types. In other words, they can reverse any object that has sequence interface protocols. Here they are working on lists, strings, and tuples:

```
% python
>>> from rev2 import *
>>> reverse([1,2,3]), ireverse([1,2,3])
([3, 2, 1], [3, 2, 1])
>>> reverse("spam"), ireverse("spam")
('maps', 'maps')
>>> reverse((1.2, 2.3, 3.4)), ireverse((1.2, 2.3, 3.4))
((3.4, 2.3, 1.2), (3.4, 2.3, 1.2))
```

Permuting Sequences

The functions defined in Example 20-23 shuffle sequences in a number of ways:

- permute constructs a list with all valid permutations of any sequence.
- subset constructs a list with all valid permutations of a specific length.
- combo works like subset, but order doesn't matter: permutations of the same items are filtered out.

These results are useful in a variety of algorithms: searches, statistical analysis, and more. For instance, one way to find an optimal ordering for items is to put them in a list, generate all possible permutations, and simply test each one in turn. All three of the functions make use of the generic sequence slicing tricks of the reversal functions in the prior section so that the result list contains sequences of the same type as the one passed in (e.g., when we permute a string, we get back a list of strings).

Example 20-23. PP3E\Dstruct\Classics\permcomb.py

```
def permute(list):
    if not list:                              # shuffle any sequence
        return [list]                         # empty sequence
    else:
        res = []
        for i in range(len(list)):
            rest = list[:i] + list[i+1:]      # delete current node
            for x in permute(rest):           # permute the others
                res.append(list[i:i+1] + x)   # add node at front
        return res

def subset(list, size):
    if size == 0 or not list:                 # order matters here
        return [list[:0]]                     # an empty sequence
    else:
        result = []
```

Example 20-23. PP3E\Dstruct\Classics\permcomb.py (continued)

```
        for i in range(len(list)):
            pick = list[i:i+1]                      # sequence slice
            rest = list[:i] + list[i+1:]            # keep [:i] part
            for x in subset(rest, size-1):
                result.append(pick + x)
        return result

def combo(list, size):
    if size == 0 or not list:                       # order doesn't matter
        return [list[:0]]                           # xyz == yzx
    else:
        result = []
        for i in range(0, (len(list) - size) + 1):  # iff enough left
            pick = list[i:i+1]
            rest = list[i+1:]                        # drop [:i] part
            for x in combo(rest, size - 1):
                result.append(pick + x)
        return result
```

As in the reversal functions, all three of these work on any sequence object that supports len, slicing, and concatenation operations. For instance, we can use permute on instances of some of the stack classes defined at the start of this chapter; we'll get back a list of stack instance objects with shuffled nodes.

Here are our sequence shufflers in action. Permuting a list enables us to find all the ways the items can be arranged. For instance, for a four-item list, there are 24 possible permutations ($4 \times 3 \times 2 \times 1$). After picking one of the four for the first position, there are only three left to choose from for the second, and so on. Order matters: [1,2,3] is not the same as [1,3,2], so both appear in the result:

```
C:\...\PP3E\Dstruct\Classics>python
>>> from permcomb import *
>>> permute([1,2,3])
[[1, 2, 3], [1, 3, 2], [2, 1, 3], [2, 3, 1], [3, 1, 2], [3, 2, 1]]
>>> permute('abc')
['abc', 'acb', 'bac', 'bca', 'cab', 'cba']
>>> permute('help')
['help', 'hepl', 'hlep', 'hlpe', 'hpel', 'hple', 'ehlp', 'ehpl', 'elhp', 'elph',
 'ephl', 'eplh', 'lhep', 'lhpe', 'lehp', 'leph', 'lphe', 'lpeh', 'phel', 'phle',
 'pehl', 'pelh', 'plhe', 'pleh']
```

combo results are related to permutations, but a fixed-length constraint is put on the result, and order doesn't matter: abc is the same as acb, so only one is added to the result set:

```
>>> combo([1,2,3], 3)
[[1, 2, 3]]
>>> combo('abc', 3)
['abc']
>>> combo('abc', 2)
['ab', 'ac', 'bc']
```

```
>>> combo('abc', 4)
[]
>>> combo((1, 2, 3, 4), 3)
[(1, 2, 3), (1, 2, 4), (1, 3, 4), (2, 3, 4)]
>>> for i in range(0, 6): print i, combo("help", i)
...
0 ['']
1 ['h', 'e', 'l', 'p']
2 ['he', 'hl', 'hp', 'el', 'ep', 'lp']
3 ['hel', 'hep', 'hlp', 'elp']
4 ['help']
5 []
```

Finally, subset is just fixed-length permutations; order matters, so the result is larger than for combo. In fact, calling subset with the length of the sequence is identical to permute:

```
>>> subset([1,2,3], 3)
[[1, 2, 3], [1, 3, 2], [2, 1, 3], [2, 3, 1], [3, 1, 2], [3, 2, 1]]
>>> subset('abc', 3)
['abc', 'acb', 'bac', 'bca', 'cab', 'cba']
>>> for i in range(0, 6): print i, subset("help", i)
...
0 ['']
1 ['h', 'e', 'l', 'p']
2 ['he', 'hl', 'hp', 'eh', 'el', 'ep', 'lh', 'le', 'lp', 'ph', 'pe', 'pl']
3 ['hel', 'hep', 'hle', 'hlp', 'hpe', 'hpl', 'ehl', 'ehp', 'elh', 'elp', 'eph',
   'epl', 'lhe', 'lhp', 'leh', 'lep', 'lph', 'lpe', 'phe', 'phl', 'peh', 'pel',
   'plh', 'ple']
4 ['help', 'hepl', 'hlep', 'hlpe', 'hpel', 'hple', 'ehlp', 'ehpl', 'elhp',
   'elph', 'ephl', 'eplh', 'lhep', 'lhpe', 'lehp', 'leph', 'lphe', 'lpeh',
   'phel', 'phle', 'pehl', 'pelh', 'plhe', 'pleh']
5 ['help', 'hepl', 'hlep', 'hlpe', 'hpel', 'hple', 'ehlp', 'ehpl', 'elhp',
   'elph', 'ephl', 'eplh', 'lhep', 'lhpe', 'lehp', 'leph', 'lphe', 'lpeh',
   'phel', 'phle', 'pehl', 'pelh', 'plhe', 'pleh']
```

Sorting Sequences

Another staple of many systems is sorting: ordering items in a collection according to some constraint. The script in Example 20-24 defines a simple sort routine in Python, which orders a list of objects on a field. Because Python indexing is generic, the field can be an index or a key—this function can sort lists of either sequences or mappings.

Example 20-24. PP3E\Dstruct\Classics\sort1.py

```
def sort(list, field):
    res = []                            # always returns a list
    for x in list:
        i = 0
        for y in res:
            if x[field] <= y[field]: break     # list node goes here?
```

Example 20-24. PP3E\Dstruct\Classics\sort1.py (continued)

```
        i = i+1
    res[i:i] = [x]                              # insert in result slot
    return res

if __name__ == '__main__':
    table = [ {'name':'john', 'age':25}, {'name':'doe', 'age':32} ]
    print sort(table, 'name')
    print sort(table, 'age')
    table = [ ('john', 25), ('doe', 32) ]
    print sort(table, 0)
    print sort(table, 1)
```

Here is this module's self-test code in action:

```
C:\...\PP3E\Dstruct\Classics>python sort1.py
[{'age': 32, 'name': 'doe'}, {'age': 25, 'name': 'john'}]
[{'age': 25, 'name': 'john'}, {'age': 32, 'name': 'doe'}]
[('doe', 32), ('john', 25)]
[('john', 25), ('doe', 32)]
```

Adding Comparison Functions

Since functions can be passed in like any other object, we can easily allow for an optional comparison function. In the next version (Example 20-25), the second argument takes a function that should return true if its first argument should be placed before its second. A lambda is used to provide an ascending-order test by default. This sorter also returns a new sequence that is the same type as the sequence passed in, by applying the slicing techniques used in earlier sections: if you sort a tuple of nodes, you get back a tuple.

Example 20-25. PP3E\Dstruct\Classics\sort2.py

```
def sort(seq, func=(lambda x,y: x <= y)):       # default: ascending
    res = seq[:0]                               # return seq's type
    for j in range(len(seq)):
        i = 0
        for y in res:
            if func(seq[j], y): break
            i = i+1
        res = res[:i] + seq[j:j+1] + res[i:]     # seq can be immutable
    return res

if __name__ == '__main__':
    table = ({'name':'doe'}, {'name':'john'})
    print sort(list(table), (lambda x, y: x['name'] > y['name']))
    print sort(tuple(table), (lambda x, y: x['name'] <= y['name']))
    print sort('axbyzc')
```

This time, the table entries are ordered per a field comparison function passed in:

```
C:\...\PP3E\Dstruct\Classics>python sort2.py
[{'name': 'john'}, {'name': 'doe'}]
```

```
({'name': 'doe'}, {'name': 'john'})
abcxyz
```

This version also dispenses with the notion of a field altogether and lets the passed-in function handle indexing if needed. That makes this version much more general; for instance, it's also useful for sorting strings.

Data Structures Versus Python Built-Ins

Now that I've shown you all of these complicated algorithms, I need to also tell you that at least in some cases, they may not be an optimal approach. Built-in types such as lists and dictionaries are often a simpler and more efficient way to represent data. For instance:

Binary trees

> These may be useful in many applications, but Python dictionaries already provide a highly optimized, C-coded, search table tool. Indexing a dictionary by key is likely to be faster than searching a Python-coded tree structure:

```
>>> x = {}
>>> for i in [3,1,9,2,7]: x[i] = None          # insert
>>> for i in range(10): print (i, x.has_key(i)),    # lookup
(0, 0) (1, 1) (2, 1) (3, 1) (4, 0) (5, 0) (6, 0) (7, 1) (8, 0) (9, 1)
```

> Because dictionaries are built into the language, they are always available and will usually be faster than Python-based data structure implementations.

Graph algorithms

> These serve many purposes, but a purely Python-coded implementation of a very large graph might be less efficient than you want in some applications. Graph programs tend to require peak performance; using dictionaries rather than class instances to represent graphs may boost performance some, but using linked-in compiled extensions may as well.

Sorting algorithms

> These are an important part of many programs too, but Python's built-in list sort method is so fast that you would be hard-pressed to beat it in Python in most scenarios. In fact, it's generally better to convert sequences to lists first just so that you can use the built-in:[*]

```
temp = list(sequence)
temp.sort( )
...use items in temp...
```

---

[*] Recent news: in Python 2.4, the sort list method also accepts a Boolean reverse flag to reverse the result (there is no need to manually reverse after the sort), and there is a new sorted built-in function, which returns its result list and works on any iterable, not just on lists (there is no need to convert to a list to sort). Python makes lives easier over time. The underlying sort routine in Python is very good, by the way. In fact, its documentation claims that it has "supernatural performance"—not bad for a sorter.

For custom sorts, simply pass in a comparison function of your own:

```
>>> L = [{'n':3}, {'n':20}, {'n':0}, {'n':9}]
>>> L.sort( lambda x, y: cmp(x['n'], y['n']) )
>>> L
[{'n': 0}, {'n': 3}, {'n': 9}, {'n': 20}]
```

Reversal algorithms

These are generally superfluous by the same token—because Python lists provide a fast reverse method, you may be better off converting a nonlist to a list first, just so that you can run the built-in list method.

Don't misunderstand: sometimes you really do need objects that add functionality to built-in types or do something more custom. The set classes we met, for instance, add tools not directly supported by Python today, and the tuple-tree stack implementation was actually faster than one based on built-in lists for common usage patterns. Permutations are something you need to add on your own too.

Moreover, class encapsulations make it possible to change and extend object internals without impacting the rest of your system. They also support reuse much better than built-in types—types are not classes today, and they cannot be specialized directly without wrapper class logic.

Yet because Python comes with a set of built-in, flexible, and optimized datatypes, data structure implementations are often not as important in Python as they are in lesser-equipped languages such as C and C++. Before you code that new datatype, be sure to ask yourself whether a built-in type or call might be more in line with the Python way of thinking.

PyTree: A Generic Tree Object Viewer

Up to now, this chapter has been command-line-oriented. To wrap up, I want to show you a program that merges the GUI technology we studied earlier in the book with some of the data structure ideas we've met in this chapter.

This program is called PyTree, a generic tree data structure viewer written in Python with the Tkinter GUI library. PyTree sketches out the nodes of a tree on-screen as boxes connected by arrows. It also knows how to route mouse clicks on drawn tree nodes back to the tree, to trigger tree-specific actions. Because PyTree lets you visualize the structure of the tree generated by a set of parameters, it's a fun way to explore tree-based algorithms.

PyTree supports arbitrary tree types by "wrapping" real trees in interface objects. The interface objects implement a standard protocol by communicating with the underlying tree object. For the purposes of this chapter, PyTree is instrumented to display binary search trees; for the next chapter, it's also set up to render expression parse trees. New trees can be viewed by coding wrapper classes to interface to new tree types.

The GUI interfaces PyTree utilizes were covered in depth earlier in this book, so I won't go over this code in much detail here. See Part III for background details and be sure to run this program on your own computer to get a better feel for its operation. Because it is written with Python and Tkinter, it should be portable to Windows, Unix, and Macs.

Running PyTree

Before we get to the code, let's see what PyTree looks like. You can launch PyTree from the PyDemos launcher bar (see the top level of the examples distribution source tree) or by directly running the *treeview.py* file listed in Example 20-27. Figure 20-2 shows PyTree in action displaying the binary tree created by the "test1" button. Trees are sketched as labels embedded in a canvas and are connected by lines with arrows. The lines reflect parent-to-child relationships in the actual tree; PyTree attempts to lay out the tree to produce a more or less uniform display like this one.

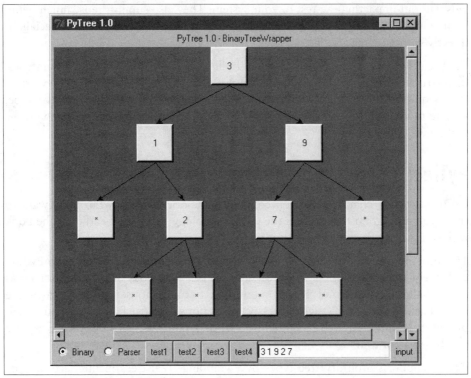

Figure 20-2. PyTree viewing a binary search tree (test1)

PyTree's window consists of a canvas with vertical and horizontal scrolls and a set of controls at the bottom: radio buttons for picking the type of tree you wish to display, a set of buttons that trigger canned tree drawing tests, and an input field for typing text to specify and generate a new tree. The set of test buttons changes if you pick the Parser radio button (you get one less test button); PyTree use widget pack_forget and pack methods to hide and show tree-specific buttons on the fly.

When you pick one of the canned test buttons, it displays in the input field the string you would type to generate the tree drawn. For binary trees, type a list of values separated by spaces and press the "input" button or the Enter key to generate a new tree; the new tree is the result of inserting the typed values from left to right. For parse trees, input an expression string in the input field instead (more on this later). Figure 20-3 shows the result of typing a set of values into the input field and submitting; the resulting binary tree shows up in the canvas.

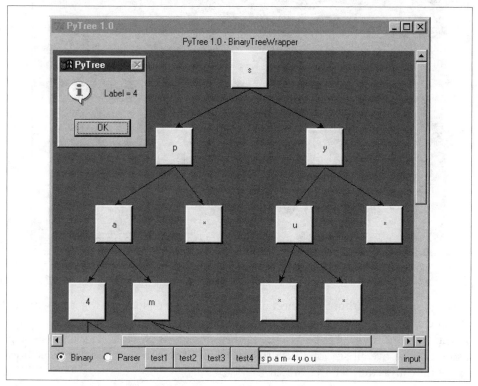

Figure 20-3. A binary tree typed manually with on-click pop up

Notice the pop up in this screenshot; left-clicking on a displayed tree node with your mouse runs whatever action a tree wrapper class defines and displays its result in the pop up. Binary trees have no action to run, so we get a default message in the pop up, but parse trees use the mouse click to evaluate the subtree rooted at the clicked node (again, more on parse trees later).

Just for fun, maximize this window and press the "test4" button—it inserts 100 numbers from zero through 99 into a new binary tree at random and displays the result. Figure 20-4 captures one portion of this tree; it's much too large to fit on one screen (or on one book page), but you can move around the tree with the canvas scroll bars.

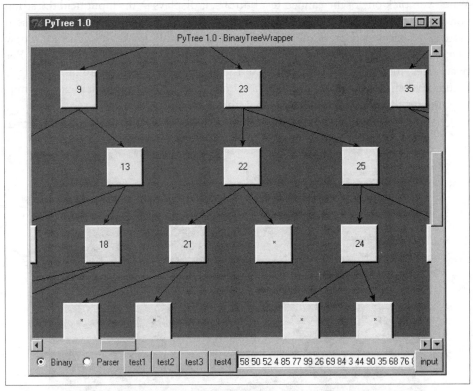

Figure 20-4. PyTree viewing a large binary search tree (test4)

PyTree uses an algorithm to connect all parents to their children in this tree without crossing their connecting lines. It does some upfront analysis to try to arrange descendents at each level to be as close to their parents as possible. This analysis step also yields the overall size of a new tree—PyTree uses it to reset the scrollable area size of the canvas for each tree drawn.

PyTree Source Code

Let's move on to the code; similar to PyForm in the prior chapter, PyTree is coded as two modules. Here, one module handles the task of sketching trees in the GUI, and another implements wrappers to interface to various tree types and extends the GUI with extra widgets.

Tree-independent GUI implementation

The module in Example 20-26 does the work of drawing trees in a canvas. It's coded to be independent of any particular tree structure—its TreeViewer class delegates to its TreeWrapper class when it needs tree-specific information for the drawing (e.g., node label text and node child links). TreeWrapper in turn expects to be subclassed for a specific kind of tree; in fact, it raises assertion errors if you try to use it without subclassing. In design terms, TreeViewer embeds a TreeWrapper; it's almost as easy to code TreeViewer subclasses per tree type, but that limits a viewer GUI to one particular kind of tree (see *treeview_subclasses.py* on the book's examples distribution for a subclassing-based alternative).

Trees are drawn in two steps: a planning traversal that builds a layout data structure that links parents and children, and a drawing step that uses the generated plan to draw and link node labels on the canvas. The two-step approach simplifies some of the logic required to lay out trees uniformly. Study Example 20-26 for more details.

Example 20-26. PP3E\Dstruct\TreeView\treeview_wrappers.py

```
#############################################################################
# PyTree: sketch arbitrary tree data structures in a scrolled canvas;
# this version uses tree wrapper classes embedded in the viewer GUI
# to support arbitrary trees (i.e., composition, not viewer subclassing);
# also adds tree node label click callbacks--run tree specific actions;
# see treeview_subclasses.py for subclass-based alternative structure;
# subclassing limits one tree viewer to one tree type, wrappers do not;
# see treeview_left.py for an alternative way to draw the tree object;
# see and run treeview.py for binary and parse tree wrapper test cases;
#############################################################################

from Tkinter import *
from tkMessageBox import showinfo

Width, Height = 350, 350                # start canvas size (reset per tree)
Rowsz = 100                             # pixels per tree row
Colsz = 100                             # pixels per tree col


####################################
# interface to tree object's nodes
####################################

class TreeWrapper:                      # subclass for a tree type
    def children(self, treenode):
        assert 0, 'children method must be specialized for tree type'
    def label(self, treenode):
        assert 0, 'label method must be specialized for tree type'
    def value(self, treenode):
        return ''
    def onClick(self, treenode):        # node label click callback
        return ''
    def onInputLine(self, line, viewer): # input line sent callback
        pass
```

Example 20-26. PP3E\Dstruct\TreeView\treeview_wrappers.py (continued)

```
##########$######################
# tree view GUI, tree independent
################################

class TreeViewer(Frame):
    def __init__(self, wrapper, parent=None, tree=None, bg='brown', fg='beige'):
        Frame.__init__(self, parent)
        self.pack(expand=YES, fill=BOTH)
        self.makeWidgets(bg)                  # build GUI: scrolled canvas
        self.master.title('PyTree 1.0')       # assume I'm run standalone
        self.wrapper = wrapper                # embed a TreeWrapper object
        self.fg = fg                          # setTreeType changes wrapper
        if tree:
            self.drawTree(tree)

    def makeWidgets(self, bg):
        self.title = Label(self, text='PyTree 1.0')
        self.canvas = Canvas(self, bg=bg, borderwidth=0)
        vbar = Scrollbar(self)
        hbar = Scrollbar(self, orient='horizontal')

        self.title.pack(side=TOP, fill=X)
        vbar.pack(side=RIGHT,  fill=Y)                # pack canvas after bars
        hbar.pack(side=BOTTOM, fill=X)
        self.canvas.pack(side=TOP, fill=BOTH, expand=YES)

        vbar.config(command=self.canvas.yview)        # call on scroll move
        hbar.config(command=self.canvas.xview)
        self.canvas.config(yscrollcommand=vbar.set)   # call on canvas move
        self.canvas.config(xscrollcommand=hbar.set)
        self.canvas.config(height=Height, width=Width)  # viewable area size

    def clearTree(self):
        mylabel = 'PyTree 1.0 - ' + self.wrapper.__class__.__name__
        self.title.config(text=mylabel)
        self.unbind_all('<Button-1>')
        self.canvas.delete('all')                     # clear events, drawing

    def drawTree(self, tree):
        self.clearTree()
        wrapper = self.wrapper
        levels, maxrow = self.planLevels(tree, wrapper)
        self.canvas.config(scrollregion=(                    # scrollable area
            0, 0, (Colsz * maxrow), (Rowsz * len(levels)) ))  # upleft, lowright
        self.drawLevels(levels, maxrow, wrapper)

    def planLevels(self, root, wrap):
        levels = []
        maxrow = 0                                    # traverse tree to
        currlevel = [(root, None)]                    # lay out rows, cols
        while currlevel:
            levels.append(currlevel)
```

Example 20-26. PP3E\Dstruct\TreeView\treeview_wrappers.py (continued)

```
            size = len(currlevel)
            if size > maxrow: maxrow = size
            nextlevel = []
            for (node, parent) in currlevel:
                if node != None:
                    children = wrap.children(node)          # list of nodes
                    if not children:
                        nextlevel.append((None, None))      # leave a hole
                    else:
                        for child in children:
                            nextlevel.append((child, node))   # parent link
            currlevel = nextlevel
        return levels, maxrow

    def drawLevels(self, levels, maxrow, wrap):
        rowpos = 0                                          # draw tree per plan
        for level in levels:                                # set click handlers
            colinc = (maxrow * Colsz) / (len(level) + 1)    # levels is treenodes
            colpos = 0
            for (node, parent) in level:
                colpos = colpos + colinc
                if node != None:
                    text = wrap.label(node)
                    more = wrap.value(node)
                    if more: text = text + '=' + more
                    win = Label(self.canvas, text=text,
                                         bg=self.fg, bd=3, relief=RAISED)
                    win.pack()
                    win.bind('<Button-1>',
                            (lambda evt, node=node: self.onClick(evt, node)))
                    self.canvas.create_window(colpos, rowpos, anchor=NW,
                            window=win, width=Colsz*.5, height=Rowsz*.5)
                    if parent != None:
                        self.canvas.create_line(
                            parent.__colpos + Colsz*.25,    # from x-y, to x-y
                            parent.__rowpos + Rowsz*.5,
                            colpos + Colsz*.25, rowpos, arrow='last', width=1)
                    node.__rowpos = rowpos
                    node.__colpos = colpos                  # mark node, private attrs
            rowpos = rowpos + Rowsz

    def onClick(self, event, node):
        label = event.widget
        wrap  = self.wrapper
        text  = 'Label = ' + wrap.label(node)               # on label click
        value = wrap.value(node)
        if value:
            text = text + '\nValue = ' + value              # add tree text if any
        result = wrap.onClick(node)                         # run tree action if any
        if result:
            text = text + '\n' + result                     # add action result
        showinfo('PyTree', text)                            # pop up std dialog
```

Example 20-26. PP3E\Dstruct\TreeView\treeview_wrappers.py (continued)

```
    def onInputLine(self, line):                    # feed text to tree wrapper
        self.wrapper.onInputLine(line, self)        # ex: parse and redraw tree

    def setTreeType(self, newTreeWrapper):          # change tree type drawn
        if self.wrapper != newTreeWrapper:          # effective on next draw
            self.wrapper = newTreeWrapper
            self.clearTree()                        # else old node, new wrapper
```

Tree wrappers and test widgets

The other half of PyTree consists of a module that defines TreeWrapper subclasses
that interface to binary and parser trees, implements canned test case buttons, and
adds the control widgets to the bottom of the PyTree window.* These control widgets were split off into this separate module (in Example 20-27) on purpose, because
the PyTree canvas might be useful as a viewer component in other GUI applications.

Example 20-27. PP3E\Dstruct\TreeView\treeview.py

```
# PyTree launcher script
# wrappers for viewing tree types in the book, plus test cases/GUI

from Tkinter import *
from treeview_wrappers import TreeWrapper, TreeViewer
from PP3E.Dstruct.Classics import btree
from PP3E.Lang.Parser import parser2


##################################################################
# binary tree wrapper
##################################################################

class BinaryTreeWrapper(TreeWrapper):                # embed binary tree in viewer
    def children(self, node):                       # adds viewer protocols
        try:                                        # to interface with tree
            return [node.left, node.right]
        except:
            return None
    def label(self, node):
        try:
            return str(node.data)
        except:
            return str(node)
    def onInputLine(self, line, viewer):            # on test entry at bottom
        items = line.split()                        # make tree from text input
        t = btree.BinaryTree()                      # draw resulting btree
        for x in items: t.insert(x)                 # no onClick handler here
```

---

* If you're looking for a coding exercise, try adding another wrapper class and radio button to view the
KeyedBinaryTree we wrote earlier in this chapter. You'll probably want to display the key in the GUI and pop
up the associated value on-clicks.

Example 20-27. PP3E\Dstruct\TreeView\treeview.py (continued)

```
        viewer.drawTree(t.tree)

###################################################################
# binary tree extension
###################################################################

class BinaryTree(btree.BinaryTree):
    def __init__(self, viewer):                # embed viewer in tree
        btree.BinaryTree.__init__(self)        # but viewer has a wrapper
        self.viewer = viewer
    def view(self):
        self.viewer.drawTree(self.tree)

###################################################################
# parse tree wrapper
###################################################################

class ParseTreeWrapper(TreeWrapper):
    def __init__(self):                        # embed parse tree in viewer
        self.dict = {}                         # adds viewer protocols
    def children(self, node):
        try:
            return [node.left, node.right]
        except:
            try:
                return [node.var, node.val]
            except:
                return None
    def label(self, node):
        for attr in ['label', 'num', 'name']:
            if hasattr(node, attr):
                return str(getattr(node, attr))
        return 'set'
    def onClick(self, node):                   # on tree label click
        try:                                   # tree-specific action
            result = node.apply(self.dict)     # evaluate subtree
            return 'Value = ' + str(result)    # show result in pop up
        except:
            return 'Value = <error>'
    def onInputLine(self, line, viewer):       # on input line
        p = parser2.Parser()                   # parse expr text
        p.lex.newtext(line)                    # draw resulting tree
        t = p.analyse()
        if t: viewer.drawTree(t)

###################################################################
# canned test cases (or type new nodelists/exprs in input field)
###################################################################

def shownodes(sequence):
    sequence = map(str, sequence)              # convert nodes to strings
    entry.delete(0, END)                       # show nodes in text field
```

Example 20-27. PP3E\Dstruct\TreeView\treeview.py (continued)

```
        entry.insert(0, ' '.join(sequence))

def test1_binary():                          # tree type is binary wrapper
    nodes = [3, 1, 9, 2, 7]                  # make a binary tree
    tree  = BinaryTree(viewer)               # embed viewer in tree
    for i in nodes: tree.insert(i)
    shownodes(nodes)                         # show nodes in input field
    tree.view()                              # sketch tree via embedded viewer

def test2_binary():
    nodes = 'badce'
    tree  = btree.BinaryTree()               # embed wrapper in viewer
    for c in nodes: tree.insert(c)           # make a binary tree
    shownodes(nodes)
    viewer.drawTree(tree.tree)               # ask viewer to draw it

def test3_binary():
    nodes = 'abcde'
    tree  = BinaryTree(viewer)
    for c in nodes: tree.insert(c)
    shownodes(nodes)
    tree.view()

def test4_binary():
    tree = BinaryTree(viewer)
    import random                            # make a big binary tree
    nodes = range(100)                       # insert 100 nodes at random
    order = []                               # and sketch in viewer
    while nodes:
        item = random.choice(nodes)
        nodes.remove(item)
        tree.insert(item)
        order.append(item)
    shownodes(order)
    tree.view()

def test_parser(expr):
    parser = parser2.Parser()                # tree type is parser wrapper
    parser.lex.newtext(expr)                 # subtrees evaluate when clicked
    tree   = parser.analyse()                # input line parses new expr
    entry.delete(0, END)                     # vars set in wrapper dictionary
    entry.insert(0, expr)                    # see lang/text chapter for parser
    if tree: viewer.drawTree(tree)

def test1_parser(): test_parser("1 + 3 * (2 * 3 + 4)")
def test2_parser(): test_parser("set temp 1 + 3 * 2 * 3 + 4")
def test3_parser(): test_parser("set result temp + ((1 + 3) * 2) * (3 + 4)")

###################################################################
# build viewer with extra widgets to test tree types
###################################################################
```

Example 20-27. PP3E\Dstruct\TreeView\treeview.py (continued)

```
if __name__ == '__main__':
    root = Tk()                                   # build a single viewer GUI
    bwrapper = BinaryTreeWrapper()                # add extras: input line, test btns
    pwrapper = ParseTreeWrapper()                 # make wrapper objects
    viewer   = TreeViewer(bwrapper, root)         # start out in binary mode

    def onRadio():
        if var.get() == 'btree':
            viewer.setTreeType(bwrapper)                  # change viewer's wrapper
            for btn in p_btns: btn.pack_forget()          # erase parser test buttons
            for btn in b_btns: btn.pack(side=LEFT)        # unhide binary buttons
        elif var.get() == 'ptree':
            viewer.setTreeType(pwrapper)
            for btn in b_btns: btn.pack_forget()
            for btn in p_btns: btn.pack(side=LEFT)

    var = StringVar()
    var.set('btree')
    Radiobutton(root, text='Binary', command=onRadio,
                      variable=var, value='btree').pack(side=LEFT)
    Radiobutton(root, text='Parser', command=onRadio,
                      variable=var, value='ptree').pack(side=LEFT)
    b_btns = []
    b_btns.append(Button(root, text='test1', command=test1_binary))
    b_btns.append(Button(root, text='test2', command=test2_binary))
    b_btns.append(Button(root, text='test3', command=test3_binary))
    b_btns.append(Button(root, text='test4', command=test4_binary))
    p_btns = []
    p_btns.append(Button(root, text='test1', command=test1_parser))
    p_btns.append(Button(root, text='test2', command=test2_parser))
    p_btns.append(Button(root, text='test3', command=test3_parser))
    onRadio()

    def onInputLine():
        line = entry.get()                # use per current tree wrapper type
        viewer.onInputLine(line)          # type a node list or expression

    Button(root, text='input', command=onInputLine).pack(side=RIGHT)
    entry = Entry(root)
    entry.pack(side=RIGHT, expand=YES, fill=X)
    entry.bind('<Return>', lambda event: onInputLine())   # button or enter key
    root.mainloop()                                        # start up the GUI
```

PyTree Does Parse Trees Too

Finally, I want to show you what happens when you click the Parser radio button in the PyTree window. The GUI changes over to an expression parse tree viewer by simply using a different tree wrapper class: the label at the top changes, the test buttons change, and input is now entered as an arithmetic expression to be parsed and sketched. Figure 20-5 shows a tree generated for the expression string displayed in the input field.

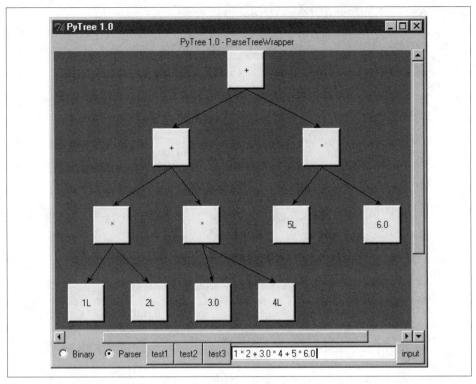

Figure 20-5. PyTree viewing an expression parse tree

PyTree is designed to be generic—it displays both binary and parse trees, but it is easy to extend for new tree types with new wrapper classes. On the GUI, you can switch between binary and parser tree types at any time by clicking the radio buttons. Input typed into the input field is always evaluated according to the current tree type. When the viewer is in parse tree mode, clicking on a node in the tree evaluates the part of the expression represented by the parse tree rooted at the node you clicked. Figure 20-6 shows the pop up you get when you click the root node of the tree displayed.

Figure 20-6. PyTree pop up after clicking a parse tree node

When viewing parse trees, PyTree becomes a sort of visual calculator—you can generate arbitrary expression trees and evaluate any part of them by clicking on nodes displayed. But at this point, there is not much more I can tell you about these kinds of trees until you move on to Chapter 21.

## CHAPTER 21

Text and Language

"See Jack Hack. Hack, Jack, Hack"

In one form or another, processing text-based information is one of the more common tasks that applications need to perform. This can include anything from scanning a text file by columns to analyzing statements in a language defined by a formal grammar. Such processing usually is called *parsing*—analyzing the structure of a text string. In this chapter, we'll explore ways to handle language and text-based information and summarize some Python development concepts in sidebars along the way.

Some of this material is advanced, but the examples are small. For instance, recursive descent parsing is illustrated with a simple example to show how it can be implemented in Python. We'll also see that it's often unnecessary to write custom parsers for each language processing task in Python. They can usually be replaced by exporting APIs for use in Python programs, and sometimes by a single built-in function call. Finally, this chapter closes by presenting PyCalc—a calculator GUI written in Python, and the last major Python coding example in this text. As we'll see, writing calculators isn't much more difficult than juggling stacks while scanning text.

Strategies for Parsing Text in Python

In the grand scheme of things, there are a variety of ways to handle text processing in Python:

- Built-in string object expressions
- String object method calls
- Regular expression matching
- Parser-generator integrations
- Handcoded and generated parsers
- Running Python code with eval and exec built-ins

For simpler tasks, Python's built-in string object is often all we really need. Python strings can be indexed, concatenated, sliced, and processed with both string method calls and built-in functions. Our emphasis in this chapter, though, is on higher-level tools and techniques for analyzing textual information. Let's briefly explore each of the other approaches with representative examples.

String Method Utilities

Python's string methods include a variety of text-processing utilities that go above and beyond string expression operators. For instance, given an instance str of the built-in string object type:

str.find(substr)
> Performs substring searches

str.replace(old, new)
> Performs substring substitutions

str.split(delim)
> Chops up a string around delimiters

str.join(seq)
> Puts substrings together with delimiters between

str.strip( )
> Removes leading and trailing whitespace

str.rstrip( )
> Removes trailing whitespace only, if any

str.rjust(width)
> Right-justifies a string in a fixed-width field

str.upper( )
> Converts to uppercase

str.isupper( )
> Tests whether the string is uppercase

str.isdigit( )
> Tests whether the string is all digit characters

str.endswith(substr)
> Tests for a substring at the end

str.startswith(substr)
> Tests for a substring at the front

This list is representative but partial, and some of these methods take additional optional arguments. For the full list of string methods, run a dir(str) call at the Python interactive prompt and run help(str.method) on any method for some quick documentation. The Python library manual also includes an exhaustive list.

Moreover, in Python today, Unicode (wide) strings fully support all normal string methods, and most of the older `string` module's functions are also now available as string object *methods*. For instance, in Python 2.0 and later, the following two expressions are equivalent:

```
string.find(aString, substr)    # original module
aString.find(substr)            # methods new in 2.0
```

However, the second form does not require callers to import the `string` module first.

As of this third edition of the book, the method call form is used everywhere, since it has been the recommended best-practice pattern for some time. If you see older code based on the module call pattern, it is a simple mapping to the newer method-based call form. The original `string` module still contains predefined constants (e.g., `string.uppercase`), as well as the new `Template` substitution interface in 2.4, and so remains useful in some contexts apart from method calls.

Templating with Replacements and Formats

Speaking of templates, as we saw when coding the web page migration scripts in Part II of this book, the string `replace` method is often adequate as a string templating tool—we can compute values and insert them at fixed positions in a string with a single `replace` call:

```
>>> template = '---$target1---$target2---'
>>> val1 = 'Spam'
>>> val2 = 'shrubbery'
>>> template = template.replace('$target1', val1)
>>> template = template.replace('$target2', val2)
>>> template
'---Spam---shrubbery---'
```

As we also saw when generating HTML code in our Common Gateway Interface (CGI) scripts in Part III of this book, the string `%` formatting operator is also a powerful templating tool—simply fill out a dictionary with values and apply substitutions to the HTML string all at once:

```
>>> template = """
... ---
... ---%(key1)s---
... ---%(key2)s---
... """
>>>
>>> vals = {}
>>> vals['key1'] = 'Spam'
>>> vals['key2'] = 'shrubbery'
>>> print template % vals

---
---Spam---
---shrubbery---
```

The 2.4 string module's `Template` feature is essentially a simplified variation of the dictionary-based format scheme, but it allows some additional call patterns:

```
>>> vals
{'key2': 'shrubbery', 'key1': 'Spam'}

>>> import string
>>> template = string.Template('---$key1---$key2---')
>>> template.substitute(vals)
'---Spam---shrubbery---'

>>> template.substitute(key1='Brian', key2='Loretta')
'---Brian---Loretta---'
```

See the library manual for more on this extension. Although the string datatype does not itself support the pattern-directed text processing that we'll meet later in this chapter, its tools are powerful enough for many tasks.

Parsing with Splits and Joins

In terms of this chapter's main focus, Python's built-in tools for splitting and joining strings around tokens turn out to be especially useful when it comes to parsing text:

str.split(delimiter?, maxsplits?)
:   Splits a string into substrings, using either whitespace substrings (tabs, spaces, newlines) or an explicitly passed string as a delimiter. maxsplits limits the number of splits performed, if passed.

delimiter.join(sequence)
:   Concatenates a sequence of substrings (e.g., list or tuple), adding the subject separator string between each.

These two are among the most powerful of string methods. As we saw earlier in Chapter 3, split chops a string into a list of substrings and join puts them back together:[*]

```
>>> 'A B C D'.split()
['A', 'B', 'C', 'D']
>>> 'A+B+C+D'.split('+')
['A', 'B', 'C', 'D']
>>> '--'.join(['a', 'b', 'c'])
'a--b--c'
```

Despite their simplicity, they can handle surprisingly complex text-parsing tasks. Moreover, string method calls are very fast because they are implemented in C language code. For instance, to quickly replace all tabs in a file with four periods, pipe the file into a script that looks like this:

```
from sys import *
stdout.write( ('.' * 4).join( stdin.read().split('\t') ) )
```

---

[*] Very early Python releases had similar tools called spitfields and joinfields; the more modern (and less verbose) split and join are the preferred way to spell these today.

The split call here divides input around tabs, and the join puts it back together with periods where tabs had been. The combination of the two calls is equivalent to using the global replacement string method call as follows:

```
stdout.write( stdin.read( ).replace('\t', '.'*4) )
```

As we'll see in the next sections, splitting strings is sufficient for many text-parsing goals.

Summing Columns in a File

Let's look at a couple of practical applications of string splits and joins. In many domains, scanning files by columns is a fairly common task. For instance, suppose you have a file containing columns of numbers output by another system, and you need to sum each column's numbers. In Python, string splitting does the job, as demonstrated by Example 21-1. As an added bonus, it's easy to make the solution a reusable tool in Python.

Example 21-1. PP3E\Lang\summer.py

```
#!/usr/local/bin/python

def summer(numCols, fileName):
    sums = [0] * numCols                    # make list of zeros
    for line in open(fileName):             # scan file's lines
        cols = line.split( )                # split up columns
        for i in range(numCols):            # around blanks/tabs
            sums[i] += eval(cols[i])        # add numbers to sums
    return sums

if __name__ == '__main__':
    import sys
    print summer(eval(sys.argv[1]), sys.argv[2])    # '% summer.py cols file'
```

Notice that we use file iterators here to read line by line, instead of calling the file readlines method explicitly (recall from Chapter 4 that iterators avoid loading the entire file into memory all at once).

As usual, you can both *import* this module and call its function and *run* it as a shell tool from the command line. The *summer.py* script calls split to make a list of strings representing the line's columns, and eval to convert column strings to numbers. Here's an input file that uses both blanks and tabs to separate columns:

```
C:\...\PP3E\Lang>type table1.txt
1       5       10      2   1.0
2       10      20      4   2.0
3       15      30      8   3
4       20      40      16  4.0
C:\...\PP3E\Lang>python summer.py 5 table1.txt
[10, 50, 100, 30, 10.0]
```

Also notice that because the summer script uses eval to convert file text to numbers, you could really store arbitrary Python expressions in the file. Here, for example, it's run on a file of Python code snippets:

```
C:\...\PP3E\Lang>type table2.txt
2      1+1        1<<1       eval("2")
16     2*2*2*2    pow(2,4)   16.0
3      len('abc') [1,2,3][2] {'spam':3}['spam']

C:\...\PP3E\Lang>python summer.py 4 table2.txt
[21, 21, 21, 21.0]
```

We'll revisit eval later in this chapter, when we explore expression evaluators. Sometimes this is more than we want—if we can't be sure that the strings that we run this way won't contain malicious code, for instance, it may be necessary to run them with limited machine access or use more restrictive conversion tools. Consider the following recoding of the summer function:

```
def summer(numCols, fileName):
    sums = [0] * numCols
    for line in open(fileName):             # use file iterators
        cols = line.split(',')              # assume comma-delimited
        nums = [int(x) for x in cols]       # use limited converter
        both = zip(sums, nums)              # avoid nested for loop
        sums = [x + y for (x, y) in both]
    return sums
```

This version uses int for its conversions from strings to support only numbers, and not arbitrary and possibly unsafe expressions. Although the first four lines of this coding are similar to the original, for variety this version also assumes the data is separated by commas rather than whitespace and runs list comprehensions and zip to avoid the nested for loop statement. This version is also substantially trickier than the original and so might be less desirable from a maintenance perspective. If its code is confusing, try adding print statements after each step to trace the results of each operation.

For related examples, also see the grid examples in Chapter 10 for another case of eval table magic at work. The summer script here is a much simpler version of that chapter's column sum logic. To remove the need to pass in a number-columns value, see also the more advanced floating-point column summer example in the "Other Uses for Dictionaries" sidebar in Chapter 2—it works by making the column number a key rather than an offset.

Parsing and Unparsing Rule Strings

Splitting comes in handy for diving text into columns, but it can also be used as a more general parsing tool—by splitting more than once on different delimiters, we can pick apart more complex text. Although such parsing can also be achieved with more powerful tools such as the regular expressions we'll meet later in this chapter, split-based parsing is simpler to code, and may run quicker.

For instance, Example 21-2 demonstrates one way that splitting and joining strings can be used to parse sentences in a simple language. It is taken from a rule-based expert system shell (holmes) that is written in Python and included in this book's examples distribution (see the top-level *Ai* examples directory). Rule strings in holmes take the form:

```
"rule <id> if <test1>, <test2>... then <conclusion1>, <conclusion2>..."
```

Tests and conclusions are conjunctions of terms ("," means "and"). Each term is a list of words or variables separated by spaces; variables start with ?. To use a rule, it is translated to an internal form—a dictionary with nested lists. To display a rule, it is translated back to the string form. For instance, given the call:

```
rules.internal_rule('rule x if a ?x, b then c, d ?x')
```

the conversion in function internal_rule proceeds as follows:

```
string = 'rule x if a ?x, b then c, d ?x'
i = ['rule x', 'a ?x, b then c, d ?x']
t = ['a ?x, b', 'c, d ?x']
r = ['', 'x']
result = {'rule':'x', 'if':[['a','?x'], ['b']], 'then':[['c'], ['d','?x']]}
```

We first split around the if, then around the then, and finally around rule. The result is the three substrings that were separated by the keywords. Test and conclusion substrings are split around "," first and spaces last. join is used to convert back (unparse) to the original string for display. Example 21-2 is the concrete implementation of this scheme.

Example 21-2. PP3E\Lang\rules.py

```python
def internal_rule(string):
    i = string.split(' if ')
    t = i[1].split(' then ')
    r = i[0].split('rule ')
    return {'rule': r[1].strip(), 'if':internal(t[0]), 'then':internal(t[1])}

def external_rule(rule):
    return ('rule '   + rule['rule']            +
            ' if '    + external(rule['if'])    +
            ' then '  + external(rule['then'])  + '.')

def internal(conjunct):
    res = []                                    # 'a b, c d'
    for clause in conjunct.split(','):          # -> ['a b', ' c d']
        res.append(clause.split())              # -> [['a','b'], ['c','d']]
    return res

def external(conjunct):
    strs = []                                   # [['a','b'], ['c','d']]
    for clause in conjunct:                      # -> ['a b', 'c d']
        strs.append(' '.join(clause))           # -> 'a b, c d'
    return ', '.join(strs)
```

Notice that we could use newer list comprehensions to gain some conciseness here. The internal function, for instance, could be recoded to simply:

```
return [clause.split( ) for clause in conjunct.split(',')]
```

to produce the desired nested lists by combining two steps into one. This form might run faster; we'll leave it to the reader to decide whether it is more difficult to understand. As usual, we can test components of this module interactively:

```
>>> import rules
>>> rules.internal('a ?x, b')
[['a', '?x'], ['b']]

>>> rules.internal_rule('rule x if a ?x, b then c, d ?x')
{'if': [['a', '?x'], ['b']], 'rule': 'x', 'then': [['c'], ['d', '?x']]}

>>> r = rules.internal_rule('rule x if a ?x, b then c, d ?x')
>>> rules.external_rule(r)
'rule x if a ?x, b then c, d ?x.'
```

Parsing by splitting strings around tokens like this takes you only so far. There is no direct support for recursive nesting of components, and syntax errors are not handled very gracefully. But for simple language tasks like this, string splitting might be enough, at least for prototyping systems. You can always add a more robust rule parser later or reimplement rules as embedded Python code or classes.

More on the holmes Expert System Shell

So how are these rules actually used? As mentioned, the rule parser we just met is part of the Python-coded holmes expert system shell. This book does not cover holmes in detail due to lack of space; see the *PP3E\AI\ExpertSystem* directory in this book's examples distribution for its code and documentation. But by way of introduction, holmes is an inference engine that performs forward and backward chaining deduction on rules that you supply. For example, the rule:

```
rule pylike if ?X likes coding, ?X likes spam then ?X likes Python
```

can be used both to prove whether someone likes Python (backward, from "then" to "if"), and to deduce that someone likes Python from a set of known facts (forward, from "if" to "then"). Deductions may span multiple rules, and rules that name the same conclusion represent alternatives. holmes also performs simple pattern-matching along the way to assign the variables that appear in rules (e.g., ?X), and it is able to explain its work.

To make all of this more concrete, let's step through a simple holmes session. The += interactive command adds a new rule to the rule base by running the rule parser, and @@ prints the current rule base:

```
C:..\PP3E\Ai\ExpertSystem\holmes\holmes>python holmes.py
-Holmes inference engine-
holmes> += rule pylike if ?X likes coding, ?X likes spam then ?X likes Python
```

Lesson 1: Prototype and Migrate

As a rule of thumb, use the string object's methods rather than things such as regular expressions whenever you can. Although this can vary from release to release, some string methods may be faster because they have less work to do.

In fact, the original implementation of these operations in the string module became substantially faster when they were moved to the C language. When you imported string, it internally replaced most of its content with functions imported from the strop C extension module; strop methods were reportedly 100 to 1,000 times faster than their Python-coded equivalents at the time (though Python has been heavily optimized since then).

The string module was originally written in Python but demands for string efficiency prompted recoding it in C. The result was dramatically faster performance for string client programs without impacting the interface. That is, string module clients became instantly faster without having to be modified for the new C-based module. A similar migration was applied to the pickle module we met in Chapter 19—the later cPickle recoding is compatible but much faster.

This is a great lesson about Python development: modules can be coded quickly in Python at first and translated to C later for efficiency if required. Because the interface to Python and C extension modules is identical (both are imported), C translations of modules are backward compatible with their Python prototypes. The only impact of the translation of such modules on clients is an improvement in performance.

There is usually no need to move every module to C for delivery of an application: you can pick and choose performance-critical modules (such as string and pickle) for translation and leave others coded in Python. Use the timing and profiling techniques discussed in Chapter 20 to isolate which modules will give the most improvement when translated to C. C-based extension modules are introduced in Part VI of this book.

Actually, in Python 2.0, the string module changed its implementation again: it is now a frontend to new string *methods*, which are able to also handle Unicode strings. As mentioned, most string functions are also available as object methods in 2.0. For instance, string.split(X) is now simply a synonym for X.split( ); both forms are still supported, but the latter is more prevalent and preferred today (and may be the only option in the future). Either way, clients of the original string module are not affected by this change—yet another lesson!

```
holmes> @@
rule pylike if ?X likes coding, ?X likes spam then ?X likes Python.
```

Now, to kick off a backward-chaining proof of a goal, use the ?- command. A proof explanation is shown here; holmes can also tell you why it is asking a question. Holmes pattern variables can show up in both rules and queries; in rules, variables provide generalization; in a query, they provide an answer:

```
holmes> ?- mel likes Python
is this true: "mel likes coding" ? y
is this true: "mel likes spam" ? y
yes: (no variables)

show proof ? yes
  "mel likes Python" by rule pylike
      "mel likes coding" by your answer
      "mel likes spam" by your answer
more solutions? n

holmes> ?- ann likes ?X
is this true: "ann likes coding" ? y
is this true: "ann likes spam" ? y
yes: ann likes Python
```

Forward chaining from a set of facts to conclusions is started with a +- command. Here, the same rule is being applied but in a different way:

```
holmes> +- chris likes spam, chris likes coding
I deduced these facts...
    chris likes Python
I started with these facts...
    chris likes spam
    chris likes coding
time: 0.0
```

More interestingly, deductions chain through multiple rules when part of a rule's "if" is mentioned in another rule's "then":

```
holmes> += rule 1 if thinks ?x then human ?x
holmes> += rule 2 if human ?x then mortal ?x
holmes> ?- mortal bob
is this true: "thinks bob" ? y
yes: (no variables)

holmes> +- thinks bob
I deduced these facts...
    human bob
    mortal bob
I started with these facts...
    thinks bob
time: 0.0
```

Finally, the @= command is used to load files of rules that implement more sophisticated knowledge bases; the rule parser is run on each rule in the file. Here is a file that encodes animal classification rules (other example files are available in the book's examples distribution, if you'd like to experiment):

```
holmes> @= ..\kbases\zoo.kb
holmes> ?- it is a penguin
is this true: "has feathers" ? why
to prove "it is a penguin" by rule 17
this was part of your original query.
is this true: "has feathers" ? y
```

```
is this true: "able to fly" ? n
is this true: "black color" ? y
yes: (no variables)
```

Type stop to end a session and help for a full commands list; see the text files in the holmes directories for more details. Holmes is an old system written before Python 1.0 (and around 1993), but it still works unchanged on all platforms.

Regular Expression Pattern Matching

Splitting and joining strings is a simple way to process text, as long as it follows the format you expect. For more general text analysis tasks, Python provides regular expression matching utilities. Regular expressions are simply strings that define *patterns* to be matched against other strings. Supply a pattern and a string and ask whether the string matches your pattern. After a match, parts of the string matched by parts of the pattern are made available to your script. That is, matches not only give a yes/no answer, but also can pick out substrings as well.

Regular expression pattern strings can be complicated (let's be honest—they can be downright gross to look at). But once you get the hang of them, they can replace larger handcoded string search routines—a single pattern string generally does the work of dozens of lines of manual string scanning code and may run much faster. They are a concise way to encode the expected structure of text and extract portions of it.

In Python, regular expressions are not part of the syntax of the Python language itself, but they are supported by extension modules that you must import to use. The modules define functions for compiling pattern strings into pattern objects, matching these objects against strings and fetching matched substrings after a match. They also provide tools for pattern-based splitting, replacing, and so on.

Beyond those generalities, Python's regular expression story is complicated a little by history:

The regex *module (old)*
> In earlier Python releases, a module called regex was the standard (and only) regular expression module. It was fast and supported patterns coded in awk, grep, and emacs styles, but it is now somewhat deprecated. (It generates a deprecation when imported today, though it will likely still be available for some time to come.)

The re *module (new)*
> Today, you should use re, a new regular expression module for Python that was introduced sometime around Python release 1.5. This module provides a much richer regular expression pattern syntax that tries to be close to that used to code patterns in the Perl language (yes, regular expressions are a feature of Perl worth emulating). For instance, re supports the notions of named groups, character classes, and *non-greedy* matches—regular expression pattern operators that match as few characters as possible (other regular expression pattern operators always match the longest possible substring).

When it was first made available, re was generally slower than regex, so you had to choose between speed and Perl-like regular expression syntax. Today, though, re has been optimized to the extent that regex no longer offers any clear advantages. Moreover, re supports a richer pattern syntax and matching of Unicode strings (strings with 16-bit-wide or wider characters for representing large character sets).

Because of this migration, I've recoded regular expression examples in this text to use the new re module rather than regex. The old regex-based versions are still available in the book's examples distribution in the directory *PP3E\lang\old-regex*. If you find yourself having to migrate old regex code, you can also find a document describing the translation steps needed at *http://www.python.org*. Both modules' interfaces are similar, but re introduces a match object and changes pattern syntax in minor ways.

Having said that, I also want to warn you that regular expressions is a complex topic that cannot be covered in depth here. If this area sparks your interest, the text *Mastering Regular Expressions*, written by Jeffrey E. F. Friedl (O'Reilly), is a good next step to take. We won't be able to go into pattern construction in much depth here.

Once you learn how to code patterns, though, the top-level interface for performing matches is straightforward. In fact, they are so easy to use that we'll jump right into an example before getting into more details.

First Examples

There are two basic ways to kick off matches: through top-level function calls and via methods of precompiled pattern objects. The latter precompiled form is quicker if you will be applying the same pattern more than once—to all lines in a text file, for instance. To demonstrate, let's do some matching on the following strings:

```
>>> text1 = 'Hello spam...World'
>>> text2 = 'Hello spam...other'
```

The match performed in the following code does not precompile: it executes an immediate match to look for all the characters between the words *Hello* and *World* in our text strings:

```
>>> import re
>>> matchobj = re.match('Hello(.*)World', text2)
>>> print matchobj
None
```

When a match fails as it does here (the text2 string doesn't end in *World*), we get back the None object, which is Boolean false if tested in an if statement.

In the pattern string we're using here (the first argument to re.match), the words *Hello* and *World* match themselves, and (.*) means any character (.) repeated zero or more times (*). The fact that it is enclosed in parentheses tells Python to save away the part of the string matched by that part of the pattern as a *group*—a matched substring. To see how, we need to make a match work:

```
>>> matchobj = re.match('Hello(.*)World', text1)
>>> print matchobj
<_sre.SRE_Match object at 0x009D6520>

>>> matchobj.group(1)
' spam...'
```

When a match succeeds, we get back a *match object*, which has interfaces for extracting matched substrings—the group(1) call returns the portion of the string matched by the first, leftmost, parenthesized portion of the pattern (our (.*)). In other words, matching is not just a yes/no answer (as already mentioned); by enclosing parts of the pattern in parentheses, it is also a way to extract matched substrings.

The interface for precompiling is similar, but the pattern is implied in the *pattern object* we get back from the compile call:

```
>>> pattobj  = re.compile('Hello(.*)World')
>>> matchobj = pattobj.match(text1)
>>> matchobj.group(1)
' spam...'
```

Again, you should precompile for speed if you will run the pattern multiple times. Here's something a bit more complex that hints at the generality of patterns. This one allows for zero or more blanks or tabs at the front ([\t]*), skips one or more after the word *Hello* ([\t]+), and allows the final word to begin with an upper- or lowercase letter ([Ww]); as you can see, patterns can handle wide variations in data:

```
>>> patt = '[ \t]*Hello[ \t]+(.*)[Ww]orld'
>>> line = ' Hello   spamworld'
>>> mobj = re.match(patt, line)
>>> mobj.group(1)
'spam'
```

In addition to the tools these examples demonstrate, there are methods for scanning ahead to find a match (search), splitting and replacing on patterns, and so on. All have analogous module and precompiled call forms. Let's dig into a few details of the module before we get to more code.

Using the re Module

The Python re module comes with functions that can search for patterns right away or make compiled pattern objects for running matches later. Pattern objects (and module search calls) in turn generate match objects, which contain information about successful matches and matched substrings. The next few sections describe the module's interfaces and some of the operators you can use to code patterns.

Module functions

The top level of the module provides functions for matching, substitution, precompiling, and so on:

compile(pattern [, flags])

Compile a regular expression pattern string into a regular expression pattern object, for later matching. See the reference manual for the flags argument's meaning.

match(pattern, string [, flags])

If zero or more characters at the start of string match the pattern string, return a corresponding match object, or None if no match is found. Roughly like a search for a pattern that begins with the ^ operator.

search(pattern, string [, flags])

Scan through string for a location matching pattern, and return a corresponding match object, or None if no match is found.

split(pattern, string [, maxsplit])

Split string by occurrences of pattern. If capturing parenthese (( )) are used in the pattern, occurrences of patterns or subpatterns are also returned.

sub(pattern, repl, string [, count])

Return the string obtained by replacing the (first count) leftmost nonoverlapping occurrences of pattern (a string or a pattern object) in string by repl (which may be a string or a function that is passed a single match object).

subn(pattern, repl, string [, count])

Same as sub, but returns a tuple: (new-string, number-of-substitutions-made).

findall(pattern, string [, flags])

Return a list of strings giving all nonoverlapping matches of pattern in string; if there are any groups in patterns, returns a list of groups.

finditer(pattern, string [, flags])

Return iterator over all nonoverlapping matches of pattern in string.

escape(string)

Return string with all nonalphanumeric characters backslashed, such that they can be compiled as a string literal.

Compiled pattern objects

At the next level, pattern objects provide similar attributes, but the pattern string is implied. The re.compile function in the previous section is useful to optimize patterns that may be matched more than once (compiled patterns match faster). Pattern objects returned by re.compile have these sorts of attributes.

```
match(string [, pos] [, endpos])
search(string [, pos] [, endpos])
split(string [, maxsplit])
sub(repl, string [, count])
subn(repl, string [, count])
findall(string [, pos [, endpos]])
finditer(string [, pos [, endpos]])
```
> Same as the re functions, but the pattern is implied, and pos and endpos give start/end string indexes for the match.

Match objects

Finally, when a match or search function or method is successful, you get back a match object (None comes back on failed matches). Match objects export a set of attributes of their own, including:

```
group(g)
group([g1, g2, ...])
```
> Return the substring that matched a parenthesized group (or groups) in the pattern. Accept group numbers or names. Group numbers start at 1; group 0 is the entire string matched by the pattern.

```
groups()
```
> Returns a tuple of all groups' substrings of the match.

```
groupdict()
```
> Returns a dictionary containing all named groups of the match.

```
start([group])
end([group])
```
> Indices of the start and end of the substring matched by group (or the entire matched string, if no group).

```
span([group])
```
> Returns the two-item tuple: (start(group),end(group)).

```
expand(template])
```
> Performs backslash group substitutions; see the Python library manual.

Regular expression patterns

Regular expression strings are built up by concatenating single-character regular expression forms, shown in Table 21-1. The longest-matching string is usually matched by each form, except for the nongreedy operators. In the table, R means any regular expression form, C is a character, and N denotes a digit.

Table 21-1. re pattern syntax

Operator	Interpretation
.	Matches any character (including newline if DOTALL flag is specified)
^	Matches start of the string (of every line in MULTILINE mode)
$	Matches end of the string (of every line in MULTILINE mode)
C	Any nonspecial character matches itself
R*	Zero or more of preceding regular expression R (as many as possible)
R+	One or more of preceding regular expression R (as many as possible)
R?	Zero or one occurrence of preceding regular expression R
R{m}	Matches exactly m copies preceding R: a{5} matches 'aaaaa'
R{m,n}	Matches from m to n repetitions of preceding regular expression R
R*?, R+?, R??, R{m,n}?	Same as *, +, and ? but matches as few characters/times as possible; these are known as *nongreedy* match operators (unlike others, they match and consume as few characters as possible)
[...]	Defines character set: e.g., [a-zA-Z] to match all letters
[^...]	Defines complemented character set: matches if char is not in set
\	Escapes special chars (e.g., *?+| ( )) and introduces special sequences
\\	Matches a literal \ (write as \\\\ in pattern, or r'\\')
\number	Matches the contents of the group of the same number: (.+) \1 matches "42 42"
R|R	Alternative: matches left or right R
RR	Concatenation: match both Rs
(R)	Matches any regular expression inside ( ), and delimits a group (retains matched substring)
(?:R)	Same but doesn't delimit a group
(?=R)	Look-ahead assertion: matches if R matches next, but doesn't consume any of the string (e.g., X (?=Y) matches X only if followed by Y)
(?!R)	Matches if R doesn't match next; negative of (?=R)
(?P<name>R)	Matches any regular expression inside ( ), and delimits a named group
(?P=name)	Matches whatever text was matched by the earlier group named name
(?#...)	A comment; ignored
(?letter)	Set mode flag; letter is one of i, L, m, s, u, x (see the library manual)
(?<=R)	Look-behind assertion: matches if the current position in the string is preceded by a match of R that ends at the current position
(?<!R)	Matches if the current position in the string is not preceded by a match for R; negative of (?<=R)
(?(id/name)yespattern|nopattern)	Will try to match with yespattern if the group with given id or name exists, else with optional nopattern

Within patterns, ranges and selections can be combined. For instance, [a-zA-Z0-9_]+ matches the longest possible string of one or more letters, digits, or underscores. Special characters can be escaped as usual in Python strings: [\t]* matches zero or more tabs and spaces (i.e., it skips whitespace).

The parenthesized grouping construct, (R), lets you extract matched substrings after a successful match. The portion of the string matched by the expression in parentheses is retained in a numbered register. It's available through the group method of a match object after a successful match.

In addition to the entries in this table, special sequences in Table 21-2 can be used in patterns too. Due to Python string rules, you sometimes must double up on backslashes (\\) or use Python raw strings (r'...') to retain backslashes in the pattern. Python ignores backslashes in normal strings if the letter following the backslash is not recognized as an escape code.

Table 21-2. re special sequences

Sequence	Interpretation
\number	Matches text of group number (numbered from 1)
\A	Matches only at the start of the string
\b	Empty string at word boundaries
\B	Empty string not at word boundaries
\d	Any decimal digit character (such as [0-9])
\D	Any nondecimal digit character (such as [^0-9])
\s	Any whitespace character (such as [\t\n\r\f\v])
\S	Any nonwhitespace character (such as [^ \t\n\r\f\v])
\w	Any alphanumeric character (uses LOCALE flag)
\W	Any nonalphanumeric character (uses LOCALE flag)
\Z	Matches only at the end of the string

Most of the standard escapes supported by Python string literals are also accepted by the regular expression parser: \a, \b, \f, \n, \r, \t, \v, \x, and \\.

The Python library manual gives additional details. But to demonstrate how the re pattern syntax is typically used, let's go back to writing some code.

Basic Patterns

To illustrate how to combine regular expression operators, we'll turn to a few short test files that match simple pattern forms. Comments in Example 21-3 describe the operations exercised; check Table 21-1 to see which operators are used in these patterns.

Example 21-3. PP3E\lang\re-basics.py

```
# literals, sets, ranges    (all print 2 = offset where pattern found)

import re                                # the one to use today

pattern, string = "A.C.", "xxABCDxx"     # nonspecial chars match themselves
matchobj = re.search(pattern, string)    # '.' means any one char
if matchobj:                             # search returns match object or None
    print matchobj.start()               # start is index where matched

pattobj  = re.compile("A.*C.*")          # 'R*' means zero or more Rs
matchobj = pattobj.search("xxABCDxx")    # compile returns pattern obj
if matchobj:                             # patt.search returns match obj
    print matchobj.start()

# selection sets
print re.search(" *A.C[DE][D-F][^G-ZE]G\t+ ?", "..ABCDEFG\t..").start()

# alternatives
print re.search("A|XB|YC|ZD", "..AYCD..").start()  # R1|R2 means R1 or R2

# word boundaries
print re.search(r"\bABCD", "..ABCD ").start()      # \b means word boundary
print re.search(r"ABCD\b", "..ABCD ").start()      # use r'...' to escape '\'
```

Notice again that there are different ways to kick off a match with re: by calling module search functions and by making compiled pattern objects. In either event, you can hang on to the resulting match object or not. All the print statements in this script show a result of 2—the offset where the pattern was found in the string. In the first test, for example, A.C. matches the ABCD at offset 2 in the search string (i.e., after the first xx):

```
C:\...\PP3E\Lang>python re-basic.py
2
2
2
2
2
2
```

In Example 21-4, parts of the pattern strings enclosed in parentheses delimit *groups*; the parts of the string they matched are available after the match.

Example 21-4. PP3E\lang\re-groups.py

```
# groups (extract substrings matched by REs in '()' parts)

import re

patt = re.compile("A(.)B(.)C(.)")                    # saves 3 substrings
mobj = patt.match("A0B1C2")                           # each '()' is a group, 1..n
print mobj.group(1), mobj.group(2), mobj.group(3)  # group() gives substring
```

Example 21-4. PP3E\lang\re-groups.py (continued)

```
patt = re.compile("A(.*)B(.*)C(.*)")              # saves 3 substrings
mobj = patt.match("A000B111C222")                 # groups( ) gives all groups
print mobj.groups( )

print re.search("(A|X)(B|Y)(C|Z)D", "..AYCD..").groups( )

patt = re.compile(r"[\t ]*#\s*define\s*([a-z0-9_]*)\s*(.*)")
mobj = patt.search(" # define   spam   1 + 2 + 3")    # parts of C #define
print mobj.groups( )                                   # \s is whitespace
```

In the first test here, for instance, the three (.) groups each match a single character, but they retain the character matched; calling group pulls out the bits matched. The second test's (.*) groups match and retain any number of characters. The last test matches C #define lines; more on this later.

```
C:\...\PP3E\Lang>python re-groups.py
0 1 2
('000', '111', '222')
('A', 'Y', 'C')
('spam', '1 + 2 + 3')
```

Finally, besides matches and substring extraction, re also includes tools for string replacement or substitution (see Example 21-5).

Example 21-5. PP3E\lang\re-subst.py

```
# substitutions (replace occurrences of patt with repl in string)

import re
print re.sub('[ABC]', '*', 'XAXAXBXBXCXC')
print re.sub('[ABC]_', '*', 'XA-XA_XB-XB_XC-XC_')
```

In the first test, all characters in the set are replaced; in the second, they must be followed by an underscore:

```
C:\...\PP3E\Lang>python re-subst.py
X*X*X*X*X*X*
XA-X*XB-X*XC-X*
```

Scanning C Header Files for Patterns

On to some realistic examples: the script in Example 21-6 puts these pattern operators to more practical use. It uses regular expressions to find #define and #include lines in C header files and extract their components. The generality of the patterns makes them detect a variety of line formats; pattern groups (the parts in parentheses) are used to extract matched substrings from a line after a match.

Example 21-6. PP3E\Lang\cheader.py

```
#! /usr/local/bin/python
import sys, re
```

Example 21-6. PP3E\Lang\cheader.py (continued)

```
pattDefine = re.compile(                                 # compile to pattobj
    '^#[\t ]*define[\t ]+([a-zA-Z0-9_]+)[\t ]*(.*)')     # "# define xxx yyy..."

pattInclude = re.compile(
    '^#[\t ]*include[\t ]+[<"]([a-zA-Z0-9_/\.]+)')       # "# include <xxx>..."

def scan(file):
    count = 0
    while 1:                                      # scan line-by-line
        line = file.readline()
        if not line: break
        count += 1
        matchobj = pattDefine.match(line)         # None if match fails
        if matchobj:
            name = matchobj.group(1)              # substrings for (...) parts
            body = matchobj.group(2)
            print count, 'defined', name, '=', body.strip()
            continue
        matchobj = pattInclude.match(line)
        if matchobj:
            start, stop = matchobj.span(1)        # start/stop indexes of (...)
            filename = line[start:stop]           # slice out of line
            print count, 'include', filename      # same as matchobj.group(1)

if len(sys.argv) == 1:
    scan(sys.stdin)                      # no args: read stdin
else:
    scan(open(sys.argv[1], 'r'))         # arg: input filename
```

To test, let's run this script on the text file in Example 21-7.

Example 21-7. PP3E\Lang\test.h

```
#ifndef TEST_H
#define TEST_H

#include <stdio.h>
#include <lib/spam.h>
#  include   "Python.h"

#define DEBUG
#define HELLO 'hello regex world'
#  define SPAM    1234

#define EGGS sunny + side + up
#define  ADDER(arg) 123 + arg
#endif
```

Notice the spaces after # in some of these lines; regular expressions are flexible enough to account for such departures from the norm. Here is the script at work;

picking out #include and #define lines and their parts. For each matched line, it prints the line number, the line type, and any matched substrings:

```
C:\...\PP3E\Lang>python cheader.py test.h
2 defined TEST_H =
4 include stdio.h
5 include lib/spam.h
6 include Python.h
8 defined DEBUG =
9 defined HELLO = 'hello regex world'
10 defined SPAM = 1234
12 defined EGGS = sunny + side + up
13 defined ADDER = (arg) 123 + arg
```

A File Pattern Search Utility

The next script searches for patterns in a set of files, much like the grep command-line program. We wrote file and directory searchers earlier in Chapter 7. Here, the file searches look for patterns rather than simple strings (see Example 21-8). The patterns are typed interactively, separated by a space, and the files to be searched are specified by an input pattern for Python's glob.glob filename expansion tool that we studied earlier.

Example 21-8. PP3E\Lang\pygrep1.py

```python
#!/usr/local/bin/python
import sys, re, glob

help_string = """
Usage options.
interactive:  % pygrep1.py
"""

def getargs():
    if len(sys.argv) == 1:
        return raw_input("patterns? >").split(), raw_input("files? >")
    else:
        try:
            return sys.argv[1], sys.argv[2]
        except:
            print help_string
            sys.exit(1)

def compile_patterns(patterns):
    res = []
    for pattstr in patterns:
        try:
            res.append(re.compile(pattstr))          # make re patt object
        except:                                      # or use re.match
            print 'pattern ignored:', pattstr
    return res
```

Example 21-8. PP3E\Lang\pygrep1.py (continued)

```
def searcher(pattfile, srchfiles):
    patts = compile_patterns(pattfile)             # compile for speed
    for file in glob.glob(srchfiles):              # all matching files
        lineno = 1                                 # glob uses re too
        print '\n[%s]' % file
        for line in open(file, 'r').readlines():   # all lines in file
            for patt in patts:
                if patt.search(line):              # try all patterns
                    print '%04d)' % lineno, line,  # match if not None
                    break
            lineno = lineno+1

if __name__ == '__main__':
    searcher(*getargs())                           # was apply(func, args)
```

Here's what a typical run of this script looks like, scanning old versions of some of the source files in this chapter; it searches all Python files in the current directory for two different patterns, compiled for speed. Notice that files are named by a pattern too—Python's glob module also uses re internally:

```
C:\...\PP3E\Lang>python pygrep1.py
patterns? >import.*string spam
files? >*.py

[cheader.py]

[finder2.py]
0002) import string, glob, os, sys

[patterns.py]
0048) mobj = patt.search(" # define  spam  1 + 2 + 3")

[pygrep1.py]

[rules.py]

[summer.py]
0002) import string

[__init__.py]
```

Advanced Language Tools

If you have a background in parsing theory, you may know that neither regular expressions nor string splitting is powerful enough to handle more complex language grammars. Roughly, regular expressions don't have the stack "memory" required by true grammars, so they cannot support arbitrary nesting of language constructs (nested if statements in a programming language, for instance). From a theoretical perspective, regular expressions are intended to handle just the first stage of parsing—separating text into components, otherwise known as *lexical analysis*. Language parsing requires more.

In most applications, the Python language itself can replace custom languages and parsers—user-entered code can be passed to Python for evaluation with tools such as eval and exec. By augmenting the system with custom modules, user code in this scenario has access to both the full Python language and any application-specific extensions required. In a sense, such systems embed Python in Python. Since this is a common application of Python, we'll revisit this approach later in this chapter.

For some sophisticated language analysis tasks, though, a full-blown parser may still be required. Since Python is built for integrating C tools, we can write integrations to traditional parser generator systems such as yacc and bison, tools that create parsers from language grammar definitions. Better yet, we could use an integration that already exists—interfaces to such common parser generators are freely available in the open source domain (run a web search in Google for up-to-date details and links).

Python-specific parsing systems also are accessible from Python's web site. Among them, the kwParsing system is a parser generator written in Python, and the SPARK toolkit is a lightweight system that employs the Earley algorithm to work around technical problems with LALR parser generation (if you don't know what that means, you probably don't need to care). Since all of these are complex tools, though, we'll skip their details in this text. Consult *http://www.python.org* for information on parser generator tools available for use in Python programs.

Even more demanding language analysis tasks require techniques developed in artificial intelligence research, such as semantic analysis and machine learning. For instance, the Natural Language Toolkit, or NLTK, is an open source suite of Python libraries and programs for symbolic and statistical natural language processing. It applies linguistic techniques to textual data, and it can be used in the development of natural language recognition software and systems.

Lesson 2: Don't Reinvent the Wheel

Speaking of parser generators, to use some of these tools in Python programs, you'll need an extension module that integrates them. The first step in such scenarios should always be to see whether the extension already exists in the public domain. Especially for common tools like these, chances are that someone else has already written an integration that you can use off-the-shelf instead of writing one from scratch.

Of course, not everyone can donate all their extension modules to the public domain, but there's a growing library of available components that you can pick up for free and a community of experts to query. Visit *http://www.python.org* for links to Python software resources. With roughly one million Python users out there as I write this book, much can be found in the prior-art department.

Of special interest to this chapter, also see Yet Another Python Parser System (YAPPS). YAPPS is a parser generator written in Python. It uses supplied grammar rules to generate human-readable Python code that implements a recursive descent parser. The parsers generated by YAPPS look much like (and are inspired by) the handcoded expression parsers shown in the next section. YAPPS creates LL(1) parsers, which are not as powerful as LALR parsers but are sufficient for many language tasks. For more on YAPPS, see *http://theory.stanford.edu/~amitp/Yapps* or search the Web at large.

Handcoded Parsers

Since Python is a general-purpose programming language, it's also reasonable to consider writing a handcoded parser. For instance, *recursive descent parsing* is a fairly well-known technique for analyzing language-based information. Since Python is a very high-level language, writing the parser itself is usually easier than it would be in a traditional language such as C or C++.

To illustrate, this section develops a custom parser for a simple grammar: it parses and evaluates arithmetic expression strings. This example also demonstrates the utility of Python as a general-purpose programming language. Although Python is often used as a frontend or rapid development language, it's also useful for the kinds of things we'd normally write in a systems development language such as C or C++.

The Expression Grammar

The grammar that our parser will recognize can be described as follows:

```
goal -> <expr> END                          [number, variable, ( ]
goal -> <assign> END                        [set]

assign -> 'set' <variable> <expr>           [set]

expr -> <factor> <expr-tail>                [number, variable, ( ]

expr-tail -> ^                              [END, ) ]
expr-tail -> '+' <factor> <expr-tail>       [+]
expr-tail -> '-' <factor> <expr-tail>       [-]

factor -> <term> <factor-tail>              [number, variable, ( ]

factor-tail -> ^                            [+, -, END, ) ]
factor-tail -> '*' <term> <factor-tail>     [*]
factor-tail -> '/' <term> <factor-tail>     [/]

term -> <number>                            [number]
term -> <variable>                          [variable]
term -> '(' <expr> ')'                      [(]

tokens: (, ), num, var, -, +, /, *, set, end
```

This is a fairly typical grammar for a simple expression language, and it allows for arbitrary expression nesting (some example expressions appear at the end of the testparser module listing in Example 21-11). Strings to be parsed are either an expression or an assignment to a variable name (set). Expressions involve numbers, variables, and the operators +, -, *, and /. Because factor is nested in expr in the grammar, * and / have higher precedence (i.e., they bind tighter) than + and -. Expressions can be enclosed in parentheses to override precedence, and all operators are left associative—that is, they group on the left (e.g., 1-2-3 is treated the same as (1-2)-3).

Tokens are just the most primitive components of the expression language. Each grammar rule earlier is followed in square brackets by a list of tokens used to select it. In recursive descent parsing, we determine the set of tokens that can possibly start a rule's substring, and we use that information to predict which rule will work ahead of time. For rules that iterate (the -tail rules), we use the set of possibly following tokens to know when to stop. Typically, tokens are recognized by a string processor (a *scanner*), and a higher-level processor (a *parser*) uses the token stream to predict and step through grammar rules and substrings.

The Parser's Code

The system is structured as two modules, holding two classes:

- The scanner handles low-level character-by-character analysis.
- The parser embeds a scanner and handles higher-level grammar analysis.

The parser is also responsible for computing the expression's value and testing the system. In this version, the parser evaluates the expression while it is being parsed. To use the system, we create a parser with an input string and call its parse method. We can also call parse again later with a new expression string.

There's a deliberate division of labor here. The scanner extracts tokens from the string, but it knows nothing about the grammar. The parser handles the grammar, but it is naive about the string itself. This modular structure keeps the code relatively simple. And it's another example of the object-oriented programming (OOP) composition relationship at work: parsers embed and delegate to scanners.

The module in Example 21-9 implements the lexical analysis task—detecting the expression's basic tokens by scanning the text string left to right on demand. Notice that this is all straightforward logic; such analysis can sometimes be performed with regular expressions instead (described earlier), but the pattern needed to detect and extract tokens in this example would be too complex and fragile for my tastes. If your tastes vary, try recoding this module with re.

Example 21-9. PP3E\Lang\Parser\scanner.py

```python
#####################################################
# the scanner (lexical analyser)
#####################################################

import string
class SyntaxError(Exception): pass          # local errors
class LexicalError(Exception): pass         # used to be strings

class Scanner:
    def __init__(self, text):
        self.next = 0
        self.text = text + '\0'

    def newtext(self, text):
        Scanner.__init__(self, text)

    def showerror(self):
        print '=> ', self.text
        print '=> ', (' ' * self.start) + '^'

    def match(self, token):
        if self.token != token:
            raise SyntaxError, [token]
        else:
            value = self.value
            if self.token != '\0':
                self.scan()                 # next token/value
            return value                    # return prior value

    def scan(self):
        self.value = None
        ix = self.next
        while self.text[ix] in string.whitespace:
            ix = ix+1
        self.start = ix

        if self.text[ix] in ['(', ')', '-', '+', '/', '*', '\0']:
            self.token = self.text[ix]
            ix = ix+1

        elif self.text[ix] in string.digits:
            str = ''
            while self.text[ix] in string.digits:
                str = str + self.text[ix]
                ix = ix+1
            if self.text[ix] == '.':
                str = str + '.'
                ix = ix+1
                while self.text[ix] in string.digits:
                    str = str + self.text[ix]
                    ix = ix+1
                self.token = 'num'
```

Example 21-9. PP3E\Lang\Parser\scanner.py (continued)

```
                    self.value = float(str)
                else:
                    self.token = 'num'
                    self.value = long(str)

            elif self.text[ix] in string.letters:
                str = ''
                while self.text[ix] in (string.digits + string.letters):
                    str = str + self.text[ix]
                    ix = ix+1
                if str.lower() == 'set':
                    self.token = 'set'
                else:
                    self.token = 'var'
                    self.value = str

            else:
                raise LexicalError
        self.next = ix
```

The parser module's class creates and embeds a scanner for its lexical chores and handles interpretation of the expression grammar's rules and evaluation of the expression's result, as shown in Example 21-10.

Example 21-10. PP3E\Lang\Parser\parser1.py

```
#########################################################
# the parser (syntax analyser, evaluates during parse)
#########################################################

class UndefinedError(Exception): pass
from scanner import Scanner, LexicalError, SyntaxError

class Parser:
    def __init__(self, text=''):
        self.lex  = Scanner(text)           # embed a scanner
        self.vars = {'pi':3.14159}          # add a variable

    def parse(self, *text):
        if text:                            # main entry-point
            self.lex.newtext(text[0])       # reuse this parser?
        try:
            self.lex.scan()                 # get first token
            self.Goal()                     # parse a sentence
        except SyntaxError:
            print 'Syntax Error at column:', self.lex.start
            self.lex.showerror()
        except LexicalError:
            print 'Lexical Error at column:', self.lex.start
            self.lex.showerror()
        except UndefinedError, name:
            print "'%s' is undefined at column:" % name, self.lex.start
```

Example 21-10. PP3E\Lang\Parser\parser1.py (continued)

```
                self.lex.showerror()

    def Goal(self):
        if self.lex.token in ['num', 'var', '(']:
            val = self.Expr()
            self.lex.match('\0')                    # expression?
            print val
        elif self.lex.token == 'set':               # set command?
            self.Assign()
            self.lex.match('\0')
        else:
            raise SyntaxError

    def Assign(self):
        self.lex.match('set')
        var = self.lex.match('var')
        val = self.Expr()
        self.vars[var] = val            # assign name in dict

    def Expr(self):
        left = self.Factor()
        while 1:
            if self.lex.token in ['\0', ')']:
                return left
            elif self.lex.token == '+':
                self.lex.scan()
                left = left + self.Factor()
            elif self.lex.token == '-':
                self.lex.scan()
                left = left - self.Factor()
            else:
                raise SyntaxError

    def Factor(self):
        left = self.Term()
        while 1:
            if self.lex.token in ['+', '-', '\0', ')']:
                return left
            elif self.lex.token == '*':
                self.lex.scan()
                left = left * self.Term()
            elif self.lex.token == '/':
                self.lex.scan()
                left = left / self.Term()
            else:
                raise SyntaxError

    def Term(self):
        if self.lex.token == 'num':
            val = self.lex.match('num')             # numbers
            return val
        elif self.lex.token == 'var':
```

Example 21-10. PP3E\Lang\Parser\parser1.py (continued)

```
            if self.vars.has_key(self.lex.value):
                val = self.vars[self.lex.value]       # look up name's value
                self.lex.scan()
                return val
            else:
                raise UndefinedError, self.lex.value
        elif self.lex.token == '(':
            self.lex.scan()
            val = self.Expr()                        # sub-expression
            self.lex.match(')')
            return val
        else:
            raise SyntaxError

if __name__ == '__main__':
    import testparser                        # self-test code
    testparser.test(Parser, 'parser1')       # test local Parser
```

If you study this code closely, you'll notice that the parser keeps a dictionary (self. vars) to manage variable names: they're stored in the dictionary on a set command and are fetched from it when they appear in an expression. Tokens are represented as strings, with an optional associated value (a numeric value for numbers and a string for variable names).

The parser uses iteration (while loops) rather than recursion for the expr-tail and factor-tail rules. Other than this optimization, the rules of the grammar map directly onto parser methods: tokens become calls to the scanner, and nested rule references become calls to other methods.

When the file *parser1.py* is run as a top-level program, its self-test code is executed, which in turn simply runs a canned test in the module shown in Example 21-11. Note that all integer math uses Python long integers (unlimited precision integers) because the scanner converts numbers to strings with long. Also notice that mixed integer/floating-point operations cast up to floating point since Python operators are used to do the actual calculations.

Example 21-11. PP3E\Lang\Parser\testparser.py

```
#####################################################
# parser test code
#####################################################

def test(ParserClass, msg):
    print msg, ParserClass
    x = ParserClass('4 / 2 + 3')                  # allow different Parser's
    x.parse()

    x.parse('3 + 4 / 2')                          # like eval('3 + 4 / 2')...
    x.parse('(3 + 4) / 2')
    x.parse('4 / (2 + 3)')
```

Example 21-11. PP3E\Lang\Parser\testparser.py (continued)

```
    x.parse('4.0 / (2 + 3)')
    x.parse('4 / (2.0 + 3)')
    x.parse('4.0 / 2 * 3')
    x.parse('(4.0 / 2) * 3')
    x.parse('4.0 / (2 * 3)')
    x.parse('(((3))) + 1')

    y = ParserClass()
    y.parse('set a 4 / 2 + 1')
    y.parse('a * 3')
    y.parse('set b 12 / a')
    y.parse('b')

    z = ParserClass()
    z.parse('set a 99')
    z.parse('set a a + 1')
    z.parse('a')

    z = ParserClass()
    z.parse('pi')
    z.parse('2 * pi')
    z.parse('1.234 + 2.1')

def interact(ParserClass):                       # command-line entry
    print ParserClass
    x = ParserClass()
    while 1:
        cmd = raw_input('Enter=> ')
        if cmd == 'stop':
            break
        x.parse(cmd)
```

Correlate the following results to print statements in the self-test module:

```
C:\...\PP3E\Lang\Parser>python parser1.py
parser1 __main__.Parser
5
5
3
0
0.8
0.8
6.0
6.0
0.666666666667
4
9
4
100
3.14159
6.28318
3.334
```

The integer results here are really long integers; in the past they printed with a trailing L (e.g., 5L), but they no longer do in recent Python releases because normal integers are automatically converted to long integers as needed (in fact, there may be no distinction between the two types at all in a future Python release). Change the Goal method to print repr(val) if you still want to see the L—repr prints objects as code.

As usual, we can also test and use the system interactively:

```
% python
>>> import parser1
>>> x = parser1.Parser()
>>> x.parse('1 + 2')
3
```

Error cases are trapped and reported:

```
>>> x.parse('1 + a')
'a' is undefined at column: 4
=>  1 + a
=>       ^
>>> x.parse('1+a+2')
'a' is undefined at column: 2
=>  1+a+2
=>     ^
>>> x.parse('1 * 2 $')
Lexical Error at column: 6
=>  1 * 2 $
=>         ^
>>> x.parse('1 * - 1')
Syntax Error at column: 4
=>  1 * - 1
=>       ^
>>> x.parse('1 * (9')
Syntax Error at column: 6
=>  1 * (9
=>         ^
```

Pathologically big numbers are handled well, because Python's built-in objects and operators are used along the way:

```
>>> x.parse('888888888888888888888888888888888888888888888888.9999999')
8.88888888889e+044
>>> x.parse('9999999999999999999999999999999999999999 + 2')
10000000000000000000000000000000000000000001
>>> x.parse('99999999999999999999999999999.88888888888 + 1.1')
1e+030
```

In addition, there is an interactive loop interface in the testparser module if you want to use the parser as a simple command-line calculator (or if you get tired of typing parser method calls). Pass the Parser class, so testparser can make one of its own:

```
>>> import testparser
>>> testparser.interact(parser1.Parser)
```

```
Enter=> 4 * 3 + 5
17
Enter=> 5 + 4 * 3
17
Enter=> (5 + 4) * 3
27
Enter=> set a 99
Enter=> set b 66
Enter=> a + b
165
Enter=> # + 1
Lexical Error at column: 0
=>  # + 1
=>  ^
Enter=> a * b + c
'c' is undefined at column: 8
=>  a * b + c
=>          ^
Enter=> a * b * + c
Syntax Error at column: 8
=>  a * b * + c
=>            ^
Enter=> a
99
Enter=> a * a * a
970299
Enter=> stop
>>>
```

Lesson 3: Divide and Conquer

As the parser system demonstrates, modular program design is almost always a major win. By using Python's program structuring tools (functions, modules, classes, and so on), big tasks can be broken down into small, manageable parts that can be coded and tested independently.

For instance, the scanner can be tested without the parser by making an instance with an input string and calling its scan or match methods repeatedly. We can even test it like this interactively, from Python's command line. By separating programs into logical components, they become easier to understand and modify. Imagine what the parser would look like if the scanner's logic was embedded rather than called.

Adding a Parse Tree Interpreter

One weakness in the parser1 program is that it embeds expression evaluation logic in the parsing logic: the result is computed while the string is being parsed. This makes evaluation quick, but it can also make it difficult to modify the code, especially in larger systems. To simplify, we could restructure the program to keep expression parsing and evaluation separate. Instead of evaluating the string, the parser can build up an intermediate representation of it that can be evaluated later. As an added incentive, building the representation separately makes it available to other analysis tools (e.g., optimizers, viewers, and so on)—they can be run as separate passes over the tree.

Example 21-12 shows a variant of parser1 that implements this idea. The parser analyzes the string and builds up a *parse tree*—that is, a tree of class instances that represents the expression and that may be evaluated in a separate step. The parse tree is built from classes that "know" how to evaluate themselves: to compute the expression, we just ask the tree to evaluate itself. Root nodes in the tree ask their children to evaluate themselves, and then combine the results by applying a single operator. In effect, evaluation in this version is simply a recursive traversal of a tree of embedded class instances constructed by the parser.

Example 21-12. PP3E\Lang\Parser\parser2.py

```
TraceDefault = False
class UndefinedError(Exception): pass
from scanner import Scanner, SyntaxError, LexicalError



#####################################################
# the interpreter (a smart objects tree)
#####################################################

class TreeNode:
    def validate(self, dict):        # default error check
        pass
    def apply(self, dict):           # default evaluator
        pass
    def trace(self, level):          # default unparser
        print '.'*level + '<empty>'

# ROOTS

class BinaryNode(TreeNode):
    def __init__(self, left, right):          # inherited methods
        self.left, self.right = left, right   # left/right branches
    def validate(self, dict):
        self.left.validate(dict)              # recurse down branches
        self.right.validate(dict)
    def trace(self, level):
        print '.'*level + '[' + self.label + ']'
        self.left.trace(level+3)
        self.right.trace(level+3)

class TimesNode(BinaryNode):
    label = '*'
    def apply(self, dict):
        return self.left.apply(dict) * self.right.apply(dict)
```

Example 21-12. PP3E\Lang\Parser\parser2.py (continued)

```python
class DivideNode(BinaryNode):
    label = '/'
    def apply(self, dict):
        return self.left.apply(dict) / self.right.apply(dict)

class PlusNode(BinaryNode):
    label = '+'
    def apply(self, dict):
        return self.left.apply(dict) + self.right.apply(dict)

class MinusNode(BinaryNode):
    label = '-'
    def apply(self, dict):
        return self.left.apply(dict) - self.right.apply(dict)

# LEAVES

class NumNode(TreeNode):
    def __init__(self, num):
        self.num = num                   # already numeric
    def apply(self, dict):               # use default validate
        return self.num
    def trace(self, level):
        print '.'*level + repr(self.num)      # as code, was `self.num`

class VarNode(TreeNode):
    def __init__(self, text, start):
        self.name   = text               # variable name
        self.column = start              # column for errors
    def validate(self, dict):
        if not dict.has_key(self.name):
            raise UndefinedError, (self.name, self.column)
    def apply(self, dict):
        return dict[self.name]           # validate before apply
    def assign(self, value, dict):
        dict[self.name] = value          # local extension
    def trace(self, level):
        print '.'*level + self.name

# COMPOSITES

class AssignNode(TreeNode):
    def __init__(self, var, val):
        self.var, self.val = var, val
    def validate(self, dict):
        self.val.validate(dict)          # don't validate var
    def apply(self, dict):
        self.var.assign( self.val.apply(dict), dict )
    def trace(self, level):
        print '.'*level + 'set '
        self.var.trace(level + 3)
        self.val.trace(level + 3)
```

Example 21-12. PP3E\Lang\Parser\parser2.py (continued)

```
####################################################
# the parser (syntax analyser, tree builder)
####################################################

class Parser:
    def __init__(self, text=''):
        self.lex      = Scanner(text)          # make a scanner
        self.vars     = {'pi':3.14159}         # add constants
        self.traceme = TraceDefault

    def parse(self, *text):                    # external interface
        if text:
            self.lex.newtext(text[0])          # reuse with new text
        tree = self.analyse()                  # parse string
        if tree:
            if self.traceme:                   # dump parse-tree?
                print; tree.trace(0)
            if self.errorCheck(tree):          # check names
                self.interpret(tree)           # evaluate tree

    def analyse(self):
        try:
            self.lex.scan()                    # get first token
            return self.Goal()                 # build a parse-tree
        except SyntaxError:
            print 'Syntax Error at column:', self.lex.start
            self.lex.showerror()
        except LexicalError:
            print 'Lexical Error at column:', self.lex.start
            self.lex.showerror()

    def errorCheck(self, tree):
        try:
            tree.validate(self.vars)           # error checker
            return 'ok'
        except UndefinedError, instance:       # args is a tuple
            varinfo = instance.args            # instance is a sequence
            print "'%s' is undefined at column: %d" % varinfo
            self.lex.start = varinfo[1]
            self.lex.showerror()               # returns None

    def interpret(self, tree):
        result = tree.apply(self.vars)         # tree evals itself
        if result != None:                     # ignore 'set' result
            print result

    def Goal(self):
        if self.lex.token in ['num', 'var', '(']:
            tree = self.Expr()
            self.lex.match('\0')
            return tree
        elif self.lex.token == 'set':
```

Example 21-12. PP3E\Lang\Parser\parser2.py (continued)

```
                tree = self.Assign( )
                self.lex.match('\0')
                return tree
            else:
                raise SyntaxError

    def Assign(self):
        self.lex.match('set')
        vartree = VarNode(self.lex.value, self.lex.start)
        self.lex.match('var')
        valtree = self.Expr( )
        return AssignNode(vartree, valtree)            # two subtrees

    def Expr(self):
        left = self.Factor( )                          # left subtree
        while 1:
            if self.lex.token in ['\0', ')']:
                return left
            elif self.lex.token == '+':
                self.lex.scan( )
                left = PlusNode(left, self.Factor( ))   # add root-node
            elif self.lex.token == '-':
                self.lex.scan( )
                left = MinusNode(left, self.Factor( ))  # grows up/right
            else:
                raise SyntaxError

    def Factor(self):
        left = self.Term( )
        while 1:
            if self.lex.token in ['+', '-', '\0', ')']:
                return left
            elif self.lex.token == '*':
                self.lex.scan( )
                left = TimesNode(left, self.Term( ))
            elif self.lex.token == '/':
                self.lex.scan( )
                left = DivideNode(left, self.Term( ))
            else:
                raise SyntaxError

    def Term(self):
        if self.lex.token == 'num':
            leaf = NumNode(self.lex.match('num'))
            return leaf
        elif self.lex.token == 'var':
            leaf = VarNode(self.lex.value, self.lex.start)
            self.lex.scan( )
            return leaf
        elif self.lex.token == '(':
            self.lex.scan( )
            tree = self.Expr( )
```

Example 21-12. PP3E\Lang\Parser\parser2.py (continued)

```
            self.lex.match(')')
            return tree
        else:
            raise SyntaxError


#####################################################
# self-test code: use my parser, parser1's tester
#####################################################

if __name__ == '__main__':
    import testparser
    testparser.test(Parser, 'parser2')    # run with Parser class here
```

When parser2 is run as a top-level program, we get the same test code output as for parser1. In fact, it reuses the same test code: both parsers pass in their parser class object to testparser.test. And since classes are objects, we can also pass this version of the parser to testparser's interactive loop: testparser.interact(parser2. Parser). The new parser's external behavior is identical to that of the original.

Notice the way we handle undefined name exceptions in errorCheck. This exception is a class instance now, not a string as in the prior edition (string exceptions are now deprecated). When exceptions derived from the built-in Exception class are used as sequences, they return the arguments passed to the exception constructor call. This doesn't quite work for string formatting, though, because it expects a real tuple—we have to call tuple( ) manually on the instance, extract the arguments with its args attribute, or write our own custom constructor to handle the state information.

Also notice that the new parser reuses the same scanner module as well. To catch errors raised by the scanner, it also imports the specific strings that identify the scanner's exceptions. Both the scanner and the parser can raise exceptions on errors (lexical errors, syntax errors, and undefined name errors). They're caught at the top level of the parser, and they end the current parse. There's no need to set and check status flags to terminate the recursion. Since math is done using long integers, floating-point numbers, and Python's operators, there's usually no need to trap numeric overflow or underflow errors. But as is, the parser doesn't handle errors such as division by zero—such errors make the parser system exit with a Python stack dump. Uncovering the cause and fix for this is left as an exercise.

Parse Tree Structure

In fact, the only real difference with this latest parser is that it builds and uses trees to evaluate an expression internally instead of evaluating as it parses. The intermediate representation of an expression is a tree of class instances, whose shape reflects the order of operator evaluation. This parser also has logic to print an indented listing of the constructed parse tree if the traceme attribute is set to True (or 1). Integers print with a trailing L here because the trace logic displays them with `repr`, indentation gives the nesting of subtrees, and binary operators list left subtrees first. For example:

```
% python
>>> import parser2
>>> p = parser2.Parser()
>>> p.traceme = 1
>>> p.parse('5 + 4 * 2')

[+]
...5L
...[*]
......4L
......2L
13L
```

When this tree is evaluated, the `apply` method recursively evaluates subtrees and applies root operators to their results. Here, * is evaluated before +, since it's lower in the tree. The `Factor` method consumes the * substring before returning a right subtree to `Expr`:

```
>>> p.parse('5 * 4 - 2')

[-]
...[*]
......5L
......4L
...2L
18L
```

In this example, * is evaluated before -. The `Factor` method loops through a substring of * and / expressions before returning the resulting left subtree to `Expr`:

```
>>> p.parse('1 + 3 * (2 * 3 + 4)')

[+]
...1L
...[*]
......3L
......[+]
.........[*]
............2L
............3L
.........4L
31L
```

Trees are made of nested class instances. From an OOP perspective, it's another way to use composition. Since tree nodes are just class instances, this tree could be created and evaluated manually too:

```
PlusNode( NumNode(1),
         TimesNode( NumNode(3),
                   PlusNode( TimesNode(NumNode(2), NumNode(3)),
                            NumNode(4) ))).apply({})
```

But we might as well let the parser build it for us (Python is not that much like Lisp, despite what you may have heard).

Exploring Parse Trees with PyTree

But wait—there is a better way to explore parse tree structures. Figure 21-1 shows the parse tree generated for the string 1 + 3 * (2 * 3 + 4), displayed in PyTree, the tree visualization GUI presented at the end of Chapter 20. This works only because the parser2 module builds the parse tree explicitly (parser1 evaluates during a parse instead), and because PyTree's code is generic and reusable.

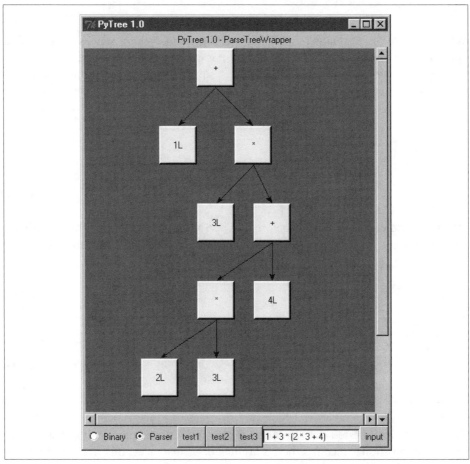

*Figure 21-1. Parse tree built for 1 + 3 * (2 * 3 + 4)*

If you read the last chapter, you'll recall that PyTree can draw most any tree data structure, but it is preconfigured to handle binary search trees and the parse trees we're studying in this chapter. You might also remember that clicking on nodes in a displayed parse tree evaluates the subtree rooted there. Figure 21-2 shows the pop up generated after clicking the tree's root node (you get different results if you click other parts of the tree because smaller subtrees are evaluated).

Figure 21-2. Clicking the root node to evaluate a tree

PyTree makes it easy to learn about and experiment with the parser. To determine the tree shape produced for a given expression, start PyTree, click on its Parser radio button, type the expression in the input field at the bottom, and press "input" (or your Enter key). The parser class is run to generate a tree from your input, and the GUI displays the result. For instance, Figure 21-3 sketches the parse tree generated if we remove the parentheses from the first expression in the input field. The root node evaluates to 23 this time, due to the different shape's evaluation order.

To generate a shape that is even more different, try introducing more parentheses to the expression and hitting the Enter key again. Figure 21-4 shows a much flatter tree structure produced by adding a few parentheses to override operator precedence. Because these parentheses change the tree shape, they also change the expression's overall result again. Figure 21-5 shows the resulting pop up after clicking the root node in this display.

Depending on the operators used within an expression, some very differently shaped trees yield the same result when evaluated. For instance, Figure 21-6 shows a more left-heavy tree generated from a different expression string that evaluates to 56 nevertheless.

Finally, Figure 21-7 shows a parsed assignment statement; clicking the set root assigns the variable spam, and clicking the node spam then evaluates to −4. If you find the parser puzzling, try running PyTree like this on your computer to get a better feel for the parsing process. (I'd like to show more example trees, but I ran out of page real estate at this point in the book.)

Parsers Versus Python

The handcoded parser programs shown earlier illustrate some interesting concepts and underscore the power of Python for general-purpose programming. Depending on your job description, they may also be typical of the sort of thing you'd write regularly in a traditional language such as C. Parsers are an important component in a

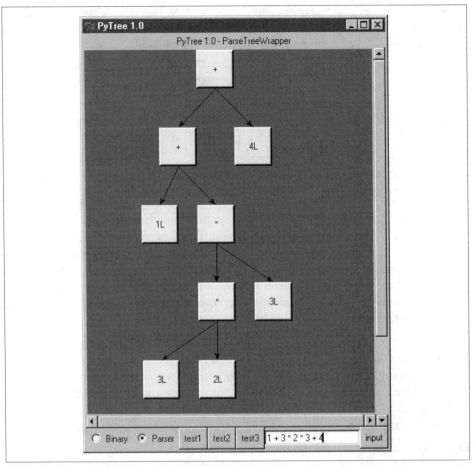

Figure 21-3. Parse tree for 1 + 3 * 2 * 3 + 4, result=23

wide variety of applications, but in some cases, they're not as necessary as you might think. Let me explain why.

So far, we started with an expression parser and added a parse tree interpreter to make the code easier to modify. As is, the parser works, but it may be slow compared to a C implementation. If the parser is used frequently, we could speed it up by moving parts to C extension modules. For instance, the scanner might be moved to C initially, since it's often called from the parser. Ultimately, we might add components to the grammar that allow expressions to access application-specific variables and functions.

All of these steps constitute good engineering. But depending on your application, this approach may not be the best one in Python. Often the easiest way to evaluate input expressions in Python is to let Python do it, by calling the eval built-in function. In fact, we can usually replace the entire expression evaluation program with one function call. The next example will demonstrate how this is done.

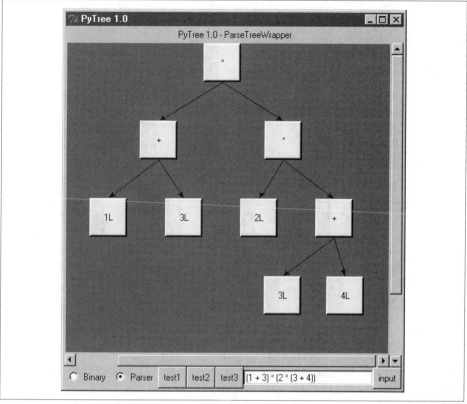

Figure 21-4. Parse tree built for (1 + 3) * (2 * (3 + 4))

Figure 21-5. Clicking and evaluating the root node

More important, the next section underscores a core idea behind the language: if you already have an extensible, embeddable, high-level language system, why invent another? Python itself can often satisfy language-based component needs.

PyCalc: A Calculator Program/Object

To wrap up this chapter, I'm going to show you a practical application for some of the parsing technology introduced in the preceding section. This section presents

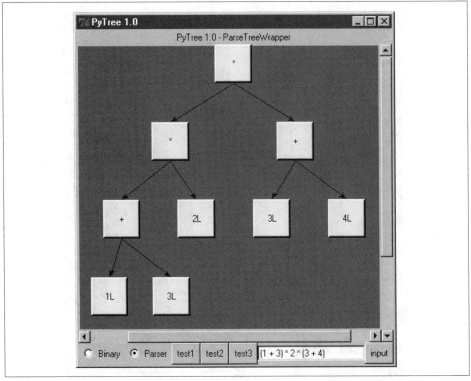

Figure 21-6. Parse tree for (1 + 3) * 2 * (3 + 4), result=56

PyCalc, a Python calculator program with a graphical interface similar to the calculator programs available on most window systems. But like most of the GUI examples in this book, PyCalc offers a few advantages over existing calculators. Because PyCalc is written in Python, it is both easily customized and widely portable across window platforms. And because it is implemented with classes, it is both a standalone program and a reusable object library.

A Simple Calculator GUI

Before I show you how to write a full-blown calculator, though, the module shown in Example 21-13 starts this discussion in simpler terms. It implements a limited calculator GUI, whose buttons just add text to the input field at the top in order to compose a Python expression string. Fetching and running the string all at once produces results. Figure 21-8 shows the window this module makes when run as a top-level script.

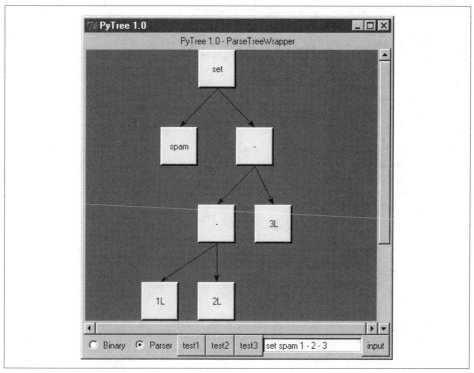

Figure 21-7. Assignment, left-grouping: "set spam 1 - 2 - 3"

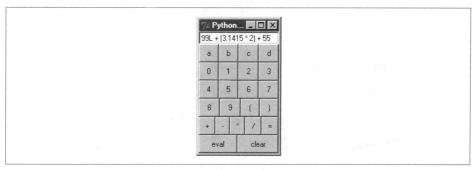

Figure 21-8. The calc0 script in action on Windows (result=160.283)

Example 21-13. PP3E\Lang\Calculator\calc0.py

```
#!/usr/local/bin/python
# a simple calculator GUI: expressions run all at once with eval/exec

from Tkinter  import *
from PP3E.Dbase.TableBrowser.guitools import frame, button, entry

class CalcGui(Frame):
    def __init__(self, parent=None):                      # an extended frame
```

Example 21-13. PP3E\Lang\Calculator\calc0.py (continued)

```
        Frame.__init__(self, parent)                # on default top-level
        self.pack(expand=YES, fill=BOTH)            # all parts expandable
        self.master.title('Python Calculator 0.1')  # 6 frames plus entry
        self.master.iconname("pcalc1")

        self.names = {}                             # namespace for variables
        text = StringVar()
        entry(self, TOP, text)

        rows = ["abcd", "0123", "4567", "89()"]
        for row in rows:
            frm = frame(self, TOP)
            for char in row:
                button(frm, LEFT, char,
                            lambda char=char: text.set(text.get() + char))

        frm = frame(self, TOP)
        for char in "+-*/=":
            button(frm, LEFT, char,
                        lambda char=char: text.set(text.get()+ ' ' + char + ' '))

        frm = frame(self, BOTTOM)
        button(frm, LEFT, 'eval',  lambda: self.eval(text) )
        button(frm, LEFT, 'clear', lambda: text.set('') )

    def eval(self, text):
        try:
            text.set(str(eval(text.get(), self.names, self.names)))    # was `x`
        except SyntaxError:
            try:
                exec(text.get(), self.names, self.names)
            except:
                text.set("ERROR")          # bad as statement too?
            else:
                text.set('')               # worked as a statement
        except:
            text.set("ERROR")              # other eval expression errors

if __name__ == '__main__': CalcGui().mainloop()
```

Building the GUI

Now, this is about as simple as a calculator can be, but it demonstrates the basics. This window comes up with buttons for entry of numbers, variable names, and operators. It is built by attaching buttons to frames: each row of buttons is a nested Frame, and the GUI itself is a Frame subclass with an attached Entry and six embedded row frames (grids would work here too). The calculator's frame, entry field, and buttons are made expandable in the imported guitools utility module.

This calculator builds up a string to pass to the Python interpreter all at once on "eval" button presses. Because you can type any Python expression or statement in the entry field, the buttons are really just a convenience. In fact, the entry field isn't much more than a command line. Try typing import sys, and then dir(sys) to display sys module attributes in the input field at the top—it's not what you normally do with a calculator, but it is demonstrative nevertheless.[*]

In CalcGui's constructor, buttons are coded as lists of strings; each string represents a row and each character in the string represents a button. Lambdas are used to save extra callback data for each button. The callback functions retain the button's character and the linked text entry variable so that the character can be added to the end of the entry widget's current string on a press.

Notice how we must pass in the loop variable as a default argument to some lambdas in this code. Recall from Chapter 8 how references within a lambda (or nested def) to names in an enclosing scope are evaluated when the nested function is called, not when it is created. When the generated function is called, enclosing scope references inside the lambda reflect their latest setting in the enclosing scope, which is not necessarily the values they held when the lambda expression ran. By contrast, defaults are evaluated at function creation time instead and so can remember the current values of loop variables. Without the defaults, each button would reflect the last iteration of the loop.

Running code strings

This module implements a GUI calculator in 45 lines of code (counting comments and blank lines). But to be honest, it cheats: expression evaluation is delegated to Python. In fact, the built-in eval and exec tools do most of the work here:

eval

> Parses, evaluates, and returns the result of a Python expression represented as a string.

exec

> Runs an arbitrary Python statement represented as a string; there's no return value because the code is a string.

Both accept optional dictionaries to be used as global and local namespaces for assigning and evaluating names used in the code strings. In the calculator, self. names becomes a symbol table for running calculator expressions. A related Python function, compile, can be used to precompile code strings to code objects before passing them to eval and exec (use it if you need to run the same string many times).

---

[*] Once again, I need to warn you about running strings like this if you can't be sure they won't cause damage. If these strings can be entered by users you cannot trust, they will have access to anything on the computer that the Python process has access to. See the Chapter 18 discussion of the (now defunct) rexec module for more on this topic.

Lesson 4: Embedding Beats Parsers

The calculator uses eval and exec to call Python's parser/interpreter at runtime instead of analyzing and evaluating expressions manually. In effect, the calculator runs embedded Python code from a Python program. This works because Python's development environment (the parser and bytecode compiler) is always a part of systems that use Python. Because there is no difference between the development and the delivery environments, Python's parser can be used by Python programs.

The net effect here is that the entire expression evaluator has been replaced with a single call to eval. In broader terms, this is a powerful technique to remember: the Python language itself can replace many small, custom languages. Besides saving development time, clients have to learn just one language, one that's potentially simple enough for end-user coding.

Furthermore, Python can take on the flavor of any application. If a language interface requires application-specific extensions, just add Python classes, or export an API for use in embedded Python code as a C extension. By evaluating Python code that uses application-specific extensions, custom parsers become almost completely unnecessary.

There's also a critical added benefit to this approach: embedded Python code has access to all the tools and features of a powerful, full-blown programming language. It can use lists, functions, classes, external modules, and even larger Python tools like Tkinter GUIs, shelve storage, multiple threads, network sockets, and web page fetches. You'd probably spend years trying to provide similar functionality in a custom language parser. Just ask Guido.

By default, a code string's namespace defaults to the caller's namespaces. If we didn't pass in dictionaries here, the strings would run in the eval method's namespace. Since the method's local namespace goes away after the method call returns, there would be no way to retain names assigned in the string. Notice the use of nested exception handlers in the eval method:

1. It first assumes the string is an expression and tries the built-in eval function.

2. If that fails due to a syntax error, it tries evaluating the string as a statement using exec.

3. Finally, if both attempts fail, it reports an error in the string (a syntax error, undefined name, and so on).

Statements and invalid expressions might be parsed twice, but the overhead doesn't matter here, and you can't tell whether a string is an expression or a statement without parsing it manually. Note that the "eval" button evaluates expressions, but = sets Python variables by running an assignment statement. Variable names are combinations of the letter keys "abcd" (or any name typed directly). They are assigned and evaluated in a dictionary used to represent the calculator's namespace.

Extending and attaching

Clients that reuse this calculator are as simple as the calculator itself. Like most class-based Tkinter GUIs, this one can be extended in subclasses—Example 21-14 customizes the simple calculator's constructor to add extra widgets.

Example 21-14. PP3E\Lang\Calculator\calc0ext.py

```
from Tkinter import *
from calc0 import CalcGui

class Inner(CalcGui):                                    # extend GUI
    def __init__(self):
        CalcGui.__init__(self)
        Label(self,  text='Calc Subclass').pack()        # add after
        Button(self, text='Quit', command=self.quit).pack()   # top implied

Inner().mainloop()
```

It can also be embedded in a container class—Example 21-15 attaches the simple calculator's widget package, along with extras, to a common parent.

Example 21-15. PP3E\Lang\Calculator\calc0emb.py

```
from Tkinter  import *
from calc0 import CalcGui                    # add parent, no master calls

class Outer:
    def __init__(self, parent):                         # embed GUI
        Label(parent, text='Calc Attachment').pack()    # side=top
        CalcGui(parent)                                 # add calc frame
        Button(parent, text='Quit', command=parent.quit).pack()

root = Tk()
Outer(root)
root.mainloop()
```

Figure 21-9 shows the result of running both of these scripts from different command lines. Both have a distinct input field at the top. This works; but to see a more practical application of such reuse techniques, we need to make the underlying calculator more practical too.

PyCalc—A Real Calculator GUI

Of course, real calculators don't usually work by building up expression strings and evaluating them all at once; that approach is really little more than a glorified Python command line. Traditionally, expressions are evaluated in piecemeal fashion as they are entered, and temporary results are displayed as soon as they are computed. Implementing this behavior requires a bit more work: expressions must be evaluated manually and in parts, instead of calling the eval function only once. But the end result is much more useful and intuitive.

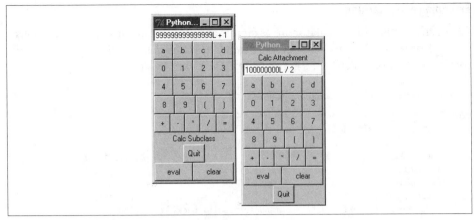

Figure 21-9. The calc0 script's object attached and extended

This section presents the implementation of PyCalc—a Python/Tkinter program that implements such a traditional calculator GUI. It touches on the subject of text and languages in two ways: it parses and evaluates expressions, and it implements a kind of stack-based language to perform the evaluation. Although its evaluation logic is more complex than the simpler calculator shown earlier, it demonstrates advanced programming techniques and serves as an interesting finale for this chapter.

Running PyCalc

As usual, let's look at the GUI before the code. You can run PyCalc from the PyGadgets and PyDemos launcher bars at the top of the examples tree, or by directly running the file *calculator.py* listed shortly (e.g., click it in a file explorer). Figure 21-10 shows PyCalc's main window. By default, it shows operand buttons in black-on-blue (and opposite for operator buttons), but font and color options can be passed into the GUI class's constructor method. Of course, that means gray-on-gray in this book, so you'll have to run PyCalc yourself to see what I mean.

Figure 21-10. PyCalc calculator at work on Windows

If you do run this, you'll notice that PyCalc implements a normal calculator model—expressions are evaluated as entered, not all at once at the end. That is, parts of an expression are computed and displayed as soon as operator precedence and manually typed parentheses allow. I'll explain how this evaluation works in a moment.

PyCalc's CalcGui class builds the GUI interface as frames of buttons much like the simple calculator of the previous section, but PyCalc adds a host of new features. Among them are another row of action buttons, inherited methods from GuiMixin (presented in Chapter 11), a new "cmd" button that pops up nonmodal dialogs for entry of arbitrary Python code, and a recent calculations history pop up. Figure 21-11 captures some of PyCalc's pop-up windows.

You may enter expressions in PyCalc by clicking buttons in the GUI, typing full expressions in command-line pop ups, or typing keys on your keyboard. PyCalc intercepts key press events and interprets them the same as corresponding button presses; typing + is like pressing the + button, the Space bar key is "clear," Enter is "eval," backspace erases a character, and ? is like pressing "help."

The command-line pop-up windows are nonmodal (you can pop up as many as you like). They accept any Python code—press the Run button or your Enter key to evaluate text in the input field. The result of evaluating this code in the calculator's

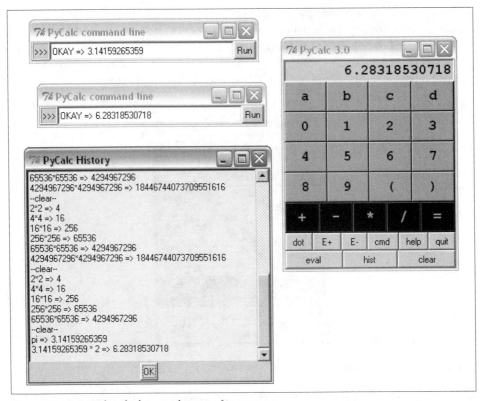

Figure 21-11. PyCalc calculator with some of its pop ups

namespace dictionary is thrown up in the main window for use in larger expressions. You can use this as an escape mechanism to employ external tools in your calculations. For instance, you can import and use functions coded in Python or C within these pop ups. The current value in the main calculator window is stored in newly opened command-line pop ups too, for use in typed expressions.

PyCalc supports long integers (unlimited precision), negatives, and floating-point numbers just because Python does. Individual operands and expressions are still evaluated with the eval built-in, which calls the Python parser/interpreter at runtime. Variable names can be assigned and referenced in the main window with the letter, =, and "eval" keys; they are assigned in the calculator's namespace dictionary (more complex variable names may be typed in command-line pop ups). Note the use of pi in the history window: PyCalc preimports names in the math and random modules into the namespace where expressions are evaluated.

Evaluating expressions with stacks

Now that you have the general idea of what PyCalc does, I need to say a little bit about how it does what it does. Most of the changes in this version involve managing the expression display and evaluating expressions. PyCalc is structured as two classes:

The `CalcGui` *class*

Manages the GUI itself. It controls input events and is in charge of the main window's display field at the top. It doesn't evaluate expressions, though; for that, it sends operators and operands entered in the GUI to an embedded instance of the `Evaluator` class.

The `Evaluator` *class*

Manages two stacks. One stack records pending *operators* (e.g., +), and one records pending *operands* (e.g., 3.141). Temporary results are computed as new operators are sent from `CalcGui` and pushed onto the operands stack.

As you can see from this, the magic of expression evaluation boils down to juggling the operator and operand stacks. In a sense, the calculator implements a little stack-based *language*, to evaluate the expressions being entered. While scanning expression strings from left to right as they are entered, operands are pushed along the way, but operators delimit operands and may trigger temporary results before they are pushed. Because it records states and performs transitions, some might use the term *state machine* to describe this calculator language implementation.

Here's the general scenario:

1. When a new operator is seen (i.e., when an operator button or key is pressed), the prior operand in the entry field is pushed onto the operands stack.

2. The operator is then added to the operators stack, but only after all pending operators of higher precedence have been popped and applied to pending operands (e.g., pressing + makes any pending * operators on the stack fire).

3. When "eval" is pressed, all remaining operators are popped and applied to all remaining operands, and the result is the last remaining value on the operands stack.

In the end, the last value on the operands stack is displayed in the calculator's entry field, ready for use in another operation. This evaluation algorithm is probably best described by working through examples. Let's step through the entry of a few expressions and watch the evaluation stacks grow.

PyCalc stack tracing is enabled with the `debugme` flag in the module; if true, the operator and operand stacks are displayed on `stdout` each time the `Evaluator` class is about to apply an operator and *reduce* (pop) the stacks. Run PyCalc with a console window to see the traces. A tuple holding the stack lists (*operators, operands*) is printed on each stack reduction; tops of stack are at the ends of the lists. For instance, here is the console output after typing and evaluating a simple string:

```
1) Entered keys: "5 * 3 + 4 <eval>" [result = 19]

(['*'], ['5', '3'])    [on '+' press: displays "15"]
(['+'], ['15', '4'])   [on 'eval' press: displays "19"]
```

Note that the pending (stacked) * subexpression is evaluated when the + is pressed: * operators bind tighter than +, so the code is evaluated immediately before the + operator is pushed. When the + button is pressed, the entry field contains 3; we push 3 onto the operands stack, reduce the * subexpression (5 * 3), push its result onto operands, push + onto operators, and continue scanning user inputs. When "eval" is pressed at the end, 4 is pushed onto operators, and the final + on operators is applied to stacked operands.

The text input field and expression stacks are integrated by the calculator class. In general, the text entry field always holds the prior operand when an operator button is pressed; the text in the entry field is pushed onto the operands stack before the operator is resolved. Because of this, we have to pop results before displaying them after "eval" or) is pressed (otherwise the results are pushed onto the stack twice— they would be both on the stack and in the display field, from which they would be immediately pushed again when the next operator is input). When an operator is seen (or "eval" or) is applied), we also have to take care to erase the entry field when the next operand's entry is started.

Expression stacks also defer operations of lower precedence as the input is scanned. In the next trace, the pending + isn't evaluated when the * button is pressed: since * binds tighter, we need to postpone the + until the * can be evaluated. The * operator isn't popped until its right operand 4 has been seen. There are two operators to pop and apply to operand stack entries on the "eval" press—the * at the top of operators is applied to the 3 and 4 at the top of operands, and then + is run on 5 and the 12 pushed for *:

```
2) "5 + 3 * 4 <eval>" [result = 17]

(['+', '*'], ['5', '3', '4'])    [on 'eval' press]
(['+'], ['5', '12'])             [displays "17"]
```

For strings of same-precedence operators such as the following, we pop and evaluate immediately as we scan left to right, instead of postponing evaluation. This results in a left-associative evaluation, in the absence of parentheses: 5+3+4 is evaluated as ((5+3)+4). For + and * operations this is irrelevant because order doesn't matter:

```
3) "5 + 3 + 4 <eval>" [result = 12]

(['+'], ['5', '3'])    [on the second '+']
(['+'], ['8', '4'])    [on 'eval']
```

The following trace is more complex. In this case, all the operators and operands are stacked (postponed) until we press the) button at the end. To make parentheses work, (is given a higher precedence than any operator and is pushed onto the operators stack to seal off lower stack reductions until the) is seen. When the) button is pressed, the parenthesized subexpression is popped and evaluated ((3 * 4), then (1 + 12)), and 13 is displayed in the entry field. On pressing "eval," the rest is evaluated

((3 * 13), (1 +39)), and the final result (40) is shown. This result in the entry field itself becomes the left operand of a future operator.

```
4) "1 + 3 * ( 1 + 3 * 4 ) <eval>" [result = 40]

(['+', '*', '(', '+', '*'], ['1', '3', '1', '3', '4'])    [on ')']
(['+', '*', '(', '+'], ['1', '3', '1', '12'])             [displays "13"]
(['+', '*'], ['1', '3', '13'])                            [on 'eval']
(['+'], ['1', '39'])
```

In fact, any temporary result can be used again: if we keep pressing an operator button without typing new operands, it's reapplied to the result of the prior press—the value in the entry field is pushed twice and applied to itself each time. Press * many times after entering 2 to see how this works (e.g., 2***). On the first *, it pushes 2 and the *. On the next *, it pushes 2 again from the entry field, pops and evaluates the stacked (2 * 2), pushes back and displays the result, and pushes the new *. And on each following *, it pushes the currently displayed result and evaluates again, computing successive squares.

Figure 21-12 shows how the two stacks look at their highest level while scanning the expression in the prior example trace. On each reduction, the top operator is applied to the top two operands and the result is pushed back for the operator below. Because of the way the two stacks are used, the effect is similar to converting the expression to a string of the form +1*3(+1*34 and evaluating it right to left. In other cases, though, parts of the expression are evaluated and displayed as temporary results along the way, so it's not simply a string conversion process.

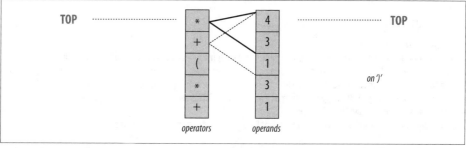

Figure 21-12. Evaluation stacks: 1 + 3 * (1 + 3 * 4)

Finally, the next example's string triggers an error. PyCalc is casual about error handling. Many errors are made impossible by the algorithm itself, but things such as unmatched parentheses still trip up the evaluator. Instead of trying to detect all possible error cases explicitly, a general try statement in the reduce method is used to catch them all: expression errors, numeric errors, undefined name errors, syntax errors, and so on.

Operands and temporary results are always stacked as strings, and each operator is applied by calling eval. When an error occurs inside an expression, a result operand of *ERROR* is pushed, which makes all remaining operators fail in eval too. *ERROR* essentially percolates to the top of the expression. At the end, it's the last operand and is displayed in the text entry field to alert you of the mistake:

```
5) "1 + 3 * ( 1 + 3 * 4 <eval>" [result = *ERROR*]

(['+', '*', '(', '+', '*'], ['1', '3', '1', '3', '4'])         [on eval]
(['+', '*', '(', '+'], ['1', '3', '1', '12'])
(['+', '*', '('], ['1', '3', '13'])
(['+', '*'], ['1', '*ERROR*'])
(['+'], ['*ERROR*'])
(['+'], ['*ERROR*', '*ERROR*'])
```

Try tracing through these and other examples in the calculator's code to get a feel for the stack-based evaluation that occurs. Once you understand the general shift/reduce (push/pop) mechanism, expression evaluation is straightforward.

PyCalc source code

Example 21-16 contains the PyCalc source module that puts these ideas to work in the context of a GUI. It's a single-file implementation (not counting utilities imported and reused). Study the source for more details; as usual, there's no substitute for interacting with the program on your own to get a better feel for its functionality.

Also see the opening comment's "to do" list for suggested areas for improvement. Like all software systems, this calculator is prone to evolve over time (and in fact it has, with each new edition of this book). Since it is written in Python, such future mutations will be easy to apply.

Example 21-16. PP3E\Lang\Calculator\calculator.py

```
#!/usr/local/bin/python
###############################################################################
# PyCalc 3.0: a Python/Tkinter calculator program and GUI component.
# evaluates expressions as they are entered, catches keyboard keys for
# expression entry; 2.0 added integrated command-line popups, a recent
# calculations history display popup, fonts and colors configuration,
# help and about popups, preimported math/random constants, and more;
#
# 3.0 changes (PP3E):
# -use 'readonly' entry state, not 'disabled', else field is greyed
#  out (fix for 2.3 Tkinter change);
# -avoid extended display precision for floats by using str( ), instead
#  of `x`/repr( ) (fix for Python change);
# -apply font to input field to make it larger;
# -use justify=right for input field so it displays on right, not left;
# -add 'E+' and 'E-' buttons (and 'E' keypress) for float exponents;
# -remove 'L' button (but still allow 'L' keypress): superfluous now,
#  because Python auto converts up if too big ('L' forced this in past);
# -use smaller font size overall;
# -use windows.py module to get a window icon;
# -auto scroll to the end in the history window
#
```

Example 21-16. PP3E\Lang\Calculator\calculator.py (continued)

```
# to do: add a commas-insertion mode, allow '**' as a operator key, allow
# '+' and 'J' inputs for complex numbers, use new decimal type for fixed
# precision floats; as is, can use 'cmd' popup windows to input and eval
# an initial complex, complex exprs, and 'E' '-' key sequences, but can't
# be input via main window; caveat: this calulator's precision, accuracy,
# and some of its behaviour, is currently bound by result of str( ) call;
#
# note that the new nested scopes simplify some lambdas here, but we have to
# use defaults to pass in some scope values in lambdas here anyhow, because
# enclosing scope names are looked up when the nested function is called, not
# when it is created (but defaults are);  when the generated function is
# called enclosing scope refs are whatever they were set to last in the
# enclosing function's block, not what they were when the lambda ran;
##############################################################################

from Tkinter  import *                                 # widgets, consts
from PP3E.Gui.Tools.guimixin import GuiMixin           # quit method
from PP3E.Dbase.TableBrowser.guitools import *         # widget builders
Fg, Bg, Font = 'black', 'skyblue', ('courier', 14, 'bold')   # default config

debugme = 1
def trace(*args):
    if debugme: print args



##############################################################################
# the main class - handles user interface;
# an extended Frame, on new Toplevel, orembedded in another container widget
##############################################################################

class CalcGui(GuiMixin, Frame):
    Operators = "+-*/="                                # button lists
    Operands  = ["abcd", "0123", "4567", "89( )"]      # customizable

    def __init__(self, parent=None, fg=Fg, bg=Bg, font=Font):
        Frame.__init__(self, parent)
        self.pack(expand=YES, fill=BOTH)               # all parts expandable
        self.eval = Evaluator( )                       # embed a stack handler
        self.text = StringVar( )                       # make a linked variable
        self.text.set("0")
        self.erase = 1                                 # clear "0" text next
        self.makeWidgets(fg, bg, font)                 # build the GUI itself
        if not parent or not isinstance(parent, Frame):
            self.master.title('PyCalc 3.0')            # title iff owns window
            self.master.iconname("PyCalc")             # ditto for key bindings
            self.master.bind('<KeyPress>', self.onKeyboard)
            self.entry.config(state='readonly')        # 3.0: not 'disabled'=grey
        else:
            self.entry.config(state='normal')
            self.entry.focus( )

    def makeWidgets(self, fg, bg, font):               # 7 frames plus text-entry
```

Example 21-16. PP3E\Lang\Calculator\calculator.py (continued)

```
            self.entry = entry(self, TOP, self.text)      # font, color configurable
            self.entry.config(font=font)                  # 3.0: make display larger
            self.entry.config(justify=RIGHT)              # 3.0: on right, not left
            for row in self.Operands:
                frm = frame(self, TOP)
                for char in row:
                    button(frm, LEFT, char,
                                lambda op=char: self.onOperand(op),
                                fg=fg, bg=bg, font=font)

            frm = frame(self, TOP)
            for char in self.Operators:
                button(frm, LEFT, char,
                            lambda op=char: self.onOperator(op),
                            fg=bg, bg=fg, font=font)

            frm = frame(self, TOP)
            button(frm, LEFT, 'dot ', lambda: self.onOperand('.'))
            button(frm, LEFT, ' E+ ', lambda: self.text.set(self.text.get()+'E+'))
            button(frm, LEFT, ' E- ', lambda: self.text.set(self.text.get()+'E-'))
            button(frm, LEFT, 'cmd ', self.onMakeCmdline)
            button(frm, LEFT, 'help', self.help)
            button(frm, LEFT, 'quit', self.quit)          # from guimixin

            frm = frame(self, BOTTOM)
            button(frm, LEFT, 'eval ', self.onEval)
            button(frm, LEFT, 'hist ', self.onHist)
            button(frm, LEFT, 'clear', self.onClear)

    def onClear(self):
        self.eval.clear()
        self.text.set('0')
        self.erase = 1

    def onEval(self):
        self.eval.shiftOpnd(self.text.get())       # last or only opnd
        self.eval.closeall()                       # apply all optrs left
        self.text.set(self.eval.popOpnd())         # need to pop: optr next?
        self.erase = 1

    def onOperand(self, char):
        if char == '(':
            self.eval.open()
            self.text.set('(')                             # clear text next
            self.erase = 1
        elif char == ')':
            self.eval.shiftOpnd(self.text.get())   # last or only nested opnd
            self.eval.close()                      # pop here too: optr next?
            self.text.set(self.eval.popOpnd())
            self.erase = 1
        else:
            if self.erase:
```

Example 21-16. PP3E\Lang\Calculator\calculator.py (continued)

```
                self.text.set(char)                    # clears last value
            else:
                self.text.set(self.text.get() + char)  # else append to opnd
            self.erase = 0

    def onOperator(self, char):
        self.eval.shiftOpnd(self.text.get())    # push opnd on left
        self.eval.shiftOptr(char)               # eval exprs to left?
        self.text.set(self.eval.topOpnd())      # push optr, show opnd|result
        self.erase = 1                          # erased on next opnd|'('

    def onMakeCmdline(self):
        new = Toplevel()                        # new top-level window
        new.title('PyCalc command line')        # arbitrary Python code
        frm = frame(new, TOP)                   # only the Entry expands
        label(frm, LEFT, '>>>').pack(expand=NO)
        var = StringVar()
        ent = entry(frm, LEFT, var, width=40)
        onButton = (lambda: self.onCmdline(var, ent))
        onReturn = (lambda event: self.onCmdline(var, ent))
        button(frm, RIGHT, 'Run', onButton).pack(expand=NO)
        ent.bind('<Return>', onReturn)
        var.set(self.text.get())

    def onCmdline(self, var, ent):              # eval cmdline pop-up input
        try:
            value = self.eval.runstring(var.get())
            var.set('OKAY')
            if value != None:                   # run in eval namespace dict
                self.text.set(value)            # expression or statement
                self.erase = 1
                var.set('OKAY => '+ value)
        except:                                 # result in calc field
            var.set('ERROR')                    # status in pop-up field
        ent.icursor(END)                        # insert point after text
        ent.select_range(0, END)                # select msg so next key deletes

    def onKeyboard(self, event):
        pressed = event.char                    # on keyboard press event
        if pressed != '':                       # pretend button was pressed
            if pressed in self.Operators:
                self.onOperator(pressed)
            else:
                for row in self.Operands:
                    if pressed in row:
                        self.onOperand(pressed)
                        break
                else:
                    if pressed == '.':
                        self.onOperand(pressed)                 # can start opnd
                    if pressed in 'LlEe':
                        self.text.set(self.text.get()+pressed) # can't: no erase
```

Example 21-16. PP3E\Lang\Calculator\calculator.py (continued)

```
                        elif pressed == '\r':
                            self.onEval()                          # enter key=eval
                        elif pressed == ' ':
                            self.onClear()                         # spacebar=clear
                        elif pressed == '\b':
                            self.text.set(self.text.get()[:-1])    # backspace
                        elif pressed == '?':
                            self.help()

    def onHist(self):
        # show recent calcs log popup
        from ScrolledText import ScrolledText
        new = Toplevel()                              # make new window
        ok = Button(new, text="OK", command=new.destroy)
        ok.pack(pady=1, side=BOTTOM)                  # pack first=clip last
        text = ScrolledText(new, bg='beige')          # add Text + scrollbar
        text.insert('0.0', self.eval.getHist())       # get Evaluator text
        text.see(END)                                 # 3.0: scroll to end
        text.pack(expand=YES, fill=BOTH)

        # new window goes away on ok press or enter key
        new.title("PyCalc History")
        new.bind("<Return>", (lambda event: new.destroy()))
        ok.focus_set()                    # make new window modal:
        new.grab_set()                    # get keyboard focus, grab app
        new.wait_window()                 # don't return till new.destroy

    def help(self):
        self.infobox('PyCalc', 'PyCalc 3.0\n'
                               'A Python/Tk calculator\n'
                               'Programming Python 3E\n'
                               'June, 2005\n'
                               '(2.0 1999, 1.0 1996)\n\n'
                               'Use mouse or keyboard to\n'
                               'input numbers and operators,\n'
                               'or type code in cmd popup')



###########################################################################
# the expression evaluator class
# embedded in and used by a CalcGui instance, to perform calculations
###########################################################################

class Evaluator:
    def __init__(self):
        self.names = {}                        # a names-space for my vars
        self.opnd, self.optr = [], []          # two empty stacks
        self.hist = []                         # my prev calcs history log
        self.runstring("from math import *")   # preimport math modules
        self.runstring("from random import *") # into calc's namespace

    def clear(self):
```

Example 21-16. PP3E\Lang\Calculator\calculator.py (continued)

```
        self.opnd, self.optr = [], []        # leave names intact
        if len(self.hist) > 64:              # don't let hist get too big
            self.hist = ['clear']
        else:
            self.hist.append('--clear--')

    def popOpnd(self):
        value = self.opnd[-1]                # pop/return top|last opnd
        self.opnd[-1:] = []                  # to display and shift next
        return value                         # or x.pop(), or del x[-1]

    def topOpnd(self):
        return self.opnd[-1]                 # top operand (end of list)

    def open(self):
        self.optr.append('(')                # treat '(' like an operator

    def close(self):                         # on ')' pop downto higest '('
        self.shiftOptr(')')                  # ok if empty: stays empty
        self.optr[-2:] = []                  # pop, or added again by optr

    def closeall(self):
        while self.optr:                     # force rest on 'eval'
            self.reduce()                    # last may be a var name
        try:
            self.opnd[0] = self.runstring(self.opnd[0])
        except:
            self.opnd[0] = '*ERROR*'         # pop else added again next:

    afterMe = {'*': ['+', '-', '(', '='],    # class member
               '/': ['+', '-', '(', '='],    # optrs to not pop for key
               '+': ['(', '='],              # if prior optr is this: push
               '-': ['(', '='],              # else: pop/eval prior optr
               ')': ['(', '='],              # all left-associative as is
               '=': ['('] }

    def shiftOpnd(self, newopnd):            # push opnd at optr, ')', eval
        self.opnd.append(newopnd)

    def shiftOptr(self, newoptr):            # apply ops with <= priority
        while (self.optr and
               self.optr[-1] not in self.afterMe[newoptr]):
            self.reduce()
        self.optr.append(newoptr)            # push this op above result
                                             # optrs assume next opnd erases
    def reduce(self):
        trace(self.optr, self.opnd)
        try:                                 # collapse the top expr
            operator     = self.optr[-1]     # pop top optr (at end)
            [left, right] = self.opnd[-2:]   # pop top 2 opnds (at end)
            self.optr[-1:] = []              # delete slice in-place
            self.opnd[-2:] = []
```

Example 21-16. PP3E\Lang\Calculator\calculator.py (continued)

```
                result = self.runstring(left + operator + right)
                if result == None:
                    result = left              # assignment? key var name
                self.opnd.append(result)       # push result string back
            except:
                self.opnd.append('*ERROR*')         # stack/number/name error

    def runstring(self, code):
        try:                                       # 3.0: not `x`
            result = str(eval(code, self.names, self.names))  # try expr: string
            self.hist.append(code + ' => ' + result)          # add to hist log
        except:
            exec code in self.names, self.names         # try stmt: None
            self.hist.append(code)
            result = None
        return result

    def getHist(self):
        return '\n'.join(self.hist)

def getCalcArgs():
    from sys import argv                      # get cmdline args in a dict
    config = {}                               # ex: -bg black -fg red
    for arg in argv[1:]:                      # font not yet supported
        if arg in ['-bg', '-fg']:             # -bg red' -> {'bg':'red'}
            try:
                config[arg[1:]] = argv[argv.index(arg) + 1]
            except:
                pass
    return config

if __name__ == '__main__':
    CalcGui(**getCalcArgs()).mainloop()     # in default toplevel window
```

Using PyCalc as a component

PyCalc serves a standalone program on my desktop, but it's also useful in the context of other GUIs. Like most of the GUI classes in this book, PyCalc can be customized with subclass extensions or embedded in a larger GUI with attachments. The module in Example 21-17 demonstrates one way to reuse PyCalc's CalcGui class by extending and embedding, similar to what was done for the simple calculator earlier.

Example 21-17. PP3E\Lang\Calculator\calculator_test.py

```
#######################################################################
# test calculator use as an extended and embedded GUI component;
#######################################################################

from Tkinter import *
from calculator import CalcGui
from PP3E.Dbase.TableBrowser.guitools import *
```

Example 21-17. PP3E\Lang\Calculator\calculator_test.py (continued)

```
def calcContainer(parent=None):
    frm = Frame(parent)
    frm.pack(expand=YES, fill=BOTH)
    Label(frm, text='Calc Container').pack(side=TOP)
    CalcGui(frm)
    Label(frm, text='Calc Container').pack(side=BOTTOM)
    return frm

class calcSubclass(CalcGui):
    def makeWidgets(self, fg, bg, font):
        Label(self, text='Calc Subclass').pack(side=TOP)
        Label(self, text='Calc Subclass').pack(side=BOTTOM)
        CalcGui.makeWidgets(self, fg, bg, font)
        #Label(self, text='Calc Subclass').pack(side=BOTTOM)

if __name__ == '__main__':
    import sys
    if len(sys.argv) == 1:                  # % calculator_test.py
        root = Tk()                         # run 3 calcs in same process
        CalcGui(Toplevel())                 # each in a new toplevel window
        calcContainer(Toplevel())
        calcSubclass(Toplevel())
        Button(root, text='quit', command=root.quit).pack()
        root.mainloop()
    if len(sys.argv) == 2:                  # % calculator_test1.py -
        CalcGui().mainloop()                # as a standalone window (default root)
    elif len(sys.argv) == 3:                # % calculator_test.py - -
        calcContainer().mainloop()          # as an embedded component
    elif len(sys.argv) == 4:                # % calculator_test.py - - -
        calcSubclass().mainloop()           # as a customized superclass
```

Figure 21-13 shows the result of running this script with no command-line arguments. We get instances of the original calculator class, plus the container and subclass classes defined in this script, all attached to new top-level windows.

These two windows on the right reuse the core PyCalc code running in the window on the left. All of these windows run in the same process (e.g., quitting one quits them all), but they all function as independent windows. Note that when running three calculators in the same process like this, each has its own distinct expression evaluation namespace because it's a class instance attribute, not a global module-level variable. Because of that, variables set in one calculator are set in that calculator only, and they don't overwrite settings made in other windows. Similarly, each calculator has its own evaluation stack manager object, such that calculations in one window don't appear in or impact other windows at all.

The two extensions in this script are artificial, of course—they simply add labels at the top and bottom of the window—but the concept is widely applicable. You could reuse the calculator's class by attaching it to any GUI that needs a calculator and customize it with subclasses arbitrarily. It's a reusable widget.

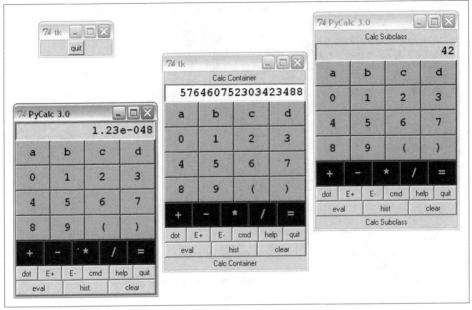

Figure 21-13. The calculator_test script: attaching and extending

Adding new buttons in new components

One obvious way to reuse the calculator is to add additional expression feature buttons—square roots, inverses, cubes, and the like. You can type such operations in the command-line pop ups, but buttons are a bit more convenient. Such features could also be added to the main calculator implementation itself, but since the set of features that will be useful may vary per user and application, a better approach may be to add them in separate extensions. For instance, the class in Example 21-18 adds a few extra buttons to PyCalc by embedding (i.e., attaching) it in a container.

Example 21-18. PP3E\Lang\Calculator\calculator_plus_emb.py

```
#######################################################################
# a container with an extra row of buttons for common operations;
# a more useful customization: adds buttons for more operations (sqrt,
# 1/x, etc.) by embedding/composition, not subclassing; new buttons are
# added after entire CalGui frame because of the packing order/options;
#######################################################################

from Tkinter import *
from calculator import CalcGui, getCalcArgs
from PP3E.Dbase.TableBrowser.guitools import frame, button, label

class CalcGuiPlus(Toplevel):
    def __init__(self, **args):
```

Example 21-18. PP3E\Lang\Calculator\calculator_plus_emb.py (continued)

```
        Toplevel.__init__(self)
        label(self, TOP, 'PyCalc Plus - Container')
        self.calc = CalcGui(self, **args)
        frm = frame(self, BOTTOM)
        extras = [('sqrt', 'sqrt(%s)'),
                  ('x^2 ', '(%s)**2'),
                  ('x^3 ', '(%s)**3'),
                  ('1/x ', '1.0/(%s)')]
        for (lab, expr) in extras:
            button(frm, LEFT, lab, (lambda expr=expr: self.onExtra(expr)) )
        button(frm, LEFT, ' pi ', self.onPi)
    def onExtra(self, expr):
        text = self.calc.text
        eval = self.calc.eval
        try:
            text.set(eval.runstring(expr % text.get()))
        except:
            text.set('ERROR')
    def onPi(self):
        self.calc.text.set(self.calc.eval.runstring('pi'))

if __name__ == '__main__':
    root = Tk()
    button(root, TOP, 'Quit', root.quit)
    CalcGuiPlus(**getCalcArgs()).mainloop()        # -bg,-fg to calcgui
```

Because PyCalc is coded as a Python class, you can always achieve a similar effect by extending PyCalc in a new subclass instead of embedding it, as shown in Example 21-19.

Example 21-19. PP3E\Lang\Calculator\calculator_plus_ext.py

```
###############################################################################
# a customization with an extra row of buttons for common operations;
# a more useful customization: adds buttons for more operations (sqrt,
# 1/x, etc.) by subclassing to extend the original class, not embedding;
# new buttons show up before frame attached to bottom be calcgui class;
###############################################################################

from Tkinter import *
from calculator import CalcGui, getCalcArgs
from PP3E.Dbase.TableBrowser.guitools import *

class CalcGuiPlus(CalcGui):
    def makeWidgets(self, *args):
        label(self, TOP, 'PyCalc Plus - Subclass')
        CalcGui.makeWidgets(self, *args)
        frm = frame(self, BOTTOM)
```

Example 21-19. PP3E\Lang\Calculator\calculator_plus_ext.py (continued)

```
        extras = [('sqrt', 'sqrt(%s)'),
                  ('x^2 ', '(%s)**2'),
                  ('x^3 ', '(%s)**3'),
                  ('1/x ', '1.0/(%s)')]
        for (lab, expr) in extras:
            button(frm, LEFT, lab, (lambda expr=expr: self.onExtra(expr)) )
        button(frm, LEFT, ' pi ', self.onPi)
    def onExtra(self, expr):
        try:
            self.text.set(self.eval.runstring(expr % self.text.get( )))
        except:
            self.text.set('ERROR')
    def onPi(self):
        self.text.set(self.eval.runstring('pi'))

if __name__ == '__main__':
    CalcGuiPlus(**getCalcArgs()).mainloop( )         # passes -bg, -fg on
```

Notice that these buttons' callbacks use 1.0/x to force float-point division to be used for inverses (integer division truncates remainders) and wrap entry field values in parentheses (to sidestep precedence issues). They could instead convert the entry's text to a number and do real math, but Python does all the work automatically when expression strings are run raw.

Also note that the buttons added by these scripts simply operate on the current value in the entry field, immediately. That's not quite the same as expression operators applied with the stacks evaluator (additional customizations are needed to make them true operators). Still, these buttons prove the point these scripts are out to make—they use PyCalc as a component, both from the outside and from below.

Finally, to test both of the extended calculator classes, as well as PyCalc configuration options, the script in Example 21-20 puts up four distinct calculator windows (this is the script run by PyDemos).

Example 21-20. PP3E\Lang\Calculator\calculator_plusplus.py

```
#!/usr/local/bin/python
from Tkinter import Tk, Button, Toplevel
import calculator, calculator_plus_ext, calculator_plus_emb

# demo all 3 calculator flavors at once
# each is a distinct calculator object and window

root=Tk( )
calculator.CalcGui(Toplevel( ))
calculator.CalcGui(Toplevel( ), fg='white', bg='purple')
calculator_plus_ext.CalcGuiPlus(Toplevel( ), fg='gold', bg='black')
```

Example 21-20. PP3E\Lang\Calculator\calculator_plusplus.py (continued)

```
calculator_plus_emb.CalcGuiPlus(fg='black', bg='red')
Button(root, text='Quit Calcs', command=root.quit).pack()
root.mainloop()
```

Figure 21-14 shows the result—four independent calculators in top-level windows within the same process. The two windows on the top represent specialized reuses of PyCalc as a component. Although it may not be obvious in this book, all four use different color schemes; calculator classes accept color and font configuration options and pass them down the call chain as needed.

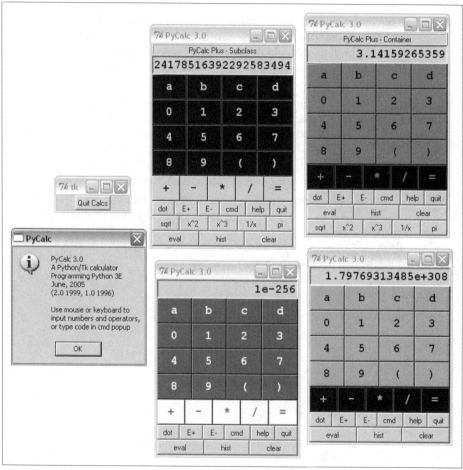

Figure 21-14. calculator_plusplus: extend, embed, and configure

As we learned earlier, these calculators could also be run as independent processes by spawning command lines with the launchmodes module we met in Chapter 5. In fact, that's how the PyGadgets and PyDemos launcher bars run calculators, so see their code for more details.

Lesson 6: Have Fun

In closing, here's a less tangible but important aspect of Python programming. A common remark among new users is that it's easy to "say what you mean" in Python without getting bogged down in complex syntax or obscure rules. It's a programmer-friendly language. In fact, it's not too uncommon for Python programs to run on the first attempt.

As we've seen in this book, there are a number of factors behind this distinction—lack of declarations, no compile steps, simple syntax, useful built-in objects, and so on. Python is specifically designed to optimize speed of development (an idea we'll expand on in Chapter 24). For many users, the end result is a remarkably expressive and responsive language, which can actually be fun to use.

For instance, the calculator programs shown earlier were first thrown together in one afternoon, starting from vague, incomplete goals. There was no analysis phase, no formal design, and no official coding stage. I typed up some ideas and they worked. Moreover, Python's interactive nature allowed me to experiment with new ideas and get immediate feedback. Since its initial development, the calculator has been polished and expanded, but the core implementation remains unchanged.

Naturally, such a laid-back programming mode doesn't work for every project. Sometimes more upfront design is warranted. For more demanding tasks, Python has modular constructs and fosters systems that can be extended in either Python or C. And a simple calculator GUI may not be what some would call "serious" software development. But maybe that's part of the point too.

## PART VI

Integration

This part of the book explores Python's interfaces for in-process communication with software components written in other programming languages. Its emphasis is on mixing Python with programs written in C and C++, but other integration techniques are also introduced along the way. This part contains two chapters that address the two primary modes of Python/C integration:

Chapter 22, *Extending Python*

> This chapter presents tools that allow Python scripts to call out to C components. C components take the form of new modules or object types. Extending is used as an optimization technique, as an escape mechanism for performing tasks outside the Python language, and as a way to leverage existing libraries. This chapter also covers SWIG—a system that automatically generates the glue code needed to export C and C++ libraries to Python scripts and hides much of the complexity underlying extensions.

Chapter 23, *Embedding Python*

> This chapter presents tools that allow C programs to execute Python scripts. These tools live in the Python runtime API—a collection of functions exposed by the Python interpreter and linked into your C/C++ program. Embedding is often used as a customization mechanism and for routing events back to Python code. This chapter concludes with a look at other integration topics and systems: Jython, COM, CORBA, and so on.

This part of the book assumes that you know how to read C programs, and it is useful mostly to developers responsible for implementing application integration layers that route control to and from Python scripts. Yet because C components are at the heart of many Python systems, a basic understanding of integration concepts can be useful even to scripters who code strictly in Python.

## CHAPTER 22

Extending Python

"I Am Lost at C"

So far in this book, we've been using Python as it comes out of the box. We have used interfaces to services outside Python, and we've coded extensions as Python modules. But we haven't added any external services beyond the built-in set. For many users, this makes perfect sense: such standalone programming is one of the main ways people apply Python. As we've seen, Python comes with batteries included—interfaces to system tools, Internet protocols, GUIs, filesystems, and much more, are already available.

But for many systems, Python's ability to integrate with C-compatible components is a crucial feature of the language. In fact, Python's role as an extension and interface language in larger systems is one of the reasons for its popularity and why it is often called a "scripting" language. Its design supports *hybrid* systems that mix components written in a variety of programming languages. Because different languages have different strengths, being able to pick and choose on a component-by-component basis is a powerful concept. You can add Python to the mix anywhere you need an easy-to-use and flexible language tool, without sacrificing raw speed where it matters.

For instance, compiled languages such as C and C++ are optimized for speed of *execution*, but are complex to program—for developers, and especially for end users. Because Python is optimized for speed of *development*, using Python scripts to control or customize software components written in C or C++ can yield more flexible systems and dramatically faster development modes. Moreover, systems designed to delegate customizations to Python scripts don't need to be shipped with full source code and don't require end users to learn complex or proprietary languages. Moving selected components of a pure Python program to C can also optimize program performance.

Integration Modes

The last two technical chapters of this book introduce Python's tools for interfacing to the outside world and discuss both its ability to be used as an embedded language tool in other systems and its interfaces for extending Python scripts with new modules and types implemented in C-compatible languages. We'll also briefly explore other integration techniques that are less C specific, such as the Component Object Model (COM) and Jython.

Our focus in these chapters is on tight integration—where control is transferred between languages by a simple, direct, and fast in-process function call. Although it is also possible to link components of an application less directly using Inter-Process Communication (IPC) and networking tools such as sockets and pipes that we explored earlier in the book, we are interested in this part of the book in more direct and efficient techniques.

When you mix Python with components written in C (or other compiled languages) either Python or C can be "on top." Because of that, there are two distinct integration modes and two distinct APIs:

The extending interface
> For running compiled C library code from Python programs

The embedding interface
> For running Python code from compiled C programs

Extending generally has three main roles: to optimize programs—recoding parts of a program in C is a last-resort performance boost; to leverage existing libraries—opening them up for use in Python code extends their reach; and to allow Python programs to do things not directly supported by the language—Python code cannot normally access devices at absolute memory addresses, for instance, but can call C functions that do. For example, the NumPy package for Python is largely an instance of extending at work: by integrating optimized numeric libraries, it turns Python into a flexible and efficient system that some compare to Matlab.

Embedding typically takes the role of customization—by running user-configurable Python code, a system can be modified without shipping or building its full source code. For instance, some game systems provide a Python customization layer that can be used to modify the game or characters. Embedding is also sometimes used to route events to Python coded handlers. Python GUI toolkits, for example, usually employ embedding.

Figure 22-1 sketches this traditional dual-mode integration model. In extending, control passes from Python through a glue layer on its way to C code. In embedding, C code processes Python objects and runs Python code by calling Python C API functions. In some models, things are not as clear-cut. For example, in the COM and CORBA systems, calls are passed through different kinds of intermediaries. Under cytpes, Python scripts make library calls rather than employing glue code. And in systems such as Pyrex, things are more different still. We will meet such alternative systems later in this part of the book. For now, our focus is on traditional Python/C integration models.

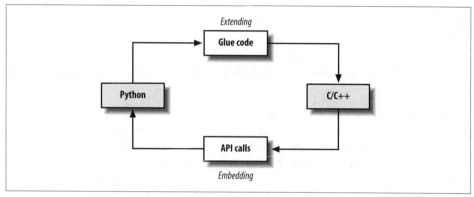

Figure 22-1. Traditional integration model

This chapter covers extending, and the next explores embedding. Although we will study these topics in isolation, keep in mind that many systems combine the two techniques. For instance, embedded Python code run from C can also import and call linked-in C extensions to interface with the enclosing application. And in call-back-based systems, C code initially accessed through extending interfaces may later use embedding techniques to run Python callback handlers on events.

For example, when we created buttons with Python's Tkinter GUI library earlier in the book, we called out to a C library through the extending API. When our GUI's user later clicked those buttons, the GUI C library caught the event and routed it to our Python functions with embedding. Although most of the details are hidden to Python code, control jumps often and freely between languages in such systems. Python has an open and reentrant architecture that lets you mix languages arbitrarily.

Presentation Notes

Before we get into details, I should also mention that Python/C integration is a big topic. In principle, the entire set of *extern* C functions in the Python system makes up its runtime interface. Because of that, these next two chapters focus on the tools commonly used to implement integration with external components—just enough to get you started.

For additional examples beyond this book and its examples distribution, see the Python source code itself; its *Modules* and *Objects* directories are a wealth of code resources. Most of the Python built-ins we have used in this book—from simple things such as integers and strings to more advanced tools such as files, system calls, Tkinter, and the DBM files underlying shelves. Their utilization of integration APIs can be studied in Python's source code distribution as models for extensions of your own.

In addition, Python's *Extending and Embedding* and *Python/C API* manuals are now reasonably complete, and they provide supplemental information to the presentation here. If you plan to do integration, you should browse these as a next step. For example, the manuals go into additional details about C extensions in threaded programs and multiple interpreters in embedded programs, which we will largely finesse here.

These chapters also assume that you know basic C programming concepts. If you don't, you won't miss much by skipping or skimming these chapters. Typically, C developers code the extending and embedding interfaces of a system, and others do the bulk of the system's programming with Python alone. But if you know enough about C programming to recognize a need for an extension language, you probably already have the required background knowledge for this chapter.

The good news in both chapters is that much of the complexity inherent in integrating Python with a static compiled language such as C can be automated with tools in the extension domain and higher-level APIs in the embedding world. For example, in this chapter we begin with a brief look at basic C API use, but then quickly move onto using the automated SWIG integration code generator in three examples and introduce alternatives such as ctypes, Pyrex, and Boost.Python at the end of the chapter. The next chapter takes a similar approach to embedding, with a basic introduction followed by a higher-level library. For now, let's get started with some extending fundamentals.

C Extensions Overview

Because Python itself is coded in C today, compiled Python extensions can be coded in any language that is C compatible in terms of call stacks and linking. That includes C, but also C++ with appropriate "extern C" declarations (which are automatically provided in Python header files). Regardless of the implementation language, the compiled Python extensions language can take two forms:

C modules
    These look and feel to their clients like Python module files

C types
    These behave like standard built-in types (numbers, lists, and so on)

Generally, C extension modules are used to implement flat function libraries, and they wind up appearing as importable modules to Python code (hence their name). C extension types are used to code objects that generate multiple instances and may optionally support expression operators much like classes. Because built-in types are really just precoded C extension types, your C extension types can do anything that built-in types can: method calls, addition, indexing, slicing, and so on.*

Moreover, C extension types today may provide a class-like interface, and so can support customization by either subclassing or coding "wrapper" classes as frontend interfaces to the type. For instance, as we saw in Chapter 20, the Python list object may now be customized by direct subclassing.

To make the interface work, both C modules and types must provide a layer of "glue" code that translates calls and data between the two languages. This layer registers C-coded operations with the Python interpreter as C function pointers. In all cases, the C layer is responsible for converting arguments passed from Python to C form and for converting results from C to Python form. Python scripts simply import C extensions and use them as though they were really coded in Python. Because C code does all the translation work, the interface is very seamless and simple in Python scripts.

C modules and types are also responsible for communicating errors back to Python, detecting errors raised by Python API calls, and managing garbage-collector reference counters on objects retained by the C layer indefinitely—Python objects held by your C code won't be garbage-collected as long as you make sure their reference counts don't fall to zero. Once coded, C modules and types may be linked to Python either statically (by rebuilding Python) or dynamically (when first imported). Thereafter, the C extension becomes another toolkit available for use in Python scripts.

A Simple C Extension Module

At least that's the short story; we need to turn to some code to make this more concrete. C types generally export a C module with a constructor function. Because of that, and because they are simpler, let's start off by studying the basics of C *module* coding with a quick example.

As mentioned, when you add new or existing C components to Python, you need to code an interface ("glue") logic layer in C that handles cross-language dispatching and data translation. The C source file in Example 22-1 shows how to code one by hand. It implements a simple C extension module named hello for use in Python scripts, with a function named message that simply returns its input string argument with extra text prepended. Python scripts will call this function as usual, but this one is coded in C, not in Python.

---

* In fact, every time you make an integer or string in Python, you generate a new C type instance object (whether you know it or not). This isn't as inefficient as you may think, though; as we'll see, type operations are dispatched through fast C pointers, and Python internally caches some integers and strings to avoid object creation when possible.

Example 22-1. PP3E\Integrate\Extend\Hello\hello.c

```c
/******************************************************************
 * A simple C extension module for Python, called "hello"; compile
 * this into a ".so" on python path, import and call hello.message;
 ******************************************************************/

#include <Python.h>
#include <string.h>

/* module functions */
static PyObject *                                  /* returns object */
message(PyObject *self, PyObject *args)            /* self unused in modules */
{                                                  /* args from Python call */
    char *fromPython, result[64];
    if (! PyArg_Parse(args, "(s)", &fromPython))   /* convert Python -> C */
        return NULL;                               /* null=raise exception */
    else {
        strcpy(result, "Hello, ");                 /* build up C string */
        strcat(result, fromPython);                /* add passed Python string */
        return Py_BuildValue("s", result);         /* convert C -> Python */
    }
}

/* registration table  */
static struct PyMethodDef hello_methods[] = {
    {"message", message, 1},        /* method name, C func ptr, always-tuple */
    {NULL, NULL}                    /* end of table marker */
};
,
/* module initializer */
void inithello( )                          /* called on first import */
{                                          /* name matters if loaded dynamically */
    (void) Py_InitModule("hello", hello_methods);   /* mod name, table ptr */
}
```

Ultimately, Python code will call this C file's message function, passing in a string object and getting back a new string object. First, though, it has to be somehow linked into the Python interpreter. To use this C file in a Python script, compile it into a dynamically loadable object file (e.g., *hello.so* on Linux, *hello.dll* under Cygwin on Windows) with a makefile like the one listed in Example 22-2, and drop the resulting object file into a directory listed on your module import search path exactly as though it were a *.py* or *.pyc* file.

Example 22-2. PP3E\Integrate\Extend\Hello\makefile.hello

```
##############################################################
# Compile hello.c into a shareable object file on Cygwin,
# to be loaded dynamically when first imported by Python.
##############################################################

PYLIB = /usr/bin
PYINC = /usr/include/python2.4
```

Example 22-2. PP3E\Integrate\Extend\Hello\makefile.hello (continued)

```
hello.dll: hello.c
        gcc hello.c -g -I$(PYINC) -shared -L$(PYLIB) -lpython2.4 -o hello.dll

clean:
        rm -f hello.dll core
```

This is a Cygwin makefile that uses gcc to compile our C code; other platforms are analogous but will vary. As mentioned in Chapter 5 in the sidebar "Forking on Windows with Cygwin," Cygwin provides a Unix-like environment and libraries on Windows. To work along with the examples here, either see *http://www.cygwin.com* for download details or change the makefiles listed per your compiler and platform requirements. Be sure to include the path to Python's install directory with -I flags to access Python include (a.k.a. header) files, as well as the path to the Python binary library file with -L flags, if needed.

Now, to use the makefile in Example 22-2 to build the extension module in Example 22-1, simply type a standard make command at your shell (the Cygwin shell is used here):

```
.../PP3E/Integrate/Extend/Hello$ make -f makefile.hello
gcc hello.c -g -I/usr/include/python2.4 -shared
                   -L/usr/bin -lpython2.4 -o hello.dll
```

This generates a shareable object file—a *.dll* under Cygwin on Windows. When compiled this way, Python automatically loads and links the C module when it is first imported by a Python script. At import time, the *.dll* binary library file will be located in a directory on the Python import search path, just like a *.py* file. Because Python always searches the current working directory on imports, this chapter's examples will run from the directory you compile them in (.) without any file copies or moves. In larger systems, you will generally place compiled extensions in a directory listed in PYTHONPATH or *.pth* files instead.

Finally, to call the C function from a Python program, simply import the module hello and call its hello.message function with a string; you'll get back a normal Python string:

```
.../PP3E/Integrate/Extend/Hello$ python
>>> import hello                          # import a C module
>>> hello.message('world')               # call a C function
'Hello, world'
>>> hello.message('extending')
'Hello, extending'
```

And that's it—you've just called an integrated C module's function from Python. The most important thing to notice here is that the C function looks exactly as if it were coded in Python. Python callers send and receive normal string objects from the call; the Python interpreter handles routing calls to the C function, and the C function itself handles Python/C data conversion chores.

In fact, there is little to distinguish hello as a C extension module at all, apart from its filename. Python code imports the module and fetches its attributes as if it had been written in Python. C extension modules even respond to dir calls as usual and have the standard module and filename attributes (though the filename doesn't end in a *.py* or *.pyc* this time around):

```
>>> dir(hello)                                    # C module attributes
['__doc__', '__file__', '__name__', 'message']

>>> hello.__name__, hello.__file__
('hello', 'hello.dll')

>>> hello.message                                 # a C function object
<built-in function message>
>>> hello                                         # a C module object
<module 'hello' from 'hello.dll'>
```

Like any module in Python, you can also access the C extension from a script file. The Python file in Example 22-3, for instance, imports and uses the C extension module.

Example 22-3. PP3E\Integrate\Extend\Hello\hellouse.py

```
import hello

print hello.message('C')
print hello.message('module ' + hello.__file__)

for i in range(3):
    print hello.message(str(i))
```

Run this script as any other—when the script first imports the module hello, Python automatically finds the C module's *.dll* object file in a directory on the module search path and links it into the process dynamically. All of this script's output represents strings returned from the C function in the file *hello.c*:

```
.../PP3E/Integrate/Extend/Hello$ python hellouse.py
Hello, C
Hello, module /cygdrive/c/.../PP3E/Integrate/Extend/Hello/hello.dll
Hello, 0
Hello, 1
Hello, 2
```

Extension Module Details

Now that I've shown you the somewhat longer story, let's fill in the rest. The next few sections go into more detail on compilation and linking, code structure, data conversions, error handling, and reference counts. These are core ideas in Python C extensions—some of which we will later learn you can often largely forget.

Compilation and Linking

You always must compile C extension files such as the *hello.c* example and somehow link them with the Python interpreter to make them accessible to Python scripts, but there is wide variability on how you might go about doing so. For example, a rule of the following form could be used to compile this C file on Linux too:

```
hello.so: hello.c
    gcc hello.c -c -g -fpic -I$(PYINC) -o hello.o
    gcc -shared hello.o -o hello.so
    rm -f hello.o
```

To compile the C file into a shareable object file on Solaris, you might instead say something like this:

```
hello.so: hello.c
    cc hello.c -c -KPIC -o hello.o
    ld -G hello.o -o hello.so
    rm hello.o
```

On other platforms, it's more different still. Because compiler options vary widely, you'll want to consult your C or C++ compiler's documentation or Python's extension manuals for platform- and compiler-specific details. The point is to determine how to compile a C source file into your platform's notion of a shareable or dynamically loaded object file. Once you have, the rest is easy; Python supports dynamic loading of C extensions on all major platforms today.

Because build details vary so widely from machine to machine (and even compiler to compiler), the build scripts in this book will take some liberties with platform details. In general, most are shown under the Cygwin Unix-like environment on Windows, partly because it is a simpler alternative to a full Linux install and partly because this writer's background is primarily in Unix development. Be sure to translate for your own context. If you use standard Windows build tools, see also the directories *PC* and *PCbuild* in Python's current source distribution for pointers.

Dynamic binding

Technically, what I've been showing you so far is called *dynamic binding*, and it represents one of two ways to link compiled C extensions with the Python interpreter. Since the alternative, *static binding*, is more complex, dynamic binding is almost always the way to go. To bind dynamically, simply follow these steps:

1. Compile *hello.c* into a shareable object file for your system (e.g., *.dll*, *.so*).
2. Put the object file in a directory on Python's module search path.

That is, once you've compiled the source code file into a shareable object file, simply copy or move the object file to a directory listed in sys.path (which includes PYTHONPATH and .pth path file settings). It will be automatically loaded and linked by the Python interpreter at runtime when the module is first imported anywhere in the

Python process—including imports from the interactive prompt, a standalone or embedded Python program, or a C API call.

Notice that the only non-static name in the *hello.c* example C file is the initialization function. Python calls this function by name after loading the object file, so its name must be a C global and should generally be of the form initX, where X is both the name of the module in Python import statements and the name passed to Py_InitModule. All other names in C extension files are arbitrary because they are accessed by C pointer, not by name (more on this later). The name of the C source file is arbitrary too—at import time, Python cares only about the compiled object file.

Static binding

Although dynamic binding is preferred in most applications, static binding allows extensions to be added to the Python interpreter in a more permanent fashion. This is more complex, though, because you must rebuild Python itself, and hence you need access to the Python source distribution (an interpreter executable won't do). Moreover, static linking of extensions is prone to change over time, so you should consult the README file at the top of Python's source distribution tree for current details.[*]

In short, though, one way to statically link the extension of Example 22-1 is to add a line such as the following:

```
hello ~/PP3E/Integrate/Extend/Hello/hello.c
```

to the Modules/Setup configuration file in the Python source code tree (change the ~ if this isn't in your home directory). Alternatively, you can copy your C file to the *Modules* directory (or add a link to it there with an ln command) and add a line to Setup, such as hello hello.c.

Then, rebuild Python itself by running a make command at the top level of the Python source tree. Python reconstructs its own makefiles to include the module you added to Setup, such that your code becomes part of the interpreter and its libraries. In fact, there's really no distinction between C extensions written by Python users and services that are a standard part of the language; Python is built with this same interface. The full format of module declaration lines looks like this:

```
<module> ... [<sourceOrObjectFile> ...] [<cpparg> ...] [<library> ...]
```

---

[*] In fact, starting with Python 2.1, the *setup.py* script at the top of the source distribution attempts to detect which modules can be built, and it automatically compiles them using the distutils system described in the next section. The *setup.py* script is run by Python's make system after building a minimal interpreter. This process doesn't always work, though, and you can still customize the configuration by editing the *Modules/Setup* file. As a more recent alternative, see also the example lines in Python's *setup.py* for xxmodule.c.

Under this scheme, the name of the module's initialization function must match the name used in the Setup file, or you'll get linking errors when you rebuild Python. The name of the source or object file doesn't have to match the module name; the leftmost name is the resulting Python module's name. This process and syntax are prone to change over time, so again, be sure to consult the README file at the top of Python's source tree.

Static versus dynamic binding

Static binding works on any platform and requires no extra makefile to compile extensions. It can be useful if you don't want to ship extensions as separate files, or if you're on a platform without dynamic linking support. Its downsides are that you need to update Python configuration files and rebuild the Python interpreter itself, so you must therefore have the full source distribution of Python to use static linking at all. Moreover, all statically linked extensions are always added to your interpreter, regardless of whether they are used by a particular program. This can needlessly increase the memory needed to run all Python programs.

With dynamic binding, you still need Python include files, but you can add C extensions even if all you have is a binary Python interpreter executable. Because extensions are separate object files, there is no need to rebuild Python itself or to access the full source distribution. And because object files are only loaded on demand in this mode, it generally makes for smaller executables too—Python loads into memory only the extensions actually imported by each program run. In other words, if you can use dynamic linking on your platform, you probably should.

Compiling with the Distutils System

As an alternative to makefiles, it's possible to specify compilation of C extensions by writing Python scripts that use tools in the Distutils package—a standard part of Python that is used to build, install, and distribute Python extensions coded in Python or C. Its larger goal is automated building of distributed packages on target machines.

We won't go into Distutils exhaustively in this text; see Python's standard distribution and installation manuals for more details. Among other things, Distutils is the de facto way to distribute larger Python packages these days. Its tools know how to install a system in the right place on target machines (usually, in Python's standard site-packages) and handle many platform-specific details that are tedious and error prone to accommodate manually.

For our purposes here, though, because Distutils also has built-in support for running common compilers on a variety of platforms (including Cygwin), it provides an alternative to makefiles for situations where the complexity of makefiles is either prohibitive or unwarranted. For example, to compile the C code in Example 22-1, we can code the makefile of Example 22-2, or we can code and run the Python script in Example 22-4.

Example 22-4. PP3E\Integrate\Extend\Hello\hellouse.py

```
# to build: python disthello.py build
# resulting dll shows up in build subdir

from distutils.core import setup, Extension
setup(ext_modules=[Extension('hello', ['hello.c'])])
```

Example 22-4 is a Python script run by Python; it is not a makefile. Moreover, there is nothing in it about a particular compiler or compiler options. Instead, the Distutils tools it employs automatically detect and run an appropriate compiler for the platform, using compiler options that are appropriate for building dynamically linked Python extensions on that platform. For the Cygwin test machine, gcc is used to generate a *.dll* dynamic library ready to be imported into a Python script—exactly like the result of the makefile in Example 22-2, but considerably simpler:

```
.../PP3E/Integrate/Extend/Hello$ python disthello.py build
running build
running build_ext
building 'hello' extension
creating build
creating build/temp.cygwin-1.5.19-i686-2.4
gcc -fno-strict-aliasing -DNDEBUG -g -O3 -Wall -Wstrict-prototypes
-I/usr/include/python2.4 -c hello.c -o build/temp.cygwin-1.5.19-i686-2.4/hello.o
hello.c:31: warning: function declaration isn't a prototype
creating build/lib.cygwin-1.5.19-i686-2.4
gcc -shared -Wl,--enable-auto-image-base build/temp.cygwin-1.5.19-i686-2.4/hello
.o -L/usr/lib/python2.4/config -lpython2.4
-o build/lib.cygwin-1.5.19-i686-2.4/hello.dll
```

The resulting binary library file shows up in the generated built subdirectory, but it's used in Python code just as before:

```
.../PP3E/Integrate/Extend/Hello$ cd build/lib.cygwin-1.5.19-i686-2.4/

.../PP3E/Integrate/Extend/Hello/build/lib.cygwin-1.5.19-i686-2.4$ ls
hello.dll

.../PP3E/Integrate/Extend/Hello/build/lib.cygwin-1.5.19-i686-2.4$ python
>>> import hello
>>> hello.__file__
'hello.dll'
>>> hello.message('distutils')
'Hello, distutils'
```

Distutils scripts can become much more complex in order to specify build options; for example, here is a slightly more verbose version of ours:

```
from distutils.core import setup, Extension
setup(name='hello',
      version='1.0',
      ext_modules=[Extension('hello', ['hello.c'])])
```

Unfortunately, further details about both Distutils and makefiles are beyond the scope of this chapter and book. Especially if you're not used to makefiles, see the

Python manuals for more details on Distutils. Makefiles are a traditional way to build code on some platforms and we will employ them in this book, but Distutils can sometimes be simpler in cases where they apply.

Anatomy of a C Extension Module

Though simple, the *hello.c* code of Example 22-1 illustrates the structure common to all C modules. Most of it is glue code, whose only purpose is to wrap the C string processing logic for use in Python scripts. In fact, although this structure can vary somewhat, this file consists of fairly typical boilerplate code:

Python header files

The C file first includes the standard *Python.h* header file (from the installed Python *Include* directory). This file defines almost every name exported by the Python API to C, and it serves as a starting point for exploring the API itself.

Method functions

The file then defines a function to be called from the Python interpreter in response to calls in Python programs. C functions receive two Python objects as input, and send either a Python object back to the interpreter as the result or a NULL to trigger an exception in the script (more on this later). In C, a PyObject* represents a generic Python object pointer; you can use more specific type names, but you don't always have to. C module functions can be declared C static (local to the file) because Python calls them by pointer, not by name.

Registration table

Near the end, the file provides an initialized table (array) that maps function *names* to function *pointers* (addresses). Names in this table become module attribute names that Python code uses to call the C functions. Pointers in this table are used by the interpreter to dispatch C function calls. In effect, the table "registers" attributes of the module. A NULL entry terminates the table.

Initialization function

Finally, the C file provides an initialization function, which Python calls the first time this module is imported into a Python program. This function calls the API function Py_InitModule to build up the new module's attribute dictionary from the entries in the registration table and create an entry for the C module on the sys.modules table (described in Chapter 3). Once so initialized, calls from Python are routed directly to the C function through the registration table's function pointers.

Data Conversions

C module functions are responsible for converting Python objects to and from C datatypes. In Example 22-1, message gets two Python input objects passed from the Python interpreter: args is a Python tuple holding the arguments passed from the

Python caller (the values listed in parentheses in a Python program), and self is ignored. It is useful only for extension types (discussed later in this chapter).

After finishing its business, the C function can return any of the following to the Python interpreter: a Python object (known in C as PyObject*), for an actual result; a Python None (known in C as Py_None), if the function returns no real result; or a C NULL pointer, to flag an error and raise a Python exception.

There are distinct API tools for handling input conversions (Python to C) and output conversions (C to Python). It's up to C functions to implement their call signatures (argument lists and types) by using these tools properly.

Python to C: using Python argument lists

When the C function is run, the arguments passed from a Python script are available in the args Python tuple object. The API function PyArg_Parse—and its cousin, PyArg_ParseTuple, which assumes it is converting a tuple object—is probably the easiest way to extract and convert passed arguments to C form.

PyArg_Parse takes a Python object, a format string, and a variable-length list of C target addresses. It converts the items in the tuple to C datatype values according to the format string, and it stores the results in the C variables whose addresses are passed in. The effect is much like C's scanf string function. For example, the hello module converts a passed-in Python string argument to a C char* using the s convert code:

```
PyArg_Parse(args, "(s)", &fromPython)      # or PyArg_ParseTuple(args, "s",...
```

To handle multiple arguments, simply string format codes together and include corresponding C targets for each code in the string. For instance, to convert an argument list holding a string, an integer, and another string to C, say this:

```
PyArg_Parse(args, "(sis)", &s1, &i, &s2)   # or PyArg_ParseTuple(args, "sis",...
```

To verify that no arguments were passed, use an empty format string like this:

```
PyArg_Parse(args, "()")
```

This API call checks that the number and types of the arguments passed from Python match the format string in the call. If there is a mismatch, it sets an exception and returns zero to C (more on errors shortly).

Python to C: using Python return values

As we'll see in Chapter 23, API functions may also return Python objects to C as results when Python is being run as an embedded language. Converting Python return values in this mode is almost the same as converting Python arguments passed to C extension functions, except that Python return values are not always tuples. To convert returned Python objects to C form, simply use PyArg_Parse. Unlike PyArg_ParseTuple, this call takes the same kinds of arguments but doesn't expect the Python object to be a tuple.

C to Python: returning values to Python

There are two ways to convert C data to Python objects: by using type-specific API functions or via the general object-builder function, Py_BuildValue. The latter is more general and is essentially the inverse of PyArg_Parse, in that Py_BuildValue converts C data to Python objects according to a format string. For instance, to make a Python string object from a C char*, the hello module uses an s convert code:

```
return Py_BuildValue("s", result)        # "result" is a C char []/*
```

More specific object constructors can be used instead:

```
return PyString_FromString(result)       # same effect
```

Both calls make a Python string object from a C character array pointer. See the now-standard Python extension and runtime API manuals for an exhaustive list of such calls available. Besides being easier to remember, though, Py_BuildValue has syntax that allows you to build lists in a single step, described next.

Common conversion codes

With a few exceptions, PyArg_Parse(Tuple) and Py_BuildValue use the same conversion codes in format strings. A list of all supported conversion codes appears in Python's extension manuals. The most commonly used are shown in Table 22-1; the tuple, list, and dictionary formats can be nested.

Table 22-1. Common Python/C data conversion codes

Format-string code	C datatype	Python object type
s	char*	String
s#	char*, int	String, length
i	int	Integer
l	long int	Integer
c	char	String
f	float	Floating-point
d	double	Floating-point
O	PyObject*	Raw (unconverted) object
O&	&converter, void*	Converted object (calls converter)
(*items*)	Targets or values	Nested tuple
[*items*]	Series of arguments/values	List
{*items*}	Series of key,value arguments	Dictionary

These codes are mostly what you'd expect (e.g., i maps between a C int and a Python integer object), but here are a few usage notes on this table's entries:

- Pass in the address of a char* for s codes when converting *to* C, not the address of a char array: Python copies out the address of an existing C string (and you must copy it to save it indefinitely on the C side: use strdup or similar).

- The 0 code is useful to pass raw Python objects between languages; once you have a raw object pointer, you can use lower-level API tools to access object attributes by name, index and slice sequences, and so on.

- The O& code lets you pass in C converter functions for custom conversions. This comes in handy for special processing to map an object to a C datatype not directly supported by conversion codes (for instance, when mapping to or from an entire C struct or C++ class instance). See the extensions manual for more details.

- The last two entries, [...] and {...}, are currently supported only by Py_BuildValue: you can construct lists and dictionaries with format strings, but you can't unpack them. Instead, the API includes type-specific routines for accessing sequence and mapping components given a raw object pointer.

PyArg_Parse supports some extra codes, which must not be nested in tuple formats ((...)):

| The remaining arguments are optional (varargs, much like the Python language's * arguments). The C targets are unchanged if arguments are missing in the Python tuple. For instance, si|sd requires two arguments but allows up to four.

:   The function name follows, for use in error messages set by the call (argument mismatches). Normally Python sets the error message to a generic string.

;   A full error message follows, running to the end of the format string.

This format code list isn't exhaustive, and the set of convert codes may expand over time; refer to Python's extension manual for further details.

Error Handling

When you write C extensions, you need to be aware that errors can occur on either side of the languages fence. The following sections address both possibilities.

Raising Python exceptions in C

C extension module functions return a C NULL value for the result object to flag an error. When control returns to Python, the NULL result triggers a normal Python exception in the Python code that called the C function. To name an exception, C code can also set the type and extra data of the exceptions it triggers. For instance, the PyErr_SetString API function sets the exception object to a Python object and sets the exception's extra data to a character string:

```
PyErr_SetString(ErrorObject, message)
```

We will use this in the next example to be more specific about exceptions raised when C detects an error. C modules may also set a built-in Python exception; for instance, returning NULL after saying this:

```
PyErr_SetString(PyExc_IndexError, "index out-of-bounds")
```

raises a standard Python `IndexError` exception with the message string data. When an error is raised inside a Python API function, both the exception object and its associated "extra data" are automatically set by Python; there is no need to set it again in the calling C function. For instance, when an argument-passing error is detected in the `PyArg_Parse` function, the `hello` stack module just returns `NULL` to propagate the exception to the enclosing Python layer, instead of setting its own message.

Detecting errors that occur in Python

Python API functions may be called from C extension functions or from an enclosing C layer when Python is embedded. In either case, C callers simply check the return value to detect errors raised in Python API functions. For pointer result functions, Python returns `NULL` pointers on errors. For integer result functions, Python generally returns a status code of -1 to flag an error and a 0 or positive value on success. (`PyArg_Parse` is an exception to this rule: it returns 0 when it detects an error.) To make your programs robust, you should check return codes for error indicators after most Python API calls; some calls can fail for reasons you may not have expected (e.g., memory overflow).

Reference Counts

The Python interpreter uses a reference-count scheme to implement garbage collection. Each Python object carries a count of the number of places it is referenced; when that count reaches zero, Python reclaims the object's memory space automatically. Normally, Python manages the reference counts for objects behind the scenes; Python programs simply make and use objects without concern for managing storage space.

When extending or embedding Python, though, integrated C code is responsible for managing the reference counts of the Python objects it uses. How important this becomes depends on how many raw Python objects a C module processes and which Python API functions it calls. In simple programs, reference counts are of minor, if any, concern; the `hello` module, for instance, makes no reference-count management calls at all.

When the API is used extensively, however, this task can become significant. In later examples, we'll see calls of these forms show up:

`Py_INCREF(obj)`
> Increments an object's reference count.

`Py_DECREF(obj)`
> Decrements an object's reference count (reclaims if zero).

`Py_XINCREF(obj)`
> Behaves similarly to `Py_INCREF(obj)`, but ignores a `NULL` object pointer.

```
Py_XDECREF(obj)
```
   Behaves similarly to py_DECREF(obj), but ignores a NULL object pointer.

C module functions are expected to return either an object with an incremented reference count or NULL to signal an error. As a general rule, API functions that create new objects increment their reference counts before returning them to C; unless a new object is to be passed back to Python, the C program that creates it should eventually decrement the object's counts. In the extending scenario, things are relatively simple; argument object reference counts need not be decremented, and new result objects are passed back to Python with their reference counts intact.

The upside of reference counts is that Python will never reclaim a Python object held by C as long as C increments the object's reference count (or doesn't decrement the count on an object it owns). Although it requires counter management calls, Python's garbage collector scheme is fairly well suited to C integration.

Other Extension Tasks: Threads

Some C extensions may be required to perform additional tasks beyond data conversion, error handling, and reference counting. For instance, long-running C extension functions in threaded applications must release and later reacquire the global interpreter lock, so as to allow Python language threads to run in parallel. See the introduction to this topic in Chapter 5 for background details. Calls to long-running tasks implemented in C extensions, for example, are normally wrapped up in two C macros:

```
Py_BEGIN_ALLOW_THREADS
...Perform a potentially blocking operation...
Py_END_ALLOW_THREADS
```

The first of these saves the thread state data structure in a local variable and releases the global lock; the second reacquires the lock and restores the thread state from the local variable. The net effect is to allow Python threads to run during the execution of the code in the enclosed block, instead of making them wait. The C code in the calling thread can run freely of and in parallel with other Python threads, as long as it doesn't reenter the Python C API until it reacquires the lock.

The API has addition thread calls, and depending on the application, there may be other C coding requirements in general. In deference to space, though, and because we're about to meet a tool that automates much of our integration work, we'll defer to Python's integration manuals for additional details.

The SWIG Integration Code Generator

But don't do that. As you can probably tell, manual coding of C extensions can become fairly involved (this is almost inevitable in C language work). I've introduced the basics in this chapter thus far so that you understand the underlying structure. But today, C extensions are usually better and more easily implemented with a tool that generates all the required integration glue code automatically. There are a variety of such tools for use in the Python world, including SIP, SWIG, and Boost.Python; we'll explore alternatives at the end of this chapter. Of these, the SWIG system is likely still the most widely used.

The Simplified Wrapper and Interface Generator (SWIG) is an open source system created by Dave Beazley and now developed by its community, much like Python. It uses C and C++ type declarations to generate complete C extension modules that integrate existing libraries for use in Python scripts. The generated C (and C++) extension modules are complete: they automatically handle data conversion, error protocols, reference-count management, and more.

That is, SWIG is a program that automatically generates all the glue code needed to plug C and C++ components into Python programs; simply run SWIG, compile its output, and your extension work is done. You still have to manage compilation and linking details, but the rest of the C extension task is largely performed by SWIG.

A Simple SWIG Example

To use SIWG, instead of writing all that C code in the prior sections, write the C function you want to use from Python without any Python integration logic at all, as though it is to be used from C alone. For instance, Example 22-5 is a recoding of Example 22-1 as a straight C function.

Example 22-5. PP3E\Integrate\Extend\HelloLib\hellolib.c

```
/**********************************************************************
 * A simple C library file, with a single function, "message",
 * which is to be made available for use in Python programs.
 * There is nothing about Python here--this C function can be
 * called from a C program, as well as Python (with glue code).
 **********************************************************************/

#include <string.h>
#include <hellolib.h>

static char result[64];                 /* this isn't exported */

char *
message(char *label)                     /* this is exported */
{
    strcpy(result, "Hello, ");           /* build up C string */
    strcat(result, label);               /* add passed-in label */
    return result;                       /* return a temporary */
}
```

While you're at it, define the usual C header file to declare the function externally, as shown in Example 22-6. This is probably overkill for such a small example, but it will prove a point.

Example 22-6. PP3E\Integrate\Extend\HelloLib\hellolib.h

```
/**********************************************************************
 * Define hellolib.c exports to the C namespace, not to Python
 * programs--the latter is defined by a method registration
 * table in a Python extension module's code, not by this .h;
 **********************************************************************/

extern char *message(char *label);
```

Now, instead of all the Python extension glue code shown in the prior sections, simply write a SWIG type declarations input file, as in Example 22-7.

Example 22-7. PP3E\Integrate\Extend\Swig\hellolib.i

```
/*****************************************************
 * Swig module description file, for a C lib file.
 * Generate by saying "swig -python hellolib.i".
 *****************************************************/

%module hellowrap

%{
#include <hellolib.h>
%}

extern char *message(char*);     /* or: %include "../HelloLib/hellolib.h"  */
                                 /* or: %include hellolib.h, and use -I arg */
```

This file spells out the C function's type signature. In general, SWIG scans files containing ANSI C and C++ declarations. Its input file can take the form of an interface description file (usually with a *.i* suffix) or a C/C++ header or source file. Interface files like this one are the most common input form; they can contain comments in C or C++ format, type declarations just like standard header files, and SWIG directives that all start with %. For example:

%module
: Sets the module's name as known to Python importers.

%{...%}
: Encloses code added to generated wrapper file verbatim.

extern *statements*
: Declare exports in normal ANSI C/C++ syntax.

%include
: Makes SWIG scan another file (-I flags give search paths).

In this example, SWIG could also be made to read the *hellolib.h* header file of Example 22-6 directly. But one of the advantages of writing special SWIG input files like *hellolib.i* is that you can pick and choose which functions are wrapped and exported to Python, and you may use directives to gain more control over the generation process.

SWIG is a utility program that you run from your build scripts; it is not a programming language, so there is not much more to show here. Simply add a step to your makefile that runs SWIG and compile its output to be linked with Python. Example 22-8 shows one way to do it on Cygwin.

Example 22-8. PP3E\Integrate\Extend\Swig\makefile.hellolib-swig

```
##################################################################
# Use SWIG to integrate hellolib.c for use in Python programs on
# Cygwin.  The DLL must have a leading "_" in its name in current
# SWIG (>1.3.13) because also makes a .py without "_" in its name.
##################################################################

PYLIB = /usr/bin
PYINC = /usr/include/python2.4
CLIB  = ../HelloLib

# the library plus its wrapper
_hellowrap.dll: hellolib_wrap.o $(CLIB)/hellolib.o
        gcc -shared hellolib_wrap.o $(CLIB)/hellolib.o \
                    -L$(PYLIB) -lpython2.4 -o $@

# generated wrapper module code
hellolib_wrap.o: hellolib_wrap.c $(CLIB)/hellolib.h
        gcc hellolib_wrap.c -g -I$(CLIB) -I$(PYINC) -c -o $@

hellolib_wrap.c: hellolib.i
        swig -python -I$(CLIB) hellolib.i

# C library code (in another directory)
$(CLIB)/hellolib.o: $(CLIB)/hellolib.c $(CLIB)/hellolib.h
        gcc $(CLIB)/hellolib.c -g -I$(CLIB) -c -o $(CLIB)/hellolib.o

clean:
        rm -f *.dll *.o *.pyc core
force:
        rm -f *.dll *.o *.pyc core hellolib_wrap.c hellowrap.py
```

When run on the *hellolib.i* input file by this makefile, SWIG generates two files:

hellolib_wrap.c
>   The generated C extension module glue code file.[*]

hellowrap.py
>   A Python module that imports the generated C extension module.

---

[*] You can wade through this generated file in the book's examples distribution if you are so inclined, though they are highly prone to change over time (in fact, the .py module generated by SWIG for this example is also new since the second edition of this book). Also see the file *PP3E\Integrate\Extend\HelloLib\hellolib_wrapper.c* in the book's examples distribution for a handcoded equivalent; it's shorter because SWIG also generates extra support code.

The former is named for the input file, and the later per the %module directive. Really, SWIG generates two modules today: it uses a combination of Python and C code to achieve the integration. Scripts ultimately import the generated Python module file, which internally imports the generated and compiled C module.

To build the C module, the makefile runs a compile after running SWIG, and then combines the result with the original C library code:

```
.../PP3E/Integrate/Extend/Swig$ make -f makefile.hellolib-swig force
rm -f *.dll *.o *.pyc core hellolib_wrap.c hellowrap.py

.../PP3E/Integrate/Extend/Swig$ ls
Environ  Shadow  hellolib.i  makefile.hellolib-swig

.../PP3E/Integrate/Extend/Swig$ make -f makefile.hellolib-swig
swig -python -I../HelloLib hellolib.i
gcc hellolib_wrap.c -g -I../HelloLib -I/usr/include/python2.4 -c
    -o hellolib_wrap.o
gcc -shared hellolib_wrap.o ../HelloLib/hellolib.o \
                    -L/usr/bin -lpython2.4 -o _hellowrap.dll

.../PP3E/Integrate/Extend/Swig$ ls
Environ  _hellowrap.dll  hellolib_wrap.c  hellowrap.py
Shadow   hellolib.i      hellolib_wrap.o  makefile.hellolib-swig
```

More specifically, the makefile runs SWIG over the input file, compiles the generated C glue code file into a *.o* object file, and then links it with *hellolib.c*'s compiled object file to produce *_hellowrap.dll*. The result is a dynamically loaded C extension module file ready to be imported by Python code. Like all modules, _hellowrap.dll must, along with hellowrap.py, be placed in a directory on your Python module search path (a period [.] will suffice if you're working in the directory where you compile).

Notice that the *.dll* file must be built with a leading underscore in its name; as of SWIG 1.3.14, this is required because SWIG also created the *.py* file of the same name without the underscore.

As usual in C development, you may have to barter with the makefile to get it to work on your system. Once you've run the makefile, though, you are finished. The generated C module is used exactly like the manually coded version shown before, except that SWIG has taken care of the complicated parts automatically:

```
.../PP3E/Integrate/Extend/Swig$ python
>>> import hellowrap                          # import glue + library file
>>> hellowrap.message('swig world')           # cwd always searched on imports
'Hello, swig world'

>>> hellowrap.__file__
'hellowrap.py'
>>> dir(hellowrap)
['__builtins__', '__doc__', '__file__', '__name__', '_hellowrap', ...]
```

In other words, once you learn how to use SWIG, you can largely forget all the integration coding details introduced in this chapter. In fact, SWIG is so adept at generating Python glue code that it's usually much easier and less error prone to code C extensions for Python as purely C- or C++-based libraries first, and later add them to Python by running their header files through SWIG, as demonstrated here.

SWIG Details

Of course, you must have SWIG before you can run SWIG; it's not part of Python itself. Unless it is already on your system, fetch SWIG off the Web and run its installer or build it from its source code. To do the latter, you'll need a C++ compiler; see SWIG's README file and web site for more details. SWIG is a command-line program and generally can be run just by saying the following:

```
swig -python hellolib.i
```

Along the way in this chapter, we'll meet a few more SWIG-based alternatives to the remaining examples. By way of introduction, here is a quick look at a few more SWIG highlights:

C++ "shadow" classes

> We'll learn how to use SWIG to integrate C++ classes for use in your Python scripts. When given C++ class declarations, SWIG generates glue code that makes C++ classes look just like Python classes in Python scripts. In fact, C++ classes *are* Python classes under SWIG; you get what SWIG calls a C++ shadow (or proxy) class that interfaces with a C++-coded extension module, which in turn talks to C++ classes using a function-based interface. Because the integration's outer layer is Python classes, those classes may be subclassed in Python and their instances processed with normal Python object syntax.

Variables

> Besides functions and C++ classes, SWIG can also wrap C global variables and constants for use in Python: they become attributes of an object named cvar inserted in generated modules (e.g., module.cvar.name fetches the value of C's variable name from a SWIG-generated wrapper module).

structs

> C structs are converted into a set of get and set *accessor* functions that are called to fetch and assign fields with a struct object pointer (e.g., module.Vector_fieldx_get(v) fetches C's Vector.fieldx from a Vector pointer v, like C's v->fieldx). Similar accessor functions are generated for data members and methods of C++ classes (the C++ class is roughly a struct with extra syntax), but the SWIG shadow class feature allows you to treat wrapped classes just like Python classes, instead of calling the lower-level accessor functions.

Other

> For C++, besides wrapping up classes and functions for use from Python, SWIG also generates code to support overloaded operators, routing of virtual method calls from C++ back to Python, templates, and much more.

Consult the SWIG Python user manual for the full scoop on its features. SWIG's feature set and implementation are both prone to change over time (e.g., its pointers are no longer strings, and Python new-style classes are employed in dual-mode proxy classes), so we'll defer to its documentation for more internals information.

Later in this chapter, we'll see SWIG in action two more times, wrapping up C environment calls and a C++ class. Although the SWIG examples in this book are simple, you should also know that SWIG handles industrial-strength libraries just as easily. For instance, Python developers have successfully used SWIG to integrate libraries as complex as Windows extensions and commonly used graphics APIs such as OpenGL.

SWIG can also generate integration code for other scripting languages such as Tcl and Perl. In fact, one of its underlying goals is to make components independent of scripting language choices—C/C++ libraries can be plugged into whatever scripting language you prefer to use (I prefer to use Python, but I might be biased). SWIG's support for things such as classes seems strongest for Python, though, probably because Python is considered to be strong in the classes department. As a language-neutral integration tool, SWIG addresses some of the same goals as systems such as COM and CORBA (described in Chapter 23), but it provides a code generation–based alternative rather than an object model.

You can find SWIG by a web search or by visiting its current home page on the Web at *http://www.swig.org*. Along with full source code, SWIG comes with outstanding documentation (including documentation specifically for Python). The documentation also describes how to build SWIG extensions with other platforms and compilers, including standard Windows without Cygwin.

Wrapping C Environment Calls

Let's move on to a more useful application of C extension modules. The handcoded C file in Example 22-9 integrates the standard C library's getenv and putenv shell environment variable calls for use in Python scripts.

Example 22-9. PP3E\Integrate\Extend\CEnviron\cenviron.c

```
/********************************************************************
 * A C extension module for Python, called "cenviron".  Wraps the
 * C library's getenv/putenv routines for use in Python programs.
 ********************************************************************/

#include <Python.h>
```

Example 22-9. PP3E\Integrate\Extend\CEnviron\cenviron.c (continued)

```c
#include <stdlib.h>
#include <string.h>

/***********************/
/* 1) module functions */
/***********************/

static PyObject *                                   /* returns object */
wrap_getenv(PyObject *self, PyObject *args)          /* self not used */
{                                                    /* args from python */
    char *varName, *varValue;
    PyObject *returnObj = NULL;                          /* null=exception */

    if (PyArg_Parse(args, "s", &varName)) {             /* Python -> C */
        varValue = getenv(varName);                     /* call C getenv */
        if (varValue != NULL)
            returnObj = Py_BuildValue("s", varValue);   /* C -> Python */
        else
            PyErr_SetString(PyExc_SystemError, "Error calling getenv");
    }
    return returnObj;
}

static PyObject *
wrap_putenv(PyObject *self, PyObject *args)
{
    char *varName, *varValue, *varAssign;
    PyObject *returnObj = NULL;

    if (PyArg_Parse(args, "(ss)", &varName, &varValue))
    {
        varAssign = malloc(strlen(varName) + strlen(varValue) + 2);
        sprintf(varAssign, "%s=%s", varName, varValue);
        if (putenv(varAssign) == 0) {
            Py_INCREF(Py_None);                      /* C call success */
            returnObj = Py_None;                     /* reference None */
        }
        else
            PyErr_SetString(PyExc_SystemError, "Error calling putenv");
    }
    return returnObj;
}

/**************************/
/* 2) registration table  */
/**************************/

static struct PyMethodDef cenviron_methods[] = {
    {"getenv", wrap_getenv},
    {"putenv", wrap_putenv},        /* method name, address */
    {NULL, NULL}
};
```

Example 22-9. PP3E\Integrate\Extend\CEnviron\cenviron.c (continued)

```
/************************/
/* 3) module initializer */
/************************/

void initcenviron()                    /* called on first import */
{
    (void) Py_InitModule("cenviron", cenviron_methods);   /* mod name, table */
}
```

This example is less useful now than it was in the first edition of this book—as we learned in Part II, not only can you fetch shell environment variables by indexing the os.environ table, but assigning to a key in this table automatically calls C's putenv to export the new setting to the C code layer in the process. That is, os.environ['key'] fetches the value of the shell variable 'key', and os.environ['key']=value assigns a variable both in Python and in C.

The second action—pushing assignments out to C—was added to Python releases after the first edition of this book was published. Besides demonstrating additional extension coding techniques, though, this example still serves a practical purpose: even today, changes made to shell variables by the C code linked into a Python process are not picked up when you index os.environ in Python code. That is, once your program starts, os.environ reflects only subsequent changes made by Python code.

Moreover, although Python now has both a putenv and a getenv call in its os module, their integration seems incomplete. Changes to os.environ call os.putenv, but direct calls to os.putenv do not update os.environ, so the two can become out of sync. And os.getenv today simply translates to an os.environ fetch, and hence will not pick up environment changes made in the process outside of Python code after startup time. This may rarely, if ever, be an issue for you, but this C extension module is not completely without purpose; to truly interface environment variables with linked-in C code, we need to call the C library routines directly.[*]

The *cenviron.c* C file in Example 22-9 creates a Python module called cenviron that does a bit more than the prior examples—it exports two functions, sets some exception descriptions explicitly, and makes a reference count call for the Python None object (it's not created anew, so we need to add a reference before passing it to Python). As before, to add this code to Python, compile and link into an object file; the Cygwin makefile in Example 22-10 builds the C source code for dynamic binding.

---

[*] This code is also open to customization (e.g., it can limit the set of shell variables read and written by checking names), but you could do the same by wrapping os.environ. In fact, because os.environ is simply a Python UserDict subclass that preloads shell variables on startup, you could *almost* add the required getenv call to load C layer changes by simply wrapping os.environ accesses in a Python class whose __getitem__ calls gentenv before passing the access off to os.environ. But you still need C's getenv call in the first place, and it's not directly available in os today.

Example 22-10. PP3E\Integrate\Extend\Cenviron\makefile.cenviron

```
#################################################################
# Compile cenviron.c into cenviron.dll--a shareable object file
# on Cygwin, which is loaded dynamically when first imported.
#################################################################

PYLIB = /usr/bin
PYINC = /usr/include/python2.4

cenviron.dll: cenviron.c
        gcc cenviron.c -g -I$(PYINC) -shared  -L$(PYLIB) -lpython2.4 -o $@

clean:
        rm -f *.pyc cenviron.dll
```

To build, type make -f makefile.cenviron at your shell. To run, make sure the *.dll* file
is in a directory on Python's module path (a period [.] works too):

```
.../PP3E/Integrate/Extend/Cenviron$ python
>>> import cenviron
>>> cenviron.getenv('USER')              # like os.environ[key] but refetched
'mark'
>>> cenviron.putenv('USER', 'gilligan')  # like os.environ[key]=value
>>> cenviron.getenv('USER')              # C sees the changes too
'gilligan'
```

As before, cenviron is a bona fide Python module object after it is imported, with all
the usual attached information:

```
>>> dir(cenviron)
['__doc__', '__file__', '__name__', 'getenv', 'putenv']
>>> cenviron.__file__
'./cenviron.dll'
>>> cenviron.__name__
'cenviron'
>>> cenviron.getenv
<built-in function getenv>
>>> cenviron
<module 'cenviron' from 'cenviron.dll'>
>>> cenviron.getenv('PYTHONPATH')
'/cygdrive/c/Mark/PP3E-cd/Examples'
```

Here is an example of the problem this module addresses (but you have to pretend
that some of these calls are made by linked-in C code, not by Python):

```
.../PP3E/Integrate/Extend/Cenviron$ python
>>> import os
>>> os.environ['USER']                   # initialized from the shell
'skipper'
>>> from cenviron import getenv, putenv  # direct C library call access
>>> getenv('USER')
'skipper'
>>> putenv('USER', 'gilligan')           # changes for C but not Python
>>> getenv('USER')
```

```
'gilligan'
>>> os.environ['USER']                          # oops--does not fetch values again
'skipper'
>>> os.getenv('USER')                           # ditto
'skipper'
```

Adding Wrapper Classes to Flat Libraries

As is, the C extension module exports a function-based interface, but you can wrap
its functions in Python code that makes the interface look any way you like. For
instance, Example 22-11 makes the functions accessible by dictionary indexing and
integrates with the os.environ object—it guarantees that the object will stay in sync
with fetches and changes made by calling our C extension functions.

Example 22-11. PP3E\Integrate\Extend\Cenviron\envmap.py

```
import os
from cenviron import getenv, putenv          # get C module's methods

class EnvMapping:                            # wrap in a Python class
    def __setitem__(self, key, value):
        os.environ[key] = value              # on writes: Env[key]=value
        putenv(key, value)                   # put in os.environ too

    def __getitem__(self, key):
        value = getenv(key)                  # on reads: Env[key]
        os.environ[key] = value              # integrity check
        return value

Env = EnvMapping()                           # make one instance
```

To use this module, clients may import its Env object using Env['var'] dictionary
syntax to refer to environment variables. And Example 22-12 exports the functions
as qualified attribute names rather than as calls—variables are referenced with Env.
var attribute syntax. The main point to notice here is that you can graft many different sorts of interface models on top of extension functions by providing Python
wrappers on top of the extension's C wrappers.

Example 22-12. PP3E\Integrate\Extend\Cenviron\envattr.py

```
import os
from cenviron import getenv, putenv          # get C module's methods

class EnvWrapper:                            # wrap in a Python class
    def __setattr__(self, name, value):
        os.environ[name] = value             # on writes: Env.name=value
        putenv(name, value)                  # put in os.environ too

    def __getattr__(self, name):
        value = getenv(name)                 # on reads: Env.name
        os.environ[name] = value             # integrity check
```

Example 22-12. PP3E\Integrate\Extend\Cenviron\envattr.py (continued)

```
      return value

Env = EnvWrapper( )                          # make one instance
```

But Don't Do That Either—SWIG

You can manually code extension modules like we just did, but you don't necessarily have to. Because this example really just wraps functions that already exist in standard C libraries, the entire *cenviron.c* C code file in Example 22-9 can be replaced with a simple SWIG input file that looks like Example 22-13.

Example 22-13. PP3E\Integrate\Extend\Swig\Environ\environ.i

```
/*************************************************************
 * Swig module description file, to generate all Python wrapper
 * code for C lib getenv/putenv calls: "swig -python environ.i".
 *************************************************************/

%module environ

extern char * getenv(const char *varname);
extern int    putenv(char *assignment);
```

And you're done. Well, almost; you still need to run this file through SWIG and compile its output. As before, simply add a SWIG step to your makefile and compile its output file into a shareable object, and you're in business. Example 22-14 is a Cygwin makefile that does the job.

Example 22-14. PP3E\Integrate\Extend\Swig\Environ\makefile.environ-swig

```
# build environ extension from SWIG generated code

PYLIB = /usr/bin
PYINC = /usr/include/python2.4

_environ.dll: environ_wrap.c
        gcc environ_wrap.c -g -I$(PYINC) -L$(PYLIB) -lpython2.4 -shared -o $@

environ_wrap.c: environ.i
        swig -python environ.i

clean:
        rm -f *.o *.dll *.pyc core environ_wrap.c environ.py
```

When run on *environ.i*, SWIG generates two files and two modules—environ.py (the Python interface module we import) and *environ_wrap.c* (the lower-level glue code module file we compile). Because the functions being wrapped here live in standard linked-in C libraries, there is nothing to combine with the generated code; this makefile simply runs SWIG and compiles the wrapper file into a C extension module, ready to be imported:

```
.../PP3E/Integrate/Extend/Swig/Environ$ make -f makefile.environ-swig
swig -python environ.i
gcc environ_wrap.c -g -I/usr/include/python2.4 -L/usr/bin -lpython2.4
    -shared -o _environ.dll
```

And now you're really done. The resulting C extension module is linked when imported, and it's used as before (except that SWIG handled all the gory bits):

```
.../PP3E/Integrate/Extend/Swig/Environ$ ls
_environ.dll  environ.py       makefile.environ-swig
environ.i     environ_wrap.c

.../PP3E/Integrate/Extend/Swig/Environ$ python
>>> import environ
>>> environ.getenv('USER')
'Mark Lutz'
>>> temp = 'USER=gilligan'              # use C lib call pattern now
>>> environ.putenv(temp)                # temp required in Cygwin
0
>>> environ.getenv('USER')
'gilligan'
>>> environ.__name__, environ.__file__, environ
('environ', 'environ.py', <module 'environ' from 'environ.py'>)
>>> dir(environ)
[ ... '_environ', 'getenv', 'putenv' ... ]
```

A C Extension Module String Stack

Let's kick it up another notch—the following C extension module implements a stack of strings for use in Python scripts. Example 22-15 demonstrates additional API calls, but it also serves as a basis of comparison. It is roughly equivalent to the Python stack module we coded earlier in Chapter 20, but it stacks only strings (not arbitrary objects), has limited string storage and stack lengths, and is written in C.

Alas, the last point makes for a complicated program listing—C code is never quite as nice to look at as equivalent Python code. C must declare variables, manage memory, implement data structures, and include lots of extra syntax. Unless you're a big fan of C, you should focus on the Python interface code in this file, not on the internals of its functions.

Example 22-15. PP3E\Integrate\Extend\Stacks\stackmod.c

```
/***************************************************
 * stackmod.c: a shared stack of character-strings;
 * a C extension module for use in Python programs;
 * linked into Python libraries or loaded on import;
 ***************************************************/
```

Example 22-15. PP3E\Integrate\Extend\Stacks\stackmod.c (continued)

```
#include "Python.h"              /* Python header files */
#include <stdio.h>               /* C header files */
#include <string.h>

static PyObject *ErrorObject;    /* locally raised exception */

#define onError(message) \
        { PyErr_SetString(ErrorObject, message); return NULL; }

/**************************************************************************
 * LOCAL LOGIC/DATA (THE STACK)
 **************************************************************************/

#define MAXCHARS 2048
#define MAXSTACK MAXCHARS

static int  top = 0;             /* index into 'stack' */
static int  len = 0;             /* size of 'strings' */
static char *stack[MAXSTACK];    /* pointers into 'strings' */
static char strings[MAXCHARS];   /* string-storage area */

/**************************************************************************
 * EXPORTED MODULE METHODS/FUNCTIONS
 **************************************************************************/

static PyObject *
stack_push(PyObject *self, PyObject *args)      /* args: (string) */
{
    char *pstr;
    if (!PyArg_ParseTuple(args, "s", &pstr))    /* convert args: Python->C */
        return NULL;                            /* NULL triggers exception */
    if (top == MAXSTACK)                         /* Python sets arg-error msg */
        onError("stack overflow")               /* iff maxstack < maxchars */
    if (len + strlen(pstr) + 1 >= MAXCHARS)
        onError("string-space overflow")
    else {
        strcpy(strings + len, pstr);            /* store in string-space */
        stack[top++] = &(strings[len]);         /* push start address */
        len += (strlen(pstr) + 1);              /* new string-space size */
        Py_INCREF(Py_None);                     /* a 'procedure' call */
        return Py_None;                         /* None: no errors */
    }
}

static PyObject *
stack_pop(PyObject *self, PyObject *args)
{                                               /* no arguments for pop */
    PyObject *pstr;
    if (!PyArg_ParseTuple(args, ""))            /* verify no args passed */
        return NULL;
    if (top == 0)
        onError("stack underflow")              /* return NULL = raise */
```

Example 22-15. PP3E\Integrate\Extend\Stacks\stackmod.c (continued)

```c
    else {
        pstr = Py_BuildValue("s", stack[--top]); /* convert result: C->Py */
        len -= (strlen(stack[top]) + 1);
        return pstr;                              /* return new Python string */
    }                                             /* pstr ref-count++ already */
}

static PyObject *
stack_top(PyObject *self, PyObject *args)     /* almost same as item(-1) */
{                                             /* but different errors */
    PyObject *result = stack_pop(self, args); /* get top string */
    if (result != NULL)
        len += (strlen(stack[top++]) + 1);    /* undo pop */
    return result;                            /* NULL or string object */
}

static PyObject *
stack_empty(PyObject *self, PyObject *args)   /* no args: '()' */
{
    if (!PyArg_ParseTuple(args, ""))          /* or PyArg_NoArgs */
        return NULL;
    return Py_BuildValue("i", top == 0);      /* Boolean: a Python int */
}

static PyObject *
stack_member(PyObject *self, PyObject *args)
{
    int i;
    char *pstr;
    if (!PyArg_ParseTuple(args, "s", &pstr))
        return NULL;
    for (i = 0; i < top; i++)                 /* find arg in stack */
        if (strcmp(pstr, stack[i]) == 0)
            return PyInt_FromLong(1);         /* send back a Python int */
    return PyInt_FromLong(0);                 /* same as Py_BuildValue("i" */
}

static PyObject *
stack_item(PyObject *self, PyObject *args)    /* return Python string or NULL */
{                                             /* inputs = (index): Python int */
    int index;
    if (!PyArg_ParseTuple(args, "i", &index))   /* convert args to C */
        return NULL;                            /* bad type or arg count? */
    if (index < 0)
        index = top + index;                    /* negative: offset from end */
    if (index < 0 || index >= top)
        onError("index out-of-bounds")          /* return NULL = 'raise' */
    else
        return Py_BuildValue("s", stack[index]); /* convert result to Python */
}                                                /* no need to INCREF new obj */

static PyObject *
```

Example 22-15. PP3E\Integrate\Extend\Stacks\stackmod.c (continued)

```
stack_len(PyObject *self, PyObject *args)       /* return a Python int or NULL */
{                                               /* no inputs */
    if (!PyArg_ParseTuple(args, ""))
        return NULL;
    return PyInt_FromLong(top);                 /* wrap in Python object */
}

static PyObject *
stack_dump(PyObject *self, PyObject *args)      /* not "print": reserved word */
{
    int i;
    if (!PyArg_ParseTuple(args, ""))
        return NULL;
    printf("[Stack:\n");
    for (i=top-1; i >= 0; i--)                  /* formatted output */
        printf("%d: '%s'\n", i, stack[i]);
    printf("]\n");
    Py_INCREF(Py_None);
    return Py_None;
}

/*****************************************************************************
 * METHOD REGISTRATION TABLE: NAME-STRING -> FUNCTION-POINTER
 *****************************************************************************/

static struct PyMethodDef stack_methods[] = {
  {"push",      stack_push,     1},             /* name, address */
  {"pop",       stack_pop,      1},             /* '1'=always tuple args */
  {"top",       stack_top,      1},
  {"empty",     stack_empty,    1},
  {"member",    stack_member,   1},
  {"item",      stack_item,     1},
  {"len",       stack_len,      1},
  {"dump",      stack_dump,     1},
  {NULL,        NULL}                           /* end, for initmodule */
};

/*****************************************************************************
 * INITIALIZATION FUNCTION (IMPORT-TIME)
 *****************************************************************************/

void
initstackmod()
{
    PyObject *m, *d;

    /* create the module and add the functions */
    m = Py_InitModule("stackmod", stack_methods);       /* registration hook */

    /* add symbolic constants to the module */
    d = PyModule_GetDict(m);
    ErrorObject = Py_BuildValue("s", "stackmod.error"); /* export exception */
```

Example 22-15. PP3E\Integrate\Extend\Stacks\stackmod.c (continued)

```
    PyDict_SetItemString(d, "error", ErrorObject);        /* add more if need */

    /* check for errors */
    if (PyErr_Occurred())
        Py_FatalError("can't initialize module stackmod");
}
```

This C extension file is compiled and statically or dynamically linked with the interpreter, just like in previous examples. The file *makefile.stack* in this book's examples distribution handles the build with a rule like this:

```
stackmod.dll: stackmod.c
        gcc stackmod.c -g -I$(PYINC) -shared -L$(PYLIB) -lpython2.4 -o $@
```

The whole point of implementing such a stack in a C extension module (apart from demonstrating API calls in a Python book) is *optimization*: in theory, this code should present a similar interface to the Python stack module we wrote earlier, but it should run considerably faster due to its C coding. The interface is roughly the same, though we've sacrificed some Python flexibility by moving to C—there are limits on size and stackable object types:

```
.../PP3E/Integrate/Extend/Stacks$ python
>>> import stackmod                       # load C module
>>> stackmod.push('new')                  # call C functions
>>> stackmod.dump()                       # dump format differs
[Stack:
0: 'new'
]
>>> for c in "SPAM": stackmod.push(c)
...
>>> stackmod.dump()
[Stack:
4: 'M'
3: 'A'
2: 'P'
1: 'S'
0: 'new'
]
>>> stackmod.len(), stackmod.top()
(5, 'M')
>>> x = stackmod.pop()
>>> x
'M'
>>> stackmod.dump()
[Stack:
3: 'A'
2: 'P'
1: 'S'
0: 'new'
]
>>> stackmod.push(99)
Traceback (most recent call last):
```

```
     File "<stdin>", line 1, in ?
   TypeError: argument 1 must be string, not int
```

Some of the C stack's type and size limitations could be removed by alternate C coding (which might eventually create something that looks and performs almost exactly like a Python built-in list). Before we check on this stack's speed, though, we'll see what can be done about also optimizing our stack *classes* with a C *type*.

But Don't Do That Either—SWIG

You can manually code extension modules like this, but you don't necessarily have to. As we saw earlier, if you instead code the stack module's functions without any notion of Python integration, they can be integrated into Python automatically by running their type signatures through SWIG. I haven't coded these functions that way here, because I also need to teach the underlying Python C extension API. But if I were asked to write a C string stack for Python in any other context, I'd probably do it with SWIG instead.

A C Extension Type String Stack

So far in this chapter, we've been dealing with C extension modules—flat function libraries. To implement multiple-instance objects in C, you need to code a C extension *type*, not a module. Like Python classes, C types generate multiple-instance objects and can overload (i.e., intercept and implement) Python expression operators and type operations. In recent Python releases, C types can also support subclassing just like Python classes.

One of the biggest drawbacks of types, though, is their size—to implement a realistically equipped C type, you need to code lots of not-very-pretty C code and fill out type descriptor tables with pointers to link up operation handlers. In fact, C extension types are so complex that I'm going to cut some details here. To give you a feel for the overall structure, Example 22-16 presents a C string stack type implementation, but with the bodies of all its functions stripped out. For the complete implementation, see this file in the book's examples distribution.

This C type roughly implements the same interface as the stack classes we met in Chapter 20, but it imposes a few limits on the stack itself. The stripped parts use the same algorithms as the C module in Example 22-15, but they operate on the passed-in self object, which now refers to the particular type instance object being processed, just as the first argument does in class methods. In types, self is a pointer to an allocated C struct that represents a type instance object.

Please note that the C API is prone to frequent changes, especially for C extension types. Although the code of this book's stack type example has been updated and retested for each edition, it may in fact not completely reflect current practice by the time you read these words.

Even as is, although it works as shown, this example does not support new, advanced C type concepts such as support for subclassing. Because this is such a volatile topic, the example was almost cut from this edition completely, but was retained in abbreviated form just to give you a sampling of the general flavor of C types. To code types of your own, you will want to explore additional resources.

For more up-to-date details on C types, consult Python's now thorough *Extending and Embedding* manual. And for more complete examples, see the *Objects* directory in the Python source distribution tree—all of Python's own datatypes are merely precoded C extension types that utilize the same interfaces and demonstrate best practice usage better than the static nature of books allows.

Of special interest, see Python 2.4's Objects/xxmodule.c for example C type code. Type descriptor layouts, described shortly, are perhaps the most prone to change over time; consult the file *Include/object.h* in the Python distribution for an up-to-date list of fields. Some new Python releases may also require that C types written to work with earlier releases be recompiled to pick up descriptor changes.

Finally, if it seems like C types are complex, transitory, and error prone, it's because they are. Because many developers will find higher-level tools such as SWIG to be more reasonable alternatives to hand-coded C types anyhow, this section is not designed to be complete.

Having said all that, the C extension type in Example 22-16 does work, and it demonstrates the basics of the model. Let's take a quick look.

Example 22-16. PP3E\Integrate\Extend\Stacks\stacktyp.c

```
/***************************************************
 * stacktyp.c: a character-string stack datatype;
 * a C extension type, for use in Python programs;
 * stacktype module clients can make multiple stacks;
 * similar to stackmod, but 'self' is the instance,
 * and we can overload sequence operators here;
 ***************************************************/

#include "Python.h"

static PyObject *ErrorObject;      /* local exception */
#define onError(message) \
        { PyErr_SetString(ErrorObject, message); return NULL; }


/**************************************************************************
 * STACK-TYPE INFORMATION
 **************************************************************************/
```

Example 22-16. PP3E\Integrate\Extend\Stacks\stacktyp.c (continued)

```c
#define MAXCHARS 2048
#define MAXSTACK MAXCHARS

typedef struct {                    /* stack instance object format */
    PyObject_HEAD                   /* Python header: ref-count + &typeobject */
    int top, len;
    char *stack[MAXSTACK];          /* per-instance state info */
    char strings[MAXCHARS];         /* same as stackmod, but multiple copies */
} stackobject;

/***************************************************************************
 * INSTANCE METHODS
 **************************************************************************/

static PyObject *               /* on "instance.push(arg)" */
stack_push(self, args)          /* 'self' is the stack instance object */
    stackobject *self;          /* 'args' are args passed to self.push method */
    PyObject    *args;
{   ...
}
static PyObject *
stack_pop(self, args)
    stackobject *self;
    PyObject    *args;          /* on "instance.pop( )" */
{   ...
}
static PyObject *
stack_top(self, args)
    stackobject *self;
    PyObject    *args;
{   ...
}
static PyObject *
stack_empty(self, args)
    stackobject *self;
    PyObject    *args;
{   ...
}
static struct PyMethodDef stack_methods[] = {    /* instance methods */
 {"push",       stack_push,     1},              /* name/address table */
 {"pop",        stack_pop,      1},              /* like list append,sort */
 {"top",        stack_top,      1},
 {"empty",      stack_empty,    1},              /* extra ops besides optrs */
 {NULL,         NULL}                            /* end, for getattr here */
};

/***************************************************************************
 * BASIC TYPE-OPERATIONS
 **************************************************************************/

static stackobject *            /* on "x = stacktype.Stack( )" */
newstackobject( )               /* instance constructor function */
```

Example 22-16. PP3E\Integrate\Extend\Stacks\stacktyp.c (continued)

```c
{   ...                             /* these don't get an 'args' input */
}
static void                   /* instance destructor function */
stack_dealloc(self)           /* when reference-count reaches zero */
    stackobject *self;
{   ...                             /* do cleanup activity */
}
static int
stack_print(self, fp, flags)
    stackobject *self;
    FILE *fp;
    int flags;                /* print self to file */
{   ...
}
static PyObject *
stack_getattr(self, name)     /* on "instance.attr" reference  */
    stackobject *self;        /* make a bound-method or member */
    char *name;
{   ...
}
static int
stack_compare(v, w)           /* on all comparisons */
    stackobject *v, *w;
{   ...
}


/***************************************************************************
 * SEQUENCE TYPE-OPERATIONS
 ***************************************************************************/

static int
stack_length(self)
    stackobject *self;              /* called on "len(instance)" */
{   ...
}
static PyObject *
stack_concat(self, other)
    stackobject *self;              /* on "instance + other" */
    PyObject    *other;             /* 'self' is the instance */
{   ...
}
static PyObject *
stack_repeat(self, n)             /* on "instance * N" */
    stackobject *self;              /* new stack = repeat self n times */
    int n;
{   ...
}
static PyObject *
stack_item(self, index)           /* on "instance[offset]", "in/for" */
    stackobject *self;              /* return the i-th item of self */
    int index;                      /* negative index pre-adjusted */
{   ...
}
```

Example 22-16. PP3E\Integrate\Extend\Stacks\stacktyp.c (continued)

```
static PyObject *
stack_slice(self, ilow, ihigh)
    stackobject *self;              /* on "instance[ilow:ihigh]" */
    int ilow, ihigh;               /* negative-adjusted, not scaled */
{   ...
}


/****************************************************************************
 * TYPE DESCRIPTORS
 ****************************************************************************/

static PySequenceMethods stack_as_sequence = {  /* sequence supplement     */
    (inquiry)        stack_length,      /* sq_length    "len(x)"    */
    (binaryfunc)     stack_concat,      /* sq_concat    "x + y"     */
    (intargfunc)     stack_repeat,      /* sq_repeat    "x * n"     */
    (intargfunc)     stack_item,        /* sq_item      "x[i], in"  */
    (intintargfunc)  stack_slice,       /* sq_slice     "x[i:j]"    */
    (intobjargproc)  0,                 /* sq_ass_item  "x[i] = v"  */
    (intintobjargproc) 0,               /* sq_ass_slice "x[i:j]=v"  */
};


/* The ob_type field must be initialized in the module init
   function to be portable to Windows without using C++. */

static PyTypeObject Stacktype = {       /* main Python type-descriptor */
  /* type header */                     /* shared by all instances */
    PyObject_HEAD_INIT(NULL)            /* was PyObject_HEAD_INIT(&PyType_Type)*/
    0,                                  /* ob_size */
    "stack",                            /* tp_name */
    sizeof(stackobject),                /* tp_basicsize */
    0,                                  /* tp_itemsize */

  /* standard methods */
    (destructor)   stack_dealloc,       /* tp_dealloc  ref-count==0  */
    (printfunc)    stack_print,         /* tp_print    "print x"     */
    (getattrfunc)  stack_getattr,       /* tp_getattr  "x.attr"      */
    (setattrfunc)  0,                   /* tp_setattr  "x.attr=v"    */
    (cmpfunc)      stack_compare,       /* tp_compare  "x > y"       */
    (reprfunc)     0,                   /* tp_repr     `x`,repr,print */

  /* type categories */
    0,                                  /* tp_as_number   +,-,*,/,%,&,>>,...*/
    &stack_as_sequence,                 /* tp_as_sequence +,[i],[i:j],len, ...*/
    0,                                  /* tp_as_mapping  [key], len, ...*/

  /* more methods */
    (hashfunc)     0,                   /* tp_hash     "dict[x]" */
    (ternaryfunc)  0,                   /* tp_call     "x()"     */
    (reprfunc)     0,                   /* tp_str      "str(x)"  */

};  /* plus others: see Python's Include/object.h, Modules/xxmodule.c */
```

Example 22-16. PP3E\Integrate\Extend\Stacks\stacktyp.c (continued)

```c
/****************************************************************************
 * MODULE LOGIC
 ****************************************************************************/

static PyObject *
stacktype_new(self, args)               /* on "x = stacktype.Stack()" */
    PyObject *self;                     /* self not used */
    PyObject *args;                     /* constructor args */
{
    if (!PyArg_ParseTuple(args, ""))    /* Module-method function */
        return NULL;
    return (PyObject *)newstackobject(); /* make a new type-instance object */
}                                        /* the hook from module to type... */

static struct PyMethodDef stacktype_methods[] = {
    {"Stack",  stacktype_new,  1},          /* one function: make a stack */
    {NULL,     NULL}                         /* end marker, for initmodule */
};

void
initstacktype()                 /* on first "import stacktype" */
{
    PyObject *m, *d;

    /* finalize type object, setting type of new type object
       here for portability to Windows without requiring C++ */
    if (PyType_Ready(&Stacktype) < 0)
        return;

    m = Py_InitModule("stacktype", stacktype_methods);   /* make the module, */
    d = PyModule_GetDict(m);                              /* with 'Stack' func */
    ErrorObject = Py_BuildValue("s", "stacktype.error");
    PyDict_SetItemString(d, "error", ErrorObject);       /* export exception */
    if (PyErr_Occurred())
        Py_FatalError("can't initialize module stacktype");

}
```

Anatomy of a C Extension Type

Although most of the file *stacktyp.c* is missing, there is enough here to illustrate the global structure common to C type implementations:

Instance struct
> The file starts off by defining a C struct called stackobject that will be used to hold per-instance state information—each generated instance object gets a newly malloc'd copy of the struct. It serves the same function as class instance attribute dictionaries, and it contains data that was saved in global variables by the C stack module of the preceding section (Example 22-15).

Instance methods

As in the module, a set of instance methods follows next; they implement method calls such as push and pop. But here, method functions process the implied instance object, passed in to the self argument. This is similar in spirit to class methods. Type instance methods are looked up in the registration table of the code listing (Example 22-16) when accessed.

Basic type operations

Next, the file defines functions to handle basic operations common to all types: creation, printing, qualification, and so on. These functions have more specific type signatures than instance method handlers. The object creation handler allocates a new stack struct and initializes its header fields; the reference count is set to 1, and its type object pointer is set to the Stacktype type descriptor that appears later in the file.

Sequence operations

Functions for handling sequence type operations come next. Stacks respond to most sequence operators: len, +, *, and [i]. Much like the __getitem__ class method, the stack_item indexing handler performs indexing, but also in membership tests and for iterator loops. These latter two work by indexing an object until an IndexError exception is caught by Python.

Type descriptors

The type descriptor tables (really, structs) that appear near the end of the file are the crux of the matter for types—Python uses these tables to dispatch an operation performed on an instance object to the corresponding C handler function in this file. In fact, everything is routed through these tables; even method attribute lookups start by running a C stack_getattr function listed in the table (which in turn looks up the attribute name in a name/function-pointer table). The main Stacktype table includes a link to the supplemental stack_as_sequence table in which sequence operation handlers are registered; types can provide such tables to register handlers for mapping, number, and sequence operation sets.

See Python's integer and dictionary objects' source code for number and mapping examples; they are analogous to the sequence type here, but their operation tables vary. Descriptor layouts, like most C API tools, are prone to change over time, and you should always consult *Include/object.h* in the Python distribution for an up-to-date list of fields.

Constructor module

Besides defining a C type, this file also creates a simple C *module* at the end that exports a stacktype.Stack constructor function, which Python scripts call to generate new stack instance objects. The initialization function for this module is the only C name in this file that is not static (local to the file); everything else is reached by following pointers—from instance to type descriptor to C handler function.

Again, see this book's examples distribution for the full C stack type implementation. But to give you the general flavor of C type methods, here is what the C type's pop function looks like; compare this with the C module's pop function to see how the self argument is used to access per-instance information in types:

```
static PyObject *
stack_pop(self, args)
    stackobject *self;
    PyObject *args;                          /* on "instance.pop()" */
{
    PyObject *pstr;
    if (!PyArg_ParseTuple(args, ""))         /* verify no args passed */
        return NULL;
    if (self->top == 0)
        onError("stack underflow")           /* return NULL = raise */
    else {
        pstr = Py_BuildValue("s", self->stack[--self->top]);
        self->len -= (strlen(self->stack[self->top]) + 1);
        return pstr;
    }
}
```

Compiling and Running

This C extension file is compiled and dynamically or statically linked like previous examples; the file *makefile.stack* in the book's examples distribution handles the build like this:

```
PYLIB = /usr/bin
PYINC = /usr/include/python2.4

stacktype.dll: stacktyp.c
        gcc stacktyp.c -g -I$(PYINC) -shared -L$(PYLIB) -lpython2.4 -o $@
```

Once compiled, you can import the C module and make and use instances of the C type that it defines much as if it were a Python class. You would normally do this from a Python script, but the interactive prompt is a convenient place to test the basics:

```
.../PP3E/Integrate/Extend/Stacks$ python
>>> import stacktype                         # import C constructor module
>>> x = stacktype.Stack()                    # make C type instance object
>>> x.push('new')                            # call C type methods
>>> x                                        # call C type print handler
[Stack:
0: 'new'
]

>>> x[0]                                      # call C type index handler
'new'
>>> y = stacktype.Stack()                    # make another type instance
>>> for c in 'SPAM': y.push(c)               # a distinct stack object
...
```

```
>>> y
[Stack:
3: 'M'
2: 'A'
1: 'P'
0: 'S'
]

>>> z = x + y                              # call C type concat handler
>>> z
[Stack:
4: 'M'
3: 'A'
2: 'P'
1: 'S'
0: 'new'
]

>>> y.pop( )
'M'
>>> len(z), z[0], z[-1]                     # for loops work too (indexing)
(5, 'new', 'M')

>>> dir( stacktype)
['Stack', '__doc__', '__file__', '__name__', 'error']
>>> stacktype.__file__
'stacktype.dll'
```

Timing the C Implementations

So how did we do on the optimization front this time? Let's resurrect that timer
module we wrote back in Example 20-6 to compare the C stack module and type of
this chapter to the Python stack module and classes we coded in Chapter 20.
Example 22-17 calculates the system time in seconds that it takes to run tests on all
of this book's stack implementations.

Example 22-17. PP3E\Integrate\Extend\Stacks\exttime.py

```
#!/usr/local/bin/python
# time the C stack module and type extensions
# versus the object chapter's Python stack implementations

from PP3E.Dstruct.Basic.timer  import test     # second count function
from PP3E.Dstruct.Basic import stack1           # Python stack module
from PP3E.Dstruct.Basic import stack2           # Python stack class: +/slice
from PP3E.Dstruct.Basic import stack3           # Python stack class: tuples
from PP3E.Dstruct.Basic import stack4           # Python stack class: append/pop
import stackmod, stacktype                       # C extension type, module

from sys import argv
rept, pushes, pops, items = 200, 200, 200, 200  # default: 200 * (600 ops)
try:
    [rept, pushes, pops, items] = map(int, argv[1:])
```

Example 22-17. PP3E\Integrate\Extend\Stacks\exttime.py (continued)

```
except: pass
print 'reps=%d * [push=%d+pop=%d+fetch=%d]' % (rept, pushes, pops, items)

def moduleops(mod):
    for i in range(pushes): mod.push('hello')   # strings only for C
    for i in range(items):  t = mod.item(i)
    for i in range(pops):   mod.pop( )

def objectops(Maker):                           # type has no init args
    x = Maker( )                                # type or class instance
    for i in range(pushes): x.push('hello')     # strings only for C
    for i in range(items):  t = x[i]
    for i in range(pops):   x.pop( )

# test modules: python/c
print "Python module:", test(rept, moduleops, stack1)
print "C ext module: ", test(rept, moduleops, stackmod), '\n'

# test objects: class/type
print "Python simple Stack:", test(rept, objectops, stack2.Stack)
print "Python tuple  Stack:", test(rept, objectops, stack3.Stack)
print "Python append Stack:", test(rept, objectops, stack4.Stack)
print "C ext type Stack:    ", test(rept, objectops, stacktype.Stack)
```

Running this script under Cygwin on Windows produces the following results (as usual, these are prone to change over time; these tests were run under Python 2.4 on a 1.2 GHz machine). As we saw before, the Python tuple stack is slightly better than the Python in-place append stack in typical use (when the stack is only pushed and popped), but it is slower when indexed. The first test here runs 200 repetitions of 200 stack pushes and pops, or 80,000 stack operations (200×400); times listed are test duration seconds:

```
.../PP3E/Integrate/Extend/Stacks$ python exttime.py 200 200 200 0
reps=200 * [push=200+pop=200+fetch=0]
Python module: 0.35
C ext module:  0.07

Python simple Stack: 0.381
Python tuple  Stack: 0.11
Python append Stack: 0.13
C ext type Stack:    0.07

.../PP3E/Integrate/Extend/Stacks$ python exttime.py 100 300 300 0
reps=100 * [push=300+pop=300+fetch=0]
Python module: 0.33
C ext module:  0.06

Python simple Stack: 0.321
Python tuple  Stack: 0.08
Python append Stack: 0.09
C ext type Stack:    0.06
```

At least when there are no indexing operations on the stack, as in these two tests (just pushes and pops), the C type is only slightly faster than the best Python stack (tuples). In fact, the difference seems trivial; it's not exactly the kind of performance issue that would generate a bug report.

The C module comes in at roughly five times faster than the Python module, but these results are flawed. The stack1 Python module tested here uses the same slow stack implementation as the Python "simple" stack (stack2). If it was recoded to use the *tuple* stack representation used in Chapter 20, its speed would be similar to the "tuple" figures listed here and almost identical to the speed of the C module in the first two tests:

```
.../PP3E/Integrate/Extend/Stacks$ python exttime.py 200 200 200 50
reps=200 * [push=200+pop=200+fetch=50]
Python module: 0.36
C ext module:  0.08

Python simple Stack: 0.401
Python tuple  Stack: 0.24
Python append Stack: 0.15
C ext type Stack:    0.08

.../PP3E/Integrate/Extend/Stacks$ python exttime.py
reps=200 * [push=200+pop=200+fetch=200]
Python module: 0.44
C ext module:  0.12

Python simple Stack: 0.431
Python tuple  Stack: 1.983
Python append Stack: 0.19
C ext type Stack:    0.1
```

But under the different usage patterns simulated in these two tests, the C type wins the race. It is about twice as fast as the best Python stack (append) when indexing is added to the test mix, as illustrated by the two preceding test runs that ran with a nonzero fetch count. Similarly, the C module would be twice as fast as the best Python module coding in this case as well.

In other words, the fastest Python stacks are essentially as good as the C stacks if you stick to pushes and pops, but the C stacks are roughly twice as fast if any indexing is performed. Moreover, since you have to pick one representation, if indexing is possible at all you would likely pick the Python append stack; assuming they represent the best case, C stacks would always be twice as fast.

Of course, the measured time differences are so small that in many applications you won't care. Even at one million iterations, the best Python stack is still less than half a second slower than the C stack type:

```
.../PP3E/Integrate/Extend/Stacks$$ python exttime.py 2000 250 250 0
reps=2000 * [push=250+pop=250+fetch=0]
Python module: 4.686
C ext module:  0.952
```

```
Python simple Stack: 4.987
Python tuple  Stack: 1.352
Python append Stack: 1.572
C ext type Stack:    0.941
```

Further, in many ways, this is not quite an apples-to-apples comparison. The C stacks are much more difficult to program, and they achieve their speed by imposing substantial functional limits (as coded, the C module and type overflow at 342 pushes: 342 * 6 > 2048). But as a rule of thumb, C extensions can not only integrate existing components for use in Python scripts, they can also optimize time-critical components of pure Python programs. In other scenarios, migration to C might yield an even larger speedup.

On the other hand, C extensions should generally be used only as a last resort. As we learned earlier, algorithms and data structures are often bigger influences on program performance than implementation language. The fact that Python-coded tuple stacks are very nearly as fast as the C stacks under common usage patterns speaks volumes about the importance of data structure representation. Installing the Psyco just-in-time compiler for Python code might erase the remaining difference completely, but we'll leave this as a suggested exercise.

Older Timing Results

Interestingly, Python grew much faster between this book's first and second editions, relative to C. In the first edition, the C type was still almost three times faster than the best Python stack (tuples), even when no indexing was performed. Today, as in the second edition, it's almost a draw. One might infer from this that C migrations have become one-third as important as they once were.

For comparison, here were the results of this script in the second edition of this book, run on a 650 MHz machine under Python 1.5.2 and Linux. The results were relatively similar, though typically six or more times slower—owing likely to both Python and machine speedups:

```
.../PP3E/Integrate/Extend/Stacks$ python exttime.py 200 200 200 0
reps=200 * [push=200+pop=200+fetch=0]
Python module: 2.09
C ext module:  0.68

Python simple Stack: 2.15
Python tuple  Stack: 0.68
Python append Stack: 1.16
C ext type Stack:    0.5

.../PP3E/Integrate/Extend/Stacks$ python exttime.py 100 300 300 0
reps=100 * [push=300+pop=300+fetch=0]
Python module: 1.86
C ext module:  0.52
```

```
Python simple Stack: 1.91
Python tuple  Stack: 0.51
Python append Stack: 0.87
C ext type Stack:    0.38

.../PP3E/Integrate/Extend/Stacks$ python exttime.py 200 200 200 50
reps=200 * [push=200+pop=200+fetch=50]
Python module: 2.17
C ext module:  0.79

Python simple Stack: 2.24
Python tuple  Stack: 1.94
Python append Stack: 1.25
C ext type Stack:    0.52

.../PP3E/Integrate/Extend/Stacks$ python exttime.py
reps=200 * [push=200+pop=200+fetch=200]
Python module: 2.42
C ext module:  1.1

Python simple Stack: 2.54
Python tuple  Stack: 19.09
Python append Stack: 1.54
C ext type Stack:    0.63
```

But Don't Do That Either—SWIG

You can code C types manually like this—and in some applications, this approach
may make sense. But you don't necessarily have to—because SWIG knows how to
generate glue code for C++ classes, you can instead *automatically* generate all the C
extension and wrapper class code required to integrate such a stack object, simply by
running SWIG over an appropriate class declaration. The wrapped C++ class provides a multiple-instance datatype much like the C extension type presented in this
section, but SWIG handles language integration details. The next section shows
how.

Wrapping C++ Classes with SWIG

One of the more clever tricks SWIG can perform is class wrapper generation. Given a
C++ class declaration and special command-line settings, SWIG generates the
following:

- A C++-coded Python extension module with accessor functions that interface
  with the C++ class's methods and members
- A Python-coded module with a wrapper class (called a "shadow" or "proxy"
  class in SWIG-speak) that interfaces with the C++ class accessor functions
  module

As before, to use SWIG in this domain, write and debug your class as though it would be used only from C++. Then, simply run SWIG in your makefile to scan the C++ class declaration and compile and link its output. The end result is that by importing the shadow class in your Python scripts, you can utilize C++ classes as though they were really coded in Python. Not only can Python programs make and use instances of the C++ class, they can also customize it by subclassing the generated shadow class.

A Simple C++ Extension Class

To see how this works, we need a C++ class. To illustrate, let's code a simple one to be used in Python scripts.* The following C++ files define a Number class with three methods (add, sub, display), a data member (data), and a constructor and destructor. Example 22-18 shows the header file.

Example 22-18. PP3E\Integrate\Extend\Swig\Shadow\number.h

```
class Number
{
public:
    Number(int start);          // constructor
    ~Number();                  // destructor
    void add(int value);        // update data member
    void sub(int value);
    int  square();              // return a value
    void display();             // print data member
    int data;
};
```

Example 22-19 is the C++ class's implementation file; each method prints a message when called to trace class operations.

Example 22-19. PP3E\Integrate\Extend\Swig\Shadow\number.cxx

```
/////////////////////////////////////////////////////////////
// implement a C++ class, to be used from Python code or not;
// caveat: cout and print usually both work, but I ran into
// an issue on Cygwin that prompted printf due to lack of time
/////////////////////////////////////////////////////////////

#include "number.h"
#include "stdio.h"                    // versus #include "iostream.h"

Number::Number(int start) {
    data = start;                     // python print goes to stdout
    printf("Number: %d\n", data);     // cout << "Number: " << data << endl;
}
```

---

* For a more direct comparison, you could translate the stack type in Example 22-15 to a C++ class too, but that yields much more C++ code than I care to show in this Python book.

Example 22-19. PP3E\Integrate\Extend\Swig\Shadow\number.cxx (continued)

```
Number::~Number( ) {
    printf("~Number: %d\n", data);
}

void Number::add(int value) {
    data += value;
    printf("add %d\n", value);
}

void Number::sub(int value) {
    data -= value;
    printf("sub %d\n", value);
}

int Number::square( ) {
    printf("Square = ");
    return data * data;
}

void Number::display( ) {
    printf("Number = %d\n", data);
}
```

Just so that you can compare languages, the following is how this class is used in a C++ program. Example 22-20 makes a Number object, calls its methods, and fetches and sets its data attribute directly (C++ distinguishes between "members" and "methods," while they're usually both called "attributes" in Python).

Example 22-20. PP3E\Integrate\Extend\Swig\Shadow\main.cxx

```
#include "iostream.h"
#include "number.h"

main( )
{
    Number *num;
    num = new Number(1);          // make a C++ class instance
    num->add(4);                  // call its methods
    num->display( );
    num->sub(2);
    num->display( );
    cout << num->square( ) << endl;

    num->data = 99;               // set C++ data member
    cout << num->data << endl;    // fetch C++ data member
    num->display( );
    cout << num << endl;          // print raw instance ptr
    delete num;                   // run destructor
}
```

You can use the g++ command-line C++ compiler program to compile and run this code on Cygwin (it's the same on Linux). If you don't use a similar system, you'll have to extrapolate (there are far too many C++ compiler differences to list here). Type the compile command directly or use the cxxtest target in this directory's makefile, and then run the purely C++ program created:

```
.../PP3E/Integrate/Extend/Swig/Shadow$ make -f makefile.number-swig cxxtest
g++ main.cxx number.cxx -Wno-deprecated

.../PP3E/Integrate/Extend/Swig/Shadow$ ./a.exe
Number: 1
add 4
Number = 5
sub 2
Number = 3
Square = 9
99
Number = 99
0x4a0248
~Number: 99
```

Wrapping the C++ Class with SWIG

Let's get back to Python. To use the C++ Number class of the preceding section in Python scripts, you need to code or generate a glue logic layer between the two languages, just as in prior C extension examples. To generate that layer automatically, write a SWIG input file like the one shown in Example 22-21.

Example 22-21. PP3E\Integrate\Extend\Swig\Shadow\number.i

```
/*******************************************************
 * Swig module description file for wrapping a C++ class.
 * Generate by saying "swig -python -shadow number.i".
 * The C module is generated in file number_wrap.c; here,
 * module 'number' refers to the number.py shadow class.
 *******************************************************/

%module number

%{
#include "number.h"
%}

%include number.h
```

This interface file simply directs SWIG to read the C++ class's type signature information from the included *number.h* header file. SWIG uses the class declaration to generate two different Python modules again:

number_wrap.cxx
    A C++ extension module with class accessor functions.

number.py

A Python shadow class module that wraps accessor functions.

The former must be compiled into a binary library. The latter imports and uses the former and is the file that Python scripts ultimately import. As for simple functions, SWIG achieves the integration with a combination of Python and C++ code.

After running SWIG, the Cygwin makefile shown in Example 22-22 combines the generated number_wrap.cxx C++ wrapper code module with the C++ class implementation file to create a _number.dll—a dynamically loaded extension module that must be in a directory on your Python module search path when imported from a Python script, along with the generated number.py.

As before, the compiled C extension module must be named with a leading underscore in SWIG today: _number.dll, rather than the numberc.dll format used by earlier releases. The shadow class module number.py internally imports _number.dll.

Example 22-22. PP3E\Integrate\Extend\Swig\Shadow\makefile.number-swig

```
#########################################################################
# Use SWIG to integrate the number.h C++ class for use in Python programs.
# Note: name "_number.dll" matters, because shadow class imports _number.
#########################################################################

PYLIB = /usr/bin
PYINC = /usr/include/python2.4

all: _number.dll number.py

# wrapper + real class
_number.dll: number_wrap.o number.o
        g++ -shared number_wrap.o number.o -L$(PYLIB) -lpython2.4 -o $@

# generated class wrapper module(s)
number_wrap.o: number_wrap.cxx number.h
        g++ number_wrap.cxx -c -g -I$(PYINC)

number_wrap.cxx: number.i
        swig -c++ -python -shadow number.i

number.py: number.i
        swig -c++ -python -shadow number.i

# wrapped C++ class code
number.o: number.cxx number.h
        g++ -c -g number.cxx -Wno-deprecated

# non Python test
cxxtest:
        g++ main.cxx number.cxx -Wno-deprecated

clean:
```

Example 22-22. PP3E\Integrate\Extend\Swig\Shadow\makefile.number-swig (continued)

```
        rm -f *.pyc *.o *.dll core a.exe
force:
        rm -f *.pyc *.o *.dll core a.exe \
                number_wrap.doc number_wrap.cxx number.py
```

As usual, run this makefile to generate and compile the necessary glue code into an extension module that can be imported by Python programs:

```
.../PP3E/Integrate/Extend/Swig/Shadow$ make -f makefile.number-swig
swig -c++ -python -shadow number.i
g++ number_wrap.cxx -c -g -I/usr/include/python2.4
g++ -c -g number.cxx -Wno-deprecated
g++ -shared number_wrap.o number.o -L/usr/bin -lpython2.4 -o _number.dll
```

Using the C++ Class in Python

Once the glue code is generated and compiled, Python scripts can access the C++ class as though it were coded in Python. In fact, it is—the shadow class on top of the extension module is generated Python code. Example 22-23 repeats the *main.cxx* file's class tests; here, though, the C++ class is being utilized from the Python programming language.

Example 22-23. PP3E\Integrate\Extend\Swig\Shadow\main.py

```
from number import Number      # use C++ class in Python (shadow class)
                              # runs same tests as main.cxx C++ file
num = Number(1)               # make a C++ class object in Python
num.add(4)                    # call its methods from Python
num.display()                 # num saves the C++ 'this' pointer
num.sub(2)
num.display()
res = num.square()             # converted C++ return value
print res

num.data = 99                 # set C++ data member, generated __setattr__
print num.data                # get C++ data member, generated __getattr__
num.display()
print num                     # runs repr in shadow/proxy class
del num                       # runs C++ destructor automatically
```

Because the C++ class and its wrappers are automatically loaded when imported by the number shadow class, you run this script like any other:

```
.../PP3E/Integrate/Extend/Swig/Shadow$ python main.py
Number: 1
add 4
Number = 5
sub 2
Number = 3
Square = 9
99
```

```
Number = 99
<number.Number; proxy of C++ Number instance at _b0974700_p_Number>
~Number: 99
```

This output is mostly coming from the C++ class's methods and is the same as the *main.cxx* results shown in Example 22-20 (less the instance output format; it's a Python shadow class instance now).

Using the low-level extension module

If you really want to use the generated accessor functions module, you can, as shown in Example 22-24. This version runs the C++ extension module directly without the shadow class, to demonstrate how the shadow class maps calls back to C++.

Example 22-24. PP3E\Integrate\Extend\Swig\Shadow\main_low.py

```
from _number import *          # same test as main.cxx
                              # use low-level C accessor function interface

num = new_Number(1)
Number_add(num, 4)            # pass C++ 'this' pointer explicitly
Number_display(num)          # use accessor functions in the C module
Number_sub(num, 2)
Number_display(num)
print Number_square(num)

Number_data_set(num, 99)
print Number_data_get(num)
Number_display(num)
print num
delete_Number(num)
```

This script generates essentially the same output as *main.py*, though the C++ class instance is something lower level than the proxy class here:

```
.../PP3E/Integrate/Extend/Swig/Shadow$ python main_low.py
Number: 1
add 4
Number = 5
sub 2
Number = 3
Square = 9
99
Number = 99
<Swig Object at _400d4900_p_Number>
~Number: 99
```

Subclassing the C++ class in Python

Using the extension module directly works, but there is no obvious advantage to moving from the shadow class to functions here. By using the shadow class, you get both an object-based interface to C++ and a customizable Python object. For instance, the Python module shown in Example 22-25 extends the C++ class, adding an extra print statement to the C++ add method and defining a brand-new mul method. Because the shadow class is pure Python, this works naturally.

Example 22-25. PP3E\Integrate\Extend\Swig\Shadow\main_subclass.py

```python
from number import Number      # sublass C++ class in Python (shadow class)

class MyNumber(Number):
    def add(self, other):
        print 'in Python add...'
        Number.add(self, other)
    def mul(self, other):
        print 'in Python mul...'
        self.data = self.data * other

num = MyNumber(1)             # same test as main.cxx
num.add(4)                    # using Python subclass of shadow class
num.display()                 # add() is specialized in Python
num.sub(2)
num.display()
print num.square()

num.data = 99
print num.data
num.display()

num.mul(2)                    # mul() is implemented in Python
num.display()
print num                     # repr from shadow superclass
del num
```

Now we get extra messages out of add calls, and mul changes the C++ class's data member automatically when it assigns self.data—Python code extends C++ code:

```
.../PP3E/Integrate/Extend/Swig/Shadow$ python main_subclass.py
Number: 1
in Python add...
add 4
Number = 5
sub 2
Number = 3
Square = 9
99
Number = 99
in Python mul...
Number = 198
<__main__.MyNumber; proxy of C++ Number instance at _580d4900_p_Number>
~Number: 198
```

In other words, SWIG makes it easy to use C++ class libraries as base classes in your Python scripts. Among other things, this allows us to leverage existing C++ class libraries in Python scripts and optimize by coding parts of class hierarchies in C++ when needed.

Exploring the wrappers interactively

As usual, you can import the C++ class interactively to experiment with it some more:

```
.../PP3E/Integrate/Extend/Swig/Shadow$ python
>>> import _number
>>> _number.__file__                    # the C++ class plus generated glue module
'_number.dll'
>>> import number                       # the generated Python shadow class module
>>> number.__file__
'number.pyc'

>>> x = number.Number(2)                # make a C++ class instance in Python
Number: 2
>>> y = number.Number(4)                # make another C++ object
Number: 4
>>> x, y
(<number.Number; proxy of C++ Number instance at _a0764900_p_Number>,
 <number.Number; proxy of C++ Number instance at _508b4900_p_Number>)

>>> x.display()                         # call C++ method (like C++ x->display())
Number = 2
>>> x.add(y.data)                       # fetch C++ data member, call C++ method
add 4
>>> x.display()
Number = 6

>>> y.data = x.data + y.data + 32       # set C++ data member
>>> y.display()                         # y records the C++ this pointer
Number = 42

>>> y.square()                          # method with return value
Square = 1764
>>> t = y.square()
Square = >>>
>>> t, type(t)
(1764, <type 'int'>)
```

Naturally, this example uses a small C++ class to underscore the basics, but even at this level, the seamlessness of the Python-to-C++ integration we get from SWIG is astonishing. Python code uses C++ members and methods as though they are Python code. Moreover, this integration transparency still applies once we step up to more realistic C++ class libraries.

So what's the catch? Nothing much, really, but if you start using SWIG in earnest, the biggest downside may be that SWIG cannot handle every feature of C++ today. If your classes use some esoteric C++ tools (and there are many), you may need to handcode simplified class type declarations for SWIG instead of running SWIG over the original class header files. SWIG development is ongoing, so you should consult the SWIG manuals and web site for more details on these and other topics.

In return for any such trade-offs, though, SWIG can completely obviate the need to code glue layers to access C and C++ libraries from Python scripts. If you have ever coded such layers by hand in the past, you already know that this is a *very* big win.

If you do go the handcoded route, though, consult Python's standard extension manuals for more details on both API calls used in this and the next chapter, as well as additional extension tools we don't have space to cover in this text. C extensions can run the gamut from short SWIG input files to code that is staunchly wedded to the internals of the Python interpreter; as a rule of thumb, the former survives the ravages of time much better than the latter.

Other Extending Tools

In closing the extending topic, I should mention that there are alternatives to SWIG, some of which have a loyal user base of their own. This section briefly introduces some of the more popular tools in this domain; as usual, search the Web for more details on these and more. All of the following are currently third-party tools that must be installed separately like SWIG, though Python 2.5 is scheduled to incorporate the ctypes extension as a standard library module by the time you read this.

SIP

> Just as a sip is a smaller swig in the drinking world, so too is the SIP system a lighter alternative to SWIG in the Python world (in fact, it was named on purpose for the joke). According to its web page, SIP makes it easy to create Python bindings for C and C++ libraries. Originally developed to create the PyQt Python bindings for the Qt toolkit, it can be used to create bindings for any C or C++ library. SIP includes a code generator and a Python support module.

> Much like SWIG, the code generator processes a set of specification files and generates C or C++ code, which is compiled to create the bindings extension module. The SIP Python module provides support functions to the automatically generated code. Unlike SWIG, SIP is specifically designed for bringing together Python and C/C++; SWIG also generates wrappers for many other scripting languages.

ctypes

> The ctypes system is a foreign function interface (FFI) module for Python. It allows Python scripts to access and call compiled functions in a binary library file directly and dynamically, by writing dispatch code in Python instead of generating or writing the integration C wrapper code we've studied in this chapter.

> According to its web site, ctypes allows Python to call functions exposed from DLLs and shared libraries and has facilities to create, access, and manipulate complex C datatypes in Python. The net effect is to wrap libraries in pure

Python. It is also possible to implement C callback functions in pure Python; ctypes now includes an experimental code generator feature that allows automatic creation of library wrappers from C header files. ctypes works on Windows, Mac OS X, Linux, Solaris, FreeBSD, and OpenBSD. It may run on additional systems, provided that the libffi package it employs is supported. For Windows, ctypes contains a ctypes.com package, which allows Python code to call and implement custom COM interfaces.

Boost.Python

The Boost.Python system is a C++ library that enables seamless interoperability between C++ and the Python programming language through an IDL-like model. Using it, developers generally write a small amount of C++ wrapper code to create a shared library for use in Python scripts. Boost.Python handles references, callbacks, type mappings, and cleanup tasks. Because it is designed to wrap C++ interfaces nonintrusively, C++ code need not be changed to be wrapped. Like other tools, this makes the system useful for wrapping existing libraries, as well as developing new extensions from scratch.

Writing interface code for large libraries can be more tedious than the generation approaches of SWIG and SIP, but it's easier than manually wrapping libraries and may afford greater control than a fully automated wrapping tool. In addition, the Pyste system provides a Boost.Python code generator, in which users specify classes and functions to be exported using a simple interface file, which is Python code. Pyste uses GCCXML to parse all the headers and extract the necessary information to generate C++ code.

Pyrex

Pyrex is a language specifically for writing Python extension modules. It lets you write code that mixes Python and C datatypes anyway you want, and it compiles it into a C extension for Python. In principle, developers need not deal with the Python/C API at all, because Pyrex takes care of things such as error-checking and reference counts automatically.

Technically, Pyrex is a distinct language that is Python-like, with extensions for mixing in C datatype declarations. However, almost any Python code is also valid Pyrex code. The Pyrex compiler converts Python code into C code, which makes calls to the Python/C API. In this aspect, Pyrex is similar to the older Python2C conversion project. By combining Python and C code, Pyrex offers a very different approach than the integration code generation or coding schemes of other systems.

CXX

The CXX system is roughly a C++ version of Python's usual C API, which handles reference counters, exception translation, and much of the type checking and cleanup inherent in handcoded C++ extensions. As such, CXX lets you focus on the application-specific parts of your code. CXX also exposes parts of the C++ Standard Template Library containers to be compatible with Python lists and tuples.

Modulator

Finally, the Modulator system is a simple Python-coded GUI that generates skeleton boilerplate code for C extension modules and types. Users select components to be supported in the GUI, and Modulator generates the initial C code; simply edit to insert type-specific parts of extension functions. Modulator is available in the *Tools* directory of the Python source distribution.

At the end of the next chapter, we will return to extending in the context of integration at large, and we'll compare Python C integration techniques to very different approaches such as COM, CORBA, and Jython. First, though, we need to shift our perspective 180 degrees to explore the other mode of Python/C integration discussed in the next chapter: embedding.

Mixing Python and C++

Python's standard implementation is currently coded in C, so all the normal rules about mixing C programs with C++ programs apply to the Python interpreter. In fact, there is nothing special about Python in this context, but here are a few pointers.

When embedding Python in a C++ program, there are no special rules to follow. Simply link in the Python library and call its functions from C++. Python's header files automatically wrap themselves in extern "C" {...} declarations to suppress C++ name mangling. Hence, the Python library looks like any other C component to C++; there is no need to recompile Python itself with a C++ compiler.

When extending Python with C++ components, Python header files are still C++ friendly, so Python API calls in C++ extensions work like any other C++-to-C call. But be sure to wrap the parts of your extension code made visible to Python with extern "C" declarations so that they may be called by Python's C code. For example, to wrap a C++ class, SWIG generates a C++ extension module that declares its initialization function this way, though the rest of the module is pure C++.

The only other potential complication involves C++ static or global object constructor methods when extending. If Python (a C program) is at the top level of a system, such C++ constructors may not be run when the system starts up. This behavior may vary per compiler, but if your C++ objects are not initialized on startup, make sure that your main program is linked by your C++ compiler, not by C.

If you are interested in Python/C++ integration in general, be sure to consult the C++ Special Interest Group (SIG) pages at *http://www.python.org* for information about work in this domain. The CXX system, for instance, makes it easier to extend Python with C++.

## CHAPTER 23

Embedding Python

"Add Python. Mix Well. Repeat."

In the prior chapter, we explored half of the Python/C integration picture: calling C services from Python. This mode lets programmers speed up operations by moving them to C, and to utilize external libraries by wrapping them in C extension modules and types. But the inverse can be just as useful: calling Python from C. By delegating selected components of an application to embedded Python code, we can open them up to onsite changes without having to ship a system's code.

This chapter tells this other half of the Python/C integration tale. It introduces the Python C interfaces that make it possible for programs written in C-compatible languages to run Python program code. In this mode, Python acts as an embedded control language (what some call a "macro" language). Although embedding is mostly presented in isolation here, keep in mind that Python's integration support is best viewed as a whole. A system's structure usually determines an appropriate integration approach: C extensions, embedded code calls, or both. To wrap up, this chapter concludes by discussing a handful of larger integration platforms, such as Component Object Model (COM) and Jython, which present broader component integration possibilities.

C Embedding API Overview

The first thing you should know about Python's embedded-call API is that it is less structured than the extension interfaces. Embedding Python in C may require a bit more creativity on your part than extending: you must pick tools from a general collection of calls to implement the Python integration instead of coding to a boilerplate structure. The upside of this loose structure is that programs can combine embedding calls and strategies to build up arbitrary integration architectures.

The lack of a more rigid model for embedding is largely the result of a less clear-cut goal. When *extending* Python, there is a distinct separation for Python and C responsibilities and a clear structure for the integration. C modules and types are required to fit the Python module/type model by conforming to standard extension structures. This makes the integration seamless for Python clients: C extensions look like Python objects and handle most of the work.

But when Python is *embedded*, the structure isn't as obvious; because C is the enclosing level, there is no clear way to know what model the embedded Python code should fit. C may want to run objects fetched from modules, strings fetched from files or parsed out of documents, and so on. Instead of deciding what C can and cannot do, Python provides a collection of general embedding interface tools, which you use and structure according to your embedding goals.

Most of these tools correspond to tools available to Python programs. Table 23-1 lists some of the more common API calls used for embedding, as well as their Python equivalents. In general, if you can figure out how to accomplish your embedding goals in pure Python code, you can probably find C API tools that achieve the same results.

Table 23-1. Common API functions

C API call	Python equivalent
PyImport_ImportModule	import module, __import__
PyImport_ReloadModule	reload(module)
PyImport_GetModuleDict	sys.modules
PyModule_GetDict	module.__dict__
PyDict_GetItemString	dict[key]
PyDict_SetItemString	dict[key]=val
PyDict_New	dict={}
PyObject_GetAttrString	getattr(obj, attr)
PyObject_SetAttrString	setattr(obj, attr, val)
PyEval_CallObject	funcobj(*argstuple), apply
PyRun_String	eval(exprstr), exec stmtstr
PyRun_File	execfile(filename)

Because embedding relies on API call selection, becoming familiar with the Python C API is fundamental to the embedding task. This chapter presents a handful of representative embedding examples and discusses common API calls, but it does not provide a comprehensive list of all tools in the API. Once you've mastered the examples here, you'll probably need to consult Python's integration manuals for more details on available calls in this domain. As mentioned in the preceding chapter, Python offers two standard manuals for C/C++ integration programmers: *Extending and Embedding*, an integration tutorial; and *Python/C API*, the Python runtime library reference.

You can find the most recent releases of these manuals at *http://www.python.org*. Beyond this chapter, these manuals are likely to be your best resource for up-to-date and complete Python API tool information.

What Is Embedded Code?

Before we jump into details, let's get a handle on some of the core ideas in the embedding domain. When this book speaks of "embedded" Python code, it simply means any Python program structure that can be executed from C with a direct in-process function call interface. Generally speaking, embedded Python code can take a variety of forms:

Code strings
> C programs can represent Python programs as character strings and run them as either expressions or statements (such as eval and exec).

Callable objects
> C programs can load or reference Python callable objects such as functions, methods, and classes, and call them with argument list objects (such as apply and the newer func(*pargs, *kargs)).

Code files
> C programs can execute entire Python program files by importing modules and running script files through the API or general system calls (e.g., popen).

The Python binary library is usually what is physically embedded in the C program; the actual Python code run from C can come from a wide variety of sources:

- Code strings might be loaded from files, obtained from an interactive user, fetched from persistent databases and shelves, parsed out of HTML or XML files, read over sockets, built or hardcoded in a C program, passed to C extension functions from Python registration code, and so on.

- Callable objects might be fetched from Python modules, returned from other Python API calls, passed to C extension functions from Python registration code, and so on.

- Code files simply exist as files, modules, and executable scripts.

Registration is a technique commonly used in callback scenarios that we will explore in more detail later in this chapter. But especially for strings of code, there are as many possible sources as there are for C character strings. For example, C programs can construct arbitrary Python code dynamically by building and running strings.

Finally, once you have some Python code to run, you need a way to communicate with it: the Python code may need to use inputs passed in from the C layer and may want to generate outputs to communicate results back to C. In fact, embedding generally becomes interesting only when the embedded code has access to the enclosing C layer. Usually, the form of the embedded code suggests its communication media:

- Code strings that are Python expressions return an expression result as their output. Both inputs and outputs can take the form of global variables in the namespace in which a code string is run; C may set variables to serve as input, run Python code, and fetch variables as the code's result. Inputs and outputs can also be passed with exported C *extension function calls*—Python code may use C module or type interfaces that we met in the preceding chapter to get or set variables in the enclosing C layer. Communications schemes are often combined; for instance, C may preassign global names to objects that export state and interface calls to the embedded Python code.*

- Callable objects may accept inputs as function arguments and produce results as function return values. Passed-in mutable arguments (e.g., lists, dictionaries, class instances) can be used as both input and output for the embedded code—changes made in Python are retained in objects held by C. Objects can also make use of the global variable and C extension functions interface techniques described for strings to communicate with C.

- Code files can communicate with most of the same techniques as code strings; when run as separate programs, files can also employ Inter-Process Communication (IPC) techniques.

Naturally, all embedded code forms can also communicate with C using general system-level tools: files, sockets, pipes, and so on. These techniques are generally less direct and slower, though. Here, we are still interested in in-process function call integration.

Basic Embedding Techniques

As you can probably tell from the preceding overview, there is much flexibility in the embedding domain. To illustrate common embedding techniques in action, this section presents a handful of short C programs that run Python code in one form or another. Most of these examples make use of the simple Python module file shown in Example 23-1.

---

* If you want a concrete example, flip back to the discussion of Active Scripting in Chapter 18. This system fetches Python code embedded in an HTML web page file, assigns global variables in a namespace to objects that give access to the web browser's environment, and runs the Python code in the namespace where the objects were assigned. I worked on a project where we did something similar, but Python code was embedded in XML documents, and objects that were preassigned to globals in the code's namespace represented widgets in a GUI.

Example 23-1. PP3E\Integrate\Embed\Basics\usermod.py

```
##########################################################
# C runs Python code in this module in embedded mode.
# Such a file can be changed without changing the C layer.
# There is just standard Python code (C does conversions).
# You can also run code in standard modules like string.
##########################################################

message = 'The meaning of life...'

def transform(input):
    input = input.replace('life', 'Python')
    return input.upper( )
```

If you know any Python at all, you probably know that this file defines a string and a function; the function returns whatever it is passed with string substitution and uppercase conversions applied. It's easy to use from Python:

```
.../PP3E/Integrate/Embed/Basics$ python
>>> import usermod                              # import a module
>>> usermod.message                             # fetch a string
'The meaning of life...'
>>> usermod.transform(usermod.message)          # call a function
'THE MEANING OF PYTHON...'
```

With a little Python API wizardry, it's not much more difficult to use this module the same way in C.

Running Simple Code Strings

Perhaps the simplest way to run Python code from C is by calling the PyRun_ SimpleString API function. With it, C programs can execute Python programs represented as C character string arrays. This call is also very limited: all code runs in the same namespace (the module __main__), the code strings must be Python statements (not expressions), and there is no direct way to communicate inputs or outputs with the Python code run.

Still, it's a simple place to start. Moreover, when augmented with an imported C extension module that the embedded Python code can use to communicate with the enclosing C layer, this technique can satisfy many embedding goals. To demonstrate the basics, the C program in Example 23-2 runs Python code to accomplish the same results as the interactive session listed in the prior section.

Example 23-2. PP3E\Integrate\Embed\Basics\embed-simple.c

```
/*****************************************************
 * simple code strings: C acts like the interactive
 * prompt, code runs in __main__, no output sent to C;
 *****************************************************/
```

Example 23-2. PP3E\Integrate\Embed\Basics\embed-simple.c (continued)

```
#include <Python.h>    /* standard API def */

main( ) {
    printf("embed-simple\n");
    Py_Initialize( );
    PyRun_SimpleString("import usermod");                /* load .py file */
    PyRun_SimpleString("print usermod.message");         /* on Python path */
    PyRun_SimpleString("x = usermod.message");           /* compile and run */
    PyRun_SimpleString("print usermod.transform(x)");
}
```

The first thing you should notice here is that when Python is embedded, C programs always call `Py_Initialize` to initialize linked-in Python libraries before using any other API functions. The rest of this code is straightforward—C submits hardcoded strings to Python that are roughly what we typed interactively. Internally, `PyRun_SimpleString` invokes the Python compiler and interpreter to run the strings sent from C; as usual, the Python compiler is always available in systems that contain Python.

Compiling and running

To build a standalone executable from this C source file, you need to link its compiled form with the Python library file. In this chapter, "library" usually means the binary library file that is generated when Python is compiled, not the Python source code library.

Today, everything in Python that you need in C is compiled into a single Python library file when the interpreter is built (e.g., *libpython2.4.dll* on Cygwin). The program's `main` function comes from your C code, and depending on your platform and the extensions installed in your Python, you may also need to link any external libraries referenced by the Python library.

Assuming no extra extension libraries are needed, Example 23-3 is a minimal makefile for building the C program in Example 23-2 under Cygwin on Windows. Again, makefile details vary per platform, but see Python manuals for hints. This makefile uses the Python include-files path to find *Python.h* in the compile step and adds the Python library file to the final link step to make API calls available to the C program.

Example 23-3. PP3E\Integrate\Embed\Basics\makefile.1

```
# a Cygwin makefile that builds a C executable that embeds
# Python, assuming no external module libs must be linked in;
# uses Python header files, links in the Python lib file;
# both may be in other dirs (e.g., /usr) in your install;

PYLIB = /usr/bin
PYINC = /usr/include/python2.4
```

Example 23-3. PP3E\Integrate\Embed\Basics\makefile.1 (continued)

```
embed-simple: embed-simple.o
        gcc embed-simple.o -L$(PYLIB) -lpython2.4 -g -o embed-simple

embed-simple.o: embed-simple.c
        gcc embed-simple.c -c -g -I$(PYINC)
```

To build a program with this file, launch make on it as usual:

```
.../PP3E/Integrate/Embed/Basics$ make -f makefile.1
gcc embed-simple.c -c -g -I/usr/include/python2.4
gcc embed-simple.o -L/usr/bin -lpython2.4 -g -o embed-simple
```

Things may not be quite this simple in practice, though, at least not without some coaxing. The makefile in Example 23-4 is the one I actually used to build all of this section's C programs on Cygwin.

Example 23-4. PP3E\Integrate\Embed\Basics\makefile.basics

```
# cygwin makefile to build all 5
# basic embedding examples at once

PYLIB = /usr/bin
PYINC = /usr/include/python2.4

BASICS = embed-simple.exe    \
         embed-string.exe    \
         embed-object.exe    \
         embed-dict.exe      \
         embed-bytecode.exe

all:    $(BASICS)

embed%.exe: embed%.o
        gcc embed$*.o -L$(PYLIB) -lpython2.4 -g -o $@

embed%.o: embed%.c
        gcc embed$*.c -c -g -I$(PYINC)

clean:
        rm -f *.o *.pyc $(BASICS) core
```

On some platforms, you may need to also link in other libraries because the Python library file used may have been built with external dependencies enabled and required. In fact, you may have to link in arbitrarily many more externals for your Python library, and frankly, chasing down all the linker dependencies can be tedious. Required libraries may vary per platform and Python install, so there isn't a lot of advice I can offer to make this process simple (this is C, after all). The standard C development techniques will apply.

One thing to note is that on some platforms, if you're going to do much embedding work and you run into external dependency issues, you might want to build Python on your machine from its source with all unnecessary extensions *disabled* in the Modules/Setup file (or the top-level setup.py Distutils script in more recent releases). This produces a Python library with minimal external requirements, which links much more easily.

For example, if your embedded code won't be building GUIs, Tkinter can simply be removed from the library; see the README file at the top of Python's source distribution for details. You can also find a list of external libraries referenced from your Python in the generated makefiles located in the Python source tree. In any event, the good news is that you need to resolve linker dependencies only once.

Once you've gotten the makefile to work, run it to build the C program with Python libraries linked in:

```
.../PP3E/Integrate/Embed/Basics$ make -f makefile.basics clean
rm -f *.o *.pyc embed-simple.exe embed-string.exe embed-object.exe embed-dict.ex
e embed-bytecode.exe core

.../PP3E/Integrate/Embed/Basics$ make -f makefile.basics
gcc embed-simple.c -c -g -I/usr/include/python2.4
gcc embed-simple.o -L/usr/bin -lpython2.4 -g -o embed-simple.exe
...lines deleted...
gcc embed-bytecode.c -c -g -I/usr/include/python2.4
gcc embed-bytecode.o -L/usr/bin -lpython2.4 -g -o embed-bytecode.exe
rm embed-dict.o embed-object.o embed-simple.o embed-bytecode.o embed-string.o
```

After building, run the resulting C program as usual, regardless of how this works in your platform:*

```
.../PP3E/Integrate/Embed/Basics$ embed-simple
embed-simple
The meaning of life...
THE MEANING OF PYTHON...
```

Most of this output is produced by Python print statements sent from C to the linked-in Python library. It's as if C has become an interactive Python programmer.

Naturally, strings of Python code run by C probably would not be hardcoded in a C program file like this. They might instead be loaded from a text file or GUI, extracted from HTML or XML files, fetched from a persistent database or socket, and so on. With such external sources, the Python code strings that are run from C could be changed arbitrarily without having to recompile the C program that runs them. They may even be changed onsite, and by end users of a system. To make the most of code strings, though, we need to move on to more flexible API tools.

---

* Under Python 2.4 and Cygwin on Windows, I had to first set my PYTHONPATH to include the current directory in order to run the embedding examples under Python 2.4 and Cygwin, with the shell command export PYTHONPATH=.. I also had to use the shell command ./embed-simple to execute the program due to my system path setting. Your mileage may vary; if you have trouble, try running the embedded Python commands import sys and print sys.path from C to see what Python's path looks like, and take a look at the *Python/C API* manual for more on path configuration for embedded applications.

Running Code Strings with Results and Namespaces

Example 23-5 uses the following API calls to run code strings that return expression results back to C:

Py_Initialize
> Initializes linked-in Python libraries as before

PyImport_ImportModule
> Imports a Python module and returns a pointer to it

PyModule_GetDict
> Fetches a module's attribute dictionary object

PyRun_String
> Runs a string of code in explicit namespaces

PyObject_SetAttrString
> Assigns an object attribute by namestring

PyArg_Parse
> Converts a Python return value object to C form

The import calls are used to fetch the namespace of the usermod module listed in Example 23-1 earlier so that code strings can be run there directly (and will have access to names defined in that module without qualifications). Py_Import_ImportModule is like a Python import statement, but the imported module object is returned to C; it is not assigned to a Python variable name. As a result, it's probably more similar to the Python __import__ built-in function.

The PyRun_String call is the one that actually runs code here, though. It takes a code string, a parser mode flag, and dictionary object pointers to serve as the global and local namespaces for running the code string. The mode flag can be Py_eval_input to run an expression, or Py_file_input to run a statement; when running an expression, the result of evaluating the expression is returned from this call (it comes back as a PyObject* object pointer). The two namespace dictionary pointer arguments allow you to distinguish global and local scopes, but they are typically passed the same dictionary such that code runs in a single namespace.*

Example 23-5. PP3E\Integrate\Embed\Basics\embed-string.c

```
/* code-strings with results and namespaces */

#include <Python.h>

main( ) {
```

---

* A related function lets you run *files* of code but is not demonstrated in this chapter: PyObject* PyRun_File(FILE *fp, char *filename, mode, globals, locals). Because you can always load a file's text and run it as a single code string with PyRun_String, the PyRun_File call is not always necessary. In such multiline code strings, the \n character terminates lines and indentation groups blocks as usual.

Example 23-5. PP3E\Integrate\Embed\Basics\embed-string.c (continued)

```
    char *cstr;
    PyObject *pstr, *pmod, *pdict;
    printf("embed-string\n");
    Py_Initialize();

    /* get usermod.message */
    pmod  = PyImport_ImportModule("usermod");
    pdict = PyModule_GetDict(pmod);
    pstr  = PyRun_String("message", Py_eval_input, pdict, pdict);

    /* convert to C */
    PyArg_Parse(pstr, "s", &cstr);
    printf("%s\n", cstr);

    /* assign usermod.X */
    PyObject_SetAttrString(pmod, "X", pstr);

    /* print usermod.transform(X) */
    (void) PyRun_String("print transform(X)", Py_file_input, pdict, pdict);
    Py_DECREF(pmod);
    Py_DECREF(pstr);
}
```

When compiled and run, this file produces the same result as its predecessor:

```
.../PP3E/Integrate/Embed/Basics$ embed-string
embed-string
The meaning of life...
THE MEANING OF PYTHON...
```

But very different work goes into producing this output. This time, C fetches, converts, and prints the value of the Python module's message attribute directly by running a string expression and assigning a global variable (X) within the module's namespace to serve as input for a Python print statement string.

Because the string execution call in this version lets you specify namespaces, you can better partition the embedded code your system runs—each grouping can have a distinct namespace to avoid overwriting other groups' variables. And because this call returns a result, you can better communicate with the embedded code; expression results are outputs, and assignments to globals in the namespace in which code runs can serve as inputs.

Before we move on, I need to explain two coding issues here. First, this program also decrements the reference count on objects passed to it from Python, using the Py_DECREF call introduced in Chapter 22. These calls are not strictly needed here (the objects' space is reclaimed when the programs exits anyhow), but they demonstrate how embedding interfaces must manage reference counts when Python passes their ownership to C. If this was a function called from a larger system, for instance, you would generally want to decrement the count to allow Python to reclaim the objects.

Second, in a realistic program, you should generally test the return values of *all* the API calls in this program immediately to detect errors (e.g., import failure). Error tests are omitted in this section's example to keep the code simple, but they will appear in later code listings and should be included in your programs to make them more robust.

Calling Python Objects

The last two sections dealt with running strings of code, but it's easy for C programs to deal in terms of Python objects too. Example 23-6 accomplishes the same task as Examples 23-2 and 23-5, but it uses other API tools to interact with objects in the Python module directly:

PyImport_ImportModule
> Imports the module from C as before

PyObject_GetAttrString
> Fetches an object's attribute value by name

PyEval_CallObject
> Calls a Python function (or class, or method)

PyArg_Parse
> Converts Python objects to C values

Py_BuildValue
> Converts C values to Python objects

We met both of the data conversion functions in Chapter 22. The PyEval_CallObject call in this version of the example is the key call here: it runs the imported function with a tuple of arguments, much like the Python apply built-in function and newer func(*args) call syntax. The Python function's return value comes back to C as a PyObject*, a generic Python object pointer.

Example 23-6. PP3E\Integrate\Embed\Basics\embed-object.c

```
/* fetch and call objects in modules */

#include <Python.h>

main( ) {
    char *cstr;
    PyObject *pstr, *pmod, *pfunc, *pargs;
    printf("embed-object\n");
    Py_Initialize( );

    /* get usermod.message */
    pmod = PyImport_ImportModule("usermod");
    pstr = PyObject_GetAttrString(pmod, "message");

    /* convert string to C */
```

Example 23-6. PP3E\Integrate\Embed\Basics\embed-object.c (continued)

```
    PyArg_Parse(pstr, "s", &cstr);
    printf("%s\n", cstr);
    Py_DECREF(pstr);

    /* call usermod.transform(usermod.message) */
    pfunc = PyObject_GetAttrString(pmod, "transform");
    pargs = Py_BuildValue("(s)", cstr);
    pstr  = PyEval_CallObject(pfunc, pargs);
    PyArg_Parse(pstr, "s", &cstr);
    printf("%s\n", cstr);

    /* free owned objects */
    Py_DECREF(pmod);
    Py_DECREF(pstr);
    Py_DECREF(pfunc);        /* not really needed in main() */
    Py_DECREF(pargs);        /* since all memory goes away  */
}
```

When compiled and run, the result is the same again:

```
.../PP3E/Integrate/Embed/Basics$ embed-object
embed-object
The meaning of life...
THE MEANING OF PYTHON...
```

But this output is generated by C this time—first, by fetching the Python module's message attribute value, and then by fetching and calling the module's transform function object directly and printing its return value that is sent back to C. Input to the transform function is a function argument here, not a preset global variable. Notice that message is fetched as a module attribute this time, instead of by running its name as a code string; there is often more than one way to accomplish the same goals with different API calls.

Running functions in modules like this is a simple way to structure embedding; code in the module file can be changed arbitrarily without having to recompile the C program that runs it. It also provides a direct communication model: inputs and outputs to Python code can take the form of function arguments and return values.

Running Strings in Dictionaries

When we used PyRun_String earlier to run expressions with results, code was executed in the namespace of an existing Python module. However, sometimes it's more convenient to create a brand-new namespace for running code strings that is independent of any existing module files. The C file in Example 23-7 shows how; the new namespace is created as a new Python dictionary object, and a handful of new API calls are employed in the process:

PyDict_New
    Makes a new empty dictionary object

PyDict_SetItemString
> Assigns to a dictionary's key

PyDict_GetItemString
> Fetches (indexes) a dictionary value by key

PyRun_String
> Runs a code string in namespaces, as before

PyEval_GetBuiltins
> Gets the built-in scope's module

The main trick here is the new dictionary. Inputs and outputs for the embedded code strings are mapped to this dictionary by passing it as the code's namespace dictionaries in the PyRun_String call. The net effect is that the C program in Example 23-7 works exactly like this Python code:

```
>>> d = {}
>>> d['Y'] = 2
>>> exec 'X = 99' in d, d
>>> exec 'X = X + Y' in d, d
>>> print d['X']
101
```

But here, each Python operation is replaced by a C API call.

Example 23-7. PP3E\Integrate\Embed\Basics\embed-dict.c

```c
/**************************************************
 * make a new dictionary for code string namespace;
 **************************************************/

#include <Python.h>

main() {
    int cval;
    PyObject *pdict, *pval;
    printf("embed-dict\n");
    Py_Initialize();

    /* make a new namespace */
    pdict = PyDict_New();
    PyDict_SetItemString(pdict, "__builtins__", PyEval_GetBuiltins());

    PyDict_SetItemString(pdict, "Y", PyInt_FromLong(2));    /* dict['Y'] = 2    */
    PyRun_String("X = 99",  Py_file_input, pdict, pdict);   /* run statements   */
    PyRun_String("X = X+Y", Py_file_input, pdict, pdict);   /* same X and Y     */
    pval = PyDict_GetItemString(pdict, "X");               /* fetch dict['X']  */

    PyArg_Parse(pval, "i", &cval);                          /* convert to C */
    printf("%d\n", cval);                                   /* result=101 */
    Py_DECREF(pdict);
}
```

When compiled and run, this C program creates this sort of output:

```
.../PP3E/Integrate/Embed/Basics$ embed-dict
embed-dict
101
```

The output is different this time: it reflects the value of the Python variable X assigned by the embedded Python code strings and fetched by C. In general, C can fetch module attributes either by calling PyObject_GetAttrString with the module or by using PyDict_GetItemString to index the module's attribute dictionary (expression strings work too, but they are less direct). Here, there is no module at all, so dictionary indexing is used to access the code's namespace in C.

Besides allowing you to partition code string namespaces independent of any Python module files on the underlying system, this scheme provides a natural communication mechanism. Values that are stored in the new dictionary before code is run serve as inputs, and names assigned by the embedded code can later be fetched out of the dictionary to serve as code outputs. For instance, the variable Y in the second string run refers to a name set to 2 by C; X is assigned by the Python code and fetched later by C code as the printed result.

There is one subtlety: dictionaries that serve as namespaces for running code are generally required to have a __builtins__ link to the built-in scope searched last for name lookups, set with code of this form:

```
PyDict_SetItemString(pdict, "__builtins__", PyEval_GetBuiltins());
```

This is esoteric, and it is normally handled by Python internally for modules. For raw dictionaries, though, we are responsible for setting the link manually.

Precompiling Strings to Bytecode

When you call Python function objects from C, you are actually running the already compiled bytecode associated with the object (e.g., a function body). When running strings, Python must compile the string before running it. Because compilation is a slow process, this can be a substantial overhead if you run a code string more than once. Instead, precompile the string to a bytecode object to be run later, using the API calls illustrated in Example 23-8:[*]

Py_CompileString
    Compiles a string of code and returns a bytecode object

PyEval_EvalCode
    Runs a compiled bytecode object

---

[*] In case you've forgotten: *bytecode* is simply an intermediate representation for already compiled program code in the current standard Python implementation. It's a low-level binary format that can be quickly interpreted by the Python runtime system. Bytecode is usually generated automatically when you import a module, but there may be no notion of an import when running raw strings from C.

The first of these takes the mode flag that is normally passed to PyRun_String, as well as a second string argument that is used only in error messages. The second takes two namespace dictionaries. These two API calls are used in Example 23-8 to compile and execute three strings of Python code in turn.

Example 23-8. PP3E\Integrate\Embed\Basics\embed-bytecode.c

```
/* precompile code strings to bytecode objects */

#include <Python.h>
#include <compile.h>
#include <eval.h>

main( ) {
    int i;
    char *cval;
    PyObject *pcode1, *pcode2, *pcode3, *presult, *pdict;
    char *codestr1, *codestr2, *codestr3;
    printf("embed-bytecode\n");

    Py_Initialize( );
    codestr1 = "import usermod\nprint usermod.message";     /* statements */
    codestr2 = "usermod.transform(usermod.message)";        /* expression */
    codestr3 = "print '%d:%d' % (X, X ** 2),";              /* use input X */

    /* make new namespace dictionary */
    pdict = PyDict_New( );
    if (pdict == NULL) return -1;
    PyDict_SetItemString(pdict, "__builtins__", PyEval_GetBuiltins( ));

    /* precompile strings of code to bytecode objects */
    pcode1 = Py_CompileString(codestr1, "<embed>", Py_file_input);
    pcode2 = Py_CompileString(codestr2, "<embed>", Py_eval_input);
    pcode3 = Py_CompileString(codestr3, "<embed>", Py_file_input);

    /* run compiled bytecode in namespace dict */
    if (pcode1 && pcode2 && pcode3) {
        (void)    PyEval_EvalCode((PyCodeObject *)pcode1, pdict, pdict);
        presult = PyEval_EvalCode((PyCodeObject *)pcode2, pdict, pdict);
        PyArg_Parse(presult, "s", &cval);
        printf("%s\n", cval);
        Py_DECREF(presult);

        /* rerun code object repeatedly */
        for (i = 0; i <= 10; i++) {
            PyDict_SetItemString(pdict, "X", PyInt_FromLong(i));
            (void) PyEval_EvalCode((PyCodeObject *)pcode3, pdict, pdict);
        }
        printf("\n");
    }
}
```

Example 23-8. PP3E\Integrate\Embed\Basics\embed-bytecode.c (continued)

```
    /* free referenced objects */
    Py_XDECREF(pdict);
    Py_XDECREF(pcode1);
    Py_XDECREF(pcode2);
    Py_XDECREF(pcode3);
}
```

This program combines a variety of techniques that we've already seen. The namespace in which the compiled code strings run, for instance, is a newly created dictionary (not an existing module object), and inputs for code strings are passed as preset variables in the namespace. When built and executed, the first part of the output is similar to previous examples in this section, but the last line represents running the same precompiled code string 11 times:

```
.../PP3E/Integrate/Embed/Basics$ embed-bytecode
embed-bytecode
The meaning of life...
THE MEANING OF PYTHON...
0:0 1:1 2:4 3:9 4:16 5:25 6:36 7:49 8:64 9:81 10:100
```

If your system executes strings multiple times, it is a major speedup to precompile to bytecode in this fashion.

Registering Callback Handler Objects

In the examples thus far, C has been running and calling Python code from a standard main program flow of control. That's not always the way programs work, though; in some cases, programs are modeled on an *event-driven* architecture in which code is executed only in response to some sort of event. The event might be an end user clicking a button in a GUI, the operating system delivering a signal, or simply software running an action associated with an entry in a table.

In any event (pun accidental), program code in such an architecture is typically structured as *callback handlers*—chunks of code dispatched by event-processing logic. It's easy to use embedded Python code to implement callback handlers in such a system; in fact, the event-processing layer can simply use the embedded-call API tools we saw earlier in this chapter to run Python handlers.

The only new trick in this model is how to make the C layer know what code should be run for each event. Handlers must somehow be registered to C to associate them with future events. In general, there is a wide variety of ways to achieve this code/event association; for instance, C programs can:

- Fetch and call *functions* by event name from one or more *module* files
- Fetch and run code *strings* associated with event names in a *database*

- Extract and run code associated with event *tags* in HTML or XML[*]
- Run Python code that calls back to C to tell it what should be run

And so on. Really, any place you can associate objects or strings with identifiers is a potential callback registration mechanism. Some of these techniques have advantages all their own. For instance, callbacks fetched from module files support dynamic reloading (reload works on modules but does not update objects held directly). And none of the first three schemes requires users to code special Python programs that do nothing but register handlers to be run later.

It is perhaps more common, though, to register callback handlers with the last approach: letting Python code register handlers with C by calling back to C through extension interfaces. Although this scheme is not without trade-offs, it can provide a natural and direct model in scenarios where callbacks are associated with a large number of objects.

For instance, consider a GUI constructed by building a tree of widget objects in Python scripts. If each widget object in the tree can have an associated event handler, it may be easier to register handlers by simply calling methods of widgets in the tree. Associating handlers with widget objects in a separate structure such as a module file or an HTML file requires extra cross-reference work to keep the handlers in sync with the tree.[†]

The following C and Python files demonstrate the basic coding techniques used to implement explicitly registered callback handlers. The C file in Example 23-9 implements interfaces for registering Python handlers, as well as code to run those handlers in response to events:

Event router
> The Route_Event function responds to an event by calling a Python function object previously passed from Python to C.

Callback registration
> The Register_Handler function saves a passed-in Python function object pointer in a C global variable. Python calls Register_Handler through a simple cregister C extension module created by this file.

---

[*] If C chooses to do so, it might even run embedded Python code that uses Python's standard HTML and XML processing tools to parse out the embedded code associated with an event tag. See the Python library manual for details on these parsers.

[†] If you're looking for a more realistic example of Python callback handlers, see the Tkinter GUI system used extensively in this book. Tkinter uses both extending and embedding. Its *extending* interface (widget objects) is used to register Python callback handlers, which are later run with *embedding* interfaces in response to GUI events. You can study Tkinter's implementation in the Python source distribution for more details, though its Tk library interface logic makes it a somewhat challenging read.

Event trigger

To simulate real-world events, the `Trigger_Event` function can be called from Python through the generated C module to trigger an event.

In other words, this example uses both the embedding and the extending interfaces we've already met to register and invoke Python event handler code.

Example 23-9. PP3E\Integrate\Mixed\Regist\cregister.c

```c
#include <Python.h>
#include <stdlib.h>

/*********************************************/
/* 1) code to route events to Python object    */
/* note that we could run strings here instead */
/*********************************************/

static PyObject *Handler = NULL;        /* keep Python object in C */

void Route_Event(char *label, int count)
{
    char *cres;
    PyObject *args, *pres;

    /* call Python handler */
    args = Py_BuildValue("(si)", label, count);    /* make arg-list */
    pres = PyEval_CallObject(Handler, args);       /* apply: run a call */
    Py_DECREF(args);                               /* add error checks */

    if (pres != NULL) {
        /* use and decref handler result */
        PyArg_Parse(pres, "s", &cres);
        printf("%s\n", cres);
        Py_DECREF(pres);
    }
}

/***********************************************************/
/* 2) python extension module to register handlers    */
/* python imports this module to set handler objects */
/***********************************************************/

static PyObject *
Register_Handler(PyObject *self, PyObject *args)
{
    /* save Python callable object */
    Py_XDECREF(Handler);                 /* called before? */
    PyArg_Parse(args, "O", &Handler);    /* one argument? */
    Py_XINCREF(Handler);                 /* add a reference */
    Py_INCREF(Py_None);                  /* return 'None': success */
    return Py_None;
}
```

Example 23-9. PP3E\Integrate\Mixed\Regist\cregister.c (continued)

```c
static PyObject *
Trigger_Event(PyObject *self, PyObject *args)
{
    /* let Python simulate event caught by C */
    static count = 0;
    Route_Event("spam", count++);
    Py_INCREF(Py_None);
    return Py_None;
}

static struct PyMethodDef cregister_methods[] = {
    {"setHandler",   Register_Handler},      /* name, address */
    {"triggerEvent", Trigger_Event},
    {NULL, NULL}
};

void initcregister()                     /* this is called by Python  */
{                                        /* on first "import cregister" */
    (void) Py_InitModule("cregister", cregister_methods);
}
```

Ultimately, this C file is an extension module for Python, not a standalone C program that embeds Python (though C could just as well be on top). To compile it into a dynamically loaded module file, run the makefile in Example 23-10 on Cygwin (and use something similar on other platforms). As we learned in the last chapter, the resulting *cregister.dll* file will be loaded when first imported by a Python script if it is placed in a directory on Python's module search path (e.g., . or PYTHONPATH settings).

Example 23-10. PP3E\Integrate\Mixed\Regist\makefile.regist

```
#######################################################################
# Cygwin makefile that builds cregister.dll. a dynamically loaded
# C extension module (shareable), which is imported by register.py
#######################################################################

PYLIB = /usr/bin
PYINC = /usr/include/python2.4

CMODS = cregister.dll

all: $(CMODS)

cregister.dll: cregister.c
	gcc cregister.c -g -I$(PYINC) -shared -L$(PYLIB) -lpython2.4 -o $@

clean:
	rm -f *.pyc $(CMODS)
```

Now that we have a C extension module set to register and dispatch Python handlers, all we need are some Python handlers. The Python module shown in

Example 23-11 defines two callback handler functions and imports the C extension module to register handlers and trigger events.

Example 23-11. PP3E\Integrate\Mixed\Regist\register.py

```
#################################x###################
# register for and handle event callbacks from C;
# compile C code, and run with 'python register.py'
#####################################################


#
# C calls these Python functions;
# handle an event, return a result
#

def callback1(label, count):
    return 'callback1 => %s number %i' % (label, count)

def callback2(label, count):
    return 'callback2 => ' +  label * count


#
# Python calls a C extension module
# to register handlers, trigger events
#

import cregister

print '\nTest1:'
cregister.setHandler(callback1)
for i in range(3):
    cregister.triggerEvent()            # simulate events caught by C layer

print '\nTest2:'
cregister.setHandler(callback2)
for i in range(3):
    cregister.triggerEvent()            # routes these events to callback2
```

That's it—the Python/C callback integration is set to go. To kick off the system, run the Python script; it registers one handler function, forces three events to be triggered, and then changes the event handler and does it again:

```
.../PP3E/Integration/Mixed/Regist$ make -f makefile.regist
gcc cregister.c -g -I/usr/include/python2.4 -shared -L/usr/bin -lpython2.4
-o cregister.dll

.../PP3E/Integration/Mixed/Regist$ python register.py

Test1:
callback1 => spam number 0
callback1 => spam number 1
callback1 => spam number 2
```

```
Test2:
callback2 => spamspamspam
callback2 => spamspamspamspam
callback2 => spamspamspamspamspam
```

This output is printed by the C event router function, but its content is the return values of the handler functions in the Python module. Actually, something pretty wild is going on under the hood. When Python forces an event to trigger, control flows between languages like this:

1. From Python to the C event router function
2. From the C event router function to the Python handler function
3. Back to the C event router function (where the output is printed)
4. And finally back to the Python script

That is, we jump from Python to C to Python and back again. Along the way, control passes through both extending and embedding interfaces. When the Python callback handler is running, two Python levels are active, and one C level in the middle. Luckily, this just works; Python's API is reentrant, so you don't need to be concerned about having multiple Python interpreter levels active at the same time. Each level runs different code and operates independently.

Using Python Classes in C

In the previous chapter, we saw how to use C++ classes in Python by wrapping them with SWIG. But what about going the other way—using Python classes from other languages? It turns out that this is really just a matter of applying interfaces already shown.

Recall that Python scripts generate class instance objects by *calling* class objects as though they were functions. To do it from C (or C++), simply follow the same steps: import a class from a module (or elsewhere), build an arguments tuple, and call it to generate an instance using the same C API tools you use to call Python functions. Once you've got an instance, you can fetch attributes and methods with the same tools you use to fetch globals out of a module.

To illustrate how this works in practice, Example 23-12 defines a simple Python class in a module that we can utilize from C.

Example 23-12. PP3E\Integrate\Embed\ApiClients\module.py

```python
# call this class from C to make objects

class klass:
    def method(self, x, y):
        return "brave %s %s" % (x, y)   # run me from C
```

This is nearly as simple as it gets, but it's enough to illustrate the basics. As usual, make sure that this module is on your Python search path (e.g., in the current directory, or one listed on your PYTHONPATH setting), or else the import call to access it from C will fail, just as it would in a Python script. Now, here is how you might make use of this Python class from a Python program:

```
...\PP3E\Integrate\Embed\ApiClients$ python
>>> import module                            # import the file
>>> object = module.klass( )                 # make class instance
>>> result = object.method('sir', 'robin')   # call class method
>>> print result
brave sir robin
```

This is fairly easy in Python. You can do all of these operations in C too, but it takes a bit more code. The C file in Example 23-13 implements these steps by arranging calls to the appropriate Python API tools.

Example 23-13. PP3E\Integrate\Embed\ApiClients\objects-low.c

```c
#include <Python.h>
#include <stdio.h>

main( ) {
  /* run objects with low-level calls */
  char *arg1="sir", *arg2="robin", *cstr;
  PyObject *pmod, *pclass, *pargs, *pinst, *pmeth, *pres;

  /* instance = module.klass( ) */
  Py_Initialize( );
  pmod   = PyImport_ImportModule("module");          /* fetch module */
  pclass = PyObject_GetAttrString(pmod, "klass");    /* fetch module.class */
  Py_DECREF(pmod);

  pargs  = Py_BuildValue("( )");
  pinst  = PyEval_CallObject(pclass, pargs);         /* call class( ) */
  Py_DECREF(pclass);
  Py_DECREF(pargs);

  /* result = instance.method(x,y) */
  pmeth  = PyObject_GetAttrString(pinst, "method");  /* fetch bound method */
  Py_DECREF(pinst);
  pargs  = Py_BuildValue("(ss)", arg1, arg2);        /* convert to Python */
  pres   = PyEval_CallObject(pmeth, pargs);          /* call method(x,y) */
  Py_DECREF(pmeth);
  Py_DECREF(pargs);

  PyArg_Parse(pres, "s", &cstr);                     /* convert to C */
  printf("%s\n", cstr);
  Py_DECREF(pres);
}
```

Step through this source file for more details; it's mostly a matter of figuring out how you would accomplish the task in Python, and then calling equivalent C functions in the Python API. To build this source into a C executable program, run the makefile in the file's directory (it's analogous to makefiles we've already seen, so we'll omit it here—see the book's examples distribution package for a listing). After compiling, run it as you would any other C program:

```
.../PP3E/Integrate/Embed/ApiClients$ objects-low
brave sir robin
```

This output might seem anticlimactic, but it actually reflects the return values sent back to C by the class method in the file *module.py*. C did a lot of work to get this little string: it imported the module, fetched the class, made an instance, and fetched and called the instance method, performing data conversions and reference count management every step of the way. In return for all the work, C gets to use the techniques shown in this file to reuse *any* Python class.

Of course, this example would be more complex in practice. As mentioned earlier, you generally need to check the return value of every Python API call to make sure it didn't fail. The module import call in this C code, for instance, can fail easily if the module isn't on the search path; if you don't trap the NULL pointer result, your program will almost certainly crash when it tries to use the pointer (at least eventually). Example 23-14 is a recoding of Example 23-13 with full error-checking; it's big, but it's robust.

Example 23-14. PP3E\Integrate\Embed\ApiClients\objects-err-low.c

```c
#include <Python.h>
#include <stdio.h>
#define error(msg) do { printf("%s\n", msg); exit(1); } while (1)

main( ) {
    /* run objects with low-level calls and full error checking */
    char *arg1="sir", *arg2="robin", *cstr;
    PyObject *pmod, *pclass, *pargs, *pinst, *pmeth, *pres;

    /* instance = module.klass( ) */
    Py_Initialize( );
    pmod = PyImport_ImportModule("module");          /* fetch module */
    if (pmod == NULL)
        error("Can't load module");

    pclass = PyObject_GetAttrString(pmod, "klass");  /* fetch module.class */
    Py_DECREF(pmod);
    if (pclass == NULL)
        error("Can't get module.klass");

    pargs = Py_BuildValue("( )");
    if (pargs == NULL) {
        Py_DECREF(pclass);
        error("Can't build arguments list");
    }
    pinst = PyEval_CallObject(pclass, pargs);         /* call class( ) */
```

```
  Py_DECREF(pclass);
  Py_DECREF(pargs);
  if (pinst == NULL)
      error("Error calling module.klass( )");

  /* result = instance.method(x,y) */
  pmeth = PyObject_GetAttrString(pinst, "method"); /* fetch bound method */
  Py_DECREF(pinst);
  if (pmeth == NULL)
      error("Can't fetch klass.method");

  pargs = Py_BuildValue("(ss)", arg1, arg2);        /* convert to Python */
  if (pargs == NULL) {
      Py_DECREF(pmeth);
      error("Can't build arguments list");
  }
  pres = PyEval_CallObject(pmeth, pargs);           /* call method(x,y) */
  Py_DECREF(pmeth);
  Py_DECREF(pargs);
  if (pres == NULL)
      error("Error calling klass.method");

  if (!PyArg_Parse(pres, "s", &cstr))               /* convert to C */
      error("Can't convert klass.method result");
  printf("%s\n", cstr);
  Py_DECREF(pres);
}
```

A High-Level Embedding API: ppembed

As you can probably tell from Example 23-14, embedded-mode integration code can very quickly become as complicated as extending code for nontrivial use. Today, no automation solution solves the embedding problem as well as SWIG addresses extending. Because embedding does not impose the kind of structure that extension modules and types provide, it's much more of an open-ended problem; what automates one embedding strategy might be completely useless in another.

With a little upfront work, though, you can still automate common embedding tasks by wrapping up calls in higher-level APIs that make assumptions about common use cases. These APIs could handle things such as error detection, reference counts, data conversions, and so on. One such API, *ppembed*, is available in this book's examples distribution. It merely combines existing tools in Python's standard C API to provide a set of easier-to-use calls for running Python programs from C.

Running Objects with ppembed

For instance, Example 23-15 demonstrates how to recode *objects-err-low.c* in Example 23-14, by linking ppembed's library files with your program.

Example 23-15. PP3E\Integrate\Embed\ApiClients\object-api.c

```
#include <stdio.h>
#include "ppembed.h"

main () {                                      /* with ppembed high-level api */
  int failflag;
  PyObject *pinst;
  char *arg1="sir", *arg2="robin", *cstr;

  failflag = PP_Run_Function("module", "klass", "O", &pinst, "()") ||
              PP_Run_Method(pinst, "method", "s", &cstr, "(ss)", arg1, arg2);

  printf("%s\n", (!failflag) ? cstr : "Can't call objects");
  Py_XDECREF(pinst); free(cstr);
}
```

This file uses two ppembed calls (the names that start with PP) to make the class instance and call its method. Because ppembed handles error checks, reference counts, data conversions, and so on, there isn't much else to do here. When this program is run and linked with ppembed library code, it works like the original, but it is much easier to read, write, and debug:

```
.../PP3E/Integrate/Embed/ApiClients$ objects-api
brave sir robin
```

See the book's examples distribution for the makefile used to build this program; because it's similar to what we've seen and may vary widely on your system, we'll omit further build details in this chapter.

Running Code Strings with ppembed

The ppembed API provides higher-level calls for most of the embedding techniques we've seen in this chapter. For example, the C program in Example 23-16 runs code strings to make the (now rarely used) string module capitalize a simple text.

Example 23-16. PP3E\Integrate\Embed\ApiClients\codestring-low.c

```
#include <Python.h>              /* standard API defs  */
void error(char *msg) { printf("%s\n", msg); exit(1); }

main( ) {
    /* run strings with low-level calls */
    char *cstr;
    PyObject *pstr, *pmod, *pdict;                  /* with error tests */
    Py_Initialize( );

    /* result = string.upper('spam') + '!' */
    pmod = PyImport_ImportModule("string");        /* fetch module */
    if (pmod == NULL)                              /* for namespace */
        error("Can't import module");
```

```
    pdict = PyModule_GetDict(pmod);                /* string.__dict__ */
    Py_DECREF(pmod);
    if (pdict == NULL)
        error("Can't get module dict");

    pstr = PyRun_String("upper('spam') + '!'", Py_eval_input, pdict, pdict);
    if (pstr == NULL)
        error("Error while running string");

    /* convert result to C */
    if (!PyArg_Parse(pstr, "s", &cstr))
        error("Bad result type");
    printf("%s\n", cstr);
    Py_DECREF(pstr);          /* free exported objects, not pdict */
}
```

This C program file includes politically correct error tests after each API call. When run, it prints the result returned by running an uppercase conversion call in the namespace of the Python string module:

```
.../PP3E/Integrate/Embed/ApiClients$ codestring-low
SPAM!
```

You can implement such integrations by calling Python API functions directly, but you don't necessarily have to. With a higher-level embedding API such as ppembed, the task can be noticeably simpler, as shown in Example 23-17.

Example 23-17. PP3E\Integrate\Embed\ApiClients\codestring-api.c

```
#include "ppembed.h"
#include <stdio.h>
                                         /* with ppembed high-level API */
main( ) {
    char *cstr;
    int err = PP_Run_Codestr(
                    PP_EXPRESSION,                       /* expr or stmt?  */
                    "upper('spam') + '!'", "string",    /* code, module   */
                    "s", &cstr);                         /* expr result    */
    printf("%s\n", (!err) ? cstr : "Can't run string"); /* and free(cstr) */
}
```

When linked with the ppembed library code, this version produces the same result as the former. Like most higher-level APIs, ppembed makes some usage mode assumptions that are not universally applicable; when they match the embedding task at hand, though, such wrapper calls can cut much clutter from programs that need to run embedded Python code.

Running Customizable Validations

Our examples so far have been intentionally simple, but embedded Python code can do useful work as well. For instance, the C program in Example 23-18 calls ppembed functions to run a string of Python code fetched from a file that performs validation tests on inventory data. To save space, I'm not going to list all the components used by this example (you can find all of its source files and makefiles in the book's examples distribution package). Still, this file shows the embedding portions relevant to this chapter: it sets variables in the Python code's namespace to serve as input, runs the Python code, and then fetches names out of the code's namespace as results.[*]

Example 23-18. PP3E\Integrate\Embed\Inventory\order-string.c

```c
/* run embedded code-string validations */

#include <ppembed.h>
#include <stdio.h>
#include <string.h>
#include "ordersfile.h"

run_user_validation( )
{                                       /* Python is initialized automatically */
    int i, status, nbytes;              /* caveat: should check status everywhere */
    char script[4096];                  /* caveat: should malloc a big-enough block */
    char *errors, *warnings;
    FILE *file;

    file = fopen("validate1.py", "r");      /* customizable validations */
    nbytes = fread(script, 1, 4096, file);  /* load Python file text */
    script[nbytes] = '\0';

    status = PP_Make_Dummy_Module("orders"); /* application's own namespace */
    for (i=0; i < numorders; i++) {          /* like making a new dictionary */
        printf("\n%d (%d, %d, '%s')\n",
            i, orders[i].product, orders[i].quantity, orders[i].buyer);

        PP_Set_Global("orders", "PRODUCT",  "i", orders[i].product);   /* int */
        PP_Set_Global("orders", "QUANTITY", "i", orders[i].quantity);  /* int */
        PP_Set_Global("orders", "BUYER",    "s", orders[i].buyer);     /* str */

        status = PP_Run_Codestr(PP_STATEMENT, script, "orders", "", NULL);
        if (status == -1) {
            printf("Python error during validation.\n");
            PyErr_Print( );  /* show traceback */
```

---

[*] This is more or less the kind of structure used when Python is embedded in HTML files in contexts such as the Active Scripting extension described in Chapter 18, except that the globals set here (e.g., PRODUCT) become names preset to web browser objects, and the code is extracted from a web page. It is not fetched from a text file with a known name.

Example 23-18. PP3E\Integrate\Embed\Inventory\order-string.c (continued)

```
        continue;
    }

    PP_Get_Global("orders", "ERRORS",   "s", &errors);    /* can split */
    PP_Get_Global("orders", "WARNINGS", "s", &warnings);  /* on blanks */

    printf("errors:   %s\n", strlen(errors)? errors : "none");
    printf("warnings: %s\n", strlen(warnings)? warnings : "none");
    free(errors); free(warnings);
    PP_Run_Function("inventory", "print_files", "", NULL, "()");
    }
}

main(int argc, char **argv)    /* C is on top, Python is embedded */
{                              /* but Python can use C extensions too */
    run_user_validation();     /* don't need sys.argv in embedded code */
}
```

There are a couple of things worth noticing here. First, in practice, this program might fetch the Python code file's name or path from configurable shell variables; here, it is loaded from the current directory. Second, you could also code this program by using straight API calls rather than ppembed, but each of the PP calls here would then grow into a chunk of more complex code. As coded, you can compile and link this file with Python and ppembed library files to build a program. The Python code run by the resulting C program lives in Example 23-19; it uses preset globals and is assumed to set globals to send result strings back to C.

Example 23-19. PP3E\Integrate\Embed\Inventory\validate1.py

```python
# embedded validation code, run from C
# input vars:  PRODUCT, QUANTITY, BUYER
# output vars: ERRORS, WARNINGS

import string           # all Python tools are available to embedded code
import inventory        # plus C extensions, Python modules, classes,..
msgs, errs = [], []     # warning, error message lists

def validate_order():
    if PRODUCT not in inventory.skus():     # this function could be imported
        errs.append('bad-product')          # from a user-defined module too
    elif QUANTITY > inventory.stock(PRODUCT):
        errs.append('check-quantity')
    else:
        inventory.reduce(PRODUCT, QUANTITY)
        if inventory.stock(PRODUCT) / QUANTITY < 2:
            msgs.append('reorder-soon:' + repr(PRODUCT))

first, last = BUYER[0], BUYER[1:]       # code is changeable onsite:
if first not in string.uppercase:       # this file is run as one long
    errs.append('buyer-name:' + first)  # code string, with input and
if BUYER not in inventory.buyers():     # output vars used by the C app
```

Example 23-19. PP3E\Integrate\Embed\Inventory\validate1.py (continued)

```
    msgs.append('new-buyer-added')
    inventory.add_buyer(BUYER)
validate_order()

ERRORS   = ' '.join(errs)      # add a space between messages
WARNINGS = ' '.join(msgs)      # pass out as strings: "" == none
```

Don't sweat the details in this code; some components it uses are not listed here either (see the book's examples distribution for the full implementation). The thing you should notice, though, is that this code file can contain any kind of Python code—it can define functions and classes, use sockets and threads, and so on. When you embed Python, you get a full-featured extension language for free. Perhaps even more importantly, because this file is Python code, it can be changed arbitrarily without having to recompile the C program. Such flexibility is especially useful after a system has been shipped and installed.

Running function-based validations

As discussed earlier, there are a variety of ways to structure embedded Python code. For instance, you can implement similar flexibility by delegating actions to Python functions fetched from module files, as illustrated in Example 23-20.

Example 23-20. PP3E\Integrate\Embed\Inventory\order-func.c

```c
/* run embedded module-function validations */

#include <ppembed.h>
#include <stdio.h>
#include <string.h>
#include "ordersfile.h"

run_user_validation() {
    int i, status;              /* should check status everywhere */
    char *errors, *warnings;    /* no file/string or namespace here */
    PyObject *results;

    for (i=0; i < numorders; i++) {
        printf("\n%d (%d, %d, '%s')\n",
            i, orders[i].product, orders[i].quantity, orders[i].buyer);

        status = PP_Run_Function(                   /* validate2.validate(p,q,b) */
                    "validate2", "validate",
                    "O",            &results,
                    "(iis)",        orders[i].product,
                                    orders[i].quantity, orders[i].buyer);
        if (status == -1) {
            printf("Python error during validation.\n");
            PyErr_Print();  /* show traceback */
            continue;
        }
```

Example 23-20. PP3E\Integrate\Embed\Inventory\order-func.c (continued)

```
        PyArg_Parse(results, "(ss)", &warnings, &errors);
        printf("errors:    %s\n", strlen(errors)? errors : "none");
        printf("warnings: %s\n", strlen(warnings)? warnings : "none");
        Py_DECREF(results);  /* ok to free strings */
        PP_Run_Function("inventory", "print_files", "", NULL, "()");
    }
}

main(int argc, char **argv) {
    run_user_validation();
}
```

The difference here is that the Python code file (shown in Example 23-21) is imported and so must live on the Python module search path. It also is assumed to contain functions, not a simple list of statements. Strings can live anywhere—files, databases, web pages, and so on—and may be simpler for end users to code. But assuming that the extra requirements of module functions are not prohibitive, functions provide a natural communication model in the form of arguments and return values.

Example 23-21. PP3E\Integrate\Embed\Inventory\validate2.py

```
# embedded validation code, run from C
# input = args, output = return value tuple

import string
import inventory

def validate(product, quantity, buyer):        # function called by name
    msgs, errs = [], []                         # via mod/func name strings
    first, last = buyer[0], buyer[1:]
    if first not in string.uppercase:           # or not first.isupper()
        errs.append('buyer-name:' + first)
    if buyer not in inventory.buyers():
        msgs.append('new-buyer-added')
        inventory.add_buyer(buyer)
    validate_order(product, quantity, errs, msgs)   # mutable list args
    return ' '.join(msgs), ' '.join(errs)           # use "(ss)" format

def validate_order(product, quantity, errs, msgs):
    if product not in inventory.skus():
        errs.append('bad-product')
    elif quantity > inventory.stock(product):
        errs.append('check-quantity')
    else:
        inventory.reduce(product, quantity)
        if inventory.stock(product) / quantity < 2:
            msgs.append('reorder-soon:' + repr(product))
```

Other validation components

For another API use case, the file *order-bytecode.c* in the book's source distribution shows how to utilize ppembed's convenience functions to precompile strings to byte-code for speed. It's similar to Example 23-18, but it calls `PP_Compile_Codestr` to compile and `PP_Run_Bytecode` to run.

For reference, the database used by the validations code was initially prototyped for testing with the Python module inventory.py (see Example 23-22).

Example 23-22. PP3E\Integrate\Embed\Inventory\inventory.py

```
# simulate inventory/buyer databases while prototyping

Inventory = { 111: 10,        # "sku (product#) : quantity"
              555: 1,         # would usually be a file or shelve:
              444: 100,       # the operations below could work on
              222: 5 }        # an open shelve (or DBM file) too...

Skus = Inventory.keys()       # cache keys if they won't change

def skus():           return Skus
def stock(sku):       return Inventory[sku]
def reduce(sku, qty): Inventory[sku] = Inventory[sku] - qty

Buyers = ['GRossum', 'JOusterhout', 'LWall']   # or keys() of a shelve|DBM file

def buyers():         return Buyers
def add_buyer(buyer): Buyers.append(buyer)

def print_files():
    print Inventory, Buyers     # check effect of updates
```

And the list of orders to process was simulated with the C header file *ordersfile.h* (see Example 23-23).

Example 23-23. PP3E\Integrate\Embed\Inventory\ordersfile.h

```
/* simulated file/dbase of orders to be filled */

struct {
    int product;        /* or use a string if key is structured: */
    int quantity;       /* Python code can split it up as needed */
    char *buyer;        /* by convention, first-initial+last */
} orders[] =
{
    {111, 2, "GRossum"     },    /* this would usually be an orders file */
    {222, 5, "LWall"       },    /* which the Python code could read too */
    {333, 3, "JOusterhout" },
    {222, 1, "4Spam"       },
    {222, 0, "LTorvalds"   },    /* the script might live in a database too */
    {444, 9, "ERaymond"    }
};
int numorders = 6;
```

Both of these serve for prototyping, but are intended to be replaced with real database and file interfaces in later mutations of the system. See the *WithDbase* subdirectory in the book's source distribution for more on this thread. See also the Python-coded equivalents of the C files listed in this section; they were initially prototyped in Python too.

And finally, here is the output produced the C string–based program in Example 23-18 when using the prototyping components listed in this section. The output is printed by C, but it reflects the results of the Python-coded validations it runs:[*]

```
.../PP3E/Integrate/Embed/Inventory$ ./order-string

0 (111, 2, 'GRossum')
errors:   none
warnings: none
{555: 1, 444: 100, 222: 5, 111: 8} ['GRossum', 'JOusterhout', 'LWall']

1 (222, 5, 'LWall')
errors:   none
warnings: reorder-soon:222
{555: 1, 444: 100, 222: 0, 111: 8} ['GRossum', 'JOusterhout', 'LWall']

2 (333, 3, 'JOusterhout')
errors:   bad-product
warnings: none
{555: 1, 444: 100, 222: 0, 111: 8} ['GRossum', 'JOusterhout', 'LWall']

3 (222, 1, '4Spam')
errors:   buyer-name:4 check-quantity
warnings: new-buyer-added
{555: 1, 444: 100, 222: 0, 111: 8} ['GRossum', 'JOusterhout', 'LWall', '4Spam']

4 (222, 0, 'LTorvalds')
Python error during validation.
Traceback (most recent call last):
  File "<string>", line 25, in ?
  File "<string>", line 16, in validate_order
ZeroDivisionError: integer division or modulo by zero

5 (444, 9, 'ERaymond')
errors:   none
warnings: new-buyer-added
{555: 1, 444: 91, 222: 0, 111: 8} ['GRossum', 'JOusterhout', 'LWall', '4Spam',
'LTorvalds', 'ERaymond']
```

The function-based output is similar, but more details are printed for the exception (function calls are active; they are not a single string). Trace through the Python and

---

[*] Note that to get this example to work under Cygwin on Windows, I had to run the Python file through dos2unix to convert line-end characters; as always, your platform may vary.

C code files to see how orders are validated and applied to inventory. This output is a bit cryptic because the system is still a work in progress at this stage. One of the nice features of Python, though, is that it enables such incremental development. In fact, with its integration interfaces, we can simulate future components in either Python or C.

ppembed Implementation

The ppembed API originally appeared as an example in the first edition of this book. Since then, it has been utilized in real systems and has become too large to present here in its entirety. For instance, ppembed also supports debugging embedded code (by routing it to the pdb debugger module), dynamically reloading modules containing embedded code, and other features too complex to illustrate usefully here.

But if you are interested in studying another example of Python embedding calls in action, ppembed's full source code and makefile live in this book's examples distribution:

> *PP3E\Integration\Embed\HighLevelApi*

This API serves as a supplemental example of advanced embedding techniques. As a sample of the kinds of tools you can build to simplify embedding, the ppembed API's header file is shown in Example 23-24. You are invited to study, use, copy, and improve its code as you like.

Or you can simply write an API of your own; the main point to take from this section is that embedding programs need to be complicated only if you stick with the Python runtime API as shipped. By adding convenience functions such as those in ppembed, embedding can be as simple as you make it. It also makes your C programs immune to changes in the Python C core; ideally, only the API must change if Python ever does. In fact, the third edition of this book proved this point: one of the utilities in the API had to be patched for a change in the Python/C API, but only one update was required.

Be sure to also see the file *abstract.h* in the Python *include* directory if you are in the market for higher-level interfaces. That file provides generic type operation calls that make it easy to do things like creating, filling, indexing, slicing, and concatenating Python objects referenced by pointer from C. Also see the corresponding implementation file, *abstract.c*, as well as the Python built-in module and type implementations in the Python source distribution for more examples of lower-level object access. Once you have a Python object pointer in C, you can do all sorts of type-specific things to Python inputs and outputs.

Example 23-24. PP3E\Integrate\Embed\HighLevelApi\ppembed.h

```
/****************************************************************************
 * PPEMBED, VERSION 2.1
 * AN ENHANCED PYTHON EMBEDDED-CALL INTERFACE
 *
 * Wraps Python's runtime embedding API functions for easy use.
 * Most utilities assume the call is qualified by an enclosing module
 * (namespace). The module can be a filename reference or a dummy module
 * created to provide a namespace for fileless strings. These routines
 * automate debugging, module (re)loading, input/output conversions, etc.
 *
 * Python is automatically initialized when the first API call occurs.
 * Input/output conversions use the standard Python conversion format
 * codes (described in the C API manual).  Errors are flagged as either
 * a -1 int, or a NULL pointer result.  Exported names use a PP_ prefix
 * to minimize clashes; names in the built-in Python API use Py prefixes
 * instead (alas, there is no "import" equivalent in C, just "from*").
 * Also note that the varargs code here may not be portable to certain
 * C compilers; to do it portably, see the text or file 'vararg.txt'
 * here, or search for string STDARG in Python's source code files.
 *
 * New in version 2.1 (3rd Edition): minor fix for a change in the
 * Python C API: ppembed-callables.c call to _PyTuple_Resize -- added
 * code to manually move args to the right because the original
 * isSticky argument is now gone;
 *
 * New in version 2.0 (2nd Edition): names now have a PP_ prefix,
 * files renamed, compiles to a single file, fixed pdb retval bug
 * for strings, char* results returned by the "s" convert code now
 * point to new char arrays which the caller should free( ) when no
 * longer needed (this was a potential bug in prior version).  Also
 * added new API interfaces for fetching exception info after errors,
 * precompiling code strings to byte code, and calling simple objects.
 *
 * Also fully supports Python 1.5 module package imports: module names
 * in this API can take the form "package.package.[...].module", where
 * Python maps the package names to a nested directories path in your
 * filesystem hierarchy;  package dirs all contain __init__.py files,
 * and the leftmost one is in a directory found on PYTHONPATH. This
 * API's dynamic reload feature also works for modules in packages;
 * Python stores the full pathname in the sys.modules dictionary.
 *
 * Caveats: there is no support for advanced things like threading or
 * restricted execution mode here, but such things may be added with
 * extra Python API calls external to this API (see the Python/C API
 * manual for C-level threading calls; see modules rexec and bastion
 * in the library manual for restricted mode details).  For threading,
 * you may also be able to get by with C threads and distinct Python
 * namespaces per Python code segments, or Python language threads
 * started by Python code run from C (see the Python thread module).
 *
 * Note that Python can only reload Python modules, not C extensions,
 * but it's okay to leave the dynamic reload flag on even if you might
```

Example 23-24. PP3E\Integrate\Embed\HighLevelApi\ppembed.h (continued)

```
 * access dynamically loaded C extension modules--in 1.5.2, Python
 * simply resets C extension modules to their initial attribute state
 * when reloaded, but doesn't actually reload the C extension file.
 *********************************************************************/

#ifndef PPEMBED_H
#define PPEMBED_H

#ifdef __cplusplus
extern "C" {             /* a C library, but callable from C++ */
#endif

#include <stdio.h>
#include <Python.h>

extern int PP_RELOAD;    /* 1=reload py modules when attributes referenced */
extern int PP_DEBUG;     /* 1=start debugger when string/function/member run */

typedef enum {
    PP_EXPRESSION,       /* which kind of code-string */
    PP_STATEMENT         /* expressions and statements differ */
} PPStringModes;


/************************************************/
/*  ppembed-modules.c: load,access module objects  */
/************************************************/

extern char     *PP_Init(char *modname);
extern int       PP_Make_Dummy_Module(char *modname);
extern PyObject *PP_Load_Module(char *modname);
extern PyObject *PP_Load_Attribute(char *modname, char *attrname);
extern int       PP_Run_Command_Line(char *prompt);


/*********************************************************/
/*  ppembed-globals.c: read,write module-level variables  */
/*********************************************************/

extern int
    PP_Convert_Result(PyObject *presult, char *resFormat, void *resTarget);

extern int
    PP_Get_Global(char *modname, char *varname, char *resfmt, void *cresult);

extern int
    PP_Set_Global(char *modname, char *varname, char *valfmt, ... /*val*/);


/************************************************/
/*  ppembed-strings.c: run strings of Python code  */
/************************************************/
```

Example 23-24. PP3E\Integrate\Embed\HighLevelApi\ppembed.h (continued)

```
extern int                                         /* run C string of code */
    PP_Run_Codestr(PPStringModes mode,             /* code=expr or stmt?  */
                char *code,   char *modname,        /* codestr, modnamespace */
                char *resfmt, void *cresult);       /* result type, target */

extern PyObject*
    PP_Debug_Codestr(PPStringModes mode,           /* run string in pdb */
                char *codestring, PyObject *moddict);

extern PyObject *
    PP_Compile_Codestr(PPStringModes mode,
                    char *codestr);                 /* precompile to bytecode */

extern int
    PP_Run_Bytecode(PyObject *codeobj,             /* run a bytecode object */
                char    *modname,
                char    *resfmt, void *restarget);

extern PyObject *                                   /* run bytecode under pdb */
    PP_Debug_Bytecode(PyObject *codeobject, PyObject *moddict);


/******************************************************/
/*  ppembed-callables.c: call functions, classes, etc. */
/******************************************************/

extern int                                          /* mod.func(args) */
    PP_Run_Function(char *modname, char *funcname,  /* func|classname */
                char *resfmt,  void *cresult,        /* result target  */
                char *argfmt,  ... /* arg, arg... */ ); /* input arguments*/

extern PyObject*
    PP_Debug_Function(PyObject *func, PyObject *args);   /* call func in pdb */

extern int
    PP_Run_Known_Callable(PyObject *object,             /* func|class|method */
                    char *resfmt, void *restarget,  /* skip module fetch */
                    char *argfmt, ... /* arg,.. */ );


/************************************************************/
/*  ppembed-attributes.c: run object methods, access members  */
/************************************************************/

extern int
    PP_Run_Method(PyObject *pobject, char *method,    /* uses Debug_Function */
                char *resfmt,  void *cresult,        /* output */
                char *argfmt,  ... /* arg, arg... */ );   /* inputs */

extern int
    PP_Get_Member(PyObject *pobject, char *attrname,
                char *resfmt,  void *cresult);            /* output */
```

Example 23-24. PP3E\Integrate\Embed\HighLevelApi\ppembed.h (continued)

```
extern int
    PP_Set_Member(PyObject *pobject, char *attrname,
                      char *valfmt, ... /* val, val... */ );    /* input */


/********************************************************/
/* ppembed-errors.c: get exception data after API error */
/********************************************************/

extern void PP_Fetch_Error_Text();    /* fetch (and clear) exception */

extern char PP_last_error_type[];     /* exception name text */
extern char PP_last_error_info[];     /* exception data text */
extern char PP_last_error_trace[];    /* exception traceback text */

extern PyObject *PP_last_traceback;   /* saved exception traceback object */


#ifdef __cplusplus
}
#endif

#endif /* !PPEMBED_H */
```

Other Integration Examples (External)

While writing this chapter, I ran out of space before I ran out of examples. Besides the ppembed API example described in the last section, you can find a handful of additional Python/C integration self-study examples in this book's examples distribution:

PP3E\Integration\Embed\Inventory
> The full implementation of the validation examples listed earlier. This case study uses the ppembed API to run embedded Python order validations, both as embedded code strings and as functions fetched from modules. The inventory is implemented with and without shelves and pickle files for data persistence.

PP3E\Integration\Mixed\Exports
> A tool for exporting C variables for use in embedded Python programs.

PP3E\Integration\Embed\TestApi
> A ppembed test program, shown with and without package import paths to identify modules.

Some of these are large C examples that are probably better studied than listed.

Other Integration Topics

In this book, the term *integration* has largely meant mixing Python with components written in C or C++ (or other C-compatible languages) in extending and embedding modes. But from a broader perspective, integration also includes any other technology that lets us mix Python components into larger systems. This last section briefly looks at a handful of integration technologies beyond the C API tools we've seen in this part of the book.

Jython: Java Integration

We met Jython in Chapter 18 but it is worth another mention in the context of integration at large. As we saw earlier, Jython supports two kinds of integration:

- Jython uses Java's *reflection API* to allow Python programs to call out to Java class libraries automatically (extending). The Java reflection API provides Java type information at runtime and serves the same purpose as the glue code we've generated to plug C libraries into Python in this part of the book. In Jython, however, this runtime type information allows largely automated resolution of Java calls in Python scripts—no glue code has to be written or generated.

- Jython also provides a Java `PythonInterpreter` class API that allows Java programs to run Python code in a namespace (embedding), much like the C API tools we've used to run Python code strings from C programs. In addition, because Jython implements all Python objects as instances of a Java `PyObject` class, it is straightforward for the Java layer that encloses embedded Python code to process Python objects.

In other words, Jython allows Python to be both extended and embedded in Java, much like the C integration strategies we've seen in this part of the book. By adding a simpler scripting language to Java applications, Jython serves many of the same roles as the C integration tools we've studied. With the addition of the Jython system, Python may be integrated with any C-compatible program by using C API tools, as well as any Java-compatible program by using Jython.

Although Jython provides a remarkably seamless integration model, Python code runs slower in the Jython implementation, and its reliance on Java class libraries and execution environments introduces Java dependencies that may be a concern in some Python-oriented development scenarios. See Chapter 18 for more Jython details; for the full story, read the documentation available online at *http://www.jython.org*.

IronPython: C#/.NET Integration

Much like Jython, the emerging IronPython implementation of the Python language promises to provide seamless integration between Python code and software components written for the .NET framework. Although .NET is a Microsoft Windows initiative, the Mono open source implementation of .NET for Linux provides .NET functionality in a cross-platform fashion. Like Jython, IronPython compiles Python source code to the .NET systems bytecode format and runs programs on the system's runtime engine. As a result, integration with external components is similarly seamless.

Also like Jython, the net effect is to provide Python as an easy-to-use scripting language for C#/.NET-base applications, and a rapid development tool that complements C#. For more details on IronPython, as well as its alternatives such as Python.NET, do a web search on Google.com or visit Python's home page at *http://www.python.org*.

COM Integration on Windows

We briefly discussed Python's support for the COM object model on Windows when we explored Active Scripting in Chapter 18, but it's really a general integration tool that is useful apart from the Internet too.

Recall that COM defines a standard and language-neutral object model with which components written in a variety of programming languages may integrate and communicate. Python's PyWin32 Windows extension package tools allow Python programs to implement both server and client in the COM interface model.

As such, it provides a powerful way to integrate Python programs with programs written in other COM-aware languages such as Visual Basic, Delphi, Visual C++, PowerBuilder, and even other Python programs. Python scripts can also use COM calls to script popular Microsoft applications such as Word and Excel, since these systems register COM object interfaces of their own.

On the downside, COM implies a level of dispatch indirection and is a Windows-only solution at this writing. As a result, it is not as fast or as portable as some of the lower-level integration schemes we've studied in this part of the book (linked-in, in-process, and direct calls between Python and C-compatible language components). For nontrivial use, COM is also considered to be a large system, and further details about it are well beyond the scope of this book.

For more information on COM support and other Windows extensions, refer to Chapter 18 in this book, and to O'Reilly's *Python Programming on Win32*, by Mark Hammond and Andy Robinson. That book also describes how to use Windows compilers to do Python/C integration in much more detail than is possible here; for instance, it shows how to use Visual C++ tools to compile and link Python C/C++ integration layer code. The basic C code behind low-level extending and embedding on Windows is the same as shown in this book, but compiling and linking details vary.

CORBA Integration

There is also much open source support for using Python in the context of a CORBA-based application. *CORBA* stands for the Common Object Request Broker; it's a language-neutral way to distribute systems among communicating components, which speak through an object model architecture. As such, it represents another way to integrate Python components into a larger system.

Python's CORBA support includes the public domain systems OmniORB, ILU, and fnorb (see *http://www.python.org* or do a web search for pointers). The OMG (Object Management Group, responsible for directing CORBA growth) has also played host to an effort to elect Python as the standard scripting language for CORBA-based systems. Python is an ideal language for programming distributed objects, and it is being used in such a role by many companies around the world.

Like COM, CORBA is a large system—too large for us to even scratch the surface in this text. For more details, search Python's web site for CORBA-related materials.

Other Languages

In the public domain, you'll also find direct support for mixing Python with other compiled languages. For example, the f2py and PyFort systems provide integration with FORTRAN code, and other tools provide access to languages such as Delphi and Objective-C. The PyObjC project, for instance, aims to provide a bridge between Python and Objective-C, the most important usage of which is writing Cocoa GUI applications on Mac OS X in Python. Search the Web for details on other language-integration tools.

Network-Based Integration Protocols

Finally, there is also support in the Python world for Internet-based data transport protocols, including SOAP, XML-RPC, and even basic HTTP. Some of these support the notion of Python as an implementation language for web services. These are distributed models, generally designed for integration across a network, rather than in-process calls. XML-RPC is supported by a standard library module in Python, but search the Web for more details on these protocols.

Integration Versus Optimization

Given so many integration options, choosing among them can be puzzling. For instance, when should you choose something like COM over writing C extension modules? As usual, it depends on why you're interested in mixing external components into your Python programs in the first place.

Basically, frameworks such as Jython, IronPython, COM, and CORBA allow Python scripts to leverage existing libraries of software components, and they do a great job of addressing goals such as code reuse and integration. However, they say almost nothing about optimization: integrated components are not necessarily faster than the Python equivalents.

On the other hand, Python extension modules and types coded in a compiled language such as C serve two roles: they too can be used to integrate existing components, but they also tend to be a better approach when it comes to boosting system performance. In closing, here are a few words of context.

Framework roles

Frameworks such as COM and CORBA can perhaps be understood as alternatives to the Python/C integration techniques we met in this part of the book. For example, packaging Python logic as a COM *server* makes it available for something akin to *embedding*—many languages (including C) can access it using the COM client-side interfaces we met in Chapter 18. And as we saw earlier, Jython allows Java to embed and run Python code and objects through a Java class interface.

Furthermore, frameworks allow Python scripts to use existing component libraries: standard Java class libraries in Jython, COM server libraries on Windows, and so on. In such a role, the external libraries exposed by such frameworks are more or less analogous to Python extension modules. For instance, Python scripts that use COM client interfaces to access an external object are acting much like importers of C extension modules (albeit through the COM indirection layer).

Extension module roles

Python's C API is designed to serve in many of the same roles. As we've seen, C extension modules can serve as code reuse and integration tools too—it's straightforward to plug existing C and C++ libraries into Python with SWIG. In most cases, we simply generate and import the glue code created with SWIG to make almost any existing compiled library available for use in Python scripts.

In fact, as we saw in the preceding chapter, it's so easy to plug in libraries with SWIG that extensions are usually best coded first as simple C/C++ libraries and later wrapped for use in Python with SWIG. Adding a COM layer to an existing C library may or may not be as straightforward, but it will clearly be less portable—COM is currently a Windows-only technology. Moreover, Python's embedding API allows other languages to run Python code, much like client-side interfaces in COM.

One of the primary reasons for writing C extension modules in the first place, though, is *optimization*: key parts of Python applications may be implemented or recoded as C or C++ extension modules to speed up the system at large (as in the last chapter's stack examples). Moving such components to compiled extension modules not only improves system performance, but also is completely seamless—module interfaces in Python look the same no matter what programming language implements the module.

Picking an integration technology

By contrast, Jython, COM, and CORBA do not deal directly with optimization goals at all; they serve only to integrate. For instance, Jython allows Python scripts to automatically access Java libraries, but it generally mandates that non-Python extensions be coded in the Java language that is itself usually interpreted and is no speed demon. COM and CORBA focus on the interfaces between components and leave the component implementation language ambiguous by design. Exporting a Python class as a COM server, for instance, can make its tools widely reusable on Windows but has little to do with performance improvement.

Because of their different focus, frameworks are not quite replacements for the more direct Python/C extension modules and types we've studied in these last two chapters, and they are less direct (and hence likely slower) than Python's C embedding API. It's possible to mix-and-match approaches, but the combinations are rarely any better than their parts. For example, although C libraries can be added to Java with its native call interface, it's neither a secure nor a straightforward undertaking. And while C libraries can also be wrapped as COM servers to make them visible to Python scripts on Windows, the end result will probably be slower and no less complex than a more directly linked-in Python extension module.

As you can see, there are a lot of options in the integration domain. Perhaps the best parting advice I can give you is simply that different tools are meant for different tasks. C extension modules and types are ideal at optimizing systems and integrating libraries, but frameworks offer other ways to integrate components—Jython for mixing in Java tools, COM for reusing and publishing objects on Windows, and so on. As always, your mileage may vary.

## PART VII

The End

This last part of the book wraps up with a single short chapter:

Chapter 24, *Conclusion: Python and the Development Cycle*
This chapter discusses Python's roles and scope. It returns to some of the broader ideas that were introduced in Chapter 1, with the added perspective afforded by the rest of the book. Much of this chapter is philosophical in nature, but it underscores some of the main reasons for using a tool like Python.

Note that there are no reference appendixes here. For additional reference resources, consult the Python standard manuals available online, or commercially published reference books such as O'Reilly's *Python Pocket Reference*, by Mark Lutz, and *Python in a Nutshell*, by Alex Martelli, as well as *Python Essential Reference*, by David M. Beazley (Sams).

For additional Python core language material, see O'Reilly's *Learning Python*, by Mark Lutz. And for help on other Python-related topics, see the resources available at Python's official web site, *http://www.python.org*, or search the Web using your favorite web search engine.

Conclusion: Python and the Development Cycle

"That's the End of the Book, Now Here's the Meaning of Life"

Well, the meaning of Python, anyway. In the introduction to this book, I promised that we'd return to the issue of Python's roles after seeing how it is used in practice. So in closing, here are some subjective comments on the broader implications of the language. Most of this conclusion remains unchanged since the first edition of this book was penned in 1995, but so are the factors that pushed Python into the development spotlight.

As I mentioned in the first chapter, Python's focus is on concepts such as *quality*, *productivity*, *portability*, and *integration*. I hope that this book has demonstrated some of the benefits of that focus in action. Along the way, we've seen Python applied to systems programming, GUI development, Internet scripting, database and text processing, and more. And we've witnessed firsthand the application of the language to realistically scaled tasks. I hope you've also had some fun; that, too, is part of the Python story.

In this conclusion, I wish now to return to the forest after our long walk among the trees—to revisit Python's roles in more concrete terms. In particular, Python's role as a prototyping tool can profoundly affect the development cycle.

"Something's Wrong with the Way We Program Computers"

This has to be one of the most overused lines in the business. Still, given time to ponder the big picture, most of us would probably agree that we're not quite "there" yet. Over the last few decades, the computer software industry has made significant progress on streamlining the development task (anyone remember dropping punch cards?). But at the same time, the cost of developing potentially useful computer applications is often still high enough to make them impractical.

Moreover, systems built using modern tools and paradigms are often delivered far behind schedule. Software engineering remains largely defiant of the sort of quantitative measurements employed in other engineering fields. In the software world, it's not uncommon to take one's best time estimate for a new project and multiply by a factor of two or three to account for unforeseen overheads in the development task. This situation is clearly unsatisfactory for software managers, developers, and end users.

The "Gilligan Factor"

It has been suggested, tongue in cheek, that if there were a patron saint of software engineers, the honor would fall on none other than Gilligan, the character in the pervasively popular American television show of the 1960s, *Gilligan's Island*. Gilligan is the enigmatic, sneaker-clad first mate, widely held to be responsible for the shipwreck that stranded the now-residents of the island.

To be sure, Gilligan's situation seems oddly familiar. Stranded on a desert island with only the most meager of modern technological comforts, Gilligan and his cohorts must resort to scratching out a living using the resources naturally available. In episode after episode, we observe the Professor developing exquisitely intricate tools for doing the business of life on their remote island, only to be foiled in the implementation phase by the ever-bungling Gilligan.

But clearly it was never poor Gilligan's fault. How could one possibly be expected to implement designs for such sophisticated applications as home appliances and telecommunications devices, given the rudimentary technologies available in such an environment? He simply lacked the proper tools. For all we know, Gilligan may have had the capacity for engineering on the grandest level. But you can't get there with bananas and coconuts.

And pathologically, time after time, Gilligan wound up inadvertently sabotaging the best of the Professor's plans: misusing, abusing, and eventually destroying his inventions. If he could just pedal his makeshift stationary bicycle faster and faster (he was led to believe), all would be well. But in the end, inevitably, the coconuts were sent hurling into the air, the palm branches came crashing down around his head, and poor Gilligan was blamed once again for the failure of the technology.

Dramatic though this image may be, some observers would consider it a striking metaphor for the software industry. Like Gilligan, we software engineers are often asked to perform tasks with arguably inappropriate tools. Like Gilligan, our intentions are sound, but technology can hold us back. And like poor Gilligan, we inevitably must bear the brunt of management's wrath when our systems are delivered behind schedule. You can't get there with bananas and coconuts....

Doing the Right Thing

Of course, the Gilligan factor is an exaggeration, added for comic effect. But few would argue that the bottleneck between ideas and working systems has disappeared completely. Even today, the cost of developing software far exceeds the cost of computer hardware. And when software is finally delivered, it often comes with failure rates that would be laughable in other engineering domains. Why must programming be so complex?

Let's consider the situation carefully. By and large, the root of the complexity in developing software isn't related to the role it's supposed to perform—usually this is a well-defined, real-world process. Rather, it stems from the mapping of real-world tasks onto computer-executable models. And this mapping is performed in the context of programming languages and tools.

The path toward easing the software bottleneck must therefore lie, at least partially, in optimizing the act of programming itself by deploying the right tools. Given this realistic scope, there's much that can be done now—there are a number of purely artificial overheads inherent in our current tools.

The Static Language Build Cycle

Using traditional static languages, there is an unavoidable overhead in moving from coded programs to working systems: compile and link steps add a built-in delay to the development process. In some environments, it's common to spend many hours each week just waiting for a static language application's build cycle to finish. Given that modern development practice involves an iterative process of building, testing, and rebuilding, such delays can be expensive and demoralizing (if not physically painful).

Of course, this varies from shop to shop, and in some domains the demand for performance justifies build-cycle delays. But I've worked in C++ environments where programmers joked about having to go to lunch whenever they recompiled their systems. Except they weren't really joking.

Artificial Complexities

With many traditional programming tools, you can easily lose focus: the very act of programming becomes so complex that the real-world goal of the program is obscured. Traditional languages divert valuable attention to syntactic issues and development of bookkeeping code. Obviously, complexity isn't an end in itself; it must be clearly warranted. Yet some of our current tools are so complex that the language itself makes the task harder and lengthens the development process.

One Language Does Not Fit All

Many traditional languages implicitly encourage homogeneous, single-language systems. By making integration complex, they impede the use of multiple-language tools. As a result, instead of being able to select the right tool for the task at hand, developers are often compelled to use the same language for every component of an application. Since no language is good at everything, this constraint inevitably sacrifices both product functionality and programmer productivity.

Until our machines are as clever at taking directions as we are (arguably, not the most rational of goals), the task of programming won't go away. But for the time being, we can make substantial progress by making the mechanics of that task easier. This topic is what I want to talk about now.

Enter Python

If this book has achieved its goals, you should by now have a good understanding of why Python has been called a "next-generation scripting language." Compared with similar tools, it has some critical distinctions that we're finally in a position to summarize:

Tcl

> Like Tcl, Python can be used as an embedded extension language. Unlike Tcl, Python is also a full-featured programming language. For many, Python's data structure tools and support for programming-in-the-large make it useful in more domains. Tcl demonstrated the utility of integrating interpreted languages with C modules. Python provides similar functionality plus a powerful, object-oriented language; it's not just a command string processor.

Perl

> Like Perl, Python can be used for writing shell tools, making it easy to use system services. Unlike Perl, Python has a simple, readable syntax and a remarkably coherent design. For some, this makes Python easier to use and a better choice for programs that must be reused or maintained by others. Without question, Perl is a powerful system administration tool. But once we move beyond processing text and files, Python's features become attractive.

Scheme/Lisp

> Like Scheme (and Lisp), Python supports dynamic typing, incremental development, and metaprogramming; it exposes the interpreter's state and supports runtime program construction. Unlike Lisp, Python has a procedural syntax that is familiar to users of mainstream languages such as C and Pascal. If extensions are to be coded by end users, this can be a major advantage.

Smalltalk

Like Smalltalk, Python supports object-oriented programming (OOP) in the context of a highly dynamic language. Unlike Smalltalk, Python doesn't extend the object system to include fundamental program control flow constructs. Users need not come to grips with the concept of if statements as message-receiving objects to use Python—Python is more conventional.

Icon

Like Icon, Python supports a variety of high-level datatypes and operations such as lists, dictionaries, and slicing. Unlike Icon, Python is fundamentally simple. Programmers (and end users) don't need to master esoteric concepts such as backtracking just to get started.

BASIC

Like modern structured BASIC dialects, Python has an interpretive/interactive nature. Unlike most BASICs, Python includes standard support for advanced programming features such as classes, modules, exceptions, high-level datatypes, and general C integration. And unlike Visual Basic, Python provides a cross-platform solution, which is not controlled by a commercially vested company.

Java

Like Java, Python is a general-purpose language, supports OOP, exceptions, and modular design, and compiles to a portable bytecode format. Unlike Java, Python's simple syntax and built-in datatypes make development much more rapid. Python programs are typically one-third to one-fifth the size of the equivalent Java program.

C/C++

Like C and C++, Python is a general-purpose language and can be used for long-term strategic system development tasks. Unlike compiled languages in general, Python also works well in tactical mode, as a rapid development language. Python programs are smaller, simpler, and more flexible than those written in compiled languages. For instance, because Python code does not constrain datatypes or sizes, it both is more concise and can be applied in a broader range of contexts. (For more on this comparison, see the sidebar "Why Not Just Use C or C++?" in Chapter 1.)

All of these languages (and others) have merit and unique strengths of their own—in fact, Python borrowed most of its features from languages such as these. It's not Python's goal to replace every other language; different tasks require different tools, and mixed-language development is one of Python's main ideas. But Python's blend of advanced programming constructs and integration tools make it a natural choice for the problem domains we've talked about in this book, and many more.

But What About That Bottleneck?

Back to our original question: how can the act of writing software be made easier? At some level, Python is really "just another computer language." It's certainly true that Python the language doesn't represent much that's radically new from a theoretical point of view. So why should we be excited about Python when so many languages have been tried already?

What makes Python of interest, and what may be its larger contribution to the development world, is not its syntax or semantics, but its world view: Python's combination of tools makes rapid development a realistic goal. In a nutshell, Python fosters rapid development by providing features like these:

- Fast build-cycle turnaround
- A very high-level, object-oriented language
- Integration facilities to enable mixed-language development

Specifically, Python attacks the software development bottleneck on four fronts, described in the following sections.

Python Provides Immediate Turnaround

Python's development cycle is dramatically shorter than that of traditional tools. In Python, there are no compile or link steps—Python programs simply import modules at runtime and use the objects they contain. Because of this, Python programs run immediately after changes are made. And in cases where dynamic module reloading can be used, it's even possible to change and reload parts of a running program without stopping it at all. Figure 24-1 shows Python's impact on the development cycle.

Because Python is interpreted, there's a rapid turnaround after program changes. And because Python's parser is embedded in Python-based systems, it's easy to modify programs at runtime. For example, we saw how GUI programs developed with Python allow developers to change the code that handles a button press while the GUI remains active; the effect of the code change may be observed immediately when the button is pressed again. There's no need to stop and rebuild.

More generally, the entire development process in Python is an exercise in rapid prototyping. Python lends itself to experimental and interactive program development, and it encourages developing systems incrementally by testing components in isolation and putting them together later. In fact, we've seen that we can switch from testing components (unit tests) to testing whole systems (integration tests) arbitrarily, as illustrated in Figure 24-2.

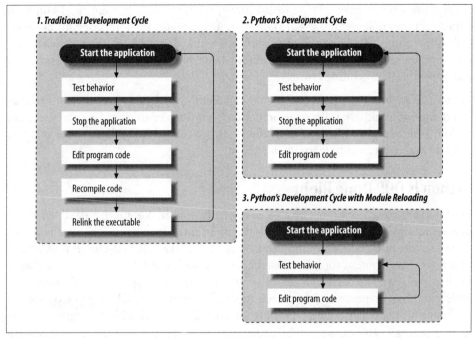

Figure 24-1. Development cycles

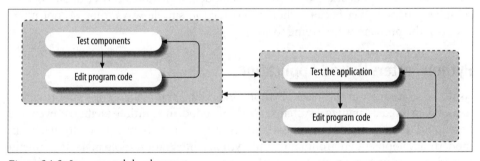

Figure 24-2. Incremental development

Python Is "Executable Pseudocode"

Python's very high-level nature means there's less for us to program and manage. The lack of compile and link steps isn't really enough to address the development-cycle bottleneck by itself. For instance, a C or C++ interpreter might provide fast turnaround but would still be almost useless for rapid development: the language is too complex and low level.

But because Python is also a simple language, coding is dramatically faster too. For example, its dynamic typing, built-in objects, and garbage collection eliminate much of the manual bookkeeping code required in lower-level languages such as C and

C++. Since things such as type declarations, memory management, and common data structure implementations are conspicuously absent, Python programs are typically a fraction of the size of their C and C++ equivalents. There's less to write and read, and there are fewer interactions among language components, and thus there is less opportunity for coding errors.

Because most bookkeeping code is missing, Python programs are easier to understand and more closely reflect the actual problem they're intended to address. And Python's high-level nature not only allows algorithms to be realized more quickly, but also makes it easier to learn the language.

Python Is OOP Done Right

For OOP to be useful, it must be easy to apply. Python makes OOP a flexible tool by delivering it in a dynamic language. More importantly, its class mechanism is a simplified subset of C++'s; this simplification is what makes OOP useful in the context of a rapid-development tool. For instance, when we looked at data structure classes in this book, we saw that Python's dynamic typing let us apply a single class to a variety of object types; we didn't need to write variants for each supported type. In exchange for not constraining types, Python code becomes flexible and agile.

In fact, Python's OOP is so easy to use that there's really no reason not to apply it in most parts of an application. Python's class model has features powerful enough for complex programs, yet because they're provided in simple ways, they do not interfere with the problem we're trying to solve.

Python Fosters Hybrid Applications

As we've seen earlier in this book, Python's extending and embedding support makes it useful in mixed-language systems. Without good integration facilities, even the best rapid-development language is a "closed box" and is not generally useful in modern development environments. But Python's integration tools make it usable in hybrid, multicomponent applications. As one consequence, systems can simultaneously utilize the strengths of Python for rapid development and of traditional languages such as C for rapid execution.

While it's possible and common to use Python as a standalone tool, it doesn't impose this mode. Instead, Python encourages an integrated approach to application development. By supporting arbitrary mixtures of Python and traditional languages, Python fosters a spectrum of development paradigms, ranging from pure prototyping to pure efficiency. Figure 24-3 shows the abstract case.

As we move to the left extreme of the spectrum, we optimize speed of development. Moving to the right side optimizes speed of execution. And somewhere in between is an optimum mix for any given project. With Python, not only can we pick the proper

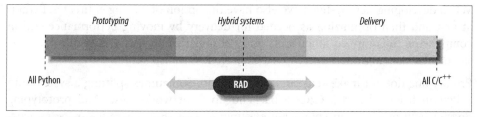

Figure 24-3. The development mode "slider"

mix for our project, but we can also later move the RAD slider in the picture arbitrarily as our needs change:

Going to the right

    Projects can be started on the left end of the scale in Python and gradually moved toward the right, module by module, as needed to optimize performance for delivery.

Going to the left

    Similarly, we can move strategic parts of existing C or C++ applications on the right end of the scale to Python, to support end-user programming and customization on the left end of the scale.

This flexibility of development modes is crucial in realistic environments. Python is optimized for speed of development, but that alone isn't always enough. By themselves, neither C nor Python is adequate to address the development bottleneck; together, they can do much more. As shown in Figure 24-4, for instance, apart from standalone use, one of Python's most common roles splits systems into frontend components that can benefit from Python's ease of use and backend modules that require the efficiency of static languages such as C, C++, or FORTRAN.

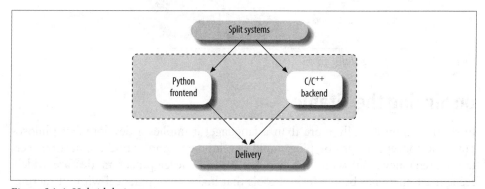

Figure 24-4. Hybrid designs

Whether we add Python frontend interfaces to existing systems or design them in early on, such a division of labor can open up a system to its users without exposing its internals.

When developing new systems, we also have the option of writing entirely in Python at first and then optimizing as needed for delivery by moving performance-critical components to compiled languages. And because Python and C modules look the same to clients, migration to compiled extensions is transparent.

Prototyping doesn't make sense in every scenario. Sometimes splitting a system into a Python frontend and a C/C++ backend up front works best. And prototyping doesn't help much when enhancing existing systems. But where it can be applied, early prototyping can be a major asset. By prototyping in Python first, we can show results more quickly. Perhaps more critically, end users can be closely involved in the early stages of the process, as sketched in Figure 24-5. The result is systems that more closely reflect their original requirements.

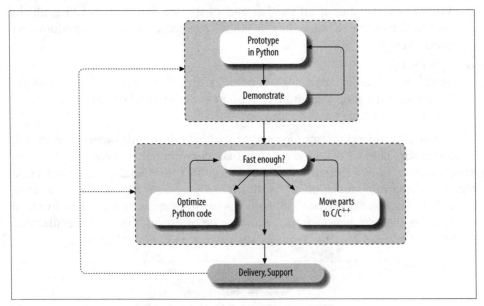

Figure 24-5. Prototyping with Python

On Sinking the Titanic

In short, Python is really more than a language; it implies a development philosophy. The concepts of prototyping, rapid development, and hybrid applications certainly aren't new. But while the benefits of such development modes are widely recognized, there has been a lack of tools that make them practical without sacrificing programming power. This is one of the main gaps that Python's design fills: *Python provides a simple but powerful rapid development language, along with the integration tools needed to apply it in realistic development environments.*

This combination arguably makes Python unique among similar tools. For instance, Tcl is a good integration tool but not a full-blown language; Perl is a powerful system administration language but a weak integration tool. But Python's marriage of a powerful dynamic language and integration opens the door to fundamentally faster development modes. With Python, it's no longer necessary to choose between fast development and fast execution.

By now, it should be clear that a single programming language can't satisfy all our development goals. In fact, our needs are sometimes contradictory: the goals of efficiency and flexibility will probably always clash. Given the high cost of making software, the choice between development and execution speed is crucial. Although machine cycles are cheaper than programmers, we can't yet ignore efficiency completely.

But with a tool like Python, we don't need to decide between the two goals at all. Just as a carpenter wouldn't drive a nail with a chainsaw, software engineers are now empowered to use the right tool for the task at hand: Python when speed of development matters, compiled languages when efficiency dominates, and combinations of the two when our goals are not absolute.

Moreover, we don't have to sacrifice code reuse or rewrite exhaustively for delivery when applying rapid development with Python. We can have our rapid development cake and eat it too:

Reusability
> Because Python is a high-level, object-oriented language, it encourages writing reusable software and well-designed systems.

Deliverability
> Because Python is designed for use in mixed-language systems, we don't have to move to more efficient languages all at once.

In many scenarios, a system's frontend and infrastructure may be written in Python for ease of development and modification, but the kernel is still written in C or C++ for efficiency. Python has been called the tip of the iceberg in such systems—the part visible to end users of a package, as captured in Figure 24-6.

Such an architecture uses the best of both worlds: it can be extended by adding more Python code or by writing C extension modules, depending on performance requirements. But this is just one of many mixed-language development scenarios:

System interfaces
> Packaging libraries as Python extension modules makes them more accessible.

End-user customization
> Delegating logic to embedded Python code provides for onsite changes.

Pure prototyping
> Python prototypes can be moved to C all at once or piecemeal.

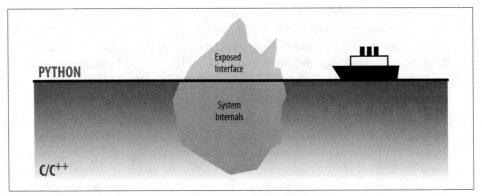

Figure 24-6. "Sinking the Titanic" with mixed-language systems

Legacy code migration
　　Moving existing code from C to Python makes it simpler and more flexible.

Standalone use
　　Of course, using Python all by itself leverages its existing library of tools.

Python's design lets us apply it in whatever way makes sense for each project.

So What's "Python: The Sequel"?

As we've seen in this book, Python is a multifaceted tool, useful in a wide variety of domains. What can we say about Python to sum up here? In terms of some of its best attributes, the Python language is:

- General purpose
- Object-oriented
- Interpreted
- Very high level
- Openly designed
- Widely portable
- Freely available
- Refreshingly coherent

Python is useful for both standalone development and extension work, and it is optimized to boost *developer productivity* on many fronts. But the real meaning of Python is really up to you, the reader. Since Python is a general-purpose tool, what it "is" depends on how you choose to use it.

In the Final Analysis . . .

I hope this book has taught you something about Python, both the language and its roles. Beyond this text, there is really no substitute for doing some original Python programming. Be sure to grab a reference source or two to help you along the way.

The task of programming computers will probably always be challenging. Perhaps happily, there will continue to be a need for intelligent software engineers, skilled at translating real-world tasks into computer-executable form, at least for the foreseeable future. After all, if it were too easy, none of us would get paid.

But current development practice and tools make our tasks unnecessarily difficult: many of the obstacles faced by software developers are purely artificial. We have come far in our quest to improve the speed of computers; the time has come to focus our attention on improving the speed of development. In an era of constantly shrinking schedules, productivity must be paramount.

Python, as a mixed-paradigm tool, has the potential to foster development modes that simultaneously leverage the benefits of rapid development and of traditional languages. While Python won't solve all the problems of the software industry, it offers hope for making programming simpler, faster, and at least a little more enjoyable.

It may not get us off that island altogether, but it sure beats bananas and coconuts.

Postscript to the Second Edition (2000)

One of the luxuries of updating a book like this is that you get an opportunity to debate yourself, or at least your opinions, from years past. With the benefit of five years' retrospect, I'd like to add a few comments to the original conclusion.

Integration Isn't Everything

The conclusion for this book's first edition stressed the importance of Python's role as an integration tool. Although the themes underscored there are still valid, I should point out that not all Python applications rely explicitly on the ability to be mixed with components written in other languages. Many developers now use Python in standalone mode, either not having or not noticing integration layers.

For instance, developers who code Common Gateway Interface (CGI) Internet scripts with Python often code in pure Python. Somewhere down the call chain, C libraries are called (to access sockets, databases, and so on), but Python coders often don't need to care. In fact, this has proven to be true in my own recent experience as well. While working on the new GUI, system, and Internet examples for this edition, I worked purely in Python for long periods of time. A few months later I also worked on a Python/C++ integration framework, but this integration project was entirely separate from the pure Python book examples programming effort. Many projects are implemented in Python alone.

That is not to say that Python's integration potential is not one of its most profound attributes—indeed, most Python systems *are* composed of combinations of Python and C. However, in many cases, the integration layer is implemented once by a handful of advanced developers, while others perform the bulk of the programming in Python alone. If you're fortunate enough to count yourself among the latter group, Python's overall ease of use may seem more crucial than its integration role.

The End of the Java Wars

In 1995, the Python community perceived a conflict between Java and Python in terms of competition for developer mindshare—hence the sidebar "Python Versus Java: Round 1?" in the first edition. Since then, this has become virtually a nonissue; I've even deleted this sidebar completely.

This cooling of hostilities has come about partly because Java's role is now better understood: Java is recognized as a systems development language, not as a scripting language. That is essentially what the sidebar proposed. Java's complexity is on the order of C++'s (from which it is derived), making it impractical for scripting work, where short development cycles are at a premium. This is by design—Java is meant for tasks where the extra complexity may make sense. Given the great disparity in their roles, the Python/Java conflict has fizzled.

The truce has also been called on account of the new Jython implementation of Python. Jython was described in Chapter 18; in short, it integrates Python and Java programs such that applications can be developed as hybrids: parts can be coded in Python when scripting is warranted and in Java for performance-intensive parts. This is exactly the argument made for C/C++ integration in the conclusion of the first edition; thanks to Jython, the same reasoning behind hybrid systems now applies to Java-based applications.

The claims made by the old Java sidebar are still true—Python is simpler, more open, and easier to learn and apply. But that is as it should be: as a scripting language, Python naturally complements systems languages such as Java and C++ instead of competing with them. There are still some who would argue that Python is better suited for many applications now coded in Java. But just as for Python and C and C++, Python and Java seem to work best as a team.

It's also worth noting that as I write these words, Microsoft has just announced a new, proprietary language called C# that seems to be intended as a substitute for Java in Microsoft's systems language offerings. Moreover, a new Python port to the C#/.NET environment has been announced as well. See Chapter 18 for details—this port is roughly to C# what Jython is to Java. Time will tell whether C# and Java will do battle for mindshare. But given that Python integrates with both, the outcome of these clashes between megacompanies is largely irrelevant; Pythonistas can watch calmly from the sidelines this time around.

We're Not Off That Island Yet

As I mentioned in the Preface to this edition, Python has come far in the last five years. Companies around the world have adopted it, and Python now boasts a user base estimated at half a million strong. Yet for all the progress, there is still work to be done, both in improving and popularizing Python and in simplifying software development in general.

As I travel around the world teaching Python classes at companies and organizations, I still meet many people who are utterly frustrated with the development tools they are required to use in their jobs. Some even change jobs (or careers) because of such frustrations. Even well after the onset of the Internet revolution, development is still harder than it needs to be.

On the other hand, I also meet people who find Python so much fun to use, they can't imagine going back to their old ways. They use Python both on and off the job for the pure pleasure of programming.

Five years from now, I hope to report that I meet many more people in the latter category than in the former. After all, Guido may have appeared on the covers of *Linux Journal* and *Dr. Dobb's* since the first edition of this book, but we still have a bit more work to do before he makes the cover of *Rolling Stone*.

Postscript to the Third Edition (2006)

And now here I am in the future again, so I get to add a few more words.

Proof of Concept

Some 5 years after writing the second edition of this book, and 10 years after the first, perhaps the most obvious thing worth adding to this original conclusion today is proof of concept: Python's success over the years seems validation of the simplicity and mixed-language themes that Python, and this conclusion, originally advocated. By all accounts, Python has been a greater success than most of its pioneers ever imagined.

See Chapter 1 for some statistics on this front—Python is now a mainstream language, widely used in very successful projects and organizations, and often in the context of hybrid architectures. In fact, the question today is not who is using Python, but who is *not*; it shows up in some fashion in virtually every substantial development organization. Moreover, all signs point to continued growth in years to come; as I write these words, Python's popularity is roughly doubling each year.

Today I meet many more people than ever before who are able to use Python. Programming may indeed always be a challenge, but Python has shown that the language used, and the mixture of languages used, can greatly reduce the difficulty of that challenge. People enjoy using Python—so much so that many of them would find it difficult to go back to using something as tedious and complex as C++.

Integration Today

Another trend that has become clear in recent years is that many people are indeed using Python in a *hybrid* role. GIS and graphical modeling systems, for example, often generate Python code to render models created in a user interface. And many people still plug C and C++ libraries into their Pythons; for instance, hardware testing is often structured as low-level device libraries made accessible to Python scripts—the classic integration model. Newer systems, such as the IronPython port to the .NET/Mono framework, open up new integration possibilities for the future.

I should add again, though, that integration with other components is not required to leverage the flexibility of this language. Many successful Python-based systems are all, or mostly, Python code. Ultimately, every realistic Python program does run linked-in code (even opening a file or network socket invokes a C library function in standard Python), but many systems never integrate user-coded, compiled language libraries. Python code is fast and capable enough to be used for most applications standalone.

Quality Counts

So how, then, does one define Python's contribution to the software field? Perhaps its emphasis on simplicity—on *limiting interactions* in your code—is at least as important as its integration focus. This theme makes Python much less difficult and error prone to use than other tools, but it also goes to the core of the software engineering task.

Although it is a richly creative endeavor, developing software is fundamentally an act of engineering, not art. Computer programs and paintings, for example, have very different roles, and they should be created in very different ways. In art, freedom of expression is paramount. One creates a painting for purely aesthetic and often very personal purposes, without expecting the next artist to modify or build upon their work later.

But as anyone who has worked in this field for even a few years knows only too well, in engineering, unconstrained freedom of expression can be a liability. In engineering, we need predictability, simplicity, and a limited set of possible interactions. In engineering, maintaining and modifying a creation is usually just as important as building it in the first place. And in engineering, making your system complex for the sake of complexity is not a reasonable goal. It doesn't matter how clever a system's code is, if it cannot be understood and changed by others.

The Python language has always taken the complexity issue head-on, in terms of both syntax and overall design. Its syntax model encourages and enforces readable code, and most of the language follows from a small and simple set of core principles. Python does offer alternatives, but there is usually one obvious way to accomplish a task, and a relatively small set of ways that language features interact. Simplicity, explicitness, and lack of exceptional cases permeate the language's design.

That is, *magic is frowned on* in both the Python language and its community, because magic is simply not good engineering. This is in sharp contrast to many other languages, especially in the scripting realm. And this philosophy is much of what makes Python code easier to use and understand and it is a large part of what makes Python programmers so productive. If you can understand someone else's code well enough to reuse it, part of your job is already done.

But at the end of the day, something even more profound seems to be at work. After watching Python inspire people for some 13 years, I have come to believe that Python's real legacy, if it is to have one, is just what I stated in the sidebar at the end of this edition's first chapter: it has almost forced software developers to think about *quality* issues that they may have not otherwise considered. In hindsight, it seems almost deliberate—by attempting to be a "better" tool, Python has stirred developers to consider the very term. And by addressing quality among an ever-larger audience, Python has, in its way, helped to improve the state of the software field at large.

Not bad, for a little language from Amsterdam.

A Morality Tale of Perl Versus Python

(The following was posted recently to the *rec.humor.funny* Usenet newsgroup by Larry Hastings, and it is reprinted here with the original author's permission. I don't necessarily condone language wars; OK?)

This has been percolating in the back of my mind for a while. It's a scene from *The Empire Strikes Back*, reinterpreted to serve a valuable moral lesson for aspiring programmers.

EXTERIOR: DAGOBAH—DAY

With Yoda strapped to his back, Luke climbs up one of the many thick vines that grow in the swamp until he reaches the Dagobah statistics lab. Panting heavily, he continues his exercises—grepping, installing new packages, logging in as root, and writing replacements for two-year-old shell scripts in Python.

YODA: Code! Yes. A programmer's strength flows from code maintainability. But beware of Perl. Terse syntax . . . more than one way to do it . . . default variables. The dark side of code maintainability are they. Easily they flow, quick to join you when code you write. If once you start down the dark path, forever will it dominate your destiny, consume you it will.

LUKE: Is Perl better than Python?

YODA: No . . . no . . . no. Quicker, easier, more seductive.

LUKE: But how will I know why Python is better than Perl?

YODA: You will know. When your code you try to read six months from now.

Index

We'd like to hear your suggestions for improving our indexes. Send email to *index@oreilly.com*.

E

R

radiobuttons, 456, 460
    callback handlers, 458
    command option, 456, 460
    configuring, 419
    dialogs, 427
    Entry widgets, 448
    HTML forms, adding to, 1001
    Message widgets, 448
    value attribute, 460
    variable option, 456
    variables, 463
    variables and, 462
    windows, top-level, 422
random module
    GIF files, 481
raw_input(), 815
re module, 1346, 1348
    functions, 1349
re.compile(), 1349
re.match(), 1349
re.search(), 1349
re.split(), 1349
re.sub(), 1349
re.subn(), 1349
read(), Unpickler class, 1203
readable code, 4
reading files, iterators and, 146–148
readlines method, 296
readlines(), 158
reapChildren(), 737
record dictionaries, 1239
records, lists, 25
recursion
    os.path.walk, 169
    os.walk, 169
redirectedGuiFunc function, 605
redirectedGuiFunc(), 605
redirectedGuiShellCmd function, 605
redirection
    to files, 125–126
    to objects, 134–137
    coding alternatives, 129
    pipes and, 127–128
    print statements, 139
    reading keyboard input, 130–134
    StreamApp class, 259
    streams to widgets, 605
    user interaction and, 130
    using for packing scripts, 608
refactoring uploads/downloads, 795–803

reference count management, 1421
regex module, 1346
    migrating code using, 1347
Register_Handler(), 1479
registering methods, 1417
regression test script, 251–253
regular expressions, 1346
    compiled pattern objects, 1349
    match objects, 1350
    patterns, 1350
    re module, 1348
    vs. string module, 1344
relational algebra, adding to sets, 1303
reload(), 609
    callback handlers and, 610
ReplaceVisitor class, 323
replies, web interface, text format, 77
return values, 1418
reusable tools, 307
reusing downloads/uploads, 795–803
rfc822 module, 719
    email client, 904
rotor module, 1109
rule strings, 1342
running code, 19

S

scales, 465–468
    command option, 465
    labels, 466
    linking, 468
    variables, 467
scheduled callbacks, 559
Scheme, Python compared to, 1510
scripting
    Internet, 17, 711
    overview, 90
scripting languages, 3
scripts
    CGI, 979
    client-side, 766
        email, 808
        files, transferring over Internet, 767
        newsgroups, 862
        PyMailGUI, 876
        web sites, accessing, 866
    executable
        Unix, 120
    execution, context, 113–114
    format, persistence, 38
    Jython, compared to Java, 1153

T

Table class (HTMLgen), 1147
tables on web pages
    adding, 982
    laying out forms, 994
    tags, 984, 994
Tcl language, 416
Tcl/Tk, 416, 1510
TCP objects, 723
TCP/IP, 710
    socket module, 719
tear-offs, menus, 501
Telnet, 786
telnetlib module, 719
templates, web pages, forward link files, 248
testing
    GuiMaker self-test, 592
    mixin methods, 586
    persistence, 35
    regression test script, 251–253
    sequence permutations, 1319
    set classes, 1296
    set functions, 1295
text
    advanced operations, 527
    clipboard and, 524
    composition, inheritance and, 526
    editing, 522
    files
        distinguishing from binary, 789
        uploading, 793
    labels, 420
    processing, 1336
        parser generators, 1357
        regular expressions, 1346
        rule strings, 1342
        summing columns, 1340
        utilities, 1337
    ScrolledText class, 586
    widgets, 517
text editors, PyEdit
    example, 638–657
text widget, programming, 519
thread module, 92, 185–193
threading module, 193–195
threads, 176, 183
    C API, 201
    exits, 191, 206–208
    function calls, 184
    GIL and, 184, 197–201
    GUIs and, 198, 560, 616–624
    memory and, 183

performance and, 183
portability and, 184
queues, 184
synchronization, 184
threading servers, 742
thumbnails
    PIL, 489–498
    scrollable, 536
    scrolling, 497
tic-tac-toe game, 700–704
time module, 92
time.sleep()
    client requests, 734
    servers, multiplexing, 751
time.strftime(), 825
time/date formatting, 825
timer module, 1290, 1299
time-slicing, 747
titles, top-level windows, 426
Tix, Tkinter and, 373
Tk library, 416
tkFileDialog module, 434
Tkinter, 60, 367, 371
    animation techniques, 564
    Button class, 387
    callback handlers, user-defined, 389–401
    callbacks, protocols, 399
    canvas widgets, 529
    checkbuttons, 456–460
        adding to HTML forms, 1001
        configuring, 419
        dialogs, 427
        Entry widget, 448
        Message widget, 448
        variables and, 458
        windows, top-level, 422
    classes, container, 412
    coding, 377–380
    coding alternatives, 380
    documentation, 372–373
    events, binding, 400
    extensions, 373–374
    FTP client frontend, 757
    Grail and, 1161
    grids, 543
    IDLE and, 374
    images, 478–483
    listboxes, 511
    menus, 499, 593
    object viewers, 1323
        persistent, 1257
    pack widget method, 378

---

text in, escaping, 1024
web sites, accessing, 869
Zope
    invoking functions through, 1134
    mapping into calls on objects by, 1133
user interaction, adding to CGI scripts, 986
users
    groups, 13
    growth of, 9
    input, 64
    stream redirection and, 130
uses of Python, 17
utilities
    email browser, 1106
        external components, 1106
        POP interface, 1107
    scripts
        persistence, 40
    text processing, 1337
uu module, 719

V

van Rossum, Guido, 8
variables
    checkbuttons, 458
    radio buttons, 462, 463
    scales, 467
    shell
        changing, 121
        faking inputs on forms with, 1039
        fetching, 119–121
Vaults of Parnassus, 8
visitors
    copied directory trees, 343
    fixers and, 329–332

W

walking directories, 159–164
    trees, 164–170
Web
    applications, trade-offs, 1122
    CGI scripts and, 963
    client/server architecture, 964
    servers, 717
web browsers, 732
    launching
        command lines and, 280
        function calls, 282
        portably, 277–284
    multimedia, viewing in, 283

web interface, 70
    CGI, 70–73
    query strings, 76–77
    reply text format, 77
    urllib, 76–77
    web server, 73–76
web pages, 972
    cgi module, parsing user input, 989
    CGI scripts and, 977
    email
        forwarding, 1098
        passwords, 1081, 1100
        replying to, 1098
        selecting, 1082
        sending, 1073
        viewing, 1090
    forms on, 964
        changing, 1003
        hidden fields in, 1020
        laying out with tables, 994
        mocking up inputs, 1024
        reusable, 1034
        selection list, 1020
        tags, 986
    forward-link, generating, 247–250
    graphics on, adding, 982
    HTMLgen, 1145
    modules, 719
    opening, remote servers, 282
    sharing objects between, 1030
    tables on
        adding, 982
        tags, 994
    templates
        forward-link files, 248
        Zope and, 1132
web servers, 717
    email client and, 1125
    finding Python on, 981
    uploading client files to, 1053
    web interface, 73–76
web sites
    accessing, 866
        httplib module, 866
        urllib module, 869
    downloading, 786
        deleting files when, 788
    from CGI scripts
        email, 1080
        root page, 1070
    mirroring, 786

About the Author

Mark Lutz is the world leader in Python training, the author of Python's earliest and best-selling texts, and a pioneering figure in the Python community.

Mark is also the author of the O'Reilly book *Python Pocket Reference*, and coauthor of *Learning Python*, all currently in second or third editions. Involved with Python since 1992, he started writing Python books in 1995 and began teaching Python classes in 1997. As of mid-2006, he has instructed more than 170 Python training sessions.

In addition, he holds B.S. and M.S. degrees in computer science from the University of Wisconsin, and over the last two decades has worked on compilers, programming tools, scripting applications, and assorted client/server systems.

Whenever Mark gets a break from spreading the Python word, he leads an ordinary, average life in Colorado. Mark can be reached by email at *lutz@rmi.net*, or on the Web at *http://www.rmi.net/~lutz*.

Colophon

The animal on the cover of *Programming Python* is an African rock python, one of approximately 18 species of python. Pythons are nonvenomous constrictor snakes that live in tropical regions of Africa, Asia, Australia, and some Pacific Islands. Pythons live mainly on the ground, but they are also excellent swimmers and climbers. Both male and female pythons retain vestiges of their ancestral hind legs. The male python uses these vestiges, or spurs, when courting a female.

The python kills its prey by suffocation. While the snake's sharp teeth grip and hold the prey in place, the python's long body coils around its victim's chest, constricting tighter each time it breathes out. They feed primarily on mammals and birds. Python attacks on humans are extremely rare.

The cover image is a 19th-century engraving from the *Dover Pictorial Archive*. The cover font is Adobe ITC Garamond. The text font is Linotype Birka; the heading font is Adobe Myriad Condensed; and the code font is LucasFont's TheSans Mono Condensed.

Better than e-books

Buy *Programming Python*, 3rd Edition, and access the digital edition FREE on Safari for 45 days.

Go to www.oreilly.com/go/safarienabled
and type in coupon code 2ZJR-BAVK-NX4P-51KB-1AWV

Search
thousands of
top tech books

Download
whole chapters

Cut and Paste
code examples

Find
answers fast

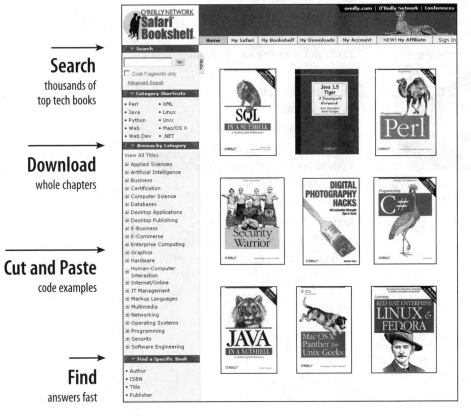

Search Safari! The premier electronic reference
library for programmers and IT professionals.

Related Titles from O'Reilly

Scripting Languages

Essential PHP Security

Exploring Expect

Jython Essentials

Learning Python, *2nd Edition*

PHP 5 Essentials

PHP Cookbook, *2nd Edition*

PHP Hacks

PHP in a Nutshell

PHP Pocket Reference, *2nd Edition*

Programming PHP, *2nd Edition*

Programming Python, *3rd Edition*

Python & XML

Python Cookbook, *2nd Edition*

Python in a Nutshell, *2nd Edition*

Python Pocket Reference, *3rd Edition*

Python Standard Library

Ruby in a Nutshell

Ruby on Rails: Up and Running

Twisted: A Developer's Notebook

Web Database Applications with PHP and MySQL, *2nd Edition*

Our books are available at most retail and online bookstores.

To order direct: 1-800-998-9938 • *order@oreilly.com* • *www.oreilly.com*

Online editions of most O'Reilly titles are available by subscription at *safari.oreilly.com*

The O'Reilly Advantage

Stay Current and Save Money